Pearson International Edition

Java™
HOW TO PROGRAM
EIGHTH EDITION

P9-AFK-161

CYBER
CLASSROOM
STUDENT
ACCESS
CARD

Thank you for purchasing a new copy of the International Edition of *Java How to Program* Eighth Edition, by Deitel and Deitel. The access code below provides you with full access to the Cyber Classroom that accompanies this text. You will now have full access to all student support areas, including:

- Hours of detailed, expert descriptions of thousands of lines of code that help to reinforce important concepts.
- An abundance of self-assessment material, including practice exams, hundreds of programming exercises, and self-review questions and answers.
- A lab manual featuring lab exercises as well as pre- and post-lab activities.
- Student solutions to approximately half of the exercises in the textbook.

To access the *Java How to Program Cyber Classroom* for the first time:

You will need to register online using a computer with an Internet connection and a Web browser. The registration process takes just a few minutes and only needs to be completed once.

1. Go to http://int.prenhall.com/deitel/
2. Find the appropriate title and click "**Access the Cyber Classroom**"
3. Click "**register**" under the student area.
4. Use a coin to scratch off the gray coating below and reveal your student access code.
   ** *Do not use a knife or other sharp object, which can damage the code.*

5. On the registration page, enter your student access code. Do not type the dashes. You can use lower or uppercase letters.
6. Follow the on-screen instructions. If you need help during the online registration process, simply click the **Need Help?** icon.
7. Once your personal Login Name and Password are confirmed, you can begin using the *Java How to Program Cyber Classroom*!

To login to the *Java How to Program Cyber Classroom* for the first time after you register:

Please visit http://int.prenhall.com/deitel/ and click "**Access the Cyber Classroom**" under the appropriate book title. Click "login" under the student section.
When prompted, provide your login name and password created during the registration process.

Note to Instructors: For access to Instructor Resources, contact your Prentice Hall Sales Representative.

IMPORTANT The access code on this page can only be used once to establish a subscription to the *Java How to Program Cyber Classroom*. If this access code has already been scratched off, it may no longer be valid. If this is the case, you can purchase a subscription by going to http://int.prenhall.com/deitel/, and clicking on "Purchase" under the appropriate book title.

PEARSON

Pearson Education International

Java™

HOW TO PROGRAM

EIGHTH EDITION

Pearson International Edition

108 1300
020590

Deitel® Ser

How To Program Series

Java How to Program, 8/E

C++ How to Program, 6/E

Visual C++® 2008 How to Program, 2/E

C How to Program, 5/E

Internet & World Wide Web How to Program, 4/E

Visual Basic® 2008 How to Program

Visual C#® 2008 How to Program, 3/E

Small Java™ How to Program, 6/E

Small C++ How to Program, 5/E

Simply Series

Simply C++: An Application-Driven
Tutorial Approach

Simply Java™ Programming: An
Application-Driven Tutorial
Approach

Simply C#: An Application-Driven
Tutorial Approach

Simply Visual Basic® 2008, 3/E: An
Application-Driven Tutorial
Approach

CourseSmart Web Books

www.deitel.com/books/CourseSmart.html

C++ How to Program, 5/E & 6/E

Java How to Program, 6/E, 7/E & 8/E

Simply C++: An Application-Driven
Tutorial Approach

Simply Visual Basic 2008: An
Application-Driven Tutorial
Approach, 3/E

Small C++ How to Program, 5/E

Small Java How to Program, 6/E

Visual Basic 2008 How to Program

Visual C# 2008 How to Program, 3/E

ies Page

Deitel® Developer Series

AJAX, Rich Internet Applications and
   Web Development for Programmers

C++ for Programmers

C# 2008 for Programmers, 3/E

Java for Programmers

Javascript for Programmers

LiveLessons Video Learning Products

www.deitel.com/books/LiveLessons/

Java Fundamentals Parts 1 and 2

C# Fundamentals Parts 1 and 2

C++ Fundamentals Parts 1 and 2

JavaScript Fundamentals Parts 1 and 2

To follow the Deitel publishing program, please register for the free *Deitel® Buzz Online* e-mail newsletter at:

      www.deitel.com/newsletter/subscribe.html

To communicate with the authors, send e-mail to:

      deitel@deitel.com

For information on government and corporate *Dive-Into® Series* on-site seminars offered by Deitel & Associates, Inc. worldwide, visit:

      www.deitel.com/training/

or write to

      deitel@deitel.com

For continuing updates on Prentice Hall/Deitel publications visit:

      www.deitel.com
      www.prenhall.com/deitel

Check out our Resource Centers for valuable web resources that will help you master Java, other important programming languages, software and Internet- and web-related topics:

      www.deitel.com/ResourceCenters.html

Vice President and Editorial Director, ECS: *Marcia J. Horton*
Associate Editor: *Carole Snyder*
Supervisor/Editorial Assistant: *Dolores Mars*
Director of Team-Based Project Management: *Vince O'Brien*
Senior Managing Editor: *Scott Disanno*
Managing Editor: *Robert Engelhardt*
A/V Production Editor: *Greg Dulles*
Art Director: *Kristine Carney*
Cover Design: *Abbey S. Deitel, Harvey M. Deitel, Francesco Santalucia, Kristine Carney*
Interior Design: *Harvey M. Deitel, Kristine Carney*
Manufacturing Manager: *Alexis Heydt-Long*
Manufacturing Buyer: *Lisa McDowell*
Director of Marketing: *Margaret Waples*
Marketing Manager: *Erin Davis*

PEARSON
Prentice
Hall

© 2010 by Pearson Education, Inc.
Upper Saddle River, New Jersey 07458

Printed in the United States of America

10 9 8 7 6 5 4 3 2 1

ISBN-10: 0-13-136483-9

ISBN-13: 978-0-13-136483-7

Pearson Education Ltd., *London*
Pearson Education Australia Pty. Ltd., *Sydney*
Pearson Education Singapore, Pte. Ltd.
Pearson Education North Asia Ltd., *Hong Kong*
Pearson Education Canada, Inc., *Toronto*
Pearson Educación de Mexico, S.A. de C.V.
Pearson Education–Japan, *Tokyo*
Pearson Education Malaysia, Pte. Ltd.
Pearson Education, Inc., *Upper Saddle River, New Jersey*

Java™

HOW TO PROGRAM

EIGHTH EDITION

Pearson International Edition

Paul Deitel
Deitel & Associates, Inc.

Harvey Deitel
Deitel & Associates, Inc.

PEARSON

Prentice
Hall

Upper Saddle River, New Jersey 07458

Trademarks

DEITEL, the double-thumbs-up bug and DIVE INTO are registered trademarks of Deitel and Associates, Inc.

JavaScript, Java and all Java-based marks are trademarks or registered trademarks of Sun Microsystems, Inc. in the United States and other countries.

Microsoft, Internet Explorer and the Windows logo are either registered trademarks or trademarks of Microsoft Corporation in the United States and/or other countries.

UNIX is a registered trademark of The Open Group.

Apache is a trademark of The Apache Software Foundation.

CSS, XHTML and XML are registered trademarks of the World Wide Web Consortium.

Firefox is a registered trademark of the Mozilla Foundation.

Google is a trademark of Google, Inc.

Web 2.0 is a service mark of CMP Media.

Throughout this book, trademarks are used. Rather than put a trademark symbol in every occurrence of a trademarked name, we state that we are using the names in an editorial fashion only and to the benefit of the trademark owner, with no intention of infringement of the trademark.

In memory of

Kristen Nygaard, co-inventor of Simula, the world's first object-oriented programming language.

Paul and Harvey Deitel

Deitel Resource Centers

Our Resource Centers focus on the vast amounts of free content available online. Find resources, downloads, tutorials, documentation, books, e-books, journals, articles, blogs, RSS feeds and more on many of today's hottest programming and technology topics. For the most up-to-date list of our Resource Centers, visit:

www.deitel.com/ResourceCenters.html

Let us know what other Resource Centers you'd like to see! Also, please register for the free *Deitel®* *Buzz Online* e-mail newsletter at:

www.deitel.com/newsletter/subscribe.html

Computer Science
Functional Programming
Regular Expressions

Programming
ASP.NET 3.5
Adobe Flex
Ajax
Apex
ASP.NET Ajax
ASP.NET
C
C++
C++ Boost Libraries
C++ Game Programming
C#
Code Search Engines and Code Sites
Computer Game Programming
CSS 2.1
Dojo
Facebook Developer Platform
Flash 9
Functional Programming
Java
Java Certification and Assessment Testing
Java Design Patterns
Java EE 5
Java SE 6
Java SE 7 (Dolphin) Resource Center
JavaFX
JavaScript
JSON
Microsoft LINQ
Microsoft Popfly
.NET
.NET 3.0
.NET 3.5
OpenGL
Perl
PHP
Programming Projects
Python
Regular Expressions
Ruby
Ruby on Rails

Silverlight
Visual Basic
Visual C++
Visual Studio Team System
Web 3D Technologies
Web Services
Windows Presentation Foundation
XHTML
XML

Games and Game Programming
Computer Game Programming
Computer Games
Mobile Gaming
Sudoku

Internet Business
Affiliate Programs
Competitive Analysis
Facebook Social Ads
Google AdSense
Google Analytics
Google Services
Internet Advertising
Internet Business Initiative
Internet Public Relations
Link Building
Location-Based Services
Online Lead Generation
Podcasting
Search Engine Optimization
Selling Digital Content
Sitemaps
Web Analytics
Website Monetization
YouTube and AdSense

Java
Java
Java Certification and Assessment Testing
Java Design Patterns
Java EE 5
Java SE 6

Java SE 7 (Dolphin) Resource Center
JavaFX

Microsoft
ASP.NET
ASP.NET 3.5
ASP.NET Ajax
C#
DotNetNuke (DNN)
Internet Explorer 7 (IE7)
Microsoft LINQ
.NET
.NET 3.0
.NET 3.5
SharePoint
Silverlight
Visual Basic
Visual C++
Visual Studio Team System
Windows Presentation Foundation
Windows Vista
Microsoft Popfly

Open Source & LAMP Stack
Apache
DotNetNuke (DNN)
Eclipse
Firefox
Linux
MySQL
Open Source
Perl
PHP
Python
Ruby

Software
Apache
DotNetNuke (DNN)
Eclipse
Firefox
Internet Explorer 7 (IE7)
Linux
MySQL
Open Source
Search Engines

SharePoint
Skype
Web Servers
Wikis
Windows Vista

Web 2.0
Alert Services
Attention Economy
Blogging
Building Web Communities
Community Generated Content
Facebook Developer Platform
Facebook Social Ads
Google Base
Google Video
Google Web Toolkit (GWT)
Internet Video
Joost
Location-Based Services
Mashups
Microformats
Recommender Systems
RSS
Social Graph
Social Media
Social Networking
Software as a Service (SaaS)
Virtual Worlds
Web 2.0
Web 3.0
Widgets

Dive Into® Web 2.0 eBook
Web 2 eBook

Other Topics
Computer Games
Computing Jobs
Gadgets and Gizmos
Ring Tones
Sudoku

Contents

3   Introduction to Classes and Objects   72

4   Control Statements: Part I   106

5   Control Statements: Part 2   156

9 Object-Oriented Programming: Inheritance 365

10 Object-Oriented Programming: Polymorphism 400

11 Exception Handling 443

12 ATM Case Study, Part 1: Object-Oriented Design with the UML 476

15 Graphics and Java 2D™   640

16 Strings, Characters and Regular Expressions   681

17 Files, Streams and Object Serialization   728

18 Recursion 778

19 Searching, Sorting and Big O 811

20 Generic Collections 841

21 Generic Classes and Methods 886

22 Custom Generic Data Structures 917

27   Networking   1131

28   Accessing Databases with JDBC   1184

29 JavaServer™ Faces Web Applications   1247

30 Ajax-Enabled JavaServer™ Faces Web Applications   1313

N Bit Manipulation · LV

O Labeled break and continue Statements · LXIX

P UML 2: Additional Diagram Types · LXXII

Q Design Patterns · LXXIV

Index · 1466

Preface

Live in fragments no longer, only connect.
—Edgar Morgan Foster

Welcome to Java and *Java How to Program, Eighth Edition*! This book presents leading-edge computing technologies for students, instructors, software developers and IT professionals.

We use the Deitel signature "live-code approach," presenting most concepts in the context of complete working Java programs, rather than using code snippets. Each code example is immediately followed by one or more sample executions. All the source code is available at www.deitel.com/books/jhtp8/.

At Deitel & Associates, we write programming-language textbooks and professional books for Pearson/Prentice Hall, deliver corporate training courses worldwide and develop Web 2.0 Internet businesses. We have updated the previous edition of this book based on recent changes to the Java language and the evolving preferred ways of teaching and learning programming. All of the chapters have been significantly tuned.

New and Updated Features

Here are the updates we've made for *Java How to Program, 8/e:*

- The book has a new interior design that graphically organizes, clarifies and highlights the information and enhances the book's pedagogy.

- We updated the entire book to Java Standard Edition 6 Update 11 and carefully audited the manuscript against the *Java Language Specification*.

- We added the "Making a Difference" exercises set: Students *want* to make a difference. We're encouraging them to associate computers and the Internet with solving problems that really matter to individuals, communities, countries and the world. We hope that our new exercises encourage students to think for themselves as they explore complex social issues. These exercises are not intended to make a political statement. They are meant to increase awareness of important issues the world is facing. Students should approach these issues in the context of their own values, politics and beliefs. Many of the new exercises require students to do research on the web—and weave the results into their problem-solving process. Here's a list of the 34 new "Making a Difference" exercises:

Test Drive: Carbon Footprint Calculator	World Population Growth Calculator
Test Drive: Body Mass Index Calculator	Car Pool Savings Calculator
Attributes of Hybrid Vehicles	Target Heart Rate Calculator
Gender Neutrality	Computerization of Health Records
Body Mass Index Calculator	Enforcing Privacy with Cryptography

World Population Growth
Global Warming Facts Quiz
Tax Plan Alternatives; The "Fair Tax"
Computer-Assisted Instruction
Computer-Assisted Instruction: Reducing
   Student Fatigue
Computer-Assisted Instruction:
   Monitoring Student Performance
Computer Assisted Instruction:
   Difficulty Levels
Computer-Assisted Instruction: Varying
   the Types of Problems
Polling
Air Traffic Control
Carbon Footprint Interface: Polymorphism

Ecofont
Typing Tutor: Tuning a Crucial Skill in
   the Computer Age
Large Type Displays for People with
   Low Vision
Cooking with Healthier Ingredients
Spam Scanner
Phishing Scanner
Accessibility Project: Speech Synthesis
Accessibility Project: Speech
   Recognition
Project: Simbad Robotics Simulator
SPAM Scanner Web Service
SMS Web Service
Gender Neutrality Web Service

- We tuned the optional Object-Oriented Design/UML 2 automated teller machine (ATM) case study and reorganized it into two optional chapters (12 and 13) that present the ATM's design and complete code implementation. The ATM is a nice business example that all students can relate to. In our experience, teaching these two chapters as a unit helps students tie together many of the object-oriented concepts they learn in Chapters 1–10. A key concept in object-oriented programming is the interactions among objects. In most programming textbooks, the code examples create and use one or two objects. The ATM gives students the opportunity to study interactions of *many* objects that provide the functionality of a substantial system. Chapters 12 and 13 provide complete solutions to *all* of their exercises. Previously, the case study was distributed through Chapters 2–8, 10 and an appendix. For instructors who wish to cover the case study in a distributed manner, for each section in Chapters 12 and 13, we indicate after which early chapter that section can be covered.

- We reinforced our early classes and objects pedagogy, paying careful attention to the guidance of the college instructors on our review teams to ensure that we got the conceptual level right. The treatment of OOP is clear and accessible. We introduce the basic concepts and terminology of object technology in Chapter 1. Students develop their first customized classes and objects in Chapter 3. Presenting objects and classes early gets students "thinking about objects" immediately and mastering these concepts more thoroughly.

- We reordered our presentation of data structures. We now begin with generic class ArrayList in Chapter 7. Because students will understand basic generics concepts so early in the book, our later data structures discussions provide a deeper treatment of generic collections—showing how to use the built-in collections of the Java API. We then show how to implement generic methods and classes. Finally, we show how to build custom generic data structures.

- We added coverage of Java Web Start and the Java Network Launch Protocol (JNLP), which enable *both* applets *and* applications to be launched via a web browser. In addition, the user can install them as shortcuts on the desktop to execute them in the future without revisiting the website. Programs can also request the user's permission to access local system resources such as files—enabling you to develop more robust applets and applications that execute safely using Java's sandbox security model, which applies to downloaded code.

- We reordered several chapters to facilitate teaching the book in modules. The dependencies chart (page xxx) was updated to reflect the new modularization.

- We've added many links to online documentation where students can learn more about a class or topic. And we've added many links to the Deitel Java-related Resource Centers available at `www.deitel.com/ResourceCenters.html`.

- Chapter 7 now covers class `Arrays`—which contains methods for performing common array manipulations—and class `ArrayList`—which implements a dynamically resizable array-like data structure. This follows our philosophy of *using existing classes before learning how to define your own classes*.

- We now introduce class `BigInteger` for arbitrarily large integer values in Chapter 18, Recursion.

- We carefully tuned all the chapters with a focus on increasing clarity and simplicity, eliminating redundancy, reducing page count (this new edition is 90 in-book pages shorter than the previous one), and improving pedagogy and modular organization.

- We've replaced all uses of `StringTokenizer` with the recommended `String` method `split` throughout the book. Class `StringTokenizer` is still discussed, primarily for backward compatibility with legacy code.

- We include an alphabetized list of the important terms defined in each chapter with the page number of the term's defining occurrence. Defining occurrences are also highlighted in the index with a **bold, maroon** page number.

All of this has been carefully reviewed by 24 distinguished academics and industry developers who worked with us on *Java How to Program, 8/e*.

We believe that this book and its support materials will give students and professionals an informative, interesting, challenging and entertaining Java educational experience. We provide a suite of ancillary materials that will help instructors maximize their students' learning experience.

As you read the book, if you have questions, send an e-mail to `deitel@deitel.com`; we'll respond promptly. For updates on this book and the status of all supporting Java software, and for the latest news on all Deitel publications and services, visit `www.deitel.com`. Sign up at `www.deitel.com/newsletter/subscribe.html` for the free *Deitel® Buzz Online* e-mail newsletter, and check out our growing list of Java and related Resource Centers at `www.deitel.com/ResourceCenters.html`. Each week we announce our latest Resource Centers in the newsletter.

Other Features

Other features of *Java How to Program, 8/e*, include:

- We audited the presentation against the ACM/IEEE curriculum recommendations and the Computer Science Advanced Placement Examination.

- The early classes and objects presentation features `Time`, `Employee` and `GradeBook` class case studies that weave their way through multiple sections and chapters, gradually introducing deeper OO concepts.

- Instructors teaching introductory courses have a broad choice of the amount of GUI and graphics to cover—from none, to a ten-brief-sections introductory sequence, to a deep treatment in Chapters 14, 15 and 25, and Appendix I.

- Our object-oriented programming and design presentations use the *UML™ (Unified Modeling Language™)*—the industry-standard graphical language for modeling object-oriented systems.

- We provide several substantial object-oriented web programming case studies.

- Chapter 28, Accessing Databases with JDBC, covers JDBC 4 and uses the Java DB/Apache Derby and MySQL database management systems. The chapter features an OO case study on developing a database-driven address book that demonstrates prepared statements and JDBC 4's automatic driver discovery.

- Chapter 29, JavaServer™ Faces Web Applications, and Chapter 30, Ajax-Enabled JavaServer™ Faces Web Applications, introduce JavaServer Faces (JSF) technology and use it with Netbeans 6.5 to build web applications quickly and easily. Chapter 29 includes examples on building web application GUIs, handling events, validating forms and session tracking. Chapter 30 discusses developing Ajax-enabled web applications, using JavaServer Faces technology. The chapter features a database-driven multitier web address book application that allows users to add and search for contacts. This Ajax-enabled application gives the reader a nice sense of Web 2.0 software development. The application uses Ajax-enabled JSF components to suggest contact names while the user types a name to locate.

- Chapter 31, Web Services, uses a tools-based approach to creating and consuming SOAP- *and* REST-based web services. Case studies include developing blackjack and airline reservation web services.

- We use a new tools-based approach for rapidly developing web applications; all the tools are available free for download.

- We provide 100+ Resource Centers (www.deitel.com/resourcecenters.html) to support our academic and professional readers. Their topics include Java SE 6, Java, Java Assessment and Certification, Java Design Patterns, Java EE 5, Code Search Engines and Code Sites, Game Programming, Programming Projects and many more. Sign up at www.deitel.com/newsletter/subscribe.html for the free *Deitel® Buzz Online* e-mail newsletter—each week we announce our latest Resource Center(s) and include other items of interest to our readers.

- We discuss key software engineering community concepts, such as Web 2.0, Ajax, SaaS (Software as a Service), web services, open-source software, design patterns, mashups, refactoring, agile software development, rapid prototyping and more.

- We completely reworked Chapter 26, Multithreading [special thanks to Brian Goetz and Joseph Bowbeer—co-authors of *Java Concurrency in Practice,* Addison-Wesley, 2006].

- We discuss the SwingWorker class for developing multithreaded user interfaces.

- We discuss the GroupLayout layout manager in the context of the GUI design tool in the NetBeans IDE.

- We present `JTable` sorting and filtering capabilities which allow the user to re-sort the data in a `JTable` and filter it by regular expressions.

- We discuss the `StringBuilder` class, which performs better than `StringBuffer` in non-threaded applications.

- We present annotations, which greatly reduce the amount of code you have to write to build applications.

Optional Case Study: Using the UML 2 to Develop an Object-Oriented ATM Design

UML 2 has become the preferred graphical modeling language for designing object-oriented systems. We use UML activity diagrams (in preference to flowcharts) to demonstrate the flow of control in each of Java's control statements, and we use UML class diagrams to visually represent classes and their inheritance relationships.

We include an optional (but highly recommended) case study on object-oriented design using the UML. The case study has been reviewed through many editions by a distinguished team of OOD/UML academics and industry professionals, including leaders in the field from Rational (the creators of the UML) and the Object Management Group (responsible for evolving the UML). In the case study, we design and fully implement the software for a simple automated teller machine (ATM). The optional Software Engineering Case Study in Chapters 12 and 13 presents a carefully paced introduction to object-oriented design using the UML.

We introduce a simple, concise subset of the UML 2, then guide the reader through a first design experience intended for the novice. The case study is not an exercise; rather, it's an end-to-end learning experience that concludes with a detailed walkthrough of the complete Java code. Chapters 12 and 13 help students develop an object-oriented design to complement the object-oriented programming concepts they've learned in Chapters 1 through 11.

At the end of Chapter 1, we introduce basic concepts and terminology of OOD. In Chapter 12, we consider more substantial issues, as we undertake a challenging problem with the techniques of OOD. We analyze a typical requirements document that specifies a system to be built, determine the objects needed to implement that system, determine the attributes these objects need to have, determine the behaviors these objects need to exhibit, and specify how the objects must interact with one another to meet the system requirements. In Chapter 13, we include a complete Java code implementation of the object-oriented system that we designed in Chapter 12.

This case study helps prepare students for the kinds of substantial projects they'll encounter in industry. We employ a carefully developed, incremental object-oriented design process to produce a UML 2 model for our ATM system. From this design, we produce a substantial working Java implementation using key object-oriented programming notions, including classes, objects, encapsulation, visibility, composition, inheritance and polymorphism.

Dependency Chart

The chart on the next page shows the dependencies among the chapters to help instructors plan their syllabi. *Java How to Program, 8/e,* is appropriate for a variety of programming courses at various levels, most notably CS 1 and CS 2 courses and introductory course

Chapter Dependency Chart

[*Note:* Arrows pointing into a chapter indicate that chapter's dependencies. Some chapters have multiple dependencies.]

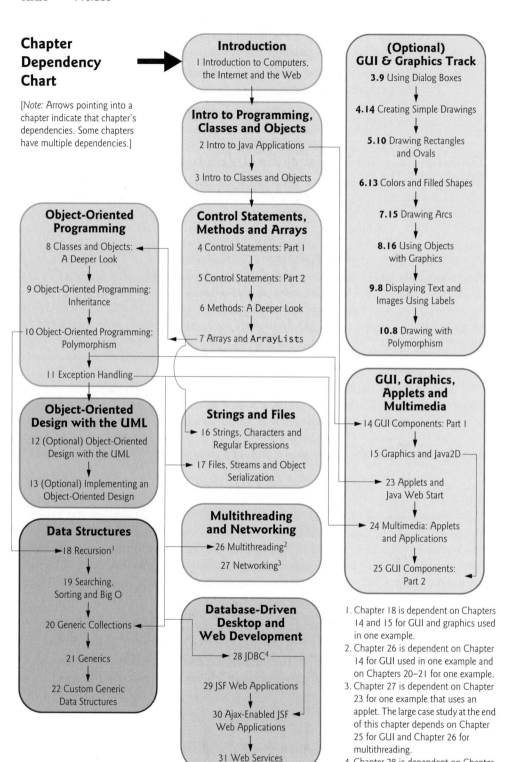

Introduction
1 Introduction to Computers, the Internet and the Web

Intro to Programming, Classes and Objects
2 Intro to Java Applications
3 Intro to Classes and Objects

Control Statements, Methods and Arrays
4 Control Statements: Part 1
5 Control Statements: Part 2
6 Methods: A Deeper Look
7 Arrays and `ArrayLists`

Object-Oriented Programming
8 Classes and Objects: A Deeper Look
9 Object-Oriented Programming: Inheritance
10 Object-Oriented Programming: Polymorphism
11 Exception Handling

Object-Oriented Design with the UML
12 (Optional) Object-Oriented Design with the UML
13 (Optional) Implementing an Object-Oriented Design

Data Structures
18 Recursion[1]
19 Searching, Sorting and Big O
20 Generic Collections
21 Generics
22 Custom Generic Data Structures

Strings and Files
16 Strings, Characters and Regular Expressions
17 Files, Streams and Object Serialization

Multithreading and Networking
26 Multithreading[2]
27 Networking[3]

Database-Driven Desktop and Web Development
28 JDBC[4]
29 JSF Web Applications
30 Ajax-Enabled JSF Web Applications
31 Web Services

(Optional) GUI & Graphics Track
3.9 Using Dialog Boxes
4.14 Creating Simple Drawings
5.10 Drawing Rectangles and Ovals
6.13 Colors and Filled Shapes
7.15 Drawing Arcs
8.16 Using Objects with Graphics
9.8 Displaying Text and Images Using Labels
10.8 Drawing with Polymorphism

GUI, Graphics, Applets and Multimedia
14 GUI Components: Part 1
15 Graphics and Java2D
23 Applets and Java Web Start
24 Multimedia: Applets and Applications
25 GUI Components: Part 2

1. Chapter 18 is dependent on Chapters 14 and 15 for GUI and graphics used in one example.
2. Chapter 26 is dependent on Chapter 14 for GUI used in one example and on Chapters 20–21 for one example.
3. Chapter 27 is dependent on Chapter 23 for one example that uses an applet. The large case study at the end of this chapter depends on Chapter 25 for GUI and Chapter 26 for multithreading.
4. Chapter 28 is dependent on Chapter 14 for GUI used in one example.

sequences in related disciplines. The book has a clearly delineated, modular organization. Chapters 1–11 and 14–17 form an accessible elementary programming sequence with a solid introduction to object-oriented programming. Optional Chapters 12–13 form an accessible introduction to object-oriented design with the UML. The GUI and Graphics Track and Chapters 14, 15, 23, 24 and 25 form a substantial GUI, graphics and multimedia sequence. Chapters 18–22 form a nice data-structures sequence. Chapters 26–27 form a solid introduction to multithreading and Internet networking. Chapters 28–31 form a clear database-intensive web development sequence.

Syllabus Assistance

We're happy to assist instructors designing syllabi based on *Java How to Program, 8/e*. You can reach us by email (deitel@deitel.com) or phone (1 978 823-0130). We'll respond promptly.

Teaching Approach

Java How to Program, 8/e, contains a rich collection of examples. The book concentrates on the principles of good software engineering and stresses program clarity. We teach by example. We are educators who teach leading-edge programming languages and software-related topics in government, industry, military and academic classrooms worldwide.

Live-Code Approach. *Java How to Program, 8/e,* is loaded with "live-code" examples. By this we mean that each new concept is presented in the context of a complete working Java application, followed immediately by one or more actual executions showing the program's inputs and outputs.

Syntax Coloring. For readability, we syntax color all the Java code, similar to the way most Java integrated-development environments and code editors syntax color code. Our syntax-coloring conventions are as follows:

```
comments appear in green
keywords appear in dark blue
errors appear in red
constants and literal values appear in light blue
all other code appears in black
```

Code Highlighting. We place yellow rectangles around key code segments.

Using Fonts for Emphasis. We place the key terms and the index's page reference for each defining occurrence in **bold maroon** text for easier reference. We emphasize on-screen components in the **bold Helvetica** font (e.g., the **File** menu) and emphasize Java program text in the Lucida font (for example, int x = 5;).

Web Access. All of the source-code examples for *Java How to Program, 8/e,* are available for download from:

```
www.deitel.com/books/jhtp8
```

Objectives. Each chapter begins with a statement of objectives.

Quotations. The learning objectives are followed by quotations. We hope that you enjoy relating these to the chapter material.

Illustrations/Figures. Abundant charts, tables, line drawings, programs and program output are included. We model the flow of control in control statements with UML activity diagrams. UML class diagrams model the fields, constructors and methods of classes. We make extensive use of six major UML diagram types in the optional OOD/UML 2 ATM case study.

Programming Tips. We include programming tips to help you focus on important aspects of program development. These tips and practices represent the best we've gleaned from a combined seven decades of programming and teaching experience.

Good Programming Practice

The Good Programming Practices *call attention to techniques that will help you produce programs that are clearer, more understandable and more maintainable.*

Common Programming Error

Pointing out these Common Programming Errors *reduces the likelihood that you'll make them.*

Error-Prevention Tip

These tips contain suggestions for exposing bugs and removing them from your programs; many describe aspects of Java that prevent bugs from getting into programs in the first place.

Performance Tip

These tips highlight opportunities for making your programs run faster or minimizing the amount of memory that they occupy.

Portability Tip

The Portability Tips *help you write code that will run on a variety of platforms.*

Software Engineering Observation

The Software Engineering Observations *highlight architectural and design issues that affect the construction of software systems, especially large-scale systems.*

Look-and-Feel Observation

The Look-and-Feel Observations *highlight graphical-user-interface conventions. These observations help you design attractive, user-friendly graphical user interfaces that conform to industry norms.*

Wrap-Up Section. Each chapter ends with a "wrap-up" section that recaps the chapter content and transitions to the next chapter.

Summary Bullets. Each chapter ends with additional pedagogical devices. We present a section-by-section, bullet-list-style summary of the chapter.

Terminology. We include an alphabetized list of the important terms defined in each chapter with the page number of the term's defining occurrence. Defining occurrences are also highlighted in the index with a **bold, maroon** page number.

Self-Review Exercises and Answers. Extensive self-review exercises *and* answers are included for self-study. All of the exercises in the optional ATM case study are fully solved.

Exercises. Each chapter concludes with a substantial set of exercises, including simple recall of important terminology and concepts; identifying the errors in code samples; writing individual program statements; writing small portions of methods and Java classes; writing complete methods, Java classes and programs; and building major term projects. Instructors can use these exercises to form homework assignments, short quizzes, major examinations and term projects. [*NOTE:* **Please do not write to us requesting access to the Pearson Instructor's Resource Center. Access is limited strictly to college instructors teaching from the book. Instructors may obtain access only through their Pearson representatives.**] Be sure to check out our Programming Projects Resource Center (http://www.deitel.com/ProgrammingProjects/) for lots of additional exercise and project possibilities.

Thousands of Index Entries. We have included an extensive index, which is especially useful when you use the book as a reference.

Student Resources Included with *Java How to Program, 8/e*

Many Java development tools are available for purchase, but you need none of these to get started with Java. For Windows systems, all the software you'll need for this book is available free for download from the web or on the accompanying CD. For other platforms, all the software you'll need for this book is generally available free for download from the web. We wrote most of the examples in *Java How to Program, 8/e,* using the free Java Standard Edition Development Kit (JDK) 6. The current JDK version (and separately its documentation) can be downloaded from Sun's Java website java.sun.com/javase/downloads/index.jsp. Mac OS X users can download Java from developer.apple.com/java. In several chapters, we also used the Netbeans IDE. Netbeans is available as a bundle with the JDK from the preceding Sun Java website, or you can download it separately from www.netbeans.org/downloads/index.html. The Eclipse IDE can be downloaded from www.eclipse.org/downloads/. MySQL can be downloaded from dev.mysql.com/downloads/, and MySQL Connector/J from dev.mysql.com/downloads/connector/j/5.1.html. You can find additional resources and software downloads in our Java SE 6 Resource Center at:

> www.deitel.com/JavaSE6Mustang/

The CD that accompanies *Java How to Program, 8/e,* contains versions of the following software packages for use on Microsoft® Windows®:

- Java™ SE Development Kit (JDK) 6 Update 11—which was used to create and test all the programs in the book.

- Eclipse IDE for Java EE Developers 3.4.1.

- NetBeans™ IDE Version 6.5 All Bundle.

- MySQL® 5.0 Community Server version 5.0.67.

- MySQL® Connector/J version 5.1.7.

Netbeans and Eclipse are integrated development environments (IDEs) for developing all types of Java applications. MySQL and MySQL Connector/J are provided for the database applications in Chapters 28–31. All of these tools are downloadable for other platforms also, as we discuss in Before You Begin, after this Preface.

The CD also contains a web page with links to the Deitel & Associates, Inc., website and the Pearson website. This web page can be loaded into a web browser to afford quick access to all the resources.

Java Multimedia Cyber Classroom, 8/e

Java How to Program, 8/e, includes a free, web-based, video-intensive interactive multimedia ancillary to the book—the *Java Multimedia Cyber Classroom, 8/e*—available with new books purchased from Pearson. Our web-based *Cyber Classroom* includes video walkthroughs of all the code examples in Chapters 1–11 and some of the code examples in Chapters 14 and 17, solutions to about half of the exercises in the book, a lab manual and more. For more information about the web-based *Cyber Classroom*, please visit

```
http://int.prenhall.com/deitel/
```

Students like the *Cyber Classroom's* interactivity and reference capabilities. Professors tell us that their students enjoy using the *Cyber Classroom* and consequently spend more time on the courses, mastering more of the material than in textbook-only courses. Instructors may want to explicitly weave *Cyber Classroom* assignments into their syllabi.

Instructor Resources for Java How to Program, 8/e

The Pearson *Instructor's Resource Center* contains

- the *Solutions Manual* with solutions to most of the end-of-chapter exercises,
- a *Test Item File* of multiple-choice questions (approximately two per book section) and
- PowerPoint® slides containing all the code and figures in the text, plus bulleted items that summarize the key points in the text. Instructors can customize the slides.

If you are not already a registered faculty member, contact your Pearson representative or visit www.pearsonhighered.com/educator/replocator/.

Pearson offers many different products around the world to facilitate learning. In countries outside the United States, some products and services related to this textbook may not be available due to copyright and/or permissions restrictions. If you have questions, you can contact your local office by visiting www.pearsonhighered.com/international or you can contact your local Pearson representative.

Computer Science AP Courses

Java How to Program, 8/e, is a suitable textbook for teaching AP Computer Science classes and for preparing students to take the AP exam.

Deitel® Buzz Online Free E-mail Newsletter

Each week, the *Deitel® Buzz Online* announces our latest Resource Center(s) and includes commentary on industry trends and developments, links to free articles and resources from our published books and upcoming publications, product-release schedules, errata, challenges, anecdotes, information on our corporate instructor-led training courses and more. It's also a good way to keep posted about issues related to *Java How to Program, 8/e.* To subscribe, visit

```
www.deitel.com/newsletter/subscribe.html
```

The Deitel Online Resource Centers

Our website www.deitel.com provides more than 100 Resource Centers on various topics including programming languages, software development, Web 2.0, Internet business and open-source projects—see the list of Resource Centers in the first few pages of this book and visit www.deitel.com/ResourceCenters.html. The Resource Centers evolve out of the research we do to support our books and business endeavors. We've found many exceptional resources online, including tutorials, documentation, software downloads, articles, blogs, podcasts, videos, code samples, books, e-books and more—most of them are free. Each week we announce our latest Resource Centers in our newsletter, the *Deitel®️ Buzz Online* (www.deitel.com/newsletter/subscribe.html). Some of the Resource Centers you might find helpful while studying this book are Java SE 6, Java, Java Assessment and Certification, Java Design Patterns, Java EE 5, Code Search Engines and Code Sites, Game Programming, Programming Projects and many more.

Acknowledgments

It's a pleasure to acknowledge the efforts of people whose names do not appear on the cover, but whose hard work, cooperation, friendship and understanding were crucial to the book's production. Many people at Deitel & Associates, Inc., devoted long hours to this project—thanks especially to Abbey Deitel and Barbara Deitel.

We would also like to thank the participants of our Honors Internship Program who contributed to this new edition—Nicholas Doiron, an Electrical and Computer Engineering major at Carnegie Mellon University; and Matthew Pearson, a Computer Science major at Cornell University.

We are fortunate to have worked on this project with the talented and dedicated team of publishing professionals at Pearson. We appreciate the extraordinary efforts of Marcia Horton, Editorial Director of Pearson's Engineering and Computer Science Division. Carole Snyder and Dolores Mars did an extraordinary job recruiting the book's review team and managing the review process. Francesco Santalucia (an independent artist) and Kristine Carney of Pearson did a wonderful job designing the book's cover—we provided the concept, and they made it happen. Scott Disanno and Robert Engelhardt did a marvelous job managing the book's production. Our marketing manager Erin Davis and her boss Margaret Waples did a great job marketing the book through academic and professional channels.

Java How to Program, 8/e *Reviewers*

We wish to acknowledge the efforts of our reviewers. Adhering to a tight time schedule, they scrutinized the text and the programs and provided countless suggestions for improving the accuracy and completeness of the presentation:

Sun Microsystems Reviewers:
- Lance Andersen
- Soundararajan Angusamy
- Lawrence Prem Kumar
- Simon Ritter
- Sang Shin
- Alexander Zuev

Academic Reviewers:
- William E. Duncan (Louisiana State University)
- Diana Franklin (University of California, Santa Barbara)
- Edward F. Gehringer (North Carolina State University)
- Ric Heishman (George Mason University)
- Patty Kraft (San Diego State University)
- Manjeet Rege, Ph.D. (Rochester Institute of Technology)
- Tim Margush (University of Akron)
- Sue McFarland Metzger (Villanova University)
- Shyamal Mitra (The University of Texas at Austin)
- Susan Rodger (Duke University)
- Amr Sabry (Indiana University)
- Monica Sweat (Georgia Tech)

Industry Reviewers:
- Joseph Bowbeer (Consultant)
- Peter Pilgrim (Lloyds TSB)
- José Antonio González Seco (Parliament of Andalusia)
- S. Sivakumar (Astra Infotech Private Limited)
- Raghavan "Rags" Srinivas (Intuit)
- Vinod Varma (Astra Infotech Private Limited)

Well, there you have it! Java is a powerful programming language that will help you write programs quickly and effectively. It scales nicely into the realm of enterprise systems development to help organizations build their business-critical and mission-critical information systems. As you read the book, we would sincerely appreciate your comments, criticisms, corrections and suggestions for improving the text. Please address all correspondence to:

```
deitel@deitel.com
```

We'll respond promptly, and post corrections and clarifications on:

```
www.deitel.com/books/jHTP8/
```

We hope you enjoy reading *Java How to Program, 8/e*, as much as we enjoyed writing it!

Paul J. Deitel
Dr. Harvey M. Deitel

About the Authors

Paul J. Deitel, CEO and Chief Technical Officer of Deitel & Associates, Inc., is a graduate of MIT's Sloan School of Management, where he studied Information Technology. He holds the Java Certified Programmer and Java Certified Developer certifications and has been designated by Sun Microsystems as a Java Champion. Through Deitel & Associates, Inc., he has delivered Java, C, C++, C#, Visual Basic and Internet programming courses to industry clients, including Cisco, IBM, Sun Microsystems, Dell, Lucent Technologies, Fidelity, NASA at the Kennedy Space Center, the National Severe Storm Laboratory, White Sands Missile Range, Rogue Wave Software, Boeing, Stratus, Cambridge Technology Partners, Open Environment Corporation, One Wave, Hyperion Software, Adra Systems, Entergy, CableData Systems, Nortel Networks, Puma, iRobot, Invensys and many more. He has also lectured on Java and C++ for the Boston Chapter of the Association for Computing Machinery. He and his co-author, Dr. Harvey M. Deitel, are the world's best-selling programming-language textbook authors.

Dr. Harvey M. Deitel, Chairman and Chief Strategy Officer of Deitel & Associates, Inc., has 48 years of academic and industry experience in the computer field. Dr. Deitel earned B.S. and M.S. degrees from MIT and a Ph.D. from Boston University. He has 20 years of college teaching experience, including earning tenure and serving as the Chairman of the Computer Science Department at Boston College before founding Deitel & Associates, Inc., with his son, Paul J. Deitel. He and Paul are the co-authors of dozens of books and multimedia packages and they are writing many more. With translations published in Traditional Chinese, Simplified Chinese, Japanese, German, Russian, Spanish, Korean, French, Polish, Italian, Portuguese, Greek, Urdu and Turkish, the Deitels' texts have earned international recognition. Dr. Deitel has delivered hundreds of professional seminars to major corporations, academic institutions, government organizations and the military.

About Deitel & Associates, Inc.

Deitel & Associates, Inc., is an internationally recognized corporate training and authoring organization specializing in computer programming languages, Internet and web software technology, object-technology education and Internet business development through its Web 2.0 Internet Business Initiative. The company provides instructor-led courses on major programming languages and platforms, such as Java™, C++, C, Visual C#®, Visual Basic®, Visual C++®, XML®, Python®, object technology, Internet and web programming, and a growing list of additional programming and software-development related courses. The founders of Deitel & Associates, Inc., are Paul J. Deitel and Dr. Harvey M. Deitel. The company's clients include many of the world's largest companies, government agencies, branches of the military, and academic institutions. Through its 33-year publishing partnership with Prentice Hall/Pearson, Deitel & Associates, Inc., publishes leading-edge programming textbooks, professional books, interactive multimedia *Cyber Classrooms*, *LiveLessons* DVD-based and web-based video courses, and e-content for popular course-management systems. Deitel & Associates, Inc., and the authors can be reached via e-mail at:

```
deitel@deitel.com
```

To learn more about Deitel & Associates, Inc., its publications and its worldwide *Dive Into® Series* Corporate Training curriculum delivered at client locations worldwide, visit:

```
www.deitel.com/training/
```

and subscribe to the free *Deitel® Buzz Online* e-mail newsletter at:

```
www.deitel.com/newsletter/subscribe.html
```

Individuals wishing to purchase Deitel books, and *LiveLessons* DVD and web-based training courses can do so through www.deitel.com. Bulk orders by corporations, the government, the military and academic institutions should be placed directly with Pearson. For more information, visit www.prenhall.com/mischtm/support.html#order.

Check out the growing list of online Deitel Resource Centers at:

```
www.deitel.com/resourcecenters.html
```

Individuals wishing to purchase Deitel publications can do so through:

```
www.deitel.com/books/index.html
```

Bulk orders by corporations, the government, the military and academic institutions should be placed directly with Pearson. For more information, visit

```
www.prenhall.com/mischtm/support.html#order
```

Before You Begin

This section contains information you should review before using this book and instructions to ensure that your computer is set up properly for use with this book. We'll post updates (if any) to this Before You Begin section on the book's website:

www.deitel.com/books/jhtp8/

Font and Naming Conventions

We use fonts to distinguish between on-screen components (such as menu names and menu items) and Java code or commands. Our convention is to emphasize on-screen components in a sans-serif bold **Helvetica** font (for example, **File** menu) and to emphasize Java code and commands in a sans-serif Lucida font (for example, System.out.println()).

Software and Hardware System Requirements

The interface to the contents of the CD that accompanies this book is designed to start automatically through the AUTORUN.EXE file (the CD is for use on Microsoft® Windows® systems). If a startup screen does not appear when you insert the CD into your computer, double click the welcome.htm file to launch the Student CD's interface, or refer to the file readme.txt on the CD. On the welcome.htm page, click the **Software** link at the bottom of the page to view the software and hardware system requirements. Please read these requirements carefully before installing the software on the CD.

The CD that accompanies *Java How to Program, 8/e* contains versions of the following software packages for use on Microsoft® Windows®:

- Java™ SE Development Kit (JDK) 6 Update 11—which was used to create and test all the programs in the book.
- Eclipse IDE for Java EE Developers 3.4.1.
- NetBeans™ IDE Version 6.5 All Bundle.
- MySQL® 5.0 Community Server/v5.0.67.
- MySQL® Connector/J Version 5.1.7.

Netbeans and Eclipse are integrated development environments (IDEs) for developing all types of Java applications. MySQL and MySQL Connector/J are provided for the database applications in Chapters 28–31. All of these tools are downloadable for other platforms as well, which we discuss in the next section.

Installing the Software

The CD includes the software required to compile and execute the examples in *Java How To Program, 8/e* on the Windows platform. For other platforms, you can download the software. Mac OS X users can learn about using Java on a Mac at

```
developer.apple.com/java/
```

Linux users can get the latest Java SE Development Kit from

```
java.sun.com/javase/downloads/index.jsp
```

Installation Instructions and Installers

On the left side of the CD's software and hardware requirements page there are links to the installation instructions for each software package for the Windows operating system. Each installation-instructions page contains a link to the corresponding software package's installer. You can also launch these installers directly from the CD's software folder. Follow the installation instructions carefully for each software package. Before you can run the applications in *Java How To Program, 8/e* or build your own applications, you must install the Java Standard Edition Development Kit (JDK) 6 or a Java development tool, such as the NetBeans (which requires the JDK) or Eclipse integrated development environments (IDEs). NetBeans is required for Chapters 29–31. Eclipse is optional for use with this book. We provide videos to help you get started with NetBeans and Eclipse at

```
www.deitel.com/books/jhtp8/
```

These videos discuss:

- creating single-file programs,
- creating multi-file programs,
- how the IDEs manage files, directories and Java packages,
- using the debugger,
- and using third party Java libraries.

Downloads for Other Platforms

The software on the CD is also available for other platforms:

- Netbeans bundled with the JDK: `java.sun.com/javase/downloads/index.jsp`
- Netbeans without the JDK bundle: `www.netbeans.org/downloads/index.html`
- Eclipse: `www.eclipse.org/downloads/`
- MySQL Community Edition: `dev.mysql.com/downloads/`
- MySQL Connector/J: `dev.mysql.com/downloads/connector/j/5.1.html`.

Obtaining the Code Examples

The examples for *Java How to Program, 8/e* are available for download at

```
www.deitel.com/books/jhtp8/
```

If you are not already registered at our website, go to www.deitel.com and click the **Register** link below our logo in the upper-left corner of the page. Fill in your information. There is no charge to register, and we do not share your information with anyone. We send you only account-management e-mails unless you register separately for our free *Deitel®* *Buzz Online* e-mail newsletter at www.deitel.com/newsletter/subscribe.html. After registering, you'll receive a confirmation e-mail with your verification code. *You'll need this code to sign in at www.deitel.com for the first time.* Configure your e-mail client to allow e-mails from deitel.com to ensure that the confirmation email is not filtered as junk mail.

Next, go to www.deitel.com and sign in using the **Login** link below our logo in the upper-left corner of the page. Go to www.deitel.com/books/jhtp8/. Click the **Examples** link to download the Examples.zip file to your computer. Write down the location where you choose to save the file on your computer.

We assume the examples are located at C:\Examples on your computer. Extract the contents of Examples.zip using a tool such as WinZip (www.winzip.com) or the built-in capabilities of Windows XP and Windows Vista (or a similar tool on other platforms).

Setting the PATH Environment Variable

The PATH environment variable on your computer designates which directories the computer searches when looking for applications, such as the applications that enable you to compile and run your Java applications (called javac and java, respectively). *Carefully follow the installation instructions for Java on your platform to ensure that you set the PATH environment variable correctly.*

If you do not set the PATH variable correctly, when you use the JDK's tools, you'll receive a message like:

```
'java' is not recognized as an internal or external command,
operable program or batch file.
```

In this case, go back to the installation instructions for setting the PATH and recheck your steps. If you've downloaded a newer version of the JDK, you may need to change the name of the JDK's installation directory in the PATH variable.

Setting the CLASSPATH Environment Variable

If you attempt to run a Java program and receive a message like

```
Exception in thread "main" java.lang.NoClassDefFoundError: YourClass
```

then your system has a CLASSPATH environment variable that must be modified. To fix the preceding error, follow the steps in setting the PATH environment variable, to locate the CLASSPATH variable, then edit the variable's value to include the local directory—typically represented as a dot (.). On Windows add

```
.;
```

at the beginning of the CLASSPATH's value (with no spaces before or after these characters). On other platforms, replace the semicolon with the appropriate path separator characters—often a colon (:)

Java's New Nimbus Look-and-Feel

As of Java SE 6 update 10, Java comes bundled with a new, elegant, cross-platform look-and-feel known as Nimbus. For programs with graphical user interfaces, we've configured our systems to use Nimbus as the default look-and-feel.

To set Nimbus as the default for all Java applications, you must create a text file named `swing.properties` in the `lib` folder of both your JDK installation folder and your JRE installation folder. Place the following line of code in the file:

```
swing.defaultlaf=com.sun.java.swing.plaf.nimbus.NimbusLookAndFeel
```

For more information on locating these installation folders visit java.sun.com/javase/6/webnotes/install/index.html. [*Note:* In addition to the standalone JRE, there is a JRE nested in your JDK's installation folder. If you are using an IDE that depends on the JDK (e.g., NetBeans), you may also need to place the `swing.properties` file in the nested `jre` folder's `lib` folder.]

You are now ready to begin your Java studies with *Java How to Program, 8/e*. We hope you enjoy the book!

Our life is frittered away by detail. ... Simplify, simplify.
—Henry David Thoreau

The chief merit of language is clearness.
—Galen

My object all sublime I shall achieve in time.
—W. S. Gilbert

He had a wonderful talent for packing thought close, and rendering it portable.
—Thomas B. Macaulay

Egad, I think the interpreter is the hardest to be understood of the two!
—Richard Brinsley Sheridan

Man is still the most extraordinary computer of all.
—John F. Kennedy

Introduction to Computers, the Internet and the Web

Objectives

In this chapter you'll learn:

- Basic computer hardware, software and networking concepts.
- Basic object-technology concepts, such as classes, objects, attributes, behaviors, encapsulation and inheritance.
- The different types of programming languages and which languages are most widely used.
- A typical Java program-development environment.
- Java's role in developing distributed client/server applications for the Internet and the web.
- The history of the UML—the industry-standard object-oriented design language.
- The history of the Internet and the World Wide Web through Web 2.0.
- To test-drive Java applications.
- Some key recent software technologies.

1.1 Introduction

Welcome to Java—a powerful computer programming language that is fun for novices to learn and appropriate for experienced programmers to use in building substantial enterprise information systems. *Java How to Program, Eighth Edition*, is an effective learning tool for each of these audiences.

Pedagogy
The core of the book emphasizes achieving program *clarity* through the proven techniques of *object-oriented programming*. Nonprogrammers will learn programming the right way from the beginning. The presentation is clear, straightforward and abundantly illustrated. It includes hundreds of Java programs and shows the outputs produced when they are run on a computer. We teach Java features in the context of complete working Java programs—we call this the **live-code approach**. The example programs can be downloaded from www.deitel.com/books/jhtp8/ or www.prenhall.com/deitel (see the Before You Begin section after the Preface).

Fundamentals
The early chapters introduce the fundamentals of computers, computer programming and the Java programming language, providing a solid foundation for the deeper treatment of Java in the later chapters. Experienced programmers tend to read the early chapters quickly and find the treatment of Java in the later chapters rigorous and challenging.

Most people are familiar with the exciting tasks computers perform. Using this textbook, you'll learn to write instructions commanding computers to perform those tasks. Software (i.e., the instructions you write) hardware (i.e., computers). Java, developed by Sun Microsystems, is one of today's most popular languages for developing software.

Evolution of Computing and Programming

Computer use is increasing in almost every field of endeavor. Computing costs are dropping dramatically, owing to rapid developments in both hardware and software technologies. Computers that might have filled large rooms and cost millions of dollars decades ago can now be inscribed on silicon chips smaller than a fingernail, costing perhaps a few dollars each. Fortunately, silicon is one of the most abundant materials on earth—it's an ingredient in common sand. Silicon-chip technology has made computing so economical that more than a billion general-purpose computers are in use worldwide, helping people in business, industry and government and in their personal lives. The number could easily double in the next few years.

Over the years, many programmers learned the methodology called structured programming. You'll learn structured programming and an exciting newer methodology, **object-oriented programming**. Why do we teach both? Object orientation is the key programming methodology used by programmers today. You'll create and work with many software objects in this text. But you'll discover that their internal structure is often built using structured-programming techniques. Also, the logic of manipulating objects is occasionally expressed with structured programming.

Language of Choice for Networked Applications

Java has become the language of choice for implementing Internet-based applications and software for devices that communicate over a network. Stereos and other devices in homes are often networked together by Java technology. There are now billions of Java-enabled mobile phones and handheld devices! Java is the preferred language for meeting many organizations' enterprisewide programming needs.

Java has evolved so rapidly that this eighth edition of *Java How to Program*—based on **Java Standard Edition (Java SE)** 6, Update 11—was published just 13 years after the first edition. Java is used in such a broad spectrum of applications that it has two other editions. The **Java Enterprise Edition (Java EE)** is geared toward developing large-scale, distributed networking applications and web-based applications—we discuss several Java EE features later in the book. The **Java Micro Edition (Java ME)** is geared toward developing applications for small, memory-constrained devices, such as cell phones, pagers and PDAs.

Staying in Touch with the Authors

If you'd like to communicate with us, please send e-mail to deitel@deitel.com. We'll respond promptly. To keep up to date with Java developments at Deitel & Associates, register for our free e-mail newsletter, the *Deitel® Buzz Online,* at

    www.deitel.com/newsletter/subscribe.html

For lots of additional Java material, visit our growing list of Java Resource Centers at www.deitel.com/ResourceCenters.html. We hope that you'll enjoy learning with *Java How to Program, Eighth Edition.*

1.2 Computers: Hardware and Software

A **computer** is a device that can perform computations and make logical decisions phenomenally faster than human beings can. Many of today's personal computers can perform billions of calculations in one second. A person operating a calculator could not perform that many calculations in a lifetime. (Points to ponder: How would you know whether the person added that many numbers correctly? How would you know whether the computer added the numbers correctly?) **Supercomputers** are already performing *thousands of trillions (quadrillions)* of instructions per second! To put that in perspective, a quadrillion-instruction-per-second computer can perform more than 100,000 calculations per second for every person on the planet!

Computers process **data** under the control of sets of instructions called **computer programs**. These programs guide the computer through orderly sets of actions specified by people called **computer programmers**.

A computer consists of various devices referred to as **hardware** (e.g., the keyboard, screen, mouse, disks, memory, DVD, CD-ROM and processing units). The programs that run on a computer are referred to as **software**. Hardware costs have been declining dramatically in recent years, to the point that personal computers have become a commodity. In this book, you'll learn proven methodologies that can reduce software-development costs—object-oriented programming and (in our optional Software Engineering Case Study in Chapters 12–13) object-oriented design.

1.3 Computer Organization

Regardless of differences in physical appearance, virtually every computer may be envisioned as divided into various **logical units** or sections:

1. *Input unit.* This "receiving" section obtains information (data and computer programs) from **input devices** and places it at the disposal of the other units so that it can be processed. Most information is entered into computers through keyboards and mouse devices. Information also can be entered in many other ways, including by speaking to your computer, scanning images and barcodes, reading from secondary storage devices (like hard drives, CD drives, DVD drives and USB drives—also called "thumb drives") and having your computer receive information from the Internet (such as when you download videos from YouTube™, e-books from Amazon, and the like).

2. *Output unit.* This "shipping" section takes information that the computer has processed and places it on various **output devices** to make it available for use outside the computer. Most information that is output from computers today is displayed on screens, printed on paper, played on audio players (such as Apple's popular iPods), or used to control other devices. Computers also can output their information to networks, such as the Internet.

3. *Memory unit.* This rapid-access, relatively low-capacity "warehouse" section retains information that has been entered through the input unit, making it immediately available for processing when needed. The memory unit also retains processed information until it can be placed on output devices by the output unit. Information in the memory unit is **volatile**—it's typically lost when the computer's power is turned off. The memory unit is often called either **memory** or **primary memory**.

4. *Arithmetic and logic unit (ALU).* This "manufacturing" section performs calculations, such as addition, subtraction, multiplication and division. It also contains the decision mechanisms that allow the computer, for example, to compare two

items from the memory unit to determine whether they are equal. In today's systems, the ALU is usually implemented as part of the next logical unit, the CPU.

5. *Central processing unit (CPU).* This "administrative" section coordinates and supervises the operation of the other sections. The CPU tells the input unit when information should be read into the memory unit, tells the ALU when information from the memory unit should be used in calculations and tells the output unit when to send information from the memory unit to certain output devices. Many of today's computers have multiple CPUs and, hence, can perform many operations simultaneously—such computers are called **multiprocessors**. A **multicore processor** implements multiprocessing on a single integrated circuit chip—for example a dual-core processor has two CPUs and a quad-core processor has four CPUs.

6. *Secondary storage unit.* This is the long-term, high-capacity "warehousing" section. Programs or data not actively being used by the other units normally are placed on secondary storage devices (e.g., your hard drive) until they are again needed, possibly hours, days, months or even years later. Therefore, information on secondary storage devices is said to be **persistent**—it is preserved even when the computer's power is turned off. Secondary storage information takes much longer to access than information in primary memory, but the cost per unit of secondary storage is much less than that of primary memory. Examples of secondary storage devices include CDs, DVDs and flash drives (sometimes called memory sticks), which can hold hundreds of millions to billions of characters.

1.4 Early Operating Systems

Early computers could perform only one **job** or **task** at a time. This is often called single-user **batch processing** and was the norm in the 1950s. The computer ran a single program while processing data in groups or **batches**. Users generally submitted their jobs to a computer center on decks of punched cards and often waited hours or even days before printouts were returned to their desks.

Software **operating systems** were developed to make using computers more convenient. Early operating systems smoothed and speeded up the transition between jobs, increasing the amount of work, or **throughput**, computers could process in a given time.

As computers became more powerful, it became evident that single-user batch processing was inefficient, because so much time was spent waiting for slow input/output devices to complete their tasks. The idea was conceived that many jobs or tasks could *share* the resources of the computer to achieve better utilization. This is called **multiprogramming**. Multiprogramming involves the simultaneous operation of many jobs that are competing to share the computer's resources.

In the 1960s, several groups in industry and the universities pioneered **timesharing** operating systems. Timesharing is a special case of multiprogramming in which users access the computer through terminals, typically devices with keyboards and screens. Dozens or even hundreds of users share the computer at once. The computer actually does not run all the jobs simultaneously. Rather, it runs a small portion of one user's job, then moves on to service the next user, perhaps providing service to each user several times per second. Thus, the users' programs *appear* to be running simultaneously. An advantage of timesharing is that user requests receive almost immediate responses.

1.5 Personal, Distributed and Client/Server Computing

In 1977, Apple Computer popularized **personal computing**. Computers became so economical that people could buy them for their own personal or business use. In 1981, IBM, the world's largest computer vendor, introduced the IBM Personal Computer. This quickly legitimized personal computing in business, industry and government organizations.

These computers were "standalone" units—people transported disks back and forth between them to share information (a mode of transfer often called "sneakernet"). Although early personal computers were not powerful enough to support several simultaneous users, these machines could be linked together in computer networks, sometimes over telephone lines and sometimes in **local area networks** (**LANs**) within an organization. This led to the phenomenon of **distributed computing**, in which an organization's computing, instead of being performed only at some central installation, is distributed over networks to the sites where the organization's work is performed. Personal computers were powerful enough to handle the computing requirements of individual users as well as the basic communications tasks of passing information between computers electronically.

Today's personal computers are as powerful as the million-dollar machines of just a few decades ago. The most powerful desktop machines—called **workstations**—provide individual users with enormous capabilities. Information is shared easily across computer networks, where computers called **servers** store data that may be used by **client** computers distributed throughout the network—hence the term **client/server computing**. Java has become widely used for writing software for computer networking and for distributed client/server applications. Today's popular operating systems, such as Linux, Apple's Mac OS X (pronounced "O-S ten") and Microsoft Windows, provide the kinds of capabilities needed today.

1.6 The Internet and the World Wide Web

The **Internet**—a global network of computers—has its roots in the 1960s, when funding was supplied by the U.S. Department of Defense. Originally designed to connect the main computer systems of about a dozen universities and research organizations, the Internet today is accessible by billions of computers and computer-controlled devices worldwide.

With the introduction of the **World Wide Web**—which allows computer users to locate and view multimedia-based documents on almost any subject over the Internet—the Internet has exploded into one of the world's premier communication mechanisms.

In the past, most computer applications ran on computers that were not connected to one another. Today's applications can be written to communicate among the world's computers. The Internet, by mixing computing and communications technologies, makes people's work easier. It makes information instantly and conveniently accessible worldwide. It enables individuals and local small businesses to get worldwide exposure. It's changing the way business is done. People can search for the best prices on virtually any product or service. Special-interest communities can stay in touch with one another. Researchers can be made instantly aware of the latest breakthroughs.

Java How to Program, Eighth Edition, presents programming techniques that allow Java applications to use the Internet and the web to interact with other applications. These capabilities and others allow you to develop the kind of enterprise-level distributed applications that are used in industry today. Java applications can be written to execute portably on every major type of computer, greatly reducing the time and cost of systems development.

1.7 **Machine Languages, Assembly Languages and High-Level Languages**

Programmers write instructions in various programming languages, some directly understandable by computers and others requiring intermediate **translation** steps. Hundreds of such languages are in use today. These may be divided into three general types:

1. Machine languages
2. Assembly languages
3. High-level languages

Any computer can directly understand only its own **machine language**. This is the computer's "natural language," defined by its hardware design. Machine languages generally consist of strings of numbers (ultimately reduced to 1s and 0s) that instruct computers to perform their most elementary operations one at a time. Machine languages are **machine dependent** (a particular machine language can be used on only one type of computer). Such languages are cumbersome for humans. For example, here is a section of an early machine-language program that adds overtime pay to base pay and stores the result in gross pay:

```
+1300042774
+1400593419
+1200274027
```

Programming in machine-language was simply too slow and tedious a process for most programmers. Instead of using the strings of numbers that computers could directly understand, programmers began using Englishlike abbreviations to represent elementary operations. These abbreviations formed the basis of **assembly languages**. **Translator programs** called **assemblers** were developed to convert early assembly-language programs to machine language at computer speeds. The following section of an assembly-language program also adds overtime pay to base pay and stores the result in gross pay:

```
load    basepay
add     overpay
store   grosspay
```

Although such code is clearer to humans, it's incomprehensible to computers until translated to machine language.

Computer usage increased rapidly with the advent of assembly languages, but programmers still had to use many instructions to accomplish even the simplest tasks. To speed the programming process, **high-level languages** were developed in which single statements could be written to accomplish substantial tasks. Translator programs called **compilers** convert high-level language programs into machine language. High-level languages allow you to write instructions that look almost like everyday English and contain commonly used mathematical notations. A payroll program written in a high-level language might contain a statement such as

```
grossPay = basePay + overTimePay
```

From the programmer's standpoint, high-level languages are preferable to machine and assembly languages. C, C++, Microsoft's .NET languages (e.g., Visual Basic, Visual C++ and C#) are among the most widely used high-level programming languages; Java is by far *the* most widely used.

Compiling a high-level language program into machine language can take a considerable amount of computer time. **Interpreter** programs were developed to execute high-level language programs directly (without the delay of compilation), although slower than compiled programs run. We'll say more about how interpreters work in Section 1.13, where you'll learn that Java uses a clever mixture of compilation and interpretation to ultimately run programs. Exercises 7.30–7.32 (in the Special Section: Building Your Own Computer) guide you through the process of building an interpreter program.

1.8 History of C and C++

Java evolved from C++, which evolved from C, which evolved from BCPL and B. BCPL was developed in 1967 by Martin Richards as a language for writing operating-systems software and compilers. Ken Thompson modeled many features in his language B after their counterparts in BCPL, using B to create early versions of the UNIX operating system at Bell Laboratories in 1970.

C—originally implemented in 1972—was evolved from B by Dennis Ritchie at Bell Laboratories. It initially became widely known as the UNIX operating system's development language. Today, most of the code for general-purpose operating systems (e.g., those found in notebooks, desktops, workstations and small servers) is written in C or C++.

C++, an extension of C, was developed by Bjarne Stroustrup in the early 1980s at Bell Laboratories. C++ provides a number of features that "spruce up" the C language, but more important, it provides capabilities for *object-oriented programming* (discussed in more detail in Section 1.16 and throughout this book). C++ is a hybrid language—it's possible to program in either a C-like style, an object-oriented style or both.

Building software quickly, correctly and economically remains an elusive goal at a time when demands for new and more powerful software are soaring. *Objects*, or more precisely—as we'll see in Section 1.16—the classes objects come from, are essentially reusable software components. There are date objects, time objects, audio objects, video objects, automobile objects, people objects and so on. In fact, almost any noun can be represented as a software object in terms of **attributes** (e.g., name, color and size) and **behaviors** (e.g., calculating, moving and communicating). Software developers are discovering that using a modular, object-oriented design and implementation approach can make software-development groups much more productive than was possible with earlier popular techniques like structured programming. Object-oriented programs are often easier to understand, correct and modify. Java is the world's most widely used object-oriented programming language.

1.9 History of Java

The microprocessor revolution's most important contribution to date is that it made possible the development of personal computers, which now number more than a billion worldwide. Personal computers have profoundly affected people's lives and the ways organizations conduct and manage their business.

Microprocessors are having a profound impact in intelligent consumer-electronic devices. Recognizing this, Sun Microsystems in 1991 funded an internal corporate research project, which resulted in a C++-based language that its creator, James Gosling, called Oak after an oak tree outside his window at Sun. It was later discovered that there already was a computer language by that name. When a group of Sun people visited a local coffee shop, the name Java was suggested, and it stuck.

The research project ran into some difficulties. The marketplace for intelligent consumer-electronic devices was not developing as quickly as Sun had anticipated. By sheer good fortune, the web exploded in popularity in 1993, and Sun saw the potential of using Java to add **dynamic content,** such as interactivity and animations, to web pages. This breathed new life into the project.

Sun formally announced Java at an industry conference in May 1995. Java garnered the attention of the business community because of the phenomenal interest in the web. Java is now used to develop large-scale enterprise applications, to enhance the functionality of web servers (the computers that provide the content we see in our web browsers), to provide applications for consumer devices (e.g., cell phones, pagers and personal digital assistants) and for many other purposes.

1.10 Java Class Libraries

Java programs consist of pieces called **classes**. Classes include pieces called **methods** that perform tasks and return information when the tasks complete. You can create each piece you need to form your Java programs. However, most Java programmers take advantage of the rich collections of existing classes in the **Java class libraries**, which are also known as the **Java APIs (Application Programming Interfaces)**. Thus, there are really two aspects to learning the Java "world." The first is the Java language itself, so that you can program your own classes; the second is the classes in the extensive Java class libraries. Throughout this book we discuss many preexisting Java API classes. To download the Java API documentation, go to `java.sun.com/javase/downloads/`, scroll down to the **Additional Resources** section and click the **Download** button to the right of **Java SE 6 Documentation**.

Software Engineering Observation 1.1

Use a building-block approach to creating your programs. Avoid reinventing the wheel—use existing pieces wherever possible. This software reuse *is a key benefit of object-oriented programming.*

We include many **Software Engineering Observations** throughout the book to explain concepts that affect and improve the overall architecture and quality of software systems. We also highlight other kinds of tips, including:

- **Good Programming Practices** (to help you write programs that are clearer, more understandable, more maintainable and easier to test and **debug**—i.e., remove programming errors),

- **Common Programming Errors** (problems to watch out for and avoid),

- **Performance Tips** (techniques for writing programs that run faster and use less memory),

- **Portability Tips** (techniques to help you write programs that can run, with little or no modification, on a variety of computers—these tips also include general observations about how Java achieves its high degree of portability),

- **Error-Prevention Tips** (techniques for removing bugs from your programs and, more important, techniques for writing bug-free programs in the first place) and

- **Look-and-Feel Observations** (techniques to help you design the "look" and "feel" of your applications' user interfaces for appearance and ease of use).

Many of these are only guidelines. You'll, no doubt, develop your own preferred programming style.

Software Engineering Observation 1.2
When programming in Java, you'll typically use the following building blocks: classes and methods from class libraries, classes and methods you create yourself and classes and methods that others create and make available to you.

The advantage of creating your own classes and methods is that you know exactly how they work and you can examine the Java code. The disadvantage is the time-consuming and potentially complex effort that is required.

Performance Tip 1.1
Using Java API classes and methods instead of writing your own versions can improve program performance, because they are carefully written to perform efficiently. This technique also shortens program development time.

Portability Tip 1.1
Using classes and methods from the Java API instead of writing your own improves program portability, because they are included in every Java implementation.

1.11 Fortran, COBOL, Pascal and Ada

Hundreds of high-level languages have been developed, but only a few have achieved broad acceptance. **Fortran** (FORmula TRANslator) was developed by IBM Corporation in the mid-1950s to be used for scientific and engineering applications that require complex mathematical computations. Fortran is still widely used in engineering applications.

COBOL (COmmon Business Oriented Language) was developed in the late 1950s by computer manufacturers, the U.S. government and industrial computer users. COBOL is used for commercial applications that require precise and efficient manipulation of large amounts of data. Much business software is still programmed in COBOL.

During the 1960s, many large software-development efforts encountered severe difficulties. Software deliveries were typically late, costs greatly exceeded budgets and the finished products were unreliable. People began to realize that software development was a far more complex activity than they had imagined. Research in the 1960s resulted in the evolution of **structured programming**—a disciplined approach to writing programs that are clearer, easier to test and debug and easier to modify than large programs produced with previous techniques.

One of the more tangible results of this research was the development of the Pascal programming language by Professor Niklaus Wirth in 1971. Named after the seventeenth-century mathematician and philosopher Blaise Pascal, it was designed for teaching structured programming in academic environments and rapidly became the preferred programming language in most colleges.

The **Ada** programming language was developed under the sponsorship of the U.S. Department of Defense (DOD) during the 1970s and early 1980s. The DOD wanted a single language that would fill most of its needs. The Ada language was named after Lady

Ada Lovelace, daughter of the poet Lord Byron. Lady Lovelace is credited with writing the world's first computer program in the early 1800s (for the Analytical Engine mechanical computing device designed by Charles Babbage). One important capability of Ada, called **multitasking**, allows programmers to specify that many activities in a program are to occur in parallel. Java, through a technique called *multithreading* (which we discuss in Chapter 26), also enables programmers to write programs with parallel activities.

1.12 BASIC, Visual Basic, Visual C++, C# and .NET

The **BASIC** (Beginner's All-Purpose Symbolic Instruction Code) programming language was developed in the mid-1960s at Dartmouth College as a means of writing simple programs. BASIC's primary purpose was to familiarize novices with programming techniques.

Microsoft's **Visual Basic** language was introduced in the early 1990s to simplify the development of Microsoft Windows applications and is one of the world's most popular programming languages.

Microsoft's latest development tools are part of its corporatewide strategy for integrating the Internet and the web into computer applications. This strategy is implemented in Microsoft's **.NET platform**, which provides developers with the capabilities they need to create and run computer applications that can execute on computers distributed across the Internet. Microsoft's three primary programming languages are Visual Basic (based on the original BASIC), **Visual C++** (based on C++) and **C#** (based on C++ and Java, and developed expressly for the .NET platform). Developers using .NET can write software components in the language they are most familiar with, then form applications by combining those components with others written in any .NET language.

1.13 Typical Java Development Environment

We now explain the commonly used steps in creating and executing a Java application using a Java development environment (illustrated in Fig. 1.1).

Java programs normally go through five phases—edit, compile, load, verify and execute. We discuss these phases in the context of the Java SE Development Kit 6 (JDK6) from Sun Microsystems, Inc. You can download the most up-to-date JDK and its documentation from `java.sun.com/javase/downloads/`. *Carefully follow the installation instructions for the JDK provided in the* Before You Begin *section of this book to ensure that you set up your computer properly to compile and execute Java programs.* You may also want to visit Sun's New to Java Center at:

```
java.sun.com/new2java/
```

[*Note:* This website provides installation instructions for Windows, Linux and Mac OS X. If you are not using one of these operating systems, refer to the documentation for your system's Java environment or ask your instructor how to accomplish these tasks based on your computer's operating system. If you encounter a problem with this link or any others referenced in this book, please check `www.deitel.com/books/jhtp8/` for errata and please notify us by e-mail at `deitel@deitel.com`.]

Phase 1: Creating a Program
Phase 1 consists of editing a file with an **editor program** (normally known simply as an **editor**). You type a Java program (typically referred to as **source code**) using the editor,

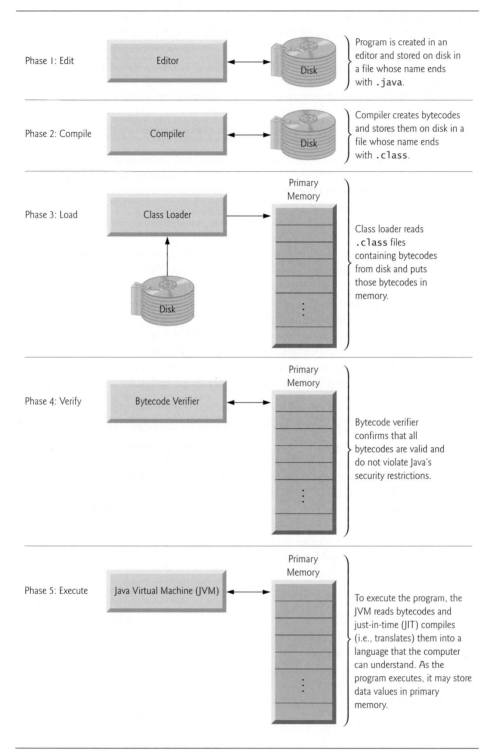

Fig. 1.1 | Typical Java development environment.

make any necessary corrections and save the program on a secondary storage device, such as your hard drive. A file name ending with the **.java extension** indicates that the file contains Java source code. We assume that you know how to edit a file.

Two editors widely used on Linux systems are vi and emacs. On Windows, Notepad will suffice. Many freeware and shareware editors are also available online, including Edit-Plus (www.editplus.com), TextPad (www.textpad.com) and jEdit (www.jedit.org).

For organizations that develop substantial information systems, **integrated development environments (IDEs)** are available from many major software suppliers. IDEs provide tools that support the software-development process, including editors for writing and editing programs and debuggers for locating **logic errors**—errors that cause programs to execute incorrectly. Popular IDEs include Eclipse (www.eclipse.org), NetBeans (www.netbeans.org), JBuilder (www.codegear.com), JCreator (www.jcreator.com), BlueJ (www.bluej.org) and jGRASP (www.jgrasp.org).

Phase 2: Compiling a Java Program into Bytecodes
In Phase 2, you use the command **javac** (the **Java compiler**) to **compile** a program. For example, to compile a program called Welcome.java, you'd type

```
javac Welcome.java
```

in the command window of your system (i.e., the **Command Prompt** in Windows, the **shell prompt** in Linux or the **Terminal application** in Mac OS X). If the program compiles, the compiler produces a **.class** file called Welcome.class that contains the compiled version of the program.

The Java compiler translates Java source code into **bytecodes** that represent the tasks to execute in the execution phase (Phase 5). Bytecodes are executed by the **Java Virtual Machine (JVM)**—a part of the JDK and the foundation of the Java platform. A **virtual machine (VM)** is a software application that simulates a computer but hides the underlying operating system and hardware from the programs that interact with it. If the same VM is implemented on many computer platforms, applications that it executes can be used on all those platforms. The JVM is one of the most widely used virtual machines. Microsoft's .NET uses a similar virtual-machine architecture.

Unlike machine language, which is dependent on specific computer hardware, bytecodes are platform independent—they do not depend on a particular hardware platform. So, Java's bytecodes are **portable**—without recompiling the source code, the same bytecodes can execute on any platform containing a JVM that understands the version of Java in which the bytecodes were compiled. The JVM is invoked by the **java** command. For example, to execute a Java application called Welcome, you'd type the command

```
java Welcome
```

in a command window to invoke the JVM, which would then initiate the steps necessary to execute the application. This begins Phase 3.

Phase 3: Loading a Program into Memory
In Phase 3, the JVM places the program in memory to execute it—this is known as **loading**. The JVM's **class loader** takes the .class files containing the program's bytecodes and transfers them to primary memory. The class loader also loads any of the .class files provided by Java that your program uses. The .class files can be loaded from a disk on your system or over a network (e.g., your local college or company network, or the Internet).

Phase 4: Bytecode Verification

In Phase 4, as the classes are loaded, the **bytecode verifier** examines their bytecodes to ensure that they are valid and do not violate Java's security restrictions. Java enforces strong security to make sure that Java programs arriving over the network do not damage your files or your system (as computer viruses and worms might).

Phase 5: Execution

In Phase 5, the JVM executes the program's bytecodes, thus performing the actions specified by the program. In early Java versions, the JVM was simply an interpreter for Java bytecodes. This caused most Java programs to execute slowly, because the JVM would interpret and execute one bytecode at a time. Today's JVMs typically execute bytecodes using a combination of interpretation and so-called **just-in-time (JIT) compilation**. In this process, the JVM analyzes the bytecodes as they are interpreted, searching for **hot spots**—parts of the bytecodes that execute frequently. For these parts, a **just-in-time (JIT) compiler**—known as the **Java HotSpot compiler**—translates the bytecodes into the underlying computer's machine language. When the JVM encounters these compiled parts again, the faster machine-language code executes. Thus Java programs actually go through two compilation phases—one in which source code is translated into bytecodes (for portability across JVMs on different computer platforms) and a second in which, during execution, the bytecodes are translated into machine language for the actual computer on which the program executes.

Problems That May Occur at Execution Time

Programs might not work on the first try. Each of the preceding phases can fail because of various errors that we'll discuss throughout this book. For example, an executing program might try to divide by zero (an illegal operation for whole-number arithmetic in Java). This would cause the Java program to display an error message. If this occurred, you'd have to return to the edit phase, make the necessary corrections and proceed through the remaining phases again to determine that the corrections fixed the problem(s). [*Note:* Most programs in Java input or output data. When we say that a program displays a message, we normally mean that it displays that message on your computer's screen. Messages and other data may be output to other devices, such as disks and hardcopy printers, or even to a network for transmission to other computers.]

Common Programming Error 1.1

*Errors such as division by zero occur as a program runs, so they are called **runtime errors** or **execution-time errors**. Fatal runtime errors cause programs to terminate immediately without having successfully performed their jobs. Nonfatal runtime errors allow programs to run to completion, often producing incorrect results.*

1.14 Notes about Java and *Java How to Program, Eighth Edition*

Java is a powerful programming language. Experienced programmers sometimes take pride in creating weird, contorted, convoluted usage of a language. This is a poor programming practice. It makes programs more difficult to read, more likely to behave strangely, more difficult to test and debug, and more difficult to adapt to changing requirements. This book stresses *clarity.* The following is our first Good Programming Practice tip.

Good Programming Practice 1.1

Write your Java programs in a simple and straightforward manner. This is sometimes referred to as KIS ("keep it simple"). Do not "stretch" the language by trying bizarre usages.

You've heard that Java is a portable language and that programs written in Java can run on many different computers. In general, *portability is an elusive goal.*

Portability Tip 1.2

Although it's easier to write portable programs in Java than in most other programming languages, differences between compilers, JVMs and computers can make portability difficult to achieve. Simply writing programs in Java does not guarantee portability.

Error-Prevention Tip 1.1

Always test your Java programs on all systems on which you intend to run them, to ensure that they'll work correctly for their intended audiences.

You can find a web-based version of the Java API documentation at `java.sun.com/javase/6/docs/api/index.html`, or you can download this documentation to your own computer from `java.sun.com/javase/downloads/`. For additional technical details on many aspects of Java development, visit `java.sun.com/reference/docs/index.html`.

Good Programming Practice 1.2

Read the documentation for the version of Java you're using. Refer to it frequently to be sure you're aware of the rich collection of Java features and are using them correctly.

1.15 Test-Driving a Java Application

In this section, you'll run and interact with your first Java application. You'll begin by running an ATM application that simulates the transactions that take place when you use an ATM machine (e.g., withdrawing money, making deposits and checking your account balances). You'll learn how to build this application in the optional, object-oriented case study included in Chapters 12–13. Figure 1.10 at the end of this section suggests other interesting applications that you may also want to test-drive. For the purpose of this section, we assume you're running Microsoft Windows.[1]

In the following steps, you'll run the application and perform various transactions. The elements and functionality you see here are typical of what you'll learn to program in this book. [*Note:* We use fonts to distinguish between features you see on a screen (e.g., the **Command Prompt**) and elements that are not directly related to a screen. Our convention is to emphasize screen features like titles and menus (e.g., the **File** menu) in a semibold **sans-serif Helvetica** font and to emphasize nonscreen elements, such as file names or input (e.g., `ProgramName.java`) in a sans-serif `Lucida` font. As you've already noticed, the defining occurrence of each key term in the text is set in **bold maroon**. In the figures in this section, we highlight in yellow the user input required by each step and point out significant parts of the application. To make these features more visible, we've changed the background color of the **Command Prompt** windows to white and the foreground color to black.]

---

1. At `www.deitel.com/books/jhtp8/`, we provide a Linux version of this test-drive. We also provide links to videos that help you get started with several popular integrated development environments (IDEs), including Eclipse and NetBeans.

1. ***Checking your setup.*** Read the *Before You Begin* section of the book to confirm that you've set up Java properly on your computer and that you've copied the book's examples to your hard drive.

2. ***Locating the completed application.*** Open a **Command Prompt** window. This can be done by selecting **Start > All Programs > Accessories > Command Prompt**. Change to the ATM application directory by typing cd C:\examples\ch01\ATM, then press *Enter* (Fig. 1.2). The command cd is used to change directories.

Fig. 1.2 | Opening a **Command Prompt** and changing directories.

3. ***Running the ATM application.*** Type the command java ATMCaseStudy (Fig. 1.3) and press *Enter*. Recall that the java command, followed by the name of the application's .class file (in this case, ATMCaseStudy), executes the application. Specifying the .class extension when using the java command results in an error. [*Note:* Java commands are case sensitive. It's important to type the name of this application with a capital A, T and M in "ATM," a capital C in "Case" and a capital S in "Study." Otherwise, the application will not execute.] If you receive the error message, "Exception in thread "main" java.lang.NoClass-DefFoundError: ATMCaseStudy," your system has a CLASSPATH problem. Please refer to the *Before You Begin* section of the book for instructions to help you fix this problem.

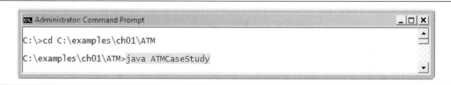

Fig. 1.3 | Using the java command to execute the ATM application.

4. ***Entering an account number.*** When the application first executes, it displays a "Welcome!" greeting and prompts you for an account number. Type 12345 at the "Please enter your account number:" prompt (Fig. 1.4) and press *Enter*.

5. ***Entering a PIN.*** Once a valid account number is entered, the application displays the prompt "Enter your PIN:". Type "54321" as your valid PIN (Personal Identification Number) and press *Enter*. The ATM main menu containing a list of options will be displayed (Fig. 1.5).

6. ***Viewing the account balance.*** Select option 1, "View my balance", from the ATM menu (Fig. 1.6). The application then displays two numbers—the Avail-

ATM welcome message   Enter account number prompt

```
Administrator: Command Prompt - java ATMCaseStudy        _ □ ×
C:\examples\ch01\ATM>java ATMCaseStudy
Welcome!
Please enter your account number: 12345
```

Fig. 1.4 | Prompting the user for an account number.

Enter valid PIN   ATM main menu

```
Administrator: Command Prompt - java ATMCaseStudy        _ □ ×
Welcome!

Please enter your account number: 12345

Enter your PIN: 54321

Main menu:
1 - View my balance
2 - Withdraw cash
3 - Deposit funds
4 - Exit

Enter a choice:
```

Fig. 1.5 | Entering a valid PIN number and displaying the ATM application's main menu.

able balance ($1000.00) and the Total balance ($1200.00). The available balance is the maximum amount of money in your account which is available for withdrawal at a given time. In some cases, certain funds, such as recent deposits, are not immediately available for the user to withdraw, so the available balance may be less than the total balance, as it is here. After the account-balance information is shown, the application's main menu is displayed again.

Account-balance information

```
Administrator: Command Prompt - java ATMCaseStudy        _ □ ×
Enter a choice: 1

Balance Information:
 - Available balance: $1,000.00
 - Total balance:     $1,200.00

Main menu:
1 - View my balance
2 - Withdraw cash
3 - Deposit funds
4 - Exit

Enter a choice:
```

Fig. 1.6 | ATM application displaying user account-balance information.

7. *Withdrawing money from the account.* Select option 2, "Withdraw cash", from the application menu. You're then presented (Fig. 1.7) with a list of dollar

amounts (e.g., 20, 40, 60, 100 and 200). You are also given the option to cancel the transaction and return to the main menu. Withdraw $100 by selecting option 4. The application displays "Please take your cash now." and returns to the main menu. [*Note:* Unfortunately, this application only *simulates* the behavior of a real ATM and thus does not actually dispense money.]

ATM withdrawal menu

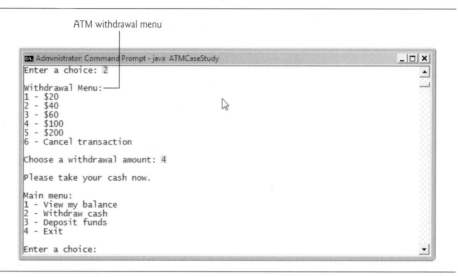

Fig. 1.7 | Withdrawing money from the account and returning to the main menu.

8. *Confirming that the account information has been updated.* From the main menu, select option 1 again to view your current account balance (Fig. 1.8). Note that both the available balance and the total balance have been updated to reflect your withdrawal transaction.

Confirming updated account-balance
information after withdrawal transaction

Fig. 1.8 | Checking the new balance.

9. *Ending the transaction.* To end your current ATM session, select option 4, "Exit" from the main menu (Fig. 1.9). The ATM will exit the system and display a good-

bye message to the user. The application will then return to its original prompt, asking for the next user's account number.

ATM goodbye message   Account-number prompt for next user

Fig. 1.9 | Ending an ATM transaction session.

10. ***Exiting the ATM application and closing the* Command Prompt *window.*** Most applications provide an option to exit and return to the **Command Prompt** directory from which the application was run. A real ATM does not provide a user with the option to turn off the ATM machine. Rather, when a user has completed all desired transactions and chosen the menu option to exit, the ATM resets itself and displays a prompt for the next user's account number. As Fig. 1.9 illustrates, the ATM application here behaves similarly. Choosing the menu option to exit ends only the current user's ATM session, not the entire ATM application. To actually exit the ATM application, click the close (**x**) button in the upper-right corner of the **Command Prompt** window. Closing the window causes the running application to terminate.

Java How to Program, 8/e *Applications to Test-Drive*
Figure 1.10 lists a few of the hundreds of applications found in the book's examples and exercises. These programs introduce many of the powerful and fun features of Java. Run these programs to see more of the types of applications you'll learn how to build in this book. The examples folder for this chapter contains all the files required to run each application. Simply type the commands listed in Fig. 1.10 in a **Command Prompt** window.

Application name	Chapter location	Commands to run
Tic-Tac-Toe	Chapter 8	`cd C:\examples\ch01\Tic-Tac-Toe` `java TicTacToeTest`
Guessing Game	Chapter 14	`cd C:\examples\ch01\GuessGame` `java GuessGame`
Logo Animator	Chapter 24	`cd C:\examples\ch01\LogoAnimator` `java LogoAnimator`
Bouncing Ball	Chapter 26	`cd C:\examples\ch01\BouncingBall` `java BouncingBall`

Fig. 1.10 | Additional *Java How to Program, 8/e,* applications to test-drive.

1.16 Software Engineering Case Study: Introduction to Object Technology and the UML

Now we begin our early introduction to object orientation, a natural way of thinking about the world and writing computer programs. Chapters 12–13 present a carefully paced introduction to object-oriented design. Our goal here is to help you develop an object-oriented way of thinking and to introduce you to the **Unified Modeling Language™** (**UML™**)—a graphical language that allows people who design software systems to use an industry-standard notation to represent them.

In this only required section, we introduce object-oriented concepts and terminology. The optional sections in Chapters 12–13 present an object-oriented design and implementation of the software for a simple automated teller machine (ATM). The Software Engineering Case Study Sections 12.2–12.7

- analyze a typical requirements document that describes a software system (the ATM) to be built
- determine the objects required to implement that system
- determine the attributes the objects will have
- determine the behaviors these objects will exhibit
- specify how the objects interact with one another to meet the system requirements.

Sections 13.2–13.3 modify and enhance the design presented in Sections 12.2–12.7. Section 13.4 contains a complete, working Java implementation of the object-oriented ATM software system.

You'll experience a concise, yet solid introduction to object-oriented design with the UML. Also, you'll sharpen your code-reading skills by touring the complete, carefully written and well-documented Java implementation of the ATM in Section 13.4.

Basic Object-Technology Concepts

We begin our introduction to object orientation with some key terminology. Everywhere you look in the real world you see **objects**—people, animals, plants, cars, planes, buildings, computers and so on. Humans think in terms of objects. Telephones, houses, traffic lights, microwave ovens and water coolers are just a few more objects. Computer programs, such as the Java programs you'll read in this book and the ones you'll write, are composed of lots of interacting software objects.

We sometimes divide objects into two categories: animate and inanimate. Animate objects are "alive" in some sense—they move around and do things. Inanimate objects, on the other hand, do not move on their own. Objects of both types, however, have some things in common. They all have **attributes** (e.g., size, shape, color and weight), and they all exhibit **behaviors** (e.g., a ball rolls, bounces, inflates and deflates; a baby cries, sleeps, crawls, walks and blinks; a car accelerates, brakes and turns; a towel absorbs water). We'll study the kinds of attributes and behaviors that software objects have.

Humans learn about existing objects by studying their attributes and observing their behaviors. Different objects can have similar attributes and can exhibit similar behaviors. Comparisons can be made, for example, between babies and adults and between humans and chimpanzees.

Object-oriented design (OOD) models software in terms similar to those that people use to describe real-world objects. It takes advantage of **class** relationships, where objects of a certain class, such as a class of vehicles, have the same characteristics—cars, trucks, little red wagons and roller skates have much in common. OOD also takes advantage of **inheritance** relationships, where new classes of objects are derived by absorbing characteristics of existing classes and adding unique characteristics of their own. An object of class "convertible" certainly has the characteristics of the more general class "automobile," but more specifically, the roof goes up and down.

Object-oriented design provides a natural and intuitive way to view the software design process—namely, modeling objects by their attributes and behaviors, just as we describe real-world objects. OOD also models communication between objects. Just as people send messages to one another (e.g., a sergeant commands a soldier to stand at attention), objects also communicate via messages. A bank-account object may receive a message to decrease its balance by a certain amount because the customer has withdrawn that amount of money.

OOD **encapsulates** (i.e., wraps) attributes and **operations** (behaviors) into objects—an object's attributes and operations are intimately tied together. Objects have the property of **information hiding**. This means that objects may know how to communicate with one another across well-defined **interfaces**, but normally they are not allowed to know how other objects are implemented—implementation details are hidden within the objects themselves. We can drive a car effectively, for instance, without knowing the details of how engines, transmissions, brakes and exhaust systems work internally—as long as we know how to use the accelerator pedal, the brake pedal, the wheel and so on. Information hiding, as we'll see, is crucial to good software engineering.

Languages like Java are **object oriented**. Programming in such a language, called **object-oriented programming (OOP)**, allows you to implement an object-oriented design as a working system. Languages like C, on the other hand, are **procedural**, so programming tends to be **action oriented**. In C, the unit of programming is the **function**. Groups of actions that perform some common task are formed into functions, and functions are grouped to form programs. In Java, the unit of programming is the class from which objects are eventually **instantiated** (created). Java classes contain **methods** (which implement operations and are similar to functions in C) as well as **fields** (which implement attributes).

Java programmers concentrate on creating classes. Each class contains fields and the set of methods that manipulate the fields and provide services to **clients** (i.e., other classes that use the class). The programmer uses existing classes as the building blocks for constructing new classes.

Classes are to objects as blueprints are to houses. Just as we can build many houses from one blueprint, we can instantiate (create) many objects from one class. You cannot cook meals in the kitchen of a blueprint; you can cook meals in the kitchen of a house.

Classes can have relationships with other classes. For example, in an object-oriented design of a bank, the "bank teller" class needs to relate to the "customer" class, the "cash drawer" class, the "safe" class, and so on. These relationships are called **associations**.

Packaging software as classes makes it possible for future software systems to **reuse** the classes. Groups of related classes are often packaged as reusable **components**. Just as realtors often say that the three most important factors affecting the price of real estate are "location, location and location," people in the software community often say that the three most important factors affecting the future of software development are "reuse, reuse and reuse." Reuse of existing classes when building new classes and programs saves time and effort. Reuse also helps you build more reliable and effective systems, because existing classes and components often have gone through extensive testing, debugging and performance tuning.

With object technology, you can build much of the software you'll need by combining classes, just as automobile manufacturers combine interchangeable parts. Each new class you create will have the potential to become a "software asset" that you and other programmers can use to speed and enhance the quality of future software-development efforts.

Introduction to Object-Oriented Analysis and Design (OOAD)

Soon you'll be writing programs in Java. How will you create the code for your programs? Perhaps, like many programmers, you'll simply turn on your computer and start typing. This approach may work for small programs (like the ones we present in the early chapters of the book), but what if you were asked to create a software system to control thousands of automated teller machines for a major bank? Or suppose you were asked to work on a team of 1,000 software developers building the next U.S. air traffic control system? For projects so large and complex, you should not simply sit down and start writing programs.

To create the best solutions, you should follow a detailed process for **analyzing** your project's **requirements** (i.e., determining *what* the system is supposed to do) and developing a **design** that satisfies them (i.e., deciding *how* the system should do it). Ideally, you'd go through this process and carefully review the design (or have your design reviewed by other software professionals) before writing any code. If this process involves analyzing and designing your system from an object-oriented point of view, it's called an **object-oriented analysis and design (OOAD) process**. Experienced programmers know that analysis and design can save many hours by helping them to avoid an ill-planned system-development approach that has to be abandoned part way through its implementation, possibly wasting considerable time, money and effort.

OOAD is the generic term for the process of analyzing a problem and developing an approach for solving it. Small problems like the ones discussed in these first few chapters do not require an exhaustive OOAD process. It may be sufficient to write **pseudocode** before we begin writing Java code. Pseudocode is an informal means of expressing program logic. It's not actually a programming language, but we can use it as a kind of outline to guide us as we write our code. We introduce pseudocode in Chapter 4.

As problems and the groups of people solving them increase in size, the methods of OOAD become more appropriate than pseudocode. Ideally, a group should agree on a strictly defined process for solving its problem and a uniform way of communicating the results of that process to one another. Although many different OOAD processes exist, a single graphical language for communicating the results of *any* OOAD process has come into wide use. This language, known as the Unified Modeling Language (UML), was developed in the mid-1990s under the initial direction of three software methodologists—Grady Booch, James Rumbaugh and Ivar Jacobson.

History of the UML

In the 1980s, increasing numbers of organizations began using OOP to build their applications, and a need developed for a standard OOAD process. Many methodologists—including Booch, Rumbaugh and Jacobson—individually produced and promoted separate processes to satisfy this need. Each process had its own notation, or "language" (in the form of graphical diagrams), to convey the results of analysis and design.

By the early 1990s, different organizations, and even divisions within the same organization, were using their own unique processes and notations. At the same time, these organizations also wanted to use software tools that would support their particular processes. Software vendors found it difficult and costly to provide tools for so many processes. A standard notation and standard processes were needed.

In 1994, James Rumbaugh joined Grady Booch at Rational Software Corporation (now a division of IBM), and the two began working to unify their popular processes. They soon were joined by Ivar Jacobson. In 1996, the group released early versions of the UML to the software engineering community and requested feedback. Around the same time, an organization known as the **Object Management Group™ (OMG™)** invited submissions for a common modeling language. The OMG (`www.omg.org`) is a nonprofit organization that promotes the standardization of object-oriented technologies by issuing guidelines and specifications, such as the UML. Several corporations—among them HP, IBM, Microsoft, Oracle and Rational Software—had already recognized the need for a common modeling language. In response to the OMG's request for proposals, these companies formed **UML Partners**—the consortium that developed the UML version 1.1 and submitted it to the OMG. The OMG accepted the proposal and, in 1997, assumed responsibility for the continuing maintenance and revision of the UML. We present UML 2 terminology and notation throughout this book.

What Is the UML?

The UML is now the most widely used graphical representation scheme for modeling object-oriented systems. It has indeed unified the various popular notational schemes. Those who design systems use the language (in the form of diagrams) to model their systems.

An attractive feature of the UML is its flexibility. It is **extensible** (i.e., capable of being enhanced with new features) and is independent of any particular OOAD process. UML modelers are free to use various processes in designing systems, but all developers can now express their designs with one standard set of graphical notations.

The UML is a complex, feature-rich graphical language. We present our first UML diagrams in Chapters 3 and 4. In our (optional) ATM Software Engineering Case Study in Chapters 12–13 we present a simple, concise subset of the UML's features. We then use this subset to guide you through a first design experience with the UML, intended for novice object-oriented programmers in first- or second-semester programming courses. For more information about the UML, visit our UML Resource Center at `www.deitel.com/UML/`.

Section 1.16 Self-Review Exercises

1.1 List three examples of real-world objects that we did not mention. For each object, list several attributes and behaviors.

1.2 Pseudocode is _____.
 a) another term for OOAD
 b) a programming language used to display UML diagrams
 c) an informal means of expressing program logic
 d) a graphical representation scheme for modeling object-oriented systems

1.3 The UML is used primarily to _____.
 a) test object-oriented systems
 b) design object-oriented systems
 c) implement object-oriented systems
 d) Both a and b

Answers to Section 1.16 Self-Review Exercises

1.1 [*Note:* Answers may vary.] a) A television's attributes include the size of the screen, the number of colors it can display, its current channel and its current volume. A television turns on and off, changes channels, displays video and plays sounds. b) A coffee maker's attributes include the maximum volume of water it can hold, the time required to brew a pot of coffee and the temperature of the heating plate under the coffee pot. A coffee maker turns on and off, brews coffee and heats coffee. c) A turtle's attributes include its age, the size of its shell and its weight. A turtle walks, retreats into its shell, emerges from its shell and eats vegetation.

1.2   c.

1.3   b.

1.17 Web 2.0

The web literally exploded in the mid-to-late 1990s, but the "dot com" economic bust brought hard times in the early 2000s. The resurgence that began in 2004 or so has been named **Web 2.0**. The first Web 2.0 Conference was held in 2004. A year into its life, the term "Web 2.0" garnered about 10 million hits on the **Google** search engine, growing to 60 million a year later. Google is widely regarded as the signature company of Web 2.0. Some others are Craigslist (free classified listings), Flickr (photo sharing), del.icio.us (social bookmarking), YouTube (video sharing), MySpace and FaceBook (social networking), Salesforce (business software offered as online services), Second Life (a virtual world), Skype (Internet telephony) and Wikipedia (a free online encyclopedia).

At Deitel & Associates, we launched our Web 2.0-based **Internet Business Initiative** in 2005. We research the key technologies of Web 2.0 and use them to build Internet businesses. We sharing our research in the form of Resource Centers at www.deitel.com/resourcecenters.html. Each week, we announce the latest Resource Centers in our newsletter, the *Deitel® Buzz Online* (www.deitel.com/newsletter/subscribe.html). Each lists many links to mostly free content and software on the Internet.

We include in this book a substantial treatment of **web services** (Chapter 31) and introduce the new applications-development methodology of **mashups** in which you can rapidly develop powerful and intriguing applications by combining complementary web services and other forms of information feeds of two or more organizations. A popular mashup is www.housingmaps.com, which combines the real estate listings provided by www.craigslist.org with the mapping capabilities of **Google Maps** to offer maps that show the locations of apartments for rent in a given area.

Ajax is one of the premier Web 2.0 technologies. Though the term's use exploded in 2005, it just names a group of technologies and programming techniques that have been in use since the late 1990s. Ajax helps Internet-based applications perform like desktop applications—a difficult task, given that such applications suffer transmission delays as data is shuttled back and forth between your computer and other computers on the Internet. Using Ajax, applications like Google Maps have achieved excellent performance and approach the look-and-feel of desktop applications. Although we don't discuss "raw" Ajax programming (which is quite complex) in this text, we do show in Chapter 30 how to build Ajax-enabled applications using JavaServer Faces (JSF) Ajax-enabled components.

Blogs are websites (currently 100+ million of them) that are like online diaries, with the most recent entries appearing first. Bloggers quickly post their opinions about news, product releases, political candidates, controversial issues, and just about everything else.

The collection of all blogs and the blogging community is called the **blogosphere** and is becoming increasingly influential. **Technorati** and **Google Blog Search** are two of the popular blog search engines.

RSS feeds enable sites to push information to subscribers. A common use of RSS feeds is to deliver the latest blog postings to people who subscribe to blogs. The RSS information flows on the Internet are growing exponentially.

Web 3.0 is another name for the next generation of the web, also called the **Semantic Web**. Web 1.0 was almost purely HTML-based. Web 2.0 is making increasing use of XML, especially in technologies like RSS feeds and web services. Web 3.0 will make deep use of XML, creating a "web of meaning." If you're a student looking for a great research paper or thesis topic, or an entrepreneur looking for business opportunities, check out our Web 3.0 Resource Center.

To follow the latest developments in Web 2.0, read `www.techcrunch.com` and `www.slashdot.org` and check out the growing list of Internet- and web-related Resource Centers at `www.deitel.com/resourcecenters.html`.

1.18 Software Technologies

In this section, we discuss a number of software engineering buzzwords that you'll hear in the software-development community. We've created Resource Centers on most of these topics, with more on the way.

Agile Software Development is a set of methodologies that try to get software implemented quickly using fewer resources than previous methodologies. Check out the Agile Alliance (`www.agilealliance.org`) and the Agile Manifesto (`www.agilemanifesto.org`).

Refactoring involves reworking code to make it clearer and easier to maintain while preserving its functionality. It's widely employed with agile development methodologies. Many refactoring tools are available to do major portions of the reworking automatically.

Design patterns are proven architectures for constructing flexible and maintainable object-oriented software (see Appendix Q). The field of design patterns tries to enumerate those recurring patterns, encouraging software designers to reuse them to develop better-quality software with less time, money and effort.

Game programming is a fun and challenging career for software developers. The computer game business is already larger than the first-run movie business. College courses and even majors are now devoted to the sophisticated techniques used in game programming. Check out our Game Programming and Programming Projects Resource Centers.

Open-source software is a software-development style that departs from the proprietary development that dominated software's early years. With open-source development, individuals and companies contribute their efforts in developing, maintaining and evolving software in exchange for the right to use that software for their own purposes, typically at no charge. Open-source code generally gets scrutinized by a much larger audience than proprietary software, so errors often get removed faster. Open-source also encourages more innovation. Sun has open sourced the Sun implementation of the Java Development Kit. Some organizations you'll hear a lot about in the open-source community are the Eclipse Foundation (the Eclipse IDE is popular for Java software development), the Mozilla Foundation (creators of the Firefox web browser), the Apache Software Foundation (creators of the Apache web server) and SourceForge (which provides the tools for managing open-source projects and currently has over 100,000 open-source projects under development).

Linux is an open-source operating system and one of the greatest successes of the open-source movement. **MySQL** is an open-source database management system. **PHP** is the most popular open-source server-side Internet "scripting" language for developing Internet-based applications. **LAMP** is an acronym for the set of open-source technologies that many developers used to build web applications—it stands for Linux, Apache, MySQL and PHP (or Perl or Python—two other languages used for similar purposes).

Ruby on Rails combines the scripting language Ruby with the Rails web application framework developed by the company 37Signals. Their book, *Getting Real*, is a must read for today's web application developers; read it free at `gettingreal.37signals.com/toc.php`. Many Ruby on Rails developers have reported significant productivity gains over using other languages when developing database-intensive web applications.

Software has generally been viewed as a product; most software still is offered this way. If you want to run an application, you buy a software package from a software vendor. You then install that software on your computer and run it as needed. As new versions of the software appear, you upgrade your software, often at significant expense. This process can become cumbersome for organizations with tens of thousands of systems that must be maintained on a diverse array of computer equipment. With **Software as a Service (SAAS)** the software runs on servers elsewhere on the Internet. When that server is updated, all clients worldwide see the new capabilities; no local installation is needed. You access the service through a browser. Browsers are quite portable, so you can run the same applications on different kinds of computers from anywhere in the world. Salesforce.com, Google, and Microsoft's Office Live and Windows Live all offer SAAS.

1.19 Wrap-Up

This chapter introduced basic hardware, software and communications concepts and basic object-technology concepts, including classes, objects, attributes, behaviors, encapsulation and inheritance. We discussed the different types of programming languages and which specific languages are most widely used. You learned the steps for creating and executing a Java application using Sun's JDK 6. The chapter explored the history of the Internet and the World Wide Web up to the Web 2.0 phenomenon, and Java's role in developing distributed client/server applications for the Internet and the web. You also learned about the history and purpose of the UML—the industry-standard graphical language for modeling object-oriented software systems. You "test-drove" one or more sample Java applications similar to those you'll learn to program in this book. We discussed a number of important recent software technologies.

In Chapter 2, you'll create your first Java applications. You'll see examples that show how programs display messages and obtain information from the user for processing. You'll use Java's primitive data types and arithmetic operators. You'll use Java's equality and relational operators to write simple decision-making statements. We'll analyze and explain each example to help you ease into Java programming.

1.20 Web Resources

This section lists many sites that will be useful to you as you learn Java. The sites include Java resources, Java development tools for students and professionals, and our own websites where you can find downloads and resources associated with this book.

Deitel & Associates Websites

www.deitel.com
Contains updates, corrections and additional resources for all Deitel publications.

www.deitel.com/newsletter/subscribe.html
Subscribe to the free *Deitel® Buzz Online* e-mail newsletter to follow the Deitel & Associates publishing program, including updates and errata to this book.

www.deitel.com/books/jhtp8/
The Deitel & Associates site for *Java How to Program, Eighth Edition*. Here you'll find links to the book's examples and other resources.

Deitel Java and Related Resource Centers

www.deitel.com/Java/
Our Java Resource Center focuses on the enormous amount of Java free content available online. Start your search here for tools, integrated development environments (IDEs), resources, downloads, tutorials, documentation, books, e-books, journals, articles, blogs and more that will help you develop Java applications.

www.deitel.com/JavaSE6Mustang/
Our Java SE 6 (Mustang) Resource Center is your guide to the latest release of Java. The site includes the best resources we found online to help you get started with Java SE 6 development.

www.deitel.com/CodeSearchEngines/
Our Code Search Engines and Code Sites Resource Center includes resources developers use to find source code online.

www.deitel.com/ProgrammingProjects/
Our Programming Projects Resource Center is your online guide to great ideas for student programming projects.

Editors and Integrated Development Environments

www.eclipse.org
The Eclipse development environment can be used to develop code in any programming language. You can download the environment and several Java plug-ins to develop your Java programs.

www.netbeans.org
The NetBeans IDE is one of the most widely used, freely distributed Java development tools.

www.blueJ.org
BlueJ is a free tool designed to help teach object-oriented Java to new programmers.

www.jgrasp.org
jGRASP is a "lighter weight" integrated development environment that was developed at Auburn University. The tool also displays visual representations of Java programs to aid comprehension.

www.jcreator.com
JCreator is a popular Java IDE. JCreator Lite Edition is available as a free download. A 30-day trial version of JCreator Pro Edition is also available.

www.textpad.com
TextPad is an editor that also enables you to compile and run your Java programs.

www.editplus.com
EditPlus is an editor that can be configured to compile and run your Java programs.

www.jedit.org
jEdit is an editor that is written in Java and can be used with many programming languages.

Summary

Section 1.1 Introduction
- Java has become the language of choice for implementing Internet-based applications and software for devices that communicate over a network.
- Java Enterprise Edition (Java EE) is geared toward developing large-scale, distributed networking applications and web-based applications.
- Java Micro Edition (Java ME) is geared toward developing applications for small, memory-constrained devices, such as cell phones, pagers and PDAs.

Section 1.2 Computers: Hardware and Software
- A computer is a device that can perform computations and make logical decisions phenomenally faster than human beings can.
- Computers process data under the control of sets of instructions called computer programs. Programs guide computers through actions specified by people called computer programmers.
- A computer consists of various devices referred to as hardware. The programs that run on a computer are referred to as software.

Section 1.3 Computer Organization
- Virtually every computer may be envisioned as divided into six logical units or sections.
- The input unit obtains information from input devices and places this information at the disposal of the other units so that it can be processed.
- The output unit takes information that the computer has processed and places it on various output devices to make it available for use outside the computer.
- The memory unit is the rapid-access, relatively low-capacity "warehouse" section of the computer. It retains information that has been entered through the input unit, making it immediately available for processing when needed. It also retains processed information until it can be placed on output devices by the output unit.
- The arithmetic and logic unit (ALU) is responsible for performing calculations (such as addition, subtraction, multiplication and division) and making decisions.
- The central processing unit (CPU) coordinates and supervises the operation of the other sections. The CPU tells the input unit when information should be read into the memory unit, tells the ALU when information from the memory unit should be used in calculations and tells the output unit when to send information from the memory unit to certain output devices.
- Multiprocessors have multiple CPUs and, hence, can perform many operations simultaneously.
- A multi-core processor implements multiprocessing on a single integrated circuit chip—for example a dual-core processor has two CPUs and a quad-core processor has four CPUs.
- The secondary storage unit is the long-term, high-capacity "warehousing" section of the computer. Programs or data not actively being used by the other units normally are placed on secondary storage devices until they are again needed.

Section 1.4 Early Operating Systems
- Early computers could perform only one job or task at a time.
- Operating systems were developed to make using computers more convenient.
- Multiprogramming involves the simultaneous operation of many jobs.
- With timesharing, the computer runs a small portion of one user's job, then moves on to service the next user, perhaps providing service to each user several times per second.

Section 1.5 Personal, Distributed and Client/Server Computing
- In 1977, Apple Computer popularized personal computing.
- In 1981, IBM, the world's largest computer vendor, introduced the IBM Personal Computer, which quickly legitimized personal computing in business, industry and government.
- In distributed computing, instead of being performed only at a central computer, computing is distributed over networks to the sites where the organization's work is performed.
- Servers store data that may be used by client computers distributed throughout the network, hence the term client/server computing.
- Java has become widely used for writing software for computer networking and for distributed client/server applications.

Section 1.6 The Internet and the World Wide Web
- The Internet is accessible by more than a billion computers and computer-controlled devices.
- With the introduction of the World Wide Web the Internet has exploded into one of the world's premier communication mechanisms.

Section 1.7 Machine Languages, Assembly Languages and High-Level Languages
- Any computer can directly understand only its own machine language.
- Machine language is the "natural language" of a computer.
- Machine languages generally consist of strings of numbers (ultimately reduced to 1s and 0s) that instruct computers to perform their most elementary operations one at a time.
- Machine languages are machine dependent.
- Programmers began using Englishlike abbreviations to represent elementary operations. These abbreviations formed the basis of assembly languages.
- Translator programs called assemblers were developed to convert early assembly-language programs to machine language at computer speeds.
- To speed the programming process, high-level languages were developed in which single statements could be written to accomplish substantial tasks.
- Translator programs called compilers convert high-level language programs into machine language.
- High-level languages allow you to write instructions that look almost like everyday English and contain commonly used mathematical notations.
- Java is by far the most widely used high-level language.
- Compiling a high-level language program into machine language can take a considerable amount of computer time. Interpreter programs were developed to execute high-level language programs directly (without the delay of compilation), although slower than compiled programs run.

Section 1.8 History of C and C++
- Java evolved from C++, which evolved from C, which evolved from BCPL and B.
- The C language was developed by Dennis Ritchie at Bell Laboratories. It initially became widely known as the development language of the UNIX operating system.
- C++, an extension of C, was developed by Bjarne Stroustrup in the early 1980s at Bell Laboratories. C++ provides a number of features that "spruce up" the C language, and capabilities for object-oriented programming.

Section 1.9 History of Java
- Java is used to develop large-scale enterprise applications, to enhance the functionality of web servers, to provide applications for consumer devices and for many other purposes.

• Java programs consist of pieces called classes. Classes include pieces called methods that perform tasks and return information when the tasks are completed.

Section 1.10 Java Class Libraries
• Most Java programmers take advantage of the rich collections of existing classes in the Java class libraries, also known as the Java APIs (Application Programming Interfaces).

• The advantage of creating your own classes and methods is that you know how they work and can examine the code. The disadvantage is the time-consuming and potentially complex effort.

Section 1.11 Fortran, COBOL, Pascal and Ada
• Fortran (FORmula TRANslator) was developed by IBM Corporation in the mid-1950s for use in scientific and engineering applications that require complex mathematical computations.

• COBOL (COmmon Business Oriented Language) is used for commercial applications that require precise and efficient manipulation of large amounts of data.

• Research in the 1960s resulted in structured programming—an approach to writing programs that are clearer, and easier to test, debug and modify than those produced with earlier techniques.

• Pascal was designed for teaching structured programming in academic environments and rapidly became the preferred programming language in most colleges.

• The Ada programming language was developed under the sponsorship of the U.S. Department of Defense (DOD) to fill most of its needs. An Ada capability called multitasking allows programmers to specify that activities are to occur in parallel. Java, through a technique called *multithreading*, also enables programmers to write programs with parallel activities.

Section 1.12 BASIC, Visual Basic, Visual C++, C# and .NET
• BASIC was developed in the mid-1960s for writing simple programs.

• Microsoft's Visual Basic language simplifies the development of Windows applications.

• Microsoft's .NET platform integrates the Internet and the web into computer applications.

Section 1.13 Typical Java Development Environment
• Java programs normally go through five phases—edit, compile, load, verify and execute.

• Phase 1 consists of editing a file with an editor. You type a program using the editor, make corrections and save the program on a secondary storage device, such as your hard drive.

• A file name ending with the `.java` extension indicates that the file contains Java source code.

• Integrated development environments (IDEs) provide tools that support software development, including editors for writing and editing programs and debuggers for locating logic errors.

• In Phase 2, the programmer uses the command `javac` to compile a program.

• If a program compiles, the compiler produces a `.class` file that contains the compiled program.

• The Java compiler translates Java source code into bytecodes that represent the tasks to be executed. Bytecodes are executed by the Java Virtual Machine (JVM).

• In Phase 3, loading, the class loader takes the `.class` files containing the program's bytecodes and transfers them to primary memory.

• In Phase 4, as the classes are loaded, the bytecode verifier examines their bytecodes to ensure that they are valid and do not violate Java's security restrictions.

• In Phase 5, the JVM executes the program's bytecodes.

Section 1.14 Notes about Java and Java How to Program, Eighth Edition
• Portability is an elusive goal. Simply writing programs in Java does not guarantee portability.

Section 1.15 Test-Driving a Java Application
- In this section, you ran and interacted with your first Java application.

Section 1.16 Software Engineering Case Study: Introduction to Object Technology and the UML
- The Unified Modeling Language (UML) is a graphical language that allows people who build systems to represent their object-oriented designs in a common notation.
- Object-oriented design (OOD) models software components in terms of real-world objects.
- Objects have the property of information hiding—objects of one class are normally not allowed to know how objects of other classes are implemented.
- Object-oriented programming (OOP) implements object-oriented designs.
- Java programmers concentrate on creating their own user-defined types called classes. Each class contains data as well as methods that manipulate that data and provide services to clients.
- The data components of a class are attributes or fields; the operation components are methods.
- Classes can have relationships with other classes; these relationships are called associations.
- Packaging software as classes makes it possible for future software systems to reuse the classes.
- An instance of a class is called an object.
- The process of analyzing and designing a system from an object-oriented point of view is called object-oriented analysis and design (OOAD).

Section 1.17 Web 2.0
- The resurgence of the web that began in 2004 or so has been named Web 2.0.
- Mashups enable you to rapidly develop powerful and intriguing applications by combining complementary web services and other forms of information feeds of two or more organizations.
- Ajax helps Internet-based applications perform like desktop applications—a difficult task, given that such applications suffer transmission delays as data is shuttled back and forth between your computer and other computers on the Internet.
- Blogs are websites that are like online diaries, with the most recent entries appearing first.
- RSS feeds enable sites to push information to subscribers.
- Web 3.0 is another name for the next generation of the web, also called the Semantic Web. Web 3.0 will make deep use of XML, creating a "web of meaning."

Section 1.18 Software Technologies
- Agile Software Development is a set of methodologies that try to get software implemented quickly using fewer resources than previous methodologies.
- Refactoring involves reworking code to make it clearer and easier to maintain while preserving its functionality.
- Design patterns are proven architectures for constructing flexible and maintainable object-oriented software.
- Game programming is a fun and challenging career for software developers. College courses and even majors are devoted to the sophisticated software techniques used in game programming.
- With open-source development, individuals and companies contribute their efforts in developing, maintaining and evolving software in exchange for the right to use that software for their own purposes, typically at no charge. Open-source code generally gets scrutinized by a much larger audience than proprietary software, so errors often get removed faster. Open-source also encourages more innovation.

- Linux is an open-source operating system and one of the greatest successes of the open-source movement. MySQL is an open-source database management system. PHP is the most popular open-source server-side Internet "scripting" language for developing Internet-based applications. LAMP is an acronym for the set of open-source technologies that many developers used to build web applications—it stands for Linux, Apache, MySQL and PHP (or Perl or Python—two other languages used for similar purposes).

- Ruby on Rails combines the scripting language Ruby with the Rails web application framework developed by the company 37Signals. Many Ruby on Rails developers have reported productivity gains over using other languages when developing database-intensive web applications.

- With Software as a Service (SAAS) the software runs on servers elsewhere on the Internet. You access the service through a browser. Browsers are quite portable, so you can run the same applications on different kinds of computers from anywhere in the world.

Terminology

action oriented 21
Ada programming language 10
Agile Software Development 25
Ajax 24
analyzing a project's requirements 22
application programming interface (API) 9
arithmetic and logic unit (ALU) 4
assembler 7
assembly language 7
association 21
attribute of a class 8
attribute of an object 20
BASIC (Beginner's All-Purpose Symbolic Instruction Code) 11
batch processing 5
behavior of a class 8
behavior of an object 20
blogosphere 25
blogs 24
bytecode 13
bytecode verifier 14
C# programming language 11
central processing unit (CPU) 5
class 9, 21
.class file 13
class loader 13
client computer 6
client of a class 21
client/server computing 6
COBOL (COmmon Business Oriented Language) 10
Command Prompt 13
Common Programming Error 9
compile a program 13
compiler 7
component 21
computer 3

computer program 4
computer programmer 4
data 4
debug 9
design patterns 25
design process 22
distributed computing 6
dynamic content 9
editor 11
encapsulation 21
Error-Prevention Tip 9
execution-time error 14
extensible language 23
fatal error 14
field 21
Fortran (FORmula TRANslator) 10
function 21
Game programming 25
Good Programming Practices 9
Google 24
Google Blog Search 25
Google Maps 24
hardware 4
high-level language 7
hot spots in bytecode 14
information hiding 21
inheritance 21
input device 4
input unit 4
instantiate 21
integrated development environment 13
interface 21
Internet 6
Internet Business Initiative 24
Java applications programming interface (API) 9
Java class libraries 9

Self-Review Exercises

1.1   Fill in the blanks in each of the following statements:
    a) The company that popularized personal computing was _____.
    b) The computer that made personal computing legitimate in business and industry was the _____.

c) Computers process data under the control of sets of instructions called _____.

d) The key logical units of the computer are the _____, _____, _____, _____, _____ and _____.

e) The three types of languages discussed in the chapter are _____, _____ and _____.

f) The programs that translate high-level language programs into machine language are called _____.

g) The _____ allows computer users to locate and view multimedia-based documents on almost any subject over the Internet.

h) _____ allows a Java program to perform multiple activities in parallel.

1.2 Fill in the blanks in each of the following sentences about the Java environment:

a) The _____ command from the JDK executes a Java application.

b) The _____ command from the JDK compiles a Java program.

c) A Java program file must end with the _____ file extension.

d) When a Java program is compiled, the file produced by the compiler ends with the _____ file extension.

e) The file produced by the Java compiler contains _____ that are executed by the Java Virtual Machine.

1.3 Fill in the blanks in each of the following statements (based on Section 1.16):

a) Objects have the property of _____—although objects may know how to communicate with one another across well-defined interfaces, they normally are not allowed to know how other objects are implemented.

b) Java programmers concentrate on creating _____, which contain fields and the set of methods that manipulate those fields and provide services to clients.

c) Classes can have relationships called _____ with other classes.

d) The process of analyzing and designing a system from an object-oriented point of view is called _____.

e) OOD takes advantage of _____ relationships, where new classes of objects are derived by absorbing characteristics of existing classes, then adding unique characteristics of their own.

f) _____ is a graphical language that allows people who design software systems to use an industry-standard notation to represent them.

g) The size, shape, color and weight of an object are considered _____ of the object's class.

Answers to Self-Review Exercises

1.1 a) Apple. b) IBM Personal Computer. c) programs. d) input unit, output unit, memory unit, central processing unit, arithmetic and logic unit, secondary storage unit. e) machine languages, assembly languages, high-level languages. f) compilers. g) World Wide Web. h) Multithreading.

1.2 a) java. b) javac. c) .java. d) .class. e) bytecodes.

1.3 a) information hiding. b) classes. c) associations. d) object-oriented analysis and design (OOAD). e) inheritance. f) The Unified Modeling Language (UML). g) attributes.

Exercises

1.4 Categorize each of the following items as either hardware or software:

a) CPU

b) Java compiler

c) JVM

     d) input unit

     e) editor

1.5   What is the difference between fatal errors and nonfatal errors? Why might you prefer to experience a fatal rather than a nonfatal error?

1.6   Fill in the blanks in each of the following statements:

     a) Java programs normally go through five phases—_____, _____, _____, _____ and _____.

     b) A(n) _____ provides many tools that support the software-development process, such as editors for writing and editing programs, debuggers for locating logic errors in programs, and many other features.

     c) The command java invokes the _____, which executes Java programs.

     d) A(n) _____ is a software application that simulates a computer, but hides the underlying operating system and hardware from the programs that interact with it.

     e) A(n) _____ program can run on multiple platforms.

     f) The _____ takes the `.class` files containing the program's bytecodes and transfers them to primary memory.

     g) The _____ examines bytecodes to ensure that they are valid.

1.7   Explain the two compilation phases of Java programs.

1.8   You are probably wearing on your wrist one of the world's most common types of objects—a watch. Discuss how each of the following terms and concepts applies to the notion of a watch: object, attributes, behaviors, class, inheritance (consider, for example, an alarm clock), abstraction, modeling, messages, encapsulation, interface and information hiding.

Making a Difference

1.9   *(Test Drive: Carbon Footprint Calculator)* Some scientists believe that carbon emissions, especially from the burning of fossil fuels, contribute significantly to global warming and that this can be combatted if individuals take steps to limit their use of carbon-based fuels. Organizations and individuals are increasingly concerned about their "carbon footprints." Websites such as TerraPass

     `www.terrapass.com/carbon-footprint-calculator/`

and Carbon Footprint

     `www.carbonfootprint.com/calculator.aspx`

provide carbon footprint calculators. Test drive these calculators to determine your carbon footprint. Exercises in later chapters will ask you to program your own carbon footprint calculator. To prepare for this, research the formulas for calculating carbon footprints.

1.10   *(Test Drive: Body Mass Index Calculator)* By recent estimates, two-thirds of the people in the United States are overweight and about half of those are obese. This causes significant increases in illnesses such as diabetes and heart disease. To determine whether a person is overweight or obese, you can use a measure called the body mass index (BMI). The United States Department of Health and Human Services provides a BMI calculator at `www.nhlbisupport.com/bmi/`. Use it to calculate your own BMI. An exercise in Chapter 2 will ask you to program your own BMI calculator. To prepare for this, research the formulas for calculating BMI.

1.11   *(Attributes of Hybrid Vehicles)* In this chapter you learned the basics of classes. Now you'll begin "fleshing out" aspects of a class called "Hybrid Vehicle." Hybrid vehicles are becoming increasingly popular, because they often get much better mileage than purely gasoline-powered vehicles. Browse the web and study the features of four or five of today's popular hybrid cars, then list as many of their hybrid-related attributes as you can. For example, common attributes include city-miles-per-gallon and highway-miles-per-gallon. Also list the attributes of the batteries (type, weight, etc.).

1.12   *(Gender Neutrality)* Many people want to eliminate sexism in all forms of communication. You've been asked to create a program that can process a paragraph of text and replace gender-specific words with gender-neutral ones. Assuming that you've been given a list of gender-specific words and their gender-neutral replacements (e.g., replace "wife" by "spouse," "man" by "person," "daughter" by "child" and so on), explain the procedure you'd use to read through a paragraph of text and manually perform these replacements. How might your procedure generate a strange term like "woperchild," which is actually listed in the Urban Dictionary (www.urbandictionary.com)? In Chapter 4, you'll learn that a more formal term for "procedure" is "algorithm," and that an algorithm specifies the steps to be performed and the order in which to perform them.

What's in a name? That which we call a rose
By any other name would smell as sweet.
—William Shakespeare

When faced with a decision, I always ask, "What
would be the most fun?"
—Peggy Walker

"Take some more tea," the March Hare said to Alice,
very earnestly. "I've had nothing yet," Alice replied in
an offended tone: "so I can't take more." "You mean
you can't take less," said the Hatter: "It's very easy to
take more than nothing."
—Lewis Carroll

Introduction to Java Applications

Objectives

In this chapter you'll learn:

- To write simple Java applications.
- To use input and output statements.
- Java's primitive types.
- Basic memory concepts.
- To use arithmetic operators.
- The precedence of arithmetic operators.
- To write decision-making statements.
- To use relational and equality operators.

2.1 Introduction

In this chapter, we introduce Java application programming with simple programs to get you started with building Java programs. We begin with several examples that display messages on the screen, then demonstrate a program that obtains two numbers from a user, calculates their sum and displays the result. You'll learn how to perform arithmetic calculations and save their results for later use. The last example demonstrates decision making by showing you how to compare numbers, then display messages based on the comparison results. This chapter uses the tools from the JDK to compile and run programs. We've also posted videos at `www.deitel.com/books/jhtp8/` to help you get started with the popular Eclipse and NetBeans integrated development environments.

2.2 Our First Program in Java: Printing a Line of Text

A Java **application** is a computer program that executes when you use the **java command** to launch the Java Virtual Machine (JVM). Let's consider a simple application that displays a line of text. (Later in this section we'll discuss how to compile and run an application.) The program and its output are shown in Fig. 2.1. The output appears in the box at the end of the program. The program illustrates several important Java language features. Each program we present includes line numbers, which are not part of actual Java programs. We'll soon see that line 9 does the real work of the program—displaying the phrase `Welcome to Java Programming!` on the screen.

```java
1   // Fig. 2.1: Welcome1.java
2   // Text-printing program.
3
4   public class Welcome1
5   {
6      // main method begins execution of Java application
7      public static void main( String[] args )
8      {
9         System.out.println( "Welcome to Java Programming!" );
10     } // end method main
11  } // end class Welcome1
```

```
Welcome to Java Programming!
```

Fig. 2.1 | Text-printing program.

Commenting Your Programs
Line 1

```
// Fig. 2.1: Welcome1.java
```

begins with **//**, indicating that the line is a **comment**. You insert comments to **document programs** and improve their readability. The Java compiler ignores comments, so they do not cause the computer to perform any action when the program is run. By convention, we begin every program with a comment indicating the figure number and file name.

A comment that begins with **//** is an **end-of-line comment**—it terminates at the end of the line on which it appears. An end-of-line comment also can begin in the middle of a line and continue until the end of that line (as in lines 10 and 11). Another kind of comment, called a **traditional comment**, can be spread over several lines as in

```
/* This is a traditional comment. It
   can be split over multiple lines */
```

This type of comment begins with **/*** and ends with ***/**. All text between the delimiters is ignored by the compiler. Java incorporated traditional comments and end-of-line comments from the C and C++ programming languages, respectively. In this book, we use only **//** comments.

Java also provides **Javadoc comments** that are delimited by **/**** and ***/**. As with traditional comments, all text between the Javadoc comment delimiters is ignored by the compiler. Javadoc comments enable you to embed program documentation directly in your programs. Such comments are the preferred Java documenting format in industry. The **javadoc utility program** (part of the Java SE Development Kit) reads Javadoc comments and uses them to prepare your program's documentation in HTML format. We demonstrate Javadoc comments and the `javadoc` utility in Appendix M, Creating Documentation with `javadoc`.

Line 2

```
// Text-printing program.
```

is a comment that describes the purpose of the program.

Common Programming Error 2.1

*Forgetting one of the delimiters of a traditional or Javadoc comment is a syntax error. The syntax of a programming language specifies the rules for creating proper programs in that language, similar to how a natural language's grammar rules specify sentence structure. A syntax error occurs when the compiler encounters code that violates Java's language rules (i.e., its syntax). In this case, the compiler issues an error message and prevents your program from compiling. Syntax errors are also called **compiler errors**, **compile-time errors** or **compilation errors**, because the compiler detects them during the compilation phase.*

Good Programming Practice 2.1

Some organizations require that every program begin with a comment that states the purpose of the program and the author, date and time when the program was last modified.

Using Blank Lines
Line 3 is a blank line. Blank lines and space characters make programs easier to read. Together, blank lines, spaces and tabs are known as **white space** (or whitespace). White space is ignored by the compiler.

Good Programming Practice 2.2
Use blank lines and spaces to enhance program readability.

Declaring a Class
Line 4

```
public class Welcome1
```

begins a **class declaration** for class Welcome1. Every Java program consists of at least one class that you (the programmer) define. These are known as **programmer-defined classes**. The **class keyword** introduces a class declaration and is immediately followed by the **class name** (Welcome1). **Keywords** (sometimes called **reserved words**) are reserved for use by Java and are always spelled with all lowercase letters. The complete list of keywords is shown in Appendix C.

By convention, class names begin with a capital letter and capitalize the first letter of each word they include (e.g., SampleClassName). A class name is an **identifier**—a series of characters consisting of letters, digits, underscores (_) and dollar signs ($) that does not begin with a digit and does not contain spaces. Some valid identifiers are Welcome1, $value, _value, m_inputField1 and button7. The name 7button is not a valid identifier because it begins with a digit, and the name input field is not a valid identifier because it contains a space. Normally, an identifier that does not begin with a capital letter is not a class name. Java is **case sensitive**—uppercase and lowercase letters are distinct—so a1 and A1 are different (but both valid) identifiers.

Good Programming Practice 2.3
By convention, begin each class name identifier with a capital letter and start each subsequent word in the identifier with a capital letter.

Common Programming Error 2.2
Java is case sensitive. Not using the proper uppercase and lowercase letters for an identifier normally causes a compilation error.

In Chapters 2–7, every class we define begins with the **public** keyword. For now, we simply require this keyword. For our application, the file name is Welcome1.java. You'll learn more about public and non-public classes in Chapter 8.

Common Programming Error 2.3
A public class must be placed in a file that has the same name as the class (in terms of both spelling and capitalization) plus the .java extension; otherwise, a compilation error occurs. For example, public class Welcome must be placed in a file named Welcome.java.

A **left brace** (at line 5 in this program), {, begins the **body** of every class declaration. A corresponding **right brace** (at line 11), }, must end each class declaration. Note that lines 6–10 are indented. This indentation is one of the spacing conventions mentioned earlier.

Error-Prevention Tip 2.1
When you type an opening left brace, {, immediately type the closing right brace, }, then reposition the cursor between the braces and indent to begin typing the body. This practice helps prevent errors due to missing braces. Many IDEs insert the braces for you.

Good Programming Practice 2.4

Indent the entire body of each class declaration one "level" between the left brace and the right brace that delimit the body of the class. This format emphasizes the class declaration's structure and makes it easier to read.

Good Programming Practice 2.5

Many IDEs insert indentation for you in all the right places. The Tab *key may also be used to create indents, but tab stops vary among text editors. We recommend using three spaces to form a level of indent.*

Common Programming Error 2.4

It's a syntax error if braces do not occur in matching pairs.

Declaring a Method
Line 6

```
// main method begins execution of Java application
```

is an end-of-line comment indicating the purpose of lines 7–10 of the program. Line 7

```
public static void main( String[] args )
```

is the starting point of every Java application. The **parentheses** after the identifier main indicate that it's a program building block called a **method**. Java class declarations normally contain one or more methods. For a Java application, one of the methods must be called main and must be defined as shown in line 7; otherwise, the JVM will not execute the application. Methods perform tasks and can return information when they complete their tasks. Keyword **void** indicates that this method will not return any information. Later, we'll see how a method can return information. For now, simply mimic main's first line in your Java applications. In line 7, the String[] args in parentheses is a required part of the method main's declaration. We discuss this in Chapter 7.

The left brace in line 8 begins the **body of the method declaration**. A corresponding right brace must end the method declaration's body (line 10). Note that line 9 in the method body is indented between the braces.

Good Programming Practice 2.6

Indent the entire body of each method declaration one "level" between the braces that define the body of the method. This makes the structure of the method stand out and makes the method declaration easier to read.

Performing Output with **System.out.println**
Line 9

```
System.out.println( "Welcome to Java Programming!" );
```

instructs the computer to perform an action—namely, to print the **string** of characters contained between the double quotation marks (but not the quotation marks themselves). A string is sometimes called a **character string** or a **string literal**. White-space characters in strings are not ignored by the compiler. Strings cannot span multiple lines of code.

The **System.out** object is known as the **standard output object**. It allows Java applications to display strings in the **command window** from which the Java application executes. In recent versions of Microsoft Windows, the command window is the **Command Prompt**. In UNIX/Linux/Mac OS X, the command window is called a **terminal window** or a **shell**. Many programmers refer to the command window simply as the **command line**.

Method **System.out.println** displays (or prints) a line of text in the command window. The string in the parentheses in line 9 is the **argument** to the method. When System.out.println completes its task, it positions the output cursor (the location where the next character will be displayed) at the beginning of the next line in the command window. (This is similar to when a user presses the *Enter* key while typing in a text editor—the cursor appears at the beginning of the next line in the document.)

The entire line 9, including System.out.println, the argument "Welcome to Java Programming!" in the parentheses and the **semicolon** (;), is called a **statement**. Most statements end with a semicolon. When the statement in line 9 executes, it displays Welcome to Java Programming! in the command window. A method typically contains one or more statements that perform the method's task.

Common Programming Error 2.5

When a semicolon is required to end a statement, omitting the semicolon is a syntax error.

Error-Prevention Tip 2.2

When learning how to program, sometimes it's helpful to "break" a working program so you can familiarize yourself with the compiler's syntax-error messages. These messages do not always state the exact problem in the code. When you encounter such syntax-error messages, you'll have an idea of what caused the error. [Try removing a semicolon or brace from the program of Fig. 2.1, then recompile the program to see the error messages generated by the omission.]

Error-Prevention Tip 2.3

When the compiler reports a syntax error, the error may not be on the line indicated by the error message. First, check the line for which the error was reported. If that line does not contain syntax errors, check several preceding lines.

Using End-of-Line Comments on Right Braces for Readability
We include an end-of-line comment after a closing brace that ends a method declaration and after a closing brace that ends a class declaration. For example, line 10

```
} // end method main
```

indicates the closing brace of method main, and line 11

```
} // end class Welcome1
```

indicates the closing brace of class Welcome1. Each comment indicates the method or class that the right brace terminates.

Good Programming Practice 2.7

To improve program readability, follow the closing brace of a method body or class declaration with a comment indicating the method or class declaration to which the brace belongs.

Compiling and Executing Your First Java Application

We're now ready to compile and execute our program. We assume you're using the Sun Microsystems' Java SE Development Kit (JDK) 6 Update 10 (or higher), not an IDE. Our Java Resource Centers at www.deitel.com/ResourceCenters.html provide links to tutorials that help you get started with several popular Java development tools, including Net-Beans™, Eclipse™ and others. We've also posted NetBeans and Eclipse videos at www.deitel.com/books/jhtp8/ to help you get started using these popular IDEs.

To prepare to compile the program, open a command window and change to the directory where the program is stored. Many operating systems use the command cd to change directories. For example,

```
cd c:\examples\ch02\fig02_01
```

changes to the fig02_01 directory on Windows. The command

```
cd ~/examples/ch02/fig02_01
```

changes to the fig02_01 directory on UNIX/Linux/Max OS X.

To compile the program, type

```
javac Welcome1.java
```

If the program contains no syntax errors, the preceding command creates a new file called Welcome1.class (known as the **class file** for Welcome1) containing the platform-independent Java bytecodes that represent our application. When we use the java command to execute the application on a given platform, these bytecodes will be translated by the JVM into instructions that are understood by the underlying operating system.

Error-Prevention Tip 2.4

When attempting to compile a program, if you receive a message such as "bad command or filename," "javac: command not found" or "'javac' is not recognized as an internal or external command, operable program or batch file," then your Java software installation was not completed properly. If you are using the JDK, this indicates that the system's PATH environment variable was not set properly. Please carefully review the installation instructions in the Before You Begin section of this book. On some systems, after correcting the PATH, you may need to reboot your computer or open a new command window for these settings to take effect.

Error-Prevention Tip 2.5

Each syntax-error message contains the file name and line number where the error occurred. For example, Welcome1.java:6 indicates that an error occurred in the file Welcome1.java at line 6. The remainder of the error message provides information about the syntax error.

Error-Prevention Tip 2.6

The compiler error message "class Welcome1 is public, should be declared in a file named Welcome1.java" indicates that the file name does not exactly match the name of the public class in the file or that you typed the class name incorrectly when compiling the class.

Figure 2.2 shows the program of Fig. 2.1 executing in a Microsoft® Windows Vista® **Command Prompt** window. To execute the program, type java Welcome1. This launches the JVM, which loads the `.class` file for class `Welcome1`. Note that the `.class` file-name extension is omitted from the preceding command; otherwise, the JVM will not execute the program. The JVM calls method `main`. Next, the statement at line 9 of `main` displays `"Welcome to Java Programming!"` [*Note:* Many environments show command prompts with black backgrounds and white text. We adjusted these settings in our environment to make our screen captures more readable.]

Fig. 2.2 | Executing `Welcome1` from the **Command Prompt**.

 Error-Prevention Tip 2.7

When attempting to run a Java program, if you receive a message such as "Exception in thread "main" java.lang.NoClassDefFoundError: Welcome1," your CLASSPATH environment variable has not been set properly. Please carefully review the installation instructions in the Before You Begin section of this book. On some systems, you may need to reboot your computer or open a new command window after configuring the CLASSPATH.

2.3 Modifying Our First Java Program

In this section, we modify the example in Fig. 2.1 to print text on one line by using multiple statements and to print text on several lines by using a single statement.

Displaying a Single Line of Text with Multiple Statements
`Welcome to Java Programming!` can be displayed several ways. Class `Welcome2`, shown in Fig. 2.3, uses two statements to produce the same output as that shown in Fig. 2.1. From this point forward, we highlight the new and key features in each code listing, as shown in lines 9–10 of this program.

The program is similar to Fig. 2.1, so we discuss only the changes here. Line 2

```
// Printing a line of text with multiple statements.
```

is an end-of-line comment stating the purpose of this program. Line 4 begins the `Welcome2` class declaration. Lines 9–10 of method `main`

```
System.out.print( "Welcome to " );
System.out.println( "Java Programming!" );
```

display one line of text in the command window. The first statement uses `System.out`'s method `print` to display a string. Unlike `println`, after displaying its argument, `print` does not position the output cursor at the beginning of the next line in the command

```
 1    // Fig. 2.3: Welcome2.java
 2    // Printing a line of text with multiple statements.
 3
 4    public class Welcome2
 5    {
 6       // main method begins execution of Java application
 7       public static void main( String[] args )
 8       {
 9          System.out.print( "Welcome to " );
10          System.out.println( "Java Programming!" );
11       } // end method main
12    } // end class Welcome2
```

```
Welcome to Java Programming!
```

Fig. 2.3 | Printing a line of text with multiple statements.

window—the next character the program displays will appear immediately after the last character that print displays. Thus, line 10 positions the first character in its argument (the letter "J") immediately after the last character that line 9 displays (the space character before the string's closing double-quote character). Each print or println statement resumes displaying characters from where the last print or println statement stopped displaying characters.

Displaying Multiple Lines of Text with a Single Statement

A single statement can display multiple lines by using **newline characters**, which indicate to System.out's print and println methods when to position the output cursor at the beginning of the next line in the command window. Like blank lines, space characters and tab characters, newline characters are white-space characters. Figure 2.4 outputs four lines of text, using newline characters to determine when to begin each new line. Most of the program is identical to those in Fig. 2.1 and Fig. 2.3, so we discuss only the changes here.

```
 1    // Fig. 2.4: Welcome3.java
 2    // Printing multiple lines of text with a single statement.
 3
 4    public class Welcome3
 5    {
 6       // main method begins execution of Java application
 7       public static void main( String[] args )
 8       {
 9          System.out.println( "Welcome\nto\nJava\nProgramming!" );
10       } // end method main
11    } // end class Welcome3
```

```
Welcome
to
Java
Programming!
```

Fig. 2.4 | Printing multiple lines of text with a single statement.

Line 2

```
// Printing multiple lines of text with a single statement.
```

is a comment stating the program's purpose. Line 4 begins the `Welcome3` class declaration.
Line 9

```
System.out.println( "Welcome\nto\nJava\nProgramming!" );
```

displays four separate lines of text in the command window. Normally, the characters in a string are displayed exactly as they appear in the double quotes. Note, however, that the two characters \ and n (repeated three times in the statement) do not appear on the screen. The **backslash** (\) is called an **escape character**. It indicates to System.out's print and println methods that a "special character" is to be output. When a backslash appears in a string of characters, Java combines the next character with the backslash to form an **escape sequence**. The escape sequence \n represents the newline character. When a newline character appears in a string being output with System.out, the newline character causes the screen's output cursor to move to the beginning of the next line in the command window. Figure 2.5 lists several common escape sequences and describes how they affect the display of characters in the command window. For the complete list of escape sequences, visit java.sun.com/docs/books/jls/third_edition/html/lexical.html#3.10.6.

Escape sequence	Description
\n	Newline. Position the screen cursor at the beginning of the next line.
\t	Horizontal tab. Move the screen cursor to the next tab stop.
\r	Carriage return. Position the screen cursor at the beginning of the current line—do not advance to the next line. Any characters output after the carriage return overwrite the characters previously output on that line.
\\	Backslash. Used to print a backslash character.

\"	Double quote. Used to print a double-quote character. For example,
	`System.out.println( "\"in quotes\"" );`
	displays
	`"in quotes"`

Fig. 2.5 | Some common escape sequences.

2.4 Displaying Text with `printf`

The **System.out.printf** method (f means "formatted") displays formatted data. Figure 2.6 uses this method to output the strings "Welcome to" and "Java Programming!".
Lines 9–10

```
System.out.printf( "%s\n%s\n",
    "Welcome to", "Java Programming!" );
```

call method System.out.printf to display the program's output. The method call specifies three arguments. When a method requires multiple arguments, the arguments are placed in a **comma-separated list**.

```
 1   // Fig. 2.6: Welcome4.java
 2   // Displaying multiple lines with method System.out.printf.
 3
 4   public class Welcome4
 5   {
 6      // main method begins execution of Java application
 7      public static void main( String[] args )
 8      {
 9         System.out.printf( "%s\n%s\n",
10            "Welcome to", "Java Programming!" );
11      } // end method main
12   } // end class Welcome4
```

```
Welcome to
Java Programming!
```

Fig. 2.6 | Displaying multiple lines with method `System.out.printf`.

Good Programming Practice 2.8
Place a space after each comma (,) in an argument list to make programs more readable.

Lines 9–10 represent only one statement. Java allows large statements to be split over many lines. We indent line 10 to indicate that it's a continuation of line 9. Note that you cannot split a statement in the middle of an identifier or in the middle of a string.

Common Programming Error 2.6
Splitting a statement in the middle of an identifier or a string is a syntax error.

Method `printf`'s first argument is a **format string** that may consist of **fixed text** and **format specifiers**. Fixed text is output by `printf` just as it would be by `print` or `println`. Each format specifier is a placeholder for a value and specifies the type of data to output. Format specifiers also may include optional formatting information.

Format specifiers begin with a percent sign (%) and are followed by a character that represents the data type. For example, the format specifier **%s** is a placeholder for a string. The format string in line 9 specifies that `printf` should output two strings, each followed by a newline character. At the first format specifier's position, `printf` substitutes the value of the first argument after the format string. At each subsequent format specifier's position, `printf` substitutes the value of the next argument in the argument list. So this example substitutes "Welcome to" for the first %s and "Java Programming!" for the second %s. The output shows that two lines of text are displayed.

We introduce various formatting features as they are needed in our examples. Appendix G presents the details of formatting output with `printf`.

2.5 Another Application: Adding Integers

Our next application reads (or inputs) two **integers** (whole numbers, like –22, 7, 0 and 1024) typed by a user at the keyboard, computes the sum of the values and displays the result. This program must keep track of the numbers supplied by the user for the calculation later in the program. Programs remember numbers and other data in the computer's memory and access that data through program elements called **variables**. The program of Fig. 2.7 demonstrates these concepts. In the sample output, we use bold text to identify the user's input (i.e., **45** and **72**).

```
 1   // Fig. 2.7: Addition.java
 2   // Addition program that displays the sum of two numbers.
 3   import java.util.Scanner; // program uses class Scanner
 4
 5   public class Addition
 6   {
 7      // main method begins execution of Java application
 8      public static void main( String[] args )
 9      {
10         // create a Scanner to obtain input from the command window
11         Scanner input = new Scanner( System.in );
12
13         int number1; // first number to add
14         int number2; // second number to add
15         int sum; // sum of number1 and number2
16
17         System.out.print( "Enter first integer: " ); // prompt
18         number1 = input.nextInt(); // read first number from user
19
20         System.out.print( "Enter second integer: " ); // prompt
21         number2 = input.nextInt(); // read second number from user
22
23         sum = number1 + number2; // add numbers, then store total in sum
24
25         System.out.printf( "Sum is %d\n", sum ); // display sum
26      } // end method main
27   } // end class Addition
```

```
Enter first integer: 45
Enter second integer: 72
Sum is 117
```

Fig. 2.7 | Addition program that displays the sum of two numbers.

Lines 1–2

```
// Fig. 2.7: Addition.java
// Addition program that displays the sum of two numbers.
```

state the figure number, file name and purpose of the program. Line 3

```
import java.util.Scanner; // program uses class Scanner
```

is an **import declaration** that helps the compiler locate a class that is used in this program. A great strength of Java is its rich set of predefined classes that you can reuse rather than "reinventing the wheel." These classes are grouped into **packages**—named groups of related classes—and are collectively referred to as the **Java class library**, or the **Java Application Programming Interface (Java API)**. You use import declarations to identify the predefined classes used in a Java program. The import declaration in line 3 indicates that this example uses Java's predefined Scanner class (discussed shortly) from package **java.util**.

Common Programming Error 2.7

All `import` declarations must appear before the first class declaration in the file. Placing an `import` declaration inside a class declaration's body or after a class declaration is a syntax error.

Error-Prevention Tip 2.8

Forgetting to include an `import` declaration for a class used in your program typically results in a compilation error containing a message such as "`cannot find symbol.`" When this occurs, check that you provided the proper `import` declarations and that the names in the `import` declarations are spelled correctly, including proper use of uppercase and lowercase letters.

Line 5

```
public class Addition
```

begins the declaration of class `Addition`. The file name for this `public` class must be `Addition.java`. Remember that the body of each class declaration starts with an opening left brace (line 6) and ends with a closing right brace (line 27).

The application begins execution with method `main` (lines 8–26). The left brace (line 9) marks the beginning of `main`'s body, and the corresponding right brace (line 26) marks the end of `main`'s body. Note that method `main` is indented one level in the body of class `Addition` and that the code in the body of `main` is indented another level for readability.

Line 11

```
Scanner input = new Scanner( System.in );
```

is a **variable declaration statement** that specifies the name (`input`) and type (`Scanner`) of a variable that is used in this program. A variable is a location in the computer's memory where a value can be stored for use later in a program. All Java variables must be declared with a **name** and a **type** before they can be used. A variable's name enables the program to access the value of the variable in memory. A variable's name can be any valid identifier. (Identifier naming requirements are given in Section 2.2.) A variable's type specifies what kind of information is stored at that location in memory. Like other statements, declaration statements end with a semicolon (`;`).

The declaration in line 11 specifies that the variable named `input` is of type `Scanner`. A **Scanner** enables a program to read data (e.g., numbers) for use in a program. The data can come from many sources, such as the user at the keyboard or a file on disk. Before using a `Scanner`, you must create it and specify the source of the data.

The equals sign (=) in line 11 indicates that `Scanner` variable `input` should be **initialized** (i.e., prepared for use in the program) in its declaration with the result of the expression `new Scanner(System.in)` to the right of the equals sign. This expression uses the **new** keyword to create a `Scanner` object that reads characters typed by the user at the keyboard. The **standard input object, System.in**, enables applications to read bytes of information typed by the user. The `Scanner` object translates these bytes into types (like `int`s) that can be used in a program.

The variable declaration statements at lines 13–15

```
int number1; // first number to add
int number2; // second number to add
int sum; // sum of number1 and number2
```

declare that variables number1, number2 and sum hold data of type **int**—they can hold integer values (whole numbers such as 72, –1127 and 0). These variables are not yet initialized. The range of values for an int is –2,147,483,648 to +2,147,483,647. [*Note:* Actual int values may not contain commas.] We'll soon discuss types **float** and **double**, for holding real numbers, and type **char**, for holding character data. Real numbers contain decimal points, such as 3.4, 0.0 and –11.19. Variables of type char represent individual characters, such as an uppercase letter (e.g., A), a digit (e.g., 7), a special character (e.g., * or %) or an escape sequence (e.g., the newline character, \n). The types int, float, double and char are called **primitive types**. Primitive-type names are keywords and must appear in all lowercase letters. Appendix D, summarizes the characteristics of the eight primitive types (boolean, byte, char, short, int, long, float and double).

Several variables of the same type may be declared in one declaration with the variable names separated by commas (i.e., a comma-separated list of variable names). For example, lines 13–15 can also be written as a single statement as follows:

```
int number1, // first number to add
    number2, // second number to add
    sum; // sum of number1 and number2
```

Good Programming Practice 2.9

Declare each variable on a separate line. This format allows a descriptive comment to be easily inserted next to each declaration.

Good Programming Practice 2.10

*Choosing meaningful variable names helps a program to be **self-documenting** (i.e., one can understand the program simply by reading it rather than by reading manuals or viewing an excessive number of comments).*

Good Programming Practice 2.11

By convention, variable-name identifiers begin with a lowercase letter, and every word in the name after the first word begins with a capital letter. For example, variable-name identifier firstNumber starts its second word, Number, with a capital N.

Line 17

```
System.out.print( "Enter first integer: " ); // prompt
```

uses System.out.print to display the message "Enter first integer: ". This message is called a **prompt** because it directs the user to take a specific action. We used method print here rather than println so that the user's input appears on the same line as the prompt. Recall from Section 2.2 that identifiers starting with capital letters typically represent class names. So, System is a class. Class System is part of package **java.lang**. Notice that class System is not imported with an import declaration at the beginning of the program.

Software Engineering Observation 2.1

By default, package java.lang is imported in every Java program; thus, classes in java.lang are the only ones in the Java API that do not require an import declaration.

Line 18

```
number1 = input.nextInt(); // read first number from user
```

uses Scanner object input's nextInt method to obtain an integer from the user at the keyboard. At this point the program waits for the user to type the number and press the *Enter* key to submit the number to the program.

Our program assumes that the user enters a valid integer value. If not, a runtime logic error will occur and the program will terminate. Chapter 11, Exception Handling, discusses how to make your programs more robust by enabling them to handle such errors. This is also known as making your program fault tolerant.

In line 18, the result of the call to method nextInt (an int value) is placed in variable number1 by using the **assignment operator**, =. The statement is read as "number1 gets the value of input.nextInt()." Operator = is called a **binary operator**, because it has two **operands**—number1 and the result of the method call input.nextInt(). This statement is called an assignment statement, because it assigns a value to a variable. Everything to the right of the assignment operator, =, is always evaluated before the assignment is performed.

Good Programming Practice 2.12

Place spaces on either side of a binary operator to make it stand out and make the program more readable.

Line 20

```
System.out.print( "Enter second integer: " ); // prompt
```

prompts the user to input the second integer.
Line 21

```
number2 = input.nextInt(); // read second number from user
```

reads the second integer and assigns it to variable number2.
Line 23

```
sum = number1 + number2; // add numbers then store total in sum
```

is an assignment statement that calculates the sum of the variables number1 and number2 then assigns the result to variable sum by using the assignment operator, =. The statement is read as "sum gets the value of number1 + number2." In general, calculations are performed in assignment statements. When the program encounters the addition operation, it uses the values stored in the variables number1 and number2 to perform the calculation. In the preceding statement, the addition operator is a binary operator—its two operands are the variables number1 and number2. Portions of statements that contain calculations are called **expressions**. In fact, an expression is any portion of a statement that has a value associated with it. For example, the value of the expression number1 + number2 is the sum of the numbers. Similarly, the value of the expression input.nextInt() is the integer typed by the user.

After the calculation has been performed, line 25

```
System.out.printf( "Sum is %d\n", sum ); // display sum
```

uses method System.out.printf to display the sum. The format specifier **%d** is a placeholder for an int value (in this case the value of sum)—the letter d stands for "decimal integer." Note that other than the %d format specifier, the remaining characters in the format string are all fixed text. So method printf displays "Sum is ", followed by the value of sum (in the position of the %d format specifier) and a newline.

Note that calculations can also be performed inside `printf` statements. We could have combined the statements at lines 23 and 25 into the statement

```
System.out.printf( "Sum is %d\n", ( number1 + number2 ) );
```

The parentheses around the expression `number1 + number2` are not required—they are included to emphasize that the value of the entire expression is output in the position of the `%d` format specifier.

Java API Documentation

For each new Java API class we use, we indicate the package in which it's located. This information helps you locate descriptions of each package and class in the Java API documentation. A web-based version of this documentation can be found at

```
java.sun.com/javase/6/docs/api/
```

You can download this documentation from

```
java.sun.com/javase/downloads
```

Appendix E shows how to use this documentation.

2.6 Memory Concepts

Variable names such as `number1`, `number2` and `sum` actually correspond to locations in the computer's memory. Every variable has a **name**, a **type**, a **size** (in bytes) and a **value**.

In the addition program of Fig. 2.7, when the following statement (line 18) executes:

```
number1 = input.nextInt(); // read first number from user
```

the number typed by the user is placed into a memory location corresponding to the name `number1`. Suppose that the user enters 45. The computer places that integer value into location `number1` (Fig. 2.8), replacing the previous value (if any) in that location. The previous value is lost.

number1	45

Fig. 2.8 | Memory location showing the name and value of variable `number1`.

When the statement (line 21)

```
number2 = input.nextInt(); // read second number from user
```

executes, suppose that the user enters 72. The computer places that integer value into location `number2`. The memory now appears as shown in Fig. 2.9.

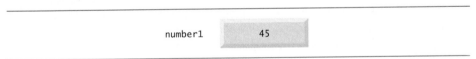

number1	45
number2	72

Fig. 2.9 | Memory locations after storing values for `number1` and `number2`.

After the program of Fig. 2.7 obtains values for number1 and number2, it adds the values and places the total into variable sum. The statement (line 23)

```
sum = number1 + number2; // add numbers, then store total in sum
```

performs the addition, then replaces any previous value in sum. After sum has been calculated, memory appears as shown in Fig. 2.10. Note that the values of number1 and number2 appear exactly as they did before they were used in the calculation of sum. These values were used, but not destroyed, as the computer performed the calculation. Thus, when a value is read from a memory location, the process is nondestructive.

number1	45
number2	72
sum	117

Fig. 2.10 | Memory locations after storing the sum of number1 and number2.

2.7 Arithmetic

Most programs perform arithmetic calculations. The **arithmetic operators** are summarized in Fig. 2.11. Note the use of various special symbols not used in algebra. The **asterisk** (*) indicates multiplication, and the percent sign (%) is the **remainder operator**, which we'll discuss shortly. The arithmetic operators in Fig. 2.11 are binary operators because they each operate on two operands. For example, the expression f + 7 contains the binary operator + and the two operands f and 7.

Java operation	Operator	Algebraic expression	Java expression
Addition	+	$f + 7$	f + 7
Subtraction	–	$p - c$	p - c
Multiplication	*	bm	b * m
Division	/	x/y or $\frac{x}{y}$ or $x \div y$	x / y
Remainder	%	$r \bmod s$	r % s

Fig. 2.11 | Arithmetic operators.

Integer division yields an integer quotient—for example, the expression 7 / 4 evaluates to 1, and the expression 17 / 5 evaluates to 3. Any fractional part in integer division is simply discarded (i.e., truncated)—no rounding occurs. Java provides the remainder operator, %, which yields the remainder after division. The expression x % y yields the remainder after x is divided by y. Thus, 7 % 4 yields 3, and 17 % 5 yields 2. This operator is most commonly used with integer operands but can also be used with other arithmetic types. In this chapter's exercises and in later chapters, we consider several interesting applications of the remainder operator, such as determining whether one number is a multiple of another.

Arithmetic Expressions in Straight-Line Form
Arithmetic expressions in Java must be written in **straight-line form** to facilitate entering programs into the computer. Thus, expressions such as "a divided by b" must be written as a / b, so that all constants, variables and operators appear in a straight line. The following algebraic notation is generally not acceptable to compilers:

$$\frac{a}{b}$$

Parentheses for Grouping Subexpressions
Parentheses are used to group terms in Java expressions in the same manner as in algebraic expressions. For example, to multiply a times the quantity b + c, we write

```
a * ( b + c )
```

If an expression contains **nested parentheses**, such as

```
( ( a + b ) * c )
```

the expression in the innermost set of parentheses (a + b in this case) is evaluated first.

Rules of Operator Precedence
Java applies the operators in arithmetic expressions in a precise sequence determined by the following **rules of operator precedence**, which are generally the same as those followed in algebra (Fig. 2.12):

1. Multiplication, division and remainder operations are applied first. If an expression contains several such operations, they are applied from left to right. Multiplication, division and remainder operators have the same level of precedence.

2. Addition and subtraction operations are applied next. If an expression contains several such operations, the operators are applied from left to right. Addition and subtraction operators have the same level of precedence.

These rules enable Java to apply operators in the correct order.[1] When we say that operators are applied from left to right, we are referring to their **associativity**. Some operators associate from right to left. Figure 2.12 summarizes these rules of operator precedence. A complete precedence chart is included in Appendix A.

Operator(s)	Operation(s)	Order of evaluation (precedence)
* / %	Multiplication Division Remainder	Evaluated first. If there are several operators of this type, they are evaluated from left to right.
+ -	Addition Subtraction	Evaluated next. If there are several operators of this type, they are evaluated from left to right.
=	Assignment	Evaluated last.

Fig. 2.12 | Precedence of arithmetic operators.

---

1. We use simple examples to explain the order of evaluation of expressions. Subtle issues occur in the more complex expressions you'll encounter later in the book. For more information on order of evaluation, see Chapter 15 of *The Java™ Language Specification* (java.sun.com/docs/books/jls/).

Sample Algebraic and Java Expressions

Now let's consider several expressions in light of the rules of operator precedence. Each example lists an algebraic expression and its Java equivalent. The following is an example of an arithmetic mean (average) of five terms:

Algebra: $m = \dfrac{a + b + c + d + e}{5}$

Java: m = (a + b + c + d + e) / 5;

The parentheses are required because division has higher precedence than addition. The entire quantity (a + b + c + d + e) is to be divided by 5. If the parentheses are erroneously omitted, we obtain a + b + c + d + e / 5, which evaluates as

$$a + b + c + d + \frac{e}{5}$$

The following is an example of the equation of a straight line:

Algebra: $y = mx + b$

Java: y = m * x + b;

No parentheses are required. The multiplication operator is applied first because multiplication has a higher precedence than addition. The assignment occurs last because it has a lower precedence than multiplication or addition.

The following example contains remainder (%), multiplication, division, addition and subtraction operations:

Algebra: $z = pr\%q + w/x - y$

Java: z = p * r % q + w / x - y;
 　　　　　　　 6　　1　　2　　4　　3　　5

The circled numbers under the statement indicate the order in which Java applies the operators. The *, % and / operations are evaluated first in left-to-right order (i.e., they associate from left to right), because they have higher precedence than + and -. The + and - operations are evaluated next. These operations are also applied from left to right. The assignment (=) operaton is evaluated last.

Evaluation of a Second-Degree Polynomial

To develop a better understanding of the rules of operator precedence, consider the evaluation of an assignment expression that includes a second-degree polynomial $ax^2 + bx + c$:

y = a * x * x + b * x + c;
 6　　1　　2　　4　　3　　5

In this statement, the multiplication operations are evaluated first in left-to-right order (i.e., they associate from left to right), because they have higher precedence than addition. The addition operations are evaluated next and are applied from left to right. There is no arithmetic operator for exponentiation in Java, so x^2 is represented as x * x. Section 5.4 shows an alternative for performing exponentiation. Suppose that a, b, c and x in the preceding second-degree polynomial are initialized (given values) as follows: a = 2, b = 3, c = 7 and x = 5. Figure 2.13 illustrates the order in which the operators are applied.

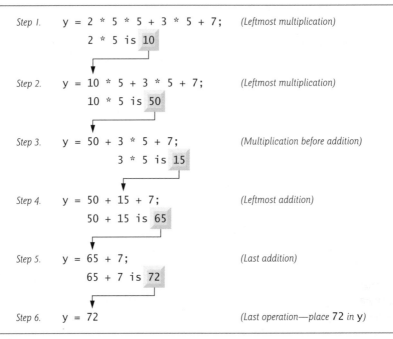

Step 1. y = 2 * 5 * 5 + 3 * 5 + 7;   *(Leftmost multiplication)*

      2 * 5 is 10

Step 2. y = 10 * 5 + 3 * 5 + 7;   *(Leftmost multiplication)*

      10 * 5 is 50

Step 3. y = 50 + 3 * 5 + 7;   *(Multiplication before addition)*

      3 * 5 is 15

Step 4. y = 50 + 15 + 7;   *(Leftmost addition)*

      50 + 15 is 65

Step 5. y = 65 + 7;   *(Last addition)*

      65 + 7 is 72

Step 6. y = 72   *(Last operation—place 72 in y)*

Fig. 2.13 | Order in which a second-degree polynomial is evaluated.

As in algebra, it's acceptable to place **redundant parentheses** (unnecessary parentheses) in an expression to make the expression clearer. For example, the preceding statement might be parenthesized as follows:

```
y = ( a * x * x ) + ( b * x ) + c;
```

> **Good Programming Practice 2.13**
> *Using redundant parentheses in complex arithmetic expressions can make them easier to read.*

2.8 Decision Making: Equality and Relational Operators

A **condition** is an expression that can be **true** or **false**. This section introduces Java's **if selection statement** that allows a program to make a **decision** based on a condition's value. For example, the condition "grade is greater than or equal to 60" determines whether a student passed a test. If the condition in an `if` statement is true, the body of the `if` statement executes. If the condition is false, the body does not execute. We'll see an example shortly.

Conditions in `if` statements can be formed by using the **equality operators** (`==` and `!=`) and **relational operators** (`>`, `<`, `>=` and `<=`) summarized in Fig. 2.14. Both equality operators have the same level of precedence, which is lower than that of the relational operators. The equality operators associate from left to right. The relational operators all have the same level of precedence and also associate from left to right.

Fig. 2.15 uses six `if` statements to compare two integers input by the user. If the condition in any of these `if` statements is true, the output statement associated with that `if`

Standard algebraic equality or relational operator	Java equality or relational operator	Sample Java condition	Meaning of Java condition
Equality operators			
=	==	x == y	x is equal to y
≠	!=	x != y	x is not equal to y
Relational operators			
>	>	x > y	x is greater than y
<	<	x < y	x is less than y
≥	>=	x >= y	x is greater than or equal to y
≤	<=	x <= y	x is less than or equal to y

Fig. 2.14 | Equality and relational operators.

statement executes; otherwise, the statement is skipped. The program uses a Scanner to input the two integers from the user and store them in variables number1 and number2. Then the program compares the numbers and displays the results of the comparisons that are true. We show three sample outputs.

```java
1   // Fig. 2.15: Comparison.java
2   // Compare integers using if statements, relational operators
3   // and equality operators.
4   import java.util.Scanner; // program uses class Scanner
5
6   public class Comparison
7   {
8      // main method begins execution of Java application
9      public static void main( String[] args )
10     {
11        // create Scanner to obtain input from command window
12        Scanner input = new Scanner( System.in );
13
14        int number1; // first number to compare
15        int number2; // second number to compare
16
17        System.out.print( "Enter first integer: " ); // prompt
18        number1 = input.nextInt(); // read first number from user
19
20        System.out.print( "Enter second integer: " ); // prompt
21        number2 = input.nextInt(); // read second number from user
22
23        if ( number1 == number2 )
24           System.out.printf( "%d == %d\n", number1, number2 );
25
26        if ( number1 != number2 )
27           System.out.printf( "%d != %d\n", number1, number2 );
```

Fig. 2.15 | Compare integers using if statements, relational operators and equality operators. (Part 1 of 2.)

```
28
29        if ( number1 < number2 )
30           System.out.printf( "%d < %d\n", number1, number2 );
31
32        if ( number1 > number2 )
33           System.out.printf( "%d > %d\n", number1, number2 );
34
35        if ( number1 <= number2 )
36           System.out.printf( "%d <= %d\n", number1, number2 );
37
38        if ( number1 >= number2 )
39           System.out.printf( "%d >= %d\n", number1, number2 );
40     } // end method main
41  } // end class Comparison
```

```
Enter first integer: 777
Enter second integer: 777
777 == 777
777 <= 777
777 >= 777
```

```
Enter first integer: 1000
Enter second integer: 2000
1000 != 2000
1000 < 2000
1000 <= 2000
```

```
Enter first integer: 2000
Enter second integer: 1000
2000 != 1000
2000 > 1000
2000 >= 1000
```

Fig. 2.15 | Compare integers using if statements, relational operators and equality operators. (Part 2 of 2.)

The declaration of class Comparison begins at line 6

```
public class Comparison
```

The class's main method (lines 9–40) begins the execution of the program. Line 12

```
Scanner input = new Scanner( System.in );
```

declares Scanner variable input and assigns it a Scanner that inputs data from the standard input (i.e., the keyboard).

Lines 14–15

```
int number1; // first number to compare
int number2; // second number to compare
```

declare the int variables used to store the values input from the user.

Lines 17–18

```
System.out.print( "Enter first integer: " ); // prompt
number1 = input.nextInt(); // read first number from user
```

prompt the user to enter the first integer and input the value, respectively. The input value is stored in variable `number1`.

Lines 20–21

```
System.out.print( "Enter second integer: " ); // prompt
number2 = input.nextInt(); // read second number from user
```

prompt the user to enter the second integer and input the value, respectively. The input value is stored in variable `number2`.

Lines 23–24

```
if ( number1 == number2 )
    System.out.printf( "%d == %d\n", number1, number2 );
```

compare the values of `number1` and `number2` to determine whether they're equal. An `if` statement always begins with keyword `if`, followed by a condition in parentheses. An `if` statement expects one statement in its body, but may contain multiple statements if they are enclosed in a set of braces ({}). The indentation of the body statement shown here is not required, but it improves the program's readability by emphasizing that the statement in line 24 is part of the `if` statement that begins at line 23. Line 24 executes only if the numbers stored in variables `number1` and `number2` are equal (i.e., the condition is true). The `if` statements in lines 26–27, 29–30, 32–33, 35–36 and 38–39 compare `number1` and `number2` with the operators `!=`, `<`, `>`, `<=` and `>=`, respectively. If the condition in any of the `if` statements is true, the corresponding body statement executes.

Common Programming Error 2.8
Forgetting the left and/or right parentheses for the condition in an `if` statement is a syntax error—the parentheses are required.

Common Programming Error 2.9
Confusing the equality operator, `==`, with the assignment operator, `=`, can cause a logic error or a syntax error. The equality operator should be read as "is equal to," and the assignment operator should be read as "gets" or "gets the value of." To avoid confusion, some people read the equality operator as "double equals" or "equals equals."

Good Programming Practice 2.14
Placing only one statement per line in a program enhances program readability.

Note that there is no semicolon (;) at the end of the first line of each `if` statement. Such a semicolon would result in a logic error at execution time. For example,

```
if ( number1 == number2 ); // logic error
    System.out.printf( "%d == %d\n", number1, number2 );
```

would actually be interpreted by Java as

```
if ( number1 == number2 )
    ; // empty statement
System.out.printf( "%d == %d\n", number1, number2 );
```

where the semicolon on the line by itself—called the **empty statement**—is the statement to execute if the condition in the if statement is true. When the empty statement executes, no task is performed in the program. The program then continues with the output statement, which always executes, regardless of whether the condition is true or false, because the output statement is not part of the if statement.

Common Programming Error 2.10
Placing a semicolon immediately after the right parenthesis of the condition in an if statement is normally a logic error.

Note the use of white space in Fig. 2.15. Recall that white space is normally ignored by the compiler. So, statements may be split over several lines and may be spaced according to your preferences without affecting the meaning of a program. It's incorrect to split identifiers and strings. Ideally, statements should be kept small, but this is not always possible.

Good Programming Practice 2.15
A lengthy statement can be spread over several lines. If a single statement must be split across lines, choose breaking points that make sense, such as after a comma in a comma-separated list, or after an operator in a lengthy expression. If a statement is split across two or more lines, indent all subsequent lines until the end of the statement.

Figure 2.16 shows the operators discussed so far in decreasing order of precedence. All these operators, with the exception of the assignment operator, =, associate from left to right. Addition is left associative, so an expression like x + y + z is evaluated as if it had been written as (x + y) + z. The assignment operator, =, associates from right to left, so an expression like x = y = 0 is evaluated as if it had been written as x = (y = 0), which first assigns the value 0 to variable y, then assigns the result of that assignment, 0, to x.

Operators				Associativity	Type
*	/	%		left to right	multiplicative
+	-			left to right	additive
<	<=	>	>=	left to right	relational
==	!=			left to right	equality
=				right to left	assignment

Fig. 2.16 | Precedence and associativity of operators discussed.

Good Programming Practice 2.16
Refer to the operator precedence chart (Appendix A) when writing expressions containing many operators. Confirm that the operations in the expression are performed in the order you expect. If you are uncertain about the order of evaluation in a complex expression, use parentheses to force the order, exactly as you'd do in algebraic expressions.

2.9 Wrap-Up

You learned many important features of Java in this chapter, including displaying data on the screen in a **Command Prompt**, inputting data from the keyboard, performing calculations and making decisions. The applications presented here were meant to introduce you to basic programming concepts. As you'll see in Chapter 3, Java applications typically contain just a few lines of code in method main—these statements normally create the objects that perform the work of the application. In Chapter 3, you'll learn how to implement your own classes and use objects of those classes in applications.

Summary

Section 2.2 Our First Program in Java: Printing a Line of Text

- A Java application is a computer program that executes when you use the java command to launch the JVM.
- Comments document programs and improve their readability. They're ignored by the compiler.
- A comment that begins with // is called an end-of-line comment—it terminates at the end of the line on which it appears.
- Traditional comments can be spread over several lines and are delimited by /* and */.
- Javadoc comments, delimited by /** and */, enable you to embed program documentation in your code. The javadoc utility program generates HTML pages based on these comments.
- A syntax error (also called a compiler error, compile-time error or compilation error) occurs when the compiler encounters code that violates Java's language rules. This is similar to a grammar error in a natural language.
- Blank lines, space characters and tab characters are known as white space. White space makes programs easier to read and is ignored by the compiler.
- Every program that you create consists of at least one programmer-defined class.
- Keywords are reserved for use by Java and are always spelled with all lowercase letters.
- Keyword class introduces a class declaration and is immediately followed by the class name.
- By convention, all class names in Java begin with a capital letter and capitalize the first letter of each word they include (e.g., SampleClassName).
- A Java class name is an identifier—a series of characters consisting of letters, digits, underscores (_) and dollar signs ($) that does not begin with a digit and does not contain spaces.
- Java is case sensitive—that is, uppercase and lowercase letters are distinct.
- The body of every class declaration is delimited by braces, { and }.
- A public class declaration must be saved in a file with the same name as the class followed by the ".java" file-name extension.
- Method main is the starting point of every Java application and must begin with

```
public static void main( String[] args )
```

  otherwise, the JVM will not execute the application.
- Methods perform tasks and return information when they complete their tasks. Keyword void indicates that a method will perform a task but will not return any information.
- Statements instruct the computer to perform actions.
- A string in double quotes is sometimes called a character string or a string literal.
- The standard output object (System.out) displays characters in the command window.
- Method System.out.println displays its argument in the command window followed by a new-line character to position the output cursor to the beginning of the next line.

- You compile a program with the command javac. If the program contains no syntax errors, a class file containing the Java bytecodes that represent the application is created. These bytecodes are interpreted by the JVM when we execute the program.

- To run an application, type java followed by the name of the class that contains main.

Section 2.3 Modifying Our First Java Program
- System.out.print displays its argument and positions the output cursor immediately after the last character displayed.

- A backslash (\) in a string is an escape character. Java combines the next character with the backslash to form an escape sequence. The escape sequence \n represents the newline character.

Section 2.4 Displaying Text with **printf**
- System.out.printf method (f means "formatted") displays formatted data.

- Method printf's first argument is a format string that may consist of fixed text and format specifiers. Each format specifier is a placeholder for a value and specifies the type of data to output.

- Format specifiers begin with a percent sign (%) and are followed by a character that represents the data type. The format specifier %s is a placeholder for a string.

- Each format specifier is replaced with the value of the corresponding argument that appears after the format string.

Section 2.5 Another Application: Adding Integers
- An import declaration helps the compiler locate a class that is used in a program.

- Java's rich set of predefined classes are grouped into packages—named groups of classes.

- Collectively, Java's packages are referred to as the Java class library, or the Java Application Programming Interface (Java API).

- A variable is a location in the computer's memory where a value can be stored for use later in a program. All variables must be declared with a name and a type before they can be used.

- A variable's name enables the program to access the value of the variable in memory.

- A Scanner (package java.util) enables a program to read data for use in a program. Before a Scanner can be used, the program must create it and specify the source of the data.

- Variables should be initialized to prepare them for use in a program.

- The expression new Scanner(System.in) creates a Scanner that reads from the standard input object (System.in)—normally the keyboard.

- Data type int is used to declare variables that will hold integer values. The range of values for an int is –2,147,483,648 to +2,147,483,647.

- Types float and double specify real numbers with decimal points, such as 3.4 and –11.19.

- Variables of type char represent individual characters, such as an uppercase letter (e.g., A), a digit (e.g., 7), a special character (e.g., * or %) or an escape sequence (e.g., newline, \n).

- Types such as int, float, double and char are primitive types. Primitive-type names are keywords; thus, they must appear in all lowercase letters.

- A prompt directs the user to take a specific action.

- Scanner method nextInt obtains an integer for use in a program.

- The assignment operator, =, enables the program to give a value to a variable. Operator = is called a binary operator because it has two operands.

- Portions of statements that have values are called expressions.

- The format specifier %d is a placeholder for an int value.

Section 2.6 Memory Concepts

- Variable names correspond to locations in the computer's memory. Every variable has a name, a type, a size and a value.

- A value that is placed in a memory location replaces the location's previous value, which is lost.

Section 2.7 Arithmetic

- The arithmetic operators are + (addition), - (subtraction), * (multiplication), / (division) and % (remainder).

- Integer division yields an integer quotient.

- The remainder operator, %, yields the remainder after division.

- Arithmetic expressions must be written in straight-line form.

- If an expression contains nested parentheses, the innermost set of parentheses is evaluated first.

- Java applies the operators in arithmetic expressions in a precise sequence determined by the rules of operator precedence.

- When we say that operators are applied from left to right, we are referring to their associativity. Some operators associate from right to left.

- Redundant parentheses in an expression can make an expression clearer.

Section 2.8 Decision Making: Equality and Relational Operators

- The if statement makes a decision based on a condition's value (true or false).

- Conditions in if statements can be formed by using the equality (== and !=) and relational (>, <, >= and <=) operators.

- An if statement begins with keyword if followed by a condition in parentheses and expects one statement in its body.

- The empty statement is a statement that does not perform a task.

Terminology

!= ("is not equal to") operator 56
%d format specifier 51
%s format specifier 47
< ("less than") operator 56
<= ("less than or equal to") operator 56
== ("is equal to") operator 56
> ("greater than") operator 56
>= ("greater than or equal to") operator 56
addition operator (+) 53
application 38
argument 42
arithmetic operators (*, /, %, + and -) 53
assignment operator (=) 51
associativity of operators 54
asterisk (*) 53
backslash (\) escape character 46
binary operator 51
body of a class declaration 40
body of a method declaration 41
case sensitive 40
cd 43
char primitive type 50

character string 41
class declaration 40
class file 43
class keyword 40
class name 40
comma-separated list 46
command line 42
command window 42
comment 39
compilation error 39
compile-time error 39
compiler error 39
condition 56
decision 56
division operator (/) 53
document programs 39
double primitive type 50
empty statement (;) 60
end-of-line comment (//) 39
equality operators 56
escape character 46
escape sequence 46

Self-Review Exercises

2.1 Fill in the blanks in each of the following statements:

a) A(n) _____ begins the body of every method, and a(n) _____ ends the body of every method.

b) The _____ statement is used to make decisions.

c) _____ begins an end-of-line comment.

d) _____, _____ and _____ are called white space.

e) _____ are reserved for use by Java.

f) Java applications begin execution at method _____.

g) Methods _____, _____ and _____ display information in a command window.

2.2 State whether each of the following is *true* or *false*. If *false*, explain why.

a) Comments cause the computer to print the text after the // on the screen when the program executes.

b) All variables must be given a type when they are declared.
c) Java considers the variables number and NuMbEr to be identical.
d) The remainder operator (%) can be used only with integer operands.
e) The arithmetic operators *, /, %, + and - all have the same level of precedence.

2.3 Write statements to accomplish each of the following tasks:
a) Declare variables c, thisIsAVariable, q76354 and number to be of type int.
b) Prompt the user to enter an integer.
c) Input an integer and assign the result to int variable value. Assume Scanner variable input can be used to read a value from the keyboard.
d) Print "This is a Java program" on one line in the command window. Use method System.out.println.
e) Print "This is a Java program" on two lines in the command window. The first line should end with Java. Use method System.out.println.
f) Print "This is a Java program" on two lines in the command window. The first line should end with Java. Use method System.out.printf and two %s format specifiers.
g) If the variable number is not equal to 7, display "The variable number is not equal to 7".

2.4 Identify and correct the errors in each of the following statements:
a) `if ( c < 7 );`
   `    System.out.println( "c is less than 7" );`
b) `if ( c => 7 )`
   `    System.out.println( "c is equal to or greater than 7" );`

2.5 Write declarations, statements or comments that accomplish each of the following tasks:
a) State that a program will calculate the product of three integers.
b) Create a Scanner called input that reads values from the standard input.
c) Declare the variables x, y, z and result to be of type int.
d) Prompt the user to enter the first integer.
e) Read the first integer from the user and store it in the variable x.
f) Prompt the user to enter the second integer.
g) Read the second integer from the user and store it in the variable y.
h) Prompt the user to enter the third integer.
i) Read the third integer from the user and store it in the variable z.
j) Compute the product of the three integers contained in variables x, y and z, and assign the result to the variable result.
k) Display the message "Product is" followed by the value of the variable result.

2.6 Using the statements you wrote in Exercise 2.5, write a complete program that calculates and prints the product of three integers.

Answers to Self-Review Exercises

2.1 a) left brace ({), right brace (}). b) if. c) //. d) Space characters, newlines and tabs. e) Keywords. f) main. g) System.out.print, System.out.println and System.out.printf.

2.2 a) False. Comments do not cause any action to be performed when the program executes. They are used to document programs and improve their readability.
b) True.
c) False. Java is case sensitive, so these variables are distinct.
d) False. The remainder operator can also be used with noninteger operands in Java.
e) False. The operators *, / and % are on the same level of precedence, and the operators + and - are on a lower level of precedence.

2.3 a) `int c, thisIsAVariable, q76354, number;`
   or

```
        int c;
        int thisIsAVariable;
        int q76354;
        int number;
```
b) `System.out.print( "Enter an integer: " );`
c) `value = input.nextInt();`
d) `System.out.println( "This is a Java program" );`
e) `System.out.println( "This is a Java\nprogram" );`
f) `System.out.printf( "%s\n%s\n", "This is a Java", "program" );`
g) ```
   if (number != 7)
       System.out.println("The variable number is not equal to 7");
   ```

**2.4**  a) Error: Semicolon after the right parenthesis of the condition ( c < 7 ) in the `if`.
Correction: Remove the semicolon after the right parenthesis. [*Note:* As a result, the
output statement will execute regardless of whether the condition in the `if` is true.]

b) Error: The relational operator `=>` is incorrect. Correction: Change `=>` to `>=`.

**2.5**  a) `// Calculate the product of three integers`
b) `Scanner input = new Scanner( System.in );`
c) `int x, y, z, result;`
or
```
int x;
int y;
int z;
int result;
```
d) `System.out.print( "Enter first integer: " );`
e) `x = input.nextInt();`
f) `System.out.print( "Enter second integer: " );`
g) `y = input.nextInt();`
h) `System.out.print( "Enter third integer: " );`
i) `z = input.nextInt();`
j) `result = x * y * z;`
k) `System.out.printf( "Product is %d\n", result );`

**2.6**  The solution to Self-Review Exercise 2.6 is as follows:

```
 1 // Ex. 2.6: Product.java
 2 // Calculate the product of three integers.
 3 import java.util.Scanner; // program uses Scanner
 4
 5 public class Product
 6 {
 7   public static void main(String[] args)
 8   {
 9   // create Scanner to obtain input from command window
10   Scanner input = new Scanner(System.in);
11
12   int x; // first number input by user
13   int y; // second number input by user
14   int z; // third number input by user
15   int result; // product of numbers
16
17   System.out.print("Enter first integer: "); // prompt for input
18   x = input.nextInt(); // read first integer
19
20   System.out.print("Enter second integer: "); // prompt for input
21   y = input.nextInt(); // read second integer
```
```

```
22
23          System.out.print( "Enter third integer: " ); // prompt for input
24          z = input.nextInt(); // read third integer
25
26          result = x * y * z; // calculate product of numbers
27
28          System.out.printf( "Product is %d\n", result );
29     } // end method main
30 } // end class Product
```

```
Enter first integer: 10
Enter second integer: 20
Enter third integer: 30
Product is 6000
```

Exercises

2.7   Write Java statements that accomplish each of the following tasks:
   a) Display the message "Enter an integer: ", leaving the cursor on the same line.
   b) Assign the product of variables b and c to variable a.
   c) State that a program performs a sample payroll calculation (i.e., use text that helps to document a program).

2.8   Assuming that x = 2 and y = 3, what does each of the following statements display?
   a) System.out.printf("x = %d\n", x);
   b) System.out.printf("Value of %d + %d is %d\n", x, x, (x + x));
   c) System.out.printf("x =");
   d) System.out.printf("%d = %d\n", (x + y), (y + x));

2.9   Given that $y = ax^3 + 7$, which of the following are correct Java statements for this equation?
   a) y = a * x * x * x + 7;
   b) y = a * x * x * (x + 7);
   c) y = (a * x) * x * (x + 7);
   d) y = (a * x) * x * x + 7;
   e) y = a * (x * x * x) + 7;
   f) y = a * x * (x * x + 7);

2.10   Write an application that displays the numbers 1 to 4 on the same line, with each pair of adjacent numbers separated by one space. Write the program using the following techniques:
   a) Use one System.out.println statement.
   b) Use four System.out.print statements.
   c) Use one System.out.printf statement.

2.11   *(Arithmetic)* Write an application that asks the user to enter two integers, obtains them from the user and prints their sum, product, difference and quotient (division). Use the techniques shown in Fig. 2.7.

2.12   *(Comparing Integers)* Write an application that asks the user to enter two integers, obtains them from the user and displays the larger number followed by the words "is larger". If the numbers are equal, print the message "These numbers are equal". Use the techniques shown in Fig. 2.15.

2.13   *(Arithmetic, Smallest and Largest)* Write an application that inputs three integers from the user and displays the sum, average, product, smallest and largest of the numbers. Use the techniques shown in Fig. 2.15. [*Note:* The calculation of the average in this exercise should result in an integer representation of the average. So, if the sum of the values is 7, the average should be 2, not 2.3333....]

2.14   What does the following code print?

```
System.out.println( "*\n**\n***\n****\n*****" );
```

2.15   What does the following code print?

```
System.out.println( "*" );
System.out.println( "***" );
System.out.println( "*****" );
System.out.println( "****" );
System.out.println( "**" );
```

2.16   What does the following code print?

```
System.out.print( "*" );
System.out.print( "***" );
System.out.print( "*****" );
System.out.print( "****" );
System.out.println( "**" );
```

2.17   What does the following code print?

```
System.out.print( "*" );
System.out.println( "***" );
System.out.println( "*****" );
System.out.print( "****" );
System.out.println( "**" );
```

2.18   What does the following code print?

```
System.out.printf( "%s\n%s\n%s\n", "*", "***", "*****" );
```

2.19   *(Largest and Smallest Integers)* Write an application that reads five integers, and determines and prints the largest and smallest integers in the group. Use only the programming techniques you learned in this chapter.

2.20   *(Odd or Even)* Write an application that reads an integer and determines and prints whether it's odd or even. [*Hint:* Use the remainder operator. An even number is a multiple of 2. Any multiple of 2 leaves a remainder of 0 when divided by 2.]

2.21   *(Multiples)* Write an application that reads two integers, determines whether the first is a multiple of the second and prints the result. [*Hint:* Use the remainder operator.]

2.22   *(Diameter, Circumference and Area of a Circle)* Here's a peek ahead. In this chapter, you learned about integers and the type int. Java can also represent floating-point numbers that contain decimal points, such as 3.14159. Write an application that inputs from the user the radius of a circle as an integer and prints the circle's diameter, circumference and area using the floating-point value 3.14159 for π. Use the techniques shown in Fig. 2.7. [*Note:* You may also use the predefined constant Math.PI for the value of π. This constant is more precise than the value 3.14159. Class Math is defined in package java.lang. Classes in that package are imported automatically, so you do not need to import class Math to use it.] Use the following formulas (r is the radius):

diameter = 2*r*
circumference = 2π*r*
area = πr^2

Do not store the results of each calculation in a variable. Rather, specify each calculation as the value that will be output in a System.out.printf statement. Note that the values produced by the circumference and area calculations are floating-point numbers. Such values can be output with the format specifier %f in a System.out.printf statement. You'll learn more about floating-point numbers in Chapter 3.

2.23   *(Separating the Digits in an Integer)* Write an application that inputs one number consisting of five digits from the user, separates the number into its individual digits and prints the digits separated from one another by three spaces each. For example, if the user types in the number 42339, the program should print

```
4   2   3   3   9
```

Assume that the user enters the correct number of digits. What happens when you execute the program and type a number with more than five digits? What happens when you execute the program and type a number with fewer than five digits? [*Hint:* It's possible to do this exercise with the techniques you learned in this chapter. You'll need to use both division and remainder operations to "pick off" each digit.]

2.24   *(Table of Squares and Cubes)* Using only the programming techniques you learned in this chapter, write an application that calculates the squares and cubes of the numbers from 0 to 10 and prints the resulting values in table format, as shown below. [*Note:* This program does not require any input from the user.]

```
number  square  cube
0       0       0
1       1       1
2       4       8
3       9       27
4       16      64
5       25      125
6       36      216
7       49      343
8       64      512
9       81      729
10      100     1000
```

2.25   *(Negative, Positive and Zero Values)* Write a program that inputs five numbers and determines and prints the number of negative numbers input, the number of positive numbers input and the number of zeros input.

Making a Difference

2.26   *(Body Mass Index Calculator)* We introduced the body mass index (BMI) calculator in Exercise 1.12. The formulas for calculating BMI are

$$BMI = \frac{weightInPounds \times 703}{heightInInches \times heightInInches}$$

or

$$BMI = \frac{weightInKilograms}{heightInMeters \times heightInMeters}$$

Create a BMI calculator application that reads the user's weight in pounds and height in inches (or, if you prefer, the user's weight in kilograms and height in meters), then calculates and displays the user's body mass index. Also, the application should display the following information from the Department of Health and Human Services/National Institutes of Health so the user can evaluate his/her BMI:

```
BMI VALUES
Underweight: less than 18.5
Normal:      between 18.5 and 24.9
Overweight:  between 25 and 29.9
Obese:       30 or greater
```

[*Note:* In this chapter, you learned to use the int type to represent whole numbers. The BMI calculations when done with int values will both produce whole-number results. In Chapter 3 you'll learn to use the double type to represent numbers with decimal points. When the BMI calculations are performed with doubles, they'll both produce numbers with decimal points—these are called "floating-point" numbers.]

2.27   *(World Population Growth Calculator)* Use the web to determine the current world population and the annual world population growth rate. Write an application that inputs these values, then displays the estimated world population after one, two, three, four and five years.

2.28   *(Car-Pool Savings Calculator)* Research several car-pooling websites. Create an application that calculates your daily driving cost, so that you can estimate how much money could be saved by car pooling, which also has other advantages such as reducing carbon emissions and reducing traffic congestion. The application should input the following information and display the user's cost per day of driving to work:

    a)   Total miles driven per day.
    b)   Cost per gallon of gasoline.
    c)   Average miles per gallon.
    d)   Parking fees per day.
    e)   Tolls per day.

3

> You'll see something new.
> Two things. And I call them
> Thing One and Thing Two.
> —Dr. Theodor Seuss Geisel

> Nothing can have value without being an object of
> utility.
> —Karl Marx

> Your public servants serve you right.
> —Adlai E. Stevenson

> Knowing how to answer one who speaks,
> To reply to one who sends a message.
> —Amenemope

Introduction to Classes and Objects

Objectives

In this chapter you'll learn:

- What classes, objects, methods and instance variables are.
- How to declare a class and use it to create an object.
- How to declare methods in a class to implement the class's behaviors.
- How to declare instance variables in a class to implement the class's attributes.
- How to call an object's methods to make those methods perform their tasks.
- The differences between instance variables of a class and local variables of a method.
- How to use a constructor to ensure that an object's data is initialized when the object is created.
- The differences between primitive and reference types.

Outline

3.1 Introduction

We introduced the basic terminology and concepts of object-oriented programming in Section 1.16. Typically, the applications you develop in this book will consist of two or more classes, each containing one or more methods. If you become part of a development team in industry, you might work on applications that contain hundreds, or even thousands, of classes. In this chapter, we present a simple framework for organizing object-oriented applications in Java.

First, we motivate the notion of classes with a real-world example. Then we present five complete working applications to demonstrate creating and using your own classes. The first four of these examples begin our case study on developing a grade book class that instructors can use to maintain student test scores. This case study is enhanced in Chapters 4, 5 and 7. The last example in the chapter introduces floating-point numbers—that is, numbers containing decimal points—in the context of a bank account class that maintains a customer's balance.

3.2 Classes, Objects, Methods and Instance Variables

Let's begin with a simple analogy to help you understand classes and their contents. Suppose you want to drive a car and make it go faster by pressing down on its accelerator pedal. What must happen before you can do this? Well, before you can drive a car, someone has to design it. A car typically begins as engineering drawings, similar to the blueprints used to design a house. These engineering drawings include the design for an accelerator pedal to make the car go faster. The pedal "hides" from the driver the complex mechanisms that actually make the car go faster, just as the brake pedal "hides" the mechanisms that slow the car and the steering wheel "hides" the mechanisms that turn the car. This enables people with little or no knowledge of how engines work to drive a car easily.

Unfortunately, you cannot drive a car's engineering drawings. Before you can drive a car, it must be built from the engineering drawings that describe it. A completed car has an actual accelerator pedal to make the car go faster, but even that's not enough—the car won't accelerate on its own, so the driver must press the accelerator pedal.

Now let's use our car example to introduce the key programming concepts of this section. Performing a task in a program requires a method. The method describes the mechanisms that actually perform its tasks. The method hides from its user the complex tasks that it performs, just as the accelerator pedal of a car hides from the driver the complex mechanisms of making the car go faster. In Java, we begin by creating a program unit called a class to house a method, just as a car's engineering drawings house the design of an accelerator pedal. In a class, you provide one or more methods that are designed to perform the class's tasks. For example, a class that represents a bank account might contain one method to deposit money to an account, another to withdraw money from an account and a third to inquire what the current balance is.

Just as you cannot drive an engineering drawing of a car, you cannot "drive" a class. Just as someone has to build a car from its engineering drawings before you can actually drive a car, you must build an object of a class before you can get a program to perform the tasks the class describes how to do. That is one reason Java is known as an object-oriented programming language.

When you drive a car, pressing its gas pedal sends a message to the car to perform a task—that is, make the car go faster. Similarly, you **send messages** to an object—each message is implemented as a **method call** that tells a method of the object to perform its task.

Thus far, we've used the car analogy to introduce classes, objects and methods. A car, in addition to it's capabilities, also has many attributes, such as its color, the number of doors, the amount of gas in its tank, its current speed and its total miles driven (i.e., its odometer reading). Like the car's capabilities, these attributes are represented as part of a car's design in its engineering diagrams. As you drive a car, these attributes are always associated with the car. Every car maintains its own attributes. For example, each car knows how much gas is in its own gas tank, but not how much is in the tanks of other cars. Similarly, an object has attributes that are carried with the object as it's used in a program. These attributes are specified as part of the object's class. For example, a bank account object has a balance attribute that represents the amount of money in the account. Each bank account object knows the balance in the account it represents, but not the balances of the other accounts in the bank. Attributes are specified by the class's **instance variables**.

Overview of This Chapter's Examples

The remainder of this chapter presents examples that demonstrate the concepts we introduced in the context of the car analogy. The first four examples incrementally build a GradeBook class to demonstrate these concepts:

1. The first example presents a GradeBook class with one method that simply displays a welcome message when it's called. We then show how to create an object of that class and call the method so that it displays the welcome message.

2. The second example enhances the first by allowing the method to receive a course name as an argument and by displaying the name as part of the welcome message.

3. The third example shows how to store the course name in a GradeBook object. For this version of the class, we also show how to use methods to set the course name and obtain the course name.

4. The fourth example demonstrates how the data in a GradeBook object can be initialized when the object is created.

The last example presents an Account class that reinforces the concepts presented in the first four examples and introduces floating-point numbers. The Account class represents a bank account and maintains its balance as a floating-point number. The class contains two methods—one that credits a deposit to the account, thus increasing the balance, and another that retrieves the balance. The class's constructor allows the balance of each `Account` object to be initialized as the object is created. We create two `Account` objects and make deposits into each to show that each object maintains its own balance. The example also demonstrates how to input and display floating-point numbers.

3.3 Declaring a Class with a Method and Instantiating an Object of a Class

In Sections 2.5 and 2.8, you created an object of the existing class `Scanner`, then used that object to read data from the keyboard. In this section, you create a new class, then use it to create an object. We begin with an example that consists of classes `GradeBook` (Fig. 3.1) and `GradeBookTest` (Fig. 3.2). Class `GradeBook` (declared in file `GradeBook.java`) will be used to display a message on the screen (Fig. 3.2) welcoming the instructor to the grade book application. Class `GradeBookTest` (declared in file `GradeBookTest.java`) is an application class in which the `main` method will use an object of class `GradeBook`. Each class declaration that begins with keyword `public` must be stored in a file that has the same name as the class and ends with the `.java` file-name extension. Thus, classes `GradeBook` and `GradeBookTest` must be declared in separate files, because each class is declared public. As we'll discuss, starting in Chapter 8, there are other ways to declare classes.

Common Programming Error 3.1
Declaring more than one `public` class in the same file is a compilation error.

Class *GradeBook*
The `GradeBook` class declaration (Fig. 3.1) contains a `displayMessage` method (lines 7–10) that displays a message on the screen. Recall that a class is like a blueprint—we'll need to make an object of this class and call its method to execute line 9 and display the message.

```
 1   // Fig. 3.1: GradeBook.java
 2   // Class declaration with one method.
 3
 4   public class GradeBook
 5   {
 6      // display a welcome message to the GradeBook user
 7      public void displayMessage()
 8      {
 9         System.out.println( "Welcome to the Grade Book!" );
10      } // end method displayMessage
11   } // end class GradeBook
```

Fig. 3.1 | Class declaration with one method.

The class declaration begins in line 4. The keyword `public` is an **access modifier**. For now, we'll simply declare every class `public`. Every class declaration contains keyword `class` followed immediately by the class's name. Every class's body is enclosed in a pair of left and right braces, as in lines 5 and 11 of class `GradeBook`.

In Chapter 2, each class we declared had one method named `main`. Class `GradeBook` also has one method—`displayMessage` (lines 7–10). Recall that `main` is a special method that is always called automatically by the Java Virtual Machine (JVM) when you execute an application. Most methods do not get called automatically. As you'll soon see, you must call method displayMessage explicitly to tell it to perform its task.

The method declaration begins with keyword public to indicate that the method is "available to the public"—it can be called from methods of other classes. Next is the method's **return type**, which specifies the type of data the method returns after performing its task. The return type void indicates that this method will perform a task but will *not* return (i.e., give back) any information to its **calling method** when it completes its task. You've already used methods that return information—for example, in Chapter 2 you used Scanner method nextInt to input an integer typed by the user at the keyboard. When nextInt reads a value from the user, it returns that value for use in the program.

The name of the method, displayMessage, follows the return type. By convention, method names begin with a lowercase first letter and subsequent words in the name begin with a capital letter. The parentheses after the method name indicate that this is a method. Empty parentheses, as in line 7, indicate that this method does not require additional information to perform its task. Line 7 is commonly referred to as the **method header**. Every method's body is delimited by left and right braces, as in lines 8 and 10.

The body of a method contains one or more statements that perform the method's task. In this case, the method contains one statement (line 9) that displays the message "Welcome to the Grade Book!" followed by a newline in the command window. After this statement executes, the method has completed its task.

Next, we'd like to use class GradeBook in an application. As you learned in Chapter 2, method main begins the execution of every application. A class that contains method main begins the execution of a Java application. Class GradeBook is not an application because it does not contain main. Therefore, if you try to execute GradeBook by typing java Grade-Book in the command window, you'll receive an error message like:

```
Exception in thread "main" java.lang.NoSuchMethodError: main
```

This was not a problem in Chapter 2, because every class you declared had a main method. To fix this problem, we must either declare a separate class that contains a main method or place a main method in class GradeBook. To help you prepare for the larger programs you'll encounter later in this book and in industry, we use a separate class (GradeBookTest in this example) containing method main to test each new class we create in this chapter. Some programmers refer to such a class as a driver class.

Class *GradeBookTest*

The GradeBookTest class declaration (Fig. 3.2) contains the main method that will control our application's execution. The GradeBookTest class declaration begins in line 4 and ends in line 15. The class contains only a main method, which is typical of many classes that begin an application's execution.

```
1   // Fig. 3.2: GradeBookTest.java
2   // Creating a GradeBook object and calling its displayMessage method.
3
4   public class GradeBookTest
5   {
```

Fig. 3.2 | Creating a GradeBook object and calling its displayMessage method. (Part I of 2.)

```
 6      // main method begins program execution
 7      public static void main( String[] args )
 8      {
 9         // create a GradeBook object and assign it to myGradeBook
10         GradeBook myGradeBook = new GradeBook();
11
12         // call myGradeBook's displayMessage method
13         myGradeBook.displayMessage();
14      } // end main
15   } // end class GradeBookTest
```

```
Welcome to the Grade Book!
```

Fig. 3.2 | Creating a GradeBook object and calling its displayMessage method. (Part 2 of 2.)

Lines 7–14 declare method main. A key part of enabling the JVM to locate and call method main to begin the application's execution is the static keyword (line 7), which indicates that main is a static method. A static method is special, because it can be called without first creating an object of the class in which the method is declared. We thoroughly explain static methods in Chapter 6, Methods: A Deeper Look.

In this application, we'd like to call class GradeBook's displayMessage method to display the welcome message in the command window. Typically, you cannot call a method that belongs to another class until you create an object of that class, as shown in line 10. We begin by declaring variable myGradeBook. Note that the variable's type is GradeBook— the class we declared in Fig. 3.1. Each new class you create becomes a new type that can be used to declare variables and create objects. You can declare new class types as needed; this is one reason why Java is known as an **extensible language**.

Variable myGradeBook is initialized with the result of the **class instance creation expression** new GradeBook(). Keyword **new** creates a new object of the class specified to the right of the keyword (i.e., GradeBook). The parentheses to the right of GradeBook are required. As you'll learn in Section 3.7, those parentheses in combination with a class name represent a call to a **constructor**, which is similar to a method but is used only at the time an object is created to initialize the object's data. In that section you'll see that data can be placed in the parentheses to specify initial values for the object's data. For now, we simply leave the parentheses empty.

Just as we can use object System.out to call methods print, printf and println, we can use object myGradeBook to call method displayMessage. Line 13 calls the method displayMessage (lines 7–10 of Fig. 3.1) using myGradeBook followed by a **dot separator** (.), the method name displayMessage and an empty set of parentheses. This call causes the displayMessage method to perform its task. This method call differs from those in Chapter 2 that displayed information in a command window—each of those method calls provided arguments that specified the data to display. At the beginning of line 13, "myGradeBook." indicates that main should use the myGradeBook object that was created in line 10. Line 7 of Fig. 3.1 indicates that method displayMessage has an empty parameter list—that is, displayMessage does not require additional information to perform its task. For this reason, the method call (line 13 of Fig. 3.2) specifies an empty set of parentheses after the method name to indicate that no arguments are being passed to method displayMessage. When method displayMessage completes its task, method main continues executing at line 14. This is the end of method main, so the program terminates.

Note that any class can contain a main method. The JVM invokes the main method only in the class used to execute the application. If an application has multiple classes that contain main, then one that is invoked is the one in the class named in the java command.

Compiling an Application with Multiple Classes

You must compile the classes in Fig. 3.1 and Fig. 3.2 before you can execute the application. First, change to the directory that contains the application's source-code files. Next, type the command

```
javac GradeBook.java GradeBookTest.java
```

to compile both classes at once. If the directory containing the application includes only this application's files, you can compile all the classes in the directory with the command

```
javac *.java
```

The asterisk (*) in *.java indicates that all files in the current directory that end with the file-name extension ".java" should be compiled.

UML Class Diagram for Class GradeBook

Figure 3.3 presents a **UML class diagram** for class GradeBook of Fig. 3.1. Recall from Section 1.16 that the UML is a graphical language used by programmers to represent object-oriented systems in a standardized manner. In the UML, each class is modeled in a class diagram as a rectangle with three **compartments**. The top one contains the name of the class centered horizontally in boldface type. The middle compartment contains the class's attributes, which correspond to instance variables (discussed in Section 3.5) in Java. In Fig. 3.3, the middle compartment is empty, because this GradeBook class does not have any attributes. The bottom compartment contains the class's **operations**, which correspond to methods in Java. The UML models operations by listing the operation name preceded by an access modifier (in this case +) and followed by a set of parentheses. Class GradeBook has one method, displayMessage, so the bottom compartment of Fig. 3.3 lists one operation with this name. Method displayMessage does not require additional information to perform its tasks, so the parentheses following the method name in the class diagram are empty, just as they were in the method's declaration in line 7 of Fig. 3.1. The plus sign (+) in front of the operation name indicates that displayMessage is a public operation in the UML (i.e., a public method in Java). We'll often use UML class diagrams to summarize a class's attributes and operations.

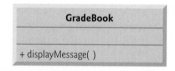

Fig. 3.3 | UML class diagram indicating that class GradeBook has a public displayMessage operation.

3.4 Declaring a Method with a Parameter

In our car analogy from Section 3.2, we discussed the fact that pressing a car's gas pedal sends a message to the car to perform a task—make the car go faster. But how fast should the car accelerate? As you know, the farther down you press the pedal, the faster the car accelerates. So the message to the car actually includes the task to perform and additional information that helps the car perform the task. This additional information is known as a **parameter**—the value of the parameter helps the car determine how fast to accelerate. Similarly, a method can require one or more parameters that represent additional information it needs to perform its task. Parameters are defined in a comma-separated **parameter list**, which is located in the parentheses that follow the method name. Each parameter must specify a type and an identifier. The parameter list may contain any number of parameters, including none at all. Empty parentheses following the method name (as in Fig. 3.1, line 7) indicate that a method does not require any parameters.

A method call supplies values—called arguments—for each of the method's parameters. For example, the method System.out.println requires an argument that specifies the data to output in a command window. Similarly, to make a deposit into a bank account, a deposit method specifies a parameter that represents the deposit amount. When the deposit method is called, an argument value representing the deposit amount is assigned to the method's parameter. The method then makes a deposit of that amount.

Our next example declares class GradeBook (Fig. 3.4) with a displayMessage method that displays the course name as part of the welcome message. (See the sample execution in Fig. 3.5.) The new displayMessage method requires a parameter that represents the course name to output.

```
1   // Fig. 3.4: GradeBook.java
2   // Class declaration with a method that has a parameter.
3
4   public class GradeBook
5   {
6      // display a welcome message to the GradeBook user
7      public void displayMessage( String courseName )
8      {
9         System.out.printf( "Welcome to the grade book for\n%s!\n",
10           courseName );
11     } // end method displayMessage
12  } // end class GradeBook
```

Fig. 3.4 | Class declaration with one method that has a parameter.

```
1   // Fig. 3.5: GradeBookTest.java
2   // Create GradeBook object and pass a String to
3   // its displayMessage method.
4   import java.util.Scanner; // program uses Scanner
5
6   public class GradeBookTest
7   {
8      // main method begins program execution
9      public static void main( String[] args )
10     {
11        // create Scanner to obtain input from command window
12        Scanner input = new Scanner( System.in );
```

Fig. 3.5 | Creating a GradeBook object and passing a String to its displayMessage method. (Part 1 of 2.)

```
13
14      // create a GradeBook object and assign it to myGradeBook
15      GradeBook myGradeBook = new GradeBook();
16
17      // prompt for and input course name
18      System.out.println( "Please enter the course name:" );
19      String nameOfCourse = input.nextLine(); // read a line of text
20      System.out.println(); // outputs a blank line
21
22      // call myGradeBook's displayMessage method
23      // and pass nameOfCourse as an argument
24      myGradeBook.displayMessage( nameOfCourse );
25   } // end main
26 } // end class GradeBookTest
```

```
Please enter the course name:
CS101 Introduction to Java Programming

Welcome to the grade book for
CS101 Introduction to Java Programming!
```

Fig. 3.5 | Creating a GradeBook object and passing a String to its displayMessage method. (Part 2 of 2.)

Before discussing the new features of class GradeBook, let's see how the new class is used from the main method of class GradeBookTest (Fig. 3.5). Line 12 creates a Scanner named input for reading the course name from the user. Line 15 creates an object of class GradeBook and assigns it to variable myGradeBook. Line 18 prompts the user to enter a course name. Line 19 reads the name from the user and assigns it to the nameOfCourse variable, using Scanner method **nextLine** to perform the input. The user types the course name and presses *Enter* to submit the course name to the program. Note that pressing *Enter* inserts a newline character at the end of the characters typed by the user. Method nextLine reads characters typed by the user until the newline character is encountered, then returns a String containing the characters up to, but not including, the newline. The newline character is discarded. Class Scanner also provides a similar method—**next**—that reads individual words. When the user presses *Enter* after typing input, method next reads characters until a white-space character (such as a space, tab or newline) is encountered, then returns a String containing the characters up to, but not including, the white-space character (which is discarded). All information after the first white-space character is not lost—it can be read by other statements that call the Scanner's methods later in the program. Line 20 outputs a blank line.

Line 24 calls myGradeBooks's displayMessage method. The variable nameOfCourse in parentheses is the *argument* that is passed to method displayMessage so that the method can perform its task. The value of variable nameOfCourse in main becomes the value of method displayMessage's *parameter* courseName in line 7 of Fig. 3.4. When you execute this application, notice that method displayMessage outputs the name you type as part of the welcome message (Fig. 3.5).

More on Arguments and Parameters
In Fig. 3.4, displayMessage's parameter list (line 7) declares one parameter indicating that the method requires a String to perform its task. When the method is called, the ar-

gument value in the call is assigned to the corresponding parameter (in this case, course-Name) in the method header. Then, the method body uses the value of the courseName parameter. Lines 9–10 of Fig. 3.4 display parameter courseName's value, using the %s format specifier in printf's format string. Note that the parameter variable's name (course-Name in Fig. 3.4, line 7) can be the same or different from the argument variable's name (nameOfCourse in Fig. 3.5, line 24).

The number of arguments in a method call must match the number of parameters in the parameter list of the method's declaration. Also, the argument types in the method call must be "consistent with" the types of the corresponding parameters in the method's declaration. (As you'll learn in subsequent chapters, an argument's type and its corresponding parameter's type are not always required to be identical.) In our example, the method call passes one argument of type String (nameOfCourse is declared as a String in line 19 of Fig. 3.5) and the method declaration specifies one parameter of type String (courseName is declared as a String in line 7 of Fig. 3.4). So in this example the type of the argument in the method call exactly matches the type of the parameter in the method header.

Common Programming Error 3.2

A compilation error occurs if the number of arguments in a method call does not match the number of parameters in the method declaration.

Common Programming Error 3.3

A compilation error occurs if the type of any argument in a method call is not consistent with the type of the corresponding parameter in the method declaration.

Updated UML Class Diagram for Class GradeBook

The UML class diagram of Fig. 3.6 models class GradeBook of Fig. 3.4. Like Fig. 3.1, this GradeBook class contains public operation displayMessage. However, this version of displayMessage has a parameter. The UML models a parameter a bit differently from Java by listing the parameter name, followed by a colon and the parameter type in the parentheses following the operation name. The UML has its own data types similar to those of Java (but, as you'll see, not all the UML data types have the same names as the corresponding Java types). The UML type String does correspond to the Java type String. GradeBook method displayMessage (Fig. 3.4) has a String parameter named courseName, so Fig. 3.6 lists courseName : String between the parentheses following displayMessage.

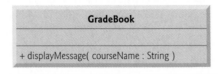

Fig. 3.6 | UML class diagram indicating that class GradeBook has a displayMessage operation with a courseName parameter of UML type String.

Notes on import Declarations

Notice the import declaration in Fig. 3.5 (line 4). This indicates to the compiler that the program uses class Scanner. Why do we need to import class Scanner, but not classes

System, String or GradeBook? Classes System and String are in package java.lang, which is implicitly imported into every Java program, so all programs can use that package's classes without explicitly importing them. Most other classes you'll use in Java programs must be imported explicitly.

There is a special relationship between classes that are compiled in the same directory on disk, like classes GradeBook and GradeBookTest. By default, such classes are considered to be in the same package—known as the **default package**. Classes in the same package are implicitly imported into the source-code files of other classes in the same package. Thus, an import declaration is not required when one class in a package uses another in the same package—such as when class GradeBookTest uses class GradeBook.

The import declaration in line 4 is not required if we always refer to class Scanner as java.util.Scanner, which includes the full package name and class name. This is known as the class's **fully qualified class name**. For example, line 12 could be written as

```
java.util.Scanner input = new java.util.Scanner( System.in );
```

Software Engineering Observation 3.1

The Java compiler does not require import declarations in a Java source-code file if the fully qualified class name is specified every time a class name is used in the source code. Most Java programmers prefer to use import declarations.

3.5 Instance Variables, *set* Methods and *get* Methods

In Chapter 2, we declared all of an application's variables in the application's main method. Variables declared in the body of a particular method are known as **local variables** and can be used only in that method. When that method terminates, the values of its local variables are lost. Recall from Section 3.2 that an object has attributes that are carried with the object as it's used in a program. Such attributes exist before a method is called on an object and after the method completes execution.

A class normally consists of one or more methods that manipulate the attributes that belong to a particular object of the class. Attributes are represented as variables in a class declaration. Such variables are called **fields** and are declared inside a class declaration but outside the bodies of the class's method declarations. When each object of a class maintains its own copy of an attribute, the field that represents the attribute is also known as an **instance variable**—each object (instance) of the class has a separate instance of the variable in memory. The example in this section demonstrates a GradeBook class that contains a courseName instance variable to represent a particular GradeBook object's course name.

GradeBook* Class with an Instance Variable, a set *Method and a* get *Method
In our next application (Figs. 3.7–3.8), class GradeBook (Fig. 3.7) maintains the course name as an instance variable so that it can be used or modified at any time during an application's execution. The class contains three methods—setCourseName, getCourseName and displayMessage. Method setCourseName stores a course name in a GradeBook. Method getCourseName obtains a GradeBook's course name. Method displayMessage, which now specifies no parameters, still displays a welcome message that includes the course name; as you'll see, the method now obtains the course name by calling another method in the same class—getCourseName.

```
 1   // Fig. 3.7: GradeBook.java
 2   // GradeBook class that contains a courseName instance variable
 3   // and methods to set and get its value.
 4
 5   public class GradeBook
 6   {
 7      private String courseName; // course name for this GradeBook
 8
 9      // method to set the course name
10      public void setCourseName( String name )
11      {
12         courseName = name; // store the course name
13      } // end method setCourseName
14
15      // method to retrieve the course name
16      public String getCourseName()
17      {
18         return courseName;
19      } // end method getCourseName
20
21      // display a welcome message to the GradeBook user
22      public void displayMessage()
23      {
24         // calls getCourseName to get the name of
25         // the course this GradeBook represents
26         System.out.printf( "Welcome to the grade book for\n%s!\n",
27            getCourseName() );
28      } // end method displayMessage
29   } // end class GradeBook
```

Fig. 3.7 | GradeBook class that contains a `courseName` instance variable and methods to set and get its value.

A typical instructor teaches more than one course, each with its own course name. Line 7 declares that `courseName` is a variable of type `String`. Because the variable is declared in the body of the class but outside the bodies of the class's methods (lines 10–13, 16–19 and 22–28), line 7 is a declaration for an instance variable. Every instance (i.e., object) of class `GradeBook` contains one copy of each instance variable. For example, if there are two `GradeBook` objects, each object has its own copy of `courseName` (one per object). A benefit of making `courseName` an instance variable is that all the methods of the class (in this case, `GradeBook`) can manipulate any instance variables that appear in the class (in this case, `courseName`).

Access Modifiers *public and private*
Most instance-variable declarations are preceded with the keyword `private` (as in line 7). Like `public`, keyword **private** is an access modifier. Variables or methods declared with access modifier `private` are accessible only to methods of the class in which they are declared. Thus, variable `courseName` can be used only in methods `setCourseName`, `getCourseName` and `displayMessage` of (every object of) class `GradeBook`.

Declaring instance variables with access modifier `private` is known as **data hiding** or information hiding. When a program creates (instantiates) an object of class `GradeBook`, variable `courseName` is encapsulated (hidden) in the object and can be accessed only by methods of the object's class. This prevents courseName from being modified accidentally by a class in another part of the program. In class GradeBook, methods setCourseName and getCourseName manipulate the instance variable courseName.

Software Engineering Observation 3.2

Precede each field and method declaration with an access modifier. Generally, instance variables should be declared private and methods public. (We'll see that it's appropriate to declare certain methods private, if they'll be accessed only by other methods of the class.)

Good Programming Practice 3.1

We prefer to list a class's fields first, so that, as you read the code, you see the names and types of the variables before they're used in the class's methods. You can list the class's fields anywhere in the class outside its method declarations, but scattering them tends to lead to hard-to-read code.

Good Programming Practice 3.2

Place a blank line between method declarations to separate the methods and enhance program readability.

Methods *setCourseName* and *getCourseName*

Method setCourseName (lines 10–13) does not return any data when it completes its task, so its return type is void. The method receives one parameter—name—which represents the course name that will be passed to the method as an argument. Line 12 assigns name to instance variable courseName.

Method getCourseName (lines 16–19) returns a particular GradeBook object's courseName. The method has an empty parameter list, so it does not require additional information to perform its task. The method specifies that it returns a String—this is the method's return type. When a method that specifies a return type other than void is called and completes its task, the method returns a result to its calling method. For example, when you go to an automated teller machine (ATM) and request your account balance, you expect the ATM to give you back a value that represents your balance. Similarly, when a statement calls method getCourseName on a GradeBook object, the statement expects to receive the GradeBook's course name (in this case, a String, as specified in the method declaration's return type).

The **return** statement in line 18 passes the value of instance variable courseName back to the statement that calls method getCourseName. Consider, method displayMessage's line 27, which calls method getCourseName. When the value is returned, the statement in lines 26–27 uses that value to output the course name. Similarly, if you have a method square that returns the square of its argument, you'd expect the statement

```
int result = square( 2 );
```

to return 4 from method square and assign 4 to the variable result. If you have a method maximum that returns the largest of three integer arguments, you'd expect the statement

```
int biggest = maximum( 27, 114, 51 );
```

to return 114 from method maximum and assign 114 to variable biggest.

Note that the statements in lines 12 and 18 each use courseName even though it was not declared in any of the methods. We can use courseName in GradeBook's methods because courseName is an instance variable of the class. Also note that the order in which methods are declared in a class does not determine when they are called at execution time. So method getCourseName could be declared before method setCourseName.

Method displayMessage

Method displayMessage (lines 22–28) does not return any data when it completes its task, so its return type is void. The method does not receive parameters, so the parameter list is empty. Lines 26–27 output a welcome message that includes the value of instance variable courseName, which is returned by the call to method getCourseName in line 27. Notice that one method of a class (displayMessage in this case) can call another method of the same class by using just the method name (getCourseName in this case). Once again, we need to create an object of class GradeBook and call its methods before the welcome message can be displayed.

GradeBookTest Class That Demonstrates Class GradeBook

Class GradeBookTest (Fig. 3.8) creates one object of class GradeBook and demonstrates its methods. Line 14 creates a GradeBook object and assigns it to local variable myGradeBook of type GradeBook. Lines 17–18 display the initial course name calling the object's getCourse-Name method. Note that the first line of the output shows the name "null." Unlike local variables, which are not automatically initialized, every field has a **default initial value**—a value provided by Java when you do not specify the field's initial value. Thus, fields are not required to be explicitly initialized before they are used in a program—unless they must be initialized to values other than their default values. The default value for a field of type String (like courseName in this example) is null, which we say more about in Section 3.6.

```java
1   // Fig. 3.8: GradeBookTest.java
2   // Creating and manipulating a GradeBook object.
3   import java.util.Scanner; // program uses Scanner
4
5   public class GradeBookTest
6   {
7      // main method begins program execution
8      public static void main( String[] args )
9      {
10        // create Scanner to obtain input from command window
11        Scanner input = new Scanner( System.in );
12
13        // create a GradeBook object and assign it to myGradeBook
14        GradeBook myGradeBook = new GradeBook();
15
16        // display initial value of courseName
17        System.out.printf( "Initial course name is: %s\n\n",
18           myGradeBook.getCourseName() );
19
20        // prompt for and read course name
21        System.out.println( "Please enter the course name:" );
22        String theName = input.nextLine(); // read a line of text
23        myGradeBook.setCourseName( theName ); // set the course name
24        System.out.println(); // outputs a blank line
25
```

Fig. 3.8 | Creating and manipulating a GradeBook object. (Part 1 of 2.)

```
26          // display welcome message after specifying course name
27          myGradeBook.displayMessage();
28      } // end main
29  } // end class GradeBookTest
```

```
Initial course name is: null

Please enter the course name:
CS101 Introduction to Java Programming

Welcome to the grade book for
CS101 Introduction to Java Programming!
```

Fig. 3.8 | Creating and manipulating a GradeBook object. (Part 2 of 2.)

Line 21 prompts the user to enter a course name. Local String variable theName (declared in line 22) is initialized with the course name entered by the user, which is returned by the call to the nextLine method of the Scanner object input. Line 23 calls object myGradeBook's setCourseName method and supplies theName as the method's argument. When the method is called, the argument's value is assigned to parameter name (line 10, Fig. 3.7) of method setCourseName (lines 10–13, Fig. 3.7). Then the parameter's value is assigned to instance variable courseName (line 12, Fig. 3.7). Line 24 (Fig. 3.8) skips a line in the output, then line 27 calls object myGradeBook's displayMessage method to display the welcome message containing the course name.

set *and* get *Methods*
A class's private fields can be manipulated only by the class's methods. So a **client of an object**—that is, any class that calls the object's methods—calls the class's public methods to manipulate the private fields of an object of the class. This is why the statements in method main (Fig. 3.8) call the setCourseName, getCourseName and displayMessage methods on a GradeBook object. Classes often provide public methods to allow clients to *set* (i.e., assign values to) or *get* (i.e., obtain the values of) private instance variables. The names of these methods need not begin with *set* or *get*, but this naming convention is recommended and is required for special Java software components called JavaBeans that can simplify programming in many Java integrated development environments (IDEs). The method that *sets* instance variable courseName in this example is called setCourseName, and the method that *gets* the value of courseName is called getCourseName.

GradeBook UML Class Diagram with an Instance Variable and set *and* get *Methods*
Figure 3.9 contains an updated UML class diagram for the version of class GradeBook in Fig. 3.7. This diagram models class GradeBook's instance variable courseName as an attribute in the middle compartment of the class. The UML represents instance variables as attributes by listing the attribute name, followed by a colon and the attribute type. The UML type of attribute courseName is String. Instance variable courseName is private in Java, so the class diagram lists a minus sign (–) access modifier in front of the corresponding attribute's name. Class GradeBook contains three public methods, so the class diagram lists three operations in the third compartment. Recall that the plus sign (+) before each operation name indicates that the operation is public. Operation setCourseName has a String parameter called name. The UML indicates the return type of an operation by placing a colon and the return type after the parentheses following the operation name. Meth-

od getCourseName of class GradeBook (Fig. 3.7) has a String return type in Java, so the class diagram shows a String return type in the UML. Note that operations setCourse-Name and displayMessage do not return values (i.e., they return void in Java), so the UML class diagram does not specify a return type after the parentheses of these operations.

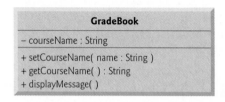

| **GradeBook** |
| – courseName : String |
| + setCourseName(name : String)
+ getCourseName( ) : String
+ displayMessage( ) |

Fig. 3.9 | UML class diagram indicating that class GradeBook has a private courseName attribute of UML type String and three public operations—setCourseName (with a name parameter of UML type String), getCourseName (which returns UML type String) and displayMessage.

3.6 Primitive Types vs. Reference Types

Java's types are divided into primitive types and **reference types**. The primitive types are boolean, byte, char, short, int, long, float and double. All nonprimitive types are reference types, so classes, which specify the types of objects, are reference types.

A primitive-type variable can store exactly one value of its declared type at a time. For example, an int variable can store one whole number (such as 7) at a time. When another value is assigned to that variable, its initial value is replaced. Primitive-type instance variables are initialized by default—variables of types byte, char, short, int, long, float and double are initialized to 0, and variables of type boolean are initialized to false. You can specify your own initial value for a primitive-type variable by assigning the variable a value in its declaration. Recall that local variables are *not* initialized by default.

Error-Prevention Tip 3.1
An attempt to use an uninitialized local variable causes a compilation error.

Programs use variables of reference types (normally called **references**) to store the locations of objects in the computer's memory. Such a variable is said to **refer to an object** in the program. Objects that are referenced may each contain many instance variables and methods. Line 14 of Fig. 3.8 creates an object of class GradeBook, and the variable myGradeBook contains a reference to that GradeBook object. Reference-type instance variables are initialized by default to the value null—a reserved word that represents a "reference to nothing." This is why the first call to getCourseName in line 18 of Fig. 3.8 returned null—the value of courseName had not been set, so the default initial value null was returned. The complete list of reserved words and keywords is listed in Appendix C.

When using an object of another class, a reference to the object is required to **invoke** (i.e., call) its methods. In the application of Fig. 3.8, the statements in method main use the variable myGradeBook to send messages to the GradeBook object. These messages are calls to methods (like setCourseName and getCourseName) that enable the program to interact with the GradeBook object. For example, the statement in line 23 uses myGrade-

Book to send the setCourseName message to the GradeBook object. The message includes the argument that setCourseName requires to perform its task. The GradeBook object uses this information to set the courseName instance variable. Note that primitive-type variables do not refer to objects, so such variables cannot be used to invoke methods.

Software Engineering Observation 3.3

A variable's declared type (e.g., int, double or GradeBook) indicates whether the variable is of a primitive or a reference type. If a variable's type is not one of the eight primitive types, then it's a reference type.

3.7 Initializing Objects with Constructors

As mentioned in Section 3.5, when an object of class GradeBook (Fig. 3.7) is created, its instance variable courseName is initialized to null by default. What if you want to provide a course name when you create a GradeBook object? Each class you declare can provide a special method called a constructor that can be used to initialize an object of a class when the object is created. In fact, Java requires a constructor call for *every* object that is created. Keyword new requests memory from the system to store an object, then calls the corresponding class's constructor to initialize the object. The call is indicated by the parentheses after the class name. A constructor *must* have the same name as the class. For example, line 14 of Fig. 3.8 first uses new to create a GradeBook object. The empty parentheses after "new GradeBook" indicate a call to the class's constructor without arguments. By default, the compiler provides a **default constructor** with no parameters in any class that does not explicitly include a constructor. When a class has only the default constructor, its instance variables are initialized to their default values.

When you declare a class, you can provide your own constructor to specify custom initialization for objects of your class. For example, you might want to specify a course name for a GradeBook object when the object is created, as in

```
GradeBook myGradeBook =
    new GradeBook( "CS101 Introduction to Java Programming" );
```

In this case, the argument "CS101 Introduction to Java Programming" is passed to the GradeBook object's constructor and used to initialize the courseName. The preceding statement requires that the class provide a constructor with a String parameter. Figure 3.10 contains a modified GradeBook class with such a constructor.

```
 1   // Fig. 3.10: GradeBook.java
 2   // GradeBook class with a constructor to initialize the course name.
 3
 4   public class GradeBook
 5   {
 6      private String courseName; // course name for this GradeBook
 7
 8      // constructor initializes courseName with String argument
 9      public GradeBook( String name )
10      {
11         courseName = name; // initializes courseName
12      } // end constructor
```

Fig. 3.10 | GradeBook class with a constructor to initialize the course name. (Part 1 of 2.)

```
13
14      // method to set the course name
15      public void setCourseName( String name )
16      {
17         courseName = name; // store the course name
18      } // end method setCourseName
19
20      // method to retrieve the course name
21      public String getCourseName()
22      {
23         return courseName;
24      } // end method getCourseName
25
26      // display a welcome message to the GradeBook user
27      public void displayMessage()
28      {
29         // this statement calls getCourseName to get the
30         // name of the course this GradeBook represents
31         System.out.printf( "Welcome to the grade book for\n%s!\n",
32            getCourseName() );
33      } // end method displayMessage
34   } // end class GradeBook
```

Fig. 3.10 | GradeBook class with a constructor to initialize the course name. (Part 2 of 2.)

Lines 9–12 declare GradeBook's constructor. Like a method, a constructor's parameter list specifies the data it requires to perform its task. When you create a new object (as we'll do in Fig. 3.11), this data is placed in the parentheses that follow the class name. Line 9 indicates that the constructor has a String parameter called name. The name passed to the constructor is assigned to instance variable courseName in line 11.

Figure 3.11 initializes GradeBook objects using the constructor. Lines 11–12 create and initialize the GradeBook object gradeBook1. The GradeBook constructor is called with the argument "CS101 Introduction to Java Programming" to initialize the course name. The class instance creation expression in lines 11–12 returns a reference to the new object, which is assigned to the variable gradeBook1. Lines 13–14 repeat this process, this time passing the argument "CS102 Data Structures in Java" to initialize the course name for gradeBook2. Lines 17–20 use each object's getCourseName method to obtain the course names and show that they were initialized when the objects were created. The output confirms that each GradeBook maintains its own copy of instance variable courseName.

```
1   // Fig. 3.11: GradeBookTest.java
2   // GradeBook constructor used to specify the course name at the
3   // time each GradeBook object is created.
4
5   public class GradeBookTest
6   {
7      // main method begins program execution
8      public static void main( String[] args )
9      {
```

Fig. 3.11 | GradeBook constructor used to specify the course name at the time each GradeBook object is created. (Part 1 of 2.)

```
10          // create GradeBook object
11          GradeBook gradeBook1 = new GradeBook(
12             "CS101 Introduction to Java Programming" );
13          GradeBook gradeBook2 = new GradeBook(
14             "CS102 Data Structures in Java" );
15
16          // display initial value of courseName for each GradeBook
17          System.out.printf( "gradeBook1 course name is: %s\n",
18             gradeBook1.getCourseName() );
19          System.out.printf( "gradeBook2 course name is: %s\n",
20             gradeBook2.getCourseName() );
21       } // end main
22    } // end class GradeBookTest
```

```
gradeBook1 course name is: CS101 Introduction to Java Programming
gradeBook2 course name is: CS102 Data Structures in Java
```

Fig. 3.11 | GradeBook constructor used to specify the course name at the time each GradeBook object is created. (Part 2 of 2.)

An important difference between constructors and methods is that constructors cannot return values, so they cannot specify a return type (not even void). Normally, constructors are declared public. If a class does not include a constructor, the class's instance variables are initialized to their default values. *If you declare any constructors for a class, the Java compiler will not create a default constructor for that class.* Thus, we can no longer create a GradeBook object with new GradeBook() as we did in the earlier examples.

Error-Prevention Tip 3.2
Unless default initialization of your class's instance variables is acceptable, provide a constructor to ensure that your class's instance variables are properly initialized with meaningful values when each new object of your class is created.

Adding the Constructor to Class **GradeBook**'s *UML Class Diagram*
The UML class diagram of Fig. 3.12 models class GradeBook of Fig. 3.10, which has a constructor that has a name parameter of type String. Like operations, the UML models constructors in the third compartment of a class in a class diagram. To distinguish a constructor from a class's operations, the UML requires that the word "constructor" be placed between **guillemets** (« **and** ») before the constructor's name. It's customary to list constructors before other operations in the third compartment.

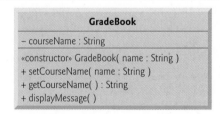

Fig. 3.12 | UML class diagram indicating that class GradeBook has a constructor that has a name parameter of UML type String.

Constructors with Multiple Parameters

Sometimes you'll want to initialize objects with multiple pieces of data. For example, Exercise 3.8 asks you to store the course name *and* the instructor's name in a GradeBook object. In this case, the GradeBook's constructor would be modified to receive two Strings, as in

```
public GradeBook( String courseName, String instructorName )
```

and you'd call the GradeBook constructor as follows:

```
GradeBook gradeBook = new GradeBook(
    "CS101 Introduction to Java Programming", "Sue Green" );
```

3.8 Floating-Point Numbers and Type double

We now depart temporarily from our GradeBook case study to declare an Account class that maintains the balance of a bank account. Most account balances are not whole numbers (e.g., 0, –22 and 1024). For this reason, class Account represents the account balance as a **floating-point number** (i.e., a number with a decimal point, such as 7.33, 0.0975 or 1000.12345). Java provides two primitive types for storing floating-point numbers in memory—float and double. The primary difference between them is that double variables can store numbers with larger magnitude and finer detail (i.e., more digits to the right of the decimal point—also known as the number's **precision**) than float variables.

Floating-Point Number Precision and Memory Requirements

Variables of type **float** represent **single-precision floating-point numbers** and can represent up to seven significant digits. Variables of type **double** represent **double-precision floating-point numbers**. These require twice as much memory as float variables and provide 15 significant digits—approximately double the precision of float variables. For the range of values required by most programs, variables of type float should suffice, but you can use double to "play it safe." In some applications, even variables of type double will be inadequate. Most programmers represent floating-point numbers with type double. In fact, Java treats all floating-point numbers you type in a program's source code (such as 7.33 and 0.0975) as double values by default. Such values in the source code are known as **floating-point literals**. See Appendix D, Primitive Types, for the ranges of values for floats and doubles.

Although floating-point numbers are not always 100% precise, they have numerous applications. For example, when we speak of a "normal" body temperature of 98.6, we do not need to be precise to a large number of digits. When we read the temperature on a thermometer as 98.6, it may actually be 98.5999473210643. Calling this number simply 98.6 is fine for most applications involving body temperatures. Owing to the imprecise nature of floating-point numbers, type double is preferred over type float, because double variables can represent floating-point numbers more accurately. For this reason, we primarily use type double throughout the book. For precise floating-point numbers, Java provides class BigDecimal (package java.math).

Floating-point numbers also arise as a result of division. In conventional arithmetic, when we divide 10 by 3, the result is 3.3333333…, with the sequence of 3s repeating infinitely. The computer allocates only a fixed amount of space to hold such a value, so clearly the stored floating-point value can be only an approximation.

Common Programming Error 3.4
Using floating-point numbers in a manner that assumes they are represented precisely can lead to incorrect results.

Account *Class with an Instance Variable of Type* double

Our next application (Figs. 3.13–3.14) contains a class named Account (Fig. 3.13) that maintains the balance of a bank account. A typical bank services many accounts, each with its own balance, so line 7 declares an instance variable named balance of type double. Variable balance is an instance variable because it's declared in the body of the class but outside the class's method declarations (lines 10–16, 19–22 and 25–28). Every instance (i.e., object) of class Account contains its own copy of balance.

```java
1   // Fig. 3.13: Account.java
2   // Account class with a constructor to validate and
3   // initialize instance variable balance of type double.
4
5   public class Account
6   {
7      private double balance; // instance variable that stores the balance
8
9      // constructor
10     public Account( double initialBalance )
11     {
12        // validate that initialBalance is greater than 0.0;
13        // if it is not, balance is initialized to the default value 0.0
14        if ( initialBalance > 0.0 )
15           balance = initialBalance;
16     } // end Account constructor
17
18     // credit (add) an amount to the account
19     public void credit( double amount )
20     {
21        balance = balance + amount; // add amount to balance
22     } // end method credit
23
24     // return the account balance
25     public double getBalance()
26     {
27        return balance; // gives the value of balance to the calling method
28     } // end method getBalance
29  } // end class Account
```

Fig. 3.13 | Account class with a constructor to validate and initialize instance variable balance of type double.

The class has a constructor and two methods. It's common for someone opening an account to deposit money immediately, so the constructor (lines 10–16) receives a parameter initialBalance of type double that represents the starting balance. Lines 14–15 ensure that initialBalance is greater than 0.0. If so, initialBalance's value is assigned to instance variable balance. Otherwise, balance remains at 0.0—its default initial value.

Method credit (lines 19–22) does not return any data when it completes its task, so its return type is void. The method receives one parameter named amount—a double value that will be added to the balance. Line 21 adds amount to the current value of bal-ance, then assigns the result to balance (thus replacing the prior balance amount).

Method getBalance (lines 25–28) allows clients of the class (i.e., other classes that use this class) to obtain the value of a particular Account object's balance. The method specifies return type double and an empty parameter list.

Once again, note that the statements in lines 15, 21 and 27 use instance variable bal-ance even though it was not declared in any of the methods. We can use balance in these methods because it's an instance variable of the class.

AccountTest Class to Use Class Account

Class AccountTest (Fig. 3.14) creates two Account objects (lines 10–11) and initializes them with 50.00 and -7.53, respectively. Lines 14–17 output the balance in each Account by calling the Account's getBalance method. When method getBalance is called for account1 from line 15, the value of account1's balance is returned from line 27 of Fig. 3.13 and displayed by the System.out.printf statement (Fig. 3.14, lines 14–15). Similarly, when method getBalance is called for account2 from line 17, the value of the account2's balance is returned from line 27 of Fig. 3.13 and displayed by the System.out.printf statement (Fig. 3.14, lines 16–17). Note that the balance of account2 is 0.00, because the constructor ensured that the account could not begin with a negative balance. The value is output by printf with the format specifier %.2f. The format specifier %f is used to output values of type float or double. The .2 between % and f represents the number of decimal places (2) that should be output to the right of the decimal point in the floating-point number—also known as the number's **precision**. Any floating-point value output with %.2f will be rounded to the hundredths position—for example, 123.457 would be rounded to 123.46, 27.333 would be rounded to 27.33 and 123.455 would be rounded to 123.46.

```
1   // Fig. 3.14: AccountTest.java
2   // Inputting and outputting floating-point numbers with Account objects.
3   import java.util.Scanner;
4
5   public class AccountTest
6   {
7      // main method begins execution of Java application
8      public static void main( String[] args )
9      {
10         Account account1 = new Account( 50.00 ); // create Account object
11         Account account2 = new Account( -7.53 ); // create Account object
12
13         // display initial balance of each object
14         System.out.printf( "account1 balance: $%.2f\n",
15            account1.getBalance() );
16         System.out.printf( "account2 balance: $%.2f\n\n",
17            account2.getBalance() );
18
19         // create Scanner to obtain input from command window
20         Scanner input = new Scanner( System.in );
21         double depositAmount; // deposit amount read from user
22
```

Fig. 3.14 | Inputting and outputting floating-point numbers with Account objects. (Part 1 of 2.)

```
23          System.out.print( "Enter deposit amount for account1: " ); // prompt
24          depositAmount = input.nextDouble(); // obtain user input
25          System.out.printf( "\nadding %.2f to account1 balance\n\n",
26             depositAmount );
27          account1.credit( depositAmount ); // add to account1 balance
28
29          // display balances
30          System.out.printf( "account1 balance: $%.2f\n",
31             account1.getBalance() );
32          System.out.printf( "account2 balance: $%.2f\n\n",
33             account2.getBalance() );
34
35          System.out.print( "Enter deposit amount for account2: " ); // prompt
36          depositAmount = input.nextDouble(); // obtain user input
37          System.out.printf( "\nadding %.2f to account2 balance\n\n",
38             depositAmount );
39          account2.credit( depositAmount ); // add to account2 balance
40
41          // display balances
42          System.out.printf( "account1 balance: $%.2f\n",
43             account1.getBalance() );
44          System.out.printf( "account2 balance: $%.2f\n",
45             account2.getBalance() );
46       } // end main
47    } // end class AccountTest
```

```
account1 balance: $50.00
account2 balance: $0.00

Enter deposit amount for account1: 25.53

adding 25.53 to account1 balance

account1 balance: $75.53
account2 balance: $0.00

Enter deposit amount for account2: 123.45

adding 123.45 to account2 balance

account1 balance: $75.53
account2 balance: $123.45
```

Fig. 3.14 | Inputting and outputting floating-point numbers with Account objects. (Part 2 of 2.)

Line 21 declares local variable depositAmount to store each deposit amount entered by the user. Unlike the instance variable balance in class Account, local variable depositAmount in main is not initialized to 0.0 by default. However, this variable does not need to be initialized here, because its value will be determined by the user's input.

Line 23 prompts the user to enter a deposit amount for account1. Line 24 obtains the input from the user by calling Scanner object input's **nextDouble** method, which returns a double value entered by the user. Lines 25–26 display the deposit amount. Line 27 calls object account1's credit method and supplies depositAmount as the method's argument. When the method is called, the argument's value is assigned to parameter amount (line 19 of Fig. 3.13) of method credit (lines 19–22 of Fig. 3.13); then method credit adds that value to the balance (line 21 of Fig. 3.13). Lines 30–33 (Fig. 3.14) output the balances of both Accounts again to show that only account1's balance changed.

Line 35 prompts the user to enter a deposit amount for account2. Line 36 obtains the input from the user by calling Scanner object input's nextDouble method. Lines 37–38 display the deposit amount. Line 39 calls object account2's credit method and supplies depositAmount as the method's argument; then method credit adds that value to the balance. Finally, lines 42–45 output the balances of both Accounts again to show that only account2's balance changed.

UML Class Diagram for Class Account

The UML class diagram in Fig. 3.15 models class Account of Fig. 3.13. The diagram models the private attribute balance with UML type Double to correspond to the class's instance variable balance of Java type double. The diagram models class Account's constructor with a parameter initialBalance of UML type Double in the third compartment of the class. The class's two public methods are modeled as operations in the third compartment as well. The diagram models operation credit with an amount parameter of UML type Double (because the corresponding method has an amount parameter of Java type double) and operation getBalance with a return type of Double (because the corresponding Java method returns a double value).

Account

– balance : Double

«constructor» Account(initialBalance : Double)
+ credit(amount : Double)
+ getBalance( ) : Double

Fig. 3.15 | UML class diagram indicating that class Account has a private balance attribute of UML type Double, a constructor (with a parameter of UML type Double) and two public operations—credit (with an amount parameter of UML type Double) and getBalance (returns UML type Double).

3.9 (Optional) GUI and Graphics Case Study: Using Dialog Boxes

This optional case study is designed for those who want to begin learning Java's powerful capabilities for creating graphical user interfaces (GUIs) and graphics early in the book, before the main discussions of these topics in Chapter 14, GUI Components: Part 1, Chapter 15, Graphics and Java 2D™, and Chapter 25, GUI Components: Part 2.

The GUI and Graphics Case Study appears in 10 brief sections (see Fig. 3.16). Each section introduces several new concepts and provides examples with screen captures that show sample interactions and results. In the first few sections, you'll create your first graphical applications. In subsequent sections, you'll use object-oriented programming concepts to create an application that draws a variety of shapes. When we formally introduce GUIs in Chapter 14, we use the mouse to choose exactly which shapes to draw and where to draw them. In Chapter 15, we add capabilities of the Java 2D graphics API to draw the shapes with different line thicknesses and fills. We hope you find this case study informative and entertaining.

Fig. 3.16 | Summary of the GUI and Graphics Case Study in each chapter.

Displaying Text in a Dialog Box

The programs presented thus far display output in the command window. Many applications use windows or **dialog boxes** (also called **dialogs**) to display output. Web browsers such as Mozilla Firefox and Microsoft Internet Explorer display web pages in their own windows. E-mail programs allow you to type and read messages in a window. Typically, dialog boxes are windows in which programs display important messages to users. Class **JOptionPane** provides prebuilt dialog boxes that enable programs to display windows containing messages—such windows are called **message dialogs**. Figure 3.17 displays the String "Welcome\nto\nJava" in a message dialog.

```
1   // Fig. 3.17: Dialog1.java
2   // Printing multiple lines in dialog box.
3   import javax.swing.JOptionPane; // import class JOptionPane
4
5   public class Dialog1
6   {
7      public static void main( String[] args )
8      {
9         // display a dialog with a message
10        JOptionPane.showMessageDialog( null, "Welcome\nto\nJava" );
11     } // end main
12   } // end class Dialog1
```

Fig. 3.17 | Using JOptionPane to display multiple lines in a dialog box.

Line 3 indicates that the program uses class JOptionPane from package **javax.swing**. This package contains many classes that help you create **graphical user interfaces (GUIs)**.

GUI components facilitate data entry by a program's user and presentation of outputs to the user. Line 10 calls JOptionPane method **showMessageDialog** to display a dialog box containing a message. The method requires two arguments. The first helps the Java application determine where to position the dialog box. A dialog is typically displayed from a GUI application with its own window. The first argument refers to that window (known as the parent window) and causes the dialog to appear centered over the application's window. If the first argument is null, the dialog box is displayed at the center of your screen. The second argument is the String to display in the dialog box.

Introducing static Methods

JOptionPane method showMessageDialog is a so-called **static method**. Such methods often define frequently used tasks. For example, many programs display dialog boxes, and the code to do this is the same each time. Rather than requiring you to "reinvent the wheel" and create code to display a dialog, the designers of class JOptionPane declared a static method that performs this task for you. A static method is typically called by using its class name followed by a dot (.) and the method name, as in

     ClassName.*methodName*(*arguments*)

Notice that you do not create an object of class JOptionPane to use its static method showMessageDialog. We discuss static methods in more detail in Chapter 6.

Entering Text in a Dialog

Figure 3.18 uses another predefined JOptionPane dialog called an **input dialog** that allows the user to enter data into a program. The program asks for the user's name, and responds with a message dialog containing a greeting and the name that the user entered.

Lines 10–11 use JOptionPane method **showInputDialog** to display an input dialog containing a prompt and a field (known as a **text field**) in which the user can enter text. Method showInputDialog's argument is the prompt that indicates what the user should enter. The user types characters in the text field, then clicks the **OK** button or presses the *Enter* key to return the String to the program. Method showInputDialog (line 11) returns a String containing the characters typed by the user. We store the String in variable name (line 10). [*Note:* If you press the dialog's **Cancel** button or press the *Esc* key, the method returns null and the program displays the word "null" as the name.]

Lines 14–15 use static String method **format** to return a String containing a greeting with the user's name. Method format works like method System.out.printf, except that format returns the formatted String rather than displaying it in a command window. Line 18 displays the greeting in a message dialog, just as we did in Fig. 3.17.

```
1    // Fig. 3.18: NameDialog.java
2    // Basic input with a dialog box.
3    import javax.swing.JOptionPane;
4
5    public class NameDialog
6    {
7       public static void main( String[] args )
8       {
```

Fig. 3.18 | Obtaining user input from a dialog. (Part 1 of 2.)

```
 9        // prompt user to enter name
10        String name =
11           JOptionPane.showInputDialog( "What is your name?" );
12
13        // create the message
14        String message =
15           String.format( "Welcome, %s, to Java Programming!", name );
16
17        // display the message to welcome the user by name
18        JOptionPane.showMessageDialog( null, message );
19     } // end main
20  } // end class NameDialog
```

 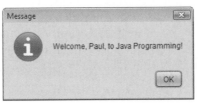

Fig. 3.18 | Obtaining user input from a dialog. (Part 2 of 2.)

GUI and Graphics Case Study Exercise

3.1 Modify the addition program in Fig. 2.7 to use dialog-based input and output with the methods of class JOptionPane. Since method showInputDialog returns a String, you must convert the String the user enters to an int for use in calculations. The Integer class's static method parseInt takes a String argument representing an integer (e.g., the result of JOptionPane.showInputDialog) and returns the value as an int. Method parseInt is a static method of class Integer (from package java.lang). Note that if the String does not contain a valid integer, the program will terminate with an error.

3.10 Wrap-Up

In this chapter, you learned the basic concepts of classes, objects, methods and instance variables—these will be used in most Java applications you create. In particular, you learned how to declare instance variables of a class to maintain data for each object of the class, and how to declare methods that operate on that data. You learned how to call a method to tell it to perform its task and how to pass information to methods as arguments. You learned the difference between a local variable of a method and an instance variable of a class and that only instance variables are initialized automatically. You also learned how to use a class's constructor to specify the initial values for an object's instance variables. Throughout the chapter, you saw how the UML can be used to create class diagrams that model the constructors, methods and attributes of classes. Finally, you learned about floating-point numbers—how to store them with variables of primitive type double, how to input them with a Scanner object and how to format them with printf and format specifier %f for display purposes. In the next chapter we begin our introduction to control statements, which specify the order in which a program's actions are performed. You'll use these in your methods to specify how they should perform their tasks.

Summary

Section 3.2 Classes, Objects, Methods and Instance Variables

- Performing a task in a program requires a method. Inside the method you put the mechanisms that make the method do its tasks.

- The program unit that houses a method is called a class. A class may contain one or more methods that are designed to perform the class's tasks.

- A method can perform a task and return a result.

- A class can be used to create an instance of the class called an object.

- A method call tells a method to perform its task.

- Each method can specify parameters that represent additional information the method requires to perform its task correctly. A method call supplies arguments for the method's parameters.

- An object has attributes that are carried with the object as it's used in a program. These attributes are specified as part of the object's class. Attributes are specified in classes by fields.

Section 3.3 Declaring a Class with a Method and Instantiating an Object of a Class

- Each class declaration that begins with the access modifier public must be stored in a file that has exactly the same name as the class and ends with the .java file-name extension.

- Every class declaration contains keyword class followed immediately by the class's name.

- A method declaration that begins with keyword public indicates that the method can be called by other classes declared outside the class declaration.

- Keyword void indicates that a method will perform a task but will not return any information.

- By convention, method names begin with a lowercase first letter and all subsequent words in the name begin with a capital first letter.

- Empty parentheses following a method name indicate that the method does not require any parameters to perform its task.

- Every method's body is delimited by left and right braces ({ and }).

- The method's body contains statements that perform the method's task. After the statements execute, the method has completed its task.

- When you attempt to execute a class, Java looks for the class's main method to begin execution.

- Typically, you cannot call a method of another class until you create an object of that class.

- Class instance creation expressions beginning with keyword new create new objects.

- To call a method of an object, follow the variable name with a dot separator (.), the method name and a set of parentheses containing the method's arguments.

- In the UML, each class is modeled in a class diagram as a rectangle with three compartments. The top one contains the class's name centered horizontally in boldface. The middle one contains the class's attributes, which correspond to fields in Java. The bottom one contains the class's operations, which correspond to methods and constructors in Java.

- The UML models operations by listing the operation name followed by a set of parentheses. A plus sign (+) in front of the operation name indicates that the operation is a public one in the UML (i.e., a public method in Java).

Section 3.4 Declaring a Method with a Parameter

- Methods often require additional information to perform their tasks. Such additional information is provided to methods via arguments in method calls.

- Scanner method nextLine reads characters until a newline character is encountered, then returns the characters as a String.

- Scanner method next reads characters until any white-space character is encountered, then returns the characters as a String.
- A method that requires data to perform its task must specify this in its declaration by placing additional information in the method's parameter list.
- Each parameter must specify both a type and an identifier.
- At the time a method is called, its arguments are assigned to its parameters. Then the method body uses the parameter variables to access the argument values.
- A method specifies multiple parameters in a comma-separated list.
- The number of arguments in the method call must match the number of parameters in the method declaration's parameter list. Also, the argument types in the method call must be consistent with the types of the corresponding parameters in the method's declaration.
- Class String is in package java.lang, which is imported implicitly into all source-code files.
- There's a special relationship between classes that are compiled in the same directory on disk. By default, such classes are considered to be in the same package. Classes in the same package are implicitly imported into the source-code files of other classes in the same package.
- import declarations are not required if you always use fully qualified class names.
- The UML models a parameter of an operation by listing the parameter name, followed by a colon and the parameter type between the parentheses following the operation name.
- The UML has its own data types similar to those of Java. Not all the UML data types have the same names as the corresponding Java types.
- The UML type String corresponds to the Java type String.

Section 3.5 Instance Variables, set *Methods and* get *Methods*
- Variables declared in a method's body are local variables and can be used only in that method.
- A class normally consists of one or more methods that manipulate the attributes (data) that belong to a particular object of the class. Such variables are called fields and are declared inside a class declaration but outside the bodies of the class's method declarations.
- When each object of a class maintains its own copy of an attribute, the corresponding field is known as an instance variable.
- Variables or methods declared with access modifier private are accessible only to methods of the class in which they are declared.
- Declaring instance variables with access modifier private is known as data hiding.
- A benefit of fields is that all the methods of the class can use the fields. Another distinction between a field and a local variable is that a field has a default initial value provided by Java when you do not specify the field's initial value, but a local variable does not.
- The default value for a field of type String (or any other reference type) is null.
- When a method that specifies a return type is called and completes its task, the method returns a result to its calling method.
- Classes often provide public methods to allow the class's clients to *set* or *get* private instance variables. The names of these methods need not begin with *set* or *get*, but this naming convention is recommended and is required for special Java software components called JavaBeans.
- The UML represents instance variables as an attribute name, followed by a colon and the type.
- Private attributes are preceded by a minus sign (–) in the UML.
- The UML indicates an operation's return type by placing a colon and the return type after the parentheses following the operation name.
- UML class diagrams do not specify return types for operations that do not return values.

Section 3.6 Primitive Types vs. Reference Types

- Types in Java are divided into two categories—primitive types and reference types. The primitive types are `boolean`, `byte`, `char`, `short`, `int`, `long`, `float` and `double`. All other types are reference types, so classes, which specify the types of objects, are reference types.

- A primitive-type variable can store exactly one value of its declared type at a time.

- Primitive-type instance variables are initialized by default. Variables of types `byte`, `char`, `short`, `int`, `long`, `float` and `double` are initialized to 0. Variables of type `boolean` are initialized to `false`.

- Programs use variables of reference types (called references) to store the location of an object in the computer's memory. Such variables refer to objects in the program. The object that is referenced may contain many instance variables and methods.

- Reference-type fields are initialized by default to the value `null`.

- A reference to an object is required to invoke an object's instance methods. A primitive-type variable does not refer to an object and therefore cannot be used to invoke a method.

Section 3.7 Initializing Objects with Constructors

- Keyword `new` requests memory from the system to store an object, then calls the corresponding class's constructor to initialize the object.

- A constructor can be used to initialize an object of a class when the object is created.

- Constructors can specify parameters but cannot specify return types.

- If a class does not define constructors, the compiler provides a default constructor with no parameters, and the class's instance variables are initialized to their default values.

- Like operations, the UML models constructors in the third compartment of a class diagram. To distinguish a constructor from a class's operations, the UML places the word "constructor" between guillemets (« and ») before the constructor's name.

Section 3.8 Floating-Point Numbers and Type *double*

- A floating-point number is a number with a decimal point, such as 7.33, 0.0975 or 1000.12345. Java provides two primitive types for storing floating-point numbers in memory—`float` and `double`. The primary difference between these types is that `double` variables can store numbers with larger magnitude and finer detail (known as the number's precision) than `float` variables.

- Variables of type `float` represent single-precision floating-point numbers and have seven significant digits. Variables of type `double` represent double-precision floating-point numbers. These require twice as much memory as `float` variables and provide 15 significant digits—approximately double the precision of `float` variables.

- Floating-point literals are of type `double` by default.

- `Scanner` method `nextDouble` returns a `double` value.

- The format specifier `%f` is used to output values of type `float` or `double`. The format specifier `%.2f` specifies that two digits of precision should be output to the right of the decimal point in the floating-point number.

- The default value for a field of type `double` is `0.0`, and the default value for a field of type `int` is `0`.

Terminology

Self-Review Exercises

3.1 Fill in the blanks in each of the following:

a) A house is to a blueprint as a(n) _____ is to a class.

b) Each class declaration that begins with keyword _____ must be stored in a file that has exactly the same name as the class and ends with the .java file-name extension.

c) Keyword _____ in a class declaration is followed immediately by the class's name.

d) Keyword _____ requests memory from the system to store an object, then calls the corresponding class's constructor to initialize the object.

e) Each parameter must specify both a(n) _____ and a(n) _____.

f) By default, classes that are compiled in the same directory are considered to be in the same package, known as the _____.

g) When each object of a class maintains its own copy of an attribute, the field that represents the attribute is also known as a(n) _____.

h) Java provides two primitive types for storing floating-point numbers in memory: _____ and _____.

i) Variables of type double represent _____ floating-point numbers.

j) Scanner method _____ returns a double value.

k) Keyword public is an access _____.

l) Return type _____ indicates that a method will not return a value.

m) Scanner method _____ reads characters until a newline character is encountered, then returns those characters as a String.

n) Class String is in package _____.

o) A(n) _____ is not required if you always refer to a class with its fully qualified class name.

p) A(n) _____ is a number with a decimal point, such as 7.33, 0.0975 or 1000.12345.

q) Variables of type float represent _____ floating-point numbers.

r) The format specifier _____ is used to output values of type float or double.

s) Types in Java are divided into two categories—_____ types and _____ types.

3.2 State whether each of the following is *true* or *false*. If *false*, explain why.

a) By convention, method names begin with an uppercase first letter, and all subsequent words in the name begin with a capital first letter.

b) An import declaration is not required when one class in a package uses another in the same package.

c) Empty parentheses following a method name in a method declaration indicate that the method does not require any parameters to perform its task.

d) Variables or methods declared with access modifier `private` are accessible only to methods of the class in which they are declared.

e) A primitive-type variable can be used to invoke a method.

f) Variables declared in the body of a particular method are known as instance variables and can be used in all methods of the class.

g) Every method's body is delimited by left and right braces (`{` and `}`).

h) Primitive-type local variables are initialized by default.

i) Reference-type instance variables are initialized by default to the value `null`.

j) Any class that contains `public static void main( String[] args )` can be used to execute an application.

k) The number of arguments in the method call must match the number of parameters in the method declaration's parameter list.

l) Floating-point values that appear in source code are known as floating-point literals and are type `float` by default.

3.3 What is the difference between a local variable and a field?

3.4 Explain the purpose of a method parameter. What is the difference between a parameter and an argument?

Answers to Self-Review Exercises

3.1 a) object. b) `public`. c) `class`. d) `new`. e) type, name. f) default package. g) instance variable. h) `float`, `double`. i) double-precision. j) `nextDouble`. k) modifier. l) `void`. m) `nextLine`. n) `java.lang`. o) `import` declaration. p) floating-point number. q) single-precision. r) `%f`. s) primitive, reference.

3.2 a) False. By convention, method names begin with a lowercase first letter and all subsequent words in the name begin with a capital first letter. b) True. c) True. d) True. e) False. A primitive-type variable cannot be used to invoke a method—a reference to an object is required to invoke the object's methods. f) False. Such variables are called local variables and can be used only in the method in which they are declared. g) True. h) False. Primitive-type instance variables are initialized by default. Each local variable must explicitly be assigned a value. i) True. j) True. k) True. l) False. Such literals are of type `double` by default.

3.3 A local variable is declared in the body of a method and can be used only from the point at which it is declared through the end of the method declaration. A field is declared in a class, but not in the body of any of the class's methods. Also, fields are accessible to all methods of the class. (We'll see an exception to this in Chapter 8, Classes and Objects: A Deeper Look.)

3.4 A parameter represents additional information that a method requires to perform its task. Each parameter required by a method is specified in the method's declaration. An argument is the actual value for a method parameter. When a method is called, the argument values are passed to the corresponding parameters of the method so that it can perform its task.

Exercises

3.5 What is a default constructor? How are an object's instance variables initialized if a class has only a default constructor?

3.6 Most classes need to be imported before they can be used in an application. Why is every application allowed to use classes `System` and `String` without first importing them?

3.7   Explain why a class might provide a *set* method and a *get* method for an instance variable.

3.8   *(Modified GradeBook Class)* Modify class GradeBook (Fig. 3.10) as follows:
  a) Include a String instance variable that represents the name of the course's instructor.
  b) Provide a *set* method to change the instructor's name and a *get* method to retrieve it.
  c) Modify the constructor to specify two parameters—one for the course name and one for the instructor's name.
  d) Modify method displayMessage to output the welcome message and course name, followed by "This course is presented by: " and the instructor's name.

Use your modified class in a test application that demonstrates the class's new capabilities.

3.9   *(Modified Account Class)* Modify class Account (Fig. 3.13) to provide a method called debit that withdraws money from an Account. Ensure that the debit amount does not exceed the Account's balance. If it does, the balance should be left unchanged and the method should print a message indicating "Debit amount exceeded account balance." Modify class AccountTest (Fig. 3.14) to test method debit.

3.10   *(Employee Class)* Create a class called Employee that includes three instance variables—a first name (type String), a last name (type String) and a monthly salary (double). Provide a constructor that initializes the three instance variables. Provide a *set* and a *get* method for each instance variable. If the monthly salary is not positive, do not set its value. Write a test application named EmployeeTest that demonstrates class Employee's capabilities. Create two Employee objects and display each object's *yearly* salary. Then give each Employee a 10% raise and display each Employee's yearly salary again.

Making a Difference

3.11   *(Target-Heart-Rate Calculator)* While exercising, you can use a heart-rate monitor to see that your heart rate stays within a safe range suggested by your trainers and doctors. According to the American Heart Association (AHA) (www.americanheart.org/presenter.jhtml?identifier=4736), the formula for calculating your *maximum heart rate* in beats per minute is 220 minus your age in years. Your *target heart rate* is a range that is 50–85% of your maximum heart rate. [*Note:* These formulas are estimates provided by the AHA. Maximum and target heart rates may vary based on the health, fitness and gender of the individual. Always consult a physician or qualified health care professional before beginning or modifying an exercise program.] Create a class called HeartRates. The class attributes should include the person's first name, last name and date of birth (consisting of separate attributes for the month, day and year of birth). Your class should have a constructor that receives this data as parameters. For each attribute provide *set* and *get* methods. The class also should include a method that calculates and returns the person's age (in years), a method that calculates and returns the person's maximum heart rate and a method that calculates and returns the person's target heart rate. Write a Java application that prompts for the person's information, instantiates an object of class HeartRates and prints the information from that object—including the person's first name, last name and date of birth—then calculates and prints the person's age in (years), maximum heart rate and target-heart-rate range.

3.12   *(Computerization of Health Records)* A health care issue that has been in the news lately is the computerization of health records. This possibility is being approached cautiously because of sensitive privacy and security concerns, among others. [We address such concerns in later exercises.] Computerizing health records could make it easier for patients to share their health profiles and histories among their various health care professionals. This could improve the quality of health care, help avoid drug conflicts and erroneous drug prescriptions, reduce costs and in emergencies, could save lives. In this exercise, you'll design a "starter" HealthProfile class for a person. The class attributes should include the person's first name, last name, gender, date of birth (consisting of separate attributes for the month, day and year of birth), height (in inches) and weight (in pounds). Your class should have a constructor that receives this data. For each attribute, provide *set* and *get* methods. The class also should include methods that calculate and return the user's age in years, maximum heart rate and target-heart-rate range (see Exercise 3.11), and body mass index (BMI; see Exercise 2.26). Write a Java application that prompts for the person's information, instantiates an object of class HealthProfile for that person and prints the information from that object—including the person's first name, last name, gender, date of birth, height and weight—then calculates and prints the person's age in years, BMI, maximum heart rate and target-heart-rate range. It should also display the "BMI values" chart from Exercise 2.26.

Let's all move one place on.
—Lewis Carroll

The wheel is come full circle.
—William Shakespeare

How many apples fell on Newton's head before he took the hint!
—Robert Frost

All the evolution we know of proceeds from the vague to the definite.
—Charles Sanders Peirce

Control Statements: Part 1

Objectives

In this chapter you'll learn:

- To use basic problem-solving techniques.
- To develop algorithms through the process of top-down, stepwise refinement using pseudocode.
- To use the `if` and `if...else` selection statements to choose among alternative actions.
- To use the `while` repetition statement to execute statements in a program repeatedly.
- To use counter-controlled repetition and sentinel-controlled repetition.
- To use the compound assignment, increment and decrement operators.
- The portability of primitive data types.

4.1 Introduction

Before writing a program to solve a problem, you should have a thorough understanding of the problem and a carefully planned approach to solving it. When writing a program, you also should understand the types of building blocks that are available and employ proven program-construction techniques. In this chapter and in Chapter 5, Control Statements: Part 2, we discuss these issues in our presentation of the theory and principles of structured programming. The concepts presented here are crucial in building classes and manipulating objects.

In this chapter, we introduce Java's if, if...else and while statements, three of the building blocks that allow you to specify the logic required for methods to perform their tasks. We devote a portion of this chapter (and Chapters 5 and 7) to further developing the GradeBook class introduced in Chapter 3. In particular, we add a method to the GradeBook class that uses control statements to calculate the average of a set of student grades. Another example demonstrates additional ways to combine control statements to solve a similar problem. We introduce Java's compound assignment, increment and decrement operators. Finally, we discuss the portability of Java's primitive types.

4.2 Algorithms

Any computing problem can be solved by executing a series of actions in a specific order. A procedure for solving a problem in terms of

1. the **actions** to execute and

2. the **order** in which these actions execute

is called an **algorithm**. The following example demonstrates that correctly specifying the order in which the actions execute is important.

Consider the "rise-and-shine algorithm" followed by one executive for getting out of bed and going to work: (1) Get out of bed; (2) take off pajamas; (3) take a shower; (4) get dressed; (5) eat breakfast; (6) carpool to work. This routine gets the executive to work well prepared to make critical decisions. Suppose that the same steps are performed in a slightly different order: (1) Get out of bed; (2) take off pajamas; (3) get dressed; (4) take a shower;

(5) eat breakfast; (6) carpool to work. In this case, our executive shows up for work soaking wet. Specifying the order in which statements (actions) execute in a program is called **program control**. This chapter investigates program control using Java's **control statements**.

4.3 Pseudocode

Pseudocode is an informal language that helps you develop algorithms without having to worry about the strict details of Java language syntax. The pseudocode we present is particularly useful for developing algorithms that will be converted to structured portions of Java programs. Pseudocode is similar to everyday English—it's convenient and user friendly, but it's not an actual computer programming language. You'll see an algorithm written in pseudocode in Fig. 4.5.

Pseudocode does not execute on computers. Rather, it helps you "think out" a program before attempting to write it in a programming language, such as Java. This chapter provides several examples of how to use pseudocode to develop Java programs.

The style of pseudocode we present consists purely of characters, so you can type pseudocode conveniently, using any text-editor program. A carefully prepared pseudocode program can easily be converted to a corresponding Java program.

Pseudocode normally describes only statements representing the actions that occur after you convert a program from pseudocode to Java and the program is run on a computer. Such actions might include input, output or calculations. We typically do not include variable declarations in our pseudocode, but some programmers choose to list variables and mention their purposes at the beginning of their pseudocode.

4.4 Control Structures

Normally, statements in a program are executed one after the other in the order in which they are written. This process is called **sequential execution**. Various Java statements, which we'll soon discuss, enable you to specify that the next statement to execute is not necessarily the next one in sequence. This is called **transfer of control**.

During the 1960s, it became clear that the indiscriminate use of transfers of control was the root of much difficulty experienced by software development groups. The blame was pointed at the **goto statement** (used in most programming languages of the time), which allows the programmer to specify a transfer of control to one of a wide range of destinations in a program. The term **structured programming** became almost synonymous with "goto elimination." [*Note:* Java does not have a goto statement; however, the word goto is reserved by Java and should not be used as an identifier in programs.]

The research of Bohm and Jacopini[1] had demonstrated that programs could be written *without* any goto statements. The challenge of the era for programmers was to shift their styles to "goto-less programming." Not until the 1970s did most programmers start taking structured programming seriously. The results were impressive. Software development groups reported shorter development times, more frequent on-time delivery of systems and more frequent within-budget completion of software projects. The key to these successes was that structured programs were clearer, easier to debug and modify, and more likely to be bug free in the first place.

---

1. Bohm, C., and G. Jacopini, "Flow Diagrams, Turing Machines, and Languages with Only Two Formation Rules," *Communications of the ACM*, Vol. 9, No. 5, May 1966, pp. 336–371.

Bohm and Jacopini's work demonstrated that all programs could be written in terms of only three control structures—the **sequence structure**, the **selection structure** and the **repetition structure**. When we introduce Java's control structure implementations, we'll refer to them in the terminology of the *Java Language Specification* as "control statements."

Sequence Structure in Java

The sequence structure is built into Java. Unless directed otherwise, the computer executes Java statements one after the other in the order in which they're written—that is, in sequence. The **activity diagram** in Fig. 4.1 illustrates a typical sequence structure in which two calculations are performed in order. Java lets you have as many actions as you want in a sequence structure. As we'll soon see, anywhere a single action may be placed, we may place several actions in sequence.

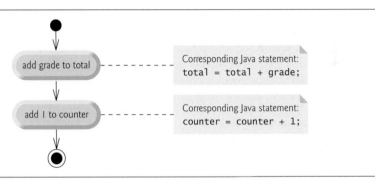

Fig. 4.1 | Sequence structure activity diagram.

A UML activity diagram models the **workflow** (also called the **activity**) of a portion of a software system. Such workflows may include a portion of an algorithm, like the sequence structure in Fig. 4.1. Activity diagrams are composed of symbols, such as **action-state symbols** (rectangles with their left and right sides replaced with outward arcs), **diamonds** and **small circles**. These symbols are connected by **transition arrows**, which represent the flow of the activity—that is, the order in which the actions should occur.

Like pseudocode, activity diagrams help you develop and represent algorithms, although many programmers prefer pseudocode. Activity diagrams clearly show how control structures operate. We use the UML in this chapter and Chapter 5 to show control flow in control statements. In Chapters 12–13, we use the UML in a real-world automated-teller machine case study.

Consider the sequence structure activity diagram in Fig. 4.1. It contains two **action states** that represent actions to perform. Each action state contains an **action expression**—for example, "add grade to total" or "add 1 to counter"—that specifies a particular action to perform. Other actions might include calculations or input/output operations. The arrows in the activity diagram represent **transitions**, which indicate the order in which the actions represented by the action states occur. The program that implements the activities illustrated by the diagram in Fig. 4.1 first adds `grade` to `total`, then adds 1 to `counter`.

The **solid circle** at the top of the activity diagram represents the **initial state**—the beginning of the workflow before the program performs the modeled actions. The **solid circle surrounded by a hollow circle** that appears at the bottom of the diagram represents the **final state**—the end of the workflow after the program performs its actions.

Figure 4.1 also includes rectangles with the upper-right corners folded over. These are UML **notes** (like comments in Java)—explanatory remarks that describe the purpose of symbols in the diagram. Figure 4.1 uses UML notes to show the Java code associated with each action state. A **dotted line** connects each note with the element it describes. Activity diagrams normally do not show the Java code that implements the activity. We do this here to illustrate how the diagram relates to Java code. For more information on the UML, see our optional case study (Chapters 12–13) or visit `www.uml.org`.

Selection Statements in Java
Java has three types of **selection statements** (discussed in this chapter and Chapter 5). The `if` statement either performs (selects) an action, if a condition is true, or skips it, if the condition is false. The `if...else` statement performs an action if a condition is true and performs a different action if the condition is false. The `switch` statement (Chapter 5) performs one of many different actions, depending on the value of an expression.

The `if` statement is a **single-selection statement** because it selects or ignores a single action (or, as we'll soon see, a single group of actions). The `if...else` statement is called a **double-selection statement** because it selects between two different actions (or groups of actions). The `switch` statement is called a **multiple-selection statement** because it selects among many different actions (or groups of actions).

Repetition Statements in Java
Java provides three **repetition statements** (also called **looping statements**) that enable programs to perform statements repeatedly as long as a condition (called the **loop-continuation condition**) remains true. The repetition statements are the `while`, `do...while` and `for` statements. (Chapter 5 presents the `do...while` and `for` statements.) The `while` and `for` statements perform the action (or group of actions) in their bodies zero or more times—if the loop-continuation condition is initially false, the action (or group of actions) will not execute. The `do...while` statement performs the action (or group of actions) in its body one or more times. The words `if`, `else`, `switch`, `while`, `do` and `for` are Java keywords. A complete list of Java keywords appears in Appendix C.

Summary of Control Statements in Java
Java has only three kinds of control structures, which from this point forward we refer to as control statements: the sequence statement, selection statements (three types) and repetition statements (three types). Every program is formed by combining as many of these statements as is appropriate for the algorithm the program implements. We can model each control statement as an activity diagram. Like Fig. 4.1, each diagram contains an initial state and a final state that represent a control statement's entry point and exit point, respectively. **Single-entry/single-exit control statements** make it easy to build programs—we simply connect the exit point of one to the entry point of the next. We call this **control-statement stacking**. We'll learn that there is only one other way in which control statements may be connected—**control-statement nesting**—in which one control statement appears inside another. Thus, algorithms in Java programs are constructed from only three kinds of control statements, combined in only two ways. This is the essence of simplicity.

4.5 `if` Single-Selection Statement

Programs use selection statements to choose among alternative courses of action. For example, suppose that the passing grade on an exam is 60. The pseudocode statement

> *If student's grade is greater than or equal to 60*
> *Print "Passed"*

determines whether the condition "student's grade is greater than or equal to 60" is true. If so, "Passed" is printed, and the next pseudocode statement in order is "performed." (Remember, pseudocode is not a real programming language.) If the condition is false, the *Print* statement is ignored, and the next pseudocode statement in order is performed. The indentation of the second line of this selection statement is optional, but recommended, because it emphasizes the inherent structure of structured programs.

The preceding pseudocode *If* statement may be written in Java as

```java
if ( studentGrade >= 60 )
    System.out.println( "Passed" );
```

Note that the Java code corresponds closely to the pseudocode. This is one of the properties of pseudocode that makes it such a useful program development tool.

Figure 4.2 illustrates the single-selection if statement. This figure contains the most important symbol in an activity diagram—the diamond, or **decision symbol**, which indicates that a decision is to be made. The workflow continues along a path determined by the symbol's associated **guard conditions**, which can be true or false. Each transition arrow emerging from a decision symbol has a guard condition (specified in square brackets next to the arrow). If a guard condition is true, the workflow enters the action state to which the transition arrow points. In Fig. 4.2, if the grade is greater than or equal to 60, the program prints "Passed," then transitions to the activity's final state. If the grade is less than 60, the program immediately transitions to the final state without displaying a message.

Fig. 4.2 | if single-selection statement UML activity diagram.

The if statement is a single-entry/single-exit control statement. We'll see that the activity diagrams for the remaining control statements also contain initial states, transition arrows, action states that indicate actions to perform, decision symbols (with associated guard conditions) that indicate decisions to be made, and final states.

Envision seven bins, each containing only one type of Java control statement. The control statements are all empty. Your task is to assemble a program from as many of each type of control statement as the algorithm demands, combining them in only two possible ways (stacking or nesting), then filling in the action states and decisions with action expressions and guard conditions appropriate for the algorithm. We'll discuss the variety of ways in which actions and decisions can be written.

4.6 if...else Double-Selection Statement

The if single-selection statement performs an indicated action only when the condition is true; otherwise, the action is skipped. The **if...else double-selection statement** allows you to specify an action to perform when the condition is true and a different action when the condition is false. For example, the pseudocode statement

> *If student's grade is greater than or equal to 60*
>   *Print "Passed"*
> *Else*
>   *Print "Failed"*

prints "Passed" if the student's grade is greater than or equal to 60, but prints "Failed" if it's less than 60. In either case, after printing occurs, the next pseudocode statement in sequence is "performed."

The preceding *If...Else* pseudocode statement can be written in Java as

```java
if ( grade >= 60 )
    System.out.println( "Passed" );
else
    System.out.println( "Failed" );
```

Note that the body of the `else` is also indented. Whatever indentation convention you choose should be applied consistently throughout your programs.

Good Programming Practice 4.1
Indent both body statements of an `if...else` *statement.*

Good Programming Practice 4.2
If there are several levels of indentation, each level should be indented the same additional amount of space.

Figure 4.3 illustrates the flow of control in the `if...else` statement. Once again, the symbols in the UML activity diagram (besides the initial state, transition arrows and final state) represent action states and decisions.

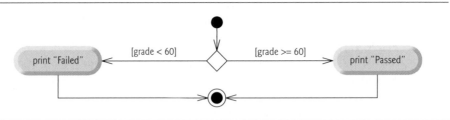

Fig. 4.3 | `if...else` double-selection statement UML activity diagram.

Conditional Operator (?:)

Java provides the **conditional operator** (**?:**) that can be used in place of an `if...else` statement. This is Java's only **ternary operator** (operator that takes three operands). Together, the operands and the ?: symbol form a **conditional expression.** The first operand (to the left of the ?) is a **boolean expression** (i.e., a condition that evaluates to a `boolean` value—**true** or **false**), the second operand (between the ? and :) is the value of the conditional expression if the boolean expression is `true` and the third operand (to the right of the :) is the value of the conditional expression if the boolean expression evaluates to false. For example, the statement

```
System.out.println( studentGrade >= 60 ? "Passed" : "Failed" );
```

prints the value of println's conditional-expression argument. The conditional expression in this statement evaluates to the string "Passed" if the boolean expression student-Grade >= 60 is true and to the string "Failed" if it is false. Thus, this statement with the conditional operator performs essentially the same function as the if...else statement shown earlier in this section. The precedence of the conditional operator is low, so the entire conditional expression is normally placed in parentheses. We'll see that conditional expressions can be used in some situations where if...else statements cannot.

Good Programming Practice 4.3

Conditional expressions are more difficult to read than if...else statements and should be used to replace only simple if...else statements that choose between two values.

Nested *if...else* Statements

A program can test multiple cases by placing if...else statements inside other if...else statements to create **nested if...else statements**. For example, the following pseudocode represents a nested if...else that prints A for exam grades greater than or equal to 90, B for grades 80 to 89, C for grades 70 to 79, D for grades 60 to 69 and F for all other grades:

> *If student's grade is greater than or equal to 90*
> > *Print "A"*
>
> *else*
> > *If student's grade is greater than or equal to 80*
> > > *Print "B"*
> >
> > *else*
> > > *If student's grade is greater than or equal to 70*
> > > > *Print "C"*
> > >
> > > *else*
> > > > *If student's grade is greater than or equal to 60*
> > > > > *Print "D"*
> > > >
> > > > *else*
> > > > > *Print "F"*

This pseudocode may be written in Java as

```
if ( studentGrade >= 90 )
    System.out.println( "A" );
else
    if ( studentGrade >= 80 )
        System.out.println( "B" );
    else
        if ( studentGrade >= 70 )
            System.out.println( "C" );
        else
            if ( studentGrade >= 60 )
                System.out.println( "D" );
            else
                System.out.println( "F" );
```

If variable `studentGrade` is greater than or equal to 90, the first four conditions in the nested `if...else` statement will be true, but only the statement in the `if` part of the first `if...else` statement will execute. After that statement executes, the `else` part of the "outermost" `if...else` statement is skipped. Most Java programmers prefer to write the preceding nested `if...else` statement as

```
if ( studentGrade >= 90 )
    System.out.println( "A" );
else if ( studentGrade >= 80 )
    System.out.println( "B" );
else if ( studentGrade >= 70 )
    System.out.println( "C" );
else if ( studentGrade >= 60 )
    System.out.println( "D" );
else
    System.out.println( "F" );
```

The two forms are identical except for the spacing and indentation, which the compiler ignores. The latter form is popular because it avoids deep indentation of the code to the right. Such indentation often leaves little room on a line of source code, forcing lines to be split.

Dangling-*else* Problem

The Java compiler always associates an `else` with the immediately preceding `if` unless told to do otherwise by the placement of braces (`{` and `}`). This behavior can lead to what is referred to as the **dangling-else problem**. For example,

```
if ( x > 5 )
    if ( y > 5 )
        System.out.println( "x and y are > 5" );
else
    System.out.println( "x is <= 5" );
```

appears to indicate that if x is greater than 5, the nested `if` statement determines whether y is also greater than 5. If so, the string `"x and y are > 5"` is output. Otherwise, it appears that if x is not greater than 5, the `else` part of the `if...else` outputs the string `"x is <= 5"`. Beware! This nested `if...else` statement does not execute as it appears. The compiler actually interprets the statement as

```
if ( x > 5 )
    if ( y > 5 )
        System.out.println( "x and y are > 5" );
    else
        System.out.println( "x is <= 5" );
```

in which the body of the first `if` is a nested `if...else`. The outer `if` statement tests whether x is greater than 5. If so, execution continues by testing whether y is also greater than 5. If the second condition is true, the proper string—`"x and y are > 5"`—is displayed. However, if the second condition is false, the string `"x is <= 5"` is displayed, even though we know that x is greater than 5. Equally bad, if the outer `if` statement's condition is false, the inner `if...else` is skipped and nothing is displayed.

To force the nested `if...else` statement to execute as it was originally intended, we must write it as follows:

```
if ( x > 5 )
{
   if ( y > 5 )
      System.out.println( "x and y are > 5" );
}
else
   System.out.println( "x is <= 5" );
```

The braces indicate that the second if is in the body of the first and that the else is associated with the *first* if. Exercises 4.24–4.25 investigate the dangling-else problem further.

Blocks

The if statement normally expects only one statement in its body. To include several statements in the body of an if (or the body of an else for an if...else statement), enclose the statements in braces. Statements contained in a pair of braces form a **block**. A block can be placed anywhere in a program that a single statement can be placed.

The following example includes a block in the else part of an if...else statement:

```
if ( grade >= 60 )
   System.out.println( "Passed" );
else
{
   System.out.println( "Failed" );
   System.out.println( "You must take this course again." );
}
```

In this case, if grade is less than 60, the program executes both statements in the body of the else and prints

```
Failed.
You must take this course again.
```

Note the braces surrounding the two statements in the else clause. These braces are important. Without the braces, the statement

```
System.out.println( "You must take this course again." );
```

would be outside the body of the else part of the if...else statement and would execute *regardless* of whether the grade was less than 60.

Syntax errors (e.g., when one brace in a block is left out of the program) are caught by the compiler. A **logic error** (e.g., when both braces in a block are left out of the program) has its effect at execution time. A **fatal logic error** causes a program to fail and terminate prematurely. A **nonfatal logic error** allows a program to continue executing but causes it to produce incorrect results.

Common Programming Error 4.1

Forgetting one or both of the braces that delimit a block can lead to syntax or logic errors.

Good Programming Practice 4.4

Always using braces in an if...else (or other) control statement helps prevent their accidental omission, especially when adding statements to the if part or the else part at a later time. To avoid omitting one or both of the braces, type the beginning and ending braces of blocks before typing the individual statements within the braces.

Just as a block can be placed anywhere a single statement can be placed, it's also possible to have an empty statement. Recall from Section 2.8 that the empty statement is represented by placing a semicolon (;) where a statement would normally be.

Common Programming Error 4.2

Placing a semicolon after the condition in an if or if...else statement leads to a logic error in single-selection if statements and a syntax error in double-selection if...else statements (when the if-part contains an actual body statement).

4.7 while Repetition Statement

A **repetition** (or **looping**) **statement** allows you to specify that a program should repeat an action while some condition remains true. The pseudocode statement

> *While there are more items on my shopping list*
> *Purchase next item and cross it off my list*

describes the repetition that occurs during a shopping trip. The condition "there are more items on my shopping list" may be true or false. If it's true, then the action "Purchase next item and cross it off my list" is performed. This action will be performed repeatedly while the condition remains true. The statement(s) contained in the *While* repetition statement constitute its body, which may be a single statement or a block. Eventually, the condition will become false (when the last item on the shopping list has been purchased and crossed off). At this point, the repetition terminates, and the first statement after the repetition statement executes.

As an example of Java's **while repetition statement**, consider a program segment designed to find the first power of 3 larger than 100. Suppose that the int variable product is initialized to 3. When the following while statement finishes executing, product contains the result:

```
while ( product <= 100 )
   product = 3 * product;
```

When this while statement begins execution, the value of variable product is 3. Each iteration of the while statement multiplies product by 3, so product takes on the values 9, 27, 81 and 243 successively. When variable product becomes 243, the while-statement condition—product <= 100—becomes false. This terminates the repetition, so the final value of product is 243. At this point, program execution continues with the next statement after the while statement.

Common Programming Error 4.3

*Not providing, in the body of a while statement, an action that eventually causes the condition in the while to become false normally results in a logic error called an **infinite loop** (the loop never terminates).*

The UML activity diagram in Fig. 4.4 illustrates the flow of control in the preceding while statement. Once again, the symbols in the diagram (besides the initial state, transition arrows, a final state and three notes) represent an action state and a decision. This diagram also introduces the UML's **merge symbol**. The UML represents both the merge symbol and the decision symbol as diamonds. The merge symbol joins two flows of activity into one. In this diagram, the merge symbol joins the transitions from the initial state and from the action state, so they both flow into the decision that determines whether the loop should begin (or continue) executing. The decision and merge symbols can be distinguished by the number of "incoming" and "outgoing" transition arrows. A decision symbol has one transition arrow pointing to the diamond and two or more pointing out from it to indicate possible transitions from that point. In addition, each transition arrow pointing out of a decision symbol has a guard condition next to it. A merge symbol has two or more transition arrows pointing to the diamond and only one pointing from the diamond, to indicate multiple activity flows merging to continue the activity. None of the transition arrows associated with a merge symbol has a guard condition.

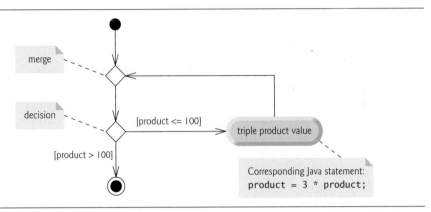

Fig. 4.4 | `while` repetition statement UML activity diagram.

Figure 4.4 clearly shows the repetition of the `while` statement discussed earlier in this section. The transition arrow emerging from the action state points back to the merge, from which program flow transitions back to the decision that is tested at the beginning of each iteration of the loop. The loop continues to execute until the guard condition `product > 100` becomes true. Then the `while` statement exits (reaches its final state), and control passes to the next statement in sequence in the program.

4.8 Formulating Algorithms: Counter-Controlled Repetition

To illustrate how algorithms are developed, we modify the `GradeBook` class of Chapter 3 to solve two variations of a problem that averages student grades. Consider the following problem statement:

> *A class of ten students took a quiz. The grades (integers in the range 0 to 100) for this quiz are available to you. Determine the class average on the quiz.*

The class average is equal to the sum of the grades divided by the number of students. The algorithm for solving this problem on a computer must input each grade, keep track of the total of all grades input, perform the averaging calculation and print the result.

Pseudocode Algorithm with Counter-Controlled Repetition
Let's use pseudocode to list the actions to execute and specify the order in which they should execute. We use **counter-controlled repetition** to input the grades one at a time.

This technique uses a variable called a **counter** (or **control variable**) to control the number of times a set of statements will execute. Counter-controlled repetition is often called **definite repetition**, because the number of repetitions is known before the loop begins executing. In this example, repetition terminates when the counter exceeds 10. This section presents a fully developed pseudocode algorithm (Fig. 4.5) and a version of class Grade-Book (Fig. 4.6) that implements the algorithm in a Java method. We then present an application (Fig. 4.7) that demonstrates the algorithm in action. In Section 4.9, we demonstrate how to use pseudocode to develop such an algorithm from scratch.

> **Software Engineering Observation 4.1**
>
> *Experience has shown that the most difficult part of solving a problem on a computer is developing the algorithm for the solution. Once a correct algorithm has been specified, producing a working Java program from the algorithm is usually straightforward.*

Note the references in the algorithm of Fig. 4.5 to a total and a counter. A **total** is a variable used to accumulate the sum of several values. A counter is a variable used to count—in this case, the grade counter indicates which of the 10 grades is about to be entered by the user. Variables used to store totals are normally initialized to zero before being used in a program.

1	*Set total to zero*
2	*Set grade counter to one*
3	
4	*While grade counter is less than or equal to ten*
5	*Prompt the user to enter the next grade*
6	*Input the next grade*
7	*Add the grade into the total*
8	*Add one to the grade counter*
9	
10	*Set the class average to the total divided by ten*
11	*Print the class average*

Fig. 4.5 | Pseudocode algorithm that uses counter-controlled repetition to solve the class-average problem.

Implementing Counter-Controlled Repetition in Class GradeBook

Class GradeBook (Fig. 4.6) contains a constructor (lines 11–14) that assigns a value to the class's instance variable courseName (declared in line 8). Lines 17–20, 23–26 and 29–34 declare methods setCourseName, getCourseName and displayMessage, respectively. Lines 37–66 declare method determineClassAverage, which implements the class-averaging algorithm described by the pseudocode in Fig. 4.5.

```
1   // Fig. 4.6: GradeBook.java
2   // GradeBook class that solves class-average problem using
3   // counter-controlled repetition.
4   import java.util.Scanner; // program uses class Scanner
5
```

Fig. 4.6 | Counter-controlled repetition: class-average problem. (Part 1 of 3.)

```
6   public class GradeBook
7   {
8      private String courseName; // name of course this GradeBook represents
9
10     // constructor initializes courseName
11     public GradeBook( String name )
12     {
13        courseName = name; // initializes courseName
14     } // end constructor
15
16     // method to set the course name
17     public void setCourseName( String name )
18     {
19        courseName = name; // store the course name
20     } // end method setCourseName
21
22     // method to retrieve the course name
23     public String getCourseName()
24     {
25        return courseName;
26     } // end method getCourseName
27
28     // display a welcome message to the GradeBook user
29     public void displayMessage()
30     {
31        // getCourseName gets the name of the course
32        System.out.printf( "Welcome to the grade book for\n%s!\n\n",
33           getCourseName() );
34     } // end method displayMessage
35
36     // determine class average based on 10 grades entered by user
37     public void determineClassAverage()
38     {
39        // create Scanner to obtain input from command window
40        Scanner input = new Scanner( System.in );
41
42        int total; // sum of grades entered by user
43        int gradeCounter; // number of the grade to be entered next
44        int grade; // grade value entered by user
45        int average; // average of grades
46
47        // initialization phase
48        total = 0; // initialize total
49        gradeCounter = 1; // initialize loop counter
50
51        // processing phase
52        while ( gradeCounter <= 10 ) // loop 10 times
53        {
54           System.out.print( "Enter grade: " ); // prompt
55           grade = input.nextInt(); // input next grade
56           total = total + grade; // add grade to total
57           gradeCounter = gradeCounter + 1; // increment counter by 1
58        } // end while
59
```

Fig. 4.6 | Counter-controlled repetition: class-average problem. (Part 2 of 3.)

```
60              // termination phase
61              average = total / 10; // integer division yields integer result
62
63              // display total and average of grades
64              System.out.printf( "\nTotal of all 10 grades is %d\n", total );
65              System.out.printf( "Class average is %d\n", average );
66          } // end method determineClassAverage
67      } // end class GradeBook
```

Fig. 4.6 | Counter-controlled repetition: class-average problem. (Part 3 of 3.)

Line 40 declares and initializes Scanner variable input, which is used to read values entered by the user. Lines 42–45 declare local variables total, gradeCounter, grade and average to be of type int. Variable grade stores the user input.

Note that the declarations (in lines 42–45) appear in the body of method determine-ClassAverage. Recall that variables declared in a method body are local variables and can be used only from the line of their declaration to the closing right brace of the method declaration. A local variable's declaration must appear before the variable is used in that method. A local variable cannot be accessed outside the method in which it's declared.

In this chapter, class GradeBook simply reads and processes a set of grades. The averaging calculation is performed in method determineClassAverage using local variables—we do not preserve any information about student grades in instance variables of the class.

The assignments (in lines 48–49) initialize total to 0 and gradeCounter to 1. Note that these initializations occur before the variables are used in calculations. Variables grade and average (for the user input and calculated average, respectively) need not be initialized here—their values will be assigned as they are input or calculated later in the method.

Common Programming Error 4.4
Using the value of a local variable before it's initialized results in a compilation error. All local variables must be initialized before their values are used in expressions.

Error-Prevention Tip 4.1
Initialize each counter and total, either in its declaration or in an assignment statement. Totals are normally initialized to 0. Counters are normally initialized to 0 or 1, depending on how they're used (we'll show examples of when to use 0 and when to use 1).

Line 52 indicates that the while statement should continue looping (also called **iterating**) as long as gradeCounter's value is less than or equal to 10. While this condition remains true, the while statement repeatedly executes the statements between the braces that delimit its body (lines 54–57).

Line 54 displays the prompt "Enter grade: ". Line 55 reads the grade entered by the user and assigns it to variable grade. Then line 56 adds the new grade entered by the user to the total and assigns the result to total, which replaces its previous value.

Line 57 adds 1 to gradeCounter to indicate that the program has processed a grade and is ready to input the next grade from the user. Incrementing gradeCounter eventually causes it to exceed 10. Then the loop terminates, because its condition (line 52) becomes false.

When the loop terminates, line 61 performs the averaging calculation and assigns its result to the variable average. Line 64 uses System.out's printf method to display the text "Total of all 10 grades is " followed by variable total's value. Line 65 then uses printf to display the text "Class average is " followed by variable average's value. After reaching line 66, method determineClassAverage returns control to the calling method (i.e., main in GradeBookTest of Fig. 4.7).

Class *GradeBookTest*

Class GradeBookTest (Fig. 4.7) creates an object of class GradeBook (Fig. 4.6) and demonstrates its capabilities. Lines 10–11 of Fig. 4.7 create a new GradeBook object and assign it to variable myGradeBook. The String in line 11 is passed to the GradeBook constructor (lines 11–14 of Fig. 4.6). Line 13 calls myGradeBook's displayMessage method to display a welcome message to the user. Line 14 then calls myGradeBook's determineClassAverage method to allow the user to enter 10 grades, for which the method then calculates and prints the average—the method performs the algorithm shown in Fig. 4.5.

```
1   // Fig. 4.7: GradeBookTest.java
2   // Create GradeBook object and invoke its determineClassAverage method.
3
4   public class GradeBookTest
5   {
6      public static void main( String[] args )
7      {
8         // create GradeBook object myGradeBook and
9         // pass course name to constructor
10        GradeBook myGradeBook = new GradeBook(
11           "CS101 Introduction to Java Programming" );
12
13        myGradeBook.displayMessage(); // display welcome message
14        myGradeBook.determineClassAverage(); // find average of 10 grades
15     } // end main
16  } // end class GradeBookTest
```

```
Welcome to the grade book for
CS101 Introduction to Java Programming!

Enter grade: 67
Enter grade: 78
Enter grade: 89
Enter grade: 67
Enter grade: 87
Enter grade: 98
Enter grade: 93
Enter grade: 85
Enter grade: 82
Enter grade: 100

Total of all 10 grades is 846
Class average is 84
```

Fig. 4.7 | GradeBookTest class creates an object of class GradeBook (Fig. 4.6) and invokes its determineClassAverage method.

Notes on Integer Division and Truncation

The averaging calculation performed by method determineClassAverage in response to the method call at line 14 in Fig. 4.7 produces an integer result. The program's output indicates that the sum of the grade values in the sample execution is 846, which, when divided by 10, should yield the floating-point number 84.6. However, the result of the calculation `total / 10` (line 61 of Fig. 4.6) is the integer 84, because `total` and 10 are both integers. Dividing two integers results in **integer division**—any fractional part of the calculation is lost (i.e., **truncated**). In the next section we'll see how to obtain a floating-point result from the averaging calculation.

Common Programming Error 4.5

Assuming that integer division rounds (rather than truncates) can lead to incorrect results. For example, 7 ÷ 4, which yields 1.75 in conventional arithmetic, truncates to 1 in integer arithmetic, rather than rounding to 2.

4.9 Formulating Algorithms: Sentinel-Controlled Repetition

Let's generalize Section 4.8's class-average problem. Consider the following problem:

> *Develop a class-averaging program that processes grades for an arbitrary number of students each time it is run.*

In the previous class-average example, the problem statement specified the number of students, so the number of grades (10) was known in advance. In this example, no indication is given of how many grades the user will enter during the program's execution. The program must process an arbitrary number of grades. How can it determine when to stop the input of grades? How will it know when to calculate and print the class average?

One way to solve this problem is to use a special value called a **sentinel value** (also called a **signal value**, a **dummy value** or a **flag value**) to indicate "end of data entry." The user enters grades until all legitimate grades have been entered. The user then types the sentinel value to indicate that no more grades will be entered. **Sentinel-controlled repetition** is often called **indefinite repetition** because the number of repetitions is not known before the loop begins executing.

Clearly, a sentinel value must be chosen that cannot be confused with an acceptable input value. Grades on a quiz are nonnegative integers, so –1 is an acceptable sentinel value for this problem. Thus, a run of the class-average program might process a stream of inputs such as 95, 96, 75, 74, 89 and –1. The program would then compute and print the class average for the grades 95, 96, 75, 74 and 89; since –1 is the sentinel value, it should not enter into the averaging calculation.

Common Programming Error 4.6

Choosing a sentinel value that is also a legitimate data value is a logic error.

Developing the Pseudocode Algorithm with Top-Down, Stepwise Refinement: The Top and First Refinement

We approach this class-average program with a technique called **top-down, stepwise refinement**, which is essential to the development of well-structured programs. We begin with a pseudocode representation of the **top**—a single statement that conveys the overall function of the program:

Determine the class average for the quiz

The top is, in effect, a *complete* representation of a program. Unfortunately, the top rarely conveys sufficient detail from which to write a Java program. So we now begin the refinement process. We divide the top into a series of smaller tasks and list these in the order in which they'll be performed. This results in the following **first refinement**:

Initialize variables
Input, sum and count the quiz grades
Calculate and print the class average

This refinement uses only the sequence structure—the steps listed should execute in order, one after the other.

Software Engineering Observation 4.2

Each refinement, as well as the top itself, is a complete specification of the algorithm—only the level of detail varies.

Software Engineering Observation 4.3

Many programs can be divided logically into three phases: an initialization phase that initializes the variables; a processing phase that inputs data values and adjusts program variables accordingly; and a termination phase that calculates and outputs the final results.

Proceeding to the Second Refinement
The preceding Software Engineering Observation is often all you need for the first refinement in the top-down process. To proceed to the next level of refinement—that is, the **second refinement**—we commit to specific variables. In this example, we need a running total of the numbers, a count of how many numbers have been processed, a variable to receive the value of each grade as it's input by the user and a variable to hold the calculated average. The pseudocode statement

Initialize variables

can be refined as follows:

Initialize total to zero
Initialize counter to zero

Only the variables *total* and *counter* need to be initialized before they're used. The variables *average* and *grade* (for the calculated average and the user input, respectively) need not be initialized, because their values will be replaced as they're calculated or input.

The pseudocode statement

Input, sum and count the quiz grades

requires a repetition structure (i.e., a loop) that successively inputs each grade. We do not know in advance how many grades are to be processed, so we'll use sentinel-controlled repetition. The user enters grades one at a time. After entering the last grade, the user enters the sentinel value. The program tests for the sentinel value after each grade is input and terminates the loop when the user enters the sentinel value. The second refinement of the preceding pseudocode statement is then

> *Prompt the user to enter the first grade*
> *Input the first grade (possibly the sentinel)*
>
> *While the user has not yet entered the sentinel*
>   *Add this grade into the running total*
>   *Add one to the grade counter*
>   *Prompt the user to enter the next grade*
>   *Input the next grade (possibly the sentinel)*

In pseudocode, we do not use braces around the statements that form the body of the *While* structure. We simply indent the statements under the *While* to show that they belong to the *While*. Again, pseudocode is only an informal program development aid.

The pseudocode statement

> *Calculate and print the class average*

can be refined as follows:

> *If the counter is not equal to zero*
>   *Set the average to the total divided by the counter*
>   *Print the average*
> *else*
>   *Print "No grades were entered"*

We are careful here to test for the possibility of division by zero—a logic error that, if undetected, would cause the program to fail or produce invalid output. The complete second refinement of the pseudocode for the class-average problem is shown in Fig. 4.8.

Error-Prevention Tip 4.2

When performing division by an expression whose value could be zero, test for this and handle it (e.g., print an error message) rather than allow the error to occur.

---

1   *Initialize total to zero*
2   *Initialize counter to zero*
3
4   *Prompt the user to enter the first grade*
5   *Input the first grade (possibly the sentinel)*
6
7   *While the user has not yet entered the sentinel*
8   *Add this grade into the running total*
9   *Add one to the grade counter*
10   *Prompt the user to enter the next grade*
11   *Input the next grade (possibly the sentinel)*
12
13   *If the counter is not equal to zero*
14   *Set the average to the total divided by the counter*
15   *Print the average*
16   *else*
17   *Print "No grades were entered"*

Fig. 4.8 | Class-average problem pseudocode algorithm with sentinel-controlled repetition.

In Fig. 4.5 and Fig. 4.8, we included blank lines and indentation in the pseudocode to make it more readable. The blank lines separate the algorithms into their phases and set off control statements; the indentation emphasizes the bodies of the control statements.

The pseudocode algorithm in Fig. 4.8 solves the more general class-average problem. This algorithm was developed after two refinements. Sometimes more are needed.

Software Engineering Observation 4.4

Terminate the top-down, stepwise refinement process when you've specified the pseudocode algorithm in sufficient detail for you to convert the pseudocode to Java. Normally, implementing the Java program is then straightforward.

Software Engineering Observation 4.5

Some programmers do not use program development tools like pseudocode. They feel that their ultimate goal is to solve the problem on a computer and that writing pseudocode merely delays the production of final outputs. Although this may work for simple and familiar problems, it can lead to serious errors and delays in large, complex projects.

Implementing Sentinel-Controlled Repetition in Class *GradeBook*

Figure 4.9 shows the Java class GradeBook containing method determineClassAverage that implements the pseudocode algorithm of Fig. 4.8. Although each grade is an integer, the averaging calculation is likely to produce a number with a decimal point—in other words, a real (i.e., floating-point) number. The type int cannot represent such a number, so this class uses type double to do so.

```java
// Fig. 4.9: GradeBook.java
// GradeBook class that solves class-average program using
// sentinel-controlled repetition.
import java.util.Scanner; // program uses class Scanner

public class GradeBook
{
   private String courseName; // name of course this GradeBook represents

   // constructor initializes courseName
   public GradeBook( String name )
   {
      courseName = name; // initializes courseName
   } // end constructor

   // method to set the course name
   public void setCourseName( String name )
   {
      courseName = name; // store the course name
   } // end method setCourseName

   // method to retrieve the course name
   public String getCourseName()
   {
      return courseName;
   } // end method getCourseName
```

Fig. 4.9 | Sentinel-controlled repetition: Class-average problem. (Part 1 of 3.)

```
27
28     // display a welcome message to the GradeBook user
29     public void displayMessage()
30     {
31        // getCourseName gets the name of the course
32        System.out.printf( "Welcome to the grade book for\n%s!\n\n",
33           getCourseName() );
34     } // end method displayMessage
35
36     // determine the average of an arbitrary number of grades
37     public void determineClassAverage()
38     {
39        // create Scanner to obtain input from command window
40        Scanner input = new Scanner( System.in );
41
42        int total; // sum of grades
43        int gradeCounter; // number of grades entered
44        int grade; // grade value
45        double average; // number with decimal point for average
46
47        // initialization phase
48        total = 0; // initialize total
49        gradeCounter = 0; // initialize loop counter
50
51        // processing phase
52        // prompt for input and read grade from user
53        System.out.print( "Enter grade or -1 to quit: " );
54        grade = input.nextInt();
55
56        // loop until sentinel value read from user
57        while ( grade != -1 )
58        {
59           total = total + grade; // add grade to total
60           gradeCounter = gradeCounter + 1; // increment counter
61
62           // prompt for input and read next grade from user
63           System.out.print( "Enter grade or -1 to quit: " );
64           grade = input.nextInt();
65        } // end while
66
67        // termination phase
68        // if user entered at least one grade...
69        if ( gradeCounter != 0 )
70        {
71           // calculate average of all grades entered
72           average = (double) total / gradeCounter;
73
74           // display total and average (with two digits of precision)
75           System.out.printf( "\nTotal of the %d grades entered is %d\n",
76              gradeCounter, total );
77           System.out.printf( "Class average is %.2f\n", average );
78        } // end if
```

Fig. 4.9 | Sentinel-controlled repetition: Class-average problem. (Part 2 of 3.)

```
79          else // no grades were entered, so output appropriate message
80             System.out.println( "No grades were entered" );
81       } // end method determineClassAverage
82    } // end class GradeBook
```

Fig. 4.9 | Sentinel-controlled repetition: Class-average problem. (Part 3 of 3.)

In this example, we see that control statements may be stacked on top of one another (in sequence). The `while` statement (lines 57–65) is followed in sequence by an `if...else` statement (lines 69–80). Much of the code in this program is identical to that in Fig. 4.6, so we concentrate on the new concepts.

Line 45 declares `double` variable `average`, which allows us to store the class average as a floating-point number. Line 49 initializes `gradeCounter` to 0, because no grades have been entered yet. Remember that this program uses sentinel-controlled repetition to input the grades. To keep an accurate record of the number of grades entered, the program increments `gradeCounter` only when the user enters a valid grade.

Program Logic for Sentinel-Controlled Repetition vs. Counter-Controlled Repetition
Compare the program logic for sentinel-controlled repetition in this application with that for counter-controlled repetition in Fig. 4.6. In counter-controlled repetition, each iteration of the `while` statement (e.g., lines 52–58 of Fig. 4.6) reads a value from the user, for the specified number of iterations. In sentinel-controlled repetition, the program reads the first value (lines 53–54 of Fig. 4.9) before reaching the `while`. This value determines whether the program's flow of control should enter the body of the `while`. If the condition of the `while` is false, the user entered the sentinel value, so the body of the `while` does not execute (i.e., no grades were entered). If, on the other hand, the condition is true, the body begins execution, and the loop adds the `grade` value to the `total` (line 59). Then lines 63–64 in the loop body input the next value from the user. Next, program control reaches the closing right brace of the loop body at line 65, so execution continues with the test of the `while`'s condition (line 57). The condition uses the most recent `grade` input by the user to determine whether the loop body should execute again. Note that the value of variable `grade` is always input from the user immediately before the program tests the `while` condition. This allows the program to determine whether the value just input is the sentinel value *before* the program processes that value (i.e., adds it to the `total`). If the sentinel value is input, the loop terminates, and the program does not add –1 to the `total`.

Good Programming Practice 4.5
In a sentinel-controlled loop, the prompts requesting data should remind the user of the sentinel.

After the loop terminates, the `if...else` statement at lines 69–80 executes. The condition at line 69 determines whether any grades were input. If none were input, the `else` part (lines 79–80) of the `if...else` statement executes and displays the message `"No grades were entered"` and the method returns control to the calling method.

Notice the `while` statement's block in Fig. 4.9 (lines 58–65). Without the braces, the loop would consider its body to be only the first statement, which adds the `grade` to the `total`. The last three statements in the block would fall outside the loop body, causing the computer to interpret the code incorrectly as follows:

```
while ( grade != -1 )
   total = total + grade; // add grade to total
gradeCounter = gradeCounter + 1; // increment counter

// prompt for input and read next grade from user
System.out.print( "Enter grade or -1 to quit: " );
grade = input.nextInt();
```

The preceding code would cause an infinite loop in the program if the user did not input the sentinel -1 at line 54 (before the while statement).

Common Programming Error 4.7

Omitting the braces that delimit a block can lead to logic errors, such as infinite loops. To prevent this problem, some programmers enclose the body of every control statement in braces, even if the body contains only a single statement.

Explicitly and Implicitly Converting Between Primitive Types

If at least one grade was entered, line 72 of Fig. 4.9 calculates the average of the grades. Recall from Fig. 4.6 that integer division yields an integer result. Even though variable average is declared as a double (line 45), the calculation

```
average = total / gradeCounter;
```

loses the fractional part of the quotient before the result of the division is assigned to average. This occurs because total and gradeCounter are both integers, and integer division yields an integer result. To perform a floating-point calculation with integer values, we must temporarily treat these values as floating-point numbers for use in the calculation. Java provides the **unary cast operator** to accomplish this task. Line 72 uses the **(double)** cast operator—a unary operator—to create a *temporary* floating-point copy of its operand total (which appears to the right of the operator). Using a cast operator in this manner is called **explicit conversion** or **type cast**. The value stored in total is still an integer.

The calculation now consists of a floating-point value (the temporary double version of total) divided by the integer gradeCounter. Java knows how to evaluate only arithmetic expressions in which the operands' types are identical. To ensure that the operands are of the same type, Java performs an operation called **promotion** (or **implicit conversion**) on selected operands. For example, in an expression containing values of the types int and double, the int values are promoted to double values for use in the expression. In this example, the value of gradeCounter is promoted to type double, then the floating-point division is performed and the result of the calculation is assigned to average. As long as the (double) cast operator is applied to any variable in the calculation, the calculation will yield a double result. Later in this chapter, we discuss all the primitive types. You'll learn more about the promotion rules in Section 6.7.

Common Programming Error 4.8

A cast operator can be used to convert between primitive numeric types, such as int and double, and between related reference types (as we discuss in Chapter 10, Object-Oriented Programming: Polymorphism). Casting to the wrong type may cause compilation errors or runtime errors.

Cast operators are available for any type. The cast operator is formed by placing parentheses around the name of a type. The operator is a **unary operator** (i.e., an operator that takes only one operand). Java also supports unary versions of the plus (+) and minus (–)

operators, so the programmer can write expressions like -7 or +5. Cast operators associate from right to left and have the same precedence as other unary operators, such as unary + and unary -. This precedence is one level higher than that of the **multiplicative operators** *, / and %. (See the operator precedence chart in Appendix A.) We indicate the cast operator with the notation (*type*) in our precedence charts, to indicate that any type name can be used to form a cast operator.

Line 77 displays the class average. In this example, we display the class average rounded to the nearest hundredth. The format specifier %.2f in printf's format control string (line 77) indicates that variable average's value should be displayed with two digits of precision to the right of the decimal point—indicated by .2 in the format specifier. The three grades entered during the sample execution of class GradeBookTest (Fig. 4.10) total 257, which yields the average 85.666666.... Method printf uses the precision in the format specifier to round the value to the specified number of digits. In this program, the average is rounded to the hundredths position and the average is displayed as 85.67.

```java
1   // Fig. 4.10: GradeBookTest.java
2   // Create GradeBook object and invoke its determineClassAverage method.
3
4   public class GradeBookTest
5   {
6      public static void main( String[] args )
7      {
8         // create GradeBook object myGradeBook and
9         // pass course name to constructor
10        GradeBook myGradeBook = new GradeBook(
11           "CS101 Introduction to Java Programming" );
12
13        myGradeBook.displayMessage(); // display welcome message
14        myGradeBook.determineClassAverage(); // find average of grades
15     } // end main
16  } // end class GradeBookTest
```

```
Welcome to the grade book for
CS101 Introduction to Java Programming!

Enter grade or -1 to quit: 97
Enter grade or -1 to quit: 88
Enter grade or -1 to quit: 72
Enter grade or -1 to quit: -1

Total of the 3 grades entered is 257
Class average is 85.67
```

Fig. 4.10 | GradeBookTest class creates an object of class GradeBook (Fig. 4.9) and invokes its determineClassAverage method.

4.10 Formulating Algorithms: Nested Control Statements

For the next example, we once again formulate an algorithm by using pseudocode and top-down, stepwise refinement, and write a corresponding Java program. We've seen that control statements can be stacked on top of one another (in sequence). In this case study, we examine the only other structured way control statements can be connected—namely, by **nesting** one control statement within another.

Consider the following problem statement:

> *A college offers a course that prepares students for the state licensing exam for real estate brokers. Last year, ten of the students who completed this course took the exam. The college wants to know how well its students did on the exam. You've been asked to write a program to summarize the results. You've been given a list of these 10 students. Next to each name is written a 1 if the student passed the exam or a 2 if the student failed.*
>
> *Your program should analyze the results of the exam as follows:*
>
> *1. Input each test result (i.e., a 1 or a 2). Display the message "Enter result" on the screen each time the program requests another test result.*
>
> *2. Count the number of test results of each type.*
>
> *3. Display a summary of the test results, indicating the number of students who passed and the number who failed.*
>
> *4. If more than eight students passed the exam, print the message "Bonus to instructor!"*

After reading the problem statement carefully, we make the following observations:

1. The program must process test results for 10 students. A counter-controlled loop can be used, because the number of test results is known in advance.

2. Each test result has a numeric value—either a 1 or a 2. Each time it reads a test result, the program must determine whether it is a 1 or a 2. We test for a 1 in our algorithm. If the number is not a 1, we assume that it's a 2. (Exercise 4.23 considers the consequences of this assumption.)

3. Two counters are used to keep track of the exam results—one to count the number of students who passed the exam and one to count the number who failed.

4. After the program has processed all the results, it must decide whether more than eight students passed the exam.

Let's proceed with top-down, stepwise refinement. We begin with a pseudocode representation of the top:

> *Analyze exam results and decide whether tuition should be raised*

Once again, the top is a *complete* representation of the program, but several refinements are likely to be needed before the pseudocode can evolve naturally into a Java program.

Our first refinement is

> *Initialize variables*
> *Input the 10 exam results, and count passes and failures*
> *Print a summary of the exam results and decide whether tuition should be raised*

Here, too, even though we have a complete representation of the entire program, further refinement is necessary. We now commit to specific variables. Counters are needed to record the passes and failures, a counter will be used to control the looping process and a variable is needed to store the user input. The variable in which the user input will be stored is not initialized at the start of the algorithm, because its value is read from the user during each iteration of the loop.

The pseudocode statement

> *Initialize variables*

can be refined as follows:

> *Initialize passes to zero*
> *Initialize failures to zero*
> *Initialize student counter to one*

Notice that only the counters are initialized at the start of the algorithm.
The pseudocode statement

> *Input the 10 exam results, and count passes and failures*

requires a loop that successively inputs the result of each exam. We know in advance that there are precisely 10 exam results, so counter-controlled looping is appropriate. Inside the loop (i.e., nested within the loop), a double-selection structure will determine whether each exam result is a pass or a failure and will increment the appropriate counter. The refinement of the preceding pseudocode statement is then

> *While student counter is less than or equal to 10*
> *Prompt the user to enter the next exam result*
> *Input the next exam result*
>
> *If the student passed*
> *Add one to passes*
> *Else*
> *Add one to failures*
>
> *Add one to student counter*

We use blank lines to isolate the *If…Else* control structure, which improves readability.
The pseudocode statement

> *Print a summary of the exam results and decide whether tuition should be raised*

can be refined as follows:

> *Print the number of passes*
> *Print the number of failures*
>
> *If more than eight students passed*
> *Print "Bonus to instructor!"*

Complete Second Refinement of Pseudocode and Conversion to Class **Analysis**

The complete second refinement appears in Fig. 4.11. Notice that blank lines are also used to set off the *While* structure for program readability. This pseudocode is now sufficiently refined for conversion to Java.

---

1   *Initialize passes to zero*
2   *Initialize failures to zero*
3   *Initialize student counter to one*

Fig. 4.11 | Pseudocode for examination-results problem. (Part 1 of 2.)

```
 4
 5    While student counter is less than or equal to 10
 6        Prompt the user to enter the next exam result
 7        Input the next exam result
 8
 9        If the student passed
10            Add one to passes
11        Else
12            Add one to failures
13
14        Add one to student counter
15
16    Print the number of passes
17    Print the number of failures
18
19    If more than eight students passed
20        Print "Bonus to instructor!"
```

Fig. 4.11 | Pseudocode for examination-results problem. (Part 2 of 2.)

The Java class that implements the pseudocode algorithm and two sample executions are shown in Fig. 4.12. Lines 13–16 of main declare the variables that method processExamResults of class Analysis uses to process the examination results. Several of these declarations use Java's ability to incorporate variable initialization into declarations (passes is assigned 0, failures 0 and studentCounter 1). Looping programs may require initialization at the beginning of each repetition—normally performed by assignment statements rather than in declarations.

Error-Prevention Tip 4.3

Initializing local variables when they are declared helps you avoid any compilation errors that might arise from attempts to use uninitialized variables. While Java does not require that local-variable initializations be incorporated into declarations, it does require that local variables be initialized before their values are used in an expression.

The while statement (lines 19–33) loops 10 times. During each iteration, the loop inputs and processes one exam result. Notice that the if...else statement (lines 26–29) for processing each result is nested in the while statement. If the result is 1, the if...else statement increments passes; otherwise, it assumes the result is 2 and increments failures. Line 32 increments studentCounter before the loop condition is tested again at line 19. After 10 values have been input, the loop terminates and line 36 displays the number of passes and failures. The if statement at lines 39–40 determines whether more than eight students passed the exam and, if so, outputs the message "Bonus to instructor!".

```
1    // Fig. 4.12: Analysis.java
2    // Analysis of examination results.
3    import java.util.Scanner; // class uses class Scanner
```

Fig. 4.12 | Nested control structures: Examination-results problem. (Part 1 of 3.)

```
4
5   public class Analysis
6   {
7      public static void main( String[] args )
8      {
9         // create Scanner to obtain input from command window
10        Scanner input = new Scanner( System.in );
11
12        // initializing variables in declarations
13        int passes = 0; // number of passes
14        int failures = 0; // number of failures
15        int studentCounter = 1; // student counter
16        int result; // one exam result (obtains value from user)
17
18        // process 10 students using counter-controlled loop
19        while ( studentCounter <= 10 )
20        {
21           // prompt user for input and obtain value from user
22           System.out.print( "Enter result (1 = pass, 2 = fail): " );
23           result = input.nextInt();
24
25           // if...else nested in while
26           if ( result == 1 )          // if result 1,
27              passes = passes + 1;     // increment passes;
28           else                        // else result is not 1, so
29              failures = failures + 1; // increment failures
30
31           // increment studentCounter so loop eventually terminates
32           studentCounter = studentCounter + 1;
33        } // end while
34
35        // termination phase; prepare and display results
36        System.out.printf( "Passed: %d\nFailed: %d\n", passes, failures );
37
38        // determine whether more than 8 students passed
39        if ( passes > 8 )
40           System.out.println( "Bonus to instructor!" );
41     } // end main
42  } // end class Analysis
```

```
Enter result (1 = pass, 2 = fail): 1
Enter result (1 = pass, 2 = fail): 2
Enter result (1 = pass, 2 = fail): 1
Enter result (1 = pass, 2 = fail): 1
Enter result (1 = pass, 2 = fail): 1
Enter result (1 = pass, 2 = fail): 1
Enter result (1 = pass, 2 = fail): 1
Enter result (1 = pass, 2 = fail): 1
Enter result (1 = pass, 2 = fail): 1
Enter result (1 = pass, 2 = fail): 1
Passed: 9
Failed: 1
Bonus to instructor!
```

Fig. 4.12 | Nested control structures: Examination-results problem. (Part 2 of 3.)

```
Enter result (1 = pass, 2 = fail): 1
Enter result (1 = pass, 2 = fail): 2
Enter result (1 = pass, 2 = fail): 1
Enter result (1 = pass, 2 = fail): 2
Enter result (1 = pass, 2 = fail): 1
Enter result (1 = pass, 2 = fail): 2
Enter result (1 = pass, 2 = fail): 2
Enter result (1 = pass, 2 = fail): 1
Enter result (1 = pass, 2 = fail): 1
Enter result (1 = pass, 2 = fail): 1
Passed: 6
Failed: 4
```

Fig. 4.12 | Nested control structures: Examination-results problem. (Part 3 of 3.)

Figure 4.12 shows the input and output from two sample excutions of the program. During the first sample execution, the condition at line 39 of method main is true—more than eight students passed the exam, so the program outputs a message indicating that the instructor should receive a bonus.

4.11 Compound Assignment Operators

The **compound assignment operators** abbreviate assignment expressions. Statements like

> *variable = variable   operator   expression*;

where *operator* is one of the binary operators +, -, *, / or % (or others we discuss later in the text) can be written in the form

> *variable   operator=   expression*;

For example, you can abbreviate the statement

```
c = c + 3;
```

with the **addition compound assignment operator, +=**, as

```
c += 3;
```

The += operator adds the value of the expression on its right to the value of the variable on its left and stores the result in the variable on the left of the operator. Thus, the assignment expression c += 3 adds 3 to c. Figure 4.13 shows the arithmetic compound assignment operators, sample expressions using the operators and explanations of what the operators do.

Assignment operator	Sample expression	Explanation	Assigns
Assume: int c = 3, d = 5, e = 4, f = 6, g = 12;			
+=	c += 7	c = c + 7	10 to c
-=	d -= 4	d = d - 4	1 to d
*=	e *= 5	e = e * 5	20 to e
/=	f /= 3	f = f / 3	2 to f
%=	g %= 9	g = g % 9	3 to g

Fig. 4.13 | Arithmetic compound assignment operators.

4.12 Increment and Decrement Operators

Java provides two unary operators for adding 1 to or subtracting 1 from the value of a numeric variable. These are the unary **increment operator**, ++, and the unary **decrement operator**, --, which are summarized in Fig. 4.14. A program can increment by 1 the value of a variable called c using the increment operator, ++, rather than the expression c = c + 1 or c += 1. An increment or decrement operator that is prefixed to (placed before) a variable is referred to as the **prefix increment** or **prefix decrement operator**, respectively. An increment or decrement operator that is postfixed to (placed after) a variable is referred to as the **postfix increment** or **postfix decrement operator**, respectively.

Operator	Operator name	Sample expression	Explanation
++	prefix increment	++a	Increment a by 1, then use the new value of a in the expression in which a resides.
++	postfix increment	a++	Use the current value of a in the expression in which a resides, then increment a by 1.
--	prefix decrement	--b	Decrement b by 1, then use the new value of b in the expression in which b resides.
--	postfix decrement	b--	Use the current value of b in the expression in which b resides, then decrement b by 1.

Fig. 4.14 | Increment and decrement operators.

Using the prefix increment (or decrement) operator to add (or subtract) 1 from a variable is known as **preincrementing** (or **predecrementing**) the variable. Preincrementing (or predecrementing) a variable causes the variable to be incremented (decremented) by 1; then the new value of the variable is used in the expression in which it appears. Using the postfix increment (or decrement) operator to add (or subtract) 1 from a variable is known as **postincrementing** (or **postdecrementing**) the variable. This causes the current value of the variable to be used in the expression in which it appears; then the variable's value is incremented (decremented) by 1.

Good Programming Practice 4.6
Unlike binary operators, the unary increment and decrement operators should be placed next to their operands, with no intervening spaces.

Figure 4.15 demonstrates the difference between the prefix increment and postfix increment versions of the ++ increment operator. The decrement operator (--) works similarly. Note that this example contains only one class, with method main performing all the class's work. In this chapter and in Chapter 3, you've seen examples consisting of two classes—one class containing methods that perform useful tasks and one containing method main, which creates an object of the other class and calls its methods. In this example, we simply want to show the mechanics of the ++ operator, so we use only one class declaration containing method main. Occasionally, when it does not make sense to try to create a reusable class to demonstrate a simple concept, we'll use a "mechanical" example contained entirely within the main method of a single class.

```
1   // Fig. 4.15: Increment.java
2   // Prefix increment and postfix increment operators.
3
4   public class Increment
5   {
6      public static void main( String[] args )
7      {
8         int c;
9
10        // demonstrate postfix increment operator
11        c = 5; // assign 5 to c
12        System.out.println( c );   // prints 5
13        System.out.println( c++ ); // prints 5 then postincrements
14        System.out.println( c );   // prints 6
15
16        System.out.println(); // skip a line
17
18        // demonstrate prefix increment operator
19        c = 5; // assign 5 to c
20        System.out.println( c );   // prints 5
21        System.out.println( ++c ); // preincrements then prints 6
22        System.out.println( c );   // prints 6
23     } // end main
24  } // end class Increment
```

```
5
5
6

5
6
6
```

Fig. 4.15 | Preincrementing and postincrementing.

Line 11 initializes the variable c to 5, and line 12 outputs c's initial value. Line 13 outputs the value of the expression c++. This expression postincrements the variable c, so c's original value (5) is output, then c's value is incremented (to 6). Thus, line 13 outputs c's initial value (5) again. Line 14 outputs c's new value (6) to prove that the variable's value was indeed incremented in line 13.

Line 19 resets c's value to 5, and line 20 outputs c's value. Line 21 outputs the value of the expression ++c. This expression preincrements c, so its value is incremented; then the new value (6) is output. Line 22 outputs c's value again to show that the value of c is still 6 after line 21 executes.

The arithmetic compound assignment operators and the increment and decrement operators can be used to simplify program statements. For example, the three assignment statements in Fig. 4.12 (lines 27, 29 and 32)

```
passes = passes + 1;
failures = failures + 1;
studentCounter = studentCounter + 1;
```

can be written more concisely with compound assignment operators as

```
passes += 1;
failures += 1;
studentCounter += 1;
```

with prefix increment operators as

```
++passes;
++failures;
++studentCounter;
```

or with postfix increment operators as

```
passes++;
failures++;
studentCounter++;
```

When incrementing or decrementing a variable in a statement by itself, the prefix increment and postfix increment forms have the same effect, and the prefix decrement and postfix decrement forms have the same effect. It's only when a variable appears in the context of a larger expression that preincrementing and postincrementing the variable have different effects (and similarly for predecrementing and postdecrementing).

Common Programming Error 4.9

Attempting to use the increment or decrement operator on an expression other than one to which a value can be assigned is a syntax error. For example, writing ++(x + 1) is a syntax error, because (x + 1) is not a variable.

Figure 4.16 shows the precedence and associativity of the operators we've introduced. They are shown from top to bottom in decreasing order of precedence. The second column describes the associativity of the operators at each level of precedence. The conditional operator (?:); the unary operators increment (++), decrement (--), plus (+) and minus (-); the cast operators and the assignment operators =, +=, -=, *=, /= and %= associate from right to left. All the other operators in the operator precedence chart in Fig. 4.16 associate from left to right. The third column lists the type of each group of operators.

Operators					Associativity	Type
++ --					right to left	unary postfix
++ -- + - (*type*)					right to left	unary prefix
* / %					left to right	multiplicative
+ -					left to right	additive
< <= > >=					left to right	relational
== !=					left to right	equality
?:					right to left	conditional
= += -= *= /= %=					right to left	assignment

Fig. 4.16 | Precedence and associativity of the operators discussed so far.

4.13 Primitive Types

The table in Appendix D lists the eight primitive types in Java. Like its predecessor languages C and C++, Java requires all variables to have a type. For this reason, Java is referred to as a **strongly typed language**.

In C and C++, programmers frequently have to write separate versions of programs to support different computer platforms, because the primitive types are not guaranteed to be identical from computer to computer. For example, an int value on one machine might be represented by 16 bits (2 bytes) of memory, and on another machine by 32 bits (4 bytes) of memory. In Java, int values are always 32 bits (4 bytes).

 Portability Tip 4.1
The primitive types in Java are portable across all computer platforms that support Java.

Each type in Appendix D is listed with its size in bits (there are eight bits to a byte) and its range of values. Because the designers of Java want to ensure portability, they use internationally recognized standards for both character formats (Unicode; for more information, visit www.unicode.org) and floating-point numbers (IEEE 754; for more information, visit grouper.ieee.org/groups/754/).

Recall from Section 3.5 that variables of primitive types declared outside of a method as fields of a class are automatically assigned default values unless explicitly initialized. Instance variables of types char, byte, short, int, long, float and double are all given the value 0 by default. Instance variables of type boolean are given the value false by default. Reference-type instance variables are initialized by default to the value null.

4.14 (Optional) GUI and Graphics Case Study: Creating Simple Drawings

An appealing feature of Java is its graphics support, which enables programmers to visually enhance their applications. This section introduces one of Java's graphical capabilities—drawing lines. It also covers the basics of creating a window to display a drawing on the computer screen.

Java's Coordinate System
To draw in Java, you must understand Java's **coordinate system** (Fig. 4.17), a scheme for identifying points on the screen. By default, the upper-left corner of a GUI component

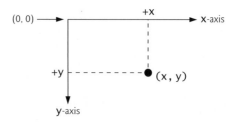

Fig. 4.17 | Java coordinate system. Units are measured in pixels.

has the coordinates (0, 0). A coordinate pair is composed of an *x*-coordinate (the **horizontal coordinate**) and a *y*-coordinate (the **vertical coordinate**). The *x*-coordinate is the horizontal location moving from left to right. The *y*-coordinate is the vertical location moving from top to bottom. The *x*-axis describes every horizontal coordinate, and the *y*-axis every vertical coordinate.

Coordinates indicate where graphics should be displayed on a screen. Coordinate units are measured in **pixels**. The term pixel stands for "picture element." A pixel is a display monitor's smallest unit of resolution.

First Drawing Application

Our first drawing application simply draws two lines. Class DrawPanel (Fig. 4.18) performs the actual drawing, while class DrawPanelTest (Fig. 4.19) creates a window to display the drawing. In class DrawPanel, the import statements in lines 3–4 allow us to use class **Graphics** (from package java.awt), which provides various methods for drawing text and shapes onto the screen, and class **JPanel** (from package javax.swing), which provides an area on which we can draw.

```java
1  // Fig. 4.18: DrawPanel.java
2  // Using drawLine to connect the corners of a panel.
3  import java.awt.Graphics;
4  import javax.swing.JPanel;
5
6  public class DrawPanel extends JPanel
7  {
8     // draws an X from the corners of the panel
9     public void paintComponent( Graphics g )
10    {
11       // call paintComponent to ensure the panel displays correctly
12       super.paintComponent( g );
13
14       int width = getWidth(); // total width
15       int height = getHeight(); // total height
16
17       // draw a line from the upper-left to the lower-right
18       g.drawLine( 0, 0, width, height );
19
20       // draw a line from the lower-left to the upper-right
21       g.drawLine( 0, height, width, 0 );
22    } // end method paintComponent
23 } // end class DrawPanel
```

Fig. 4.18 | Using drawLine to connect the corners of a panel.

```java
1  // Fig. 4.19: DrawPanelTest.java
2  // Application to display a DrawPanel.
3  import javax.swing.JFrame;
4
5  public class DrawPanelTest
6  {
```

Fig. 4.19 | Creating JFrame to display DrawPanel. (Part 1 of 2.)

```
7    public static void main( String[] args )
8    {
9       // create a panel that contains our drawing
10      DrawPanel panel = new DrawPanel();
11
12      // create a new frame to hold the panel
13      JFrame application = new JFrame();
14
15      // set the frame to exit when it is closed
16      application.setDefaultCloseOperation( JFrame.EXIT_ON_CLOSE );
17
18      application.add( panel ); // add the panel to the frame
19      application.setSize( 250, 250 ); // set the size of the frame
20      application.setVisible( true ); // make the frame visible
21   } // end main
22 } // end class DrawPanelTest
```

Fig. 4.19 | Creating JFrame to display DrawPanel. (Part 2 of 2.)

Line 6 uses the keyword **extends** to indicate that class DrawPanel is an enhanced type of JPanel. The keyword extends represents a so-called inheritance relationship in which our new class DrawPanel begins with the existing members (data and methods) from class JPanel. The class from which DrawPanel **inherits**, JPanel, appears to the right of keyword extends. In this inheritance relationship, JPanel is called the **superclass** and DrawPanel is called the **subclass**. This results in a DrawPanel class that has the attributes (data) and behaviors (methods) of class JPanel as well as the new features we are adding in our Draw-Panel class declaration—specifically, the ability to draw two lines along the diagonals of the panel. Inheritance is explained in detail in Chapter 9. For now, you should mimic our DrawPanel class when creating your own graphics programs.

Method paintComponent
Every JPanel, including our DrawPanel, has a **paintComponent** method (lines 9–22), which the system automatically calls every time it needs to display the JPanel. Method paintComponent must be declared as shown in line 9—otherwise, the system will not call it. This method is called when a JPanel is first displayed on the screen, when it's covered then uncovered by a window on the screen and when the window in which it appears is resized. Method paintComponent requires one argument, a Graphics object, that is provided by the system when it calls paintComponent.

The first statement in every paintComponent method you create should always be

```
super.paintComponent( g );
```

which ensures that the panel is properly rendered before we begin drawing on it. Next, lines 14–15 call methods that class DrawPanel inherits from JPanel. Because DrawPanel extends JPanel, DrawPanel can use any public methods of JPanel. Methods **getWidth** and **getHeight** return the JPanel's width and height, respectively. Lines 14–15 store these values in the local variables width and height. Finally, lines 18 and 21 use the Graphics variable g to call method **drawLine** to draw the two lines. Method drawLine draws a line between two points represented by its four arguments. The first two arguments are the *x*- and *y*-coordinates for one endpoint, and the last two arguments are the coordinates for the other endpoint. If you resize the window, the lines will scale accordingly, because the arguments are based on the width and height of the panel. Resizing the window in this application causes the system to call paintComponent to redraw the DrawPanel's contents.

Class *DrawPanelTest*

To display the DrawPanel on the screen, you must place it in a window. You create a window with an object of class **JFrame**. In DrawPanelTest.java (Fig. 4.19), line 3 imports class JFrame from package javax.swing. Line 10 in main creates a DrawPanel object, which contains our drawing, and line 13 creates a new JFrame that can hold and display our panel. Line 16 calls JFrame method **setDefaultCloseOperation** with the argument **JFrame.EXIT_ON_CLOSE** to indicate that the application should terminate when the user closes the window. Line 18 uses class JFrame's **add method** to attach the DrawPanel to the JFrame. Line 19 sets the size of the JFrame. Method **setSize** takes two parameters that represent the width and height of the JFrame, respectively. Finally, line 20 displays the JFrame by calling its **setVisible method** with the argument true. When the JFrame is displayed, the DrawPanel's paintComponent method (lines 9–22 of Fig. 4.18) is implicitly called, and the two lines are drawn (see the sample outputs in Fig. 4.19). Try resizing the window to see that the lines always draw based on the window's current width and height.

GUI and Graphics Case Study Exercises

4.1 Using loops and control statements to draw lines can lead to many interesting designs.
 a) Create the design in the left screen capture of Fig. 4.20. This design draws lines from the top-left corner, fanning them out until they cover the upper-left half of the panel. One approach is to divide the width and height into an equal number of steps (we found 15 steps worked well). The first endpoint of a line will always be in the top-left corner (0, 0). The second endpoint can be found by starting at the bottom-left corner and moving up one vertical step and right one horizontal step. Draw a line between the two endpoints. Continue moving up and to the right one step to find each successive endpoint. The figure should scale accordingly as you resize the window.
 b) Modify your answer in part (a) to have lines fan out from all four corners, as shown in the right screen capture of Fig. 4.20. Lines from opposite corners should intersect along the middle.

4.2 Figure 4.21 displays two additional designs created using while loops and drawLine.
 a) Create the design in the left screen capture of Fig. 4.21. Begin by dividing each edge into an equal number of increments (we chose 15 again). The first line starts in the top-left corner and ends one step right on the bottom edge. For each successive line, move down one increment on the left edge and right one increment on the bottom edge. Continue drawing lines until you reach the bottom-right corner. The figure should scale as you resize the window so that the endpoints always touch the edges.
 b) Modify your answer in part (a) to mirror the design in all four corners, as shown in the right screen capture of Fig. 4.21.

Fig. 4.20 | Lines fanning from a corner.

Fig. 4.21 | Line art with loops and `drawLine`.

4.15 Wrap-Up

This chapter presented basic problem-solving strategies that programmers use in building classes and developing methods for these classes. We demonstrated how to construct an algorithm (i.e., an approach to solving a problem), then how to refine the algorithm through several phases of pseudocode development, resulting in Java code that can be executed as part of a method. The chapter showed how to use top-down, stepwise refinement to plan out the specific actions that a method must perform and the order in which the method must perform these actions.

Only three types of control structures—sequence, selection and repetition—are needed to develop any problem-solving algorithm. Specifically, this chapter demonstrated the `if` single-selection statement, the `if...else` double-selection statement and the `while` repetition statement. These are some of the building blocks used to construct solutions to many problems. We used control-statement stacking to total and compute the average of a set of student grades with counter- and sentinel-controlled repetition, and we used control-statement nesting to analyze and make decisions based on a set of exam results. We introduced Java's compound assignment operators and its increment and decrement operators. Finally, we discussed the primitive types available to Java programmers. In Chapter 5, we continue our discussion of control statements, introducing the `for`, `do...while` and `switch` statements.

Summary

Section 4.1 Introduction
- Before writing a program to solve a problem, you must have a thorough understanding of the problem and a carefully planned approach to solving it. You must also understand the building blocks that are available and to employ proven program-construction techniques.

Section 4.2 Algorithms
- Any computing problem can be solved by executing a series of actions in a specific order.
- A procedure for solving a problem in terms of the actions to execute and the order in which they execute is called an algorithm.
- Specifying the order in which statements execute in a program is called program control.

Section 4.3 Pseudocode
- Pseudocode is an informal language that helps programmers develop algorithms without having to worry about the strict details of Java language syntax.
- Pseudocode is similar to everyday English—it's convenient and user friendly, but it's not an actual computer programming language.
- Pseudocode helps the programmer "think out" a program before attempting to write it in a programming language, such as Java.
- Carefully prepared pseudocode can easily be converted to a corresponding Java program.

Section 4.4 Control Structures
- Normally, statements in a program are executed one after the other in the order in which they are written. This process is called sequential execution.
- Various Java statements enable the programmer to specify that the next statement to execute is not necessarily the next one in sequence. This is called transfer of control.
- Bohm and Jacopini demonstrated that all programs could be written in terms of only three control structures—the sequence structure, the selection structure and the repetition structure.
- The term "control structures" comes from the field of computer science. The *Java Language Specification* refers to "control structures" as "control statements."
- The sequence structure is built into Java. Unless directed otherwise, the computer executes Java statements one after the other in the order in which they are written—that is, in sequence.
- Anywhere a single action may be placed, several actions may be placed in sequence.
- Activity diagrams are part of the UML. An activity diagram models the workflow (also called the activity) of a portion of a software system.
- Activity diagrams are composed of symbols—such as action-state symbols, diamonds and small circles—that are connected by transition arrows, which represent the flow of the activity.
- Action states contain action expressions that specify particular actions to perform.
- The arrows in an activity diagram represent transitions, which indicate the order in which the actions represented by the action states occur.
- The solid circle located at the top of an activity diagram represents the activity's initial state—the beginning of the workflow before the program performs the modeled actions.
- The solid circle surrounded by a hollow circle that appears at the bottom of the diagram represents the final state—the end of the workflow after the program performs its actions.
- Rectangles with their upper-right corners folded over are UML notes—explanatory remarks that describe the purpose of symbols in the diagram.

- Java has three types of selection statements.
- The `if` single-selection statement selects or ignores a single action or a single group of actions.
- The `if...else` double-selection statement selects between two actions or groups of actions.
- The `switch` statement is called a multiple-selection statement because it selects among many different actions or groups of actions.
- Java provides the `while`, `do...while` and `for` repetition (looping) statements that enable programs to perform statements repeatedly as long as a loop-continuation condition remains true.
- The `while` and `for` statements perform the action(s) in their bodies zero or more times—if the loop-continuation condition is initially false, the action(s) will not execute. The `do...while` statement performs the action(s) in its body one or more times.
- The words `if`, `else`, `switch`, `while`, `do` and `for` are Java keywords. Keywords cannot be used as identifiers, such as variable names.
- Every program is formed by combining as many sequence, selection and repetition statements as is appropriate for the algorithm the program implements.
- Single-entry/single-exit control statements are attached to one another by connecting the exit point of one to the entry point of the next. This is known as control-statement stacking.
- A control statement may also be nested inside another control statement.

Section 4.5 `if` Single-Selection Statement
- Programs use selection statements to choose among alternative courses of action.
- The single-selection `if` statement's activity diagram contains the diamond symbol, which indicates that a decision is to be made. The workflow follows a path determined by the symbol's associated guard conditions. If a guard condition is true, the workflow enters the action state to which the corresponding transition arrow points.
- The `if` statement is a single-entry/single-exit control statement.

Section 4.6 `if...else` Double-Selection Statement
- The `if` single-selection statement performs an indicated action only when the condition is `true`.
- The `if...else` double-selection statement performs one action when the condition is true and a different action when the condition is false.
- The conditional operator (`?:`) is Java's only ternary operator—it takes three operands. Together, the operands and the `?:` symbol form a conditional expression.
- A program can test multiple cases with nested `if...else` statements.
- The Java compiler associates an `else` with the immediately preceding `if` unless told to do otherwise by the placement of braces.
- The `if` statement expects one statement in its body. To include several statements in the body of an `if` (or the body of an `else` for an `if...else` statement), enclose the statements in braces.
- A block of statements can be placed anywhere in a program that a single statement can be placed.
- A logic error has its effect at execution time. A fatal logic error causes a program to fail and terminate prematurely. A nonfatal logic error allows a program to continue executing, but causes the program to produce incorrect results.
- Just as a block can be placed anywhere a single statement can be placed, you can also use an empty statement, represented by placing a semicolon (`;`) where a statement would normally be.

Section 4.7 `while` Repetition Statement
- The `while` repetition statement allows the programmer to specify that a program should repeat an action while some condition remains true.

- The UML's merge symbol joins two flows of activity into one.
- The decision and merge symbols can be distinguished by the number of "incoming" and "outgoing" transition arrows. A decision symbol has one transition arrow pointing to the diamond and two or more transition arrows pointing out from the diamond to indicate possible transitions from that point. Each transition arrow pointing out of a decision symbol has a guard condition. A merge symbol has two or more transition arrows pointing to the diamond and only one transition arrow pointing from the diamond, to indicate multiple activity flows merging to continue the activity. None of the transition arrows associated with a merge symbol has a guard condition.

Section 4.8 Formulating Algorithms: Counter-Controlled Repetition
- Counter-controlled repetition uses a variable called a counter (or control variable) to control the number of times a set of statements execute.
- Counter-controlled repetition is often called definite repetition, because the number of repetitions is known before the loop begins executing.
- A total is a variable used to accumulate the sum of several values. Variables used to store totals are normally initialized to zero before being used in a program.
- A local variable's declaration must appear before the variable is used in that method. A local variable cannot be accessed outside the method in which it's declared.
- Dividing two integers results in integer division—the calculation's fractional part is truncated.

Section 4.9 Formulating Algorithms: Sentinel-Controlled Repetition
- In sentinel-controlled repetition, a special value called a sentinel value (also called a signal value, a dummy value or a flag value) is used to indicate "end of data entry."
- A sentinel value must be chosen that cannot be confused with an acceptable input value.
- Top-down, stepwise refinement is essential to the development of well-structured programs.
- Division by zero is a logic error.
- To perform a floating-point calculation with integer values, cast one of the integers to type double.
- Java knows how to evaluate only arithmetic expressions in which the operands' types are identical. To ensure this, Java performs an operation called promotion on selected operands.
- The unary cast operator is formed by placing parentheses around the name of a type.

Section 4.11 Compound Assignment Operators
- The compound assignment operators abbreviate assignment expressions. Statements of the form

   variable = *variable   operator   expression*;

   where *operator* is one of the binary operators +, -, *, / or %, can be written in the form

   variable   operator= *expression*;

- The += operator adds the value of the expression on the right of the operator to the value of the variable on the left of the operator and stores the result in the variable on the left of the operator.

Section 4.12 Increment and Decrement Operators
- The unary increment operator, ++, and the unary decrement operator, --, add 1 to or subtract 1 from the value of a numeric variable.
- An increment or decrement operator that is prefixed to a variable is the prefix increment or prefix decrement operator, respectively. An increment or decrement operator that is postfixed to a variable is the postfix increment or postfix decrement operator, respectively.
- Using the prefix increment or decrement operator to add or subtract 1 is known as preincrementing or predecrementing, respectively.

- Preincrementing or predecrementing a variable causes the variable to be incremented or decremented by 1; then the new value of the variable is used in the expression in which it appears.
- Using the postfix increment or decrement operator to add or subtract 1 is known as postincrementing or postdecrementing, respectively.
- Postincrementing or postdecrementing the variable causes its value to be used in the expression in which it appears; then the variable's value is incremented or decremented by 1.
- When incrementing or decrementing a variable in a statement by itself, the prefix and postfix increment have the same effect, and the prefix and postfix decrement have the same effect.

Section 4.13 Primitive Types
- Java requires all variables to have a type. Thus, Java is referred to as a strongly typed language.
- Java uses Unicode characters and IEEE 754 floating-point numbers.

Terminology

--, decrement operator 135
?:, conditional operator 112
++, increment operator 135
+=, addition compound assignment operator 134
action 107
action expression (in the UML) 109
action state (in the UML) 109
action-state symbol (in the UML) 109
activity (in the UML) 109
activity diagram (in the UML) 109
addition compound assignment operator, += 134
algorithm 107
arithmetic compound assignment operator: +=, -=, *=, /= and %= 134
block 115
boolean expression 112
cast operator, (*type*) 128
compound assignment operator 134
conditional expression 112
conditional operator, ?: 112
control statement 108
control-statement nesting 110
control-statement stacking 110
control variable 118
counter 118
counter-controlled repetition 117
dangling-else problem 114
decision symbol (in the UML) 111
decrement operator, -- 135
definite repetition 118
diamond symbol (in the UML) 109
dotted line (in the UML) 110
(double) cast operator 128
double-selection statement 110

dummy value 122
explicit conversion 128
false 112
fatal logic error 115
final state (in the UML) 109
first refinement 123
flag value 122
goto statement 108
guard condition (in the UML) 111
if...else double-selection statement 111
implicit conversion 128
increment operator, ++ 135
indefinite repetition 122
infinite loop 116
initial state (in the UML) 109
integer division 122
iteration 120
logic error 115
loop-continuation condition 110
looping statement 110, 116
merge symbol 116
multiple-selection statement 110
multiplicative operators 129
nested control statements 130
nested if...else statements 113
nonfatal logic error 115
notes (in the UML) 110
order in which actions should execute 107
postdecrement a variable 135
postfix decrement operator 135
postfix increment operator 135
postincrement a variable 135
predecrement a variable 135
prefix decrement operator 135
prefix increment operator 135
preincrement a variable 135

Self-Review Exercises

4.1 Fill in the blanks in each of the following statements:

a) All programs can be written in terms of three types of control structures: _____, _____ and _____.

b) The _____ statement is used to execute one action when a condition is true and another when that condition is false.

c) Repeating a set of instructions a specific number of times is called _____ repetition.

d) When it's not known in advance how many times a set of statements will be repeated, a(n) _____ value can be used to terminate the repetition.

e) The _____ structure is built into Java—by default, statements execute in the order they appear.

f) Instance variables of types char, byte, short, int, long, float and double are all given the value _____ by default.

g) Java is a(n) _____ language—it requires all variables to have a type.

h) If the increment operator is _____ to a variable, first the variable is incremented by 1, then its new value is used in the expression.

4.2 State whether each of the following is *true* or *false*. If *false*, explain why.

a) An algorithm is a procedure for solving a problem in terms of the actions to execute and the order in which they execute.

b) A set of statements contained within a pair of parentheses is called a block.

c) A selection statement specifies that an action is to be repeated while some condition remains true.

d) A nested control statement appears in the body of another control statement.

e) Java provides the arithmetic compound assignment operators +=, -=, *=, /= and %= for abbreviating assignment expressions.

f) The primitive types (boolean, char, byte, short, int, long, float and double) are portable across only Windows platforms.

g) Specifying the order in which statements (actions) execute in a program is called program control.

h) The unary cast operator (double) creates a temporary integer copy of its operand.

i) Instance variables of type boolean are given the value true by default.

j) Pseudocode helps a programmer think out a program before attempting to write it in a programming language.

4.3   Write four different Java statements that each add 1 to integer variable x.

4.4   Write Java statements to accomplish each of the following tasks:
a) Use one statement to assign the sum of x and y to z, then increment x by 1.
b) Test whether variable count is greater than 10. If it is, print "Count is greater than 10".
c) Use one statement to decrement the variable x by 1, then subtract it from variable total and store the result in variable total.
d) Calculate the remainder after q is divided by divisor, and assign the result to q. Write this statement in two different ways.

4.5   Write a Java statement to accomplish each of the following tasks:
a) Declare variables sum and x to be of type int.
b) Assign 1 to variable x.
c) Assign 0 to variable sum.
d) Add variable x to variable sum, and assign the result to variable sum.
e) Print "The sum is: ", followed by the value of variable sum.

4.6   Combine the statements that you wrote in Exercise 4.5 into a Java application that calculates and prints the sum of the integers from 1 to 10. Use a while statement to loop through the calculation and increment statements. The loop should terminate when the value of x becomes 11.

4.7   Determine the value of the variables in the statement product *= x++; after the calculation is performed. Assume that all variables are type int and initially have the value 5.

4.8   Identify and correct the errors in each of the following sets of code:
a)
```
while ( c <= 5 )
  {
     product *= c;
     ++c;
```
b)
```
if ( gender == 1 )
     System.out.println( "Woman" );
  else;
     System.out.println( "Man" );
```

4.9   What is wrong with the following while statement?
```
while ( z >= 0 )
   sum += z;
```

Answers to Self-Review Exercises

4.1   a) sequence, selection, repetition. b) if...else. c) counter-controlled (or definite). d) sentinel, signal, flag or dummy. e) sequence. f) 0 (zero). g) strongly typed. h) prefixed.

4.2   a) True. b) False. A set of statements contained within a pair of braces ({ and }) is called a block. c) False. A repetition statement specifies that an action is to be repeated while some condition remains true. d) True. e) True. f) False. The primitive types (boolean, char, byte, short, int, long, float and double) are portable across all computer platforms that support Java. g) True. h) False. The unary cast operator (double) creates a temporary floating-point copy of its operand. i) False. Instance variables of type boolean are given the value false by default. j) True.

4.3
```
x = x + 1;
x += 1;
++x;
x++;
```

4.4   a) z = x++ + y;
       b) if (count > 10)
              System.out.println("Count is greater than 10");

c) `total -= --x;`
d) `q %= divisor;`
   `q = q % divisor;`

4.5 a) `int sum;`
        `int x;`
   b) `x = 1;`
   c) `sum = 0;`
   d) `sum += x;` or `sum = sum + x;`
   e) `System.out.printf( "The sum is: %d\n", sum );`

4.6 The program is as follows:

```
1   // Exercise 4.6: Calculate.java
2   // Calculate the sum of the integers from 1 to 10
3   public class Calculate
4   {
5      public static void main( String[] args )
6      {
7         int sum;
8         int x;
9
10        x = 1;   // initialize x to 1 for counting
11        sum = 0; // initialize sum to 0 for totaling
12
13        while ( x <= 10 ) // while x is less than or equal to 10
14        {
15           sum += x; // add x to sum
16           ++x; // increment x
17        } // end while
18
19        System.out.printf( "The sum is: %d\n", sum );
20     } // end main
21  } // end class Calculate
```

```
The sum is: 55
```

4.7 product = 25, x = 6

4.8 a) Error: The closing right brace of the `while` statement's body is missing.
        Correction: Add a closing right brace after the statement `++c;`.
   b) Error: The semicolon after `else` results in a logic error. The second output statement will always be executed.
        Correction: Remove the semicolon after `else`.

4.9 The value of the variable z is never changed in the `while` statement. Therefore, if the loop-continuation condition (z >= 0) is true, an infinite loop is created. To prevent an infinite loop from occurring, z must be decremented so that it eventually becomes less than 0.

Exercises

4.10 Compare and contrast the `if` single-selection statement and the `while` repetition statement. How are these two statements similar? How are they different?

4.11 Explain what happens when a Java program attempts to divide one integer by another. What happens to the fractional part of the calculation? How can a programmer avoid that outcome?

4.12 Describe the two ways in which control statements can be combined.

4.13   What type of repetition would be appropriate for calculating the sum of the first 100 positive integers? What type of repetition would be appropriate for calculating the sum of an arbitrary number of positive integers? Briefly describe how each of these tasks could be performed.

4.14   What is the difference between preincrementing and postincrementing a variable?

4.15   What does the following program print?

```
1   // Exercise 4.15: Mystery.java
2   public class Mystery
3   {
4      public static void main( String[] args )
5      {
6         int y;
7         int x = 1;
8         int total = 0;
9
10        while ( x <= 10 )
11        {
12           y = x * x;
13           System.out.println( y );
14           total += y;
15           ++x;
16        } // end while
17
18        System.out.printf( "Total is %d\n", total );
19     } // end main
20  } // end class Mystery
```

For Exercise 4.16 through Exercise 4.19, perform each of the following steps:
   a) Read the problem statement.
   b) Formulate the algorithm using pseudocode and top-down, stepwise refinement.
   c) Write a Java program.
   d) Test, debug and execute the Java program.
   e) Process three complete sets of data.

4.16   *(Gas Mileage)* Drivers are concerned with the mileage their automobiles get. One driver has kept track of several tankfuls of gasoline by recording the miles driven and gallons used for each tankful. Develop a Java application that will input the miles driven and gallons used (both as integers) for each tankful. The program should calculate and display the miles per gallon obtained for each tankful and print the combined miles per gallon obtained for all tankfuls up to this point. All averaging calculations should produce floating-point results. Use class Scanner and sentinel-controlled repetition to obtain the data from the user.

4.17   *(Credit Limit Calculator)* Develop a Java application that determines whether any of several department-store customers has exceeded the credit limit on a charge account. For each customer, the following facts are available:
   a) account number
   b) balance at the beginning of the month
   c) total of all items charged by the customer this month
   d) total of all credits applied to the customer's account this month
   e) allowed credit limit.

The program should input all these facts as integers, calculate the new balance (= *beginning balance + charges – credits*), display the new balance and determine whether the new balance exceeds the customer's credit limit. For those customers whose credit limit is exceeded, the program should display the message "Credit limit exceeded".

4.18 *(Sales Commission Calculator)* A large company pays its salespeople on a commission basis. The salespeople receive $200 per week plus 9% of their gross sales for that week. For example, a salesperson who sells $5000 worth of merchandise in a week receives $200 plus 9% of $5000, or a total of $650. You've been supplied with a list of the items sold by each salesperson. The values of these items are as follows:

Item	Value
1	239.99
2	129.75
3	99.95
4	350.89

Develop a Java application that inputs one salesperson's items sold for last week and calculates and displays that salesperson's earnings. There is no limit to the number of items that can be sold.

4.19 *(Salary Calculator)* Develop a Java application that determines the gross pay for each of three employees. The company pays straight time for the first 40 hours worked by each employee and time and a half for all hours worked in excess of 40. You are given a list of the employees, their number of hours worked last week and their hourly rates. Your program should input this information for each employee, then determine and display the employee's gross pay. Use class Scanner to input the data.

4.20 *(Find the Largest Number)* The process of finding the largest value is used frequently in computer applications. For example, a program that determines the winner of a sales contest would input the number of units sold by each salesperson. The salesperson who sells the most units wins the contest. Write a pseudocode program, then a Java application that inputs a series of 10 integers and determines and prints the largest integer. Your program should use at least the following three variables:

a) counter: A counter to count to 10 (i.e., to keep track of how many numbers have been input and to determine when all 10 numbers have been processed).

b) number: The integer most recently input by the user.

c) largest: The largest number found so far.

4.21 *(Tabular Output)* Write a Java application that uses looping to print the following table of values:

N	10*N	100*N	1000*N
1	10	100	1000
2	20	200	2000
3	30	300	3000
4	40	400	4000
5	50	500	5000

4.22 *(Find the Two Largest Numbers)* Using an approach similar to that for Exercise 4.20, find the *two* largest values of the 10 values entered. [*Note:* You may input each number only once.]

4.23 *(Validating User Input)* Modify the program in Fig. 4.12 to validate its inputs. For any input, if the value entered is other than 1 or 2, keep looping until the user enters a correct value.

4.24 *(Dangling-else Problem)* Determine the output for each of the given sets of code when x is 9 and y is 11 and when x is 11 and y is 9. Note that the compiler ignores the indentation in a Java program. Also, the Java compiler always associates an else with the immediately preceding if unless told to do otherwise by the placement of braces ({}). On first glance, the programmer may not be sure which if a particular else matches—this situation is referred to as the "dangling-else problem." We've eliminated the indentation from the following code to make the problem more challenging. [*Hint:* Apply the indentation conventions you've learned.]

a)
```
if ( x < 10 )
if ( y > 10 )
System.out.println( "*****" );
else
System.out.println( "#####" );
System.out.println( "$$$$$" );
```

b)
```
if ( x < 10 )
{
if ( y > 10 )
System.out.println( "*****" );
}
else
{
System.out.println( "#####" );
System.out.println( "$$$$$" );
}
```

4.25 *(Another Dangling-else Problem)* Modify the given code to produce the output shown in each part of the problem. Use proper indentation techniques. Make no changes other than inserting braces and changing the indentation of the code. The compiler ignores indentation in a Java program. We've eliminated the indentation from the given code to make the problem more challenging. [*Note:* It's possible that no modification is necessary for some of the parts.]

```
if ( y == 8 )
if ( x == 5 )
System.out.println( "@@@@@" );
else
System.out.println( "#####" );
System.out.println( "$$$$$" );
System.out.println( "&&&&&" );
```

a) Assuming that x = 5 and y = 8, the following output is produced:

```
@@@@@
$$$$$
&&&&&
```

b) Assuming that x = 5 and y = 8, the following output is produced:

```
@@@@@
```

c) Assuming that x = 5 and y = 8, the following output is produced:

```
@@@@@
```

d) Assuming that x = 5 and y = 7, the following output is produced. [*Note:* The last three output statements after the else are all part of a block.]

```
#####
$$$$$
&&&&&
```

4.26 *(Square of Asterisks)* Write an application that prompts the user to enter the size of the side of a square, then displays a hollow square of that size made of asterisks. Your program should work for squares of all side lengths between 1 and 20.

4.27 *(Palindromes)* A palindrome is a sequence of characters that reads the same backward as forward. For example, each of the following five-digit integers is a palindrome: 12321, 55555, 45554 and 11611. Write an application that reads in a five-digit integer and determines whether it's a palindrome. If the number is not five digits long, display an error message and allow the user to enter a new value.

4.28 *(Printing the Decimal Equivalent of a Binary Number)* Write an application that inputs an integer containing only 0s and 1s (i.e., a binary integer) and prints its decimal equivalent. [*Hint:* Use the remainder and division operators to pick off the binary number's digits one at a time, from right to left. In the decimal number system, the rightmost digit has a positional value of 1 and the next digit to the left a positional value of 10, then 100, then 1000, and so on. The decimal number 234 can be interpreted as 4 * 1 + 3 * 10 + 2 * 100. In the binary number system, the rightmost digit has a positional value of 1, the next digit to the left a positional value of 2, then 4, then 8, and so on. The decimal equivalent of binary 1101 is 1 * 1 + 0 * 2 + 1 * 4 + 1 * 8, or 1 + 0 + 4 + 8 or, 13.]

4.29 *(Checkerboard Pattern of Asterisks)* Write an application that uses only the output statements

```
System.out.print( "* " );
System.out.print( "  " );
System.out.println();
```

to display the checkerboard pattern that follows. Note that a `System.out.println` method call with no arguments causes the program to output a single newline character. [*Hint:* Repetition statements are required.]

```
* * * * * * * *
 * * * * * * * *
* * * * * * * *
 * * * * * * * *
* * * * * * * *
 * * * * * * * *
* * * * * * * *
 * * * * * * * *
```

4.30 *(Multiples of 2 with an Infinite Loop)* Write an application that keeps displaying in the command window the multiples of the integer 2—namely, 2, 4, 8, 16, 32, 64, and so on. Your loop should not terminate (i.e., it should create an infinite loop). What happens when you run this program?

4.31 What is wrong with the following statement? Provide the correct statement to add one to the sum of x and y.

```
System.out.println( ++(x + y) );
```

4.32 *(Sides of a Triangle)* Write an application that reads three nonzero values entered by the user and determines and prints whether they could represent the sides of a triangle.

4.33 *(Sides of a Right Triangle)* Write an application that reads three nonzero integers and determines and prints whether they could represent the sides of a right triangle.

4.34 *(Factorial)* The factorial of a nonnegative integer n is written as $n!$ (pronounced "n factorial") and is defined as follows:

$$n! = n \cdot (n - 1) \cdot (n - 2) \cdot \ldots \cdot 1 \quad \text{(for values of } n \text{ greater than or equal to 1)}$$

and

$$n! = 1 \quad \text{(for } n = 0)$$

For example, $5! = 5 \cdot 4 \cdot 3 \cdot 2 \cdot 1$, which is 120.

    a) Write an application that reads a nonnegative integer and computes and prints its factorial.

    b) Write an application that estimates the value of the mathematical constant e by using the following formula. Allow the user to enter the number of terms to calculate.

$$e = 1 + \frac{1}{1!} + \frac{1}{2!} + \frac{1}{3!} + ..$$

    c) Write an application that computes the value of e^x by using the following formula. Allow the user to enter the number of terms to calculate.

$$e^x = 1 + \frac{x}{1!} + \frac{x^2}{2!} + \frac{x^3}{3!} + ...$$

Making a Difference

4.35 *(Enforcing Privacy with Cryptography)* The explosive growth of Internet communications and data storage on Internet-connected computers has greatly increased privacy concerns. The field of cryptography is concerned with coding data to make it difficult (and hopefully—with the most advanced schemes—impossible) for unauthorized users to read. In this exercise you'll investigate a simple scheme for encrypting and decrypting data. A company that wants to send data over the Internet has asked you to write a program that will encrypt it so that it may be transmitted more securely. All the data is transmitted as four-digit integers. Your application should read a four-digit integer entered by the user and encrypt it as follows: Replace each digit with the result of adding 7 to the digit and getting the remainder after dividing the new value by 10. Then swap the first digit with the third, and swap the second digit with the fourth. Then print the encrypted integer. Write a separate application that inputs an encrypted four-digit integer and decrypts it (by reversing the encryption scheme) to form the original number. [*Optional reading project:* Research "public key cryptography" in general and the PGP (Pretty Good Privacy) specific public key scheme. You may also want to investigate the RSA scheme, which is widely used in industrial-strength applications.]

4.36 *(World Population Growth)* World population has grown considerably over the centuries. Continued growth could eventually challenge the limits of breathable air, drinkable water, arable cropland and other limited resources. There is evidence that growth has been slowing in recent years and that world population could peak some time this century, then start to decline.

For this exercise, research world population growth issues online. *Be sure to investigate various viewpoints.* Get estimates for the current world population and its growth rate (the percentage by which it is likely to increase this year). Write a program that calculates world population growth each year for the next 75 years, *using the simplifying assumption that the current growth rate will stay constant.* Print the results in a table. The first column should display the year from year 1 to year 75. The second column should display the anticipated world population at the end of that year. The third column should display the numerical increase in the world population that would occur that year. Using your results, determine the year in which the population would be double what it is today, if this year's growth rate were to persist.

5

*Not everything that can be counted counts, and not
every thing that counts can be counted.*
—Albert Einstein

Who can control his fate?
—William Shakespeare

The used key is always bright.
—Benjamin Franklin

*Intelligence … is the faculty of making artificial
objects, especially tools to make tools.*
—Henri Bergson

*Every advantage in the past is judged in the light of the
final issue.*
—Demosthenes

Control Statements: Part 2

Objectives

In this chapter you'll learn:

- The essentials of counter-controlled repetition.
- To use the **for** and **do**...**while** repetition statements to execute statements in a program repeatedly.
- To understand multiple selection using the **switch** selection statement.
- To use the **break** and **continue** program control statements to alter the flow of control.
- To use the logical operators to form complex conditional expressions in control statements.

5.1 Introduction

This chapter continues our presentation of structured programming theory and principles by introducing all but one of Java's remaining control statements. We demonstrate Java's for, do...while and switch statements. Through a series of short examples using while and for, we explore the essentials of counter-controlled repetition. We create a version of class GradeBook that uses a switch statement to count the number of A, B, C, D and F grade equivalents in a set of numeric grades entered by the user. We introduce the break and continue program-control statements. We discuss Java's logical operators, which enable you to use more complex conditional expressions in control statements. Finally, we summarize Java's control statements and the proven problem-solving techniques presented in this chapter and Chapter 4.

5.2 Essentials of Counter-Controlled Repetition

This section uses the while repetition statement introduced in Chapter 4 to formalize the elements required to perform counter-controlled repetition. Counter-controlled repetition requires

1. a **control variable** (or loop counter)

2. the **initial value** of the control variable

3. the **increment** (or **decrement**) by which the control variable is modified each time through the loop (also known as **each iteration of the loop**)

4. the **loop-continuation condition** that determines if looping should continue.

To see these elements of counter-controlled repetition, consider the application of Fig. 5.1, which uses a loop to display the numbers from 1 through 10.

```
1   // Fig. 5.1: WhileCounter.java
2   // Counter-controlled repetition with the while repetition statement.
3
4   public class WhileCounter
5   {
6      public static void main( String[] args )
7      {
```

Fig. 5.1 | Counter-controlled repetition with the while repetition statement. (Part 1 of 2.)

```
8        int counter = 1; // declare and initialize control variable
9
10       while ( counter <= 10 ) // loop-continuation condition
11       {
12          System.out.printf( "%d  ", counter );
13          ++counter; // increment control variable by 1
14       } // end while
15
16       System.out.println(); // output a newline
17    } // end main
18 } // end class WhileCounter
```

```
1  2  3  4  5  6  7  8  9  10
```

Fig. 5.1 | Counter-controlled repetition with the `while` repetition statement. (Part 2 of 2.)

In Fig. 5.1, the elements of counter-controlled repetition are defined in lines 8, 10 and 13. Line 8 declares the control variable (`counter`) as an `int`, reserves space for it in memory and sets its initial value to 1. Variable `counter` could also have been declared and initialized with the following local-variable declaration and assignment statements:

```
int counter; // declare counter
counter = 1; // initialize counter to 1
```

Line 12 displays control variable `counter`'s value during each iteration of the loop. Line 13 increments the control variable by 1 for each iteration of the loop. The loop-continuation condition in the `while` (line 10) tests whether the value of the control variable is less than or equal to 10 (the final value for which the condition is `true`). Note that the program performs the body of this `while` even when the control variable is 10. The loop terminates when the control variable exceeds 10 (i.e., `counter` becomes 11).

Common Programming Error 5.1

Because floating-point values may be approximate, controlling loops with floating-point variables may result in imprecise counter values and inaccurate termination tests.

Error-Prevention Tip 5.1

Use integers to control counting loops.

Good Programming Practice 5.1

Place blank lines above and below repetition and selection control statements, and indent the statement bodies to enhance readability.

The program in Fig. 5.1 can be made more concise by initializing `counter` to 0 in line 8 and preincrementing `counter` in the `while` condition as follows:

```
while ( ++counter <= 10 ) // loop-continuation condition
   System.out.printf( "%d  ", counter );
```

This code saves a statement (and eliminates the need for braces around the loop's body), because the `while` condition performs the increment before testing the condition. (Recall from Section 4.12 that the precedence of ++ is higher than that of <=.) Coding in such a condensed fashion takes practice, might make code more difficult to read, debug, modify and maintain, and typically should be avoided.

Software Engineering Observation 5.1
"Keep it simple" is good advice for most of the code you'll write.

5.3 for Repetition Statement

Section 5.2 presented the essentials of counter-controlled repetition. The while statement can be used to implement any counter-controlled loop. Java also provides the **for repetition statement**, which specifies the counter-controlled-repetition details in a single line of code. Figure 5.2 reimplements the application of Fig. 5.1 using for.

```
 1  // Fig. 5.2: ForCounter.java
 2  // Counter-controlled repetition with the for repetition statement.
 3
 4  public class ForCounter
 5  {
 6     public static void main( String[] args )
 7     {
 8        // for statement header includes initialization,
 9        // loop-continuation condition and increment
10        for ( int counter = 1; counter <= 10; counter++ )
11           System.out.printf( "%d  ", counter );
12
13        System.out.println(); // output a newline
14     } // end main
15  } // end class ForCounter
```

```
1  2  3  4  5  6  7  8  9  10
```

Fig. 5.2 | Counter-controlled repetition with the for repetition statement.

The application's main method operates as follows: When the for statement (lines 10–11) begins executing, the control variable counter is declared and initialized to 1. (Recall from Section 5.2 that the first two elements of counter-controlled repetition are the control variable and its initial value.) Next, the program checks the loop-continuation condition, counter <= 10, which is between the two required semicolons. Because the initial value of counter is 1, the condition initially is true. Therefore, the body statement (line 11) displays control variable counter's value, namely 1. After executing the loop's body, the program increments counter in the expression counter++, which appears to the right of the second semicolon. Then the loop-continuation test is performed again to determine whether the program should continue with the next iteration of the loop. At this point, the control-variable value is 2, so the condition is still true (the final value is not exceeded)—thus, the program performs the body statement again (i.e., the next iteration of the loop). This process continues until the numbers 1 through 10 have been displayed and the counter's value becomes 11, causing the loop-continuation test to fail and repetition to terminate (at line 11, after 10 repetitions of the loop body). Then the program performs the first statement after the for—in this case, line 13.

Note that Fig. 5.2 uses (in line 10) the loop-continuation condition `counter <= 10`. If you incorrectly specified `counter < 10` as the condition, the loop would iterate only nine times. This is a common logic error called an **off-by-one error**.

Common Programming Error 5.2

Using an incorrect relational operator or an incorrect final value of a loop counter in the loop-continuation condition of a repetition statement can cause an off-by-one error.

Error-Prevention Tip 5.2

Using the final value in the condition of a while or for statement and using the <= relational operator helps avoid off-by-one errors. For a loop that prints the values 1 to 10, the loop-continuation condition should be counter <= 10 rather than counter < 10 (which causes an off-by-one error) or counter < 11 (which is correct). Many programmers prefer so-called zero-based counting, in which to count 10 times, counter would be initialized to zero and the loop-continuation test would be counter < 10.

Figure 5.3 takes a closer look at the `for` statement in Fig. 5.2. The `for`'s first line (including the keyword `for` and everything in parentheses after `for`)—line 10 in Fig. 5.2—is sometimes called the **for statement header**. Note that the `for` header "does it all"—it specifies each item needed for counter-controlled repetition with a control variable. If there is more than one statement in the body of the `for`, braces are required to define the body of the loop.

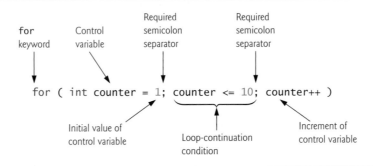

Fig. 5.3 | for statement header components.

The general format of the `for` statement is

```
for ( initialization; loopContinuationCondition; increment )
    statement
```

where the *initialization* expression names the loop's control variable and optionally provides its initial value, *loopContinuationCondition* determines whether the loop should continue executing and *increment* modifies the control variable's value (possibly an increment or decrement), so that the loop-continuation condition eventually becomes false. The two semicolons in the `for` header are required.

Common Programming Error 5.3

Using commas instead of the two required semicolons in a for header is a syntax error.

In most cases, the `for` statement can be represented with an equivalent `while` statement as follows:

```
initialization;
while ( loopContinuationCondition )
{
    statement
    increment;
}
```

In Section 5.7, we show a case in which a `for` statement cannot be represented with an equivalent `while` statement.

Typically, `for` statements are used for counter-controlled repetition and `while` statements for sentinel-controlled repetition. However, `while` and `for` can each be used for either repetition type.

If the *initialization* expression in the `for` header declares the control variable (i.e., the control variable's type is specified before the variable name, as in Fig. 5.2), the control variable can be used only in that `for` statement—it will not exist outside it. This restricted use is known as the variable's **scope**. The scope of a variable defines where it can be used in a program. For example, a local variable can be used only in the method that declares it and only from the point of declaration through the end of the method. Scope is discussed in detail in Chapter 6, Methods: A Deeper Look.

Common Programming Error 5.4

When a `for` statement's control variable is declared in the initialization section of the `for`'s header, using the control variable after the `for`'s body is a compilation error.

All three expressions in a `for` header are optional. If the *loopContinuationCondition* is omitted, Java assumes that the loop-continuation condition is always true, thus creating an infinite loop. You might omit the *initialization* expression if the program initializes the control variable before the loop. You might omit the *increment* expression if the program calculates the increment with statements in the loop's body or if no increment is needed. The increment expression in a `for` acts as if it were a standalone statement at the end of the `for`'s body. Therefore, the expressions

```
counter = counter + 1
counter += 1
++counter
counter++
```

are equivalent increment expressions in a `for` statement. Many programmers prefer counter++ because it's concise and because a `for` loop evaluates its increment expression after its body executes. Therefore, the postfix increment form seems more natural. In this case, the variable being incremented does not appear in a larger expression, so preincrementing and postincrementing actually have the same effect.

Performance Tip 5.1

There is a slight performance advantage to preincrementing, but if you choose to post-increment because it seems more natural (as in a `for` header), optimizing compilers will typically generate Java bytecode that uses the more efficient form anyway. So you should use the idiom with which you feel most comfortable in these situations.

Common Programming Error 5.5

Placing a semicolon immediately to the right of the right parenthesis of a for header makes that for's body an empty statement. This is normally a logic error.

Error-Prevention Tip 5.3

Infinite loops occur when the loop-continuation condition in a repetition statement never becomes false. To prevent this situation in a counter-controlled loop, ensure that the control variable is incremented (or decremented) during each iteration of the loop. In a sentinel-controlled loop, ensure that the sentinel value is able to be input.

The initialization, loop-continuation condition and increment portions of a for statement can contain arithmetic expressions. For example, assume that x = 2 and y = 10. If x and y are not modified in the body of the loop, the statement

```
for ( int j = x; j <= 4 * x * y; j += y / x )
```

is equivalent to the statement

```
for ( int j = 2; j <= 80; j += 5 )
```

The increment of a for statement may also be negative, in which case it's really a decrement, and the loop counts downward.

If the loop-continuation condition is initially false, the program does not execute the for statement's body. Instead, execution proceeds with the statement following the for.

Programs frequently display the control-variable value or use it in calculations in the loop body, but this use is not required. The control variable is commonly used to control repetition without being mentioned in the body of the for.

Error-Prevention Tip 5.4

Although the value of the control variable can be changed in the body of a for loop, avoid doing so, because this practice can lead to subtle errors.

The for statement's UML activity diagram is similar to that of the while statement (Fig. 4.4). Figure 5.4 shows the activity diagram of the for statement in Fig. 5.2. The diagram makes it clear that initialization occurs *once* before the loop-continuation test is evaluated the first time, and that incrementing occurs *each* time through the loop after the body statement executes.

5.4 Examples Using the for Statement

The following examples show techniques for varying the control variable in a for statement. In each case, we write the appropriate for header. Note the change in the relational operator for loops that decrement the control variable.

a) Vary the control variable from 1 to 100 in increments of 1.

```
for ( int i = 1; i <= 100; i++ )
```

b) Vary the control variable from 100 to 1 in decrements of 1.

```
for ( int i = 100; i >= 1; i-- )
```

c) Vary the control variable from 7 to 77 in increments of 7.

```
for ( int i = 7; i <= 77; i += 7 )
```

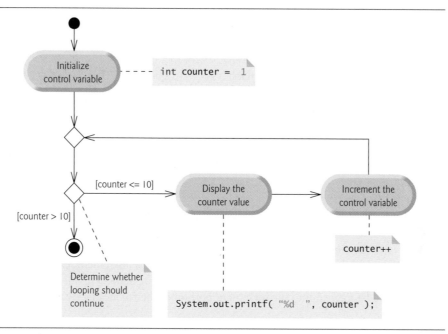

Fig. 5.4 | UML activity diagram for the for statement in Fig. 5.2.

d) Vary the control variable from 20 to 2 in decrements of 2.

```
for ( int i = 20; i >= 2; i -= 2 )
```

e) Vary the control variable over the values 2, 5, 8, 11, 14, 17, 20.

```
for ( int i = 2; i <= 20; i += 3 )
```

f) Vary the control variable over the values 99, 88, 77, 66, 55, 44, 33, 22, 11, 0.

```
for ( int i = 99; i >= 0; i -= 11 )
```

 Common Programming Error 5.6
Using an incorrect relational operator in the loop-continuation condition of a loop that counts downward (e.g., using i <= 1 instead of i >= 1 in a loop counting down to 1) is usually a logic error.

Application: Summing the Even Integers from 2 to 20
We now consider two sample applications that demonstrate simple uses of for. The application in Fig. 5.5 uses a for statement to sum the even integers from 2 to 20 and store the result in an int variable called total.

```java
1  // Fig. 5.5: Sum.java
2  // Summing integers with the for statement.
3
4  public class Sum
5  {
```

Fig. 5.5 | Summing integers with the for statement. (Part 1 of 2.)

```
 6      public static void main( String[] args )
 7      {
 8         int total = 0; // initialize total
 9
10         // total even integers from 2 through 20
11         for ( int number = 2; number <= 20; number += 2 )
12            total += number;
13
14         System.out.printf( "Sum is %d\n", total ); // display results
15      } // end main
16   } // end class Sum
```

```
Sum is 110
```

Fig. 5.5 | Summing integers with the for statement. (Part 2 of 2.)

The *initialization* and *increment* expressions can be comma-separated lists that enable you to use multiple initialization expressions or multiple increment expressions. For example, *although this is discouraged*, the body of the for statement in lines 11–12 of Fig. 5.5 could be merged into the increment portion of the for header by using a comma as follows:

```
for ( int number = 2; number <= 20; total += number, number += 2 )
   ; // empty statement
```

Good Programming Practice 5.2

For readability limit the size of control-statement headers to a single line if possible.

Application: Compound-Interest Calculations

The next application uses the for statement to compute compound interest. Consider the following problem:

> *A person invests $1000 in a savings account yielding 5% interest. Assuming that all the interest is left on deposit, calculate and print the amount of money in the account at the end of each year for 10 years. Use the following formula to determine the amounts:*
>
> $$a = p\,(1 + r)^n$$
>
> *where*
>
> p is the original amount invested (i.e., the principal)
> r is the annual interest rate (e.g., use 0.05 for 5%)
> n is the number of years
> a is the amount on deposit at the end of the nth year.

The solution to this problem (Fig. 5.6) involves a loop that performs the indicated calculation for each of the 10 years the money remains on deposit. Lines 8–10 in method main declare double variables amount, principal and rate, and initialize principal to 1000.0 and rate to 0.05. Java treats floating-point constants like 1000.0 and 0.05 as type double. Similarly, Java treats whole-number constants like 7 and -22 as type int.

```
 1   // Fig. 5.6: Interest.java
 2   // Compound-interest calculations with for.
 3
 4   public class Interest
 5   {
 6      public static void main( String[] args )
 7      {
 8         double amount; // amount on deposit at end of each year
 9         double principal = 1000.0; // initial amount before interest
10         double rate = 0.05; // interest rate
11
12         // display headers
13         System.out.printf( "%s%20s\n", "Year", "Amount on deposit" );
14
15         // calculate amount on deposit for each of ten years
16         for ( int year = 1; year <= 10; year++ )
17         {
18            // calculate new amount for specified year
19            amount = principal * Math.pow( 1.0 + rate, year );
20
21            // display the year and the amount
22            System.out.printf( "%4d%,20.2f\n", year, amount );
23         } // end for
24      } // end main
25   } // end class Interest
```

```
Year      Amount on deposit
   1             1,050.00
   2             1,102.50
   3             1,157.63
   4             1,215.51
   5             1,276.28
   6             1,340.10
   7             1,407.10
   8             1,477.46
   9             1,551.33
  10             1,628.89
```

Fig. 5.6 | Compound-interest calculations with for.

Formatting Strings with Field Widths and Justification

Line 13 outputs the headers for this application's two columns of output. The first column displays the year, and the second column the amount on deposit at the end of that year. Note that we use the format specifier %20s to output the String "Amount on Deposit". The integer 20 between the % and the conversion character s indicates that the value output should be displayed with a **field width** of 20—that is, printf displays the value with at least 20 character positions. If the value to be output is less than 20 character positions wide (17 characters in this example), the value is **right justified** in the field by default. If the year value to be output were more than four character positions wide, the field width would be extended to the right to accommodate the entire value—this would push the amount field to the right, upsetting the neat columns of our tabular output. To indicate that values should be output **left justified**, simply precede the field width with the **minus sign (–) formatting flag** (e.g., %-20s).

Performing the Interest Calculations

The for statement (lines 16–23) executes its body 10 times, varying control variable year from 1 to 10 in increments of 1. This loop terminates when control variable year becomes 11. (Note that year represents *n* in the problem statement.)

Classes provide methods that perform common tasks on objects. In fact, most methods must be called on a specific object. For example, to output text in Fig. 5.6, line 13 calls method printf on the System.out object. Many classes also provide methods that perform common tasks and do not require objects. These are called static methods. For example, Java does not include an exponentiation operator, so the designers of Java's Math class defined static method pow for raising a value to a power. You can call a static method by specifying the class name followed by a dot (.) and the method name, as in

> *ClassName*.*methodName*(*arguments*)

In Chapter 6, you'll learn how to implement static methods in your own classes.

We use static method **pow** of class **Math** to perform the compound-interest calculation in Fig. 5.6. Math.pow(*x*, *y*) calculates the value of *x* raised to the *y*th power. The method receives two double arguments and returns a double value. Line 19 performs the calculation $a = p(1 + r)^n$, where *a* is amount, *p* is principal, *r* is rate and *n* is year. Note that the Math class is defined in package java.lang, so you do not need to import class Math to use it.

Note that the body of the for statement contains the calculation 1.0 + rate, which appears as an argument to the Math.pow method. In fact, this calculation produces the same result each time through the loop, so repeating it every iteration of the loop is wasteful.

Performance Tip 5.2

In loops, avoid calculations for which the result never changes—such calculations should typically be placed before the loop. [Note: Many of today's sophisticated optimizing compilers will place such calculations outside loops in the compiled code.]

Formatting Floating-Point Numbers

After each calculation, line 22 outputs the year and the amount on deposit at the end of that year. The year is output in a field width of four characters (as specified by %4d). The amount is output as a floating-point number with the format specifier %,20.2f. The **comma (,) formatting flag** indicates that the floating-point value should be output with a **grouping separator**. The actual separator used is specific to the user's locale (i.e., country). For example, in the United States, the number will be output using commas to separate every three digits and a decimal point to separate the fractional part of the number, as in 1,234.45. The number 20 in the format specification indicates that the value should be output right justified in a field width of 20 characters. The .2 specifies the formatted number's precision—in this case, the number is rounded to the nearest hundredth and output with two digits to the right of the decimal point.

A Warning about Displaying Rounded Values

We declared variables amount, principal and rate to be of type double in this example. We are dealing with fractional parts of dollars and thus need a type that allows decimal points in its values. Unfortunately, floating-point numbers can cause trouble. Here is a simple explanation of what can go wrong when using double (or float) to represent dollar amounts (assuming that dollar amounts are displayed with two digits to the right of the decimal point): Two `double` dollar amounts stored in the machine could be 14.234 (which would normally be rounded to 14.23 for display purposes) and 18.673 (which would normally be rounded to 18.67 for display purposes). When these amounts are added, they produce the internal sum 32.907, which would normally be rounded to 32.91 for display purposes. Thus, your output could appear as

```
     14.23
   + 18.67
   -------
     32.91
```

but a person adding the individual numbers as displayed would expect the sum to be 32.90. You've been warned!

Error-Prevention Tip 5.5

Do not use variables of type `double` *(or* `float`*) to perform precise monetary calculations. The imprecision of floating-point numbers can cause errors. In the exercises, you'll learn how to use integers to perform precise monetary calculations. Java also provides class* `java.math.BigDecimal` *to perform precise monetary calculations. For more information, see* `java.sun.com/javase/6/docs/api/java/math/BigDecimal.html`*.*

5.5 do...while Repetition Statement

The **do...while repetition statement** is similar to the `while` statement. In the `while`, the program tests the loop-continuation condition at the beginning of the loop, before executing the loop's body; if the condition is false, the body never executes. The do...while statement tests the loop-continuation condition *after* executing the loop's body; therefore, the body always executes at least once. When a do...while statement terminates, execution continues with the next statement in sequence. Figure 5.7 uses a do...while (lines 10–14) to output the numbers 1–10.

```java
1   // Fig. 5.7: DoWhileTest.java
2   // do...while repetition statement.
3
4   public class DoWhileTest
5   {
6      public static void main( String[] args )
7      {
8         int counter = 1; // initialize counter
9
10        do
11        {
12           System.out.printf( "%d  ", counter );
13           ++counter;
14        } while ( counter <= 10 ); // end do...while
15
16        System.out.println(); // outputs a newline
17     } // end main
18  } // end class DoWhileTest
```

Fig. 5.7 | do...while repetition statement. (Part 1 of 2.)

```
1   2   3   4   5   6   7   8   9   10
```

Fig. 5.7 | do...while repetition statement. (Part 2 of 2.)

Line 8 declares and initializes control variable counter. Upon entering the do...while statement, line 12 outputs counter's value and line 13 increments counter. Then the program evaluates the loop-continuation test at the bottom of the loop (line 14). If the condition is true, the loop continues from the first body statement in the do...while (line 12). If the condition is false, the loop terminates and the program continues with the next statement after the loop.

Figure 5.8 contains the UML activity diagram for the do...while statement. This diagram makes it clear that the loop-continuation condition is not evaluated until after the loop performs the action state at least once. Compare this activity diagram with that of the while statement (Fig. 4.4).

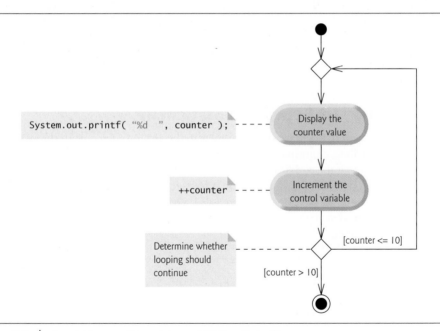

Fig. 5.8 | do...while repetition statement UML activity diagram.

It isn't necessary to use braces in the do...while repetition statement if there's only one statement in the body. However, most programmers include the braces, to avoid confusion between the while and do...while statements. For example,

```
while ( condition )
```

is normally the first line of a while statement. A do...while statement with no braces around a single-statement body appears as:

```
do
    statement
while ( condition );
```

which can be confusing. A reader may misinterpret the last line—while(*condition*);— as a while statement containing an empty statement (the semicolon by itself). Thus, the do...while statement with one body statement is usually written as follows:

```
do
{
   statement
} while ( condition );
```

Good Programming Practice 5.3

Always include braces in a do...while statement, even if they're not necessary. This helps eliminate ambiguity between the while statement and a do...while statement containing only one statement.

5.6 switch Multiple-Selection Statement

Chapter 4 discussed the if single-selection statement and the if...else double-selection statement. The **switch multiple-selection statement** performs different actions based on the possible values of a **constant integral expression** of type byte, short, int or char.

GradeBook Class with switch Statement to Count A, B, C, D and F Grades
Figure 5.9 enhances class GradeBook from Chapters 3–4. The new version we now present not only calculates the average of a set of numeric grades entered by the user, but uses a switch statement to determine whether each grade is the equivalent of an A, B, C, D or F and to increment the appropriate grade counter. The class also displays a summary of the number of students who received each grade. Refer to Fig. 5.10 for sample input and output of the GradeBookTest application that uses class GradeBook to process a set of grades.

```
 1   // Fig. 5.9: GradeBook.java
 2   // GradeBook class uses switch statement to count letter grades.
 3   import java.util.Scanner; // program uses class Scanner
 4
 5   public class GradeBook
 6   {
 7      private String courseName; // name of course this GradeBook represents
 8      // int instance variables are initialized to 0 by default
 9      private int total; // sum of grades
10      private int gradeCounter; // number of grades entered
11      private int aCount; // count of A grades
12      private int bCount; // count of B grades
13      private int cCount; // count of C grades
14      private int dCount; // count of D grades
15      private int fCount; // count of F grades
16
17      // constructor initializes courseName;
18      public GradeBook( String name )
19      {
20         courseName = name; // initializes courseName
21      } // end constructor
22
```

Fig. 5.9 | GradeBook class uses switch statement to count letter grades. (Part 1 of 3.)

```
23      // method to set the course name
24      public void setCourseName( String name )
25      {
26         courseName = name; // store the course name
27      } // end method setCourseName
28
29      // method to retrieve the course name
30      public String getCourseName()
31      {
32         return courseName;
33      } // end method getCourseName
34
35      // display a welcome message to the GradeBook user
36      public void displayMessage()
37      {
38         // getCourseName gets the name of the course
39         System.out.printf( "Welcome to the grade book for\n%s!\n\n",
40            getCourseName() );
41      } // end method displayMessage
42
43      // input arbitrary number of grades from user
44      public void inputGrades()
45      {
46         Scanner input = new Scanner( System.in );
47
48         int grade; // grade entered by user
49
50         System.out.printf( "%s\n%s\n    %s\n    %s\n",
51            "Enter the integer grades in the range 0-100.",
52            "Type the end-of-file indicator to terminate input:",
53            "On UNIX/Linux/Mac OS X type <Ctrl> d then press Enter",
54            "On Windows type <Ctrl> z then press Enter" );
55
56         // loop until user enters the end-of-file indicator
57         while ( input.hasNext() )
58         {
59            grade = input.nextInt(); // read grade
60            total += grade; // add grade to total
61            ++gradeCounter; // increment number of grades
62
63            // call method to increment appropriate counter
64            incrementLetterGradeCounter( grade );
65         } // end while
66      } // end method inputGrades
67
68      // add 1 to appropriate counter for specified grade
69      private void incrementLetterGradeCounter( int grade )
70      {
71         // determine which grade was entered
72         switch ( grade / 10 )
73         {
74            case 9:  // grade was between 90
75            case 10: // and 100, inclusive
76               ++aCount; // increment aCount
```

Fig. 5.9 | GradeBook class uses switch statement to count letter grades. (Part 2 of 3.)

```
77              break; // necessary to exit switch
78
79          case 8: // grade was between 80 and 89
80              ++bCount; // increment bCount
81              break; // exit switch
82
83          case 7: // grade was between 70 and 79
84              ++cCount; // increment cCount
85              break; // exit switch
86
87          case 6: // grade was between 60 and 69
88              ++dCount; // increment dCount
89              break; // exit switch
90
91          default: // grade was less than 60
92              ++fCount; // increment fCount
93              break; // optional; will exit switch anyway
94      } // end switch
95   } // end method incrementLetterGradeCounter
96
97   // display a report based on the grades entered by user
98   public void displayGradeReport()
99   {
100      System.out.println( "\nGrade Report:" );
101
102      // if user entered at least one grade...
103      if ( gradeCounter != 0 )
104      {
105          // calculate average of all grades entered
106          double average = (double) total / gradeCounter;
107
108          // output summary of results
109          System.out.printf( "Total of the %d grades entered is %d\n",
110              gradeCounter, total );
111          System.out.printf( "Class average is %.2f\n", average );
112          System.out.printf( "%s\n%s%d\n%s%d\n%s%d\n%s%d\n%s%d\n",
113              "Number of students who received each grade:",
114              "A: ", aCount,   // display number of A grades
115              "B: ", bCount,   // display number of B grades
116              "C: ", cCount,   // display number of C grades
117              "D: ", dCount,   // display number of D grades
118              "F: ", fCount ); // display number of F grades
119      } // end if
120      else // no grades were entered, so output appropriate message
121          System.out.println( "No grades were entered" );
122   } // end method displayGradeReport
123 } // end class GradeBook
```

Fig. 5.9 | GradeBook class uses switch statement to count letter grades. (Part 3 of 3.)

Like earlier versions of the class, class GradeBook (Fig. 5.9) declares instance variable courseName (line 7) and contains methods setCourseName (lines 24–27), getCourseName (lines 30–33) and displayMessage (lines 36–41), which set the course name, store the course name and display a welcome message to the user, respectively. The class also contains a constructor (lines 18–21) that initializes the course name.

Class GradeBook also declares instance variables total (line 9) and gradeCounter (line 10), which keep track of the sum of the grades entered by the user and the number of grades entered, respectively. Lines 11–15 declare counter variables for each grade category. Class GradeBook maintains total, gradeCounter and the five letter-grade counters as instance variables so that they can be used or modified in any of the class's methods. Note that the class's constructor (lines 18–21) sets only the course name, because the remaining seven instance variables are ints and are initialized to 0 by default.

Class GradeBook (Fig. 5.9) contains three additional methods—inputGrades, incrementLetterGradeCounter and displayGradeReport. Method inputGrades (lines 44–66) reads an arbitrary number of integer grades from the user using sentinel-controlled repetition and updates instance variables total and gradeCounter. This method calls method incrementLetterGradeCounter (lines 69–95) to update the appropriate letter-grade counter for each grade entered. Method displayGradeReport (lines 98–122) outputs a report containing the total of all grades entered, the average of the grades and the number of students who received each letter grade. Let's examine these methods in more detail.

Method inputGrades

Line 48 in method inputGrades declares variable grade, which will store the user's input. Lines 50–54 prompt the user to enter integer grades and to type the end-of-file indicator to terminate the input. The **end-of-file indicator** is a system-dependent keystroke combination which the user enters to indicate that there is no more data to input. In Chapter 17, Files, Streams and Object Serialization, we'll see how the end-of-file indicator is used when a program reads its input from a file.

On UNIX/Linux/Mac OS X systems, end-of-file is entered by typing the sequence

<Ctrl> d

on a line by itself. This notation means to simultaneously press both the *Ctrl* key and the *d* key. On Windows systems, end-of-file can be entered by typing

<Ctrl> z

[*Note:* On some systems, you must press *Enter* after typing the end-of-file key sequence. Also, Windows typically displays the characters ^Z on the screen when the end-of-file indicator is typed, as is shown in the output of Fig. 5.10.]

Portability Tip 5.1

The keystroke combinations for entering end-of-file are system dependent.

The while statement (lines 57–65) obtains the user input. The condition at line 57 calls Scanner method **hasNext** to determine whether there is more data to input. This method returns the boolean value true if there is more data; otherwise, it returns false. The returned value is then used as the value of the condition in the while statement. As long as the end-of-file indicator has not been typed, method hasNext will return true.

Line 59 inputs a grade value from the user. Line 60 uses the += operator to add grade to total. Line 61 increments gradeCounter. The class's displayGradeReport method uses these variables to compute the average of the grades. Line 64 calls the class's incrementLetterGradeCounter method (declared in lines 69–95) to increment the appropriate letter-grade counter based on the numeric grade entered.

Method incrementLetterGradeCounter

Method incrementLetterGradeCounter contains a switch statement (lines 72–94) that determines which counter to increment. We assume that the user enters a valid grade in the range 0–100. A grade in the range 90–100 represents A, 80–89 represents B, 70–79 represents C, 60–69 represents D and 0–59 represents F. The switch statement consists of a block that contains a sequence of **case labels** and an optional **default case**. These are used in this example to determine which counter to increment based on the grade.

When the flow of control reaches the switch, the program evaluates the expression in the parentheses (grade / 10) following keyword switch. This is the switch's **controlling expression**. The program compares the controlling expression's value (which must evaluate to an integral value of type byte, char, short or int) with each case label. The controlling expression in line 72 performs integer division, which truncates the fractional part of the result. Thus, when we divide a value from 0 to 100 by 10, the result is always a value from 0 to 10. We use several of these values in our case labels. For example, if the user enters the integer 85, the controlling expression evaluates to 8. The switch compares 8 with each case label. If a match occurs (case 8: at line 79), the program executes that case's statements. For the integer 8, line 80 increments bCount, because a grade in the 80s is a B. The **break statement** (line 81) causes program control to proceed with the first statement after the switch—in this program, we reach the end of method incrementLetterGradeCounter's body, so the method terminates and control returns to line 65 in method inputGrades (the first line after the call to incrementLetterGradeCounter). Line 65 is the end of a while loop's body, so control flows to the while's condition (line 57) to determine whether the loop should continue executing.

The cases in our switch explicitly test for the values 10, 9, 8, 7 and 6. Note the cases at lines 74–75 that test for the values 9 and 10 (both of which represent the grade A). Listing cases consecutively in this manner with no statements between them enables the cases to perform the same set of statements—when the controlling expression evaluates to 9 or 10, the statements in lines 76–77 will execute. The switch statement does not provide a mechanism for testing ranges of values, so every value you need to test must be listed in a separate case label. Note that each case can have multiple statements. The switch statement differs from other control statements in that it does not require braces around multiple statements in a case.

Without break statements, each time a match occurs in the switch, the statements for that case and subsequent cases execute until a break statement or the end of the switch is encountered. This is often referred to as "falling through" to the statements in subsequent cases. (This feature is perfect for writing a concise program that displays the iterative song "The Twelve Days of Christmas" in Exercise 5.24.)

 Common Programming Error 5.7
Forgetting a break statement when one is needed in a switch is a logic error.

If no match occurs between the controlling expression's value and a case label, the default case (lines 91–93) executes. We use the default case in this example to process all controlling-expression values that are less than 6—that is, all failing grades. If no match occurs and the switch does not contain a default case, program control simply continues with the first statement after the switch.

GradeBookTest Class That Demonstrates Class GradeBook

Class GradeBookTest (Fig. 5.10) creates a GradeBook object (lines 10–11). Line 13 invokes the object's displayMessage method to output a welcome message to the user. Line 14 invokes the object's inputGrades method to read a set of grades from the user and keep track of the sum of all the grades entered and the number of grades. Recall that method inputGrades also calls method incrementLetterGradeCounter to keep track of the number of students who received each letter grade. Line 15 invokes method displayGradeReport of class GradeBook, which outputs a report based on the grades entered (as in the input/output window in Fig. 5.10). Line 103 of class GradeBook (Fig. 5.9) determines whether the user entered at least one grade—this helps us avoid dividing by zero. If so, line 106 calculates the average of the grades. Lines 109–118 then output the total of all the grades, the class average and the number of students who received each letter grade. If no grades were entered, line 121 outputs an appropriate message. The output in Fig. 5.10 shows a sample grade report based on 10 grades.

```java
1    // Fig. 5.10: GradeBookTest.java
2    // Create GradeBook object, input grades and display grade report.
3
4    public class GradeBookTest
5    {
6       public static void main( String[] args )
7       {
8          // create GradeBook object myGradeBook and
9          // pass course name to constructor
10         GradeBook myGradeBook = new GradeBook(
11            "CS101 Introduction to Java Programming" );
12
13         myGradeBook.displayMessage(); // display welcome message
14         myGradeBook.inputGrades(); // read grades from user
15         myGradeBook.displayGradeReport(); // display report based on grades
16      } // end main
17   } // end class GradeBookTest
```

```
Welcome to the grade book for
CS101 Introduction to Java Programming!

Enter the integer grades in the range 0-100.
Type the end-of-file indicator to terminate input:
   On UNIX/Linux/Mac OS X type <Ctrl> d then press Enter
   On Windows type <Ctrl> z then press Enter
99
92
45
57
63
71
76
85
90
100
^Z
```

Fig. 5.10 | GradeBookTest creates a GradeBook object and invokes its methods. (Part 1 of 2.)

```
Grade Report:
Total of the 10 grades entered is 778
Class average is 77.80
Number of students who received each grade:
A: 4
B: 1
C: 2
D: 1
F: 2
```

Fig. 5.10 | GradeBookTest creates a GradeBook object and invokes its methods. (Part 2 of 2.)

Note that class GradeBookTest (Fig. 5.10) does not directly call GradeBook method incrementLetterGradeCounter (lines 69–95 of Fig. 5.9). This method is used exclusively by method inputGrades of class GradeBook to update the appropriate letter-grade counter as each new grade is entered by the user. Method incrementLetterGradeCounter exists solely to support the operations of GradeBook's other methods so it is declared private.

Software Engineering Observation 5.2

*Recall from Chapter 3 that methods declared with access modifier private can be called only by other methods of the class in which the private methods are declared. Such methods are commonly referred to as **utility methods** or **helper methods** because they are typically used to support the operation of the class's other methods.*

switch *Statement UML Activity Diagram*

Figure 5.11 shows the UML activity diagram for the general switch statement. Most switch statements use a break in each case to terminate the switch statement after processing the case. Figure 5.11 emphasizes this by including break statements in the activity diagram. The diagram makes it clear that the break statement at the end of a case causes control to exit the switch statement immediately.

The break statement is not required for the switch's last case (or the optional default case, when it appears last), because execution continues with the next statement after the switch.

Software Engineering Observation 5.3

Provide a default case in switch statements. Including a default case focuses you on the need to process exceptional conditions.

Good Programming Practice 5.4

Although each case and the default case in a switch can occur in any order, place the default case last. When the default case is listed last, the break for that case is not required.

Notes on the Expression in Each **case** of a **switch**

When using the switch statement, remember that each case must contain a constant integral expression—that is, any combination of integer constants that evaluates to a constant integer value (e.g., –7, 0 or 221). An integer constant is simply an integer value. In addition, you can use **character constants**—specific characters in single quotes, such as 'A', '7' or '$'—which represent the integer values of characters. (Appendix B, shows the

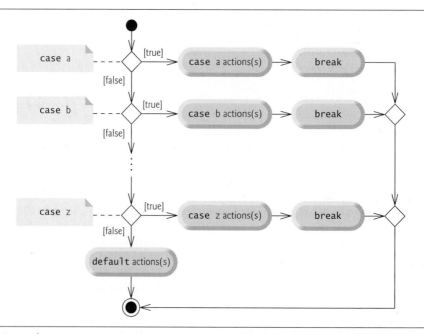

Fig. 5.11 | `switch` multiple-selection statement UML activity diagram with `break` statements.

integer values of the characters in the ASCII character set, which is a subset of the Unicode character set used by Java.)

The expression in each `case` can also be a **constant variable**—a variable that contains a value which does not change for the entire program. Such a variable is declared with keyword `final` (discussed in Chapter 6). Java has a feature called enumerations, which we also present in Chapter 6. Enumeration constants can also be used in `case` labels. In Chapter 10, Object-Oriented Programming: Polymorphism, we present a more elegant way to implement `switch` logic—we use a technique called polymorphism to create programs that are often clearer, easier to maintain and easier to extend than programs using `switch` logic.

5.7 `break` and `continue` Statements

In addition to selection and repetition statements, Java provides statements `break` and **continue** (presented in this section and Appendix O) to alter the flow of control. The preceding section showed how `break` can be used to terminate a `switch` statement's execution. This section discusses how to use `break` in repetition statements.

`break` Statement

The `break` statement, when executed in a `while`, `for`, `do...while` or `switch`, causes immediate exit from that statement. Execution continues with the first statement after the control statement. Common uses of the `break` statement are to escape early from a loop or to skip the remainder of a `switch` (as in Fig. 5.9). Figure 5.12 demonstrates a `break` statement exiting a `for`.

```
 1   // Fig. 5.12: BreakTest.java
 2   // break statement exiting a for statement.
 3   public class BreakTest
 4   {
 5      public static void main( String[] args )
 6      {
 7         int count; // control variable also used after loop terminates
 8
 9         for ( count = 1; count <= 10; count++ ) // loop 10 times
10         {
11            if ( count == 5 ) // if count is 5,
12               break;          // terminate loop
13
14            System.out.printf( "%d ", count );
15         } // end for
16
17         System.out.printf( "\nBroke out of loop at count = %d\n", count );
18      } // end main
19   } // end class BreakTest
```

```
1 2 3 4
Broke out of loop at count = 5
```

Fig. 5.12 | break statement exiting a for statement.

When the if statement nested at line 11 in the for statement (lines 9–15) detects that count is 5, the break statement at line 12 executes. This terminates the for statement, and the program proceeds to line 17 (immediately after the for statement), which displays a message indicating the value of the control variable when the loop terminated. The loop fully executes its body only four times instead of 10.

continue *Statement*

The continue statement, when executed in a while, for or do...while, skips the remaining statements in the loop body and proceeds with the next iteration of the loop. In while and do...while statements, the program evaluates the loop-continuation test immediately after the continue statement executes. In a for statement, the increment expression executes, then the program evaluates the loop-continuation test.

```
 1   // Fig. 5.13: ContinueTest.java
 2   // continue statement terminating an iteration of a for statement.
 3   public class ContinueTest
 4   {
 5      public static void main( String[] args )
 6      {
 7         for ( int count = 1; count <= 10; count++ ) // loop 10 times
 8         {
 9            if ( count == 5 ) // if count is 5,
10               continue; // skip remaining code in loop
11
12            System.out.printf( "%d ", count );
13         } // end for
```

Fig. 5.13 | continue statement terminating an iteration of a for statement. (Part 1 of 2.)

```
14
15          System.out.println( "\nUsed continue to skip printing 5" );
16      } // end main
17  } // end class ContinueTest
```

```
1 2 3 4 6 7 8 9 10
Used continue to skip printing 5
```

Fig. 5.13 | continue statement terminating an iteration of a for statement. (Part 2 of 2.)

Figure 5.13 uses continue to skip the statement at line 12 when the nested if (line 9) determines that count's value is 5. When the continue statement executes, program control continues with the increment of the control variable in the for statement (line 7).

In Section 5.3, we stated that while could be used in most cases in place of for. This is not the case when the increment expression in the while follows a continue statement. In this case, the increment does not execute before the program evaluates the repetition-continuation condition, so the while does not execute in the same manner as the for.

Software Engineering Observation 5.4
Some programmers feel that break and continue violate structured programming. Since the same effects are achievable with structured programming techniques, these programmers do not use break or continue.

Software Engineering Observation 5.5
There is a tension between achieving quality software engineering and achieving the best-performing software. Often, one of these goals is achieved at the expense of the other. For all but the most performance-intensive situations, apply the following rule of thumb: First, make your code simple and correct; then make it fast and small, but only if necessary.

5.8 Logical Operators

The if, if...else, while, do...while and for statements each require a condition to determine how to continue a program's flow of control. So far, we've studied only simple conditions, such as count <= 10, number != sentinelValue and total > 1000. Simple conditions are expressed in terms of the relational operators >, <, >= and <= and the equality operators == and !=, and each expression tests only one condition. To test multiple conditions in the process of making a decision, we performed these tests in separate statements or in nested if or if...else statements. Sometimes, control statements require more complex conditions to determine a program's flow of control.

Java's **logical operators** enable you to form more complex conditions by combining simple conditions. The logical operators are && (conditional AND), || (conditional OR), & (boolean logical AND), | (boolean logical inclusive OR), ∧ (boolean logical exclusive OR) and ! (logical NOT). [*Note:* The &, | and ∧ operators are also bitwise operators when they are applied to integral operands. We discuss the bitwise operators in Appendix N.]

Conditional AND (&&) Operator
Suppose we wish to ensure at some point in a program that two conditions are *both* true before we choose a certain path of execution. In this case, we can use the **&& (conditional AND)** operator, as follows:

```
if ( gender == FEMALE && age >= 65 )
   ++seniorFemales;
```

This `if` statement contains two simple conditions. The condition `gender == FEMALE` compares variable `gender` to the constant `FEMALE` to determine whether a person is female. The condition `age >= 65` might be evaluated to determine whether a person is a senior citizen. The `if` statement considers the combined condition

```
gender == FEMALE && age >= 65
```

which is true if and only if both simple conditions are true. In this case, the `if` statement's body increments `seniorFemales` by 1. If either or both of the simple conditions are false, the program skips the increment. Some programmers find that the preceding combined condition is more readable when redundant parentheses are added, as in:

```
( gender == FEMALE ) && ( age >= 65 )
```

The table in Fig. 5.14 summarizes the `&&` operator. The table shows all four possible combinations of `false` and `true` values for *expression1* and *expression2*. Such tables are called **truth tables**. Java evaluates to `false` or `true` all expressions that include relational operators, equality operators or logical operators.

expression1	expression2	expression1 && expression2
false	false	false
false	true	false
true	false	false
true	true	true

Fig. 5.14 │ `&&` (conditional AND) operator truth table.

Conditional OR (││) Operator

Now suppose we wish to ensure that either *or* both of two conditions are true before we choose a certain path of execution. In this case, we use the `││` (**conditional OR**) operator, as in the following program segment:

```
if ( ( semesterAverage >= 90 ) || ( finalExam >= 90 ) )
   System.out.println ( "Student grade is A" );
```

This statement also contains two simple conditions. The condition `semesterAverage >= 90` evaluates to determine whether the student deserves an A in the course because of a solid performance throughout the semester. The condition `finalExam >= 90` evaluates to determine whether the student deserves an A in the course because of an outstanding performance on the final exam. The `if` statement then considers the combined condition

```
( semesterAverage >= 90 ) || ( finalExam >= 90 )
```

and awards the student an A if either or both of the simple conditions are true. The only time the message `"Student grade is A"` is *not* printed is when both of the simple conditions are false. Figure 5.15 is a truth table for operator conditional OR (`││`). Operator `&&` has a higher precedence than operator `││`. Both operators associate from left to right.

expression1	expression2	expression1 || expression2
false	false	false
false	true	true
true	false	true
true	true	true

Fig. 5.15 | \|\| (conditional OR) operator truth table.

Short-Circuit Evaluation of Complex Conditions

The parts of an expression containing && or \|\| operators are evaluated only until it's known whether the condition is true or false. Thus, evaluation of the expression

```
( gender == FEMALE ) && ( age >= 65 )
```

stops immediately if gender is not equal to FEMALE (i.e., the entire expression is false) and continues if gender *is* equal to FEMALE (i.e., the entire expression could still be true if the condition age >= 65 is true). This feature of conditional AND and conditional OR expressions is called **short-circuit evaluation**.

Common Programming Error 5.8

In expressions using operator &&, a condition—we'll call this the dependent condition— may require another condition to be true for the evaluation of the dependent condition to be meaningful. In this case, the dependent condition should be placed after the other condition, or an error might occur. For example, in the expression (i != 0) && (10 / i == 2), the second condition must appear after the first condition, or a divide-by-zero error might occur.

Boolean Logical AND (&) and Boolean Logical Inclusive OR (|) Operators

The **boolean logical AND (&)** and **boolean logical inclusive OR (|)** operators are identical to the && and \|\| operators, except that the & and | operators *always* evaluate both of their operands (i.e., they do not perform short-circuit evaluation). So, the expression

```
( gender == 1 ) & ( age >= 65 )
```

evaluates age >= 65 regardless of whether gender is equal to 1. This is useful if the right operand of the boolean logical AND or boolean logical inclusive OR operator has a required **side effect**—a modification of a variable's value. For example, the expression

```
( birthday == true ) | ( ++age >= 65 )
```

guarantees that the condition ++age >= 65 will be evaluated. Thus, the variable age is incremented, regardless of whether the overall expression is true or false.

Error-Prevention Tip 5.6

For clarity, avoid expressions with side effects in conditions. The side effects may look clever, but they can make it harder to understand code and can lead to subtle logic errors.

Boolean Logical Exclusive OR (^)

A simple condition containing the **boolean logical exclusive OR (^)** operator is true *if and only if one of its operands is* true *and the other is* false. If both are true or both are false, the entire condition is false. Figure 5.16 is a truth table for the boolean logical exclusive OR operator (∧). This operator is guaranteed to evaluate both of its operands.

expression1	expression2	expression1 ∧ expression2
false	false	false
false	true	true
true	false	true
true	true	false

Fig. 5.16 | ∧ (boolean logical exclusive OR) operator truth table.

Logical Negation (!) Operator

The ! (**logical NOT**, also called **logical negation** or **logical complement**) operator "reverses" the meaning of a condition. Unlike the logical operators &&, ||, &, | and ∧, which are binary operators that combine two conditions, the logical negation operator is a unary operator that has only a single condition as an operand. The logical negation operator is placed before a condition to choose a path of execution if the original condition (without the logical negation operator) is false, as in the program segment

```
if ( ! ( grade == sentinelValue ) )
    System.out.printf( "The next grade is %d\n", grade );
```

which executes the printf call only if grade is not equal to sentinelValue. The parentheses around the condition grade == sentinelValue are needed because the logical negation operator has a higher precedence than the equality operator.

In most cases, you can avoid using logical negation by expressing the condition differently with an appropriate relational or equality operator. For example, the previous statement may also be written as follows:

```
if ( grade != sentinelValue )
    System.out.printf( "The next grade is %d\n", grade );
```

This flexibility can help you express a condition in a more convenient manner. Figure 5.17 is a truth table for the logical negation operator.

expression	!expression
false	true
true	false

Fig. 5.17 | ! (logical negation, or logical NOT) operator truth table.

Logical Operators Example

Figure 5.18 produces the truth tables discussed in this section. The output shows the boolean expression that was evaluated and its result. Note that we used the **%b format specifier** to display the word "true" or the word "false" based on a boolean expression's value. Lines 9–13 produce the truth table for &&. Lines 16–20 produce the truth table for ||. Lines 23–27 produce the truth table for &. Lines 30–35 produce the truth table for |. Lines 38–43 produce the truth table for ∧. Lines 46–47 produce the truth table for !.

```java
1   // Fig. 5.18: LogicalOperators.java
2   // Logical operators.
3
4   public class LogicalOperators
5   {
6      public static void main( String[] args )
7      {
8         // create truth table for && (conditional AND) operator
9         System.out.printf( "%s\n%s: %b\n%s: %b\n%s: %b\n%s: %b\n\n",
10           "Conditional AND (&&)", "false && false", ( false && false ),
11           "false && true", ( false && true ),
12           "true && false", ( true && false ),
13           "true && true", ( true && true ) );
14
15        // create truth table for || (conditional OR) operator
16        System.out.printf( "%s\n%s: %b\n%s: %b\n%s: %b\n%s: %b\n\n",
17           "Conditional OR (||)", "false || false", ( false || false ),
18           "false || true", ( false || true ),
19           "true || false", ( true || false ),
20           "true || true", ( true || true ) );
21
22        // create truth table for & (boolean logical AND) operator
23        System.out.printf( "%s\n%s: %b\n%s: %b\n%s: %b\n%s: %b\n\n",
24           "Boolean logical AND (&)", "false & false", ( false & false ),
25           "false & true", ( false & true ),
26           "true & false", ( true & false ),
27           "true & true", ( true & true ) );
28
29        // create truth table for | (boolean logical inclusive OR) operator
30        System.out.printf( "%s\n%s: %b\n%s: %b\n%s: %b\n%s: %b\n\n",
31           "Boolean logical inclusive OR (|)",
32           "false | false", ( false | false ),
33           "false | true", ( false | true ),
34           "true | false", ( true | false ),
35           "true | true", ( true | true ) );
36
37        // create truth table for ∧ (boolean logical exclusive OR) operator
38        System.out.printf( "%s\n%s: %b\n%s: %b\n%s: %b\n%s: %b\n\n",
39           "Boolean logical exclusive OR (∧)",
40           "false ∧ false", ( false ∧ false ),
41           "false ∧ true", ( false ∧ true ),
42           "true ∧ false", ( true ∧ false ),
43           "true ∧ true", ( true ∧ true ) );
44
45        // create truth table for ! (logical negation) operator
46        System.out.printf( "%s\n%s: %b\n%s: %b\n", "Logical NOT (!)",
47           "!false", ( !false ), "!true", ( !true ) );
48     } // end main
49  } // end class LogicalOperators
```

Fig. 5.18 | Logical operators. (Part 1 of 2.)

```
Conditional AND (&&)
false && false: false
false && true: false
true && false: false
true && true: true

Conditional OR (||)
false || false: false
false || true: true
true || false: true
true || true: true

Boolean logical AND (&)
false & false: false
false & true: false
true & false: false
true & true: true

Boolean logical inclusive OR (|)
false | false: false
false | true: true
true | false: true
true | true: true

Boolean logical exclusive OR (^)
false ^ false: false
false ^ true: true
true ^ false: true
true ^ true: false

Logical NOT (!)
!false: true
!true: false
```

Fig. 5.18 │ Logical operators. (Part 2 of 2.)

Figure 5.19 shows the precedence and associativity of the Java operators introduced so far. The operators are shown from top to bottom in decreasing order of precedence.

Operators	Associativity	Type
++ --	right to left	unary postfix
++ -- + - ! (*type*)	right to left	unary prefix
* / %	left to right	multiplicative
+ -	left to right	additive
< <= > >=	left to right	relational
== !=	left to right	equality

Fig. 5.19 │ Precedence/associativity of the operators discussed so far. (Part 1 of 2.)

Operators	Associativity	Type
&	left to right	boolean logical AND
^	left to right	boolean logical exclusive OR
|	left to right	boolean logical inclusive OR
&&	left to right	conditional AND
||	left to right	conditional OR
?:	right to left	conditional
= += -= *= /= %=	right to left	assignment

Fig. 5.19 | Precedence/associativity of the operators discussed so far. (Part 2 of 2.)

5.9 Structured Programming Summary

Just as architects design buildings by employing the collective wisdom of their profession, so should programmers design programs. Our field is much younger than architecture, and our collective wisdom is considerably sparser. We've learned that structured programming produces programs that are easier than unstructured programs to understand, test, debug, modify and even prove correct in a mathematical sense.

Figure 5.20 uses UML activity diagrams to summarize Java's control statements. The initial and final states indicate the single entry point and the single exit point of each control statement. Arbitrarily connecting individual symbols in an activity diagram can lead to unstructured programs. Therefore, the programming profession has chosen a limited set of control statements that can be combined in only two simple ways to build structured programs.

For simplicity, Java includes only single-entry/single-exit control statements—there is only one way to enter and only one way to exit each control statement. Connecting control statements in sequence to form structured programs is simple. The final state of one control statement is connected to the initial state of the next—that is, the control statements are placed one after another in a program in sequence. We call this control-statement stacking. The rules for forming structured programs also allow for control statements to be nested.

Figure 5.21 shows the rules for forming structured programs. The rules assume that action states may be used to indicate any action. The rules also assume that we begin with the simplest activity diagram (Fig. 5.22) consisting of only an initial state, an action state, a final state and transition arrows.

Applying the rules in Fig. 5.21 always results in a properly structured activity diagram with a neat, building-block appearance. For example, repeatedly applying rule 2 to the simplest activity diagram results in an activity diagram containing many action states in sequence (Fig. 5.23). Rule 2 generates a stack of control statements, so let's call rule 2 the **stacking rule**. [*Note:* The vertical dashed lines in Fig. 5.23 are not part of the UML. We use them to separate the four activity diagrams that demonstrate rule 2 of Fig. 5.21 being applied.]

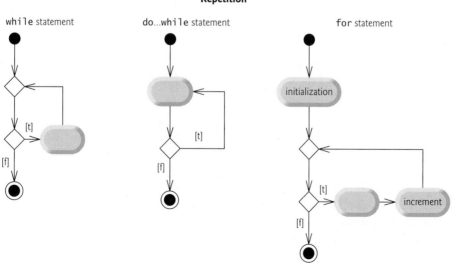

Fig. 5.20 | Java's single-entry/single-exit sequence, selection and repetition statements.

Rules for forming structured programs

1. Begin with the simplest activity diagram (Fig. 5.22).
2. Any action state can be replaced by two action states in sequence.
3. Any action state can be replaced by any control statement (sequence of action states, if, if...else, switch, while, do...while or for).
4. Rules 2 and 3 can be applied as often as you like and in any order.

Fig. 5.21 | Rules for forming structured programs.

Fig. 5.22 | Simplest activity diagram.

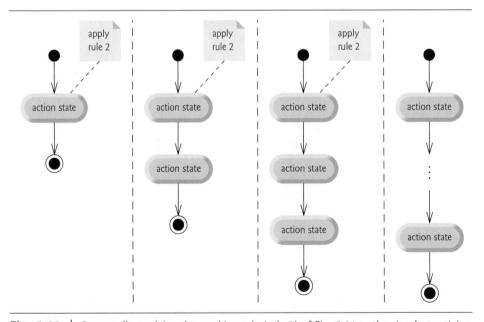

Fig. 5.23 | Repeatedly applying the stacking rule (rule 2) of Fig. 5.21 to the simplest activity diagram.

Rule 3 is called the **nesting rule**. Repeatedly applying rule 3 to the simplest activity diagram results in an activity diagram with neatly nested control statements. For example, in Fig. 5.24, the action state in the simplest activity diagram is replaced with a double-selection (if...else) statement. Then rule 3 is applied again to the action states in the double-selection statement, replacing each with a double-selection statement. The dashed action-state symbol around each double-selection statement represents the action state that was replaced. [*Note:* The dashed arrows and dashed action-state symbols shown in Fig. 5.24 are not part of the UML. They are used here to illustrate that any action state can be replaced with a control statement.]

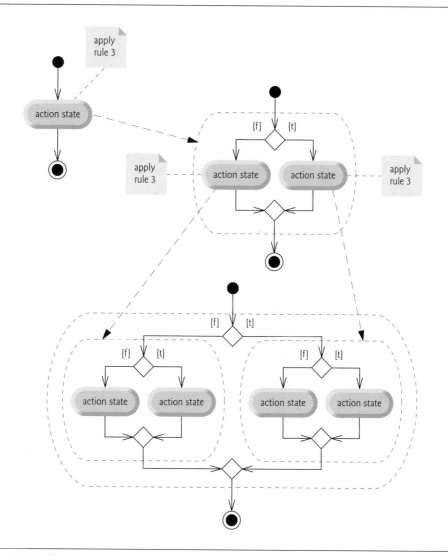

Fig. 5.24 | Repeatedly applying the nesting rule (rule 3) of Fig. 5.21 to the simplest activity diagram.

Rule 4 generates larger, more involved and more deeply nested statements. The diagrams that emerge from applying the rules in Fig. 5.21 constitute the set of all possible structured activity diagrams and hence the set of all possible structured programs. The beauty of the structured approach is that we use only seven simple single-entry/single-exit control statements and assemble them in only two simple ways.

If the rules in Fig. 5.21 are followed, an "unstructured' activity diagram (like the one in Fig. 5.25) cannot be created. If you are uncertain about whether a particular diagram is structured, apply the rules of Fig. 5.21 in reverse to reduce the diagram to the simplest activity diagram. If you can reduce it, the original diagram is structured; otherwise, it's not.

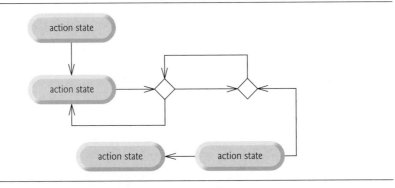

Fig. 5.25 | "Unstructured" activity diagram.

Structured programming promotes simplicity. Bohm and Jacopini have given us the result that only three forms of control are needed to implement an algorithm:

- Sequence
- Selection
- Repetition

The sequence structure is trivial. Simply list the statements to execute in the order in which they should execute. Selection is implemented in one of three ways:

- `if` statement (single selection)
- `if...else` statement (double selection)
- `switch` statement (multiple selection)

In fact, it's straightforward to prove that the simple `if` statement is sufficient to provide any form of selection—everything that can be done with the `if...else` statement and the `switch` statement can be implemented by combining `if` statements (although perhaps not as clearly and efficiently).

Repetition is implemented in one of three ways:

- `while` statement
- `do...while` statement
- `for` statement

[*Note:* There is a fourth repetition statement—the enhanced `for` statement—that we discuss in Section 7.6.] It's straightforward to prove that the `while` statement is sufficient to provide any form of repetition. Everything that can be done with `do...while` and `for` can be done with the `while` statement (although perhaps not as conveniently).

Combining these results illustrates that any form of control ever needed in a Java program can be expressed in terms of

- sequence
- if statement (selection)
- while statement (repetition)

and that these can be combined in only two ways—stacking and nesting. Indeed, structured programming is the essence of simplicity.

5.10 (Optional) GUI and Graphics Case Study: Drawing Rectangles and Ovals

This section demonstrates drawing rectangles and ovals, using the Graphics methods **drawRect** and **drawOval**, respectively. These methods are demonstrated in Fig. 5.26.

```java
1   // Fig. 5.26: Shapes.java
2   // Demonstrates drawing different shapes.
3   import java.awt.Graphics;
4   import javax.swing.JPanel;
5
6   public class Shapes extends JPanel
7   {
8      private int choice; // user's choice of which shape to draw
9
10     // constructor sets the user's choice
11     public Shapes( int userChoice )
12     {
13        choice = userChoice;
14     } // end Shapes constructor
15
16     // draws a cascade of shapes starting from the top-left corner
17     public void paintComponent( Graphics g )
18     {
19        super.paintComponent( g );
20
21        for ( int i = 0; i < 10; i++ )
22        {
23           // pick the shape based on the user's choice
24           switch ( choice )
25           {
26              case 1: // draw rectangles
27                 g.drawRect( 10 + i * 10, 10 + i * 10,
28                    50 + i * 10, 50 + i * 10 );
29                 break;
30              case 2: // draw ovals
31                 g.drawOval( 10 + i * 10, 10 + i * 10,
32                    50 + i * 10, 50 + i * 10 );
33                 break;
34           } // end switch
35        } // end for
36     } // end method paintComponent
37  } // end class Shapes
```

Fig. 5.26 | Drawing a cascade of shapes based on the user's choice.

Line 6 begins the class declaration for Shapes, which extends JPanel. Instance variable choice, declared in line 8, determines whether paintComponent should draw rectangles or ovals. The Shapes constructor at lines 11–14 initializes choice with the value passed in parameter userChoice.

Method paintComponent (lines 17–36) performs the actual drawing. Remember, the first statement in every paintComponent method should be a call to super.paintComponent, as in line 19. Lines 21–35 loop 10 times to draw 10 shapes. The nested switch statement (lines 24–34) chooses between drawing rectangles and drawing ovals.

If choice is 1, then the program draws rectangles. Lines 27–28 call Graphics method drawRect. Method drawRect requires four arguments. The first two represent the *x*- and *y*-coordinates of the upper-left corner of the rectangle; the next two represent the rectangle's width and height. In this example, we start at a position 10 pixels down and 10 pixels right of the top-left corner, and every iteration of the loop moves the upper-left corner another 10 pixels down and to the right. The width and the height of the rectangle start at 50 pixels and increase by 10 pixels in each iteration.

If choice is 2, the program draws ovals. It creates an imaginary rectangle called a **bounding rectangle** and places inside it an oval that touches the midpoints of all four sides. Method drawOval (lines 31–32) requires the same four arguments as method drawRect. The arguments specify the position and size of the bounding rectangle for the oval. The values passed to drawOval in this example are exactly the same as those passed to drawRect in lines 27–28. Since the width and height of the bounding rectangle are identical in this example, lines 27–28 draw a circle. As an exercise, try modifying the program to draw both rectangles and ovals to see how drawOval and drawRect are related.

*Class **ShapesTest***
Figure 5.27 is responsible for handling input from the user and creating a window to display the appropriate drawing based on the user's response. Line 3 imports JFrame to handle the display, and line 4 imports JOptionPane to handle the input.

```
1   // Fig. 5.27: ShapesTest.java
2   // Test application that displays class Shapes.
3   import javax.swing.JFrame;
4   import javax.swing.JOptionPane;
5
6   public class ShapesTest
7   {
8      public static void main( String[] args )
9      {
10         // obtain user's choice
11         String input = JOptionPane.showInputDialog(
12            "Enter 1 to draw rectangles\n" +
13            "Enter 2 to draw ovals" );
14
15         int choice = Integer.parseInt( input ); // convert input to int
16
17         // create the panel with the user's input
18         Shapes panel = new Shapes( choice );
```

Fig. 5.27 | Obtaining user input and creating a JFrame to display Shapes. (Part 1 of 2.)

```
19
20       JFrame application = new JFrame(); // creates a new JFrame
21
22       application.setDefaultCloseOperation( JFrame.EXIT_ON_CLOSE );
23       application.add( panel ); // add the panel to the frame
24       application.setSize( 300, 300 ); // set the desired size
25       application.setVisible( true ); // show the frame
26    } // end main
27 } // end class ShapesTest
```

Fig. 5.27 | Obtaining user input and creating a JFrame to display Shapes. (Part 2 of 2.)

Lines 11–13 prompt the user with an input dialog and store the user's response in variable input. Line 15 uses Integer method parseInt to convert the String entered by the user to an int and stores the result in variable choice. Line 18 creates a Shapes object, with the user's choice passed as an argument to the constructor. Lines 20–25 perform the standard operations that create and set up a window in this case study—create a frame, set it to exit the application when closed, add the drawing to the frame, set the frame size and make it visible.

GUI and Graphics Case Study Exercises

5.1   Draw 12 concentric circles in the center of a JPanel (Fig. 5.28). The innermost circle should have a radius of 10 pixels, and each successive circle should have a radius 10 pixels larger than the previous one. Begin by finding the center of the JPanel. To get the upper-left corner of a circle, move up one radius and to the left one radius from the center. The width and height of the bounding rectangle are both the same as the circle's diameter (i.e., twice the radius).

Fig. 5.28 | Drawing concentric circles.

5.2 Modify Exercise 5.15 from the end-of-chapter exercises to read input using dialogs and to display the bar chart using rectangles of varying lengths.

5.11 Wrap-Up

In this chapter, we completed our introduction to Java's control statements, which enable you to control the flow of execution in methods. Chapter 4 discussed Java's if, if...else and while statements. The current chapter demonstrated Java's remaining control statements—for, do...while and switch. We showed that any algorithm can be developed using combinations of the sequence structure (i.e., statements listed in the order in which they should execute), the three types of selection statements—if, if...else and switch—and the three types of repetition statements—while, do...while and for. In this chapter and Chapter 4, we discussed how you can combine these building blocks to utilize proven program-construction and problem-solving techniques. This chapter also introduced Java's logical operators, which enable you to use more complex conditional expressions in control statements.

In Chapter 3, we introduced the basic concepts of objects, classes and methods. Chapter 4 and Chapter 5 introduced the types of control statements that you can use to specify program logic in methods. In Chapter 6, we examine methods in greater depth.

Summary

Section 5.2 Essentials of Counter-Controlled Repetition
- Counter-controlled repetition requires a control variable (or loop counter), the initial value of the control variable, the increment (or decrement) by which the control variable is modified each time through the loop (also known as each iteration of the loop) and the loop-continuation condition that determines whether looping should continue.
- You can declare a variable and initialize it in the same statement.

Section 5.3 **for** Repetition Statement
- The while statement can be used to implement any counter-controlled loop.
- The for statement specifies the details of counter-controlled repetition in a single line of code.

- When the for statement begins executing, its control variable is declared and initialized. Next, the program checks the loop-continuation condition. If the condition is initially true, the body executes. After executing the loop's body, the increment expression executes. Then the loop-continuation test is performed again to determine whether the program should continue with the next iteration of the loop.

- The general format of the for statement is

    for (*initialization*; *loopContinuationCondition*; *increment*)
        statement

  where the *initialization* expression names the loop's control variable and provides its initial value, *loopContinuationCondition* determines whether the loop should continue executing and *increment* modifies the control variable's value, so that the loop-continuation condition eventually becomes false. The two semicolons in the for header are required.

- Most for statements can be represented with equivalent while statements as follows:

    initialization;
    while (*loopContinuationCondition*)
    {
        statement
        increment;
    }

- Typically, for statements are used for counter-controlled repetition and while statements for sentinel-controlled repetition.

- If the *initialization* expression in the for header declares the control variable, the control variable can be used only in that for statement—it will not exist outside the for statement.

- The expressions in a for header are optional. If the *loopContinuationCondition* is omitted, Java assumes that it's always true, thus creating an infinite loop. You might omit the *initialization* expression if the control variable is initialized before the loop. You might omit the *increment* expression if the increment is calculated with statements in the loop's body or if no increment is needed.

- The increment expression in a for acts as if it's a standalone statement at the end of the for's body.

- A for statement can count downward by using a negative increment (i.e., a decrement).

- If the loop-continuation condition is initially false, the program does not execute the for statement's body. Instead, execution proceeds with the statement following the for.

Section 5.4 Examples Using the **for** Statement

- Java treats floating-point constants like 1000.0 and 0.05 as type double. Similarly, Java treats whole-number constants like 7 and -22 as type int.

- The format specifier %4s outputs a String in a field width of 4—that is, printf displays the value with at least 4 character positions. If the value to be output is less than 4 character positions wide, the value is right justified in the field by default. If the value is greater than 4 character positions wide, the field width expands to accommodate the appropriate number of characters. To left justify the value, use a negative integer to specify the field width.

- Math.pow(*x*, *y*) calculates the value of *x* raised to the *y*th power. The method receives two double arguments and returns a double value.

- The comma (,) formatting flag in a format specifier (e.g., %,20.2f) indicates that a floating-point value should be output with a grouping separator. The actual separator used is specific to the user's locale (i.e., country). In the United States, the number will have commas separating every three digits and a decimal point separating the fractional part of the number, as in 1,234.45.

- The . in a format specifier (e.g., %,20.2f) indicates that the integer to its right is the number's precision.

Section 5.5 do...while *Repetition Statement*

- The do...while statement is similar to the while statement. In the while, the program tests the loop-continuation condition at the beginning of the loop, before executing its body; if the condition is false, the body never executes. The do...while statement tests the loop-continuation condition *after* executing the loop's body; therefore, the body always executes at least once.

- It's not necessary to use braces in the do...while repetition statement if there is only one statement in the body. Most programmers include the braces, to avoid confusion between the while and do...while statements.

Section 5.6 switch *Multiple-Selection Statement*

- The switch statement performs different actions based on the possible values of a constant integral expression (i.e., a constant value of type byte, short, int or char, but not long).

- The end-of-file indicator is a system-dependent keystroke combination that terminates user input. On UNIX/Linux/Mac OS X systems, end-of-file is entered by typing the sequence *<Ctrl>* *d* on a line by itself. This notation means to simultaneously press both the *Ctrl* key and the *d* key. On Windows systems, enter end-of-file by typing *<Ctrl> z*.

- Scanner method hasNext determines whether there is more data to input. This method returns the boolean value true if there is more data; otherwise, it returns false. As long as the end-of-file indicator has not been typed, method hasNext will return true.

- The switch statement consists of a block that contains a sequence of case labels and an optional default case.

- When the flow of control reaches a switch, the program evaluates the switch's controlling expression and compares its value with each case label. If a match occurs, the program executes the statements for that case.

- Listing cases consecutively with no statements between them enables the cases to perform the same set of statements.

- Every value you wish to test in a switch must be listed in a separate case label.

- Each case can have multiple statements, and these are not required to be placed in braces.

- Without break statements, each time a match occurs in the switch, the statements for that case and subsequent cases execute until a break statement or the end of the switch is encountered.

- If no match occurs between the controlling expression's value and a case label, the optional default case executes. If no match occurs and the switch does not contain a default case, program control simply continues with the first statement after the switch.

Section 5.7 break *and* continue *Statements*

- The break statement, when executed in a while, for, do...while or switch, causes immediate exit from that statement. Execution continues with the first statement after the control statement.

- The continue statement, when executed in a while, for or do...while, skips the remaining statements in the loop body and proceeds with the next iteration of the loop. In while and do...while statements, the program evaluates the loop-continuation test immediately. In a for statement, the increment expression executes, then the program evaluates the loop-continuation test.

Section 5.8 *Logical Operators*

- Simple conditions are expressed in terms of the relational operators >, <, >= and <= and the equality operators == and !=, and each expression tests only one condition.

- Logical operators enable you to form more complex conditions by combining simple conditions. The logical operators are && (conditional AND), || (conditional OR), & (boolean logical AND), | (boolean logical inclusive OR), ∧ (boolean logical exclusive OR) and ! (logical NOT).

- To ensure that two conditions are *both* true, use the && (conditional AND) operator. If either or both of the simple conditions are false, the entire expression is false.

- To ensure that either *or* both of two conditions are true, use the || (conditional OR) operator, which evaluates to true if either or both of its simple conditions are true.

- A condition using && or || operators uses short-circuit evaluation—they are evaluated only until it's known whether the condition is true or false.

- The boolean logical AND (&) and boolean logical inclusive OR (|) operators work identically to the && (conditional AND) and || (conditional OR) operators, but always evaluate both operands.

- A simple condition containing the boolean logical exclusive OR (^) operator is true *if and only if one of its operands is* true *and the other is* false. If both operands are true or both are false, the entire condition is false. This operator is also guaranteed to evaluate both of its operands.

- The unary ! (logical NOT) operator "reverses" the value of a condition.

Terminology

Self-Review Exercises

5.1 Fill in the blanks in each of the following statements:

a) Typically, _____ statements are used for counter-controlled repetition and _____ statements for sentinel-controlled repetition.

b) The do...while statement tests the loop-continuation condition _____ executing the loop's body; therefore, the body always executes at least once.

c) The _____ statement selects among multiple actions based on the possible values of an integer variable or expression.

d) The _____ statement, when executed in a repetition statement, skips the remaining statements in the loop body and proceeds with the next iteration of the loop.

e) The _____ operator can be used to ensure that two conditions are *both* true before choosing a certain path of execution.

f) If the loop-continuation condition in a `for` header is initially _____, the program does not execute the `for` statement's body.

g) Methods that perform common tasks and do not require objects are called _____ methods.

5.2 State whether each of the following is *true* or *false*. If *false*, explain why.

a) The `default` case is required in the `switch` selection statement.

b) The `break` statement is required in the last case of a `switch` selection statement.

c) The expression ((x > y) && (a < b)) is true if either x > y is true or a < b is true.

d) An expression containing the || operator is true if either or both of its operands are true.

e) The comma (,) formatting flag in a format specifier (e.g., %,20.2f) indicates that a value should be output with a thousands separator.

f) To test for a range of values in a `switch` statement, use a hyphen (–) between the start and end values of the range in a `case` label.

g) Listing cases consecutively with no statements between them enables the cases to perform the same set of statements.

5.3 Write a Java statement or a set of Java statements to accomplish each of the following tasks:

a) Sum the odd integers between 1 and 99, using a `for` statement. Assume that the integer variables `sum` and `count` have been declared.

b) Calculate the value of 2.5 raised to the power of 3, using the `pow` method.

c) Print the integers from 1 to 20, using a `while` loop and the counter variable `i`. Assume that the variable `i` has been declared, but not initialized. Print only five integers per line. [*Hint:* Use the calculation i % 5. When the value of this expression is 0, print a newline character; otherwise, print a tab character. Assume that this code is an application. Use the `System.out.println()` method to output the newline character, and use the `System.out.print( '\t' )` method to output the tab character.]

d) Repeat part (c), using a `for` statement.

5.4 Find the error in each of the following code segments, and explain how to correct it:

a)
```
i = 1;

while ( i <= 10 );
   i++;

}
```

b)
```
for ( k = 0.1; k != 1.0; k += 0.1 )
    System.out.println( k );
```

c)
```
switch ( n )
   {
      case 1:
         System.out.println( "The number is 1" );
      case 2:
         System.out.println( "The number is 2" );
         break;
      default:
         System.out.println( "The number is not 1 or 2" );
         break;
   }
```

d) The following code should print the values 1 to 10:
```
n = 1;
while ( n < 10 )
    System.out.println( n++ );
```

Answers to Self-Review Exercises

5.1   a) `for`, `while`. b) after. c) `switch`. d) `continue`. e) `&&` (conditional AND). f) `false`. g) `static`.

5.2   a) False. The `default` case is optional. If no default action is needed, then there is no need for a `default` case. b) False. The `break` statement is used to exit the `switch` statement. The `break` statement is not required for the last case in a `switch` statement. c) False. Both of the relational expressions must be true for the entire expression to be true when using the `&&` operator. d) True. e) True. f) False. The `switch` statement does not provide a mechanism for testing ranges of values, so every value that must be tested should be listed in a separate case label. g) True.

5.3   a)
```
sum = 0;
    for ( count = 1; count <= 99; count += 2 )
        sum += count;
```
b) `double result = Math.pow( 2.5, 3 );`
c)
```
i = 1;

while ( i <= 20 )
{
    System.out.print( i );

    if ( i % 5 == 0 )
        System.out.println();
    else
        System.out.print( '\t' );

    ++i;
}
```
d)
```
for ( i = 1; i <= 20; i++ )
{
    System.out.print( i );

    if ( i % 5 == 0 )
        System.out.println();
    else
        System.out.print( '\t' );
}
```

5.4   a) Error: The semicolon after the `while` header causes an infinite loop, and there is a missing left brace.
     Correction: Replace the semicolon by a {, or remove both the ; and the }.
     b) Error: Using a floating-point number to control a `for` statement may not work, because floating-point numbers are represented only approximately by most computers.
     Correction: Use an integer, and perform the proper calculation in order to get the values you desire:
```
for ( k = 1; k != 10; k++ )
    System.out.println( (double) k / 10 );
```

c) Error: The missing code is the break statement in the statements for the first case. Correction: Add a break statement at the end of the statements for the first case. Note that this omission is not necessarily an error if you want the statement of case 2: to execute every time the case 1: statement executes.

d) Error: An improper relational operator is used in the while's continuation condition. Correction: Use <= rather than <, or change 10 to 11.

Exercises

5.5   Describe the four basic elements of counter-controlled repetition.

5.6   Compare and contrast the while and for repetition statements.

5.7   Discuss a situation in which it would be more appropriate to use a do...while statement than a while statement. Explain why.

5.8   Compare and contrast the break and continue statements.

5.9   What does the following program do?

```
 1   // Exercise 5.10: Printing.java
 2   public class Printing
 3   {
 4      public static void main( String[] args )
 5      {
 6         for ( int i = 1; i <= 10; i++ )
 7         {
 8            for ( int j = 1; j <= 5; j++ )
 9               System.out.print( '@' );
10
11            System.out.println();
12         } // end outer for
13      } // end main
14   } // end class Printing
```

5.10   *(Find the Smallest Value)* Write an application that finds the smallest of several integers. Assume that the first value read specifies the number of values to input from the user.

5.11   *(Calculating the Product of Odd Integers)* Write an application that calculates the product of the odd integers from 1 to 15.

5.12   *(Factorials)* *Factorials* are used frequently in probability problems. The factorial of a positive integer *n* (written *n!* and pronounced "*n* factorial") is equal to the product of the positive integers from 1 to *n*. Write an application that calculates the factorials of 1 through 20. Use type long. Display the results in tabular format. What difficulty might prevent you from calculating the factorial of 100?

5.13   *(Modified Compound Interest Program)* Modify the compound-interest application of Fig. 5.6 to repeat its steps for interest rates of 5%, 6%, 7%, 8%, 9% and 10%. Use a for loop to vary the interest rate.

5.14   *(Triangle Printing Program)* Write an application that displays the following patterns separately, one below the other. Use for loops to generate the patterns. All asterisks (*) should be printed by a single statement of the form System.out.print('*'); which causes the asterisks to print side by side. A statement of the form System.out.println(); can be used to move to the next line. A statement of the form System.out.print(' '); can be used to display a space for the last two patterns. There should be no other output statements in the program. [*Hint:* The last two patterns require that each line begin with an appropriate number of blank spaces.]

(a)	(b)	(c)	(d)
*	**********	**********	*
**	*********	*********	**
***	********	********	***
****	*******	*******	****
*****	******	******	*****
******	*****	*****	******
*******	****	****	*******
********	***	***	********
*********	**	**	*********
**********	*	*	**********

5.15   *(Bar Chart Printing Program)* One interesting application of computers is to display graphs and bar charts. Write an application that reads five numbers between 1 and 30. For each number that is read, your program should display the same number of adjacent asterisks. For example, if your program reads the number 7, it should display *******. Display the bars of asterisks *after* you read all five numbers.

5.16   *(Calculating Sales)* An online retailer sells five products whose retail prices are as follows: Product 1, $2.98; product 2, $4.50; product 3, $9.98; product 4, $4.49 and product 5, $6.87. Write an application that reads a series of pairs of numbers as follows:

a)   product number

b)   quantity sold

Your program should use a `switch` statement to determine the retail price for each product. It should calculate and display the total retail value of all products sold. Use a sentinel-controlled loop to determine when the program should stop looping and display the final results.

5.17   *(Modified Compound Interest Program)* Modify the application in Fig. 5.6 to use only integers to calculate the compound interest. [*Hint:* Treat all monetary amounts as integral numbers of pennies. Then break the result into its dollars and cents portions by using the division and remainder operations, respectively. Insert a period between the dollars and the cents portions.]

5.18   Assume that i = 1, j = 2, k = 3 and m = 2. What does each of the following statements print?

a)   `System.out.println( i == 1 );`

b)   `System.out.println( j == 3 );`

c)   `System.out.println( ( i >= 1 ) && ( j < 4 ) );`

d)   `System.out.println( ( m <= 99 ) & ( k < m ) );`

e)   `System.out.println( ( j >= i ) || ( k == m ) );`

f)   `System.out.println( ( k + m < j ) | ( 3 - j >= k ) );`

g)   `System.out.println( !( k > m ) );`

5.19   *(Calculating the Value of π)* Calculate the value of π from the infinite series

$$\pi = 4 - \frac{4}{3} + \frac{4}{5} - \frac{4}{7} + \frac{4}{9} - \frac{4}{11} + \cdots$$

Print a table that shows the value of π approximated by computing the first 200,000 terms of this series. How many terms do you have to use before you first get a value that begins with 3.14159?

5.20   *(Modified Triangle Printing Program)* Modify Exercise 5.14 to combine your code from the four separate triangles of asterisks such that all four patterns print side by side. [*Hint:* Make clever use of nested `for` loops.]

5.21   *(Diamond Printing Program)* Write an application that prints the following diamond shape. You may use output statements that print a single asterisk (*), a single space or a single newline character. Maximize your use of repetition (with nested `for` statements), and minimize the number of output statements.

```
      *
     ***
    *****
   *******
  *********
   *******
    *****
     ***
      *
```

5.22   *(Modified Diamond Printing Program)* Modify the application you wrote in Exercise 5.21 to read an odd number in the range 1 to 19 to specify the number of rows in the diamond. Your program should then display a diamond of the appropriate size.

5.23   Describe in general how you'd remove any continue statement from a loop in a program and replace it with some structured equivalent. Use the technique you develop here to remove the continue statement from the program in Fig. 5.13.

5.24   *("The Twelve Days of Christmas" Song)* Write an application that uses repetition and switch statements to print the song "The Twelve Days of Christmas." One switch statement should be used to print the day ("first," "second," and so on). A separate switch statement should be used to print the remainder of each verse. Visit the website en.wikipedia.org/wiki/The_Twelve_Days_of_Christmas_(song) for the lyrics of the song.

Making a Difference

5.25   *(Global Warming Facts Quiz)* The controversial issue of global warming has been widely publicized by the film "An Inconvenient Truth," featuring former Vice President Al Gore. Mr. Gore and a U.N. network of scientists, the Intergovernmental Panel on Climate Change, shared the 2007 Nobel Peace Prize in recognition of "their efforts to build up and disseminate greater knowledge about man-made climate change." Research *both* sides of the global warming issue online (you might want to search for phrases like "global warming skeptics"). Create a five-question multiple-choice quiz on global warming, each question having four possible answers (numbered 1–4). Be objective and try to fairly represent both sides of the issue. Next, write an application that administers the quiz, calculates the number of correct answers (zero through five) and returns a message to the user. If the user correctly answers five questions, print "Excellent"; if four, print "Very good"; if three or fewer, print "Time to brush up on your knowledge of global warming," and include a list of some of the websites where you found your facts.

5.26   *(Tax Plan Alternatives; The "FairTax")* There are many proposals to make taxation fairer. Check out the FairTax initiative in the United States at

   www.fairtax.org/site/PageServer?pagename=calculator

Research how the proposed FairTax works. One suggestion is to eliminate income taxes and most other taxes in favor of a 23% consumption tax on all products and services that you buy. Some FairTax opponents question the 23% figure and say that because of the way the tax is calculated, it would be more accurate to say the rate is 30%—check this carefully. Write a program that prompts the user to enter expenses in various expense categories they have (e.g., housing, food, clothing, transportation, education, health care, vacations), then prints the estimated FairTax that person would pay.

6

*The greatest invention of the nineteenth century was
the invention of the method of invention.*
—Alfred North Whitehead

Call me Ishmael.
—Herman Melville

When you call me that, smile!
—Owen Wister

Answer me in one word.
—William Shakespeare

O! call back yesterday, bid time return.
—William Shakespeare

There is a point at which methods devour themselves.
—Frantz Fanon

Methods: A Deeper Look

Objectives

In this chapter you'll learn:

- How **static** methods and fields are associated with an entire class rather than specific instances of the class.
- To use common **Math** methods available in the Java API.
- To understand the mechanisms for passing information between methods.
- How the method call/return mechanism is supported by the method-call stack and activation records.
- How packages group related classes.
- How to use random-number generation to implement game-playing applications.
- How the visibility of declarations is limited to specific regions of programs.
- What method overloading is and how to create overloaded methods.

6.1 Introduction

Experience has shown that the best way to develop and maintain a large program is to construct it from small, simple pieces, or **modules**. This technique is called **divide and conquer**. We introduced methods in Chapter 3. In this chapter, we study methods in more depth. We emphasize how to declare and use methods to facilitate the design, implementation, operation and maintenance of large programs.

You'll see that it's possible for certain methods, called `static` methods, to be called without the need for an object of the class to exist. You'll learn how to declare a method with more than one parameter. You'll also learn how Java is able to keep track of which method is currently executing, how local variables of methods are maintained in memory and how a method knows where to return after it completes execution.

We'll take a brief diversion into simulation techniques with random-number generation and develop a version of the casino dice game called craps that uses most of the programming techniques you've used to this point in the book. In addition, you'll learn how to declare values that cannot change (i.e., constants) in your programs.

Many of the classes you'll use or create while developing applications will have more than one method of the same name. This technique, called overloading, is used to implement methods that perform similar tasks for arguments of different types or for different numbers of arguments.

We continue our discussion of methods in Chapter 18, Recursion. Recursion provides an intriguing way of thinking about methods and algorithms.

6.2 Program Modules in Java

Three kinds of modules exist in Java—methods, classes and packages. Java programs are written by combining new methods and classes that you write with predefined methods and classes available in the **Java Application Programming Interface** (also referred to as the **Java API** or **Java class library**) and in various other class libraries. Related classes are typically grouped into packages so that they can be imported into programs and reused.

You'll learn how to group your own classes into packages in Chapter 8. The Java API provides a rich collection of predefined classes that contain methods for performing common mathematical calculations, string manipulations, character manipulations, input/output operations, database operations, networking operations, file processing, error checking and many other useful tasks.

Software Engineering Observation 6.1

Familiarize yourself with the rich collection of classes and methods provided by the Java API (java.sun.com/javase/6/docs/api/). In Section 6.8, we present an overview of several common packages. In Appendix E, we explain how to navigate the Java API documentation. Don't reinvent the wheel. When possible, reuse Java API classes and methods. This reduces program development time and avoids introducing programming errors.

Methods (called **functions** or **procedures** in some languages) help you modularize a program by separating its tasks into self-contained units. You've declared methods in every program you've written. The statements in the method bodies are written only once, are hidden from other methods and can be reused from several locations in a program.

One motivation for modularizing a program into methods is the divide-and-conquer approach, which makes program development more manageable by constructing programs from small, simple pieces. Another is **software reusability**—using existing methods as building blocks to create new programs. Often, you can create programs mostly from standardized methods rather than by building customized code. For example, in earlier programs, we did not define how to read data values from the keyboard—Java provides these capabilities in class Scanner. A third motivation is to avoid repeating code. Dividing a program into meaningful methods makes the program easier to debug and maintain.

Software Engineering Observation 6.2

To promote software reusability, every method should be limited to performing a single, well-defined task, and the name of the method should express that task effectively.

Error-Prevention Tip 6.1

A method that performs one task is easier to test and debug than one that performs many tasks.

Software Engineering Observation 6.3

If you cannot choose a concise name that expresses a method's task, your method might be attempting to perform too many tasks. Break such a method into several smaller methods.

As you know, a method is invoked by a method call, and when the called method completes its task, it returns either a result or simply control to the caller. An analogy to this program structure is the hierarchical form of management (Fig. 6.1). A boss (the caller) asks a worker (the called method) to perform a task and report back (return) the results after completing the task. The boss method does not know how the worker method performs its designated tasks. The worker may also call other worker methods, unbeknown to the boss. This "hiding" of implementation details promotes good software engineering. Figure 6.1 shows the boss method communicating with several worker methods in a hierarchical manner. The boss method divides its responsibilities among the various worker methods. Note that worker1 acts as a "boss method" to worker4 and worker5.

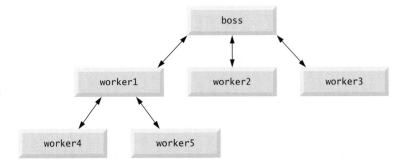

Fig. 6.1 | Hierarchical boss-method/worker-method relationship.

6.3 static Methods, static Fields and Class Math

Although most methods execute in response to method calls on specific objects, this is not always the case. Sometimes a method performs a task that does not depend on the contents of any object. Such a method applies to the class in which it's declared as a whole and is known as a static method or a **class method**. It's common for classes to contain convenient static methods to perform common tasks. For example, recall that we used static method pow of class Math to raise a value to a power in Fig. 5.6. To declare a method as static, place the keyword static before the return type in the method's declaration. You can call any static method by specifying the name of the class in which the method is declared, followed by a dot (.) and the method name, as in

> *ClassName.methodName(arguments)*

We use various Math class methods here to present the concept of static methods. Class Math provides a collection of methods that enable you to perform common mathematical calculations. For example, you can calculate the square root of 900.0 with the static method call

> `Math.sqrt( 900.0 )`

The preceding expression evaluates to 30.0. Method sqrt takes an argument of type double and returns a result of type double. To output the value of the preceding method call in the command window, you might write the statement

> `System.out.println( Math.sqrt( 900.0 ) );`

In this statement, the value that sqrt returns becomes the argument to method println. Note that there was no need to create a Math object before calling method sqrt. Also note that *all* Math class methods are static—therefore, each is called by preceding the name of the method with the class name Math and the dot (.) separator.

Software Engineering Observation 6.4

Class Math is part of the java.lang package, which is implicitly imported by the compiler, so it's not necessary to import class Math to use its methods.

Method arguments may be constants, variables or expressions. If c = 13.0, d = 3.0 and f = 4.0, then the statement

```
        System.out.println( Math.sqrt( c + d * f ) );
```

calculates and prints the square root of 13.0 + 3.0 * 4.0 = 25.0—namely, 5.0. Figure 6.2 summarizes several Math class methods. In the figure, *x* and *y* are of type double.

Method	Description	Example
abs(*x*)	absolute value of *x*	abs(23.7) is 23.7 abs(0.0) is 0.0 abs(-23.7) is 23.7
ceil(*x*)	rounds *x* to the smallest integer not less than *x*	ceil(9.2) is 10.0 ceil(-9.8) is -9.0
cos(*x*)	trigonometric cosine of *x* (*x* in radians)	cos(0.0) is 1.0
exp(*x*)	exponential method *e*ˣ	exp(1.0) is 2.71828 exp(2.0) is 7.38906
floor(*x*)	rounds *x* to the largest integer not greater than *x*	floor(9.2) is 9.0 floor(-9.8) is -10.0
log(*x*)	natural logarithm of *x* (base *e*)	log(Math.E) is 1.0 log(Math.E * Math.E) is 2.0
max(*x*, *y*)	larger value of *x* and *y*	max(2.3, 12.7) is 12.7 max(-2.3, -12.7) is -2.3
min(*x*, *y*)	smaller value of *x* and *y*	min(2.3, 12.7) is 2.3 min(-2.3, -12.7) is -12.7
pow(*x*, *y*)	*x* raised to the power *y* (i.e., *x*ʸ)	pow(2.0, 7.0) is 128.0 pow(9.0, 0.5) is 3.0
sin(*x*)	trigonometric sine of *x* (*x* in radians)	sin(0.0) is 0.0
sqrt(*x*)	square root of *x*	sqrt(900.0) is 30.0
tan(*x*)	trigonometric tangent of *x* (*x* in radians)	tan(0.0) is 0.0

Fig. 6.2 | Math class methods.

Math Class Constants PI and E

Class Math declares two fields that represent commonly used mathematical constants— **Math.PI** and **Math.E**. Math.PI (3.141592653589793) is the ratio of a circle's circumference to its diameter. Math.E (2.718281828459045) is the base value for natural logarithms (calculated with static Math method log). These fields are declared in class Math with the modifiers public, final and static. Making them public allows you to use these fields in your own classes. Any field declared with keyword **final** is constant—its value cannot change after the field is initialized. PI and E are declared final because their values never change. Making these fields static allows them to be accessed via the class name Math and a dot (.) separator, just like class Math's methods. Recall from Section 3.5 that when each object of a class maintains its own copy of an attribute, the field that represents the attribute is also known as an instance variable—each object (instance) of the class has a separate instance of the variable in memory. There are fields for which each object of a class does not have a separate instance of the field. That is the case with static fields, which are also known as **class variables**. When objects of a class containing static fields are created, all the objects of that class share one copy of the class's static fields. Together the class variables (i.e., static variables) and instance variables represent the fields of a class. You'll learn more about static fields in Section 8.11.

Why Is Method main Declared static?

Why must main be declared static? When you execute the Java Virtual Machine (JVM) with the java command, the JVM attempts to invoke the main method of the class you specify—when no objects of the class have been created. Declaring main as static allows the JVM to invoke main without creating an instance of the class. When you execute your application, you specify its class name as an argument to the command java, as in

> java *ClassName argument1 argument2 …*

The JVM loads the class specified by *ClassName* and uses that class name to invoke method main. In the preceding command, *ClassName* is a **command-line argument** to the JVM that tells it which class to execute. Following the *ClassName*, you can also specify a list of Strings (separated by spaces) as command-line arguments that the JVM will pass to your application. Such arguments might be used to specify options (e.g., a file name) to run the application. As you'll learn in Chapter 7, Arrays and ArrayLists, your application can access those command-line arguments and use them to customize the application.

6.4 Declaring Methods with Multiple Parameters

The application in Figs. 6.3–6.4 uses a method called maximum to determine and return the largest of three double values. Class MaximumFinderTest's main method (lines 7–11 of Fig. 6.4) creates MaximumFinder object (line 9) and calls its determineMaximum method (line 10) to produce the program's output. In method determineMaximum (Fig. 6.3), lines 14–18 prompt the user to enter three double values, and read them from the user. Line 21 calls method maximum (declared in lines 28–41) to determine the largest of the three it receives as arguments. When method maximum returns the result to line 21, the program assigns maximum's return value to local variable result. Then line 24 outputs the maximum value. At the end of this section, we'll discuss the use of operator + in line 24.

```
 1   // Fig. 6.3: MaximumFinder.java
 2   // Programmer-declared method maximum with three double parameters.
 3   import java.util.Scanner;
 4
 5   public class MaximumFinder
 6   {
 7      // obtain three floating-point values and locate the maximum value
 8      public void determineMaximum()
 9      {
10         // create Scanner for input from command window
11         Scanner input = new Scanner( System.in );
12
13         // prompt for and input three floating-point values
14         System.out.print(
15            "Enter three floating-point values separated by spaces: " );
16         double number1 = input.nextDouble(); // read first double
17         double number2 = input.nextDouble(); // read second double
18         double number3 = input.nextDouble(); // read third double
```

Fig. 6.3 | Programmer-declared method maximum with three double parameters. (Part 1 of 2.)

```
19
20          // determine the maximum value
21          double result = maximum( number1, number2, number3 );
22
23          // display maximum value
24          System.out.println( "Maximum is: " + result );
25       } // end method determineMaximum
26
27       // returns the maximum of its three double parameters
28       public double maximum( double x, double y, double z )
29       {
30          double maximumValue = x; // assume x is the largest to start
31
32          // determine whether y is greater than maximumValue
33          if ( y > maximumValue )
34             maximumValue = y;
35
36          // determine whether z is greater than maximumValue
37          if ( z > maximumValue )
38             maximumValue = z;
39
40          return maximumValue;
41       } // end method maximum
42    } // end class MaximumFinder
```

Fig. 6.3 | Programmer-declared method maximum with three double parameters. (Part 2 of 2.)

```
1    // Fig. 6.4: MaximumFinderTest.java
2    // Application to test class MaximumFinder.
3
4    public class MaximumFinderTest
5    {
6       // application starting point
7       public static void main( String[] args )
8       {
9          MaximumFinder maximumFinder = new MaximumFinder();
10         maximumFinder.determineMaximum();
11      } // end main
12   } // end class MaximumFinderTest
```

```
Enter three floating-point values separated by spaces: 9.35 2.74 5.1
Maximum is: 9.35
```

```
Enter three floating-point values separated by spaces: 5.8 12.45 8.32
Maximum is: 12.45
```

```
Enter three floating-point values separated by spaces: 6.46 4.12 10.54
Maximum is: 10.54
```

Fig. 6.4 | Application to test class MaximumFinder.

Consider maximum's declaration (lines 28–41). Line 28 indicates that the method returns a double value, that the method's name is maximum and that the method requires three double parameters (x, y and z) to accomplish its task. Note that multiple parameters are specified as a comma-separated list. When maximum is called from line 21, the parameters x, y and z are initialized with the values of arguments number1, number2 and number3, respectively. There must be one argument in the method call for each parameter (sometimes called a **formal parameter**) in the method declaration. Also, each argument must be consistent with the type of the corresponding parameter. For example, a parameter of type double can receive values like 7.35, 22 or –0.03456, but not Strings like "hello" nor the boolean values true or false. Section 6.7 discusses the argument types that can be provided in a method call for each parameter of a primitive type.

To determine the maximum value, we begin with the assumption that parameter x contains the largest value, so line 30 declares local variable maximumValue and initializes it with the value of parameter x. Of course, it's possible that parameter y or z contains the actual largest value, so we must compare each of these values with maximumValue. The if statement at lines 33–34 determines whether y is greater than maximumValue. If so, line 34 assigns y to maximumValue. The if statement at lines 37–38 determines whether z is greater than maximumValue. If so, line 38 assigns z to maximumValue. At this point the largest of the three values resides in maximumValue, so line 40 returns that value to line 21. When program control returns to the point in the program where maximum was called, maximum's parameters x, y and z no longer exist in memory.

Software Engineering Observation 6.5
Methods can return at most one value, but the returned value could be a reference to an object that contains many values.

Software Engineering Observation 6.6
Variables should be declared as fields of a class only if they are required for use in more than one method of the class or if the program should save their values between calls to the class's methods.

Common Programming Error 6.1
Declaring method parameters of the same type as float x, y instead of float x, float y is a syntax error—a type is required for each parameter in the parameter list.

Implementing Method **maximum** *by Reusing Method* **Math.max**
The entire body of our maximum method could also be implemented with two calls to Math.max, as follows:

```
return Math.max( x, Math.max( y, z ) );
```

The first call to Math.max specifies arguments x and Math.max(y, z). Before any method can be called, its arguments must be evaluated to determine their values. If an argument is a method call, the method call must be performed to determine its return value. So, in the preceding statement, Math.max(y, z) is evaluated to determine the maximum of y and z. Then the result is passed as the second argument to the other call to Math.max, which returns the larger of its two arguments. This is a good example of software reuse—we find the largest of three values by reusing Math.max, which finds the largest of two values. Note how concise this code is compared to lines 30–38 of Fig. 6.3.

Assembling Strings with String Concatenation

Java allows you to assemble String objects into larger strings by using operators + or +=. This is known as **string concatenation**. When both operands of operator + are String objects, operator + creates a new String object in which the characters of the right operand are placed at the end of those in the left operand—e.g., the expression "hello " + "there" creates the String "hello there".

In line 24 of Fig. 6.3, the expression "Maximum is: " + result uses operator + with operands of types String and double. Every primitive value and object in Java has a String representation. When one of the + operator's operands is a String, the other is converted to a String, then the two are concatenated. In line 24, the double value is converted to its String representation and placed at the end of the String "Maximum is: ". If there are any trailing zeros in a double value, these will be discarded when the number is converted to a String, for example 9.3500 would be represented as 9.35.

For primitive values used in String concatenation, the primitive values are converted to Strings. If a boolean is concatenated with a String, the boolean is converted to the String "true" or "false". All objects have a toString method that returns a String representation of the object. (We discuss toString in more detail subsequent chapters.) When an object is concatenated with a String, the object's toString method is implicitly called to obtain the String representation of the object.

Programmers sometimes prefer to break large String literals into several smaller Strings and place them on multiple lines of code for readability. In this case, the Strings can be reassembled using concatenation. We discuss the details of Strings in Chapter 16, Strings, Characters and Regular Expressions.

Common Programming Error 6.2

It's a syntax error to break a String literal across lines. If necessary, you can split a String into several smaller Strings and use concatenation to form the desired String.

Common Programming Error 6.3

Confusing the + operator used for string concatenation with the + operator used for addition can lead to strange results. Java evaluates the operands of an operator from left to right. For example, if integer variable y has the value 5, the expression "y + 2 = " + y + 2 results in the string "y + 2 = 52", not "y + 2 = 7", because first the value of y (5) is concatenated to the string "y + 2 = ", then the value 2 is concatenated to the new larger string "y + 2 = 5". The expression "y + 2 = " + (y + 2) produces the desired result "y + 2 = 7".

6.5 Notes on Declaring and Using Methods

There are three ways to call a method:

1. Using a method name by itself to call another method of the same class—such as maximum(number1, number2, number3) in line 21 of Fig. 6.3.

2. Using a variable that contains a reference to an object, followed by a dot (.) and the method name to call a method of the referenced object—such as the method call in line 10 of Fig. 6.4, maximumFinder.determineMaximum(), which calls a method of class MaximumFinder from the main method of MaximumFinderTest.

3. Using the class name and a dot (.) to call a static method of a class—such as Math.sqrt(900.0) in Section 6.3.

A non-`static` method can call any method of the same class directly (i.e., using the method name by itself) and can manipulate any of the class's fields directly. On the other hand, a `static` method can call only other `static` methods of the same class directly and can manipulate only `static` fields in the same class directly. To access the class's non-`static` members, a `static` method must use a reference to an object of the class. Recall that `static` methods relate to a class as a whole, whereas non-`static` methods are associated with a specific class instance (object) and may manipulate the object's instance variables. Many objects of a class, each with its own copies of the instance variables, may exist at the same time. Suppose a `static` method were to invoke a non-`static` method directly. How would the method know which object's instance variables to manipulate? What would happen if no objects of the class existed when the non-`static` method was invoked? Clearly, this would be problematic. So, Java does not allow a `static` method to access non-`static` members of the same class directly.

There are three ways to return control to the statement that calls a method. If the method does not return a result, control returns when the program flow reaches the method-ending right brace or when the statement

```
return;
```

is executed. If the method returns a result, the statement

```
return expression;
```

evaluates the *expression*, then returns the result to the caller.

Common Programming Error 6.4
Declaring a method outside the body of a class declaration or inside the body of another method is a syntax error.

Common Programming Error 6.5
Omitting the return-value-type, *possibly* void, *in a method declaration is a syntax error.*

Common Programming Error 6.6
Placing a semicolon after the right parenthesis enclosing the parameter list of a method declaration is a syntax error.

Common Programming Error 6.7
Redeclaring a parameter as a local variable in the method's body is a compilation error.

Common Programming Error 6.8
Forgetting to return a value from a method that should return a value is a compilation error. If a return type other than void *is specified, the method must contain a* return *statement that returns a value consistent with the method's return type. Returning a value from a method whose return type has been declared* void *is a compilation error.*

6.6 Method-Call Stack and Activation Records

To understand how Java performs method calls, we first need to consider a data structure (i.e., collection of related data items) known as a **stack**. You can think of a stack as analogous to a pile of dishes. When a dish is placed on the pile, it's normally placed at the top (referred to as **pushing** the dish onto the stack). Similarly, when a dish is removed from the pile, it's always removed from the top (referred to as **popping** the dish off the stack). Stacks are known as **last-in, first-out (LIFO) data structures**—the last item pushed (inserted) on the stack is the first item popped (removed) from the stack.

When a program calls a method, the called method must know how to return to its caller, so the return address of the calling method is pushed onto the **program-execution stack** (sometimes referred to as the **method-call stack**). If a series of method calls occurs, the successive return addresses are pushed onto the stack in last-in, first-out order so that each method can return to its caller.

The program-execution stack also contains the memory for the local variables used in each invocation of a method during a program's execution. This data, stored as a portion of the program-execution stack, is known as the **activation record** or **stack frame** of the method call. When a method call is made, the activation record for that method call is pushed onto the program-execution stack. When the method returns to its caller, the activation record for this method call is popped off the stack and those local variables are no longer known to the program. If a local variable holding a reference to an object is the only variable in the program with a reference to that object, when the activation record containing that local variable is popped off the stack, the object can no longer be accessed by the program and will eventually be deleted from memory by the JVM during "garbage collection." We discuss garbage collection in Section 8.10.

Of course, the amount of memory in a computer is finite, so only a certain amount of memory can be used to store activation records on the program execution stack. If more method calls occur than can have their activation records stored on the program-execution stack, an error known as a **stack overflow** occurs.

6.7 Argument Promotion and Casting

Another important feature of method calls is **argument promotion**—converting an argument's value, if possible, to the type that the method expects to receive in its corresponding parameter. For example, a program can call Math method sqrt with an integer argument even though the method expects to receive a double argument (but, as we'll soon see, not vice versa). The statement

```
System.out.println( Math.sqrt( 4 ) );
```

correctly evaluates Math.sqrt(4) and prints the value 2.0. The method declaration's parameter list causes Java to convert the int value 4 to the double value 4.0 before passing the value to method sqrt. Attempting these conversions may lead to compilation errors if Java's **promotion rules** are not satisfied. The promotion rules specify which conversions are allowed—that is, which conversions can be performed without losing data. In the sqrt example above, an int is converted to a double without changing its value. However, converting a double to an int truncates the fractional part of the double value—thus, part of the value is lost. Converting large integer types to small integer types (e.g., long to int, or int to short) may also result in changed values.

The promotion rules apply to expressions containing values of two or more primitive types and to primitive-type values passed as arguments to methods. Each value is promoted to the "highest" type in the expression. Actually, the expression uses a temporary copy of each value—the types of the original values remain unchanged. Figure 6.5 lists the primitive types and the types to which each can be promoted. Note that the valid promotions for a given type are always to a type higher in the table. For example, an int can be promoted to the higher types long, float and double.

Type	Valid promotions
double	None
float	double
long	float or double
int	long, float or double
char	int, long, float or double
short	int, long, float or double (but not char)
byte	short, int, long, float or double (but not char)
boolean	None (boolean values are not considered to be numbers in Java)

Fig. 6.5 | Promotions allowed for primitive types.

Converting values to types lower in the table of Fig. 6.5 will result in different values if the lower type cannot represent the value of the higher type (e.g., the int value 2000000 cannot be represented as a short, and any floating-point number with digits after its decimal point cannot be represented in an integer type such as long, int or short). Therefore, in cases where information may be lost due to conversion, the Java compiler requires you to use a cast operator (introduced in Section 4.9) to explicitly force the conversion to occur—otherwise a compilation error occurs. This enables you to "take control" from the compiler. You essentially say, "I know this conversion might cause loss of information, but for my purposes here, that's fine." Suppose method square calculates the square of an integer and thus requires an int argument. To call square with a double argument named doubleValue, we would be required to write the method call as

```
square( (int) doubleValue )
```

This method call explicitly casts (converts) a *copy* of variable doubleValue's value to an integer for use in method square. Thus, if doubleValue's value is 4.5, the method receives the value 4 and returns 16, not 20.25.

Common Programming Error 6.9

Converting a primitive-type value to another primitive type may change the value if the new type is not a valid promotion. For example, converting a floating-point value to an integer value may introduce truncation errors (loss of the fractional part) into the result.

6.8 Java API Packages

As you've seen, Java contains many predefined classes that are grouped into categories of related classes called packages. Together, these are known as the Java Application Programming Interface (Java API), or the Java class library. A great strength of Java is the Java API's thousands of classes. Some key Java API packages are described in Fig. 6.6, which represents only a small portion of the reusable components in the Java API.

Package	Description
java.applet	The **Java Applet Package** contains a class and several interfaces required to create Java applets—programs that execute in web browsers. Applets are discussed in Chapter 23, Applets and Java Web Start; interfaces are discussed in Chapter 10, Object-Oriented Programming: Polymorphism.)
java.awt	The **Java Abstract Window Toolkit Package** contains the classes and interfaces required to create and manipulate GUIs in early versions of Java. In current versions of Java, the Swing GUI components of the javax.swing packages are typically used instead. (Some elements of the java.awt package are discussed in Chapter 14, GUI Components: Part 1, Chapter 15, Graphics and Java 2D™, and Chapter 25, GUI Components: Part 2.)
java.awt.event	The **Java Abstract Window Toolkit Event Package** contains classes and interfaces that enable event handling for GUI components in both the java.awt and javax.swing packages. (See Chapter 14, GUI Components: Part 1 and Chapter 25, GUI Components: Part 2.)
java.awt.geom	The **Java 2D Shapes Package** contains classes and interfaces for working with Java's advanced two-dimensional graphics capabilities. (See Chapter 15, Graphics and Java 2D™.)
java.io	The **Java Input/Output Package** contains classes and interfaces that enable programs to input and output data. (See Chapter 17, Files, Streams and Object Serialization.)
java.lang	The **Java Language Package** contains classes and interfaces (discussed bookwide) that are required by many Java programs. This package is imported by the compiler into all programs.
java.net	The **Java Networking Package** contains classes and interfaces that enable programs to communicate via computer networks like the Internet. (See Chapter 27, Networking.)
java.sql	The **JDBC Package** contains classes and interfaces for working with databases. (See Chapter 28, Accessing Databases with JDBC.)
java.text	The **Java Text Package** contains classes and interfaces that enable programs to manipulate numbers, dates, characters and strings. The package provides internationalization capabilities that enable a program to be customized to locales (e.g., a program may display strings in different languages, based on the user's country).
java.util	The **Java Utilities Package** contains utility classes and interfaces that enable such actions as date and time manipulations, random-number processing (class Random) and the storing and processing of large amounts of data. (See Chapter 20, Generic Collections.)
java.util.concurrent	The **Java Concurrency Package** contains utility classes and interfaces for implementing programs that can perform multiple tasks in parallel. (See Chapter 26, Multithreading.)

Fig. 6.6 | Java API packages (a subset). (Part 1 of 2.)

Package	Description
`javax.media`	The **Java Media Framework Package** contains classes and interfaces for working with Java's multimedia capabilities. (See Chapter 24, Multimedia: Applets and Applications.)
`javax.swing`	The **Java Swing GUI Components Package** contains classes and interfaces for Java's Swing GUI components that provide support for portable GUIs. (See Chapter 14, GUI Components: Part 1 and Chapter 25, GUI Components: Part 2.)
`javax.swing.event`	The **Java Swing Event Package** contains classes and interfaces that enable event handling (e.g., responding to button clicks) for GUI components in package `javax.swing`. (See Chapter 14, GUI Components: Part 1 and Chapter 25, GUI Components: Part 2.)
`javax.xml.ws`	The **JAX-WS Package** contains classes and interfaces for working with web services in Java. (See Chapter 31, Web Services.)

Fig. 6.6 | Java API packages (a subset). (Part 2 of 2.)

The set of packages available in Java SE 6 is quite large. In addition to those summarized in Fig. 6.6, Java SE 6 includes packages for complex graphics, advanced graphical user interfaces, printing, advanced networking, security, database processing, multimedia, accessibility (for people with disabilities), concurrent programming, cryptography, XML processing and many other capabilities. For an overview of the packages in Java SE 6, visit

```
java.sun.com/javase/6/docs/api/overview-summary.html
```

Many other packages are also available for download at `java.sun.com`.

You can locate additional information about a predefined Java class's methods in the Java API documentation at `java.sun.com/javase/6/docs/api/`. When you visit this site, click the **Index** link to see an alphabetical listing of all the classes and methods in the Java API. Locate the class name and click its link to see the online description of the class. Click the **METHOD** link to see a table of the class's methods. Each `static` method will be listed with the word "`static`" preceding the method's return type.

6.9 Case Study: Random-Number Generation

We now take a brief diversion into a popular type of programming application—simulation and game playing. In this and the next section, we develop a nicely structured game-playing program with multiple methods. The program uses most of the control statements presented thus far in the book and introduces several new programming concepts.

There is something in the air of a casino that invigorates people—from the high rollers at the plush mahogany-and-felt craps tables to the quarter poppers at the one-armed bandits. It's the **element of chance**, the possibility that luck will convert a pocketful of money into a mountain of wealth. The element of chance can be introduced in a program via an object of class **Random** (package `java.util`) or via the `static` method random of class `Math`. Objects of class Random can produce random `boolean`, `byte`, `float`, `double`, `int`, `long` and Gaussian values, whereas `Math` method `random` can produce only `double` values in the range $0.0 \leq x < 1.0$, where x is the value returned by method `random`. In the next several examples, we use objects of class Random to produce random values.

A new random-number generator object can be created as follows:

```
Random randomNumbers = new Random();
```

It can then be used to generate random `boolean`, `byte`, `float`, `double`, `int`, `long` and Gaussian values—we discuss only random `int` values here. For more information on the `Random` class, see `java.sun.com/javase/6/docs/api/java/util/Random.html`.

Consider the following statement:

```
int randomValue = randomNumbers.nextInt();
```

Random method **nextInt** generates a random `int` value in the range –2,147,483,648 to +2,147,483,647, inclusive. If it truly produces values at random, then every value in the range should have an equal chance (or probability) of being chosen each time `nextInt` is called. The numbers are actually **pseudorandom numbers**—a sequence of values produced by a complex mathematical calculation. The calculation uses the current time of day (which, of course, changes constantly) to **seed** the random-number generator such that each execution of a program yields a different sequence of random values.

The range of values produced directly by method `nextInt` often differs from the range of values required in a particular Java application. For example, a program that simulates coin tossing might require only 0 for "heads" and 1 for "tails." A program that simulates the rolling of a six-sided die might require random integers in the range 1–6. A program that randomly predicts the next type of spaceship (out of four possibilities) that will fly across the horizon in a video game might require random integers in the range 1–4. For cases like these, class `Random` provides another version of method `nextInt` that receives an `int` argument and returns a value from 0 up to, but not including, the argument's value. For example, for coin tossing, the following statement returns 0 or 1.

```
int randomValue = randomNumbers.nextInt( 2 );
```

Rolling a Six-Sided Die

To demonstrate random numbers, let's develop a program that simulates 20 rolls of a six-sided die and displays the value of each roll. We begin by using `nextInt` to produce random values in the range 0–5, as follows:

```
face = randomNumbers.nextInt( 6 );
```

The argument 6—called the **scaling factor**—represents the number of unique values that `nextInt` should produce (in this case six—0, 1, 2, 3, 4 and 5). This manipulation is called **scaling** the range of values produced by `Random` method `nextInt`.

A six-sided die has the numbers 1–6 on its faces, not 0–5. So we **shift** the range of numbers produced by adding a **shifting value**—in this case 1—to our previous result, as in

```
face = 1 + randomNumbers.nextInt( 6 );
```

The shifting value (1) specifies the first value in the desired range of random integers. The preceding statement assigns `face` a random integer in the range 1–6.

Figure 6.7 shows two sample outputs which confirm that the results of the preceding calculation are integers in the range 1–6, and that each run of the program can produce a different sequence of random numbers. Line 3 imports class `Random` from the `java.util` package. Line 9 creates the `Random` object `randomNumbers` to produce random values. Line 16 executes 20 times in a loop to roll the die. The `if` statement (lines 21–22) in the loop starts a new line of output after every five numbers.

```
 1   // Fig. 6.7: RandomIntegers.java
 2   // Shifted and scaled random integers.
 3   import java.util.Random; // program uses class Random
 4
 5   public class RandomIntegers
 6   {
 7      public static void main( String[] args )
 8      {
 9         Random randomNumbers = new Random(); // random number generator
10         int face; // stores each random integer generated
11
12         // loop 20 times
13         for ( int counter = 1; counter <= 20; counter++ )
14         {
15            // pick random integer from 1 to 6
16            face = 1 + randomNumbers.nextInt( 6 );
17
18            System.out.printf( "%d  ", face ); // display generated value
19
20            // if counter is divisible by 5, start a new line of output
21            if ( counter % 5 == 0 )
22               System.out.println();
23         } // end for
24      } // end main
25   } // end class RandomIntegers
```

```
1  5  3  6  2
5  2  6  5  2
4  4  4  2  6
3  1  6  2  2
```

```
6  5  4  2  6
1  2  5  1  3
6  3  2  2  1
6  4  2  6  4
```

Fig. 6.7 | Shifted and scaled random integers.

Rolling a Six-Sided Die 6000 Times

To show that the numbers produced by `nextInt` occur with approximately equal likelihood, let's simulate 6000 rolls of a die with the application in Fig. 6.8. Each integer from 1 to 6 should appear approximately 1000 times.

```
 1   // Fig. 6.8: RollDie.java
 2   // Roll a six-sided die 6000 times.
 3   import java.util.Random;
 4
 5   public class RollDie
 6   {
 7      public static void main( String[] args )
 8      {
```

Fig. 6.8 | Rolling a six-sided die 6000 times. (Part 1 of 3.)

```
 9          Random randomNumbers = new Random(); // random number generator
10
11          int frequency1 = 0; // maintains count of 1s rolled
12          int frequency2 = 0; // count of 2s rolled
13          int frequency3 = 0; // count of 3s rolled
14          int frequency4 = 0; // count of 4s rolled
15          int frequency5 = 0; // count of 5s rolled
16          int frequency6 = 0; // count of 6s rolled
17
18          int face; // stores most recently rolled value
19
20          // tally counts for 6000 rolls of a die
21          for ( int roll = 1; roll <= 6000; roll++ )
22          {
23             face = 1 + randomNumbers.nextInt( 6 ); // number from 1 to 6
24
25             // determine roll value 1-6 and increment appropriate counter
26             switch ( face )
27             {
28                case 1:
29                   ++frequency1; // increment the 1s counter
30                   break;
31                case 2:
32                   ++frequency2; // increment the 2s counter
33                   break;
34                case 3:
35                   ++frequency3; // increment the 3s counter
36                   break;
37                case 4:
38                   ++frequency4; // increment the 4s counter
39                   break;
40                case 5:
41                   ++frequency5; // increment the 5s counter
42                   break;
43                case 6:
44                   ++frequency6; // increment the 6s counter
45                   break; // optional at end of switch
46             } // end switch
47          } // end for
48
49          System.out.println( "Face\tFrequency" ); // output headers
50          System.out.printf( "1\t%d\n2\t%d\n3\t%d\n4\t%d\n5\t%d\n6\t%d\n",
51             frequency1, frequency2, frequency3, frequency4,
52             frequency5, frequency6 );
53       } // end main
54    } // end class RollDie
```

Face	Frequency
1	982
2	1001
3	1015
4	1005
5	1009
6	988

Fig. 6.8 | Rolling a six-sided die 6000 times. (Part 2 of 3.)

Face	Frequency
1	1029
2	994
3	1017
4	1007
5	972
6	981

Fig. 6.8 | Rolling a six-sided die 6000 times. (Part 3 of 3.)

As the sample outputs show, scaling and shifting the values produced by nextInt enables the program to simulate rolling a six-sided die. The application uses nested control statements (the switch is nested inside the for) to determine the number of times each side of the die appears. The for statement (lines 21–47) iterates 6000 times. During each iteration, line 23 produces a random value from 1 to 6. That value is then used as the controlling expression (line 26) of the switch statement (lines 26–46). Based on the face value, the switch statement increments one of the six counter variables during each iteration of the loop. When we study arrays in Chapter 7, we'll show an elegant way to replace the entire switch statement in this program with a single statement! Note that this switch statement has no default case, because we have a case for every possible die value that the expression in line 23 could produce. Run the program, and observe the results. As you'll see, every time you run this program, it produces different results.

6.9.1 Generalized Scaling and Shifting of Random Numbers

Previously, we simulated the rolling of a six-sided die with the statement

```
face = 1 + randomNumbers.nextInt( 6 );
```

This statement always assigns to variable face an integer in the range $1 \leq face \leq 6$. The width of this range (i.e., the number of consecutive integers in the range) is 6, and the starting number in the range is 1. Referring to the preceding statement, we see that the width of the range is determined by the number 6 that is passed as an argument to Random method nextInt, and the starting number of the range is the number 1 that is added to randomNumberGenerator.nextInt(6). We can generalize this result as

```
number = shiftingValue + randomNumbers.nextInt( scalingFactor );
```

where *shiftingValue* specifies the first number in the desired range of consecutive integers and *scalingFactor* specifies how many numbers are in the range.

It's also possible to choose integers at random from sets of values other than ranges of consecutive integers. For example, to obtain a random value from the sequence 2, 5, 8, 11 and 14, you could use the statement

```
number = 2 + 3 * randomNumbers.nextInt( 5 );
```

In this case, randomNumberGenerator.nextInt(5) produces values in the range 0–4. Each value produced is multiplied by 3 to produce a number in the sequence 0, 3, 6, 9 and 12. We add 2 to that value to shift the range of values and obtain a value from the sequence 2, 5, 8, 11 and 14. We can generalize this result as

```
number = shiftingValue +
    differenceBetweenValues * randomNumbers.nextInt( scalingFactor );
```

where *shiftingValue* specifies the first number in the desired range of values, *difference-BetweenValues* represents the constant difference between consecutive numbers in the sequence and *scalingFactor* specifies how many numbers are in the range.

6.9.2 Random-Number Repeatability for Testing and Debugging

Class `Random`'s methods actually generate pseudorandom numbers based on complex mathematical calculations—the sequence of numbers appears to be random. The calculation that produces the numbers uses the time of day as a **seed value** to change the sequence's starting point. Each new `Random` object seeds itself with a value based on the computer system's clock at the time the object is created, enabling each execution of a program to produce a different sequence of random numbers.

When debugging an application, it's sometimes useful to repeat the exact same sequence of pseudorandom numbers during each execution of the program. This repeatability enables you to prove that your application is working for a specific sequence of random numbers before you test the program with different sequences of random numbers. When repeatability is important, you can create a `Random` object as follows:

```
Random randomNumbers = new Random( seedValue );
```

The `seedValue` argument (of type `long`) seeds the random-number calculation. If the same `seedValue` is used every time, the `Random` object produces the same sequence of numbers. You can set a `Random` object's seed at any time during program execution by calling the object's `set` method, as in

```
randomNumbers.set( seedValue );
```

Error-Prevention Tip 6.2

While developing a program, create the `Random` object with a specific seed value to produce a repeatable sequence of numbers each time the program executes. If a logic error occurs, fix the error and test the program again with the same seed value—this allows you to reconstruct the same sequence of numbers that caused the error. Once the logic errors have been removed, create the `Random` object without using a seed value, causing the `Random` object to generate a new sequence of random numbers each time the program executes.

6.10 Case Study: A Game of Chance; Introducing Enumerations

A popular game of chance is a dice game known as craps, which is played in casinos and back alleys throughout the world. The rules of the game are straightforward:

> *You roll two dice. Each die has six faces, which contain one, two, three, four, five and six spots, respectively. After the dice have come to rest, the sum of the spots on the two upward faces is calculated. If the sum is 7 or 11 on the first throw, you win. If the sum is 2, 3 or 12 on the first throw (called "craps"), you lose (i.e., the "house" wins). If the sum is 4, 5, 6, 8, 9 or 10 on the first throw, that sum becomes your "point." To win, you must continue rolling the dice until you "make your point" (i.e., roll that same point value). You lose by rolling a 7 before making your point.*

The application in Fig. 6.9 and Fig. 6.10 simulates the game of craps, using methods to implement the game's logic. In class `CrapsTest`'s `main` method (Fig. 6.10), line 8 creates an object of class `Craps` (Fig. 6.9) and line 9 calls its `play` method to start the game. The play method (Fig. 6.9, lines 21–65) calls the rollDice method (Fig. 6.9, lines 68–81) as necessary to roll the dice and compute their sum. The sample outputs (Fig. 6.10) show winning and losing on the first roll, and winning and losing on a subsequent roll.

```java
1   // Fig. 6.9: Craps.java
2   // Craps class simulates the dice game craps.
3   import java.util.Random;
4
5   public class Craps
6   {
7      // create random number generator for use in method rollDice
8      private static final Random randomNumbers = new Random();
9
10     // enumeration with constants that represent the game status
11     private enum Status { CONTINUE, WON, LOST };
12
13     // constants that represent common rolls of the dice
14     private static final int SNAKE_EYES = 2;
15     private static final int TREY = 3;
16     private static final int SEVEN = 7;
17     private static final int YO_LEVEN = 11;
18     private static final int BOX_CARS = 12;
19
20     // plays one game of craps
21     public void play()
22     {
23        int myPoint = 0; // point if no win or loss on first roll
24        Status gameStatus; // can contain CONTINUE, WON or LOST
25
26        int sumOfDice = rollDice(); // first roll of the dice
27
28        // determine game status and point based on first roll
29        switch ( sumOfDice )
30        {
31           case SEVEN: // win with 7 on first roll
32           case YO_LEVEN: // win with 11 on first roll
33              gameStatus = Status.WON;
34              break;
35           case SNAKE_EYES: // lose with 2 on first roll
36           case TREY: // lose with 3 on first roll
37           case BOX_CARS: // lose with 12 on first roll
38              gameStatus = Status.LOST;
39              break;
40           default: // did not win or lose, so remember point
41              gameStatus = Status.CONTINUE; // game is not over
42              myPoint = sumOfDice; // remember the point
43              System.out.printf( "Point is %d\n", myPoint );
44              break; // optional at end of switch
45        } // end switch
46
47        // while game is not complete
48        while ( gameStatus == Status.CONTINUE ) // not WON or LOST
49        {
```

Fig. 6.9 | Craps class simulates the dice game craps. (Part 1 of 2.)

```
50              sumOfDice = rollDice(); // roll dice again
51
52              // determine game status
53              if ( sumOfDice == myPoint ) // win by making point
54                 gameStatus = Status.WON;
55              else
56                 if ( sumOfDice == SEVEN ) // lose by rolling 7 before point
57                    gameStatus = Status.LOST;
58           } // end while
59
60           // display won or lost message
61           if ( gameStatus == Status.WON )
62              System.out.println( "Player wins" );
63           else
64              System.out.println( "Player loses" );
65        } // end method play
66
67        // roll dice, calculate sum and display results
68        public int rollDice()
69        {
70           // pick random die values
71           int die1 = 1 + randomNumbers.nextInt( 6 ); // first die roll
72           int die2 = 1 + randomNumbers.nextInt( 6 ); // second die roll
73
74           int sum = die1 + die2; // sum of die values
75
76           // display results of this roll
77           System.out.printf( "Player rolled %d + %d = %d\n",
78              die1, die2, sum );
79
80           return sum; // return sum of dice
81        } // end method rollDice
82     } // end class Craps
```

Fig. 6.9 | Craps class simulates the dice game craps. (Part 2 of 2.)

```
1    // Fig. 6.10: CrapsTest.java
2    // Application to test class Craps.
3
4    public class CrapsTest
5    {
6       public static void main( String[] args )
7       {
8          Craps game = new Craps();
9          game.play(); // play one game of craps
10      } // end main
11   } // end class CrapsTest
```

```
Player rolled 5 + 6 = 11
Player wins
```

Fig. 6.10 | Application to test class Craps. (Part 1 of 2.)

```
Player rolled 5 + 4 = 9
Point is 9
Player rolled 2 + 2 = 4
Player rolled 2 + 6 = 8
Player rolled 4 + 2 = 6
Player rolled 3 + 6 = 9
Player wins
```

```
Player rolled 1 + 2 = 3
Player loses
```

```
Player rolled 2 + 6 = 8
Point is 8
Player rolled 5 + 1 = 6
Player rolled 2 + 1 = 3
Player rolled 1 + 6 = 7
Player loses
```

Fig. 6.10 | Application to test class Craps. (Part 2 of 2.)

Method `rollDice`

In the rules of the game, the player must roll two dice on the first roll and must do the same on all subsequent rolls. We declare method rollDice (Fig. 6.9, lines 68–81) to roll the dice and compute and print their sum. Method rollDice is declared once, but it's called from two places (lines 26 and 50) in method play, which contains the logic for one complete game of craps. Method rollDice takes no arguments, so it has an empty parameter list. Each time it's called, rollDice returns the sum of the dice, so the return type int is indicated in the method header (line 68). Although lines 71 and 72 look the same (except for the die names), they do not necessarily produce the same result. Each of these statements produces a random value in the range 1–6. Note that randomNumbers (used in lines 71–72) is not declared in the method. Instead it's declared as a private static final variable of the class and initialized in line 8. This enables us to create one Random object that is reused in each call to rollDice. Since this object is static, it would also be shared by all instances of class Craps in the program

Method play's Local Variables

The game is reasonably involved. The player may win or lose on the first roll, or may win or lose on any subsequent roll. Method play (lines 21–65) uses local variable myPoint (line 23) to store the "point" if the player does not win or lose on the first roll, local variable gameStatus (line 24) to keep track of the overall game status and local variable sumOfDice (line 26) to hold the sum of the dice for the most recent roll. Note that myPoint is initialized to 0 to ensure that the application will compile. If you do not initialize myPoint, the compiler issues an error, because myPoint is not assigned a value in every case of the switch statement, and thus the program could try to use myPoint before it is assigned a value. By contrast, gameStatus *is* assigned a value in *every* case of the switch statement—thus, it's guaranteed to be initialized before it's used and does not need to be initialized.

enum *Type* **Status**

Local variable gameStatus (line 24) is declared to be of a new type called Status (declared at line 11). Type Status is a private member of class Craps, because Status will be used only in that class. Status is a type called an **enumeration**, which, in its simplest form, declares a set of constants represented by identifiers. An enumeration is a special kind of class that is introduced by the keyword **enum** and a type name (in this case, Status). As with classes, braces delimit an enum declaration's body. Inside the braces is a comma-separated list of **enumeration constants**, each representing a unique value. The identifiers in an enum must be unique. (You'll learn more about enumerations in Chapter 8.)

Good Programming Practice 6.1

Use only uppercase letters in the names of enumeration constants. This makes the constants stand out and reminds you that enumeration constants are not variables.

Variables of type Status can be assigned only the three constants declared in the enumeration (line 11) or a compilation error will occur. When the game is won, the program sets local variable gameStatus to Status.WON (lines 33 and 54). When the game is lost, the program sets local variable gameStatus to Status.LOST (lines 38 and 57). Otherwise, the program sets local variable gameStatus to Status.CONTINUE (line 41) to indicate that the game is not over and the dice must be rolled again.

Good Programming Practice 6.2

Using enumeration constants (like Status.WON, Status.LOST and Status.CONTINUE) rather than literal values (such as 0, 1 and 2) makes programs easier to read and maintain.

Logic of the **play** *Method*

Line 26 in method play calls rollDice, which picks two random values from 1 to 6, displays the values of the first die, the second die and the sum of the dice, and returns the sum. Method play next enters the switch statement at lines 29–45, which uses the sumOfDice value from line 26 to determine whether the game has been won or lost, or whether it should continue with another roll. The sums of the dice that would result in a win or loss on the first roll are declared as public static final int constants in lines 14–18. These are used in the cases of the switch statement. The identifier names use casino parlance for these sums. Note that these constants, like enum constants, are declared with all capital letters by convention, to make them stand out in the program. Lines 31–34 determine whether the player won on the first roll with SEVEN (7) or YO_LEVEN (11). Lines 35–39 determine whether the player lost on the first roll with SNAKE_EYES (2), TREY (3), or BOX_CARS (12). After the first roll, if the game is not over, the default case (lines 40–44) sets gameStatus to Status.CONTINUE, saves sumOfDice in myPoint and displays the point.

If we're still trying to "make our point" (i.e., the game is continuing from a prior roll), lines 48–58 execute. Line 50 rolls the dice again. If sumOfDice matches myPoint (line 53), line 54 sets gameStatus to Status.WON, then the loop terminates because the game is complete. If sumOfDice is SEVEN (line 56), line 57 sets gameStatus to Status.LOST, and the loop terminates because the game is complete. When the game completes, lines 61–64 display a message indicating whether the player won or lost, and the program terminates.

Note the use of the various program-control mechanisms we've discussed. The Craps class in concert with class CrapsTest uses three methods—main, play (called from main) and rollDice (called twice from play)—and the switch, while, if...else and nested if control statements. Note also the use of multiple `case` labels in the `switch` statement to execute the same statements for sums of SEVEN and YO_LEVEN (lines 31–32) and for sums of SNAKE_EYES, TREY and BOX_CARS (lines 35–37).

Why Some Constants Are Not Defined as *enum* Constants

You might be wondering why we declared the sums of the dice as `public final static int` constants rather than as `enum` constants. The answer lies in the fact that the program must compare the `int` variable `sumOfDice` (line 26) to these constants to determine the outcome of each roll. Suppose we were to declare `enum Sum` containing constants (e.g., `Sum.SNAKE_EYES`) representing the five sums used in the game, then use these constants in the `cases` of the `switch` statement (lines 29–45). Doing so would prevent us from using `sumOfDice` as the `switch` statement's controlling expression, because Java does not allow an `int` to be compared to an enumeration constant. To achieve the same functionality as the current program, we would have to use a variable `currentSum` of type `Sum` as the `switch`'s controlling expression. Unfortunately, Java does not provide an easy way to convert an `int` value to a particular `enum` constant. Translating an `int` into an `enum` constant could be done with a separate `switch` statement. Clearly this would be cumbersome and not improve the readability of the program (thus defeating the purpose of using an `enum`).

6.11 Scope of Declarations

You've seen declarations of various Java entities, such as classes, methods, variables and parameters. Declarations introduce names that can be used to refer to such Java entities. The **scope** of a declaration is the portion of the program that can refer to the declared entity by its name. Such an entity is said to be "in scope" for that portion of the program. This section introduces several important scope issues. (For more scope information, see the *Java Language Specification, Section 6.3: Scope of a Declaration*, at `java.sun.com/docs/books/jls/third_edition/html/names.html#103228`.)

The basic scope rules are as follows:

1. The scope of a parameter declaration is the body of the method in which the declaration appears.

2. The scope of a local-variable declaration is from the point at which the declaration appears to the end of that block.

3. The scope of a local-variable declaration that appears in the initialization section of a `for` statement's header is the body of the `for` statement and the other expressions in the header.

4. A method or field's scope is the entire body of the class. This enables non-`static` methods of a class to use the fields and other methods of the class.

Any block may contain variable declarations. If a local variable or parameter in a method has the same name as a field of the class, the field is "hidden" until the block terminates execution—this is called **shadowing**. In Chapter 8, we discuss how to access shadowed fields.

Common Programming Error 6.10

A compilation error occurs when a local variable is declared more than once in a method.

Error-Prevention Tip 6.3

Use different names for fields and local variables to help prevent subtle logic errors that occur when a method is called and a local variable of the method shadows a field in the class.

The application in Fig. 6.11 and Fig. 6.12 demonstrates scoping issues with fields and local variables. When the application begins execution, class `ScopeTest`'s `main` method (Fig. 6.12, lines 7–11) creates an object of class `Scope` (line 9) and calls the object's `begin` method (line 11) to produce the program's output (shown in Fig. 6.12).

```java
1   // Fig. 6.11: Scope.java
2   // Scope class demonstrates field and local variable scopes.
3
4   public class Scope
5   {
6      // field that is accessible to all methods of this class
7      private int x = 1;
8
9      // method begin creates and initializes local variable x
10     // and calls methods useLocalVariable and useField
11     public void begin()
12     {
13        int x = 5; // method's local variable x shadows field x
14
15        System.out.printf( "local x in method begin is %d\n", x );
16
17        useLocalVariable(); // useLocalVariable has local x
18        useField(); // useField uses class Scope's field x
19        useLocalVariable(); // useLocalVariable reinitializes local x
20        useField(); // class Scope's field x retains its value
21
22        System.out.printf( "\nlocal x in method begin is %d\n", x );
23     } // end method begin
24
25     // create and initialize local variable x during each call
26     public void useLocalVariable()
27     {
28        int x = 25; // initialized each time useLocalVariable is called
29
30        System.out.printf(
31           "\nlocal x on entering method useLocalVariable is %d\n", x );
32        ++x; // modifies this method's local variable x
33        System.out.printf(
34           "local x before exiting method useLocalVariable is %d\n", x );
35     } // end method useLocalVariable
36
37     // modify class Scope's field x during each call
38     public void useField()
39     {
40        System.out.printf(
41           "\nfield x on entering method useField is %d\n", x );
42        x *= 10; // modifies class Scope's field x
```

Fig. 6.11 | `Scope` class demonstrating scopes of a field and local variables. (Part 1 of 2.)

```
43              System.out.printf(
44                  "field x before exiting method useField is %d\n", x );
45      } // end method useField
46  } // end class Scope
```

Fig. 6.11 | Scope class demonstrating scopes of a field and local variables. (Part 2 of 2.)

```
 1  // Fig. 6.12: ScopeTest.java
 2  // Application to test class Scope.
 3
 4  public class ScopeTest
 5  {
 6      // application starting point
 7      public static void main( String[] args )
 8      {
 9          Scope testScope = new Scope();
10          testScope.begin();
11      } // end main
12  } // end class ScopeTest
```

```
local x in method begin is 5

local x on entering method useLocalVariable is 25
local x before exiting method useLocalVariable is 26

field x on entering method useField is 1
field x before exiting method useField is 10

local x on entering method useLocalVariable is 25
local x before exiting method useLocalVariable is 26

field x on entering method useField is 10
field x before exiting method useField is 100

local x in method begin is 5
```

Fig. 6.12 | Application to test class Scope.

In class Scope, line 7 declares and initializes the field x to 1. This field is shadowed (hidden) in any block (or method) that declares a local variable named x. Method begin (lines 11–23) declares a local variable x (line 13) and initializes it to 5. This local variable's value is output to show that the field x (whose value is 1) is shadowed in method begin. The program declares two other methods—useLocalVariable (lines 26–35) and use-Field (lines 38–45)—that each take no arguments and return no results. Method begin calls each method twice (lines 17–20). Method useLocalVariable declares local variable x (line 28). When useLocalVariable is first called (line 17), it creates local variable x and initializes it to 25 (line 28), outputs the value of x (lines 30–31), increments x (line 32) and outputs the value of x again (lines 33–34). When useLocalVariable is called a second time (line 19), it recreates local variable x and re-initializes it to 25, so the output of each useLocalVariable call is identical.

Method useField does not declare any local variables. Therefore, when it refers to x, field x (line 7) of the class is used. When method useField is first called (line 18), it outputs the value (1) of field x (lines 40–41), multiplies the field x by 10 (line 42) and outputs the value (10) of field x again (lines 43–44) before returning. The next time method use-Field is called (line 20), the field has its modified value (10), so the method outputs 10, then 100. Finally, in method begin, the program outputs the value of local variable x again (line 22) to show that none of the method calls modified begin's local variable x, because the methods all referred to variables named x in other scopes.

6.12 Method Overloading

Methods of the same name can be declared in the same class, as long as they have different sets of parameters (determined by the number, types and order of the parameters)—this is called **method overloading**. When an overloaded method is called, the Java compiler selects the appropriate method by examining the number, types and order of the arguments in the call. Method overloading is commonly used to create several methods with the same name that perform the same or similar tasks, but on different types or different numbers of arguments. For example, Math methods abs, min and max (summarized in Section 6.3) are overloaded with four versions each:

1. One with two double parameters.

2. One with two float parameters.

3. One with two int parameters.

4. One with two long parameters.

Our next example demonstrates declaring and invoking overloaded methods. We present examples of overloaded constructors in Chapter 8.

Declaring Overloaded Methods
In our class MethodOverload (Fig. 6.13), we include two overloaded versions of a method called square—one that calculates the square of an int (and returns an int) and one that calculates the square of a double (and returns a double). Although these methods have the same name and similar parameter lists and bodies, think of them simply as *different* methods. It may help to think of the method names as "square of int" and "square of double," respectively. When the application begins execution, class MethodOverloadTest's main method (Fig. 6.14, lines 6–10) creates an object of class MethodOverload (line 8) and calls the object's method testOverloadedMethods (line 9) to produce the output (Fig. 6.14).

```
 1    // Fig. 6.13: MethodOverload.java
 2    // Overloaded method declarations.
 3
 4    public class MethodOverload
 5    {
 6       // test overloaded square methods
 7       public void testOverloadedMethods()
 8       {
 9          System.out.printf( "Square of integer 7 is %d\n", square( 7 ) );
10          System.out.printf( "Square of double 7.5 is %f\n", square( 7.5 ) );
11       } // end method testOverloadedMethods
12
```

Fig. 6.13 | Overloaded method declarations. (Part 1 of 2.)

```
13      // square method with int argument
14      public int square( int intValue )
15      {
16         System.out.printf( "\nCalled square with int argument: %d\n",
17            intValue );
18         return intValue * intValue;
19      } // end method square with int argument
20
21      // square method with double argument
22      public double square( double doubleValue )
23      {
24         System.out.printf( "\nCalled square with double argument: %f\n",
25            doubleValue );
26         return doubleValue * doubleValue;
27      } // end method square with double argument
28   } // end class MethodOverload
```

Fig. 6.13 | Overloaded method declarations. (Part 2 of 2.)

```
1    // Fig. 6.14: MethodOverloadTest.java
2    // Application to test class MethodOverload.
3
4    public class MethodOverloadTest
5    {
6       public static void main( String[] args )
7       {
8          MethodOverload methodOverload = new MethodOverload();
9          methodOverload.testOverloadedMethods();
10      } // end main
11   } // end class MethodOverloadTest
```

```
Called square with int argument: 7
Square of integer 7 is 49

Called square with double argument: 7.500000
Square of double 7.5 is 56.250000
```

Fig. 6.14 | Application to test class MethodOverload.

In Fig. 6.13, line 9 invokes method square with the argument 7. Literal integer values are treated as type int, so the method call in line 9 invokes the version of square at lines 14–19 that specifies an int parameter. Similarly, line 10 invokes method square with the argument 7.5. Literal floating-point values are treated as type double, so the method call in line 10 invokes the version of square at lines 22–27 that specifies a double parameter. Each method first outputs a line of text to prove that the proper method was called in each case. Note that the values in lines 10 and 24 are displayed with the format specifier %f and that we did not specify a precision in either case. By default, floating-point values are displayed with six digits of precision if the precision is not specified in the format specifier.

Distinguishing Between Overloaded Methods
The compiler distinguishes overloaded methods by their **signature**—a combination of the method's name and the number, types and order of its parameters. If the compiler looked only at method names during compilation, the code in Fig. 6.13 would be ambiguous—

the compiler would not know how to distinguish between the two `square` methods (lines 14–19 and 22–27). Internally, the compiler uses longer method names that include the original method name, the types of each parameter and the exact order of the parameters to determine whether the methods in a class are unique in that class.

For example, in Fig. 6.13, the compiler might use the logical name "square of int" for the `square` method that specifies an `int` parameter and "square of double" for the `square` method that specifies a `double` parameter (the actual names the compiler uses are messier). If `method1`'s declaration begins as

```
void method1( int a, float b )
```

then the compiler might use the logical name "`method1` of `int` and `float`." If the parameters are specified as

```
void method1( float a, int b )
```

then the compiler might use the logical name "`method1` of `float` and `int`." Note that the order of the parameter types is important—the compiler considers the preceding two `method1` headers to be distinct.

Return Types of Overloaded Methods

In discussing the logical names of methods used by the compiler, we did not mention the return types of the methods. *Method calls cannot be distinguished by return type.* If you had overloaded methods that differed only by their return types and you called one of the methods in a standalone statement as in:

```
square( 2 );
```

the compiler would not be able to determine the version of the method to call, because the return value is ignored. Figure 6.15 illustrates the compiler errors generated when two methods have the same signature and different return types. Overloaded methods can have different return types if the methods have different parameter lists. Also, overloaded methods need not have the same number of parameters.

 Common Programming Error 6.11

Declaring overloaded methods with identical parameter lists is a compilation error regardless of whether the return types are different.

```java
1   // Fig. 6.15: MethodOverloadError.java
2   // Overloaded methods with identical signatures
3   // cause compilation errors, even if return types are different.
4
5   public class MethodOverloadError
6   {
7      // declaration of method square with int argument
8      public int square( int x )
9      {
10        return x * x;
11     }
```

Fig. 6.15 | Overloaded method declarations with identical signatures cause compilation errors, even if the return types are different. (Part 1 of 2.)

```
12
13     // second declaration of method square with int argument
14     // causes compilation error even though return types are different
15     public double square( int y )
16     {
17        return y * y;
18     }
19  } // end class MethodOverloadError
```

```
MethodOverloadError.java:15: square(int) is already defined in
MethodOverloadError
    public double square( int y )
                  ^
1 error
```

Fig. 6.15 | Overloaded method declarations with identical signatures cause compilation errors, even if the return types are different. (Part 2 of 2.)

6.13 (Optional) GUI and Graphics Case Study: Colors and Filled Shapes

Although you can create many interesting designs with just lines and basic shapes, class Graphics provides many more capabilities. The next two features we introduce are colors and filled shapes. Adding color enriches the drawings a user sees on the computer screen. Shapes can be filled with solid colors.

Colors displayed on computer screens are defined by their red, green, and blue components (called **RGB values**) that have integer values from 0 to 255. The higher the value of a component color, the richer that shade will be in the final color. Java uses class **Color** in package java.awt to represent colors using their RGB values. For convenience, class Color (java.sun.com/javase/6/docs/api/java/awt/Color.html) contains 13 predefined static Color objects—BLACK, BLUE, CYAN, DARK_GRAY, GRAY, GREEN, LIGHT_GRAY, MAGENTA, ORANGE, PINK, RED, WHITE and YELLOW. Each can be accessed via the class name and a dot (.) as in Color.RED. Class Color also contains a constructor of the form:

```
public Color( int r, int g, int b )
```

so you can create custom colors by specifying the red, green and blue component values.

Graphics methods **fillRect** and **fillOval** draw filled rectangles and ovals, respectively. These have the same parameters as drawRect and drawOval; the first two are the coordinates for the upper-left corner of the shape, while the next two determine the width and height. The example in Fig. 6.16 and Fig. 6.17 demonstrates colors and filled shapes by drawing and displaying a yellow smiley face on the screen.

```
1  // Fig. 6.16: DrawSmiley.java
2  // Demonstrates filled shapes.
3  import java.awt.Color;
4  import java.awt.Graphics;
5  import javax.swing.JPanel;
6
```

Fig. 6.16 | Drawing a smiley face using colors and filled shapes. (Part 1 of 2.)

```
 7
 8  {
 9     public void paintComponent( Graphics g )
10     {
11        super.paintComponent( g );
12
13        // draw the face
14        g.setColor( Color.YELLOW );
15        g.fillOval( 10, 10, 200, 200 );
16
17        // draw the eyes
18        g.setColor( Color.BLACK );
19        g.fillOval( 55, 65, 30, 30 );
20        g.fillOval( 135, 65, 30, 30 );
21
22        // draw the mouth
23        g.fillOval( 50, 110, 120, 60 );
24
25        // "touch up" the mouth into a smile
26        g.setColor( Color.YELLOW );
27        g.fillRect( 50, 110, 120, 30 );
28        g.fillOval( 50, 120, 120, 40 );
29     } // end method paintComponent
30  } // end class DrawSmiley
```

Fig. 6.16 | Drawing a smiley face using colors and filled shapes. (Part 2 of 2.)

The import statements in lines 3–5 of Fig. 6.16 import classes Color, Graphics and JPanel. Class DrawSmiley (lines 7–30) uses class Color to specify drawing colors, and uses class Graphics to draw. Class JPanel again provides the area in which we draw. Line 14 in method paintComponent uses Graphics method **setColor** to set the current drawing color to Color.YELLOW. Method setColor requires one argument, the Color to set as the drawing color. In this case, we use the predefined object Color.YELLOW. Line 15 draws a circle with diameter 200 to represent the face—when the width and height arguments are identical, method fillOval draws a circle. Next, line 18 sets the color to Color.Black, and lines 19–20 draw the eyes. Line 23 draws the mouth as an oval, but this is not quite what we want. To create a happy face, we'll "touch up" the mouth. Line 26 sets the color to Color.YELLOW, so any shapes we draw will blend in with the face. Line 27 draws a rectangle that is half the mouth's height. This "erases" the top half of the mouth, leaving just the bottom half. To create a better smile, line 28 draws another oval to slightly cover the upper portion of the mouth. Class DrawSmileyTest (Fig. 6.17) creates and displays a JFrame containing the drawing. When the JFrame is displayed, the system calls method paintComponent to draw the smiley face.

```
1  // Fig. 6.17: DrawSmileyTest.java
2  // Test application that displays a smiley face.
3  import javax.swing.JFrame;
4
5  public class DrawSmileyTest
6  {
```

Fig. 6.17 | Creating JFrame to display a smiley face. (Part 1 of 2.)

```
 7      public static void main( String[] args )
 8      {
 9         DrawSmiley panel = new DrawSmiley();
10         JFrame application = new JFrame();
11
12         application.setDefaultCloseOperation( JFrame.EXIT_ON_CLOSE );
13         application.add( panel );
14         application.setSize( 230, 250 );
15         application.setVisible( true );
16      } // end main
17   } // end class DrawSmileyTest
```

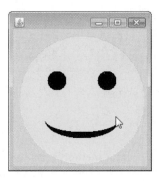

Fig. 6.17 | Creating `JFrame` to display a smiley face. (Part 2 of 2.)

GUI and Graphics Case Study Exercises

6.1   Using method `fillOval`, draw a bull's-eye that alternates between two random colors, as in Fig. 6.18. Use the constructor `Color( int r, int g, int b )` with random arguments to generate random colors.

Fig. 6.18 | A bull's-eye with two alternating, random colors.

6.2   Create a program that draws 10 random filled shapes in random colors, positions and sizes (Fig. 6.19). Method `paintComponent` should contain a loop that iterates 10 times. In each iteration, the loop should determine whether to draw a filled rectangle or an oval, create a random color and choose coordinates and dimensions at random. The coordinates should be chosen based on the panel's width and height. Lengths of sides should be limited to half the width or height of the window.

Fig. 6.19 | Randomly generated shapes.

6.14 Wrap-Up

In this chapter, you learned more about method declarations. You also learned the difference between non-static and static methods and how to call static methods by preceding the method name with the name of the class in which it appears and the dot (.) separator. You learned how to use operators + and += to perform string concatenations. We discussed how the method-call stack and activation records keep track of the methods that have been called and where each method must return to when it completes its task. We also discussed Java's promotion rules for converting implicitly between primitive types and how to perform explicit conversions with cast operators. Next, you learned about some of the commonly used packages in the Java API.

You saw how to declare named constants using both enum types and public static final variables. You used class Random to generate random numbers for simulations. You also learned about the scope of fields and local variables in a class. Finally, you learned that multiple methods in one class can be overloaded by providing methods with the same name and different signatures. Such methods can be used to perform the same or similar tasks using different types or different numbers of parameters.

In Chapter 7, you'll learn how to maintain lists and tables of data in arrays. You'll see a more elegant implementation of the application that rolls a die 6000 times and two enhanced versions of our GradeBook case study that you studied in Chapters 3–5. You'll also learn how to access an application's command-line arguments that are passed to method main when an application begins execution.

Summary

Section 6.1 Introduction

- Experience has shown that the best way to develop and maintain a large program is to construct it from small, simple pieces, or modules. This technique is called divide and conquer.

Section 6.2 Program Modules in Java

- Methods are declared within classes. Classes are typically grouped into packages so they can be imported and reused.

- Methods allow you to modularize a program by separating its tasks into self-contained units. The statements in a method are written only once and hidden from other methods.

- Using existing methods as building blocks to create new programs is a form of software reusability that allows you to avoid repeating code within a program.

Section 6.3 `static` Methods, `static` Fields and Class `Math`

- A method call specifies the name of the method to call and provides the arguments that the called method requires to perform its task. When the method call completes, the method returns either a result, or simply control, to its caller.

- A class may contain `static` methods to perform common tasks that do not require an object of the class. Any data a `static` method might require to perform its tasks can be sent to the method as arguments in a method call. A `static` method is called by specifying the name of the class in which the method is declared followed by a dot (.) and the method name, as in

  ClassName.methodName(arguments)

- Class `Math` provides `static` methods for performing common mathematical calculations.

- The constant `Math.PI` (3.141592653589793) is the ratio of a circle's circumference to its diameter. The constant `Math.E` (2.718281828459045) is the base value for natural logarithms (calculated with `static` `Math` method `log`).

- `Math.PI` and `Math.E` are declared with the modifiers `public`, `final` and `static`. Making them `public` allows you to use these fields in your own classes. A field declared with keyword `final` is constant—its value cannot be changed after it's initialized. Both `PI` and `E` are declared `final` because their values never change. Making these fields `static` allows them to be accessed via the class name `Math` and a dot (.) separator, just like class `Math`'s methods.

- All the objects of a class share one copy of the class's `static` fields. Together the class variables and instance variables represent the fields of a class.

- When you execute the Java Virtual Machine (JVM) with the `java` command, the JVM loads the class you specify and uses that class name to invoke method `main`. You can specify additional command-line arguments that the JVM will pass to your application.

- You can place a `main` method in every class you declare—only the `main` method in the class you use to execute the application will be called by the `java` command.

Section 6.4 Declaring Methods with Multiple Parameters

- When a method is called, the program makes a copy of the method's argument values and assigns them to the method's corresponding parameters. When program control returns to the point in the program where the method was called, the method's parameters are removed from memory.

- A method can return at most one value, but the returned value could be a reference to an object that contains many values.

- Variables should be declared as fields of a class only if they are required for use in more than one method of the class or if the program should save their values between calls to the class's methods.

Section 6.5 Notes on Declaring and Using Methods

- There are three ways to call a method—using a method name by itself to call another method of the same class; using a variable that contains a reference to an object, followed by a dot (.) and the method name to call a method of the referenced object; and using the class name and a dot (.) to call a `static` method of a class.

- There are three ways to return control to a statement that calls a method. If the method does not return a result, control returns when the program flow reaches the method-ending right brace or when the statement

      return;

  is executed. If the method returns a result, the statement

      return *expression*;

  evaluates the *expression*, then immediately returns the resulting value to the caller.
- When a method has more than one parameter, the parameters are specified as a comma-separated list. There must be one argument in the method call for each parameter in the method declaration. Also, each argument must be consistent with the type of the corresponding parameter. If a method does not accept arguments, the parameter list is empty.
- Strings can be concatenated using operator +, which places the characters of the right operand at the end of those in the left operand.
- Every primitive value and object in Java has a String representation. When an object is concatenated with a String, the object is converted to a String, then the two Strings are concatenated.
- If a boolean is concatenated with a String, the word "true" or the word "false" is used to represent the boolean value.
- All objects in Java have a special method named toString that returns a String representation of the object's contents. When an object is concatenated with a String, the JVM implicitly calls the object's toString method to obtain the string representation of the object.
- Programmers sometimes break large String literals into several smaller Strings and place them on multiple lines of code for readability, then reassemble the Strings using concatenation.

Section 6.6 Method-Call Stack and Activation Records
- Stacks are known as last-in, first-out (LIFO) data structures—the last item pushed (inserted) on the stack is the first item popped (removed) from the stack.
- A called method must know how to return to its caller, so the return address of the calling method is pushed onto the program-execution stack when the method is called. If a series of method calls occurs, the successive return addresses are pushed onto the stack in last-in, first-out order so that the last method to execute will be the first to return to its caller.
- The program-execution stack contains the memory for the local variables used in each invocation of a method during a program's execution. This data is known as the method call's activation record or stack frame. When a method call is made, the activation record for that method call is pushed onto the program-execution stack. When the method returns to its caller, its activation record call is popped off the stack and the local variables are no longer known to the program. If such a local variable holds the only reference to an object, the object can no longer be accessed by the program and will eventually be deleted from memory during "garbage collection."
- The amount of memory in a computer is finite, so only a certain amount of memory can be used to store activation records on the program-execution stack. If there are more method calls than can have their activation records stored on the program-execution stack, an error known as a stack overflow occurs. The application will compile correctly, but its execution causes a stack overflow.

Section 6.7 Argument Promotion and Casting
- Argument promotion converts an argument's value to the type that the method expects to receive in its corresponding parameter.
- Promotion rules apply to expressions containing values of two or more primitive types and to primitive-type values passed as arguments to methods. Each value is promoted to the "highest"

type in the expression. In cases where information may be lost due to conversion, the Java compiler requires you to use a cast operator to explicitly force the conversion to occur.

Section 6.9 Case Study: Random-Number Generation

- Objects of class Random (package java.util) can produce random int, long, float or double values. Math method random can produce double values in the range $0.0 \le x < 1.0$, where x is the value returned by method random.

- Random method nextInt generates a random int value in the range $-2,147,483,648$ to $+2,147,483,647$. The values returned by nextInt are actually pseudorandom numbers—a sequence of values produced by a complex mathematical calculation. That calculation uses the current time of day to seed the random-number generator such that each execution of a program yields a different sequence of random values.

- Class Random provides another version of method nextInt that receives an int argument and returns a value from 0 up to, but not including, the argument's value.

- Random numbers in a range can be generated with

      number = *shiftingValue* + randomNumbers.nextInt(*scalingFactor*);

  where *shiftingValue* specifies the first number in the desired range of consecutive integers, and *scalingFactor* specifies how many numbers are in the range.

- Random numbers can be chosen from nonconsecutive integer ranges, as in

      number = *shiftingValue* +
          differenceBetweenValues * randomNumbers.nextInt(*scalingFactor*);

  where *shiftingValue* specifies the first number in the range of values, *differenceBetweenValues* represents the difference between consecutive numbers in the sequence and *scalingFactor* specifies how many numbers are in the range.

- For debugging, it's sometimes useful to repeat the sequence of pseudorandom numbers during each program execution. To do so, pass a long integer value to the Random object's constructor. Using the same seed every time the program executes, produces the same sequence of numbers.

Section 6.10 Case Study: A Game of Chance; Introducing Enumerations

- An enumeration is introduced by the keyword enum and a type name. As with any class, braces ({ and }) delimit the body of an enum declaration. Inside the braces is a comma-separated list of enumeration constants, each representing a unique value. The identifiers in an enum must be unique. Variables of an enum type can be assigned only constants of that enum type.

- Constants can also be declared as public final static variables. Such constants are declared with all capital letters by convention to make them stand out in the program.

Section 6.11 Scope of Declarations

- Scope is the portion of the program in which an entity, such as a variable or a method, can be referred to by its name. Such an entity is said to be "in scope" for that portion of the program.

- The scope of a parameter declaration is the body of the method in which the declaration appears.

- The scope of a local-variable declaration is from the point at which the declaration appears to the end of that block.

- The scope of a local-variable declaration that appears in the initialization section of a for statement's header is the body of the for statement and the other expressions in the header.

- The scope of a method or field of a class is the entire body of the class. This enables a class's methods to use simple names to call the class's other methods and to access the class's fields.

- Any block may contain variable declarations. If a local variable or parameter in a method has the same name as a field, the field is shadowed until the block terminates execution.

Section 6.12 Method Overloading

- Java allows several methods of the same name to be declared in a class, as long as the methods have different sets of parameters (determined by the number, order and types of the parameters). This technique is called method overloading.

- Overloaded methods are distinguished by their signatures—combinations of the methods' names and the number, types and order of their parameters. Methods cannot be distinguished by return type.

Terminology

activation record 212
argument promotion 212
class method 205
class variable 206
command-line argument 207
divide and conquer 203
element of chance 215
enum keyword 224
enumeration 224
enumeration constant 224
final keyword 206
formal parameter 209
function 204
Java API 203
Java Application Programming Interface 203
Java class library 203
last-in, first-out (LIFO) data structure 212
Math.E 206
Math.PI 206
method 228
method-call stack 212
method overloading 228
module 203

nextInt method of class Random 216
pop off a stack 212
procedure 204
program execution stack 212
promotion rules for primitive types 212
pseudorandom numbers 216
push onto a stack 212
Random class 215
scale a range of values (random numbers) 216
scaling factor (random numbers) 216
scope of a declaration 225
seed the random-number generator 216
seed value (random numbers) 220
shadow a field 225
shift a range of numbers (random numbers) 216
shifting value (random numbers) 216
signature of a method 229
software reusability 204
stack 211
stack frame 212
stack overflow 212
string concatenation 210

Self-Review Exercises

6.1   Fill in the blanks in each of the following statements:

a) A method is invoked with a(n) _____.

b) A variable known only within the method in which it's declared is called a(n) _____.

c) The _____ statement in a called method can be used to pass the value of an expression back to the calling method.

d) The keyword _____ indicates that a method does not return a value.

e) Data can be added or removed only from the _____ of a stack.

f) Stacks are known as _____ data structures—the last item pushed (inserted) on the stack is the first item popped (removed) from the stack.

g) The three ways to return control from a called method to a caller are _____, _____ and _____.

h) An object of class _____ produces random numbers.

i) The program-execution stack contains the memory for local variables on each invocation of a method during a program's execution. This data, stored as a portion of the program-execution stack, is known as the _____ or _____ of the method call.

    j) If there are more method calls than can be stored on the program-execution stack, an error known as a(n) _____ occurs.

    k) The _____ of a declaration is the portion of a program that can refer to the entity in the declaration by name.

    l) It's possible to have several methods with the same name that each operate on different types or numbers of arguments. This feature is called method _____.

    m) The program-execution stack is also referred to as the _____ stack.

6.2 For the class Craps in Fig. 6.9, state the scope of each of the following entities:
    a) the variable randomNumbers.
    b) the variable die1.
    c) the method rollDice.
    d) the method play.
    e) the variable sumOfDice.

6.3 Write an application that tests whether the examples of the Math class method calls shown in Fig. 6.2 actually produce the indicated results.

6.4 Give the method header for each of the following methods:
    a) Method hypotenuse, which takes two double-precision, floating-point arguments side1 and side2 and returns a double-precision, floating-point result.
    b) Method smallest, which takes three integers x, y and z and returns an integer.
    c) Method instructions, which does not take any arguments and does not return a value. [*Note:* Such methods are commonly used to display instructions to a user.]
    d) Method intToFloat, which takes an integer argument number and returns a floating-point result.

6.5 Find the error in each of the following program segments. Explain how to correct the error.
    a)
```java
void g()
{
    System.out.println( "Inside method g" );

    void h()
    {
        System.out.println( "Inside method h" );
    }
}
```
    b)
```java
int sum( int x, int y )
{
    int result;
    result = x + y;
}
```
    c)
```java
void f( float a );
{
    float a;
    System.out.println( a );
}
```
    d)
```java
void product()
{
    int a = 6, b = 5, c = 4, result;
    result = a * b * c;
    System.out.printf( "Result is %d\n", result );
    return result;
}
```

6.6   Write a complete Java application to prompt the user for the `double` radius of a sphere, and call method `sphereVolume` to calculate and display the volume of the sphere. Use the following statement to calculate the volume:

```
double volume = ( 4.0 / 3.0 ) * Math.PI * Math.pow( radius, 3 )
```

Answers to Self-Review Exercises

6.1   a) method call. b) local variable. c) return. d) void. e) top. f) last-in, first-out (LIFO). g) return; or return *expression*; or encountering the closing right brace of a method. h) Random. i) activation record, stack frame. j) stack overflow. k) scope. l) method overloading. m) method call.

6.2   a) class body. b) block that defines method `rollDice`'s body. c) class body. d) class body. e) block that defines method `play`'s body.

6.3   The following solution demonstrates the Math class methods in Fig. 6.2:

```
 1   // Exercise 6.3: MathTest.java
 2   // Testing the Math class methods.
 3
 4   public class MathTest
 5   {
 6      public static void main( String[] args )
 7      {
 8         System.out.printf( "Math.abs( 23.7 ) = %f\n", Math.abs( 23.7 ) );
 9         System.out.printf( "Math.abs( 0.0 ) = %f\n", Math.abs( 0.0 ) );
10         System.out.printf( "Math.abs( -23.7 ) = %f\n", Math.abs( -23.7 ) );
11         System.out.printf( "Math.ceil( 9.2 ) = %f\n", Math.ceil( 9.2 ) );
12         System.out.printf( "Math.ceil( -9.8 ) = %f\n", Math.ceil( -9.8 ) );
13         System.out.printf( "Math.cos( 0.0 ) = %f\n", Math.cos( 0.0 ) );
14         System.out.printf( "Math.exp( 1.0 ) = %f\n", Math.exp( 1.0 ) );
15         System.out.printf( "Math.exp( 2.0 ) = %f\n", Math.exp( 2.0 ) );
16         System.out.printf( "Math.floor( 9.2 ) = %f\n", Math.floor( 9.2 ) );
17         System.out.printf( "Math.floor( -9.8 ) = %f\n",
18            Math.floor( -9.8 ) );
19         System.out.printf( "Math.log( Math.E ) = %f\n",
20            Math.log( Math.E ) );
21         System.out.printf( "Math.log( Math.E * Math.E ) = %f\n",
22            Math.log( Math.E * Math.E ) );
23         System.out.printf( "Math.max( 2.3, 12.7 ) = %f\n",
24            Math.max( 2.3, 12.7 ) );
25         System.out.printf( "Math.max( -2.3, -12.7 ) = %f\n",
26            Math.max( -2.3, -12.7 ) );
27         System.out.printf( "Math.min( 2.3, 12.7 ) = %f\n",
28            Math.min( 2.3, 12.7 ) );
29         System.out.printf( "Math.min( -2.3, -12.7 ) = %f\n",
30            Math.min( -2.3, -12.7 ) );
31         System.out.printf( "Math.pow( 2.0, 7.0 ) = %f\n",
32            Math.pow( 2.0, 7.0 ) );
33         System.out.printf( "Math.pow( 9.0, 0.5 ) = %f\n",
34            Math.pow( 9.0, 0.5 ) );
35         System.out.printf( "Math.sin( 0.0 ) = %f\n", Math.sin( 0.0 ) );
36         System.out.printf( "Math.sqrt( 900.0 ) = %f\n",
37            Math.sqrt( 900.0 ) );
38         System.out.printf( "Math.tan( 0.0 ) = %f\n", Math.tan( 0.0 ) );
39      } // end main
40   } // end class MathTest
```

```
Math.abs( 23.7 ) = 23.700000
Math.abs( 0.0 ) = 0.000000
Math.abs( -23.7 ) = 23.700000
Math.ceil( 9.2 ) = 10.000000
Math.ceil( -9.8 ) = -9.000000
Math.cos( 0.0 ) = 1.000000
Math.exp( 1.0 ) = 2.718282
Math.exp( 2.0 ) = 7.389056
Math.floor( 9.2 ) = 9.000000
Math.floor( -9.8 ) = -10.000000
Math.log( Math.E ) = 1.000000
Math.log( Math.E * Math.E ) = 2.000000
Math.max( 2.3, 12.7 ) = 12.700000
Math.max( -2.3, -12.7 ) = -2.300000
Math.min( 2.3, 12.7 ) = 2.300000
Math.min( -2.3, -12.7 ) = -12.700000
Math.pow( 2.0, 7.0 ) = 128.000000
Math.pow( 9.0, 0.5 ) = 3.000000
Math.sin( 0.0 ) = 0.000000
Math.sqrt( 900.0 ) = 30.000000
Math.tan( 0.0 ) = 0.000000
```

6.4   a) `double hypotenuse( double side1, double side2 )`

        b) `int smallest( int x, int y, int z )`

        c) `void instructions()`

        d) `float intToFloat( int number )`

6.5   a) Error: Method h is declared within method g.

           Correction: Move the declaration of h outside the declaration of g.

        b) Error: The method is supposed to return an integer, but does not.

           Correction: Delete the variable `result`, and place the statement

               `return x + y;`

           in the method, or add the following statement at the end of the method body:

               `return result;`

        c) Error: The semicolon after the right parenthesis of the parameter list is incorrect, and the parameter a should not be redeclared in the method.

           Correction: Delete the semicolon after the right parenthesis of the parameter list, and delete the declaration `float a;`.

        d) Error: The method returns a value when it's not supposed to.

           Correction: Change the return type from `void` to `int`.

6.6   The following solution calculates the volume of a sphere, using the radius entered by the user:

```
 1   // Exercise 6.6: Sphere.java
 2   // Calculate the volume of a sphere.
 3   import java.util.Scanner;
 4
 5   public class Sphere
 6   {
 7      // obtain radius from user and display volume of sphere
 8      public void determineSphereVolume()
 9      {
10         Scanner input = new Scanner( System.in );
11
12         System.out.print( "Enter radius of sphere: " );
13         double radius = input.nextDouble();
14
15         System.out.printf( "Volume is %f\n", sphereVolume( radius ) );
16      } // end method determineSphereVolume
17
```

```
18      // calculate and return sphere volume
19      public double sphereVolume( double radius )
20      {
21          double volume = ( 4.0 / 3.0 ) * Math.PI * Math.pow( radius, 3 );
22          return volume;
23      } // end method sphereVolume
24   } // end class Sphere
```

```
1    // Exercise 6.6: SphereTest.java
2    // Calculate the volume of a sphere.
3
4    public class SphereTest
5    {
6        // application starting point
7        public static void main( String[] args )
8        {
9            Sphere mySphere = new Sphere();
10           mySphere.determineSphereVolume();
11       } // end main
12   } // end class SphereTest
```

```
Enter radius of sphere: 4
Volume is 268.082573
```

Exercises

6.7 What is the value of x after each of the following statements is executed?
a) x = Math.abs(7.5);
b) x = Math.floor(7.5);
c) x = Math.abs(0.0);
d) x = Math.ceil(0.0);
e) x = Math.abs(-6.4);
f) x = Math.ceil(-6.4);
g) x = Math.ceil(-Math.abs(-8 + Math.floor(-5.5)));

6.8 *(Parking Charges)* A parking garage charges a $2.00 minimum fee to park for up to three hours. The garage charges an additional $0.50 per hour for each hour *or part thereof* in excess of three hours. The maximum charge for any given 24-hour period is $10.00. Assume that no car parks for longer than 24 hours at a time. Write an application that calculates and displays the parking charges for each customer who parked in the garage yesterday. You should enter the hours parked for each customer. The program should display the charge for the current customer and should calculate and display the running total of yesterday's receipts. It should use the method calculateCharges to determine the charge for each customer.

6.9 *(Rounding Numbers)* Math.floor can be used to round values to the nearest integer—e.g.,

    y = Math.floor(x + 0.5);

will round the number x to the nearest integer and assign the result to y. Write an application that reads double values and uses the preceding statement to round each of the numbers to the nearest integer. For each number processed, display both the original number and the rounded number.

6.10 Answer each of the following questions:
a) What does it mean to choose numbers "at random"?
b) Why is the nextInt method of class Random useful for simulating games of chance?
c) Why is it often necessary to scale or shift the values produced by a Random object?
d) Why is computerized simulation of real-world situations a useful technique?

6.11   Write statements that assign random integers to the variable n in the following ranges:
a) $1 \leq n \leq 2$.
b) $1 \leq n \leq 100$.
c) $0 \leq n \leq 9$.
d) $1000 \leq n \leq 1112$.
e) $-1 \leq n \leq 1$.
f) $-3 \leq n \leq 11$.

6.12   For each of the following sets of integers, write a single statement that will display a number at random from the set:
a) 2, 4, 6, 8, 10.
b) 3, 5, 7, 9, 11.
c) 6, 10, 14, 18, 22.

6.13   *(Exponentiation)* Write a method `integerPower(base, exponent)` that returns the value of

$$base^{\,exponent}$$

For example, `integerPower(3, 4)` calculates 3^4 (or 3 * 3 * 3 * 3). Assume that `exponent` is a positive, nonzero integer and that `base` is an integer. Method `integerPower` should use a `for` or `while` statement to control the calculation. Do not use any `Math` class methods. Incorporate this method into an application that reads integer values for `base` and `exponent` and performs the calculation with the `integerPower` method.

6.14   *(Multiples)* Write a method `isMultiple` that determines, for a pair of integers, whether the second integer is a multiple of the first. The method should take two integer arguments and return `true` if the second is a multiple of the first and `false` otherwise. [*Hint:* Use the remainder operator.] Incorporate this method into an application that inputs a series of pairs of integers (one pair at a time) and determines whether the second value in each pair is a multiple of the first.

6.15   *(Even or Odd)* Write a method `isEven` that uses the remainder operator (%) to determine whether an integer is even. The method should take an integer argument and return `true` if the integer is even and `false` otherwise. Incorporate this method into an application that inputs a sequence of integers (one at a time) and determines whether each is even or odd.

6.16   *(Displaying a Square of Asterisks)* Write a method `squareOfAsterisks` that displays a solid square (the same number of rows and columns) of asterisks whose side is specified in integer parameter `side`. For example, if `side` is 4, the method should display

```
****
****
****
****
```

Incorporate this method into an application that reads an integer value for `side` from the user and outputs the asterisks with the `squareOfAsterisks` method.

6.17   *(Displaying a Square of Any Character)* Modify the method created in Exercise 6.16 to receive a second parameter of type `char` called `fillCharacter`. Form the square using the char provided as an argument. Thus, if `side` is 5 and `fillCharacter` is #, the method should display

```
#####
#####
#####
#####
#####
```

Use the following statement (in which `input` is a `Scanner` object) to read a character from the user at the keyboard:

```
char fill = input.next().charAt( 0 );
```

6.18 *(Circle Area)* Write an application that prompts the user for the radius of a circle and uses a method called `circleArea` to calculate the area of the circle.

6.19 *(Separating Digits)* Write methods that accomplish each of the following tasks:
a) Calculate the integer part of the quotient when integer a is divided by integer b.
b) Calculate the integer remainder when integer a is divided by integer b.
c) Use the methods developed in parts (a) and (b) to write a method `displayDigits` that receives an integer between 1 and 99999 and displays it as a sequence of digits, separating each pair of digits by two spaces. For example, the integer 4562 should appear as

   4 5 6 2

Incorporate the methods into an application that inputs an integer and calls `displayDigits` by passing the method the integer entered. Display the results.

6.20 *(Temperature Conversions)* Implement the following integer methods:
a) Method `celsius` returns the Celsius equivalent of a Fahrenheit temperature, using the calculation

   `celsius = 5.0 / 9.0 * ( fahrenheit - 32 );`

b) Method `fahrenheit` returns the Fahrenheit equivalent of a Celsius temperature, using the calculation

   `fahrenheit = 9.0 / 5.0 * celsius + 32;`

c) Use the methods from parts (a) and (b) to write an application that enables the user either to enter a Fahrenheit temperature and display the Celsius equivalent or to enter a Celsius temperature and display the Fahrenheit equivalent.

6.21 *(Find the Minimum)* Write a method `minimum3` that returns the smallest of three floating-point numbers. Use the `Math.min` method to implement `minimum3`. Incorporate the method into an application that reads three values from the user, determines the smallest value and displays the result.

6.22 *(Perfect Numbers)* An integer number is said to be a *perfect number* if its factors, including 1 (but not the number itself), sum to the number. For example, 6 is a perfect number, because 6 = 1 + 2 + 3. Write a method `isPerfect` that determines if parameter `number` is a perfect number. Use this method in an application that displays all the perfect numbers between 1 and 1000. Display the factors of each perfect number to confirm that the number is indeed perfect. Challenge the computing power of your computer by testing numbers much larger than 1000. Display the results.

6.23 *(Reversing Digits)* Write a method that takes an integer value and returns the number with its digits reversed. For example, given the number 7631, the method should return 1367. Incorporate the method into an application that reads a value from the user and displays the result.

6.24 *(Greatest Common Divisor)* The *greatest common divisor* (*GCD*) of two integers is the largest integer that evenly divides each of the two numbers. Write a method `gcd` that returns the greatest common divisor of two integers. [*Hint:* You might want to use Euclid's algorithm. You can find information about the algorithm at `en.wikipedia.org/wiki/Euclidean_algorithm`.] Incorporate the method into an application that reads two values from the user and displays the result.

6.25 Write a method `qualityPoints` that inputs a student's average and returns 4 if the student's average is 90–100, 3 if the average is 80–89, 2 if the average is 70–79, 1 if the average is 60–69 and 0 if the average is lower than 60. Incorporate the method into an application that reads a value from the user and displays the result.

6.26 *(Coin Tossing)* Write an application that simulates coin tossing. Let the program toss a coin each time the user chooses the "Toss Coin" menu option. Count the number of times each side of the coin appears. Display the results. The program should call a separate method `flip` that takes no arguments and returns a value from a `Coin` enum (HEADS and TAILS). [*Note:* If the program realistically simulates coin tossing, each side of the coin should appear approximately half the time.]

6.27   *(Guess the Number)* Write an application that plays "guess the number" as follows: Your program chooses the number to be guessed by selecting a random integer in the range 1 to 1000. The application displays the prompt Guess a number between 1 and 1000. The player inputs a first guess. If the player's guess is incorrect, your program should display Too high. Try again. or Too low. Try again. to help the player "zero in" on the correct answer. The program should prompt the user for the next guess. When the user enters the correct answer, display Congratulations. You guessed the number!, and allow the user to choose whether to play again. [*Note:* The guessing technique employed in this problem is similar to a binary search, which is discussed in Chapter 19, Searching, Sorting and Big O.]

6.28   *(Guess the Number Modification)* Modify the program of Exercise 6.27 to count the number of guesses the player makes. If the number is 10 or fewer, display Either you know the secret or you got lucky! If the player guesses the number in 10 tries, display Aha! You know the secret! If the player makes more than 10 guesses, display You should be able to do better! Why should it take no more than 10 guesses? Well, with each "good guess," the player should be able to eliminate half of the numbers, then half of the remaining numbers, and so on.

6.29   *(Distance Between Points)* Write method distance to calculate the distance between two points (*x1*, *y1*) and (*x2*, *y2*). All numbers and return values should be of type double. Incorporate this method into an application that enables the user to enter the coordinates of the points.

6.30   *(Craps Game Modification)* Modify the craps program of Fig. 6.9 to allow wagering. Initialize variable bankBalance to 1000 dollars. Prompt the player to enter a wager. Check that wager is less than or equal to bankBalance, and if it's not, have the user reenter wager until a valid wager is entered. After a correct wager is entered, run one game of craps. If the player wins, increase bankBalance by wager and display the new bankBalance. If the player loses, decrease bankBalance by wager, display the new bankBalance, check whether bankBalance has become zero and, if so, display the message "Sorry. You busted!" As the game progresses, display various messages to create some "chatter," such as "Oh, you're going for broke, huh?" or "Aw c'mon, take a chance!" or "You're up big. Now's the time to cash in your chips!". Implement the "chatter" as a separate method that randomly chooses the string to display.

6.31   *(Table of Binary, Octal and Hexadecimal Numbers)* Write an application that displays a table of the binary, octal and hexadecimal equivalents of the decimal numbers in the range 1 through 256. If you are not familiar with these number systems, read Appendix H first.

Making a Difference

As computer costs decline, it becomes feasible for every student, regardless of economic circumstance, to have a computer and use it in school. This creates exciting possibilities for improving the educational experience of all students worldwide as suggested by the next five exercises. [*Note:* Check out initiatives such as the One Laptop Per Child Project (www.laptop.org). Also, research "green" laptops—what are some key "going green" characteristics of these devices? Look into the Electronic Product Environmental Assessment Tool (www.epeat.net) which can help you assess the "greenness" of desktops, notebooks and monitors to help you decide which products to purchase.]

6.32   *(Computer-Assisted Instruction)* The use of computers in education is referred to as *computer-assisted instruction* (*CAI*). Write a program that will help an elementary school student learn multiplication. Use a Random object to produce two positive one-digit integers. The program should then prompt the user with a question, such as

        How much is 6 times 7?

The student then inputs the answer. Next, the program checks the student's answer. If it's correct, display the message "Very good!" and ask another multiplication question. If the answer is wrong, display the message "No. Please try again." and let the student try the same question repeatedly until the student finally gets it right. A separate method should be used to generate each new question. This method should be called once when the application begins execution and each time the user answers the question correctly.

6.33 *(Computer-Assisted Instruction: Reducing Student Fatigue)* One problem in CAI environments is student fatigue. This can be reduced by varying the computer's responses to hold the student's attention. Modify the program of Exercise 6.32 so that various comments are displayed for each answer as follows:

Possible responses to a correct answer:

```
Very good!
Excellent!
Nice work!
Keep up the good work!
```

Possible responses to an incorrect answer:

```
No. Please try again.
Wrong. Try once more.
Don't give up!
No. Keep trying.
```

Use random-number generation to choose a number from 1 to 4 that will be used to select one of the four appropriate responses to each correct or incorrect answer. Use a switch statement to issue the responses.

6.34 *(Computer-Assisted Instruction: Monitoring Student Performance)* More sophisticated computer-assisted instruction systems monitor the student's performance over a period of time. The decision to begin a new topic is often based on the student's success with previous topics. Modify the program of Exercise 6.33 to count the number of correct and incorrect responses typed by the student. After the student types 10 answers, your program should calculate the percentage that are correct. If the percentage is lower than 75%, display "Please ask your teacher for extra help.", then reset the program so another student can try it. If the percentage is 75% or higher, display "Congratulations, you are ready to go to the next level!", then reset the program so another student can try it.

6.35 *(Computer-Assisted Instruction: Difficulty Levels)* Exercise 6.32 through Exercise 6.34 developed a computer-assisted instruction program to help teach an elementary school student multiplication. Modify the program to allow the user to enter a difficulty level. At a difficulty level of 1, the program should use only single-digit numbers in the problems; at a difficulty level of 2, numbers as large as two digits, and so on.

6.36 *(Computer-Assisted Instruction: Varying the Types of Problems)* Modify the program of Exercise 6.35 to allow the user to pick a type of arithmetic problem to study. An option of 1 means addition problems only, 2 means subtraction problems only, 3 means multiplication problems only, 4 means division problems only and 5 means a random mixture of all these types.

7

Now go, write it before them in a table, and note it in
a book.
—Isaiah 30:8

To go beyond is as wrong as to fall short.
—Confucius

Begin at the beginning, … and go on till you come to
the end: then stop.
—Lewis Carroll

Arrays and ArrayLists

Objectives

In this chapter you'll learn:

- What arrays are.

- To use arrays to store data in and retrieve data from lists and tables of values.

- To declare arrays, initialize arrays and refer to individual elements of arrays.

- To use the enhanced **for** statement to iterate through arrays.

- To pass arrays to methods.

- To declare and manipulate multidimensional arrays.

- To write methods that use variable-length argument lists.

- To read command-line arguments into a program.

7.1 Introduction

This chapter introduces **data structures**—collections of related data items. **Arrays** are data structures consisting of related data items of the same type. Arrays make it convenient to process related groups of values. Arrays remain the same length once they are created, although an array variable may be reassigned such that it refers to a new array of a different length. We study data structures in depth in Chapters 20–22.

After discussing how arrays are declared, created and initialized, we present practical examples that demonstrate common array manipulations. We also present a case study that examines how arrays can help simulate the shuffling and dealing of playing cards in a card-game application. We introduce Java's enhanced for statement, which allows a program to access the data in an array more easily than does the counter-controlled for statement presented in Section 5.3. We enhance the GradeBook case study from Chapters 3–5. In particular, we use arrays to enable the class to maintain a set of grades in memory and analyze student grades from multiple exams. We show how to use variable-length argument lists to create methods that can be called with varying numbers of arguments, and we demonstrate how to process command-line arguments in method main. Next, we present some common array manipulations with static methods of class Arrays from the java.util package.

Although commonly used, arrays have limited capabilities. For instance, you must specify an array's size, and if at execution time you wish to modify it, you must do so manually by creating a new array. At the end of this chapter, we introduce one of Java's prebuilt data structures from the Java API's collection classes. These offer greater capabilities than traditional arrays. They are reusable, reliable, powerful and efficient and have been carefully designed and tested to ensure quality and performance. We focus on the ArrayList collection. ArrayLists are similar to arrays but provide additional functionality, such as **dynamic resizing**—they automatically increase their size at execution time to accommodate additional elements.

7.2 Arrays

An array is a group of variables (called **elements** or **components**) containing values that all have the same type. Arrays are objects, so they are considered reference types. As you'll soon see, what we typically think of as an array is actually a reference to an array object in memory. The elements of an array can be either primitive types or reference types (including arrays, as we'll see in Section 7.9). To refer to a particular element in an array, we specify the name of the reference to the array and the position number of the element in the array. The position number of the element is called the element's **index** or **subscript**.

Figure 7.1 shows a logical representation of an integer array called c. This array contains 12 elements. A program refers to any one of these elements with an **array-access expression** that includes the name of the array followed by the index of the particular element in **square brackets ([])**. The first element in every array has **index zero** and is sometimes called the **zeroth element**. Thus, the elements of array c are c[0], c[1], c[2] and so on. The highest index in array c is 11, which is 1 less than 12—the number of elements in the array. Array names follow the same conventions as other variable names.

Fig. 7.1 | A 12-element array.

An index must be a nonnegative integer. A program can use an expression as an index. For example, if we assume that variable a is 5 and variable b is 6, then the statement

```
c[ a + b ] += 2;
```

adds 2 to array element c[11]. Note that an indexed array name is an array-access expression. Such expressions can be used on the left side of an assignment to place a new value into an array element.

Common Programming Error 7.1

An index must be an int value or a value of a type that can be promoted to int—namely, byte, short or char, but not long; otherwise, a compilation error occurs.

Let's examine array c in Fig. 7.1 more closely. The **name** of the array is c. Every array object knows its own length and stores it in a **length instance variable**. The expression c.length accesses array c's length field to determine the length of the array. Note that, even though the length instance variable of an array is public, it cannot be changed because it's a final variable. This array's 12 elements are referred to as c[0], c[1], c[2], ..., c[11]. The value of c[0] is -45, the value of c[1] is 6, the value of c[2] is 0, the value of c[7] is 62 and the value of c[11] is 78. To calculate the sum of the values contained in the first three elements of array c and store the result in variable sum, we would write

```
sum = c[ 0 ] + c[ 1 ] + c[ 2 ];
```

To divide the value of c[6] by 2 and assign the result to the variable x, we would write

```
x = c[ 6 ] / 2;
```

7.3 Declaring and Creating Arrays

Array objects occupy space in memory. Like other objects, arrays are created with keyword new. To create an array object, you specify the type of the array elements and the number of elements as part of an **array-creation expression** that uses keyword new. Such an expression returns a reference that can be stored in an array variable. The following declaration and array-creation expression create an array object containing 12 int elements and store the array's reference in array variable c:

```
int[] c = new int[ 12 ];
```

This expression can be used to create the array shown in Fig. 7.1. This task also can be performed in two steps as follows:

```
int[] c; // declare the array variable
c = new int[ 12 ]; // create the array; assign to array variable
```

In the declaration, the square brackets following the type indicate that c is a variable that will refer to an array (i.e., the variable will store an array reference). In the assignment statement, the array variable c receives the reference to a new array of 12 int elements. When an array is created, each element of the array receives a default value—zero for the numeric primitive-type elements, false for boolean elements and null for references. As you'll soon see, you can provide nondefault initial element values when you create an array.

 Common Programming Error 7.2
In an array declaration, specifying the number of elements in the square brackets of the declaration (e.g., int[12] c;) is a syntax error.

A program can create several arrays in a single declaration. The following declaration reserves 100 elements for b and 27 elements for x:

```
String[] b = new String[ 100 ], x = new String[ 27 ];
```

When type of the array and the square brackets are combined at the beginning of the declaration, all the identifiers in the declaration are array variables. In this case, variables b and x refer to String arrays. For readability, we prefer to declare only one variable per declaration. The preceding declaration is equivalent to:

```
String[] b = new String[ 100 ]; // create array b
String[] x = new String[ 27 ]; // create array x
```

Good Programming Practice 7.1

For readability, declare only one variable per declaration. Keep each declaration on a separate line, and include a comment describing the variable being declared.

When only one variable is declared in each declaration, the square brackets can be placed either after the type or after the array variable name, as in:

```
String b[] = new String[ 100 ]; // create array b
String x[] = new String[ 27 ]; // create array x
```

Common Programming Error 7.3

Declaring multiple array variables in a single declaration can lead to subtle errors. Consider the declaration int[] a, b, c;. If a, b and c should be declared as array variables, then this declaration is correct—placing square brackets directly following the type indicates that all the identifiers in the declaration are array variables. However, if only a is intended to be an array variable, and b and c are intended to be individual int variables, then this declaration is incorrect—the declaration int a[], b, c; would achieve the desired result.

A program can declare arrays of any type. Every element of a primitive-type array contains a value of the array's declared element type. Similarly, in an array of a reference type, every element is a reference to an object of the array's declared element type. For example, every element of an int array is an int value, and every element of a String array is a reference to a String object.

7.4 Examples Using Arrays

This section presents several examples that demonstrate declaring arrays, creating arrays, initializing arrays and manipulating array elements.

Creating and Initializing an Array
The application of Fig. 7.2 uses keyword new to create an array of 10 int elements, which are initially zero (the default for int variables).

```
 1  // Fig. 7.2: InitArray.java
 2  // Initializing the elements of an array to default values of zero.
 3
 4  public class InitArray
 5  {
 6     public static void main( String[] args )
 7     {
 8        int[] array; // declare array named array
 9
10        array = new int[ 10 ]; // create the array object
11
12        System.out.printf( "%s%8s\n", "Index", "Value" ); // column headings
13
```

Fig. 7.2 | Initializing the elements of an array to default values of zero. (Part 1 of 2.)

```
14          // output each array element's value
15          for ( int counter = 0; counter < array.length; counter++ )
16              System.out.printf( "%5d%8d\n", counter, array[ counter ] );
17      } // end main
18  } // end class InitArray
```

```
Index    Value
   0        0
   1        0
   2        0
   3        0
   4        0
   5        0
   6        0
   7        0
   8        0
   9        0
```

Fig. 7.2 | Initializing the elements of an array to default values of zero. (Part 2 of 2.)

Line 8 declares array—a reference capable of referring to an array of int elements. Line 10 creates the array object and assigns its reference to variable array. Line 12 outputs the column headings. The first column contains the index (0–9) of each array element, and the second column contains the default value (0) of each array element.

The for statement in lines 15–16 outputs the index number (represented by counter) and the value of each array element (represented by array[counter]). Note that the loop-control variable counter is initially 0—index values start at 0, so using zero-based counting allows the loop to access every element of the array. The for's loop-continuation condition uses the expression array.length (line 15) to determine the length of the array. In this example, the length of the array is 10, so the loop continues executing as long as the value of control variable counter is less than 10. The highest index value of a 10-element array is 9, so using the less-than operator in the loop-continuation condition guarantees that the loop does not attempt to access an element beyond the end of the array (i.e., during the final iteration of the loop, counter is 9). We'll soon see what Java does when it encounters such an out-of-range index at execution time.

Using an Array Initializer
You can create an array and initialize its elements with an **array initializer**—a comma-separated list of expressions (called an **initializer list**) enclosed in braces. In this case, the array length is determined by the number of elements in the initializer list. For example,

```
int[] n = { 10, 20, 30, 40, 50 };
```

creates a five-element array with index values 0–4. Element n[0] is initialized to 10, n[1] is initialized to 20, and so on. When the compiler encounters an array declaration that includes an initializer list, it counts the number of initializers in the list to determine the size of the array, then sets up the appropriate new operation "behind the scenes."

The application in Fig. 7.3 initializes an integer array with 10 values (line 9) and displays the array in tabular format. The code for displaying the array elements (lines 14–15) is identical to that in Fig. 7.2 (lines 15–16).

```
 1   // Fig. 7.3: InitArray.java
 2   // Initializing the elements of an array with an array initializer.
 3
 4   public class InitArray
 5   {
 6      public static void main( String[] args )
 7      {
 8         // initializer list specifies the value for each element
 9         int[] array = { 32, 27, 64, 18, 95, 14, 90, 70, 60, 37 };
10
11         System.out.printf( "%s%8s\n", "Index", "Value" ); // column headings
12
13         // output each array element's value
14         for ( int counter = 0; counter < array.length; counter++ )
15            System.out.printf( "%5d%8d\n", counter, array[ counter ] );
16      } // end main
17   } // end class InitArray
```

```
Index   Value
    0      32
    1      27
    2      64
    3      18
    4      95
    5      14
    6      90
    7      70
    8      60
    9      37
```

Fig. 7.3 | Initializing the elements of an array with an array initializer.

Calculating the Values to Store in an Array

The application in Fig. 7.4 creates a 10-element array and assigns to each element one of the even integers from 2 to 20 (2, 4, 6, ..., 20). Then the application displays the array in tabular format. The for statement at lines 12–13 calculates an array element's value by multiplying the current value of the control variable counter by 2, then adding 2.

```
 1   // Fig. 7.4: InitArray.java
 2   // Calculating values to be placed into elements of an array.
 3
 4   public class InitArray
 5   {
 6      public static void main( String[] args )
 7      {
 8         final int ARRAY_LENGTH = 10; // declare constant
 9         int[] array = new int[ ARRAY_LENGTH ]; // create array
10
11         // calculate value for each array element
12         for ( int counter = 0; counter < array.length; counter++ )
13            array[ counter ] = 2 + 2 * counter;
14
```

Fig. 7.4 | Calculating the values to be placed into the elements of an array. (Part 1 of 2.)

```
15            System.out.printf( "%s%8s\n", "Index", "Value" ); // column headings
16
17            // output each array element's value
18            for ( int counter = 0; counter < array.length; counter++ )
19                System.out.printf( "%5d%8d\n", counter, array[ counter ] );
20        } // end main
21   } // end class InitArray
```

```
Index   Value
    0       2
    1       4
    2       6
    3       8
    4      10
    5      12
    6      14
    7      16
    8      18
    9      20
```

Fig. 7.4 | Calculating the values to be placed into the elements of an array. (Part 2 of 2.)

Line 8 uses the modifier final to declare the constant variable ARRAY_LENGTH with the value 10. Constant variables must be initialized before they are used and cannot be modified thereafter. If you attempt to modify a final variable after it's initialized in its declaration (as in line 8), the compiler issues an error message like

> cannot assign a value to final variable *variableName*

If an attempt is made to access the value of a final variable before it's initialized, the compiler issues an error message like

> variable *variableName* might not have been initialized

Good Programming Practice 7.2

*Constant variables also are called **named constants**. They often make programs more readable than programs that use literal values (e.g., 10)—a named constant such as ARRAY_LENGTH clearly indicates its purpose, whereas a literal value could have different meanings based on its context.*

Common Programming Error 7.4

Assigning a value to a constant variable after it has been initialized is a compilation error.

Common Programming Error 7.5

Attempting to use a constant before it's initialized is a compilation error.

Summing the Elements of an Array

Often, the elements of an array represent a series of values to be used in a calculation. If, for example, they represent exam grades, a professor may wish to total the elements of the array and use that sum to calculate the class average for the exam. The GradeBook examples in Figs. 7.14 and 7.18 use this technique.

Figure 7.5 sums the values contained in a 10-element integer array. The program declares, creates and initializes the array at line 8. The for statement performs the calculations. [*Note:* The values supplied as array initializers are often read into a program rather than specified in an initializer list. For example, an application could input the values from a user or from a file on disk (as discussed in Chapter 17, Files, Streams and Object Serialization). Reading the data into a program (rather than "hand coding" it into the program) makes the program more reusable, because it can be used with different sets of data.]

```
1   // Fig. 7.5: SumArray.java
2   // Computing the sum of the elements of an array.
3
4   public class SumArray
5   {
6      public static void main( String[] args )
7      {
8         int[] array = { 87, 68, 94, 100, 83, 78, 85, 91, 76, 87 };
9         int total = 0;
10
11         // add each element's value to total
12         for ( int counter = 0; counter < array.length; counter++ )
13            total += array[ counter ];
14
15         System.out.printf( "Total of array elements: %d\n", total );
16      } // end main
17   } // end class SumArray
```

```
Total of array elements: 849
```

Fig. 7.5 | Computing the sum of the elements of an array.

Using Bar Charts to Display Array Data Graphically

Many programs present data to users in a graphical manner. For example, numeric values are often displayed as bars in a bar chart. In such a chart, longer bars represent proportionally larger numeric values. One simple way to display numeric data graphically is with a bar chart that shows each numeric value as a bar of asterisks (*).

Professors often like to examine the distribution of grades on an exam. A professor might graph the number of grades in each of several categories to visualize the grade distribution. Suppose the grades on an exam were 87, 68, 94, 100, 83, 78, 85, 91, 76 and 87. Note that they include one grade of 100, two grades in the 90s, four grades in the 80s, two grades in the 70s, one grade in the 60s and no grades below 60. Our next application (Fig. 7.6) stores this grade distribution data in an array of 11 elements, each corresponding to a category of grades. For example, array[0] indicates the number of grades in the range 0–9, array[7] the number of grades in the range 70–79 and array[10] the number of 100 grades. The GradeBook classes later in the chapter (Figs. 7.14 and 7.18) contain code that calculates these grade frequencies based on a set of grades. For now, we manually create the array with the given grade frequencies.

The application reads the numbers from the array and graphs the information as a bar chart. It displays each grade range followed by a bar of asterisks indicating the number of grades in that range. To label each bar, lines 16–20 output a grade range (e.g., "70-79: ") based on the current value of counter. When counter is 10, line 17 outputs 100 with a field width of 5, followed by a colon and a space, to align the label "100: " with the other bar labels. The nested for statement (lines 23–24) outputs the bars. Note the loop-continuation condition at line 23 (stars < array[counter]). Each time the program reaches the inner for, the loop counts from 0 up to array[counter], thus using a value in array to determine the number of asterisks to display. In this example, no students received a grade below 60, so array[0]–array[5] contain zeroes, and no asterisks are displayed next to the first six grade ranges. In line 19, the format specifier %02d indicates that an int value should be formatted as a field of two digits. The **0 flag** in the format specifier displays a leading 0 for values with fewer digits than the field width (2).

```java
1   // Fig. 7.6: BarChart.java
2   // Bar chart printing program.
3
4   public class BarChart
5   {
6      public static void main( String[] args )
7      {
8         int[] array = { 0, 0, 0, 0, 0, 0, 1, 2, 4, 2, 1 };
9
10        System.out.println( "Grade distribution:" );
11
12        // for each array element, output a bar of the chart
13        for ( int counter = 0; counter < array.length; counter++ )
14        {
15           // output bar label ( "00-09: ", ..., "90-99: ", "100: " )
16           if ( counter == 10 )
17              System.out.printf( "%5d: ", 100 );
18           else
19              System.out.printf( "%02d-%02d: ",
20                 counter * 10, counter * 10 + 9  );
21
22           // print bar of asterisks
23           for ( int stars = 0; stars < array[ counter ]; stars++ )
24              System.out.print( "*" );
25
26           System.out.println(); // start a new line of output
27        } // end outer for
28     } // end main
29  } // end class BarChart
```

```
Grade distribution:
00-09:
10-19:
20-29:
30-39:
40-49:
50-59:
60-69: *
70-79: **
80-89: ****
90-99: **
  100: *
```

Fig. 7.6 | Bar chart printing program.

Using the Elements of an Array as Counters

Sometimes, programs use counter variables to summarize data, such as the results of a survey. In Fig. 6.8, we used separate counters in our die-rolling program to track the number of occurrences of each side of a six-sided die as the program rolled the die 6000 times. An array version of this application is shown in Fig. 7.7.

```java
1   // Fig. 7.7: RollDie.java
2   // Die-rolling program using arrays instead of switch.
3   import java.util.Random;
4
5   public class RollDie
6   {
7      public static void main( String[] args )
8      {
9         Random randomNumbers = new Random(); // random number generator
10        int[] frequency = new int[ 7 ]; // array of frequency counters
11
12        // roll die 6000 times; use die value as frequency index
13        for ( int roll = 1; roll <= 6000; roll++ )
14           ++frequency[ 1 + randomNumbers.nextInt( 6 ) ];
15
16        System.out.printf( "%s%10s\n", "Face", "Frequency" );
17
18        // output each array element's value
19        for ( int face = 1; face < frequency.length; face++ )
20           System.out.printf( "%4d%10d\n", face, frequency[ face ] );
21     } // end main
22  } // end class RollDie
```

```
Face Frequency
   1       988
   2       963
   3      1018
   4      1041
   5       978
   6      1012
```

Fig. 7.7 | Die-rolling program using arrays instead of switch.

Figure 7.7 uses the array frequency (line 10) to count the occurrences of each side of the die. *The single statement in line 14 of this program replaces lines 23–46 of Fig. 6.8.* Line 14 uses the random value to determine which frequency element to increment during each iteration of the loop. The calculation in line 14 produces random numbers from 1 to 6, so the array frequency must be large enough to store six counters. However, we use a seven-element array in which we ignore frequency[0]—it's more logical to have the face value 1 increment frequency[1] than frequency[0]. Thus, each face value is used as an index for array frequency. In line 14, the calculation inside the square brackets evaluates first to determine which element of the array to increment, then the ++ operator adds one to that element. We also replaced lines 50–52 from Fig. 6.8 by looping through array frequency to output the results (lines 19–20).

Using Arrays to Analyze Survey Results

Figure 7.8 uses arrays to summarize the results of data collected in a survey:

> *Forty students were asked to rate the quality of the food in the student cafeteria on a scale of 1 to 10 (where 1 means awful and 10 means excellent). Place the 40 responses in an integer array, and summarize the results of the poll.*

This is a typical array-processing application. We wish to summarize the number of responses of each type (i.e., 1 through 10). The array responses (lines 9–11) is a 40-element int array of the survey responses. We use an 11-element array frequency (line 12) to count the number of occurrences of each response (1 to 10). Each element is initialized to zero by default. As in Fig. 7.7, we ignore frequency[0].

```java
1   // Fig. 7.8: StudentPoll.java
2   // Poll analysis program.
3
4   public class StudentPoll
5   {
6      public static void main( String[] args )
7      {
8         // array of survey responses
9         int[] responses = { 1, 2, 6, 4, 8, 5, 9, 7, 8, 10, 1, 6, 3, 8, 6,
10           10, 3, 8, 2, 7, 6, 5, 7, 6, 8, 6, 7, 5, 6, 6, 5, 6, 7, 5, 6,
11           4, 8, 6, 8, 10 };
12        int[] frequency = new int[ 11 ]; // array of frequency counters
13
14        // for each answer, select responses element and use that value
15        // as frequency index to determine element to increment
16        for ( int answer = 0; answer < responses.length; answer++ )
17           ++frequency[ responses[ answer ] ];
18
19        System.out.printf( "%s%10s", "Rating", "Frequency" );
20
21        // output each array element's value
22        for ( int rating = 1; rating < frequency.length; rating++ )
23           System.out.printf( "%d%10d", rating, frequency[ rating ] );
24     } // end main
25  } // end class StudentPoll
```

```
Rating Frequency
     1         2
     2         2
     3         2
     4         2
     5         5
     6        11
     7         5
     8         7
     9         1
    10         3
```

Fig. 7.8 | Poll analysis program.

The for loop at lines 16–17 takes the responses one at a time from array responses and increments one of the 10 counters in the frequency array (frequency[1] to frequency[10]). The key statement in the loop is line 17, which increments the appropriate frequency counter, depending on the value of `responses[answer]`.

Let's consider several iterations of the `for` loop. When control variable `answer` is 0, the value of `responses[answer]` is the value of `responses[0]` (i.e., 1), so the program interprets `++frequency[responses[answer]]` as

```
++frequency[ 1 ]
```

which increments the value in array element 1. To evaluate the expression, start with the value in the innermost set of square brackets (`answer`). Once you know `answer`'s value (which is the value of the loop control variable in line 16), plug it into the expression and evaluate the next outer set of square brackets (i.e., `responses[answer]`, which is a value selected from the `responses` array in lines 9–11). Then use the resulting value as the index for the `frequency` array to specify which counter to increment.

When `answer` is 1, `responses[answer]` is the value of `responses[1]` (2), so the program interprets `++frequency[responses[answer]]` as

```
++frequency[ 2 ]
```

which increments array element 2.

When `answer` is 2, `responses[answer]` is the value of `responses[2]` (6), so the program interprets `++frequency[responses[answer]]` as

```
++frequency[ 6 ]
```

which increments array element 6, and so on. Regardless of the number of responses processed in the survey, the program requires only an 11-element array (ignoring element zero) to summarize the results, because all the response values are between 1 and 10 and the index values for an 11-element array are 0 through 10.

If the data in the `responses` array had contained invalid values, such as 13, the program would have attempted to add 1 to `frequency[13]`, which is outside the bounds of the array. Java doesn't allow this. When a Java program executes, the JVM checks array indices to ensure that they are greater than or equal to 0 and less than the length of the array—this is called **bounds checking**. If a program uses an invalid index, Java generates a so-called exception to indicate that an error occurred in the program at execution time. A control statement can be used to prevent such an "out-of-bounds" error from occurring. For example, the condition in a control statement could determine whether an index is valid before allowing it to be used in an array-access expression.

Error-Prevention Tip 7.1

An exception indicates that an error has occurred in a program. You often can write code to recover from an exception and continue program execution, rather than abnormally terminating the program. When a program attempts to access an element outside the array bounds, an `ArrayIndexOutOfBoundsException` occurs. Exception handling is discussed in Chapter 11.

Error-Prevention Tip 7.2

When writing code to loop through an array, ensure that the array index is always greater than or equal to 0 and less than the length of the array. The loop-continuation condition should prevent accessing elements outside this range.

7.5 Case Study: Card Shuffling and Dealing Simulation

The examples in the chapter thus far have used arrays containing elements of primitive types. Recall from Section 7.2 that the elements of an array can be either primitive types or reference types. This section uses random-number generation and an array of reference-type elements, namely objects representing playing cards, to develop a class that simulates card shuffling and dealing. This class can then be used to implement applications that play specific card games. The exercises at the end of the chapter use the classes developed here to build a simple poker application.

We first develop class Card (Fig. 7.9), which represents a playing card that has a face (e.g., "Ace", "Deuce", "Three", ..., "Jack", "Queen", "King") and a suit (e.g., "Hearts", "Diamonds", "Clubs", "Spades"). Next, we develop the DeckOfCards class (Fig. 7.10), which creates a deck of 52 playing cards in which each element is a Card object. We then build a test application (Fig. 7.11) that demonstrates class DeckOfCards's card shuffling and dealing capabilities.

Class Card

Class Card (Fig. 7.9) contains two String instance variables—face and suit—that are used to store references to the face name and suit name for a specific Card. The constructor for the class (lines 10–14) receives two Strings that it uses to initialize face and suit. Method toString (lines 17–20) creates a String consisting of the face of the card, the String " of " and the suit of the card. Card's toString method can be invoked explicitly to obtain a string representation of a Card object (e.g., "Ace of Spades"). The toString method of an object is called implicitly when the object is used where a String is expected (e.g., when printf outputs the object as a String using the %s format specifier or when the object is concatenated to a String using the + operator). For this behavior to occur, toString must be declared with the header shown in Fig. 7.9.

```java
 1   // Fig. 7.9: Card.java
 2   // Card class represents a playing card.
 3
 4   public class Card
 5   {
 6      private String face; // face of card ("Ace", "Deuce", ...)
 7      private String suit; // suit of card ("Hearts", "Diamonds", ...)
 8
 9      // two-argument constructor initializes card's face and suit
10      public Card( String cardFace, String cardSuit )
11      {
12         face = cardFace; // initialize face of card
13         suit = cardSuit; // initialize suit of card
14      } // end two-argument Card constructor
15
16      // return String representation of Card
17      public String toString()
18      {
19         return face + " of " + suit;
20      } // end method toString
21   } // end class Card
```

Fig. 7.9 | Card class represents a playing card.

*Class **DeckOfCards***

Class DeckOfCards (Fig. 7.10) declares as an instance variable a Card array named deck (line 7). Note that an array of a reference type is declared like any other array. Class DeckOfCards also declares an integer instance variable currentCard (line 8) representing the next Card to be dealt from the deck array and a named constant NUMBER_OF_CARDS (line 9) indicating the number of Cards in the deck (52).

```
1   // Fig. 7.10: DeckOfCards.java
2   // DeckOfCards class represents a deck of playing cards.
3   import java.util.Random;
4
5   public class DeckOfCards
6   {
7      private Card[] deck; // array of Card objects
8      private int currentCard; // index of next Card to be dealt
9      private static final int NUMBER_OF_CARDS = 52; // constant # of Cards
10     // random number generator
11     private static final Random randomNumbers = new Random();
12
13     // constructor fills deck of Cards
14     public DeckOfCards()
15     {
16        String[] faces = { "Ace", "Deuce", "Three", "Four", "Five", "Six",
17           "Seven", "Eight", "Nine", "Ten", "Jack", "Queen", "King" };
18        String[] suits = { "Hearts", "Diamonds", "Clubs", "Spades" };
19
20        deck = new Card[ NUMBER_OF_CARDS ]; // create array of Card objects
21        currentCard = 0; // set currentCard so first Card dealt is deck[ 0 ]
22
23        // populate deck with Card objects
24        for ( int count = 0; count < deck.length; count++ )
25           deck[ count ] =
26              new Card( faces[ count % 13 ], suits[ count / 13 ] );
27     } // end DeckOfCards constructor
28
29     // shuffle deck of Cards with one-pass algorithm
30     public void shuffle()
31     {
32        // after shuffling, dealing should start at deck[ 0 ] again
33        currentCard = 0; // reinitialize currentCard
34
35        // for each Card, pick another random Card and swap them
36        for ( int first = 0; first < deck.length; first++ )
37        {
38           // select a random number between 0 and 51
39           int second =  randomNumbers.nextInt( NUMBER_OF_CARDS );
40
41           // swap current Card with randomly selected Card
42           Card temp = deck[ first ];
43           deck[ first ] = deck[ second ];
44           deck[ second ] = temp;
45        } // end for
46     } // end method shuffle
```

Fig. 7.10 | DeckOfCards class represents a deck of playing cards. (Part 1 of 2.)

```
47
48        // deal one Card
49        public Card dealCard()
50        {
51            // determine whether Cards remain to be dealt
52            if ( currentCard < deck.length )
53                return deck[ currentCard++ ]; // return current Card in array
54            else
55                return null; // return null to indicate that all Cards were dealt
56        } // end method dealCard
57    } // end class DeckOfCards
```

Fig. 7.10 | DeckOfCards class represents a deck of playing cards. (Part 2 of 2.)

The class's constructor instantiates the deck array (line 20) with NUMBER_OF_CARDS (52) elements. When first created, the elements of the deck array are null by default, so the constructor uses a for statement (lines 24–26) to fill the deck array with Cards. The for statement initializes control variable count to 0 and loops while count is less than deck.length, causing count to take on each integer value from 0 to 51 (the indices of the deck array). Each Card is instantiated and initialized with two Strings—one from the faces array (which contains the Strings "Ace" through "King") and one from the suits array (which contains the Strings "Hearts", "Diamonds", "Clubs" and "Spades"). The calculation count % 13 always results in a value from 0 to 12 (the 13 indices of the faces array in lines 16–17), and the calculation count / 13 always results in a value from 0 to 3 (the four indices of the suits array in line 18). When the deck array is initialized, it contains the Cards with faces "Ace" through "King" in order for each suit ("Hearts" then "Diamonds" then "Clubs" then "Spades"). Note that we use arrays of Strings to represent the faces and suits in this example. In Exercise 7.29, we ask you to modify this example to use arrays of enumeration constants to represent the faces and suits.

Method shuffle (lines 30–46) shuffles the Cards in the deck. The method loops through all 52 Cards (array indices 0 to 51). For each Card, a number between 0 and 51 is picked randomly to select another Card. Next, the current Card object and the randomly selected Card object are swapped in the array. This exchange is performed by the three assignments in lines 42–44. The extra variable temp temporarily stores one of the two Card objects being swapped. The swap cannot be performed with only the two statements

```
deck[ first ] = deck[ second ];
deck[ second ] = deck[ first ];
```

If deck[first] is the "Ace" of "Spades" and deck[second] is the "Queen" of "Hearts", after the first assignment, both array elements contain the "Queen" of "Hearts" and the "Ace" of "Spades" is lost—hence, the extra variable temp is needed. After the for loop terminates, the Card objects are randomly ordered. A total of only 52 swaps are made in a single pass of the entire array, and the array of Card objects is shuffled!

Method dealCard (lines 49–56) deals one Card in the array. Recall that currentCard indicates the index of the next Card to be dealt (i.e., the Card at the top of the deck). Thus, line 52 compares currentCard to the length of the deck array. If the deck is not empty (i.e., currentCard is less than 52), line 53 returns the "top" Card and postincrements currentCard to prepare for the next call to dealCard—otherwise, null is returned. Recall from Chapter 3 that null represents a "reference to nothing."

Shuffling and Dealing Cards

Figure 7.11 demonstrates class `DeckOfCards` (Fig. 7.10). Line 9 creates a `DeckOfCards` object named `myDeckOfCards`. Recall that the `DeckOfCards` constructor creates the deck with the 52 `Card` objects in order by suit and face. Line 10 invokes `myDeckOfCards`'s `shuffle` method to rearrange the `Card` objects. Lines 13–20 deal all 52 `Cards` and print them in four columns of 13 `Cards` each. Line 16 deals one `Card` object by invoking `myDeckOf-Cards`'s `dealCard` method, then displays the `Card` left justified in a field of 19 characters. When a `Card` is output as a `String`, the `Card`'s `toString` method (lines 17–20 of Fig. 7.9) is implicitly invoked. Lines 18–19 start a new line after every four `Cards`.

```java
1   // Fig. 7.11: DeckOfCardsTest.java
2   // Card shuffling and dealing.
3
4   public class DeckOfCardsTest
5   {
6      // execute application
7      public static void main( String[] args )
8      {
9         DeckOfCards myDeckOfCards = new DeckOfCards();
10        myDeckOfCards.shuffle(); // place Cards in random order
11
12        // print all 52 Cards in the order in which they are dealt
13        for ( int i = 1; i <= 52; i++ )
14        {
15           // deal and display a Card
16           System.out.printf( "%-19s", myDeckOfCards.dealCard() );
17
18           if ( i % 4 == 0 ) // output newline every 4 cards
19              System.out.println();
20        } // end for
21     } // end main
22  } // end class DeckOfCardsTest
```

Six of Spades	Eight of Spades	Six of Clubs	Nine of Hearts
Queen of Hearts	Seven of Clubs	Nine of Spades	King of Hearts
Three of Diamonds	Deuce of Clubs	Ace of Hearts	Ten of Spades
Four of Spades	Ace of Clubs	Seven of Diamonds	Four of Hearts
Three of Clubs	Deuce of Hearts	Five of Spades	Jack of Diamonds
King of Clubs	Ten of Hearts	Three of Hearts	Six of Diamonds
Queen of Clubs	Eight of Diamonds	Deuce of Diamonds	Ten of Diamonds
Three of Spades	King of Diamonds	Nine of Clubs	Six of Hearts
Ace of Spades	Four of Diamonds	Seven of Hearts	Eight of Clubs
Deuce of Spades	Eight of Hearts	Five of Hearts	Queen of Spades
Jack of Hearts	Seven of Spades	Four of Clubs	Nine of Diamonds
Ace of Diamonds	Queen of Diamonds	Five of Clubs	King of Spades
Five of Diamonds	Ten of Clubs	Jack of Spades	Jack of Clubs

Fig. 7.11 | Card shuffling and dealing.

7.6 Enhanced for Statement

The **enhanced for statement** iterates through the elements of an array without using a counter, thus avoiding the possibility of "stepping outside" the array. We show how to use the enhanced for statement with the Java API's prebuilt data structures (called collections) in Section 7.14. The syntax of an enhanced for statement is:

```
for ( parameter : arrayName )
   statement
```

where *parameter* has a type and an identifier (e.g., int number), and *arrayName* is the array through which to iterate. The type of the parameter must be consistent with the type of the elements in the array. As the next example illustrates, the identifier represents successive values in the array on successive iterations of the loop.

Figure 7.12 uses the enhanced for statement (lines 12–13) to sum the integers in an array of student grades. The enhanced for's parameter is of type int, because array contains int values—the loop selects one int value from the array during each iteration. The enhanced for statement iterates through successive values in the array one by one. The statement's header can be read as "for each iteration, assign the next element of array to int variable number, then execute the following statement." Thus, for each iteration, identifier number represents an int value in array. Lines 12–13 are equivalent to the following counter-controlled repetition used in lines 12–13 of Fig. 7.5 to total the integers in array:

```
for ( int counter = 0; counter < array.length; counter++ )
   total += array[ counter ];
```

```
1   // Fig. 7.12: EnhancedForTest.java
2   // Using enhanced for statement to total integers in an array.
3
4   public class EnhancedForTest
5   {
6      public static void main( String[] args )
7      {
8         int[] array = { 87, 68, 94, 100, 83, 78, 85, 91, 76, 87 };
9         int total = 0;
10
11         // add each element's value to total
12         for ( int number : array )
13            total += number;
14
15         System.out.printf( "Total of array elements: %d\n", total );
16      } // end main
17   } // end class EnhancedForTest
```

```
Total of array elements: 849
```

Fig. 7.12 | Using the enhanced for statement to total integers in an array.

The enhanced for statement simplifies the code for iterating through an array. Note, however, that the enhanced for statement can be used only to obtain array elements—it cannot be used to modify elements. If your program needs to modify elements, use the traditional counter-controlled for statement.

The enhanced for statement can be used in place of the counter-controlled for statement whenever code looping through an array does not require access to the counter indicating the index of the current array element. For example, totaling the integers in an array requires access only to the element values—the index of each element is irrelevant. However, if a program must use a counter for some reason other than simply to loop through an array (e.g., to print an index number next to each array element value, as in the examples earlier in this chapter), use the counter-controlled `for` statement.

7.7 Passing Arrays to Methods

This section demonstrates how to pass arrays and individual array elements as arguments to methods. To pass an array argument to a method, specify the name of the array without any brackets. For example, if array `hourlyTemperatures` is declared as

```
double[] hourlyTemperatures = new double[ 24 ];
```

then the method call

```
modifyArray( hourlyTemperatures );
```

passes the reference of array `hourlyTemperatures` to method `modifyArray`. Every array object "knows" its own length (via its `length` field). Thus, when we pass an array object's reference into a method, we need not pass the array length as an additional argument.

For a method to receive an array reference through a method call, the method's parameter list must specify an array parameter. For example, the method header for method `modifyArray` might be written as

```
void modifyArray( double[] b )
```

indicating that `modifyArray` receives the reference of a `double` array in parameter b. The method call passes array `hourlyTemperature`'s reference, so when the called method uses the array variable b, it refers to the same array object as `hourlyTemperatures` in the caller.

When an argument to a method is an entire array or an individual array element of a reference type, the called method receives a copy of the reference. However, when an argument to a method is an individual array element of a primitive type, the called method receives a copy of the element's value. Such primitive values are called **scalars** or **scalar quantities**. To pass an individual array element to a method, use the indexed name of the array element as an argument in the method call.

Figure 7.13 demonstrates the difference between passing an entire array and passing a primitive-type array element to a method. Notice that `main` invokes static methods `modifyArray` (line 19) and `modifyElement` (line 30) directly. Recall from Section 6.5 that a `static` method of a class can invoke other `static` methods of the same class directly.

```
1    // Fig. 7.13: PassArray.java
2    // Passing arrays and individual array elements to methods.
3
4    public class PassArray
5    {
6       // main creates array and calls modifyArray and modifyElement
7       public static void main( String[] args )
8       {
9          int[] array = { 1, 2, 3, 4, 5 };
10
```

Fig. 7.13 | Passing arrays and individual array elements to methods. (Part 1 of 2.)

```
11      System.out.println(
12         "Effects of passing reference to entire array:\n" +
13         "The values of the original array are:" );
14
15      // output original array elements
16      for ( int value : array )
17         System.out.printf( "   %d", value );
18
19      modifyArray( array ); // pass array reference
20      System.out.println( "\n\nThe values of the modified array are:" );
21
22      // output modified array elements
23      for ( int value : array )
24         System.out.printf( "   %d", value );
25
26      System.out.printf(
27         "\n\nEffects of passing array element value:\n" +
28         "array[3] before modifyElement: %d\n", array[ 3 ] );
29
30      modifyElement( array[ 3 ] ); // attempt to modify array[ 3 ]
31      System.out.printf(
32         "array[3] after modifyElement: %d\n", array[ 3 ] );
33   } // end main
34
35   // multiply each element of an array by 2
36   public static void modifyArray( int[] array2 )
37   {
38      for ( int counter = 0; counter < array2.length; counter++ )
39         array2[ counter ] *= 2;
40   } // end method modifyArray
41
42   // multiply argument by 2
43   public static void modifyElement( int element )
44   {
45      element *= 2;
46      System.out.printf(
47         "Value of element in modifyElement: %d\n", element );
48   } // end method modifyElement
49 } // end class PassArray
```

```
Effects of passing reference to entire array:
The values of the original array are:
   1   2   3   4   5

The values of the modified array are:
   2   4   6   8   10

Effects of passing array element value:
array[3] before modifyElement: 8
Value of element in modifyElement: 16
array[3] after modifyElement: 8
```

Fig. 7.13 | Passing arrays and individual array elements to methods. (Part 2 of 2.)

The enhanced for statement at lines 16–17 outputs the five int elements of array. Line 19 invokes method modifyArray, passing array as an argument. Method modify-

Array (lines 36–40) receives a copy of `array`'s reference and uses the reference to multiply each of `array`'s elements by 2. To prove that `array`'s elements were modified, lines 23–24 output the five elements of `array` again. As the output shows, method `modifyArray` doubled the value of each element. Note that we could not use the enhanced `for` statement in lines 38–39 because we are modifying the array's elements.

Figure 7.13 next demonstrates that when a copy of an individual primitive-type array element is passed to a method, modifying the copy in the called method does not affect the original value of that element in the calling method's array. Lines 26–28 output the value of `array[3]` before invoking method `modifyElement`. Remember that the value of this element is now 8 after it was modified in the call to `modifyArray`. Line 30 calls method `modifyElement` and passes `array[3]` as an argument. Remember that `array[3]` is actually one `int` value (8) in `array`. Therefore, the program passes a copy of the value of `array[3]`. Method `modifyElement` (lines 43–48) multiplies the value received as an argument by 2, stores the result in its parameter `element`, then outputs the value of `element` (16). Since method parameters, like local variables, cease to exist when the method in which they are declared completes execution, the method parameter `element` is destroyed when method `modifyElement` terminates. When the program returns control to `main`, lines 31–32 output the unmodified value of `array[3]` (i.e., 8).

Notes on Passing Arguments to Methods
The preceding example demonstrated how arrays and primitive-type array elements are passed as arguments to methods. We now take a closer look at how arguments in general are passed to methods. Two ways to pass arguments in method calls in many programming languages are **pass-by-value** and **pass-by-reference** (also called **call-by-value** and **call-by-reference**). When an argument is passed by value, a copy of the argument's *value* is passed to the called method. The called method works exclusively with the copy. Changes to the called method's copy do not affect the original variable's value in the caller.

When an argument is passed by reference, the called method can access the argument's value in the caller directly and modify that data, if necessary. Pass-by-reference improves performance by eliminating the need to copy possibly large amounts of data.

Unlike some other languages, Java does not allow programmers to choose pass-by-value or pass-by-reference—all arguments are passed by value. A method call can pass two types of values to a method—copies of primitive values (e.g., values of type `int` and `double`) and copies of references to objects. Objects themselves cannot be passed to methods. When a method modifies a primitive-type parameter, changes to the parameter have no effect on the original argument value in the calling method. For example, when line 30 in `main` of Fig. 7.13 passes `array[3]` to method `modifyElement`, the statement in line 45 that doubles the value of parameter `element` has no effect on the value of `array[3]` in `main`. This is also true for reference-type parameters. If you modify a reference-type parameter so that it refers to another object, only the parameter refers to the new object—the reference stored in the caller's variable still refers to the original object.

Although an object's reference is passed by value, a method can still interact with the referenced object by calling its `public` methods using the copy of the object's reference. Since the reference stored in the parameter is a copy of the reference that was passed as an argument, the parameter in the called method and the argument in the calling method refer to the same object in memory. For example, in Fig. 7.13, both parameter `array2` in method `modifyArray` and variable `array` in `main` refer to the same array object in memory. Any changes made using the parameter `array2` are carried out on the object that `array` references in the calling method. In Fig. 7.13, the changes made in modifyArray using array2 affect the contents of the array object referenced by array in main. Thus, with a reference to an object, the called method can manipulate the caller's object directly.

Performance Tip 7.1

Passing arrays by reference makes sense for performance reasons. If arrays were passed by value, a copy of each element would be passed. For large, frequently passed arrays, this would waste time and consume considerable storage for the copies of the arrays.

7.8 Case Study: Class GradeBook Using an Array to Store Grades

Previous versions of class GradeBook process a set of grades entered by the user, but do not maintain the individual grade values in instance variables of the class. Thus, repeat calculations require the user to reenter the same grades. One way to solve this problem would be to store each grade entered in an individual instance of the class. For example, we could create instance variables grade1, grade2, ..., grade10 in class GradeBook to store 10 student grades. But this would make the code to total the grades and determine the class average cumbersome, and the class would not be able to process any more than 10 grades at a time. We solve this problem by storing grades in an array.

*Storing Student Grades in an Array in Class **GradeBook***
Class GradeBook (Fig. 7.14) uses an array of ints to store several students' grades on a single exam. This eliminates the need to repeatedly input the same set of grades. Array grades is declared as an instance variable (line 7), so each GradeBook object maintains its own set of grades. The constructor (lines 10–14) has two parameters—the name of the course and an array of grades. When an application (e.g., class GradeBookTest in Fig. 7.15) creates a GradeBook object, the application passes an existing int array to the constructor, which assigns the array's reference to instance variable grades (line 13). The grades array's size is determined by the length of the array that is passed to the constructor. Thus, a GradeBook object can process a variable number of grades. The grade values in the passed array could have been input from a user or read from a file on disk (as discussed in Chapter 17). In our test application, we initialize an array with grade values (Fig. 7.15, line 10). Once the grades are stored in instance variable grades of class GradeBook, all the class's methods can access the elements of grades as often as needed to perform various calculations.

```
 1    // Fig. 7.14: GradeBook.java
 2    // GradeBook class using an array to store test grades.
 3
 4    public class GradeBook
 5    {
 6       private String courseName; // name of course this GradeBook represents
 7       private int[] grades; // array of student grades
 8
 9       // two-argument constructor initializes courseName and grades array
10       public GradeBook( String name, int[] gradesArray )
11       {
```

Fig. 7.14 | GradeBook class using an array to store test grades. (Part 1 of 4.)

```
12          courseName = name; // initialize courseName
13          grades = gradesArray; // store grades
14      } // end two-argument GradeBook constructor
15
16      // method to set the course name
17      public void setCourseName( String name )
18      {
19          courseName = name; // store the course name
20      } // end method setCourseName
21
22      // method to retrieve the course name
23      public String getCourseName()
24      {
25          return courseName;
26      } // end method getCourseName
27
28      // display a welcome message to the GradeBook user
29      public void displayMessage()
30      {
31          // getCourseName gets the name of the course
32          System.out.printf( "Welcome to the grade book for\n%s!\n\n",
33              getCourseName() );
34      } // end method displayMessage
35
36      // perform various operations on the data
37      public void processGrades()
38      {
39          // output grades array
40          outputGrades();
41
42          // call method getAverage to calculate the average grade
43          System.out.printf( "\nClass average is %.2f\n", getAverage() );
44
45          // call methods getMinimum and getMaximum
46          System.out.printf( "Lowest grade is %d\nHighest grade is %d\n\n",
47              getMinimum(), getMaximum() );
48
49          // call outputBarChart to print grade distribution chart
50          outputBarChart();
51      } // end method processGrades
52
53      // find minimum grade
54      public int getMinimum()
55      {
56          int lowGrade = grades[ 0 ]; // assume grades[ 0 ] is smallest
57
58          // loop through grades array
59          for ( int grade : grades )
60          {
61              // if grade lower than lowGrade, assign it to lowGrade
62              if ( grade < lowGrade )
63                  lowGrade = grade; // new lowest grade
64          } // end for
65
```

Fig. 7.14 | GradeBook class using an array to store test grades. (Part 2 of 4.)

```
66          return lowGrade; // return lowest grade
67       } // end method getMinimum
68
69       // find maximum grade
70       public int getMaximum()
71       {
72          int highGrade = grades[ 0 ]; // assume grades[ 0 ] is largest
73
74          // loop through grades array
75          for ( int grade : grades )
76          {
77             // if grade greater than highGrade, assign it to highGrade
78             if ( grade > highGrade )
79                highGrade = grade; // new highest grade
80          } // end for
81
82          return highGrade; // return highest grade
83       } // end method getMaximum
84
85       // determine average grade for test
86       public double getAverage()
87       {
88          int total = 0; // initialize total
89
90          // sum grades for one student
91          for ( int grade : grades )
92             total += grade;
93
94          // return average of grades
95          return (double) total / grades.length;
96       } // end method getAverage
97
98       // output bar chart displaying grade distribution
99       public void outputBarChart()
100      {
101         System.out.println( "Grade distribution:" );
102
103         // stores frequency of grades in each range of 10 grades
104         int[] frequency = new int[ 11 ];
105
106         // for each grade, increment the appropriate frequency
107         for ( int grade : grades )
108            ++frequency[ grade / 10 ];
109
110         // for each grade frequency, print bar in chart
111         for ( int count = 0; count < frequency.length; count++ )
112         {
113            // output bar label ( "00-09: ", ..., "90-99: ", "100: " )
114            if ( count == 10 )
115               System.out.printf( "%5d: ", 100 );
116            else
117               System.out.printf( "%02d-%02d: ",
118                  count * 10, count * 10 + 9 );
119
```

Fig. 7.14 | GradeBook class using an array to store test grades. (Part 3 of 4.)

```
120              // print bar of asterisks
121              for ( int stars = 0; stars < frequency[ count ]; stars++ )
122                 System.out.print( "*" );
123
124              System.out.println(); // start a new line of output
125           } // end outer for
126        } // end method outputBarChart
127
128        // output the contents of the grades array
129        public void outputGrades()
130        {
131           System.out.println( "The grades are:\n" );
132
133           // output each student's grade
134           for ( int student = 0; student < grades.length; student++ )
135              System.out.printf( "Student %2d: %3d\n",
136                 student + 1, grades[ student ] );
137        } // end method outputGrades
138     } // end class GradeBook
```

Fig. 7.14 | GradeBook class using an array to store test grades. (Part 4 of 4.)

Method processGrades (lines 37–51) contains a series of method calls that output a report summarizing the grades. Line 40 calls method outputGrades to print the contents of the array grades. Lines 134–136 in method outputGrades use a for statement to output the students' grades. A counter-controlled for must be used in this case, because lines 135–136 use counter variable student's value to output each grade next to a particular student number (see output in Fig. 7.15). Although array indices start at 0, a professor would typically number students starting at 1. Thus, lines 135–136 output student + 1 as the student number to produce grade labels "Student 1: ", "Student 2: ", and so on.

Method processGrades next calls method getAverage (line 43) to obtain the average of the grades in the array. Method getAverage (lines 86–96) uses an enhanced for statement to total the values in array grades before calculating the average. The parameter in the enhanced for's header (e.g., int grade) indicates that for each iteration, the int variable grade takes on a value in the array grades. Note that the averaging calculation in line 95 uses grades.length to determine the number of grades being averaged.

Lines 46–47 in method processGrades calls methods getMinimum and getMaximum to determine the lowest and highest grades of any student on the exam, respectively. Each of these methods uses an enhanced for statement to loop through array grades. Lines 59–64 in method getMinimum loop through the array. Lines 62–63 compare each grade to lowGrade; if a grade is less than lowGrade, lowGrade is set to that grade. When line 66 executes, lowGrade contains the lowest grade in the array. Method getMaximum (lines 70–83) works similarly to method getMinimum.

Finally, line 50 in method processGrades calls method outputBarChart to print a distribution chart of the grade data using a technique similar to that in Fig. 7.6. In that example, we manually calculated the number of grades in each category (i.e., 0–9, 10–19, …, 90–99 and 100) by simply looking at a set of grades. In this example, lines 107–108 use a technique similar to that in Figs. 7.7 and 7.8 to calculate the frequency of grades in each category. Line 104 declares and creates array frequency of 11 ints to store the frequency of grades in each grade category. For each grade in array grades, lines 107–108 increment the appropriate element of the `frequency` array. To determine which element to increment, line 108 divides the current `grade` by 10 using integer division. For example, if grade is 85, line 108 increments `frequency[8]` to update the count of grades in the range 80–89. Lines 111–125 next print the bar chart (see Fig. 7.15) based on the values in array `frequency`. Like lines 23–24 of Fig. 7.6, lines 121–122 of Fig. 7.14 use a value in array `frequency` to determine the number of asterisks to display in each bar.

Class *GradeBookTest* That Demonstrates Class *GradeBook*

The application of Fig. 7.15 creates an object of class `GradeBook` (Fig. 7.14) using the `int` array `gradesArray` (declared and initialized in line 10). Lines 12–13 pass a course name and `gradesArray` to the `GradeBook` constructor. Line 14 displays a welcome message, and line 15 invokes the `GradeBook` object's `processGrades` method. The output summarizes the 10 grades in `myGradeBook`.

Software Engineering Observation 7.1

A test harness (or test application) is responsible for creating an object of the class being tested and providing it with data. This data could come from any of several sources. Test data can be placed directly into an array with an array initializer, it can come from the user at the keyboard, it can come from a file (as you'll see in Chapter 17), or it can come from a network (as you'll see in Chapter 27). After passing this data to the class's constructor to instantiate the object, the test harness should call upon the object to test its methods and manipulate its data. Gathering data in the test harness like this allows the class to manipulate data from several sources.

```java
 1  // Fig. 7.15: GradeBookTest.java
 2  // GradeBookTest creates a GradeBook object using an array of grades,
 3  // then invokes method processGrades to analyze them.
 4  public class GradeBookTest
 5  {
 6     // main method begins program execution
 7     public static void main( String[] args )
 8     {
 9        // array of student grades
10        int[] gradesArray = { 87, 68, 94, 100, 83, 78, 85, 91, 76, 87 };
11
12        GradeBook myGradeBook = new GradeBook(
13           "CS101 Introduction to Java Programming", gradesArray );
14        myGradeBook.displayMessage();
15        myGradeBook.processGrades();
16     } // end main
17  } // end class GradeBookTest
```

```
Welcome to the grade book for
CS101 Introduction to Java Programming!

The grades are:

Student  1:  87
Student  2:  68
```

Fig. 7.15 | GradeBookTest creates a GradeBook object using an array of grades, then invokes method processGrades to analyze them. (Part I of 2.)

```
Student  3:  94
Student  4: 100
Student  5:  83
Student  6:  78
Student  7:  85
Student  8:  91
Student  9:  76
Student 10:  87

Class average is 84.90
Lowest grade is 68
Highest grade is 100

Grade distribution:
00-09:
10-19:
20-29:
30-39:
40-49:
50-59:
60-69: *
70-79: **
80-89: ****
90-99: **
  100: *
```

Fig. 7.15 | GradeBookTest creates a GradeBook object using an array of grades, then invokes method processGrades to analyze them. (Part 2 of 2.)

7.9 Multidimensional Arrays

Multidimensional arrays with two dimensions are often used to represent tables of values consisting of information arranged in rows and columns. To identify a particular table element, we must specify two indices. By convention, the first identifies the element's row and the second its column. Arrays that require two indices to identify a particular element are called **two-dimensional arrays**. (Multidimensional arrays can have more than two dimensions.) Java does not support multidimensional arrays directly, but it does allow you to specify one-dimensional arrays whose elements are also one-dimensional arrays, thus achieving the same effect. Figure 7.16 illustrates a two-dimensional array named a that contains three rows and four columns (i.e., a three-by-four array). In general, an array with m rows and n columns is called an m-**by-**n **array**.

Every element in array a is identified in Fig. 7.16 by an array-access expression of the form a[row][column]; a is the name of the array, and row and column are the indices that uniquely identify each element in array a by row and column number. Note that the names of the elements in row 0 all have a first index of 0, and the names of the elements in column 3 all have a second index of 3.

Arrays of One-Dimensional Arrays

Like one-dimensional arrays, multidimensional arrays can be initialized with array initializers in declarations. A two-dimensional array b with two rows and two columns could be declared and initialized with **nested array initializers** as follows:

```
int[][] b = { { 1, 2 }, { 3, 4 } };
```

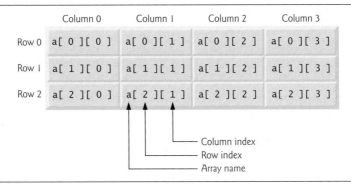

Fig. 7.16 | Two-dimensional array with three rows and four columns.

The initial values are grouped by row in braces. So 1 and 2 initialize b[0][0] and b[0][1], respectively, and 3 and 4 initialize b[1][0] and b[1][1], respectively. The compiler counts the number of nested array initializers (represented by sets of braces within the outer braces) to determine the number of rows in array b. The compiler counts the initializer values in the nested array initializer for a row to determine the number of columns in that row. As we'll see momentarily, this means that rows can have different lengths.

Multidimensional arrays are maintained as arrays of one-dimensional arrays. Therefore array b in the preceding declaration is actually composed of two separate one-dimensional arrays—one containing the values in the first nested initializer list { 1, 2 } and one containing the values in the second nested initializer list { 3, 4 }. Thus, array b itself is an array of two elements, each a one-dimensional array of int values.

Two-Dimensional Arrays with Rows of Different Lengths
The manner in which multidimensional arrays are represented makes them quite flexible. In fact, the lengths of the rows in array b are not required to be the same. For example,

```
int[][] b = { { 1, 2 }, { 3, 4, 5 } };
```

creates integer array b with two elements (determined by the number of nested array initializers) that represent the rows of the two-dimensional array. Each element of b is a reference to a one-dimensional array of int variables. The int array for row 0 is a one-dimensional array with two elements (1 and 2), and the int array for row 1 is a one-dimensional array with three elements (3, 4 and 5).

Creating Two-Dimensional Arrays with Array-Creation Expressions
A multidimensional array with the same number of columns in every row can be created with an array-creation expression. For example, the following lines declare array b and assign it a reference to a three-by-four array:

```
int[][] b = new int[ 3 ][ 4 ];
```

In this case, we use the literal values 3 and 4 to specify the number of rows and number of columns, respectively, but this is not required. Programs can also use variables to specify array dimensions, because new creates arrays at execution time—not at compile time. As with one-dimensional arrays, the elements of a multidimensional array are initialized when the array object is created.

A multidimensional array in which each row has a different number of columns can be created as follows:

```
int[][] b = new int[ 2 ][ ];    // create 2 rows
b[ 0 ] = new int[ 5 ]; // create 5 columns for row 0
b[ 1 ] = new int[ 3 ]; // create 3 columns for row 1
```

The preceding statements create a two-dimensional array with two rows. Row 0 has five columns, and row 1 has three columns.

Two-Dimensional Array Example: Displaying Element Values

Figure 7.17 demonstrates initializing two-dimensional arrays with array initializers and using nested for loops to **traverse** the arrays (i.e., manipulate every element of each array). Class `InitArray`'s main declares two arrays. The declaration of `array1` (line 9) uses nested array initializers to initialize the first row to the values 1, 2 and 3, and the second row to the values 4, 5 and 6. The declaration of `array2` (line 10) uses nested initializers of different lengths. In this case, the first row is initialized to two elements with the values 1 and 2, respectively. The second row is initialized to one element with the value 3. The third row is initialized to three elements with the values 4, 5 and 6, respectively.

```java
 1   // Fig. 7.17: InitArray.java
 2   // Initializing two-dimensional arrays.
 3
 4   public class InitArray
 5   {
 6      // create and output two-dimensional arrays
 7      public static void main( String[] args )
 8      {
 9         int[][] array1 = { { 1, 2, 3 }, { 4, 5, 6 } };
10         int[][] array2 = { { 1, 2 }, { 3 }, { 4, 5, 6 } };
11
12         System.out.println( "Values in array1 by row are" );
13         outputArray( array1 ); // displays array1 by row
14
15         System.out.println( "\nValues in array2 by row are" );
16         outputArray( array2 ); // displays array2 by row
17      } // end main
18
19      // output rows and columns of a two-dimensional array
20      public static void outputArray( int[][] array )
21      {
22         // loop through array's rows
23         for ( int row = 0; row < array.length; row++ )
24         {
25            // loop through columns of current row
26            for ( int column = 0; column < array[ row ].length; column++ )
27               System.out.printf( "%d  ", array[ row ][ column ] );
28
29            System.out.println(); // start new line of output
30         } // end outer for
31      } // end method outputArray
32   } // end class InitArray
```

Fig. 7.17 | Initializing two-dimensional arrays. (Part 1 of 2.)

```
Values in array1 by row are
1  2  3
4  5  6

Values in array2 by row are
1  2
3
4  5  6
```

Fig. 7.17 | Initializing two-dimensional arrays. (Part 2 of 2.)

Lines 13 and 16 call method `outputArray` (lines 20–31) to output the elements of `array1` and `array2`, respectively. Method `outputArray`'s parameter—`int[][] array`—indicates that the method receives a two-dimensional array. The `for` statement (lines 23–30) outputs the rows of a two-dimensional array. In the loop-continuation condition of the outer `for` statement, the expression `array.length` determines the number of rows in the array. In the inner `for` statement, the expression `array[row].length` determines the number of columns in the current row of the array. This condition enables the loop to determine the exact number of columns in each row.

Common Multidimensional-Array Manipulations Performed with `for` Statements
Many common array manipulations use `for` statements. As an example, the following `for` statement sets all the elements in row 2 of array a in Fig. 7.16 to zero:

```
for ( int column = 0; column < a[ 2 ].length; column++)
    a[ 2 ][ column ] = 0;
```

We specified row 2; therefore, we know that the first index is always 2 (0 is the first row, and 1 is the second row). This `for` loop varies only the second index (i.e., the column index). If row 2 of array a contains four elements, then the preceding `for` statement is equivalent to the assignment statements

```
a[ 2 ][ 0 ] = 0;
a[ 2 ][ 1 ] = 0;
a[ 2 ][ 2 ] = 0;
a[ 2 ][ 3 ] = 0;
```

The following nested `for` statement totals the values of all the elements in array a:

```
int total = 0;
for ( int row = 0; row < a.length; row++ )
{
    for ( int column = 0; column < a[ row ].length; column++ )
        total += a[ row ][ column ];
} // end outer for
```

These nested `for` statements total the array elements one row at a time. The outer `for` statement begins by setting the row index to 0 so that the first row's elements can be totaled by the inner `for` statement. The outer `for` then increments row to 1 so that the second row can be totaled. Then, the outer `for` increments row to 2 so that the third row can be totaled. The variable `total` can be displayed when the outer `for` statement terminates. In the next example, we show how to process a two-dimensional array in a similar manner using nested enhanced `for` statements.

7.10 Case Study: Class GradeBook Using a Two-Dimensional Array

In Section 7.8, we presented class GradeBook (Fig. 7.14), which used a one-dimensional array to store student grades on a single exam. In most semesters, students take several exams. Professors are likely to want to analyze grades across the entire semester, both for a single student and for the class as a whole.

Storing Student Grades in a Two-Dimensional Array in Class **GradeBook**
Figure 7.18 contains a version of class GradeBook that uses a two-dimensional array grades to store the grades of a number of students on multiple exams. Each row of the array represents a single student's grades for the entire course, and each column represents the grades of all the students who took a particular exam. An application such as Grade-BookTest (Fig. 7.19) passes the array as an argument to the GradeBook constructor. In this example, we use a ten-by-three array containing ten students' grades on three exams. Five methods perform array manipulations to process the grades. Each method is similar to its counterpart in the earlier one-dimensional array version of class GradeBook (Fig. 7.14). Method getMinimum (lines 52–70) determines the lowest grade of any student for the semester. Method getMaximum (lines 73–91) determines the highest grade of any student for the semester. Method getAverage (lines 94–104) determines a particular student's semester average. Method outputBarChart (lines 107–137) outputs a bar chart of the distribution of all student grades for the semester. Method outputGrades (lines 140–164) outputs the two-dimensional array in a tabular format, along with each student's semester average.

```
 1   // Fig. 7.18: GradeBook.java
 2   // GradeBook class using a two-dimensional array to store grades.
 3
 4   public class GradeBook
 5   {
 6      private String courseName; // name of course this grade book represents
 7      private int[][] grades; // two-dimensional array of student grades
 8
 9      // two-argument constructor initializes courseName and grades array
10      public GradeBook( String name, int[][] gradesArray )
11      {
12         courseName = name; // initialize courseName
13         grades = gradesArray; // store grades
14      } // end two-argument GradeBook constructor
15
16      // method to set the course name
17      public void setCourseName( String name )
18      {
19         courseName = name; // store the course name
20      } // end method setCourseName
21
22      // method to retrieve the course name
23      public String getCourseName()
24      {
25         return courseName;
26      } // end method getCourseName
```

Fig. 7.18 | GradeBook class using a two-dimensional array to store grades. (Part 1 of 4.)

```
27
28      // display a welcome message to the GradeBook user
29      public void displayMessage()
30      {
31         // getCourseName gets the name of the course
32         System.out.printf( "Welcome to the grade book for\n%s!\n\n",
33            getCourseName() );
34      } // end method displayMessage
35
36      // perform various operations on the data
37      public void processGrades()
38      {
39         // output grades array
40         outputGrades();
41
42         // call methods getMinimum and getMaximum
43         System.out.printf( "\n%s %d\n%s %d\n\n",
44            "Lowest grade in the grade book is", getMinimum(),
45            "Highest grade in the grade book is", getMaximum() );
46
47         // output grade distribution chart of all grades on all tests
48         outputBarChart();
49      } // end method processGrades
50
51      // find minimum grade
52      public int getMinimum()
53      {
54         // assume first element of grades array is smallest
55         int lowGrade = grades[ 0 ][ 0 ];
56
57         // loop through rows of grades array
58         for ( int[] studentGrades : grades )
59         {
60            // loop through columns of current row
61            for ( int grade : studentGrades )
62            {
63               // if grade less than lowGrade, assign it to lowGrade
64               if ( grade < lowGrade )
65                  lowGrade = grade;
66            } // end inner for
67         } // end outer for
68
69         return lowGrade; // return lowest grade
70      } // end method getMinimum
71
72      // find maximum grade
73      public int getMaximum()
74      {
75         // assume first element of grades array is largest
76         int highGrade = grades[ 0 ][ 0 ];
77
78         // loop through rows of grades array
79         for ( int[] studentGrades : grades )
80         {
```

Fig. 7.18 | GradeBook class using a two-dimensional array to store grades. (Part 2 of 4.)

```
81            // loop through columns of current row
82            for ( int grade : studentGrades )
83            {
84               // if grade greater than highGrade, assign it to highGrade
85               if ( grade > highGrade )
86                  highGrade = grade;
87            } // end inner for
88         } // end outer for
89
90         return highGrade; // return highest grade
91      } // end method getMaximum
92
93      // determine average grade for particular set of grades
94      public double getAverage( int[] setOfGrades )
95      {
96         int total = 0; // initialize total
97
98         // sum grades for one student
99         for ( int grade : setOfGrades )
100            total += grade;
101
102        // return average of grades
103        return (double) total / setOfGrades.length;
104     } // end method getAverage
105
106     // output bar chart displaying overall grade distribution
107     public void outputBarChart()
108     {
109        System.out.println( "Overall grade distribution:" );
110
111        // stores frequency of grades in each range of 10 grades
112        int[] frequency = new int[ 11 ];
113
114        // for each grade in GradeBook, increment the appropriate frequency
115        for ( int[] studentGrades : grades )
116        {
117           for ( int grade : studentGrades )
118              ++frequency[ grade / 10 ];
119        } // end outer for
120
121        // for each grade frequency, print bar in chart
122        for ( int count = 0; count < frequency.length; count++ )
123        {
124           // output bar label ( "00-09: ", ..., "90-99: ", "100: " )
125           if ( count == 10 )
126              System.out.printf( "%5d: ", 100 );
127           else
128              System.out.printf( "%02d-%02d: ",
129                 count * 10, count * 10 + 9  );
130
131           // print bar of asterisks
132           for ( int stars = 0; stars < frequency[ count ]; stars++ )
133              System.out.print( "*" );
134
```

Fig. 7.18 | GradeBook class using a two-dimensional array to store grades. (Part 3 of 4.)

```
135                System.out.println(); // start a new line of output
136        } // end outer for
137    } // end method outputBarChart
138
139    // output the contents of the grades array
140    public void outputGrades()
141    {
142        System.out.println( "The grades are:\n" );
143        System.out.print( "                 " ); // align column heads
144
145        // create a column heading for each of the tests
146        for ( int test = 0; test < grades[ 0 ].length; test++ )
147            System.out.printf( "Test %d  ", test + 1 );
148
149        System.out.println( "Average" ); // student average column heading
150
151        // create rows/columns of text representing array grades
152        for ( int student = 0; student < grades.length; student++ )
153        {
154            System.out.printf( "Student %2d", student + 1 );
155
156            for ( int test : grades[ student ] ) // output student's grades
157                System.out.printf( "%8d", test );
158
159            // call method getAverage to calculate student's average grade;
160            // pass row of grades as the argument to getAverage
161            double average = getAverage( grades[ student ] );
162            System.out.printf( "%9.2f\n", average );
163        } // end outer for
164    } // end method outputGrades
165 } // end class GradeBook
```

Fig. 7.18 | GradeBook class using a two-dimensional array to store grades. (Part 4 of 4.)

Methods getMinimum and getMaximum

Methods getMinimum, getMaximum, outputBarChart and outputGrades each loop through array grades by using nested for statements—for example, the nested enhanced for statement from the declaration of method getMinimum (lines 58–67). The outer enhanced for statement iterates through the two-dimensional array grades, assigning successive rows to parameter studentGrades on successive iterations. The square brackets following the parameter name indicate that studentGrades refers to a one-dimensional int array—namely, a row in array grades containing one student's grades. To find the lowest overall grade, the inner for statement compares the elements of the current one-dimensional array studentGrades to variable lowGrade. For example, on the first iteration of the outer for, row 0 of grades is assigned to parameter studentGrades. The inner enhanced for statement then loops through studentGrades and compares each grade value with lowGrade. If a grade is less than lowGrade, lowGrade is set to that grade. On the second iteration of the outer enhanced for statement, row 1 of grades is assigned to studentGrades, and the elements of this row are compared with variable lowGrade. This repeats until all rows of grades have been traversed. When execution of the nested statement is complete, lowGrade contains the lowest grade in the two-dimensional array. Method getMaximum works similarly to method getMinimum.

Method `outputBarChart`

Method `outputBarChart` in Fig. 7.18 is nearly identical to the one in Fig. 7.14. However, to output the overall grade distribution for a whole semester, the method here uses nested enhanced `for` statements (lines 115–119) to create the one-dimensional array `frequency` based on all the grades in the two-dimensional array. The rest of the code in each of the two `outputBarChart` methods that displays the chart is identical.

Method `outputGrades`

Method `outputGrades` (lines 140–164) uses nested `for` statements to output values of the array `grades` and each student's semester average. The output (Fig. 7.19) shows the result, which resembles the tabular format of a professor's physical grade book. Lines 146–147 print the column headings for each test. We use a counter-controlled `for` statement here so that we can identify each test with a number. Similarly, the `for` statement in lines 152–163 first outputs a row label using a counter variable to identify each student (line 154). Although array indices start at 0, lines 147 and 154 output `test + 1` and `student + 1`, respectively, to produce test and student numbers starting at 1 (see Fig. 7.19). The inner `for` statement (lines 156–157) uses the outer `for` statement's counter variable `student` to loop through a specific row of array `grades` and output each student's test grade. Note that an enhanced `for` statement can be nested in a counter-controlled `for` statement, and vice versa. Finally, line 161 obtains each student's semester average by passing the current row of `grades` (i.e., `grades[student]`) to method `getAverage`.

Method `getAverage`

Method `getAverage` (lines 94–104) takes one argument—a one-dimensional array of test results for a particular student. When line 161 calls `getAverage`, the argument is `grades[student]`, which specifies that a particular row of the two-dimensional array `grades` should be passed to `getAverage`. For example, based on the array created in Fig. 7.19, the argument `grades[1]` represents the three values (a one-dimensional array of grades) stored in row 1 of the two-dimensional array `grades`. Recall that a two-dimensional array is one whose elements are one-dimensional arrays. Method `getAverage` calculates the sum of the array elements, divides the total by the number of test results and returns the floating-point result as a `double` value (line 103).

Class `GradeBookTest` That Demonstrates Class `GradeBook`

Figure 7.19 creates an object of class `GradeBook` (Fig. 7.18) using the two-dimensional array of `int`s named `gradesArray` (declared and initialized in lines 10–19). Lines 21–22 pass a course name and `gradesArray` to the `GradeBook` constructor. Lines 23–24 then invoke `myGradeBook`'s `displayMessage` and `processGrades` methods to display a welcome message and obtain a report summarizing the students' grades for the semester, respectively.

```
1   // Fig. 7.19: GradeBookTest.java
2   // GradeBookTest creates GradeBook object using a two-dimensional array
3   // of grades, then invokes method proctessGrades to analyze them.
4   public class GradeBookTest
5   {
```

Fig. 7.19 | `GradeBookTest` creates `GradeBook` object using a two-dimensional array of grades, then invokes method `processGrades` to analyze them. (Part I of 2.)

```
 6      // main method begins program execution
 7      public static void main( String[] args )
 8      {
 9         // two-dimensional array of student grades
10         int[][] gradesArray = { { 87, 96, 70 },
11                                 { 68, 87, 90 },
12                                 { 94, 100, 90 },
13                                 { 100, 81, 82 },
14                                 { 83, 65, 85 },
15                                 { 78, 87, 65 },
16                                 { 85, 75, 83 },
17                                 { 91, 94, 100 },
18                                 { 76, 72, 84 },
19                                 { 87, 93, 73 } };
20
21         GradeBook myGradeBook = new GradeBook(
22            "CS101 Introduction to Java Programming", gradesArray );
23         myGradeBook.displayMessage();
24         myGradeBook.processGrades();
25      } // end main
26  } // end class GradeBookTest
```

```
Welcome to the grade book for
CS101 Introduction to Java Programming!

The grades are:

            Test 1  Test 2  Test 3  Average
Student  1      87      96      70    84.33
Student  2      68      87      90    81.67
Student  3      94     100      90    94.67
Student  4     100      81      82    87.67
Student  5      83      65      85    77.67
Student  6      78      87      65    76.67
Student  7      85      75      83    81.00
Student  8      91      94     100    95.00
Student  9      76      72      84    77.33
Student 10      87      93      73    84.33

Lowest grade in the grade book is 65
Highest grade in the grade book is 100

Overall grade distribution:
00-09:
10-19:
20-29:
30-39:
40-49:
50-59:
60-69: ***
70-79: ******
80-89: ***********
90-99: *******
  100: ***
```

Fig. 7.19 | GradeBookTest creates GradeBook object using a two-dimensional array of grades, then invokes method processGrades to analyze them. (Part 2 of 2.)

7.11 Variable-Length Argument Lists

With **variable-length argument lists**, you can create methods that receive an unspecified number of arguments. A type followed by an **ellipsis** (...) in a method's parameter list indicates that the method receives a variable number of arguments of that particular type. This use of the ellipsis can occur only once in a parameter list, and the ellipsis, together with its type, must be placed at the end of the parameter list. While you can use method overloading and array passing to accomplish much of what is accomplished with variable-length argument lists, using an ellipsis in a method's parameter list is more concise.

Figure 7.20 demonstrates method average (lines 7–16), which receives a variable-length sequence of doubles. Java treats the variable-length argument list as an array whose elements are all of the same type. Hence, the method body can manipulate the parameter numbers as an array of doubles. Lines 12–13 use the enhanced for loop to walk through the array and calculate the total of the doubles in the array. Line 15 accesses numbers.length to obtain the size of the numbers array for use in the averaging calculation. Lines 29, 31 and 33 in main call method average with two, three and four arguments, respectively. Method average has a variable-length argument list (line 7), so it can average as many double arguments as the caller passes. The output shows that each call to method average returns the correct value.

```java
1   // Fig. 7.20: VarargsTest.java
2   // Using variable-length argument lists.
3
4   public class VarargsTest
5   {
6      // calculate average
7      public static double average( double... numbers )
8      {
9         double total = 0.0; // initialize total
10
11         // calculate total using the enhanced for statement
12         for ( double d : numbers )
13            total += d;
14
15         return total / numbers.length;
16      } // end method average
17
18      public static void main( String[] args )
19      {
20         double d1 = 10.0;
21         double d2 = 20.0;
22         double d3 = 30.0;
23         double d4 = 40.0;
24
25         System.out.printf( "d1 = %.1f\nd2 = %.1f\nd3 = %.1f\nd4 = %.1f\n\n",
26            d1, d2, d3, d4 );
27
28         System.out.printf( "Average of d1 and d2 is %.1f\n",
29            average( d1, d2 ) );
```

Fig. 7.20 | Using variable-length argument lists. (Part 1 of 2.)

```
30          System.out.printf( "Average of d1, d2 and d3 is %.1f\n",
31            average( d1, d2, d3 ) );
32          System.out.printf( "Average of d1, d2, d3 and d4 is %.1f\n",
33            average( d1, d2, d3, d4 ) );
34      } // end main
35  } // end class VarargsTest
```

```
d1 = 10.0
d2 = 20.0
d3 = 30.0
d4 = 40.0

Average of d1 and d2 is 15.0
Average of d1, d2 and d3 is 20.0
Average of d1, d2, d3 and d4 is 25.0
```

Fig. 7.20 | Using variable-length argument lists. (Part 2 of 2.)

Common Programming Error 7.6

Placing an ellipsis indicating a variable-length argument list in the middle of a parameter list is a syntax error. An ellipsis may be placed only at the end of the parameter list.

7.12 Using Command-Line Arguments

On many systems it's possible to pass arguments from the command line (these are known as **command-line arguments**) to an application by including a parameter of type String[] (i.e., an array of Strings) in the parameter list of main, exactly as we've done in every application in the book. By convention, this parameter is named args. When an application is executed using the java command, Java passes the command-line arguments that appear after the class name in the java command to the application's main method as Strings in the array args. The number of command-line arguments is obtained by accessing the array's length attribute. For example, the command "java MyClass a b" passes two command-line arguments, a and b, to application MyClass. Note that command-line arguments are separated by white space, not commas. When this command executes, MyClass's main method receives the two-element array args (i.e., args.length is 2) in which args[0] contains the String "a" and args[1] contains the String "b". Common uses of command-line arguments include passing options and file names to applications.

Figure 7.21 uses three command-line arguments to initialize an array. When the program executes, if args.length is not 3, the program prints an error message and terminates (lines 9–12). Otherwise, lines 14–32 initialize and display the array based on the values of the command-line arguments.

```
1   // Fig. 7.21: InitArray.java
2   // Initializing an array using command-line arguments.
3
4   public class InitArray
5   {
```

Fig. 7.21 | Initializing an array using command-line arguments. (Part 1 of 2.)

```
 6     public static void main( String[] args )
 7     {
 8        // check number of command-line arguments
 9        if ( args.length != 3 )
10           System.out.println(
11              "Error: Please re-enter the entire command, including\n" +
12              "an array size, initial value and increment." );
13        else
14        {
15           // get array size from first command-line argument
16           int arrayLength = Integer.parseInt( args[ 0 ] );
17           int[] array = new int[ arrayLength ]; // create array
18
19           // get initial value and increment from command-line arguments
20           int initialValue = Integer.parseInt( args[ 1 ] );
21           int increment = Integer.parseInt( args[ 2 ] );
22
23           // calculate value for each array element
24           for ( int counter = 0; counter < array.length; counter++ )
25              array[ counter ] = initialValue + increment * counter;
26
27           System.out.printf( "%s%8s\n", "Index", "Value" );
28
29           // display array index and value
30           for ( int counter = 0; counter < array.length; counter++ )
31              System.out.printf( "%5d%8d\n", counter, array[ counter ] );
32        } // end else
33     } // end main
34  } // end class InitArray
```

```
java InitArray
Error: Please re-enter the entire command, including
an array size, initial value and increment.
```

```
java InitArray 5 0 4
Index    Value
    0        0
    1        4
    2        8
    3       12
    4       16
```

```
java InitArray 8 1 2
Index    Value
    0        1
    1        3
    2        5
    3        7
    4        9
    5       11
    6       13
    7       15
```

Fig. 7.21 | Initializing an array using command-line arguments. (Part 2 of 2.)

The command-line arguments become available to main as Strings in args. Line 16 gets args[0]—a String that specifies the array size—and converts it to an int value that the program uses to create the array in line 17. The static method parseInt of class Integer converts its String argument to an int.

Lines 20–21 convert the args[1] and args[2] command-line arguments to int values and store them in initialValue and increment, respectively. Lines 24–25 calculate the value for each array element.

The output of the first execution shows that the application received an insufficient number of command-line arguments. The second execution uses command-line arguments 5, 0 and 4 to specify the size of the array (5), the value of the first element (0) and the increment of each value in the array (4), respectively. The corresponding output shows that these values create an array containing the integers 0, 4, 8, 12 and 16. The output from the third execution shows that the command-line arguments 8, 1 and 2 produce an array whose 8 elements are the nonnegative odd integers from 1 to 15.

7.13 Class Arrays

Class **Arrays** helps you avoid reinventing the wheel by providing static methods for common array manipulations. These methods include **sort** for sorting an array (i.e., arranging elements into increasing order), **binarySearch** for searching an array (i.e., determining whether an array contains a specific value and, if so, where the value is located), **equals** for comparing arrays and **fill** for placing values into an array. These methods are overloaded for primitive-type arrays and for arrays of objects. Our focus in this section is on using the built-in capabilities provided by the Java API. Chapter 19, Searching, Sorting and Big O shows how to implement your own sorting and searching algorithms, which are of great interest to computer science researchers and students.

Figure 7.22 uses Arrays methods sort, binarySearch, equals and fill, and shows how to copy arrays with class System's static **arraycopy method**. In main, line 11 sorts the elements of array doubleArray. The static method sort of class Arrays orders the array's elements in *ascending* order by default. We discuss how to sort in *descending* order later in the chapter. Overloaded versions of sort allow you to sort a specific range of elements. Lines 12–15 output the sorted array.

```java
1   // Fig. 7.22: ArrayManipulations.java
2   // Arrays class methods and System.arraycopy.
3   import java.util.Arrays;
4
5   public class ArrayManipulations
6   {
7      public static void main( String[] args )
8      {
9         // sort doubleArray into ascending order
10        double[] doubleArray = { 8.4, 9.3, 0.2, 7.9, 3.4 };
11        Arrays.sort( doubleArray );
12        System.out.printf( "\ndoubleArray: " );
13
```

Fig. 7.22 | Arrays class methods. (Part 1 of 3.)

```
14          for ( double value : doubleArray )
15              System.out.printf( "%.1f ", value );
16
17          // fill 10-element array with 7s
18          int[] filledIntArray = new int[ 10 ];
19          Arrays.fill( filledIntArray, 7 );
20          displayArray( filledIntArray, "filledIntArray" );
21
22          // copy array intArray into array intArrayCopy
23          int[] intArray = { 1, 2, 3, 4, 5, 6 };
24          int[] intArrayCopy = new int[ intArray.length ];
25          System.arraycopy( intArray, 0, intArrayCopy, 0, intArray.length );
26          displayArray( intArray, "intArray" );
27          displayArray( intArrayCopy, "intArrayCopy" );
28
29          // compare intArray and intArrayCopy for equality
30          boolean b = Arrays.equals( intArray, intArrayCopy );
31          System.out.printf( "\n\nintArray %s intArrayCopy\n",
32              ( b ? "==" : "!=" ) );
33
34          // compare intArray and filledIntArray for equality
35          b = Arrays.equals( intArray, filledIntArray );
36          System.out.printf( "intArray %s filledIntArray\n",
37              ( b ? "==" : "!=" ) );
38
39          // search intArray for the value 5
40          int location = Arrays.binarySearch( intArray, 5 );
41
42          if ( location >= 0 )
43              System.out.printf(
44                  "Found 5 at element %d in intArray\n", location );
45          else
46              System.out.println( "5 not found in intArray" );
47
48          // search intArray for the value 8763
49          location = Arrays.binarySearch( intArray, 8763 );
50
51          if ( location >= 0 )
52              System.out.printf(
53                  "Found 8763 at element %d in intArray\n", location );
54          else
55              System.out.println( "8763 not found in intArray" );
56      } // end main
57
58      // output values in each array
59      public static void displayArray( int[] array, String description )
60      {
61          System.out.printf( "\n%s: ", description );
62
63          for ( int value : array )
64              System.out.printf( "%d ", value );
65      } // end method displayArray
66  } // end class ArrayManipulations
```

Fig. 7.22 | `Arrays` class methods. (Part 2 of 3.)

```
doubleArray: 0.2 3.4 7.9 8.4 9.3
filledIntArray: 7 7 7 7 7 7 7 7 7 7
intArray: 1 2 3 4 5 6
intArrayCopy: 1 2 3 4 5 6

intArray == intArrayCopy
intArray != filledIntArray
Found 5 at element 4 in intArray
8763 not found in intArray
```

Fig. 7.22 | Arrays class methods. (Part 3 of 3.)

Line 19 calls static method fill of class Arrays to populate all 10 elements of filledIntArray with 7s. Overloaded versions of fill allow you to populate a specific range of elements with the same value. Line 20 calls our class's displayArray method (declared at lines 59–65) to output the contents of filledIntArray.

Line 25 copies the elements of intArray into intArrayCopy. The first argument (intArray) passed to System method arraycopy is the array from which elements are to be copied. The second argument (0) is the index that specifies the starting point in the range of elements to copy from the array. This value can be any valid array index. The third argument (intArrayCopy) specifies the destination array that will store the copy. The fourth argument (0) specifies the index in the destination array where the first copied element should be stored. The last argument specifies the number of elements to copy from the array in the first argument. In this case, we copy all the elements in the array.

Lines 30 and 35 call static method equals of class Arrays to determine whether all the elements of two arrays are equivalent. If the arrays contain the same elements in the same order, the method returns true; otherwise, it returns false.

Lines 40 and 49 call static method binarySearch of class Arrays to perform a binary search on intArray, using the second argument (5 and 8763, respectively) as the key. If value is found, binarySearch returns the index of the element; otherwise, binarySearch returns a negative value. The negative value returned is based on the search key's insertion point—the index where the key would be inserted in the array if we were performing an insert operation. After binarySearch determines the insertion point, it changes its sign to negative and subtracts 1 to obtain the return value. For example, in Fig. 7.22, the insertion point for the value 8763 is the element with index 6 in the array. Method binarySearch changes the insertion point to –6, subtracts 1 from it and returns the value –7. Subtracting 1 from the insertion point guarantees that method binarySearch returns positive values (>= 0) if and only if the key is found. This return value is useful for inserting elements in a sorted array. Chapter 19 discusses binary searching in detail.

Common Programming Error 7.7

Passing an unsorted array to binarySearch is a logic error—the value returned is undefined.

7.14 Introduction to Collections and Class ArrayList

The Java API provides several predefined data structures, called **collections**, used to store groups of related objects. These classes provide efficient methods that organize, store and

retrieve your data without requiring knowledge of how the data is being stored. This reduces application-development time.

You've used arrays to store sequences of objects. Arrays do not automatically change
their size at execution time to accommodate additional elements. The collection class
ArrayList<T> (from package `java.util`) provides a convenient solution to this
problem—it can dynamically change its size to accommodate more elements. The T is a
placeholder—when declaring a new `ArrayList`, replace it with the type of elements that
you want the `ArrayList` to hold. This is similar to specifying the type when declaring an
array, except that only nonprimitive types can be used with these collection classes. For
example,

```
ArrayList< String > list;
```

declares `list` as an `ArrayList` collection that can store only `Strings`. Classes with this
kind of placeholder that can be used with any type are called **generic classes**. Additional
generic collection classes and generics are discussed in Chapters 20 and 21, respectively.
Figure 7.23 shows some common methods of class `ArrayList<T>`.

Method	Description
add	Adds an element to the end of the `ArrayList`.
clear	Removes all the elements from the `ArrayList`.
contains	Returns true if the `ArrayList` contains the specified element; otherwise, returns false.
get	Returns the element at the specified index.
indexOf	Returns the index of the first occurrence of the specified element in the `ArrayList`.
remove	Removes the first occurrence of the specified value.
remove	Removes the element at the specified index.
size	Returns the number of elements stored in the `ArrayList`.
trimToSize	Trims the capacity of the `ArrayList` to current number of elements.

Fig. 7.23 | Some methods and properties of class `ArrayList<T>`.

Figure 7.24 demonstrates some common `ArrayList` capabilities. Line 10 creates a
new empty `ArrayList` of `Strings` with an initial capacity of 10 elements. The capacity
indicates how many items the `ArrayList` can hold without growing. `ArrayList` is implemented using an array behind the scenes. When the `ArrayList` grows, it must create a
larger internal array and copy each element to the new array. This is a time-consuming
operation. It would be inefficient for the `ArrayList` to grow each time an element is
added. Instead, it grows only when an element is added *and* the number of elements is
equal to the capacity—i.e., there is no space for the new element.

The **add** method adds elements to the `ArrayList` (lines 12–13). The add method with
one argument appends its argument to the end of the `ArrayList`. The add method with
two arguments inserts a new element at the specified position. The first argument is an
index. As with arrays, collection indices start at zero. The second argument is the value that
is to insert at that index. All elements at the specified index and above are shifted up by
one position. This is usually slower than adding an element to the end of the `ArrayList`.

```java
 1    // Fig. 7.24: ArrayListCollection.java
 2    // Generic ArrayList collection demonstration.
 3    import java.util.ArrayList;
 4
 5    public class ArrayListCollection
 6    {
 7       public static void main( String[] args )
 8       {
 9          // create a new ArrayList of Strings
10          ArrayList< String > items = new ArrayList< String >();
11
12          items.add( "red" ); // append an item to the list
13          items.add( 0, "yellow" ); // insert the value at index 0
14
15          // header
16          System.out.print(
17             "Display list contents with counter-controlled loop:" );
18
19          // display the colors in the list
20          for ( int i = 0; i < items.size(); i++ )
21             System.out.printf( " %s", items.get( i ) );
22
23          // display colors using foreach in the display method
24          display( items,
25             "\nDisplay list contents with enhanced for statement:" );
26
27          items.add( "green" ); // add "green" to the end of the list
28          items.add( "yellow" ); // add "yellow" to the end of the list
29          display( items, "List with two new elements:" );
30
31          items.remove( "yellow" ); // remove the first "yellow"
32          display( items, "Remove first instance of yellow:" );
33
34          items.remove( 1 ); // remove item at index 1
35          display( items, "Remove second list element (green):" );
36
37          // check if a value is in the List
38          System.out.printf( "\"red\" is %sin the list\n",
39             items.contains( "red" ) ? "": "not " );
40
41          // display number of elements in the List
42          System.out.printf( "Size: %s\n", items.size() );
43       } // end main
44
45       // display the ArrayList's elements on the console
46       public static void display( ArrayList< String > items, String header )
47       {
48          System.out.print( header ); // display header
49
50          // display each element in items
51          for ( String item : items )
52             System.out.printf( " %s", item );
53
```

Fig. 7.24 | Generic ArrayList<T> collection demonstration. (Part 1 of 2.)

```
54          System.out.println(); // display end of line
55       } // end method display
56    } // end class ArrayListCollection
```

```
Display list contents with counter-controlled loop: yellow red
Display list contents with enhanced for statement: yellow red
List with two new elements: yellow red green yellow
Remove first instance of yellow: red green yellow
Remove second list element (green): red yellow
"red" is in the list
Size: 2
```

Fig. 7.24 | Generic `ArrayList<T>` collection demonstration. (Part 2 of 2.)

Lines 20–21 display the items in the `ArrayList`. The **size** method returns the number of elements currently in the `ArrayList`. `ArrayLists` method **get** (line 21) obtains the element at a specified index. Lines 24–25 display the elements again by invoking method display (defined at lines 46–55). Lines 27–28 add two more elements to the `ArrayList`, then line 29 displays the elements again to confirm that the two elements were added to the end of the collection.

The **remove** method is used to remove an element with a specific value (line 31). Note that it removes only the first such element. If no such element is in the `ArrayList`, remove does nothing. An overloaded version of the method removes the element at the specified index (line 34). When an element is removed through either of these methods, all elements above that index are shifted down by one.

Line 39 uses the **contains** method to check if an item is in the `ArrayList`. The contains method returns true if the element is found in the `ArrayList`, and false otherwise. The method compares its argument to each element of the `ArrayList` in order, so using contains on a large `ArrayList` is inefficient. Line 42 displays the `ArrayList`'s size.

7.15 (Optional) GUI and Graphics Case Study: Drawing Arcs

Using Java's graphics features, we can create complex drawings that would be more tedious to code line by line. In Figs. 7.25–7.26, we use arrays and repetition statements to draw a rainbow by using `Graphics` method `fillArc`. Drawing arcs in Java is similar to drawing ovals—an arc is simply a section of an oval.

Figure 7.25 begins with the usual `import` statements for creating drawings (lines 3–5). Lines 10–11 declare and create two new color constants—VIOLET and INDIGO. As you may know, the colors of a rainbow are red, orange, yellow, green, blue, indigo and violet. Java has predefined constants only for the first five colors. Lines 15–17 initialize an array with the colors of the rainbow, starting with the innermost arcs first. The array begins with two Color.WHITE elements, which, as you'll soon see, are for drawing the empty arcs at the center of the rainbow. Note that the instance variables can be initialized when they are declared, as shown in lines 10–17. The constructor (lines 20–23) contains a single statement that calls method **setBackground** (which is inherited from class JPanel) with the parameter Color.WHITE. Method setBackground takes a single Color argument and sets the background of the component to that color.

```
 1   // Fig. 7.25: DrawRainbow.java
 2   // Demonstrates using colors in an array.
 3   import java.awt.Color;
 4   import java.awt.Graphics;
 5   import javax.swing.JPanel;
 6
 7   public class DrawRainbow extends JPanel
 8   {
 9      // define indigo and violet
10      private final static Color VIOLET = new Color( 128, 0, 128 );
11      private final static Color INDIGO = new Color( 75, 0, 130 );
12
13      // colors to use in the rainbow, starting from the innermost
14      // The two white entries result in an empty arc in the center
15      private Color[] colors =
16         { Color.WHITE, Color.WHITE, VIOLET, INDIGO, Color.BLUE,
17           Color.GREEN, Color.YELLOW, Color.ORANGE, Color.RED };
18
19      // constructor
20      public DrawRainbow()
21      {
22         setBackground( Color.WHITE ); // set the background to white
23      } // end DrawRainbow constructor
24
25      // draws a rainbow using concentric arcs
26      public void paintComponent( Graphics g )
27      {
28         super.paintComponent( g );
29
30         int radius = 20; // radius of an arc
31
32         // draw the rainbow near the bottom-center
33         int centerX = getWidth() / 2;
34         int centerY = getHeight() - 10;
35
36         // draws filled arcs starting with the outermost
37         for ( int counter = colors.length; counter > 0; counter-- )
38         {
39            // set the color for the current arc
40            g.setColor( colors[ counter - 1 ] );
41
42            // fill the arc from 0 to 180 degrees
43            g.fillArc( centerX - counter * radius,
44               centerY - counter * radius,
45               counter * radius * 2, counter * radius * 2, 0, 180 );
46         } // end for
47      } // end method paintComponent
48   } // end class DrawRainbow
```

Fig. 7.25 | Drawing a rainbow using arcs and an array of colors.

Line 30 in paintComponent declares local variable radius, which determines the radius of each arc. Local variables centerX and centerY (lines 33–34) determine the location of the midpoint on the base of the rainbow. The loop at lines 37–46 uses control variable counter to count backward from the end of the array, drawing the largest arcs first and placing each successive smaller arc on top of the previous one. Line 40 sets the color to draw the current arc from the array. The reason we have `Color.WHITE` entries at the beginning of the array is to create the empty arc in the center. Otherwise, the center of the rainbow would just be a solid violet semicircle. [*Note:* You can change the individual colors and the number of entries in the array to create new designs.]

The `fillArc` method call at lines 43–45 draws a filled semicircle. Method `fillArc` requires six parameters. The first four represent the bounding rectangle in which the arc will be drawn. The first two of these specify the coordinates for the upper-left corner of the bounding rectangle, and the next two specify its width and height. The fifth parameter is the starting angle on the oval, and the sixth specifies the **sweep**, or the amount of arc to cover. The starting angle and sweep are measured in degrees, with zero degrees pointing right. A positive sweep draws the arc counterclockwise, while a negative sweep draws the arc clockwise. A method similar to `fillArc` is **drawArc**—it requires the same parameters as `fillArc`, but draws the edge of the arc rather than filling it.

Class `DrawRainbowTest` (Fig. 7.26) creates and sets up a `JFrame` to display the rainbow. Once the program makes the `JFrame` visible, the system calls the `paintComponent` method in class `DrawRainbow` to draw the rainbow on the screen.

```java
 1   // Fig. 7.26: DrawRainbowTest.java
 2   // Test application to display a rainbow.
 3   import javax.swing.JFrame;
 4
 5   public class DrawRainbowTest
 6   {
 7      public static void main( String[] args )
 8      {
 9         DrawRainbow panel = new DrawRainbow();
10         JFrame application = new JFrame();
11
12         application.setDefaultCloseOperation( JFrame.EXIT_ON_CLOSE );
13         application.add( panel );
14         application.setSize( 400, 250 );
15         application.setVisible( true );
16      } // end main
17   } // end class DrawRainbowTest
```

Fig. 7.26 | Creating `JFrame` to display a rainbow.

GUI and Graphics Case Study Exercise

7.1   (*Drawing Spirals*) In this exercise, you'll draw spirals with methods drawLine and drawArc.

a)   Draw a square-shaped spiral (as in the left screen capture of Fig. 7.27), centered on the panel, using method drawLine. One technique is to use a loop that increases the line length after drawing every second line. The direction in which to draw the next line should follow a distinct pattern, such as down, left, up, right.

b)   Draw a circular spiral (as in the right screen capture of Fig. 7.27), using method drawArc to draw one semicircle at a time. Each successive semicircle should have a larger radius (as specified by the bounding rectangle's width) and should continue drawing where the previous semicircle finished.

Fig. 7.27 | Drawing a spiral using drawLine (left) and drawArc (right).

7.16 **Wrap-Up**

This chapter began our introduction to data structures, exploring the use of arrays to store data in and retrieve data from lists and tables of values. The chapter examples demonstrated how to declare an array, initialize an array and refer to individual elements of an array. The chapter introduced the enhanced for statement to iterate through arrays. We also illustrated how to pass arrays to methods and how to declare and manipulate multidimensional arrays. Finally, the chapter showed how to write methods that use variable-length argument lists and how to read arguments passed to a program from the command line.

We introduced the ArrayList<T> generic collection, which provides all the functionality and performance of arrays, along with other useful capabilities such as dynamic resizing. We used the add methods to add new items to the end of an ArrayList and to insert items in an ArrayList. The remove method was used to remove the first occurrence of a specified item, and an overloaded version of remove was used to remove an item at a specified index. We used the size method to obtain number of items in the ArrayList.

We continue our coverage of data structures in Chapter 20, Generic Collections. Chapter 20 introduces the Java Collections Framework, which uses generics to allow programmers to specify the exact types of objects that a particular data structure will store. Chapter 20 also introduces Java's other predefined data structures. The Collections API provides class Arrays, which contains utility methods for array manipulation. Chapter 20 uses several static methods of class Arrays to perform such manipulations as sorting and searching the data in an array. You'll be able to use some of the Arrays methods discussed in Chapter 20 after reading the current chapter, but some of the Arrays methods require knowledge of concepts presented later in the book. Chapter 21, presents the topic of generics, which provide the means to create general models of methods and classes that can be declared once, but used with many different data types. Chapter 22, Custom Generic Data Structures, shows how to build dynamic data structures, such as lists, queues, stacks and trees, that can grow and shrink as programs execute.

We've now introduced the basic concepts of classes, objects, control statements, methods, arrays and collections. In Chapter 8, we take a deeper look at classes and objects.

Summary

Section 7.1 Introduction
- Arrays are data structures consisting of related data items of the same type. Arrays are fixed-length entities—they remain the same length once they are created, although an array variable may be reassigned the reference of a new array of a different length.

Section 7.2 Arrays
- An array is a group of variables (called elements or components) containing values that all have the same type. Arrays are objects, so they are considered reference types.
- A program refers to any one of an array's elements with an array-access expression that includes the name of the array followed by the index of the particular element in square brackets (`[]`).
- The first element in every array has index zero and is sometimes called the zeroth element.
- An index must be a nonnegative integer. A program can use an expression as an index.
- An array object knows its own length and stores this information in a `length` instance variable.

Section 7.3 Declaring and Creating Arrays
- To create an array object, specify the array's element type and the number of elements as part of an array-creation expression that uses keyword `new`.
- When an array is created, each element receives a default value—zero for numeric primitive-type elements, `false` for boolean elements and `null` for references.
- In an array declaration, the type and the square brackets can be combined at the beginning of the declaration to indicate that all the identifiers in the declaration are array variables.
- Every element of a primitive-type array contains a variable of the array's declared type. Every element of a reference-type array is a reference to an object of the array's declared type.

Section 7.4 Examples Using Arrays
- A program can create an array and initialize its elements with an array initializer.
- Constant variables are declared with keyword `final`, must be initialized before they are used and cannot be modified thereafter.
- When a Java program executes, the JVM checks array indices to ensure that they are greater than or equal to 0 and less than the array's length. If a program uses an invalid index, Java generates a so-called exception to indicate that an error occurred in the program at execution time.

Section 7.5 Case Study: Card Shuffling and Dealing Simulation
- The `toString` method of an object is called implicitly when the object is used where a `String` is expected (e.g., when `printf` outputs the object as a `String` using the `%s` format specifier or when the object is concatenated to a `String` using the + operator).

Section 7.6 Enhanced **for** Statement

- The enhanced for statement allows you to iterate through the elements of an array or a collection without using a counter. The syntax of an enhanced for statement is:

  ```
  for ( parameter : arrayName )
      statement
  ```

  where *parameter* has a type and an identifier (e.g., int number), and *arrayName* is the array through which to iterate.
- The enhanced for statement cannot be used to modify elements in an array. If a program needs to modify elements, use the traditional counter-controlled for statement.

Section 7.7 Passing Arrays to Methods

- When an argument is passed by value, a copy of the argument's value is made and passed to the called method. The called method works exclusively with the copy.
- When an argument is passed by reference, the called method can access the argument's value in the caller directly and possibly modify it.
- Java does not allow programmers to choose between pass-by-value and pass-by-reference—all arguments are passed by value. A method call can pass two types of values to a method—copies of primitive values and copies of references to objects. Although an object's reference is passed by value, a method can still interact with the referenced object by calling its public methods using the copy of the object's reference.
- To pass an object reference to a method, simply specify in the method call the name of the variable that refers to the object.
- When you pass an array or an individual array element of a reference type to a method, the called method receives a copy of the array or element's reference. When you pass an individual element of a primitive type, the called method receives a copy of the element's value.
- To pass an individual array element to a method, use the indexed name of the array as an argument in the method call.

Section 7.9 Multidimensional Arrays

- Multidimensional arrays with two dimensions are often used to represent tables of values consisting of information arranged in rows and columns.
- Arrays that require two indices to identify a particular element are called two-dimensional arrays. An array with *m* rows and *n* columns is called an *m*-by-*n* array. A two-dimensional array can be initialized with an array initializer of the form

  ```
  arrayType[][] arrayName = { { row1 initializer }, { row2 initializer }, ... };
  ```
- Multidimensional arrays are maintained as arrays of separate one-dimensional arrays. As a result, the lengths of the rows in a two-dimensional array are not required to be the same.
- A multidimensional array with the same number of columns in every row can be created with an array-creation expression of the form

  ```
  arrayType[][] arrayName = new arrayType[ numRows ][ numColumns ];
  ```

Section 7.11 Variable-Length Argument Lists

- An argument type followed by an ellipsis (...) in a method's parameter list indicates that the method receives a variable number of arguments of that particular type. The ellipsis can occur only once in a method's parameter list, and it must be at the end of the parameter list.
- A variable-length argument list is treated as an array within the method body. The number of arguments in the array can be obtained using the array's length field.

Section 7.12 Using Command-Line Arguments

- Passing arguments to `main` from the command line is achieved by including a parameter of type `String[]` in the parameter list of `main`. By convention, `main`'s parameter is named `args`.

- Java passes the command-line arguments that appear after the class name in the `java` command to the application's `main` method as `Strings` in the array `args`. The number of arguments passed in from the command line is obtained by accessing the array's `length` attribute.

Section 7.13 Class `Arrays`

- Class `Arrays` provides `static` methods that pefore common array manipulations, including `sort` to sort an array, `binarySearch` to search a sorted array, `equals` to compare arrays and `fill` to place items in an array.

- Class `System`'s `arraycopy` method enables you to copy the elements of one array into another.

Section 7.14 Introduction to Collections and Class `ArrayList`

- The Java API's collection classes provide efficient methods that organize, store and retrieve data without requiring knowledge of how the data is being stored.

- An `ArrayList<T>` is similar to an array, but can be dynamically resized.

- The `add` method with one argument appends an element to the end of an `ArrayList`.

- The `add` method with two arguments inserts a new element at a specified position in an `ArrayList`.

- The `size` method returns the number of elements currently in an `ArrayList`.

- The `remove` method with a reference to an object as an argument removes the first element that matches the argument's value.

- The `remove` method with an integer argument removes the element at the specified index and all elements above that index are shifted down by one.

- The `contains` method returns `true` if the element is found in the `ArrayList`, and `false` otherwise.

Terminology

Self-Review Exercises

7.1   Fill in the blank(s) in each of the following statements:
a) Lists and tables of values can be stored in _____.
b) An array is a group of _____ (called elements or components) containing values that all have the same _____.
c) The _____ allows programmers to iterate through the elements in an array without using a counter.
d) The number used to refer to a particular array element is called the element's _____.
e) An array that uses two indices is referred to as a(n) _____ array.
f) Use the enhanced `for` statement _____ to walk through `double` array `numbers`.
g) Command-line arguments are stored in _____.
h) Use the expression _____ to receive the total number of arguments in a command line. Assume that command-line arguments are stored in `String[] args`.
i) Given the command `java MyClass test`, the first command-line argument is _____.
j) A(n) _____ in the parameter list of a method indicates that the method can receive a variable number of arguments.

7.2   Determine whether each of the following is *true* or *false*. If *false*, explain why.
a) An array can store many different types of values.
b) An array index should normally be of type `float`.
c) An individual array element that is passed to a method and modified in that method will contain the modified value when the called method completes execution.
d) Command-line arguments are separated by commas.

7.3   Perform the following tasks for an array called `fractions`:
a) Declare a constant `ARRAY_SIZE` that is initialized to 10.
b) Declare an array with `ARRAY_SIZE` elements of type `double`, and initialize the elements to 0.
c) Refer to array element 4.
d) Assign the value `1.667` to array element 9.
e) Assign the value `3.333` to array element 6.
f) Sum all the elements of the array, using a `for` statement. Declare the integer variable x as a control variable for the loop.

7.4   Perform the following tasks for an array called `table`:
a) Declare and create the array as an integer array that has three rows and three columns. Assume that the constant `ARRAY_SIZE` has been declared to be 3.
b) How many elements does the array contain?
c) Use a `for` statement to initialize each element of the array to the sum of its indices. Assume that the integer variables x and y are declared as control variables.

7.5   Find and correct the error in each of the following program segments:
a) `final int ARRAY_SIZE = 5;`
   `ARRAY_SIZE = 10;`
b) Assume `int[] b = new int[ 10 ];`
   `for ( int i = 0; i <= b.length; i++ )`
     `b[ i ] = 1;`
c) Assume `int[][] a = { { 1, 2 }, { 3, 4 } };`
     `a[ 1, 1 ] = 5;`

Answers to Self-Review Exercises

7.1   a) arrays. b) variables, type. c) enhanced `for` statement. d) index (or subscript or position number). e) two-dimensional. f) `for ( double d : numbers )`. g) an array of `String`s, called `args` by convention. h) `args.length`. i) `test`. j) ellipsis (`...`).

7.2   a)   False. An array can store only values of the same type.

 b)   False. An array index must be an integer or an integer expression.

 c)   For individual primitive-type elements of an array: False. A called method receives and manipulates a copy of the value of such an element, so modifications do not affect the original value. If the reference of an array is passed to a method, however, modifications to the array elements made in the called method are indeed reflected in the original. For individual elements of a reference type: True. A called method receives a copy of the reference of such an element, and changes to the referenced object will be reflected in the original array element.

 d)   False. Command-line arguments are separated by white space.

7.3   a)   `final int ARRAY_SIZE = 10;`

 b)   `double[] fractions = new double[ ARRAY_SIZE ];`

 c)   `fractions[ 4 ]`

 d)   `fractions[ 9 ] = 1.667;`

 e)   `fractions[ 6 ] = 3.333;`

 f)   `double total = 0.0;`
```
for ( int x = 0; x < fractions.length; x++ )
    total += fractions[ x ];
```

7.4   a)   `int[][] table = new int[ ARRAY_SIZE ][ ARRAY_SIZE ];`

 b)   Nine.

 c)
```
for ( int x = 0; x < table.length; x++ )
    for ( int y = 0; y < table[ x ].length; y++ )
        table[ x ][ y ] = x + y;
```

7.5   a)   Error: Assigning a value to a constant after it has been initialized.
 Correction: Assign the correct value to the constant in a `final int ARRAY_SIZE` declaration or declare another variable.

 b)   Error: Referencing an array element outside the bounds of the array (`b[10]`).
 Correction: Change the `<=` operator to `<`.

 c)   Error: Array indexing is performed incorrectly.
 Correction: Change the statement to `a[ 1 ][ 1 ] = 5;`.

Exercises

7.6   Fill in the blanks in each of the following statements:

 a)   One-dimensional array p contains four elements. The names of those elements are _____, _____, _____ and _____.

 b)   Naming an array, stating its type and specifying the number of dimensions in the array is called _____ the array.

 c)   In a two-dimensional array, the first index identifies the _____ of an element and the second index identifies the _____ of an element.

 d)   An *m*-by-*n* array contains _____ rows, _____ columns and _____ elements.

 e)   The name of the element in row 3 and column 5 of array d is _____.

7.7   Consider a two-by-three integer array t.

 a)   Write a statement that declares and creates t.

 b)   How many rows does t have?

 c)   How many columns does t have?

 d)   How many elements does t have?

 e)   Write access expressions for all the elements in row 1 of t.

 f)   Write access expressions for all the elements in column 2 of t.

 g)   Write a single statement that sets the element of t in row 0 and column 1 to zero.

 h)   Write individual statements to initialize each element of t to zero.

    i) Write a nested `for` statement that initializes each element of t to zero.

    j) Write a nested `for` statement that inputs the values for the elements of t from the user.

    k) Write a series of statements that determines and displays the smallest value in t.

    l) Write a single `printf` statement that displays the elements of the first row of t.

    m) Write a statement that totals the elements of the third column of t. Do not use repetition.

    n) Write a series of statements that displays the contents of t in tabular format. List the column indices as headings across the top, and list the row indices at the left of each row.

7.8   *(Sales Commissions)* Use a one-dimensional array to solve the following problem: A company pays its salespeople on a commission basis. The salespeople receive $200 per week plus 9% of their gross sales for that week. For example, a salesperson who grosses $5000 in sales in a week receives $200 plus 9% of $5000, or a total of $650. Write an application (using an array of counters) that determines how many of the salespeople earned salaries in each of the following ranges (assume that each salesperson's salary is truncated to an integer amount):

    a) $200–299
    b) $300–399
    c) $400–499
    d) $500–599
    e) $600–699
    f) $700–799
    g) $800–899
    h) $900–999
    i) $1000 and over

Summarize the results in tabular format.

7.9   Write statements that perform the following one-dimensional-array operations:

    a) Set the 10 elements of integer array `counts` to zero.

    b) Add one to each of the 15 elements of integer array `bonus`.

    c) Display the five values of integer array `bestScores` in column format.

7.10   *(Duplicate Elimination)* Use a one-dimensional array to solve the following problem: Write an application that inputs five numbers, each between 10 and 100, inclusive. As each number is read, display it only if it's not a duplicate of a number already read. Provide for the "worst case," in which all five numbers are different. Use the smallest possible array to solve this problem. Display the complete set of unique values input after the user enters each new value.

7.11   Write an application that calculates the product of a series of integers that are passed to method `product` using a variable-length argument list. Test your method with several calls, each with a different number of arguments.

7.12   Rewrite Fig. 7.2 so that the size of the array is specified by the first command-line argument. If no command-line argument is supplied, use 10 as the default size of the array.

7.13   Write an application that uses an enhanced `for` statement to sum the `double` values passed by the command-line arguments. [*Hint:* Use the `static` method `parseDouble` of class `Double` to convert a `String` to a `double` value.]

7.14   *(Airline Reservations System)* A small airline has just purchased a computer for its new automated reservations system. You've been asked to develop the new system. You are to write an application to assign seats on each flight of the airline's only plane (capacity: 10 seats).

    Your application should display the following alternatives: `Please type 1 for First Class` and `Please type 2 for Economy`. If the user types 1, your application should assign a seat in the first-class section (seats 1–5). If the user types 2, your application should assign a seat in the economy section (seats 6–10). Your application should then display a boarding pass indicating the person's seat number and whether it's in the first-class or economy section of the plane.

Use a one-dimensional array of primitive type boolean to represent the seating chart of the plane. Initialize all the elements of the array to false to indicate that all the seats are empty. As each seat is assigned, set the corresponding element of the array to true to indicate that the seat is no longer available.

Your application should never assign a seat that has already been assigned. When the economy section is full, your application should ask the person if it's acceptable to be placed in the first-class section (and vice versa). If yes, make the appropriate seat assignment. If no, display the message "Next flight leaves in 3 hours."

7.15 *(Total Sales)* Use a two-dimensional array to solve the following problem: A company has four salespeople (1 to 4) who sell five different products (1 to 5). Once a day, each salesperson passes in a slip for each type of product sold. Each slip contains the following:

    a) The salesperson number
    b) The product number
    c) The total dollar value of that product sold that day

Thus, each salesperson passes in between 0 and 5 sales slips per day. Assume that the information from all the slips for last month is available. Write an application that will read all this information for last month's sales and summarize the total sales by salesperson and by product. All totals should be stored in the two-dimensional array sales. After processing all the information for last month, display the results in tabular format, with each column representing a particular salesperson and each row representing a particular product. Cross-total each row to get the total sales of each product for last month. Cross-total each column to get the total sales by salesperson for last month. Your tabular output should include these cross-totals to the right of the totaled rows and to the bottom of the totaled columns.

7.16 *(Turtle Graphics)* The Logo language made the concept of *turtle graphics* famous. Imagine a mechanical turtle that walks around the room under the control of a Java application. The turtle holds a pen in one of two positions, up or down. While the pen is down, the turtle traces out shapes as it moves, and while the pen is up, the turtle moves about freely without writing anything. In this problem, you'll simulate the operation of the turtle and create a computerized sketchpad.

Use a 20-by-20 array floor that is initialized to zeros. Read commands from an array that contains them. Keep track of the current position of the turtle at all times and whether the pen is currently up or down. Assume that the turtle always starts at position (0, 0) of the floor with its pen up. The set of turtle commands your application must process are shown in Fig. 7.28.

Command	Meaning
1	Pen up
2	Pen down
3	Turn right
4	Turn left
5,10	Move forward 10 spaces (replace 10 for a different number of spaces)
6	Display the 20-by-20 array
9	End of data (sentinel)

Fig. 7.28 | Turtle graphics commands.

```
2
5,12
3
5,12
3
5,12
3
5,12
1
6
9
```

As the turtle moves with the pen down, set the appropriate elements of array floor to 1s. When the 6 command (display the array) is given, wherever there is a 1 in the array, display an asterisk or any character you choose. Wherever there is a 0, display a blank.

Write an application to implement the turtle graphics capabilities discussed here. Write several turtle graphics programs to draw interesting shapes. Add other commands to increase the power of your turtle graphics language.

7.17   *(Knight's Tour)* An interesting puzzler for chess buffs is the Knight's Tour problem, originally proposed by the mathematician Euler. Can the knight piece move around an empty chessboard and touch each of the 64 squares once and only once? We study this intriguing problem in depth here.

The knight makes only L-shaped moves (two spaces in one direction and one space in a perpendicular direction). Thus, as shown in Fig. 7.29, from a square near the middle of an empty chessboard, the knight (labeled K) can make eight different moves (numbered 0 through 7).

Fig. 7.29 | The eight possible moves of the knight.

a) Draw an eight-by-eight chessboard on a sheet of paper, and attempt a Knight's Tour by hand. Put a 1 in the starting square, a 2 in the second square, a 3 in the third, and so on. Before starting the tour, estimate how far you think you'll get, remembering that a full tour consists of 64 moves. How far did you get? Was this close to your estimate?

b) Now let's develop an application that will move the knight around a chessboard. The board is represented by an eight-by-eight two-dimensional array board. Each square is initialized to zero. We describe each of the eight possible moves in terms of its horizontal and vertical components. For example, a move of type 0, as shown in Fig. 7.29, consists of moving two squares horizontally to the right and one square vertically upward. A move of type 2 consists of moving one square horizontally to the left and two squares vertically upward. Horizontal moves to the left and vertical moves upward are indicated with negative numbers. The eight moves may be described by two one-dimensional arrays, horizontal and vertical, as follows:

```
horizontal[ 0 ] = 2          vertical[ 0 ] = -1
horizontal[ 1 ] = 1          vertical[ 1 ] = -2
horizontal[ 2 ] = -1         vertical[ 2 ] = -2
horizontal[ 3 ] = -2         vertical[ 3 ] = -1
horizontal[ 4 ] = -2         vertical[ 4 ] = 1
horizontal[ 5 ] = -1         vertical[ 5 ] = 2
horizontal[ 6 ] = 1          vertical[ 6 ] = 2
horizontal[ 7 ] = 2          vertical[ 7 ] = 1
```

Let the variables `currentRow` and `currentColumn` indicate the row and column, respectively, of the knight's current position. To make a move of type `moveNumber`, where `moveNumber` is between 0 and 7, your application should use the statements

```
currentRow += vertical[ moveNumber ];
currentColumn += horizontal[ moveNumber ];
```

Write an application to move the knight around the chessboard. Keep a counter that varies from 1 to 64. Record the latest count in each square the knight moves to. Test each potential move to see if the knight has already visited that square. Test every potential move to ensure that the knight does not land off the chessboard. Run the application. How many moves did the knight make?

c) After attempting to write and run a Knight's Tour application, you've probably developed some valuable insights. We'll use these insights to develop a *heuristic* (i.e., a common-sense rule) for moving the knight. Heuristics do not guarantee success, but a carefully developed heuristic greatly improves the chance of success. You may have observed that the outer squares are more troublesome than the squares nearer the center of the board. In fact, the most troublesome or inaccessible squares are the four corners.

Intuition may suggest that you should attempt to move the knight to the most troublesome squares first and leave open those that are easiest to get to, so that when the board gets congested near the end of the tour, there will be a greater chance of success.

We could develop an "accessibility heuristic" by classifying each of the squares according to how accessible it is and always moving the knight (using the knight's L-shaped moves) to the most inaccessible square. We label a two-dimensional array `accessibility` with numbers indicating from how many squares each particular square is accessible. On a blank chessboard, each of the 16 squares nearest the center is rated as 8, each corner square is rated as 2, and the other squares have accessibility numbers of 3, 4 or 6 as follows:

```
2  3  4  4  4  4  3  2
3  4  6  6  6  6  4  3
4  6  8  8  8  8  6  4
4  6  8  8  8  8  6  4
4  6  8  8  8  8  6  4
4  6  8  8  8  8  6  4
3  4  6  6  6  6  4  3
2  3  4  4  4  4  3  2
```

Write a new version of the Knight's Tour, using the accessibility heuristic. The knight should always move to the square with the lowest accessibility number. In case of a tie, the knight may move to any of the tied squares. Therefore, the tour may begin in any of the four corners. [*Note:* As the knight moves around the chessboard, your application should reduce the accessibility numbers as more squares become occupied. In this way, at any given time during the tour, each available square's accessibility number will remain equal to precisely the number of squares from which that square may be reached.] Run this version of your application. Did you get a full tour? Modify the application to run 64 tours, one starting from each square of the chessboard. How many full tours did you get?

d) Write a version of the Knight's Tour application that, when encountering a tie between two or more squares, decides what square to choose by looking ahead to those squares reachable from the "tied" squares. Your application should move to the tied square for which the next move would arrive at a square with the lowest accessibility number.

7.18 *(Knight's Tour: Brute-Force Approaches)* In part (c) of Exercise 7.17, we developed a solution to the Knight's Tour problem. The approach used, called the "accessibility heuristic," generates many solutions and executes efficiently.

As computers continue to increase in power, we'll be able to solve more problems with sheer computer power and relatively unsophisticated algorithms. Let's call this approach "brute-force" problem solving.

a) Use random-number generation to enable the knight to walk around the chessboard (in its legitimate L-shaped moves) at random. Your application should run one tour and display the final chessboard. How far did the knight get?

b) Most likely, the application in part (a) produced a relatively short tour. Now modify your application to attempt 1000 tours. Use a one-dimensional array to keep track of the number of tours of each length. When your application finishes attempting the 1000 tours, it should display this information in neat tabular format. What was the best result?

c) Most likely, the application in part (b) gave you some "respectable" tours, but no full tours. Now let your application run until it produces a full tour. [*Caution:* This version of the application could run for hours on a powerful computer.] Once again, keep a table of the number of tours of each length, and display this table when the first full tour is found. How many tours did your application attempt before producing a full tour? How much time did it take?

d) Compare the brute-force version of the Knight's Tour with the accessibility-heuristic version. Which required a more careful study of the problem? Which algorithm was more difficult to develop? Which required more computer power? Could we be certain (in advance) of obtaining a full tour with the accessibility-heuristic approach? Could we be certain (in advance) of obtaining a full tour with the brute-force approach? Argue the pros and cons of brute-force problem solving in general.

7.19 *(Eight Queens)* Another puzzler for chess buffs is the Eight Queens problem, which asks the following: Is it possible to place eight queens on an empty chessboard so that no queen is "attacking" any other (i.e., no two queens are in the same row, in the same column or along the same diagonal)? Use the thinking developed in Exercise 7.17 to formulate a heuristic for solving the Eight Queens problem. Run your application. [*Hint:* It's possible to assign a value to each square of the chessboard to indicate how many squares of an empty chessboard are "eliminated" if a queen is placed in that square. Each of the corners would be assigned the value 22, as demonstrated by Fig. 7.30. Once these "elimination numbers" are placed in all 64 squares, an appropriate heuristic might be as follows: Place the next queen in the square with the smallest elimination number. Why is this strategy intuitively appealing?]

Fig. 7.30 | The 22 squares eliminated by placing a queen in the upper left corner.

7.20 *(Eight Queens: Brute-Force Approaches)* In this exercise, you'll develop several brute-force approaches to solving the Eight Queens problem introduced in Exercise 7.19.
a) Use the random brute-force technique developed in Exercise 7.18 to solve the Eight Queens problem.
b) Use an exhaustive technique (i.e., try all possible combinations of eight queens on the chessboard) to solve the Eight Queens problem.
c) Why might the exhaustive brute-force approach not be appropriate for solving the Knight's Tour problem?
d) Compare and contrast the random brute-force and exhaustive brute-force approaches.

7.21 *(Knight's Tour: Closed-Tour Test)* In the Knight's Tour (Exercise 7.17), a full tour occurs when the knight makes 64 moves, touching each square of the chessboard once and only once. A closed tour occurs when the 64th move is one move away from the square in which the knight started the tour. Modify the application you wrote in Exercise 7.17 to test for a closed tour if a full tour has occurred.

7.22 *(Sieve of Eratosthenes)* A prime number is any integer greater than 1 that is evenly divisible only by itself and 1. The Sieve of Eratosthenes is a method of finding prime numbers. It operates as follows:
a) Create a primitive-type `boolean` array with all elements initialized to `true`. Array elements with prime indices will remain `true`. All other array elements will eventually be set to `false`.
b) Starting with array index 2, determine whether a given element is `true`. If so, loop through the remainder of the array and set to `false` every element whose index is a multiple of the index for the element with value `true`. Then continue the process with the next element with value `true`. For array index 2, all elements beyond element 2 in the array that have indices which are multiples of 2 (indices 4, 6, 8, 10, etc.) will be set to `false`; for array index 3, all elements beyond element 3 in the array that have indices which are multiples of 3 (indices 6, 9, 12, 15, etc.) will be set to `false`; and so on.

When this process completes, the array elements that are still `true` indicate that the index is a prime number. These indices can be displayed. Write an application that uses an array of 1000 elements to determine and display the prime numbers between 2 and 999. Ignore array elements 0 and 1.

7.23 *(Simulation: The Tortoise and the Hare)* In this problem, you'll re-create the classic race of the tortoise and the hare. You'll use random-number generation to develop a simulation of this memorable event.

Our contenders begin the race at square 1 of 70 squares. Each square represents a possible position along the race course. The finish line is at square 70. The first contender to reach or pass square 70 is rewarded with a pail of fresh carrots and lettuce. The course weaves its way up the side of a slippery mountain, so occasionally the contenders lose ground.

A clock ticks once per second. With each tick of the clock, your application should adjust the position of the animals according to the rules in Fig. 7.31. Use variables to keep track of the positions of the animals (i.e., position numbers are 1–70). Start each animal at position 1 (the "starting gate"). If an animal slips left before square 1, move it back to square 1.

Animal	Move type	Percentage of the time	Actual move
Tortoise	Fast plod	50%	3 squares to the right
	Slip	20%	6 squares to the left
	Slow plod	30%	1 square to the right
Hare	Sleep	20%	No move at all
	Big hop	20%	9 squares to the right
	Big slip	10%	12 squares to the left
	Small hop	30%	1 square to the right
	Small slip	20%	2 squares to the left

Fig. 7.31 | Rules for adjusting the positions of the tortoise and the hare.

Generate the percentages in Fig. 7.31 by producing a random integer i in the range $1 \le i \le 10$. For the tortoise, perform a "fast plod" when $1 \le i \le 5$, a "slip" when $6 \le i \le 7$ or a "slow plod" when $8 \le i \le 10$. Use a similar technique to move the hare.

Begin the race by displaying

```
BANG !!!!!
AND THEY'RE OFF !!!!!
```

Then, for each tick of the clock (i.e., each repetition of a loop), display a 70-position line showing the letter T in the position of the tortoise and the letter H in the position of the hare. Occasionally, the contenders will land on the same square. In this case, the tortoise bites the hare, and your application should display OUCH!!! beginning at that position. All output positions other than the T, the H or the OUCH!!! (in case of a tie) should be blank.

After each line is displayed, test for whether either animal has reached or passed square 70. If so, display the winner and terminate the simulation. If the tortoise wins, display TORTOISE WINS!!! YAY!!! If the hare wins, display Hare wins. Yuch. If both animals win on the same tick of the clock, you may want to favor the tortoise (the "underdog"), or you may want to display It's a tie. If neither animal wins, perform the loop again to simulate the next tick of the clock. When you are ready to run your application, assemble a group of fans to watch the race. You'll be amazed at how involved your audience gets!

Later in the book, we introduce a number of Java capabilities, such as graphics, images, animation, sound and multithreading. As you study those features, you might enjoy enhancing your tortoise-and-hare contest simulation.

7.24 *(Fibonacci Series)* The Fibonacci series

0, 1, 1, 2, 3, 5, 8, 13, 21, ...

begins with the terms 0 and 1 and has the property that each succeeding term is the sum of the two preceding terms.

    a) Write a method fibonacci(n) that calculates the nth Fibonacci number. Incorporate this method into an application that enables the user to enter the value of n.

b) Determine the largest Fibonacci number that can be displayed on your system.

c) Modify the application you wrote in part (a) to use `double` instead of `int` to calculate and return Fibonacci numbers, and use this modified application to repeat part (b).

Exercises 7.25–7.28 are reasonably challenging. Once you've done them, you ought to be able to implement most popular card games easily.

7.25 *(Card Shuffling and Dealing)* Modify the application of Fig. 7.11 to deal a five-card poker hand. Then modify class `DeckOfCards` of Fig. 7.10 to include methods that determine whether a hand contains

a) a pair

b) two pairs

c) three of a kind (e.g., three jacks)

d) four of a kind (e.g., four aces)

e) a flush (i.e., all five cards of the same suit)

f) a straight (i.e., five cards of consecutive face values)

g) a full house (i.e., two cards of one face value and three cards of another face value)

[*Hint:* Add methods `getFace` and `getSuit` to class `Card` of Fig. 7.9.]

7.26 *(Card Shuffling and Dealing)* Use the methods developed in Exercise 7.25 to write an application that deals two five-card poker hands, evaluates each hand and determines which is better.

7.27 *(Card Shuffling and Dealing)* Modify the application developed in Exercise 7.26 so that it can simulate the dealer. The dealer's five-card hand is dealt "face down," so the player cannot see it. The application should then evaluate the dealer's hand, and, based on the quality of the hand, the dealer should draw one, two or three more cards to replace the corresponding number of unneeded cards in the original hand. The application should then reevaluate the dealer's hand. [*Caution:* This is a difficult problem!]

7.28 *(Card Shuffling and Dealing)* Modify the application developed in Exercise 7.27 so that it can handle the dealer's hand automatically, but the player is allowed to decide which cards of the player's hand to replace. The application should then evaluate both hands and determine who wins. Now use this new application to play 20 games against the computer. Who wins more games, you or the computer? Have a friend play 20 games against the computer. Who wins more games? Based on the results of these games, refine your poker-playing application. (This, too, is a difficult problem.) Play 20 more games. Does your modified application play a better game?

7.29 *(Card Shuffling and Dealing)* Modify the application of Figs. 7.9–7.11 to use `Face` and `Suit` enumerations to represent the faces and suits of the cards. Declare each of these enumerations as a `public` type in its own source-code file. Each `Card` should have a `Face` and a `Suit` instance variable. These should be initialized by the `Card` constructor. In class `DeckOfCards`, create an array of `Faces` that is initialized with the names of the constants in the `Face` enumeration and an array of `Suits` that is initialized with the names of the constants in the `Suit` enumeration. [*Note:* When you output an enumeration constant as a `String`, the name of the constant is displayed.]

Special Section: Building Your Own Computer

In the next several problems, we take a temporary diversion from the world of high-level language programming to "peel open" a computer and look at its internal structure. We introduce machine-language programming and write several machine-language programs. To make this an especially valuable experience, we then build a computer (through the technique of software-based *simulation*) on which you can execute your machine-language programs.

7.30 *(Machine-Language Programming)* Let's create a computer called the Simpletron. As its name implies, it's a simple, but powerful, machine. The Simpletron runs programs written in the only language it directly understands: Simpletron Machine Language (SML).

The Simpletron contains an *accumulator*—a special register in which information is put before the Simpletron uses that information in calculations or examines it in various ways. All the information in the Simpletron is handled in terms of *words*. A word is a signed four-digit decimal number, such as +3364, -1293, +0007 and -0001. The Simpletron is equipped with a 100-word memory, and these words are referenced by their location numbers 00, 01, ..., 99.

Before running an SML program, we must *load*, or place, the program into memory. The first instruction (or statement) of every SML program is always placed in location 00. The simulator will start executing at this location.

Each instruction written in SML occupies one word of the Simpletron's memory (and hence instructions are signed four-digit decimal numbers). We shall assume that the sign of an SML instruction is always plus, but the sign of a data word may be either plus or minus. Each location in the Simpletron's memory may contain an instruction, a data value used by a program or an unused (and hence undefined) area of memory. The first two digits of each SML instruction are the *operation code* specifying the operation to be performed. SML operation codes are summarized in Fig. 7.32.

Operation code	Meaning
Input/output operations:	
`final int READ = 10;`	Read a word from the keyboard into a specific location in memory.
`final int WRITE = 11;`	Write a word from a specific location in memory to the screen.
Load/store operations:	
`final int LOAD = 20;`	Load a word from a specific location in memory into the accumulator.
`final int STORE = 21;`	Store a word from the accumulator into a specific location in memory.
Arithmetic operations:	
`final int ADD = 30;`	Add a word from a specific location in memory to the word in the accumulator (leave the result in the accumulator).
`final int SUBTRACT = 31;`	Subtract a word from a specific location in memory from the word in the accumulator (leave the result in the accumulator).
`final int DIVIDE = 32;`	Divide a word from a specific location in memory into the word in the accumulator (leave result in the accumulator).
`final int MULTIPLY = 33;`	Multiply a word from a specific location in memory by the word in the accumulator (leave the result in the accumulator).
Transfer-of-control operations:	
`final int BRANCH = 40;`	Branch to a specific location in memory.
`final int BRANCHNEG = 41;`	Branch to a specific location in memory if the accumulator is negative.
`final int BRANCHZERO = 42;`	Branch to a specific location in memory if the accumulator is zero.
`final int HALT = 43;`	Halt. The program has completed its task.

Fig. 7.32 | Simpletron Machine Language (SML) operation codes.

The last two digits of an SML instruction are the *operand*—the address of the memory location containing the word to which the operation applies. Let's consider several simple SML programs.

The first SML program (Fig. 7.33) reads two numbers from the keyboard and computes and displays their sum. The instruction +1007 reads the first number from the keyboard and places it into location 07 (which has been initialized to 0). Then instruction +1008 reads the next number into location 08. The *load* instruction, +2007, puts the first number into the accumulator, and the *add* instruction, +3008, adds the second number to the number in the accumulator. *All SML arithmetic instructions leave their results in the accumulator.* The *store* instruction, +2109, places the result back into memory location 09, from which the *write* instruction, +1109, takes the number and displays it (as a signed four-digit decimal number). The *halt* instruction, +4300, terminates execution.

Location	Number	Instruction
00	+1007	(Read A)
01	+1008	(Read B)
02	+2007	(Load A)
03	+3008	(Add B)
04	+2109	(Store C)
05	+1109	(Write C)
06	+4300	(Halt)
07	+0000	(Variable A)
08	+0000	(Variable B)
09	+0000	(Result C)

Fig. 7.33 | SML program that reads two integers and computes their sum.

The second SML program (Fig. 7.34) reads two numbers from the keyboard and determines and displays the larger value. Note the use of the instruction +4107 as a conditional transfer of control, much the same as Java's `if` statement.

Location	Number	Instruction
00	+1009	(Read A)
01	+1010	(Read B)
02	+2009	(Load A)
03	+3110	(Subtract B)
04	+4107	(Branch negative to 07)
05	+1109	(Write A)
06	+4300	(Halt)
07	+1110	(Write B)
08	+4300	(Halt)
09	+0000	(Variable A)
10	+0000	(Variable B)

Fig. 7.34 | SML program that reads two integers and determines the larger.

Now write SML programs to accomplish each of the following tasks:

a) Use a sentinel-controlled loop to read 10 positive numbers. Compute and display their sum.

b) Use a counter-controlled loop to read seven numbers, some positive and some negative, and compute and display their average.

c) Read a series of numbers, and determine and display the largest number. The first number read indicates how many numbers should be processed.

7.31   *(Computer Simulator)* In this problem, you are going to build your own computer. No, you'll not be soldering components together. Rather, you'll use the powerful technique of *software-based simulation* to create an object-oriented *software model* of the Simpletron of Exercise 7.30. Your Simpletron simulator will turn the computer you are using into a Simpletron, and you'll actually be able to run, test and debug the SML programs you wrote in Exercise 7.30.

When you run your Simpletron simulator, it should begin by displaying:

```
*** Welcome to Simpletron! ***
*** Please enter your program one instruction    ***
*** (or data word) at a time. I will display     ***
*** the location number and a question mark (?) ***
*** You then type the word for that location.    ***
*** Type -99999 to stop entering your program.   ***
```

Your application should simulate the memory of the Simpletron with a one-dimensional array memory that has 100 elements. Now assume that the simulator is running, and let's examine the dialog as we enter the program of Fig. 7.34 (Exercise 7.30):

```
00 ? +1009
01 ? +1010
02 ? +2009
03 ? +3110
04 ? +4107
05 ? +1109
06 ? +4300
07 ? +1110
08 ? +4300
09 ? +0000
10 ? +0000
11 ? -99999
```

Your program should display the memory location followed by a question mark. Each value to the right of a question mark is input by the user. When the sentinel value -99999 is input, the program should display the following:

```
*** Program loading completed ***
*** Program execution begins   ***
```

The SML program has now been placed (or loaded) in array memory. Now the Simpletron executes the SML program. Execution begins with the instruction in location 00 and, as in Java, continues sequentially, unless directed to some other part of the program by a transfer of control.

Use the variable accumulator to represent the accumulator register. Use the variable instructionCounter to keep track of the location in memory that contains the instruction being performed. Use the variable operationCode to indicate the operation currently being performed (i.e., the left two digits of the instruction word). Use the variable operand to indicate the memory location on which the current instruction operates. Thus, operand is the rightmost two digits of the instruction currently being performed. Do not execute instructions directly from memory. Rather, transfer the next instruction to be performed from memory to a variable called instructionRegister. Then "pick off" the left two digits and place them in operationCode, and "pick off" the right two digits and place them in operand. When the Simpletron begins execution, the special registers are all initialized to zero.

Now, let's "walk through" execution of the first SML instruction, +1009 in memory location 00. This procedure is called an *instruction-execution cycle*.

The `instructionCounter` tells us the location of the next instruction to be performed. We *fetch* the contents of that location from `memory` by using the Java statement

```
instructionRegister = memory[ instructionCounter ];
```

The operation code and the operand are extracted from the instruction register by the statements

```
operationCode = instructionRegister / 100;
operand = instructionRegister % 100;
```

Now the Simpletron must determine that the operation code is actually a *read* (versus a *write*, a *load*, and so on). A `switch` differentiates among the 12 operations of SML. In the `switch` statement, the behavior of various SML instructions is simulated as shown in Fig. 7.35. We discuss branch instructions shortly and leave the others to you.

Instruction	Description
read:	Display the prompt `"Enter an integer"`, then input the integer and store it in location `memory[operand]`.
load:	`accumulator = memory[ operand ];`
add:	`accumulator += memory[ operand ];`
halt:	This instruction displays the message `*** Simpletron execution terminated ***`

Fig. 7.35 | Behavior of several SML instructions in the Simpletron.

When the SML program completes execution, the name and contents of each register as well as the complete contents of memory should be displayed. Such a printout is often called a computer dump (no, a computer dump is not a place where old computers go). To help you program your dump method, a sample dump format is shown in Fig. 7.36. Note that a dump after executing a Simpletron program would show the actual values of instructions and data values at the moment execution terminated.

```
REGISTERS:
accumulator          +0000
instructionCounter      00
instructionRegister  +0000
operationCode           00
operand                 00

MEMORY:
        0     1     2     3     4     5     6     7     8     9
 0  +0000 +0000 +0000 +0000 +0000 +0000 +0000 +0000 +0000 +0000
10  +0000 +0000 +0000 +0000 +0000 +0000 +0000 +0000 +0000 +0000
20  +0000 +0000 +0000 +0000 +0000 +0000 +0000 +0000 +0000 +0000
30  +0000 +0000 +0000 +0000 +0000 +0000 +0000 +0000 +0000 +0000
40  +0000 +0000 +0000 +0000 +0000 +0000 +0000 +0000 +0000 +0000
50  +0000 +0000 +0000 +0000 +0000 +0000 +0000 +0000 +0000 +0000
60  +0000 +0000 +0000 +0000 +0000 +0000 +0000 +0000 +0000 +0000
70  +0000 +0000 +0000 +0000 +0000 +0000 +0000 +0000 +0000 +0000
80  +0000 +0000 +0000 +0000 +0000 +0000 +0000 +0000 +0000 +0000
90  +0000 +0000 +0000 +0000 +0000 +0000 +0000 +0000 +0000 +0000
```

Fig. 7.36 | A sample dump.

Let's proceed with the execution of our program's first instruction—namely, the +1009 in location 00. As we've indicated, the `switch` statement simulates this task by prompting the user to enter a value, reading the value and storing it in memory location `memory[ operand ]`. The value is then read into location 09.

At this point, simulation of the first instruction is completed. All that remains is to prepare the Simpletron to execute the next instruction. Since the instruction just performed was not a transfer of control, we need merely increment the instruction-counter register as follows:

```
instructionCounter++;
```

This action completes the simulated execution of the first instruction. The entire process (i.e., the instruction-execution cycle) begins anew with the fetch of the next instruction to execute.

Now let's consider how the branching instructions—the transfers of control—are simulated. All we need to do is adjust the value in the instruction counter appropriately. Therefore, the unconditional branch instruction (40) is simulated within the `switch` as

```
instructionCounter = operand;
```

The conditional "branch if accumulator is zero" instruction is simulated as

```
if ( accumulator == 0 )
    instructionCounter = operand;
```

At this point, you should implement your Simpletron simulator and run each of the SML programs you wrote in Exercise 7.30. If you desire, you may embellish SML with additional features and provide for these features in your simulator.

Your simulator should check for various types of errors. During the program-loading phase, for example, each number the user types into the Simpletron's `memory` must be in the range -9999 to +9999. Your simulator should test that each number entered is in this range and, if not, keep prompting the user to re-enter the number until the user enters a correct number.

During the execution phase, your simulator should check for various serious errors, such as attempts to divide by zero, attempts to execute invalid operation codes, and accumulator overflows (i.e., arithmetic operations resulting in values larger than +9999 or smaller than -9999). Such serious errors are called *fatal errors*. When a fatal error is detected, your simulator should display an error message, such as

```
*** Attempt to divide by zero ***
*** Simpletron execution abnormally terminated ***
```

and should display a full computer dump in the format we discussed previously. This treatment will help the user locate the error in the program.

7.32 *(Simpletron Simulator Modifications)* In Exercise 7.31, you wrote a software simulation of a computer that executes programs written in Simpletron Machine Language (SML). In this exercise, we propose several modifications and enhancements to the Simpletron Simulator. In the exercises of Chapter 22, we propose building a compiler that converts programs written in a high-level programming language (a variation of Basic) to Simpletron Machine Language. Some of the following modifications and enhancements may be required to execute the programs produced by the compiler:

a) Extend the Simpletron Simulator's memory to contain 1000 memory locations to enable the Simpletron to handle larger programs.

b) Allow the simulator to perform remainder calculations. This modification requires an additional SML instruction.

c) Allow the simulator to perform exponentiation calculations. This modification requires an additional SML instruction.

d) Modify the simulator to use hexadecimal rather than integer values to represent SML instructions.

e) Modify the simulator to allow output of a newline. This modification requires an additional SML instruction.

f) Modify the simulator to process floating-point values in addition to integer values.

g) Modify the simulator to handle string input. [*Hint:* Each Simpletron word can be divided into two groups, each holding a two-digit integer. Each two-digit integer represents the ASCII (see Appendix B) decimal equivalent of a character. Add a machine-language instruction that will input a string and store the string, beginning at a specific Simpletron memory location. The first half of the word at that location will be a count of the number of characters in the string (i.e., the length of the string). Each succeeding half-word contains one ASCII character expressed as two decimal digits. The machine-language instruction converts each character into its ASCII equivalent and assigns it to a half-word.]

h) Modify the simulator to handle output of strings stored in the format of part (g). [*Hint:* Add a machine-language instruction that will display a string, beginning at a certain Simpletron memory location. The first half of the word at that location is a count of the number of characters in the string (i.e., the length of the string). Each succeeding half-word contains one ASCII character expressed as two decimal digits. The machine-language instruction checks the length and displays the string by translating each two-digit number into its equivalent character.]

Making a Difference

7.33 *(Polling)* The Internet and the web are enabling more people to network, join a cause, voice opinions, and so on. The presidential candidates in 2008 used the Internet intensively to get out their messages and raise money for their campaigns. In this exercise, you'll write a simple polling program that allows users to rate five social-consciousness issues from 1 (least important) to 10 (most important). Pick five causes that are important to you (e.g., political issues, global environmental issues). Use a one-dimensional array topics (of type String) to store the five causes. To summarize the survey responses, use a 5-row, 10-column two-dimensional array responses (of type int), each row corresponding to an element in the topics array. When the program runs, it should ask the user to rate each issue. Have your friends and family respond to the survey. Then have the program display a summary of the results, including:

a) A tabular report with the five topics down the left side and the 10 ratings across the top, listing in each column the number of ratings received for each topic.

b) To the right of each row, show the average of the ratings for that issue.

c) Which issue received the highest point total? Display both the issue and the point total.

d) Which issue received the lowest point total? Display both the issue and the point total.

Instead of this absurd division into sexes, they ought to class people as static and dynamic.
—Evelyn Waugh

Is it a world to hide virtues in?
—William Shakespeare

But what, to serve our private ends, Forbids the cheating of our friends?
—Charles Churchill

This above all: to thine own self be true.
—William Shakespeare

Don't be "consistent," but be simply true.
—Oliver Wendell Holmes, Jr.

Classes and Objects: A Deeper Look

Objectives

In this chapter you'll learn:

- Encapsulation and data hiding.
- To use keyword `this`.
- To use `static` variables and methods.
- To import `static` members of a class.
- To use the `enum` type to create sets of constants with unique identifiers.
- To declare `enum` constants with parameters.
- To organize classes in packages to promote reuse.

8.1   Introduction

We now take a deeper look at building classes, controlling access to members of a class and creating constructors. We discuss composition—a capability that allows a class to have references to objects of other classes as members. We reexamine the use of *set* and *get* methods. Recall that Section 6.10 introduced the basic enum type to declare a set of constants. In this chapter, we discuss the relationship between enum types and classes, demonstrating that an enum, like a class, can be declared in its own file with constructors, methods and fields. The chapter also discusses `static` class members and `final` instance variables in detail. We investigate issues such as software reusability, data abstraction and encapsulation. Finally, we explain how to organize classes in packages to help manage large applications and promote reuse, then show a special relationship between classes in the same package.

Chapter 9, Object-Oriented Programming: Inheritance, and Chapter 10, Object-Oriented Programming: Polymorphism, introduce two additional key object-oriented programming technologies.

8.2   `Time` Class Case Study

Our first example consists of two classes—`Time1` (Fig. 8.1) and `Time1Test` (Fig. 8.2). Class `Time1` represents the time of day. Class `Time1Test` is an application class in which the main method creates one object of class `Time1` and invokes its methods. These classes must be declared in separate files because they are both `public` classes. The output of this program appears in Fig. 8.2.

Time1 Class Declaration
Class `Time1`'s `private int` instance variables `hour`, `minute` and `second` (Fig. 8.1, lines 6–8) represent the time in universal-time format (24-hour clock format in which hours are in the range 0–23). Class `Time1` contains `public` methods `setTime` (lines 12–17), `toUniversalString` (lines 20–23) and `toString` (lines 26–31). These methods are also called the **public services** or the **public interface** that the class provides to its clients.

```
1   // Fig. 8.1: Time1.java
2   // Time1 class declaration maintains the time in 24-hour format.
3
4   public class Time1
5   {
6      private int hour;   // 0 - 23
7      private int minute; // 0 - 59
8      private int second; // 0 - 59
9
10     // set a new time value using universal time; ensure that
11     // the data remains consistent by setting invalid values to zero
12     public void setTime( int h, int m, int s )
13     {
14        hour = ( ( h >= 0 && h < 24 ) ? h : 0 ); // validate hour
15        minute = ( ( m >= 0 && m < 60 ) ? m : 0 ); // validate minute
16        second = ( ( s >= 0 && s < 60 ) ? s : 0 ); // validate second
17     } // end method setTime
18
19     // convert to String in universal-time format (HH:MM:SS)
20     public String toUniversalString()
21     {
22        return String.format( "%02d:%02d:%02d", hour, minute, second );
23     } // end method toUniversalString
24
25     // convert to String in standard-time format (H:MM:SS AM or PM)
26     public String toString()
27     {
28        return String.format( "%d:%02d:%02d %s",
29           ( ( hour == 0 || hour == 12 ) ? 12 : hour % 12 ),
30           minute, second, ( hour < 12 ? "AM" : "PM" ) );
31     } // end method toString
32  } // end class Time1
```

Fig. 8.1 | `Time1` class declaration maintains the time in 24-hour format.

Default Constructor

In this example, class `Time1` does not declare a constructor, so the class has a default constructor that is supplied by the compiler. Each instance variable implicitly receives the default value 0 for an `int`. Note that instance variables also can be initialized when they are declared in the class body, using the same initialization syntax as with a local variable.

Method `setTime` *and Maintaining Consistent Data*

Method `setTime` (lines 12–17) is a `public` method that declares three `int` parameters and uses them to set the time. A conditional expression tests each argument for validity to determine whether it is in a specified range. For example, the `hour` value (line 14) must be greater than or equal to 0 and less than 24, because universal-time format represents hours as integers from 0 to 23 (e.g., 1 PM is hour 13 and 11 PM is hour 23; midnight is hour 0 and noon is hour 12). Similarly, `minute` and `second` values (lines 15 and 16) must be greater than or equal to 0 and less than 60. Any values outside these ranges are set to zero to ensure that a `Time1` object always contains *consistent data*—that is, the object's data values are always kept in range, even if the values provided as arguments to method `setTime` were *incorrect*. In this example, zero is a consistent value for `hour`, `minute` and `second`. In fact, when you create a Time1 object, its hour, minute and second are all set to zero by default; thus, a Time1 object contains consistent data from the moment it is created.

Correct vs. Consistent Values

It's important to distinguish between a *correct* value and a *consistent* value. A consistent value for minute must be in the range 0 to 59. A correct value for minute in a particular application, such as simply telling time, would be the actual minute at that time of day. Suppose you are setting the time on a watch. If the actual time is 17 minutes after the hour and you accidently set the watch to 19 minutes after, the 19 is a *consistent* value (0 to 59) but not a *correct* value. If you set the watch to 17 minutes after the hour, then 17 is a correct value—and a correct value is *always* a consistent value.

We've designed our setTime method so that when it receives an inconsistent value, it sets the corresponding instance variable to zero. This is certainly a *consistent* value, but it's unlikely to be *correct*. Is there a better approach? We could simply leave the object in its current state, without changing the instance variable. Given that Time objects begin in a consistent state (with hour, minute and second set to zero) and that the setTime method would reject any inconsistent values, the object would always be *guaranteed* to be in a consistent state. Often that state would be the object's last correct state, which some designers feel is superior to setting the instance variables to zero.

Potential Problems

A problem with the approaches discussed so far is that they do not inform the client code of inconsistent values. We could have the setTime return a value such as true if all the values are consistent and false if any of the values are inconsistent. The caller would check the return value, and if it were false, would attempt to set the time again. A problem with this approach is that some Java technologies (such as JavaBeans) require that the *set* methods return void. In Chapter 11, Exception Handling, you'll learn elegant techniques that enable your methods to indicate when inconsistent values are received.

Methods *toUniversalString* and *toString*

Method toUniversalString (lines 20–23) takes no arguments and returns a String in universal-time format, consisting of two digits each for the hour, minute and second. For example, if the time were 1:30:07 PM, the method would return 13:30:07. Line 22 uses static method **format** of class String to return a String containing the formatted hour, minute and second values, each with two digits and possibly a leading 0 (specified with the 0 flag). Method format is similar to method System.out.printf except that format returns a formatted String rather than displaying it in a command window. The formatted String is returned by method toUniversalString.

Method toString (lines 26–31) takes no arguments and returns a String in standard-time format, consisting of the hour, minute and second values separated by colons and followed by AM or PM (e.g., 1:27:06 PM). Like method toUniversalString, method toString uses static String method format to format the minute and second as two-digit values, with leading zeros if necessary. Line 29 uses a conditional operator (?:) to determine the value for hour in the String—if the hour is 0 or 12 (AM or PM), it appears as 12; otherwise, it appears as a value from 1 to 11. The conditional operator in line 30 determines whether AM or PM will be returned as part of the String.

Recall from Section 6.5 that all objects in Java have a toString method that returns a String representation of the object. We chose to return a String containing the time in standard-time format. Method `toString` can be called implicitly whenever a `Time1` object appears in the code where a `String` is needed, such as the value to output with a `%s` format specifier in a call to `System.out.printf`.

Using Class *Time1*

As you learned in Chapter 3, each class you declare represents a new type in Java. Therefore, after declaring class `Time1`, we can use it as a type in declarations such as

```
Time1 sunset; // sunset can hold a reference to a Time1 object
```

The `Time1Test` application class (Fig. 8.2) uses class `Time1`. Line 9 declares and creates a `Time1` object and assigns it to local variable `time`. Note that `new` implicitly invokes class `Time1`'s default constructor, since `Time1` does not declare any constructors. Lines 12–16 output the time first in universal-time format (by invoking `time`'s `toUniversalString` method in line 13), then in standard-time format (by explicitly invoking `time`'s `toString` method in line 15) to confirm that the `Time1` object was initialized properly.

```java
1   // Fig. 8.2: Time1Test.java
2   // Time1 object used in an application.
3
4   public class Time1Test
5   {
6      public static void main( String[] args )
7      {
8         // create and initialize a Time1 object
9         Time1 time = new Time1(); // invokes Time1 constructor
10
11        // output string representations of the time
12        System.out.print( "The initial universal time is: " );
13        System.out.println( time.toUniversalString() );
14        System.out.print( "The initial standard time is: " );
15        System.out.println( time.toString() );
16        System.out.println(); // output a blank line
17
18        // change time and output updated time
19        time.setTime( 13, 27, 6 );
20        System.out.print( "Universal time after setTime is: " );
21        System.out.println( time.toUniversalString() );
22        System.out.print( "Standard time after setTime is: " );
23        System.out.println( time.toString() );
24        System.out.println(); // output a blank line
25
26        // set time with invalid values; output updated time
27        time.setTime( 99, 99, 99 );
28        System.out.println( "After attempting invalid settings:" );
29        System.out.print( "Universal time: " );
30        System.out.println( time.toUniversalString() );
31        System.out.print( "Standard time: " );
32        System.out.println( time.toString() );
33     } // end main
34  } // end class Time1Test
```

Fig. 8.2 | Time1 object used in an application. (Part 1 of 2.)

```
The initial universal time is: 00:00:00
The initial standard time is: 12:00:00 AM

Universal time after setTime is: 13:27:06
Standard time after setTime is: 1:27:06 PM

After attempting invalid settings:
Universal time: 00:00:00
Standard time: 12:00:00 AM
```

Fig. 8.2 | `Time1` object used in an application. (Part 2 of 2.)

Line 19 invokes method `setTime` of the `time` object to change the time. Then lines 20–24 output the time again in both formats to confirm that it was set correctly.

To illustrate that it maintains the object in a consistent state, line 27 calls method `setTime` with inconsistent arguments of 99 for the `hour`, `minute` and `second`. Lines 28–32 output the time again in both formats to confirm the object's consistent state, then the program terminates. The last two lines of the output show that the time is reset to midnight—the initial value of a `Time1` object—after an attempt to set the time with three out-of-range values.

Notes on the *Time1 Class Declaration*

Consider several issues of class design with respect to class `Time1`. The instance variables `hour`, `minute` and `second` are each declared `private`. The actual data representation used within the class is of no concern to the class's clients. For example, it would be perfectly reasonable for `Time1` to represent the time internally as the number of seconds since midnight or the number of minutes and seconds since midnight. Clients could use the same `public` methods and get the same results without being aware of this. (Exercise 8.5 asks you to represent the time in class `Time1` as the number of seconds since midnight and show that indeed no change is visible to the clients of the class.)

Software Engineering Observation 8.1

Classes simplify programming, because the client can use only the `public` methods exposed by the class. Such methods are usually client oriented rather than implementation oriented. Clients are neither aware of, nor involved in, a class's implementation. Clients generally care about what the class does but not how the class does it.

Software Engineering Observation 8.2

Interfaces change less frequently than implementations. When an implementation changes, implementation-dependent code must change accordingly. Hiding the implementation reduces the possibility that other program parts will become dependent on class implementation details.

8.3 **Controlling Access to Members**

The access modifiers `public` and `private` control access to a class's variables and methods. In Chapter 9, we'll introduce the additional access modifier `protected`. As we stated in Section 8.2, the primary purpose of `public` methods is to present to the class's clients a view of the services the class provides (the class's `public` interface). Clients need not be concerned with how the class accomplishes its tasks. For this reason, the class's `private` variables and `private` methods (i.e., its implementation details) are not accessible to its clients.

Figure 8.3 demonstrates that private class members are not accessible outside the class. Lines 9–11 attempt to access directly the private instance variables hour, minute and second of the Time1 object time. When this program is compiled, the compiler generates error messages that these private members are not accessible. [*Note:* This program assumes that the Time1 class from Fig. 8.1 is used.]

Common Programming Error 8.1

An attempt by a method that is not a member of a class to access a private member of that class is a compilation error.

```
1   // Fig. 8.3: MemberAccessTest.java
2   // Private members of class Time1 are not accessible.
3   public class MemberAccessTest
4   {
5      public static void main( String[] args )
6      {
7         Time1 time = new Time1(); // create and initialize Time1 object
8
9         time.hour = 7; // error: hour has private access in Time1
10        time.minute = 15; // error: minute has private access in Time1
11        time.second = 30; // error: second has private access in Time1
12     } // end main
13  } // end class MemberAccessTest
```

```
MemberAccessTest.java:9: hour has private access in Time1
      time.hour = 7; // error: hour has private access in Time1
          ^
MemberAccessTest.java:10: minute has private access in Time1
      time.minute = 15; // error: minute has private access in Time1
          ^
MemberAccessTest.java:11: second has private access in Time1
      time.second = 30; // error: second has private access in Time1
          ^
3 errors
```

Fig. 8.3 | Private members of class Time1 are not accessible.

8.4 Referring to the Current Object's Members with the this Reference

Every object can access a reference to itself with keyword **this** (sometimes called the **this reference**). When a non-static method is called for a particular object, the method's body implicitly uses keyword this to refer to the object's instance variables and other methods. This enables the class's code to know which object should be manipulated. As you'll see in Fig. 8.4, you can also use keyword this explicitly in a non-static method's body. Section 8.5 shows another interesting use of keyword this. Section 8.11 explains why keyword this cannot be used in a static method.

We now demonstrate implicit and explicit use of the this reference (Fig. 8.4). Note that this example is the first in which we declare two classes in one file—class ThisTest is declared in lines 4–11, and class SimpleTime is declared in lines 14–47. We do this to demonstrate that when you compile a `.java` file containing more than one class, the compiler produces a separate class file with the `.class` extension for every compiled class. In this case, two separate files are produced—`SimpleTime.class` and `ThisTest.class`. When one source-code (`.java`) file contains multiple class declarations, the compiler places both class files for those classes in the same directory. Note also in Fig. 8.4 that only class `ThisTest` is declared `public`. A source-code file can contain only one `public` class—otherwise, a compilation error occurs. Non-`public` classes can be used only by other classes in the same package. So, in this example, class `SimpleTime` can be used only by class `ThisTest`.

```java
1   // Fig. 8.4: ThisTest.java
2   // this used implicitly and explicitly to refer to members of an object.
3
4   public class ThisTest
5   {
6      public static void main( String[] args )
7      {
8         SimpleTime time = new SimpleTime( 15, 30, 19 );
9         System.out.println( time.buildString() );
10     } // end main
11  } // end class ThisTest
12
13  // class SimpleTime demonstrates the "this" reference
14  class SimpleTime
15  {
16     private int hour; // 0-23
17     private int minute; // 0-59
18     private int second; // 0-59
19
20     // if the constructor uses parameter names identical to
21     // instance variable names the "this" reference is
22     // required to distinguish between names
23     public SimpleTime( int hour, int minute, int second )
24     {
25        this.hour = hour; // set "this" object's hour
26        this.minute = minute; // set "this" object's minute
27        this.second = second; // set "this" object's second
28     } // end SimpleTime constructor
29
30     // use explicit and implicit "this" to call toUniversalString
31     public String buildString()
32     {
33        return String.format( "%24s: %s\n%24s: %s",
34           "this.toUniversalString()", this.toUniversalString(),
35           "toUniversalString()", toUniversalString() );
36     } // end method buildString
37
38     // convert to String in universal-time format (HH:MM:SS)
39     public String toUniversalString()
40     {
41        // "this" is not required here to access instance variables,
42        // because method does not have local variables with same
43        // names as instance variables
```

Fig. 8.4 | `this` used implicitly and explicitly to refer to members of an object. (Part 1 of 2.)

```
44              return String.format( "%02d:%02d:%02d",
45                  this.hour, this.minute, this.second );
46          } // end method toUniversalString
47     } // end class SimpleTime
```

```
this.toUniversalString(): 15:30:19
    toUniversalString(): 15:30:19
```

Fig. 8.4 | this used implicitly and explicitly to refer to members of an object. (Part 2 of 2.)

Class SimpleTime (lines 14–47) declares three private instance variables—hour, minute and second (lines 16–18). The constructor (lines 23–28) receives three int arguments to initialize a SimpleTime object. Note that we used parameter names for the constructor (line 23) that are identical to the class's instance-variable names (lines 16–18). We don't recommend this practice, but we did it here to shadow (hide) the corresponding instance variables so that we could illustrate a case in which explicit use of the this reference is required. If a method contains a local variable with the same name as a field, that method will refer to the local variable rather than the field. In this case, the local variable shadows the field in the method's scope. However, the method can use the this reference to refer to the shadowed field explicitly, as shown on the left sides of the assignments in lines 25–27 for SimpleTime's shadowed instance variables.

Method buildString (lines 31–36) returns a String created by a statement that uses the this reference explicitly and implicitly. Line 34 uses it explicitly to call method toUniversalString. Line 35 it implicitly to call the same method. Note that both lines perform the same task. You typically will not use this explicitly to reference other methods within the current object. Also, note that line 45 in method toUniversalString explicitly uses the this reference to access each instance variable. This is not necessary here, because the method does not have any local variables that shadow the instance variables of the class.

Common Programming Error 8.2

It's often a logic error when a method contains a parameter or local variable that has the same name as a field of the class. In this case, use reference this if you wish to access the field of the class—otherwise, the method parameter or local variable will be referenced.

Error-Prevention Tip 8.1

Avoid method-parameter names or local-variable names that conflict with field names. This helps prevent subtle, hard-to-locate bugs.

Performance Tip 8.1

Java conserves storage by maintaining only one copy of each method per class—this method is invoked by every object of the class. Each object, on the other hand, has its own copy of the class's instance variables (i.e., non-static fields). Each method of the class implicitly uses this to determine the specific object of the class to manipulate.

Application class ThisTest (lines 4–11) demonstrates class SimpleTime. Line 8 creates an instance of class SimpleTime and invokes its constructor. Line 9 invokes the object's buildString method, then displays the results.

8.5 Time Class Case Study: Overloaded Constructors

As you know, you can declare your own constructor to specify how objects of a class should be initialized. Next, we demonstrate a class with several **overloaded constructors** that enable objects of that class to be initialized in different ways. To overload constructors, simply provide multiple constructor declarations with different signatures. Recall from Section 6.12 that the compiler differentiates signatures by the *number* of parameters, the *types* of the parameters and the *order* of the parameter types in each signature.

Class *Time2* with Overloaded Constructors

The default constructor for class Time1 (Fig. 8.1) initialized hour, minute and second to their default 0 values (which is midnight in universal time). The default constructor does not enable the class's clients to initialize the time with specific nonzero values. Class Time2 (Fig. 8.5) contains five overloaded constructors that provide convenient ways to initialize objects of the new class Time2. Each constructor initializes the object to begin in a consistent state. In this program, four of the constructors invoke a fifth, which in turn calls method setTime to ensure that the value supplied for hour is in the range 0 to 23, and the values for minute and second are each in the range 0 to 59. If a value is out of range, it's set to zero by setTime (once again ensuring that each instance variable remains in a consistent state). The compiler invokes the appropriate constructor by matching the number, types and order of the types of the arguments specified in the constructor call with the number, types and order of the types of the parameters specified in each constructor declaration. Note that class Time2 also provides *set* and *get* methods for each instance variable.

```
1   // Fig. 8.5: Time2.java
2   // Time2 class declaration with overloaded constructors.
3
4   public class Time2
5   {
6      private int hour;   // 0 - 23
7      private int minute; // 0 - 59
8      private int second; // 0 - 59
9
10     // Time2 no-argument constructor: initializes each instance variable
11     // to zero; ensures that Time2 objects start in a consistent state
12     public Time2()
13     {
14        this( 0, 0, 0 ); // invoke Time2 constructor with three arguments
15     } // end Time2 no-argument constructor
16
17     // Time2 constructor: hour supplied, minute and second defaulted to 0
18     public Time2( int h )
19     {
20        this( h, 0, 0 ); // invoke Time2 constructor with three arguments
21     } // end Time2 one-argument constructor
22
23     // Time2 constructor: hour and minute supplied, second defaulted to 0
24     public Time2( int h, int m )
25     {
```

Fig. 8.5 | Time2 class with overloaded constructors. (Part 1 of 3.)

```
26          this( h, m, 0 ); // invoke Time2 constructor with three arguments
27       } // end Time2 two-argument constructor
28
29       // Time2 constructor: hour, minute and second supplied
30       public Time2( int h, int m, int s )
31       {
32          setTime( h, m, s ); // invoke setTime to validate time
33       } // end Time2 three-argument constructor
34
35       // Time2 constructor: another Time2 object supplied
36       public Time2( Time2 time )
37       {
38          // invoke Time2 three-argument constructor
39          this( time.getHour(), time.getMinute(), time.getSecond() );
40       } // end Time2 constructor with a Time2 object argument
41
42       // Set Methods
43       // set a new time value using universal time; ensure that
44       // the data remains consistent by setting invalid values to zero
45       public void setTime( int h, int m, int s )
46       {
47          setHour( h ); // set the hour
48          setMinute( m ); // set the minute
49          setSecond( s ); // set the second
50       } // end method setTime
51
52       // validate and set hour
53       public void setHour( int h )
54       {
55          hour = ( ( h >= 0 && h < 24 ) ? h : 0 );
56       } // end method setHour
57
58       // validate and set minute
59       public void setMinute( int m )
60       {
61          minute = ( ( m >= 0 && m < 60 ) ? m : 0 );
62       } // end method setMinute
63
64       // validate and set second
65       public void setSecond( int s )
66       {
67          second = ( ( s >= 0 && s < 60 ) ? s : 0 );
68       } // end method setSecond
69
70       // Get Methods
71       // get hour value
72       public int getHour()
73       {
74          return hour;
75       } // end method getHour
76
77       // get minute value
78       public int getMinute()
79       {
```

Fig. 8.5 | Time2 class with overloaded constructors. (Part 2 of 3.)

```
80          return minute;
81       } // end method getMinute
82
83       // get second value
84       public int getSecond()
85       {
86          return second;
87       } // end method getSecond
88
89       // convert to String in universal-time format (HH:MM:SS)
90       public String toUniversalString()
91       {
92          return String.format(
93             "%02d:%02d:%02d", getHour(), getMinute(), getSecond() );
94       } // end method toUniversalString
95
96       // convert to String in standard-time format (H:MM:SS AM or PM)
97       public String toString()
98       {
99          return String.format( "%d:%02d:%02d %s",
100             ( (getHour() == 0 || getHour() == 12) ? 12 : getHour() % 12 ),
101             getMinute(), getSecond(), ( getHour() < 12 ? "AM" : "PM" ) );
102       } // end method toString
103    } // end class Time2
```

Fig. 8.5 | Time2 class with overloaded constructors. (Part 3 of 3.)

Class *Time2's Constructors*

Lines 12–15 declare a so-called **no-argument constructor** that is invoked without arguments. Once you declare any constructors in a class, the compiler will not provide a default constructor. This no-argument constructor ensures that class Time2's clients can create Time2 objects with default values. Such a constructor simply initializes the object as specified in the constructor's body. In the body, we introduce a use of the this reference that is allowed only as the first statement in a constructor's body. Line 14 uses this in method-call syntax to invoke the Time2 constructor that takes three arguments (lines 30–33). The no-argument constructor passes values of 0 for the hour, minute and second to the constructor with three parameters. Using the this reference as shown here is a popular way to reuse initialization code provided by another of the class's constructors rather than defining similar code in the no-argument constructor's body. We use this syntax in four of the five Time2 constructors to make the class easier to maintain and modify. If we need to change how objects of class Time2 are initialized, only the constructor that the class's other constructors call will need to be modified. In fact, even that constructor might not need modification in this example. That constructor simply calls the setTime method to perform the actual initialization, so it's possible that the changes the class might require would be localized to the *set* methods.

Common Programming Error 8.3

It's a syntax error when this is used in a constructor's body to call another constructor of the same class if that call is not the first statement in the constructor. It's also a syntax error when a method attempts to invoke a constructor directly via this.

Lines 18–21 declare a `Time2` constructor with a single `int` parameter representing the hour, which is passed with 0 for the `minute` and `second` to the constructor at lines 30–33. Lines 24–27 declare a `Time2` constructor that receives two `int` parameters representing the hour and `minute`, which are passed with 0 for the `second` to the constructor at lines 30–33. Like the no-argument constructor, each of these constructors invokes the constructor at lines 30–33 to minimize code duplication. Lines 30–33 declare the `Time2` constructor that receives three `int` parameters representing the hour, `minute` and `second`. This constructor calls `setTime` to initialize the instance variables to consistent values.

Common Programming Error 8.4

A constructor can call methods of the class. Be aware that the instance variables might not yet be in a consistent state, because the constructor is in the process of initializing the object. Using instance variables before they have been initialized properly is a logic error.

Lines 36–40 declare a `Time2` constructor that receives a reference to another `Time2` object. In this case, the values from the `Time2` argument are passed to the three-argument constructor at lines 30–33 to initialize the hour, `minute` and `second`. Note that line 39 could have directly accessed the hour, `minute` and `second` values of the constructor's argument `time` with the expressions `time.hour`, `time.minute` and `time.second`—even though hour, `minute` and `second` are declared as `private` variables of class `Time2`. This is due to a special relationship between objects of the same class. We'll see in a moment why it's preferable to use the *get* methods.

Software Engineering Observation 8.3

When one object of a class has a reference to another object of the same class, the first object can access all the second object's data and methods (including those that are `private`).

Notes Regarding Class `Time2`'s Set and Get Methods and Constructors

Note that `Time2`'s *set* and *get* methods are called throughout the class. In particular, method `setTime` calls methods `setHour`, `setMinute` and `setSecond` in lines 47–49, and methods `toUniversalString` and `toString` call methods `getHour`, `getMinute` and `getSecond` in line 93 and lines 100–101, respectively. In each case, these methods could have accessed the class's private data directly without calling the *set* and *get* methods. However, consider changing the representation of the time from three `int` values (requiring 12 bytes of memory) to a single `int` value representing the total number of seconds that have elapsed since midnight (requiring only 4 bytes of memory). If we made such a change, only the bodies of the methods that access the `private` data directly would need to change—in particular, the individual *set* and *get* methods for the hour, `minute` and `second`. There would be no need to modify the bodies of methods `setTime`, `toUniversalString` or `toString` because they do not access the data directly. Designing the class in this manner reduces the likelihood of programming errors when altering the class's implementation.

Similarly, each `Time2` constructor could be written to include a copy of the appropriate statements from methods `setHour`, `setMinute` and `setSecond`. Doing so may be slightly more efficient, because the extra constructor call and call to `setTime` are eliminated. However, duplicating statements in multiple methods or constructors makes changing the class's internal data representation more difficult. Having the `Time2` constructors call the constructor with three arguments (or even call `setTime` directly) requires any changes to the implementation of `setTime` to be made only once. Also, the compiler can optimize programs by removing calls to simple methods and replacing them with the expanded code of their declarations—a technique known as **inlining the code**, which improves program performance.

> ### Software Engineering Observation 8.4
> *When implementing a method of a class, use the class's set and get methods to access the class's `private` data. This simplifies code maintenance and reduces the likelihood of errors.*

Using Class Time2's Overloaded Constructors

Class `Time2Test` (Fig. 8.6) invokes the overloaded `Time2` constructors (lines 8–13). Line 8 invokes the no-argument constructor (Fig. 8.5, lines 12–15). Lines 9–13 of the program demonstrate passing arguments to the other `Time2` constructors. Line 9 invokes the constructor at lines 18–21 of Fig. 8.5. Line 10 invokes the constructor at lines 24–27 of Fig. 8.5. Lines 11–12 invoke the constructor at lines 30–33 of Fig. 8.5. Line 13 invokes the constructor at lines 36–40 of Fig. 8.5. The application displays the `String` representation of each `Time2` object to confirm that it was initialized properly.

```
 1   // Fig. 8.6: Time2Test.java
 2   // Overloaded constructors used to initialize Time2 objects.
 3
 4   public class Time2Test
 5   {
 6      public static void main( String[] args )
 7      {
 8         Time2 t1 = new Time2(); // 00:00:00
 9         Time2 t2 = new Time2( 2 ); // 02:00:00
10         Time2 t3 = new Time2( 21, 34 ); // 21:34:00
11         Time2 t4 = new Time2( 12, 25, 42 ); // 12:25:42
12         Time2 t5 = new Time2( 27, 74, 99 ); // 00:00:00
13         Time2 t6 = new Time2( t4 ); // 12:25:42
14
15         System.out.println( "Constructed with:" );
16         System.out.println( "t1: all arguments defaulted" );
17         System.out.printf( "   %s\n", t1.toUniversalString() );
18         System.out.printf( "   %s\n", t1.toString() );
19
20         System.out.println(
21            "t2: hour specified; minute and second defaulted" );
22         System.out.printf( "   %s\n", t2.toUniversalString() );
23         System.out.printf( "   %s\n", t2.toString() );
24
25         System.out.println(
26            "t3: hour and minute specified; second defaulted" );
27         System.out.printf( "   %s\n", t3.toUniversalString() );
28         System.out.printf( "   %s\n", t3.toString() );
29
30         System.out.println( "t4: hour, minute and second specified" );
31         System.out.printf( "   %s\n", t4.toUniversalString() );
32         System.out.printf( "   %s\n", t4.toString() );
33
34         System.out.println( "t5: all invalid values specified" );
```

Fig. 8.6 | Overloaded constructors used to initialize `Time2` objects. (Part 1 of 2.)

```
35          System.out.printf( "    %s\n", t5.toUniversalString() );
36          System.out.printf( "    %s\n", t5.toString() );
37
38          System.out.println( "t6: Time2 object t4 specified" );
39          System.out.printf( "    %s\n", t6.toUniversalString() );
40          System.out.printf( "    %s\n", t6.toString() );
41      } // end main
42  } // end class Time2Test
```

```
t1: all arguments defaulted
   00:00:00
   12:00:00 AM
t2: hour specified; minute and second defaulted
   02:00:00
   2:00:00 AM
t3: hour and minute specified; second defaulted
   21:34:00
   9:34:00 PM
t4: hour, minute and second specified
   12:25:42
   12:25:42 PM
t5: all invalid values specified
   00:00:00
   12:00:00 AM
t6: Time2 object t4 specified
   12:25:42
   12:25:42 PM
```

Fig. 8.6 | Overloaded constructors used to initialize `Time2` objects. (Part 2 of 2.)

8.6 Default and No-Argument Constructors

Every class must have at least one constructor. If you do not provide any constructors in a class's declaration, the compiler creates a default constructor that takes no arguments when it's invoked. The default constructor initializes the instance variables to the initial values specified in their declarations or to their default values (zero for primitive numeric types, `false` for `boolean` values and `null` for references). In Section 9.4.1, you'll learn that the default constructor performs another task also.

If your class declares constructors, the compiler will not create a default constructor. In this case, you must declare a no-argument constructor if default initialization is required. Like a default constructor, a no-argument constructor is invoked with empty parentheses. Note that the `Time2` no-argument constructor (lines 12–15 of Fig. 8.5) explicitly initializes a `Time2` object by passing to the three-argument constructor 0 for each parameter. Since 0 is the default value for `int` instance variables, the no-argument constructor in this example could actually be declared with an empty body. In this case, each instance variable would receive its default value when the no-argument constructor was called. If we omit the no-argument constructor, clients of this class would not be able to create a `Time2` object with the expression `new Time2()`.

Common Programming Error 8.5

A compilation error occurs if a program attempts to initialize an object of a class by passing the wrong number or types of arguments to the class's constructor.

Software Engineering Observation 8.5

Java allows other methods of the class besides its constructors to have the same name as the class and to specify return types. Such methods are not constructors and will not be called when an object of the class is instantiated. Java determines which methods are constructors by locating those that have the same name as the class and do not specify a return type.

8.7 Notes on *Set* and *Get* Methods

As you know, a class's `private` fields can be manipulated only by its methods. A typical manipulation might be the adjustment of a customer's bank balance (e.g., a `private` instance variable of a class `BankAccount`) by a method `computeInterest`. Classes often provide `public` methods to allow clients of the class to *set* (i.e., assign values to) or *get* (i.e., obtain the values of) `private` instance variables.

As a naming example, a method that sets instance variable `interestRate` would typically be named `setInterestRate` and a method that gets the `interestRate` would typically be called `getInterestRate`. *Set* methods are also commonly called **mutator methods**, because they typically change an object's state—i.e., modify the values of instance variables. *Get* methods are also commonly called **accessor methods** or **query methods**.

Set *and* Get *Methods vs.* `public` *Data*

It would seem that providing *set* and *get* capabilities is essentially the same as making the instance variables `public`. This is one of the subtleties that makes Java so desirable for software engineering. A `public` instance variable can be read or written by any method that has a reference to an object that contains that variable. If an instance variable is declared `private`, a `public` *get* method certainly allows other methods to access the it, but the *get* method can control how the client can access it. For example, a *get* method might control the format of the data it returns and thus shield the client code from the actual data representation. A `public` *set* method can—and should—carefully scrutinize attempts to modify the variable's value to ensure that the new value is consistent for that data item. For example, an attempt to *set* the day of the month to 37 would be rejected, an attempt to *set* a person's weight to a negative value would be rejected, and so on. Thus, although *set* and *get* methods provide access to `private` data, the access is restricted by the implementation of the methods. This helps promote good software engineering.

Validity Checking in Set *Methods*

The benefits of data integrity do not follow automatically simply because instance variables are declared `private`—you must provide validity checking. Java enables you to design better programs in a convenient manner. A class's *set* methods could return values indicating that attempts were made to assign invalid data to objects of the class. A client of the class could test the return value of a *set* method to determine whether the client's attempt to modify the object was successful and to take appropriate action. Typically, however, *set* methods have `void` return type and use exception handling to indicate attempts to assign invalid data. We discuss exception handling in detail in Chapter 11.

Software Engineering Observation 8.6

When appropriate, provide `public` *methods to change and retrieve the values of* `private` *instance variables. This architecture helps hide the implementation of a class from its clients, which improves program modifiability.*

Error-Prevention Tip 8.2

Using set *and* get *methods helps you create classes that are easier to debug and maintain. If only one method performs a particular task, such as setting the hour in a* Time2 *object, it's easier to debug and maintain the class. If the* hour *is not being set properly, the code that actually modifies instance variable* hour *is localized to one method's body—*setHour. *Thus, your debugging efforts can be focused on method* setHour.

Predicate Methods

Another common use for accessor methods is to test whether a condition is true or false—such methods are often called **predicate methods.** An example would be class ArrayList's isEmpty method, which returns true if the ArrayList is empty. A program might test isEmpty before attempting to read another item from an ArrayList.

8.8 Composition

A class can have references to objects of other classes as members. This is called **composition** and is sometimes referred to as a *has-a* relationship. For example, an AlarmClock object needs to know the current time and the time when it's supposed to sound its alarm, so it's reasonable to include two references to Time objects in an AlarmClock object.

Our example of composition contains three classes—Date (Fig. 8.7), Employee (Fig. 8.8) and EmployeeTest (Fig. 8.9). Class Date (Fig. 8.7) declares instance variables month, day and year (lines 6–8) to represent a date. The constructor receives three int parameters. Line 14 invokes utility method checkMonth (lines 23–33) to validate the month—an out-of-range value is set to 1 to maintain a consistent state. Line 15 assumes that the value for year is correct and does not validate it. Line 16 invokes utility method checkDay (lines 36–52) to validate the value for day based on the current month and year. Lines 42–43 determine whether the day is correct based on the number of days in the particular month. If the day is not correct, lines 46–47 determine whether the month is February, the day is 29 and the year is a leap year. If lines 42–48 do not return a correct value for day, line 51 returns 1 to maintain the Date in a consistent state. Note that lines 18–19 in the constructor output the this reference as a String. Since this is a reference to the current Date object, the object's toString method (lines 55–58) is called implicitly to obtain the object's String representation.

```
1   // Fig. 8.7: Date.java
2   // Date class declaration.
3
4   public class Date
5   {
6      private int month; // 1-12
7      private int day; // 1-31 based on month
8      private int year; // any year
9
10     // constructor: call checkMonth to confirm proper value for month;
11     // call checkDay to confirm proper value for day
12     public Date( int theMonth, int theDay, int theYear )
13     {
```

Fig. 8.7 | Date class declaration. (Part 1 of 2.)

```
14          month = checkMonth( theMonth ); // validate month
15          year = theYear; // could validate year
16          day = checkDay( theDay ); // validate day
17
18          System.out.printf(
19              "Date object constructor for date %s\n", this );
20       } // end Date constructor
21
22       // utility method to confirm proper month value
23       private int checkMonth( int testMonth )
24       {
25          if ( testMonth > 0 && testMonth <= 12 ) // validate month
26             return testMonth;
27          else // month is invalid
28          {
29             System.out.printf(
30                "Invalid month (%d) set to 1.", testMonth );
31             return 1; // maintain object in consistent state
32          } // end else
33       } // end method checkMonth
34
35       // utility method to confirm proper day value based on month and year
36       private int checkDay( int testDay )
37       {
38          int[] daysPerMonth =
39             { 0, 31, 28, 31, 30, 31, 30, 31, 31, 30, 31, 30, 31 };
40
41          // check if day in range for month
42          if ( testDay > 0 && testDay <= daysPerMonth[ month ] )
43             return testDay;
44
45          // check for leap year
46          if ( month == 2 && testDay == 29 && ( year % 400 == 0 ||
47             ( year % 4 == 0 && year % 100 != 0 ) ) )
48             return testDay;
49
50          System.out.printf( "Invalid day (%d) set to 1.", testDay );
51          return 1;  // maintain object in consistent state
52       } // end method checkDay
53
54       // return a String of the form month/day/year
55       public String toString()
56       {
57          return String.format( "%d/%d/%d", month, day, year );
58       } // end method toString
59    } // end class Date
```

Fig. 8.7 | Date class declaration. (Part 2 of 2.)

Class Employee (Fig. 8.8) has instance variables firstName, lastName, birthDate and hireDate. Members firstName and lastName (lines 6–7) are references to String objects. Members birthDate and hireDate (lines 8–9) are references to Date objects. This demonstrates that a class can have as instance variables references to objects of other classes. The Employee constructor (lines 12–19) takes four parameters—first, last, dateOf-Birth and dateOfHire. The objects referenced by the parameters are assigned to the

Employee object's instance variables. Note that when class Employee's toString method is called, it returns a String containing the employee's name and the String representations of the two Date objects. Each of these Strings is obtained with an implicit call to the Date class's toString method.

```java
1   // Fig. 8.8: Employee.java
2   // Employee class with references to other objects.
3
4   public class Employee
5   {
6      private String firstName;
7      private String lastName;
8      private Date birthDate;
9      private Date hireDate;
10
11     // constructor to initialize name, birth date and hire date
12     public Employee( String first, String last, Date dateOfBirth,
13        Date dateOfHire )
14     {
15        firstName = first;
16        lastName = last;
17        birthDate = dateOfBirth;
18        hireDate = dateOfHire;
19     } // end Employee constructor
20
21     // convert Employee to String format
22     public String toString()
23     {
24        return String.format( "%s, %s  Hired: %s  Birthday: %s",
25           lastName, firstName, hireDate, birthDate );
26     } // end method toString
27  } // end class Employee
```

Fig. 8.8 | Employee class with references to other objects.

Class EmployeeTest (Fig. 8.9) creates two Date objects (lines 8–9) to represent an Employee's birthday and hire date, respectively. Line 10 creates an Employee and initializes its instance variables by passing to the constructor two Strings (representing the Employee's first and last names) and two Date objects (representing the birthday and hire date). Line 12 implicitly invokes the Employee's toString method to display the values of its instance variables and demonstrate that the object was initialized properly.

```java
1   // Fig. 8.9: EmployeeTest.java
2   // Composition demonstration.
3
4   public class EmployeeTest
5   {
6      public static void main( String[] args )
7      {
8         Date birth = new Date( 7, 24, 1949 );
9         Date hire = new Date( 3, 12, 1988 );
```

Fig. 8.9 | Composition demonstration. (Part 1 of 2.)

```
10          Employee employee = new Employee( "Bob", "Blue", birth, hire );
11
12          System.out.println( employee );
13    } // end main
14  } // end class EmployeeTest
```

```
Date object constructor for date 7/24/1949
Date object constructor for date 3/12/1988
Blue, Bob  Hired: 3/12/1988  Birthday: 7/24/1949
```

Fig. 8.9 | Composition demonstration. (Part 2 of 2.)

8.9 Enumerations

In Fig. 6.9 (Craps.java) we introduced the basic enum type, which defines a set of constants represented as unique identifiers. In that program the enum constants represented the game's status. In this section we discuss the relationship between enum types and classes. Like classes, all enum types are reference types. An enum type is declared with an **enum declaration**, which is a comma-separated list of enum constants—the declaration may optionally include other components of traditional classes, such as constructors, fields and methods. Each enum declaration declares an enum class with the following restrictions:

1. enum constants are implicitly final, because they declare constants that shouldn't be modified.

2. enum constants are implicitly static.

3. Any attempt to create an object of an enum type with operator new results in a compilation error.

The enum constants can be used anywhere constants can be used, such as in the case labels of switch statements and to control enhanced for statements.

Figure 8.10 illustrates how to declare instance variables, a constructor and methods in an enum type. The enum declaration (lines 5–37) contains two parts—the enum constants and the other members of the enum type. The first part (lines 8–13) declares six enum constants. Each is optionally followed by arguments which are passed to the **enum constructor** (lines 20–24). Like the constructors you've seen in classes, an enum constructor can specify any number of parameters and can be overloaded. In this example, the enum constructor has two String parameters, hence each enum constant is followed by parentheses containing two String arguments. The second part (lines 16–36) declares the other members of the enum type—two instance variables (lines 16–17), a constructor (lines 20–24) and two methods (lines 27–30 and 33–36).

```
1  // Fig. 8.10: Book.java
2  // Declaring an enum type with constructor and explicit instance fields
3  // and accessors for these fields
```

Fig. 8.10 | Declaring an **enum** type with constructor and explicit instance fields and accessors for these fields. (Part 1 of 2.)

```
 4
 5   public enum Book
 6   {
 7      // declare constants of enum type
 8      JHTP( "Java How to Program", "2010" ),
 9      CHTP( "C How to Program", "2007" ),
10      IW3HTP( "Internet & World Wide Web How to Program", "2008" ),
11      CPPHTP( "C++ How to Program", "2008" ),
12      VBHTP( "Visual Basic 2008 How to Program", "2009" ),
13      CSHARPHTP( "Visual C# 2008 How to Program", "2009" );
14
15      // instance fields
16      private final String title; // book title
17      private final String copyrightYear; // copyright year
18
19      // enum constructor
20      Book( String bookTitle, String year )
21      {
22         title = bookTitle;
23         copyrightYear = year;
24      } // end enum Book constructor
25
26      // accessor for field title
27      public String getTitle()
28      {
29         return title;
30      } // end method getTitle
31
32      // accessor for field copyrightYear
33      public String getCopyrightYear()
34      {
35         return copyrightYear;
36      } // end method getCopyrightYear
37   } // end enum Book
```

Fig. 8.10 | Declaring an enum type with constructor and explicit instance fields and accessors for these fields. (Part 2 of 2.)

Lines 16–17 declare the instance variables title and copyrightYear. Each enum constant in Book is actually an object of type Book that has its own copy of instance variables title and copyrightYear. The constructor (lines 20–24) takes two String parameters, one that specifies the book's title and one that specifies its copyright year. Lines 22–23 assign these parameters to the instance variables. Lines 27–36 declare two methods, which return the book title and copyright year, respectively.

Figure 8.11 tests the enum type Book and illustrates how to iterate through a range of enum constants. For every enum, the compiler generates the static method **values** (called in line 12) that returns an array of the enum's constants in the order they were declared. Lines 12–14 use the enhanced for statement to display all the constants declared in the enum Book. Line 14 invokes the enum Book's getTitle and getCopyrightYear methods to get the title and copyright year associated with the constant. Note that when an enum constant is converted to a String (e.g., book in line 13), the constant's identifier is used as the String representation (e.g., JHTP for the first enum constant).

```
I    // Fig. 8.11: EnumTest.java
2    // Testing enum type Book.
3    import java.util.EnumSet;
4
5    public class EnumTest
6    {
7       public static void main( String[] args )
8       {
9          System.out.println( "All books:\n" );
10
11         // print all books in enum Book
12         for ( Book book : Book.values() )
13            System.out.printf( "%-10s%-45s%s\n", book,
14               book.getTitle(), book.getCopyrightYear() );
15
16         System.out.println( "\nDisplay a range of enum constants:\n" );
17
18         // print first four books
19         for ( Book book : EnumSet.range( Book.JHTP, Book.CPPHTP ) )
20            System.out.printf( "%-10s%-45s%s\n", book,
21               book.getTitle(), book.getCopyrightYear() );
22      } // end main
23   } // end class EnumTest
```

```
All books:

JHTP       Java How to Program                            2010
CHTP       C How to Program                               2007
IW3HTP     Internet & World Wide Web How to Program       2008
CPPHTP     C++ How to Program                             2008
VBHTP      Visual Basic 2008 How to Program               2009
CSHARPHTP  Visual C# 2008 How to Program                  2009

Display a range of enum constants:

JHTP       Java How to Program                            2010
CHTP       C How to Program                               2007
IW3HTP     Internet & World Wide Web How to Program       2008
CPPHTP     C++ How to Program                             2008
```

Fig. 8.11 | Testing an enum type.

Lines 19–21 use the static method **range** of class **EnumSet** (declared in package java.util) to display a range of the enum Book's constants. Method range takes two parameters—the first and the last enum constants in the range—and returns an EnumSet that contains all the constants between these two constants, inclusive. For example, the expression EnumSet.range(Book.JHTP, Book.CPPHTP) returns an EnumSet containing Book.JHTP, Book.CHTP, Book.IW3HTP and Book.CPPHTP. The enhanced for statement can be used with an EnumSet just as it can with an array, so lines 12–14 use it to display the title and copyright year of every book in the EnumSet. Class EnumSet provides several other static methods for creating sets of enum constants from the same enum type. For more information on class EnumSet, visit java.sun.com/javase/6/docs/api/java/util/EnumSet.html.

Common Programming Error 8.6

In an enum *declaration, it's a syntax error to declare* enum *constants after the* enum *type's constructors, fields and methods.*

8.10 Garbage Collection and Method finalize

Every class in Java has the methods of class Object (package java.lang), one of which is the finalize method. This method is rarely used because it can cause performance problems and there is some uncertainty as to whether it will get called. Nevertheless, because finalize is part of every class, we discuss it here to help you understand its intended purpose. The complete details of the finalize method are beyond the scope of this book, and most programmers should not use it—you'll soon see why. You'll learn more about class Object in Chapter 9.

Every object uses system resources, such as memory. We need a disciplined way to give resources back to the system when they're no longer needed; otherwise, "resource leaks" might occur that would prevent them from being reused by your program or possibly by other programs. The JVM performs automatic **garbage collection** to reclaim the memory occupied by objects that are no longer used. When there are no more references to an object, the object is eligible to be collected. This typically occurs when the JVM executes its **garbage collector**. So, memory leaks that are common in other languages like C and C++ (because memory is not automatically reclaimed in those languages) are less likely in Java, but some can still happen in subtle ways. Other types of resource leaks can occur. For example, an application may open a file on disk to modify its contents. If it does not close the file, the application must terminate before any other application can use it.

The **finalize method** is called by the garbage collector to perform **termination housekeeping** on an object just before the garbage collector reclaims the object's memory. Method finalize does not take parameters and has return type void. A problem with method finalize is that the garbage collector is not guaranteed to execute at a specified time. In fact, the garbage collector may never execute before a program terminates. Thus, it's unclear if, or when, method finalize will be called. For this reason, most programmers should avoid method finalize.

Software Engineering Observation 8.7

A class that uses system resources, such as files on disk, should provide a method that programmers can call to release resources when they are no longer needed in a program. Many Java API classes provide close *or* dispose *methods for this purpose. For example, class* Scanner *(java.sun.com/javase/6/docs/api/java/util/Scanner.html) has a* close *method.*

8.11 static Class Members

Every object has its own copy of all the instance variables of the class. In certain cases, only one copy of a particular variable should be shared by all objects of a class. A **static field**—called a **class variable**—is used in such cases. A static variable represents **classwide information**—all objects of the class share the same piece of data. The declaration of a static variable begins with the keyword static.

Let's motivate static data with an example. Suppose that we have a video game with Martians and other space creatures. Each Martian tends to be brave and willing to attack other space creatures when the Martian is aware that at least four other Martians are present. If fewer than five Martians are present, each of them becomes cowardly. Thus, each Martian needs to know the martianCount. We could endow class Martian with martianCount as an instance variable. If we do this, then every Martian will have a separate copy of the instance variable, and every time we create a new Martian, we'll have to update the instance variable martianCount in every Martian object. This wastes space with the redundant copies, wastes time in updating the separate copies and is error prone. Instead, we declare martianCount to be static, making martianCount classwide data. Every Martian can see the martianCount as if it were an instance variable of class Martian, but only one copy of the static martianCount is maintained. This saves space. We save time by having the Martian constructor increment the static martianCount—there is only one copy, so we do not have to increment separate copies for each Martian object.

Software Engineering Observation 8.8
Use a static variable when all objects of a class must use the same copy of the variable.

Static variables have class scope. We can access a class's public static members through a reference to any object of the class, or by qualifying the member name with the class name and a dot (.), as in Math.random(). A class's private static class members can be accessed by client code only through methods of the class. Actually, static class members exist even when no objects of the class exist—they are available as soon as the class is loaded into memory at execution time. To access a public static member when no objects of the class exist (and even when they do), prefix the class name and a dot (.) to the static member, as in Math.PI. To access a private static member when no objects of the class exist, provide a public static method and call it by qualifying its name with the class name and a dot.

Software Engineering Observation 8.9
Static class variables and methods exist, and can be used, even if no objects of that class have been instantiated.

A static method cannot access non-static class members, because a static method can be called even when no objects of the class have been instantiated. For the same reason, the this reference cannot be used in a static method. The this reference must refer to a specific object of the class, and when a static method is called, there might not be any objects of its class in memory.

Common Programming Error 8.7
A compilation error occurs if a static method calls an instance (non-static) method in the same class by using only the method name. Similarly, a compilation error occurs if a static method attempts to access an instance variable in the same class by using only the variable name.

Common Programming Error 8.8
Referring to this in a static method is a syntax error.

Tracking the Number of Employee Objects That Have Been Created

Our next program declares two classes—Employee (Fig. 8.12) and EmployeeTest (Fig. 8.13). Class Employee declares private static variable count (Fig. 8.12, line 9) and public static method getCount (lines 36–39). The static variable count is initialized to zero in line 9. If a static variable is not initialized, the compiler assigns it a default value—in this case 0, the default value for type int. Variable count maintains a count of the number of objects of class Employee that have been created so far.

```
1   // Fig. 8.12: Employee.java
2   // Static variable used to maintain a count of the number of
3   // Employee objects in memory.
4
5   public class Employee
6   {
7      private String firstName;
8      private String lastName;
9      private static int count = 0; // number of Employees created
10
11     // initialize Employee, add 1 to static count and
12     // output String indicating that constructor was called
13     public Employee( String first, String last )
14     {
15        firstName = first;
16        lastName = last;
17
18        ++count;  // increment static count of employees
19        System.out.printf( "Employee constructor: %s %s; count = %d\n",
20           firstName, lastName, count );
21     } // end Employee constructor
22
23     // get first name
24     public String getFirstName()
25     {
26        return firstName;
27     } // end method getFirstName
28
29     // get last name
30     public String getLastName()
31     {
32        return lastName;
33     } // end method getLastName
34
35     // static method to get static count value
36     public static int getCount()
37     {
38        return count;
39     } // end method getCount
40  } // end class Employee
```

Fig. 8.12 | static variable used to maintain a count of the number of Employee objects in memory.

When Employee objects exist, variable count can be used in any method of an Employee object—this example increments count in the constructor (line 18). The public static method getCount (lines 36–39) returns the number of Employee objects that have been created so far. When no objects of class Employee exist, client code can access variable count by calling method getCount via the class name, as in Employee.getCount(). When objects exist, method getCount can also be called via any reference to an Employee object.

Good Programming Practice 8.1

Invoke every static method by using the class name and a dot (.) to emphasize that the method being called is a static method.

EmployeeTest method main (Fig. 8.13) instantiates two Employee objects (lines 13–14). When each Employee object's constructor is invoked, lines 15–16 of Fig. 8.12 assign the Employee's first name and last name to instance variables firstName and lastName. Note that these two statements do not make copies of the original String arguments. Actually, String objects in Java are **immutable**—they cannot be modified after they are created. Therefore, it's safe to have many references to one String object. This is not normally the case for objects of most other classes in Java. If String objects are immutable, you might wonder why are we able to use operators + and += to concatenate String objects. String-concatenation operations actually result in a new Strings object containing the concatenated values. The original String objects are not modified.

```
1   // Fig. 8.13: EmployeeTest.java
2   // Static member demonstration.
3
4   public class EmployeeTest
5   {
6      public static void main( String[] args )
7      {
8         // show that count is 0 before creating Employees
9         System.out.printf( "Employees before instantiation: %d\n",
10           Employee.getCount() );
11
12        // create two Employees; count should be 2
13        Employee e1 = new Employee( "Susan", "Baker" );
14        Employee e2 = new Employee( "Bob", "Blue" );
15
16        // show that count is 2 after creating two Employees
17        System.out.println( "\nEmployees after instantiation: " );
18        System.out.printf( "via e1.getCount(): %d\n", e1.getCount() );
19        System.out.printf( "via e2.getCount(): %d\n", e2.getCount() );
20        System.out.printf( "via Employee.getCount(): %d\n",
21           Employee.getCount() );
22
23        // get names of Employees
24        System.out.printf( "\nEmployee 1: %s %s\nEmployee 2: %s %s\n",
25           e1.getFirstName(), e1.getLastName(),
26           e2.getFirstName(), e2.getLastName() );
27
28        // in this example, there is only one reference to each Employee,
29        // so the following two statements indicate that these objects
30        // are eligible for garbage collection
```

Fig. 8.13 | static member demonstration. (Part 1 of 2.)

```
31          e1 = null;
32          e2 = null;
33      } // end main
34   } // end class EmployeeTest
```

```
Employees before instantiation: 0
Employee constructor: Susan Baker; count = 1
Employee constructor: Bob Blue; count = 2

Employees after instantiation:
via e1.getCount(): 2
via e2.getCount(): 2
via Employee.getCount(): 2

Employee 1: Susan Baker
Employee 2: Bob Blue
```

Fig. 8.13 | static member demonstration. (Part 2 of 2.)

When main has finished using the two Employee objects, the references e1 and e2 are set to null at lines 31–32. At this point, references e1 and e2 no longer refer to the objects that were instantiated in lines 13–14. The objects become "eligible for garbage collection" because there are no more references to them in the program.

Eventually, the garbage collector might reclaim the memory for these objects (or the operating system will reclaim the memory when the program terminates). The JVM does not guarantee when, or even whether, the garbage collector will execute. When the garbage collector does execute, it's possible that no objects or only a subset of the eligible objects will be collected.

8.12 static Import

In Section 6.3, you learned about the static fields and methods of class Math. We invoked class Math's static fields and methods by preceding each with the class name Math and a dot (.). A **static import** declaration enables you to import the static members of a class or interface so you can access them via their unqualified names in your class—the class name and a dot (.) are not required to use an imported static member.

A static import declaration has two forms—one that imports a particular static member (which is known as **single static import**) and one that imports all static members of a class (which is known as **static import on demand**). The following syntax imports a particular static member:

```
import static packageName.ClassName.staticMemberName;
```

where *packageName* is the package of the class (e.g., java.lang), *ClassName* is the name of the class (e.g., Math) and *staticMemberName* is the name of the static field or method (e.g., PI or abs). The following syntax imports all static members of a class:

```
import static packageName.ClassName.*;
```

where *packageName* is the package of the class (e.g., java.lang) and *ClassName* is the name of the class (e.g., Math). The asterisk (*) indicates that *all* static members of the specified class should be available for use in the class(es) declared in the file. Note that static import declarations import only static class members. Regular import statements should be used to specify the classes used in a program.

Figure 8.14 demonstrates a static import. Line 3 is a static import declaration, which imports all static fields and methods of class Math from package java.lang. Lines 9–12 access the Math class's static field E (line 11) and the static methods sqrt (line 9), ceil (line 10), log (line 11) and cos (line 12) without preceding the field name or method names with class name Math and a dot.

```
1   // Fig. 8.14: StaticImportTest.java
2   // Static import of Math class methods.
3   import static java.lang.Math.*;
4
5   public class StaticImportTest
6   {
7      public static void main( String[] args )
8      {
9         System.out.printf( "sqrt( 900.0 ) = %.1f\n", sqrt( 900.0 ) );
10        System.out.printf( "ceil( -9.8 ) = %.1f\n", ceil( -9.8 ) );
11        System.out.printf( "log( E ) = %.1f\n", log( E ) );
12        System.out.printf( "cos( 0.0 ) = %.1f\n", cos( 0.0 ) );
13     } // end main
14  } // end class StaticImportTest
```

```
sqrt( 900.0 ) = 30.0
ceil( -9.8 ) = -9.0
log( E ) = 1.0
cos( 0.0 ) = 1.0
```

Fig. 8.14 | Static import of Math class methods.

Common Programming Error 8.9

A compilation error occurs if a program attempts to import from two or more classes static methods that have the same signature or from static fields that have the same name.

8.13 final Instance Variables

The **principle of least privilege** is fundamental to good software engineering. In the context of an application, it states that code should be granted only the amount of privilege and access that it needs to accomplish its designated task, but no more. This makes your programs more robust by preventing code from accidentally (or maliciously) modifying variable values and calling methods that should not be accessible.

Let's see how this principle applies to instance variables. Some of them need to be modifiable and some do not. You can use the keyword final to specify that a variable is not modifiable (i.e., it's a constant) and that any attempt to modify it is an error. For example,

```
private final int INCREMENT;
```

declares a final (constant) instance variable INCREMENT of type int. Although such variables can be initialized when they are declared, this is not required. They can be initialized by each of the class's constructors so that each object of the class has a different value.

Software Engineering Observation 8.10

Declaring an instance variable as final helps enforce the principle of least privilege. If an instance variable should not be modified, declare it to be final to prevent modification.

Our next example contains two classes—class Increment (Fig. 8.15) and class IncrementTest (Fig. 8.16). Class Increment contains a final int instance variable named INCREMENT (Fig. 8.15, line 7). Note that INCREMENT is not initialized in its declaration, so it must be initialized by the class's constructor (lines 10–13). If the class provided multiple constructors, every one would be required to initialize the final variable. The constructor receives int parameter incrementValue and assigns its value to INCREMENT (line 12). A final variable cannot be modified by assignment after it's initialized. Application class IncrementTest creates an object of class Increment (Fig. 8.16, line 8) and provides as the argument to the constructor the value 5 to be assigned to the constant INCREMENT.

```java
1   // Fig. 8.15: Increment.java
2   // final instance variable in a class.
3
4   public class Increment
5   {
6      private int total = 0; // total of all increments
7      private final int INCREMENT; // constant variable (uninitialized)
8
9      // constructor initializes final instance variable INCREMENT
10     public Increment( int incrementValue )
11     {
12        INCREMENT = incrementValue; // initialize constant variable (once)
13     } // end Increment constructor
14
15     // add INCREMENT to total
16     public void addIncrementToTotal()
17     {
18        total += INCREMENT;
19     } // end method addIncrementToTotal
20
21     // return String representation of an Increment object's data
22     public String toString()
23     {
24        return String.format( "total = %d", total );
25     } // end method toString
26  } // end class Increment
```

Fig. 8.15 | final instance variable in a class.

```java
1   // Fig. 8.16: IncrementTest.java
2   // final variable initialized with a constructor argument.
3
4   public class IncrementTest
5   {
6      public static void main( String[] args )
7      {
```

Fig. 8.16 | final variable initialized with a constructor argument. (Part I of 2.)

```
 8          Increment value = new Increment( 5 );
 9
10          System.out.printf( "Before incrementing: %s\n\n", value );
11
12          for ( int i = 1; i <= 3; i++ )
13          {
14             value.addIncrementToTotal();
15             System.out.printf( "After increment %d: %s\n", i, value );
16          } // end for
17      } // end main
18  } // end class IncrementTest
```

```
Before incrementing: total = 0

After increment 1: total = 5
After increment 2: total = 10
After increment 3: total = 15
```

Fig. 8.16 | final variable initialized with a constructor argument. (Part 2 of 2.)

Common Programming Error 8.10

Attempting to modify a final instance variable after it's initialized is a compilation error.

Error-Prevention Tip 8.3

Attempts to modify a final instance variable are caught at compilation time rather than causing execution-time errors. It's always preferable to get bugs out at compilation time, if possible, rather than allow them to slip through to execution time (where studies have found that repair is often many times more expensive).

Software Engineering Observation 8.11

A final field should also be declared static if it's initialized in its declaration to a value that is the same for all objects of the class. After this initialization, its value can never change. Therefore, we don't need a separate copy of the field for every object of the class. Making the field static enables all objects of the class to share the final field.

If a final variable is not initialized, a compilation error occurs. To demonstrate this, we placed line 12 of Fig. 8.15 in a comment and recompiled the class. Figure 8.17 shows the error message produced by the compiler.

```
Increment.java:13: variable INCREMENT might not have been initialized
    } // end Increment constructor
    ^
1 error
```

Fig. 8.17 | final variable INCREMENT must be initialized.

Common Programming Error 8.11

Not initializing a final instance variable in its declaration or in every constructor of the class yields a compilation error indicating that the variable might not have been initialized.

8.14 Time Class Case Study: Creating Packages

We've seen in almost every example in the text that classes from preexisting libraries, such as the Java API, can be imported into a Java program. Each class in the Java API belongs to a package that contains a group of related classes. These packages are defined once, but can be imported into many programs. As applications become more complex, packages help programmers manage the complexity of application components. Packages also facilitate software reuse by enabling programs to import classes from other packages (as we've done in most examples), rather than copying the classes into each program that uses them. Another benefit of packages is that they provide a convention for unique class names, which helps prevent class-name conflicts (discussed later in this section). This section introduces how to create your own packages.

Steps for Declaring a Reusable Class
Before a class can be imported into multiple applications, it must be placed in a package to make it reusable. Figure 8.18 shows how to specify the package in which a class should be placed. Figure 8.19 shows how to import our packaged class so that it can be used in an application. The steps for creating a reusable class are:

1. Declare a public class. If the class is not public, it can be used only by other classes in the same package.

2. Choose a unique package name and add a **package declaration** to the source-code file for the reusable class declaration. In each Java source-code file there can be only one package declaration, and it must precede all other declarations and statements. Note that comments are not statements, so comments can be placed before a package statement in a file. [*Note:* If no package statement is provided, the class is placed in the so-called default package and is accessible only to other classes in the default package that are located in the same directory. All prior programs in this book that had two or more classes, used this default package.]

3. Compile the class so that it's placed in the appropriate package directory.

4. Import the reusable class into a program and use the class.

*Steps 1 and 2: Creating a **public** Class and Adding the **package** Statement*
For *Step 1*, we modify the public class Time1 declared in Fig. 8.1. The new version is shown in Fig. 8.18. No modifications have been made to the implementation of the class, so we'll not discuss its implementation details again here.

For *Step 2*, we add a package declaration (line 3) that declares a package named com.deitel.jhtp.ch08. Placing a package declaration at the beginning of a Java source file indicates that the class declared in the file is part of the specified package. Only package declarations, import declarations and comments can appear outside the braces of a class declaration. A Java source-code file must have the following order:

1. a package declaration (if any),

2. import declarations (if any), then

3. class declarations.

Only one of the class declarations in a particular file can be public. Other classes in the file are placed in the package and can be used only by the other classes in the package. Non-public classes are in a package to support the reusable classes in the package.

```
 1   // Fig. 8.18: Time1.java
 2   // Time1 class declaration maintains the time in 24-hour format.
 3   package com.deitel.jhtp.ch08;
 4
 5   public class Time1
 6   {
 7      private int hour;   // 0 - 23
 8      private int minute; // 0 - 59
 9      private int second; // 0 - 59
10
11      // set a new time value using universal time; ensure that
12      // the data remains consistent by setting invalid values to zero
13      public void setTime( int h, int m, int s )
14      {
15         hour   = ( ( h >= 0 && h < 24 ) ? h : 0 ); // validate hour
16         minute = ( ( m >= 0 && m < 60 ) ? m : 0 ); // validate minute
17         second = ( ( s >= 0 && s < 60 ) ? s : 0 ); // validate second
18      } // end method setTime
19
20      // convert to String in universal-time format (HH:MM:SS)
21      public String toUniversalString()
22      {
23         return String.format( "%02d:%02d:%02d", hour, minute, second );
24      } // end method toUniversalString
25
26      // convert to String in standard-time format (H:MM:SS AM or PM)
27      public String toString()
28      {
29         return String.format( "%d:%02d:%02d %s",
30            ( ( hour == 0 || hour == 12 ) ? 12 : hour % 12 ),
31            minute, second, ( hour < 12 ? "AM" : "PM" ) );
32      } // end method toString
33   } // end class Time1
```

Fig. 8.18 | Packaging class Time1 for reuse.

In an effort to provide unique names for every package, Sun Microsystems specifies a convention that you should follow. Every package name should start with your Internet domain name in reverse order. For example, our domain name is deitel.com, so our package names begin with com.deitel. For the domain name *yourcollege*.edu, the package name should begin with edu.*yourcollege*. After the domain name is reversed, you can choose any other names you want for your package. If you are part of a company with many divisions or a university with many schools, you may want to use the name of your division or school as the next name in the package. We chose to use jhtp as the next name in our package name to indicate that this class is from *Java How to Program*. The last name in our package name specifies that this package is for Chapter 8 (ch08).

Step 3: Compiling the Packaged Class
Step 3 is to compile the class so that it's stored in the appropriate package. When a Java file containing a package declaration is compiled, the resulting class file is placed in the directory specified by the declaration. The package declaration in Fig. 8.18 indicates that class Time1 should be placed in the directory

```
com
    deitel
        jhtp
            ch08
```

The directory names in the package declaration specify the exact location of the classes in the package.

When compiling a class in a package, the javac command-line option **-d** causes the javac compiler to create appropriate directories based on the class's package declaration. The option also specifies where the directories should be stored. For example, in a command window, we used the compilation command

```
javac -d . Time1.java
```

to specify that the first directory in our package name should be placed in the current directory. The period (.) after -d in the preceding command represents the current directory on the Windows, UNIX, Linux and Mac OS X operating systems (and several others as well). After execution of the compilation command, the current directory contains a directory called com, com contains a directory called deitel, deitel contains a directory called jhtp and jhtp contains a directory called ch08. In the ch08 directory, you can find the file Time1.class. [*Note:* If you do not use the -d option, then you must copy or move the class file to the appropriate package directory after compiling it.]

The package name is part of the **fully qualified class name**, so the name of class Time1 is actually com.deitel.jhtp.ch08.Time1. You can use this fully qualified name in your programs, or you can import the class and use its **simple name** (the class name by itself—Time1) in the program. If another package also contains a Time1 class, the fully qualified class names can be used to distinguish between the classes in the program and prevent a **name conflict** (also called a **name collision**).

Step 4: Importing the Reusable Class

Once the class is compiled and stored in its package, the class can be imported into programs (*Step 4*). In the Time1PackageTest application of Fig. 8.19, line 3 specifies that class Time1 should be imported for use in class Time1PackageTest. Class Time1PackageTest is in the default package because the class's .java file does not contain a package declaration. Since the two classes are in different packages, the import at line 3 is required so that class Time1PackageTest can use class Time1.

```
 1   // Fig. 8.19: Time1PackageTest.java
 2   // Time1 object used in an application.
 3   import com.deitel.jhtp.ch08.Time1; // import class Time1
 4
 5   public class Time1PackageTest
 6   {
 7      public static void main( String[] args )
 8      {
 9         // create and initialize a Time1 object
10         Time1 time = new Time1(); // calls Time1 constructor
11
12         // output string representations of the time
13         System.out.print( "The initial universal time is: " );
```

Fig. 8.19 | Time1 object used in an application. (Part 1 of 2.)

```
14          System.out.println( time.toUniversalString() );
15          System.out.print( "The initial standard time is: " );
16          System.out.println( time.toString() );
17          System.out.println(); // output a blank line
18
19          // change time and output updated time
20          time.setTime( 13, 27, 6 );
21          System.out.print( "Universal time after setTime is: " );
22          System.out.println( time.toUniversalString() );
23          System.out.print( "Standard time after setTime is: " );
24          System.out.println( time.toString() );
25          System.out.println(); // output a blank line
26
27          // set time with invalid values; output updated time
28          time.setTime( 99, 99, 99 );
29          System.out.println( "After attempting invalid settings:" );
30          System.out.print( "Universal time: " );
31          System.out.println( time.toUniversalString() );
32          System.out.print( "Standard time: " );
33          System.out.println( time.toString() );
34       } // end main
35    } // end class Time1PackageTest
```

```
The initial universal time is: 00:00:00
The initial standard time is: 12:00:00 AM

Universal time after setTime is: 13:27:06
Standard time after setTime is: 1:27:06 PM

After attempting invalid settings:
Universal time: 00:00:00
Standard time: 12:00:00 AM
```

Fig. 8.19 | Time1 object used in an application. (Part 2 of 2.)

Line 3 is known as a **single-type-import declaration**—that is, the import declaration specifies one class to import. When your program uses multiple classes from the same package, you can import those classes with a single import declaration. For example, the import declaration

```
import java.util.*; // import classes from package java.util
```

uses an asterisk (*) at the end of the import declaration to inform the compiler that all public classes from the java.util package are available for use in the program. This is known as a **type-import-on-demand declaration**. Only the classes from package java.util that are used in the program are loaded by the JVM. The preceding import allows you to use the simple name of any class from the java.util package in the program. Throughout this book, we use single-type-import declarations for clarity.

Common Programming Error 8.12

Using the import declaration import java.; causes a compilation error. You must specify the exact name of the package from which you want to import classes.*

Specifying the Classpath During Compilation
When compiling Time1PackageTest, javac must locate the .class file for Time1 to ensure that class Time1PackageTest uses class Time1 correctly. The compiler uses a special object called a **class loader** to locate the classes it needs. The class loader begins by searching the standard Java classes that are bundled with the JDK. Then it searches for **optional packages**. Java provides an **extension mechanism** that enables new (optional) packages to be added to Java for development and execution purposes. [*Note:* The extension mechanism is beyond the scope of this book. For more information, visit java.sun.com/javase/6/docs/technotes/guides/extensions/.] If the class is not found in the standard Java classes or in the extension classes, the class loader searches the **classpath**, which contains a list of locations in which classes are stored. The classpath consists of a list of directories or **archive files**, each separated by a **directory separator**—a semicolon (;) on Windows or a colon (:) on UNIX/Linux/Mac OS X. Archive files are individual files that contain directories of other files, typically in a compressed format. For example, the standard classes used by your programs are contained in the archive file rt.jar, which is installed with the JDK. Archive files normally end with the .jar or .zip file-name extensions. The directories and archive files specified in the classpath contain the classes you wish to make available to the Java compiler and the JVM.

By default, the classpath consists only of the current directory. However, the classpath can be modified by

1. providing the **-classpath** option to the javac compiler or
2. setting the **CLASSPATH environment variable** (a special variable that you define and the operating system maintains so that applications can search for classes in the specified locations).

For more information on the classpath, visit java.sun.com/javase/6/docs/technotes/tools/index.html#general. The section entitled "General Information" contains information on setting the classpath for UNIX/Linux and Windows.

Common Programming Error 8.13
Specifying an explicit classpath eliminates the current directory from the classpath. This prevents classes in the current directory (including packages in the current directory) from loading properly. If classes must be loaded from the current directory, include a dot (.) in the classpath to specify the current directory.

Software Engineering Observation 8.12
In general, it's a better practice to use the -classpath option of the compiler, rather than the CLASSPATH environment variable, to specify the classpath for a program. This enables each application to have its own classpath.

Error-Prevention Tip 8.4
Specifying the classpath with the CLASSPATH environment variable can cause subtle and difficult-to-locate errors in programs that use different versions of the same package.

For Figs. 8.18–8.19, we didn't specify an explicit classpath. Thus, to locate the classes in the com.deitel.jhtp.ch08 package from this example, the class loader looks in the current directory for the first name in the package—com—then navigates the directory structure. Directory com contains the subdirectory deitel, deitel contains the subdirectory jhtp, and jhtp contains subdirectory ch08. In the ch08 directory is the file Time1.class, which is loaded by the class loader to ensure that the class is used properly in our program.

Specifying the Classpath When Executing an Application
When you execute an application, the JVM must be able to locate the .class files of the classes used in that application. Like the compiler, the java command uses a class loader that searches the standard classes and extension classes first, then searches the classpath (the current directory by default). The classpath can be specified explicitly by using either of the techniques discussed for the compiler. As with the compiler, it's better to specify an individual program's classpath via command-line JVM options. You can specify the classpath in the java command via the **-classpath** or **-cp** command-line options, followed by a list of directories or archive files separated by semicolons (;) on Microsoft Windows or by colons (:) on UNIX/Linux/Mac OS X. Again, if classes must be loaded from the current directory, be sure to include a dot (.) in the classpath to specify the current directory.

8.15 **Package Access**

If no access modifier (public, protected or private—protected is discussed in Chapter 9) is specified for a method or variable when it's declared in a class, the method or variable is considered to have **package access**. In a program that consists of one class declaration, this has no specific effect. However, if a program uses multiple classes from the same package (i.e., a group of related classes), these classes can access each other's package-access members directly through references to objects of the appropriate classes, or in the case of static members through the class name. Package access is rarely used.

The application in Fig. 8.20 demonstrates package access. The application contains two classes in one source-code file—the PackageDataTest application class (lines 5–21) and the PackageData class (lines 24–41). When you compile this program, the compiler produces two separate .class files—PackageDataTest.class and PackageData.class. The compiler places the two .class files in the same directory, so the classes are considered to be part of the same package. Consequently, class PackageDataTest is allowed to modify the package-access data of PackageData objects. Note that you can also place class PackageData (lines 24–41) in a separate source code file. As long as both classes are compiled in the same directory on disk, the package-access relationship will still work.

```
 1   // Fig. 8.20: PackageDataTest.java
 2   // Package-access members of a class are accessible by other classes
 3   // in the same package.
 4
 5   public class PackageDataTest
 6   {
 7      public static void main( String[] args )
 8      {
 9         PackageData packageData = new PackageData();
10
11         // output String representation of packageData
12         System.out.printf( "After instantiation:\n%s\n", packageData );
```

Fig. 8.20 | Package-access members of a class are accessible by other classes in the same package. (Part 1 of 2.)

```
13
14          // change package access data in packageData object
15          packageData.number = 77;
16          packageData.string = "Goodbye";
17
18          // output String representation of packageData
19          System.out.printf( "\nAfter changing values:\n%s\n", packageData );
20       } // end main
21    } // end class PackageDataTest
22
23    // class with package access instance variables
24    class PackageData
25    {
26       int number; // package-access instance variable
27       String string; // package-access instance variable
28
29       // constructor
30       public PackageData()
31       {
32          number = 0;
33          string = "Hello";
34       } // end PackageData constructor
35
36       // return PackageData object String representation
37       public String toString()
38       {
39          return String.format( "number: %d; string: %s", number, string );
40       } // end method toString
41    } // end class PackageData
```

```
After instantiation:
number: 0; string: Hello

After changing values:
number: 77; string: Goodbye
```

Fig. 8.20 | Package-access members of a class are accessible by other classes in the same package. (Part 2 of 2.)

In the `PackageData` class declaration, lines 26–27 declare the instance variables `number` and `string` with no access modifiers—therefore, these are package-access instance variables. The `PackageDataTest` application's `main` method creates an instance of the `PackageData` class (line 9) to demonstrate the ability to modify the `PackageData` instance variables directly (as shown in lines 15–16). The results of the modification can be seen in the output window.

8.16 (Optional) GUI and Graphics Case Study: Using Objects with Graphics

Most of the graphics you've seen to this point did not vary with each program execution. Exercise 6.2 in Section 6.13 asked you to create a program that generated shapes and colors at random. In that exercise, the drawing changed every time the system called paint-

Component to redraw the panel. To create a more consistent drawing that remains the same each time it is drawn, we must store information about the displayed shapes so that we can reproduce them each time the system calls paintComponent. To do this, we'll create a set of shape classes that store information about each shape. We'll make these classes "smart" by allowing objects of these classes to draw themselves by using a Graphics object.

Class *MyLine*

Figure 8.21 declares class MyLine, which has all these capabilities. Class MyLine imports Color and Graphics (lines 3–4). Lines 8–11 declare instance variables for the coordinates needed to draw a line, and line 12 declares the instance variable that stores the color of the line. The constructor at lines 15–22 takes five parameters, one for each instance variable that it initializes. Method draw at lines 25–29 requires a Graphics object and uses it to draw the line in the proper color and at the proper coordinates.

```java
1   // Fig. 8.21: MyLine.java
2   // Declaration of class MyLine.
3   import java.awt.Color;
4   import java.awt.Graphics;
5
6   public class MyLine
7   {
8      private int x1; // x-coordinate of first endpoint
9      private int y1; // y-coordinate of first endpoint
10     private int x2; // x-coordinate of second endpoint
11     private int y2; // y-coordinate of second endpoint
12     private Color myColor; // color of this shape
13
14     // constructor with input values
15     public MyLine( int x1, int y1, int x2, int y2, Color color )
16     {
17        this.x1 = x1; // set x-coordinate of first endpoint
18        this.y1 = y1; // set y-coordinate of first endpoint
19        this.x2 = x2; // set x-coordinate of second endpoint
20        this.y2 = y2; // set y-coordinate of second endpoint
21        myColor = color; // set the color
22     } // end MyLine constructor
23
24     // Draw the line in the specified color
25     public void draw( Graphics g )
26     {
27        g.setColor( myColor );
28        g.drawLine( x1, y1, x2, y2 );
29     } // end method draw
30  } // end class MyLine
```

Fig. 8.21 | MyLine class represents a line.

Class *DrawPanel*

In Fig. 8.22, we declare class DrawPanel, which will generate random objects of class MyLine. Line 12 declares a MyLine array to store the lines to draw. Inside the constructor (lines 15–37), line 17 sets the background color to Color.WHITE. Line 19 creates the array with a random length between 5 and 9. The loop at lines 22–36 creates a new MyLine for every element in the array. Lines 25–28 generate random coordinates for each line's endpoints, and lines 31–32 generate a random color for the line. Line 35 creates a new MyLine object with the randomly generated values and stores it in the array.

```java
1   // Fig. 8.22: DrawPanel.java
2   // Program that uses class MyLine
3   // to draw random lines.
4   import java.awt.Color;
5   import java.awt.Graphics;
6   import java.util.Random;
7   import javax.swing.JPanel;
8
9   public class DrawPanel extends JPanel
10  {
11     private Random randomNumbers = new Random();
12     private MyLine[] lines; // array of lines
13
14     // constructor, creates a panel with random shapes
15     public DrawPanel()
16     {
17        setBackground( Color.WHITE );
18
19        lines = new MyLine[ 5 + randomNumbers.nextInt( 5 ) ];
20
21        // create lines
22        for ( int count = 0; count < lines.length; count++ )
23        {
24           // generate random coordinates
25           int x1 = randomNumbers.nextInt( 300 );
26           int y1 = randomNumbers.nextInt( 300 );
27           int x2 = randomNumbers.nextInt( 300 );
28           int y2 = randomNumbers.nextInt( 300 );
29
30           // generate a random color
31           Color color = new Color( randomNumbers.nextInt( 256 ),
32              randomNumbers.nextInt( 256 ), randomNumbers.nextInt( 256 ) );
33
34           // add the line to the list of lines to be displayed
35           lines[ count ] = new MyLine( x1, y1, x2, y2, color );
36        } // end for
37     } // end DrawPanel constructor
38
39     // for each shape array, draw the individual shapes
40     public void paintComponent( Graphics g )
41     {
42        super.paintComponent( g );
43
44        // draw the lines
45        for ( MyLine line : lines )
46           line.draw( g );
47     } // end method paintComponent
48  } // end class DrawPanel
```

Fig. 8.22 | Creating random MyLine objects.

Method paintComponent iterates through the MyLine objects in array lines using an enhanced for statement (lines 45–46). Each iteration calls the draw method of the current MyLine object and passes it the Graphics object for drawing on the panel.

Class *TestDraw*

Class TestDraw in Fig. 8.23 sets up a new window to display our drawing. Since we are setting the coordinates for the lines only once in the constructor, the drawing does not change if paintComponent is called to refresh the drawing on the screen.

```
1   // Fig. 8.23: TestDraw.java
2   // Creating a JFrame to display a DrawPanel.
3   import javax.swing.JFrame;
4
5   public class TestDraw
6   {
7      public static void main( String[] args )
8      {
9         DrawPanel panel = new DrawPanel();
10        JFrame application = new JFrame();
11
12        application.setDefaultCloseOperation( JFrame.EXIT_ON_CLOSE );
13        application.add( panel );
14        application.setSize( 300, 300 );
15        application.setVisible( true );
16     } // end main
17  } // end class TestDraw
```

Fig. 8.23 | Creating a JFrame to display a DrawPanel.

GUI and Graphics Case Study Exercise

8.1   Extend the program in Figs. 8.21–8.23 to randomly draw rectangles and ovals. Create classes MyRectangle and MyOval. Both of these classes should include *x1, y1, x2, y2* coordinates, a color and a boolean flag to determine whether the shape is a filled shape. Declare a constructor in each class with arguments for initializing all the instance variables. To help draw rectangles and ovals, each class should provide methods getUpperLeftX, getUpperLeftY, getWidth and getHeight that calculate the upper-left *x*-coordinate, upper-left *y*-coordinate, width and height, respectively. The upper-left *x*-coordinate is the smaller of the two *x*-coordinate values, the upper-left *y*-coordinate is the smaller of the two *y*-coordinate values, the width is the absolute value of the difference between the two *x*-coordinate values, and the height is the absolute value of the difference between the two *y*-coordinate values.

Class DrawPanel, which extends JPanel and handles the creation of the shapes, should declare three arrays, one for each shape type. The length of each array should be a random number between 1 and 5. The constructor of class DrawPanel will fill each of the arrays with shapes of random position, size, color and fill.

In addition, modify all three shape classes to include the following:

a) A constructor with no arguments that sets all the coordinates of the shape to 0, the color of the shape to Color.BLACK, and the filled property to false (MyRectangle and MyOval only).

b) *Set* methods for the instance variables in each class. The methods that set a coordinate value should verify that the argument is greater than or equal to zero before setting the coordinate—if it's not, they should set the coordinate to zero. The constructor should call the *set* methods rather than initialize the local variables directly.

c) *Get* methods for the instance variables in each class. Method draw should reference the coordinates by the *get* methods rather than access them directly.

8.17 Wrap-Up

In this chapter, we presented additional class concepts. The Time class case study presented a complete class declaration consisting of private data, overloaded public constructors for initialization flexibility, *set* and *get* methods for manipulating the class's data, and methods that returned String representations of a Time object in two different formats. You also learned that every class can declare a toString method that returns a String representation of an object of the class and that method toString can be called implicitly whenever an object of a class appears in the code where a String is expected.

You learned that the this reference is used implicitly in a class's non-static methods to access the class's instance variables and other non-static methods. You also saw explicit uses of the this reference to access the class's members (including shadowed fields) and how to use keyword this in a constructor to call another constructor of the class.

We discussed the differences between default constructors provided by the compiler and no-argument constructors provided by the programmer. You learned that a class can have references to objects of other classes as members—a concept known as composition. You saw the enum class type and learned how it can be used to create a set of constants for use in a program. You learned about Java's garbage-collection capability and how it (unpredictably) reclaims the memory of objects that are no longer used. The chapter explained the motivation for static fields in a class and demonstrated how to declare and use static fields and methods in your own classes. You also learned how to declare and initialize final variables.

You learned how to package your own classes for reuse and how to import those classes into an application. Finally, you learned that fields declared without an access modifier are given package access by default. You saw the relationship between classes in the same package that allows each class in a package to access the package-access members of other classes in the package.

In the next chapter, you'll learn about an important aspect of object-oriented programming in Java—inheritance. You'll see that all classes in Java are related directly or indirectly to the class called Object. You'll also begin to understand how the relationships between classes enable you to build more powerful applications.

Summary

Section 8.2 *Time Class Case Study*
- The `public` methods of a class are also known as the class's `public` services or `public` interface. They present to the class's clients a view of the services the class provides.
- A class's `private` members are not accessible to the class's clients.
- An object that contains consistent data has data values that are always kept in range.
- A value passed to a method to modify an instance variable is a consistent value if it is in the instance variable's allowed range. A correct value is always a consistent value, but a consistent value is not correct if a method receives an out-of-range value and sets it to a consistent value to maintain the object in a consistent state.
- `String` class `static` method `format` is similar to method `System.out.printf` except that `format` returns a formatted `String` rather than displaying it in a command window.
- All objects in Java have a `toString` method that returns a `String` representation of the object. Method `toString` is called implicitly when an object appears in code where a `String` is needed.

Section 8.3 *Controlling Access to Members*
- The access modifiers `public` and `private` control access to a class's variables and methods.
- The primary purpose of `public` methods is to present to the class's clients a view of the services the class provides. Clients need not be concerned with how the class accomplishes its tasks.
- A class's `private` variables and `private` methods (i.e., its implementation details) are not accessible to its clients.

Section 8.4 *Referring to the Current Object's Members with the* `this` *Reference*
- A non-`static` method of an object implicitly uses keyword `this` to refer to the object's instance variables and other methods. Keyword `this` can also be used explicitly.
- The compiler produces a separate file with the `.class` extension for every compiled class.
- If a local variable has the same name as a class's field, the local variable shadows the field. You can use the `this` reference in a method to refer to the shadowed field explicitly.

Section 8.5 *Time Class Case Study: Overloaded Constructors*
- Overloaded constructors enable objects of a class to be initialized in different ways. The compiler differentiates overloaded constructors by their signatures.
- To call one contructor of a class from another of the same class, you can use the `this` keyword followed by parentheses containing the constructor arguments. Such a constructor call must appear as the first statement in the constructor's body.

Section 8.6 *Default and No-Argument Constructors*
- If no constructors are provided in a class, the compiler creates a default constructor.
- If a class declares constructors, the compiler will not create a default constructor. In this case, you must declare a no-argument constructor if default initialization is required.

Section 8.7 *Notes on* Set *and* Get *Methods*
- *Set* methods are commonly called mutator methods because they typically change a value. *Get* methods are commonly called accessor methods or query methods. A predicate method tests whether a condition is true or false.

Section 8.8 *Composition*
- A class can have references to objects of other classes as members. This is called composition and is sometimes referred to as a *has-a* relationship.

Section 8.9 Enumerations

- All enum types are reference types. An enum type is declared with an enum declaration, which is a comma-separated list of enum constants. The declaration may optionally include other components of traditional classes, such as constructors, fields and methods.

- enum constants are implicitly final, because they declare constants that should not be modified.

- enum constants are implicitly static.

- Any attempt to create an object of an enum type with operator new results in a compilation error.

- enum constants can be used anywhere constants can be used, such as in the case labels of switch statements and to control enhanced for statements.

- Each enum constant in an enum declaration is optionally followed by arguments which are passed to the enum constructor.

- For every enum, the compiler generates a static method called values that returns an array of the enum's constants in the order in which they were declared.

- EnumSet static method range receives the first and last enum constants in a range and returns an EnumSet that contains all the constants between these two constants, inclusive.

Section 8.10 Garbage Collection and Method `finalize`

- Every class in Java has the methods of class Object, one of which is the finalize method.

- The Java Virtual Machine (JVM) performs automatic garbage collection to reclaim the memory occupied by objects that are no longer in use. When there are no more references to an object, the object is eligible for garbage collection. The memory for such an object can be reclaimed when the JVM executes its garbage collector.

- The finalize method is called by the garbage collector just before it reclaims the object's memory. Method finalize does not take parameters and has return type void.

- The garbage collector may never execute before a program terminates. Thus, it's unclear whether, or when, method finalize will be called.

Section 8.11 `static` Class Members

- A static variable represents classwide information that is shared among all objects of the class.

- Static variables have class scope. A class's public static members can be accessed through a reference to any object of the class, or they can be accessed by qualifying the member name with the class name and a dot (.). Client code can access a class's private static class members only through methods of the class.

- static class members exist as soon as the class is loaded into memory.

- A method declared static cannot access non-static class members, because a static method can be called even when no objects of the class have been instantiated.

- The this reference cannot be used in a static method.

Section 8.12 `static` Import

- A static import declaration enables programmers to refer to imported static members without the class name and a dot (.). A single static import declaration imports one static member, and a static import on demand imports all static members of a class.

Section 8.13 `final` Instance Variables

- In the context of an application, the principle of least privilege states that code should be granted only the amount of privilege and access that the code needs to accomplish its designated task.

- Keyword final specifies that a variable is not modifiable. Such variables must be initialized when they are declared or by each of a class's constructors.

Section 8.14 *Time Class Case Study: Creating Packages*

- Each class in the Java API belongs to a package that contains a group of related classes. Packages help manage the complexity of application components and facilitate software reuse.

- Packages provide a convention for unique class names that helps prevent class-name conflicts.

- Before a class can be imported into multiple applications, it must be placed in a package. There can be only one package declaration in each Java source-code file, and it must precede all other declarations and statements in the file.

- Every package name should start with your Internet domain name in reverse order. After the domain name is reversed, you can choose any other names you want for your package.

- When compiling a class in a package, the javac command-line option -d specifies where to store the package and causes the compiler to create the package's directories if they do not exist.

- The package name is part of the fully qualified class name. This helps prevent name conflicts.

- A single-type-import declaration specifies one class to import. A type-import-on-demand declaration imports only the classes that the program uses from a particular package.

- The compiler uses a class loader to locate the classes it needs in the classpath. The classpath consists of a list of directories or archive files, each separated by a directory separator.

- The classpath for the compiler and JVM can be specified by providing the -classpath option to the javac or java command, or by setting the CLASSPATH environment variable. If classes must be loaded from the current directory, include a dot (.) in the classpath.

Section 8.15 *Package Access*

- If no access modifier is specified for a method or variable when it's declared in a class, the method or variable is considered to have package access.

Terminology

accessor method 331
archive file in classpath 350
class loader 350
class variable 338
classpath 350
-classpath command line option to java 351
-classpath command line option to javac 350
CLASSPATH environment variable 350
classwide information 338
composition 332
-cp command line option to java 351
-d compiler option 348
directory separator in classpath 350
enum constructor 335
enum declaration 335
EnumSet class 337
extension mechanism 350
finalize method 338
format method of class String 319
fully qualified class name 348
garbage collection 338
garbage collector 338
has-a relationship 332

immutable object 341
inlining method calls 329
mutator method 331
name collision 348
name conflict 348
no-argument constructor 327
optional package 350
overloaded constructors 325
package access 351
package declaration 346
predicate method 332
principle of least privilege 343
public interface of a class 317
public services of a class 317
query method 331
range method of EnumSet 337
simple name of a class 348
single static import 342
single-type-import declaration 349
static 342
static field 338
static import 342
static import on demand 342

termination housekeeping 338
this keyword 322
this reference 322

type-import-on-demand declaration 349
values method of an enum 336

Self-Review Exercises

8.1 Fill in the blanks in each of the following statements:

a) When compiling a class in a package, the javac command-line option _____ speci-fies where to store the package and causes the compiler to create the package's directo-ries if they do not exist.

b) String class static method _____ is similar to method System.out.printf, but re-turns a formatted String rather than displaying a String in a command window.

c) If a method contains a local variable with the same name as one of its class's fields, the local variable _____ the field in that method's scope.

d) The _____ method is called by the garbage collector just before it reclaims an object's memory.

e) A(n) _____ declaration specifies one class to import.

f) If a class declares constructors, the compiler will not create a(n) _____.

g) An object's _____ method is called implicitly when an object appears in code where a String is needed.

h) *Get* methods are commonly called _____ or _____.

i) A(n) _____ method tests whether a condition is true or false.

j) For every enum, the compiler generates a static method called _____ that returns an array of the enum's constants in the order in which they were declared.

k) Composition is sometimes referred to as a(n) _____ relationship.

l) A(n) _____ declaration contains a comma-separated list of constants.

m) A(n) _____ variable represents classwide information that is shared by all the objects of the class.

n) A(n) _____ declaration imports one static member.

o) The _____ states that code should be granted only the amount of privilege and access that it needs to accomplish its designated task.

p) Keyword _____ specifies that a variable is not modifiable.

q) There can be only one _____ in a Java source-code file, and it must precede all other declarations and statements in the file.

r) A(n) _____ declaration imports only the classes that the program uses from a partic-ular package.

s) The compiler uses a(n) _____ to locate the classes it needs in the classpath.

t) The classpath for the compiler and JVM can be specified with the _____ option to the javac or java command, or by setting the _____ environment variable.

u) *Set* methods are commonly called _____ because they typically change a value.

v) A(n) _____ imports all static members of a class.

w) The public methods of a class are also known as the class's _____ or _____.

x) In an object, _____ data is data values that is always kept in range.

Answers to Self-Review Exercises

8.1 a) -d. b) format. c) shadows. d) finalize. e) single-type-import. f) default constructor. g) toString. h) accessor methods, query methods. i) predicate. j) values. k) *has-a*. l) enum. m) stat-ic. n) single static import. o) principle of least privilege. p) final. q) package declaration. r) type-import-on-demand. s) class loader. t) -classpath, CLASSPATH. u) mutator methods. v) static im-port on demand. w) public services, public interface. x) consistent.

Exercises

8.2   Explain the notion of package access in Java. Explain the negative aspects of package access.

8.3   What happens when a return type, even void, is specified for a constructor?

8.4   *(Rectangle Class)* Create a class Rectangle with attributes length and width, each of which defaults to 1. Provide methods that calculate the rectangle's perimeter and area. It has *set* and *get* methods for both length and width. The *set* methods should verify that length and width are each floating-point numbers larger than 0.0 and less than 20.0. Write a program to test class Rectangle.

8.5   *(Modifying the Internal Data Representation of a Class)* It would be perfectly reasonable for the Time2 class of Fig. 8.5 to represent the time internally as the number of seconds since midnight rather than the three integer values hour, minute and second. Clients could use the same public methods and get the same results. Modify the Time2 class of Fig. 8.5 to implement the Time2 as the number of seconds since midnight and show that no change is visible to the clients of the class.

8.6   *(Enhancing Class Time2)* Modify class Time2 of Fig. 8.5 to include a tick method that increments the time stored in a Time2 object by one second. Provide method incrementMinute to increment the minute by one and method incrementHour to increment the hour by one. The Time2 object should always remain in a consistent state. Write a program that tests the tick method, the incrementMinute method and the incrementHour method to ensure that they work correctly. Be sure to test the following cases:
    a)   incrementing into the next minute,
    b)   incrementing into the next hour and
    c)   incrementing into the next day (i.e., 11:59:59 PM to 12:00:00 AM).

8.7   *(Enhancing Class Date)* Modify class Date of Fig. 8.7 to perform error checking on the initializer values for instance variables month, day and year (currently it validates only the month and day). Provide a method nextDay to increment the day by one. The Date object should remain in a consistent state. Write a program that tests method nextDay in a loop that prints the date during each iteration to illustrate that the method works correctly. Test the following cases:
    a)   incrementing into the next month and
    b)   incrementing into the next year.

8.8   *(Returning Error Indicators from Methods)* Modify the *set* methods in class Time2 of Fig. 8.5 to return appropriate error values if an attempt is made to set one of the instance variables hour, minute or second of an object of class Time2 to an invalid value. [*Hint:* Use boolean return types on each method.] Write a program that tests these new *set* methods and outputs error messages when incorrect values are supplied.

8.9   Write an enum type TrafficLight, whose constants (RED, GREEN, YELLOW) take one parameter—the duration of the light. Write a program to test the TrafficLight enum so that it displays the enum constants and their durations.

8.10   *(Complex Numbers)* Create a class called Complex for performing arithmetic with complex numbers. Complex numbers have the form

   *realPart + imaginaryPart * i*

where *i* is

   $\sqrt{-1}$

Write a program to test your class. Use floating-point variables to represent the private data of the class. Provide a constructor that enables an object of this class to be initialized when it's declared.

Provide a no-argument constructor with default values in case no initializers are provided. Provide `public` methods that perform the following operations:

a) Add two `Complex` numbers: The real parts are added together and the imaginary parts are added together.

b) Subtract two `Complex` numbers: The real part of the right operand is subtracted from the real part of the left operand, and the imaginary part of the right operand is subtracted from the imaginary part of the left operand.

c) Print `Complex` numbers in the form (a, b), where a is the real part and b is the imaginary part.

8.11 *(Date and Time Class)* Create class `DateAndTime` that combines the modified `Time2` class of Exercise 8.6 and the modified `Date` class of Exercise 8.7. Modify method `incrementHour` to call method `nextDay` if the time is incremented into the next day. Modify methods `toString` and `toUniversalString` to output the date in addition to the time. Write a program to test the new class `DateAndTime`. Specifically, test incrementing the time to the next day.

8.12 *(Set of Integers)* Create class `IntegerSet`. Each `IntegerSet` object can hold integers in the range 0–100. The set is represented by an array of `boolean`s. Array element a[i] is `true` if integer *i* is in the set. Array element a[j] is `false` if integer *j* is not in the set. The no-argument constructor initializes the array to the "empty set" (i.e., a all `false` values).

Provide the following methods: Method `union` creates a set that is the set-theoretic union of two existing sets (i.e., an element of the new set's array is set to `true` if that element is `true` in either or both of the existing sets—otherwise, the new set's element is set to `false`). Method `intersection` creates a set which is the set-theoretic intersection of two existing sets (i.e., an element of the new set's array is set to `false` if that element is `false` in either or both of the existing sets—otherwise, the new set's element is set to `true`). Method `insertElement` inserts a new integer *k* into a set (by setting a[k] to `true`). Method `deleteElement` deletes integer *m* (by setting a[m] to `false`). Method `toString` returns a `String` containing a set as a list of numbers separated by spaces. Include only those elements that are present in the set. Use `---` to represent an empty set. Method `isEqualTo` determines whether two sets are equal. Write a program to test class `IntegerSet`. Instantiate several `IntegerSet` objects. Test that all your methods work properly.

8.13 *(Date Class)* Create class `Date` with the following capabilities:

a) Output the date in multiple formats, such as

```
MM/DD/YYYY
June 14, 1992
DDD YYYY
```

b) Use overloaded constructors to create `Date` objects initialized with dates of the formats in part (a). In the first case the constructor should receive three integer values. In the second case it should receive a `String` and two integer values. In the third case it should receive two integer values, the first of which represents the day number in the year. [*Hint:* To convert the `String` representation of the month to a numeric value, compare `Strings` using the `equals` method. For example, if s1 and s2 are `Strings`, the method call s1.equals(s2) returns `true` if the `Strings` are identical and otherwise returns `false`.]

8.14 *(Rational Numbers)* Create a class called `Rational` for performing arithmetic with fractions. Write a program to test your class. Use integer variables to represent the `private` instance variables of the class—the numerator and the denominator. Provide a constructor that enables an object of this class to be initialized when it's declared. The constructor should store the fraction in reduced form. The fraction is equivalent to 1/2 and would be stored in the object as 1 in the numerator and 2 in the denomina-tor. Provide a no-argument constructor with default values in case no initializers are provided. Provide public methods that perform each of the following operations:

a) Add two Rational numbers: The result of the addition should be stored in reduced form.

b) Subtract two Rational numbers: The result of the subtraction should be stored in re-duced form.

c) Multiply two Rational numbers: The result of the multiplication should be stored in reduced form.

d) Divide two Rational numbers: The result of the division should be stored in reduced form.

e) Return a String representation of a Rational number in the form a/b, where a is the numerator and b is the denominator.

f) Return a String representation of a Rational number in floating-point format. (Consider providing formatting capabilities that enable the user of the class to specify the number of digits of precision to the right of the decimal point.)

Making a Difference

8.15 *(Air Traffic Control)* Every day, according to the National Air Traffic Controllers Association (www.natca.org/mediacenter/bythenumbers.msp), there are more than 87,000 flights in the United States, including commercial flights, cargo flights, and so on, and the long-term trend is that air traffic activity will increase along with the population. As air traffic grows, so do the challenges to air traffic controllers, who monitor the flights and provide instructions to the pilots to ensure safety in the skies.

In this exercise, you'll create a Flight class that could be used in a simple air-traffic-control simulator. The application's main method will act as air traffic control. Visit sites such as

    www.howstuffworks.com/air-traffic-control.htm

to research how the air-traffic-control system works. Then identify some key attributes of a Flight in an air-traffic-control system. Think about the different states a plane could be in from the time it's parked at an airport gate until it arrives at its destination—parked, taxiing, waiting to take off, taking off, climbing, and so on. Use a FlightStatus enumeration to represent these states. The attributes might include the plane's make and model, current air speed, current altitude, direction, carrier, departure time, estimated arrival time, origin and destination. The origin and destination should be specified using standard three-letter airport codes, such as BOS for Boston and LAX for Los Angeles (these codes are available at world-airport-codes.com). Provide *set* and *get* methods to manipulate these and any other attributes you identify. Next, identify the class's behaviors and implement them as methods of the class. Include behaviors such as changeAltitude, reduceSpeed and beginLandingApproach. The Flight constructor should initialize a Flight's attributes. You should also provide a toString method that returns a String representation of a Flight's current status (e.g., parked at the gate, taxiing, taking off, changing altitude). This String should include all of the object's instance-variable values.

When the application executes, main will display the message, "Air Traffic Control Simulator", then will create and interact with three Flight objects representing planes that are currently flying or preparing to fly. For simplicity, the Flight's confirmation of each action will be a message displayed on the screen when the appropriate method is called on the object. For example, if you call a flight's changeAltitude method, the method should:

a) Display a message containing the airline, flight number, "changing altitude", the cur-rent altitude and the new altitude.

b) Change the state of the status instance variable to CHANGING_ALTITUDE.

c) Change the value of the newAltitude instance variable.

In main, create and initialize three Flight objects that are in different states—for example, one could be at the gate, one could be preparing for takeoff and one could be preparing for landing. The main method should send messages to (invoke methods on) the Flight objects. As a Flight object receives each message, it should display a confirmation message from the method being called—such as "[Airline name] [Flight number] changing altitude from 20000 to 25000 feet." The method should also update the appropriate state information in the Flight object. For example, if Air Traffic Control sends a message like "[Airline] [flight number] descend to 12000 feet," the program should execute a method call like flight1.changeAltitude(12000), which would display a confirmation message and would set instance variable newAltitude to 12000. [*Note:* Assume the Flight's currentAltitude instance variable is being set automatically by the plane's altimeter.]

Object-Oriented Programming: Inheritance

Objectives

In this chapter you'll learn:

- How inheritance promotes software reusability.
- The notions of superclasses and subclasses.
- To use keyword **extends** to create a class that inherits attributes and behaviors from another class.
- To use access modifier **protected** to give subclass methods access to superclass members.
- To access superclass members with **super**.
- How constructors are used in inheritance hierarchies.
- The methods of class **Object**, the direct or indirect superclass of all classes in Java.

9.1 Introduction

This chapter continues our discussion of object-oriented programming (OOP) by introducing one of its primary capabilities—**inheritance**, which is a form of software reuse in which a new class is created by absorbing an existing class's members and embellishing them with new or modified capabilities. With inheritance, you can save time during program development by basing new classes on existing proven and debugged high-quality software. This also increases the likelihood that a system will be implemented and maintained effectively.

When creating a class, rather than declaring completely new members, you can designate that the new class should inherit the members of an existing class. The existing class is called the **superclass**, and the new class is the **subclass.** (The C++ programming language refers to the superclass as the **base class** and the subclass as the **derived class**.) Each subclass can become a superclass for future subclasses.

A subclass can add its own fields and methods. Therefore, a subclass is more specific than its superclass and represents a more specialized group of objects. The subclass exhibits the behaviors of its superclass and can add behaviors that are specific to the subclass. This is why inheritance is sometimes referred to as **specialization**.

The **direct superclass** is the superclass from which the subclass explicitly inherits. An **indirect superclass** is any class above the direct superclass in the **class hierarchy**, which defines the inheritance relationships between classes. In Java, the class hierarchy begins with class Object (in package java.lang), which *every* class in Java directly or indirectly **extends** (or "inherits from"). Section 9.7 lists the methods of class Object that are inherited by all other Java classes. Java supports only **single inheritance**, in which each class is derived from exactly one direct superclass. Unlike C++, Java does not support multiple inheritance (which occurs when a class is derived from more than one direct superclass). Chapter 10, Object-Oriented Programming: Polymorphism, explains how to use Java interfaces to realize many of the benefits of multiple inheritance while avoiding the associated problems.

We distinguish between the *is-a* **relationship** and the *has-a* **relationship**. *Is-a* represents inheritance. In an *is-a* relationship, an object of a subclass can also be treated as an object of its superclass. For example, a car *is a* vehicle. By contrast, *has-a* represents composition (see Chapter 8). In a *has-a* relationship, an object contains as members references to other objects. For example, a car *has a* steering wheel (and a car object has a reference to a steering wheel object).

New classes can inherit from classes in **class libraries**. Organizations develop their own class libraries and can take advantage of others available worldwide. Some day, most new software likely will be constructed from **standardized reusable components**, just as automobiles and most computer hardware are constructed today. This will facilitate the development of more powerful, abundant and economical software.

9.2 Superclasses and Subclasses

Often, an object of one class *is an* object of another class as well. For example, in geometry, a rectangle *is a* quadrilateral—a four-sided shape—as are squares, parallelograms and trapezoids. Thus, in Java, class `Rectangle` can be said to inherit from class `Quadrilateral`. In this context, class `Quadrilateral` is a superclass and class `Rectangle` is a subclass. A rectangle *is a* specific type of quadrilateral, but it's incorrect to claim that every quadrilateral *is a* rectangle—the quadrilateral could be a parallelogram or some other shape. Figure 9.1 lists several simple examples of superclasses and subclasses—note that superclasses tend to be "more general" and subclasses "more specific."

Because every subclass object *is an* object of its superclass, and one superclass can have many subclasses, the set of objects represented by a superclass is typically larger than the set of objects represented by any of its subclasses. For example, the superclass `Vehicle` represents all vehicles, including cars, trucks, boats, bicycles and so on. By contrast, subclass `Car` represents a smaller, more specific subset of vehicles.

Superclass	Subclasses
Student	GraduateStudent, UndergraduateStudent
Shape	Circle, Triangle, Rectangle, Sphere, Cube
Loan	CarLoan, HomeImprovementLoan, MortgageLoan
Employee	Faculty, Staff
BankAccount	CheckingAccount, SavingsAccount

Fig. 9.1 | Inheritance examples.

Inheritance relationships form treelike hierarchical structures. A superclass exists in a hierarchical relationship with its subclasses. Let's develop a sample class hierarchy (Fig. 9.2), also called an **inheritance hierarchy**. A university community has thousands of members, including employees, students and alumni. Employees are either faculty or staff members. Faculty members are either administrators (e.g., deans and department chairpersons) or teachers. Note that the hierarchy could contain many other classes. For example, students can be graduate or undergraduate students. Undergraduate students can be freshmen, sophomores, juniors or seniors.

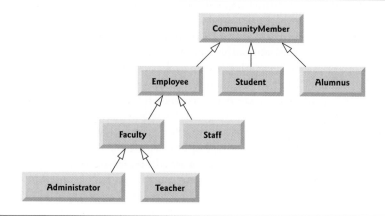

Fig. 9.2 | Inheritance hierarchy for university CommunityMembers.

Each arrow in the hierarchy represents an *is-a* relationship. As we follow the arrows upward in this class hierarchy, we can state, for instance, that "an Employee *is a* CommunityMember" and "a Teacher *is a* Faculty member." CommunityMember is the direct superclass of Employee, Student and Alumnus and is an indirect superclass of all the other classes in the diagram. Starting from the bottom, you can follow the arrows and apply the *is-a* relationship up to the topmost superclass. For example, an Administrator *is a* Faculty member, *is an* Employee, *is a* CommunityMember and, of course, *is an* Object.

Now consider the Shape inheritance hierarchy in Fig. 9.3. This hierarchy begins with superclass Shape, which is extended by subclasses TwoDimensionalShape and ThreeDimensionalShape—Shapes are either TwoDimensionalShapes or ThreeDimensionalShapes. The third level of this hierarchy contains specific types of TwoDimensionalShapes and ThreeDimensionalShapes. As in Fig. 9.2, we can follow the arrows from the bottom of the diagram to the topmost superclass in this class hierarchy to identify several *is-a* relationships. For instance, a Triangle *is a* TwoDimensionalShape and *is a* Shape, while a Sphere *is a* ThreeDimensionalShape and *is a* Shape. Note that this hierarchy could contain many other classes. For example, ellipses and trapezoids are TwoDimensionalShapes.

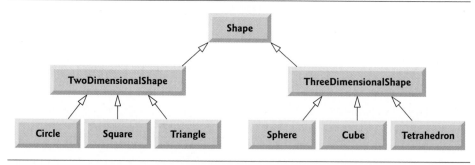

Fig. 9.3 | Inheritance hierarchy for Shapes.

Not every class relationship is an inheritance relationship. In Chapter 8, we discussed the *has-a* relationship, in which classes have members that are references to objects of other classes. Such relationships create classes by composition of existing classes. For example, given the classes Employee, BirthDate and TelephoneNumber, it's improper to say that an Employee *is a* BirthDate or that an Employee *is a* TelephoneNumber. However, an Employee *has a* BirthDate, and an Employee *has a* TelephoneNumber.

It's possible to treat superclass objects and subclass objects similarly—their commonalities are expressed in the members of the superclass. Objects of all classes that extend a common superclass can be treated as objects of that superclass (i.e., such objects have an *is-a* relationship with the superclass). Later in this chapter and in Chapter 10, Object-Oriented Programming: Polymorphism, we consider many examples that take advantage of the *is-a* relationship.

One problem with inheritance is that a subclass can inherit methods that it does not need or should not have. Even when a superclass method is appropriate for a subclass, that subclass often needs a customized version of the method. In such cases, the subclass can **override** (redefine) the superclass method with an appropriate implementation, as we'll see often in the chapter's code examples.

9.3 protected Members

Chapter 8 discussed access modifiers public and private. A class's public members are accessible wherever the program has a reference to an object of that class or one of its subclasses. A class's private members are accessible only within the class itself. In this section, we introduce access modifier **protected**. Using protected access offers an intermediate level of access between public and private. A superclass's protected members can be accessed by members of that superclass, by members of its subclasses and by members of other classes in the same package—protected members also have package access.

All public and protected superclass members retain their original access modifier when they become members of the subclass—public members of the superclass become public members of the subclass, and protected members of the superclass become protected members of the subclass. A superclass's private members are not accessible outside the class itself. Rather, they are hidden in its subclasses and can be accessed only through the public or protected methods inherited from the superclass.

Subclass methods can refer to public and protected members inherited from the superclass simply by using the member names. When a subclass method overrides an inherited superclass method, the superclass method can be accessed from the subclass by preceding the superclass method name with keyword **super** and a dot (.) separator. We discuss accessing overridden members of the superclass in Section 9.4.

Software Engineering Observation 9.1
Methods of a subclass cannot directly access private members of their superclass. A subclass can change the state of private superclass instance variables only through non-private methods provided in the superclass and inherited by the subclass.

Software Engineering Observation 9.2
Declaring private instance variables helps you test, debug and correctly modify systems. If a subclass could access its superclass's private instance variables, classes that inherit from that subclass could access the instance variables as well. This would propagate access to what should be private instance variables, and the benefits of information hiding would be lost.

9.4 Relationship between Superclasses and Subclasses

We now use an inheritance hierarchy containing types of employees in a company's payroll application to discuss the relationship between a superclass and its subclass. In this company, commission employees (who will be represented as objects of a superclass) are paid a percentage of their sales, while base-salaried commission employees (who will be represented as objects of a subclass) receive a base salary *plus* a percentage of their sales.

We divide our discussion of the relationship between these classes into five examples. The first declares class CommissionEmployee, which directly inherits from class Object and declares as private instance variables a first name, last name, social security number, commission rate and gross (i.e., total) sales amount.

The second example declares class BasePlusCommissionEmployee, which also directly inherits from class Object and declares as private instance variables a first name, last name, social security number, commission rate, gross sales amount and base salary. We create this class by writing every line of code the class requires—we'll soon see that it's much more efficient to create it by inheriting from class CommissionEmployee.

The third example declares a new BasePlusCommissionEmployee class that extends class CommissionEmployee (i.e., a BasePlusCommissionEmployee *is a* CommissionEmployee who also has a base salary). This software reuse lets us *write less code* when developing the new subclass. In this example, class BasePlusCommissionEmployee attempts to access class CommissionEmployee's private members—this results in compilation errors, because the subclass cannot access the superclass's private instance variables.

The fourth example shows that if CommissionEmployee's instance variables are declared as protected, the BasePlusCommissionEmployee subclass can access that data directly. Both BasePlusCommissionEmployee classes contain identical functionality, but we show how the inherited version is easier to create and manage.

After we discuss the convenience of using protected instance variables, we create the fifth example, which sets the CommissionEmployee instance variables back to private to enforce good software engineering. Then we show how the BasePlusCommissionEmployee subclass can use CommissionEmployee's public methods to manipulate (in a controlled manner) the private instance variables inherited from CommissionEmployee.

9.4.1 Creating and Using a CommissionEmployee Class

We begin by declaring class CommissionEmployee (Fig. 9.4). Line 4 begins the class declaration and indicates that class CommissionEmployee **extends** (i.e., inherits from) class **Object** (from package java.lang). This causes class CommissionEmployee to inherit the class Object's methods—class Object does not have any fields. If you don't explicitly specify which class a new class extends, the class extends Object implicitly. For this reason, you typically will not include "extends Object" in your code—we do so in this example only for demonstration purposes.

```
1   // Fig. 9.4: CommissionEmployee.java
2   // CommissionEmployee class represents an employee paid a
3   // percentage of gross sales.
```

Fig. 9.4 | CommissionEmployee class represents an employee paid a percentage of gross sales. (Part 1 of 3.)

```
4  public class CommissionEmployee extends Object
5  {
6     private String firstName;
7     private String lastName;
8     private String socialSecurityNumber;
9     private double grossSales; // gross weekly sales
10    private double commissionRate; // commission percentage
11
12    // five-argument constructor
13    public CommissionEmployee( String first, String last, String ssn,
14       double sales, double rate )
15    {
16       // implicit call to Object constructor occurs here
17       firstName = first;
18       lastName = last;
19       socialSecurityNumber = ssn;
20       setGrossSales( sales ); // validate and store gross sales
21       setCommissionRate( rate ); // validate and store commission rate
22    } // end five-argument CommissionEmployee constructor
23
24    // set first name
25    public void setFirstName( String first )
26    {
27       firstName = first; // should validate
28    } // end method setFirstName
29
30    // return first name
31    public String getFirstName()
32    {
33       return firstName;
34    } // end method getFirstName
35
36    // set last name
37    public void setLastName( String last )
38    {
39       lastName = last; // should validate
40    } // end method setLastName
41
42    // return last name
43    public String getLastName()
44    {
45       return lastName;
46    } // end method getLastName
47
48    // set social security number
49    public void setSocialSecurityNumber( String ssn )
50    {
51       socialSecurityNumber = ssn; // should validate
52    } // end method setSocialSecurityNumber
53
54    // return social security number
55    public String getSocialSecurityNumber()
56    {
```

Fig. 9.4 | CommissionEmployee class represents an employee paid a percentage of gross sales. (Part 2 of 3.)

```
57          return socialSecurityNumber;
58       } // end method getSocialSecurityNumber
59
60       // set gross sales amount
61       public void setGrossSales( double sales )
62       {
63          grossSales = ( sales < 0.0 ) ? 0.0 : sales;
64       } // end method setGrossSales
65
66       // return gross sales amount
67       public double getGrossSales()
68       {
69          return grossSales;
70       } // end method getGrossSales
71
72       // set commission rate
73       public void setCommissionRate( double rate )
74       {
75          commissionRate = ( rate > 0.0 && rate < 1.0 ) ? rate : 0.0;
76       } // end method setCommissionRate
77
78       // return commission rate
79       public double getCommissionRate()
80       {
81          return commissionRate;
82       } // end method getCommissionRate
83
84       // calculate earnings
85       public double earnings()
86       {
87          return commissionRate * grossSales;
88       } // end method earnings
89
90       // return String representation of CommissionEmployee object
91       @Override // indicates that this method overrides a superclass method
92       public String toString()
93       {
94          return String.format( "%s: %s %s\n%s: %s\n%s: %.2f\n%s: %.2f",
95             "commission employee", firstName, lastName,
96             "social security number", socialSecurityNumber,
97             "gross sales", grossSales,
98             "commission rate", commissionRate );
99       } // end method toString
100   } // end class CommissionEmployee
```

Fig. 9.4 | CommissionEmployee class represents an employee paid a percentage of gross sales. (Part 3 of 3.)

Overview of Class *CommissionEmployee's Methods and Instance Variables*

Class CommissionEmployee's public services include a constructor (lines 13–22) and methods earnings (lines 85–88) and toString (lines 91–99). Lines 25–82 declare public *get* and *set* methods for the class's instance variables (declared in lines 6–10) firstName, lastName, socialSecurityNumber, grossSales and commissionRate. The class declares its instance variables as private, so objects of other classes cannot directly access these variables. Declaring instance variables as private and providing *get* and *set* methods to manipulate and validate them helps enforce good software engineering. Methods set-GrossSales and setCommissionRate, for example, validate their arguments before assigning the values to instance variables grossSales and commissionRate. In a real-world, business-critical application, we'd also perform validation in the class's other *set* methods.

Class CommissionEmployee's Constructor
Constructors are not inherited, so class CommissionEmployee does not inherit class Object's constructor. However, a superclass's constructors are still available to subclasses. In fact, the first task of any subclass constructor is to call its direct superclass's constructor, either explicitly or implicitly (if no constructor call is specified), to ensure that the instance variables inherited from the superclass are initialized properly. In this example, class CommissionEmployee's constructor calls class Object's constructor implicitly. The syntax for calling a superclass constructor explicitly is discussed in Section 9.4.3. If the code does not include an explicit call to the superclass constructor, Java implicitly calls the superclass's default or no-argument constructor. The comment in line 16 of Fig. 9.4 indicates where the implicit call to the superclass Object's default constructor is made (you do not write the code for this call). Object's default (empty) constructor does nothing. Note that even if a class does not have constructors, the default constructor that the compiler implicitly declares for the class will call the superclass's default or no-argument constructor.

After the implicit call to Object's constructor, lines 17–21 of CommissionEmployee's constructor assign values to the class's instance variables. Note that we do not validate the values of arguments first, last and ssn before assigning them to the corresponding instance variables. We could validate the first and last names—perhaps to ensure that they are of a reasonable length. Similarly, a social security number could be validated to ensure that it contains nine digits, with or without dashes (e.g., 123-45-6789 or 123456789).

Class CommissionEmployee's earnings Method
Method earnings (lines 85–88) calculates a CommissionEmployee's earnings. Line 87 multiplies the commissionRate by the grossSales and returns the result.

Class CommissionEmployee's toString Method and the @Override Annotation
Method toString (lines 91–99) is special—it's one of the methods that every class inherits directly or indirectly from class Object (summarized in Section 9.7). Method toString returns a String representing an object. It's called implicitly whenever an object must be converted to a String representation, such as when an object is output by printf or String method format using the %s format specifier. Class Object's toString method returns a String that includes the name of the object's class. It's primarily a placeholder that can be overridden by a subclass to specify an appropriate String representation of the data in a subclass object. Method toString of class CommissionEmployee overrides (redefines) class Object's toString method. When invoked, CommissionEmployee's toString method uses String method format to return a String containing information about the CommissionEmployee. To override a superclass method, a subclass must declare a method with the same signature (method name, number of parameters, parameter types and order of parameter types) as the superclass method—Object's toString method takes no parameters, so CommissionEmployee declares toString with no parameters.

Line 91 uses the **@Override annotation** to indicate that method toString should override a superclass method. Annotations have several purposes. For example, when you attempt to override a superclass method, common errors include naming the subclass method incorrectly, or using the wrong number or types of parameters in the parameter list. Each of these problems creates an unintentional overload of the superclass method. If you then attempt to call the method on a subclass object, the superclass's version is invoked and the subclass version is ignored—potentially leading to subtle logic errors. When the compiler encounters a method declared with @Override, it compares the method's signature with the superclass's method signatures. If there is not an exact match, the compiler issues an error message, such as "method does not override or implement a method from a supertype." This indicates that you've accidentally overloaded a superclass method. You can then fix your method's signature so that it matches one in the superclass.

As you'll see when we discuss web applications and web services in Chapters 29–31, annotations can also add complex support code to your classes to simplify the development process and can be used by servers to configure certain aspects of web applications.

Common Programming Error 9.1

Using an incorrect method signature when attempting to override a superclass method causes an unintentional method overload that can lead to subtle logic errors.

Error-Prevention Tip 9.1

Declare overridden methods with the @Override annotation to ensure at compilation time that you defined their signatures correctly. It's always better to find errors at compile time rather than at runtime.

Common Programming Error 9.2

It's a syntax error to override a method with a more restricted access modifier—a public method of the superclass cannot become a protected or private method in the subclass; a protected method of the superclass cannot become a private method in the subclass. Doing so would break the is-a relationship in which it's required that all subclass objects be able to respond to method calls that are made to public methods declared in the superclass. If a public method, for example, could be overridden as a protected or private method, the subclass objects would not be able to respond to the same method calls as superclass objects. Once a method is declared public in a superclass, the method remains public for all that class's direct and indirect subclasses.

Class *CommissionEmployeeTest*

Figure 9.5 tests class CommissionEmployee. Lines 9–10 instantiate a CommissionEmployee object and invoke CommissionEmployee's constructor (lines 13–22 of Fig. 9.4) to initialize it with "Sue" as the first name, "Jones" as the last name, "222-22-2222" as the social security number, 10000 as the gross sales amount and .06 as the commission rate. Lines 15–24 use CommissionEmployee's *get* methods to retrieve the object's instance-variable values for output. Lines 26–27 invoke the object's methods setGrossSales and setCommissionRate to change the values of instance variables grossSales and commissionRate. Lines 29–30 output the String representation of the updated CommissionEmployee. Note that when an object is output using the %s format specifier, the object's toString method is invoked implicitly to obtain the object's String representation. [*Note:* In this chapter, we do not use the earnings methods of our classes; however, these methods are used extensively in Chapter 10.]

```
1   // Fig. 9.5: CommissionEmployeeTest.java
2   // CommissionEmployee class test program.
3
4   public class CommissionEmployeeTest
5   {
6      public static void main( String[] args )
7      {
8         // instantiate CommissionEmployee object
9         CommissionEmployee employee = new CommissionEmployee(
10           "Sue", "Jones", "222-22-2222", 10000, .06 );
11
12        // get commission employee data
13        System.out.println(
14           "Employee information obtained by get methods: \n" );
15        System.out.printf( "%s %s\n", "First name is",
16           employee.getFirstName() );
17        System.out.printf( "%s %s\n", "Last name is",
18           employee.getLastName() );
19        System.out.printf( "%s %s\n", "Social security number is",
20           employee.getSocialSecurityNumber() );
21        System.out.printf( "%s %.2f\n", "Gross sales is",
22           employee.getGrossSales() );
23        System.out.printf( "%s %.2f\n", "Commission rate is",
24           employee.getCommissionRate() );
25
26        employee.setGrossSales( 500 ); // set gross sales
27        employee.setCommissionRate( .1 ); // set commission rate
28
29        System.out.printf( "\n%s:\n\n%s\n",
30           "Updated employee information obtained by toString", employee );
31     } // end main
32  } // end class CommissionEmployeeTest
```

```
Employee information obtained by get methods:

First name is Sue
Last name is Jones
Social security number is 222-22-2222
Gross sales is 10000.00
Commission rate is 0.06

Updated employee information obtained by toString:

commission employee: Sue Jones
social security number: 222-22-2222
gross sales: 500.00
commission rate: 0.10
```

Fig. 9.5 | CommissionEmployee class test program.

9.4.2 Creating and Using a BasePlusCommissionEmployee Class

We now discuss the second part of our introduction to inheritance by declaring and testing (a completely new and independent) class BasePlusCommissionEmployee (Fig. 9.6), which contains a first name, last name, social security number, gross sales amount, commission rate *and* base salary. Class BasePlusCommissionEmployee's public services include a BasePlusCommissionEmployee constructor (lines 15–25) and methods earnings (lines 100–103) and toString (lines 106–115). Lines 28–97 declare public *get* and *set* methods for the class's private instance variables (declared in lines 7–12) firstName, lastName, socialSecurityNumber, grossSales, commissionRate *and* baseSalary. These variables and methods encapsulate all the necessary features of a base-salaried commission employee. Note the similarity between this class and class CommissionEmployee (Fig. 9.4)—in this example, we'll not yet exploit that similarity.

```java
1   // Fig. 9.6: BasePlusCommissionEmployee.java
2   // BasePlusCommissionEmployee class represents an employee that receives
3   // a base salary in addition to commission.
4
5   public class BasePlusCommissionEmployee
6   {
7      private String firstName;
8      private String lastName;
9      private String socialSecurityNumber;
10     private double grossSales; // gross weekly sales
11     private double commissionRate; // commission percentage
12     private double baseSalary; // base salary per week
13
14     // six-argument constructor
15     public BasePlusCommissionEmployee( String first, String last,
16        String ssn, double sales, double rate, double salary )
17     {
18        // implicit call to Object constructor occurs here
19        firstName = first;
20        lastName = last;
21        socialSecurityNumber = ssn;
22        setGrossSales( sales ); // validate and store gross sales
23        setCommissionRate( rate ); // validate and store commission rate
24        setBaseSalary( salary ); // validate and store base salary
25     } // end six-argument BasePlusCommissionEmployee constructor
26
27     // set first name
28     public void setFirstName( String first )
29     {
30        firstName = first; // should validate
31     } // end method setFirstName
32
33     // return first name
34     public String getFirstName()
35     {
36        return firstName;
37     } // end method getFirstName
38
39     // set last name
40     public void setLastName( String last )
41     {
42        lastName = last; // should validate
43     } // end method setLastName
44
```

Fig. 9.6 | BasePlusCommissionEmployee class represents an employee who receives a base salary in addition to a commission. (Part 1 of 3.)

```
45        // return last name
46        public String getLastName()
47        {
48           return lastName;
49        } // end method getLastName
50
51        // set social security number
52        public void setSocialSecurityNumber( String ssn )
53        {
54           socialSecurityNumber = ssn; // should validate
55        } // end method setSocialSecurityNumber
56
57        // return social security number
58        public String getSocialSecurityNumber()
59        {
60           return socialSecurityNumber;
61        } // end method getSocialSecurityNumber
62
63        // set gross sales amount
64        public void setGrossSales( double sales )
65        {
66           grossSales = ( sales < 0.0 ) ? 0.0 : sales;
67        } // end method setGrossSales
68
69        // return gross sales amount
70        public double getGrossSales()
71        {
72           return grossSales;
73        } // end method getGrossSales
74
75        // set commission rate
76        public void setCommissionRate( double rate )
77        {
78           commissionRate = ( rate > 0.0 && rate < 1.0 ) ? rate : 0.0;
79        } // end method setCommissionRate
80
81        // return commission rate
82        public double getCommissionRate()
83        {
84           return commissionRate;
85        } // end method getCommissionRate
86
87        // set base salary
88        public void setBaseSalary( double salary )
89        {
90           baseSalary = ( salary < 0.0 ) ? 0.0 : salary;
91        } // end method setBaseSalary
92
93        // return base salary
94        public double getBaseSalary()
95        {
96           return baseSalary;
97        } // end method getBaseSalary
```

Fig. 9.6 | BasePlusCommissionEmployee class represents an employee who receives a base salary in addition to a commission. (Part 2 of 3.)

```
 98
 99    // calculate earnings
100    public double earnings()
101    {
102       return baseSalary + ( commissionRate * grossSales );
103    } // end method earnings
104
105    // return String representation of BasePlusCommissionEmployee
106    @Override // indicates that this method overrides a superclass method
107    public String toString()
108    {
109       return String.format(
110          "%s: %s %s\n%s: %s\n%s: %.2f\n%s: %.2f\n%s: %.2f",
111          "base-salaried commission employee", firstName, lastName,
112          "social security number", socialSecurityNumber,
113          "gross sales", grossSales, "commission rate", commissionRate,
114          "base salary", baseSalary );
115    } // end method toString
116 } // end class BasePlusCommissionEmployee
```

Fig. 9.6 | BasePlusCommissionEmployee class represents an employee who receives a base salary in addition to a commission. (Part 3 of 3.)

Note that class BasePlusCommissionEmployee does not specify "extends Object" in line 5, so the class implicitly extends Object. Also, like class CommissionEmployee's constructor (lines 13–22 of Fig. 9.4), class BasePlusCommissionEmployee's constructor invokes class Object's default constructor implicitly, as noted in the comment in line 18.

Class BasePlusCommissionEmployee's earnings method (lines 100–103) returns the result of adding the BasePlusCommissionEmployee's base salary to the product of the commission rate and the employee's gross sales.

Class BasePlusCommissionEmployee overrides Object method toString to return a String containing the BasePlusCommissionEmployee's information. Once again, we use format specifier %.2f to format the gross sales, commission rate and base salary with two digits of precision to the right of the decimal point (line 110).

*Testing Class **BasePlusCommissionEmployee***
Figure 9.7 tests class BasePlusCommissionEmployee. Lines 9–11 create a BasePlusCommissionEmployee object and pass "Bob", "Lewis", "333-33-3333", 5000, .04 and 300 to the constructor as the first name, last name, social security number, gross sales, commission rate and base salary, respectively. Lines 16–27 use BasePlusCommissionEmployee's *get* methods to retrieve the values of the object's instance variables for output. Line 29 invokes the object's setBaseSalary method to change the base salary. Method setBaseSalary (Fig. 9.6, lines 88–91) ensures that instance variable baseSalary is not assigned a negative value, because an employee's base salary cannot be negative. Lines 31–33 of Fig. 9.7 invoke method toString explicitly to get the object's String representation.

```
 1  // Fig. 9.7: BasePlusCommissionEmployeeTest.java
 2  // BasePlusCommissionEmployee test program.
 3
```

Fig. 9.7 | BasePlusCommissionEmployee test program. (Part 1 of 2.)

```
 4   public class BasePlusCommissionEmployeeTest
 5   {
 6      public static void main( String[] args )
 7      {
 8         // instantiate BasePlusCommissionEmployee object
 9         BasePlusCommissionEmployee employee =
10            new BasePlusCommissionEmployee(
11            "Bob", "Lewis", "333-33-3333", 5000, .04, 300 );
12
13         // get base-salaried commission employee data
14         System.out.println(
15            "Employee information obtained by get methods: \n" );
16         System.out.printf( "%s %s\n", "First name is",
17            employee.getFirstName() );
18         System.out.printf( "%s %s\n", "Last name is",
19            employee.getLastName() );
20         System.out.printf( "%s %s\n", "Social security number is",
21            employee.getSocialSecurityNumber() );
22         System.out.printf( "%s %.2f\n", "Gross sales is",
23            employee.getGrossSales() );
24         System.out.printf( "%s %.2f\n", "Commission rate is",
25            employee.getCommissionRate() );
26         System.out.printf( "%s %.2f\n", "Base salary is",
27            employee.getBaseSalary() );
28
29         employee.setBaseSalary( 1000 ); // set base salary
30
31         System.out.printf( "\n%s:\n\n%s\n",
32            "Updated employee information obtained by toString",
33            employee.toString() );
34      } // end main
35   } // end class BasePlusCommissionEmployeeTest
```

```
Employee information obtained by get methods:

First name is Bob
Last name is Lewis
Social security number is 333-33-3333
Gross sales is 5000.00
Commission rate is 0.04
Base salary is 300.00

Updated employee information obtained by toString:

base-salaried commission employee: Bob Lewis
social security number: 333-33-3333
gross sales: 5000.00
commission rate: 0.04
base salary: 1000.00
```

Fig. 9.7 | BasePlusCommissionEmployee test program. (Part 2 of 2.)

*Notes on Class **BasePlusCommissionEmployee***

Much of class BasePlusCommissionEmployee's code (Fig. 9.6) is similar, or identical, to that of class CommissionEmployee (Fig. 9.4). For example, private instance variables firstName and lastName and methods setFirstName, getFirstName, setLastName and getLastName are identical to those of class CommissionEmployee. The classes also both contain private instance variables socialSecurityNumber, commissionRate and gross-Sales, and corresponding *get* and *set* methods. In addition, the BasePlusCommissionEmployee constructor is almost identical to that of class CommissionEmployee, except that BasePlusCommissionEmployee's constructor also sets the baseSalary. The other additions to class BasePlusCommissionEmployee are private instance variable baseSalary and methods setBaseSalary and getBaseSalary. Class BasePlusCommissionEmployee's toString method is nearly identical to that of class CommissionEmployee except that BasePlusCommissionEmployee's toString also outputs instance variable baseSalary with two digits of precision to the right of the decimal point.

We literally *copied* code from class CommissionEmployee and *pasted* it into class BasePlusCommissionEmployee, then modified class BasePlusCommissionEmployee to include a base salary and methods that manipulate the base salary. This "copy-and-paste" approach is often error prone and time consuming. Worse yet, it spreads copies of the same code throughout a system, creating a code-maintenance nightmare. Is there a way to "absorb" the instance variables and methods of one class in a way that makes them part of other classes without duplicating code? Next we answer this question, using a more elegant approach to building classes that emphasizes the benefits of inheritance.

Software Engineering Observation 9.3

With inheritance, the common instance variables and methods of all the classes in the hierarchy are declared in a superclass. When changes are made for these common features in the superclass— subclasses then inherit the changes. Without inheritance, changes would need to be made to all the source-code files that contain a copy of the code in question.

9.4.3 Creating a CommissionEmployee-BasePlusCommissionEmployee Inheritance Hierarchy

Now we declare a new BasePlusCommissionEmployee class (Fig. 9.8), which extends class CommissionEmployee (Fig. 9.4). A BasePlusCommissionEmployee object *is a* CommissionEmployee, because inheritance passes on class CommissionEmployee's capabilities. Class BasePlusCommissionEmployee also has instance variable baseSalary (Fig. 9.8, line 6). Keyword extends (line 4) indicates inheritance. Subclass BasePlusCommissionEmployee inherits CommissionEmployee's instance variables and methods—recall that only the superclass's public and protected members are directly accessible in the subclass. The CommissionEmployee constructor is not inherited. So, the public BasePlusCommissionEmployee services include its constructor (lines 9–16), public methods inherited from CommissionEmployee, method setBaseSalary (lines 19–22), method getBaseSalary (lines 25–28), method earnings (lines 31–36) and method toString (lines 39–49). Methods earnings and toString override the corresponding methods in class CommissionEmployee because the superclass versions of these methods do not properly calculate a BasePlusCommissionEmployee's earnings or return an appropriate String representation.

```
1   // Fig. 9.8: BasePlusCommissionEmployee.java
2   // private superclass members cannot be accessed in a subclass.
3
```

Fig. 9.8 | private superclass members cannot be accessed in a subclass. (Part 1 of 3.)

```
4   public class BasePlusCommissionEmployee extends CommissionEmployee
5   {
6      private double baseSalary; // base salary per week
7
8      // six-argument constructor
9      public BasePlusCommissionEmployee( String first, String last,
10        String ssn, double sales, double rate, double salary )
11     {
12        // explicit call to superclass CommissionEmployee constructor
13        super( first, last, ssn, sales, rate );
14
15        setBaseSalary( salary ); // validate and store base salary
16     } // end six-argument BasePlusCommissionEmployee constructor
17
18     // set base salary
19     public void setBaseSalary( double salary )
20     {
21        baseSalary = ( salary < 0.0 ) ? 0.0 : salary;
22     } // end method setBaseSalary
23
24     // return base salary
25     public double getBaseSalary()
26     {
27        return baseSalary;
28     } // end method getBaseSalary
29
30     // calculate earnings
31     @Override // indicates that this method overrides a superclass method
32     public double earnings()
33     {
34        // not allowed: commissionRate and grossSales private in superclass
35        return baseSalary + ( commissionRate * grossSales );
36     } // end method earnings
37
38     // return String representation of BasePlusCommissionEmployee
39     @Override // indicates that this method overrides a superclass method
40     public String toString()
41     {
42        // not allowed: attempts to access private superclass members
43        return String.format(
44           "%s: %s %s\n%s: %s\n%s: %.2f\n%s: %.2f\n%s: %.2f",
45           "base-salaried commission employee", firstName, lastName,
46           "social security number", socialSecurityNumber,
47           "gross sales", grossSales, "commission rate", commissionRate,
48           "base salary", baseSalary );
49     } // end method toString
50  } // end class BasePlusCommissionEmployee
```

```
BasePlusCommissionEmployee.java:35: commissionRate has private access in
CommissionEmployee
      return baseSalary + ( commissionRate * grossSales );
                            ^
```

(continued...)

Fig. 9.8 | private superclass members cannot be accessed in a subclass. (Part 2 of 3.)

```
BasePlusCommissionEmployee.java:35: grossSales has private access in
CommissionEmployee
      return baseSalary + ( commissionRate * grossSales );
                                              ^
BasePlusCommissionEmployee.java:45: firstName has private access in
CommissionEmployee
         "base-salaried commission employee", firstName, lastName,
                                               ^
BasePlusCommissionEmployee.java:45: lastName has private access in
CommissionEmployee
         "base-salaried commission employee", firstName, lastName,
                                                          ^
BasePlusCommissionEmployee.java:46: socialSecurityNumber has private access in
CommissionEmployee
         "social security number", socialSecurityNumber,
                                   ^
BasePlusCommissionEmployee.java:47: grossSales has private access in
CommissionEmployee
         "gross sales", grossSales, "commission rate", commissionRate,
                        ^
BasePlusCommissionEmployee.java:47: commissionRate has private access in
CommissionEmployee
         "gross sales", grossSales, "commission rate", commissionRate,
                                                       ^
7 errors
```

Fig. 9.8 | `private` superclass members cannot be accessed in a subclass. (Part 3 of 3.)

Each subclass constructor must implicitly or explicitly call its superclass constructor to initialize the instance variables inherited from the superclass. Line 13 in BasePlusCommissionEmployee's six-argument constructor (lines 9–16) explicitly calls class CommissionEmployee's five-argument constructor (declared at lines 13–22 of Fig. 9.4) to initialize the superclass portion of a BasePlusCommissionEmployee object (i.e., variables firstName, lastName, socialSecurityNumber, grossSales and commissionRate). We do this by using the **superclass constructor call syntax**—keyword super, followed by a set of parentheses containing the superclass constructor arguments. The arguments first, last, ssn, sales and rate are used to initialize superclass members firstName, lastName, socialSecurityNumber, grossSales and commissionRate, respectively. If BasePlusCommissionEmployee's constructor did not invoke the superclass's constructor explicitly, Java would attempt to invoke the superclass's no-argument or default constructor. Class CommissionEmployee does not have such a constructor, so the compiler would issue an error. The explicit superclass constructor call in line 13 of Fig. 9.8 must be the first statement in the subclass constructor's body. When a superclass contains a no-argument constructor, you can use super() to call that constructor explicitly, but this is rarely done.

Common Programming Error 9.3

A compilation error occurs if a subclass constructor calls a superclass constructor with arguments that do not match the number and types of parameters in one of the superclass's constructors.

The compiler generates errors for line 35 of Fig. 9.8 because superclass CommissionEmployee's instance variables commissionRate and grossSales are private—subclass BasePlusCommissionEmployee's methods are not allowed to access superclass CommissionEmployee's private instance variables. Note that we used red text in Fig. 9.8 to indicate erroneous code. The compiler issues additional errors at lines 45–47 of BasePlusCommissionEmployee's toString method for the same reason. The errors in BasePlusCommissionEmployee could have been prevented by using the *get* methods inherited from class CommissionEmployee. For example, line 35 could have used getCommissionRate and getGrossSales to access CommissionEmployee's private instance variables commissionRate and grossSales, respectively. Lines 45–47 also could have used appropriate *get* methods to retrieve the values of the superclass's instance variables.

9.4.4 CommissionEmployee–BasePlusCommissionEmployee Inheritance Hierarchy Using protected Instance Variables

To enable class BasePlusCommissionEmployee to directly access superclass instance variables firstName, lastName, socialSecurityNumber, grossSales and commissionRate, we can declare those members as protected in the superclass. As we discussed in Section 9.3, a superclass's protected members *are* accessible by all subclasses of that superclass. In the new CommissionEmployee class, we modified only lines 6–10 to declare the instance variables with the protected access modifier as follows:

```
protected String firstName;
protected String lastName;
protected String socialSecurityNumber;
protected double grossSales; // gross weekly sales
protected double commissionRate; // commission percentage
```

The rest of the class declaration (which is not shown here) is identical to that of Fig. 9.4.

We could have declared CommissionEmployee's instance variables public to enable subclass BasePlusCommissionEmployee to access them. However, declaring public instance variables is poor software engineering because it allows unrestricted access to the instance variables, greatly increasing the chance of errors. With protected instance variables, the subclass gets access to the instance variables, but classes that are not subclasses and classes that are not in the same package cannot access these variables directly—recall that protected class members are also visible to other classes in the same package.

Class BasePlusCommissionEmployee
Class BasePlusCommissionEmployee (Fig. 9.9) extends the new version of class CommissionEmployee with protected instance variables. BasePlusCommissionEmployee objects inherit CommissionEmployee's protected instance variables firstName, lastName, socialSecurityNumber, grossSales and commissionRate—all these variables are now protected members of BasePlusCommissionEmployee. As a result, the compiler does not generate errors when compiling line 33 of method earnings and lines 42–44 of method toString. If another class extends this version of class BasePlusCommissionEmployee, the new subclass also can access the protected members.

```
1   // Fig. 9.9: BasePlusCommissionEmployee.java
2   // BasePlusCommissionEmployee inherits protected instance
3   // variables from CommissionEmployee.
```

Fig. 9.9 | BasePlusCommissionEmployee inherits protected instance variables from CommissionEmployee. (Part 1 of 2.)

```
4
5   public class BasePlusCommissionEmployee extends CommissionEmployee
6   {
7      private double baseSalary; // base salary per week
8
9      // six-argument constructor
10     public BasePlusCommissionEmployee( String first, String last,
11        String ssn, double sales, double rate, double salary )
12     {
13        super( first, last, ssn, sales, rate );
14        setBaseSalary( salary ); // validate and store base salary
15     } // end six-argument BasePlusCommissionEmployee constructor
16
17     // set base salary
18     public void setBaseSalary( double salary )
19     {
20        baseSalary = ( salary < 0.0 ) ? 0.0 : salary;
21     } // end method setBaseSalary
22
23     // return base salary
24     public double getBaseSalary()
25     {
26        return baseSalary;
27     } // end method getBaseSalary
28
29     // calculate earnings
30     @Override // indicates that this method overrides a superclass method
31     public double earnings()
32     {
33        return baseSalary + ( commissionRate * grossSales );
34     } // end method earnings
35
36     // return String representation of BasePlusCommissionEmployee
37     @Override // indicates that this method overrides a superclass method
38     public String toString()
39     {
40        return String.format(
41           "%s: %s %s\n%s: %s\n%s: %.2f\n%s: %.2f\n%s: %.2f",
42           "base-salaried commission employee", firstName, lastName,
43           "social security number", socialSecurityNumber,
44           "gross sales", grossSales, "commission rate", commissionRate,
45           "base salary", baseSalary );
46     } // end method toString
47  } // end class BasePlusCommissionEmployee
```

Fig. 9.9 | BasePlusCommissionEmployee inherits **protected** instance variables from CommissionEmployee. (Part 2 of 2.)

When you create a BasePlusCommissionEmployee object, it contains all instance variables declared in the class hierarchy to that point—i.e., those from classes Object, CommissionEmployee and BasePlusCommissionEmployee. Class BasePlusCommissionEmployee does not inherit class CommissionEmployee's constructor. However, class BasePlusCommissionEmployee's six-argument constructor (lines 10–15) calls class CommissionEmployee's five-argument constructor explicitly to initialize the instance variables that

BasePlusCommissionEmployee inherited from class CommissionEmployee. Similarly, class CommissionEmployee's constructor calls class Object's constructor. BasePlusCommissionEmployee's constructor must do this explicitly because CommissionEmployee does not provide a no-argument constructor that could be invoked implicitly.

Testing Class *BasePlusCommissionEmployee*

The BasePlusCommissionEmployeeTest class for this example is identical to that of Fig. 9.7 and produces the same output, so we do not show it here. Although the version of class BasePlusCommissionEmployee in Fig. 9.6 does not use inheritance and the version in Fig. 9.9 does, *both classes provide the same functionality*. The source code in Fig. 9.9 (47 lines) is considerably shorter than that in Fig. 9.6 (116 lines), because most of Base-PlusCommissionEmployee's functionality is now inherited from CommissionEmployee—there is now only one copy of the CommissionEmployee functionality. This makes the code easier to maintain, modify and debug, because the code related to a commission employee exists only in class CommissionEmployee.

Notes on Using *protected* Instance Variables

In this example, we declared superclass instance variables as protected so that subclasses could access them. Inheriting protected instance variables slightly increases performance, because we can directly access the variables in the subclass without incurring the overhead of a *set* or *get* method call. In most cases, however, it's better to use private instance variables to encourage proper software engineering, and leave code optimization issues to the compiler. Your code will be easier to maintain, modify and debug.

Using protected instance variables creates several potential problems. First, the subclass object can set an inherited variable's value directly without using a *set* method. Therefore, a subclass object can assign an invalid value to the variable, possibly leaving the object in an inconsistent state. For example, if we were to declare CommissionEmployee's instance variable grossSales as protected, a subclass object (e.g., BasePlusCommissionEmployee) could then assign a negative value to grossSales. Another problem with using protected instance variables is that subclass methods are more likely to be written so that they depend on the superclass's data implementation. In practice, subclasses should depend only on the superclass services (i.e., non-private methods) and not on the superclass data implementation. With protected instance variables in the superclass, we may need to modify all the subclasses of the superclass if the superclass implementation changes. For example, if for some reason we were to change the names of instance variables firstName and lastName to first and last, then we would have to do so for all occurrences in which a subclass directly references superclass instance variables firstName and lastName. In such a case, the software is said to be **fragile** or **brittle**, because a small change in the superclass can "break" subclass implementation. You should be able to change the superclass implementation while still providing the same services to the subclasses. Of course, if the superclass services change, we must reimplement our subclasses. A third problem is that a class's protected members are visible to all classes in the same package as the class containing the protected members—this is not always desirable.

Software Engineering Observation 9.4

Use the protected *access modifier when a superclass should provide a method only to its subclasses and other classes in the same package, but not to other clients.*

Software Engineering Observation 9.5

Declaring superclass instance variables private *(as opposed to* protected*) enables the superclass implementation of these instance variables to change without affecting subclass implementations.*

Error-Prevention Tip 9.2

When possible, do not include protected *instance variables in a superclass. Instead, include non-private methods that access* private *instance variables. This will help ensure that objects of the class maintain consistent states.*

9.4.5 CommissionEmployee–BasePlusCommissionEmployee Inheritance Hierarchy Using private Instance Variables

Let's reexamine our hierarchy once more, this time using good software engineering practices. Class CommissionEmployee (Fig. 9.10) declares instance variables firstName, lastName, socialSecurityNumber, grossSales and commissionRate as private (lines 6–10) and provides public methods setFirstName, getFirstName, setLastName, getLastName, setSocialSecurityNumber, getSocialSecurityNumber, setGrossSales, getGrossSales, setCommissionRate, getCommissionRate, earnings and toString for manipulating these values. Note that methods earnings (lines 85–88) and toString (lines 91–99) use the class's *get* methods to obtain the values of its instance variables. If we decide to change the instance-variable names, the earnings and toString declarations will not require modification—only the bodies of the *get* and *set* methods that directly manipulate the instance variables will need to change. Note that these changes occur solely within the superclass—no changes to the subclass are needed. Localizing the effects of changes like this is a good software engineering practice. Subclass BasePlusCommissionEmployee (Fig. 9.11) inherits CommissionEmployee's non-private methods and can access the private superclass members via those methods.

```
1   // Fig. 9.10: CommissionEmployee.java
2   // CommissionEmployee class uses methods to manipulate its
3   // private instance variables.
4   public class CommissionEmployee
5   {
6      private String firstName;
7      private String lastName;
8      private String socialSecurityNumber;
9      private double grossSales; // gross weekly sales
10     private double commissionRate; // commission percentage
11
12     // five-argument constructor
13     public CommissionEmployee( String first, String last, String ssn,
14        double sales, double rate )
15     {
16        // implicit call to Object constructor occurs here
17        firstName = first;
18        lastName = last;
19        socialSecurityNumber = ssn;
```

Fig. 9.10 | CommissionEmployee class uses methods to manipulate its private instance variables. (Part 1 of 3.)

```
20          setGrossSales( sales ); // validate and store gross sales
21          setCommissionRate( rate ); // validate and store commission rate
22       } // end five-argument CommissionEmployee constructor
23
24       // set first name
25       public void setFirstName( String first )
26       {
27          firstName = first; // should validate
28       } // end method setFirstName
29
30       // return first name
31       public String getFirstName()
32       {
33          return firstName;
34       } // end method getFirstName
35
36       // set last name
37       public void setLastName( String last )
38       {
39          lastName = last; // should validate
40       } // end method setLastName
41
42       // return last name
43       public String getLastName()
44       {
45          return lastName;
46       } // end method getLastName
47
48       // set social security number
49       public void setSocialSecurityNumber( String ssn )
50       {
51          socialSecurityNumber = ssn; // should validate
52       } // end method setSocialSecurityNumber
53
54       // return social security number
55       public String getSocialSecurityNumber()
56       {
57          return socialSecurityNumber;
58       } // end method getSocialSecurityNumber
59
60       // set gross sales amount
61       public void setGrossSales( double sales )
62       {
63          grossSales = ( sales < 0.0 ) ? 0.0 : sales;
64       } // end method setGrossSales
65
66       // return gross sales amount
67       public double getGrossSales()
68       {
69          return grossSales;
70       } // end method getGrossSales
71
```

Fig. 9.10 | CommissionEmployee class uses methods to manipulate its `private` instance variables. (Part 2 of 3.)

```
72      // set commission rate
73      public void setCommissionRate( double rate )
74      {
75         commissionRate = ( rate > 0.0 && rate < 1.0 ) ? rate : 0.0;
76      } // end method setCommissionRate
77
78      // return commission rate
79      public double getCommissionRate()
80      {
81         return commissionRate;
82      } // end method getCommissionRate
83
84      // calculate earnings
85      public double earnings()
86      {
87         return getCommissionRate() * getGrossSales();
88      } // end method earnings
89
90      // return String representation of CommissionEmployee object
91      @Override // indicates that this method overrides a superclass method
92      public String toString()
93      {
94         return String.format( "%s: %s %s\n%s: %s\n%s: %.2f\n%s: %.2f",
95            "commission employee", getFirstName(), getLastName(),
96            "social security number", getSocialSecurityNumber(),
97            "gross sales", getGrossSales(),
98            "commission rate", getCommissionRate() );
99      } // end method toString
100  } // end class CommissionEmployee
```

Fig. 9.10 | CommissionEmployee class uses methods to manipulate its private instance variables. (Part 3 of 3.)

Class BasePlusCommissionEmployee (Fig. 9.11) has several changes that distinguish it from Fig. 9.9. Methods earnings (Fig. 9.11, lines 31–35) and toString (lines 38–43) each invoke method getBaseSalary to obtain the base salary value, rather than accessing baseSalary directly. If we decide to rename instance variable baseSalary, only the bodies of method setBaseSalary and getBaseSalary will need to change.

```
1   // Fig. 9.11: BasePlusCommissionEmployee.java
2   // BasePlusCommissionEmployee class inherits from CommissionEmployee
3   // and accesses the superclass's private data via inherited
4   // public methods.
5
6   public class BasePlusCommissionEmployee extends CommissionEmployee
7   {
8      private double baseSalary; // base salary per week
9
```

Fig. 9.11 | BasePlusCommissionEmployee class inherits from CommissionEmployee and accesses the superclass's private data via inherited public methods. (Part 1 of 2.)

```
10        // six-argument constructor
11        public BasePlusCommissionEmployee( String first, String last,
12           String ssn, double sales, double rate, double salary )
13        {
14           super( first, last, ssn, sales, rate );
15           setBaseSalary( salary ); // validate and store base salary
16        } // end six-argument BasePlusCommissionEmployee constructor
17
18        // set base salary
19        public void setBaseSalary( double salary )
20        {
21           baseSalary = ( salary < 0.0 ) ? 0.0 : salary;
22        } // end method setBaseSalary
23
24        // return base salary
25        public double getBaseSalary()
26        {
27           return baseSalary;
28        } // end method getBaseSalary
29
30        // calculate earnings
31        @Override // indicates that this method overrides a superclass method
32        public double earnings()
33        {
34           return getBaseSalary() + super.earnings();
35        } // end method earnings
36
37        // return String representation of BasePlusCommissionEmployee
38        @Override // indicates that this method overrides a superclass method
39        public String toString()
40        {
41           return String.format( "%s %s\n%s: %.2f", "base-salaried",
42              super.toString(), "base salary", getBaseSalary() );
43        } // end method toString
44     } // end class BasePlusCommissionEmployee
```

Fig. 9.11 | BasePlusCommissionEmployee class inherits from CommissionEmployee and accesses the superclass's private data via inherited public methods. (Part 2 of 2.)

Class *BasePlusCommissionEmployee's earnings Method*

Method earnings (Fig. 9.11, lines 31–35) overrides class CommissionEmployee's earnings method (Fig. 9.10, lines 85–88) to calculate a base-salaried commission employee's earnings. The new version obtains the portion of the earnings based on commission alone by calling CommissionEmployee's earnings method with super.earnings() (Fig. 9.11, line 34). BasePlusCommissionEmployee's earnings method then adds the base salary to this value to calculate the total earnings. Note the syntax used to invoke an overridden superclass method from a subclass—place the keyword super and a dot (.) separator before the superclass method name. This method invocation is a good software engineering practice—if a method performs all or some of the actions needed by another method, call that method rather than duplicate its code. By having BasePlusCommissionEmployee's earnings method invoke CommissionEmployee's earnings method to calculate part of a Base-PlusCommissionEmployee object's earnings, we avoid duplicating the code and reduce code-maintenance problems. If we did not use "super." then BasePlusCommissionEmployee's earnings method would call itself rather than the superclass version. This would result in a phenomenon we study in Chapter 18 called infinite recursion, which would eventually cause the method call stack to overflow—a fatal runtime error.

> **Common Programming Error 9.4**
>
> *When a superclass method is overridden in a subclass, the subclass version often calls the superclass version to do a portion of the work. Failure to prefix the superclass method name with the keyword super and a dot (.) separator when calling the superclass's method causes the subclass method to call itself, potentially creating an error called infinite recursion. Recursion, used correctly, is a powerful capability discussed in Chapter 18, Recursion.*

Class *BasePlusCommissionEmployee's* **toString** Method

Similarly, BasePlusCommissionEmployee's toString method (Fig. 9.11, lines 38–43) overrides class CommissionEmployee's toString method (Fig. 9.10, lines 91–99) to return a String representation that is appropriate for a base-salaried commission employee. The new version creates part of a BasePlusCommissionEmployee object's String representation (i.e., the String "commission employee" and the values of class CommissionEmployee's private instance variables) by calling CommissionEmployee's toString method with the expression super.toString() (Fig. 9.11, line 42). BasePlusCommissionEmployee's toString method then outputs the remainder of a BasePlusCommissionEmployee object's String representation (i.e., the value of class BasePlusCommissionEmployee's base salary).

Testing Class *BasePlusCommissionEmployee*

Class BasePlusCommissionEmployeeTest performs the same manipulations on a BasePlusCommissionEmployee object as in Fig. 9.7 and produces the same output, so we do not show it here. Although each BasePlusCommissionEmployee class you've seen behaves identically, the version in Fig. 9.11 is the best engineered. By using inheritance and by calling methods that hide the data and ensure consistency, we've efficiently and effectively constructed a well-engineered class.

Summary of the Inheritance Examples in Sections 9.4.1–9.4.5

You've now seen a set of examples that were designed to teach good software engineering with inheritance. You used the keyword extends to create a subclass using inheritance, used protected superclass members to enable a subclass to access inherited superclass instance variables, and overrode superclass methods to provide versions that are more appropriate for subclass objects. In addition, you applied software engineering techniques from Chapter 8 and this chapter to create classes that are easy to maintain, modify and debug.

9.5 Constructors in Subclasses

As we explained in the preceding section, instantiating a subclass object begins a chain of constructor calls in which the subclass constructor, before performing its own tasks, invokes its direct superclass's constructor either explicitly via the super reference or implicitly calling the superclass's default constructor or no-argument constructor. Similarly, if the superclass is derived from another class—as is, of course, every class except Object—the superclass constructor invokes the constructor of the next class up the hierarchy, and so on. The last constructor called in the chain is *always* the constructor for class Object. The original subclass constructor's body finishes executing last. Each superclass's constructor manipulates the superclass instance variables that the subclass object inherits. For example, consider again the `CommissionEmployee`–`BasePlusCommissionEmployee` hierarchy from Fig. 9.10 and Fig. 9.11. When a program creates a `BasePlusCommissionEmployee` object, its constructor is called. That constructor calls `CommissionEmployee`'s constructor, which in turn calls `Object`'s constructor. Class `Object`'s constructor has an empty body, so it immediately returns control to `CommissionEmployee`'s constructor, which then initializes the `CommissionEmployee` `private` instance variables that are part of the `BasePlusCommissionEmployee` object. When `CommissionEmployee`'s constructor completes execution, it returns control to `BasePlusCommissionEmployee`'s constructor, which initializes the `BasePlusCommissionEmployee` object's `baseSalary`.

Software Engineering Observation 9.6

When a program creates a subclass object, the subclass constructor immediately calls the superclass constructor (explicitly, via `super`, or implicitly). The superclass constructor's body executes to initialize the superclass's instance variables that are part of the subclass object, then the subclass constructor's body executes to initialize the subclass-only instance variables. Java ensures that even if a constructor does not assign a value to an instance variable, the variable is still initialized to its default value (e.g., 0 for primitive numeric types, `false` for `boolean`s, `null` for references).

9.6 Software Engineering with Inheritance

When you extend a class, the new class inherits the superclass's members—though the `private` superclass members are hidden in the new class. You can customize the new class to meet your needs by including additional members and by overriding superclass members. Doing this does not require the subclass programmer to change (or even have access to) the superclass's source code. Java simply requires access to the superclass's `.class` file so it can compile and execute any program that uses or extends the superclass. This powerful capability is attractive to independent software vendors (ISVs), who can develop proprietary classes for sale or license and make them available to users in bytecode format. Users then can derive new classes from these library classes rapidly and without accessing the ISVs' proprietary source code.

Software Engineering Observation 9.7

Although inheriting from a class does not require access to the class's source code, developers often insist on seeing the source code to understand how the class is implemented. Developers in industry want to ensure that they are extending a solid class—for example, a class that performs well and is implemented robustly and securely.

It's sometimes difficult to appreciate the scope of the problems faced by designers who work on large-scale software projects. People experienced with such projects say that effective software reuse improves the software-development process. Object-oriented programming facilitates software reuse, often significantly shortening development time.

The availability of substantial and useful class libraries delivers the maximum benefits of software reuse through inheritance. The standard Java class libraries that are shipped with Java tend to be rather general purpose, encouraging broad software reuse. Many other class libraries exist.

Reading subclass declarations can be confusing, because inherited members are not declared explicitly in the subclasses but are nevertheless present in them. A similar problem exists in documenting subclass members.

Software Engineering Observation 9.8

At the design stage in an object-oriented system, you'll often find that certain classes are closely related. You should "factor out" common instance variables and methods and place them in a superclass. Then use inheritance to develop subclasses, specializing them with capabilities beyond those inherited from the superclass.

Software Engineering Observation 9.9

Declaring a subclass does not affect its superclass's source code. Inheritance preserves the integrity of the superclass.

Software Engineering Observation 9.10

Just as designers of non-object-oriented systems should avoid method proliferation, designers of object-oriented systems should avoid class proliferation. Such proliferation creates management problems and can hinder software reusability, because in a huge class library it becomes difficult to locate the most appropriate classes. The alternative is to create fewer classes that provide more substantial functionality, but such classes might prove cumbersome.

Performance Tip 9.1

If subclasses are larger than they need to be (i.e., contain too much functionality), memory and processing resources might be wasted. Extend the superclass that contains the functionality closest to what you need.

9.7 Object Class

As we discussed earlier in this chapter, all classes in Java inherit directly or indirectly from the Object class (package java.lang), so its 11 methods are inherited by all other classes. Figure 9.12 summarizes Object's methods.

Method	Description
clone	This protected method, which takes no arguments and returns an Object reference, makes a copy of the object on which it's called. The default implementation performs a so-called **shallow copy**—instance-variable values in one object are copied into another object of the same type. For reference types, only the references are copied. A typical overridden clone method's implementation would perform a **deep copy** that creates a new object for each reference-type instance variable. Implementing clone correctly is difficult. For this reason, its use is discouraged. Many industry experts suggest that object serialization should be used instead. We discuss object serialization in Chapter 17, Files, Streams and Object Serialization.
equals	This method compares two objects for equality and returns true if they are equal and false otherwise. The method takes any Object as an argument. When objects of a particular class must be compared for equality, the class should override method equals to compare the *contents* of the two objects.

Fig. 9.12 | Object methods. (Part 1 of 2.)

Method	Description
equals *(cont.)*	For the requirements of implementing this method, refer to the method's documentation at java.sun.com/javase/6/docs/api/java/lang/ Object.html# equals(java.lang.Object). The default equals implementation uses operator == to determine whether two references *refer to the same object* in memory. Section 16.3.3 demonstrates class String's equals method and differentiates between comparing String objects with == and with equals.
finalize	This protected method (introduced in Section 8.10) is called by the garbage collector to perform termination housekeeping on an object just before the garbage collector reclaims the object's memory. Recall that it's unclear whether, or when, method finalize will be called. For this reason, most programmers should avoid method finalize.
getClass	Every object in Java knows its own type at execution time. Method get-Class (used in Sections 10.5, 14.5 and 24.3) returns an object of class Class (package java.lang) that contains information about the object's type, such as its class name (returned by Class method getName). For more about class Class visit java.sun.com/javase/6/docs/api/java/lang/Class.html.
hashCode	Hashcodes are int values that are useful for high-speed storage and retrieval of information stored in a data structure that is known as a hashtable (discussed in Section 20.11). This method is also called as part of class Object's default toString method implementation.
wait, notify, notifyAll	Methods notify, notifyAll and the three overloaded versions of wait are related to multithreading, which is discussed in Chapter 26.
toString	This method (introduced in Section 9.4.1) returns a String representation of an object. The default implementation of this method returns the package name and class name of the object's class followed by a hexadecimal representation of the value returned by the object's hashCode method.

Fig. 9.12 | Object methods. (Part 2 of 2.)

We discuss several Object methods throughout this book (as indicated in Fig. 9.12). You can learn more about Object's methods in Object's online API documentation and in *The Java Tutorial* at the following sites:

```
java.sun.com/javase/6/docs/api/java/lang/Object.html
java.sun.com/docs/books/tutorial/java/IandI/objectclass.html
```

Recall from Chapter 7 that arrays are objects. As a result, like all other objects, arrays inherit the members of class Object. Note that every array has an overridden clone method that copies the array. However, if the array stores references to objects, the objects are not copied—a shallow copy is performed. For more information about the relationship between arrays and class Object, see *Java Language Specification,* Chapter 10, at

```
java.sun.com/docs/books/jls/third_edition/html/arrays.html
```

9.8 (Optional) GUI and Graphics Case Study: Displaying Text and Images Using Labels

Programs often use labels when they need to display information or instructions to the user in a graphical user interface. **Labels** are a convenient way of identifying GUI components on the screen and keeping the user informed about the current state of the program. In Java, an object of class **JLabel** (from package javax.swing) can display text, an image or both. The example in Fig. 9.13 demonstrates several JLabel features, including a plain text label, an image label and a label with both text and an image.

```java
 1   // Fig 9.13: LabelDemo.java
 2   // Demonstrates the use of labels.
 3   import java.awt.BorderLayout;
 4   import javax.swing.ImageIcon;
 5   import javax.swing.JLabel;
 6   import javax.swing.JFrame;
 7
 8   public class LabelDemo
 9   {
10      public static void main( String[] args )
11      {
12         // Create a label with plain text
13         JLabel northLabel = new JLabel( "North" );
14
15         // create an icon from an image so we can put it on a JLabel
16         ImageIcon labelIcon = new ImageIcon( "GUItip.gif" );
17
18         // create a label with an Icon instead of text
19         JLabel centerLabel = new JLabel( labelIcon );
20
21         // create another label with an Icon
22         JLabel southLabel = new JLabel( labelIcon );
23
24         // set the label to display text (as well as an icon)
25         southLabel.setText( "South" );
26
27         // create a frame to hold the labels
28         JFrame application = new JFrame();
29
30         application.setDefaultCloseOperation( JFrame.EXIT_ON_CLOSE );
31
32         // add the labels to the frame; the second argument specifies
33         // where on the frame to add the label
34         application.add( northLabel, BorderLayout.NORTH );
35         application.add( centerLabel, BorderLayout.CENTER );
36         application.add( southLabel, BorderLayout.SOUTH );
37
38         application.setSize( 300, 300 ); // set the size of the frame
39         application.setVisible( true ); // show the frame
40      } // end main
41   } // end class LabelDemo
```

Fig. 9.13 | JLabel with text and with images. (Part 1 of 2.)

Fig. 9.13 | JLabel with text and with images. (Part 2 of 2.)

Lines 3–6 import the classes we need to display JLabels. BorderLayout from package java.awt contains constants that specify where we can place GUI components in the JFrame. Class **ImageIcon** represents an image that can be displayed on a JLabel, and class JFrame represents the window that will contain all the labels.

Line 13 creates a JLabel that displays its constructor argument—the string "North". Line 16 declares local variable labelIcon and assigns it a new ImageIcon. The constructor for ImageIcon receives a String that specifies the path to the image. Since we specify only a file name, Java assumes that it's in the same directory as class LabelDemo. ImageIcon can load images in GIF, JPEG and PNG image formats. Line 19 declares and initializes local variable centerLabel with a JLabel that displays the labelIcon. Line 22 declares and initializes local variable southLabel with a JLabel similar to the one in line 19. However, line 25 calls method **setText** to change the text the label displays. Method setText can be called on any JLabel to change its text. This JLabel displays both the icon and the text.

Line 28 creates the JFrame that displays the JLabels, and line 30 indicates that the program should terminate when the JFrame is closed. We attach the labels to the JFrame in lines 34–36 by calling an overloaded version of method add that takes two parameters. The first parameter is the component we want to attach, and the second is the region in which it should be placed. Each JFrame has an associated **layout** that helps the JFrame position the GUI components that are attached to it. The default layout for a JFrame is known as a **BorderLayout** and has five regions—NORTH (top), SOUTH (bottom), EAST (right side), WEST (left side) and CENTER. Each of these is declared as a constant in class Border-Layout. When calling method add with one argument, the JFrame places the component in the CENTER automatically. If a position already contains a component, then the new component takes its place. Lines 38 and 39 set the size of the JFrame and make it visible on screen.

GUI and Graphics Case Study Exercise

9.1   Modify GUI and Graphics Case Study Exercise 8.1 to include a JLabel as a status bar that displays counts representing the number of each shape displayed. Class DrawPanel should declare a method that returns a String containing the status text. In main, first create the DrawPanel, then create the JLabel with the status text as an argument to the JLabel's constructor. Attach the JLabel to the SOUTH region of the JFrame, as shown in Fig. 9.14.

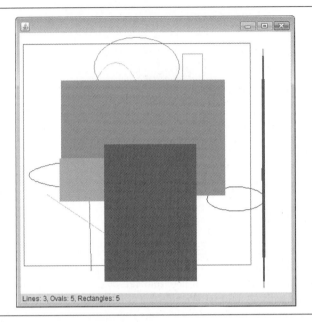

Fig. 9.14 | `JLabel` displaying shape statistics.

9.9 Wrap-Up

This chapter introduced inheritance—the ability to create classes by absorbing an existing class's members and embellishing them with new capabilities. You learned the notions of superclasses and subclasses and used keyword `extends` to create a subclass that inherits members from a superclass. We showed how to use the `@Override` annotation to prevent unintended overloading by indicating that a method overrides a superclass method. We introduced the access modifier `protected`; subclass methods can directly access `protected` superclass members. You learned how to use `super` to access overridden superclass members. You also saw how constructors are used in inheritance hierarchies. Finally, you learned about class `Object`'s methods, the direct or indirect superclass of all java classes.

In Chapter 10, Object-Oriented Programming: Polymorphism, we build on our discussion of inheritance by introducing polymorphism—an object-oriented concept that enables us to write programs that conveniently handle, in a more general manner, objects of a wide variety of classes related by inheritance. After studying Chapter 10, you'll be familiar with classes, objects, encapsulation, inheritance and polymorphism—the key technologies of object-oriented programming.

Summary

Section 9.1 Introduction

- Inheritance reduces program-development time.

- The direct superclass of a subclass (specified by the keyword `extends` in the first line of a class declaration) is the superclass from which the subclass inherits. An indirect superclass of a subclass is two or more levels up the class hierarchy from that subclass.

- In single inheritance, a class is derived from one direct superclass. In multiple inheritance, a class is derived from more than one direct superclass. Java does not support multiple inheritance.

- A subclass is more specific than its superclass and represents a smaller group of objects.

- Every object of a subclass is also an object of that class's superclass. However, a superclass object is not an object of its class's subclasses.

- An *is-a* relationship represents inheritance. In an *is-a* relationship, an object of a subclass also can be treated as an object of its superclass.

- A *has-a* relationship represents composition. In a *has-a* relationship, a class object contains references to objects of other classes.

Section 9.2 Superclasses and Subclasses
- Single-inheritance relationships form treelike hierarchical structures—a superclass exists in a hierarchical relationship with its subclasses.

Section 9.3 **protected** Members
- A superclass's `public` members are accessible wherever the program has a reference to an object of that superclass or one of its subclasses.

- A superclass's `private` members can be accessed directly only within the superclass's declaration.

- A superclass's `protected` members have an intermediate level of protection between `public` and `private` access. They can be accessed by members of the superclass, by members of its subclasses and by members of other classes in the same package.

- A superclass's `private` members are hidden in its subclasses and can be accessed only through the `public` or `protected` methods inherited from the superclass.

- When a subclass method overrides a superclass method, the superclass method can be accessed from the subclass if the superclass method name is preceded by `super` and a dot (`.`) separator.

Section 9.4 Relationship between Superclasses and Subclasses
- A subclass cannot access the `private` members of its superclass—allowing this would violate the encapsulation of the superclass. A subclass can, however, access the non-`private` members of its superclass.

- A subclass can invoke a constructor of its superclass by using the keyword `super`, followed by a set of parentheses containing the superclass constructor arguments. This must appear as the first statement in the subclass constructor's body.

- A superclass method can be overridden in a subclass to declare an appropriate implementation for the subclass.

- The annotation `@Override` indicates that a method should override a superclass method. When the compiler encounters a method declared with `@Override`, it compares the method's signature with the superclass's method signatures. If there is not an exact match, the compiler issues an error message, such as "method does not override or implement a method from a supertype."

- Method `toString` takes no arguments and returns a `String`. The `Object` class's `toString` method is normally overridden by a subclass.

- When an object is output using the `%s` format specifier, the object's `toString` method is called implicitly to obtain its `String` representation.

Section 9.5 Constructors in Subclasses
- The first task of any subclass constructor is to call its direct superclass's constructor, either explicitly or implicitly, to ensure that the instance variables inherited from the superclass are initialized.

Section 9.6 Software Engineering with Inheritance
- Declaring instance variables private, while providing non-private methods to manipulate and perform validation, helps enforce good software engineering.

Section 9.7 Object Class
- See the table of class Object's methods in Fig. 9.12.

Terminology

base class 366
brittle software 385
class hierarchy 366
deep copy 392
derived class 366
direct superclass 366
extend a class 366
extends keyword 370
fragile software 385
has-a relationship 367
indirect superclass 366
inheritance 366
inheritance hierarchy 367
is-a relationship 367

Object class 370
override a superclass method 369
@Override annotation 373
protected access modifier 369
reusable software components 367
shallow copy 392
single inheritance 366
specialization 366
standardized reusable component 367
subclass 366
super keyword 369
superclass 366
superclass constructor call syntax 382

Self-Review Exercises

9.1 Fill in the blanks in each of the following statements:
a) _____ is a form of software reusability in which new classes acquire the members of existing classes and embellish those classes with new capabilities.
b) A superclass's _____ members can be accessed in the superclass declaration *and* in subclass declarations.
c) In a(n) _____ relationship, an object of a subclass can also be treated as an object of its superclass.
d) In a(n) _____ relationship, a class object has references to objects of other classes as members.
e) In single inheritance, a class exists in a(n) _____ relationship with its subclasses.
f) A superclass's _____ members are accessible anywhere that the program has a reference to an object of that superclass or to an object of one of its subclasses.
g) When an object of a subclass is instantiated, a superclass _____ is called implicitly or explicitly.
h) Subclass constructors can call superclass constructors via the _____ keyword.

9.2 State whether each of the following is *true* or *false*. If a statement is *false*, explain why.
a) Superclass constructors are not inherited by subclasses.
b) A *has-a* relationship is implemented via inheritance.
c) A Car class has an *is-a* relationship with the SteeringWheel and Brakes classes.
d) When a subclass redefines a superclass method by using the same signature, the subclass is said to overload that superclass method.

Answers to Self-Review Exercises

9.1   a) Inheritance. b) public and protected. c) *is-a* or inheritance. d) *has-a* or composition. e) hierarchical. f) public. g) constructor. h) super.

9.2   a) True. b) False. A *has-a* relationship is implemented via composition. An *is-a* relationship is implemented via inheritance. c) False. This is an example of a *has-a* relationship. Class Car has an *is-a* relationship with class Vehicle. d) False. This is known as overriding, not overloading—an overloaded method has the same name, but a different signature.

Exercises

9.3   Many programs written with inheritance could be written with composition instead, and vice versa. Rewrite class BasePlusCommissionEmployee (Fig. 9.11) of the CommissionEmployee–BasePlusCommissionEmployee hierarchy to use composition rather than inheritance.

9.4   Discuss the ways in which inheritance promotes software reuse, saves time during program development and helps prevent errors.

9.5   The world of shapes is much richer than the shapes included in the inheritance hierarchy of Fig. 9.3. Write down all the shapes you can think of—both two-dimensional and three-dimensional—and form them into a more complete Shape hierarchy with as many levels as possible. Your hierarchy should have class Shape at the top. Classes TwoDimensionalShape and ThreeDimensionalShape should extend Shape. Add additional subclasses, such as Quadrilateral and Sphere, at their correct locations in the hierarchy as necessary.

9.6   Some programmers prefer not to use protected access, because they believe it breaks the encapsulation of the superclass. Discuss the relative merits of using protected access vs. using private access in superclasses.

9.7   Write an inheritance hierarchy for classes Quadrilateral, Trapezoid, Parallelogram, Rectangle and Square. Use Quadrilateral as the superclass of the hierarchy. Create and use a Point class to represent the points in each shape. Make the hierarchy as deep (i.e., as many levels) as possible. Specify the instance variables and methods for each class. The private instance variables of Quadrilateral should be the *x-y* coordinate pairs for the four endpoints of the Quadrilateral. Write a program that instantiates objects of your classes and outputs each object's area (except Quadrilateral).

*One Ring to rule them all, One Ring to find them,
One Ring to bring them all and in the darkness bind
them.*
—John Ronald Reuel Tolkien

General propositions do not decide concrete cases.
—Oliver Wendell Holmes

*A philosopher of imposing stature doesn't think in a
vacuum. Even his most abstract ideas are, to some
extent, conditioned by what is or is not known in the
time when he lives.*
—Alfred North Whitehead

Why art thou cast down, O my soul?
—Psalms 42:5

Object-Oriented
Programming: Polymorphism

Objectives

In this chapter you'll learn:

- The concept of polymorphism.
- To use overridden methods to effect polymorphism.
- To distinguish between abstract and concrete classes.
- To declare abstract methods to create abstract classes.
- How polymorphism makes systems extensible and maintainable.
- To determine an object's type at execution time.
- To declare and implement interfaces.

10.1 Introduction

We continue our study of object-oriented programming by explaining and demonstrating **polymorphism** with inheritance hierarchies. Polymorphism enables you to "program in the general" rather than "program in the specific." In particular, polymorphism enables you to write programs that process objects that share the same superclass (either directly or indirectly) as if they're all objects of the superclass; this can simplify programming.

Consider the following example of polymorphism. Suppose we create a program that simulates the movement of several types of animals for a biological study. Classes Fish, Frog and Bird represent the three types of animals under investigation. Imagine that each class extends superclass Animal, which contains a method move and maintains an animal's current location as *x-y* coordinates. Each subclass implements method move. Our program maintains an Animal array containing references to objects of the various Animal subclasses. To simulate the animals' movements, the program sends each object the same message once per second—namely, move. However, each specific type of Animal responds to a move message in a unique way—a Fish might swim three feet, a Frog might jump five feet and a Bird might fly ten feet. The program issues the *same* message (i.e., move) to each animal object, but each object knows how to modify its *x-y* coordinates appropriately for its *specific* type of movement. Relying on each object to know how to "do the right thing" (i.e., do what is appropriate for that type of object) in response to the same method call is the key concept of polymorphism. The same message (in this case, move) sent to a variety of objects has "many forms" of results—hence the term polymorphism.

Implementing for Extensibility
With polymorphism, we can design and implement systems that are easily extensible—new classes can be added with little or no modification to the general portions of the pro-

gram, as long as the new classes are part of the inheritance hierarchy that the program processes generically. The only parts of a program that must be altered to accommodate new classes are those that require direct knowledge of the new classes that we add to the hierarchy. For example, if we extend class Animal to create class Tortoise (which might respond to a move message by crawling one inch), we need to write only the Tortoise class and the part of the simulation that instantiates a Tortoise object. The portions of the simulation that process each Animal generically can remain the same.

Chapter Overview

This chapter has several parts. First, we discuss common examples of polymorphism. We then provide a small example demonstrating polymorphic behavior. We use superclass references to manipulate both superclass objects and subclass objects polymorphically.

We then present a case study that revisits the employee hierarchy of Section 9.4.5. We develop a simple payroll application that polymorphically calculates the weekly pay of several different types of employees using each employee's earnings method. Though the earnings of each type of employee are calculated in a specific way, polymorphism allows us to process the employees "in the general." In the case study, we enlarge the hierarchy to include two new classes—SalariedEmployee (for people paid a fixed weekly salary) and HourlyEmployee (for people paid an hourly salary and "time-and-a-half" for overtime). We declare a common set of functionality for all the classes in the updated hierarchy in an "abstract" class, Employee, from which "concrete"classes SalariedEmployee, HourlyEmployee and CommissionEmployee inherit directly and "concrete" class BasePlusCommissionEmployee inherits indirectly. As you'll soon see, when we invoke each employee's earnings method off a superclass Employee reference, the correct earnings subclass calculation is performed, due to Java's polymorphic capabilities.

Programming in the Specific

Occasionally, when performing polymorphic processing, we need to program "in the specific." Our Employee case study demonstrates that a program can determine the type of an object at *execution* time and act on that object accordingly. In the case study, we've decided that BasePlusCommissionEmployees should receive 10% raises on their base salaries. So, we use these capabilities to determine whether a particular employee object *is a* BasePlusCommissionEmployee. If so, we increase that employee's base salary by 10%.

Interfaces

The chapter continues with an introduction to Java interfaces. An interface describes a set of methods that can be called on an object, but does not provide concrete implementations for all the methods. You can declare classes that **implement** (i.e., provide concrete implementations for the methods of) one or more interfaces. Each interface method must be declared in all the classes that explicitly implement the interface. Once a class implements an interface, all objects of that class have an *is-a* relationship with the interface type, and all objects of the class are guaranteed to provide the functionality described by the interface. This is true of all subclasses of that class as well.

Interfaces are particularly useful for assigning common functionality to possibly unrelated classes. This allows objects of unrelated classes to be processed polymorphically—objects of classes that implement the same interface can respond to all of the interface method calls. To demonstrate creating and using interfaces, we modify our payroll application to create a general accounts payable application that can calculate payments due for company employees and invoice amounts to be billed for purchased goods. As you'll see, interfaces enable polymorphic capabilities similar to those possible with inheritance.

10.2 Polymorphism Examples

We now consider several additional examples of polymorphism.

Quadrilaterals

If class `Rectangle` is derived from class `Quadrilateral`, then a `Rectangle` object is a more specific version of a `Quadrilateral`. Any operation (e.g., calculating the perimeter or the area) that can be performed on a `Quadrilateral` can also be performed on a `Rectangle`. These operations can also be performed on other `Quadrilaterals`, such as `Squares`, `Parallelograms` and `Trapezoids`. The polymorphism occurs when a program invokes a method through a superclass `Quadrilateral` variable—at execution time, the correct subclass version of the method is called, based on the type of the reference stored in the superclass variable. You'll see a simple code example that illustrates this process in Section 10.3.

Space Objects in a Video Game

Suppose we design a video game that manipulates objects of classes `Martian`, `Venusian`, `Plutonian`, `SpaceShip` and `LaserBeam`. Imagine that each class inherits from the superclass `SpaceObject`, which contains method `draw`. Each subclass implements this method. A screen manager maintains a collection (e.g., a `SpaceObject` array) of references to objects of the various classes. To refresh the screen, the screen manager periodically sends each object the same message—namely, `draw`. However, each object responds in a unique way. For example, a `Martian` object might draw itself in red with green eyes and the appropriate number of antennae. A `SpaceShip` object might draw itself as a bright silver flying saucer. A `LaserBeam` object might draw itself as a bright red beam across the screen. Again, the *same* message (in this case, `draw`) sent to a variety of objects has "many forms" of results.

A screen manager might use polymorphism to facilitate adding new classes to a system with minimal modifications to the system's code. Suppose that we want to add `Mercurian` objects to our video game. To do so, we'd build a class `Mercurian` that extends `SpaceObject` and provides its own `draw` method implementation. When `Mercurian` objects appear in the `SpaceObject` collection, the screen manager code invokes method `draw`, exactly as it does for every other object in the collection, regardless of its type. So the new `Mercurian` objects simply "plug right in" without any modification of the screen manager code by the programmer. Thus, without modifying the system (other than to build new classes and modify the code that creates new objects), you can use polymorphism to conveniently include additional types that were not envisioned when the system was created.

Software Engineering Observation 10.1
Polymorphism enables you to deal in generalities and let the execution-time environment handle the specifics. You can command objects to behave in manners appropriate to those objects, without knowing their types (as long as the objects belong to the same inheritance hierarchy).

Software Engineering Observation 10.2
Polymorphism promotes extensibility: Software that invokes polymorphic behavior is independent of the object types to which messages are sent. New object types that can respond to existing method calls can be incorporated into a system without modifying the base system. Only client code that instantiates new objects must be modified to accommodate new types.

10.3 Demonstrating Polymorphic Behavior

Section 9.4 created a class hierarchy, in which class BasePlusCommissionEmployee inherited from CommissionEmployee. The examples in that section manipulated Commission-Employee and BasePlusCommissionEmployee objects by using references to them to invoke their methods—we aimed superclass variables at superclass objects and subclass variables at subclass objects. These assignments are natural and straightforward—superclass variables are intended to refer to superclass objects, and subclass variables are intended to refer to subclass objects. However, as you'll soon see, other assignments are possible.

In the next example, we aim a superclass reference at a subclass object. We then show how invoking a method on a subclass object via a superclass reference invokes the subclass functionality—the type of the *referenced object*, not the type of the *variable*, determines which method is called. This example demonstrates that an object of a subclass can be treated as an object of its superclass, enabling various interesting manipulations. A program can create an array of superclass variables that refer to objects of many subclass types. This is allowed because each subclass object *is an* object of its superclass. For instance, we can assign the reference of a BasePlusCommissionEmployee object to a superclass CommissionEmployee variable, because a BasePlusCommissionEmployee *is a* Commission-Employee—we can treat a BasePlusCommissionEmployee as a CommissionEmployee.

As you'll learn later in the chapter, you cannot treat a superclass object as a subclass object, because a superclass object is *not* an object of any of its subclasses. For example, we cannot assign the reference of a CommissionEmployee object to a subclass BasePlusCommissionEmployee variable, because a CommissionEmployee is not a BasePlusCommission-Employee—a CommissionEmployee does not have a baseSalary instance variable and does not have methods setBaseSalary and getBaseSalary. The *is-a* relationship applies only *up the hierarchy* from a subclass to its direct (and indirect) superclasses, and not vice versa (i.e., not down the hierarchy from a superclass to its subclasses).

The Java compiler *does* allow the assignment of a superclass reference to a subclass variable if we explicitly cast the superclass reference to the subclass type—a technique we discuss in Section 10.5. Why would we ever want to perform such an assignment? A superclass reference can be used to invoke only the methods declared in the superclass—attempting to invoke subclass-only methods through a superclass reference results in compilation errors. If a program needs to perform a subclass-specific operation on a subclass object referenced by a superclass variable, the program must first cast the superclass reference to a subclass reference through a technique known as **downcasting**. This enables the program to invoke subclass methods that are not in the superclass. We show a downcasting example in Section 10.5.

The example in Fig. 10.1 demonstrates three ways to use superclass and subclass variables to store references to superclass and subclass objects. The first two are straightforward—as in Section 9.4, we assign a superclass reference to a superclass variable, and we assign a subclass reference to a subclass variable. Then we demonstrate the relationship between subclasses and superclasses (i.e., the *is-a* relationship) by assigning a subclass reference to a superclass variable. [*Note:* This program uses classes CommissionEmployee and BasePlusCommissionEmployee from Fig. 9.10 and Fig. 9.11, respectively.]

In Fig. 10.1, lines 10–11 create a CommissionEmployee object and assign its reference to a CommissionEmployee variable. Lines 14–16 create a BasePlusCommissionEmployee object and assign its reference to a BasePlusCommissionEmployee variable. These assignments are natural—for example, a CommissionEmployee variable's primary purpose is to hold a reference to a CommissionEmployee object. Lines 19–21 use commissionEmployee to invoke toString explicitly. Because commissionEmployee refers to a CommissionEmployee object, superclass CommissionEmployee's version of toString is called. Similarly, lines 24–27 use basePlusCommissionEmployee to invoke toString explicitly on the BasePlusCommissionEmployee object. This invokes subclass BasePlusCommissionEmployee's version of toString.

```java
 1   // Fig. 10.1: PolymorphismTest.java
 2   // Assigning superclass and subclass references to superclass and
 3   // subclass variables.
 4
 5   public class PolymorphismTest
 6   {
 7      public static void main( String[] args )
 8      {
 9         // assign superclass reference to superclass variable
10         CommissionEmployee commissionEmployee = new CommissionEmployee(
11            "Sue", "Jones", "222-22-2222", 10000, .06 );
12
13         // assign subclass reference to subclass variable
14         BasePlusCommissionEmployee basePlusCommissionEmployee =
15            new BasePlusCommissionEmployee(
16            "Bob", "Lewis", "333-33-3333", 5000, .04, 300 );
17
18         // invoke toString on superclass object using superclass variable
19         System.out.printf( "%s %s:\n\n%s\n\n",
20            "Call CommissionEmployee's toString with superclass reference ",
21            "to superclass object", commissionEmployee.toString() );
22
23         // invoke toString on subclass object using subclass variable
24         System.out.printf( "%s %s:\n\n%s\n\n",
25            "Call BasePlusCommissionEmployee's toString with subclass",
26            "reference to subclass object",
27            basePlusCommissionEmployee.toString() );
28
29         // invoke toString on subclass object using superclass variable
30         CommissionEmployee commissionEmployee2 =
31            basePlusCommissionEmployee;
32         System.out.printf( "%s %s:\n\n%s\n",
33            "Call BasePlusCommissionEmployee's toString with superclass",
34            "reference to subclass object", commissionEmployee2.toString() );
35      } // end main
36   } // end class PolymorphismTest
```

```
Call CommissionEmployee's toString with superclass reference to superclass ob-
ject:

commission employee: Sue Jones
social security number: 222-22-2222
gross sales: 10000.00
commission rate: 0.06
```

Fig. 10.1 | Assigning superclass and subclass references to superclass and subclass variables. (Part 1 of 2.)

```
Call BasePlusCommissionEmployee's toString with subclass reference to
subclass object:

base-salaried commission employee: Bob Lewis
social security number: 333-33-3333
gross sales: 5000.00
commission rate: 0.04
base salary: 300.00

Call BasePlusCommissionEmployee's toString with superclass reference to
subclass object:

base-salaried commission employee: Bob Lewis
social security number: 333-33-3333
gross sales: 5000.00
commission rate: 0.04
base salary: 300.00
```

Fig. 10.1 | Assigning superclass and subclass references to superclass and subclass variables. (Part 2 of 2.)

Lines 30–31 then assign the reference of subclass object basePlusCommissionEmployee to a superclass CommissionEmployee variable, which lines 32–34 use to invoke method toString. *When a superclass variable contains a reference to a subclass object, and that reference is used to call a method, the subclass version of the method is called.* Hence, commissionEmployee2.toString() in line 34 actually calls class BasePlusCommissionEmployee's toString method. The Java compiler allows this "crossover" because an object of a subclass *is an* object of its superclass (but not vice versa). When the compiler encounters a method call made through a variable, the compiler determines if the method can be called by checking the variable's class type. If that class contains the proper method declaration (or inherits one), the call is compiled. At execution time, the type of the object to which the variable refers determines the actual method to use. This process, called dynamic binding, is discussed in detail in Section 10.5.

10.4 Abstract Classes and Methods

When we think of a class, we assume that programs will create objects of that type. Sometimes it's useful to declare classes—called **abstract classes**—for which you never intend to create objects. Because they are used only as superclasses in inheritance hierarchies, we refer to them as **abstract superclasses**. These classes cannot be used to instantiate objects, because, as we'll soon see, abstract classes are incomplete. Subclasses must declare the "missing pieces" to become "concrete" classes, from which you can instantiate objects. Otherwise, these subclasses, too, will be abstract. We demonstrate abstract classes in Section 10.5.

Purpose of Abstract Classes
An abstract class's purpose is to provide an appropriate superclass from which other classes can inherit and thus share a common design. In the Shape hierarchy of Fig. 9.3, for example, subclasses inherit the notion of what it means to be a Shape—perhaps common attributes such as location, color and borderThickness, and behaviors such as draw, move, resize and changeColor. Classes that can be used to instantiate objects are called **concrete classes**. Such classes provide implementations of every method they declare (some of the implementations can be inherited). For example, we could derive concrete classes Circle,

Square and Triangle from abstract superclass TwoDimensionalShape. Similarly, we could derive concrete classes Sphere, Cube and Tetrahedron from abstract superclass ThreeDimensionalShape. Abstract superclasses are too general to create real objects—they specify only what is common among subclasses. We need to be more specific before we can create objects. For example, if you send the draw message to abstract class TwoDimensionalShape, it knows that two-dimensional shapes should be drawable, but it does not know what specific shape to draw, so it cannot implement a real draw method. Concrete classes provide the specifics that make it reasonable to instantiate objects.

Not all hierarchies contain abstract classes. However, programmers often write client code that uses only abstract superclass types to reduce client code's dependencies on a range of subclass types. For example, you can write a method with a parameter of an abstract superclass type. When called, such a method can receive an object of any concrete class that directly or indirectly extends the superclass specified as the parameter's type.

Abstract classes sometimes constitute several levels of a hierarchy. For example, the Shape hierarchy of Fig. 9.3 begins with abstract class Shape. On the next level of the hierarchy are abstract classes TwoDimensionalShape and ThreeDimensionalShape. The next level of the hierarchy declares concrete classes for TwoDimensionalShapes (Circle, Square and Triangle) and for ThreeDimensionalShapes (Sphere, Cube and Tetrahedron).

Declaring an Abstract Class and Abstract Methods

You make a class abstract by declaring it with keyword **abstract**. An abstract class normally contains one or more **abstract methods**. An abstract method is one with keyword abstract in its declaration, as in

```
public abstract void draw(); // abstract method
```

Abstract methods do not provide implementations. A class that contains any abstract methods must be explicitly declared as an abstract class even if that class contains some concrete (nonabstract) methods. Each concrete subclass of an abstract superclass also must provide concrete implementations of each of the superclass's abstract methods. Constructors and static methods cannot be declared abstract. Constructors are not inherited, so an abstract constructor could never be implemented. Though non-private static methods are inherited, they cannot be overridden. Since abstract methods are meant to be overridden so that they can process objects based on their types, it would not make sense to declare a static method as abstract.

Software Engineering Observation 10.3
An abstract class declares common attributes and behaviors (both abstract and concrete) of the various classes in a class hierarchy. An abstract class typically contains one or more abstract methods that subclasses must override if they are to be concrete. The instance variables and concrete methods of an abstract class are subject to the normal rules of inheritance.

Common Programming Error 10.1
Attempting to instantiate an object of an abstract class is a compilation error.

Common Programming Error 10.2
Failure to implement a superclass's abstract methods in a subclass is a compilation error unless the subclass is also declared abstract.

Using Abstract Classes to Declare Variables

Although we cannot instantiate objects of abstract superclasses, you'll soon see that we *can* use abstract superclasses to declare variables that can hold references to objects of any concrete class derived from those abstract superclasses. Programs typically use such variables to manipulate subclass objects polymorphically. You also can use abstract superclass names to invoke static methods declared in those abstract superclasses.

Consider another application of polymorphism. A drawing program needs to display many shapes, including types of new shapes that you will add to the system after writing the drawing program. The drawing program might need to display shapes, such as Circles, Triangles, Rectangles or others, that derive from abstract class Shape. The drawing program uses Shape variables to manage the objects that are displayed. To draw any object in this inheritance hierarchy, the drawing program uses a superclass Shape variable containing a reference to the subclass object to invoke the object's draw method. This method is declared abstract in superclass Shape, so each concrete subclass *must* implement method draw in a manner specific to that shape—each object in the Shape inheritance hierarchy *knows how to draw itself.* The drawing program does not have to worry about the type of each object or whether the program has ever encountered objects of that type.

Layered Software Systems

Polymorphism is particularly effective for implementing so-called layered software systems. In operating systems, for example, each type of physical device could operate quite differently from the others. Even so, commands to read or write data from and to devices may have a certain uniformity. For each device, the operating system uses a piece of software called a device driver to control all communication between the system and the device. The write message sent to a device-driver object needs to be interpreted specifically in the context of that driver and how it manipulates devices of a specific type. However, the write call itself really is no different from the write to any other device in the system—place some number of bytes from memory onto that device. An object-oriented operating system might use an abstract superclass to provide an "interface" appropriate for all device drivers. Then, through inheritance from that abstract superclass, subclasses are formed that all behave similarly. The device-driver methods are declared as abstract methods in the abstract superclass. The implementations of these abstract methods are provided in the subclasses that correspond to the specific types of device drivers. New devices are always being developed, often long after the operating system has been released. When you buy a new device, it comes with a device driver provided by the device vendor. The device is immediately operational after you connect it to your computer and install the driver. This is another elegant example of how polymorphism makes systems extensible.

10.5 Case Study: Payroll System Using Polymorphism

This section reexamines the CommissionEmployee-BasePlusCommissionEmployee hierarchy that we explored throughout Section 9.4. Now we use an abstract method and polymorphism to perform payroll calculations based on the type of inheritance hierarchy headed by an employee. We create an enhanced employee inheritance hierarchy to meet the following requirements:

A company pays its employees on a weekly basis. The employees are of four types: Salaried employees are paid a fixed weekly salary regardless of the number of hours worked, hourly employees are paid by the hour and receive overtime pay (i.e., 1.5 times their

*hourly salary rate) for all hours worked in excess of 40 hours, commission employees
are paid a percentage of their sales and base-salaried commission employees receive a
base salary plus a percentage of their sales. For the current pay period, the company has
decided to reward salaried-commission employees by adding 10% to their base salaries. The company wants to write a Java application that performs its payroll calculations polymorphically.*

We use abstract class Employee to represent the general concept of an employee. The
classes that extend Employee are SalariedEmployee, CommissionEmployee and Hourly-
Employee. Class BasePlusCommissionEmployee—which extends CommissionEmployee—
represents the last employee type. The UML class diagram in Fig. 10.2 shows the inheritance hierarchy for our polymorphic employee-payroll application. Note that abstract class
name Employee is italicized—a convention of the UML.

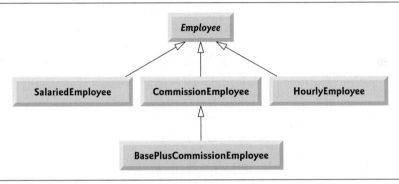

Fig. 10.2 | Employee hierarchy UML class diagram.

Abstract superclass Employee declares the "interface" to the hierarchy—that is, the set
of methods that a program can invoke on all Employee objects. We use the term "interface"
here in a general sense to refer to the various ways programs can communicate with objects
of any Employee subclass. Be careful not to confuse the general notion of an "interface"
with the formal notion of a Java interface, the subject of Section 10.7. Each employee,
regardless of the way his or her earnings are calculated, has a first name, a last name and a
social security number, so private instance variables firstName, lastName and social-
SecurityNumber appear in abstract superclass Employee.

The following sections implement the Employee class hierarchy of Fig. 10.2. The first
section implements abstract superclass Employee. The next four sections each implement
one of the concrete classes. The last section implements a test program that builds objects
of all these classes and processes those objects polymorphically.

10.5.1 Abstract Superclass Employee

Class Employee (Fig. 10.4) provides methods earnings and toString, in addition to the
get and *set* methods that manipulate Employee's instance variables. An earnings method
certainly applies generically to all employees. But each earnings calculation depends on the
employee's class. So we declare earnings as abstract in superclass Employee because a default implementation does not make sense for that method—there is not enough information to determine what amount earnings should return. Each subclass overrides earnings
with an appropriate implementation. To calculate an employee's earnings, the program as-

signs to a superclass `Employee` variable a reference to the employee's object, then invokes the `earnings` method on that variable. We maintain an array of `Employee` variables, each holding a reference to an `Employee` object. (Of course, there cannot be `Employee` objects, because `Employee` is an abstract class. Because of inheritance, however, all objects of all subclasses of `Employee` may nevertheless be thought of as `Employee` objects.) The program will iterate through the array and call method `earnings` for each `Employee` object. Java processes these method calls polymorphically. Including `earnings` as an `abstract` method in `Employee` enables the calls to `earnings` through `Employee` variables to compile and forces every direct concrete subclass of `Employee` to override `earnings`.

Method `toString` in class `Employee` returns a `String` containing the first name, last name and social security number of the employee. As we'll see, each subclass of `Employee` overrides method `toString` to create a `String` representation of an object of that class that contains the employee's type (e.g., `"salaried employee:"`) followed by the rest of the employee's information.

The diagram in Fig. 10.3 shows each of the five classes in the hierarchy down the left side and methods `earnings` and `toString` across the top. For each class, the diagram shows the desired results of each method. We do not list superclass `Employee`'s *get* and *set* methods because they are not overridden in any of the subclasses—each of these methods is inherited and used "as is" by each subclass.

	earnings	toString
Employee	abstract	*firstName lastName* `social security number:` *SSN*
Salaried- Employee	`weeklySalary`	`salaried employee:` *firstName lastName* `social security number:` *SSN* `weekly salary:` *weeklysalary*

Hourly-
Employee
	`if (hours <= 40)`
	  `wage * hours`
	`else if (hours > 40)`
	`{`
	  `40 * wage +`
	  `( hours - 40 ) *`
	  `wage * 1.5`
	`}`
		`hourly employee:` *firstName lastName*
		`social security number:` *SSN*
		`hourly wage:` *wage*`; hours worked:` *hours*

Commission- Employee	`commissionRate *` `grossSales`	`commission employee:` *firstName lastName* `social security number:` *SSN* `gross sales:` *grossSales*`;` `commission rate:` *commissionRate*

BasePlus-
Commission-
Employee
	`(commissionRate *`
	`grossSales) +`
	`baseSalary`
		`base salaried commission employee:`
		  firstName lastName
		`social security number:` *SSN*
		`gross sales:` *grossSales*`;`
		`commission rate:` *commissionRate*`;`
		`base salary:` *baseSalary*

Fig. 10.3 | Polymorphic interface for the `Employee` hierarchy classes.

Let's consider class Employee's declaration (Fig. 10.4). The class includes a constructor that takes the first name, last name and social security number as arguments (lines 11–16); *get* methods that return the first name, last name and social security number (lines 25–28, 37–40 and 49–52, respectively); *set* methods that set the first name, last name and social security number (lines 19–22, 31–34 and 43–46, respectively); method toString (lines 55–60), which returns the String representation of an Employee; and abstract method earnings (line 63), which will be implemented by each of the concrete subclasses. Note that the Employee constructor does not validate the social security number in this example. Normally, such validation should be provided.

```java
1   // Fig. 10.4: Employee.java
2   // Employee abstract superclass.
3
4   public abstract class Employee
5   {
6      private String firstName;
7      private String lastName;
8      private String socialSecurityNumber;
9
10     // three-argument constructor
11     public Employee( String first, String last, String ssn )
12     {
13        firstName = first;
14        lastName = last;
15        socialSecurityNumber = ssn;
16     } // end three-argument Employee constructor
17
18     // set first name
19     public void setFirstName( String first )
20     {
21        firstName = first; // should validate
22     } // end method setFirstName
23
24     // return first name
25     public String getFirstName()
26     {
27        return firstName;
28     } // end method getFirstName
29
30     // set last name
31     public void setLastName( String last )
32     {
33        lastName = last; // should validate
34     } // end method setLastName
35
36     // return last name
37     public String getLastName()
38     {
39        return lastName;
40     } // end method getLastName
41
```

Fig. 10.4 | Employee abstract superclass. (Part I of 2.)

```
42      // set social security number
43      public void setSocialSecurityNumber( String ssn )
44      {
45         socialSecurityNumber = ssn; // should validate
46      } // end method setSocialSecurityNumber
47
48      // return social security number
49      public String getSocialSecurityNumber()
50      {
51         return socialSecurityNumber;
52      } // end method getSocialSecurityNumber
53
54      // return String representation of Employee object
55      @Override
56      public String toString()
57      {
58         return String.format( "%s %s\nsocial security number: %s",
59            getFirstName(), getLastName(), getSocialSecurityNumber() );
60      } // end method toString
61
62      // abstract method overridden by concrete subclasses
63      public abstract double earnings(); // no implementation here
64   } // end abstract class Employee
```

Fig. 10.4 | Employee abstract superclass. (Part 2 of 2.)

Why did we decide to declare earnings as an abstract method? It simply does not make sense to provide an implementation of this method in class Employee. We cannot calculate the earnings for a general Employee—we first must know the specific type of Employee to determine the appropriate earnings calculation. By declaring this method abstract, we indicate that each concrete subclass *must* provide an appropriate earnings implementation and that a program will be able to use superclass Employee variables to invoke method earnings polymorphically for any type of Employee.

10.5.2 Concrete Subclass SalariedEmployee

Class SalariedEmployee (Fig. 10.5) extends class Employee (line 4) and overrides abstract method earnings (lines 29–33), which makes SalariedEmployee a concrete class. The class includes a constructor (lines 9–14) that takes a first name, a last name, a social security number and a weekly salary as arguments; a *set* method to assign a new nonnegative value to instance variable weeklySalary (lines 17–20); a *get* method to return weeklySalary's value (lines 23–26); a method earnings (lines 29–33) to calculate a SalariedEmployee's earnings; and a method toString (lines 36–41), which returns a String including the employee's type, namely, "salaried employee: " followed by employee-specific information produced by superclass Employee's toString method and SalariedEmployee's getWeeklySalary method. Class SalariedEmployee's constructor passes the first name, last name and social security number to the Employee constructor (line 12) to initialize the private instance variables not inherited from the superclass. Method earnings overrides Employee's abstract method earnings to provide a concrete implementation that returns the SalariedEmployee's weekly salary. If we do not implement earnings, class SalariedEmployee must be declared abstract—otherwise, class SalariedEmployee will not compile. Of course, we want SalariedEmployee here to be a concrete class in this example.

```java
 1  // Fig. 10.5: SalariedEmployee.java
 2  // SalariedEmployee concrete class extends abstract class Employee.
 3
 4  public class SalariedEmployee extends Employee
 5  {
 6     private double weeklySalary;
 7
 8     // four-argument constructor
 9     public SalariedEmployee( String first, String last, String ssn,
10        double salary )
11     {
12        super( first, last, ssn ); // pass to Employee constructor
13        setWeeklySalary( salary ); // validate and store salary
14     } // end four-argument SalariedEmployee constructor
15
16     // set salary
17     public void setWeeklySalary( double salary )
18     {
19        weeklySalary = salary < 0.0 ? 0.0 : salary;
20     } // end method setWeeklySalary
21
22     // return salary
23     public double getWeeklySalary()
24     {
25        return weeklySalary;
26     } // end method getWeeklySalary
27
28     // calculate earnings; override abstract method earnings in Employee
29     @Override
30     public double earnings()
31     {
32        return getWeeklySalary();
33     } // end method earnings
34
35     // return String representation of SalariedEmployee object
36     @Override
37     public String toString()
38     {
39        return String.format( "salaried employee: %s\n%s: $%,.2f",
40           super.toString(), "weekly salary", getWeeklySalary() );
41     } // end method toString
42  } // end class SalariedEmployee
```

Fig. 10.5 | SalariedEmployee concrete class extends abstract class Employee.

Method toString (lines 36–41) of class SalariedEmployee overrides Employee method toString. If class SalariedEmployee did not override toString, SalariedEmployee would have inherited the Employee version of toString. In that case, SalariedEmployee's toString method would simply return the employee's full name and social security number, which does not adequately represent a SalariedEmployee. To produce a complete String representation of a SalariedEmployee, the subclass's toString method returns "salaried employee: " followed by the superclass Employee-specific information (i.e., first name, last name and social security number) obtained by invoking the superclass's toString method (line 40)—this is a nice example of code reuse. The String representation of a SalariedEmployee also contains the employee's weekly salary obtained by invoking the class's getWeeklySalary method.

10.5.3 Concrete Subclass HourlyEmployee

Class HourlyEmployee (Fig. 10.6) also extends Employee (line 4). The class includes a constructor (lines 10–16) that takes as arguments a first name, a last name, a social security number, an hourly wage and the number of hours worked. Lines 19–22 and 31–35 declare *set* methods that assign new values to instance variables wage and hours, respectively. Method setWage (lines 19–22) ensures that wage is nonnegative, and method setHours (lines 31–35) ensures that hours is between 0 and 168 (the total number of hours in a week) inclusive. Class HourlyEmployee also includes *get* methods (lines 25–28 and 38–41) to return the values of wage and hours, respectively; a method earnings (lines 44–51) to calculate an HourlyEmployee's earnings; and a method toString (lines 54–60), which returns a String containing the employee's type ("hourly employee: ") and the employee-specific information. Note that the HourlyEmployee constructor, like the SalariedEmployee constructor, passes the first name, last name and social security number to the superclass Employee constructor (line 13) to initialize the private instance variables. In addition, method toString calls superclass method toString (line 58) to obtain the Employee-specific information (i.e., first name, last name and social security number)—this is another nice example of code reuse.

```
1   // Fig. 10.6: HourlyEmployee.java
2   // HourlyEmployee class extends Employee.
3
4   public class HourlyEmployee extends Employee
5   {
6      private double wage; // wage per hour
7      private double hours; // hours worked for week
8
9      // five-argument constructor
10     public HourlyEmployee( String first, String last, String ssn,
11        double hourlyWage, double hoursWorked )
12     {
13        super( first, last, ssn );
14        setWage( hourlyWage ); // validate hourly wage
15        setHours( hoursWorked ); // validate hours worked
16     } // end five-argument HourlyEmployee constructor
17
18     // set wage
19     public void setWage( double hourlyWage )
20     {
21        wage = ( hourlyWage < 0.0 ) ? 0.0 : hourlyWage;
22     } // end method setWage
23
```

Fig. 10.6 | HourlyEmployee class derived from Employee. (Part 1 of 2.)

```
24      // return wage
25      public double getWage()
26      {
27         return wage;
28      } // end method getWage
29
30      // set hours worked
31      public void setHours( double hoursWorked )
32      {
33         hours = ( ( hoursWorked >= 0.0 ) && ( hoursWorked <= 168.0 ) ) ?
34            hoursWorked : 0.0;
35      } // end method setHours
36
37      // return hours worked
38      public double getHours()
39      {
40         return hours;
41      } // end method getHours
42
43      // calculate earnings; override abstract method earnings in Employee
44      @Override
45      public double earnings()
46      {
47         if ( getHours() <= 40 ) // no overtime
48            return getWage() * getHours();
49         else
50            return 40 * getWage() + ( gethours() - 40 ) * getWage() * 1.5;
51      } // end method earnings
52
53      // return String representation of HourlyEmployee object
54      @Override
55      public String toString()
56      {
57         return String.format( "hourly employee: %s\n%s: $%,.2f; %s: %,.2f",
58            super.toString(), "hourly wage", getWage(),
59            "hours worked", getHours() );
60      } // end method toString
61   } // end class HourlyEmployee
```

Fig. 10.6 | `HourlyEmployee` class derived from `Employee`. (Part 2 of 2.)

10.5.4 Concrete Subclass CommissionEmployee

Class `CommissionEmployee` (Fig. 10.7) extends class `Employee` (line 4). The class includes a constructor (lines 10–16) that takes a first name, a last name, a social security number, a sales amount and a commission rate; *set* methods (lines 19–22 and 31–34) to assign new values to instance variables `commissionRate` and `grossSales`, respectively; *get* methods (lines 25–28 and 37–40) that retrieve the values of these instance variables; method earnings (lines 43–47) to calculate a `CommissionEmployee`'s earnings; and method `toString` (lines 50–57), which returns the employee's type, namely, `"commission employee: "` and employee-specific information. The constructor also passes the first name, last name and social security number to `Employee`'s constructor (line 13) to initialize `Employee`'s private instance variables. Method `toString` calls superclass method `toString` (line 54) to obtain the `Employee`-specific information (i.e., first name, last name and social security number).

```java
1   // Fig. 10.7: CommissionEmployee.java
2   // CommissionEmployee class extends Employee.
3
4   public class CommissionEmployee extends Employee
5   {
6      private double grossSales; // gross weekly sales
7      private double commissionRate; // commission percentage
8
9      // five-argument constructor
10     public CommissionEmployee( String first, String last, String ssn,
11        double sales, double rate )
12     {
13        super( first, last, ssn );
14        setGrossSales( sales );
15        setCommissionRate( rate );
16     } // end five-argument CommissionEmployee constructor
17
18     // set commission rate
19     public void setCommissionRate( double rate )
20     {
21        commissionRate = ( rate > 0.0 && rate < 1.0 ) ? rate : 0.0;
22     } // end method setCommissionRate
23
24     // return commission rate
25     public double getCommissionRate()
26     {
27        return commissionRate;
28     } // end method getCommissionRate
29
30     // set gross sales amount
31     public void setGrossSales( double sales )
32     {
33        grossSales = ( sales < 0.0 ) ? 0.0 : sales;
34     } // end method setGrossSales
35
36     // return gross sales amount
37     public double getGrossSales()
38     {
39        return grossSales;
40     } // end method getGrossSales
41
42     // calculate earnings; override abstract method earnings in Employee
43     @Override
44     public double earnings()
45     {
46        return getCommissionRate() * getGrossSales();
47     } // end method earnings
48
49     // return String representation of CommissionEmployee object
50     @Override
51     public String toString()
52     {
53        return String.format( "%s: %s\n%s: $%,.2f; %s: %.2f",
54           "commission employee", super.toString(),
```

Fig. 10.7 | CommissionEmployee class derived from Employee. (Part I of 2.)

```
55            "gross sales", getGrossSales(),
56            "commission rate", getCommissionRate() );
57      } // end method toString
58 } // end class CommissionEmployee
```

Fig. 10.7 | CommissionEmployee class derived from Employee. (Part 2 of 2.)

10.5.5 Indirect Concrete Subclass BasePlusCommissionEmployee

Class BasePlusCommissionEmployee (Fig. 10.8) extends class CommissionEmployee (line 4) and therefore is an indirect subclass of class Employee. Class BasePlusCommission-Employee has a constructor (lines 9–14) that takes as arguments a first name, a last name, a social security number, a sales amount, a commission rate and a base salary. It then passes the first name, last name, social security number, sales amount and commission rate to the CommissionEmployee constructor (line 12) to initialize the inherited members. Base-PlusCommissionEmployee also contains a *set* method (lines 17–20) to assign a new value to instance variable baseSalary and a *get* method (lines 23–26) to return baseSalary's value. Method earnings (lines 29–33) calculates a BasePlusCommissionEmployee's earnings. Note that line 32 in method earnings calls superclass CommissionEmployee's earnings method to calculate the commission-based portion of the employee's earnings. This is a nice example of code reuse. BasePlusCommissionEmployee's toString method (lines 36–42) creates a String representation of a BasePlusCommissionEmployee that contains "base-salaried", followed by the String obtained by invoking superclass Commission-Employee's toString method (another example of code reuse), then the base salary. The result is a String beginning with "base-salaried commission employee" followed by the rest of the BasePlusCommissionEmployee's information. Recall that CommissionEmploy-ee's toString obtains the employee's first name, last name and social security number by invoking the toString method of its superclass (i.e., Employee)—yet another example of code reuse. Note that BasePlusCommissionEmployee's toString initiates a chain of method calls that span all three levels of the Employee hierarchy.

```
1  // Fig. 10.8: BasePlusCommissionEmployee.java
2  // BasePlusCommissionEmployee class extends CommissionEmployee.
3
4  public class BasePlusCommissionEmployee extends CommissionEmployee
5  {
6     private double baseSalary; // base salary per week
7
8     // six-argument constructor
9     public BasePlusCommissionEmployee( String first, String last,
10       String ssn, double sales, double rate, double salary )
11    {
12       super( first, last, ssn, sales, rate );
13       setBaseSalary( salary ); // validate and store base salary
14    } // end six-argument BasePlusCommissionEmployee constructor
15
16    // set base salary
17    public void setBaseSalary( double salary )
18    {
```

Fig. 10.8 | BasePlusCommissionEmployee class extends CommissionEmployee. (Part 1 of 2.)

```
19           baseSalary = ( salary < 0.0 ) ? 0.0 : salary; // non-negative
20        } // end method setBaseSalary
21
22        // return base salary
23        public double getBaseSalary()
24        {
25           return baseSalary;
26        } // end method getBaseSalary
27
28        // calculate earnings; override method earnings in CommissionEmployee
29        @Override
30        public double earnings()
31        {
32           return getBaseSalary() + super.earnings();
33        } // end method earnings
34
35        // return String representation of BasePlusCommissionEmployee object
36        @Override
37        public String toString()
38        {
39           return String.format( "%s %s; %s: $%,.2f",
40              "base-salaried", super.toString(),
41              "base salary", getBaseSalary() );
42        } // end method toString
43     } // end class BasePlusCommissionEmployee
```

Fig. 10.8 │ BasePlusCommissionEmployee class extends CommissionEmployee. (Part 2 of 2.)

10.5.6 Polymorphic Processing, Operator instanceof and Downcasting

To test our Employee hierarchy, the application in Fig. 10.9 creates an object of each of the four concrete classes SalariedEmployee, HourlyEmployee, CommissionEmployee and BasePlusCommissionEmployee. The program manipulates these objects nonpolymorphically, via variables of each object's own type, then polymorphically, using an array of Employee variables. While processing the objects polymorphically, the program increases the base salary of each BasePlusCommissionEmployee by 10%—this requires *determining the object's type at execution time.* Finally, the program polymorphically determines and outputs the type of each object in the Employee array. Lines 9–18 create objects of each of the four concrete Employee subclasses. Lines 22–30 output the String representation and earnings of each of these objects nonpolymorphically. Note that each object's toString method is called implicitly by printf when the object is output as a String with the %s format specifier.

```
1     // Fig. 10.9: PayrollSystemTest.java
2     // Employee hierarchy test program.
3
4     public class PayrollSystemTest
5     {
6        public static void main( String[] args )
7        {
```

Fig. 10.9 │ Employee hierarchy test program. (Part 1 of 4.)

```
8      // create subclass objects
9      SalariedEmployee salariedEmployee =
10        new SalariedEmployee( "John", "Smith", "111-11-1111", 800.00 );
11     HourlyEmployee hourlyEmployee =
12        new HourlyEmployee( "Karen", "Price", "222-22-2222", 16.75, 40 );
13     CommissionEmployee commissionEmployee =
14        new CommissionEmployee(
15        "Sue", "Jones", "333-33-3333", 10000, .06 );
16     BasePlusCommissionEmployee basePlusCommissionEmployee =
17        new BasePlusCommissionEmployee(
18        "Bob", "Lewis", "444-44-4444", 5000, .04, 300 );
19
20     System.out.println( "Employees processed individually:\n" );
21
22     System.out.printf( "%s\n%s: $%,.2f\n\n",
23        salariedEmployee, "earned", salariedEmployee.earnings() );
24     System.out.printf( "%s\n%s: $%,.2f\n\n",
25        hourlyEmployee, "earned", hourlyEmployee.earnings() );
26     System.out.printf( "%s\n%s: $%,.2f\n\n",
27        commissionEmployee, "earned", commissionEmployee.earnings() );
28     System.out.printf( "%s\n%s: $%,.2f\n\n",
29        basePlusCommissionEmployee,
30        "earned", basePlusCommissionEmployee.earnings() );
31
32     // create four-element Employee array
33     Employee[] employees = new Employee[ 4 ];
34
35     // initialize array with Employees
36     employees[ 0 ] = salariedEmployee;
37     employees[ 1 ] = hourlyEmployee;
38     employees[ 2 ] = commissionEmployee;
39     employees[ 3 ] = basePlusCommissionEmployee;
40
41     System.out.println( "Employees processed polymorphically:\n" );
42
43     // generically process each element in array employees
44     for ( Employee currentEmployee : employees )
45     {
46        System.out.println( currentEmployee ); // invokes toString
47
48        // determine whether element is a BasePlusCommissionEmployee
49        if ( currentEmployee instanceof BasePlusCommissionEmployee )
50        {
51           // downcast Employee reference to
52           // BasePlusCommissionEmployee reference
53           BasePlusCommissionEmployee employee =
54              ( BasePlusCommissionEmployee ) currentEmployee;
55
56           employee.setBaseSalary( 1.10 * employee.getBaseSalary() );
57
58           System.out.printf(
59              "new base salary with 10%% increase is: $%,.2f\n",
60              employee.getBaseSalary() );
61        } // end if
```

Fig. 10.9 | Employee hierarchy test program. (Part 2 of 4.)

```
62
63              System.out.printf(
64                  "earned $%,.2f\n\n", currentEmployee.earnings() );
65          } // end for
66
67          // get type name of each object in employees array
68          for ( int j = 0; j < employees.length; j++ )
69              System.out.printf( "Employee %d is a %s\n", j,
70                  employees[ j ].getClass().getName() );
71      } // end main
72  } // end class PayrollSystemTest
```

```
Employees processed individually:

salaried employee: John Smith
social security number: 111-11-1111
weekly salary: $800.00
earned: $800.00

hourly employee: Karen Price
social security number: 222-22-2222
hourly wage: $16.75; hours worked: 40.00
earned: $670.00

commission employee: Sue Jones
social security number: 333-33-3333
gross sales: $10,000.00; commission rate: 0.06
earned: $600.00

base-salaried commission employee: Bob Lewis
social security number: 444-44-4444
gross sales: $5,000.00; commission rate: 0.04; base salary: $300.00
earned: $500.00

Employees processed polymorphically:

salaried employee: John Smith
social security number: 111-11-1111
weekly salary: $800.00
earned $800.00

hourly employee: Karen Price
social security number: 222-22-2222
hourly wage: $16.75; hours worked: 40.00
earned $670.00

commission employee: Sue Jones
social security number: 333-33-3333
gross sales: $10,000.00; commission rate: 0.06
earned $600.00

base-salaried commission employee: Bob Lewis
social security number: 444-44-4444
gross sales: $5,000.00; commission rate: 0.04; base salary: $300.00
new base salary with 10% increase is: $330.00
earned $530.00
```

Fig. 10.9 | Employee hierarchy test program. (Part 3 of 4.)

```
Employee 0 is a SalariedEmployee
Employee 1 is a HourlyEmployee
Employee 2 is a CommissionEmployee
Employee 3 is a BasePlusCommissionEmployee
```

Fig. 10.9 | Employee hierarchy test program. (Part 4 of 4.)

Creating the Array of *Employees*

Line 33 declares employees and assigns it an array of four Employee variables. Line 36 assigns the reference to a SalariedEmployee object to employees[0]. Line 37 assigns the reference to an HourlyEmployee object to employees[1]. Line 38 assigns the reference to a CommissionEmployee object to employees[2]. Line 39 assigns the reference to a BasePlusCommissionEmployee object to employee[3]. These assignments are allowed, because a SalariedEmployee *is an* Employee, an HourlyEmployee *is an* Employee, a CommissionEmployee *is an* Employee and a BasePlusCommissionEmployee *is an* Employee. Therefore, we can assign the references of SalariedEmployee, HourlyEmployee, CommissionEmployee and BasePlusCommissionEmployee objects to superclass Employee variables, *even though Employee is an abstract class.*

Polymorphically Processing *Employees*

Lines 44–65 iterate through array employees and invoke methods toString and earnings with Employee variable currentEmployee, which is assigned the reference to a different Employee in the array on each iteration. The output illustrates that the appropriate methods for each class are indeed invoked. All calls to method toString and earnings are resolved at execution time, based on the type of the object to which currentEmployee refers. This process is known as **dynamic binding** or **late binding**. For example, line 46 implicitly invokes method toString of the object to which currentEmployee refers. As a result of dynamic binding, Java decides which class's toString method to call *at execution time rather than at compile time.* Note that only the methods of class Employee can be called via an Employee variable (and Employee, of course, includes the methods of class Object). A superclass reference can be used to invoke only methods of the superclass—the subclass method implementations are invoked polymorphically.

Performing Type-Specific Operations on *BasePlusCommissionEmployees*

We perform special processing on BasePlusCommissionEmployee objects—as we encounter these objects, we increase their base salary by 10%. When processing objects polymorphically, we typically do not need to worry about the "specifics," but to adjust the base salary, we do have to determine the specific type of Employee object at execution time. Line 49 uses the **instanceof** operator to determine whether a particular Employee object's type is BasePlusCommissionEmployee. The condition in line 49 is true if the object referenced by currentEmployee *is a* BasePlusCommissionEmployee. This would also be true for any object of a BasePlusCommissionEmployee subclass because of the *is-a* relationship a subclass has with its superclass. Lines 53–54 downcast currentEmployee from type Employee to type BasePlusCommissionEmployee—this cast is allowed only if the object has an *is-a* relationship with BasePlusCommissionEmployee. The condition at line 49 ensures that this is the case. This cast is required if we are to invoke subclass BasePlusCommissionEmployee methods getBaseSalary and setBaseSalary on the current Employee object—

as you'll see momentarily, attempting to invoke a subclass-only method directly on a superclass reference is a compilation error.

Common Programming Error 10.3
Assigning a superclass variable to a subclass variable (without an explicit cast) is a compilation error.

Software Engineering Observation 10.4
If at execution time the reference of a subclass object has been assigned to a variable of one of its direct or indirect superclasses, it's acceptable to downcast the reference stored in that superclass variable back to a reference of the subclass type. Before performing such a cast, use the instanceof *operator to ensure that the object is indeed an object of an appropriate subclass type.*

Common Programming Error 10.4
When downcasting an object, a ClassCastException *occurs if at execution time the object does not have an* is-a *relationship with the type specified in the cast operator. A reference can be cast only to its own type or to the type of one of its superclasses.*

If the instanceof expression in line 49 is true, lines 53–60 perform the special processing required for the BasePlusCommissionEmployee object. Using BasePlusCommissionEmployee variable employee, line 56 invokes subclass-only methods getBaseSalary and setBaseSalary to retrieve and update the employee's base salary with the 10% raise.

Calling **earnings** *Polymorphically*
Lines 63–64 invoke method earnings on currentEmployee, which polymorphically calls the appropriate subclass object's earnings method. Obtaining the earnings of the SalariedEmployee, HourlyEmployee and CommissionEmployee polymorphically in lines 63–64 produces the same results as obtaining these employees' earnings individually in lines 22–27. The earnings amount obtained for the BasePlusCommissionEmployee in lines 63–64 is higher than that obtained in lines 28–30, due to the 10% increase in its base salary.

Polymorphically Processing **Employees**
Lines 68–70 display each employee's type as a String. Every object in Java knows its own class and can access this information through the **getClass** method, which all classes inherit from class Object. The getClass method returns an object of type **Class** (from package java.lang), which contains information about the object's type, including its class name. Line 70 invokes getClass on the current object to get its runtime class. The result of the getClass call is used to invoke **getName** to get the object's class name. To learn more about class Class, see its online documentation at java.sun.com/javase/6/docs/api/java/lang/Class.html.

Avoiding Compilation Errors with Downcasting
In the previous example, we avoided several compilation errors by downcasting an Employee variable to a BasePlusCommissionEmployee variable in lines 53–54. If you remove the cast operator (BasePlusCommissionEmployee) from line 54 and attempt to assign Employee variable currentEmployee directly to BasePlusCommissionEmployee variable employee, you'll receive an "incompatible types" compilation error. This error indicates that the attempt to assign the reference of superclass object currentEmployee to subclass variable employee is not allowed. The compiler prevents this assignment because a Com-

missionEmployee is not a BasePlusCommissionEmployee—the *is-a* relationship applies only between the subclass and its superclasses, not vice versa.

Similarly, if lines 56 and 60 used superclass variable currentEmployee to invoke subclass-only methods getBaseSalary and setBaseSalary, we'd receive "cannot find symbol" compilation errors on these lines. Attempting to invoke subclass-only methods via a superclass variable is not allowed—even though lines 56 and 60 execute only if instanceof in line 49 returns true to indicate that currentEmployee holds a reference to a BasePlusCommissionEmployee object. Using a superclass Employee variable, we can invoke only methods found in class Employee—earnings, toString and Employee's *get* and *set* methods.

Software Engineering Observation 10.5

Although the actual method that is called depends on the runtime type of the object to which a variable refers, a variable can be used to invoke only those methods that are members of that variable's type, which the compiler verifies.

10.5.7 Summary of the Allowed Assignments Between Superclass and Subclass Variables

Now that you've seen a complete application that processes diverse subclass objects polymorphically, we summarize what you can and cannot do with superclass and subclass objects and variables. Although a subclass object also *is a* superclass object, the two objects are nevertheless different. As discussed previously, subclass objects can be treated as if they were superclass objects. But because the subclass can have additional subclass-only members, assigning a superclass reference to a subclass variable is not allowed without an explicit cast—such an assignment would leave the subclass members undefined for the superclass object.

We've discussed four ways to assign superclass and subclass references to variables of superclass and subclass types:

1. Assigning a superclass reference to a superclass variable is straightforward.

2. Assigning a subclass reference to a subclass variable is straightforward.

3. Assigning a subclass reference to a superclass variable is safe, because the subclass object *is an* object of its superclass. However, the superclass variable can be used to refer only to superclass members. If this code refers to subclass-only members through the superclass variable, the compiler reports errors.

4. Attempting to assign a superclass reference to a subclass variable is a compilation error. To avoid this error, the superclass reference must be cast to a subclass type explicitly. At *execution time*, if the object to which the reference refers is not a subclass object, an exception will occur. (For more on exception handling, see Chapter 11.) You should use the instanceof operator to ensure that such a cast is performed only if the object is a subclass object.

10.6 final Methods and Classes

We saw in Sections 6.3 and 6.10 that variables can be declared final to indicate that they cannot be modified after they're initialized—such variables represent constant values. It's also possible to declare methods, method parameters and classes with the final modifier.

Final Methods Cannot Be Overridden

A **final method** in a superclass cannot be overridden in a subclass. Methods that are declared private are implicitly final, because it's not possible to override them in a subclass. Methods that are declared static are also implicitly final. A final method's declaration can never change, so all subclasses use the same method implementation, and calls to final methods are resolved at compile time—this is known as **static binding**.

Final Classes Cannot Be Superclasses

A **final class** that is declared final cannot be a superclass (i.e., a class cannot extend a final class). All methods in a final class are implicitly final. Class String is an example of a final class. If you were allowed to create a subclass of String, objects of that subclass could be used wherever Strings are expected. Since class String cannot be extended, programs that use Strings can rely on the functionality of String objects as specified in the Java API. Making the class final also prevents programmers from creating subclasses that might bypass security restrictions. For more insights on the use of keyword final, visit

> java.sun.com/docs/books/tutorial/java/IandI/final.html

and

> www.ibm.com/developerworks/java/library/j-jtp1029.html

Common Programming Error 10.5

Attempting to declare a subclass of a final class is a compilation error.

Software Engineering Observation 10.6

In the Java API, the vast majority of classes are not declared final. This enables inheritance and polymorphism. However, in some cases, it's important to declare classes final—typically for security reasons.

10.7 Case Study: Creating and Using Interfaces

Our next example (Figs. 10.11–10.15) reexamines the payroll system of Section 10.5. Suppose that the company involved wishes to perform several accounting operations in a single accounts payable application—in addition to calculating the earnings that must be paid to each employee, the company must also calculate the payment due on each of several invoices (i.e., bills for goods purchased). Though applied to unrelated things (i.e., employees and invoices), both operations have to do with obtaining some kind of payment amount. For an employee, the payment refers to the employee's earnings. For an invoice, the payment refers to the total cost of the goods listed on the invoice. Can we calculate such different things as the payments due for employees and invoices in a single application polymorphically? Does Java offer a capability requiring that unrelated classes implement a set of common methods (e.g., a method that calculates a payment amount)? Java **interfaces** offer exactly this capability.

Standardizing Interactions

Interfaces define and standardize the ways in which things such as people and systems can interact with one another. For example, the controls on a radio serve as an interface between radio users and a radio's internal components. The controls allow users to perform only a limited set of operations (e.g., change the station, adjust the volume, choose between AM and FM), and different radios may implement the controls in different ways (e.g., using push buttons, dials, voice commands). The interface specifies *what* operations a radio must permit users to perform but does not specify *how* the operations are performed.

Software Objects Communicate Via Interfaces

Software objects also communicate via interfaces. A Java interface describes a set of methods that can be called on an object to tell it, for example, to perform some task or return some piece of information. The next example introduces an interface named `Payable` to describe the functionality of any object that must be capable of being paid and thus must offer a method to determine the proper payment amount due. An **interface declaration** begins with the keyword **interface** and contains only constants and `abstract` methods. Unlike classes, all interface members must be `public`, and *interfaces may not specify any implementation details*, such as concrete method declarations and instance variables. All methods declared in an interface are implicitly `public abstract` methods, and all fields are implicitly `public`, `static` and `final`. [*Note:* As of Java SE 5, it became a better programming practice to declare sets of constants as enumerations with keyword enum. See Section 6.10 for an introduction to enum and Section 8.9 for additional enum details.]

Good Programming Practice 10.1

According to Chapter 9 of the Java Language Specification, *it's proper style to declare an interface's methods without keywords* `public` *and* `abstract`, *because they are redundant in interface method declarations. Similarly, constants should be declared without keywords* `public`, `static` *and* `final`, *because they, too, are redundant.*

Using an Interface

To use an interface, a concrete class must specify that it **implements** the interface and must declare each method in the interface with the signature specified in the interface declaration. To specify that a class implements an interface add the `implements` keyword and the name of the interface to the end of your class declaration's first line. A class that does not implement all the methods of the interface is an abstract class and must be declared `abstract`. Implementing an interface is like signing a contract with the compiler that states, "I will declare all the methods specified by the interface or I will declare my class `abstract`."

Common Programming Error 10.6

Failing to implement any method of an interface in a concrete class that `implements` *the interface results in a compilation error indicating that the class must be declared* `abstract`.

Relating Disparate Types

An interface is often used when disparate (i.e., unrelated) classes need to share common methods and constants. This allows objects of unrelated classes to be processed polymorphically—objects of classes that implement the same interface can respond to the same method calls. You can create an interface that describes the desired functionality, then implement this interface in any classes that require that functionality. For example, in the accounts payable application developed in this section, we implement interface `Payable` in any class that must be able to calculate a payment amount (e.g., `Employee`, `Invoice`).

Interfaces vs. Abstract Classes

An interface is often used in place of an abstract class when there is no default implementation to inherit—that is, no fields and no default method implementations. Like public abstract classes, interfaces are typically public types. Like a public class, a public interface must be declared in a file with the same name as the interface and the .java file-name extension.

Tagging Interfaces

We'll see in Chapter 17, Files, Streams and Object Serialization, the notion of "tagging interfaces"—empty interfaces that have *no* methods or constant values. They are used to add *is-a* relationships to classes. For example, in Chapter 17 we'll discuss a Java mechanism called object serialization, which can convert objects to byte representations and can convert those byte representations back to objects. To enable this mechanism to work with your objects, you simply have to mark them as Serializable by adding implements Serializable to the end of your class declaration's first line. Then, all the objects of your class have the *is-a* relationship with Serializable.

10.7.1 Developing a Payable Hierarchy

To build an application that can determine payments for employees and invoices alike, we first create interface Payable, which contains method getPaymentAmount that returns a double amount that must be paid for an object of any class that implements the interface. Method getPaymentAmount is a general-purpose version of method earnings of the Employee hierarchy—method earnings calculates a payment amount specifically for an Employee, while getPaymentAmount can be applied to a broad range of unrelated objects. After declaring interface Payable, we introduce class Invoice, which implements interface Payable. We then modify class Employee such that it also implements interface Payable. Finally, we update Employee subclass SalariedEmployee to "fit" into the Payable hierarchy by renaming SalariedEmployee method earnings as getPaymentAmount.

 Good Programming Practice 10.2

When declaring a method in an interface, choose a method name that describes the method's purpose in a general manner, because the method may be implemented by many unrelated classes.

Classes Invoice and Employee both represent things for which the company must be able to calculate a payment amount. Both classes implement the Payable interface, so a program can invoke method getPaymentAmount on Invoice objects and Employee objects alike. As we'll soon see, this enables the polymorphic processing of Invoices and Employees required for the company's accounts payable application.

The UML class diagram in Fig. 10.10 shows the hierarchy used in our accounts payable application. The hierarchy begins with interface Payable. The UML distinguishes an interface from other classes by placing the word "interface" in guillemets (« and ») above the interface name. The UML expresses the relationship between a class and an interface through a relationship known as **realization**. A class is said to "realize," or implement, the methods of an interface. A class diagram models a realization as a dashed arrow with a hollow arrowhead pointing from the implementing class to the interface. The diagram in Fig. 10.10 indicates that classes Invoice and Employee each realize (i.e., implement) interface `Payable`. Note that, as in the class diagram of Fig. 10.2, class `Employee` appears in italics, indicating that it's an abstract class. Concrete class `SalariedEmployee` extends `Employee` and *inherits its superclass's realization relationship* with interface `Payable`.

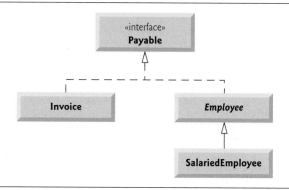

Fig. 10.10 | `Payable` interface hierarchy UML class diagram.

10.7.2 Interface Payable

The declaration of interface `Payable` begins in Fig. 10.11 at line 4. Interface `Payable` contains `public abstract` method `getPaymentAmount` (line 6). Note that the method is not explicitly declared `public` or `abstract`. Interface methods are always `public` and `abstract`, so they do not need to be declared as such. Interface `Payable` has only one method—interfaces can have any number of methods. In addition, method `getPaymentAmount` has no parameters, but interface methods *can* have parameters. Note that interfaces may also contain fields that are implicitly `final` and `static`.

```
1   // Fig. 10.11: Payable.java
2   // Payable interface declaration.
3
4   public interface Payable
5   {
6      double getPaymentAmount(); // calculate payment; no implementation
7   } // end interface Payable
```

Fig. 10.11 | `Payable` interface declaration.

10.7.3 Class Invoice

We now create class `Invoice` (Fig. 10.12) to represent a simple invoice that contains billing information for only one kind of part. The class declares `private` instance variables `partNumber`, `partDescription`, `quantity` and `pricePerItem` (in lines 6–9) that indicate the part number, a description of the part, the quantity of the part ordered and the price per item. Class `Invoice` also contains a constructor (lines 12–19), *get* and *set* methods (lines 22–67) that manipulate the class's instance variables and a `toString` method (lines 70–76) that returns a `String` representation of an `Invoice` object. Note that methods `setQuantity` (lines 46–49) and `setPricePerItem` (lines 58–61) ensure that `quantity` and `pricePerItem` obtain only nonnegative values.

```
1   // Fig. 10.12: Invoice.java
2   // Invoice class implements Payable.
3
4   public class Invoice implements Payable
5   {
6      private String partNumber;
7      private String partDescription;
8      private int quantity;
9      private double pricePerItem;
10
11     // four-argument constructor
12     public Invoice( String part, String description, int count,
13        double price )
14     {
15        partNumber = part;
16        partDescription = description;
17        setQuantity( count ); // validate and store quantity
18        setPricePerItem( price ); // validate and store price per item
19     } // end four-argument Invoice constructor
20
21     // set part number
22     public void setPartNumber( String part )
23     {
24        partNumber = part; // should validate
25     } // end method setPartNumber
26
27     // get part number
28     public String getPartNumber()
29     {
30        return partNumber;
31     } // end method getPartNumber
32
33     // set description
34     public void setPartDescription( String description )
35     {
36        partDescription = description; // should validate
37     } // end method setPartDescription
38
39     // get description
40     public String getPartDescription()
41     {
42        return partDescription;
43     } // end method getPartDescription
44
45     // set quantity
46     public void setQuantity( int count )
47     {
48        quantity = ( count < 0 ) ? 0 : count; // quantity cannot be negative
49     } // end method setQuantity
50
51     // get quantity
52     public int getQuantity()
53     {
```

Fig. 10.12 | Invoice class that implements Payable. (Part 1 of 2.)

```
54        return quantity;
55    } // end method getQuantity
56
57    // set price per item
58    public void setPricePerItem( double price )
59    {
60        pricePerItem = ( price < 0.0 ) ? 0.0 : price; // validate price
61    } // end method setPricePerItem
62
63    // get price per item
64    public double getPricePerItem()
65    {
66        return pricePerItem;
67    } // end method getPricePerItem
68
69    // return String representation of Invoice object
70    @Override
71    public String toString()
72    {
73        return String.format( "%s: \n%s: %s (%s) \n%s: %d \n%s: $%,.2f",
74            "invoice", "part number", getPartNumber(), getPartDescription(),
75            "quantity", getQuantity(), "price per item", getPricePerItem() );
76    } // end method toString
77
78    // method required to carry out contract with interface Payable
79    @Override
80    public double getPaymentAmount()
81    {
82        return getQuantity() * getPricePerItem(); // calculate total cost
83    } // end method getPaymentAmount
84 } // end class Invoice
```

Fig. 10.12 | Invoice class that implements Payable. (Part 2 of 2.)

Line 4 indicates that class Invoice implements interface Payable. Like all classes, class Invoice also implicitly extends Object. Java does not allow subclasses to inherit from more than one superclass, but it allows a class to inherit from one superclass and implement as many interfaces as it needs. To implement more than one interface, use a comma-separated list of interface names after keyword implements in the class declaration, as in:

> public class *ClassName* extends *SuperclassName* implements *FirstInterface*,
> *SecondInterface*, ...

Software Engineering Observation 10.7

All objects of a class that implement multiple interfaces have the is-a *relationship with each implemented interface type.*

Class Invoice implements the one method in interface Payable—method getPaymentAmount is declared in lines 79–83. The method calculates the total payment required to pay the invoice. The method multiplies the values of quantity and pricePerItem (obtained through the appropriate *get* methods) and returns the result (line 82). This method satisfies the implementation requirement for this method in interface Payable—we've fulfilled the interface contract with the compiler.

10.7.4 Modifying Class Employee to Implement Interface Payable

We now modify class Employee such that it implements interface Payable. Figure 10.13 contains the modified class, which is identical to that of Fig. 10.4 with two exceptions. First, line 4 of Fig. 10.13 indicates that class Employee now implements interface Payable. So we must rename earnings to getPaymentAmount throughout the Employee hierarchy. As with method earnings in the version of class Employee in Fig. 10.4, however, it does not make sense to implement method getPaymentAmount in class Employee because we cannot calculate the earnings payment owed to a general Employee—we must first know the specific type of Employee. In Fig. 10.4, we declared method earnings as abstract for this reason, so class Employee had to be declared abstract. This forced each Employee concrete subclass to override earnings with an implementation.

In Fig. 10.13, we handle this situation differently. Recall that when a class implements an interface, it makes a contract with the compiler stating either that the class will implement each of the methods in the interface or that the class will be declared abstract. If the latter option is chosen, we do not need to declare the interface methods as abstract in the abstract class—they are already implicitly declared as such in the interface. Any concrete subclass of the abstract class must implement the interface methods to fulfill the superclass's contract with the compiler. If the subclass does not do so, it too must be declared abstract. As indicated by the comments in lines 62–63, class Employee of Fig. 10.13 does not implement method getPaymentAmount, so the class is declared abstract. Each direct Employee subclass inherits the superclass's contract to implement method getPaymentAmount and thus must implement this method to become a concrete class for which objects can be instantiated. A class that extends one of Employee's concrete subclasses will inherit an implementation of getPaymentAmount and thus will also be a concrete class.

```java
1   // Fig. 10.13: Employee.java
2   // Employee abstract superclass implements Payable.
3
4   public abstract class Employee implements Payable
5   {
6      private String firstName;
7      private String lastName;
8      private String socialSecurityNumber;
9
10     // three-argument constructor
11     public Employee( String first, String last, String ssn )
12     {
13        firstName = first;
14        lastName = last;
15        socialSecurityNumber = ssn;
16     } // end three-argument Employee constructor
17
18     // set first name
19     public void setFirstName( String first )
20     {
21        firstName = first; // should validate
22     } // end method setFirstName
```

Fig. 10.13 | Employee class that implements Payable. (Part 1 of 2.)

```
23
24       // return first name
25       public String getFirstName()
26       {
27          return firstName;
28       } // end method getFirstName
29
30       // set last name
31       public void setLastName( String last )
32       {
33          lastName = last; // should validate
34       } // end method setLastName
35
36       // return last name
37       public String getLastName()
38       {
39          return lastName;
40       } // end method getLastName
41
42       // set social security number
43       public void setSocialSecurityNumber( String ssn )
44       {
45          socialSecurityNumber = ssn; // should validate
46       } // end method setSocialSecurityNumber
47
48       // return social security number
49       public String getSocialSecurityNumber()
50       {
51          return socialSecurityNumber;
52       } // end method getSocialSecurityNumber
53
54       // return String representation of Employee object
55       @Override
56       public String toString()
57       {
58          return String.format( "%s %s\nsocial security number: %s",
59             getFirstName(), getLastName(), getSocialSecurityNumber() );
60       } // end method toString
61
62       // Note: We do not implement Payable method getPaymentAmount here so
63       // this class must be declared abstract to avoid a compilation error.
64   } // end abstract class Employee
```

Fig. 10.13 | Employee class that implements Payable. (Part 2 of 2.)

10.7.5 Modifying Class SalariedEmployee for Use in the Payable Hierarchy

Figure 10.14 contains a modified SalariedEmployee class that extends Employee and fulfills superclass Employee's contract to implement Payable method getPaymentAmount. This version of SalariedEmployee is identical to that of Fig. 10.5, but it replaces method earnings with method getPaymentAmount (lines 30–34). Recall that the Payable version of the method has a more general name to be applicable to possibly disparate classes. The remaining Employee subclasses (e.g., HourlyEmployee, CommissionEmployee and BasePlusCommissionEmployee) also must be modified to contain method getPaymentAmount in place of earnings to reflect the fact that Employee now implements Payable. We leave these modifications as an exercise (Exercise 10.8) and use only SalariedEmployee in our test program here. Exercise 10.9 asks you to implement interface Payable in the entire Employee class hierarchy of Figs. 10.4–10.9 without modifying the Employee subclasses.

```
 1    // Fig. 10.14: SalariedEmployee.java
 2    // SalariedEmployee class extends Employee, which implements Payable.
 3
 4    public class SalariedEmployee extends Employee
 5    {
 6       private double weeklySalary;
 7
 8       // four-argument constructor
 9       public SalariedEmployee( String first, String last, String ssn,
10          double salary )
11       {
12          super( first, last, ssn ); // pass to Employee constructor
13          setWeeklySalary( salary ); // validate and store salary
14       } // end four-argument SalariedEmployee constructor
15
16       // set salary
17       public void setWeeklySalary( double salary )
18       {
19          weeklySalary = salary < 0.0 ? 0.0 : salary;
20       } // end method setWeeklySalary
21
22       // return salary
23       public double getWeeklySalary()
24       {
25          return weeklySalary;
26       } // end method getWeeklySalary
27
28       // calculate earnings; implement interface Payable method that was
29       // abstract in superclass Employee
30       @Override
31       public double getPaymentAmount()
32       {
33          return getWeeklySalary();
34       } // end method getPaymentAmount
35
36       // return String representation of SalariedEmployee object
37       @Override
38       public String toString()
39       {
40          return String.format( "salaried employee: %s\n%s: $%,.2f",
41             super.toString(), "weekly salary", getWeeklySalary() );
42       } // end method toString
43    } // end class SalariedEmployee
```

Fig. 10.14 | SalariedEmployee class that implements interface Payable method getPaymentAmount.

When a class implements an interface, the same *is-a* relationship provided by inheritance applies. Class Employee implements Payable, so we can say that an Employee *is a*

Payable. In fact, objects of any classes that extend Employee are also Payable objects. SalariedEmployee objects, for instance, are Payable objects. Objects of any subclasses of the class that implements the interface can also be thought of as objects of the interface type. Thus, just as we can assign the reference of a SalariedEmployee object to a superclass Employee variable, we can assign the reference of a SalariedEmployee object to an interface Payable variable. Invoice implements Payable, so an Invoice object also *is a* Payable object, and we can assign the reference of an Invoice object to a Payable variable.

Software Engineering Observation 10.8
When a method parameter is declared with a superclass or interface type, the method processes the object received as an argument polymorphically.

Software Engineering Observation 10.9
Using a superclass reference, we can polymorphically invoke any method declared in the superclass and its superclasses (e.g., class Object). Using an interface reference, we can polymorphically invoke any method declared in the interface, its superinterfaces (one interface can extend another) and in class Object—a variable of an interface type must refer to an object to call methods, and all objects have the methods of class Object.

10.7.6 Using Interface Payable to Process Invoices and Employees Polymorphically

PayableInterfaceTest (Fig. 10.15) illustrates that interface Payable can be used to process a set of Invoices and Employees polymorphically in a single application. Line 9 declares payableObjects and assigns it an array of four Payable variables. Lines 12–13 assign the references of Invoice objects to the first two elements of payableObjects. Lines 14–17 then assign the references of SalariedEmployee objects to the remaining two elements of payableObjects. These assignments are allowed because an Invoice *is a* Payable, a SalariedEmployee *is an* Employee and an Employee *is a* Payable. Lines 23–29 use the enhanced for statement to polymorphically process each Payable object in payableObjects, printing the object as a String, along with the payment amount due. Note that line 27 invokes method toString via a Payable interface reference, even though toString is not declared in interface Payable—all references (including those of interface types) refer to objects that extend Object and therefore have a toString method. (Note that toString also can be invoked implicitly here.) Line 28 invokes Payable method getPaymentAmount to obtain the payment amount for each object in payableObjects, regardless of the actual type of the object. The output reveals that the method calls in lines 27–28 invoke the appropriate class's implementation of methods toString and getPaymentAmount. For instance, when currentPayable refers to an Invoice during the first iteration of the for loop, class Invoice's toString and getPaymentAmount execute.

```
1   // Fig. 10.15: PayableInterfaceTest.java
2   // Tests interface Payable.
3
```

Fig. 10.15 | Payable interface test program processing Invoices and Employees polymorphically. (Part 1 of 2.)

```
4   public class PayableInterfaceTest
5   {
6      public static void main( String[] args )
7      {
8         // create four-element Payable array
9         Payable[] payableObjects = new Payable[ 4 ];
10
11        // populate array with objects that implement Payable
12        payableObjects[ 0 ] = new Invoice( "01234", "seat", 2, 375.00 );
13        payableObjects[ 1 ] = new Invoice( "56789", "tire", 4, 79.95 );
14        payableObjects[ 2 ] =
15           new SalariedEmployee( "John", "Smith", "111-11-1111", 800.00 );
16        payableObjects[ 3 ] =
17           new SalariedEmployee( "Lisa", "Barnes", "888-88-8888", 1200.00 );
18
19        System.out.println(
20           "Invoices and Employees processed polymorphically:\n" );
21
22        // generically process each element in array payableObjects
23        for ( Payable currentPayable : payableObjects )
24        {
25           // output currentPayable and its appropriate payment amount
26           System.out.printf( "%s \n%s: $%,.2f\n\n",
27              currentPayable.toString(),
28              "payment due", currentPayable.getPaymentAmount() );
29        } // end for
30     } // end main
31  } // end class PayableInterfaceTest
```

```
Invoices and Employees processed polymorphically:

invoice:
part number: 01234 (seat)
quantity: 2
price per item: $375.00
payment due: $750.00

invoice:
part number: 56789 (tire)
quantity: 4
price per item: $79.95
payment due: $319.80

salaried employee: John Smith
social security number: 111-11-1111
weekly salary: $800.00
payment due: $800.00

salaried employee: Lisa Barnes
social security number: 888-88-8888
weekly salary: $1,200.00
payment due: $1,200.00
```

Fig. 10.15 | Payable interface test program processing Invoices and Employees polymorphically. (Part 2 of 2.)

10.7.7 Common Interfaces of the Java API

In this section, we overview several common interfaces found in the Java API. The power and flexibility of interfaces is used frequently throughout the Java API. These interfaces are implemented and used in the same manner as the interfaces you create (e.g., interface Payable in Section 10.7.2). The Java API's interfaces enable you to use your own classes within the frameworks provided by Java, such as comparing objects of your own types and creating tasks that can execute concurrently with other tasks in the same program. Figure 10.16 presents a brief overview of a few of the more popular interfaces of the Java API that we use in *Java How to Program, Eighth Edition.*

Interface	Description
Comparable	Java contains several comparison operators (e.g., <, <=, >, >=, ==, !=) that allow you to compare primitive values. However, these operators cannot be used to compare objects. Interface Comparable is used to allow objects of a class that implements the interface to be compared to one another. Interface Comparable is commonly used for ordering objects in a collection such as an array. We use Comparable in Chapter 20, Generic Collections, and Chapter 21, Generic Classes and Methods.
Serializable	An interface used to identify classes whose objects can be written to (i.e., serialized) or read from (i.e., deserialized) some type of storage (e.g., file on disk, database field) or transmitted across a network. We use Serializable in Chapter 17, Files, Streams and Object Serialization, and Chapter 27, Networking.
Runnable	Implemented by any class for which objects of that class should be able to execute in parallel using a technique called multi-threading (discussed in Chapter 26, Multithreading). The interface contains one method, run, which describes the behavior of an object when executed.
GUI event-listener interfaces	You work with graphical user interfaces (GUIs) every day. In your web browser, you might type the address of a website to visit, or you might click a button to return to a previous site. The browser responds to your interaction and performs the desired task. Your interaction is known as an event, and the code that the browser uses to respond to an event is known as an event handler. In Chapter 14, GUI Components: Part 1, and Chapter 25, GUI Components: Part 2, you'll learn how to build GUIs and event handlers that respond to user interactions. Event handlers are declared in classes that implement an appropriate event-listener interface. Each event-listener interface specifies one or more methods that must be implemented to respond to user interactions.
SwingConstants	Contains a set of constants used in GUI programming to position GUI elements on the screen. We explore GUI programming in Chapters 14 and 25.

Fig. 10.16 | Common interfaces of the Java API.

10.8 (Optional) GUI and Graphics Case Study: Drawing with Polymorphism

You may have noticed in the drawing program created in GUI and Graphics Case Study Exercise 8.1 (and modified in GUI and Graphics Case Study Exercise 9.1) that shape classes have many similarities. Using inheritance, we can "factor out" the common features from all three classes and place them in a single shape superclass. Then, using variables of the superclass type, we can manipulate objects of all three shape types polymorphically. Removing the redundancy in the code will result in a smaller, more flexible program that is easier to maintain.

GUI and Graphics Case Study Exercises

10.1 Modify the MyLine, MyOval and MyRectangle classes of GUI and Graphics Case Study Exercise 8.1 and Exercise 9.1 to create the class hierarchy in Fig. 10.17. Classes of the MyShape hierarchy should be "smart" shape classes that know how to draw themselves (if provided with a Graphics object that tells them where to draw). Once the program creates an object from this hierarchy, it can manipulate it polymorphically for the rest of its lifetime as a MyShape.

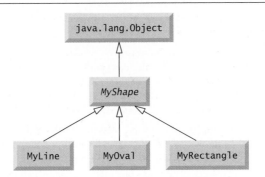

Fig. 10.17 | MyShape hierarchy.

In your solution, class MyShape in Fig. 10.17 *must* be abstract. Since MyShape represents any shape in general, you cannot implement a draw method without knowing exactly what shape it is. The data representing the coordinates and color of the shapes in the hierarchy should be declared as private members of class MyShape. In addition to the common data, class MyShape should declare the following methods:

a) A no-argument constructor that sets all the coordinates of the shape to 0 and the color to Color.BLACK.

b) A constructor that initializes the coordinates and color to the values of the arguments supplied.

c) *Set* methods for the individual coordinates and color that allow the programmer to set any piece of data independently for a shape in the hierarchy.

d) *Get* methods for the individual coordinates and color that allow the programmer to retrieve any piece of data independently for a shape in the hierarchy.

e) The abstract method

```
public abstract void draw( Graphics g );
```

which will be called from the program's paintComponent method to draw a shape on the screen.

To ensure proper encapsulation, all data in class MyShape must be private. This requires declaring proper *set* and *get* methods to manipulate the data. Class MyLine should provide a no-argument constructor and a constructor with arguments for the coordinates and color. Classes MyOval and MyRectangle should provide a no-argument constructor and a constructor with arguments for the coordinates, color and determining whether the shape is filled. The no-argument constructor should, in addition to setting the default values, set the shape to be an unfilled shape.

You can draw lines, rectangles and ovals if you know two points in space. Lines require *x1, y1, x2* and *y2* coordinates. The drawLine method of the Graphics class will connect the two points supplied with a line. If you have the same four coordinate values (*x1, y1, x2* and *y2*) for ovals and rectangles, you can calculate the four arguments needed to draw them. Each requires an upper-left *x*-coordinate value (the smaller of the two *x*-coordinate values), an upper-left *y*-coordinate value (the smaller of the two *y*-coordinate values), a *width* (the absolute value of the difference between the two *x*-coordinate values) and a *height* (the absolute value of the difference between the two *y*-coordinate values). Rectangles and ovals should also have a filled flag that determines whether to draw the shape as a filled shape.

There should be no MyLine, MyOval or MyRectangle variables in the program—only MyShape variables that contain references to MyLine, MyOval and MyRectangle objects. The program should generate random shapes and store them in an array of type MyShape. Method paintComponent should walk through the MyShape array and draw every shape (i.e., polymorphically calling every shape's draw method).

Allow the user to specify (via an input dialog) the number of shapes to generate. The program will then generate and display the shapes along with a status bar that informs the user how many of each shape were created.

10.2 *(Drawing Application Modification)* In Exercise 10.1, you created a MyShape hierarchy in which classes MyLine, MyOval and MyRectangle extend MyShape directly. If your hierarchy was properly designed, you should be able to see the similarities between the MyOval and MyRectangle classes. Redesign and reimplement the code for the MyOval and MyRectangle classes to "factor out" the common features into the abstract class MyBoundedShape to produce the hierarchy in Fig. 10.18.

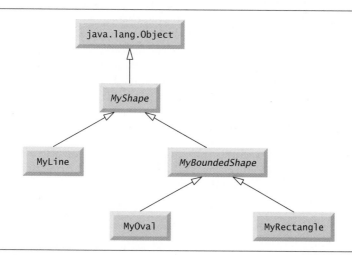

Fig. 10.18 | MyShape hierarchy with MyBoundedShape.

Class MyBoundedShape should declare two constructors that mimic those of class MyShape, only with an added parameter to set whether the shape is filled. Class MyBoundedShape should also declare *get* and *set* methods for manipulating the filled flag and methods that calculate the upper-left *x*-coordinate, upper-left *y*-coordinate, width and height. Remember, the values needed to draw an oval or a rectangle can be calculated from two *(x, y)* coordinates. If designed properly, the new MyOval and MyRectangle classes should each have two constructors and a draw method.

10.9 Wrap-Up

This chapter introduced polymorphism—the ability to process objects that share the same superclass in a class hierarchy as if they are all objects of the superclass. The chapter discussed how polymorphism makes systems extensible and maintainable, then demonstrated how to use overridden methods to effect polymorphic behavior. We introduced abstract classes, which allow you to provide an appropriate superclass from which other classes can inherit. You learned that an abstract class can declare abstract methods that each subclass must implement to become a concrete class and that a program can use variables of an abstract class to invoke the subclasses' implementations of abstract methods polymorphically. You also learned how to determine an object's type at execution time. We discussed the concepts of final methods and classes. Finally, the chapter discussed declaring and implementing an interface as another way to achieve polymorphic behavior.

You should now be familiar with classes, objects, encapsulation, inheritance, interfaces and polymorphism—the most essential aspects of object-oriented programming.

In the next chapter, you'll learn about exceptions, useful for handling errors during a program's execution. Exception handling provides for more robust programs.

Summary

Section 10.1 Introduction

- Polymorphism enables us to write programs that process objects that share the same superclass in a class hierarchy as if they are all objects of the superclass; this can simplify programming.

- With polymorphism, we can design and implement systems that are easily extensible—new classes can be added with little or no modification to the general portions of the program, as long as the new classes are part of the same inheritance hierarchy. The only parts of a program that must be altered to accommodate new classes are those that require direct knowledge of the new classes that you add to the hierarchy.

Section 10.3 Demonstrating Polymorphic Behavior

- When the compiler encounters a method call made through a variable, the compiler determines if the method can be called by checking the variable's class type. If that class contains the proper method declaration (or inherits one), the call is compiled. At execution time, the type of the object to which the variable refers determines the actual method to use.

Section 10.4 Abstract Classes and Methods

- Abstract classes cannot be used to instantiate objects, because they are incomplete.

- The primary purpose of an abstract class is to provide an appropriate superclass from which other classes can inherit and thus share a common design.

- Classes that can be used to instantiate objects are called concrete classes. Such classes provide implementations of every method they declare (some of the implementations can be inherited).

- Not all inheritance hierarchies contain abstract classes. However, programmers often write client code that uses only abstract superclass types to reduce client code's dependencies on a range of specific subclass types.

- Abstract classes sometimes constitute several levels of a hierarchy.

- You make a class abstract by declaring it with keyword `abstract`. An abstract class normally contains one or more abstract methods.

- Abstract methods do not provide implementations.

- A class that contains any abstract methods must be declared as an abstract class even if it contains some concrete methods. Each concrete subclass of an abstract superclass must provide concrete implementations of each of the superclass's abstract methods.

- Constructors and `static` methods cannot be declared `abstract`.

- You *can* use abstract superclasses to declare variables that can hold references to objects of any concrete class derived from those abstract superclasses. Programs typically use such variables to manipulate subclass objects polymorphically.

- Polymorphism is particularly effective for implementing layered software systems.

Section 10.5 Case Study: Payroll System Using Polymorphism

- Including an `abstract` method in a superclass forces every direct subclass of the superclass to override the `abstract` method in order to become a concrete class. This enables the hierarchy designer to demand that each concrete subclass provide an appropriate method implementation.

- Most method calls are resolved at execution time, based on the type of the object being manipulated. This process is known as dynamic binding or late binding.

- A superclass variable can be used to invoke only methods declared in the superclass (and the superclass can invoke overridden versions of these in the subclass).

- The `instanceof` operator can be used to determine whether a particular object's type has the *is-a* relationship with a specific type.

- Every object in Java knows its own class and can access it through method `getClass`, which all classes inherit from class `Object`. Method `getClass` returns an object of type `Class` (package `java.lang`), which contains information about the object's type, including its class name.

- The *is-a* relationship applies only between the subclass and its superclasses, not vice versa.

Section 10.6 `final` Methods and Classes

- A method that is declared `final` in a superclass cannot be overridden in a subclass.

- Methods declared `private` are implicitly `final`, because you can't override them in a subclass.

- Methods that are declared `static` are implicitly `final`.

- A `final` method's declaration can never change, so all subclasses use the same method implementation, and calls to `final` methods are resolved at compile time—this is known as static binding.

- Since the compiler knows that `final` methods cannot be overridden, it can optimize programs by removing calls to `final` methods and replacing them with the expanded code of their declarations at each method-call location—a technique known as inlining the code.

- A class that is declared `final` cannot be a superclass.

- All methods in a `final` class are implicitly `final`.

Section 10.7 Case Study: Creating and Using Interfaces

- An interface specifies *what* operations are allowed but not *how* the operations are performed.

- A Java interface describes a set of methods that can be called on an object.

- An interface declaration begins with the keyword `interface`.

- All interface members must be `public`, and interfaces may not specify any implementation details, such as concrete method declarations and instance variables.

- All methods declared in an interface are implicitly public abstract methods and all fields are implicitly public, static and final.

- To use an interface, a concrete class must specify that it implements the interface and must declare each interface method with the signature specified in the interface declaration. A class that does not implement all the interface's methods must be declared abstract.

- Implementing an interface is like signing a contract with the compiler that states, "I will declare all the methods specified by the interface or I will declare my class abstract."

- An interface is typically used when disparate (i.e., unrelated) classes need to share common methods and constants. This allows objects of unrelated classes to be processed polymorphically—objects of classes that implement the same interface can respond to the same method calls.

- You can create an interface that describes the desired functionality, then implement the interface in any classes that require that functionality.

- An interface is often used in place of an abstract class when there is no default implementation to inherit—that is, no instance variables and no default method implementations.

- Like public abstract classes, interfaces are typically public types, so they are normally declared in files by themselves with the same name as the interface and the .java file-name extension.

- Java does not allow subclasses to inherit from more than one superclass, but it does allow a class to inherit from a superclass and implement more than one interface.

- All objects of a class that implement multiple interfaces have the *is-a* relationship with each implemented interface type.

- An interface can declare constants. The constants are implicitly public, static and final.

Terminology

abstract class 406	getName method of class Class 422
abstract keyword 407	implement an interface 402
abstract method 407	implements keyword 425
abstract superclass 406	instanceof operator 421
Class class 422	interface 424
concrete class 406	interface declaration 425
downcasting 404	interface keyword 425
dynamic binding 421	late binding 421
final class 424	polymorphism 401
final method 424	realization in the UML 426
getClass method of class Object 422	static binding 424

Self-Review Exercises

10.1   Fill in the blanks in each of the following statements:
   a)   If a class contains at least one abstract method, it's a(n) _____ class.
   b)   Classes from which objects can be instantiated are called _____ classes.
   c)   _____ involves using a superclass variable to invoke methods on superclass and subclass objects, enabling you to "program in the general."
   d)   Methods that are not interface methods and that do not provide implementations must be declared using keyword _____.
   e)   Casting a reference stored in a superclass variable to a subclass type is called _____.

10.2   State whether each of the statements that follows is *true* or *false*. If *false*, explain why.
   a)   All methods in an abstract class must be declared as abstract methods.
   b)   Invoking a subclass-only method through a subclass variable is not allowed.
   c)   If a superclass declares an abstract method, a subclass must implement that method.

    d) An object of a class that implements an interface may be thought of as an object of that interface type.

Answers to Self-Review Exercises

10.1 a) abstract. b) concrete. c) Polymorphism. d) abstract. e) downcasting.

10.2 a) False. An abstract class can include methods with implementations and abstract methods. b) False. Trying to invoke a subclass-only method with a superclass variable is no allowed. c) False. Only a concrete subclass must implement the method. d) True.

Exercises

10.3 How does polymorphism enable you to program "in the general" rather than "in the specific"? Discuss the key advantages of programming "in the general."

10.4 How does polymorphism promote extensibility?

10.5 Compare and contrast abstract classes and interfaces. Why would you use an abstract class? Why would you use an interface?

10.6 *(Payroll System Modification)* Modify the payroll system of Figs. 10.4–10.9 to include private instance variable birthDate in class Employee. Use class Date of Fig. 8.7 to represent an employee's birthday. Add *get* methods to class Date. Assume that payroll is processed once per month. Create an array of Employee variables to store references to the various employee objects. In a loop, calculate the payroll for each Employee (polymorphically), and add a $100.00 bonus to the person's payroll amount if the current month is the one in which the Employee's birthday occurs.

10.7 *(Shape Hierarchy)* Implement the Shape hierarchy shown in Fig. 9.3. Each TwoDimensionalShape should contain method getArea to calculate the area of the two-dimensional shape. Each ThreeDimensionalShape should have methods getArea and getVolume to calculate the surface area and volume, respectively, of the three-dimensional shape. Create a program that uses an array of Shape references to objects of each concrete class in the hierarchy. The program should print a text description of the object to which each array element refers. Also, in the loop that processes all the shapes in the array, determine whether each shape is a TwoDimensionalShape or a ThreeDimensionalShape. If it's a TwoDimensionalShape, display its area. If it's a ThreeDimensionalShape, display its area and volume.

10.8 *(Accounts Payable System Modification)* In this exercise, we modify the accounts payable application of Figs. 10.11–10.15 to include the complete functionality of the payroll application of Figs. 10.4–10.9. The application should still process two Invoice objects, but now should process one object of each of the four Employee subclasses. If the object currently being processed is a BasePlusCommissionEmployee, the application should increase the BasePlusCommissionEmployee's base salary by 10%. Finally, the application should output the payment amount for each object. Complete the following steps to create the new application:

    a) Modify classes HourlyEmployee (Fig. 10.6) and CommissionEmployee (Fig. 10.7) to place them in the Payable hierarchy as subclasses of the version of Employee (Fig. 10.13) that implements Payable. [*Hint:* Change the name of method earnings to getPaymentAmount in each subclass so that the class satisfies its inherited contract with interface Payable.]

    b) Modify class BasePlusCommissionEmployee (Fig. 10.8) such that it extends the version of class CommissionEmployee created in part (a).

c) Modify PayableInterfaceTest (Fig. 10.15) to polymorphically process two Invoices, one SalariedEmployee, one HourlyEmployee, one CommissionEmployee and one BasePlusCommissionEmployee. First output a String representation of each Payable object. Next, if an object is a BasePlusCommissionEmployee, increase its base salary by 10%. Finally, output the payment amount for each Payable object.

10.9 *(Accounts Payable System Modification)* It's possible to include the functionality of the payroll application (Figs. 10.4–10.9) in the accounts payable application without modifying Employee subclasses SalariedEmployee, HourlyEmployee, CommissionEmployee or BasePlusCommissionEmplyee. To do so, you can modify class Employee (Fig. 10.4) to implement interface Payable and declare method getPaymentAmount to invoke method earnings. Method getPaymentAmount would then be inherited by the subclasses in the Employee hierarchy. When getPaymentAmount is called for a particular subclass object, it polymorphically invokes the appropriate earnings method for that subclass. Reimplement Exercise 10.8 using the original Employee hierarchy from the payroll application of Figs. 10.4–10.9. Modify class Employee as described in this exercise, and *do not* modify any of class Employee's subclasses.

Making a Difference

10.10 *(CarbonFootprint Interface: Polymorphism)* Using interfaces, as you learned in this chapter, you can specify similar behaviors for possibly disparate classes. Governments and companies worldwide are becoming increasingly concerned with carbon footprints (annual releases of carbon dioxide into the atmosphere) from buildings burning various types of fuels for heat, vehicles burning fuels for power, and the like. Many scientists blame these greenhouse gases for the phenomenon called global warming. Create three small classes unrelated by inheritance—classes Building, Car and Bicycle. Give each class some unique appropriate attributes and behaviors that it does not have in common with other classes. Write an interface CarbonFootprint with a getCarbonFootprint method. Have each of your classes implement that interface, so that its getCarbonFootprint method calculates an appropriate carbon footprint for that class (check out a few websites that explain how to calculate carbon footprints). Write an application that creates objects of each of the three classes, places references to those objects in ArrayList<CarbonFootprint>, then iterates through the ArrayList, polymorphically invoking each object's getCarbonFootprint method. For each object, print some identifying information and the object's carbon footprint.

*It is common sense to take a method and try it. If it
fails, admit it frankly and try another. But above all,
try something.*
—Franklin Delano Roosevelt

*O! throw away the worser part of it,
And live the purer with the other half.*
—William Shakespeare

*If they're running and they don't look where they're
going
I have to come out from somewhere and catch them.*
—Jerome David Salinger

*O infinite virtue! com'st thou smiling from the world's
great snare uncaught?*
—William Shakespeare

Exception Handling

Objectives

In this chapter you'll learn:

- What exceptions are.

- How exception and error handling works.

- To use `try`, `throw` and `catch` to detect, indicate and handle exceptions, respectively.

- To use the `finally` block to release resources.

- How stack unwinding enables exceptions not caught in one scope to be caught in another.

- How stack traces help in debugging.

- How exceptions are arranged in an exception-class hierarchy.

- To declare new exception classes.

- To create chained exceptions that maintain complete stack-trace information.

11.1 Introduction

In this chapter, we introduce **exception handling**. An **exception** is an indication of a problem that occurs during a program's execution. The name "exception" implies that the problem occurs infrequently. With exception handling, a program can continue executing (rather than terminating) after dealing with a problem. This helps ensure the kind of robust applications that contribute to what is called mission-critical or business-critical computing. A more severe problem could prevent a program from continuing normal execution, instead requiring it to notify the user of the problem before terminating in a controlled manner. Java enables you to deal with exception handling easily from the inception of a project. The features presented in this chapter help you write **robust** and **fault-tolerant programs** (i.e., programs that can deal with problems as they arise and continue executing). Java exception handling is based in part on Andrew Koenig's and Bjarne Stroustrup's paper, "Exception Handling for C++ (revised)."[1]

Error-Prevention Tip 11.1
Exception handling helps improve a program's fault tolerance.

In earlier chapters you've been briefly introduced to exceptions. In Chapter 7 you learned that an ArrayIndexOutOfBoundsException occurs when an attempt is made to access an element past either end of an array. Such a problem may occur, for example, if there is an "off-by-one" error in a for statement that manipulates an array. In Chapter 10 we introduced the ClassCastException, which occurs when an attempt is made to cast an object that does not have an *is-a* relationship with the type specified in the cast operator. A NullPointerException can occur when a null reference is used where an object is expected—for example, when an attempt is made to use a reference-type instance variable before it is initialized. Throughout this text you've also used class Scanner—which, as you'll see in this chapter, also may cause exceptions.

We begin with an overview of exception-handling concepts, then demonstrate basic exception-handling techniques. We show these techniques in action by handling an excep-

1. A. Koenig, and B. Stroustrup. "Exception Handling for C++ (revised)," *Proceedings of the Usenix C++ Conference*, pp. 149–176, San Francisco, April 1990.

tion that occurs when a method attempts to divide an integer by zero. Next, we introduce several classes at the top of Java's exception-handling class hierarchy. As you'll see, only classes that extend Throwable (package java.lang) directly or indirectly can be used with exception handling. We then show how to use chained exceptions. When you invoke a method that indicates an exception, you can throw another exception and chain the original one to the new one—this enables you to add application-specific information to the orginal exception. Next, we introduce preconditions and postconditions, which must be true when your methods are called and when they return, respectively. Finally, we present assertions, which you can use at development time to help debug your code.

[*Note:* If you execute the examples in this chapter from an IDE, such as Eclipse or Net-Beans, the outputs of your programs might differ from those shown here.]

11.2 Error-Handling Overview

Programs frequently test conditions to determine how program execution should proceed. Consider the following pseudocode:

> *Perform a task*
>
> *If the preceding task did not execute correctly*
>   *Perform error processing*
>
> *Perform next task*
>
> *If the preceding task did not execute correctly*
>   *Perform error processing*
>
> *...*

This pseudocode begins by performing a task; then tests whether it executed correctly. If not, we perform error processing. Otherwise, we continue with the next task. Although this form of error handling works, intermixing program and error-handling logic can make programs difficult to read, modify, maintain and debug—especially in large applications.

Performance Tip 11.1

If the potential problems occur infrequently, intermixing program and error-handling logic can degrade program performance, because the program must perform potentially frequent tests to determine whether the task executed correctly and the next task can be performed.

Exception handling enables you to remove error-handling code from the "main line" of program execution, improving program clarity and enhancing modifiability. You can decide to handle any exceptions you choose—all exceptions, all exceptions of a certain type or all exceptions of a group of related types (i.e., exception types that are related through a superclass in an inheritance hierarchy). Such flexibility reduces the likelihood that errors will be overlooked, thus making programs more robust.

11.3 Example: Divide by Zero without Exception Handling

First we demonstrate what happens when errors arise in an application that does not use exception handling. Figure 11.1 prompts the user for two integers and passes them to method quotient, which calculates the integer quotient and returns an int result. In this example, you'll see that exceptions are **thrown** (i.e., the exception occurs) when a method detects a problem and is unable to handle it. Note that quotient is declared static, so main can call it directly without creating a DivideByZeroNoExceptionHandling object.

The first of the three sample executions in Fig. 11.1 shows a successful division. In the second sample execution, the user enters the value 0 as the denominator. Notice that several lines of information are displayed in response to this invalid input. This information is known as a **stack trace**, which includes the name of the exception (java.lang.ArithmeticException) in a descriptive message that indicates the problem that occurred and the method-call stack (i.e., the call chain) at the time it occurred. The stack trace includes the path of execution that led to the exception method by method. This information helps you debug the program. The first line specifies that an ArithmeticException has occurred. The text after the name of the exception ("/ by zero") indicates that this exception occurred as a result of an attempt to divide by zero. Java does not allow division by zero in integer arithmetic. When division by zero in integer arithmetic occurs, Java throws an **ArithmeticException**. ArithmeticExceptions can arise from a number of different problems in arithmetic, so the extra data ("/ by zero") provides more specific information. [*Note:* Java *does* allow division by zero with floating-point values. Such a calculation results in the value positive or negative infinity, which is represented in Java as a floating-point value (but displays as the string Infinity or -Infinity). If 0.0 is divided by 0.0, the result is NaN (not a number), which is also represented in Java as a floating-point value (but displays as NaN).]

```java
1   // Fig. 11.1: DivideByZeroNoExceptionHandling.java
2   // Integer division without exception handling.
3   import java.util.Scanner;
4
5   public class DivideByZeroNoExceptionHandling
6   {
7      // demonstrates throwing an exception when a divide-by-zero occurs
8      public static int quotient( int numerator, int denominator )
9      {
10        return numerator / denominator; // possible division by zero
11     } // end method quotient
12
13     public static void main( String[] args )
14     {
15        Scanner scanner = new Scanner( System.in ); // scanner for input
16
17        System.out.print( "Please enter an integer numerator: " );
18        int numerator = scanner.nextInt();
19        System.out.print( "Please enter an integer denominator: " );
20        int denominator = scanner.nextInt();
21
22        int result = quotient( numerator, denominator );
23        System.out.printf(
24           "\nResult: %d / %d = %d\n", numerator, denominator, result );
25     } // end main
26  } // end class DivideByZeroNoExceptionHandling
```

Fig. 11.1 | Integer division without exception handling. (Part 1 of 2.)

```
Please enter an integer numerator: 100
Please enter an integer denominator: 7

Result: 100 / 7 = 14
```

```
Please enter an integer numerator: 100
Please enter an integer denominator: 0
Exception in thread "main" java.lang.ArithmeticException: / by zero
        at DivideByZeroNoExceptionHandling.quotient(
            DivideByZeroNoExceptionHandling.java:10)
        at DivideByZeroNoExceptionHandling.main(
            DivideByZeroNoExceptionHandling.java:22)
```

```
Please enter an integer numerator: 100
Please enter an integer denominator: hello
Exception in thread "main" java.util.InputMismatchException
        at java.util.Scanner.throwFor(Unknown Source)
        at java.util.Scanner.next(Unknown Source)
        at java.util.Scanner.nextInt(Unknown Source)
        at java.util.Scanner.nextInt(Unknown Source)
        at DivideByZeroNoExceptionHandling.main(
            DivideByZeroNoExceptionHandling.java:20)
```

Fig. 11.1 | Integer division without exception handling. (Part 2 of 2.)

Starting from the last line of the stack trace, we see that the exception was detected in line 22 of method main. Each line of the stack trace contains the class name and method (DivideByZeroNoExceptionHandling.main) followed by the file name and line number (DivideByZeroNoExceptionHandling.java:22). Moving up the stack trace, we see that the exception occurs in line 10, in method quotient. The top row of the call chain indicates the **throw point**—the initial point at which the exception occurs. The throw point of this exception is in line 10 of method quotient.

In the third execution, the user enters the string "hello" as the denominator. Notice again that a stack trace is displayed. This informs us that an InputMismatchException has occurred (package java.util). Our prior examples that read numeric values from the user assumed that the user would input a proper integer value. However, users sometimes make mistakes and input noninteger values. An **InputMismatchException** occurs when Scanner method nextInt receives a string that does not represent a valid integer. Starting from the end of the stack trace, we see that the exception was detected in line 20 of method main. Moving up the stack trace, we see that the exception occurred in method nextInt. Notice that in place of the file name and line number, we are provided with the text Unknown Source. This means that the so-called debugging symbols that provide the file-name and line number information for that method's class were not available to the JVM—this is typically the case for the classes of the Java API. Many IDEs have access to the Java API source code and will display file names in stack traces.

Notice that in the sample executions of Fig. 11.1 when exceptions occur and stack traces are displayed, the program also exits. This does not always occur in Java—sometimes a program may continue even though an exception has occurred and a stack trace has been printed. In such cases, the application may produce unexpected results. The next section demonstrates how to handle these exceptions.

In Fig. 11.1 both types of exceptions were detected in method `main`. In the next example, we'll see how to handle these exceptions to enable the program to run to normal completion.

11.4 Example: Handling ArithmeticExceptions and InputMismatchExceptions

The application in Fig. 11.2, which is based on Fig. 11.1, uses exception handling to process any `ArithmeticExceptions` and `InputMistmatchExceptions` that arise. The application still prompts the user for two integers and passes them to method `quotient`, which calculates the quotient and returns an `int` result. This version of the application uses exception handling so that if the user makes a mistake, the program catches and handles (i.e., deals with) the exception—in this case, allowing the user to try to enter the input again. Note that `quotient` is declared `static`, so `main` can call it directly without instantiating a `DivideByZeroWithExceptionHandling` object.

```
1   // Fig. 11.2: DivideByZeroWithExceptionHandling.java
2   // Handling ArithmeticExceptions and InputMismatchExceptions.
3   import java.util.InputMismatchException;
4   import java.util.Scanner;
5
6   public class DivideByZeroWithExceptionHandling
7   {
8      // demonstrates throwing an exception when a divide-by-zero occurs
9      public static int quotient( int numerator, int denominator )
10        throws ArithmeticException
11     {
12        return numerator / denominator; // possible division by zero
13     } // end method quotient
14
15     public static void main( String[] args )
16     {
17        Scanner scanner = new Scanner( System.in ); // scanner for input
18        boolean continueLoop = true; // determines if more input is needed
19
20        do
21        {
22           try // read two numbers and calculate quotient
23           {
24              System.out.print( "Please enter an integer numerator: " );
25              int numerator = scanner.nextInt();
26              System.out.print( "Please enter an integer denominator: " );
27              int denominator = scanner.nextInt();
28
29              int result = quotient( numerator, denominator );
30              System.out.printf( "\nResult: %d / %d = %d\n", numerator,
31                 denominator, result );
32              continueLoop = false; // input successful; end looping
33           } // end try
34           catch ( InputMismatchException inputMismatchException )
35           {
```

Fig. 11.2 | Handling `ArithmeticExceptions` and `InputMismatchExceptions`. (Part 1 of 2.)

```
36              System.err.printf( "\nException: %s\n",
37                  inputMismatchException );
38              scanner.nextLine(); // discard input so user can try again
39              System.out.println(
40                  "You must enter integers. Please try again.\n" );
41          } // end catch
42          catch ( ArithmeticException arithmeticException )
43          {
44              System.err.printf( "\nException: %s\n", arithmeticException );
45              System.out.println(
46                  "Zero is an invalid denominator. Please try again.\n" );
47          } // end catch
48      } while ( continueLoop ); // end do...while
49   } // end main
50 } // end class DivideByZeroWithExceptionHandling
```

```
Please enter an integer numerator: 100
Please enter an integer denominator: 7

Result: 100 / 7 = 14
```

```
Please enter an integer numerator: 100
Please enter an integer denominator: 0

Exception: java.lang.ArithmeticException: / by zero
Zero is an invalid denominator. Please try again.

Please enter an integer numerator: 100
Please enter an integer denominator: 7

Result: 100 / 7 = 14
```

```
Please enter an integer numerator: 100
Please enter an integer denominator: hello

Exception: java.util.InputMismatchException
You must enter integers. Please try again.

Please enter an integer numerator: 100
Please enter an integer denominator: 7

Result: 100 / 7 = 14
```

Fig. 11.2 | Handling `ArithmeticExceptions` and `InputMismatchExceptions`. (Part 2 of 2.)

The first sample execution in Fig. 11.2 is a successful one that does not encounter any problems. In the second execution the user enters a zero denominator, and an `Arithmet-icException` exception occurs. In the third execution the user enters the string `"hello"` as the denominator, and an `InputMismatchException` occurs. For each exception, the user is informed of the mistake and asked to try again, then is prompted for two new integers. In each sample execution, the program runs successfully to completion.

Class `InputMismatchException` is imported in line 3. Class `ArithmeticException` does not need to be imported because it's in package `java.lang`. Line 18 creates the `boolean` variable `continueLoop`, which is `true` if the user has not yet entered valid input. Lines 20–48 repeatedly ask users for input until a valid input is received.

*Enclosing Code in a **try** Block*

Lines 22–33 contain a **try block**, which encloses the code that might `throw` an exception and the code that should not execute if an exception occurs (i.e., if an exception occurs, the remaining code in the `try` block will be skipped). A `try` block consists of the keyword `try` followed by a block of code enclosed in curly braces. [*Note:* The term "try block" sometimes refers only to the block of code that follows the `try` keyword (not including the `try` keyword itself). For simplicity, we use the term "try block" to refer to the block of code that follows the `try` keyword, as well as the `try` keyword.] The statements that read the integers from the keyboard (lines 25 and 27) each use method `nextInt` to read an `int` value. Method `nextInt` throws an `InputMismatchException` if the value read in is not an integer.

The division that can cause an `ArithmeticException` is not performed in the `try` block. Rather, the call to method `quotient` (line 29) invokes the code that attempts the division (line 12); the JVM throws an `ArithmeticException` object when the denominator is zero.

Software Engineering Observation 11.1

Exceptions may surface through explicitly mentioned code in a try block, through calls to other methods, through deeply nested method calls initiated by code in a try block or from the Java Virtual Machine as it executes Java bytecodes.

Catching Exceptions

The `try` block in this example is followed by two `catch` blocks—one that handles an `InputMismatchException` (lines 34–41) and one that handles an `ArithmeticException` (lines 42–47). A **catch block** (also called a **catch clause** or **exception handler**) catches (i.e., receives) and handles an exception. A `catch` block begins with the keyword `catch` and is followed by a parameter in parentheses (called the exception parameter, discussed shortly) and a block of code enclosed in curly braces. [*Note:* The term "catch clause" is sometimes used to refer to the keyword `catch` followed by a block of code, whereas the term "catch block" refers to only the block of code following the `catch` keyword, but not including it. For simplicity, we use the term "catch block" to refer to the block of code following the `catch` keyword, as well as the keyword itself.]

At least one `catch` block or a **finally block** (discussed in Section 11.7) must immediately follow the `try` block. Each `catch` block specifies in parentheses an **exception parameter** that identifies the exception type the handler can process. When an exception occurs in a `try` block, the `catch` block that executes is the first one whose type matches the type of the exception that occurred (i.e., the type in the `catch` block matches the thrown exception type exactly or is a superclass of it). The exception parameter's name enables the `catch` block to interact with a caught exception object—e.g., to implicitly invoke the caught exception's `toString` method (as in lines 37 and 44), which displays basic information about the exception. Notice that we use the **System.err (standard error stream) object** to output error messages. By default, `System.err`'s print methods, like those of `System.out`, display data to the command prompt.

Line 38 of the first catch block calls Scanner method nextLine. Because an Input-MismatchException occurred, the call to method nextInt never successfully read in the user's data—so we read that input with a call to method nextLine. We do not do anything with the input at this point, because we know that it's invalid. Each catch block displays an error message and asks the user to try again. After either catch block terminates, the user is prompted for input. We'll soon take a deeper look at how this flow of control works in exception handling.

Common Programming Error 11.1

It's a syntax error to place code between a try block and its corresponding catch blocks.

Common Programming Error 11.2

Each catch block can have only a single parameter—specifying a comma-separated list of exception parameters is a syntax error.

An **uncaught exception** is an one for which there are no matching catch blocks. You saw uncaught exceptions in the second and third outputs of Fig. 11.1. Recall that when exceptions occurred in that example, the application terminated early (after displaying the exception's stack trace). This does not always occur as a result of uncaught exceptions. As you'll learn in Chapter 26, Multithreading, Java uses a multithreaded model of program execution. Each **thread** is a parallel activity. One program can have many threads. If a program has only one thread, an uncaught exception will cause the program to terminate. If a program has multiple threads, an uncaught exception will terminate only the thread where the exception occurred. In such programs, however, certain threads may rely on others, and if one thread terminates due to an uncaught exception, there may be adverse effects to the rest of the program.

Termination Model of Exception Handling

If an exception occurs in a try block (such as an InputMismatchException being thrown as a result of the code at line 25 of Fig. 11.2), the try block terminates immediately and program control transfers to the first of the following catch blocks in which the exception parameter's type matches the thrown exception's type. In Fig. 11.2, the first catch block catches InputMismatchExceptions (which occur if invalid input is entered) and the second catch block catches ArithmeticExceptions (which occur if an attempt is made to divide by zero). After the exception is handled, program control does not return to the throw point, because the try block has expired (and its local variables have been lost). Rather, control resumes after the last catch block. This is known as the **termination model of exception handling**. Some languages use the **resumption model of exception handling**, in which, after an exception is handled, control resumes just after the throw point.

Notice that we name our exception parameters (inputMismatchException and arithmeticException) based on their type. Java programmers often simply use the letter e as the name of their exception parameters.

Good Programming Practice 11.1

Using an exception-parameter name that reflects the parameter's type promotes clarity by reminding you of the type of exception being handled.

After executing a catch block, this program's flow of control proceeds to the first statement after the last catch block (line 48 in this case). The condition in the do...while statement is true (variable continueLoop contains its initial value of true), so control returns to the beginning of the loop and the user is once again prompted for input. This control statement will loop until valid input is entered. At that point, program control reaches line 32, which assigns false to variable continueLoop. The try block then terminates. If no exceptions are thrown in the try block, the catch blocks are skipped and control continues with the first statement after the catch blocks (we'll learn about another possibility when we discuss the finally block in Section 11.7). Now the condition for the do...while loop is false, and method main ends.

The try block and its corresponding catch and/or finally blocks form a **try statement**. Do not confuse the terms "try block" and "try statement"—the latter includes the try block as well as the following catch blocks and/or finally block.

As with any other block of code, when a try block terminates, local variables declared in the block go out of scope and are no longer accessible; thus, the local variables of a try block are not accessible in the corresponding catch blocks. When a catch block terminates, local variables declared within the catch block (including the exception parameter of that catch block) also go out of scope and are destroyed. Any remaining catch blocks in the try statement are ignored, and execution resumes at the first line of code after the try...catch sequence—this will be a finally block, if one is present.

Using the **throws** Clause

Now let's examine method quotient (Fig. 11.2, lines 9–13). The portion of the method declaration located at line 10 is known as a **throws clause**. A throws clause specifies the exceptions the method throws. This clause appears after the method's parameter list and before the method's body. It contains a comma-separated list of the exceptions that the method will throw if various problems occur. Such exceptions may be thrown by statements in the method's body or by methods called from the body. A method can throw exceptions of the classes listed in its throws clause or of their subclasses. We've added the throws clause to this application to indicate to the rest of the program that this method may throw an ArithmeticException. Clients of method quotient are thus informed that the method may throw an ArithmeticException. You'll learn more about the throws clause in Section 11.6.

 Error-Prevention Tip 11.2
Read the online API documentation for a method before using that method in a program. The documentation specifies the exceptions thrown by the method (if any) and indicates reasons why such exceptions may occur. Next, read the online API documentation for the specified exception classes. The documentation for an exception class typically contains potential reasons that such exceptions occur. Finally, provide for handling those exceptions in your program.

When line 12 executes, if the denominator is zero, the JVM throws an ArithmeticException object. This object will be caught by the catch block at lines 42–47, which displays basic information about the exception by implicitly invoking the exception's toString method, then asks the user to try again.

If the denominator is not zero, method quotient performs the division and returns the result to the point of invocation of method quotient in the try block (line 29). Lines

30–31 display the result of the calculation and line 32 sets `continueLoop` to `false`. In this case, the `try` block completes successfully, so the program skips the `catch` blocks and fails the condition at line 48, and method `main` completes execution normally.

Note that when `quotient` throws an `ArithmeticException`, `quotient` terminates and does not return a value, and `quotient`'s local variables go out of scope (and are destroyed). If `quotient` contained local variables that were references to objects and there were no other references to those objects, the objects would be marked for garbage collection. Also, when an exception occurs, the `try` block from which `quotient` was called terminates before lines 30–32 can execute. Here, too, if local variables were created in the `try` block prior to the exception's being thrown, these variables would go out of scope.

If an `InputMismatchException` is generated by lines 25 or 27, the `try` block terminates and execution continues with the `catch` block at lines 34–41. In this case, method `quotient` is not called. Then method `main` continues after the last `catch` block (line 48).

11.5 When to Use Exception Handling

Exception handling is designed to process **synchronous errors**, which occur when a statement executes. Common examples we'll see throughout the book are out-of-range array indices, arithmetic overflow (i.e., a value outside the representable range of values), division by zero, invalid method parameters, thread interruption (as we'll see in Chapter 26) and unsuccessful memory allocation (due to lack of memory). Exception handling is not designed to process problems associated with **asynchronous events** (e.g., disk I/O completions, network message arrivals, mouse clicks and keystrokes), which occur in parallel with, and independent of, the program's flow of control.

Software Engineering Observation 11.2
Incorporate your exception-handling strategy into your system from the inception of the design process. Including exception handling after a system has been implemented can be difficult.

Software Engineering Observation 11.3
Exception handling provides a single, uniform technique for processing problems. This helps programmers working on large projects understand each other's error-processing code.

Software Engineering Observation 11.4
Exception handling simplifies combining software components and enables them to work together effectively by enabling predefined components to communicate problems to application-specific components, which can then process the problems in an application-specific manner.

11.6 Java Exception Hierarchy

All Java exception classes inherit directly or indirectly from class **Exception**, forming an inheritance hierarchy. You can extend this hierarchy with your own exception classes.

Figure 11.3 shows a small portion of the inheritance hierarchy for class **Throwable** (a subclass of `Object`), which is the superclass of class `Exception`. Only `Throwable` objects can be used with the exception-handling mechanism. Class `Throwable` has two subclasses: `Exception` and `Error`. Class `Exception` and its subclasses—for instance, `RuntimeException` (package `java.lang`) and `IOException` (package `java.io`)—represent exceptional situations that can occur in a Java program and that can be caught by the application. Class **Error** and its subclasses represent abnormal situations that happen in the JVM. Errors happen infrequently and should not be caught by applications—it's usually not possible for applications to recover from Errors.

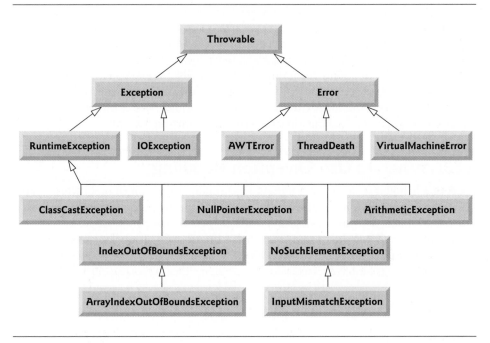

Fig. 11.3 | Portion of class Throwable's inheritance hierarchy.

The Java exception hierarchy contains hundreds of classes. Information about Java's exception classes can be found throughout the Java API. You can view Throwable's documentation at java.sun.com/javase/6/docs/api/java/lang/Throwable.html. From there, you can look at this class's subclasses to get more information about Java's Exceptions and Errors.

Checked vs. Unchecked Exceptions

Java distinguishes between **checked exceptions** and **unchecked exceptions**. This distinction is important, because the Java compiler enforces a **catch-or-declare requirement** for checked exceptions. An exception's type determines whether it is checked or unchecked. All exception types that are direct or indirect subclasses of class **RuntimeException** (package java.lang) are unchecked exceptions. These are typically caused by defects in your program's code. Examples of unchecked exceptions include ArrayIndexOutOfBoundsExceptions (discussed in Chapter 7) and ArithmeticExceptions (shown in Fig. 11.3). All classes that inherit from class Exception but not class RuntimeException are considered to be checked exceptions. Such exceptions are typically caused by conditions that are not in the control of the program—for example, in file processing, the program can't open a file because the file does not exist. Classes that inherit from class Error are considered to be unchecked.

The compiler *checks* each method call and method declaration to determine whether the method throws checked exceptions. If so, the compiler verifies that the checked exception is caught or is declared in a throws clause. We show how to catch and declare checked exceptions in the next several examples. Recall from Section 11.4 that the throws clause specifies the exceptions a method throws. Such exceptions are not caught in the method's body. To satisfy the *catch* part of the catch-or-declare requirement, the code that generates the exception must be wrapped in a try block and must provide a catch handler for the checked-exception type (or one of its superclass types). To satisfy the *declare* part of the catch-or-declare requirement, the method containing the code that generates the exception must provide a throws clause containing the checked-exception type after its parameter list and before its method body. If the catch-or-declare requirement is not satisfied, the compiler will issue an error message indicating that the exception must be caught or declared. This forces you to think about the problems that may occur when a method that throws checked exceptions is called.

Software Engineering Observation 11.5

You must deal with checked exceptions. This results in more robust code than would be created if you were able to simply ignore the exceptions.

Common Programming Error 11.3

A compilation error occurs if a method explicitly attempts to throw a checked exception (or calls another method that throws a checked exception) and that exception is not listed in that method's throws clause.

Common Programming Error 11.4

If a subclass method overrides a superclass method, it's an error for the subclass method to list more exceptions in its throws clause than the overridden superclass method does. However, a subclass's throws clause can contain a subset of a superclass's throws list.

Software Engineering Observation 11.6

If your method calls other methods that explicitly throw checked exceptions, those exceptions must be caught or declared in your method. If an exception can be handled meaningfully in a method, the method should catch the exception rather than declare it.

Unlike checked exceptions, the Java compiler does not check the code to determine whether an unchecked exception is caught or declared. Unchecked exceptions typically can be prevented by proper coding. For example, the unchecked ArithmeticException thrown by method quotient (lines 9–13) in Fig. 11.2 can be avoided if the method ensures that the denominator is not zero before attempting to perform the division. Unchecked exceptions are not required to be listed in a method's throws clause—even if they are, it's not required that such exceptions be caught by an application.

Software Engineering Observation 11.7

Although the compiler does not enforce the catch-or-declare requirement for unchecked exceptions, provide appropriate exception-handling code when it's known that such exceptions might occur. For example, a program should process the NumberFormatException from Integer method parseInt, even though NumberFormatException (an indirect subclass of RuntimeException) is an unchecked exception type. This makes your programs more robust.

Catching Subclass Exceptions

If a catch handler is written to catch superclass-type exception objects, it can also catch all objects of that class's subclasses. This enables catch to handle related errors with a concise notation and allows for polymorphic processing of related exceptions. You can certainly catch each subclass type individually if those exceptions require different processing. Catching related exceptions in one catch block makes sense only if the handling behavior is the same for all subclasses.

Only the First Matching **catch** *Executes*

If there are multiple catch blocks that match a particular exception type, only the first matching catch block executes when an exception of that type occurs. It's a compilation error to catch the *exact same type* in two different catch blocks associated with a particular try block. However, there may be several catch blocks that match an exception—i.e., several catch blocks whose types are the same as the exception type or a superclass of that type. For instance, we could follow a catch block for type ArithmeticException with a catch block for type Exception—both would match ArithmeticExceptions, but only the first matching catch block would execute.

Error-Prevention Tip 11.3

Catching subclass types individually is subject to error if you forget to test for one or more of the subclass types explicitly; catching the superclass guarantees that objects of all subclasses will be caught. Positioning a catch block for the superclass type after all other subclass catch blocks for subclasses of that superclass ensures that all subclass exceptions are eventually caught.

Common Programming Error 11.5

Placing a catch block for a superclass exception type before other catch blocks that catch subclass exception types would prevent those catch blocks from executing, so a compilation error occurs.

11.7 `finally` Block

Programs that obtain certain types of resources must return them to the system explicitly to avoid so-called **resource leaks.** In programming languages such as C and C++, the most common kind of resource leak is a memory leak. Java performs automatic garbage collection of memory no longer used by programs, thus avoiding most memory leaks. However, other types of resource leaks can occur. For example, files, database connections and network connections that are not closed properly after they're no longer needed might not be available for use in other programs.

Error-Prevention Tip 11.4

A subtle issue is that Java does not entirely eliminate memory leaks. Java will not garbage-collect an object until there are no remaining references to it. Thus, if programmers erroneously keep references to unwanted objects, memory leaks can occur. To help avoid this problem, set reference-type variables to null, when they are no longer needed.

The finally block (which consists of the finally keyword, followed by code enclosed in curly braces), sometimes referred to as the **finally clause**, is optional. If it's present, it's placed after the last catch block, as in Fig. 11.4.

```
try
{
    statements
    resource-acquisition statements
} // end try
catch ( AKindOfException exception1 )
{
    exception-handling statements
} // end catch
...
catch ( AnotherKindOfException exception2 )
{
    exception-handling statements
} // end catch
finally
{
    statements
    resource-release statements
} // end finally
```

Fig. 11.4 | A try statement with a finally block.

Java guarantees that the finally block will execute whether or not an exception is thrown in the corresponding try block. Java also guarantees that the finally block will execute if a try block exits by using a return, break or continue statement or simply by reaching its closing right brace. The finally block will *not* execute if the application exits early from a try block by calling method **System.exit**. This method, which we demonstrate in Chapter 17, immediately terminates an application.

Because a finally block almost always executes, it typically contains resource-release code. Suppose a resource is allocated in a try block. If no exception occurs, the catch blocks are skipped and control proceeds to the finally block, which frees the resource. Control then proceeds to the first statement after the finally block. If an exception occurs in the try block, the try block terminates. If the program catches the exception in one of the corresponding catch blocks, it processes the exception, then the finally block releases the resource and control proceeds to the first statement after the finally block. If the program doesn't catch the exception, the finally block still releases the resource and an attempt is made to catch the exception in a calling method.

Error-Prevention Tip 11.5
The finally block is an ideal place to release resources acquired in a try block (such as opened files), which helps eliminate resource leaks.

Performance Tip 11.2
Always release a resource explicitly and at the earliest possible moment at which it's no longer needed. This makes resources available for reuse, thus improving resource utilization.

If an exception that occurs in a try block cannot be caught by one of that try block's catch handlers, the program skips the rest of the try block and control proceeds to the finally block. Then the program passes the exception to the next outer try block—normally in the calling method—where an associated catch block might catch it. This process can occur through many levels of try blocks. Also, the exception could go uncaught.

If a catch block throws an exception, the finally block still executes. Then the exception is passed to the next outer try block—again, normally in the calling method.

Figure 11.5 demonstrates that the finally block executes even if an exception is not thrown in the corresponding try block. The program contains static methods main (lines 6–18), throwException (lines 21–44) and doesNotThrowException (lines 47–64). Methods throwException and doesNotThrowException are declared static, so main can call them directly without instantiating a UsingExceptions object.

```java
1   // Fig. 11.5: UsingExceptions.java
2   // try...catch...finally exception handling mechanism.
3
4   public class UsingExceptions
5   {
6      public static void main( String[] args )
7      {
8         try
9         {
10           throwException(); // call method throwException
11        } // end try
12        catch ( Exception exception ) // exception thrown by throwException
13        {
14           System.err.println( "Exception handled in main" );
15        } // end catch
16
17        doesNotThrowException();
18     } // end main
19
20     // demonstrate try...catch...finally
21     public static void throwException() throws Exception
22     {
23        try // throw an exception and immediately catch it
24        {
25           System.out.println( "Method throwException" );
26           throw new Exception(); // generate exception
27        } // end try
28        catch ( Exception exception ) // catch exception thrown in try
29        {
30           System.err.println(
31              "Exception handled in method throwException" );
32           throw exception; // rethrow for further processing
33
34           // code here would not be reached; would cause compilation errors
35
36        } // end catch
37        finally // executes regardless of what occurs in try...catch
38        {
39           System.err.println( "Finally executed in throwException" );
40        } // end finally
41
42        // code here would not be reached; would cause compilation errors
43
44     } // end method throwException
```

Fig. 11.5 | try...catch...finally exception-handling mechanism. (Part 1 of 2.)

```
45
46       // demonstrate finally when no exception occurs
47       public static void doesNotThrowException()
48       {
49          try // try block does not throw an exception
50          {
51             System.out.println( "Method doesNotThrowException" );
52          } // end try
53          catch ( Exception exception ) // does not execute
54          {
55             System.err.println( exception );
56          } // end catch
57          finally // executes regardless of what occurs in try...catch
58          {
59             System.err.println(
60                "Finally executed in doesNotThrowException" );
61          } // end finally
62
63          System.out.println( "End of method doesNotThrowException" );
64       } // end method doesNotThrowException
65    } // end class UsingExceptions
```

```
Method throwException
Exception handled in method throwException
Finally executed in throwException
Exception handled in main
Method doesNotThrowException
Finally executed in doesNotThrowException
End of method doesNotThrowException
```

Fig. 11.5 | try...catch...finally exception-handling mechanism. (Part 2 of 2.)

Both System.out and System.err are **streams**—a sequence of bytes. While System.out (known as the **standard output stream**) is used to display a program's output, System.err (known as the **standard error stream**) is used to display a program's errors. Output from these streams can be redirected (i.e., sent to somewhere other than the command prompt, such as to a file). Using two different streams enables you to easily separate error messages from other output. For instance, data output from System.err could be sent to a log file, while data output from System.out can be displayed on the screen. For simplicity, this chapter will not redirect output from System.err, but will display such messages to the command prompt. You'll learn more about streams in Chapter 17, Files, Streams and Object Serialization.

*Throwing Exceptions Using the **throw** Statement*
Method main (Fig. 11.5) begins executing, enters its try block and immediately calls method throwException (line 10). Method throwException throws an Exception. The statement at line 26 is known as a **throw statement**—it's executed to indicate that an exception has occurred. So far, you've only caught exceptions thrown by called methods. You can throw exceptions by using the throw statement. Just as with exceptions thrown by the Java API's methods, this indicates to client applications that an error has occurred. A throw statement specifies an object to be thrown. The operand of a throw can be of any class derived from class Throwable.

Software Engineering Observation 11.8

When toString is invoked on any Throwable object, its resulting string includes the descriptive string that was supplied to the constructor, or simply the class name if no string was supplied.

Software Engineering Observation 11.9

An object can be thrown without containing information about the problem that occurred. In this case, simply knowing that an exception of a particular type occurred may provide sufficient information for the handler to process the problem correctly.

Software Engineering Observation 11.10

Exceptions can be thrown from constructors. When an error is detected in a constructor, an exception should be thrown to avoid creating an improperly formed object.

Rethrowing Exceptions

Line 32 of Fig. 11.5 **rethrows the exception**. Exceptions are rethrown when a catch block, upon receiving an exception, decides either that it cannot process that exception or that it can only partially process it. Rethrowing an exception defers the exception handling (or perhaps a portion of it) to another catch block associated with an outer try statement. An exception is rethrown by using the **throw keyword**, followed by a reference to the exception object that was just caught. Note that exceptions cannot be rethrown from a finally block, as the exception parameter (a local variable) from the catch block no longer exists.

When a rethrow occurs, the next enclosing try block detects the rethrown exception, and that try block's catch blocks attempt to handle it. In this case, the next enclosing try block is found at lines 8–11 in method main. Before the rethrown exception is handled, however, the finally block (lines 37–40) executes. Then method main detects the rethrown exception in the try block and handles it in the catch block (lines 12–15).

Next, main calls method doesNotThrowException (line 17). No exception is thrown in doesNotThrowException's try block (lines 49–52), so the program skips the catch block (lines 53–56), but the finally block (lines 57–61) nevertheless executes. Control proceeds to the statement after the finally block (line 63). Then control returns to main and the program terminates.

Common Programming Error 11.6

If an exception has not been caught when control enters a finally block and the finally block throws an exception that is not caught in the finally block, the first exception will be lost and the exception from the finally block will be returned to the calling method.

Error-Prevention Tip 11.6

Avoid placing code that can throw an exception in a finally block. If such code is required, enclose the code in a try...catch within the finally block.

Common Programming Error 11.7

Assuming that an exception thrown from a catch block will be processed by that catch block or any other catch block associated with the same try statement can lead to logic errors.

Good Programming Practice 11.2

Java's exception-handling mechanism is intended to remove error-processing code from the main line of a program's code to improve program clarity. Do not place try...catch... finally around every statement that may throw an exception. This makes programs difficult to read. Rather, place one try block around a significant portion of your code, follow that try block with catch blocks that handle each possible exception and follow the catch blocks with a single finally block (if one is required).

11.8 Stack Unwinding

When an exception is thrown but not caught in a particular scope, the method-call stack is "unwound," and an attempt is made to catch the exception in the next outer try block. This process is called **stack unwinding**. Unwinding the method-call stack means that the method in which the exception was not caught terminates, all local variables in that method go out of scope and control returns to the statement that originally invoked that method. If a try block encloses that statement, an attempt is made to catch the exception. If a try block does not enclose that statement or if the exception is not caught, stack unwinding occurs again. Figure 11.6 demonstrates stack unwinding.

```java
1   // Fig. 11.6: UsingExceptions.java
2   // Stack unwinding.
3
4   public class UsingExceptions
5   {
6      public static void main( String[] args )
7      {
8         try // call throwException to demonstrate stack unwinding
9         {
10            throwException();
11         } // end try
12         catch ( Exception exception ) // exception thrown in throwException
13         {
14            System.err.println( "Exception handled in main" );
15         } // end catch
16      } // end main
17
18      // throwException throws exception that is not caught in this method
19      public static void throwException() throws Exception
20      {
21         try // throw an exception and catch it in main
22         {
23            System.out.println( "Method throwException" );
24            throw new Exception(); // generate exception
25         } // end try
26         catch ( RuntimeException runtimeException ) // catch incorrect type
27         {
28            System.err.println(
29               "Exception handled in method throwException" );
30         } // end catch
```

Fig. 11.6 | Stack unwinding. (Part 1 of 2.)

```
31          finally // finally block always executes
32          {
33              System.err.println( "Finally is always executed" );
34          } // end finally
35      } // end method throwException
36  } // end class UsingExceptions
```

```
Method throwException
Finally is always executed
Exception handled in main
```

Fig. 11.6 | Stack unwinding. (Part 2 of 2.)

When method main executes, line 10 in the try block calls method throwException (lines 19–35). In the try block of method throwException (lines 21–25), line 24 throws an Exception. This terminates the try block immediately, and control skips the catch block at line 26, because the type being caught (RuntimeException) is not an exact match with the thrown type (Exception) and is not a superclass of it. Method throwException terminates (but not until its finally block executes) and returns control to line 10—the point from which it was called in the program. Line 10 is in an enclosing try block. The exception has not yet been handled, so the try block terminates and an attempt is made to catch the exception at line 12. The type being caught (Exception) *does* match the thrown type. Consequently, the catch block processes the exception, and the program terminates at the end of main. If there were no matching catch blocks, and the exception is not declared in each method that throws it, a compilation error would occur. Remember that this is not always the case—for unchecked exceptions, the application will compile, but will run with unexpected results.

11.9 printStackTrace, getStackTrace and getMessage

Recall from Section 11.6 that exceptions derive from class Throwable. Class Throwable offers a **printStackTrace** method that outputs to the standard error stream the stack trace (discussed in Section 11.3). Often, this is helpful in testing and debugging. Class Throwable also provides a **getStackTrace** method that retrieves the stack-trace information that might be printed by printStackTrace. Class Throwable's **getMessage** method returns the descriptive string stored in an exception. The example in this section demonstrates these three methods.

Error-Prevention Tip 11.7
An exception that is not caught in an application causes Java's default exception handler to run. This displays the name of the exception, a descriptive message that indicates the problem that occurred and a complete execution stack trace. In an application with a single thread of execution, the application terminates. In an application with multiple threads, the thread that caused the exception terminates.

Error-Prevention Tip 11.8
Throwable method toString (inherited by all Throwable subclasses) returns a string containing the name of the exception's class and a descriptive message.

Figure 11.7 demonstrates getMessage, printStackTrace and getStackTrace. If we wanted to output the stack-trace information to streams other than the standard error stream, we could use the information returned from getStackTrace and output it to another stream or use one of the overloaded versions of method printStackTrace. Sending data to other streams is discussed in Chapter 17, Files, Streams and Object Serialization.

```
1   // Fig. 11.7: UsingExceptions.java
2   // Throwable methods getMessage, getStackTrace and printStackTrace.
3
4   public class UsingExceptions
5   {
6      public static void main( String[] args )
7      {
8         try
9         {
10           method1(); // call method1
11        } // end try
12        catch ( Exception exception ) // catch exception thrown in method1
13        {
14           System.err.printf( "%s\n\n", exception.getMessage() );
15           exception.printStackTrace(); // print exception stack trace
16
17           // obtain the stack-trace information
18           StackTraceElement[] traceElements = exception.getStackTrace();
19
20           System.out.println( "\nStack trace from getStackTrace:" );
21           System.out.println( "Class\t\tFile\t\t\tLine\tMethod" );
22
23           // loop through traceElements to get exception description
24           for ( StackTraceElement element : traceElements )
25           {
26              System.out.printf( "%s\t", element.getClassName() );
27              System.out.printf( "%s\t", element.getFileName() );
28              System.out.printf( "%s\t", element.getLineNumber() );
29              System.out.printf( "%s\n", element.getMethodName() );
30           } // end for
31        } // end catch
32     } // end main
33
34     // call method2; throw exceptions back to main
35     public static void method1() throws Exception
36     {
37        method2();
38     } // end method method1
39
40     // call method3; throw exceptions back to method1
41     public static void method2() throws Exception
42     {
43        method3();
44     } // end method method2
```

Fig. 11.7 | Throwable methods getMessage, getStackTrace and printStackTrace. (Part 1 of 2.)

```
45
46      // throw Exception back to method2
47      public static void method3() throws Exception
48      {
49         throw new Exception( "Exception thrown in method3" );
50      } // end method method3
51   } // end class UsingExceptions
```

```
Exception thrown in method3

java.lang.Exception: Exception thrown in method3
        at UsingExceptions.method3(UsingExceptions.java:49)
        at UsingExceptions.method2(UsingExceptions.java:43)
        at UsingExceptions.method1(UsingExceptions.java:37)
        at UsingExceptions.main(UsingExceptions.java:10)

Stack trace from getStackTrace:
Class               File                     Line    Method
UsingExceptions UsingExceptions.java         49      method3
UsingExceptions UsingExceptions.java         43      method2
UsingExceptions UsingExceptions.java         37      method1
UsingExceptions UsingExceptions.java         10      main
```

Fig. 11.7 | Throwable methods getMessage, getStackTrace and printStackTrace. (Part 2 of 2.)

In main, the try block (lines 8–11) calls method1 (declared at lines 35–38), which in turn calls method2 (declared at lines 41–44), which in turn calls method3 (declared at lines 47–50). Line 49 of method3 throws an Exception object—this is the throw point. Because the throw statement at line 49 is not enclosed in a try block, stack unwinding occurs— method3 terminates at line 49, then returns control to the statement in method2 that invoked method3 (i.e., line 43). Because no try block encloses line 43, stack unwinding occurs again—method2 terminates at line 43 and returns control to the statement in method1 that invoked method2 (i.e., line 37). Because no try block encloses line 37, stack unwinding occurs one more time—method1 terminates at line 37 and returns control to the statement in main that invoked method1 (i.e., line 10). The try block at lines 8–11 encloses this statement. The exception has not been handled, so the try block terminates and the first matching catch block (lines 12–31) catches and processes the exception.

Line 14 invokes the exception's getMessage method to get the exception description. Line 15 invokes the exception's printStackTrace method to output the stack trace that indicates where the exception occurred. Line 18 invokes the exception's getStackTrace method to obtain the stack-trace information as an array of **StackTraceElement** objects. Lines 24–30 get each StackTraceElement in the array and invoke its methods **getClassName**, **getFileName**, **getLineNumber** and **getMethodName** to get the class name, file name, line number and method name, respectively, for that StackTraceElement. Each StackTraceElement represents one method call on the method-call stack.

The output in Fig. 11.7 shows that the stack-trace information printed by printStackTrace follows the pattern: *className.methodName(fileName:lineNumber)*, where *className*, *methodName* and *fileName* indicate the names of the class, method and file in which the exception occurred, respectively, and the *lineNumber* indicates where in the file the exception occurred. You saw this in the output for Fig. 11.1. Method `getStackTrace` enables custom processing of the exception information. Compare the output of `print-StackTrace` with the output created from the `StackTraceElements` to see that both contain the same stack-trace information.

Software Engineering Observation 11.11

Never ignore an exception you catch. At least use `printStackTrace` to output an error message. This will inform users that a problem exists, so that they can take appropriate actions.

11.10 Chained Exceptions

Sometimes a method responds to an exception by throwing a different exception type that is specific to the current application. If a `catch` block throws a new exception, the original exception's information and stack trace are lost. Earlier Java versions provided no mechanism to wrap the original exception information with the new exception's information to provide a complete stack trace showing where the original problem occurred. This made debugging such problems particularly difficult. **Chained exceptions** enable an exception object to maintain the complete stack-trace information from the original exception. Figure 11.8 demonstrates chained exceptions.

```
1   // Fig. 11.8: UsingChainedExceptions.java
2   // Chained exceptions.
3
4   public class UsingChainedExceptions
5   {
6      public static void main( String[] args )
7      {
8         try
9         {
10           method1(); // call method1
11        } // end try
12        catch ( Exception exception ) // exceptions thrown from method1
13        {
14           exception.printStackTrace();
15        } // end catch
16     } // end main
17
18     // call method2; throw exceptions back to main
19     public static void method1() throws Exception
20     {
21        try
22        {
23           method2(); // call method2
24        } // end try
25        catch ( Exception exception ) // exception thrown from method2
26        {
27           throw new Exception( "Exception thrown in method1", exception );
28        } // end catch
29     } // end method method1
30
```

Fig. 11.8 | Chained exceptions. (Part 1 of 2.)

```
31      // call method3; throw exceptions back to method1
32      public static void method2() throws Exception
33      {
34         try
35         {
36            method3(); // call method3
37         } // end try
38         catch ( Exception exception ) // exception thrown from method3
39         {
40            throw new Exception( "Exception thrown in method2", exception );
41         } // end catch
42      } // end method method2
43
44      // throw Exception back to method2
45      public static void method3() throws Exception
46      {
47         throw new Exception( "Exception thrown in method3" );
48      } // end method method3
49   } // end class UsingChainedExceptions
```

```
java.lang.Exception: Exception thrown in method1
        at UsingChainedExceptions.method1(UsingChainedExceptions.java:27)
        at UsingChainedExceptions.main(UsingChainedExceptions.java:10)
Caused by: java.lang.Exception: Exception thrown in method2
        at UsingChainedExceptions.method2(UsingChainedExceptions.java:40)
        at UsingChainedExceptions.method1(UsingChainedExceptions.java:23)
        ... 1 more
Caused by: java.lang.Exception: Exception thrown in method3
        at UsingChainedExceptions.method3(UsingChainedExceptions.java:47)
        at UsingChainedExceptions.method2(UsingChainedExceptions.java:36)
        ... 2 more
```

Fig. 11.8 | Chained exceptions. (Part 2 of 2.)

The program consists of four methods—main (lines 6–16), method1 (lines 19–29), method2 (lines 32–42) and method3 (lines 45–48). Line 10 in method main's try block calls method1. Line 23 in method1's try block calls method2. Line 36 in method2's try block calls method3. In method3, line 47 throws a new Exception. Because this statement is not in a try block, method3 terminates, and the exception is returned to the calling method (method2) at line 36. This statement *is* in a try block; therefore, the try block terminates and the exception is caught at lines 38–41. Line 40 in the catch block throws a new exception. In this case, the Exception constructor with two arguments is called. The second argument represents the exception that was the original cause of the problem. In this program, that exception occurred at line 47. Because an exception is thrown from the catch block, method2 terminates and returns the new exception to the calling method (method1) at line 23. Once again, this statement is in a try block, so the try block terminates and the exception is caught at lines 25–28. Line 27 in the catch block throws a new exception and uses the exception that was caught as the second argument to the Exception constructor. Because an exception is thrown from the catch block, method1 terminates and returns the new exception to the calling method (main) at line 10. The try block in main terminates, and the exception is caught at lines 12–15. Line 14 prints a stack trace.

Notice in the program output that the first three lines show the most recent exception that was thrown (i.e., the one from `method1` at line 27). The next four lines indicate the exception that was thrown from `method2` at line 40. Finally, the last four lines represent the exception that was thrown from `method3` at line 47. Also notice that, as you read the output in reverse, it shows how many more chained exceptions remain.

11.11 Declaring New Exception Types

Most Java programmers use existing classes from the Java API, third-party vendors and freely available class libraries (usually downloadable from the Internet) to build Java applications. The methods of those classes typically are declared to throw appropriate exceptions when problems occur. You write code that processes these existing exceptions to make programs more robust.

If you build classes that other programmers will use, you might find it useful to declare your own exception classes that are specific to the problems that can occur when another programmer uses your reusable classes.

Software Engineering Observation 11.12

If possible, indicate exceptions from your methods by using existing exception classes, rather than creating new ones. The Java API contains many exception classes that might be suitable for the type of problems your methods need to indicate.

A new exception class must extend an existing exception class to ensure that the class can be used with the exception-handling mechanism. Like any other class, an exception class can contain fields and methods. However, a typical new exception class contains only four constructors: one that takes no arguments and passes a default error message `String` to the superclass constructor; one that receives a customized error message as a `String` and passes it to the superclass constructor; one that receives a customized error message as a `String` and a `Throwable` (for chaining exceptions) and passes both to the superclass constructor; and one that receives a `Throwable` (for chaining exceptions) and passes it to the superclass constructor.

Good Programming Practice 11.3

Associating each type of serious execution-time malfunction with an appropriately named `Exception` class improves program clarity.

Software Engineering Observation 11.13

When defining your own exception type, study the existing exception classes in the Java API and try to extend a related exception class. For example, if you are creating a new class to represent when a method attempts a division by zero, you might extend class `ArithmeticException` because division by zero occurs during arithmetic. If the existing classes are not appropriate superclasses for your new exception class, decide whether your new class should be a checked or an unchecked exception class. The new exception class should be a checked exception (i.e., extend `Exception` but not `RuntimeException`) if clients should be required to handle the exception. The client application should be able to reasonably recover from such an exception. The new exception class should extend `RuntimeException` if the client code should be able to ignore the exception (i.e., the exception is an unchecked one).

In Chapter 22, Custom Generic Data Structures, we provide an example of a custom exception class. We declare a reusable class called `List` that is capable of storing a list of references to objects. Some operations typically performed on a `List` are not allowed if the `List` is empty, such as removing an item from the front or back of the list. For this reason, some `List` methods throw exceptions of exception class `EmptyListException`.

Good Programming Practice 11.4

By convention, all exception-class names should end with the word `Exception`.

11.12 Preconditions and Postconditions

Programmers spend significant amounts of time maintaining and debugging code. To facilitate these tasks and to improve the overall design, they can specify the expected states before and after a method's execution. These states are called preconditions and postconditions, respectively.

A **precondition** must be true when a method is invoked. Preconditions describe constraints on method parameters and any other expectations the method has about the current state of a program just before it begins executing. If the preconditions are not met, then the method's behavior is undefined—it may throw an exception, proceed with an illegal value or attempt to recover from the error. You should never expect consistent behavior if the preconditions are not satisfied.

A **postcondition** is true after the method successfully returns. Postconditions describe constraints on the return value and any other side effects the method may have. When calling a method, you may assume that a method fulfills all of its postconditions. If you are writing your own method, you should document all postconditions so that others know what to expect when they call your method, and you should make certain that your method honors all its postconditions if its preconditions are indeed met.

When their preconditions or postconditions are not met, methods typically throw exceptions. As an example, examine `String` method `charAt`, which has one `int` parameter—an index in the `String`. For a precondition, method `charAt` assumes that `index` is greater than or equal to zero and less than the length of the `String`. If the precondition is met, the postcondition states that the method will return the character at the position in the `String` specified by the parameter `index`. Otherwise, the method throws an `IndexOutOfBoundsException`. We trust that method `charAt` satisfies its postcondition, provided that we meet the precondition. We need not be concerned with the details of how the method actually retrieves the character at the index.

Some programmers state the preconditions and postconditions informally as part of the general method specification, while others prefer a more formal approach by explicitly defining them. When designing your own methods, you should state the preconditions and postconditions in a comment before the method declaration in whichever manner you prefer. Stating the preconditions and postconditions before writing a method will also help guide you as you implement the method.

11.13 Assertions

When implementing and debugging a class, it's sometimes useful to state conditions that should be true at a particular point in a method. These conditions, called **assertions**, help ensure a program's validity by catching potential bugs and identifying possible logic errors during development. Preconditions and postconditions are two types of assertions. Preconditions are assertions about its state when a method is invoked, and postconditions are assertions about a program's state after a method finishes.

While assertions can be stated as comments to guide you during program development, Java includes two versions of the **assert** statement for validating assertions programatically. The assert statement evaluates a boolean expression and, if false, throws an **AssertionError** (a subclass of Error). The first form of the assert statement is

> assert *expression*;

which throws an AssertionError if *expression* is false. The second form is

> assert *expression1* : *expression2*;

which evaluates *expression1* and throws an AssertionError with *expression2* as the error message if *expression1* is false.

You can use assertions to programmatically implement preconditions and postconditions or to verify any other intermediate states that help you ensure your code is working correctly. Figure 11.9 demonstrates the assert statement. Line 11 prompts the user to enter a number between 0 and 10, then line 12 reads the number. Line 15 determines whether the user entered a number within the valid range. If the number is out of range, the assert statement reports an error; otherwise, the program proceeds normally.

```java
1   // Fig. 11.9: AssertTest.java
2   // Checking with assert that a value is within range
3   import java.util.Scanner;
4
5   public class AssertTest
6   {
7      public static void main( String[] args )
8      {
9         Scanner input = new Scanner( System.in );
10
11         System.out.print( "Enter a number between 0 and 10: " );
12         int number = input.nextInt();
13
14         // assert that the value is >= 0 and <= 10
15         assert ( number >= 0 && number <= 10 ) : "bad number: " + number;
16
17         System.out.printf( "You entered %d\n", number );
18      } // end main
19   } // end class AssertTest
```

```
Enter a number between 0 and 10: 5
You entered 5
```

```
Enter a number between 0 and 10: 50
Exception in thread "main" java.lang.AssertionError: bad number: 50
        at AssertTest.main(AssertTest.java:15)
```

Fig. 11.9 | Checking with assert that a value is within range.

You use assertions primarily for debugging and identifying logic errors in an application. You must explicitly enable assertions when executing a program, because they reduce performance and are unnecessary for the program's user. To do so, use the java command's -ea command-line option, as in

```
java -ea AssertTest
```

Users should not encounter any AssertionErrors through normal execution of a properly written program. Such errors should only indicate bugs in the implementation. As a result, you should never catch an AssertionError. Rather, you should allow the program to terminate when the error occurs, so you can see the error message, then locate and fix the source of the problem. Since application users can choose not to enable assertions at runtime, you should not use assert to indicate runtime problems in production code. Rather, you should use the exception mechanism for this purpose.

11.14 Wrap-Up

In this chapter, you learned how to use exception handling to deal with errors. You learned that exception handling enables you to remove error-handling code from the "main line" of the program's execution. We showed how to use try blocks to enclose code that may throw an exception, and how to use catch blocks to deal with exceptions that may arise. You learned about the termination model of exception handling, which dictates that after an exception is handled, program control does not return to the throw point. We discussed checked vs. unchecked exceptions, and how to specify with the throws clause the exceptions that a method might throw. You learned how to use the finally block to release resources whether or not an exception occurs. You also learned how to throw and rethrow exceptions. We showed how to obtain information about an exception using methods printStackTrace, getStackTrace and getMessage. Next, we presented chained exceptions, which allow you to wrap original exception information with new exception information. Then, we showed how to create your own exception classes. We introduced preconditions and postconditions to help programmers using your methods understand conditions that must be true when the method is called and when it returns. When preconditions and postconditions are not met, methods typically throw exceptions. Finally, we discussed the assert statement and how it can be used to help you debug your programs. In particular, assert can be used to ensure that preconditions and postconditions are met. In the next chapter, we begin our two-chapter, optional case study on object-oriented design with the UML.

Summary

Section 11.1 Introduction
• An exception is an indication of a problem that occurs during a program's execution.
• Exception handling enables programmers to create applications that can resolve exceptions.

Section 11.2 Error-Handling Overview
• Exception handling enables you to remove error-handling code from the "main line" of the program's execution, improving program clarity and enhancing modifiability.

Section 11.3 Example: Divide by Zero without Exception Handling
- Exceptions are thrown when a method detects a problem and is unable to handle it.
- An exception's stack trace includes the name of the exception in a message that indicates the problem that occurred and the complete method-call stack at the time the exception occurred.
- The point in the program at which an exception occurs is called the throw point.

Section 11.4 Example: Handling `ArithmeticExceptions` *and* `InputMismatchExceptions`
- A `try` block encloses code that might `throw` an exception and code that should not execute if that exception occurs.
- Exceptions may surface through explicitly mentioned code in a `try` block, through calls to other methods or even through deeply nested method calls initiated by code in the `try` block.
- A `catch` block begins with the keyword `catch` and an exception parameter followed by a block of code that handles the exception. This code executes when the `try` block detects the exception.
- An uncaught exception is an exception that occurs for which there are no matching `catch` blocks.
- An uncaught exception will cause a program to terminate early if that program contains only one thread. Otherwise, only the thread where the exception occurred will terminate. The rest of the program will run but possibly with adverse results.
- At least one `catch` block or a `finally` block must immediately follow the `try` block.
- A `catch` block specifies in parentheses an exception parameter identifying the exception type to handle. The parameter's name enables the `catch` block to interact with a caught exception object.
- If an exception occurs in a `try` block, the `try` block terminates immediately and program control transfers to the first `catch` block with a parameter type that matches the thrown exception's type.
- After an exception is handled, program control does not return to the throw point, because the `try` block has expired. This is known as the termination model of exception handling.
- If there are multiple matching `catch` blocks when an exception occurs, only the first is executed.
- A `throws` clause specifies a comma-separated list of exceptions that the method might throw, and appears after the method's parameter list and before the method body.

Section 11.5 When to Use Exception Handling
- Exception handling processes synchronous errors, which occur when a statement executes.
- Exception handling is not designed to process problems associated with asynchronous events, which occur in parallel with, and independent of, the program's flow of control.

Section 11.6 Java Exception Hierarchy
- All Java exception classes inherit directly or indirectly from class `Exception`.
- Programmers can extend the Java exception hierarchy with their own exception classes.
- Class `Throwable` is the superclass of class `Exception` and is therefore also the superclass of all exceptions. Only `Throwable` objects can be used with the exception-handling mechanism.
- Class `Throwable` has two subclasses: `Exception` and `Error`.
- Class `Exception` and its subclasses represent problems that could occur in a Java program and be caught by the application.
- Class `Error` and its subclasses represent problems that could happen in the Java runtime system. `Error`s happen infrequently and typically should not be caught by an application.
- Java distinguishes between two categories of exceptions: checked and unchecked.
- The Java compiler does not check to determine if an unchecked exception is caught or declared. Unchecked exceptions typically can be prevented by proper coding.

- Subclasses of `RuntimeException` represent unchecked exceptions. All exception types that inherit from class `Exception` but not from `RuntimeException` are checked.
- If a `catch` block is written to catch exception objects of a superclass type, it can also catch all objects of that class's subclasses. This allows for polymorphic processing of related exceptions.

Section 11.7 *finally block*
- Programs that obtain certain types of resources must return them to the system explicitly to avoid so-called resource leaks. Resource-release code typically is placed in a `finally` block.
- The `finally` block is optional. If it's present, it's placed after the last `catch` block.
- Java guarantees that the `finally` block will execute whether or not an exception is thrown in the corresponding `try` block or any of its corresponding `catch` blocks.
- If an exception cannot be caught by one of that `try` block's associated `catch` handlers, control proceeds to the `finally` block. Then the exception is passed to the next outer `try` block.
- If a `catch` block throws an exception, the `finally` block still executes. Then the exception is passed to the next outer `try` block.
- A `throw` statement can throw any `Throwable` object.

Section 11.8 *Stack Unwinding*
- Exceptions are rethrown when a `catch` block, upon receiving an exception, decides either that it cannot process that exception or that it can only partially process it. Rethrowing an exception defers the exception handling (or perhaps a portion of it) to another `catch` block.
- When a rethrow occurs, the next enclosing `try` block detects the rethrown exception, and that `try` block's `catch` blocks attempt to handle it.
- When an exception is thrown but not caught in a particular scope, the method-call stack is unwound, and an attempt is made to `catch` the exception in the next outer `try` statement.

Section 11.9 *printStackTrace, getStackTrace and getMessage*
- Class `Throwable` offers a `printStackTrace` method that prints the method-call stack. Often, this is helpful in testing and debugging.
- Class `Throwable` also provides a `getStackTrace` method that obtains the same stack-trace information that is printed by `printStackTrace`.
- Class `Throwable`'s `getMessage` method returns the descriptive string stored in an exception.
- Method `getStackTrace` obtains the stack-trace information as an array of `StackTraceElement` objects. Each `StackTraceElement` represents one method call on the method-call stack.
- `StackTraceElement` methods `getClassName`, `getFileName`, `getLineNumber` and `getMethodName` get the class name, file name, line number and method name, respectively.

Section 11.10 *Chained Exceptions*
- Chained exceptions enable an exception object to maintain the complete stack-trace information, including information about previous exceptions that caused the current exception.

Section 11.11 *Declaring New Exception Types*
- A new exception class must extend an existing exception class to ensure that the class can be used with the exception-handling mechanism.

Section 11.12 *Preconditions and Postconditions*
- A method's precondition is a condition that must be true when the method is invoked.
- A method's postcondition is a condition that is true after the method successfully returns.

- When designing your own methods, you should state the preconditions and postconditions in a comment before the method declaration.

Section 11.13 Assertions
- Assertions help ensure a program's validity by catching potential bugs and identifying possible logic errors.
- Java includes two versions of an assert statement for validating assertions programatically.
- To enable assertions at runtime, use the -ea switch when running the java command.

Terminology

ArithmeticException class 446
assert statement 469
assertion 468
AssertionError class 469
asynchronous event 453
catch block 450
catch clause 450
catch keyword 450
catch-or-declare requirement 454
chained exceptions 465
checked exception 454
Error class 454
exception 444
Exception class 453
exception handler 450
exception handling 444
exception parameter 450
exit method of class System 457
fault-tolerant program 444
finally block 450
finally clause 456
finally keyword 450
getClassName method of class
    StackTraceElement 464
getFileName method of class
    StackTraceElement 464
getLineNumber method of class
    StackTraceElement 464
getMessage method of class Throwable 462
getMethodName method of class
    StackTraceElement 464
getStackTrace method of class Throwable 462

InputMismatchException class 447
postcondition 468
precondition 468
printStackTrace method of class Throwable
    462
resource leak 456
resumption model of exception handling 451
rethrow an exception 460
rintStackTrace 462
robust application 444
RuntimeException class 454
stack trace 446
stack unwinding 461
StackTraceElement class 464
standard error stream 459
standard output stream 459
stream 459
synchronous error 453
termination model of exception handling 451
thread 451
throw an exception 446
throw keyword 460
throw point 447
throw statement 459
Throwable class 453
throws clause 452
throws keyword 452
try block 450
try keyword 450
try statement 452
uncaught exception 451
unchecked exception 454

Self-Review Exercises

11.1 List five common examples of exceptions.

11.2 Give several reasons why exception-handling techniques should not be used for conventional program control.

11.3 Why are exceptions particularly appropriate for dealing with errors produced by methods of classes in the Java API?

11.4 What is a "resource leak"?

11.5 If no exceptions are thrown in a try block, where does control proceed to when the try block completes execution?

11.6 Give a key advantage of using catch(Exception *exceptionName*).

11.7 Should a conventional application catch Error objects? Explain.

11.8 What happens if no catch handler matches the type of a thrown object?

11.9 What happens if several catch blocks match the type of the thrown object?

11.10 Why would a programmer specify a superclass type as the type in a catch block?

11.11 What is the key reason for using finally blocks?

11.12 What happens when a catch block throws an Exception?

11.13 What does the statement throw *exceptionReference* do in a catch block?

11.14 What happens to a local reference in a try block when that block throws an Exception?

Answers to Self-Review Exercises

11.1 Memory exhaustion, array index out of bounds, arithmetic overflow, division by zero, invalid method parameters.

11.2 (a) Exception handling is designed to handle infrequently occurring situations that often result in program termination, not situations that arise all the time. (b) Flow of control with conventional control structures is generally clearer and more efficient than with exceptions. (c) The additional exceptions can get in the way of genuine error-type exceptions. It becomes more difficult for you to keep track of the larger number of exception cases.

11.3 It's unlikely that methods of classes in the Java API could perform error processing that would meet the unique needs of all users.

11.4 A "resource leak" occurs when an executing program does not properly release a resource when it's no longer needed.

11.5 The catch blocks for that try statement are skipped, and the program resumes execution after the last catch block. If there is a finally block, it's executed first; then the program resumes execution after the finally block.

11.6 The form catch(Exception *exceptionName*) catches any type of exception thrown in a try block. An advantage is that no thrown Exception can slip by without being caught. You can then decide to handle the exception or possibly rethrow it.

11.7 Errors are usually serious problems with the underlying Java system; most programs will not want to catch Errors because they will not be able to recover from them.

11.8 This causes the search for a match to continue in the next enclosing try statement. If there is a finally block, it will be executed before the exception goes to the next enclosing try statement. If there are no enclosing try statements for which there are matching catch blocks and the exceptions are declared (or unchecked), a stack trace is printed and the current thread terminates early. If the exceptions are checked, but not caught or declared, compilation errors occur.

11.9 The first matching catch block after the try block is executed.

11.10 This enables a program to catch related types of exceptions and process them in a uniform manner. However, it's often useful to process the subclass types individually for more precise exception handling.

11.11 The finally block is the preferred means for releasing resources to prevent resource leaks.

11.12 First, control passes to the `finally` block if there is one. Then the exception will be processed by a `catch` block (if one exists) associated with an enclosing `try` block (if one exists).

11.13 It rethrows the exception for processing by an exception handler of an enclosing `try` statement, after the `finally` block of the current `try` statement executes.

11.14 The reference goes out of scope. If the referenced object becomes unreachable, the object can be garbage collected.

Exercises

11.15 List the various exceptional conditions that have occurred in programs throughout this text so far. List as many additional exceptional conditions as you can. For each of these, describe briefly how a program typically would handle the exception by using the exception-handling techniques discussed in this chapter. Typical exceptions include division by zero and array index out of bounds.

11.16 *(Catching Exceptions with Superclasses)* Use inheritance to create an exception superclass (called `ExceptionA`) and exception subclasses `ExceptionB` and `ExceptionC`, where `ExceptionB` inherits from `ExceptionA` and `ExceptionC` inherits from `ExceptionB`. Write a program to demonstrate that the `catch` block for type `ExceptionA` catches exceptions of types `ExceptionB` and `ExceptionC`.

11.17 *(Order of catch Blocks)* Write a program that shows that the order of `catch` blocks is important. If you try to catch a superclass exception type before a subclass type, the compiler should generate errors.

11.18 *(Rethrowing Exceptions)* Write a program that illustrates rethrowing an exception. Define methods `someMethod` and `someMethod2`. Method `someMethod2` should initially throw an exception. Method `someMethod` should call `someMethod2`, catch the exception and rethrow it. Call `someMethod` from method `main`, and catch the rethrown exception. Print the stack trace of this exception.

11.19 *(Catching Exceptions Using Outer Scopes)* Write a program showing that a method with its own `try` block does not have to catch every possible error generated within the `try`. Some exceptions can slip through to, and be handled in, other scopes.

Action speaks louder than words but not nearly as often.
—Mark Twain

Always design a thing by considering it in its next larger context.
—Eliel Saarinen

Oh, life is a glorious cycle of song.
—Dorothy Parker

The Wright brothers' design ... allowed them to survive long enough to learn how to fly.
—Michael Potts

ATM Case Study, Part 1: Object-Oriented Design with the UML

Objectives

In this chapter you'll learn:

- A simple object-oriented design methodology.

- What a requirements document is.

- To identify classes and class attributes from a requirements document.

- To identify objects' states, activities and operations from a requirements document.

- To determine the collaborations among objects in a system.

- To work with the UML's use case, class, state, activity, communication and sequence diagrams to graphically model an object-oriented system.

12.1 Case Study Introduction

Now we begin the optional portion of our object-oriented design and implementation case study. In this chapter and Chapter 13, you'll design and implement an object-oriented automated teller machine (ATM) software system. The case study provides you with a concise, carefully paced, complete design and implementation experience. In Sections 12.2–12.7 and 13.2–13.3, you'll perform the steps of an object-oriented design (OOD) process using the UML while relating these steps to the object-oriented concepts discussed in Chapters 2–10. In this chapter, you'll work with six popular types of UML diagrams to graphically represent the design. In Chapter 13, you'll tune the design with inheritance, then fully implement the ATM in a 673-line Java application (Section 13.4).

This is not an exercise; rather, it's an end-to-end learning experience that concludes with a detailed walkthrough of the complete Java code that implements our design. It will acquaint you with the kinds of substantial problems encountered in industry.

These chapters can be studied as a continuous unit after you've completed the introduction to object-oriented programming in Chapters 8–11. Or, you can pace the sections one at a time after Chapters 2–8 and 10. Each section of the case study begins with a note telling you the chapter after which it can be covered.

12.2 Examining the Requirements Document

[*Note:* **This section can be taught after Chapter 2.**]
We begin our design process by presenting a **requirements document** that specifies the purpose of the ATM system and *what* it must do. Throughout the case study, we refer often to this requirements document.

Requirements Document
A local bank intends to install a new automated teller machine (ATM) to allow users (i.e., bank customers) to perform basic financial transactions (Fig. 12.1). Each user can have only one account at the bank. ATM users should be able to view their account balance, withdraw cash (i.e., take money out of an account) and deposit funds (i.e., place money into an account). The user interface of the automated teller machine contains:

- a screen that displays messages to the user
- a keypad that receives numeric input from the user
- a cash dispenser that dispenses cash to the user and
- a deposit slot that receives deposit envelopes from the user.

The cash dispenser begins each day loaded with 500 $20 bills. [*Note:* Owing to the limited scope of this case study, certain elements of the ATM described here do not accurately mimic those of a real ATM. For example, a real ATM typically contains a device that reads a user's account number from an ATM card, whereas this ATM asks the user to type the account number on the keypad. A real ATM also usually prints a receipt at the end of a session, but all output from this ATM appears on the screen.]

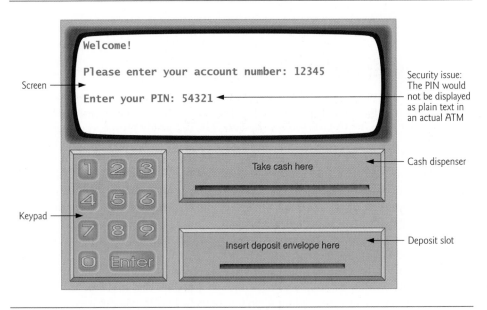

Fig. 12.1 | Automated teller machine user interface.

The bank wants you to develop software to perform the financial transactions initiated by bank customers through the ATM. The bank will integrate the software with the ATM's hardware at a later time. The software should encapsulate the functionality of the hardware devices (e.g., cash dispenser, deposit slot) within software components, but it need not concern itself with how these devices perform their duties. The ATM hardware has not been developed yet, so instead of writing your software to run on the ATM, you should develop a first version to run on a personal computer. This version should use the computer's monitor to simulate the ATM's screen, and the computer's keyboard to simulate the ATM's keypad.

An ATM session consists of authenticating a user (i.e., proving the user's identity) based on an account number and personal identification number (PIN), followed by creating and executing financial transactions. To authenticate a user and perform transactions, the ATM must interact with the bank's account information database (i.e., an organized collection of data stored on a computer; we study database access in Chapter 28). For each bank account, the database stores an account number, a PIN and a balance indicating the amount of money in the account. [*Note:* We assume that the bank plans to build only one ATM, so we need not worry about multiple ATMs accessing this database at the same time. Furthermore, we assume that the bank does not make any changes to the information in the database while a user is accessing the ATM. Also, any business system like an ATM faces reasonably complicated security issues that are beyond the scope of a first or second programming course. We make the simplifying assumption, however, that the bank trusts the ATM to access and manipulate the information in the database without significant security measures.]

Upon first approaching the ATM (assuming no one is currently using it), the user should experience the following sequence of events (shown in Fig. 12.1):

1. The screen displays Welcome! and prompts the user to enter an account number.

2. The user enters a five-digit account number using the keypad.

3. The screen prompts the user to enter the PIN (personal identification number) associated with the specified account number.

4. The user enters a five-digit PIN using the keypad.[1]

5. If the user enters a valid account number and the correct PIN for that account, the screen displays the main menu (Fig. 12.2). If the user enters an invalid account number or an incorrect PIN, the screen displays an appropriate message, then the ATM returns to *Step 1* to restart the authentication process.

Fig. 12.2 | ATM main menu.

After the ATM authenticates the user, the main menu (Fig. 12.2) should contain a numbered option for each of the three types of transactions: balance inquiry (option 1),

---

1. In this simple, command-line, text-based ATM, as you type the PIN, it appears on the screen. This is an obvious security breach—you would not want someone looking over your shoulder at an ATM and seeing your PIN displayed on the screen. In Chapter 14, we introduce the JPasswordField GUI component, which displays asterisks as the user types—making it more appropriate for entering PIN numbers and passwords. Exercise 14.12 asks you to build a GUI-based version of the ATM and to use a JPasswordField to obtain the user's PIN.

withdrawal (option 2) and deposit (option 3). It also should contain an option to allow the user to exit the system (option 4). The user then chooses either to perform a transaction (by entering 1, 2 or 3) or to exit the system (by entering 4).

If the user enters 1 to make a balance inquiry, the screen displays the user's account balance. To do so, the ATM must retrieve the balance from the bank's database.

The following steps describe what occurs when the user enters 2 to make a withdrawal:

1. The screen displays a menu (shown in Fig. 12.3) containing standard withdrawal amounts: $20 (option 1), $40 (option 2), $60 (option 3), $100 (option 4) and $200 (option 5). The menu also contains an option to allow the user to cancel the transaction (option 6).

Fig. 12.3 | ATM withdrawal menu.

2. The user enters a menu selection using the keypad.

3. If the withdrawal amount chosen is greater than the user's account balance, the screen displays a message stating this and telling the user to choose a smaller amount. The ATM then returns to *Step 1*. If the withdrawal amount chosen is less than or equal to the user's account balance (i.e., an acceptable amount), the ATM proceeds to *Step 4*. If the user chooses to cancel the transaction (option 6), the ATM displays the main menu and waits for user input.

4. If the cash dispenser contains enough cash, the ATM proceeds to *Step 5*. Otherwise, the screen displays a message indicating the problem and telling the user to choose a smaller withdrawal amount. The ATM then returns to *Step 1*.

5. The ATM debits the withdrawal amount from the user's account in the bank's database (i.e., subtracts the withdrawal amount from the user's account balance).

6. The cash dispenser dispenses the desired amount of money to the user.

7. The screen displays a message reminding the user to take the money.

The following steps describe the actions that occur when the user enters 3 (when viewing the main menu of Fig. 12.2) to make a deposit:

1. The screen prompts the user to enter a deposit amount or type 0 (zero) to cancel.

2. The user enters a deposit amount or 0 using the keypad. [*Note:* The keypad does not contain a decimal point or a dollar sign, so the user cannot type a real dollar amount (e.g., $27.25). Instead, the user must enter a deposit amount as a number of cents (e.g., 2725). The ATM then divides this number by 100 to obtain a number representing a dollar amount (e.g., 2725 ÷ 100 = 27.25).]

3. If the user specifies a deposit amount, the ATM proceeds to *Step 4*. If the user chooses to cancel the transaction (by entering 0), the ATM displays the main menu and waits for user input.

4. The screen displays a message telling the user to insert a deposit envelope.

5. If the deposit slot receives a deposit envelope within two minutes, the ATM credits the deposit amount to the user's account in the bank's database (i.e., adds the deposit amount to the user's account balance). [*Note:* This money is not immediately available for withdrawal. The bank first must physically verify the amount of cash in the deposit envelope, and any checks in the envelope must clear (i.e., money must be transferred from the check writer's account to the check recipient's account). When either of these events occurs, the bank appropriately updates the user's balance stored in its database. This occurs independently of the ATM system.] If the deposit slot does not receive a deposit envelope within this time period, the screen displays a message that the system has canceled the transaction due to inactivity. The ATM then displays the main menu and waits for user input.

After the system successfully executes a transaction, it should return to the main menu so that the user can perform additional transactions. If the user exits the system, the screen should display a thank you message, then display the welcome message for the next user.

Analyzing the ATM System

The preceding statement is a simplified example of a requirements document. Typically, such a document is the result of a detailed process of **requirements gathering**, which might include interviews with possible users of the system and specialists in fields related to the system. For example, a systems analyst who is hired to prepare a requirements document for banking software (e.g., the ATM system described here) might interview banking experts to gain a better understanding of what the software must do. The analyst would use the information gained to compile a list of **system requirements** to guide systems designers as they design the system.

The process of requirements gathering is a key task of the first stage of the software life cycle. The **software life cycle** specifies the stages through which software goes from the time it's first conceived to the time it's retired from use. These stages typically include: analysis, design, implementation, testing and debugging, deployment, maintenance and retirement. Several software life-cycle models exist, each with its own preferences and specifications for when and how often software engineers should perform each of these stages.

Waterfall models perform each stage once in succession, whereas **iterative models** may repeat one or more stages several times throughout a product's life cycle.

The analysis stage focuses on defining the problem to be solved. When designing any system, one must *solve the problem right*, but of equal importance, one must *solve the right problem*. Systems analysts collect the requirements that indicate the specific problem to solve. Our requirements document describes the requirements of our ATM system in sufficient detail that you need not go through an extensive analysis stage—it's been done for you.

To capture what a proposed system should do, developers often employ a technique known as **use case modeling**. This process identifies the **use cases** of the system, each representing a different capability that the system provides to its clients. For example, ATMs typically have several use cases, such as "View Account Balance," "Withdraw Cash," "Deposit Funds," "Transfer Funds Between Accounts" and "Buy Postage Stamps." The simplified ATM system we build in this case study allows only the first three.

Each use case describes a typical scenario for which the user uses the system. You've already read descriptions of the ATM system's use cases in the requirements document; the lists of steps required to perform each transaction type (i.e., balance inquiry, withdrawal and deposit) actually described the three use cases of our ATM—"View Account Balance," "Withdraw Cash" and "Deposit Funds," respectively.

Use Case Diagrams
We now introduce the first of several UML diagrams in the case study. We create a **use case diagram** to model the interactions between a system's clients (in this case study, bank customers) and its use cases. The goal is to show the kinds of interactions users have with a system without providing the details—these are provided in other UML diagrams (which we present throughout this case study). Use case diagrams are often accompanied by informal text that gives more detail—like the text that appears in the requirements document. Use case diagrams are produced during the analysis stage of the software life cycle. In larger systems, use case diagrams are indispensable tools that help system designers remain focused on satisfying the users' needs.

Figure 12.4 shows the use case diagram for our ATM system. The stick figure represents an **actor**, which defines the roles that an external entity—such as a person or another system—plays when interacting with the system. For our automated teller machine, the actor is a User who can view an account balance, withdraw cash and deposit funds from the ATM. The User is not an actual person, but instead comprises the roles that a real person—when playing the part of a User—can play while interacting with the ATM. Note that a use case diagram can include multiple actors. For example, the use case diagram for a real bank's ATM system might also include an actor named Administrator who refills the cash dispenser each day.

Our requirements document supplies the actors—"ATM users should be able to view their account balance, withdraw cash and deposit funds." Therefore, the actor in each of the three use cases is the user who interacts with the ATM. An external entity—a real person—plays the part of the user to perform financial transactions. Figure 12.4 shows one actor, whose name, User, appears below the actor in the diagram. The UML models each use case as an oval connected to an actor with a solid line.

Software engineers (more precisely, systems designers) must analyze the requirements document or a set of use cases and design the system before programmers implement it in

Fig. 12.4 | Use case diagram for the ATM system from the User's perspective.

a particular programming language. During the analysis stage, systems designers focus on understanding the requirements document to produce a high-level specification that describes *what* the system is supposed to do. The output of the design stage—a **design specification**—should specify clearly *how* the system should be constructed to satisfy these requirements. In the next several sections, we perform the steps of a simple object-oriented design (OOD) process on the ATM system to produce a design specification containing a collection of UML diagrams and supporting text.

The UML is designed for use with any OOD process. Many such processes exist, the best known of which is the Rational Unified Process™ (RUP) developed by Rational Software Corporation, now part of IBM. RUP is a rich process intended for designing "industrial strength" applications. For this case study, we present our own simplified design process, designed for students in first and second programming courses.

Designing the ATM System

We now begin the design stage of our ATM system. A **system** is a set of components that interact to solve a problem. For example, to perform the ATM system's designated tasks, our ATM system has a user interface (Fig. 12.1), and contains software that executes financial transactions and interacts with a database of bank account information. **System structure** describes the system's objects and their interrelationships. **System behavior** describes how the system changes as its objects interact with one another.

Every system has both structure and behavior—designers must specify both. There are several types of system structures and behaviors. For example, the interactions among objects in the system differ from those between the user and the system, yet both constitute a portion of the system behavior.

The UML 2 standard specifies 13 diagram types for documenting the system models. Each models a distinct characteristic of a system's structure or behavior—six diagrams relate to system structure, the remaining seven to system behavior. We list here only the six diagram types used in our case study—one models system structure; the other five model system behavior. We provide an overview of the remaining seven UML diagram types in Appendix P, UML 2: Additional Diagram Types.

1. **Use case diagrams,** such as the one in Fig. 12.4, model the interactions between a system and its external entities (actors) in terms of use cases (system capabilities, such as "View Account Balance," "Withdraw Cash" and "Deposit Funds").

2. **Class diagrams**, which you'll study in Section 12.3, model the classes, or "building blocks," used in a system. Each noun or "thing" described in the requirements document is a candidate to be a class in the system (e.g., `Account`, `Keypad`). Class diagrams help us specify the structural relationships between parts of the system. For example, the ATM system class diagram will specify that the ATM is physically composed of a screen, a keypad, a cash dispenser and a deposit slot.

3. **State machine diagrams**, which you'll study in Section 12.5, model the ways in which an object changes state. An object's **state** is indicated by the values of all its attributes at a given time. When an object changes state, it may behave differently in the system. For example, after validating a user's PIN, the ATM transitions from the "user not authenticated" state to the "user authenticated" state, at which point it allows the user to perform financial transactions (e.g., view account balance, withdraw cash, deposit funds).

4. **Activity diagrams**, which you'll also study in Section 12.5, model an object's **activity**—is workflow (sequence of events) during program execution. An activity diagram models the actions the object performs and specifies the order in which it performs them. For example, an activity diagram shows that the ATM must obtain the balance of the user's account (from the bank's account information database) *before* the screen can display the balance to the user.

5. **Communication diagrams** (called **collaboration diagrams** in earlier versions of the UML) model the interactions among objects in a system, with an emphasis on *what* interactions occur. You'll learn in Section 12.7 that these diagrams show which objects must interact to perform an ATM transaction. For example, the ATM must communicate with the bank's account information database to retrieve an account balance.

6. **Sequence diagrams** also model the interactions among the objects in a system, but unlike communication diagrams, they emphasize *when* interactions occur. You'll learn in Section 12.7 that these diagrams help show the order in which interactions occur in executing a financial transaction. For example, the screen prompts the user to enter a withdrawal amount before cash is dispensed.

In Section 12.3, we continue designing our ATM system by identifying the classes from the requirements document. We accomplish this by extracting key nouns and noun phrases from the requirements document. Using these classes, we develop our first draft of the class diagram that models the structure of our ATM system.

Web Resources
We've created an extensive UML Resource Center that contains many links to additional information, including introductions, tutorials, blogs, books, certification, conferences, developer tools, documentation, e-books, FAQs, forums, groups, UML in Java, podcasts, security, tools, downloads, training courses, videos and more. We encourage you to browse our UML Resource Center at `www.deitel.com/UML/` to learn more.

Self-Review Exercises for Section 12.2

12.1 Suppose we enabled a user of our ATM system to transfer money between two bank accounts. Modify the use case diagram of Fig. 12.4 to reflect this change.

12.2 _____ model the interactions among objects in a system with an emphasis on *when* these interactions occur.
   a)   Class diagrams
   b)   Sequence diagrams
   c)   Communication diagrams
   d)   Activity diagrams

12.3   Which of the following choices lists stages of a typical software life cycle in sequential order?
   a)   design, analysis, implementation, testing
   b)   design, analysis, testing, implementation
   c)   analysis, design, testing, implementation
   d)   analysis, design, implementation, testing

12.3 Identifying the Classes in a Requirements Document

[*Note:* **This section can be taught after Chapter 3.**]
Now we begin designing the ATM system. In this section, we identify the classes that are needed to build the system by analyzing the *nouns* and *noun phrases* that appear in the requirements document. We introduce UML class diagrams to model these classes. This is an important first step in defining the system's structure.

Identifying the Classes in a System
We begin our OOD process by identifying the classes required to build the ATM system. We'll eventually describe these classes using UML class diagrams and implement these classes in Java. First, we review the requirements document of Section 12.2 and identify key nouns and noun phrases to help us identify classes that comprise the ATM system. We may decide that some of these nouns and noun phrases are actually attributes of other classes in the system. We may also conclude that some of the nouns do not correspond to parts of the system and thus should not be modeled at all. Additional classes may become apparent to us as we proceed through the design process.

Figure 12.5 lists the nouns and noun phrases found in the requirements document of Section 12.2. We list them from left to right in the order in which we first encounter them. We list only the singular form of each.

Nouns and noun phrases in the ATM requirements document			
bank	money / funds	account number	ATM
screen	PIN	user	keypad
bank database	customer	cash dispenser	balance inquiry
transaction	$20 bill / cash	withdrawal	account
deposit slot	deposit	balance	deposit envelope

Fig. 12.5 | Nouns and noun phrases in the ATM requirements document.

We create classes only for the nouns and noun phrases that have significance in the ATM system. We don't model "bank" as a class, because the bank is not a part of the ATM system—the bank simply wants us to build the ATM. "Customer" and "user" also represent outside entities—they are important because they *interact* with our ATM system, but we do not need to model them as classes in the ATM software. Recall that we modeled an ATM user (i.e., a bank customer) as the actor in the use case diagram of Fig. 12.4.

We do not model "$20 bill" or "deposit envelope" as classes. These are physical objects in the real world, but they are not part of what is being automated. We can adequately represent the presence of bills in the system using an attribute of the class that models the cash dispenser. (We assign attributes to the ATM system's classes in Section 12.4.) For example, the cash dispenser maintains a count of the number of bills it contains. The requirements document does not say anything about what the system should do with deposit envelopes after it receives them. We can assume that simply acknowledging the receipt of an envelope—an operation performed by the class that models the deposit slot—is sufficient to represent the presence of an envelope in the system. (We assign operations to the ATM system's classes in Section 12.6.)

In our simplified ATM system, representing various amounts of "money," including an account's "balance," as attributes of classes seems most appropriate. Likewise, the nouns "account number" and "PIN" represent significant pieces of information in the ATM system. They are important attributes of a bank account. They do not, however, exhibit behaviors. Thus, we can most appropriately model them as attributes of an account class.

Though the requirements document frequently describes a "transaction" in a general sense, we do not model the broad notion of a financial transaction at this time. Instead, we model the three types of transactions (i.e., "balance inquiry," "withdrawal" and "deposit") as individual classes. These classes possess specific attributes needed for executing the transactions they represent. For example, a withdrawal needs to know the amount of the withdrawal. A balance inquiry, however, does not require any additional data other than the account number. Furthermore, the three transaction classes exhibit unique behaviors. A withdrawal includes dispensing cash to the user, whereas a deposit involves receiving deposit envelopes from the user. [*Note:* In Section 13.3, we "factor out" common features of all transactions into a general "transaction" class using the object-oriented concept of inheritance.]

We determine the classes for our system based on the remaining nouns and noun phrases from Fig. 12.5. Each of these refers to one or more of the following:

- ATM
- screen
- keypad
- cash dispenser
- deposit slot
- account
- bank database
- balance inquiry
- withdrawal
- deposit

The elements of this list are likely to be classes that we'll need to implement our system.

We can now model the classes in our system based on the list we've created. We capitalize class names in the design process—a UML convention—as we'll do when we write the actual Java code that implements our design. If the name of a class contains more than one word, we run the words together and capitalize each word (e.g., `MultipleWordName`). Using this convention, we create classes `ATM`, `Screen`, `Keypad`, `CashDispenser`, `Deposit-Slot`, `Account`, `BankDatabase`, `BalanceInquiry`, `Withdrawal` and `Deposit`. We construct our system using these classes as building blocks. Before we begin building the system, however, we must gain a better understanding of how the classes relate to one another.

Modeling Classes
The UML enables us to model, via **class diagrams**, the classes in the ATM system and their interrelationships. Figure 12.6 represents class `ATM`. Each class is modeled as a rectangle with three compartments. The top one contains the name of the class centered horizontally in boldface. The middle compartment contains the class's attributes. (We discuss attributes in Sections 12.4–12.5.) The bottom compartment contains the class's operations (discussed in Section 12.6). In Fig. 12.6, the middle and bottom compartments are empty because we've not yet determined this class's attributes and operations.

Fig. 12.6 | Representing a class in the UML using a class diagram.

Class diagrams also show the relationships between the classes of the system. Figure 12.7 shows how our classes `ATM` and `Withdrawal` relate to one another. For the moment, for simplicity, we choose to model only this subset of classes. We present a more complete class diagram later in this section. Notice that the rectangles representing classes in this diagram are not subdivided into compartments. The UML allows the suppression of class attributes and operations in this manner to create more readable diagrams, when appropriate. Such a diagram is said to be an **elided diagram**—one in which some information, such as the contents of the second and third compartments, is not modeled. We'll place information in these compartments in Sections 12.4–12.6.

Fig. 12.7 | Class diagram showing an association among classes.

In Fig. 12.7, the solid line that connects the two classes represents an **association**—a relationship between classes. The numbers near each end of the line are **multiplicity** values, which indicate how many objects of each class participate in the association. In this case, following the line from left to right reveals that, at any given moment, one `ATM` object participates in an association with either zero or one `Withdrawal` objects—zero if the current user is not currently performing a transaction or has requested a different type of transaction, and one if the user has requested a withdrawal. The UML can model many types of multiplicity. Figure 12.8 lists and explains the multiplicity types.

Symbol	Meaning
0	None
1	One
m	An integer value
0..1	Zero or one
m, n	m or n
$m..n$	At least m, but not more than n
*	Any nonnegative integer (zero or more)
0..*	Zero or more (identical to *)
1..*	One or more

Fig. 12.8 | Multiplicity types.

An association can be named. For example, the word Executes above the line connecting classes ATM and Withdrawal in Fig. 12.7 indicates the name of that association. This part of the diagram reads "one object of class ATM executes zero or one objects of class Withdrawal." Note that association names are *directional*, as indicated by the filled arrowhead—so it would be improper, for example, to read the preceding association from right to left as "zero or one objects of class Withdrawal execute one object of class ATM."

The word currentTransaction at the Withdrawal end of the association line in Fig. 12.7 is a **role name**, identifying the role the Withdrawal object plays in its relationship with the ATM. A role name adds meaning to an association between classes by identifying the role a class plays in the context of an association. A class can play several roles in the same system. For example, in a school personnel system, a person may play the role of "professor" when relating to students. The same person may take on the role of "colleague" when participating in an association with another professor, and "coach" when coaching student athletes. In Fig. 12.7, the role name currentTransaction indicates that the Withdrawal object participating in the Executes association with an object of class ATM represents the transaction currently being processed by the ATM. In other contexts, a Withdrawal object may take on other roles (e.g., the "previous transaction"). Notice that we do not specify a role name for the ATM end of the Executes association. Role names in class diagrams are often omitted when the meaning of an association is clear without them.

In addition to indicating simple relationships, associations can specify more complex relationships, such as objects of one class being "composed of" objects of other classes. Consider a real-world automated teller machine. What "pieces" does a manufacturer put together to build a working ATM? Our requirements document tells us that the ATM is composed of a screen, a keypad, a cash dispenser and a deposit slot.

In Fig. 12.9, the **solid diamonds** attached to the ATM class's association lines indicate that ATM has a **composition** relationship with classes Screen, Keypad, CashDispenser and DepositSlot. Composition implies a whole/part relationship. The class that has the composition symbol (the solid diamond) on its end of the association line is the whole (in this case, ATM), and the classes on the other end of the association lines are the parts—in this case, Screen, Keypad, CashDispenser and DepositSlot. The compositions in Fig. 12.9 indicate that an object of class ATM is formed from one object of class Screen, one object of class CashDispenser, one object of class Keypad and one object of class DepositSlot.

The ATM *has a* screen, a keypad, a cash dispenser and a deposit slot. (As we saw in Chapter 9, the *is-a* relationship defines inheritance. We'll see in Section 13.3 that there's a nice opportunity to use inheritance in the ATM system design.)

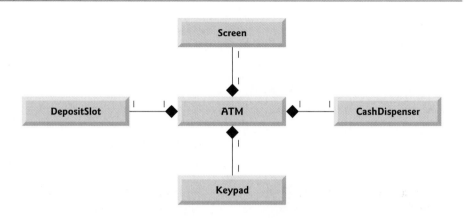

Fig. 12.9 | Class diagram showing composition relationships.

According to the UML specification (www.omg.org/technology/documents/ formal/uml.htm), composition relationships have the following properties:

1. Only one class in the relationship can represent the whole (i.e., the diamond can be placed on only one end of the association line). For example, either the screen is part of the ATM or the ATM is part of the screen, but the screen and the ATM cannot both represent the whole in the relationship.

2. The parts in the composition relationship exist only as long as the whole does, and the whole is responsible for the creation and destruction of its parts. For example, the act of constructing an ATM includes manufacturing its parts. Also, if the ATM is destroyed, its screen, keypad, cash dispenser and deposit slot are also destroyed.

3. A part may belong to only one whole at a time, although it may be removed and attached to another whole, which then assumes responsibility for the part.

The solid diamonds in our class diagrams indicate composition relationships that fulfill these properties. If a *has-a* relationship does not satisfy one or more of these criteria, the UML specifies that **hollow diamonds** be attached to the ends of association lines to indicate **aggregation**—a weaker form of composition. For example, a personal computer and a computer monitor participate in an aggregation relationship—the computer *has a* monitor, but the two parts can exist independently, and the same monitor can be attached to multiple computers at once, thus violating composition's second and third properties.

Figure 12.10 shows a class diagram for the ATM system. This diagram models most of the classes that we identified earlier in this section, as well as the associations between them that we can infer from the requirements document. [*Note:* Classes BalanceInquiry and Deposit participate in associations similar to those of class Withdrawal, so we've chosen to omit them from this diagram to keep it simple. In Section 13.3, we expand our class diagram to include all the classes in the ATM system.]

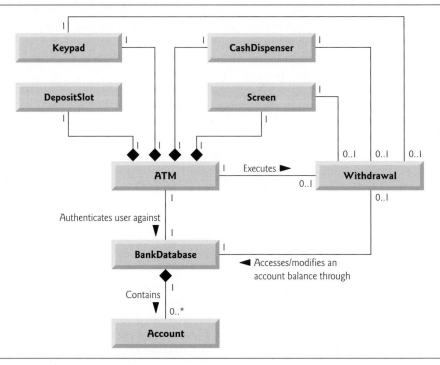

Fig. 12.10 | Class diagram for the ATM system model.

Figure 12.10 presents a graphical model of ATM system's structure. It includes classes BankDatabase and Account, and several associations that were not present in either Fig. 12.7 or Fig. 12.9. It shows that class ATM has a **one-to-one relationship** with class BankDatabase—one ATM object authenticates users against one BankDatabase object. In Fig. 12.10, we also model the fact that the bank's database contains information about many accounts—one BankDatabase object participates in a composition relationship with zero or more Account objects. The multiplicity value 0..* at the Account end of the association between class BankDatabase and class Account indicates that zero or more objects of class Account take part in the association. Class BankDatabase has a **one-to-many relationship** with class Account—the BankDatabase contains many Accounts. Similarly, class Account has a **many-to-one relationship** with class BankDatabase—there can be many Accounts stored in the BankDatabase. [*Note:* Recall from Fig. 12.8 that the multiplicity value * is identical to 0..*. We include 0..* in our class diagrams for clarity.]

Figure 12.10 also indicates that at any given time 0 or 1 Withdrawal objects can exist. If the user is performing a withdrawal, "one object of class Withdrawal accesses/modifies an account balance through one object of class BankDatabase." We could have created an association directly between class Withdrawal and class Account. The requirements document, however, states that the "ATM must interact with the bank's account information database" to perform transactions. A bank account contains sensitive information, and systems engineers must always consider the security of personal data when designing a system. Thus, only the BankDatabase can access and manipulate an account directly. All other parts of the system must interact with the database to retrieve or update account information (e.g., an account balance).

The class diagram in Fig. 12.10 also models associations between class `Withdrawal` and classes `Screen`, `CashDispenser` and `Keypad`. A withdrawal transaction includes prompting the user to choose a withdrawal amount, and receiving numeric input. These actions require the use of the screen and the keypad, respectively. Furthermore, dispensing cash to the user requires access to the cash dispenser.

Classes `BalanceInquiry` and `Deposit`, though not shown in Fig. 12.10, take part in several associations with the other classes of the ATM system. Like class `Withdrawal`, each of these classes associates with classes `ATM` and `BankDatabase`. An object of class `Balance-Inquiry` also associates with an object of class `Screen` to display the balance of an account to the user. Class `Deposit` associates with classes `Screen`, `Keypad` and `DepositSlot`. Like withdrawals, deposit transactions require use of the screen and the keypad to display prompts and receive input, respectively. To receive deposit envelopes, an object of class `Deposit` accesses the deposit slot.

We've now identified the initial classes in our ATM system—we may discover others as we proceed with the design and implementation. In Section 12.4 we determine the attributes for each of these classes, and in Section 12.5 we use these attributes to examine how the system changes over time.

Self-Review Exercises for Section 12.3

12.4 Suppose we have a class `Car` that represents a car. Think of some of the different pieces that a manufacturer would put together to produce a whole car. Create a class diagram (similar to Fig. 12.9) that models some of the composition relationships of class `Car`.

12.5 Suppose we have a class `File` that represents an electronic document in a standalone, non-networked computer represented by class `Computer`. What sort of association exists between class `Computer` and class `File`?
   a) Class `Computer` has a one-to-one relationship with class `File`.
   b) Class `Computer` has a many-to-one relationship with class `File`.
   c) Class `Computer` has a one-to-many relationship with class `File`.
   d) Class `Computer` has a many-to-many relationship with class `File`.

12.6 State whether the following statement is *true* or *false*, and if *false*, explain why: A UML diagram in which a class's second and third compartments are not modeled is said to be an elided diagram.

12.7 Modify the class diagram of Fig. 12.10 to include class `Deposit` instead of class `Withdrawal`.

12.4 Identifying Class Attributes

[*Note:* **This section can be taught after Chapter 4.**]

In Section 12.3, we began the first stage of an object-oriented design (OOD) for our ATM system—analyzing the requirements document and identifying the classes needed to implement the system. We listed the nouns and noun phrases in the requirements document and identified a class for each one that plays a significant role in the ATM system. We then modeled the classes and their relationships in a UML class diagram (Fig. 12.10).

Classes have attributes (data) and operations (behaviors). Class attributes are implemented in Java programs as fields, and class operations are implemented as methods. In this section, we determine many of the attributes needed in the ATM system. In Section 12.5 we examine how these attributes represent an object's state. In Section 12.6 we determine class operations.

Identifying Attributes

Consider the attributes of some real-world objects: A person's attributes include height, weight and whether the person is left-handed, right-handed or ambidextrous. A radio's attributes include its station, volume and AM or FM settings. A car's attributes include its speedometer and odometer readings, the amount of gas in its tank and what gear it's in. A personal computer's attributes include its manufacturer (e.g., Dell, Sun, Apple or IBM), type of screen (e.g., LCD or CRT), main memory size and hard disk size.

We can identify many attributes of the classes in our system by looking for descriptive words and phrases in the requirements document. For each such word and phrase we find that plays a significant role in the ATM system, we create an attribute and assign it to one or more of the classes identified in Section 12.3. We also create attributes to represent any additional data that a class may need, as such needs become clear throughout the design process.

Figure 12.11 lists the words or phrases from the requirements document that describe each class. We formed this list by reading the requirements document and identifying any words or phrases that refer to characteristics of the classes in the system. For example, the requirements document describes the steps taken to obtain a "withdrawal amount," so we list "amount" next to class `Withdrawal`.

Class	Descriptive words and phrases
ATM	user is authenticated
BalanceInquiry	account number
Withdrawal	account number
	amount
Deposit	account number
	amount
BankDatabase	*[no descriptive words or phrases]*
Account	account number
	PIN
	balance
Screen	*[no descriptive words or phrases]*
Keypad	*[no descriptive words or phrases]*
CashDispenser	begins each day loaded with 500 $20 bills
DepositSlot	*[no descriptive words or phrases]*

Fig. 12.11 | Descriptive words and phrases from the ATM requirements document.

Figure 12.11 leads us to create one attribute of class `ATM`. Class `ATM` maintains information about the state of the ATM. The phrase "user is authenticated" describes a state of the ATM (we introduce states in Section 12.5), so we include `userAuthenticated` as a **Boolean attribute** (i.e., an attribute that has a value of either `true` or `false`) in class `ATM`. Note that the `Boolean` attribute type in the UML is equivalent to the `boolean` type in Java. This attribute indicates whether the ATM has successfully authenticated the current user—userAuthenticated must be true for the system to allow the user to perform transactions and access account information. This attribute helps ensure the security of the data in the system.

Classes BalanceInquiry, Withdrawal and Deposit share one attribute. Each transaction involves an "account number" that corresponds to the account of the user making the transaction. We assign an integer attribute accountNumber to each transaction class to identify the account to which an object of the class applies.

Descriptive words and phrases in the requirements document also suggest some differences in the attributes required by each transaction class. The requirements document indicates that to withdraw cash or deposit funds, users must input a specific "amount" of money to be withdrawn or deposited, respectively. Thus, we assign to classes Withdrawal and Deposit an attribute amount to store the value supplied by the user. The amounts of money related to a withdrawal and a deposit are defining characteristics of these transactions that the system requires for these transactions to take place. Class BalanceInquiry, however, needs no additional data to perform its task—it requires only an account number to indicate the account whose balance should be retrieved.

Class Account has several attributes. The requirements document states that each bank account has an "account number" and "PIN," which the system uses for identifying accounts and authenticating users. We assign to class Account two integer attributes: accountNumber and pin. The requirements document also specifies that an account maintains a "balance" of the amount of money in the account and that money the user deposits does not become available for a withdrawal until the bank verifies the amount of cash in the deposit envelope, and any checks in the envelope clear. An account must still record the amount of money that a user deposits, however. Therefore, we decide that an account should represent a balance using two attributes: availableBalance and totalBalance. Attribute availableBalance tracks the amount of money that a user can withdraw from the account. Attribute totalBalance refers to the total amount of money that the user has "on deposit" (i.e., the amount of money available, plus the amount waiting to be verified or cleared). For example, suppose an ATM user deposits $50.00 into an empty account. The totalBalance attribute would increase to $50.00 to record the deposit, but the availableBalance would remain at $0.

[*Note:* We assume that the bank updates the availableBalance attribute of an Account some length of time after the ATM transaction occurs, in response to confirming that $50 worth of cash or checks was found in the deposit envelope. We assume that this update occurs through a transaction that a bank employee performs using some piece of bank software other than the ATM. Thus, we do not discuss this transaction in our case study.]

Class CashDispenser has one attribute. The requirements document states that the cash dispenser "begins each day loaded with 500 $20 bills." The cash dispenser must keep track of the number of bills it contains to determine whether enough cash is on hand to satisfy withdrawal requests. We assign to class CashDispenser an integer attribute count, which is initially set to 500.

For real problems in industry, there is no guarantee that requirements documents will be precise enough for the object-oriented systems designer to determine all the attributes or even all the classes. The need for additional classes, attributes and behaviors may become clear as the design process proceeds. As we progress through this case study, we will continue to add, modify and delete information about the classes in our system.

Modeling Attributes

The class diagram in Fig. 12.12 lists some of the attributes for the classes in our system—the descriptive words and phrases in Fig. 12.11 lead us to identify these attributes. For simplicity, Fig. 12.12 does not show the associations among classes—we showed these in Fig. 12.10. This is a common practice of systems designers when designs are being developed. Recall from Section 12.3 that in the UML, a class's attributes are placed in the middle compartment of the class's rectangle. We list each attribute's name and type separated by a colon (:), followed in some cases by an equal sign (=) and an initial value.

Consider the userAuthenticated attribute of class ATM:

```
userAuthenticated : Boolean = false
```

This attribute declaration contains three pieces of information about the attribute. The **attribute name** is userAuthenticated. The **attribute type** is Boolean. In Java, an attribute can be represented by a primitive type, such as boolean, int or double, or a reference type like a class. We've chosen to model only primitive-type attributes in Fig. 12.12—we discuss the reasoning behind this decision shortly. [*Note:* The attribute types in Fig. 12.12 are in UML notation. We'll associate the types Boolean, Integer and Double in the UML diagram with the primitive types boolean, int and double in Java, respectively.]

We can also indicate an initial value for an attribute. The userAuthenticated attribute in class ATM has an initial value of false. This indicates that the system initially does

Fig. 12.12 | Classes with attributes.

not consider the user to be authenticated. If an attribute has no initial value specified, only its name and type (separated by a colon) are shown. For example, the accountNumber attribute of class BalanceInquiry is an integer. Here we show no initial value, because the value of this attribute is a number that we do not yet know. This number will be determined at execution time based on the account number entered by the current ATM user.

Figure 12.12 does not include attributes for classes Screen, Keypad and DepositSlot. These are important components of our system, for which our design process has not yet revealed any attributes. We may discover some, however, in the remaining phases of design or when we implement these classes in Java. This is perfectly normal.

Software Engineering Observation 12.1

At early stages in the design process, classes often lack attributes (and operations). Such classes should not be eliminated, however, because attributes (and operations) may become evident in the later phases of design and implementation.

Note that Fig. 12.12 also does not include attributes for class BankDatabase. Recall that attributes in Java can be represented by either primitive types or reference types. We've chosen to include only primitive-type attributes in the class diagram in Fig. 12.12 (and in similar class diagrams throughout the case study). A reference-type attribute is modeled more clearly as an association between the class holding the reference and the class of the object to which the reference points. For example, the class diagram in Fig. 12.10 indicates that class BankDatabase participates in a composition relationship with zero or more Account objects. From this composition, we can determine that when we implement the ATM system in Java, we'll be required to create an attribute of class BankDatabase to hold references to zero or more Account objects. Similarly, we can determine reference-type attributes of class ATM that correspond to its composition relationships with classes Screen, Keypad, CashDispenser and DepositSlot. These composition-based attributes would be redundant if modeled in Fig. 12.12, because the compositions modeled in Fig. 12.10 already convey the fact that the database contains information about zero or more accounts and that an ATM is composed of a screen, keypad, cash dispenser and deposit slot. Software developers typically model these whole/part relationships as compositions rather than as attributes required to implement the relationships.

The class diagram in Fig. 12.12 provides a solid basis for the structure of our model, but the diagram is not complete. In Section 12.5 we identify the states and activities of the objects in the model, and in Section 12.6 we identify the operations that the objects perform. As we present more of the UML and object-oriented design, we'll continue to strengthen the structure of our model.

Self-Review Exercises for Section 12.4

12.8   We typically identify the attributes of the classes in our system by analyzing the _____ in the requirements document.
     a) nouns and noun phrases
     b) descriptive words and phrases
     c) verbs and verb phrases
     d) All of the above.

12.9   Which of the following is not an attribute of an airplane?
     a) length
     b) wingspan

c) fly

d) number of seats

12.10 Describe the meaning of the following attribute declaration of class `CashDispenser` in the class diagram in Fig. 12.12:

```
count : Integer = 500
```

12.5 Identifying Objects' States and Activities

[*Note:* **This section can be taught after Chapter 5.**]

In Section 12.4, we identified many of the class attributes needed to implement the ATM system and added them to the class diagram in Fig. 12.12. We now show how these attributes represent an object's state. We identify some key states that our objects may occupy and discuss how objects change state in response to various events occurring in the system. We also discuss the workflow, or **activities**, that objects perform in the ATM system, and we present the activities of `BalanceInquiry` and `Withdrawal` transaction objects.

State Machine Diagrams

Each object in a system goes through a series of states. An object's state is indicated by the values of its attributes at a given time. **State machine diagrams** (commonly called **state diagrams**) model several states of an object and show under what circumstances the object changes state. Unlike the class diagrams presented in earlier case study sections, which focused primarily on the system's structure, state diagrams model some of the system's behavior.

Figure 12.13 is a simple state diagram that models some of the states of an object of class `ATM`. The UML represents each state in a state diagram as a **rounded rectangle** with the name of the state placed inside it. A **solid circle** with an attached stick ($\rightarrow$) arrowhead designates the **initial state**. Recall that we modeled this state information as the `Boolean` attribute `userAuthenticated` in the class diagram of Fig. 12.12. This attribute is initialized to `false`, or the "User not authenticated" state, according to the state diagram.

Fig. 12.13 | State diagram for the `ATM` object.

The arrows with stick ($\rightarrow$) arrowhead indicate **transitions** between states. An object can transition from one state to another in response to various events that occur in the system. The name or description of the event that causes a transition is written near the line that corresponds to the transition. For example, the `ATM` object changes from the "User not authenticated" to the "User authenticated" state after the database authenticates the user. Recall from the requirements document that the database authenticates a user by comparing the account number and PIN entered by the user with those of an account in the database. If the user has entered a valid account number and the correct PIN, the `ATM` object transitions to the "User authenticated" state and changes its `userAuthenticated` attribute to a value of `true`. When the user exits the system by choosing the "exit" option from the main menu, the `ATM` object returns to the "User not authenticated" state.

Software Engineering Observation 12.2

Software designers do not generally create state diagrams showing every possible state and state transition for all attributes—there are simply too many of them. State diagrams typically show only key states and state transitions.

Activity Diagrams

Like a state diagram, an activity diagram models aspects of system behavior. Unlike a state diagram, an activity diagram models an object's **workflow** (sequence of events) during program execution. An activity diagram models the **actions** the object will perform and in what order. The activity diagram in Fig. 12.14 models the actions involved in executing a balance-inquiry transaction. We assume that a `BalanceInquiry` object has already been initialized and assigned a valid account number (that of the current user), so the object knows which balance to retrieve. The diagram includes the actions that occur after the user selects a balance inquiry from the main menu and before the ATM returns the user to the main menu—a `BalanceInquiry` object does not perform or initiate these actions, so we do not model them here. The diagram begins with retrieving the balance of the account from the database. Next, the `BalanceInquiry` displays the balance on the screen. This action completes the execution of the transaction. Recall that we've chosen to represent an account balance as both the `availableBalance` and `totalBalance` attributes of class `Account`, so the actions modeled in Fig. 12.14 refer to the retrieval and display of *both* balance attributes.

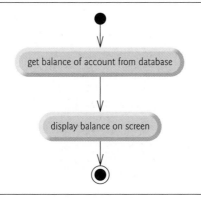

Fig. 12.14 | Activity diagram for a `BalanceInquiry` object.

The UML represents an action in an activity diagram as an action state modeled by a rectangle with its left and right sides replaced by arcs curving outward. Each action state contains an action expression—for example, "get balance of account from database"—that specifies an action to be performed. An arrow with a stick ($\rightarrow$) arrowhead connects two action states, indicating the order in which the actions represented by the action states occur. The solid circle (at the top of Fig. 12.14) represents the activity's initial state—the beginning of the workflow before the object performs the modeled actions. In this case, the transaction first executes the "get balance of account from database" action expression. The transaction then displays both balances on the screen. The solid circle enclosed in an open circle (at the bottom of Fig. 12.14) represents the final state—the end of the workflow after the object performs the modeled actions. We used UML activity diagrams to illustrate the flow of control for the control statements presented in Chapters 4–5.

Figure 12.15 shows an activity diagram for a withdrawal transaction. We assume that a Withdrawal object has been assigned a valid account number. We do not model the user

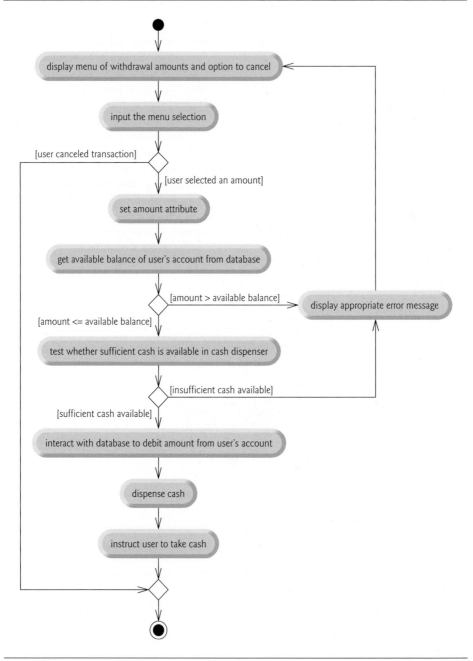

Fig. 12.15 | Activity diagram for a withdrawal transaction.

selecting a withdrawal from the main menu or the ATM returning the user to the main menu because these are not actions performed by a `Withdrawal` object. The transaction first displays a menu of standard withdrawal amounts (shown in Fig. 12.3) and an option to cancel the transaction. The transaction then receives a menu selection from the user. The activity flow now arrives at a decision (a fork indicated by the small diamond symbol). [*Note:* A decision was known as a branch in earlier versions of the UML.] This point determines the next action based on the associated guard condition (in square brackets next to the transition), which states that the transition occurs if this guard condition is met. If the user cancels the transaction by choosing the "cancel" option from the menu, the activity flow immediately skips to the final state. Note the merge (indicated by the small diamond symbol) where the cancellation flow of activity joins the main flow of activity before reaching the activity's final state. If the user selects a withdrawal amount from the menu, `Withdrawal` sets `amount` (an attribute originally modeled in Fig. 12.12) to the value chosen by the user.

After setting the withdrawal amount, the transaction retrieves the available balance of the user's account (i.e., the `availableBalance` attribute of the user's `Account` object) from the database. The activity flow then arrives at another decision. If the requested withdrawal amount exceeds the user's available balance, the system displays an appropriate error message informing the user of the problem, then returns to the beginning of the activity diagram and prompts the user to input a new amount. If the requested withdrawal amount is less than or equal to the user's available balance, the transaction proceeds. The transaction next tests whether the cash dispenser has enough cash remaining to satisfy the withdrawal request. If it does not, the transaction displays an appropriate error message, then returns to the beginning of the activity diagram and prompts the user to choose a new amount. If sufficient cash is available, the transaction interacts with the database to debit the withdrawal amount from the user's account (i.e., subtract the amount from both the `availableBalance` and `totalBalance` attributes of the user's `Account` object). The transaction then dispenses the desired amount of cash and instructs the user to take it. Finally, the main flow of activity merges with the cancellation flow of activity before reaching the final state.

We've taken the first steps in modeling the ATM software system's behavior and have shown how an object's attributes participate in performing the object's activities. In Section 12.6, we investigate the behaviors for all classes to give a more accurate interpretation of the system behavior by filling in the third compartments of the classes in our class diagram.

Self-Review Exercises for Section 12.5

12.11   State whether the following statement is *true* or *false*, and if *false*, explain why: State diagrams model structural aspects of a system.

12.12   An activity diagram models the _____ that an object performs and the order in which it performs them.
a) actions
b) attributes
c) states
d) state transitions

12.13   Based on the requirements document, create an activity diagram for a deposit transaction.

12.6 Identifying Class Operations

[*Note:* **This section can be taught after Chapter 6.**]

In this section, we determine some of the class operations (or behaviors) needed to implement the ATM system. An operation is a service that objects of a class provide to clients (users) of the class. Consider the operations of some real-world objects. A radio's operations include setting its station and volume (typically invoked by a person's adjusting the radio's controls). A car's operations include accelerating (invoked by the driver's pressing the accelerator pedal), decelerating (invoked by the driver's pressing the brake pedal or releasing the gas pedal), turning and shifting gears. Software objects can offer operations as well—for example, a software graphics object might offer operations for drawing a circle, drawing a line, drawing a square and the like. A spreadsheet software object might offer operations like printing the spreadsheet, totaling the elements in a row or column and graphing information in the spreadsheet as a bar chart or pie chart.

We can derive many of the class operations by examining the key verbs and verb phrases in the requirements document. We then relate these verbs and verb phrases to classes in our system (Fig. 12.16). The verb phrases in Fig. 12.16 help us determine the operations of each class.

Class	Verbs and verb phrases
ATM	executes financial transactions
BalanceInquiry	*[none in the requirements document]*
Withdrawal	*[none in the requirements document]*
Deposit	*[none in the requirements document]*
BankDatabase	authenticates a user, retrieves an account balance, credits a deposit amount to an account, debits a withdrawal amount from an account
Account	retrieves an account balance, credits a deposit amount to an account, debits a withdrawal amount from an account
Screen	displays a message to the user
Keypad	receives numeric input from the user
CashDispenser	dispenses cash, indicates whether it contains enough cash to satisfy a withdrawal request
DepositSlot	receives a deposit envelope

Fig. 12.16 | Verbs and verb phrases for each class in the ATM system.

Modeling Operations

To identify operations, we examine the verb phrases listed for each class in Fig. 12.16. The "executes financial transactions" phrase associated with class ATM implies that class ATM instructs transactions to execute. Therefore, classes BalanceInquiry, Withdrawal and Deposit each need an operation to provide this service to the ATM. We place this operation (which we've named execute) in the third compartment of the three transaction classes in the updated class diagram of Fig. 12.17. During an ATM session, the ATM object will invoke these transaction operations as necessary.

Fig. 12.17 | Classes in the ATM system with attributes and operations.

The UML represents operations (which are implemented as methods in Java) by listing the operation name, followed by a comma-separated list of parameters in parentheses, a colon and the return type:

operationName(parameter1, parameter2, ..., parameterN) : return type

Each parameter in the comma-separated parameter list consists of a parameter name, followed by a colon and the parameter type:

parameterName : parameterType

For the moment, we do not list the parameters of our operations—we'll identify and model some of them shortly. For some of the operations, we do not yet know the return types, so we also omit them from the diagram. These omissions are perfectly normal at this point. As our design and implementation proceed, we'll add the remaining return types.

Authenticating a User

Figure 12.16 lists the phrase "authenticates a user" next to class BankDatabase—the database is the object that contains the account information necessary to determine whether the account number and PIN entered by a user match those of an account held at the bank. Therefore, class `BankDatabase` needs an operation that provides an authentication service to the ATM. We place the operation `authenticateUser` in the third compartment of class `BankDatabase` (Fig. 12.17). However, an object of class `Account`, not class `BankDatabase`, stores the account number and PIN that must be accessed to authenticate a user, so class `Account` must provide a service to validate a PIN obtained through user input against a PIN stored in an `Account` object. Therefore, we add a `validatePIN` operation to class `Account`. Note that we specify a return type of `Boolean` for the `authenticateUser` and `validatePIN` operations. Each operation returns a value indicating either that the operation was successful in performing its task (i.e., a return value of `true`) or that it was not (i.e., a return value of `false`).

Other *BankDatabase* and *Account* Operations

Figure 12.16 lists several additional verb phrases for class `BankDatabase`: "retrieves an account balance," "credits a deposit amount to an account" and "debits a withdrawal amount from an account." Like "authenticates a user," these remaining phrases refer to services that the database must provide to the ATM, because the database holds all the account data used to authenticate a user and perform ATM transactions. However, objects of class `Account` actually perform the operations to which these phrases refer. Thus, we assign an operation to both class `BankDatabase` and class `Account` to correspond to each of these phrases. Recall from Section 12.3 that, because a bank account contains sensitive information, we do not allow the ATM to access accounts directly. The database acts as an intermediary between the ATM and the account data, thus preventing unauthorized access. As we'll see in Section 12.7, class `ATM` invokes the operations of class `BankDatabase`, each of which in turn invokes the operation with the same name in class `Account`.

Getting the Balances

The phrase "retrieves an account balance" suggests that classes `BankDatabase` and `Account` each need a `getBalance` operation. However, recall that we created two attributes in class `Account` to represent a balance—`availableBalance` and `totalBalance`. A balance inquiry requires access to both balance attributes so that it can display them to the user, but a withdrawal needs to check only the value of `availableBalance`. To allow objects in the system to obtain each balance attribute individually, we add operations `getAvailableBalance` and `getTotalBalance` to the third compartment of classes `BankDatabase` and `Account` (Fig. 12.17). We specify a return type of `Double` for these operations because the balance attributes they retrieve are of type `Double`.

Crediting and Debiting an *Account*

The phrases "credits a deposit amount to an account" and "debits a withdrawal amount from an account" indicate that classes `BankDatabase` and `Account` must perform operations to update an account during a deposit and withdrawal, respectively. We therefore assign `credit` and `debit` operations to classes `BankDatabase` and `Account`. You may recall that crediting an account (as in a deposit) adds an amount only to the `totalBalance` attribute. Debiting an account (as in a withdrawal), on the other hand, subtracts the amount from both balance attributes. We hide these implementation details inside class `Account`. This is a good example of encapsulation and information hiding.

Deposit Confirmations Performed by Another Banking System
If this were a real ATM system, classes BankDatabase and Account would also provide a set of operations to allow another banking system to update a user's account balance after either confirming or rejecting all or part of a deposit. Operation confirmDepositAmount, for example, would add an amount to the availableBalance attribute, thus making deposited funds available for withdrawal. Operation rejectDepositAmount would subtract an amount from the totalBalance attribute to indicate that a specified amount, which had recently been deposited through the ATM and added to the totalBalance, was not found in the deposit envelope. The bank would invoke this operation after determining either that the user failed to include the correct amount of cash or that any checks did not clear (i.e., they "bounced"). While adding these operations would make our system more complete, we do not include them in our class diagrams or our implementation because they are beyond the scope of the case study.

Displaying Messages
Class Screen "displays a message to the user" at various times in an ATM session. All visual output occurs through the screen of the ATM. The requirements document describes many types of messages (e.g., a welcome message, an error message, a thank you message) that the screen displays to the user. The requirements document also indicates that the screen displays prompts and menus to the user. However, a prompt is really just a message describing what the user should input next, and a menu is essentially a type of prompt consisting of a series of messages (i.e., menu options) displayed consecutively. Therefore, rather than assign class Screen an individual operation to display each type of message, prompt and menu, we simply create one operation that can display any message specified by a parameter. We place this operation (displayMessage) in the third compartment of class Screen in our class diagram (Fig. 12.17). Note that we do not worry about the parameter of this operation at this time—we model it later in this section.

Keyboard Input
From the phrase "receives numeric input from the user" listed by class Keypad in Fig. 12.16, we conclude that class Keypad should perform a getInput operation. Because the ATM's keypad, unlike a computer keyboard, contains only the numbers 0–9, we specify that this operation returns an integer value. Recall from the requirements document that in different situations the user may be required to enter a different type of number (e.g., an account number, a PIN, the number of a menu option, a deposit amount as a number of cents). Class Keypad simply obtains a numeric value for a client of the class—it does not determine whether the value meets any specific criteria. Any class that uses this operation must verify that the user entered an appropriate number in a given situation, then respond accordingly (i.e., display an error message via class Screen). [*Note:* When we implement the system, we simulate the ATM's keypad with a computer keyboard, and for simplicity we assume that the user does not enter nonnumeric input using keys on the computer keyboard that do not appear on the ATM's keypad.]

Dispensing Cash
Figure 12.16 lists "dispenses cash" for class CashDispenser. Therefore, we create operation dispenseCash and list it under class CashDispenser in Fig. 12.17. Class CashDispenser also "indicates whether it contains enough cash to satisfy a withdrawal request."

Thus, we include `isSufficientCashAvailable`, an operation that returns a value of UML type `Boolean`, in class `CashDispenser`.

Figure 12.16 also lists "receives a deposit envelope" for class `DepositSlot`. The deposit slot must indicate whether it received an envelope, so we place an operation `isEnvelopeReceived`, which returns a `Boolean` value, in the third compartment of class `DepositSlot`. [*Note:* A real hardware deposit slot would most likely send the ATM a signal to indicate that an envelope was received. We simulate this behavior, however, with an operation in class `DepositSlot` that class `ATM` can invoke to find out whether the deposit slot received an envelope.]

Class *ATM*

We do not list any operations for class `ATM` at this time. We are not yet aware of any services that class `ATM` provides to other classes in the system. When we implement the system with Java code, however, operations of this class, and additional operations of the other classes in the system, may emerge.

Identifying and Modeling Operation Parameters for Class *BankDatabase*

So far, we've not been concerned with the parameters of our operations—we've attempted to gain only a basic understanding of the operations of each class. Let's now take a closer look at some operation parameters. We identify an operation's parameters by examining what data the operation requires to perform its assigned task.

Consider `BankDatabase`'s `authenticateUser` operation. To authenticate a user, this operation must know the account number and PIN supplied by the user. So we specify that `authenticateUser` takes integer parameters `userAccountNumber` and `userPIN`, which the operation must compare to an `Account` object's account number and PIN in the database. We prefix these parameter names with "user" to avoid confusion between the operation's parameter names and class `Account`'s attribute names. We list these parameters in the class diagram in Fig. 12.18 that models only class `BankDatabase`. [*Note:* It's perfectly normal to model only one class. In this case, we're examining the parameters of this one class, so we omit the other classes. In class diagrams later in the case study, in which parameters are no longer the focus of our attention, we omit these parameters to save space. Remember, however, that the operations listed in these diagrams still have parameters.]

Fig. 12.18 | Class `BankDatabase` with operation parameters.

Recall that the UML models each parameter in an operation's comma-separated parameter list by listing the parameter name, followed by a colon and the parameter type (in UML notation). Figure 12.18 thus specifies that operation `authenticateUser` takes two parameters—userAccountNumber and userPIN, both of type Integer. When we implement the system in Java, we'll represent these parameters with int values.

Class BankDatabase operations getAvailableBalance, getTotalBalance, credit and debit also each require a userAccountNumber parameter to identify the account to which the database must apply the operations, so we include these parameters in the class diagram of Fig. 12.18. In addition, operations credit and debit each require a Double parameter amount to specify the amount of money to be credited or debited, respectively.

Identifying and Modeling Operation Parameters for Class Account
Figure 12.19 models class Account's operation parameters. Operation validatePIN requires only a userPIN parameter, which contains the user-specified PIN to be compared with the account's PIN. Like their BankDatabase counterparts, operations credit and debit in class Account each require a Double parameter amount that indicates the amount of money involved in the operation. Operations getAvailableBalance and getTotalBalance in class Account require no additional data to perform their tasks. Note that class Account's operations do not require an account-number parameter to distinguish between Accounts, because these operations can be invoked only on a specific Account object.

Fig. 12.19 | Class Account with operation parameters.

Identifying and Modeling Operation Parameters for Class Screen
Figure 12.20 models class Screen with a parameter specified for operation displayMessage. This operation requires only a String parameter message that indicates the text to be displayed. Recall that the parameter types listed in our class diagrams are in UML notation, so the String type listed in Fig. 12.20 refers to the UML type. When we implement the system in Java, we'll use the Java class String to represent this parameter.

Fig. 12.20 | Class Screen with operation parameters.

Identifying and Modeling Operation Parameters for Class CashDispenser
Figure 12.21 specifies that operation dispenseCash of class CashDispenser takes a Double parameter amount to indicate the amount of cash (in dollars) to be dispensed. Operation

isSufficientCashAvailable also takes a Double parameter amount to indicate the amount of cash in question.

Fig. 12.21 | Class CashDispenser with operation parameters.

Identifying and Modeling Operation Parameters for Other Classes
Note that we do not discuss parameters for operation execute of classes BalanceInquiry, Withdrawal and Deposit, operation getInput of class Keypad and operation isEnvelope-Received of class DepositSlot. At this point in our design process, we cannot determine whether these operations require additional data, so we leave their parameter lists empty. Later, we may decide to add parameters.

In this section, we've determined many of the operations performed by the classes in the ATM system. We've identified the parameters and return types of some of the operations. As we continue our design process, the number of operations belonging to each class may vary—we might find that new operations are needed or that some current operations are unnecessary. We also might determine that some of our class operations need additional parameters and different return types, or that some parameters are unnecessary or require different types.

Self-Review Exercises for Section 12.6

12.14 Which of the following is not a behavior?
  a) reading data from a file
  b) printing output
  c) text output
  d) obtaining input from the user

12.15 If you were to add to the ATM system an operation that returns the amount attribute of class Withdrawal, how and where would you specify this operation in the class diagram of Fig. 12.17?

12.16 Describe the meaning of the following operation listing that might appear in a class diagram for an object-oriented design of a calculator:

```
add( x : Integer, y : Integer ) : Integer
```

12.7 Indicating Collaboration Among Objects

[*Note:* **This section can be taught after Chapter 7.**]
In this section, we concentrate on the collaborations (interactions) among objects. When two objects communicate with each other to accomplish a task, they are said to **collaborate**—objects do this by invoking one another's operations. A **collaboration** consists of an object of one class sending a **message** to an object of another class. Messages are sent in Java via method calls.

In Section 12.6, we determined many of the operations of the classes in our system. In this section, we concentrate on the messages that invoke these operations. To identify the collaborations in the system, we return to the requirements document in Section 12.2. Recall that this document specifies the range of activities that occur during an ATM session (e.g., authenticating a user, performing transactions). The steps used to describe how the system must perform each of these tasks are our first indication of the collaborations in our system. As we proceed through this section and Chapter 13, we may discover additional collaborations.

Identifying the Collaborations in a System

We identify the collaborations in the system by carefully reading the sections of the requirements document that specify what the ATM should do to authenticate a user and to perform each transaction type. For each action or step described, we decide which objects in our system must interact to achieve the desired result. We identify one object as the sending object and another as the receiving object. We then select one of the receiving object's operations (identified in Section 12.6) that must be invoked by the sending object to produce the proper behavior. For example, the ATM displays a welcome message when idle. We know that an object of class `Screen` displays a message to the user via its `displayMessage` operation. Thus, we decide that the system can display a welcome message by employing a collaboration between the `ATM` and the `Screen` in which the `ATM` sends a `displayMessage` message to the `Screen` by invoking the `displayMessage` operation of class `Screen`. [*Note:* To avoid repeating the phrase "an object of class...," we refer to an object by using its class name preceded by an article (e.g., "a," "an" or "the")—for example, "the ATM" refers to an object of class `ATM`.]

Figure 12.22 lists the collaborations that can be derived from the requirements document. For each sending object, we list the collaborations in the order in which they first occur during an ATM session (i.e., the order in which they are discussed in the requirements document). We list each collaboration involving a unique sender, message and recipient only once, even though the collaborations may occur at several different times throughout an ATM session. For example, the first row in Fig. 12.22 indicates that the `ATM` collaborates with the `Screen` whenever the `ATM` needs to display a message to the user.

Let's consider the collaborations in Fig. 12.22. Before allowing a user to perform any transactions, the ATM must prompt the user to enter an account number, then to enter a PIN. It accomplishes these tasks by sending a `displayMessage` message to the `Screen`. Both actions refer to the same collaboration between the `ATM` and the `Screen`, which is already listed in Fig. 12.22. The ATM obtains input in response to a prompt by sending a `getInput` message to the `Keypad`. Next, the ATM must determine whether the user-specified account number and PIN match those of an account in the database. It does so by sending an `authenticateUser` message to the `BankDatabase`. Recall that the `BankDatabase` cannot authenticate a user directly—only the user's `Account` (i.e., the `Account` that contains the account number specified by the user) can access the user's PIN on record to authenticate the user. Figure 12.22 therefore lists a collaboration in which the `BankDatabase` sends a `validatePIN` message to an `Account`.

After the user is authenticated, the ATM displays the main menu by sending a series of `displayMessage` messages to the `Screen` and obtains input containing a menu selection by sending a `getInput` message to the `Keypad`. We've already accounted for these collaborations, so we do not add anything to Fig. 12.22. After the user chooses a type of transaction to perform, the ATM executes the transaction by sending an `execute` message to an object of the appropriate transaction class (i.e., a `BalanceInquiry`, a `Withdrawal` or a

An object of class...	sends the message...	to an object of class...
ATM	displayMessage	Screen
	getInput	Keypad
	authenticateUser	BankDatabase
	execute	BalanceInquiry
	execute	Withdrawal
	execute	Deposit
BalanceInquiry	getAvailableBalance	BankDatabase
	getTotalBalance	BankDatabase
	displayMessage	Screen
Withdrawal	displayMessage	Screen
	getInput	Keypad
	getAvailableBalance	BankDatabase
	isSufficientCashAvailable	CashDispenser
	debit	BankDatabase
	dispenseCash	CashDispenser
Deposit	displayMessage	Screen
	getInput	Keypad
	isEnvelopeReceived	DepositSlot
	credit	BankDatabase
BankDatabase	validatePIN	Account
	getAvailableBalance	Account
	getTotalBalance	Account
	debit	Account
	credit	Account

Fig. 12.22 | Collaborations in the ATM system.

Deposit). For example, if the user chooses to perform a balance inquiry, the ATM sends an execute message to a BalanceInquiry.

Further examination of the requirements document reveals the collaborations involved in executing each transaction type. A BalanceInquiry retrieves the amount of money available in the user's account by sending a getAvailableBalance message to the BankDatabase, which responds by sending a getAvailableBalance message to the user's Account. Similarly, the BalanceInquiry retrieves the amount of money on deposit by sending a getTotalBalance message to the BankDatabase, which sends the same message to the user's Account. To display both parts of the user's account balance at the same time, the BalanceInquiry sends a displayMessage message to the Screen.

A Withdrawal responds to an execute message by sending displayMessage messages to the Screen to display a menu of standard withdrawal amounts (i.e., $20, $40, $60, $100, $200). The Withdrawal sends a getInput message to the Keypad to obtain the user's selection. Next, the Withdrawal determines whether the requested amount is less than or equal to the user's account balance. The Withdrawal can obtain the amount of money available by sending a getAvailableBalance message to the BankDatabase. The Withdrawal then tests whether the cash dispenser contains enough cash by sending an isSufficientCashAvailable message to the CashDispenser. A Withdrawal sends a debit message to the BankDatabase to decrease the user's account balance. The BankDatabase in turn sends the same message to the appropriate Account, which decreases both the total-Balance and the availableBalance. To dispense the requested amount of cash, the Withdrawal sends a dispenseCash message to the CashDispenser. Finally, the Withdrawal sends a displayMessage message to the Screen, instructing the user to take the cash.

A Deposit responds to an execute message first by sending a displayMessage message to the Screen to prompt the user for a deposit amount. The Deposit sends a getInput message to the Keypad to obtain the user's input. The Deposit then sends a displayMessage message to the Screen to tell the user to insert a deposit envelope. To determine whether the deposit slot received an incoming deposit envelope, the Deposit sends an isEnvelopeReceived message to the DepositSlot. The Deposit updates the user's account by sending a credit message to the BankDatabase, which subsequently sends a credit message to the user's Account. Recall that crediting funds to an Account increases the totalBalance but not the availableBalance.

Interaction Diagrams

Now that we've identified possible collaborations between our ATM system's objects, let's graphically model these interactions using the UML. The UML provides several types of **interaction diagrams** that model the behavior of a system by modeling how objects interact. The **communication diagram** emphasizes *which objects* participate in collaborations. [*Note:* Communication diagrams were called **collaboration diagrams** in earlier versions of the UML.] Like the communication diagram, the **sequence diagram** shows collaborations among objects, but it emphasizes *when* messages are sent between objects *over time.*

Communication Diagrams

Figure 12.23 shows a communication diagram that models the ATM executing a Balance-Inquiry. Objects are modeled in the UML as rectangles containing names in the form objectName : ClassName. In this example, which involves only one object of each type, we disregard the object name and list only a colon followed by the class name. [*Note:* Specifying each object's name in a communication diagram is recommended when modeling multiple objects of the same type.] Communicating objects are connected with solid lines, and messages are passed between objects along these lines in the direction shown by arrows. The name of the message, which appears next to the arrow, is the name of an operation (i.e., a method in Java) belonging to the receiving object—think of the name as a "service" that the receiving object provides to sending objects (its clients).

Fig. 12.23 | Communication diagram of the ATM executing a balance inquiry.

The solid filled arrow represents a message—or **synchronous call**—in the UML and a method call in Java. This arrow indicates that the flow of control is from the sending object (the ATM) to the receiving object (a BalanceInquiry). Since this is a synchronous call, the sending object may not send another message, or do anything at all, until the receiving object processes the message and returns control to the sending object. The sender just waits. In Fig. 12.23, the ATM calls BalanceInquiry method execute and may not send another message until `execute` has finished and returns control to the ATM. [*Note:* If this were an **asynchronous call**, represented by a stick (⇀) arrowhead, the sending object would not have to wait for the receiving object to return control—it would continue sending additional messages immediately following the asynchronous call. Asynchronous calls are implemented in Java using a technique called multithreading, which is discussed in Chapter 26, Multithreading.]

Sequence of Messages in a Communication Diagram

Figure 12.24 shows a communication diagram that models the interactions among system objects when an object of class `BalanceInquiry` executes. We assume that the object's `accountNumber` attribute contains the account number of the current user. The collaborations in Fig. 12.24 begin after the ATM sends an `execute` message to a `BalanceInquiry` (i.e., the interaction modeled in Fig. 12.23). The number to the left of a message name indicates the order in which the message is passed. The **sequence of messages** in a communication diagram progresses in numerical order from least to greatest. In this diagram, the numbering starts with message 1 and ends with message 3. The `BalanceInquiry` first sends a `getAvailableBalance` message to the `BankDatabase` (message 1), then sends a `getTotalBalance` message to the `BankDatabase` (message 2). Within the parentheses following a message name, we can specify a comma-separated list of the names of the parameters sent with the message (i.e., arguments in a Java method call)—the `BalanceInquiry` passes attribute `accountNumber` with its messages to the `BankDatabase` to indicate which `Account`'s balance information to retrieve. Recall from Fig. 12.18 that operations `getAvailableBalance` and `getTotalBalance` of class `BankDatabase` each require a parameter to identify an account. The `BalanceInquiry` next displays the `availableBalance` and the `totalBalance` to the user by passing a `displayMessage` message to the `Screen` (message 3) that includes a parameter indicating the `message` to be displayed.

Note that Fig. 12.24 models two additional messages passing from the `BankDatabase` to an `Account` (message 1.1 and message 2.1). To provide the ATM with the two balances of the user's `Account` (as requested by messages 1 and 2), the `BankDatabase` must pass a

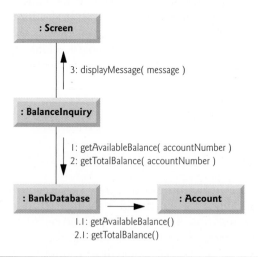

Fig. 12.24 | Communication diagram for executing a balance inquiry.

getAvailableBalance and a getTotalBalance message to the user's Account. Such messages passed within the handling of another message are called **nested messages**. The UML recommends using a decimal numbering scheme to indicate nested messages. For example, message 1.1 is the first message nested in message 1—the BankDatabase passes a getAvailableBalance message during BankDatabase's processing of a message by the same name. [*Note:* If the BankDatabase needed to pass a second nested message while processing message 1, the second message would be numbered 1.2.] A message may be passed only when all the nested messages from the previous message have been passed. For example, the BalanceInquiry passes message 3 only after messages 2 and 2.1 have been passed, in that order.

The nested numbering scheme used in communication diagrams helps clarify precisely when and in what context each message is passed. For example, if we numbered the messages in Fig. 12.24 using a flat numbering scheme (i.e., 1, 2, 3, 4, 5), someone looking at the diagram might not be able to determine that BankDatabase passes the getAvailableBalance message (message 1.1) to an Account *during* the BankDatabase's processing of message 1, as opposed to *after* completing the processing of message 1. The nested decimal numbers make it clear that the second getAvailableBalance message (message 1.1) is passed to an Account within the handling of the first getAvailableBalance message (message 1) by the BankDatabase.

Sequence Diagrams

Communication diagrams emphasize the participants in collaborations, but model their timing a bit awkwardly. A sequence diagram helps model the timing of collaborations more clearly. Figure 12.25 shows a sequence diagram modeling the sequence of interactions that occur when a Withdrawal executes. The dotted line extending down from an object's rectangle is that object's **lifeline**, which represents the progression of time. Actions occur along an object's lifeline in chronological order from top to bottom—an action near the top happens before one near the bottom.

Message passing in sequence diagrams is similar to message passing in communication diagrams. A solid arrow with a filled arrowhead extending from the sending object to the receiving object represents a message between two objects. The arrowhead points to an activation on the receiving object's lifeline. An **activation**, shown as a thin vertical rectangle, indicates that an object is executing. When an object returns control, a return message, represented as a dashed line with a stick ($\twoheadrightarrow$) arrowhead, extends from the activation of the object returning control to the activation of the object that initially sent the message. To eliminate clutter, we omit the return-message arrows—the UML allows this practice to make diagrams more readable. Like communication diagrams, sequence diagrams can indicate message parameters between the parentheses following a message name.

The sequence of messages in Fig. 12.25 begins when a Withdrawal prompts the user to choose a withdrawal amount by sending a displayMessage message to the Screen. The Withdrawal then sends a getInput message to the Keypad, which obtains input from the user. We've already modeled the control logic involved in a Withdrawal in the activity diagram of Fig. 12.15, so we do not show this logic in the sequence diagram of Fig. 12.25. Instead, we model the best-case scenario in which the balance of the user's account is greater than or equal to the chosen withdrawal amount, and the cash dispenser contains a sufficient amount of cash to satisfy the request. You can model control logic in a sequence diagram with UML frames (which are not covered in this case study). For a quick overview of UML frames, visit www.agilemodeling.com/style/frame.htm.

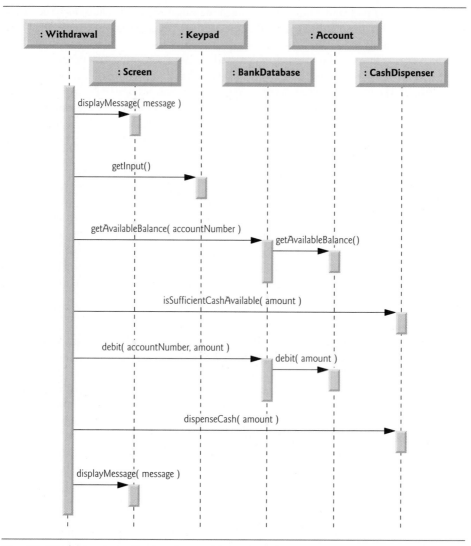

Fig. 12.25 | Sequence diagram that models a Withdrawal executing.

After obtaining a withdrawal amount, the Withdrawal sends a getAvailableBalance message to the BankDatabase, which in turn sends a getAvailableBalance message to the user's Account. Assuming that the user's account has enough money available to permit the transaction, the Withdrawal next sends an isSufficientCashAvailable message to the CashDispenser. Assuming that there is enough cash available, the Withdrawal decreases the balance of the user's account (i.e., both the totalBalance and the availableBalance) by sending a debit message to the BankDatabase. The BankDatabase responds by sending a debit message to the user's Account. Finally, the Withdrawal sends a dispenseCash message to the CashDispenser and a displayMessage message to the Screen, telling the user to remove the cash from the machine.

We've identified the collaborations among objects in the ATM system and modeled some of these collaborations using UML interaction diagrams—both communication diagrams and sequence diagrams. In Section 13.2, we enhance the structure of our model to complete a preliminary object-oriented design, then we begin implementing the ATM system in Java.

Self-Review Exercises for Section 12.7

12.17 A(n) _____ consists of an object of one class sending a message to an object of another class.
   a) association
   b) aggregation
   c) collaboration
   d) composition

12.18 Which form of interaction diagram emphasizes *what* collaborations occur? Which form emphasizes *when* collaborations occur?

12.19 Create a sequence diagram that models the interactions among objects in the ATM system that occur when a `Deposit` executes successfully, and explain the sequence of messages modeled by the diagram.

12.8 Wrap-Up

In this chapter, you learned how to work from a detailed requirements document to develop an object-oriented design. You worked with six popular types of UML diagrams to graphically model an object-oriented automated teller machine software system. In Chapter 13, we tune the design using inheritance, then completely implement the design in a 673-line Java application.

Answers to Self-Review Exercises

12.1 Figure 12.26 contains a use case diagram for a modified version of our ATM system that also allows users to transfer money between accounts.

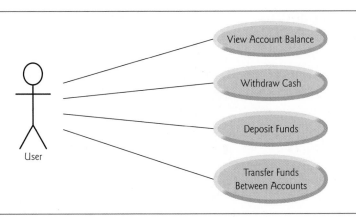

Fig. 12.26 | Use case diagram for a modified version of our ATM system that also allows users to transfer money between accounts.

12.2 b.

12.3 d.

12.4 [*Note:* Student answers may vary.] Figure 12.27 presents a class diagram that shows some of the composition relationships of a class Car.

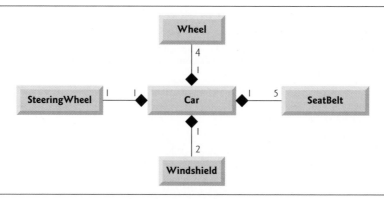

Fig. 12.27 | Class diagram showing composition relationships of a class Car.

12.5 c. [*Note:* In a computer network, this relationship could be many-to-many.]

12.6 True.

12.7 Figure 12.28 presents a class diagram for the ATM including class Deposit instead of class Withdrawal (as in Fig. 12.10). Note that Deposit does not access CashDispenser, but does access DepositSlot.

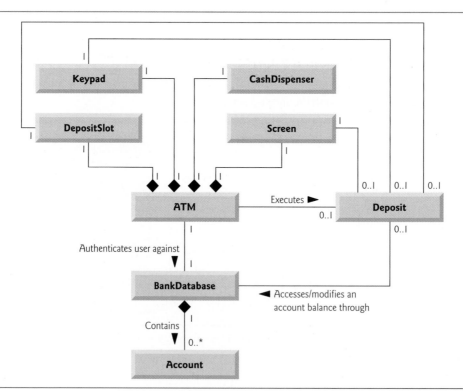

Fig. 12.28 | Class diagram for the ATM system model including class Deposit.

12.8 b.

12.9 c. Fly is an operation or behavior of an airplane, not an attribute.

12.10 This indicates that count is an Integer with an initial value of 500. This attribute keeps track of the number of bills available in the CashDispenser at any given time.

12.11 False. State diagrams model some of the behavior of a system.

12.12 a.

12.13 Figure 12.29 models the actions that occur after the user chooses the deposit option from the main menu and before the ATM returns the user to the main menu. Recall that part of receiving a deposit amount from the user involves converting an integer number of cents to a dollar amount. Also recall that crediting a deposit amount to an account increases only the totalBalance attribute of the user's Account object. The bank updates the availableBalance attribute of the user's Account object only after confirming the amount of cash in the deposit envelope and after the enclosed checks clear—this occurs independently of the ATM system.

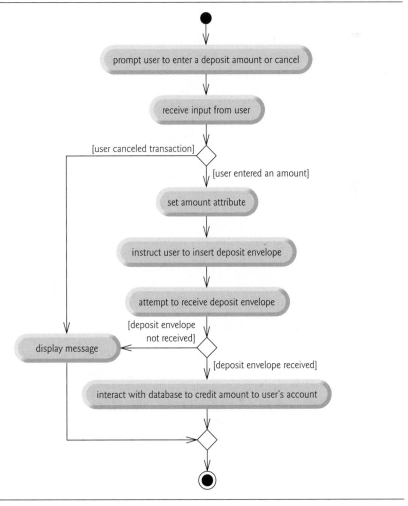

Fig. 12.29 | Activity diagram for a deposit transaction.

12.14 c.

12.15 To specify an operation that retrieves the amount attribute of class Withdrawal, the following operation listing would be placed in the operation (i.e., third) compartment of class Withdrawal:

    getAmount( ) : Double

12.16 This operation listing indicates an operation named add that takes integers x and y as parameters and returns an integer value.

12.17 c.

12.18 Communication diagrams emphasize *what* collaborations occur. Sequence diagrams emphasize *when* collaborations occur.

12.19 Figure 12.30 presents a sequence diagram that models the interactions between objects in the ATM system that occur when a Deposit executes successfully. A Deposit first sends a displayMessage message to the Screen to ask the user to enter a deposit amount. Next the Deposit sends a getInput message to the Keypad to receive input from the user. The Deposit then instructs the user to enter a deposit envelope by sending a displayMessage message to the Screen. The Deposit next sends an isEnvelopeReceived message to the DepositSlot to confirm that the deposit envelope has been received by the ATM. Finally, the Deposit increases the totalBalance attribute (but not the availableBalance attribute) of the user's Account by sending a credit message to the BankDatabase. The BankDatabase responds by sending the same message to the user's Account.

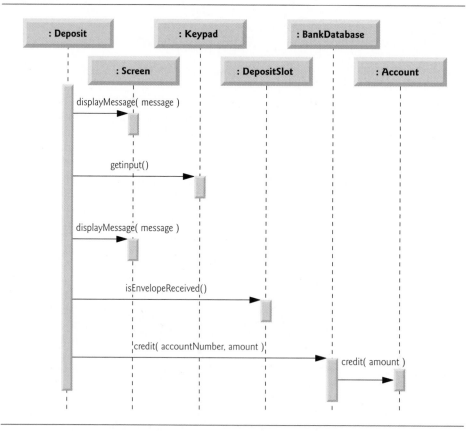

Fig. 12.30 | Sequence diagram that models a Deposit executing.

You can't work in the abstract.
—I. M. Pei

To generalize means to think.
—Georg Wilhelm Friedrich Hegel

We are all gifted. That is our inheritance.
—Ethel Waters

*Let me walk through the fields of paper
touching with my wand
dry stems and stunted
butterflies…*
—Denise Levertov

13

ATM Case Study, Part 2:
Implementing an Object-Oriented Design

Objectives

In this chapter you'll:

- Incorporate inheritance into the design of the ATM.

- Incorporate polymorphism into the design of the ATM.

- Fully implement in Java the UML-based object-oriented design of the ATM software.

- Study a detailed code walkthrough of the ATM software system that explains the implementation issues.

13.1   Introduction

In Chapter 12, we developed an object-oriented design for our ATM system. We now begin implementing our object-oriented design in Java. In Section 13.2, we show how to convert class diagrams to Java code. In Section 13.3, we tune the design with inheritance and polymorphism. Then we present a full Java code implementation of the ATM software in Section 13.4. The code is carefully commented and the discussions of the implementation are thorough and precise. Studying this application provides the opportunity for you to see a more substantial application of the kind you are likely to encounter in industry.

13.2   Starting to Program the Classes of the ATM System

[*Note:* This section can be taught after Chapter 8.]

Visibility

We now apply access modifiers to the members of our classes. We've introduced access modifiers public and private. Access modifiers determine the **visibility** or accessibility of an object's attributes and methods to other objects. Before we can begin implementing our design, we must consider which attributes and methods of our classes should be public and which should be private.

We've observed that attributes normally should be private and that methods invoked by clients of a given class should be public. Methods that are called as "utility methods" only by other methods of the class normally should be private. The UML employs **visibility markers** for modeling the visibility of attributes and operations. Public visibility is indicated by placing a plus sign (+) before an operation or an attribute, whereas a minus sign (–) indicates private visibility. Figure 13.1 shows our updated class diagram with visibility markers included. [*Note:* We do not include any operation parameters in Fig. 13.1—this is perfectly normal. Adding visibility markers does not affect the parameters already modeled in the class diagrams of Figs. 12.17–12.21.]

Fig. 13.1 | Class diagram with visibility markers.

Navigability

Before we begin implementing our design in Java, we introduce an additional UML notation. The class diagram in Fig. 13.2 further refines the relationships among classes in the ATM system by adding navigability arrows to the association lines. **Navigability arrows** (represented as arrows with stick ($\rightarrowtail$) arrowhead in the class diagram) indicate in the direction which an association can be traversed. When implementing a system designed using the UML, programmers use navigability arrows to determine which objects need references to other objects. For example, the navigability arrow pointing from class ATM to class BankDatabase indicates that we can navigate from the former to the latter, thereby enabling the ATM to invoke the BankDatabase's operations. However, since Fig. 13.2 does not contain a navigability arrow pointing from class BankDatabase to class ATM, the Bank-Database cannot access the ATM's operations. Note that associations in a class diagram that have navigability arrows at both ends or have none at all indicate **bidirectional navigability**—navigation can proceed in either direction across the association.

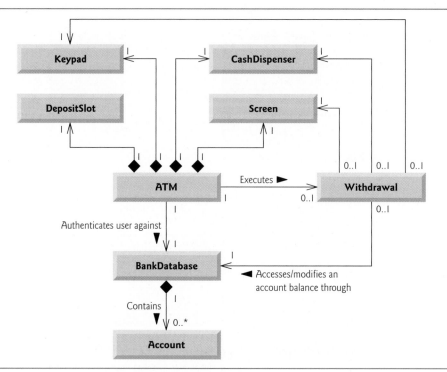

Fig. 13.2 | Class diagram with navigability arrows.

Like the class diagram of Fig. 12.10, that of Fig. 13.2 omits classes BalanceInquiry and Deposit for simplicity. The navigability of the associations in which these classes participate closely parallels that of class Withdrawal. Recall from Section 12.3 that Balance-Inquiry has an association with class Screen. We can navigate from class BalanceInquiry to class Screen along this association, but we cannot navigate from class Screen to class BalanceInquiry. Thus, if we were to model class BalanceInquiry in Fig. 13.2, we would place a navigability arrow at class Screen's end of this association. Also recall that class Deposit associates with classes Screen, Keypad and DepositSlot. We can navigate from class Deposit to each of these classes, but not vice versa. We therefore would place navigability arrows at the Screen, Keypad and DepositSlot ends of these associations. [*Note:* We model these additional classes and associations in our final class diagram in Section 13.3, after we've simplified the structure of our system by incorporating the object-oriented concept of inheritance.]

Implementing the ATM System from Its UML Design

We are now ready to begin implementing the ATM system. We first convert the classes in the diagrams of Fig. 13.1 and Fig. 13.2 into Java code. The code will represent the "skeleton" of the system. In Section 13.3, we modify the code to incorporate inheritance. In Section 13.4, we present the complete working Java code for our model.

As an example, we develop the code from our design of class Withdrawal in Fig. 13.1. We use this figure to determine the attributes and operations of the class. We use the UML model in Fig. 13.2 to determine the associations among classes. We follow the following four guidelines for each class:

1. Use the name located in the first compartment to declare the class as a `public` class with an empty no-argument constructor. We include this constructor simply as a placeholder to remind us that most classes will indeed need custom constructors. In Section 13.4, when we complete a working version of this class, we'll add any necessary arguments and code the body of the constructor as needed. For example, class `Withdrawal` yields the code in Fig. 13.3. [*Note:* If we find that the class's instance variables require only default initialization, then we'll remove the empty no-argument constructor because it's unnecessary.]

```java
1   // Class Withdrawal represents an ATM withdrawal transaction
2   public class Withdrawal
3   {
4      // no-argument constructor
5      public Withdrawal()
6      {
7      } // end no-argument Withdrawal constructor
8   } // end class Withdrawal
```

Fig. 13.3 | Java code for class `Withdrawal` based on Figs. 13.1–13.2.

2. Use the attributes located in the second compartment to declare the instance variables. For example, the `private` attributes `accountNumber` and `amount` of class `Withdrawal` yield the code in Fig. 13.4. [*Note:* The constructor of the complete working version of this class will assign values to these attributes.]

```java
1   // Class Withdrawal represents an ATM withdrawal transaction
2   public class Withdrawal
3   {
4      // attributes
5      private int accountNumber; // account to withdraw funds from
6      private double amount; // amount to withdraw
7
8      // no-argument constructor
9      public Withdrawal()
10     {
11     } // end no-argument Withdrawal constructor
12  } // end class Withdrawal
```

Fig. 13.4 | Java code for class `Withdrawal` based on Figs. 13.1–13.2.

3. Use the associations described in the class diagram to declare the references to other objects. For example, according to Fig. 13.2, `Withdrawal` can access one object of class `Screen`, one object of class `Keypad`, one object of class `CashDispenser` and one object of class `BankDatabase`. This yields the code in Fig. 13.5. [*Note:* The constructor of the complete working version of this class will initialize these instance variables with references to actual objects.]

4. Use the operations located in the third compartment of Fig. 13.1 to declare the shells of the methods. If we have not yet specified a return type for an operation, we declare the method with return type void. Refer to the class diagrams of Figs. 12.17–12.21 to declare any necessary parameters. For example, adding the public operation execute in class Withdrawal, which has an empty parameter list, yields the code in Fig. 13.6. [*Note:* We code the bodies of methods when we implement the complete system in Section 13.4.]

This concludes our discussion of the basics of generating classes from UML diagrams.

```
1   // Class Withdrawal represents an ATM withdrawal transaction
2   public class Withdrawal
3   {
4      // attributes
5      private int accountNumber; // account to withdraw funds from
6      private double amount; // amount to withdraw
7
8      // references to associated objects
9      private Screen screen; // ATM's screen
10     private Keypad keypad; // ATM's keypad
11     private CashDispenser cashDispenser; // ATM's cash dispenser
12     private BankDatabase bankDatabase; // account info database
13
14     // no-argument constructor
15     public Withdrawal()
16     {
17     } // end no-argument Withdrawal constructor
18  } // end class Withdrawal
```

Fig. 13.5 | Java code for class Withdrawal based on Figs. 13.1–13.2.

```
1   // Class Withdrawal represents an ATM withdrawal transaction
2   public class Withdrawal
3   {
4      // attributes
5      private int accountNumber; // account to withdraw funds from
6      private double amount; // amount to withdraw
7
8      // references to associated objects
9      private Screen screen; // ATM's screen
10     private Keypad keypad; // ATM's keypad
11     private CashDispenser cashDispenser; // ATM's cash dispenser
12     private BankDatabase bankDatabase; // account info database
13
14     // no-argument constructor
15     public Withdrawal()
16     {
17     } // end no-argument Withdrawal constructor
18
19     // operations
20     public void execute()
21     {
22     } // end method execute
23  } // end class Withdrawal
```

Fig. 13.6 | Java code for class Withdrawal based on Figs. 13.1–13.2.

Self-Review Exercises for Section 13.2

13.1 State whether the following statement is *true* or *false*, and if *false*, explain why: If an attribute of a class is marked with a minus sign (-) in a class diagram, the attribute is not directly accessible outside the class.

13.2 In Fig. 13.2, the association between the ATM and the Screen indicates that:
    a) we can navigate from the Screen to the ATM
    b) we can navigate from the ATM to the Screen
    c) Both (a) and (b); the association is bidirectional
    d) None of the above

13.3 Write Java code to begin implementing the design for class Keypad.

13.3 Incorporating Inheritance and Polymorphism into the ATM System

[*Note:* **This section can be taught after Chapter 10.**]

We now revisit our ATM system design to see how it might benefit from inheritance. To apply inheritance, we first look for commonality among classes in the system. We create an inheritance hierarchy to model similar (yet not identical) classes in a more elegant and efficient manner. We then modify our class diagram to incorporate the new inheritance relationships. Finally, we demonstrate how our updated design is translated into Java code.

In Section 12.3, we encountered the problem of representing a financial transaction in the system. Rather than create one class to represent all transaction types, we decided to create three individual transaction classes—BalanceInquiry, Withdrawal and Deposit—to represent the transactions that the ATM system can perform. Figure 13.7 shows the attributes and operations of classes BalanceInquiry, Withdrawal and Deposit. Note that these classes have one attribute (accountNumber) and one operation (execute) in common. Each class requires attribute accountNumber to specify the account to which the transaction applies. Each class contains operation execute, which the ATM invokes to perform the transaction. Clearly, BalanceInquiry, Withdrawal and Deposit represent *types of* transactions. Figure 13.7 reveals commonality among the transaction classes, so using inheritance to factor out the common features seems appropriate for designing classes BalanceInquiry, Withdrawal and Deposit. We place the common functionality in a superclass, Transaction, that classes BalanceInquiry, Withdrawal and Deposit extend.

Fig. 13.7 | Attributes and operations of BalanceInquiry, Withdrawal and Deposit.

Generalization

The UML specifies a relationship called a **generalization** to model inheritance. Figure 13.8 is the class diagram that models the generalization of superclass Transaction and subclasses BalanceInquiry, Withdrawal and Deposit. The arrows with triangular hollow arrowheads indicate that classes BalanceInquiry, Withdrawal and Deposit extend class Transaction. Class Transaction is said to be a generalization of classes BalanceInquiry, Withdrawal and Deposit. Class BalanceInquiry, Withdrawal and Deposit are said to be **specializations** of class Transaction.

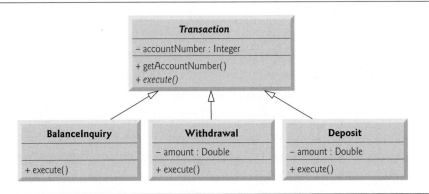

Fig. 13.8 | Class diagram modeling generalization of superclass Transaction and subclasses BalanceInquiry, Withdrawal and Deposit. Note that abstract class names (e.g., Transaction) and method names (e.g., execute in class Transaction) appear in italics.

Classes BalanceInquiry, Withdrawal and Deposit share integer attribute accountNumber, so we factor out this common attribute and place it in superclass Transaction. We no longer list accountNumber in the second compartment of each subclass, because the three subclasses inherit this attribute from Transaction. Recall, however, that subclasses cannot directly access private attributes of a superclass. We therefore include public method getAccountNumber in class Transaction. Each subclass will inherit this method, enabling the subclass to access its accountNumber as needed to execute a transaction.

According to Fig. 13.7, classes BalanceInquiry, Withdrawal and Deposit also share operation execute, so we placed public method execute in superclass Transaction. However, it does not make sense to implement execute in class Transaction, because the functionality that this method provides depends on the type of the actual transaction. We therefore declare method execute as abstract in superclass Transaction. Any class that contains at least one abstract method must also be declared abstract. This forces any subclass of Transaction that must be a concrete class (i.e., BalanceInquiry, Withdrawal and Deposit) to implement method execute. The UML requires that we place abstract class names (and abstract methods) in italics, so Transaction and its method execute appear in italics in Fig. 13.8. Note that method execute is not italicized in subclasses BalanceInquiry, Withdrawal and Deposit. Each subclass overrides superclass Transaction's execute method with a concrete implementation that performs the steps appropriate for completing that type of transaction. Note that Fig. 13.8 includes operation execute in the third compartment of classes BalanceInquiry, Withdrawal and Deposit, because each class has a different concrete implementation of the overridden method.

*Processing **Transactions** Polymorphically*

Polymorphism provides the ATM with an elegant way to execute all transactions "in the general." For example, suppose a user chooses to perform a balance inquiry. The ATM sets a Transaction reference to a new BalanceInquiry object. When the ATM uses its Transaction reference to invoke method execute, BalanceInquiry's version of execute is called.

This polymorphic approach also makes the system easily extensible. Should we wish to create a new transaction type (e.g., funds transfer or bill payment), we would just create an additional Transaction subclass that overrides the execute method with a version of the method appropriate for executing the new transaction type. We would need to make only minimal changes to the system code to allow users to choose the new transaction type from the main menu and for the ATM to instantiate and execute objects of the new subclass. The ATM could execute transactions of the new type using the current code, because it executes all transactions polymorphically using a general Transaction reference.

Recall that an abstract class like Transaction is one for which the programmer never intends to instantiate objects. An abstract class simply declares common attributes and behaviors of its subclasses in an inheritance hierarchy. Class Transaction defines the concept of what it means to be a transaction that has an account number and executes. You may wonder why we bother to include abstract method execute in class Transaction if it lacks a concrete implementation. Conceptually, we include it because it corresponds to the defining behavior of all transactions—executing. Technically, we must include method execute in superclass Transaction so that the ATM (or any other class) can polymorphically invoke each subclass's overridden version of this method through a Transaction reference. Also, from a software engineering perspective, including an abstract method in a superclass forces the implementor of the subclasses to override that method with concrete implementations in the subclasses, or else the subclasses, too, will be abstract, preventing objects of those subclasses from being instantiated.

*Additional Attribute of Classes **Withdrawal** and **Deposit***

Subclasses BalanceInquiry, Withdrawal and Deposit inherit attribute accountNumber from superclass Transaction, but classes Withdrawal and Deposit contain the additional attribute amount that distinguishes them from class BalanceInquiry. Classes Withdrawal and Deposit require this additional attribute to store the amount of money that the user wishes to withdraw or deposit. Class BalanceInquiry has no need for such an attribute and requires only an account number to execute. Even though two of the three Transaction subclasses share this attribute, we do not place it in superclass Transaction—we place only features common to all the subclasses in the superclass, otherwise subclasses could inherit attributes (and methods) that they do not need and should not have.

*Class Diagram with **Transaction** Hierarchy Incorporated*

Figure 13.9 presents an updated class diagram of our model that incorporates inheritance and introduces class Transaction. We model an association between class ATM and class Transaction to show that the ATM, at any given moment, either is executing a transaction or is not (i.e., zero or one objects of type Transaction exist in the system at a time). Because a Withdrawal is a type of Transaction, we no longer draw an association line directly between class ATM and class Withdrawal. Subclass Withdrawal inherits superclass Transaction's association with class ATM. Subclasses BalanceInquiry and Deposit inherit this association, too, so the previously omitted associations between ATM and classes BalanceInquiry and Deposit no longer exist either.

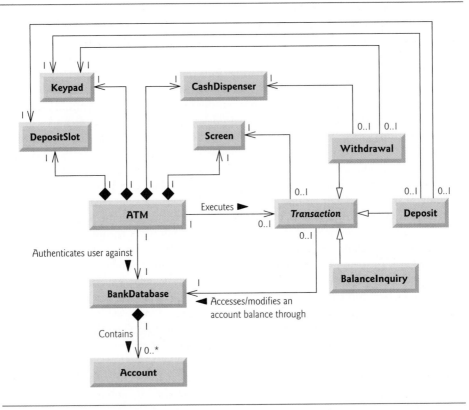

Fig. 13.9 | Class diagram of the ATM system (incorporating inheritance). Note that the abstract class name Transaction appears in italics.

We also add an association between class Transaction and the BankDatabase (Fig. 13.9). All Transactions require a reference to the BankDatabase so they can access and modify account information. Because each Transaction subclass inherits this reference, we no longer model the association between class Withdrawal and the BankDatabase. Similarly, the previously omitted associations between the BankDatabase and classes BalanceInquiry and Deposit no longer exist.

We show an association between class Transaction and the Screen. All Transactions display output to the user via the Screen. Thus, we no longer include the association previously modeled between Withdrawal and the Screen, although Withdrawal still participates in associations with the CashDispenser and the Keypad. Our class diagram incorporating inheritance also models Deposit and BalanceInquiry. We show associations between Deposit and both the DepositSlot and the Keypad. Note that class BalanceInquiry takes part in no associations other than those inherited from class Transaction—a BalanceInquiry needs to interact only with the BankDatabase and with the Screen.

Figure 13.1 showed attributes and operations with visibility markers. Now in Fig. 13.10 we present a modified class diagram that incorporates inheritance. This abbreviated diagram does not show inheritance relationships, but instead shows the attributes and methods after we've employed inheritance in our system. To save space, as we did in

Fig. 12.12, we do not include those attributes shown by associations in Fig. 13.9—we do, however, include them in the Java implementation in Section 13.4. We also omit all operation parameters, as we did in Fig. 13.1—incorporating inheritance does not affect the parameters already modeled in Figs. 12.17–12.21.

Fig. 13.10 | Class diagram with attributes and operations (incorporating inheritance). Note that the abstract class name `Transaction` and the abstract method name `execute` in class `Transaction` appear in italics.

Software Engineering Observation 13.1

A complete class diagram shows all the associations among classes and all the attributes and operations for each class. When the number of class attributes, methods and associations is substantial (as in Figs. 13.9 and 13.10), a good practice that promotes readability is to divide this information between two class diagrams—one focusing on associations and the other on attributes and methods.

13.3.1 Implementing the ATM System Design (Incorporating Inheritance)

In Section 13.2, we began implementing the ATM system design in Java code. We now modify our implementation to incorporate inheritance, using class Withdrawal as an example.

1. If a class A is a generalization of class B, then class B extends class A in the class declaration. For example, abstract superclass Transaction is a generalization of class Withdrawal. Figure 13.11 shows the declaration of class Withdrawal.

```
1   // Class Withdrawal represents an ATM withdrawal transaction
2   public class Withdrawal extends Transaction
3   {
4   } // end class Withdrawal
```

Fig. 13.11 | Java code for shell of class Withdrawal.

2. If class A is an abstract class and class B is a subclass of class A, then class B must implement the abstract methods of class A if class B is to be a concrete class. For example, class Transaction contains abstract method execute, so class Withdrawal must implement this method if we want to instantiate a Withdrawal object. Figure 13.12 is the Java code for class Withdrawal from Fig. 13.9 and Fig. 13.10. Class Withdrawal inherits field accountNumber from superclass Transaction, so Withdrawal does not need to declare this field. Class Withdrawal also inherits references to the Screen and the BankDatabase from its superclass Transaction, so we do not include these references in our code. Figure 13.10 specifies attribute amount and operation execute for class Withdrawal. Line 6 of Fig. 13.12 declares a field for attribute amount. Lines 16–19 declare the shell of a method for operation execute. Recall that subclass Withdrawal must provide a concrete implementation of the abstract method execute in superclass Transaction. The keypad and cashDispenser references (lines 7–8) are fields derived from Withdrawal's associations in Fig. 13.9. [*Note:* The constructor in the complete working version of this class will initialize these references to actual objects.]

```
1   // Withdrawal.java
2   // Generated using the class diagrams in Fig. 13.9 and Fig. 13.10
3   public class Withdrawal extends Transaction
4   {
5      // attributes
6      private double amount; // amount to withdraw
7      private Keypad keypad; // reference to keypad
8      private CashDispenser cashDispenser; // reference to cash dispenser
9
10     // no-argument constructor
11     public Withdrawal()
12     {
13     } // end no-argument Withdrawal constructor
14
```

Fig. 13.12 | Java code for class Withdrawal based on Figs. 13.9 and 13.10. (Part 1 of 2.)

```
15        // method overriding execute
16        @Override
17        public void execute()
18        {
19        } // end method execute
20   } // end class Withdrawal
```

Fig. 13.12 | Java code for class `Withdrawal` based on Figs. 13.9 and 13.10. (Part 2 of 2.)

Software Engineering Observation 13.2

Several UML modeling tools can convert UML-based designs into Java code, speeding the implementation process considerably. For more information on these tools, visit our UML Resource Center at www.deitel.com/UML/.

Congratulations on completing the case study's design portion! We implement the ATM system in Java code in Section 13.4. We recommend that you carefully read the code and its description. The code is abundantly commented and precisely follows the design with which you're now familiar. The accompanying description is carefully written to guide your understanding of the implementation based on the UML design. Mastering this code is a wonderful culminating accomplishment after studying Sections 12.2–12.7 and 13.2–13.3.

Self-Review Exercises for Section 13.3

13.4 The UML uses an arrow with a _____ to indicate a generalization relationship.
a) solid filled arrowhead
b) triangular hollow arrowhead
c) diamond-shaped hollow arrowhead
d) stick arrowhead

13.5 State whether the following statement is *true* or *false*, and if *false*, explain why: The UML requires that we underline abstract class names and method names.

13.6 Write Java code to begin implementing the design for class `Transaction` specified in Figs. 13.9 and 13.10. Be sure to include `private` reference-type attributes based on class `Transaction`'s associations. Also be sure to include `public` *get* methods that provide access to any of these `private` attributes that the subclasses require to perform their tasks.

13.4 ATM Case Study Implementation

This section contains the complete working 673-line implementation of the ATM system. We consider the classes in the order in which we identified them in Section 12.3—`ATM`, `Screen`, `Keypad`, `CashDispenser`, `DepositSlot`, `Account`, `BankDatabase`, `Transaction`, `BalanceInquiry`, `Withdrawal` and `Deposit`.

We apply the guidelines discussed in Sections 13.2–13.3 to code these classes based on how we modeled them in the UML class diagrams of Figs. 13.9 and 13.10. To develop the bodies of class methods, we refer to the activity diagrams in Section 12.5 and the communication and sequence diagrams presented in Section 12.7. Note that our ATM design does not specify all the program logic and may not specify all the attributes and operations required to complete the ATM implementation. This is a normal part of the object-oriented design process. As we implement the system, we complete the program logic and add attributes and behaviors as necessary to construct the ATM system specified by the requirements document in Section 12.2.

We conclude the discussion by presenting a Java application (ATMCaseStudy) that starts the ATM and puts the other classes in the system in use. Recall that we are developing a first version of the ATM system that runs on a personal computer and uses the computer's keyboard and monitor to approximate the ATM's keypad and screen. We also only simulate the actions of the ATM's cash dispenser and deposit slot. We attempt to implement the system, however, so that real hardware versions of these devices could be integrated without significant changes in the code.

13.4.1 Class ATM

Class ATM (Fig. 13.13) represents the ATM as a whole. Lines 6–12 implement the class's attributes. We determine all but one of these attributes from the UML class diagrams of Figs. 13.9 and 13.10. Note that we implement the UML Boolean attribute user-Authenticated in Fig. 13.10 as a boolean in Java (line 6). Line 7 declares an attribute not found in our UML design—an int attribute currentAccountNumber that keeps track of the account number of the current authenticated user. We'll soon see how the class uses this attribute. Lines 8–12 declare reference-type attributes corresponding to the ATM class's associations modeled in the class diagram of Fig. 13.9. These attributes allow the ATM to access its parts (i.e., its Screen, Keypad, CashDispenser and DepositSlot) and interact with the bank's account-information database (i.e., a BankDatabase object).

```
1   // ATM.java
2   // Represents an automated teller machine
3
4   public class ATM
5   {
6      private boolean userAuthenticated; // whether user is authenticated
7      private int currentAccountNumber; // current user's account number
8      private Screen screen; // ATM's screen
9      private Keypad keypad; // ATM's keypad
10     private CashDispenser cashDispenser; // ATM's cash dispenser
11     private DepositSlot depositSlot; // ATM's deposit slot
12     private BankDatabase bankDatabase; // account information database
13
14     // constants corresponding to main menu options
15     private static final int BALANCE_INQUIRY = 1;
16     private static final int WITHDRAWAL = 2;
17     private static final int DEPOSIT = 3;
18     private static final int EXIT = 4;
19
20     // no-argument ATM constructor initializes instance variables
21     public ATM()
22     {
23        userAuthenticated = false; // user is not authenticated to start
24        currentAccountNumber = 0; // no current account number to start
25        screen = new Screen(); // create screen
26        keypad = new Keypad(); // create keypad
27        cashDispenser = new CashDispenser(); // create cash dispenser
```

Fig. 13.13 | Class ATM represents the ATM. (Part 1 of 4.)

```
28              depositSlot = new DepositSlot(); // create deposit slot
29              bankDatabase = new BankDatabase(); // create acct info database
30         } // end no-argument ATM constructor
31
32         // start ATM
33         public void run()
34         {
35            // welcome and authenticate user; perform transactions
36            while ( true )
37            {
38               // loop while user is not yet authenticated
39               while ( !userAuthenticated )
40               {
41                  screen.displayMessageLine( "\nWelcome!" );
42                  authenticateUser(); // authenticate user
43               } // end while
44
45               performTransactions(); // user is now authenticated
46               userAuthenticated = false; // reset before next ATM session
47               currentAccountNumber = 0; // reset before next ATM session
48               screen.displayMessageLine( "\nThank you! Goodbye!" );
49            } // end while
50         } // end method run
51
52         // attempts to authenticate user against database
53         private void authenticateUser()
54         {
55            screen.displayMessage( "\nPlease enter your account number: " );
56            int accountNumber = keypad.getInput(); // input account number
57            screen.displayMessage( "\nEnter your PIN: " ); // prompt for PIN
58            int pin = keypad.getInput(); // input PIN
59
60            // set userAuthenticated to boolean value returned by database
61            userAuthenticated =
62               bankDatabase.authenticateUser( accountNumber, pin );
63
64            // check whether authentication succeeded
65            if ( userAuthenticated )
66            {
67               currentAccountNumber = accountNumber; // save user's account #
68            } // end if
69            else
70               screen.displayMessageLine(
71                  "Invalid account number or PIN. Please try again." );
72         } // end method authenticateUser
73
74         // display the main menu and perform transactions
75         private void performTransactions()
76         {
77            // local variable to store transaction currently being processed
78            Transaction currentTransaction = null;
79
80            boolean userExited = false; // user has not chosen to exit
```

Fig. 13.13 | Class ATM represents the ATM. (Part 2 of 4.)

```
81
82        // loop while user has not chosen option to exit system
83        while ( !userExited )
84        {
85           // show main menu and get user selection
86           int mainMenuSelection = displayMainMenu();
87
88           // decide how to proceed based on user's menu selection
89           switch ( mainMenuSelection )
90           {
91              // user chose to perform one of three transaction types
92              case BALANCE_INQUIRY:
93              case WITHDRAWAL:
94              case DEPOSIT:
95
96                 // initialize as new object of chosen type
97                 currentTransaction =
98                    createTransaction( mainMenuSelection );
99
100                currentTransaction.execute(); // execute transaction
101                break;
102             case EXIT: // user chose to terminate session
103                screen.displayMessageLine( "\nExiting the system..." );
104                userExited = true; // this ATM session should end
105                break;
106             default: // user did not enter an integer from 1-4
107                screen.displayMessageLine(
108                   "\nYou did not enter a valid selection. Try again." );
109                break;
110          } // end switch
111       } // end while
112    } // end method performTransactions
113
114    // display the main menu and return an input selection
115    private int displayMainMenu()
116    {
117       screen.displayMessageLine( "\nMain menu:" );
118       screen.displayMessageLine( "1 - View my balance" );
119       screen.displayMessageLine( "2 - Withdraw cash" );
120       screen.displayMessageLine( "3 - Deposit funds" );
121       screen.displayMessageLine( "4 - Exit\n" );
122       screen.displayMessage( "Enter a choice: " );
123       return keypad.getInput(); // return user's selection
124    } // end method displayMainMenu
125
126    // return object of specified Transaction subclass
127    private Transaction createTransaction( int type )
128    {
129       Transaction temp = null; // temporary Transaction variable
130
131       // determine which type of Transaction to create
132       switch ( type )
133       {
```

Fig. 13.13 | Class ATM represents the ATM. (Part 3 of 4.)

```
134              case BALANCE_INQUIRY: // create new BalanceInquiry transaction
135                 temp = new BalanceInquiry(
136                    currentAccountNumber, screen, bankDatabase );
137                 break;
138              case WITHDRAWAL: // create new Withdrawal transaction
139                 temp = new Withdrawal( currentAccountNumber, screen,
140                    bankDatabase, keypad, cashDispenser );
141                 break;
142              case DEPOSIT: // create new Deposit transaction
143                 temp = new Deposit( currentAccountNumber, screen,
144                    bankDatabase, keypad, depositSlot );
145                 break;
146           } // end switch
147
148           return temp; // return the newly created object
149        } // end method createTransaction
150  } // end class ATM
```

Fig. 13.13 | Class ATM represents the ATM. (Part 4 of 4.)

Lines 15–18 declare integer constants that correspond to the four options in the ATM's main menu (i.e., balance inquiry, withdrawal, deposit and exit). Lines 21–30 declare the constructor, which initializes the class's attributes. When an ATM object is first created, no user is authenticated, so line 23 initializes userAuthenticated to false. Likewise, line 24 initializes currentAccountNumber to 0 because there is no current user yet. Lines 25–28 instantiate new objects to represent the ATM's parts. Recall that class ATM has composition relationships with classes Screen, Keypad, CashDispenser and DepositSlot, so class ATM is responsible for their creation. Line 29 creates a new BankDatabase. [*Note:* If this were a real ATM system, the ATM class would receive a reference to an existing database object created by the bank. However, in this implementation we are only simulating the bank's database, so class ATM creates the BankDatabase object with which it interacts.]

ATM *Method* run

The class diagram of Fig. 13.10 does not list any operations for class ATM. We now implement one operation (i.e., public method) in class ATM that allows an external client of the class (i.e., class ATMCaseStudy) to tell the ATM to run. ATM method run (lines 33–50) uses an infinite loop (lines 36–49) to repeatedly welcome a user, attempt to authenticate the user and, if authentication succeeds, allow the user to perform transactions. After an authenticated user performs the desired transactions and chooses to exit, the ATM resets itself, displays a goodbye message to the user and restarts the process. We use an infinite loop here to simulate the fact that an ATM appears to run continuously until the bank turns it off (an action beyond the user's control). An ATM user has the option to exit the system but not the ability to turn off the ATM completely.

Authenticating a User

In method run's infinite loop, lines 39–43 cause the ATM to repeatedly welcome and attempt to authenticate the user as long as the user has not been authenticated (i.e., !userAuthenticated is true). Line 41 invokes method displayMessageLine of the ATM's screen to display a welcome message. Like Screen method displayMessage designed in the case study, method displayMessageLine (declared in lines 13–16 of Fig. 13.14) displays a message to the user, but this method also outputs a newline after the message. We've added this method during implementation to give class Screen's clients more control over the placement of displayed messages. Line 42 invokes class ATM's private utility method authenticateUser (declared in lines 53–72) to attempt to authenticate the user.

We refer to the requirements document to determine the steps necessary to authenticate the user before allowing transactions to occur. Line 55 of method authenticateUser invokes method displayMessage of the screen to prompt the user to enter an account number. Line 56 invokes method getInput of the keypad to obtain the user's input, then stores the integer value entered by the user in a local variable accountNumber. Method authenticateUser next prompts the user to enter a PIN (line 57), and stores the PIN input by the user in a local variable pin (line 58). Next, lines 61–62 attempt to authenticate the user by passing the accountNumber and pin entered by the user to the bankDatabase's authenticateUser method. Class ATM sets its userAuthenticated attribute to the boolean value returned by this method—userAuthenticated becomes true if authentication succeeds (i.e., accountNumber and pin match those of an existing Account in bankDatabase) and remains false otherwise. If userAuthenticated is true, line 67 saves the account number entered by the user (i.e., accountNumber) in the ATM attribute currentAccountNumber. The other ATM methods use this variable whenever an ATM session requires access to the user's account number. If userAuthenticated is false, lines 70–71 use the screen's displayMessageLine method to indicate that an invalid account number and/or PIN was entered and the user must try again. Note that we set currentAccountNumber only after authenticating the user's account number and the associated PIN—if the database could not authenticate the user, currentAccountNumber remains 0.

After method run attempts to authenticate the user (line 42), if userAuthenticated is still false, the while loop in lines 39–43 executes again. If userAuthenticated is now true, the loop terminates and control continues with line 45, which calls class ATM's utility method performTransactions.

Performing Transactions

Method performTransactions (lines 75–112) carries out an ATM session for an authenticated user. Line 78 declares a local Transaction variable to which we will assign a BalanceInquiry, Withdrawal or Deposit object representing the ATM transaction currently being processed. Note that we use a Transaction variable here to allow us to take advantage of polymorphism. Also note that we name this variable after the role name included in the class diagram of Fig. 12.7—currentTransaction. Line 80 declares another local variable—a boolean called userExited that keeps track of whether the user has chosen to exit. This variable controls a while loop (lines 83–111) that allows the user to execute an unlimited number of transactions before choosing to exit. Within this loop, line 86 displays the main menu and obtains the user's menu selection by calling an ATM utility method displayMainMenu (declared in lines 115–124). This method displays the main menu by invoking methods of the ATM's screen and returns a menu selection obtained from the user through the ATM's keypad. Line 86 stores the user's selection returned by displayMainMenu in local variable mainMenuSelection.

After obtaining a main menu selection, method performTransactions uses a switch statement (lines 89–110) to respond to the selection appropriately. If mainMenuSelection is equal to any of the three integer constants representing transaction types (i.e., if the user chose to perform a transaction), lines 97–98 call utility method createTransaction (declared in lines 127–149) to return a newly instantiated object of the type that corresponds to the selected transaction. Variable currentTransaction is assigned the reference returned by createTransaction, then line 100 invokes method execute of this transaction to execute it. We'll discuss Transaction method execute and the three Transaction subclasses shortly. We assign the Transaction variable currentTransaction an object of one of the three Transaction subclasses so that we can execute transactions polymorphically. For example, if the user chooses to perform a balance inquiry, mainMenuSelection equals BALANCE_INQUIRY, leading createTransaction to return a BalanceInquiry object. Thus, currentTransaction refers to a BalanceInquiry, and invoking currentTransaction.execute() results in BalanceInquiry's version of execute being called.

Creating a Transaction
Method createTransaction (lines 127–149) uses a switch statement (lines 132–146) to instantiate a new Transaction subclass object of the type indicated by the parameter type. Recall that method performTransactions passes mainMenuSelection to this method only when mainMenuSelection contains a value corresponding to one of the three transaction types. Therefore type is BALANCE_INQUIRY, WITHDRAWAL or DEPOSIT. Each case in the switch statement instantiates a new object by calling the appropriate Transaction subclass constructor. Each constructor has a unique parameter list, based on the specific data required to initialize the subclass object. A BalanceInquiry requires only the account number of the current user and references to the ATM's screen and the bankDatabase. In addition to these parameters, a Withdrawal requires references to the ATM's keypad and cashDispenser, and a Deposit requires references to the ATM's keypad and depositSlot. We discuss the transaction classes in more detail in Sections 13.4.8–13.4.11.

Exiting the Main Menu and Processing Invalid Selections
After executing a transaction (line 100 in performTransactions), userExited remains false and lines 83–111 repeat, returning the user to the main menu. However, if a user does not perform a transaction and instead selects the main menu option to exit, line 104 sets userExited to true, causing the condition of the while loop (!userExited) to become false. This while is the final statement of method performTransactions, so control returns to the calling method run. If the user enters an invalid main menu selection (i.e., not an integer from 1–4), lines 107–108 display an appropriate error message, userExited remains false and the user returns to the main menu to try again.

Awaiting the Next ATM User
When performTransactions returns control to method run, the user has chosen to exit the system, so lines 46–47 reset the ATM's attributes userAuthenticated and currentAccountNumber to prepare for the next ATM user. Line 48 displays a goodbye message before the ATM starts over and welcomes the next user.

13.4.2 Class Screen

Class Screen (Fig. 13.14) represents the screen of the ATM and encapsulates all aspects of displaying output to the user. Class Screen approximates a real ATM's screen with a computer monitor and outputs text messages using standard console output methods System.out.print, System.out.println and System.out.printf. In this case study, we designed class Screen to have one operation—displayMessage. For greater flexibility in displaying messages to the Screen, we now declare three Screen methods—displayMessage, displayMessageLine and displayDollarAmount.

```java
1   // Screen.java
2   // Represents the screen of the ATM
3
4   public class Screen
5   {
6      // display a message without a carriage return
7      public void displayMessage( String message )
8      {
9         System.out.print( message );
10     } // end method displayMessage
11
12     // display a message with a carriage return
13     public void displayMessageLine( String message )
14     {
15        System.out.println( message );
16     } // end method displayMessageLine
17
18     // displays a dollar amount
19     public void displayDollarAmount( double amount )
20     {
21        System.out.printf( "$%,.2f", amount );
22     } // end method displayDollarAmount
23  } // end class Screen
```

Fig. 13.14 | Class Screen represents the screen of the ATM.

Method displayMessage (lines 7–10) takes a String argument and prints it to the console. The cursor stays on the same line, making this method appropriate for displaying prompts to the user. Method displayMessageLine (lines 13–16) does the same using System.out.println, which outputs a newline to move the cursor to the next line. Finally, method displayDollarAmount (lines 19–22) outputs a properly formatted dollar amount (e.g., $1,234.56). Line 21 uses System.out.printf to output a double value formatted with commas to increase readability and two decimal places.

13.4.3 Class Keypad

Class Keypad (Fig. 13.15) represents the keypad of the ATM and is responsible for receiving all user input. Recall that we are simulating this hardware, so we use the computer's keyboard to approximate the keypad. We use class Scanner to obtain console input from the user. A computer keyboard contains many keys not found on the ATM's keypad. However, we assume that the user presses only the keys on the computer keyboard that also appear on the keypad—the keys numbered 0–9 and the *Enter* key.

```java
1   // Keypad.java
2   // Represents the keypad of the ATM
3   import java.util.Scanner; // program uses Scanner to obtain user input
4
5   public class Keypad
6   {
7      private Scanner input; // reads data from the command line
```

Fig. 13.15 | Class Keypad represents the ATM's keypad. (Part 1 of 2.)

```
 8
 9        // no-argument constructor initializes the Scanner
10        public Keypad()
11        {
12           input = new Scanner( System.in );
13        } // end no-argument Keypad constructor
14
15        // return an integer value entered by user
16        public int getInput()
17        {
18           return input.nextInt(); // we assume that user enters an integer
19        } // end method getInput
20     } // end class Keypad
```

Fig. 13.15 | Class Keypad represents the ATM's keypad. (Part 2 of 2.)

Line 3 of class Keypad imports class Scanner for use in class Keypad. Line 7 declares Scanner variable input as an instance variable. Line 12 in the constructor creates a new Scanner object that reads input from the standard input stream (System.in) and assigns the object's reference to variable input. Method getInput (declared in lines 16–19) invokes Scanner method nextInt (line 18) to return the next integer input by the user. [*Note:* Method nextInt can throw an InputMismatchException if the user enters non-integer input. Because the real ATM's keypad permits only integer input, we assume that no exception will occur and do not attempt to fix this problem. See Chapter 11, Exception Handling, for information on catching exceptions.] Recall that nextInt obtains all the input used by the ATM. Keypad's getInput method simply returns the integer input by the user. If a client of class Keypad requires input that satisfies some criteria (i.e., a number corresponding to a valid menu option), the client must perform the error checking.

13.4.4 Class CashDispenser

Class CashDispenser (Fig. 13.16) represents the cash dispenser of the ATM. Line 7 declares constant INITIAL_COUNT, which indicates the initial count of bills in the cash dispenser when the ATM starts (i.e., 500). Line 8 implements attribute count (modeled in Fig. 13.10), which keeps track of the number of bills remaining in the CashDispenser at any time. The constructor (lines 11–14) sets count to the initial count. CashDispenser has two public methods—dispenseCash (lines 17–21) and isSufficientCashAvailable (lines 24–32). The class trusts that a client (i.e., Withdrawal) calls dispenseCash only after establishing that sufficient cash is available by calling isSufficientCashAvailable. Thus, dispenseCash simply simulates dispensing the requested amount without checking whether sufficient cash is available.

```
 1     // CashDispenser.java
 2     // Represents the cash dispenser of the ATM
 3
 4     public class CashDispenser
 5     {
```

Fig. 13.16 | Class CashDispenser represents the ATM's cash dispenser. (Part 1 of 2.)

```
 6      // the default initial number of bills in the cash dispenser
 7      private final static int INITIAL_COUNT = 500;
 8      private int count; // number of $20 bills remaining
 9
10      // no-argument CashDispenser constructor initializes count to default
11      public CashDispenser()
12      {
13         count = INITIAL_COUNT; // set count attribute to default
14      } // end CashDispenser constructor
15
16      // simulates dispensing of specified amount of cash
17      public void dispenseCash( int amount )
18      {
19         int billsRequired = amount / 20; // number of $20 bills required
20         count -= billsRequired; // update the count of bills
21      } // end method dispenseCash
22
23      // indicates whether cash dispenser can dispense desired amount
24      public boolean isSufficientCashAvailable( int amount )
25      {
26         int billsRequired = amount / 20; // number of $20 bills required
27
28         if ( count >= billsRequired  )
29            return true; // enough bills available
30         else
31            return false; // not enough bills available
32      } // end method isSufficientCashAvailable
33   } // end class CashDispenser
```

Fig. 13.16 | Class CashDispenser represents the ATM's cash dispenser. (Part 2 of 2.)

Method isSufficientCashAvailable (lines 24–32) has a parameter amount that specifies the amount of cash in question. Line 26 calculates the number of $20 bills required to dispense the specified amount. The ATM allows the user to choose only withdrawal amounts that are multiples of $20, so we divide amount by 20 to obtain the number of billsRequired. Lines 28–31 return true if the CashDispenser's count is greater than or equal to billsRequired (i.e., enough bills are available) and false otherwise (i.e., not enough bills). For example, if a user wishes to withdraw $80 (i.e., billsRequired is 4), but only three bills remain (i.e., count is 3), the method returns false.

Method dispenseCash (lines 17–21) simulates cash dispensing. If our system were hooked up to a real hardware cash dispenser, this method would interact with the device to physically dispense cash. Our version of the method simply decreases the count of bills remaining by the number required to dispense the specified amount (line 20). Note that it's the responsibility of the client of the class (i.e., Withdrawal) to inform the user that cash has been dispensed—CashDispenser cannot interact directly with Screen.

13.4.5 Class DepositSlot

Class DepositSlot (Fig. 13.17) represents the ATM's deposit slot. Like class CashDispenser, class DepositSlot merely simulates the functionality of a real hardware deposit slot. DepositSlot has no attributes and only one method—isEnvelopeReceived (lines 8–11)—which indicates whether a deposit envelope was received.

```
1    // DepositSlot.java
2    // Represents the deposit slot of the ATM
3
4    public class DepositSlot
5    {
6       // indicates whether envelope was received (always returns true,
7       // because this is only a software simulation of a real deposit slot)
8       public boolean isEnvelopeReceived()
9       {
10          return true; // deposit envelope was received
11       } // end method isEnvelopeReceived
12   } // end class DepositSlot
```

Fig. 13.17 | Class DepositSlot represents the ATM's deposit slot.

Recall from the requirements document that the ATM allows the user up to two minutes to insert an envelope. The current version of method isEnvelopeReceived simply returns true immediately (line 10), because this is only a software simulation, and we assume that the user has inserted an envelope within the required time frame. If an actual hardware deposit slot were connected to our system, method isEnvelopeReceived might be implemented to wait for a maximum of two minutes to receive a signal from the hardware deposit slot indicating that the user has indeed inserted a deposit envelope. If isEnvelopeReceived were to receive such a signal within two minutes, the method would return true. If two minutes elapsed and the method still had not received a signal, then the method would return false.

13.4.6 Class Account

Class Account (Fig. 13.18) represents a bank account. Each Account has four attributes (modeled in Fig. 13.10)—accountNumber, pin, availableBalance and totalBalance. Lines 6–9 implement these attributes as private fields. Variable availableBalance represents the amount of funds available for withdrawal. Variable totalBalance represents the amount of funds available, plus the amount of deposited funds still pending confirmation or clearance.

```
1    // Account.java
2    // Represents a bank account
3
4    public class Account
5    {
6       private int accountNumber; // account number
7       private int pin; // PIN for authentication
8       private double availableBalance; // funds available for withdrawal
9       private double totalBalance; // funds available + pending deposits
10
11      // Account constructor initializes attributes
12      public Account( int theAccountNumber, int thePIN,
13         double theAvailableBalance, double theTotalBalance )
14      {
15         accountNumber = theAccountNumber;
```

Fig. 13.18 | Class Account represents a bank account. (Part 1 of 2.)

```
16            pin = thePIN;
17            availableBalance = theAvailableBalance;
18            totalBalance = theTotalBalance;
19      } // end Account constructor
20
21      // determines whether a user-specified PIN matches PIN in Account
22      public boolean validatePIN( int userPIN )
23      {
24            if ( userPIN == pin )
25                  return true;
26            else
27                  return false;
28      } // end method validatePIN
29
30      // returns available balance
31      public double getAvailableBalance()
32      {
33            return availableBalance;
34      } // end getAvailableBalance
35
36      // returns the total balance
37      public double getTotalBalance()
38      {
39            return totalBalance;
40      } // end method getTotalBalance
41
42      // credits an amount to the account
43      public void credit( double amount )
44      {
45            totalBalance += amount; // add to total balance
46      } // end method credit
47
48      // debits an amount from the account
49      public void debit( double amount )
50      {
51            availableBalance -= amount; // subtract from available balance
52            totalBalance -= amount; // subtract from total balance
53      } // end method debit
54
55      // returns account number
56      public int getAccountNumber()
57      {
58            return accountNumber;
59      } // end method getAccountNumber
60 } // end class Account
```

Fig. 13.18 | Class Account represents a bank account. (Part 2 of 2.)

The Account class has a constructor (lines 12–19) that takes an account number, the PIN established for the account, the account's initial available balance and the account's initial total balance as arguments. Lines 15–18 assign these values to the class's attributes (i.e., fields).

Method validatePIN (lines 22–28) determines whether a user-specified PIN (i.e., parameter userPIN) matches the PIN associated with the account (i.e., attribute pin).

Recall that we modeled this method's parameter userPIN in Fig. 12.19. If the two PINs match, the method returns true (line 25); otherwise, it returns false (line 27).

Methods getAvailableBalance (lines 31–34) and getTotalBalance (lines 37–40) are *get* methods that return the values of double attributes availableBalance and total-Balance, respectively.

Method credit (lines 43–46) adds an amount of money (i.e., parameter amount) to an Account as part of a deposit transaction. Note that this method adds the amount only to attribute totalBalance (line 45). The money credited to an account during a deposit does not become available immediately, so we modify only the total balance. We assume that the bank updates the available balance appropriately at a later time. Our implementation of class Account includes only methods required for carrying out ATM transactions. Therefore, we omit the methods that some other bank system would invoke to add to attribute availableBalance (to confirm a deposit) or subtract from attribute totalBalance (to reject a deposit).

Method debit (lines 49–53) subtracts an amount of money (i.e., parameter amount) from an Account as part of a withdrawal transaction. This method subtracts the amount from both attribute availableBalance (line 51) and attribute totalBalance (line 52), because a withdrawal affects both measures of an account balance.

Method getAccountNumber (lines 56–59) provides access to an Account's account-Number. We include this method in our implementation so that a client of the class (i.e., BankDatabase) can identify a particular Account. For example, BankDatabase contains many Account objects, and it can invoke this method on each of its Account objects to locate the one with a specific account number.

13.4.7 Class BankDatabase

Class BankDatabase (Fig. 13.19) models the bank's database with which the ATM interacts to access and modify a user's account information. [*Note:* We study database access in Chapter 28. For now we model the database as an array. An exercise in Chapter 28 asks you to reimplement this portion of the ATM using an actual database.]

```
 1   // BankDatabase.java
 2   // Represents the bank account information database
 3
 4   public class BankDatabase
 5   {
 6      private Account[] accounts; // array of Accounts
 7
 8      // no-argument BankDatabase constructor initializes accounts
 9      public BankDatabase()
10      {
11         accounts = new Account[ 2 ]; // just 2 accounts for testing
12         accounts[ 0 ] = new Account( 12345, 54321, 1000.0, 1200.0 );
13         accounts[ 1 ] = new Account( 98765, 56789, 200.0, 200.0 );
14      } // end no-argument BankDatabase constructor
15
```

Fig. 13.19 | Class BankDatabase represents the bank's account information database. (Part 1 of 2.)

```
16      // retrieve Account object containing specified account number
17      private Account getAccount( int accountNumber )
18      {
19         // loop through accounts searching for matching account number
20         for ( Account currentAccount : accounts )
21         {
22            // return current account if match found
23            if ( currentAccount.getAccountNumber() == accountNumber )
24               return currentAccount;
25         } // end for
26
27         return null; // if no matching account was found, return null
28      } // end method getAccount
29
30      // determine whether user-specified account number and PIN match
31      // those of an account in the database
32      public boolean authenticateUser( int userAccountNumber, int userPIN )
33      {
34         // attempt to retrieve the account with the account number
35         Account userAccount = getAccount( userAccountNumber );
36
37         // if account exists, return result of Account method validatePIN
38         if ( userAccount != null )
39            return userAccount.validatePIN( userPIN );
40         else
41            return false; // account number not found, so return false
42      } // end method authenticateUser
43
44      // return available balance of Account with specified account number
45      public double getAvailableBalance( int userAccountNumber )
46      {
47         return getAccount( userAccountNumber ).getAvailableBalance();
48      } // end method getAvailableBalance
49
50      // return total balance of Account with specified account number
51      public double getTotalBalance( int userAccountNumber )
52      {
53         return getAccount( userAccountNumber ).getTotalBalance();
54      } // end method getTotalBalance
55
56      // credit an amount to Account with specified account number
57      public void credit( int userAccountNumber, double amount )
58      {
59         getAccount( userAccountNumber ).credit( amount );
60      } // end method credit
61
62      // debit an amount from Account with specified account number
63      public void debit( int userAccountNumber, double amount )
64      {
65         getAccount( userAccountNumber ).debit( amount );
66      } // end method debit
67   } // end class BankDatabase
```

Fig. 13.19 | Class BankDatabase represents the bank's account information database. (Part 2 of 2.)

We determine one reference-type attribute for class BankDatabase based on its composition relationship with class Account. Recall from Fig. 13.9 that a BankDatabase is composed of zero or more objects of class Account. Line 6 implements attribute accounts—an array of Account objects—to implement this composition relationship. Class BankDatabase has a no-argument constructor (lines 9–14) that initializes accounts to contain a set of new Account objects. For the sake of testing the system, we declare accounts to hold just two array elements (line 11), which we instantiate as new Account objects with test data (lines 12–13). Note that the Account constructor has four parameters—the account number, the PIN assigned to the account, the initial available balance and the initial total balance. Recall that class BankDatabase serves as an intermediary between class ATM and the actual Account objects that contain a user's account information. Thus, the methods of class BankDatabase do nothing more than invoke the corresponding methods of the Account object belonging to the current ATM user.

We include private utility method getAccount (lines 17–28) to allow the BankDatabase to obtain a reference to a particular Account within array accounts. To locate the user's Account, the BankDatabase compares the value returned by method getAccountNumber for each element of accounts to a specified account number until it finds a match. Lines 20–25 traverse the accounts array. If the account number of currentAccount equals the value of parameter accountNumber, the method immediately returns the currentAccount. If no account has the given account number, then line 27 returns null.

Method authenticateUser (lines 32–42) proves or disproves the identity of an ATM user. This method takes a user-specified account number and PIN as arguments and indicates whether they match the account number and PIN of an Account in the database. Line 35 calls method getAccount, which returns either an Account with userAccountNumber as its account number or null to indicate that userAccountNumber is invalid. If getAccount returns an Account object, line 39 returns the boolean value returned by that object's validatePIN method. BankDatabase's authenticateUser method does not perform the PIN comparison itself—rather, it forwards userPIN to the Account object's validatePIN method to do so. The value returned by Account method validatePIN indicates whether the user-specified PIN matches the PIN of the user's Account, so method authenticateUser simply returns this value to the class's client (i.e., ATM).

BankDatabase trusts the ATM to invoke method authenticateUser and receive a return value of true before allowing the user to perform transactions. BankDatabase also trusts that each Transaction object created by the ATM contains the valid account number of the current authenticated user and that this is the account number passed to the remaining BankDatabase methods as argument userAccountNumber. Methods getAvailableBalance (lines 45–48), getTotalBalance (lines 51–54), credit (lines 57–60) and debit (lines 63–66) therefore simply retrieve the user's Account object with utility method getAccount, then invoke the appropriate Account method on that object. We know that the calls to getAccount from these methods will never return null, because userAccountNumber must refer to an existing Account. Methods getAvailableBalance and getTotalBalance return the values returned by the corresponding Account methods. Also note that credit and debit simply redirect parameter amount to the Account methods they invoke.

13.4.8 Class Transaction

Class Transaction (Fig. 13.20) is an abstract superclass that represents the notion of an ATM transaction. It contains the common features of subclasses BalanceInquiry, Withdrawal and Deposit. This class expands upon the "skeleton" code first developed in Section 13.3. Line 4 declares this class to be abstract. Lines 6–8 declare the class's private attributes. Recall from the class diagram of Fig. 13.10 that class Transaction contains an attribute accountNumber (line 6) that indicates the account involved in the Transaction. We derive attributes screen (line 7) and bankDatabase (line 8) from class Transaction's associations modeled in Fig. 13.9—all transactions require access to the ATM's screen and the bank's database.

```
 1   // Transaction.java
 2   // Abstract superclass Transaction represents an ATM transaction
 3
 4   public abstract class Transaction
 5   {
 6      private int accountNumber; // indicates account involved
 7      private Screen screen; // ATM's screen
 8      private BankDatabase bankDatabase; // account info database
 9
10      // Transaction constructor invoked by subclasses using super()
11      public Transaction( int userAccountNumber, Screen atmScreen,
12         BankDatabase atmBankDatabase )
13      {
14         accountNumber = userAccountNumber;
15         screen = atmScreen;
16         bankDatabase = atmBankDatabase;
17      } // end Transaction constructor
18
19      // return account number
20      public int getAccountNumber()
21      {
22         return accountNumber;
23      } // end method getAccountNumber
24
25      // return reference to screen
26      public Screen getScreen()
27      {
28         return screen;
29      } // end method getScreen
30
31      // return reference to bank database
32      public BankDatabase getBankDatabase()
33      {
34         return bankDatabase;
35      } // end method getBankDatabase
36
37      // perform the transaction (overridden by each subclass)
38      abstract public void execute();
39   } // end class Transaction
```

Fig. 13.20 | Abstract superclass Transaction represents an ATM transaction.

Class Transaction has a constructor (lines 11–17) that takes as arguments the current user's account number and references to the ATM's screen and the bank's database. Because Transaction is an abstract class, this constructor will be called only by the constructors of the Transaction subclasses.

The class has three public *get* methods—getAccountNumber (lines 20–23), get-Screen (lines 26–29) and getBankDatabase (lines 32–35). These are inherited by Transaction subclasses and used to gain access to class Transaction's private attributes.

Class Transaction also declares abstract method execute (line 38). It does not make sense to provide this method's implementation, because a generic transaction cannot be executed. So, we declare this method abstract and force each Transaction subclass to provide a concrete implementation that executes that particular type of transaction.

13.4.9 Class BalanceInquiry

Class BalanceInquiry (Fig. 13.21) extends Transaction and represents a balance-inquiry ATM transaction. BalanceInquiry does not have any attributes of its own, but it inherits Transaction attributes accountNumber, screen and bankDatabase, which are accessible through Transaction's public *get* methods. The BalanceInquiry constructor takes arguments corresponding to these attributes and simply forwards them to Transaction's constructor using super (line 10).

Class BalanceInquiry overrides Transaction's abstract method execute to provide a concrete implementation (lines 14–36) that performs the steps involved in a balance inquiry. Lines 18–19 get references to the bank database and the ATM's screen by invoking methods inherited from superclass Transaction. Lines 22–23 retrieve the available balance of the account involved by invoking method getAvailableBalance of bank-Database. Note that line 23 uses inherited method getAccountNumber to get the account number of the current user, which it then passes to getAvailableBalance. Lines 26–27 retrieve the total balance of the current user's account. Lines 30–35 display the balance information on the ATM's screen. Recall that displayDollarAmount takes a double argument and outputs it to the screen formatted as a dollar amount. For example, if a user's availableBalance is 1000.5, line 32 outputs $1,000.50. Note that line 35 inserts a blank line of output to separate the balance information from subsequent output (i.e., the main menu repeated by class ATM after executing the BalanceInquiry).

```
1   // BalanceInquiry.java
2   // Represents a balance inquiry ATM transaction
3
4   public class BalanceInquiry extends Transaction
5   {
6      // BalanceInquiry constructor
7      public BalanceInquiry( int userAccountNumber, Screen atmScreen,
8         BankDatabase atmBankDatabase )
9      {
10        super( userAccountNumber, atmScreen, atmBankDatabase );
11     } // end BalanceInquiry constructor
12
13     // performs the transaction
14     @Override
15     public void execute()
16     {
17        // get references to bank database and screen
18        BankDatabase bankDatabase = getBankDatabase();
19        Screen screen = getScreen();
```

Fig. 13.21 | Class BalanceInquiry represents a balance-inquiry ATM transaction. (Part 1 of 2.)

```
20
21        // get the available balance for the account involved
22        double availableBalance =
23           bankDatabase.getAvailableBalance( getAccountNumber() );
24
25        // get the total balance for the account involved
26        double totalBalance =
27           bankDatabase.getTotalBalance( getAccountNumber() );
28
29        // display the balance information on the screen
30        screen.displayMessageLine( "\nBalance Information:" );
31        screen.displayMessage( " - Available balance: " );
32        screen.displayDollarAmount( availableBalance );
33        screen.displayMessage( "\n - Total balance:     " );
34        screen.displayDollarAmount( totalBalance );
35        screen.displayMessageLine( "" );
36     } // end method execute
37  } // end class BalanceInquiry
```

Fig. 13.21 | Class `BalanceInquiry` represents a balance-inquiry ATM transaction. (Part 2 of 2.)

13.4.10 Class `Withdrawal`

Class `Withdrawal` (Fig. 13.22) extends `Transaction` and represents a withdrawal ATM transaction. This class expands upon the "skeleton" code for this class developed in Fig. 13.12. Recall from the class diagram of Fig. 13.10 that class `Withdrawal` has one attribute, `amount`, which line 6 implements as an `int` field. Figure 13.9 models associations between class `Withdrawal` and classes `Keypad` and `CashDispenser`, for which lines 7–8 implement reference-type attributes `keypad` and `cashDispenser`, respectively. Line 11 declares a constant corresponding to the cancel menu option. We'll soon discuss how the class uses this constant.

```
 1  // Withdrawal.java
 2  // Represents a withdrawal ATM transaction
 3
 4  public class Withdrawal extends Transaction
 5  {
 6     private int amount; // amount to withdraw
 7     private Keypad keypad; // reference to keypad
 8     private CashDispenser cashDispenser; // reference to cash dispenser
 9
10     // constant corresponding to menu option to cancel
11     private final static int CANCELED = 6;
12
13     // Withdrawal constructor
14     public Withdrawal( int userAccountNumber, Screen atmScreen,
15        BankDatabase atmBankDatabase, Keypad atmKeypad,
16        CashDispenser atmCashDispenser )
17     {
18        // initialize superclass variables
19        super( userAccountNumber, atmScreen, atmBankDatabase );
```

Fig. 13.22 | Class `Withdrawal` represents a withdrawal ATM transaction. (Part 1 of 4.)

```
20
21          // initialize references to keypad and cash dispenser
22          keypad = atmKeypad;
23          cashDispenser = atmCashDispenser;
24      } // end Withdrawal constructor
25
26      // perform transaction
27      @Override
28      public void execute()
29      {
30          boolean cashDispensed = false; // cash was not dispensed yet
31          double availableBalance; // amount available for withdrawal
32
33          // get references to bank database and screen
34          BankDatabase bankDatabase = getBankDatabase();
35          Screen screen = getScreen();
36
37          // loop until cash is dispensed or the user cancels
38          do
39          {
40              // obtain a chosen withdrawal amount from the user
41              amount = displayMenuOfAmounts();
42
43              // check whether user chose a withdrawal amount or canceled
44              if ( amount != CANCELED )
45              {
46                  // get available balance of account involved
47                  availableBalance =
48                      bankDatabase.getAvailableBalance( getAccountNumber() );
49
50                  // check whether the user has enough money in the account
51                  if ( amount <= availableBalance )
52                  {
53                      // check whether the cash dispenser has enough money
54                      if ( cashDispenser.isSufficientCashAvailable( amount ) )
55                      {
56                          // update the account involved to reflect the withdrawal
57                          bankDatabase.debit( getAccountNumber(), amount );
58
59                          cashDispenser.dispenseCash( amount ); // dispense cash
60                          cashDispensed = true; // cash was dispensed
61
62                          // instruct user to take cash
63                          screen.displayMessageLine( "\nYour cash has been" +
64                              " dispensed. Please take your cash now." );
65                      } // end if
66                      else // cash dispenser does not have enough cash
67                          screen.displayMessageLine(
68                              "\nInsufficient cash available in the ATM." +
69                              "\n\nPlease choose a smaller amount." );
70                  } // end if
71                  else // not enough money available in user's account
72                  {
```

Fig. 13.22 | Class `Withdrawal` represents a withdrawal ATM transaction. (Part 2 of 4.)

```
73                     screen.displayMessageLine(
74                        "\nInsufficient funds in your account." +
75                        "\n\nPlease choose a smaller amount." );
76                  } // end else
77               } // end if
78               else // user chose cancel menu option
79               {
80                  screen.displayMessageLine( "\nCanceling transaction..." );
81                  return; // return to main menu because user canceled
82               } // end else
83            } while ( !cashDispensed );
84
85      } // end method execute
86
87      // display a menu of withdrawal amounts and the option to cancel;
88      // return the chosen amount or 0 if the user chooses to cancel
89      private int displayMenuOfAmounts()
90      {
91         int userChoice = 0; // local variable to store return value
92
93         Screen screen = getScreen(); // get screen reference
94
95         // array of amounts to correspond to menu numbers
96         int[] amounts = { 0, 20, 40, 60, 100, 200 };
97
98         // loop while no valid choice has been made
99         while ( userChoice == 0 )
100        {
101           // display the menu
102           screen.displayMessageLine( "\nWithdrawal Menu:" );
103           screen.displayMessageLine( "1 - $20" );
104           screen.displayMessageLine( "2 - $40" );
105           screen.displayMessageLine( "3 - $60" );
106           screen.displayMessageLine( "4 - $100" );
107           screen.displayMessageLine( "5 - $200" );
108           screen.displayMessageLine( "6 - Cancel transaction" );
109           screen.displayMessage( "\nChoose a withdrawal amount: " );
110
111           int input = keypad.getInput(); // get user input through keypad
112
113           // determine how to proceed based on the input value
114           switch ( input )
115           {
116              case 1: // if the user chose a withdrawal amount
117              case 2: // (i.e., chose option 1, 2, 3, 4 or 5), return the
118              case 3: // corresponding amount from amounts array
119              case 4:
120              case 5:
121                 userChoice = amounts[ input ]; // save user's choice
122                 break;
123              case CANCELED: // the user chose to cancel
124                 userChoice = CANCELED; // save user's choice
125                 break;
```

Fig. 13.22 | Class Withdrawal represents a withdrawal ATM transaction. (Part 3 of 4.)

```
126                    default: // the user did not enter a value from 1-6
127                       screen.displayMessageLine(
128                          "\nInvalid selection. Try again." );
129                 } // end switch
130           } // end while
131
132           return userChoice; // return withdrawal amount or CANCELED
133     } // end method displayMenuOfAmounts
134 } // end class Withdrawal
```

Fig. 13.22 | Class Withdrawal represents a withdrawal ATM transaction. (Part 4 of 4.)

Class Withdrawal's constructor (lines 14–24) has five parameters. It uses super to pass parameters userAccountNumber, atmScreen and atmBankDatabase to superclass Transaction's constructor to set the attributes that Withdrawal inherits from Transaction. The constructor also takes references atmKeypad and atmCashDispenser as parameters and assigns them to reference-type attributes keypad and cashDispenser.

Class Withdrawal overrides Transaction method execute with a concrete implementation (lines 27–85) that performs the steps of a withdrawal. Line 30 declares and initializes a local boolean variable cashDispensed, which indicates whether cash has been dispensed (i.e., whether the transaction has completed successfully) and is initially false. Line 31 declares local double variable availableBalance, which will store the user's available balance during a withdrawal transaction. Lines 34–35 get references to the bank database and the ATM's screen by invoking methods inherited from superclass Transaction.

Lines 38–83 contain a do...while statement that executes its body until cash is dispensed (i.e., until cashDispensed becomes true) or until the user chooses to cancel (in which case, the loop terminates). We use this loop to continuously return the user to the start of the transaction if an error occurs (i.e., the requested withdrawal amount is greater than the user's available balance or greater than the amount of cash in the cash dispenser). Line 41 displays a menu of withdrawal amounts and obtains a user selection by calling private utility method displayMenuOfAmounts (declared in lines 89–133). This method displays the menu of amounts and returns either an int withdrawal amount or an int constant CANCELED to indicate that the user has chosen to cancel the transaction.

Method displayMenuOfAmounts (lines 89–133) first declares local variable user-Choice (initially 0) to store the value that the method will return (line 91). Line 93 gets a reference to the screen by calling method getScreen inherited from superclass Transaction. Line 96 declares an integer array of withdrawal amounts that correspond to the amounts displayed in the withdrawal menu. We ignore the first element in the array (index 0) because the menu has no option 0. The while statement at lines 99–130 repeats until userChoice takes on a value other than 0. We'll see shortly that this occurs when the user makes a valid selection from the menu. Lines 102–109 display the withdrawal menu on the screen and prompt the user to enter a choice. Line 111 obtains integer input through the keypad. The switch statement at lines 114–129 determines how to proceed based on the user's input. If the user selects a number between 1 and 5, line 121 sets userChoice to the value of the element in amounts at index input. For example, if the user enters 3 to withdraw $60, line 121 sets userChoice to the value of amounts[3] (i.e., 60). Line 122 terminates the switch. Variable userChoice no longer equals 0, so the while at lines 99–130 terminates and line 132 returns userChoice. If the user selects the cancel menu option, lines 124–125 execute, setting userChoice to CANCELED and causing the method to return this value. If the user does not enter a valid menu selection, lines 127–128 display an error message and the user is returned to the withdrawal menu.

Line 44 in method execute determines whether the user has selected a withdrawal amount or chosen to cancel. If the user cancels, lines 80–81 execute and display an appropriate message to the user before returning control to the calling method (i.e., ATM method performTransactions). If the user has chosen a withdrawal amount, lines 47–48 retrieve the available balance of the current user's Account and store it in variable availableBalance. Next, the if statement at line 51 determines whether the selected amount is less than or equal to the user's available balance. If it's not, lines 73–75 display an appropriate error message. Control then continues to the end of the do...while, and the loop repeats because cashDispensed is still false. If the user's balance is high enough, the if statement at line 54 determines whether the cash dispenser has enough money to satisfy the withdrawal request by invoking the cashDispenser's isSufficientCashAvailable method. If this method returns false, lines 67–69 display an appropriate error message and the do...while repeats. If sufficient cash is available, then the requirements for the withdrawal are satisfied, and line 57 debits amount from the user's account in the database. Lines 59–60 then instruct the cash dispenser to dispense the cash to the user and set cashDispensed to true. Finally, lines 63–64 display a message to the user that cash has been dispensed. Because cashDispensed is now true, control continues after the do...while. No additional statements appear below the loop, so the method returns control to class ATM.

13.4.11 Class Deposit

Class Deposit (Fig. 13.23) extends Transaction and represents a deposit transaction. Recall from Fig. 13.10 that class Deposit has one attribute amount, which line 6 implements as an int field. Lines 7–8 create reference-type attributes keypad and depositSlot that implement the associations between class Deposit and classes Keypad and DepositSlot modeled in Fig. 13.9. Line 9 declares a constant CANCELED that corresponds to the value a user enters to cancel. We'll soon discuss how the class uses this constant.

```
1   // Deposit.java
2   // Represents a deposit ATM transaction
3
4   public class Deposit extends Transaction
5   {
6      private double amount; // amount to deposit
7      private Keypad keypad; // reference to keypad
8      private DepositSlot depositSlot; // reference to deposit slot
9      private final static int CANCELED = 0; // constant for cancel option
10
11     // Deposit constructor
12     public Deposit( int userAccountNumber, Screen atmScreen,
13        BankDatabase atmBankDatabase, Keypad atmKeypad,
14        DepositSlot atmDepositSlot )
15     {
16        // initialize superclass variables
17        super( userAccountNumber, atmScreen, atmBankDatabase );
18
```

Fig. 13.23 | Class Deposit represents a deposit ATM transaction. (Part 1 of 3.)

```
19          // initialize references to keypad and deposit slot
20          keypad = atmKeypad;
21          depositSlot = atmDepositSlot;
22       } // end Deposit constructor
23
24       // perform transaction
25       @Override
26       public void execute()
27       {
28          BankDatabase bankDatabase = getBankDatabase(); // get reference
29          Screen screen = getScreen(); // get reference
30
31          amount = promptForDepositAmount(); // get deposit amount from user
32
33          // check whether user entered a deposit amount or canceled
34          if ( amount != CANCELED )
35          {
36             // request deposit envelope containing specified amount
37             screen.displayMessage(
38                "\nPlease insert a deposit envelope containing " );
39             screen.displayDollarAmount( amount );
40             screen.displayMessageLine( "." );
41
42             // receive deposit envelope
43             boolean envelopeReceived = depositSlot.isEnvelopeReceived();
44
45             // check whether deposit envelope was received
46             if ( envelopeReceived )
47             {
48                screen.displayMessageLine( "\nYour envelope has been " +
49                   "received.\nNOTE: The money just deposited will not " +
50                   "be available until we verify the amount of any " +
51                   "enclosed cash and your checks clear." );
52
53                // credit account to reflect the deposit
54                bankDatabase.credit( getAccountNumber(), amount );
55             } // end if
56             else // deposit envelope not received
57             {
58                screen.displayMessageLine( "\nYou did not insert an " +
59                   "envelope, so the ATM has canceled your transaction." );
60             } // end else
61          } // end if
62          else // user canceled instead of entering amount
63          {
64             screen.displayMessageLine( "\nCanceling transaction..." );
65          } // end else
66       } // end method execute
67
68       // prompt user to enter a deposit amount in cents
69       private double promptForDepositAmount()
70       {
71          Screen screen = getScreen(); // get reference to screen
72
```

Fig. 13.23 | Class Deposit represents a deposit ATM transaction. (Part 2 of 3.)

```
73          // display the prompt
74          screen.displayMessage( "\nPlease enter a deposit amount in " +
75             "CENTS (or 0 to cancel): " );
76          int input = keypad.getInput(); // receive input of deposit amount
77
78          // check whether the user canceled or entered a valid amount
79          if ( input == CANCELED )
80             return CANCELED;
81          else
82          {
83             return ( double ) input / 100; // return dollar amount
84          } // end else
85       } // end method promptForDepositAmount
86    } // end class Deposit
```

Fig. 13.23 | Class `Deposit` represents a deposit ATM transaction. (Part 3 of 3.)

Like `Withdrawal`, class `Deposit` contains a constructor (lines 12–22) that passes three parameters to superclass `Transaction`'s constructor. The constructor also has parameters `atmKeypad` and `atmDepositSlot`, which it assigns to corresponding attributes (lines 20–21).

Method `execute` (lines 25–66) overrides the `abstract` version in superclass `Transaction` with a concrete implementation that performs the steps required in a deposit transaction. Lines 28–29 get references to the database and the screen. Line 31 prompts the user to enter a deposit amount by invoking `private` utility method `promptForDepositAmount` (declared in lines 69–85) and sets attribute `amount` to the value returned. Method `promptForDepositAmount` asks the user to enter a deposit amount as an integer number of cents (because the ATM's keypad does not contain a decimal point; this is consistent with many real ATMs) and returns the `double` value representing the dollar amount to be deposited.

Line 71 in method `promptForDepositAmount` gets a reference to the ATM's screen. Lines 74–75 display a message on the screen asking the user to input a deposit amount as a number of cents or "0" to cancel the transaction. Line 76 receives the user's input from the keypad. The `if` statement at lines 79–84 determines whether the user has entered a real deposit amount or chosen to cancel. If the latter, line 80 returns the constant `CANCELED`. Otherwise, line 83 returns the deposit amount after converting from the number of cents to a dollar amount by casting `input` to a `double`, then dividing by 100. For example, if the user enters 125 as the number of cents, line 83 returns 125.0 divided by 100, or 1.25—125 cents is $1.25.

Lines 34–65 in method `execute` determine whether the user has chosen to cancel the transaction instead of entering a deposit amount. If the user cancels, line 64 displays an appropriate message, and the method returns. If the user enters a deposit amount, lines 37–40 instruct the user to insert a deposit envelope with the correct amount. Recall that `Screen` method `displayDollarAmount` outputs a `double` formatted as a dollar amount.

Line 43 sets a local `boolean` variable to the value returned by `depositSlot`'s `isEnvelopeReceived` method, indicating whether a deposit envelope has been received. Recall that we coded method `isEnvelopeReceived` (lines 8–11 of Fig. 13.17) to always return `true`, because we are simulating the functionality of the deposit slot and assume that the user always inserts an envelope. However, we code method `execute` of class `Deposit` to test for the possibility that the user does not insert an envelope—good software engineering demands that programs account for all possible return values. Thus, class `Deposit` is prepared for future versions of isEnvelopeReceived that could return false. Lines 48–54 execute if the deposit slot receives an envelope. Lines 48–51 display an appropriate message to the user. Line 54 then credits the deposit amount to the user's account in the database. Lines 58–59 will execute if the deposit slot does not receive a deposit envelope. In this case, we display a message to the user stating that the ATM has canceled the transaction. The method then returns without modifying the user's account.

13.4.12 Class ATMCaseStudy

Class ATMCaseStudy (Fig. 13.24) is a simple class that allows us to start, or "turn on," the ATM and test the implementation of our ATM system model. Class ATMCaseStudy's main method (lines 7–11) does nothing more than instantiate a new ATM object named theATM (line 9) and invoke its run method (line 10) to start the ATM.

```
1   // ATMCaseStudy.java
2   // Driver program for the ATM case study
3
4   public class ATMCaseStudy
5   {
6      // main method creates and runs the ATM
7      public static void main( String[] args )
8      {
9         ATM theATM = new ATM();
10        theATM.run();
11     } // end main
12  } // end class ATMCaseStudy
```

Fig. 13.24 | ATMCaseStudy.java starts the ATM.

13.5 Wrap-Up

In this chapter, you used inheritance to tune the design of the ATM software system, and you fully implemented the ATM in Java. Congratulations on completing the entire ATM case study! We hope you found this experience to be valuable and that it reinforced many of the object-oriented programming concepts that you've learned. In the next chapter, we take a deeper look at graphical user interfaces (GUIs).

Answers to Self-Review Exercises

13.1   True. The minus sign (–) indicates private visibility.

13.2   b.

13.3   The design for class Keypad yields the code in Fig. 13.25. Recall that class Keypad has no attributes for the moment, but attributes may become apparent as we continue the implementation. Also note that if we were designing a real ATM, method getInput would need to interact with the ATM's keypad hardware. We'll actually do input from the keyboard of a personal computer when we write the complete Java code in Section 13.4.

13.4   b.

13.5   False. The UML requires that we italicize abstract class names and method names.

13.6   The design for class Transaction yields the code in Fig. 13.26. The bodies of the class constructor and methods are completed in Section 13.4. When fully implemented, methods getScreen and getBankDatabase will return superclass Transaction's private reference attributes screen and bankDatabase, respectively. These methods allow the Transaction subclasses to access the ATM's screen and interact with the bank's database.

```
1   // Class Keypad represents an ATM's keypad
2   public class Keypad
3   {
4       // no attributes have been specified yet
5
6       // no-argument constructor
7       public Keypad()
8       {
9       } // end no-argument Keypad constructor
10
11      // operations
12      public int getInput()
13      {
14      } // end method getInput
15  } // end class Keypad
```

Fig. 13.25 | Java code for class Keypad based on Figs. 13.1–13.2.

```
1   // Abstract class Transaction represents an ATM transaction
2   public abstract class Transaction
3   {
4       // attributes
5       private int accountNumber; // indicates account involved
6       private Screen screen; // ATM's screen
7       private BankDatabase bankDatabase; // account info database
8
9       // no-argument constructor invoked by subclasses using super()
10      public Transaction()
11      {
12      } // end no-argument Transaction constructor
13
14      // return account number
15      public int getAccountNumber()
16      {
17      } // end method getAccountNumber
18
19      // return reference to screen
20      public Screen getScreen()
21      {
22      } // end method getScreen
23
24      // return reference to bank database
25      public BankDatabase getBankDatabase()
26      {
27      } // end method getBankDatabase
28
29      // abstract method overridden by subclasses
30      public abstract void execute();
31  } // end class Transaction
```

Fig. 13.26 | Java code for class Transaction based on Figs. 13.9 and 13.10.

Do you think I can listen all day to such stuff?
—Lewis Carroll

*Even a minor event in the life of a child is an event of
that child's world and thus a world event.*
—Gaston Bachelard

You pays your money and you takes your choice.
—Punch

14

GUI Components: Part 1

Objectives

In this chapter you'll learn:

■ The design principles of graphical user interfaces (GUIs).

■ How to use Java's new, elegant, cross-platform Nimbus look-and-feel.

■ To build GUIs and handle events generated by user interactions with GUIs.

■ To understand the packages containing GUI components, event-handling classes and interfaces.

■ To create and manipulate buttons, labels, lists, text fields and panels.

■ To handle mouse events and keyboard events.

■ To use layout managers to arrange GUI components

Outline

14.1 Introduction

A **graphical user interface (GUI)** presents a user-friendly mechanism for interacting with an application. A GUI (pronounced "GOO-ee") gives an application a distinctive "look" and "feel." Providing different applications with consistent, intuitive user-interface components gives users a sense of familiarity with a new application, so that they can learn it more quickly and use it more productively.

Look-and-Feel Observation 14.1
Consistent user interfaces enable a user to learn new applications faster.

GUIs are built from **GUI components**. These are sometimes called **controls** or **widgets**—short for **window gadgets**. A GUI component is an object with which the user interacts via the mouse, the keyboard or another form of input, such as voice recognition. In this chapter and Chapter 25, GUI Components: Part 2, you'll learn about many of Java's GUI components. We also cover other GUI components as they are needed throughout the rest of the book.

Many IDEs provide GUI design tools in which you can specify a component's exact size and location in a visual manner by using the mouse. The IDE generates the GUI code for you. Though this greatly simplifies creating GUIs, each IDE has different capabilities and generates different code. For this reason, we wrote the GUI code by hand.

As an example of a GUI, consider Fig. 14.1, which shows the SwingSet3 application that is available at download.java.net/javadesktop/swingset3/SwingSet3.jnlp. This application is a nice way for you to browse through the various GUI components provided by Java's Swing GUI APIs. Simply click a component name (e.g., JFrame, JTabbedPane, etc.) in the **GUI Components** area at the left of the window to see a demonstration of the GUI component in the right side of the window. The source code for each demo is shown in the text area at the bottom of the window. We've labeled a few of the GUI components in the application. At the top of the window is a **title bar** that contains the window's title. Below that is a **menu bar** containing **menus** (**File** and **View**). In the top-right region of the window is a set of **buttons**—typically, users press buttons to perform tasks. In the **GUI Components** area of the window is a **combo box**; the user can click the down arrow at the right side of the box to select from a list of items. The menus, buttons and combo box are part of the application's GUI. They enable you to interact with the application.

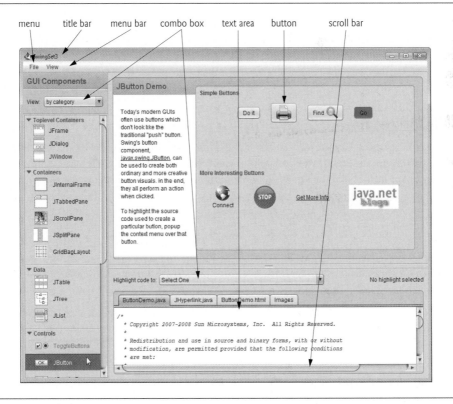

Fig. 14.1 | SwingSet3 application demonstrates many of Java's Swing GUI components.

14.2 Java's New Nimbus Look-and-Feel

As of Java SE 6 update 10, Java comes bundled with a new, elegant, cross-platform look-and-feel known as **Nimbus**. For GUI screen captures like Fig. 14.1, we've configured our systems to use Nimbus as the default look-and-feel. There are three ways that you can use Nimbus:

1. Set it as the default for all Java applications that run on your computer.

2. Set it as the look-and-feel at the time that you launch an application by passing a command-line argument to the java command.

3. Set it as the look-and-feel programatically in your application (see Section 25.6).

To set Nimbus as the default for all Java applications, you must create a text file named swing.properties in the lib folder of both your JDK installation folder and your JRE installation folder. Place the following line of code in the file:

```
swing.defaultlaf=com.sun.java.swing.plaf.nimbus.NimbusLookAndFeel
```

For more information on locating these installation folders visit java.sun.com/javase/ 6/webnotes/install/index.html. [*Note:* In addition to the standalone JRE, there is a JRE nested in your JDK's installation folder. If you are using an IDE that depends on the JDK (e.g., NetBeans), you may also need to place the swing.properties file in the nested jre folder's lib folder.]

If you prefer to select Nimbus on an application-by-application basis, place the following command-line argument after the java command and before the application's name when you run the application:

```
-Dswing.defaultlaf=com.sun.java.swing.plaf.nimbus.NimbusLookAndFeel
```

14.3 Simple GUI-Based Input/Output with JOptionPane

The applications in Chapters 2–10 display text in the command window and obtain input from the command window. Most applications you use on a daily basis use windows or **dialog boxes** (also called **dialogs**) to interact with the user. For example, an e-mail program allows you to type and read messages in a window the program provides. Typically, dialog boxes are windows in which programs display important messages to the user or obtain information from the user. Java's **JOptionPane** class (package javax.swing) provides pre-built dialog boxes for both input and output. These dialogs are displayed by invoking static JOptionPane methods. Figure 14.2 presents a simple addition application that uses two **input dialogs** to obtain integers from the user and a **message dialog** to display the sum of the integers the user enters.

```java
1   // Fig. 14.2: Addition.java
2   // Addition program that uses JOptionPane for input and output.
3   import javax.swing.JOptionPane; // program uses JOptionPane
4
5   public class Addition
6   {
7      public static void main( String[] args )
8      {
9         // obtain user input from JOptionPane input dialogs
10        String firstNumber =
11           JOptionPane.showInputDialog( "Enter first integer" );
12        String secondNumber =
13           JOptionPane.showInputDialog( "Enter second integer" );
14
```

Fig. 14.2 | Addition program that uses JOptionPane for input and output. (Part 1 of 2.)

```
15        // convert String inputs to int values for use in a calculation
16        int number1 = Integer.parseInt( firstNumber );
17        int number2 = Integer.parseInt( secondNumber );
18
19        int sum = number1 + number2; // add numbers
20
21        // display result in a JOptionPane message dialog
22        JOptionPane.showMessageDialog( null, "The sum is " + sum,
23           "Sum of Two Integers", JOptionPane.PLAIN_MESSAGE );
24     } // end method main
25  } // end class Addition
```

(a) Input dialog displayed by lines 10–11

Prompt to the user

When the user clicks **OK**, `showInputDialog` returns to the program the **100** typed by the user as a `String`. The program must convert the `String` to an `int`

Text field in which the user types a value

(b) Input dialog displayed by lines 12–13

(c) Message dialog displayed by lines 22–23

When the user clicks **OK**, the message dialog is dismissed (removed from the screen).

Fig. 14.2 | Addition program that uses `JOptionPane` for input and output. (Part 2 of 2.)

Input Dialogs

Line 3 imports class `JOptionPane`. Lines 10–11 declare the local `String` variable first-Number and assign it the result of the call to `JOptionPane` static method **showInputDialog**. This method displays an input dialog (see the first screen capture in Fig. 14.2), using the method's `String` argument (`"Enter first integer"`) as a prompt.

Look-and-Feel Observation 14.2

*The prompt in an input dialog typically uses **sentence-style capitalization**—a style that capitalizes only the first letter of the first word in the text unless the word is a proper noun (for example, Jones).*

The user types characters in the text field, then clicks **OK** or presses the *Enter* key to submit the `String` to the program. Clicking **OK** also **dismisses (hides) the dialog**. [*Note:* If you type in the text field and nothing appears, activate the text field by clicking it with the mouse.] Unlike `Scanner`, which can be used to input values of several types from the user at the keyboard, an input dialog can input only `Strings`. This is typical of most GUI components. The user can type any characters in the input dialog's text field. Our program assumes that the user enters a valid integer. If the user clicks **Cancel**, showInputDialog returns null. If the user either types a noninteger value or clicks the **Cancel** button in the input dialog, an exception will occur and the program will not operate correctly. Chapter 11, Exception Handling, discussed how to handle such errors. Lines 12–13 display another input dialog that prompts the user to enter the second integer. Note that each JOptionPane dialog that you display is a so called **modal dialog**—while the dialog is on the screen, the user cannot interact with the rest of the application.

Look-and-Feel Observation 14.3

Do not overuse modal dialogs as they can reduce the usability of your applications. Use a modal dialog only when it's necessary to prevent users from interacting with the rest of an application until they dismiss the dialog.

Converting **Strings** to **int** Values

To perform the calculation, we convert the Strings that the user entered to int values. Recall that the Integer class's static method parseInt converts its String argument to an int value. Lines 16–17 assign the converted values to local variables number1 and number2. Then, line 19 sums these values and assigns the result to local variable sum.

Message Dialogs

Lines 22–23 use JOptionPane static method **showMessageDialog** to display a message dialog (the last screen capture of Fig. 14.2) containing the sum. The first argument helps the Java application determine where to position the dialog box. A dialog is typically displayed from a GUI application with its own window. The first argument refers to that window (known as the parent window) and causes the dialog to appear centered over parent (as we'll do in Section 14.9). If the first argument is null, the dialog box is displayed at the center of your screen. The second argument is the message to display—in this case, the result of concatenating the String "The sum is " and the value of sum. The third argument—"Sum of Two Integers"—is the String that should appear in the title bar at the top of the dialog. The fourth argument—**JOptionPane.PLAIN_MESSAGE**—is the type of message dialog to display. A PLAIN_MESSAGE dialog does not display an icon to the left of the message. Class JOptionPane provides several overloaded versions of methods showInputDialog and showMessageDialog, as well as methods that display other dialog types. For complete information on class JOptionPane, visit java.sun.com/javase/6/docs/api/javax/swing/JOptionPane.html.

Look-and-Feel Observation 14.4

*The title bar of a window typically uses **book-title capitalization**—a style that capitalizes the first letter of each significant word in the text and does not end with any punctuation (for example, Capitalization in a Book Title).*

JOptionPane Message Dialog Constants

The constants that represent the message dialog types are shown in Fig. 14.3. All message dialog types except PLAIN_MESSAGE display an icon to the left of the message. These icons provide a visual indication of the message's importance to the user. Note that a QUESTION_MESSAGE icon is the default icon for an input dialog box (see Fig. 14.2).

Message dialog type	Icon	Description
ERROR_MESSAGE		Indicates an error to the user.
INFORMATION_MESSAGE		Indicates an informational message to the user.
WARNING_MESSAGE		Warns the user of a potential problem.
QUESTION_MESSAGE		Poses a question to the user. This dialog normally requires a response, such as clicking a **Yes** or a **No** button.
PLAIN_MESSAGE	no icon	A dialog that contains a message, but no icon.

Fig. 14.3 | JOptionPane static constants for message dialogs.

14.4 Overview of Swing Components

Though it's possible to perform input and output using the JOptionPane dialogs presented in Section 14.3, most GUI applications require more elaborate, customized user interfaces. The remainder of this chapter discusses many GUI components that enable application developers to create robust GUIs. Figure 14.4 lists several **Swing GUI components** from package **javax.swing** that are used to build Java GUIs. Most Swing components are pure Java components—they are written, manipulated and displayed completely in Java. They are part of the **Java Foundation Classes (JFC)**—Java's libraries for cross-platform GUI development. Visit java.sun.com/javase/technologies/desktop/ for more information on JFC and Java desktop technologies.

Component	Description
JLabel	Displays uneditable text or icons.
JTextField	Enables user to enter data from the keyboard. Can also be used to display editable or uneditable text.
JButton	Triggers an event when clicked with the mouse.
JCheckBox	Specifies an option that can be selected or not selected.
JComboBox	Provides a drop-down list of items from which the user can make a selection by clicking an item or possibly by typing into the box.
JList	Provides a list of items from which the user can make a selection by clicking on any item in the list. Multiple elements can be selected.
JPanel	Provides an area in which components can be placed and organized. Can also be used as a drawing area for graphics.

Fig. 14.4 | Some basic GUI components.

Swing vs. AWT

There are actually two sets of GUI components in Java. Before Swing was introduced in Java SE 1.2, Java GUIs were built with components from the **Abstract Window Toolkit**

(AWT) in package **java.awt**. When a Java application with an AWT GUI executes on different Java platforms, the application's GUI components display differently on each platform. Consider an application that displays an object of type Button (package java.awt). On a computer running the Microsoft Windows operating system, the Button will have the same appearance as the buttons in other Windows applications. Similarly, on a computer running the Apple Mac OS X operating system, the Button will have the same look-and-feel as the buttons in other Macintosh applications. Sometimes, the manner in which a user can interact with a particular AWT component differs between platforms.

Together, the appearance and the way in which the user interacts with the application are known as that application's **look-and-feel**. Swing GUI components allow you to specify a uniform look-and-feel for your application across all platforms or to use each platform's custom look-and-feel. An application can even change the look-and-feel during execution to enable users to choose their own preferred look-and-feel.

Portability Tip 14.1
Swing components are implemented in Java, so they are more portable and flexible than the original Java GUI components from package java.awt, which were based on the GUI components of the underlying platform. For this reason, Swing GUI components are generally preferred.

Lightweight vs. Heavyweight GUI Components

Most Swing components are not tied to actual GUI components of the underlying platform. Such GUI components are known as **lightweight components**. AWT components (many of which parallel the Swing components) are tied to the local platform and are called **heavyweight components**, because they rely on the local platform's **windowing system** to determine their functionality and their look-and-feel.

Several Swing components are heavyweight components. Like AWT components, heavyweight Swing GUI components require direct interaction with the local windowing system, which may restrict their appearance and functionality, making them less flexible than lightweight components.

Portability Tip 14.2
The look-and-feel of a GUI defined with heavyweight GUI components from package java.awt may vary across platforms. Because heavyweight components are tied to the local-platform GUI, the look-and-feel varies from platform to platform.

Superclasses of Swing's Lightweight GUI Components

The UML class diagram of Fig. 14.5 shows an inheritance hierarchy of classes from which lightweight Swing components inherit their common attributes and behaviors.

Software Engineering Observation 14.1
Study the attributes and behaviors of the classes in the class hierarchy of Fig. 14.5. These classes declare the features that are common to most Swing components.

Class **Component** (package java.awt) is a subclass of Object that declares many of the attributes and behaviors common to the GUI components in packages java.awt and javax.swing. Most GUI components extend class Component directly or indirectly. Visit java.sun.com/javase/6/docs/api/java/awt/Component.html for a complete list of these common features.

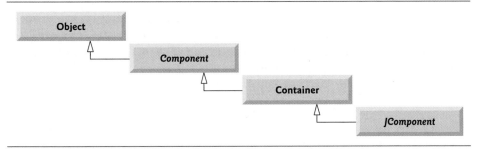

Fig. 14.5 | Common superclasses of many of the Swing components.

Class **Container** (package java.awt) is a subclass of Component. As you'll soon see, Components are attached to Containers (such as windows) so that they can be organized and displayed on the screen. Any object that *is a* Container can be used to organize other Components in a GUI. Because a Container *is a* Component, you can place Containers in other Containers to help organize a GUI. Visit java.sun.com/javase/6/docs/api/ java/awt/Container.html for a complete list of the Container features that are common to Swing lightweight components.

Class **JComponent** (package javax.swing) is a subclass of Container. JComponent is the superclass of all lightweight Swing components and declares their common attributes and behaviors. Because JComponent is a subclass of Container, all lightweight Swing components are also Containers. Some common lightweight component features supported by JComponent include:

1. A **pluggable look-and-feel** that can be used to customize the appearance of components (e.g., for use on particular platforms). You'll see an example of this in Section 25.6.

2. Shortcut keys (called **mnemonics**) for direct access to GUI components through the keyboard. You'll see an example of this in Section 25.4.

3. Common event-handling capabilities for cases where several GUI components initiate the same actions in an application.

4. Brief descriptions of a GUI component's purpose (called **tool tips**) that are displayed when the mouse cursor is positioned over the component for a short time. You'll see an example of this in the next section.

5. Support for accessibility, such as braille screen readers for the visually impaired.

6. Support for user-interface **localization**—that is, customizing the user interface to display in different languages and use local cultural conventions.

Visit java.sun.com/javase/6/docs/api/javax/swing/JComponent.html for more details on the common lightweight component features.

14.5 Displaying Text and Images in a Window

Our next example introduces a framework for building GUI applications. This framework uses several concepts that you'll see in many of our GUI applications. This is our first example in which the application appears in its own window. Most windows you'll create that can contain Swing GUI components are instances of class JFrame or a subclass of

JFrame. JFrame is an indirect subclass of class `java.awt.Window` that provides the basic attributes and behaviors of a window—a title bar at the top, and buttons to minimize, maximize and close the window. Since an application's GUI is typically specific to the application, most of our examples will consist of two classes—a subclass of JFrame that helps us demonstrate new GUI concepts and an application class in which `main` creates and displays the application's primary window.

Labeling GUI Components

A typical GUI consists of many components. In a large GUI, it can be difficult to identify the purpose of every component. So GUI designers often provide text stating each component's purpose. Such text is known as a **label** and is created with class **JLabel**—a subclass of JComponent. A JLabel displays read-only text, an image, or both text and an image. Applications rarely change a label's contents after creating it.

Look-and-Feel Observation 14.5
Text in a JLabel normally uses sentence-style capitalization.

The application of Figs. 14.6–14.7 demonstrates several JLabel features and presents the framework we use in most of our GUI examples. We did not highlight the code in this example, since most of it is new. [*Note:* There are many more features for each GUI component than we can cover in our examples. To learn the complete details of each GUI component, visit its page in the online documentation. For class JLabel, visit `java.sun.com/javase/6/docs/api/javax/swing/JLabel.html`.]

```
1   // Fig. 14.6: LabelFrame.java
2   // Demonstrating the JLabel class.
3   import java.awt.FlowLayout; // specifies how components are arranged
4   import javax.swing.JFrame; // provides basic window features
5   import javax.swing.JLabel; // displays text and images
6   import javax.swing.SwingConstants; // common constants used with Swing
7   import javax.swing.Icon; // interface used to manipulate images
8   import javax.swing.ImageIcon; // loads images
9
10  public class LabelFrame extends JFrame
11  {
12     private JLabel label1; // JLabel with just text
13     private JLabel label2; // JLabel constructed with text and icon
14     private JLabel label3; // JLabel with added text and icon
15
16     // LabelFrame constructor adds JLabels to JFrame
17     public LabelFrame()
18     {
19        super( "Testing JLabel" );
20        setLayout( new FlowLayout() ); // set frame layout
21
22        // JLabel constructor with a string argument
23        label1 = new JLabel( "Label with text" );
24        label1.setToolTipText( "This is label1" );
25        add( label1 ); // add label1 to JFrame
```

Fig. 14.6 | JLabels with text and icons. (Part 1 of 2.)

```
26
27         // JLabel constructor with string, Icon and alignment arguments
28         Icon bug = new ImageIcon( getClass().getResource(  "bug1.png" ) );
29         label2 = new JLabel( "Label with text and icon", bug,
30            SwingConstants.LEFT );
31         label2.setToolTipText( "This is label2" );
32         add( label2 ); // add label2 to JFrame
33
34         label3 = new JLabel(); // JLabel constructor no arguments
35         label3.setText( "Label with icon and text at bottom" );
36         label3.setIcon( bug ); // add icon to JLabel
37         label3.setHorizontalTextPosition( SwingConstants.CENTER );
38         label3.setVerticalTextPosition( SwingConstants.BOTTOM );
39         label3.setToolTipText( "This is label3" );
40         add( label3 ); // add label3 to JFrame
41      } // end LabelFrame constructor
42   } // end class LabelFrame
```

Fig. 14.6 | JLabels with text and icons. (Part 2 of 2.)

```
 1   // Fig. 14.7: LabelTest.java
 2   // Testing LabelFrame.
 3   import javax.swing.JFrame;
 4
 5   public class LabelTest
 6   {
 7      public static void main( String[] args )
 8      {
 9         LabelFrame labelFrame = new LabelFrame(); // create LabelFrame
10         labelFrame.setDefaultCloseOperation( JFrame.EXIT_ON_CLOSE );
11         labelFrame.setSize( 260, 180 ); // set frame size
12         labelFrame.setVisible( true ); // display frame
13      } // end main
14   } // end class LabelTest
```

Fig. 14.7 | Test class for LabelFrame.

Class LabelFrame (Fig. 14.6) is a subclass of JFrame. We'll use an instance of class LabelFrame to display a window containing three JLabels. Lines 3–8 import the classes used in class LabelFrame. The class extends JFrame to inherit the features of a window. Lines 12–14 declare the three JLabel instance variables, each of which is instantiated in the LabelFrame constructor (lines 17–41). Typically, the JFrame subclass's constructor builds the GUI that is displayed in the window when the application executes. Line 19 invokes superclass JFrame's constructor with the argument "Testing JLabel". JFrame's constructor uses this String as the text in the window's title bar.

Specifying the Layout

When building a GUI, you must attach each GUI component to a container, such as a window created with a JFrame. Also, you typically must decide where to position each GUI component. This is known as specifying the layout of the GUI components. As you'll learn at the end of this chapter and in Chapter 25, Java provides several **layout managers** that can help you position components.

Many integrated development environments provide GUI design tools in which you can specify the exact size and location of a component in a visual manner by using the mouse; then the IDE will generate the GUI code for you. Though such IDEs can greatly simplify GUI creation, they are each different in capability.

To ensure that this book's examples can be used with any IDE, we did not use an IDE to create the GUI code. For this reason, we use Java's layout managers in our GUI examples. One such layout manager is **FlowLayout**, in which GUI components are placed on a container from left to right in the order in which the program attaches them to the container. When there is no more room to fit components left to right, components continue to display left to right on the next line. If the container is resized, a FlowLayout reflows (i.e., rearranges) the components to accommodate the new width of the container, possibly with fewer or more rows of GUI components. Every container has a default layout, which we are changing for LabelFrame to a FlowLayout (line 20). Method **setLayout** is inherited into class LabelFrame indirectly from class Container. The argument to the method must be an object of a class that implements the LayoutManager interface (e.g., FlowLayout). Line 20 creates a new FlowLayout object and passes its reference as the argument to setLayout.

Creating and Attaching label1

Now that we've specified the window's layout, we can begin creating and attaching GUI components to the window. Line 23 creates a JLabel object and passes "Label with text" to the constructor. The JLabel displays this text on the screen as part of the application's GUI. Line 24 uses method **setToolTipText** (inherited by JLabel from JComponent) to specify the tool tip that is displayed when the user positions the mouse cursor over the JLabel in the GUI. You can see a sample tool tip in the second screen capture of Fig. 14.7. When you execute this application, try positioning the mouse over each JLabel to see its tool tip. Line 25 attaches label1 to the LabelFrame by passing label1 to the **add** method, which is inherited indirectly from class Container.

Common Programming Error 14.1

If you do not explicitly add a GUI component to a container, the GUI component will not be displayed when the container appears on the screen.

Look-and-Feel Observation 14.6

Use tool tips to add descriptive text to your GUI components. This text helps the user determine the GUI component's purpose in the user interface.

Creating and Attaching label2

Icons are a popular way to enhance the look-and-feel of an application and are also commonly used to indicate functionality. For examples, most of today's VCRs and DVD players use the same icon to play a tape or DVD. Several Swing components can display images. An icon is normally specified with an **Icon** argument to a constructor or to the component's **setIcon** method. An Icon is an object of any class that implements interface Icon (package javax.swing). One such class is **ImageIcon** (package javax.swing), which supports several image formats, including **Graphics Interchange Format (GIF)**, **Portable Network Graphics (PNG)** and **Joint Photographic Experts Group (JPEG)**. File names for each of these types end with .gif, .png or .jpg (or .jpeg), respectively. We discuss images in more detail in Chapter 24, Multimedia: Applets and Applications.

Line 28 declares an ImageIcon. The file bug1.png contains the image to load and store in the ImageIcon object. This image is included in the directory for this example. The ImageIcon object is assigned to Icon reference bug. Remember, class ImageIcon implements interface Icon; an ImageIcon *is an* Icon.

In line 28, the expression getClass().getResource("bug1.png") invokes method **getClass** (inherited indirectly from class Object) to retrieve a reference to the Class object that represents the LabelFrame class declaration. That reference is then used to invoke Class method **getResource**, which returns the location of the image as a URL. The ImageIcon constructor uses the URL to locate the image, then loads it into memory. As we discussed in Chapter 1, the JVM loads class declarations into memory, using a class loader. The class loader knows where each class it loads is located on disk. Method get-Resource uses the Class object's class loader to determine the location of a resource, such as an image file. In this example, the image file is stored in the same location as the Label-Frame.class file. The techniques described here enable an application to load image files from locations that are relative to LabelFrame's .class file on disk.

A JLabel can display an Icon. Lines 29–30 use another JLabel constructor to create a JLabel that displays the text "Label with text and icon" and the Icon bug created in line 28. The last constructor argument indicates that the label's contents are left justified, or left aligned (i.e., the icon and text are at the left side of the label's area on the screen). Interface **SwingConstants** (package javax.swing) declares a set of common integer constants (such as SwingConstants.LEFT) that are used with many Swing components. By default, the text appears to the right of the image when a label contains both text and an image. Note that the horizontal and vertical alignments of a JLabel can be set with methods **setHorizontalAlignment** and **setVerticalAlignment**, respectively. Line 31 specifies the tool-tip text for label2, and line 32 adds label2 to the JFrame.

Creating and Attaching *label3*

Class JLabel provides methods to change a label's appearance after it has been instantiated. Line 34 creates a JLabel and invokes its no-argument constructor. Such a label initially has no text or Icon. Line 35 uses JLabel method **setText** to set the text displayed on the label. The corresponding method **getText** retrieves the current text displayed on a label. Line 36 uses JLabel method **setIcon** to specify the Icon to display on the label. The corresponding method **getIcon** retrieves the current Icon displayed on a label. Lines 37–38 use JLabel methods **setHorizontalTextPosition** and **setVerticalTextPosition** to specify the text position in the label. In this case, the text will be centered horizontally and will appear at the bottom of the label. Thus, the Icon will appear above the text. The horizontal-position constants in SwingConstants are LEFT, CENTER and RIGHT (Fig. 14.8). The vertical-position constants in SwingConstants are TOP, CENTER and BOTTOM (Fig. 14.8). Line 39 sets the tool-tip text for label3. Line 40 adds label3 to the JFrame.

Constant	Description
Horizontal-position constants	
SwingConstants.LEFT	Place text on the left.
SwingConstants.CENTER	Place text in the center.
SwingConstants.RIGHT	Place text on the right.
Vertical-position constants	
SwingConstants.TOP	Place text at the top.
SwingConstants.CENTER	Place text in the center.
SwingConstants.BOTTOM	Place text at the bottom.

Fig. 14.8 | Positioning constants.

*Creating and Displaying a **LabelFrame** Window*
Class **LabelTest** (Fig. 14.7) creates an object of class **LabelFrame** (line 9), then specifies the default close operation for the window. By default, closing a window simply hides the window. However, when the user closes the **LabelFrame** window, we would like the application to terminate. Line 10 invokes **LabelFrame**'s **setDefaultCloseOperation** method (inherited from class **JFrame**) with constant **JFrame.EXIT_ON_CLOSE** as the argument to indicate that the program should terminate when the window is closed by the user. This line is important. Without it the application will not terminate when the user closes the window. Next, line 11 invokes **LabelFrame**'s **setSize** method to specify the width and height of the window in pixels. Finally, line 12 invokes **LabelFrame**'s **setVisible** method with the argument **true** to display the window on the screen. Try resizing the window to see how the **FlowLayout** changes the **JLabel** positions as the window width changes.

14.6 Text Fields and an Introduction to Event Handling with Nested Classes

Normally, a user interacts with an application's GUI to indicate the tasks that the application should perform. For example, when you write an e-mail in an e-mail application, clicking the **Send** button tells the application to send the e-mail to the specified e-mail addresses. GUIs are **event driven**. When the user interacts with a GUI component, the interaction—known as an **event**—drives the program to perform a task. Some common user interactions that cause an application to perform a task include clicking a button, typing in a text field, selecting an item from a menu, closing a window and moving the mouse. The code that performs a task in response to an event is called an **event handler**, and the overall process of responding to events is known as **event handling**.

Let's consider two other GUI components that can generate events—**JTextFields** and **JPasswordFields** (package javax.swing). Class JTextField extends class **JTextComponent** (package javax.swing.text), which provides many features common to Swing's text-based components. Class JPasswordField extends JTextField and adds methods that are specific to processing passwords. Each of these components is a single-line area in which the user can enter text via the keyboard. Applications can also display text in a JTextField (see the output of Fig. 14.10). A JPasswordField shows that characters are being typed as the user enters them, but hides the actual characters with an **echo character**, assuming that they represent a password that should remain known only to the user.

When the user types data into a JTextField or a JPasswordField, then presses *Enter*, an event occurs. Our next example demonstrates how a program can perform a task in response to that event. The techniques shown here are applicable to all GUI components that generate events.

The application of Figs. 14.9–14.10 uses classes JTextField and JPasswordField to create and manipulate four text fields. When the user types in one of the text fields, then presses *Enter*, the application displays a message dialog box containing the text the user typed. You can type only in the text field that is "in **focus**." A component receives the focus when the user clicks the component. This is important, because the text field with the focus is the one that generates an event when the user presses *Enter*. In this example, when the user presses *Enter* in the JPasswordField, the password is revealed. We begin by discussing the setup of the GUI, then discuss the event-handling code.

```java
 1  // Fig. 14.9: TextFieldFrame.java
 2  // Demonstrating the JTextField class.
 3  import java.awt.FlowLayout;
 4  import java.awt.event.ActionListener;
 5  import java.awt.event.ActionEvent;
 6  import javax.swing.JFrame;
 7  import javax.swing.JTextField;
 8  import javax.swing.JPasswordField;
 9  import javax.swing.JOptionPane;
10
11  public class TextFieldFrame extends JFrame
12  {
13     private JTextField textField1; // text field with set size
14     private JTextField textField2; // text field constructed with text
15     private JTextField textField3; // text field with text and size
16     private JPasswordField passwordField; // password field with text
17
18     // TextFieldFrame constructor adds JTextFields to JFrame
19     public TextFieldFrame()
20     {
21        super( "Testing JTextField and JPasswordField" );
22        setLayout( new FlowLayout() ); // set frame layout
23
24        // construct textfield with 10 columns
25        textField1 = new JTextField( 10 );
26        add( textField1 ); // add textField1 to JFrame
27
28        // construct textfield with default text
29        textField2 = new JTextField( "Enter text here" );
30        add( textField2 ); // add textField2 to JFrame
31
32        // construct textfield with default text and 21 columns
33        textField3 = new JTextField( "Uneditable text field", 21 );
34        textField3.setEditable( false ); // disable editing
35        add( textField3 ); // add textField3 to JFrame
36
```

Fig. 14.9 | JTextFields and JPasswordFields. (Part 1 of 2.)

```
37          // construct passwordfield with default text
38          passwordField = new JPasswordField( "Hidden text" );
39          add( passwordField ); // add passwordField to JFrame
40
41          // register event handlers
42          TextFieldHandler handler = new TextFieldHandler();
43          textField1.addActionListener( handler );
44          textField2.addActionListener( handler );
45          textField3.addActionListener( handler );
46          passwordField.addActionListener( handler );
47       } // end TextFieldFrame constructor
48
49       // private inner class for event handling
50       private class TextFieldHandler implements ActionListener
51       {
52          // process text field events
53          public void actionPerformed( ActionEvent event )
54          {
55             String string = ""; // declare string to display
56
57             // user pressed Enter in JTextField textField1
58             if ( event.getSource() == textField1 )
59                string = String.format( "textField1: %s",
60                   event.getActionCommand() );
61
62             // user pressed Enter in JTextField textField2
63             else if ( event.getSource() == textField2 )
64                string = String.format( "textField2: %s",
65                   event.getActionCommand() );
66
67             // user pressed Enter in JTextField textField3
68             else if ( event.getSource() == textField3 )
69                string = String.format( "textField3: %s",
70                   event.getActionCommand() );
71
72             // user pressed Enter in JTextField passwordField
73             else if ( event.getSource() == passwordField )
74                string = String.format( "passwordField: %s",
75                   event.getActionCommand() );
76
77             // display JTextField content
78             JOptionPane.showMessageDialog( null, string );
79          } // end method actionPerformed
80       } // end private inner class TextFieldHandler
81    } // end class TextFieldFrame
```

Fig. 14.9 | JTextFields and JPasswordFields. (Part 2 of 2.)

```
1    // Fig. 14.10: TextFieldTest.java
2    // Testing TextFieldFrame.
3    import javax.swing.JFrame;
4
```

Fig. 14.10 | Test class for TextFieldFrame. (Part 1 of 2.)

```
5   public class TextFieldTest
6   {
7      public static void main( String[] args )
8      {
9         TextFieldFrame textFieldFrame = new TextFieldFrame();
10        textFieldFrame.setDefaultCloseOperation( JFrame.EXIT_ON_CLOSE );
11        textFieldFrame.setSize( 350, 100 ); // set frame size
12        textFieldFrame.setVisible( true ); // display frame
13     } // end main
14  } // end class TextFieldTest
```

Fig. 14.10 | Test class for `TextFieldFrame`. (Part 2 of 2.)

Lines 3–9 import the classes and interfaces we use in this example. Class TextField-Frame extends JFrame and declares three JTextField variables and a JPasswordField variable (lines 13–16). Each of the corresponding text fields is instantiated and attached to the TextFieldFrame in the constructor (lines 19–47).

Creating the GUI
Line 22 sets the TextFieldFrame's layout to FlowLayout. Line 25 creates textField1 with 10 columns of text. A text column's width in pixels is determined by the average width of

a character in the text field's current font. When text is displayed in a text field and the text is wider than the field itself, a portion of the text at the right side is not visible. If you are typing in a text field and the cursor reaches the right edge, the text at the left edge is pushed off the left side of the field and is no longer visible. Users can use the left and right arrow keys to move through the complete text, even though the entire text is not visible at one time. Line 26 adds textField1 to the JFrame.

Line 29 creates textField2 with the initial text "Enter text here" to display in the text field. The width of the field is determined by the width of the default text specified in the constructor. Line 30 adds textField2 to the JFrame.

Line 33 creates textField3 and calls the JTextField constructor with two arguments—the default text "Uneditable text field" to display and the number of columns (21). The width of the text field is determined by the number of columns specified. Line 34 uses method **setEditable** (inherited by JTextField from class JTextComponent) to make the text field uneditable—i.e., the user cannot modify the text in the field. Line 35 adds textField3 to the JFrame.

Line 38 creates passwordField with the text "Hidden text" to display in the text field. The width of the field is determined by the width of the default text. When you execute the application, notice that the text is displayed as a string of asterisks. Line 39 adds passwordField to the JFrame.

Steps Required to Set Up Event Handling for a GUI Component

This example should display a message dialog containing the text from a text field when the user presses *Enter* in that text field. Before an application can respond to an event for a particular GUI component, you must perform several coding steps:

1. Create a class that represents the event handler.

2. Implement an appropriate interface, known as an **event-listener interface**, in the class from *Step 1*.

3. Indicate that an object of the class from *Steps 1* and *2* should be notified when the event occurs. This is known as **registering the event handler**.

Using a Nested Class to Implement an Event Handler

All the classes discussed so far were so-called **top-level classes**—that is, they were not declared inside another class. Java allows you to declare classes inside other classes—these are called **nested classes**. Nested classes can be static or non-static. Non-static nested classes are called **inner classes** and are frequently used to implement event handlers.

Before an object of an inner class can be created, there must first be an object of the top-level class that contains the inner class. This is required because an inner-class object implicitly has a reference to an object of its top-level class. There is also a special relationship between these objects—the inner-class object is allowed to directly access all the variables and methods of the outer class. A nested class that is static does not require an object of its top-level class and does not implicitly have a reference to an object of the top-level class. As you'll see in Chapter 15, Graphics and Java 2D™, the Java 2D graphics API uses static nested classes extensively.

Software Engineering Observation 14.2

An inner class is allowed to directly access all of its top-level class's variables and methods.

The event handling in this example is performed by an object of the private inner class TextFieldHandler (lines 50–80). This class is private because it will be used only to create event handlers for the text fields in top-level class TextFieldFrame. As with other class members, inner classes can be declared public, protected or private. Since event handlers tend to be specific to the application in which they are defined, they are often implemented as private inner classes or, as you'll learn in Section 14.11, as anonymous inner classes.

GUI components can generate many events in response to user interactions. Each event is represented by a class and can be processed only by the appropriate type of event handler. Normally, a component's supported events are described in the Java API documentation for that component's class and its superclasses. When the user presses *Enter* in a JTextField or JPasswordField, an **ActionEvent** (package java.awt.event) occurs. Such an event is processed by an object that implements the interface **ActionListener** (package java.awt.event). The information discussed here is available in the Java API documentation for classes JTextField and ActionEvent. Since JPasswordField is a subclass of JTextField, JPasswordField supports the same events.

To prepare to handle the events in this example, inner class TextFieldHandler implements interface ActionListener and declares the only method in that interface—actionPerformed (lines 53–79). This method specifies the tasks to perform when an ActionEvent occurs. So, inner class TextFieldHandler satisfies *Steps 1* and *2* listed earlier in this section. We'll discuss the details of method actionPerformed shortly.

Registering the Event Handler for Each Text Field

In the TextFieldFrame constructor, line 42 creates a TextFieldHandler object and assigns it to variable handler. This object's actionPerformed method will be called automatically when the user presses *Enter* in any of the GUI's text fields. However, before this can occur, the program must register this object as the event handler for each text field. Lines 43–46 are the event-registration statements that specify handler as the event handler for the three JTextFields and the JPasswordField. The application calls JTextField method **addActionListener** to register the event handler for each component. This method receives as its argument an ActionListener object, which can be an object of any class that implements ActionListener. The object handler *is an* ActionListener, because class TextFieldHandler implements ActionListener. After lines 43–46 execute, the object handler **listens for events**. Now, when the user presses *Enter* in any of these four text fields, method actionPerformed (line 53–79) in class TextFieldHandler is called to handle the event. If an event handler is not registered for a particular text field, the event that occurs when the user presses *Enter* in that text field is **consumed**—i.e., it's simply ignored by the application.

Software Engineering Observation 14.3

The event listener for an event must implement the appropriate event-listener interface.

Common Programming Error 14.2

Forgetting to register an event-handler object for a particular GUI component's event type causes events of that type to be ignored.

Details of Class **TextFieldHandler's** **actionPerformed** *Method*

In this example, we are using one event-handling object's actionPerformed method (lines 53–79) to handle the events generated by four text fields. Since we'd like to output the name of each text field's instance variable for demonstration purposes, we must determine which text field generated the event each time actionPerformed is called. The GUI component with which the user interacts is the **event source**. In this example, the event source is one of the text fields or the password field. When the user presses *Enter* while one of these GUI components has the focus, the system creates a unique ActionEvent object that contains information about the event that just occurred, such as the event source and the text in the text field. The system then passes this ActionEvent object in a method call to the event listener's actionPerformed method. In this example, we display some of that information in a message dialog. Line 55 declares the String that will be displayed. The variable is initialized with the **empty string**—a String containing no characters. The compiler requires this in case none of the branches of the nested if in lines 58–75 executes.

ActionEvent method getSource (which is inherited into ActionEvent from class EventObject and called in lines 58, 63, 68 and 73) returns a reference to the event source. The condition in line 58 asks, "Is the event source textField1?" This condition compares the references on either side of the == operator to determine if they refer to the same object. If they both refer to textField1, the program knows that the user pressed *Enter* in textField1. In this case, lines 59–60 create a String containing the message that line 78 displays in a message dialog. Line 60 uses ActionEvent method **getActionCommand** to obtain the text the user typed in the text field that generated the event.

In this example, we display the text of the password in the JPasswordField when the user presses *Enter* in that field. Sometimes it's necessary to programatically process the characters in a password. Class JPasswordField method **getPassword** returns the password's characters as an array of type char.

Class **TextFieldTest**

Class TextFieldTest (Fig. 14.10) contains the main method that executes this application and displays an object of class TextFieldFrame. When you execute the application, note that even the uneditable JTextField (textField3) can generate an ActionEvent. To test this, click the text field to give it the focus, then press *Enter*. Also note that the actual text of the password is displayed when you press *Enter* in the JPasswordField. Of course, you would normally not display the password!

This application used a single object of class TextFieldHandler as the event listener for four text fields. Starting in Section 14.10, you'll see that it's possible to declare several event-listener objects of the same type and register each object for a separate GUI component's event. This technique enables us to eliminate the if...else logic used in this example's event handler by providing separate event handlers for each component's events.

14.7 Common GUI Event Types and Listener Interfaces

In Section 14.6, you learned that information about the event that occurs when the user presses *Enter* in a text field is stored in an ActionEvent object. Many different types of events can occur when the user interacts with a GUI. The event information is stored in an object of a class that extends AWTEvent (from package java.awt). Figure 14.11 illustrates a hierarchy containing many event classes from the package **java.awt.event**. Some of these are discussed in this chapter and Chapter 25. These event types are used with both

AWT and Swing components. Additional event types that are specific to Swing GUI components are declared in package **javax.swing.event**.

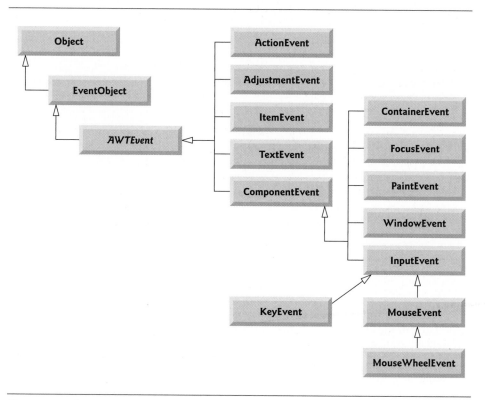

Fig. 14.11 | Some event classes of package java.awt.event.

Let's summarize the three parts to the event-handling mechanism that you saw in Section 14.6—the event source, the event object and the event listener. The event source is the GUI component with which the user interacts. The event object encapsulates information about the event that occurred, such as a reference to the event source and any event-specific information that may be required by the event listener for it to handle the event. The event listener is an object that is notified by the event source when an event occurs; in effect, it "listens" for an event, and one of its methods executes in response to the event. A method of the event listener receives an event object when the event listener is notified of the event. The event listener then uses the event object to respond to the event. This event-handling model is known as the **delegation event model**—an event's processing is delegated to an object (the event listener) in the application.

For each event-object type, there is typically a corresponding event-listener interface. An event listener for a GUI event is an object of a class that implements one or more of the event-listener interfaces from packages java.awt.event and javax.swing.event. Many of the event-listener types are common to both Swing and AWT components. Such types are declared in package java.awt.event, and some of them are shown in Fig. 14.12. Additional event-listener types that are specific to Swing components are declared in package javax.swing.event.

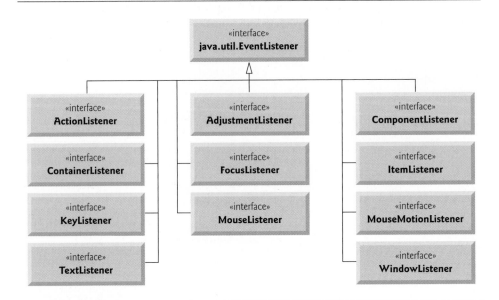

Fig. 14.12 | Some common event-listener interfaces of package `java.awt.event`.

Each event-listener interface specifies one or more event-handling methods that must be declared in the class that implements the interface. Recall from Section 10.7 that any class which implements an interface must declare all the `abstract` methods of that interface; otherwise, the class is an `abstract` class and cannot be used to create objects.

When an event occurs, the GUI component with which the user interacted notifies its registered listeners by calling each listener's appropriate event-handling method. For example, when the user presses the *Enter* key in a `JTextField`, the registered listener's `actionPerformed` method is called. How did the event handler get registered? How does the GUI component know to call `actionPerformed` rather than another event-handling method? We answer these questions and diagram the interaction in the next section.

14.8 How Event Handling Works

Let's illustrate how the event-handling mechanism works, using `textField1` from the example of Fig. 14.9. We have two remaining open questions from Section 14.7:

1. How did the event handler get registered?

2. How does the GUI component know to call `actionPerformed` rather than some other event-handling method?

The first question is answered by the event registration performed in lines 43–46 of Fig. 14.9. Figure 14.13 diagrams `JTextField` variable `textField1`, `TextFieldHandler` variable `handler` and the objects to which they refer.

Registering Events

Every `JComponent` has an instance variable called `listenerList` that refers to an object of class **EventListenerList** (package `javax.swing.event`). Each object of a `JComponent` subclass maintains references to its registered listeners in the `listenerList`. For simplicity, we've diagramed `listenerList` as an array below the `JTextField` object in Fig. 14.13.

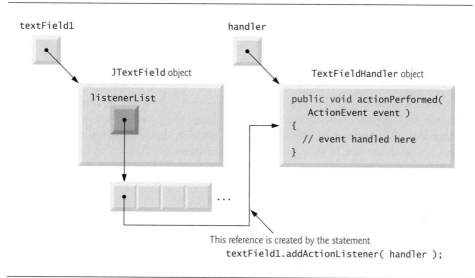

textField1

handler

JTextField object

TextFieldHandler object

listenerList

```
public void actionPerformed(
   ActionEvent event )
{
   // event handled here
}
```

. . .

This reference is created by the statement
`textField1.addActionListener( handler );`

Fig. 14.13 | Event registration for `JTextField` `textField1`.

When line 43 of Fig. 14.9

```
textField1.addActionListener( handler );
```

executes, a new entry containing a reference to the `TextFieldHandler` object is placed in `textField1`'s `listenerList`. Although not shown in the diagram, this new entry also includes the listener's type (in this case, `ActionListener`). Using this mechanism, each lightweight Swing GUI component maintains its own list of listeners that were registered to handle the component's events.

Event-Handler Invocation
The event-listener type is important in answering the second question: How does the GUI component know to call `actionPerformed` rather than another method? Every GUI component supports several event types, including **mouse events**, **key events** and others. When an event occurs, the event is **dispatched** only to the event listeners of the appropriate type. Dispatching is simply the process by which the GUI component calls an event-handling method on each of its listeners that are registered for the event type that occurred.

Each event type has one or more corresponding event-listener interfaces. For example, `ActionEvents` are handled by `ActionListeners`, **MouseEvents** are handled by **MouseListeners** and **MouseMotionListeners**, and **KeyEvents** are handled by **KeyListeners**. When an event occurs, the GUI component receives (from the JVM) a unique **event ID** specifying the event type. The GUI component uses the event ID to decide the listener type to which the event should be dispatched and to decide which method to call on each listener object. For an `ActionEvent`, the event is dispatched to every registered `ActionListener`'s `actionPerformed` method (the only method in interface `ActionListener`). For a Mouse-Event, the event is dispatched to every registered MouseListener or MouseMotionListener, depending on the mouse event that occurs. The MouseEvent's event ID determines which of the several mouse event-handling methods are called. All these decisions are handled for you by the GUI components. All you need to do is register an event handler for the particular event type that your application requires, and the GUI component will ensure that the event handler's appropriate method gets called when the event occurs. [*Note:* We discuss other event types and event-listener interfaces as they are needed with each new component we introduce.]

14.9 JButton

A **button** is a component the user clicks to trigger a specific action. A Java application can use several types of buttons, including **command buttons**, **checkboxes**, **toggle buttons** and **radio buttons**. Figure 14.14 shows the inheritance hierarchy of the Swing buttons we cover in this chapter. As you can see, all the button types are subclasses of **AbstractButton** (package javax.swing), which declares the common features of Swing buttons. In this section, we concentrate on buttons that are typically used to initiate a command.

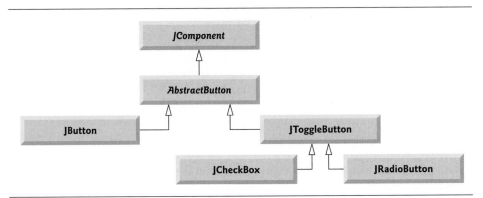

Fig. 14.14 | Swing button hierarchy.

Look-and-Feel Observation 14.7
Buttons typically use book-title capitalization.

A command button (see Fig. 14.16's output) generates an ActionEvent when the user clicks it. Command buttons are created with class **JButton**. The text on the face of a JButton is called a **button label**. A GUI can have many JButtons, but each button label typically should be unique in the portion of the GUI that is currently displayed.

Look-and-Feel Observation 14.8
Having more than one JButton with the same label makes the JButtons ambiguous to the user. Provide a unique label for each button.

The application of Figs. 14.15 and 14.16 creates two JButtons and demonstrates that JButtons support the display of Icons. Event handling for the buttons is performed by a single instance of inner class ButtonHandler (lines 39–47).

```
 1   // Fig. 14.15: ButtonFrame.java
 2   // Creating JButtons.
 3   import java.awt.FlowLayout;
 4   import java.awt.event.ActionListener;
 5   import java.awt.event.ActionEvent;
 6   import javax.swing.JFrame;
 7   import javax.swing.JButton;
 8   import javax.swing.Icon;
 9   import javax.swing.ImageIcon;
10   import javax.swing.JOptionPane;
11
12   public class ButtonFrame extends JFrame
13   {
14      private JButton plainJButton; // button with just text
15      private JButton fancyJButton; // button with icons
16
17      // ButtonFrame adds JButtons to JFrame
18      public ButtonFrame()
19      {
20         super( "Testing Buttons" );
21         setLayout( new FlowLayout() ); // set frame layout
22
23         plainJButton = new JButton( "Plain Button" ); // button with text
24         add( plainJButton ); // add plainJButton to JFrame
25
26         Icon bug1 = new ImageIcon( getClass().getResource( "bug1.gif" ) );
27         Icon bug2 = new ImageIcon( getClass().getResource( "bug2.gif" ) );
28         fancyJButton = new JButton( "Fancy Button", bug1 ); // set image
29         fancyJButton.setRolloverIcon( bug2 ); // set rollover image
30         add( fancyJButton ); // add fancyJButton to JFrame
31
32         // create new ButtonHandler for button event handling
33         ButtonHandler handler = new ButtonHandler();
34         fancyJButton.addActionListener( handler );
35         plainJButton.addActionListener( handler );
36      } // end ButtonFrame constructor
37
38      // inner class for button event handling
39      private class ButtonHandler implements ActionListener
40      {
41         // handle button event
42         public void actionPerformed( ActionEvent event )
43         {
44            JOptionPane.showMessageDialog( ButtonFrame.this, String.format(
45               "You pressed: %s", event.getActionCommand() ) );
46         } // end method actionPerformed
47      } // end private inner class ButtonHandler
48   } // end class ButtonFrame
```

Fig. 14.15 | Command buttons and action events.

Lines 14–15 declare JButton variables plainJButton and fancyJButton. The corresponding objects are instantiated in the constructor. Line 23 creates plainJButton with the button label "Plain Button". Line 24 adds the JButton to the JFrame.

```
1  // Fig. 14.16: ButtonTest.java
2  // Testing ButtonFrame.
3  import javax.swing.JFrame;
4
5  public class ButtonTest
6  {
7     public static void main( String[] args )
8     {
9        ButtonFrame buttonFrame = new ButtonFrame(); // create ButtonFrame
10       buttonFrame.setDefaultCloseOperation( JFrame.EXIT_ON_CLOSE );
11       buttonFrame.setSize( 275, 110 ); // set frame size
12       buttonFrame.setVisible( true ); // display frame
13    } // end main
14 } // end class ButtonTest
```

Fig. 14.16 | Test class for `ButtonFrame`.

A `JButton` can display an `Icon`. To provide the user with an extra level of visual inter-action with the GUI, a `JButton` can also have a **rollover Icon**—an `Icon` that is displayed when the user positions the mouse over the `JButton`. The icon on the `JButton` changes as the mouse moves in and out of the `JButton`'s area on the screen. Lines 26–27 (Fig. 14.15) create two `ImageIcon` objects that represent the default `Icon` and rollover `Icon` for the `JButton` created at line 28. Both statements assume that the image files are stored in the same directory as the application. Images are commonly placed in the same directory as the application or a subdirectory like `images`). These image files have been provided for you with the example.

Line 28 creates `fancyButton` with the text "Fancy Button" and the icon `bug1`. By default, the text is displayed to the right of the icon. Line 29 uses **setRolloverIcon** (inherited from class AbstractButton) to specify the image displayed on the JButton when the user positions the mouse over it. Line 30 adds the JButton to the JFrame.

Look-and-Feel Observation 14.9
Because class AbstractButton supports displaying text and images on a button, all subclasses of AbstractButton also support displaying text and images.

Look-and-Feel Observation 14.10
Using rollover icons for JButtons provides users with visual feedback indicating that when they click the mouse while the cursor is positioned over the JButton, an action will occur.

JButtons, like JTextFields, generate ActionEvents that can be processed by any ActionListener object. Lines 33–35 create an object of private inner class ButtonHandler and use addActionListener to register it as the event handler for each JButton. Class ButtonHandler (lines 39–47) declares actionPerformed to display a message dialog box containing the label for the button the user pressed. For a JButton event, ActionEvent method getActionCommand returns the label on the JButton.

*Accessing the **this** Reference in an Object of a Top-Level Class From an Inner Class*
When you execute this application and click one of its buttons, notice that the message dialog that appears is centered over the application's window. This occurs because the call to JOptionPane method showMessageDialog (lines 44–45 of Fig. 14.15) uses ButtonFrame.this rather than null as the first argument. When this argument is not null, it represents the so-called parent GUI component of the message dialog (in this case the application window is the parent component) and enables the dialog to be centered over that component when the dialog is displayed. ButtonFrame.this represents the this reference of the object of top-level class ButtonFrame.

Software Engineering Observation 14.4
When used in an inner class, keyword this refers to the current inner-class object being manipulated. An inner-class method can use its outer-class object's this by preceding this with the outer-class name and a dot, as in ButtonFrame.this.

14.10 Buttons That Maintain State

The Swing GUI components contain three types of **state buttons**—**JToggleButton**, **JCheckBox** and **JRadioButton**—that have on/off or true/false values. Classes JCheckBox and JRadioButton are subclasses of JToggleButton (Fig. 14.14). A JRadioButton is different from a JCheckBox in that normally several JRadioButtons are grouped together and are mutually exclusive—only one in the group can be selected at any time, just like the buttons on a car radio. We first discuss class JCheckBox.

14.10.1 JCheckBox

The application of Figs. 14.17–14.18 uses two JCheckBoxes to select the desired font style of the text displayed in a JTextField. When selected, one applies a bold style and the other an italic style. If both are selected, the style is bold and italic. When the application initially executes, neither JCheckBox is checked (i.e., they are both false), so the font is plain. Class CheckBoxTest (Fig. 14.18) contains the main method that executes this application.

```
 1   // Fig. 14.17: CheckBoxFrame.java
 2   // Creating JCheckBox buttons.
 3   import java.awt.FlowLayout;
 4   import java.awt.Font;
 5   import java.awt.event.ItemListener;
 6   import java.awt.event.ItemEvent;
 7   import javax.swing.JFrame;
 8   import javax.swing.JTextField;
 9   import javax.swing.JCheckBox;
10
11   public class CheckBoxFrame extends JFrame
12   {
13      private JTextField textField; // displays text in changing fonts
14      private JCheckBox boldJCheckBox; // to select/deselect bold
15      private JCheckBox italicJCheckBox; // to select/deselect italic
16
17      // CheckBoxFrame constructor adds JCheckBoxes to JFrame
18      public CheckBoxFrame()
19      {
20         super( "JCheckBox Test" );
21         setLayout( new FlowLayout() ); // set frame layout
22
23         // set up JTextField and set its font
24         textField = new JTextField( "Watch the font style change", 20 );
25         textField.setFont( new Font( "Serif", Font.PLAIN, 14 ) );
26         add( textField ); // add textField to JFrame
27
28         boldJCheckBox = new JCheckBox( "Bold" ); // create bold checkbox
29         italicJCheckBox = new JCheckBox( "Italic" ); // create italic
30         add( boldJCheckBox ); // add bold checkbox to JFrame
31         add( italicJCheckBox ); // add italic checkbox to JFrame
32
33         // register listeners for JCheckBoxes
34         CheckBoxHandler handler = new CheckBoxHandler();
35         boldJCheckBox.addItemListener( handler );
36         italicJCheckBox.addItemListener( handler );
37      } // end CheckBoxFrame constructor
38
39      // private inner class for ItemListener event handling
40      private class CheckBoxHandler implements ItemListener
41      {
42         // respond to checkbox events
43         public void itemStateChanged( ItemEvent event )
44         {
45            Font font = null; // stores the new Font
46
47            // determine which CheckBoxes are checked and create Font
48            if ( boldJCheckBox.isSelected() && italicJCheckBox.isSelected() )
49               font = new Font( "Serif", Font.BOLD + Font.ITALIC, 14 );
50            else if ( boldJCheckBox.isSelected() )
51               font = new Font( "Serif", Font.BOLD, 14 );
52            else if ( italicJCheckBox.isSelected() )
53               font = new Font( "Serif", Font.ITALIC, 14 );
```

Fig. 14.17 | JCheckBox buttons and item events. (Part 1 of 2.)

```
54              else
55                  font = new Font( "Serif", Font.PLAIN, 14 );
56
57              textField.setFont( font ); // set textField's font
58          } // end method itemStateChanged
59      } // end private inner class CheckBoxHandler
60  } // end class CheckBoxFrame
```

Fig. 14.17 | JCheckBox buttons and item events. (Part 2 of 2.)

```
 1  // Fig. 14.18: CheckBoxTest.java
 2  // Testing CheckBoxFrame.
 3  import javax.swing.JFrame;
 4
 5  public class CheckBoxTest
 6  {
 7      public static void main( String[] args )
 8      {
 9          CheckBoxFrame checkBoxFrame = new CheckBoxFrame();
10          checkBoxFrame.setDefaultCloseOperation( JFrame.EXIT_ON_CLOSE );
11          checkBoxFrame.setSize( 275, 100 ); // set frame size
12          checkBoxFrame.setVisible( true ); // display frame
13      } // end main
14  } // end class CheckBoxTest
```

Fig. 14.18 | Test class for CheckBoxFrame.

After the JTextField is created and initialized (Fig. 14.17, line 24), line 25 uses method **setFont** (inherited by JTextField indirectly from class Component) to set the font of the JTextField to a new object of class **Font** (package java.awt). The new Font is initialized with "Serif" (a generic font name that represents a font such as Times and is supported on all Java platforms), Font.PLAIN style and 14-point size. Next, lines 28–29 create two JCheckBox objects. The String passed to the JCheckBox constructor is the **checkbox label** that appears to the right of the JCheckBox by default.

When the user clicks a JCheckBox, an **ItemEvent** occurs. This event can be handled by an **ItemListener** object, which must implement method **itemStateChanged**. In this example, the event handling is performed by an instance of private inner class CheckBox-Handler (lines 40–59). Lines 34–36 create an instance of class CheckBoxHandler and register it with method **addItemListener** as the listener for both the JCheckBox objects.

CheckBoxHandler method itemStateChanged (lines 43–58) is called when the user clicks the boldJCheckBox or the italicJCheckBox. In this example, we don't need to know which of the two JCheckBoxes was clicked, just whether or not each one is checked.

Line 48 uses JCheckBox method **isSelected** to determine if both JCheckBoxes are selected. If so, line 49 creates a bold italic font by adding the Font constants Font.BOLD and Font.ITALIC for the font-style argument of the Font constructor. Line 50 determines whether the boldJCheckBox is selected, and if so line 51 creates a bold font. Line 52 determines whether the italicJCheckBox is selected, and if so line 53 creates an italic font. If none of the preceding conditions are true, line 55 creates a plain font using the Font constant Font.PLAIN. Finally, line 57 sets textField's new font, which changes the font in the JTextField on the screen.

Relationship Between an Inner Class and Its Top-Level Class
You may have noticed that class CheckBoxHandler used variables boldJCheckBox (Fig. 14.17, lines 48 and 50), italicJCheckBox (lines 48 and 52) and textField (line 57) even though these variables are not declared in the inner class. Recall that an inner class has a special relationship with its top-level class—it is allowed to access all the variables and methods of the top-level class. CheckBoxHandler method itemStateChanged (line 43–58) uses this relationship to determine which JCheckBoxes are checked and to set the font on the JTextField. Notice that none of the code in inner class CheckBoxHandler requires an explicit reference to the top-level class object.

14.10.2 JRadioButton

Radio buttons (declared with class JRadioButton) are similar to checkboxes in that they have two states—selected and not selected (also called deselected). However, radio buttons normally appear as a **group** in which only one button can be selected at a time (see the output of Fig. 14.20). Selecting a different radio button forces all others to be deselected. Radio buttons are used to represent **mutually exclusive options** (i.e., multiple options in the group cannot be selected at the same time). The logical relationship between radio buttons is maintained by a **ButtonGroup** object (package javax.swing), which itself is not a GUI component. A ButtonGroup object organizes a group of buttons and is not itself displayed in a user interface. Rather, the individual JRadioButton objects from the group are displayed in the GUI.

Common Programming Error 14.3

Adding a ButtonGroup object (or an object of any other class that does not derive from Component) to a container results in a compilation error.

The application of Figs. 14.19–14.20 is similar to that of Figs. 14.17–14.18. The user can alter the font style of a JTextField's text. The application uses radio buttons that permit only a single font style in the group to be selected at a time. Class RadioButtonTest (Fig. 14.20) contains the main method that executes this application.

```
1   // Fig. 14.19: RadioButtonFrame.java
2   // Creating radio buttons using ButtonGroup and JRadioButton.
3   import java.awt.FlowLayout;
4   import java.awt.Font;
5   import java.awt.event.ItemListener;
6   import java.awt.event.ItemEvent;
7   import javax.swing.JFrame;
```

Fig. 14.19 | JRadioButtons and ButtonGroups. (Part 1 of 3.)

```
 8   import javax.swing.JTextField;
 9   import javax.swing.JRadioButton;
10   import javax.swing.ButtonGroup;
11
12   public class RadioButtonFrame extends JFrame
13   {
14      private JTextField textField; // used to display font changes
15      private Font plainFont; // font for plain text
16      private Font boldFont; // font for bold text
17      private Font italicFont; // font for italic text
18      private Font boldItalicFont; // font for bold and italic text
19      private JRadioButton plainJRadioButton; // selects plain text
20      private JRadioButton boldJRadioButton; // selects bold text
21      private JRadioButton italicJRadioButton; // selects italic text
22      private JRadioButton boldItalicJRadioButton; // bold and italic
23      private ButtonGroup radioGroup; // buttongroup to hold radio buttons
24
25      // RadioButtonFrame constructor adds JRadioButtons to JFrame
26      public RadioButtonFrame()
27      {
28         super( "RadioButton Test" );
29         setLayout( new FlowLayout() ); // set frame layout
30
31         textField = new JTextField( "Watch the font style change", 25 );
32         add( textField ); // add textField to JFrame
33
34         // create radio buttons
35         plainJRadioButton = new JRadioButton( "Plain", true );
36         boldJRadioButton = new JRadioButton( "Bold", false );
37         italicJRadioButton = new JRadioButton( "Italic", false );
38         boldItalicJRadioButton = new JRadioButton( "Bold/Italic", false );
39         add( plainJRadioButton ); // add plain button to JFrame
40         add( boldJRadioButton ); // add bold button to JFrame
41         add( italicJRadioButton ); // add italic button to JFrame
42         add( boldItalicJRadioButton ); // add bold and italic button
43
44         // create logical relationship between JRadioButtons
45         radioGroup = new ButtonGroup(); // create ButtonGroup
46         radioGroup.add( plainJRadioButton ); // add plain to group
47         radioGroup.add( boldJRadioButton ); // add bold to group
48         radioGroup.add( italicJRadioButton ); // add italic to group
49         radioGroup.add( boldItalicJRadioButton ); // add bold and italic
50
51         // create font objects
52         plainFont = new Font( "Serif", Font.PLAIN, 14 );
53         boldFont = new Font( "Serif", Font.BOLD, 14 );
54         italicFont = new Font( "Serif", Font.ITALIC, 14 );
55         boldItalicFont = new Font( "Serif", Font.BOLD + Font.ITALIC, 14 );
56         textField.setFont( plainFont ); // set initial font to plain
57
58         // register events for JRadioButtons
59         plainJRadioButton.addItemListener(
60            new RadioButtonHandler( plainFont ) );
```

Fig. 14.19 | JRadioButtons and ButtonGroups. (Part 2 of 3.)

```
61      boldJRadioButton.addItemListener(
62         new RadioButtonHandler( boldFont ) );
63      italicJRadioButton.addItemListener(
64         new RadioButtonHandler( italicFont ) );
65      boldItalicJRadioButton.addItemListener(
66         new RadioButtonHandler( boldItalicFont ) );
67   } // end RadioButtonFrame constructor
68
69   // private inner class to handle radio button events
70   private class RadioButtonHandler implements ItemListener
71   {
72      private Font font; // font associated with this listener
73
74      public RadioButtonHandler( Font f )
75      {
76         font = f; // set the font of this listener
77      } // end constructor RadioButtonHandler
78
79      // handle radio button events
80      public void itemStateChanged( ItemEvent event )
81      {
82         textField.setFont( font ); // set font of textField
83      } // end method itemStateChanged
84   } // end private inner class RadioButtonHandler
85 } // end class RadioButtonFrame
```

Fig. 14.19 | JRadioButtons and ButtonGroups. (Part 3 of 3.)

```
1  // Fig. 14.20: RadioButtonTest.java
2  // Testing RadioButtonFrame.
3  import javax.swing.JFrame;
4
5  public class RadioButtonTest
6  {
7     public static void main( String[] args )
8     {
9        RadioButtonFrame radioButtonFrame = new RadioButtonFrame();
10       radioButtonFrame.setDefaultCloseOperation( JFrame.EXIT_ON_CLOSE );
11       radioButtonFrame.setSize( 300, 100 ); // set frame size
12       radioButtonFrame.setVisible( true ); // display frame
13    } // end main
14 } // end class RadioButtonTest
```

Fig. 14.20 | Test class for RadioButtonFrame.

Lines 35–42 in the constructor (Fig. 14.19) create four JRadioButton objects and add them to the JFrame. Each JRadioButton is created with a constructor call like that in line 35. This constructor specifies the label that appears to the right of the JRadioButton by default and the initial state of the JRadioButton. A true second argument indicates that the JRadioButton should appear selected when it's displayed.

Line 45 instantiates ButtonGroup object radioGroup. This object is the "glue" that forms the logical relationship between the four JRadioButton objects and allows only one of the four to be selected at a time. It's possible that no JRadioButtons in a ButtonGroup are selected, but this can occur only if no preselected JRadioButtons are added to the ButtonGroup and the user has not selected a JRadioButton yet. Lines 46–49 use ButtonGroup method **add** to associate each of the JRadioButtons with radioGroup. If more than one selected JRadioButton object is added to the group, the selected one that was added first will be selected when the GUI is displayed.

JRadioButtons, like JCheckBoxes, generate ItemEvents when they are clicked. Lines 59–66 create four instances of inner class RadioButtonHandler (declared at lines 70–84). In this example, each event-listener object is registered to handle the ItemEvent generated when the user clicks a particular JRadioButton. Notice that each RadioButtonHandler object is initialized with a particular Font object (created in lines 52–55).

Class RadioButtonHandler (line 70–84) implements interface ItemListener so it can handle ItemEvents generated by the JRadioButtons. The constructor stores the Font object it receives as an argument in the event-listener object's instance variable font (declared at line 72). When the user clicks a JRadioButton, radioGroup turns off the previously selected JRadioButton and method itemStateChanged (line 80–83) sets the font in the JTextField to the Font stored in the JRadioButton's corresponding event-listener object. Notice that line 82 of inner class RadioButtonHandler uses the top-level class's textField instance variable to set the font.

14.11 JComboBox and Using an Anonymous Inner Class for Event Handling

A combo box (sometimes called a **drop-down list**) enables the user to select one item from a list (Fig. 14.22). Combo boxes are implemented with class **JComboBox**, which extends class JComponent. JComboBoxes generate ItemEvents like JCheckBoxes and JRadioButtons. This example also demonstrates a special form of inner class that is used frequently in event handling. The application (Figs. 14.21–14.22) uses a JComboBox to provide a list of four image-file names from which the user can select one image to display. When the user selects a name, the application displays the corresponding image as an Icon on a JLabel. Class ComboBoxTest (Fig. 14.22) contains the main method that executes this application. The screen captures for this application show the JComboBox list after the selection was made to illustrate which image-file name was selected.

```
1   // Fig. 14.21: ComboBoxFrame.java
2   // JComboBox that displays a list of image names.
3   import java.awt.FlowLayout;
4   import java.awt.event.ItemListener;
5   import java.awt.event.ItemEvent;
```

Fig. 14.21 | JComboBox that displays a list of image names. (Part 1 of 2.)

```
 6   import javax.swing.JFrame;
 7   import javax.swing.JLabel;
 8   import javax.swing.JComboBox;
 9   import javax.swing.Icon;
10   import javax.swing.ImageIcon;
11
12   public class ComboBoxFrame extends JFrame
13   {
14      private JComboBox imagesJComboBox; // combobox to hold names of icons
15      private JLabel label; // label to display selected icon
16
17      private static final String[] names =
18         { "bug1.gif", "bug2.gif",  "travelbug.gif", "buganim.gif" };
19      private Icon[] icons = {
20         new ImageIcon( getClass().getResource( names[ 0 ] ) ),
21         new ImageIcon( getClass().getResource( names[ 1 ] ) ),
22         new ImageIcon( getClass().getResource( names[ 2 ] ) ),
23         new ImageIcon( getClass().getResource( names[ 3 ] ) ) };
24
25      // ComboBoxFrame constructor adds JComboBox to JFrame
26      public ComboBoxFrame()
27      {
28         super( "Testing JComboBox" );
29         setLayout( new FlowLayout() ); // set frame layout
30
31         imagesJComboBox = new JComboBox( names ); // set up JComboBox
32         imagesJComboBox.setMaximumRowCount( 3 ); // display three rows
33
34         imagesJComboBox.addItemListener(
35            new ItemListener() // anonymous inner class
36            {
37               // handle JComboBox event
38               public void itemStateChanged( ItemEvent event )
39               {
40                  // determine whether item selected
41                  if ( event.getStateChange() == ItemEvent.SELECTED )
42                     label.setIcon( icons[
43                        imagesJComboBox.getSelectedIndex() ] );
44               } // end method itemStateChanged
45            } // end anonymous inner class
46         ); // end call to addItemListener
47
48         add( imagesJComboBox ); // add combobox to JFrame
49         label = new JLabel( icons[ 0 ] ); // display first icon
50         add( label ); // add label to JFrame
51      } // end ComboBoxFrame constructor
52   } // end class ComboBoxFrame
```

Fig. 14.21 | JComboBox that displays a list of image names. (Part 2 of 2.)

```
1   // Fig. 14.22: ComboBoxTest.java
2   // Testing ComboBoxFrame.
3   import javax.swing.JFrame;
```

Fig. 14.22 | Testing ComboBoxFrame. (Part 1 of 2.)

```
4
5    public class ComboBoxTest
6    {
7       public static void main( String[] args )
8       {
9          ComboBoxFrame comboBoxFrame = new ComboBoxFrame();
10         comboBoxFrame.setDefaultCloseOperation( JFrame.EXIT_ON_CLOSE );
11         comboBoxFrame.setSize( 350, 150 ); // set frame size
12         comboBoxFrame.setVisible( true ); // display frame
13      } // end main
14   } // end class ComboBoxTest
```

Fig. 14.22 | Testing `ComboBoxFrame`. (Part 2 of 2.)

Lines 19–23 (Fig. 14.21) declare and initialize array icons with four new ImageIcon objects. String array names (lines 17–18) contains the names of the four image files that are stored in the same directory as the application.

At line 31, the constructor initializes a JComboBox object with the Strings in array names as the elements in the list. Each item in the list has an **index**. The first item is added at index 0, the next at index 1 and so forth. The first item added to a JComboBox appears as the currently selected item when the JComboBox is displayed. Other items are selected by clicking the JComboBox, then selecting an item from the list that appears.

Line 32 uses JComboBox method **setMaximumRowCount** to set the maximum number of elements that are displayed when the user clicks the JComboBox. If there are additional items, the JComboBox provides a **scrollbar** (see the first screen capture) that allows the user to scroll through all the elements in the list. The user can click the **scroll arrows** at the top and bottom of the scrollbar to move up and down through the list one element at a time, or else drag the **scroll box** in the middle of the scrollbar up and down. To drag the scroll box, position the mouse cursor on it, hold the mouse button down and move the mouse. [*Note:* In this example, the drop-down list is too short to drag the scroll box, so you can click the up and down arrows or use your mouse's wheel to scroll through the four items in the list.

Look-and-Feel Observation 14.11
Set the maximum row count for a JComboBox to a number of rows that prevents the list from expanding outside the bounds of the window in which it's used.

Line 48 attaches the JComboBox to the ComboBoxFrame's FlowLayout (set in line 29). Line 49 creates the JLabel that displays ImageIcons and initializes it with the first Image-Icon in array icons. Line 50 attaches the JLabel to the ComboBoxFrame's FlowLayout.

Using an Anonymous Inner Class for Event Handling
Lines 34–46 are one statement that declares the event listener's class, creates an object of that class and registers it as the listener for imagesJComboBox's ItemEvents. This event-listener object is an instance of an **anonymous inner class**—an inner class that is declared without a name and typically appears inside a method declaration. As with other inner classes, an anonymous inner class can access its top-level class's members. However, an anonymous inner class has limited access to the local variables of the method in which it's declared. Since an anonymous inner class has no name, one object of the anonymous inner class must be created at the point where the class is declared (starting at line 35).

Software Engineering Observation 14.5
An anonymous inner class declared in a method can access the instance variables and methods of the top-level class object that declared it, as well as the method's final local variables, but cannot access the method's non-final local variables.

Lines 34–46 are a call to imagesJComboBox's addItemListener method. The argument to this method must be an object that *is an* ItemListener (i.e., any object of a class that implements ItemListener). Lines 35–45 are a class-instance creation expression that declares an anonymous inner class and creates one object of that class. A reference to that object is then passed as the argument to addItemListener. The syntax ItemListener() after new begins the declaration of an anonymous inner class that implements interface ItemListener. This is similar to beginning a class declaration with

```
public class MyHandler implements ItemListener
```

The parentheses after ItemListener indicate a call to the default constructor of the anonymous inner class.

The opening left brace at 36 and the closing right brace at line 45 delimit the body of the anonymous inner class. Lines 38–44 declare the ItemListener's itemStateChanged method. When the user makes a selection from imagesJComboBox, this method sets label's Icon. The Icon is selected from array icons by determining the index of the selected item in the JComboBox with method **getSelectedIndex** in line 43. Note that for each item selected from a JComboBox, another item is first deselected—so two ItemEvents occur when an item is selected. We wish to display only the icon for the item the user just selected. For this reason, line 41 determines whether ItemEvent method **getStateChange** returns ItemEvent.SELECTED. If so, lines 42–43 set label's icon.

Software Engineering Observation 14.6
Like any other class, when an anonymous inner class implements an interface, the class must implement every method in the interface.

The syntax shown in lines 35–45 for creating an event handler with an anonymous inner class is similar to the code that would be generated by a Java integrated development environment (IDE). Typically, an IDE enables you to design a GUI visually, then it generates code that implements the GUI. You simply insert statements in the event-handling methods that declare how to handle each event.

14.12 JList

A list displays a series of items from which the user may select one or more items (see the output of Fig. 14.24). Lists are created with class JList, which directly extends class JComponent. Class JList supports **single-selection lists** (which allow only one item to be selected at a time) and **multiple-selection lists** (which allow any number of items to be selected). In this section, we discuss single-selection lists.

The application of Figs. 14.23–14.24 creates a JList containing 13 color names. When a color name is clicked in the JList, a **ListSelectionEvent** occurs and the application changes the background color of the application window to the selected color. Class ListTest (Fig. 14.24) contains the main method that executes this application.

```java
1   // Fig. 14.23: ListFrame.java
2   // JList that displays a list of colors.
3   import java.awt.FlowLayout;
4   import java.awt.Color;
5   import javax.swing.JFrame;
6   import javax.swing.JList;
7   import javax.swing.JScrollPane;
8   import javax.swing.event.ListSelectionListener;
9   import javax.swing.event.ListSelectionEvent;
10  import javax.swing.ListSelectionModel;
11
12  public class ListFrame extends JFrame
13  {
14     private JList colorJList; // list to display colors
15     private static final String[] colorNames = { "Black", "Blue", "Cyan",
16        "Dark Gray", "Gray", "Green", "Light Gray", "Magenta",
17        "Orange", "Pink", "Red", "White", "Yellow" };
18     private static final Color[] colors = { Color.BLACK, Color.BLUE,
19        Color.CYAN, Color.DARK_GRAY, Color.GRAY, Color.GREEN,
20        Color.LIGHT_GRAY, Color.MAGENTA, Color.ORANGE, Color.PINK,
21        Color.RED, Color.WHITE, Color.YELLOW };
22
23     // ListFrame constructor add JScrollPane containing JList to JFrame
24     public ListFrame()
25     {
26        super( "List Test" );
27        setLayout( new FlowLayout() ); // set frame layout
28
29        colorJList = new JList( colorNames ); // create with colorNames
30        colorJList.setVisibleRowCount( 5 ); // display five rows at once
31
32        // do not allow multiple selections
33        colorJList.setSelectionMode( ListSelectionModel.SINGLE_SELECTION );
```

Fig. 14.23 | JList that displays a list of colors. (Part 1 of 2.)

```
34
35        // add a JScrollPane containing JList to frame
36        add( new JScrollPane( colorJList ) );
37
38        colorJList.addListSelectionListener(
39           new ListSelectionListener() // anonymous inner class
40           {
41              // handle list selection events
42              public void valueChanged( ListSelectionEvent event )
43              {
44                 getContentPane().setBackground(
45                    colors[ colorJList.getSelectedIndex() ] );
46              } // end method valueChanged
47           } // end anonymous inner class
48        ); // end call to addListSelectionListener
49     } // end ListFrame constructor
50  } // end class ListFrame
```

Fig. 14.23 | JList that displays a list of colors. (Part 2 of 2.)

```
1   // Fig. 14.24: ListTest.java
2   // Selecting colors from a JList.
3   import javax.swing.JFrame;
4
5   public class ListTest
6   {
7      public static void main( String[] args )
8      {
9         ListFrame listFrame = new ListFrame(); // create ListFrame
10        listFrame.setDefaultCloseOperation( JFrame.EXIT_ON_CLOSE );
11        listFrame.setSize( 350, 150 ); // set frame size
12        listFrame.setVisible( true ); // display frame
13     } // end main
14  } // end class ListTest
```

Fig. 14.24 | Test class for ListFrame.

Line 29 (Fig. 14.23) creates JList object colorJList. The argument to the JList constructor is the array of Objects (in this case Strings) to display in the list. Line 30 uses JList method **setVisibleRowCount** to determine the number of items visible in the list.

Line 33 uses JList method **setSelectionMode** to specify the list's **selection mode**. Class **ListSelectionModel** (of package javax.swing) declares three constants that specify a JList's selection mode—**SINGLE_SELECTION** (which allows only one item to be selected at a time), **SINGLE_INTERVAL_SELECTION** (for a multiple-selection list that allows selection of several contiguous items) and **MULTIPLE_INTERVAL_SELECTION** (for a multiple-selection list that does not restrict the items that can be selected).

Unlike a JComboBox, a JList *does not* provide a scrollbar if there are more items in the list than the number of visible rows. In this case, a **JScrollPane** object is used to provide the scrolling capability. Line 36 adds a new instance of class JScrollPane to the JFrame. The JScrollPane constructor receives as its argument the JComponent that needs scrolling functionality (in this case, colorJList). Notice in the screen captures that a scrollbar created by the JScrollPane appears at the right side of the JList. By default, the scrollbar appears only when the number of items in the JList exceeds the number of visible items.

Lines 38–48 use JList method **addListSelectionListener** to register an object that implements **ListSelectionListener** (package javax.swing.event) as the listener for the JList's selection events. Once again, we use an instance of an anonymous inner class (lines 39–47) as the listener. In this example, when the user makes a selection from colorJList, method **valueChanged** (line 42–46) should change the background color of the ListFrame to the selected color. This is accomplished in lines 44–45. Note the use of JFrame method **getContentPane** in line 44. Each JFrame actually consists of three layers—the background, the content pane and the glass pane. The content pane appears in front of the background and is where the GUI components in the JFrame are displayed. The glass pane is used to display tool tips and other items that should appear in front of the GUI components on the screen. The content pane completely hides the background of the JFrame; thus, to change the background color behind the GUI components, you must change the content pane's background color. Method getContentPane returns a reference to the JFrame's content pane (an object of class Container). In line 44, we then use that reference to call method **setBackground**, which sets the content pane's background color to an element in the colors array. The color is selected from the array by using the selected item's index. JList method **getSelectedIndex** returns the selected item's index. As with arrays and JComboBoxes, JList indexing is zero based.

14.13 Multiple-Selection Lists

A **multiple-selection list** enables the user to select many items from a JList (see the output of Fig. 14.26). A SINGLE_INTERVAL_SELECTION list allows selecting a contiguous range of items. To do so, click the first item, then press and hold the *Shift* key while clicking the last item in the range. A MULTIPLE_INTERVAL_SELECTION list (the default) allows continuous range selection as described for a SINGLE_INTERVAL_SELECTION list. Such a list also allows miscellaneous items to be selected by pressing and holding the *Ctrl* key (sometimes called the *Control* key) while clicking each item to select. To deselect an item, press and hold the *Ctrl* key while clicking the item a second time.

The application of Figs. 14.25–14.26 uses multiple-selection lists to copy items from one JList to another. One list is a MULTIPLE_INTERVAL_SELECTION list and the other is a SINGLE_INTERVAL_SELECTION list. When you execute the application, try using the selection techniques described previously to select items in both lists.

```
1   // Fig. 14.25: MultipleSelectionFrame.java
2   // Copying items from one List to another.
3   import java.awt.FlowLayout;
```

Fig. 14.25 | JList that allows multiple selections. (Part 1 of 2.)

```
4   import java.awt.event.ActionListener;
5   import java.awt.event.ActionEvent;
6   import javax.swing.JFrame;
7   import javax.swing.JList;
8   import javax.swing.JButton;
9   import javax.swing.JScrollPane;
10  import javax.swing.ListSelectionModel;
11
12  public class MultipleSelectionFrame extends JFrame
13  {
14     private JList colorJList; // list to hold color names
15     private JList copyJList; // list to copy color names into
16     private JButton copyJButton; // button to copy selected names
17     private static final String[] colorNames = { "Black", "Blue", "Cyan",
18        "Dark Gray", "Gray", "Green", "Light Gray", "Magenta", "Orange",
19        "Pink", "Red", "White", "Yellow" };
20
21     // MultipleSelectionFrame constructor
22     public MultipleSelectionFrame()
23     {
24        super( "Multiple Selection Lists" );
25        setLayout( new FlowLayout() ); // set frame layout
26
27        colorJList = new JList( colorNames ); // holds names of all colors
28        colorJList.setVisibleRowCount( 5 ); // show five rows
29        colorJList.setSelectionMode(
30           ListSelectionModel.MULTIPLE_INTERVAL_SELECTION );
31        add( new JScrollPane( colorJList ) ); // add list with scrollpane
32
33        copyJButton = new JButton( "Copy >>>" ); // create copy button
34        copyJButton.addActionListener(
35
36           new ActionListener() // anonymous inner class
37           {
38              // handle button event
39              public void actionPerformed( ActionEvent event )
40              {
41                 // place selected values in copyJList
42                 copyJList.setListData( colorJList.getSelectedValues() );
43              } // end method actionPerformed
44           } // end anonymous inner class
45        ); // end call to addActionListener
46
47        add( copyJButton ); // add copy button to JFrame
48
49        copyJList = new JList(); // create list to hold copied color names
50        copyJList.setVisibleRowCount( 5 ); // show 5 rows
51        copyJList.setFixedCellWidth( 100 ); // set width
52        copyJList.setFixedCellHeight( 15 ); // set height
53        copyJList.setSelectionMode(
54           ListSelectionModel.SINGLE_INTERVAL_SELECTION );
55        add( new JScrollPane( copyJList ) ); // add list with scrollpane
56     } // end MultipleSelectionFrame constructor
57  } // end class MultipleSelectionFrame
```

Fig. 14.25 | JList that allows multiple selections. (Part 2 of 2.)

```
 1   // Fig. 14.26: MultipleSelectionTest.java
 2   // Testing MultipleSelectionFrame.
 3   import javax.swing.JFrame;
 4
 5   public class MultipleSelectionTest
 6   {
 7      public static void main( String[] args )
 8      {
 9         MultipleSelectionFrame multipleSelectionFrame =
10            new MultipleSelectionFrame();
11         multipleSelectionFrame.setDefaultCloseOperation(
12            JFrame.EXIT_ON_CLOSE );
13         multipleSelectionFrame.setSize( 350, 150 ); // set frame size
14         multipleSelectionFrame.setVisible( true ); // display frame
15      } // end main
16   } // end class MultipleSelectionTest
```

Fig. 14.26 | Test class for `MultipleSelectionFrame`.

Line 27 of Fig. 14.25 creates JList colorJList and initializes it with the Strings in the array colorNames. Line 28 sets the number of visible rows in colorJList to 5. Lines 29–30 specify that colorJList is a MULTIPLE_INTERVAL_SELECTION list. Line 31 adds a new JScrollPane containing colorJList to the JFrame. Lines 49–55 perform similar tasks for copyJList, which is declared as a SINGLE_INTERVAL_SELECTION list. If a JList does not contain items it will not diplay in a FlowLayout. For this reason, line 51–52 use JList methods **setFixedCellWidth** and **setFixedCellHeight** to set copyJList's width to 100 pixels and the height of each item in the JList to 15 pixels, respectively.

There are no events to indicate that a user has made multiple selections in a multiple-selection list. Normally, an event generated by another GUI component (known as an **external event**) specifies when the multiple selections in a JList should be processed. In this example, the user clicks the JButton called copyJButton to trigger the event that copies the selected items in colorJList to copyJList.

Lines 34–45 declare, create and register an ActionListener for the copyJButton. When the user clicks copyJButton, method actionPerformed (lines 39–43) uses JList method **setListData** to set the items displayed in copyJList. Line 42 calls colorJList's method **getSelectedValues**, which returns an array of Objects representing the selected items in colorJList. In this example, the returned array is passed as the argument to copyJList's setListData method.

You might be wondering why copyJList can be used in line 42 even though the application does not create the object to which it refers until line 49. Remember that method actionPerformed (lines 39–43) does not execute until the user presses the copy-JButton, which cannot occur until after the constructor completes execution and the application displays the GUI. At that point in the application's execution, copyJList is already initialized with a new JList object.

14.14 **Mouse Event Handling**

This section presents the **MouseListener** and **MouseMotionListener** event-listener interfaces for handling **mouse events**. Mouse events can be trapped for any GUI component that derives from java.awt.Component. The methods of interfaces MouseListener and MouseMotionListener are summarized in Figure 14.27. Package javax.swing.event contains interface **MouseInputListener**, which extends interfaces MouseListener and MouseMotionListener to create a single interface containing all the MouseListener and MouseMotionListener methods. The MouseListener and MouseMotionListener methods are called when the mouse interacts with a Component if appropriate event-listener objects are registered for that Component.

MouseListener and MouseMotionListener interface methods

Methods of interface MouseListener

public void mousePressed(MouseEvent event)

Called when a mouse button is pressed while the mouse cursor is on a component.

public void mouseClicked(MouseEvent event)

Called when a mouse button is pressed and released while the mouse cursor remains stationary on a component. This event is always preceded by a call to mousePressed.

public void mouseReleased(MouseEvent event)

Called when a mouse button is released after being pressed. This event is always preceded by a call to mousePressed and one or more calls to mouseDragged.

public void mouseEntered(MouseEvent event)

Called when the mouse cursor enters the bounds of a component.

public void mouseExited(MouseEvent event)

Called when the mouse cursor leaves the bounds of a component.

Methods of interface MouseMotionListener

public void mouseDragged(MouseEvent event)

Called when the mouse button is pressed while the mouse cursor is on a component and the mouse is moved while the mouse button remains pressed. This event is always preceded by a call to mousePressed. All drag events are sent to the component on which the user began to drag the mouse.

public void mouseMoved(MouseEvent event)

Called when the mouse is moved (with no mouse buttons pressed) when the mouse cursor is on a component. All move events are sent to the component over which the mouse is currently positioned.

Fig. 14.27 | MouseListener and MouseMotionListener interface methods.

Each of the mouse event-handling methods receives as an argument a **MouseEvent** object that contains information about the mouse event that occurred, including the *x*- and *y*-coordinates of the location where the event occurred. These coordinates are measured from the upper-left corner of the GUI component on which the event occurred. The *x*-coordinates start at 0 and increase from left to right. The *y*-coordinates start at 0 and increase from top to bottom. The methods and constants of class **InputEvent** (Mouse-Event's superclass) enable you to determine which mouse button the user clicked.

Software Engineering Observation 14.7

Method calls to mouseDragged are sent to the MouseMotionListener for the Component on which a mouse drag operation started. Similarly, the mouseReleased method call at the end of a drag operation is sent to the MouseListener for the Component on which the drag operation started.

Java also provides interface **MouseWheelListener** to enable applications to respond to the rotation of a mouse wheel. This interface declares method **mouseWheelMoved**, which receives a **MouseWheelEvent** as its argument. Class MouseWheelEvent (a subclass of Mouse-Event) contains methods that enable the event handler to obtain information about the amount of wheel rotation.

Tracking Mouse Events on a *JPanel*

The MouseTracker application (Figs. 14.28–14.29) demonstrates the MouseListener and MouseMotionListener interface methods. The event-handler class (lines 36–90) implements both interfaces. Note that you must declare all seven methods from these two interfaces when your class implements them both. Each mouse event in this example displays a String in the JLabel called statusBar that is attached to the bottom of the window.

```java
1   // Fig. 14.28: MouseTrackerFrame.java
2   // Demonstrating mouse events.
3   import java.awt.Color;
4   import java.awt.BorderLayout;
5   import java.awt.event.MouseListener;
6   import java.awt.event.MouseMotionListener;
7   import java.awt.event.MouseEvent;
8   import javax.swing.JFrame;
9   import javax.swing.JLabel;
10  import javax.swing.JPanel;
11
12  public class MouseTrackerFrame extends JFrame
13  {
14     private JPanel mousePanel; // panel in which mouse events will occur
15     private JLabel statusBar; // label that displays event information
16
17     // MouseTrackerFrame constructor sets up GUI and
18     // registers mouse event handlers
19     public MouseTrackerFrame()
20     {
21        super( "Demonstrating Mouse Events" );
22
23        mousePanel = new JPanel(); // create panel
24        mousePanel.setBackground( Color.WHITE ); // set background color
25        add( mousePanel, BorderLayout.CENTER ); // add panel to JFrame
26
27        statusBar = new JLabel( "Mouse outside JPanel" );
28        add( statusBar, BorderLayout.SOUTH ); // add label to JFrame
```

Fig. 14.28 | Mouse event handling. (Part 1 of 3.)

```
29
30          // create and register listener for mouse and mouse motion events
31          MouseHandler handler = new MouseHandler();
32          mousePanel.addMouseListener( handler );
33          mousePanel.addMouseMotionListener( handler );
34      } // end MouseTrackerFrame constructor
35
36      private class MouseHandler implements MouseListener,
37          MouseMotionListener
38      {
39          // MouseListener event handlers
40          // handle event when mouse released immediately after press
41          public void mouseClicked( MouseEvent event )
42          {
43              statusBar.setText( String.format( "Clicked at [%d, %d]",
44                  event.getX(), event.getY() ) );
45          } // end method mouseClicked
46
47          // handle event when mouse pressed
48          public void mousePressed( MouseEvent event )
49          {
50              statusBar.setText( String.format( "Pressed at [%d, %d]",
51                  event.getX(), event.getY() ) );
52          } // end method mousePressed
53
54          // handle event when mouse released
55          public void mouseReleased( MouseEvent event )
56          {
57              statusBar.setText( String.format( "Released at [%d, %d]",
58                  event.getX(), event.getY() ) );
59          } // end method mouseReleased
60
61          // handle event when mouse enters area
62          public void mouseEntered( MouseEvent event )
63          {
64              statusBar.setText( String.format( "Mouse entered at [%d, %d]",
65                  event.getX(), event.getY() ) );
66              mousePanel.setBackground( Color.GREEN );
67          } // end method mouseEntered
68
69          // handle event when mouse exits area
70          public void mouseExited( MouseEvent event )
71          {
72              statusBar.setText( "Mouse outside JPanel" );
73              mousePanel.setBackground( Color.WHITE );
74          } // end method mouseExited
75
76          // MouseMotionListener event handlers
77          // handle event when user drags mouse with button pressed
78          public void mouseDragged( MouseEvent event )
79          {
80              statusBar.setText( String.format( "Dragged at [%d, %d]",
81                  event.getX(), event.getY() ) );
82          } // end method mouseDragged
```

Fig. 14.28 | Mouse event handling. (Part 2 of 3.)

```
83
84          // handle event when user moves mouse
85          public void mouseMoved( MouseEvent event )
86          {
87             statusBar.setText( String.format( "Moved at [%d, %d]",
88                event.getX(), event.getY() ) );
89          } // end method mouseMoved
90       } // end inner class MouseHandler
91    } // end class MouseTrackerFrame
```

Fig. 14.28 | Mouse event handling. (Part 3 of 3.)

```
1    // Fig. 14.29: MouseTrackerFrame.java
2    // Testing MouseTrackerFrame.
3    import javax.swing.JFrame;
4
5    public class MouseTracker
6    {
7       public static void main( String[] args )
8       {
9          MouseTrackerFrame mouseTrackerFrame = new MouseTrackerFrame();
10         mouseTrackerFrame.setDefaultCloseOperation( JFrame.EXIT_ON_CLOSE );
11         mouseTrackerFrame.setSize( 300, 100 ); // set frame size
12         mouseTrackerFrame.setVisible( true ); // display frame
13      } // end main
14   } // end class MouseTracker
```

Fig. 14.29 | Test class for MouseTrackerFrame.

Line 23 in Fig. 14.28 creates JPanel mousePanel. This JPanel's mouse events will be tracked by the application. Line 24 sets mousePanel's background color to white. When the user moves the mouse into the mousePanel, the application will change mousePanel's background color to green. When the user moves the mouse out of the mousePanel, the application will change the background color back to white. Line 25 attaches mousePanel to the JFrame. As you learned in Section 14.5, you typically must specify the layout of the GUI components in a JFrame. In that section, we introduced the layout manager Flow-

Layout. Here we use the default layout of a JFrame's content pane—**BorderLayout**. This layout manager arranges components into five regions: **NORTH**, **SOUTH**, **EAST**, **WEST** and **CENTER**. NORTH corresponds to the top of the container. This example uses the CENTER and SOUTH regions. Line 25 uses a two-argument version of method add to place mousePanel in the CENTER region. The BorderLayout automatically sizes the component in the CENTER to use all the space in the JFrame that is not occupied by components in the other regions. Section 14.18.2 discusses BorderLayout in more detail.

Lines 27–28 in the constructor declare JLabel statusBar and attach it to the JFrame's SOUTH region. This JLabel occupies the width of the JFrame. The region's height is determined by the JLabel.

Line 31 creates an instance of inner class MouseHandler (lines 36–90) called handler that responds to mouse events. Lines 32–33 register handler as the listener for mouse-Panel's mouse events. Methods **addMouseListener** and **addMouseMotionListener** are inherited indirectly from class Component and can be used to register MouseListeners and MouseMotionListeners, respectively. A MouseHandler object *is a* MouseListener and *is a* MouseMotionListener because the class implements both interfaces. Note that we chose to implement both interfaces here to demonstrate a class that implements more than one interface, but we could have implemented interface MouseInputListener instead.]

When the mouse enters and exits mousePanel's area, methods mouseEntered (lines 62–67) and mouseExited (lines 70–74) are called, respectively. Method mouseEntered displays a message in the statusBar indicating that the mouse entered the JPanel and changes the background color to green. Method mouseExited displays a message in the statusBar indicating that the mouse is outside the JPanel (see the first sample output window) and changes the background color to white.

When any of the other five events occurs, it displays a message in the statusBar that includes a string containing the event and the coordinates at which it occurred. Mouse-Event methods **getX** and **getY** return the *x*- and *y*-coordinates, respectively, of the mouse at the time the event occurred.

14.15 Adapter Classes

Many event-listener interfaces, such as MouseListener and MouseMotionListener, contain multiple methods. It's not always desirable to declare every method in an event-listener interface. For instance, an application may need only the mouseClicked handler from MouseListener or the mouseDragged handler from MouseMotionListener. Interface WindowListener specifies seven window event-handling methods. For many of the listener interfaces that have multiple methods, packages java.awt.event and javax.swing.event provide event-listener adapter classes. An **adapter class** implements an interface and provides a default implementation (with an empty method body) of each method in the interface. Figure 14.30 shows several java.awt.event adapter classes and the interfaces they implement. You can extend an adapter class to inherit the default implementation of every method and subsequently override only the method(s) you need for event handling.

Software Engineering Observation 14.8

When a class implements an interface, the class has an is-a *relationship with that interface. All direct and indirect subclasses of that class inherit this interface. Thus, an object of a class that extends an event-adapter class is an object of the corresponding event-listener type (e.g., an object of a subclass of* MouseAdapter *is a* MouseListener*).*

Event-adapter class in `java.awt.event`	Implements interface
ComponentAdapter	ComponentListener
ContainerAdapter	ContainerListener
FocusAdapter	FocusListener
KeyAdapter	KeyListener
MouseAdapter	MouseListener
MouseMotionAdapter	MouseMotionListener
WindowAdapter	WindowListener

Fig. 14.30 | Event-adapter classes and the interfaces they implement in package `java.awt.event`.

Extending *MouseAdapter*

The application of Figs. 14.31–14.32 demonstrates how to determine the number of mouse clicks (i.e., the click count) and how to distinguish between the different mouse buttons. The event listener in this application is an object of inner class MouseClickHandler (lines 25–45) that extends MouseAdapter, so we can declare just the mouseClicked method we need in this example.

```java
1   // Fig. 14.31: MouseDetailsFrame.java
2   // Demonstrating mouse clicks and distinguishing between mouse buttons.
3   import java.awt.BorderLayout;
4   import java.awt.event.MouseAdapter;
5   import java.awt.event.MouseEvent;
6   import javax.swing.JFrame;
7   import javax.swing.JLabel;
8
9   public class MouseDetailsFrame extends JFrame
10  {
11     private String details; // String that is displayed in the statusBar
12     private JLabel statusBar; // JLabel that appears at bottom of window
13
14     // constructor sets title bar String and register mouse listener
15     public MouseDetailsFrame()
16     {
17        super( "Mouse clicks and buttons" );
18
19        statusBar = new JLabel( "Click the mouse" );
20        add( statusBar, BorderLayout.SOUTH );
21        addMouseListener( new MouseClickHandler() ); // add handler
22     } // end MouseDetailsFrame constructor
23
24     // inner class to handle mouse events
25     private class MouseClickHandler extends MouseAdapter
26     {
27        // handle mouse-click event and determine which button was pressed
28        public void mouseClicked( MouseEvent event )
29        {
30           int xPos = event.getX(); // get x-position of mouse
```

Fig. 14.31 | Left, center and right mouse-button clicks. (Part 1 of 2.)

```
31              int yPos = event.getY(); // get y-position of mouse
32
33              details = String.format( "Clicked %d time(s)",
34                 event.getClickCount() );
35
36              if ( event.isMetaDown() ) // right mouse button
37                 details += " with right mouse button";
38              else if ( event.isAltDown() ) // middle mouse button
39                 details += " with center mouse button";
40              else // left mouse button
41                 details += " with left mouse button";
42
43              statusBar.setText( details ); // display message in statusBar
44           } // end method mouseClicked
45        } // end private inner class MouseClickHandler
46     } // end class MouseDetailsFrame
```

Fig. 14.31 | Left, center and right mouse-button clicks. (Part 2 of 2.)

```
1   // Fig. 14.32: MouseDetails.java
2   // Testing MouseDetailsFrame.
3   import javax.swing.JFrame;
4
5   public class MouseDetails
6   {
7      public static void main( String[] args )
8      {
9         MouseDetailsFrame mouseDetailsFrame = new MouseDetailsFrame();
10        mouseDetailsFrame.setDefaultCloseOperation( JFrame.EXIT_ON_CLOSE );
11        mouseDetailsFrame.setSize( 400, 150 ); // set frame size
12        mouseDetailsFrame.setVisible( true ); // display frame
13     } // end main
14  } // end class MouseDetails
```

Fig. 14.32 | Test class for MouseDetailsFrame.

Common Programming Error 14.4

If you extend an adapter class and misspell the name of the method you are overriding, your method simply becomes another method in the class. This is a logic error that is difficult to detect, since the program will call the empty version of the method inherited from the adapter class.

A user of a Java application may be on a system with a one-, two- or three-button mouse. Java provides a mechanism to distinguish among mouse buttons. Class Mouse-Event inherits several methods from class InputEvent that can distinguish among mouse buttons on a multibutton mouse or can mimic a multibutton mouse with a combined keystroke and mouse-button click. Figure 14.33 shows the InputEvent methods used to distinguish among mouse-button clicks. Java assumes that every mouse contains a left mouse button. Thus, it's simple to test for a left-mouse-button click. However, users with a one- or two-button mouse must use a combination of keystrokes and mouse-button clicks at the same time to simulate the missing buttons on the mouse. In the case of a one- or two-button mouse, a Java application assumes that the center mouse button is clicked if the user holds down the *Alt* key and clicks the left mouse button on a two-button mouse or the only mouse button on a one-button mouse. In the case of a one-button mouse, a Java application assumes that the right mouse button is clicked if the user holds down the *Meta* key (sometimes called the *Command* key or the "Apple" key on a Mac) and clicks the mouse button.

InputEvent method	Description
isMetaDown()	Returns true when the user clicks the right mouse button on a mouse with two or three buttons. To simulate a right-mouse-button click on a one-button mouse, the user can hold down the *Meta* key on the keyboard and click the mouse button.
isAltDown()	Returns true when the user clicks the middle mouse button on a mouse with three buttons. To simulate a middle-mouse-button click on a one- or two-button mouse, the user can press the *Alt* key and click the only or left mouse button, respectively.

Fig. 14.33 | InputEvent methods that help distinguish among left-, center- and right-mouse-button clicks.

Line 21 of Fig. 14.31 registers a MouseListener for the MouseDetailsFrame. The event listener is an object of class MouseClickHandler, which extends MouseAdapter. This enables us to declare only method mouseClicked (lines 28–44). This method first captures the coordinates where the event occurred and stores them in local variables xPos and yPos (lines 30–31). Lines 33–34 create a String called details containing the number of consecutive mouse clicks, which is returned by MouseEvent method **getClickCount** at line 34. Lines 36–41 use methods **isMetaDown** and **isAltDown** to determine which mouse button the user clicked and append an appropriate String to details in each case. The resulting String is displayed in the statusBar. Class MouseDetails (Fig. 14.32) contains the main method that executes the application. Try clicking with each of your mouse's buttons repeatedly to see the click count increment.

14.16 JPanel Subclass for Drawing with the Mouse

Section 14.14 showed how to track mouse events in a JPanel. In this section, we use a JPanel as a **dedicated drawing area** in which the user can draw by dragging the mouse. In addition, this section demonstrates an event listener that extends an adapter class.

Method paintComponent

Lightweight Swing components that extend class JComponent (such as JPanel) contain method **paintComponent**, which is called when a lightweight Swing component is displayed. By overriding this method, you can specify how to draw shapes using Java's graphics capabilities. When customizing a JPanel for use as a dedicated drawing area, the subclass should override method paintComponent and call the superclass version of paintComponent as the first statement in the body of the overridden method to ensure that the component displays correctly. The reason is that subclasses of JComponent support **transparency**. To display a component correctly, the program must determine whether the component is transparent. The code that determines this is in superclass JComponent's paintComponent implementation. When a component is transparent, paintComponent will not clear its background when the program displays the component. When a component is **opaque**, paintComponent clears the component's background before the component is displayed. If the superclass version of paintComponent is not called, an opaque GUI component typically will not display correctly on the user interface. Also, if the superclass version is called after performing the customized drawing statements, the results typically will be erased. The transparency of a Swing lightweight component can be set with method **setOpaque** (a false argument indicates that the component is transparent).

Look-and-Feel Observation 14.12
Most Swing GUI components can be transparent or opaque. If a Swing GUI component is opaque, its background will be cleared when its paintComponent method is called. Only opaque components can display a customized background color. JPanel objects are opaque by default.

Error-Prevention Tip 14.1
In a JComponent subclass's paintComponent method, the first statement should always call to the superclass's paintComponent method to ensure that an object of the subclass displays correctly.

Common Programming Error 14.5
If an overridden paintComponent method does not call the superclass's version, the subclass component may not display properly. If an overridden paintComponent method calls the superclass's version after other drawing is performed, the drawing will be erased.

Defining the Custom Drawing Area

The Painter application of Figs. 14.34–14.35 demonstrates a customized subclass of JPanel that is used to create a dedicated drawing area. The application uses the mouseDragged event handler to create a simple drawing application. The user can draw pictures by dragging the mouse on the JPanel. This example does not use method mouseMoved, so our event-listener class (the anonymous inner class at lines 22–34) extends Mouse-

MotionAdapter. Since this class already declares both mouseMoved and mouseDragged, we can simply override mouseDragged to provide the event handling this application requires.

```java
1   // Fig. 14.34: PaintPanel.java
2   // Using class MouseMotionAdapter.
3   import java.awt.Point;
4   import java.awt.Graphics;
5   import java.awt.event.MouseEvent;
6   import java.awt.event.MouseMotionAdapter;
7   import javax.swing.JPanel;
8
9   public class PaintPanel extends JPanel
10  {
11     private int pointCount = 0; // count number of points
12
13     // array of 10000 java.awt.Point references
14     private Point[] points = new Point[ 10000 ];
15
16     // set up GUI and register mouse event handler
17     public PaintPanel()
18     {
19        // handle frame mouse motion event
20        addMouseMotionListener(
21
22           new MouseMotionAdapter() // anonymous inner class
23           {
24              // store drag coordinates and repaint
25              public void mouseDragged( MouseEvent event )
26              {
27                 if ( pointCount < points.length )
28                 {
29                    points[ pointCount ] = event.getPoint(); // find point
30                    pointCount++; // increment number of points in array
31                    repaint(); // repaint JFrame
32                 } // end if
33              } // end method mouseDragged
34           } // end anonymous inner class
35        ); // end call to addMouseMotionListener
36     } // end PaintPanel constructor
37
38     // draw ovals in a 4-by-4 bounding box at specified locations on window
39     public void paintComponent( Graphics g )
40     {
41        super.paintComponent( g ); // clears drawing area
42
43        // draw all points in array
44        for ( int i = 0; i < pointCount; i++ )
45           g.fillOval( points[ i ].x, points[ i ].y, 4, 4 );
46     } // end method paintComponent
47  } // end class PaintPanel
```

Fig. 14.34 | Adapter class used to implement event handlers.

Class PaintPanel (Fig. 14.34) extends JPanel to create the dedicated drawing area. Lines 3–7 import the classes used in class PaintPanel. Class **Point** (package java.awt) represents an *x-y* coordinate. We use objects of this class to store the coordinates of each mouse drag event. Class **Graphics** is used to draw.

In this example, we use an array of 10,000 Points (line 14) to store the location at which each mouse drag event occurs. As you'll see, method paintComponent uses these Points to draw. Instance variable pointCount (line 11) maintains the total number of Points captured from mouse drag events so far.

Lines 20–35 register a MouseMotionListener to listen for the PaintPanel's mouse motion events. Lines 22–34 create an object of an anonymous inner class that extends the adapter class MouseMotionAdapter. Recall that MouseMotionAdapter implements Mouse-MotionListener, so the anonymous inner class object is a MouseMotionListener. The anonymous inner class inherits default mouseMoved and mouseDragged implementations, so it already implements all the interface's methods. However, the default methods do nothing when they are called. So, we override method mouseDragged at lines 25–33 to capture the coordinates of a mouse drag event and store them as a Point object. Line 27 ensures that we store the event's coordinates only if there are still empty elements in the array. If so, line 29 invokes the MouseEvent's **getPoint** method to obtain the Point where the event occurred and stores it in the array at index pointCount. Line 30 increments the pointCount, and line 31 calls method **repaint** (inherited indirectly from class Component) to indicate that the PaintPanel should be refreshed on the screen as soon as possible with a call to the PaintPanel's paintComponent method.

Method paintComponent (lines 39–46), which receives a Graphics parameter, is called automatically any time the PaintPanel needs to be displayed on the screen (such as when the GUI is first displayed) or refreshed on the screen (such as when method repaint is called or when the GUI component was hidden by another window on the screen and subsequently becomes visible again).

Look-and-Feel Observation 14.13

Calling repaint for a Swing GUI component indicates that the component should be refreshed on the screen as soon as possible. The background of the GUI component is cleared only if the component is opaque. JComponent method setOpaque can be passed a boolean argument indicating whether the component is opaque (true) or transparent (false).

Line 41 invokes the superclass version of paintComponent to clear the PaintPanel's background (JPanels are opaque by default). Lines 44–45 draw an oval at the location specified by each Point in the array (up to the pointCount). Graphics method **fillOval** draws a solid oval. The method's four parameters represent a rectangular area (called the bounding box) in which the oval is displayed. The first two parameters are the upper-left *x*-coordinate and the upper-left *y*-coordinate of the rectangular area. The last two coordinates represent the rectangular area's width and height. Method fillOval draws the oval so it touches the middle of each side of the rectangular area. In line 45, the first two arguments are specified by using class Point's two public instance variables—x and y. The loop terminates when pointCount points have been displayed. You'll learn more Graphics features in Chapter 15.

Look-and-Feel Observation 14.14

Drawing on any GUI component is performed with coordinates that are measured from the upper-left corner (0, 0) of that GUI component, not the upper-left corner of the screen.

*Using the Custom **JPanel** in an Application*
Class Painter (Fig. 14.35) contains the main method that executes this application. Line
14 creates a PaintPanel object on which the user can drag the mouse to draw. Line 15
attaches the PaintPanel to the JFrame.

```
 1   // Fig. 14.35: Painter.java
 2   // Testing PaintPanel.
 3   import java.awt.BorderLayout;
 4   import javax.swing.JFrame;
 5   import javax.swing.JLabel;
 6
 7   public class Painter
 8   {
 9      public static void main( String[] args )
10      {
11         // create JFrame
12         JFrame application = new JFrame( "A simple paint program" );
13
14         PaintPanel paintPanel = new PaintPanel(); // create paint panel
15         application.add( paintPanel, BorderLayout.CENTER ); // in center
16
17         // create a label and place it in SOUTH of BorderLayout
18         application.add( new JLabel( "Drag the mouse to draw" ),
19            BorderLayout.SOUTH );
20
21         application.setDefaultCloseOperation( JFrame.EXIT_ON_CLOSE );
22         application.setSize( 400, 200 ); // set frame size
23         application.setVisible( true ); // display frame
24      } // end main
25   } // end class Painter
```

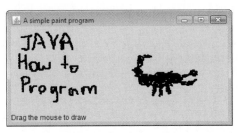

Fig. 14.35 | Test class for PaintFrame.

14.17 Key Event Handling

This section presents the KeyListener interface for handling **key events**. Key events are
generated when keys on the keyboard are pressed and released. A class that implements
KeyListener must provide declarations for methods **keyPressed**, **keyReleased** and **key-
Typed**, each of which receives a KeyEvent as its argument. Class KeyEvent is a subclass of
InputEvent. Method keyPressed is called in response to pressing any key. Method key-
Typed is called in response to pressing any key that is not an **action key**. (The action keys
are any arrow key, *Home, End, Page Up, Page Down,* any function key, etc.) Method key-
Released is called when the key is released after any keyPressed or keyTyped event.

The application of Figs. 14.36–14.37 demonstrates the KeyListener methods. Class KeyDemoFrame implements the KeyListener interface, so all three methods are declared in the application.

```java
1   // Fig. 14.36: KeyDemoFrame.java
2   // Demonstrating keystroke events.
3   import java.awt.Color;
4   import java.awt.event.KeyListener;
5   import java.awt.event.KeyEvent;
6   import javax.swing.JFrame;
7   import javax.swing.JTextArea;
8
9   public class KeyDemoFrame extends JFrame implements KeyListener
10  {
11     private String line1 = ""; // first line of textarea
12     private String line2 = ""; // second line of textarea
13     private String line3 = ""; // third line of textarea
14     private JTextArea textArea; // textarea to display output
15
16     // KeyDemoFrame constructor
17     public KeyDemoFrame()
18     {
19        super( "Demonstrating Keystroke Events" );
20
21        textArea = new JTextArea( 10, 15 ); // set up JTextArea
22        textArea.setText( "Press any key on the keyboard..." );
23        textArea.setEnabled( false ); // disable textarea
24        textArea.setDisabledTextColor( Color.BLACK ); // set text color
25        add( textArea ); // add textarea to JFrame
26
27        addKeyListener( this ); // allow frame to process key events
28     } // end KeyDemoFrame constructor
29
30     // handle press of any key
31     public void keyPressed( KeyEvent event )
32     {
33        line1 = String.format( "Key pressed: %s",
34           KeyEvent.getKeyText( event.getKeyCode() ) ); // show pressed key
35        setLines2and3( event ); // set output lines two and three
36     } // end method keyPressed
37
38     // handle release of any key
39     public void keyReleased( KeyEvent event )
40     {
41        line1 = String.format( "Key released: %s",
42           KeyEvent.getKeyText( event.getKeyCode() ) ); // show released key
43        setLines2and3( event ); // set output lines two and three
44     } // end method keyReleased
45
46     // handle press of an action key
47     public void keyTyped( KeyEvent event )
48     {
49        line1 = String.format( "Key typed: %s", event.getKeyChar() );
```

Fig. 14.36 | Key event handling. (Part 1 of 2.)

```
50          setLines2and3( event ); // set output lines two and three
51      } // end method keyTyped
52
53      // set second and third lines of output
54      private void setLines2and3( KeyEvent event )
55      {
56          line2 = String.format( "This key is %san action key",
57              ( event.isActionKey() ? "" : "not " ) );
58
59          String temp = KeyEvent.getKeyModifiersText( event.getModifiers() );
60
61          line3 = String.format( "Modifier keys pressed: %s",
62              ( temp.equals( "" ) ? "none" : temp ) ); // output modifiers
63
64          textArea.setText( String.format( "%s\n%s\n%s\n",
65              line1, line2, line3 ) ); // output three lines of text
66      } // end method setLines2and3
67  } // end class KeyDemoFrame
```

Fig. 14.36 | Key event handling. (Part 2 of 2.)

```
1   // Fig. 14.37: KeyDemo.java
2   // Testing KeyDemoFrame.
3   import javax.swing.JFrame;
4
5   public class KeyDemo
6   {
7       public static void main( String[] args )
8       {
9           KeyDemoFrame keyDemoFrame = new KeyDemoFrame();
10          keyDemoFrame.setDefaultCloseOperation( JFrame.EXIT_ON_CLOSE );
11          keyDemoFrame.setSize( 350, 100 ); // set frame size
12          keyDemoFrame.setVisible( true ); // display frame
13      } // end main
14  } // end class KeyDemo
```

Fig. 14.37 | Test class for KeyDemoFrame. (Part 1 of 2.)

Fig. 14.37 | Test class for `KeyDemoFrame`. (Part 2 of 2.)

The constructor (Fig. 14.36, lines 17–28) registers the application to handle its own key events by using method **addKeyListener** at line 27. Method `addKeyListener` is declared in class `Component`, so every subclass of `Component` can notify `KeyListener` objects of key events for that `Component`.

At line 25, the constructor adds `JTextArea textArea` (where the application's output is displayed) to the `JFrame`. A `JTextArea` is a multiline area in which you can display text. (We discuss `JTextArea`s in more detail in Section 14.20.) Notice in the screen captures that `textArea` occupies the entire window. This is due to the `JFrame`'s default `Border-Layout` (discussed in Section 14.18.2 and demonstrated in Fig. 14.41). When a single `Component` is added to a `BorderLayout`, the `Component` occupies the entire `Container`. Line 23 disables the `JTextArea` so the user cannot type in it. This causes the text in the `JTextArea` to become gray. Line 24 uses method **setDisabledTextColor** to change the text color in the `JTextArea` to black for readability.

Methods `keyPressed` (lines 31–36) and `keyReleased` (lines 39–44) use `KeyEvent` method **getKeyCode** to get the **virtual key code** of the pressed key. Class `KeyEvent` contains virtual key-code constants that represents every key on the keyboard. These constants can be compared with `getKeyCode`'s return value to test for individual keys on the keyboard. The value returned by `getKeyCode` is passed to static `KeyEvent` method **getKeyText**, which returns a string containing the name of the key that was pressed. For a complete list of virtual key constants, see the on-line documentation for class `KeyEvent` (package `java.awt.event`). Method `keyTyped` (lines 47–51) uses `KeyEvent` method **getKeyChar** (which returns a char) to get the Unicode value of the character typed.

All three event-handling methods finish by calling method `setLines2and3` (lines 54–66) and passing it the `KeyEvent` object. This method uses `KeyEvent` method **isActionKey** (line 57) to determine whether the key in the event was an action key. Also, `InputEvent` method **getModifiers** is called (line 59) to determine whether any modifier keys (such as *Shift*, *Alt* and *Ctrl*) were pressed when the key event occurred. The result of this method is passed to static `KeyEvent` method **getKeyModifiersText**, which produces a string containing the names of the pressed modifier keys.

[*Note:* If you need to test for a specific key on the keyboard, class `KeyEvent` provides a **key constant** for each one. These constants can be used from the key event handlers to determine whether a particular key was pressed. Also, to determine whether the *Alt*, *Ctrl*, *Meta* and *Shift* keys are pressed individually, `InputEvent` methods **isAltDown**, **isControlDown**, **isMetaDown** and **isShiftDown** each return a boolean indicating whether the particular key was pressed during the key event.]

14.18 Introduction to Layout Managers

Layout managers arrange GUI components in a container for presentation purposes. You can use the layout managers for basic layout capabilities instead of determining every GUI component's exact position and size. This functionality enables you to concentrate on the basic look-and-feel and lets the layout managers process most of the layout details. All layout managers implement the interface **LayoutManager** (in package java.awt). Class Container's setLayout method takes an object that implements the LayoutManager interface as an argument. There are basically three ways for you to arrange components in a GUI:

1. Absolute positioning: This provides the greatest level of control over a GUI's appearance. By setting a Container's layout to null, you can specify the absolute position of each GUI component with respect to the upper-left corner of the Container by using Component methods setSize and setLocation or setBounds. If you do this, you also must specify each GUI component's size. Programming a GUI with absolute positioning can be tedious, unless you have an integrated development environment (IDE) that can generate the code for you.

2. Layout managers: Using layout managers to position elements can be simpler and faster than creating a GUI with absolute positioning, but you lose some control over the size and the precise positioning of GUI components.

3. Visual programming in an IDE: IDEs provide tools that make it easy to create GUIs. Each IDE typically provides a **GUI design tool** that allows you to drag and drop GUI components from a tool box onto a design area. You can then position, size and align GUI components as you like. The IDE generates the Java code that creates the GUI. In addition, you can typically add event-handling code for a particular component by double-clicking the component. Some design tools also allow you to use the layout managers described in this chapter and in Chapter 25.

Look-and-Feel Observation 14.15
Most Java IDEs provide GUI design tools for visually designing a GUI; the tools then write Java code that creates the GUI. Such tools often provide greater control over the size, position and alignment of GUI components than do the built-in layout managers.

Look-and-Feel Observation 14.16
It's possible to set a Container's layout to null, which indicates that no layout manager should be used. In a Container without a layout manager, you must position and size the components in the given container and take care that, on resize events, all components are repositioned as necessary. A component's resize events can be processed by a Component-Listener.

Figure 14.38 summarizes the layout managers presented in this chapter. Others are discussed in Chapter 25 and the powerful GroupLayout layout manager is discussed in Appendix I.

Layout manager	Description
FlowLayout	Default for javax.swing.JPanel. Places components sequentially (left to right) in the order they were added. It's also possible to specify the order of the components by using the Container method add, which takes a Component and an integer index position as arguments.

Fig. 14.38 | Layout managers. (Part 1 of 2.)

Layout manager	Description
BorderLayout	Default for JFrames (and other windows). Arranges the components into five areas: NORTH, SOUTH, EAST, WEST and CENTER.
GridLayout	Arranges the components into rows and columns.

Fig. 14.38 | Layout managers. (Part 2 of 2.)

14.18.1 FlowLayout

FlowLayout is the simplest layout manager. GUI components are placed on a container from left to right in the order in which they are added to the container. When the edge of the container is reached, components continue to display on the next line. Class FlowLayout allows GUI components to be left aligned, centered (the default) and right aligned.

The application of Figs. 14.39–14.40 creates three JButton objects and adds them to the application, using a FlowLayout layout manager. The components are center aligned by default. When the user clicks **Left**, the alignment for the layout manager is changed to a left-aligned FlowLayout. When the user clicks **Right**, the alignment for the layout manager is changed to a right-aligned FlowLayout. When the user clicks **Center**, the alignment for the layout manager is changed to a center-aligned FlowLayout. Each button has its own event handler that is declared with an anonymous inner class that implements ActionListener. The sample output windows show each of the FlowLayout alignments. Also, the last sample output window shows the centered alignment after the window has been resized to a smaller width. Notice that the button **Right** flows onto a new line.

As seen previously, a container's layout is set with method setLayout of class Container. Line 25 sets the layout manager to the FlowLayout declared at line 23. Normally, the layout is set before any GUI components are added to a container.

Look-and-Feel Observation 14.17

Each individual container can have only one layout manager, but multiple containers in the same application can each use different layout managers.

```
 1   // Fig. 14.39: FlowLayoutFrame.java
 2   // Demonstrating FlowLayout alignments.
 3   import java.awt.FlowLayout;
 4   import java.awt.Container;
 5   import java.awt.event.ActionListener;
 6   import java.awt.event.ActionEvent;
 7   import javax.swing.JFrame;
 8   import javax.swing.JButton;
 9
10   public class FlowLayoutFrame extends JFrame
11   {
12      private JButton leftJButton; // button to set alignment left
13      private JButton centerJButton; // button to set alignment center
14      private JButton rightJButton; // button to set alignment right
15      private FlowLayout layout; // layout object
16      private Container container; // container to set layout
```

Fig. 14.39 | FlowLayout allows components to flow over multiple lines. (Part 1 of 3.)

```
17
18      // set up GUI and register button listeners
19      public FlowLayoutFrame()
20      {
21         super( "FlowLayout Demo" );
22
23         layout = new FlowLayout(); // create FlowLayout
24         container = getContentPane(); // get container to layout
25         setLayout( layout ); // set frame layout
26
27         // set up leftJButton and register listener
28         leftJButton = new JButton( "Left" ); // create Left button
29         add( leftJButton ); // add Left button to frame
30         leftJButton.addActionListener(
31
32            new ActionListener() // anonymous inner class
33            {
34               // process leftJButton event
35               public void actionPerformed( ActionEvent event )
36               {
37                  layout.setAlignment( FlowLayout.LEFT );
38
39                  // realign attached components
40                  layout.layoutContainer( container );
41               } // end method actionPerformed
42            } // end anonymous inner class
43         ); // end call to addActionListener
44
45         // set up centerJButton and register listener
46         centerJButton = new JButton( "Center" ); // create Center button
47         add( centerJButton ); // add Center button to frame
48         centerJButton.addActionListener(
49
50            new ActionListener() // anonymous inner class
51            {
52               // process centerJButton event
53               public void actionPerformed( ActionEvent event )
54               {
55                  layout.setAlignment( FlowLayout.CENTER );
56
57                  // realign attached components
58                  layout.layoutContainer( container );
59               } // end method actionPerformed
60            } // end anonymous inner class
61         ); // end call to addActionListener
62
63         // set up rightJButton and register listener
64         rightJButton = new JButton( "Right" ); // create Right button
65         add( rightJButton ); // add Right button to frame
66         rightJButton.addActionListener(
67
68            new ActionListener() // anonymous inner class
69            {
```

Fig. 14.39 | FlowLayout allows components to flow over multiple lines. (Part 2 of 3.)

```
70              // process rightJButton event
71              public void actionPerformed( ActionEvent event )
72              {
73                 layout.setAlignment( FlowLayout.RIGHT );
74
75                 // realign attached components
76                 layout.layoutContainer( container );
77              } // end method actionPerformed
78           } // end anonymous inner class
79        ); // end call to addActionListener
80     } // end FlowLayoutFrame constructor
81  } // end class FlowLayoutFrame
```

Fig. 14.39 | FlowLayout allows components to flow over multiple lines. (Part 3 of 3.)

```
1   // Fig. 14.40: FlowLayoutDemo.java
2   // Testing FlowLayoutFrame.
3   import javax.swing.JFrame;
4
5   public class FlowLayoutDemo
6   {
7      public static void main( String[] args )
8      {
9         FlowLayoutFrame flowLayoutFrame = new FlowLayoutFrame();
10        flowLayoutFrame.setDefaultCloseOperation( JFrame.EXIT_ON_CLOSE );
11        flowLayoutFrame.setSize( 300, 75 ); // set frame size
12        flowLayoutFrame.setVisible( true ); // display frame
13     } // end main
14  } // end class FlowLayoutDemo
```

Fig. 14.40 | Test class for FlowLayoutFrame.

Note that each button's event handler is specified with a separate anonymous inner-class object (Fig. 14.39, lines 30–43, 48–61 and 66–79, respectively) and method action-Performed in each case executes two statements. For example, line 37 in the event handler for leftJButton uses FlowLayout method **setAlignment** to change the alignment for the

FlowLayout to a left-aligned (**FlowLayout.LEFT**) FlowLayout. Line 40 uses LayoutManager interface method **layoutContainer** (which is inherited by all layout managers) to specify that the JFrame should be rearranged based on the adjusted layout. According to which button was clicked, the actionPerformed method for each button sets the FlowLayout's alignment to FlowLayout.LEFT (line 37), **FlowLayout.CENTER** (line 55) or **FlowLayout.RIGHT** (line 73).

14.18.2 BorderLayout

The BorderLayout layout manager (the default layout manager for a JFrame) arranges components into five regions: NORTH, SOUTH, EAST, WEST and CENTER. NORTH corresponds to the top of the container. Class BorderLayout extends Object and implements interface **LayoutManager2** (a subinterface of LayoutManager that adds several methods for enhanced layout processing).

A BorderLayout limits a Container to containing at most five components—one in each region. The component placed in each region can be a container to which other components are attached. The components placed in the NORTH and SOUTH regions extend horizontally to the sides of the container and are as tall as the components placed in those regions. The EAST and WEST regions expand vertically between the NORTH and SOUTH regions and are as wide as the components placed in those regions. The component placed in the CENTER region expands to fill all remaining space in the layout (which is the reason the JTextArea in Fig. 14.37 occupies the entire window). If all five regions are occupied, the entire container's space is covered by GUI components. If the NORTH or SOUTH region is not occupied, the GUI components in the EAST, CENTER and WEST regions expand vertically to fill the remaining space. If the EAST or WEST region is not occupied, the GUI component in the CENTER region expands horizontally to fill the remaining space. If the CENTER region is not occupied, the area is left empty—the other GUI components do not expand to fill the remaining space. The application of Figs. 14.41–14.42 demonstrates the BorderLayout layout manager by using five JButtons.

```
1   // Fig. 14.41: BorderLayoutFrame.java
2   // Demonstrating BorderLayout.
3   import java.awt.BorderLayout;
4   import java.awt.event.ActionListener;
5   import java.awt.event.ActionEvent;
6   import javax.swing.JFrame;
7   import javax.swing.JButton;
8
9   public class BorderLayoutFrame extends JFrame implements ActionListener
10  {
11     private JButton[] buttons; // array of buttons to hide portions
12     private static final String[] names = { "Hide North", "Hide South",
13        "Hide East", "Hide West", "Hide Center" };
14     private BorderLayout layout; // borderlayout object
15
16     // set up GUI and event handling
17     public BorderLayoutFrame()
18     {
```

Fig. 14.41 | BorderLayout containing five buttons. (Part 1 of 2.)

```
19            super( "BorderLayout Demo" );
20
21            layout = new BorderLayout( 5, 5 ); // 5 pixel gaps
22            setLayout( layout ); // set frame layout
23            buttons = new JButton[ names.length ]; // set size of array
24
25            // create JButtons and register listeners for them
26            for ( int count = 0; count < names.length; count++ )
27            {
28               buttons[ count ] = new JButton( names[ count ] );
29               buttons[ count ].addActionListener( this );
30            } // end for
31
32            add( buttons[ 0 ], BorderLayout.NORTH ); // add button to north
33            add( buttons[ 1 ], BorderLayout.SOUTH ); // add button to south
34            add( buttons[ 2 ], BorderLayout.EAST ); // add button to east
35            add( buttons[ 3 ], BorderLayout.WEST ); // add button to west
36            add( buttons[ 4 ], BorderLayout.CENTER ); // add button to center
37        } // end BorderLayoutFrame constructor
38
39        // handle button events
40        public void actionPerformed( ActionEvent event )
41        {
42            // check event source and lay out content pane correspondingly
43            for ( JButton button : buttons )
44            {
45               if ( event.getSource() == button )
46                  button.setVisible( false ); // hide button clicked
47               else
48                  button.setVisible( true ); // show other buttons
49            } // end for
50
51            layout.layoutContainer( getContentPane() ); // lay out content pane
52        } // end method actionPerformed
53     } // end class BorderLayoutFrame
```

Fig. 14.41 | BorderLayout containing five buttons. (Part 2 of 2.)

```
1   // Fig. 14.42: BorderLayoutDemo.java
2   // Testing BorderLayoutFrame.
3   import javax.swing.JFrame;
4
5   public class BorderLayoutDemo
6   {
7      public static void main( String[] args )
8      {
9         BorderLayoutFrame borderLayoutFrame = new BorderLayoutFrame();
10        borderLayoutFrame.setDefaultCloseOperation( JFrame.EXIT_ON_CLOSE );
11        borderLayoutFrame.setSize( 300, 200 ); // set frame size
12        borderLayoutFrame.setVisible( true ); // display frame
13     } // end main
14  } // end class BorderLayoutDemo
```

Fig. 14.42 | Test class for BorderLayoutFrame. (Part 1 of 2.)

Fig. 14.42 | Test class for `BorderLayoutFrame`. (Part 2 of 2.)

Line 21 of Fig. 14.41 creates a `BorderLayout`. The constructor arguments specify the number of pixels between components that are arranged horizontally (**horizontal gap space**) and between components that are arranged vertically (**vertical gap space**), respectively. The default is one pixel of gap space horizontally and vertically. Line 22 uses method `setLayout` to set the content pane's layout to `layout`.

We add `Components` to a `BorderLayout` with another version of `Container` method `add` that takes two arguments—the `Component` to add and the region in which the `Component` should appear. For example, line 32 specifies that `buttons[ 0 ]` should appear in the `NORTH` region. The components can be added in any order, but only one component should be added to each region.

Look-and-Feel Observation 14.18

If no region is specified when adding a `Component` to a `BorderLayout`, the layout manager assumes that the `Component` should be added to region `BorderLayout.CENTER`.

Common Programming Error 14.6

When more than one component is added to a region in a BorderLayout, only the last component added to that region will be displayed. There is no error that indicates this problem.

Note that class BorderLayoutFrame implements ActionListener directly in this example, so the BorderLayoutFrame will handle the events of the JButtons. For this reason, line 29 passes the this reference to the addActionListener method of each JButton. When the user clicks a particular JButton in the layout, method action-Performed (lines 40–52) executes. The enhanced for statement at lines 43–49 uses an if...else to hide the particular JButton that generated the event. Method **setVisible** (inherited into JButton from class Component) is called with a false argument (line 46) to hide the JButton. If the current JButton in the array is not the one that generated the event, method setVisible is called with a true argument (line 48) to ensure that the JButton is displayed on the screen. Line 51 uses LayoutManager method layoutContainer to recalculate the layout of the content pane. Notice in the screen captures of Fig. 14.42 that certain regions in the BorderLayout change shape as JButtons are hidden and displayed in other regions. Try resizing the application window to see how the various regions resize based on the window's width and height. For more complex layouts, group components in JPanels, each with a separate layout manager. Place the JPanels on the JFrame using either the default BorderLayout or some other layout.

14.18.3 GridLayout

The **GridLayout** layout manager divides the container into a grid so that components can be placed in rows and columns. Class GridLayout inherits directly from class Object and implements interface LayoutManager. Every Component in a GridLayout has the same width and height. Components are added to a GridLayout starting at the top-left cell of the grid and proceeding left to right until the row is full. Then the process continues left to right on the next row of the grid, and so on. The application of Figs. 14.43–14.44 demonstrates the GridLayout layout manager by using six JButtons.

```
 1   // Fig. 14.43: GridLayoutFrame.java
 2   // Demonstrating GridLayout.
 3   import java.awt.GridLayout;
 4   import java.awt.Container;
 5   import java.awt.event.ActionListener;
 6   import java.awt.event.ActionEvent;
 7   import javax.swing.JFrame;
 8   import javax.swing.JButton;
 9
10   public class GridLayoutFrame extends JFrame implements ActionListener
11   {
12      private JButton[] buttons; // array of buttons
13      private static final String[] names =
14         { "one", "two", "three", "four", "five", "six" };
15      private boolean toggle = true; // toggle between two layouts
```

Fig. 14.43 | GridLayout containing six buttons. (Part 1 of 2.)

```
16       private Container container; // frame container
17       private GridLayout gridLayout1; // first gridlayout
18       private GridLayout gridLayout2; // second gridlayout
19
20       // no-argument constructor
21       public GridLayoutFrame()
22       {
23          super( "GridLayout Demo" );
24          gridLayout1 = new GridLayout( 2, 3, 5, 5 ); // 2 by 3; gaps of 5
25          gridLayout2 = new GridLayout( 3, 2 ); // 3 by 2; no gaps
26          container = getContentPane(); // get content pane
27          setLayout( gridLayout1 ); // set JFrame layout
28          buttons = new JButton[ names.length ]; // create array of JButtons
29
30          for ( int count = 0; count < names.length; count++ )
31          {
32             buttons[ count ] = new JButton( names[ count ] );
33             buttons[ count ].addActionListener( this ); // register listener
34             add( buttons[ count ] ); // add button to JFrame
35          } // end for
36       } // end GridLayoutFrame constructor
37
38       // handle button events by toggling between layouts
39       public void actionPerformed( ActionEvent event )
40       {
41          if ( toggle )
42             container.setLayout( gridLayout2 ); // set layout to second
43          else
44             container.setLayout( gridLayout1 ); // set layout to first
45
46          toggle = !toggle; // set toggle to opposite value
47          container.validate(); // re-lay out container
48       } // end method actionPerformed
49    } // end class GridLayoutFrame
```

Fig. 14.43 | GridLayout containing six buttons. (Part 2 of 2.)

Lines 24–25 create two GridLayout objects. The GridLayout constructor used at line 24 specifies a GridLayout with 2 rows, 3 columns, 5 pixels of horizontal-gap space between Components in the grid and 5 pixels of vertical-gap space between Components in the grid. The GridLayout constructor used at line 25 specifies a GridLayout with 3 rows and 2 columns that uses the default gap space (1 pixel).

The JButton objects in this example initially are arranged using gridLayout1 (set for the content pane at line 27 with method setLayout). The first component is added to the first column of the first row. The next component is added to the second column of the first row, and so on. When a JButton is pressed, method actionPerformed (lines 39–48) is called. Every call to actionPerformed toggles the layout between gridLayout2 and gridLayout1, using boolean variable toggle to determine the next layout to set.

Line 47 shows another way to reformat a container for which the layout has changed. Container method **validate** recomputes the container's layout based on the current layout manager for the Container and the current set of displayed GUI components.

```
 1   // Fig. 14.44: GridLayoutDemo.java
 2   // Testing GridLayoutFrame.
 3   import javax.swing.JFrame;
 4
 5   public class GridLayoutDemo
 6   {
 7      public static void main( String[] args )
 8      {
 9         GridLayoutFrame gridLayoutFrame = new GridLayoutFrame();
10         gridLayoutFrame.setDefaultCloseOperation( JFrame.EXIT_ON_CLOSE );
11         gridLayoutFrame.setSize( 300, 200 ); // set frame size
12         gridLayoutFrame.setVisible( true ); // display frame
13      } // end main
14   } // end class GridLayoutDemo
```

Fig. 14.44 | Test class for `GridLayoutFrame`.

14.19 Using Panels to Manage More Complex Layouts

Complex GUIs (like Fig. 14.1) require that each component be placed in an exact location. They often consist of multiple panels, with each panel's components arranged in a specific layout. Class JPanel extends JComponent and JComponent extends class Container, so every JPanel is a Container. Thus, every JPanel may have components, including other panels, attached to it with Container method add. The application of Figs. 14.45–14.46 demonstrates how a JPanel can be used to create a more complex layout in which several JButtons are placed in the SOUTH region of a BorderLayout.

   After JPanel buttonJPanel is declared (line 11) and created (line 19), line 20 sets buttonJPanel's layout to a GridLayout of one row and five columns (there are five JButtons in array buttons). Lines 23–27 add the JButtons in the array to the JPanel. Line 26 adds the buttons directly to the JPanel—class JPanel does not have a content pane, unlike a JFrame. Line 29 uses the JFrame's default BorderLayout to add buttonJPanel to the SOUTH region. Note that the SOUTH region is as tall as the buttons on buttonJPanel. A JPanel is sized to the components it contains. As more components are added, the JPanel grows (according to the restrictions of its layout manager) to accommodate the components. Resize the window to see how the layout manager affects the size of the JButtons.

```
 1   // Fig. 14.45: PanelFrame.java
 2   // Using a JPanel to help lay out components.
 3   import java.awt.GridLayout;
 4   import java.awt.BorderLayout;
```

Fig. 14.45 | JPanel with five JButtons in a GridLayout attached to the SOUTH region of a BorderLayout. (Part 1 of 2.)

```
5   import javax.swing.JFrame;
6   import javax.swing.JPanel;
7   import javax.swing.JButton;
8
9   public class PanelFrame extends JFrame
10  {
11     private JPanel buttonJPanel; // panel to hold buttons
12     private JButton[] buttons; // array of buttons
13
14     // no-argument constructor
15     public PanelFrame()
16     {
17        super( "Panel Demo" );
18        buttons = new JButton[ 5 ]; // create buttons array
19        buttonJPanel = new JPanel(); // set up panel
20        buttonJPanel.setLayout( new GridLayout( 1, buttons.length ) );
21
22        // create and add buttons
23        for ( int count = 0; count < buttons.length; count++ )
24        {
25           buttons[ count ] = new JButton( "Button " + ( count + 1 ) );
26           buttonJPanel.add( buttons[ count ] ); // add button to panel
27        } // end for
28
29        add( buttonJPanel, BorderLayout.SOUTH ); // add panel to JFrame
30     } // end PanelFrame constructor
31  } // end class PanelFrame
```

Fig. 14.45 | JPanel with five JButtons in a GridLayout attached to the SOUTH region of a BorderLayout. (Part 2 of 2.)

```
1   // Fig. 14.46: PanelDemo.java
2   // Testing PanelFrame.
3   import javax.swing.JFrame;
4
5   public class PanelDemo extends JFrame
6   {
7      public static void main( String[] args )
8      {
9         PanelFrame panelFrame = new PanelFrame();
10        panelFrame.setDefaultCloseOperation( JFrame.EXIT_ON_CLOSE );
11        panelFrame.setSize( 450, 200 ); // set frame size
12        panelFrame.setVisible( true ); // display frame
13     } // end main
14  } // end class PanelDemo
```

Fig. 14.46 | Test class for PanelFrame.

14.20 JTextArea

A **JTextArea** provides an area for manipulating multiple lines of text. Like class JText-Field, JTextArea is a subclass of JTextComponent, which declares common methods for JTextFields, JTextAreas and several other text-based GUI components.

The application in Figs. 14.47–14.48 demonstrates JTextAreas. One JTextArea displays text that the user can select. The other is uneditable and is used to display the text the user selected in the first JTextArea. Unlike JTextFields, JTextAreas do not have action events—when you press *Enter* while typing in a JTextArea, the cursor simply moves to the next line. As with multiple-selection JLists (Section 14.13), an external event from another GUI component indicates when to process the text in a JTextArea. For example, when typing an e-mail message, you normally click a **Send** button to send the text of the message to the recipient. Similarly, when editing a document in a word processor, you normally save the file by selecting a **Save** or **Save As...** menu item. In this program, the button **Copy >>>** generates the external event that copies the selected text in the left JTextArea and displays it in the right JTextArea.

```java
 1   // Fig. 14.47: TextAreaFrame.java
 2   // Copying selected text from one textarea to another.
 3   import java.awt.event.ActionListener;
 4   import java.awt.event.ActionEvent;
 5   import javax.swing.Box;
 6   import javax.swing.JFrame;
 7   import javax.swing.JTextArea;
 8   import javax.swing.JButton;
 9   import javax.swing.JScrollPane;
10
11   public class TextAreaFrame extends JFrame
12   {
13      private JTextArea textArea1; // displays demo string
14      private JTextArea textArea2; // highlighted text is copied here
15      private JButton copyJButton; // initiates copying of text
16
17      // no-argument constructor
18      public TextAreaFrame()
19      {
20         super( "TextArea Demo" );
21         Box box = Box.createHorizontalBox(); // create box
22         String demo = "This is a demo string to\n" +
23            "illustrate copying text\nfrom one textarea to \n" +
24            "another textarea using an\nexternal event\n";
25
26         textArea1 = new JTextArea( demo, 10, 15 ); // create textarea1
27         box.add( new JScrollPane( textArea1 ) ); // add scrollpane
28
29         copyJButton = new JButton( "Copy >>>" ); // create copy button
30         box.add( copyJButton ); // add copy button to box
31         copyJButton.addActionListener(
32
33            new ActionListener() // anonymous inner class
34            {
```

Fig. 14.47 | Copying selected text from one JTextArea to another. (Part 1 of 2.)

```
35            // set text in textArea2 to selected text from textArea1
36            public void actionPerformed( ActionEvent event )
37            {
38               textArea2.setText( textArea1.getSelectedText() );
39            } // end method actionPerformed
40         } // end anonymous inner class
41      ); // end call to addActionListener
42
43      textArea2 = new JTextArea( 10, 15 ); // create second textarea
44      textArea2.setEditable( false ); // disable editing
45      box.add( new JScrollPane( textArea2 ) ); // add scrollpane
46
47      add( box ); // add box to frame
48   } // end TextAreaFrame constructor
49 } // end class TextAreaFrame
```

Fig. 14.47 | Copying selected text from one JTextArea to another. (Part 2 of 2.)

```
1  // Fig. 14.48: TextAreaDemo.java
2  // Copying selected text from one textarea to another.
3  import javax.swing.JFrame;
4
5  public class TextAreaDemo
6  {
7     public static void main( String[] args )
8     {
9        TextAreaFrame textAreaFrame = new TextAreaFrame();
10       textAreaFrame.setDefaultCloseOperation( JFrame.EXIT_ON_CLOSE );
11       textAreaFrame.setSize( 425, 200 ); // set frame size
12       textAreaFrame.setVisible( true ); // display frame
13    } // end main
14 } // end class TextAreaDemo
```

Fig. 14.48 | Test class for TextAreaFrame.

In the constructor (lines 18–48), line 21 creates a **Box** container (package javax.swing) to organize the GUI components. Box is a subclass of Container that uses a **BoxLayout** layout manager (discussed in detail in Section 25.9) to arrange the GUI components either horizontally or vertically. Box's static method **createHorizontalBox** creates a Box that arranges components from left to right in the order that they are attached.

Lines 26 and 43 create JTextAreas textArea1 and textArea2. Line 26 uses JText-Area's three-argument constructor, which takes a String representing the initial text and two ints specifying that the JTextArea has 10 rows and 15 columns. Line 43 uses JText-Area's two-argument constructor, specifying that the JTextArea has 10 rows and 15 columns. Line 26 specifies that demo should be displayed as the default JTextArea content. A JTextArea does not provide scrollbars if it cannot display its complete contents. So, line 27 creates a JScrollPane object, initializes it with textArea1 and attaches it to container box. By default, horizontal and vertical scrollbars appear as necessary in a JScrollPane.

Lines 29–41 create JButton object copyJButton with the label "Copy >>>", add copy-JButton to container box and register the event handler for copyJButton's ActionEvent. This button provides the external event that determines when the program should copy the selected text in textArea1 to textArea2. When the user clicks copyJButton, line 38 in actionPerformed indicates that method **getSelectedText** (inherited into JTextArea from JTextComponent) should return the selected text from textArea1. The user selects text by dragging the mouse over the desired text to highlight it. Method setText changes the text in textArea2 to the string returned by getSelectedText.

Lines 43–45 create textArea2, set its editable property to false and add it to container box. Line 47 adds box to the JFrame. Recall from Section 14.18 that the default layout of a JFrame is a BorderLayout and that the add method by default attaches its argument to the CENTER of the BorderLayout.

When text reaches the right edge of a JTextArea the text can wrap to the next line. This is referred to as **line wrapping**. By default, JTextArea does not wrap lines.

Look-and-Feel Observation 14.19

*To provide line wrapping functionality for a JTextArea, invoke JTextArea method **set-LineWrap** with a true argument.*

JScrollPane Scrollbar Policies

This example uses a JScrollPane to provide scrolling for a JTextArea. By default, JScrollPane displays scrollbars only if they are required. You can set the horizontal and vertical **scrollbar policies** of a JScrollPane when it's constructed. If a program has a reference to a JScrollPane, the program can use JScrollPane methods **setHorizontal-ScrollBarPolicy** and **setVerticalScrollBarPolicy** to change the scrollbar policies at any time. Class JScrollPane declares the constants

```
JScrollPane.VERTICAL_SCROLLBAR_ALWAYS
JScrollPane.HORIZONTAL_SCROLLBAR_ALWAYS
```

to indicate that a scrollbar should always appear, constants

```
JScrollPane.VERTICAL_SCROLLBAR_AS_NEEDED
JScrollPane.HORIZONTAL_SCROLLBAR_AS_NEEDED
```

to indicate that a scrollbar should appear only if necessary (the defaults) and constants

```
JScrollPane.VERTICAL_SCROLLBAR_NEVER
JScrollPane.HORIZONTAL_SCROLLBAR_NEVER
```

to indicate that a scrollbar should never appear. If the horizontal scrollbar policy is set to JScrollPane.HORIZONTAL_SCROLLBAR_NEVER, a JTextArea attached to the JScrollPane will automatically wrap lines.

14.21 Wrap-Up

In this chapter, you learned many GUI components and how to implement event handling. You also learned about nested classes, inner classes and anonymous inner classes.

You saw the special relationship between an inner-class object and an object of its top-level class. You learned how to use JOptionPane dialogs to obtain text input from the user and how to display messages to the user. You also learned how to create applications that execute in their own windows. We discussed class JFrame and components that enable a user to interact with an application. We also showed you how to display text and images to the user. You learned how to customize JPanels to create custom drawing areas, which you'll use extensively in the next chapter. You saw how to organize components on a window using layout managers and how to creating more complex GUIs by using JPanels to organize components. Finally, you learned about the JTextArea component in which a user can enter text and an application can display text. In Chapter 25, you'll learn about more advanced GUI components, such as sliders, menus and more complex layout managers. In the next chapter, you'll learn how to add graphics to your GUI application. Graphics allow you to draw shapes and text with colors and styles.

Summary

Section 14.1 Introduction
- A graphical user interface (GUI) presents a user-friendly mechanism for interacting with an application. A GUI gives an application a distinctive "look" and "feel."
- Providing different applications with consistent, intuitive user-interface components gives users a sense of familarity with a new application, so that they can learn it more quickly.
- GUIs are built from GUI components—sometimes called controls or widgets.

Section 14.2 Java's New Nimbus Look-and-Feel
- As of Java SE 6 update 10, Java comes bundled with a new, elegant, cross-platform look-and-feel known as Nimbus.
- To set Nimbus as the default for all Java applications, you must create a swing.properties text file in the lib folder of both your JDK installation folder and your JRE installation folder. Place the following line of code in the file:

      swing.defaultlaf=com.sun.java.swing.plaf.nimbus.NimbusLookAndFeel

- To select Nimbus on an application-by-application basis, place the following command-line argument after the java command and before the application's name when you run the application:

      -Dswing.defaultlaf=com.sun.java.swing.plaf.nimbus.NimbusLookAndFeel

Section 14.3 Simple GUI-Based Input/Output with **JOptionPane**
- Most applications use windows or dialog boxes (also called dialogs) to interact with the user.
- Class JOptionPane (package javax.swing) provides prebuilt dialog boxes for both input and output. JOptionPane static method showInputDialog displays an input dialog.
- A prompt typically uses sentence-style capitalization—capitalizing only the first letter of the first word in the text unless the word is a proper noun.
- An input dialog can input only input Strings. This is typical of most GUI components.
- JOptionPane static method showMessageDialog displays a message dialog.

Section 14.4 Overview of Swing Components
- Most Swing GUI components are located in package javax.swing.

- Together, the appearance and the way in which the user interacts with the application are known as that application's look-and-feel. Swing GUI components allow you to specify a uniform look-and-feel for your application across all platforms or to use each platform's custom look-and-feel.

- Lightweight Swing components are not tied to actual GUI components supported by the underlying platform on which an application executes.

- Several Swing components are heavyweight components that require direct interaction with the local windowing system, which may restrict their appearance and functionality.

- Class Component (package java.awt) declares many of the attributes and behaviors common to the GUI components in packages java.awt and javax.swing.

- Class Container (package java.awt) is a subclass of Component. Components are attached to Containers so the Components can be organized and displayed on the screen.

- Class JComponent (package javax.swing) is a subclass of Container. JComponent is the superclass of all lightweight Swing components and declares their common attributes and behaviors.

- Some common JComponent features include a pluggable look-and-feel, shortcut keys called mnemonics, tool tips, support for assistive technologies and support for user-interface localization.

Section 14.5 Displaying Text and Images in a Window

- Class JFrame provides the basic attributes and behaviors of a window.

- A JLabel displays read-only text, an image, or both text and an image. Text in a JLabel normally uses sentence-style capitalization.

- Each GUI component must be attached to a container, such as a window created with a JFrame.

- Many IDEs provide GUI design tools in which you can specify the exact size and location of a component by using the mouse; then the IDE will generate the GUI code for you.

- JComponent method setToolTipText specifies the tool tip that is displayed when the user positions the mouse cursor over a lightweight component.

- Container method add attaches a GUI component to a Container.

- Class ImageIcon supports several image formats, including GIF, PNG and JPEG.

- Method getClass (of class Object) retrieves a reference to the Class object that represents the the class declaration for the object on which the method is called.

- Class method getResource returns the location of its argument as a URL. Method getResource uses the Class object's class loader to determine the location of the resource.

- Interface SwingConstants (package javax.swing) declares common integer constants that are used with many Swing components.

- The horizontal and vertical alignments of a JLabel can be set with methods setHorizontalAlignment and setVerticalAlignment, respectively.

- JLabel method setText sets the text displayed on a label. The corresponding method getText retrieves the current text displayed on a label.

- JLabel method setIcon specifies the Icon to display on a label. The corresponding method getIcon retrieves the current Icon displayed on a label.

- JLabel methods setHorizontalTextPosition and setVerticalTextPosition specify the text position in the label.

- JFrame method setDefaultCloseOperation with constant JFrame.EXIT_ON_CLOSE as the argument indicates that the program should terminate when the window is closed by the user.

- Component method setSize specifies the width and height of a component.

- Component method setVisible with the argument true displays a JFrame on the screen.

Section 14.6 Text Fields and an Introduction to Event Handling with Nested Classes
- GUIs are event driven—when the user interacts with a GUI component, events drive the program to perform tasks.
- The code that performs a task in response to an event is called an event handler and the overall process of responding to events is known as event handling.
- Class `JTextField` extends class `JTextComponent` (package `javax.swing.text`), which provides common text-based component features. Class `JPasswordField` extends `JTextField` and adds several methods that are specific to processing passwords.
- A `JPasswordField` shows that characters are being typed as the user enters them, but hides the actual characters with echo characters.
- A component receives the focus when the user clicks the component.
- `JTextComponent` method `setEditable` can be used to make a text field uneditable.
- To respond to an event for a particular GUI component, you must: 1) Create a class that represents the event handler. 2) Implement an appropriate event-listener interface in the class from *Step 1*. 3) Indicate that an object of the class from *Steps 1* and *2* should be notified when the event occurs. This is known as registering the event handler.
- Nested classes can be `static` or `non-static`. Non-`static` nested classes are called inner classes and are frequently used for event handling.
- An object of a non-`static` inner class must be created by an object of the top-level class that contains the inner class.
- An inner-class object can directly access the instance variables and methods of its top-level class.
- A nested class that is `static` does not require an object of its top-level class and does not implicitly have a reference to an object of the top-level class.
- Pressing *Enter* in a `JTextField` or `JPasswordField` generates an `ActionEvent` (from package `java.awt.event`) that can be handled by an `ActionListener` (package `java.awt.event`).
- `JTextField` method `addActionListener` registers the event handler for that `ActionEvent` of a text field. This method receives as its argument an `ActionListener` object.
- The GUI component with which the user interacts is the event source.
- An `ActionEvent` object contains information about the event that just occurred, such as the event source and the text in the text field.
- `ActionEvent` method `getSource` returns a reference to the event source. `ActionEvent` method `getActionCommand` returns the text the user typed in a text field or the label on a `JButton`.
- `JPasswordField` method `getPassword` returns the password the user typed.

Section 14.7 Common GUI Event Types and Listener Interfaces
- Each event-object type typically has a corresponding event-listener interface that specifies one or more event-handling methods which must be declared in the class that implements the interface.

Section 14.8 How Event Handling Works
- When an event occurs, the GUI component with which the user interacted notifies its registered listeners by calling each listener's appropriate event-handling method.
- Every `JComponent` has an `EventListenerList` (package `javax.swing.event`) in which references to registered listeners are stored.
- Every GUI component supports several event types. When an event occurs, the event is dispatched only to the event listeners of the appropriate type. The GUI component receives a unique event ID specifying the event type, which it uses to decide the listener type to which the event should be dispatched and which method to call on each listener object.

Section 14.9 *JButton*

- A button is a component the user clicks to trigger an action. All the button types are subclasses of AbstractButton (package javax.swing). Button labels typically use book-title capitalization.

- Command buttons are created with class JButton.

- A JButton can display an Icon. A JButton can also have a rollover Icon—an Icon that is displayed when the user positions the mouse over the button.

- Method setRolloverIcon (of class AbstractButton) specifies the image displayed on a button when the user positions the mouse over it.

Section 14.10 Buttons That Maintain State

- There are three Swing state button types—JToggleButton, JCheckBox and JRadioButton.

- Classes JCheckBox and JRadioButton are subclasses of JToggleButton.

- Component method setFont sets the component's font to a new Font object (package java.awt).

- Clicking a JCheckBox causes an ItemEvent that can be handled by an ItemListener object (which must implement method itemStateChanged). Method addItemListener registers the listener for the ItemEvent of a JCheckBox or JRadioButton object.

- JCheckBox method isSelected determines whether a JCheckBox is selected.

- JRadioButtons are similar to JCheckBoxes in that they have two states—selected and not selected. However, radio buttons normally appear as a group in which only one button can be selected at a time. Selecting a different radio button forces all others to be deselected.

- JRadioButtons are used to represent mutually exclusive options.

- The logical relationship between JRadioButtons is maintained by a ButtonGroup object.

- ButtonGroup method add associates each JRadioButton with a ButtonGroup. If more than one selected JRadioButton object is added to a group, the selected one that was added first will be selected when the GUI is displayed.

- JRadioButtons generate ItemEvents when they are clicked.

Section 14.11 *JComboBox* and Using an Anonymous Inner Class for Event Handling

- A JComboBox provides a list of items from which the user can make a single selection. JComboBoxes generate ItemEvents.

- Each item in a JComboBox has an index. The first item added to a JComboBox appears as the currently selected item when the JComboBox is displayed. Other items are selected by clicking the JComboBox, which expands into a list from which the user can make a selection.

- JComboBox method setMaximumRowCount sets the maximum number of elements that are displayed when the user clicks the JComboBox. If there are more items, the JComboBox provides a scrollbar that allows the user to scroll through all the elements in the list.

- An anonymous inner class is a special form of inner class that is declared without a name and typically appears inside a method declaration. Since an anonymous inner class has no name, one object of the anonymous inner class must be created at the point where the class is declared.

- JComboBox method getSelectedIndex returns the index of the selected item.

Section 14.12 *JList*

- A JList displays a series of items from which the user may select one or more items. Class JList supports single-selection lists and multiple-selection lists.

- When the user clicks an item in a JList, a ListSelectionEvent occurs. JList method addListSelectionListener registers a ListSelectionListener for a JList's selection events. A ListSelectionListener (package javax.swing.event) must implement method valueChanged.

- JList method `setVisibleRowCount` specifies the number of items that are visible in the list.

- JList method `setSelectionMode` specifies a list's selection mode.

- A JList does not provide a scrollbar if there are more items in the list than the number of visible rows. In this case, a JScrollPane object can be used to provide the scrolling capability.

- JFrame method `getContentPane` returns a reference to the JFrame's content pane where GUI components are displayed.

- JList method `getSelectedIndex` returns the selected item's index.

Section 14.13 Multiple-Selection Lists
- A multiple-selection list enables the user to select many items from a JList.

- JList method `setFixedCellWidth` sets a JList's width. Method `setFixedCellHeight` sets the height of each item in a JList.

- There are no events to indicate that a user has made multiple selections in a multiple-selection list. Normally, an external event generated by another GUI component (such as a JButton) specifies when the multiple selections in a JList should be processed.

- JList method `setListData` sets the items displayed in a JList. JList method `getSelectedValues` returns an array of Objects representing the selected items in a JList.

Section 14.14 Mouse Event Handling
- The `MouseListener` and `MouseMotionListener` event-listener interfaces are used to handle mouse events. Mouse events can be trapped for any GUI component that extends Component.

- Interface `MouseInputListener` (package `javax.swing.event`) extends interfaces `MouseListener` and `MouseMotionListener` to create a single interface containing all their methods.

- Each mouse event-handling method receives a `MouseEvent` object that contains information about the event, including the x- and y-coordinates where the event occurred. Coordinates are measured from the upper-left corner of the GUI component on which the event occurred.

- The methods and constants of class `InputEvent` (MouseEvent's superclass) enable an application to determine which mouse button the user clicked.

- Interface `MouseWheelListener` enables applications to respond to the rotation of a mouse wheel.

Section 14.15 Adapter Classes
- Many event-listener interfaces contain multiple methods. For many of these interfaces, packages `java.awt.event` and `javax.swing.event` provide event-listener adapter classes. An adapter class implements an interface and provides default implementations of its methods. Extend an adapter class to inherit the default method implementations then override the method(s) you need.

- MouseEvent method `getClickCount` returns the number of consecutive mouse-button clicks. Methods `isMetaDown` and `isAltDown` determine which mouse button the user clicked.

Section 14.16 JPanel Subclass for Drawing with the Mouse
- Lightweight Swing components that extend class JComponent contain method `paintComponent`, which is called when a lightweight Swing component is displayed. By overriding this method, you can specify how to draw shapes using Java's graphics capabilities.

- When customizing a JPanel for drawing, the subclass should override method `paintComponent` and call the superclass version as the first statement in the body of the overridden method.

- Subclasses of JComponent support transparency. When a component is opaque, `paintComponent` clears the component's background before the component is displayed.

- The transparency of a Swing lightweight component can be set with method `setOpaque` (a `false` argument indicates that the component is transparent).

- Class Point (package java.awt) represents an *x-y* coordinate.
- Class Graphics is used to draw.
- MouseEvent method getPoint obtains the Point where a mouse event occurred.
- Method repaint (inherited indirectly from class Component) indicates that a component should be refreshed on the screen as soon as possible.
- Method paintComponent receives a Graphics parameter and is called automatically any time a lightweight component needs to be displayed on the screen.
- Graphics method fillOval draws a solid oval. The first two arguments are the upper-left *x*-coordinate and the upper-left *y*-coordinate of the bounding box. The last two arguments represent the bounding box's width and height.

Section 14.17 Key Event Handling
- Interface KeyListener is used to handle key events that are generated when keys on the keyboard are pressed and released. Method addKeyListener of class Component registers a KeyListener.
- KeyEvent method getKeyCode gets the virtual key code of the key that was pressed. Class KeyEvent maintains a set of virtual key-code constants that represent every key on the keyboard.
- KeyEvent method getKeyText returns a string containing the name of the key that was pressed.
- KeyEvent method getKeyChar gets the Unicode value of the character typed.
- KeyEvent method isActionKey determines whether the key in an event was an action key.
- InputEvent method getModifiers determines whether any modifier keys (such as *Shift*, *Alt* and *Ctrl*) were pressed when the key event occurred.
- KeyEvent method getKeyModifiersText produces a string containing the names of the pressed modifier keys.

Section 14.18 Introduction to Layout Managers
- Layout managers arrange GUI components in a container for presentation purposes.
- All layout managers implement the interface LayoutManager (package java.awt).
- Container method setLayout specifies the layout of a container.
- FlowLayout places components left to right in the order in which they are added to the container. When the edge of the container is reached, components continue to display on the next line. FlowLayout allows GUI components to be left aligned, centered (the default) and right aligned.
- FlowLayout method setAlignment changes the alignment for a FlowLayout.
- BorderLayout (the default for a JFrame) arranges components into five regions: NORTH, SOUTH, EAST, WEST and CENTER. NORTH corresponds to the top of the container.
- A BorderLayout limits a Container to containing at most five components—one in each region.
- GridLayout divides a container into a grid of rows and columns.
- Container method validate recomputes a container's layout based on the current layout manager for the Container and the current set of displayed GUI components.

Section 14.19 Using Panels to Manage More Complex Layouts
- Complex GUIs often consist of multiple panels, with each panel's components arranged in a specific layout. Every JPanel may have components, including other panels, attached to it with Container method add.

Section 14.20 JTextArea
- A JTextArea provides an area for manipulating multiple lines of text. JTextArea is a subclass of JTextComponent.

- Class Box is a subclass of Container that uses a BoxLayout layout manager to arrange the GUI components either horizontally or vertically.
- Box static method createHorizontalBox creates a Box that arranges components from left to right in the order that they are attached.
- Method getSelectedText returns the selected text from a JTextArea.
- You can set the horizontal and vertical scrollbar policies of a JScrollPane when it's constructed. JScrollPane methods setHorizontalScrollBarPolicy, and setVerticalScrollBarPolicy can be used to change the scrollbar policies at any time.

Terminology

Self-Review Exercises

14.1 Fill in the blanks in each of the following statements:

a) Method _____ is called when the mouse is moved with no buttons pressed and an event listener is registered to handle the event.

b) Text that cannot be modified by the user is called _____ text.

c) A(n) _____ arranges GUI components in a Container.

d) The add method for attaching GUI components is a method of class _____.

e) GUI is an acronym for _____.

f) Method _____ is used to specify the layout manager for a container.

g) A mouseDragged method call is preceded by a(n) _____ method call and followed by a(n) _____ method call.

h) Class _____ contains methods that display message dialogs and input dialogs.

i) An input dialog capable of receiving input from the user is displayed with method _____ of class _____.

j) A dialog capable of displaying a message to the user is displayed with method _____ of class _____.

k) Both `JTextFields` and `JTextAreas` directly extend class _____.

14.2   Determine whether each statement is *true* or *false*. If *false*, explain why.

a) `BorderLayout` is the default layout manager for a `JFrame`'s content pane.

b) When the mouse cursor is moved into the bounds of a GUI component, method `mouseOver` is called.

c) A `JPanel` cannot be added to another `JPanel`.

d) In a `BorderLayout`, two buttons added to the `NORTH` region will be placed side by side.

e) A maximum of five components can be added to a `BorderLayout`.

f) Inner classes are not allowed to access the members of the enclosing class.

g) A `JTextArea`'s text is always read-only.

h) Class `JTextArea` is a direct subclass of class `Component`.

14.3   Find the error(s) in each of the following statements, and explain how to correct it (them):

a) `buttonName = JButton( "Caption" );`

b) `JLabel aLabel, JLabel;    // create references`

c) `txtField = new JTextField( 50, "Default Text" );`

d) ```
setLayout(new BorderLayout());
button1 = new JButton("North Star");
button2 = new JButton("South Pole");
add(button1);
add(button2);
```

## Answers to Self-Review Exercises

**14.1**   a) mouseMoved. b) uneditable (read-only). c) layout manager. d) `Container`. e) graphical user interface. f) setLayout. g) mousePressed, mouseReleased. h) JOptionPane. i) showInputDialog, JOptionPane. j) showMessageDialog, JOptionPane. k) JTextComponent.

**14.2**   a) True.

b)  False. Method `mouseEntered` is called.

c)  False. A `JPanel` can be added to another `JPanel`, because `JPanel` is an indirect subclass of `Component`. So, a `JPanel` is a `Component`. Any `Component` can be added to a `Container`.

d)  False. Only the last button added will be displayed. Remember that only one component should be added to each region in a `BorderLayout`.

e)  True. [*Note:* Panels containing multiple components can be added to each region.]

f)  False. Inner classes have access to all members of the enclosing class declaration.

g)  False. `JTextAreas` are editable by default.

h)  False. `JTextArea` derives from class `JTextComponent`.

**14.3**   a) `new` is needed to create an object.

b)  `JLabel` is a class name and cannot be used as a variable name.

c)  The arguments passed to the constructor are reversed. The `String` must be passed first.

d)  `BorderLayout` has been set, and components are being added without specifying the region, so both are added to the center region. Proper `add` statements might be

```
add( button1, BorderLayout.NORTH );
add( button2, BorderLayout.SOUTH );
```

Exercises

14.4   Determine whether each statement is *true* or *false*. If *false*, explain why.

a) Only one layout manager can be used per `Container`.

b) GUI components can be added to a `Container` in any order in a `BorderLayout`.
```

   c) JRadioButtons provide a series of mutually exclusive options (i.e., only one can be true at a time).

   d) Graphics method setFont is used to set the font for text fields.

   e) A JList displays a scrollbar if there are more items in the list than can be displayed.

   f) A Mouse object has a method called mouseDragged.

14.5 Find any errors in each of the following lines of code, and explain how to correct them.

   a) `import javax.swing.JFrame`

   b) `panelObject.GridLayout( 8, 8 ); // set GridLayout`

   c) `container.setLayout( new FlowLayout( FlowLayout.DEFAULT ) );`

   d) `container.add( eastButton, EAST );  // BorderLayout`

14.6 Create the following GUI. You do not have to provide any functionality.

14.7 Create the following GUI. You do not have to provide any functionality.

14.8 *(Temperature Conversion)* Write a temperature-conversion application that converts from Fahrenheit to Celsius. The Fahrenheit temperature should be entered from the keyboard (via a JTextField). A JLabel should be used to display the converted temperature. Use the following formula for the conversion:

$$Celsius = \frac{5}{9} \times (\ Fahrenheit - 32 \ )$$

14.9 *(Temperature Conversion Modification)* Enhance the temperature-conversion application of Exercise 14.8 by adding the Kelvin temperature scale. The application should also allow the user to make conversions between any two scales. Use the following formula for the conversion between Kelvin and Celsius (in addition to the formula in Exercise 14.8):

$$Kelvin = Celsius + 273.15$$

14.10 *(Displaying Events)* It's often useful to display the events that occur during the execution of an application. This can help you understand when the events occur and how they are generated. Write an application that enables the user to generate and process every event discussed in this chapter. The application should provide methods from the ActionListener, ItemListener, ListSelectionListener, MouseListener, MouseMotionListener and KeyListener interfaces to display messages when the events occur. Use method toString to convert the event objects received in each event handler into Strings that can be displayed. Method toString creates a String containing all the information in the event object.

(Optional) GUI and Graphics Case Study Exercise: Expanding the Interface

14.11 *(Interactive Drawing Application)* In this exercise, you'll implement a GUI application that uses the MyShape hierarchy from the GUI case study Exercise 10.2 to create an interactive drawing application. You'll create two classes for the GUI and provide a test class that launches the application. The classes of the MyShape hierarchy require no additional changes.

The first class to create is a subclass of JPanel called DrawPanel, which represents the area on which the user draws the shapes. Class DrawPanel should have the following instance variables:

- a) An array shapes of type MyShape that will store all the shapes the user draws.
- b) An integer shapeCount that counts the number of shapes in the array.
- c) An integer shapeType that determines the type of shape to draw.
- d) A MyShape currentShape that represents the current shape the user is drawing.
- e) A Color currentColor that represents the current drawing color.
- f) A boolean filledShape that determines whether to draw a filled shape.
- g) A JLabel statusLabel that represents the status bar. The status bar will display the coordinates of the current mouse position.

Class DrawPanel should also declare the following methods:

- a) Overridden method paintComponent that draws the shapes in the array. Use instance variable shapeCount to determine how many shapes to draw. Method paintComponent should also call currentShape's draw method, provided that currentShape is not null.
- b) Set methods for the shapeType, currentColor and filledShape.
- c) Method clearLastShape should clear the last shape drawn by decrementing instance variable shapeCount. Ensure that shapeCount is never less than zero.
- d) Method clearDrawing should remove all the shapes in the current drawing by setting shapeCount to zero.

Methods clearLastShape and clearDrawing should call method repaint (inherited from JPanel) to refresh the drawing on the DrawPanel by indicating that the system should call method paintComponent.

Class DrawPanel should also provide event handling to enable the user to draw with the mouse. Create a single inner class that both extends MouseAdapter and implements MouseMotionListener to handle all mouse events in one class.

In the inner class, override method mousePressed so that it assigns currentShape a new shape of the type specified by shapeType and initializes both points to the mouse position. Next, override method mouseReleased to finish drawing the current shape and place it in the array. Set the second point of currentShape to the current mouse position and add currentShape to the array. Instance variable shapeCount determines the insertion index. Set currentShape to null and call method repaint to update the drawing with the new shape.

Override method mouseMoved to set the text of the statusLabel so that it displays the mouse coordinates—this will update the label with the coordinates every time the user moves (but does not drag) the mouse within the DrawPanel. Next, override method mouseDragged so that it sets the second point of the currentShape to the current mouse position and calls method repaint. This will allow the user to see the shape while dragging the mouse. Also, update the JLabel in mouseDragged with the current position of the mouse.

Create a constructor for DrawPanel that has a single JLabel parameter. In the constructor, initialize statusLabel with the value passed to the parameter. Also initialize array shapes with 100 entries, shapeCount to 0, shapeType to the value that represents a line, currentShape to null and currentColor to Color.BLACK. The constructor should then set the background color of the DrawPanel to Color.WHITE and register the MouseListener and MouseMotionListener so the JPanel properly handles mouse events.

Next, create a JFrame subclass called DrawFrame that provides a GUI that enables the user to control various aspects of drawing. For the layout of the DrawFrame, we recommend a BorderLayout, with the components in the NORTH region, the main drawing panel in the CENTER region, and a status bar in the SOUTH region, as in Fig. 14.49. In the top panel, create the components listed below. Each component's event handler should call the appropriate method in class DrawPanel.

a) A button to undo the last shape drawn.

b) A button to clear all shapes from the drawing.

c) A combo box for selecting the color from the 13 predefined colors.

d) A combo box for selecting the shape to draw.

e) A checkbox that specifies whether a shape should be filled or unfilled.

Declare and create the interface components in `DrawFrame`'s constructor. You'll need to create the status bar `JLabel` before you create the `DrawPanel`, so you can pass the `JLabel` as an argument to `DrawPanel`'s constructor. Finally, create a test class that initializes and displays the `DrawFrame` to execute the application.

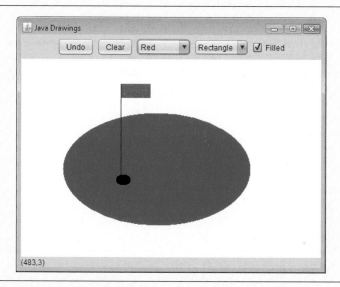

Fig. 14.49 | Interface for drawing shapes.

14.12 *(GUI-Based Version of the ATM Case Study)* Reimplement the ATM Case Study of Chapters 12–13 as a GUI-based application. Use GUI components to approximate the ATM user interface shown in Fig. 12.1. For the cash dispenser and the deposit slot use `JButtons` labeled **Remove Cash** and **Insert Envelope**. This will enable the application to receive events indicating when the user takes the cash and inserts a deposit envelope, respectively.

Making a Difference

14.13 *(Ecofont)* Ecofont (www.ecofont.eu/ecofont_en.html)—developed by SPRANQ (a Netherlands-based company)—is a free, open-source computer font designed to reduce by as much as 20% the amount of ink used for printing, thus reducing also the number of ink cartridges used and the environmental impact of the manufacturing and shipping processes (using less energy, less fuel for shipping, and so on). The font, based on sans-serif Verdana, has small circular "holes" in the letters that are not visible in smaller sizes—such as the 9- or 10-point type frequently used. Download Ecofont, then install the font file `Spranq_eco_sans_regular.ttf` using the instructions from the Ecofont website. Next, develop a GUI-based program that allows you to type in a text string to be displayed in the Ecofont. Create **Increase Font Size** and **Decrease Font Size** buttons that allow you to scale up or down by one point at a time. Start with a default font size of 9 points. As you scale up, you'll be able to see the holes in the letters more clearly. As you scale down, the holes will be less apparent. What is the smallest font size at which you begin to notice the holes?

14.14 *(Typing Tutor: Tuning a Crucial Skill in the Computer Age)* Typing quickly and correctly is an essential skill for working effectively with computers and the Internet. In this exercise, you'll build a GUI application that can help users learn to "touch type" (i.e., type correctly without looking at the keyboard). The application should display a *virtual keyboard* (Fig. 14.50) and should allow the user to watch what he or she is typing on the screen without looking at the *actual keyboard*. Use JButtons to represent the keys. As the user presses each key, the application highlights the corresponding JButton on the GUI and adds the character to a JTextArea that shows what the user has typed so far. [*Hint:* To highlight a JButton, use its setBackground method to change its background color. When the key is released, reset its original background color. You can obtain the JButton's original background color with the getBackground method before you change its color.]

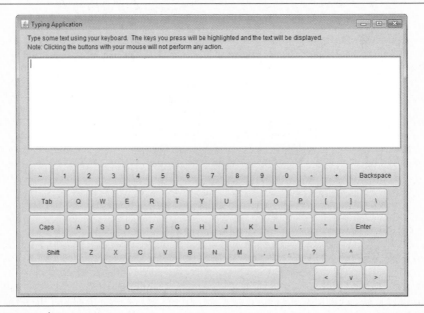

Fig. 14.50 | Typing tutor.

You can test your program by typing a pangram—a phrase that contains every letter of the alphabet at least once—such as "The quick brown fox jumped over a lazy dog." You can find other pangrams on the web.

To make the program more interesting you could monitor the user's accuracy. You could have the user type specific phrases that you've prestored in your program and that you display on the screen above the virtual keyboard. You could keep track of how many keystrokes the user types correctly and how many are typed incorrectly. You could also keep track of which keys the user is having difficulty with and display a report showing those keys.

One picture is worth ten thousand words.
—Chinese proverb

Treat nature in terms of the cylinder, the sphere, the cone, all in perspective.
—Paul Cézanne

Colors, like features, follow the changes of the emotions.
—Pablo Picasso

Nothing ever becomes real till it is experienced—even a proverb is no proverb to you till your life has illustrated it.
—John Keats

15

Graphics and Java 2D™

Objectives

In this chapter you'll learn:

- To understand graphics contexts and graphics objects.
- To manipulate colors.
- To manipulate fonts.
- To use methods of class `Graphics` to draw lines, rectangles, rectangles with rounded corners, three-dimensional rectangles, ovals, arcs and polygons.
- To use methods of class `Graphics2D` from the `Java 2D` API to draw lines, rectangles, rectangles with rounded corners, ellipses, arcs and general paths.
- To specify `Paint` and `Stroke` characteristics of shapes displayed with `Graphics2D`.

15.1 Introduction

In this chapter, we overview several of Java's capabilities for drawing two-dimensional shapes, controlling colors and controlling fonts. One of Java's initial appeals was its support for graphics that enabled programmers to visually enhance their applications. Java now contains many more sophisticated drawing capabilities as part of the Java 2D™ API. This chapter begins with an introduction to many of Java's original drawing capabilities. Next we present several of the more powerful Java 2D capabilities, such as controlling the style of lines used to draw shapes and the way shapes are filled with color and patterns.

Figure 15.1 shows a portion of the Java class hierarchy that includes several of the basic graphics classes and Java 2D API classes and interfaces covered in this chapter. Class **Color** contains methods and constants for manipulating colors. Class JComponent contains method paintComponent, which is used to draw graphics on a component. Class **Font** contains methods and constants for manipulating fonts. Class **FontMetrics** contains methods for obtaining font information. Class **Graphics** contains methods for drawing strings, lines, rectangles and other shapes. Class **Graphics2D**, which extends class Graphics, is used for drawing with the Java 2D API. Class **Polygon** contains methods for creating polygons. The bottom half of the figure lists several classes and interfaces from the Java 2D API. Class **BasicStroke** helps specify the drawing characteristics of lines. Classes **GradientPaint** and **TexturePaint** help specify the characteristics for filling shapes with colors or patterns. Classes GeneralPath, Line2D, Arc2D, Ellipse2D, Rectangle2D and RoundRectangle2D represent several Java 2D shapes. [*Note:* We begin by discussing Java's original graphics capabilities, then move on to the Java 2D API. The classes that were part of Java's original graphics capabilities are now considered to be part of the Java 2D API.]

To begin drawing in Java, we must first understand Java's **coordinate system** (Fig. 15.2), which is a scheme for identifying every point on the screen. By default, the upper-left corner of a GUI component (e.g., a window) has the coordinates (0, 0). A coordinate pair is composed of an *x*-coordinate (the **horizontal coordinate**) and a *y*-coordinate (the **vertical coordinate**). The *x*-coordinate is the horizontal distance moving right from the left of the screen. The *y*-coordinate is the vertical distance moving down from the top of the screen. The *x*-**axis** describes every horizontal coordinate, and the *y*-**axis** every vertical coordinate. The coordinates are used to indicate where graphics should be displayed on a screen. Coordinate units are measured in **pixels** (which stands for "picture element"). A pixel is a display monitor's smallest unit of resolution.

Fig. 15.1 | Classes and interfaces used in this chapter from Java's original graphics capabilities and from the Java 2D API.

Portability Tip 15.1

Different display monitors have different resolutions (i.e., the density of the pixels varies). This can cause graphics to appear in different sizes on different monitors or on the same monitor with different settings.

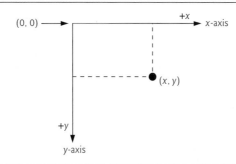

Fig. 15.2 │ Java coordinate system. Units are measured in pixels.

15.2 Graphics Contexts and Graphics Objects

A **graphics context** enables drawing on the screen. A Graphics object manages a graphics context and draws pixels on the screen that represent text and other graphical objects (e.g., lines, ellipses, rectangles and other polygons). Graphics objects contain methods for drawing, font manipulation, color manipulation and the like.

Class Graphics is an abstract class (i.e., Graphics objects cannot be instantiated). This contributes to Java's portability. Because drawing is performed differently on every platform that supports Java, there cannot be only one implementation of the drawing capabilities across all systems. For example, the graphics capabilities that enable a PC running Microsoft Windows to draw a rectangle are different from those that enable a Linux workstation to draw a rectangle—and they are both different from the graphics capabilities that enable a Macintosh to draw a rectangle. When Java is implemented on each platform, a subclass of Graphics is created that implements the drawing capabilities. This implementation is hidden by class Graphics, which supplies the interface that enables us to use graphics in a platform-independent manner.

Recall from Chapter 14 that class Component is the superclass for many of the classes in package java.awt. Class JComponent (package javax.swing), which inherits indirectly from class Component, contains a paintComponent method that can be used to draw graphics. Method paintComponent takes a Graphics object as an argument. This object is passed to the paintComponent method by the system when a lightweight Swing component needs to be repainted. The header for the paintComponent method is

```
public void paintComponent( Graphics g )
```

Parameter g receives a reference to an instance of the system-specific subclass that Graphics extends. The preceding method header should look familiar to you—it's the same one we used in some of the applications in Chapter 14. Actually, class JComponent is a superclass of JPanel. Many capabilities of class JPanel are inherited from class JComponent.

You seldom call method paintComponent directly, because drawing graphics is an event-driven process. As we mentioned in Chapter 11, Java uses a multithreaded model of program execution. Each thread is a parallel activity. Each program can have many threads. When you create a GUI-based application, one of those threads is known as the **event-dispatch thread (EDT)** and it is used to process all GUI events. All drawing and manipulation of GUI components should be performed in that thread. When a GUI application executes, the application container calls method paintComponent (in the event-dispatch thread) for each lightweight component as the GUI is displayed. For paintComponent to be called again, an event must occur (such as covering and uncovering the component with another window).

If you need paintComponent to execute (i.e., if you want to update the graphics drawn on a Swing component), you can call method **repaint**, which is inherited by all JComponents indirectly from class Component (package java.awt). Method repaint is frequently called to request a call to method paintComponent. The header for repaint is

```
public void repaint()
```

15.3 Color Control

Class Color declares methods and constants for manipulating colors in a Java program. The predeclared color constants are summarized in Fig. 15.3, and several color methods and constructors are summarized in Fig. 15.4. Note that two of the methods in Fig. 15.4 are Graphics methods that are specific to colors.

Color constant	RGB value
public final static Color RED	255, 0, 0
public final static Color GREEN	0, 255, 0
public final static Color BLUE	0, 0, 255
public final static Color ORANGE	255, 200, 0
public final static Color PINK	255, 175, 175
public final static Color CYAN	0, 255, 255
public final static Color MAGENTA	255, 0, 255
public final static Color YELLOW	255, 255, 0
public final static Color BLACK	0, 0, 0
public final static Color WHITE	255, 255, 255
public final static Color GRAY	128, 128, 128
public final static Color LIGHT_GRAY	192, 192, 192
public final static Color DARK_GRAY	64, 64, 64

Fig. 15.3 | Color constants and their RGB values.

Method	Description

Color constructors and methods

public Color(int r, int g, int b)

Creates a color based on red, green and blue components expressed as integers from 0 to 255.

public Color(float r, float g, float b)

Creates a color based on red, green and blue components expressed as floating-point values from 0.0 to 1.0.

Fig. 15.4 | Color methods and color-related Graphics methods. (Part 1 of 2.)

Method	Description

`public int getRed()`

Returns a value between 0 and 255 representing the red content.

`public int getGreen()`

Returns a value between 0 and 255 representing the green content.

`public int getBlue()`

Returns a value between 0 and 255 representing the blue content.

Graphics methods for manipulating `Color`s

`public Color getColor()`

Returns `Color` object representing current color for the graphics context.

`public void setColor( Color c )`

Sets the current color for drawing with the graphics context.

Fig. 15.4 | `Color` methods and color-related `Graphics` methods. (Part 2 of 2.)

Every color is created from a red, a green and a blue component. Together these components are called **RGB values**. All three RGB components can be integers in the range from 0 to 255, or they can be floating-point values in the range 0.0 to 1.0. The first RGB component specifies the amount of red, the second the amount of green and the third the amount of blue. The larger the RGB value, the greater the amount of that particular color. Java enables you to choose from $256 \times 256 \times 256$ (approximately 16.7 million) colors. Not all computers are capable of displaying all these colors. The computer will display the closest color it can.

Two of class `Color`'s constructors are shown in Fig. 15.4—one that takes three `int` arguments and one that takes three `float` arguments, with each argument specifying the amount of red, green and blue. The `int` values must be in the range 0–255 and the `float` values must be in the range 0.0–1.0. The new `Color` object will have the specified amounts of red, green and blue. `Color` methods **getRed**, **getGreen** and **getBlue** return integer values from 0 to 255 representing the amounts of red, green and blue, respectively. `Graphics` method **getColor** returns a `Color` object representing the current drawing color. `Graphics` method **setColor** sets the current drawing color.

Drawing in Different Colors
Figures 15.5–15.6 demonstrate several methods from Fig. 15.4 by drawing filled rectangles and `String`s in several different colors. When the application begins execution, class `ColorJPanel`'s `paintComponent` method (lines 10–37 of Fig. 15.5) is called to paint the window. Line 17 uses `Graphics` method `setColor` to set the drawing color. Method `setColor` receives a `Color` object. The expression new `Color( 255, 0, 0 )` creates a new `Color` object that represents red (red value 255, and 0 for the green and blue values). Line 18 uses `Graphics` method **fillRect** to draw a filled rectangle in the current color. Method `fillRect` draws a rectangle based on its four arguments. The first two integer values represent the upper-left *x*-coordinate and upper-left *y*-coordinate, where the `Graphics` object begins drawing the rectangle. The third and fourth arguments are nonnegative integers that represent the width and the height of the rectangle in pixels, respectively. A rectangle drawn using method `fillRect` is filled by the current color of the `Graphics` object.

```
1   // Fig. 15.5: ColorJPanel.java
2   // Demonstrating Colors.
3   import java.awt.Graphics;
4   import java.awt.Color;
5   import javax.swing.JPanel;
6
7   public class ColorJPanel extends JPanel
8   {
9      // draw rectangles and Strings in different colors
10     public void paintComponent( Graphics g )
11     {
12        super.paintComponent( g ); // call superclass's paintComponent
13
14        this.setBackground( Color.WHITE );
15
16        // set new drawing color using integers
17        g.setColor( new Color( 255, 0, 0 ) );
18        g.fillRect( 15, 25, 100, 20 );
19        g.drawString( "Current RGB: " + g.getColor(), 130, 40 );
20
21        // set new drawing color using floats
22        g.setColor( new Color( 0.50f, 0.75f, 0.0f ) );
23        g.fillRect( 15, 50, 100, 20 );
24        g.drawString( "Current RGB: " + g.getColor(), 130, 65 );
25
26        // set new drawing color using static Color objects
27        g.setColor( Color.BLUE );
28        g.fillRect( 15, 75, 100, 20 );
29        g.drawString( "Current RGB: " + g.getColor(), 130, 90 );
30
31        // display individual RGB values
32        Color color = Color.MAGENTA;
33        g.setColor( color );
34        g.fillRect( 15, 100, 100, 20 );
35        g.drawString( "RGB values: " + color.getRed() + ", " +
36           color.getGreen() + ", " + color.getBlue(), 130, 115 );
37     } // end method paintComponent
38  } // end class ColorJPanel
```

Fig. 15.5 | Color changed for drawing.

```
1   // Fig. 15.6: ShowColors.java
2   // Demonstrating Colors.
3   import javax.swing.JFrame;
4
5   public class ShowColors
6   {
7      // execute application
8      public static void main( String[] args )
9      {
10        // create frame for ColorJPanel
11        JFrame frame = new JFrame( "Using colors" );
12        frame.setDefaultCloseOperation( JFrame.EXIT_ON_CLOSE );
```

Fig. 15.6 | Creating JFrame to display colors on JPanel. (Part 1 of 2.)

```
13
14            ColorJPanel colorJPanel = new ColorJPanel(); // create ColorJPanel
15            frame.add( colorJPanel ); // add colorJPanel to frame
16            frame.setSize( 400, 180 ); // set frame size
17            frame.setVisible( true ); // display frame
18       } // end main
19   } // end class ShowColors
```

Fig. 15.6 | Creating `JFrame` to display colors on `JPanel`. (Part 2 of 2.)

Line 19 (Fig. 15.5) uses `Graphics` method **`drawString`** to draw a `String` in the current color. The expression `g.getColor()` retrieves the current color from the `Graphics` object. We then concatenate the `Color` with string `"Current RGB: "`, resulting in an implicit call to class `Color`'s `toString` method. The `String` representation of a `Color` contains the class name and package (`java.awt.Color`) and the red, green and blue values.

Look-and-Feel Observation 15.1

Everyone perceives colors differently. Choose your colors carefully to ensure that your application is readable, both for people who can perceive color and for those who are color blind. Try to avoid using many different colors in close proximity.

Lines 22–24 and 27–29 perform the same tasks again. Line 22 uses the `Color` constructor with three `float` arguments to create a dark green color (`0.50f` for red, `0.75f` for green and `0.0f` for blue). Note the syntax of the values. The letter `f` appended to a floating-point literal indicates that the literal should be treated as type `float`. Recall that by default, floating-point literals are treated as type `double`.

Line 27 sets the current drawing color to one of the predeclared `Color` constants (`Color.BLUE`). The `Color` constants are `static`, so they are created when class `Color` is loaded into memory at execution time.

The statement in lines 35–36 makes calls to `Color` methods `getRed`, `getGreen` and `getBlue` on the predeclared `Color.MAGENTA` constant. Method `main` of class `ShowColors` (lines 8–18 of Fig. 15.6) creates the `JFrame` that will contain a `ColorJPanel` object where the colors will be displayed.

Software Engineering Observation 15.1

To change the color, you must create a new `Color` object (or use one of the predeclared `Color` constants). Like `String` objects, `Color` objects are immutable (not modifiable).

Package `javax.swing` provides the **`JColorChooser`** GUI component that enables application users to select colors. The application of Figs. 15.7–15.8 demonstrates a `JColorChooser` dialog. When you click the **Change Color** button, a `JColorChooser` dialog appears. When you select a color and press the dialog's **OK** button, the background color of the application window changes.

```
1   // Fig. 15.7: ShowColors2JFrame.java
2   // Choosing colors with JColorChooser.
3   import java.awt.BorderLayout;
4   import java.awt.Color;
5   import java.awt.event.ActionEvent;
6   import java.awt.event.ActionListener;
7   import javax.swing.JButton;
8   import javax.swing.JFrame;
9   import javax.swing.JColorChooser;
10  import javax.swing.JPanel;
11
12  public class ShowColors2JFrame extends JFrame
13  {
14     private JButton changeColorJButton;
15     private Color color = Color.LIGHT_GRAY;
16     private JPanel colorJPanel;
17
18     // set up GUI
19     public ShowColors2JFrame()
20     {
21        super( "Using JColorChooser" );
22
23        // create JPanel for display color
24        colorJPanel = new JPanel();
25        colorJPanel.setBackground( color );
26
27        // set up changeColorJButton and register its event handler
28        changeColorJButton = new JButton( "Change Color" );
29        changeColorJButton.addActionListener(
30
31           new ActionListener() // anonymous inner class
32           {
33              // display JColorChooser when user clicks button
34              public void actionPerformed( ActionEvent event )
35              {
36                 color = JColorChooser.showDialog(
37                    ShowColors2JFrame.this, "Choose a color", color );
38
39                 // set default color, if no color is returned
40                 if ( color == null )
41                    color = Color.LIGHT_GRAY;
42
43                 // change content pane's background color
44                 colorJPanel.setBackground( color );
45              } // end method actionPerformed
46           } // end anonymous inner class
47        ); // end call to addActionListener
48
49        add( colorJPanel, BorderLayout.CENTER ); // add colorJPanel
50        add( changeColorJButton, BorderLayout.SOUTH ); // add button
```

Fig. 15.7 | JColorChooser dialog. (Part 1 of 2.)

```
51
52          setSize( 400, 130 ); // set frame size
53          setVisible( true ); // display frame
54      } // end ShowColor2JFrame constructor
55   } // end class ShowColors2JFrame
```

Fig. 15.7 | JColorChooser dialog. (Part 2 of 2.)

```
 1   // Fig. 15.8: ShowColors2.java
 2   // Choosing colors with JColorChooser.
 3   import javax.swing.JFrame;
 4
 5   public class ShowColors2
 6   {
 7      // execute application
 8      public static void main( String[] args )
 9      {
10         ShowColors2JFrame application = new ShowColors2JFrame();
11         application.setDefaultCloseOperation( JFrame.EXIT_ON_CLOSE );
12      } // end main
13   } // end class ShowColors2
```

(a) Initial application window.

(b) JColorChooser window.

Select a color from
one of the color
swatches.

(c) Application window after changing JPanel's
background color.

Fig. 15.8 | Choosing colors with JColorChooser.

Class JColorChooser provides static method **showDialog**, which creates a JColor-Chooser object, attaches it to a dialog box and displays the dialog. Lines 36–37 of Fig. 15.7 invoke this method to display the color chooser dialog. Method showDialog returns the selected Color object, or null if the user presses **Cancel** or closes the dialog without pressing **OK**. The method takes three arguments—a reference to its parent Component, a String to display in the title bar of the dialog and the initial selected Color for the dialog. The parent component is a reference to the window from which the dialog is displayed (in this case the JFrame, with the reference name frame). The dialog will be centered on the parent. If the parent is `null`, the dialog is centered on the screen. While the color chooser dialog is on the screen, the user cannot interact with the parent component until the dialog is dismissed. This type of dialog is called a modal dialog.

After the user selects a color, lines 40–41 determine whether `color` is `null`, and, if so, set `color` to `Color.LIGHT_GRAY`. Line 44 invokes method `setBackground` to change the background color of the `JPanel`. Method `setBackground` is one of the many `Component` methods that can be used on most GUI components. Note that the user can continue to use the **Change Color** button to change the background color of the application. Figure 15.8 contains method `main`, which executes the program.

Figure 15.8(b) shows the default `JColorChooser` dialog that allows the user to select a color from a variety of **color swatches**. Note that there are actually three tabs across the top of the dialog—**Swatches**, **HSB** and **RGB**. These represent three different ways to select a color. The **HSB** tab allows you to select a color based on **hue**, **saturation** and **brightness**—values that are used to define the amount of light in a color. We do not discuss HSB values. For more information on them, visit `whatis.techtarget.com/definition/0,,sid9_gci212262,00.html`. The **RGB** tab allows you to select a color by using sliders to select the red, green and blue components. The **HSB** and **RGB** tabs are shown in Fig. 15.9.

Fig. 15.9 | **HSB** and **RGB** tabs of the `JColorChooser` dialog.

15.4 **Manipulating Fonts**

This section introduces methods and constants for manipulating fonts. Most font methods and font constants are part of class Font. Some methods of class Font and class Graphics are summarized in Fig. 15.10.

Method or constant	Description
Font constants, constructors and methods	
public final static int PLAIN	A constant representing a plain font style.
public final static int BOLD	A constant representing a bold font style.
public final static int ITALIC	A constant representing an italic font style.
public Font(String name, int style, int size)	Creates a Font object with the specified font name, style and size.
public int getStyle()	Returns an int indicating the current font style.
public int getSize()	Returns an int indicating the current font size.
public String getName()	Returns the current font name as a string.
public String getFamily()	Returns the font's family name as a string.
public boolean isPlain()	Returns true if the font is plain, else false.
public boolean isBold()	Returns true if the font is bold, else false.
public boolean isItalic()	Returns true if the font is italic, else false.
Graphics methods for manipulating Fonts	
public Font getFont()	Returns a Font object reference representing the current font.
public void setFont(Font f)	Sets the current font to the font, style and size specified by the Font object reference f.

Fig. 15.10 | Font-related methods and constants.

Class Font's constructor takes three arguments—the **font name**, **font style** and **font size**. The font name is any font currently supported by the system on which the program is running, such as standard Java fonts Monospaced, SansSerif and Serif. The font style is **Font.PLAIN**, **Font.ITALIC** or **Font.BOLD** (each is a static field of class Font). Font styles can be used in combination (e.g., Font.ITALIC + Font.BOLD). The font size is measured in points. A **point** is 1/72 of an inch. Graphics method **setFont** sets the current drawing font—the font in which text will be displayed—to its Font argument.

> **Portability Tip 15.2**
>
> *The number of fonts varies across systems. Java provides five font names—Serif, Monospaced, SansSerif, Dialog and DialogInput—that can be used on all Java platforms. The Java runtime environment (JRE) on each platform maps these logical font names to actual fonts installed on the platform. The actual fonts used may vary by platform.*

The application of Figs. 15.11–15.12 displays text in four different fonts, with each font in a different size. Figure 15.11 uses the Font constructor to initialize Font objects (in lines 16, 20, 24 and 29) that are each passed to Graphics method setFont to change the drawing font. Each call to the Font constructor passes a font name (Serif, Monospaced or SansSerif) as a string, a font style (Font.PLAIN, Font.ITALIC or Font.BOLD) and a font size. Once Graphics method setFont is invoked, all text displayed following the call will appear in the new font until the font is changed. Each font's information is displayed in lines 17, 21, 25 and 30–31 using method drawString. Note that the coordinate passed to drawString corresponds to the lower-left corner of the baseline of the font. Line 28 changes the drawing color to red, so the next string displayed appears in red. Lines 30–31 display information about the final Font object. Method **getFont** of class Graphics returns a Font object representing the current font. Method **getName** returns the current font name as a string. Method **getSize** returns the font size in points.

Figure 15.12 contains method main, which creates a JFrame. We add a FontJPanel object to this JFrame (line 15), which displays the graphics created in Fig. 15.11.

Software Engineering Observation 15.2

To change the font, you must create a new Font object. Font objects are immutable—class Font has no set methods to change the characteristics of the current font.

```
1   // Fig. 15.11: FontJPanel.java
2   // Display strings in different fonts and colors.
3   import java.awt.Font;
4   import java.awt.Color;
5   import java.awt.Graphics;
6   import javax.swing.JPanel;
7
8   public class FontJPanel extends JPanel
9   {
10     // display Strings in different fonts and colors
11     public void paintComponent( Graphics g )
12     {
13       super.paintComponent( g ); // call superclass's paintComponent
14
15       // set font to Serif (Times), bold, 12pt and draw a string
16       g.setFont( new Font( "Serif", Font.BOLD, 12 ) );
17       g.drawString( "Serif 12 point bold.", 20, 30 );
18
19       // set font to Monospaced (Courier), italic, 24pt and draw a string
20       g.setFont( new Font( "Monospaced", Font.ITALIC, 24 ) );
21       g.drawString( "Monospaced 24 point italic.", 20, 50 );
22
23       // set font to SansSerif (Helvetica), plain, 14pt and draw a string
24       g.setFont( new Font( "SansSerif", Font.PLAIN, 14 ) );
25       g.drawString( "SansSerif 14 point plain.", 20, 70 );
26
27       // set font to Serif (Times), bold/italic, 18pt and draw a string
28       g.setColor( Color.RED );
29       g.setFont( new Font( "Serif", Font.BOLD + Font.ITALIC, 18 ) );
30       g.drawString( g.getFont().getName() + " " + g.getFont().getSize() +
31         " point bold italic.", 20, 90 );
32     } // end method paintComponent
33   } // end class FontJPanel
```

Fig. 15.11 | Graphics method setFont changes the drawing font.

```
 1   // Fig. 15.12: Fonts.java
 2   // Using fonts.
 3   import javax.swing.JFrame;
 4
 5   public class Fonts
 6   {
 7      // execute application
 8      public static void main( String[] args )
 9      {
10         // create frame for FontJPanel
11         JFrame frame = new JFrame( "Using fonts" );
12         frame.setDefaultCloseOperation( JFrame.EXIT_ON_CLOSE );
13
14         FontJPanel fontJPanel = new FontJPanel(); // create FontJPanel
15         frame.add( fontJPanel ); // add fontJPanel to frame
16         frame.setSize( 420, 150 ); // set frame size
17         frame.setVisible( true ); // display frame
18      } // end main
19   } // end class Fonts
```

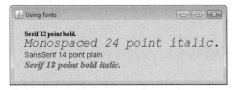

Fig. 15.12 | Creating a JFrame to display fonts.

Font Metrics

Sometimes it's necessary to get information about the current drawing font, such as its name, style and size. Several Font methods used to get font information are summarized in Fig. 15.10. Method **getStyle** returns an integer value representing the current style. The integer value returned is either Font.PLAIN, Font.ITALIC, Font.BOLD or the combination of Font.ITALIC and Font.BOLD. Method **getFamily** returns the name of the font family to which the current font belongs. The name of the font family is platform specific. Font methods are also available to test the style of the current font, and these too are summarized in Fig. 15.10. Methods **isPlain**, **isBold** and **isItalic** return true if the current font style is plain, bold or italic, respectively.

Figure 15.13 illustrates some of the common **font metrics**, which provide precise information about a font, such as **height**, **descent** (the amount a character dips below the

Fig. 15.13 | Font metrics.

baseline), **ascent** (the amount a character rises above the baseline) and **leading** (the difference between the descent of one line of text and the ascent of the line of text below it—that is, the interline spacing).

Class **FontMetrics** declares several methods for obtaining font metrics. These methods and Graphics method **getFontMetrics** are summarized in Fig. 15.14. The application of Figs. 15.15–15.16 uses the methods of Fig. 15.14 to obtain font metric information for two fonts.

Method	Description
FontMetrics methods	
public int getAscent()	Returns the ascent of a font in points.
public int getDescent()	Returns the descent of a font in points.
public int getLeading()	Returns the leading of a font in points.
public int getHeight()	Returns the height of a font in points.
Graphics methods for getting a Font's FontMetrics	
public FontMetrics getFontMetrics()	
	Returns the FontMetrics object for the current drawing Font.
public FontMetrics getFontMetrics(Font f)	
	Returns the FontMetrics object for the specified Font argument.

Fig. 15.14 | FontMetrics and Graphics methods for obtaining font metrics.

```
1   // Fig. 15.15: MetricsJPanel.java
2   // FontMetrics and Graphics methods useful for obtaining font metrics.
3   import java.awt.Font;
4   import java.awt.FontMetrics;
5   import java.awt.Graphics;
6   import javax.swing.JPanel;
7
8   public class MetricsJPanel extends JPanel
9   {
10     // display font metrics
11     public void paintComponent( Graphics g )
12     {
13        super.paintComponent( g ); // call superclass's paintComponent
14
15        g.setFont( new Font( "SansSerif", Font.BOLD, 12 ) );
16        FontMetrics metrics = g.getFontMetrics();
17        g.drawString( "Current font: " + g.getFont(), 10, 30 );
18        g.drawString( "Ascent: " + metrics.getAscent(), 10, 45 );
19        g.drawString( "Descent: " + metrics.getDescent(), 10, 60 );
20        g.drawString( "Height: " + metrics.getHeight(), 10, 75 );
21        g.drawString( "Leading: " + metrics.getLeading(), 10, 90 );
22
23        Font font = new Font( "Serif", Font.ITALIC, 14 );
24        metrics = g.getFontMetrics( font );
```

Fig. 15.15 | Font metrics. (Part 1 of 2.)

```
25        g.setFont( font );
26        g.drawString( "Current font: " + font, 10, 120 );
27        g.drawString( "Ascent: " + metrics.getAscent(), 10, 135 );
28        g.drawString( "Descent: " + metrics.getDescent(), 10, 150 );
29        g.drawString( "Height: " + metrics.getHeight(), 10, 165 );
30        g.drawString( "Leading: " + metrics.getLeading(), 10, 180 );
31     } // end method paintComponent
32  } // end class MetricsJPanel
```

Fig. 15.15 | Font metrics. (Part 2 of 2.)

```
 1  // Fig. 15.16: Metrics.java
 2  // Displaying font metrics.
 3  import javax.swing.JFrame;
 4
 5  public class Metrics
 6  {
 7     // execute application
 8     public static void main( String[] args )
 9     {
10        // create frame for MetricsJPanel
11        JFrame frame = new JFrame( "Demonstrating FontMetrics" );
12        frame.setDefaultCloseOperation( JFrame.EXIT_ON_CLOSE );
13
14        MetricsJPanel metricsJPanel = new MetricsJPanel();
15        frame.add( metricsJPanel ); // add metricsJPanel to frame
16        frame.setSize( 510, 240 ); // set frame size
17        frame.setVisible( true ); // display frame
18     } // end main
19  } // end class Metrics
```

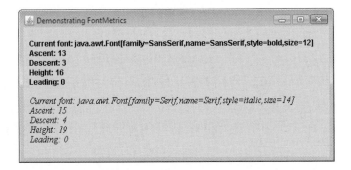

Fig. 15.16 | Creating JFrame to display font metric information.

Line 15 of Fig. 15.15 creates and sets the current drawing font to a SansSerif, bold, 12-point font. Line 16 uses Graphics method getFontMetrics to obtain the FontMetrics object for the current font. Line 17 outputs the String representation of the Font returned by g.getFont(). Lines 18–21 use FontMetric methods to obtain the ascent, descent, height and leading for the font.

Line 23 creates a new Serif, italic, 14-point font. Line 24 uses a second version of Graphics method getFontMetrics, which accepts a Font argument and returns a corresponding FontMetrics object. Lines 27–30 obtain the ascent, descent, height and leading for the font. Note that the font metrics are slightly different for the two fonts.

15.5 Drawing Lines, Rectangles and Ovals

This section presents Graphics methods for drawing lines, rectangles and ovals. The methods and their parameters are summarized in Fig. 15.17. For each drawing method that requires a width and height parameter, the width and height must be nonnegative values. Otherwise, the shape will not display.

Method	Description

`public void drawLine( int x1, int y1, int x2, int y2 )`

Draws a line between the point (x1, y1) and the point (x2, y2).

`public void drawRect( int x, int y, int width, int height )`

Draws a rectangle of the specified width and height. The rectangle's top-left corner is located at (x, y). Only the outline of the rectangle is drawn using the Graphics object's color—the body of the rectangle is not filled with this color.

`public void fillRect( int x, int y, int width, int height )`

Draws a filled rectangle in the current color with the specified width and height. The rectangle's top-left corner is located at (x, y).

`public void clearRect( int x, int y, int width, int height )`

Draws a filled rectangle with the specified width and height in the current background color. The rectangle's top-left corner is located at (x, y). This method is useful if you want to remove a portion of an image.

`public void drawRoundRect( int x, int y, int width, int height, int arcWidth, int arcHeight )`

Draws a rectangle with rounded corners in the current color with the specified width and height. The arcWidth and arcHeight determine the rounding of the corners (see Fig. 15.20). Only the outline of the shape is drawn.

`public void fillRoundRect( int x, int y, int width, int height, int arcWidth, int arcHeight )`

Draws a filled rectangle in the current color with rounded corners with the specified width and height. The arcWidth and arcHeight determine the rounding of the corners (see Fig. 15.20).

`public void draw3DRect( int x, int y, int width, int height, boolean b )`

Draws a three-dimensional rectangle in the current color with the specified width and height. The rectangle's top-left corner is located at (x, y). The rectangle appears raised when b is true and lowered when b is false. Only the outline of the shape is drawn.

`public void fill3DRect( int x, int y, int width, int height, boolean b )`

Draws a filled three-dimensional rectangle in the current color with the specified width and height. The rectangle's top-left corner is located at (x, y). The rectangle appears raised when b is true and lowered when b is false.

Fig. 15.17 | Graphics methods that draw lines, rectangles and ovals. (Part 1 of 2.)

Method	Description

`public void drawOval( int x, int y, int width, int height )`

Draws an oval in the current color with the specified width and height. The bounding rectangle's top-left corner is located at (x, y). The oval touches all four sides of the bounding rectangle at the center of each side (see Fig. 15.21). Only the outline of the shape is drawn.

`public void fillOval( int x, int y, int width, int height )`

Draws a filled oval in the current color with the specified width and height. The bounding rectangle's top-left corner is located at (x, y). The oval touches the center of all four sides of the bounding rectangle (see Fig. 15.21).

Fig. 15.17 | Graphics methods that draw lines, rectangles and ovals. (Part 2 of 2.)

The application of Figs. 15.18–15.19 demonstrates drawing a variety of lines, rectangles, three-dimensional rectangles, rounded rectangles and ovals. In Fig. 15.18, line 17 draws a red line, line 20 draws an empty blue rectangle and line 21 draws a filled blue rectangle. Methods **fillRoundRect** (line 24) and **drawRoundRect** (line 25) draw rectangles with rounded corners. Their first two arguments specify the coordinates of the upper-left corner of the **bounding rectangle**—the area in which the rounded rectangle will be drawn. Note that the upper-left corner coordinates are not the edge of the rounded rectangle, but the coordinates where the edge would be if the rectangle had square corners. The third and fourth arguments specify the width and height of the rectangle. The last two arguments determine the horizontal and vertical diameters of the arc (i.e., the arc width and arc height) used to represent the corners.

```
1   // Fig. 15.18: LinesRectsOvalsJPanel.java
2   // Drawing lines, rectangles and ovals.
3   import java.awt.Color;
4   import java.awt.Graphics;
5   import javax.swing.JPanel;
6
7   public class LinesRectsOvalsJPanel extends JPanel
8   {
9      // display various lines, rectangles and ovals
10     public void paintComponent( Graphics g )
11     {
12        super.paintComponent( g ); // call superclass's paint method
13
14        this.setBackground( Color.WHITE );
15
16        g.setColor( Color.RED );
17        g.drawLine( 5, 30, 380, 30 );
18
19        g.setColor( Color.BLUE );
20        g.drawRect( 5, 40, 90, 55 );
21        g.fillRect( 100, 40, 90, 55 );
22
```

Fig. 15.18 | Drawing lines, rectangles and ovals. (Part 1 of 2.)

```
23          g.setColor( Color.CYAN );
24          g.fillRoundRect( 195, 40, 90, 55, 50, 50 );
25          g.drawRoundRect( 290, 40, 90, 55, 20, 20 );
26
27          g.setColor( Color.GREEN );
28          g.draw3DRect( 5, 100, 90, 55, true );
29          g.fill3DRect( 100, 100, 90, 55, false );
30
31          g.setColor( Color.MAGENTA );
32          g.drawOval( 195, 100, 90, 55 );
33          g.fillOval( 290, 100, 90, 55 );
34       } // end method paintComponent
35    } // end class LinesRectsOvalsJPanel
```

Fig. 15.18 | Drawing lines, rectangles and ovals. (Part 2 of 2.)

```
1    // Fig. 15.19: LinesRectsOvals.java
2    // Drawing lines, rectangles and ovals.
3    import java.awt.Color;
4    import javax.swing.JFrame;
5
6    public class LinesRectsOvals
7    {
8       // execute application
9       public static void main( String[] args )
10      {
11         // create frame for LinesRectsOvalsJPanel
12         JFrame frame =
13            new JFrame( "Drawing lines, rectangles and ovals" );
14         frame.setDefaultCloseOperation( JFrame.EXIT_ON_CLOSE );
15
16         LinesRectsOvalsJPanel linesRectsOvalsJPanel =
17            new LinesRectsOvalsJPanel();
18         linesRectsOvalsJPanel.setBackground( Color.WHITE );
19         frame.add( linesRectsOvalsJPanel ); // add panel to frame
20         frame.setSize( 400, 210 ); // set frame size
21         frame.setVisible( true ); // display frame
22      } // end main
23   } // end class LinesRectsOvals
```

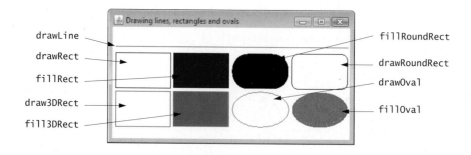

Fig. 15.19 | Creating JFrame to display lines, rectangles and ovals.

Figure 15.20 labels the arc width, arc height, width and height of a rounded rectangle. Using the same value for the arc width and arc height produces a quarter-circle at each corner. When the arc width, arc height, width and height have the same values, the result is a circle. If the values for `width` and `height` are the same and the values of `arcWidth` and `arcHeight` are 0, the result is a square.

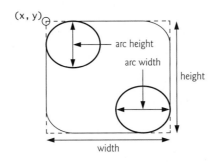

Fig. 15.20 | Arc width and arc height for rounded rectangles.

Methods **draw3DRect** (line 28) and **fill3DRect** (line 29) take the same arguments. The first two specify the top-left corner of the rectangle. The next two arguments specify the width and height of the rectangle, respectively. The last argument determines whether the rectangle is **raised** (`true`) or **lowered** (`false`). The three-dimensional effect of draw3DRect appears as two edges of the rectangle in the original color and two edges in a slightly darker color. The three-dimensional effect of fill3DRect appears as two edges of the rectangle in the original drawing color and the fill and other two edges in a slightly darker color. Raised rectangles have the original drawing color edges at the top and left of the rectangle. Lowered rectangles have the original drawing color edges at the bottom and right of the rectangle. The three-dimensional effect is difficult to see in some colors.

Methods **drawOval** and **fillOval** (Fig. 15.18, lines 32–33) take the same four arguments. The first two arguments specify the top-left coordinate of the bounding rectangle that contains the oval. The last two arguments specify the width and height of the bounding rectangle, respectively. Figure 15.21 shows an oval bounded by a rectangle. Note that the oval touches the center of all four sides of the bounding rectangle. (The bounding rectangle is not displayed on the screen.)

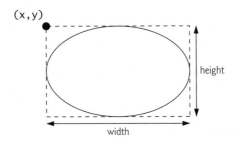

Fig. 15.21 | Oval bounded by a rectangle.

15.6 Drawing Arcs

An **arc** is drawn as a portion of an oval. Arc angles are measured in degrees. Arcs **sweep** (i.e., move along a curve) from a **starting angle** by the number of degrees specified by their **arc angle**. The starting angle indicates in degrees where the arc begins. The arc angle specifies the total number of degrees through which the arc sweeps. Figure 15.22 illustrates two arcs. The left set of axes shows an arc sweeping from zero degrees to approximately 110 degrees. Arcs that sweep in a counterclockwise direction are measured in **positive degrees**. The set of axes on the right shows an arc sweeping from zero degrees to approximately –110 degrees. Arcs that sweep in a clockwise direction are measured in **negative degrees**. Note the dashed boxes around the arcs in Fig. 15.22. When drawing an arc, we specify a bounding rectangle for an oval. The arc will sweep along part of the oval. Graphics methods **drawArc** and **fillArc** for drawing arcs are summarized in Fig. 15.23.

Fig. 15.22 | Positive and negative arc angles.

Method	Description
public void drawArc(int x, int y, int width, int height, int startAngle, int arcAngle)	
	Draws an arc relative to the bounding rectangle's top-left x- and y-coordinates with the specified width and height. The arc segment is drawn starting at startAngle and sweeps arcAngle degrees.
public void fillArc(int x, int y, int width, int height, int startAngle, int arcAngle)	
	Draws a filled arc (i.e., a sector) relative to the bounding rectangle's top-left x- and y-coordinates with the specified width and height. The arc segment is drawn starting at startAngle and sweeps arcAngle degrees.

Fig. 15.23 | Graphics methods for drawing arcs.

Figures 15.24–12.25 demonstrate the arc methods of Fig. 15.23. The application draws six arcs (three unfilled and three filled). To illustrate the bounding rectangle that helps determine where the arc appears, the first three arcs are displayed inside a red rectangle that has the same x, y, width and height arguments as the arcs.

```
 1   // Fig. 15.24: ArcsJPanel.java
 2   // Drawing arcs.
 3   import java.awt.Color;
 4   import java.awt.Graphics;
 5   import javax.swing.JPanel;
 6
 7   public class ArcsJPanel extends JPanel
 8   {
 9      // draw rectangles and arcs
10      public void paintComponent( Graphics g )
11      {
12         super.paintComponent( g ); // call superclass's paintComponent
13
14         // start at 0 and sweep 360 degrees
15         g.setColor( Color.RED );
16         g.drawRect( 15, 35, 80, 80 );
17         g.setColor( Color.BLACK );
18         g.drawArc( 15, 35, 80, 80, 0, 360 );
19
20         // start at 0 and sweep 110 degrees
21         g.setColor( Color.RED );
22         g.drawRect( 100, 35, 80, 80 );
23         g.setColor( Color.BLACK );
24         g.drawArc( 100, 35, 80, 80, 0, 110 );
25
26         // start at 0 and sweep -270 degrees
27         g.setColor( Color.RED );
28         g.drawRect( 185, 35, 80, 80 );
29         g.setColor( Color.BLACK );
30         g.drawArc( 185, 35, 80, 80, 0, -270 );
31
32         // start at 0 and sweep 360 degrees
33         g.fillArc( 15, 120, 80, 40, 0, 360 );
34
35         // start at 270 and sweep -90 degrees
36         g.fillArc( 100, 120, 80, 40, 270, -90 );
37
38         // start at 0 and sweep -270 degrees
39         g.fillArc( 185, 120, 80, 40, 0, -270 );
40      } // end method paintComponent
41   } // end class ArcsJPanel
```

Fig. 15.24 | Arcs displayed with `drawArc` and `fillArc`.

```
 1   // Fig. 15.25: DrawArcs.java
 2   // Drawing arcs.
 3   import javax.swing.JFrame;
 4
 5   public class DrawArcs
 6   {
 7      // execute application
 8      public static void main( String[] args )
 9      {
```

Fig. 15.25 | Creating `JFrame` to display arcs. (Part 1 of 2.)

```
10        // create frame for ArcsJPanel
11        JFrame frame = new JFrame( "Drawing Arcs" );
12        frame.setDefaultCloseOperation( JFrame.EXIT_ON_CLOSE );
13
14        ArcsJPanel arcsJPanel = new ArcsJPanel(); // create ArcsJPanel
15        frame.add( arcsJPanel ); // add arcsJPanel to frame
16        frame.setSize( 300, 210 ); // set frame size
17        frame.setVisible( true ); // display frame
18     } // end main
19  } // end class DrawArcs
```

Fig. 15.25 | Creating `JFrame` to display arcs. (Part 2 of 2.)

15.7 Drawing Polygons and Polylines

Polygons are closed multisided shapes composed of straight-line segments. **Polylines** are sequences of connected points. Figure 15.26 discusses methods for drawing polygons and polylines. Note that some methods require a **Polygon** object (package java.awt). Class Polygon's constructors are also described in Fig. 15.26. The application of Figs. 15.27–15.28 draws polygons and polylines.

Method	Description
Graphics methods for drawing polygons	
public void drawPolygon(int[] xPoints, int[] yPoints, int points)	
	Draws a polygon. The *x*-coordinate of each point is specified in the xPoints array, and the *y*-coordinate of each point in the yPoints array. The last argument specifies the number of points. This method draws a closed polygon. If the last point is different from the first, the polygon is closed by a line that connects the last point to the first.
public void drawPolyline(int[] xPoints, int[] yPoints, int points)	
	Draws a sequence of connected lines. The *x*-coordinate of each point is specified in the xPoints array, and the *y*-coordinate of each point in the yPoints array. The last argument specifies the number of points. If the last point is different from the first, the polyline is not closed.
public void drawPolygon(Polygon p)	
	Draws the specified polygon.

Fig. 15.26 | `Graphics` methods for polygons and class `Polygon` methods. (Part 1 of 2.)

Method	Description

`public void fillPolygon( int[] xPoints, int[] yPoints, int points )`

Draws a filled polygon. The x-coordinate of each point is specified in the xPoints array, and the y-coordinate of each point in the yPoints array. The last argument specifies the number of points. This method draws a closed polygon. If the last point is different from the first, the polygon is closed by a line that connects the last point to the first.

`public void fillPolygon( Polygon p )`

Draws the specified filled polygon. The polygon is closed.

Polygon constructors and methods

`public Polygon()`

Constructs a new polygon object. The polygon does not contain any points.

`public Polygon( int[] xValues, int[] yValues, int numberOfPoints )`

Constructs a new polygon object. The polygon has numberOfPoints sides, with each point consisting of an x-coordinate from xValues and a y-coordinate from yValues.

`public void addPoint( int x, int y )`

Adds pairs of x- and y-coordinates to the Polygon.

Fig. 15.26 | Graphics methods for polygons and class Polygon methods. (Part 2 of 2.)

```
1   // Fig. 15.27: PolygonsJPanel.java
2   // Drawing polygons.
3   import java.awt.Graphics;
4   import java.awt.Polygon;
5   import javax.swing.JPanel;
6
7   public class PolygonsJPanel extends JPanel
8   {
9      // draw polygons and polylines
10     public void paintComponent( Graphics g )
11     {
12        super.paintComponent( g ); // call superclass's paintComponent
13
14        // draw polygon with Polygon object
15        int[] xValues = { 20, 40, 50, 30, 20, 15 };
16        int[] yValues = { 50, 50, 60, 80, 80, 60 };
17        Polygon polygon1 = new Polygon( xValues, yValues, 6 );
18        g.drawPolygon( polygon1 );
19
20        // draw polylines with two arrays
21        int[] xValues2 = { 70, 90, 100, 80, 70, 65, 60 };
22        int[] yValues2 = { 100, 100, 110, 110, 130, 110, 90 };
23        g.drawPolyline( xValues2, yValues2, 7 );
24
25        // fill polygon with two arrays
26        int[] xValues3 = { 120, 140, 150, 190 };
```

Fig. 15.27 | Polygons displayed with drawPolygon and fillPolygon. (Part 1 of 2.)

```
27          int[] yValues3 = { 40, 70, 80, 60 };
28          g.fillPolygon( xValues3, yValues3, 4 );
29
30          // draw filled polygon with Polygon object
31          Polygon polygon2 = new Polygon();
32          polygon2.addPoint( 165, 135 );
33          polygon2.addPoint( 175, 150 );
34          polygon2.addPoint( 270, 200 );
35          polygon2.addPoint( 200, 220 );
36          polygon2.addPoint( 130, 180 );
37          g.fillPolygon( polygon2 );
38       } // end method paintComponent
39    } // end class PolygonsJPanel
```

Fig. 15.27 | Polygons displayed with `drawPolygon` and `fillPolygon`. (Part 2 of 2.)

```
1    // Fig. 15.28: DrawPolygons.java
2    // Drawing polygons.
3    import javax.swing.JFrame;
4
5    public class DrawPolygons
6    {
7       // execute application
8       public static void main( String[] args )
9       {
10          // create frame for PolygonsJPanel
11          JFrame frame = new JFrame( "Drawing Polygons" );
12          frame.setDefaultCloseOperation( JFrame.EXIT_ON_CLOSE );
13
14          PolygonsJPanel polygonsJPanel = new PolygonsJPanel();
15          frame.add( polygonsJPanel ); // add polygonsJPanel to frame
16          frame.setSize( 280, 270 ); // set frame size
17          frame.setVisible( true ); // display frame
18       } // end main
19    } // end class DrawPolygons
```

Fig. 15.28 | Creating `JFrame` to display polygons.

Lines 15–16 of Fig. 15.27 create two int arrays and use them to specify the points for Polygon polygon1. The Polygon constructor call in line 17 receives array xValues, which contains the *x*-coordinate of each point; array yValues, which contains the *y*-coordinate of each point and 6 (the number of points in the polygon). Line 18 displays polygon1 by passing it as an argument to Graphics method **drawPolygon**.

Lines 21–22 create two int arrays and use them to specify the points for a series of connected lines. Array xValues2 contains the *x*-coordinate of each point and array yValues2 the *y*-coordinate of each point. Line 23 uses Graphics method **drawPolyline** to display the series of connected lines specified with the arguments xValues2, yValues2 and 7 (the number of points).

Lines 26–27 create two int arrays and use them to specify the points of a polygon. Array xValues3 contains the *x*-coordinate of each point and array yValues3 the *y*-coordinate of each point. Line 28 displays a polygon by passing to Graphics method **fillPolygon** the two arrays (xValues3 and yValues3) and the number of points to draw (4).

Common Programming Error 15.1

An ArrayIndexOutOfBoundsException is thrown if the number of points specified in the third argument to method drawPolygon or method fillPolygon is greater than the number of elements in the arrays of coordinates that specify the polygon to display.

Line 31 creates Polygon polygon2 with no points. Lines 32–36 use Polygon method **addPoint** to add pairs of *x*- and *y*-coordinates to the Polygon. Line 37 displays Polygon polygon2 by passing it to Graphics method fillPolygon.

15.8 Java 2D API

The **Java 2D API** provides advanced two-dimensional graphics capabilities for programmers who require detailed and complex graphical manipulations. The API includes features for processing line art, text and images in packages java.awt, java.awt.image, java.awt.color, java.awt.font, java.awt.geom, java.awt.print and java.awt.image.renderable. The capabilities of the API are far too broad to cover in this textbook. For an overview of the capabilities, see the Java 2D demo (discussed in Chapter 23, Applets and Java Web Start) or visit java.sun.com/javase/6/docs/technotes/guides/2d. In this section, we overview several Java 2D capabilities.

Drawing with the Java 2D API is accomplished with a **Graphics2D** reference (package java.awt). Graphics2D is an abstract subclass of class Graphics, so it has all the graphics capabilities demonstrated earlier in this chapter. In fact, the actual object used to draw in every paintComponent method is an instance of a subclass of Graphics2D that is passed to method paintComponent and accessed via the superclass Graphics. To access Graphics2D capabilities, we must cast the Graphics reference (g) passed to paintComponent into a Graphics2D reference with a statement such as

```
Graphics2D g2d = ( Graphics2D ) g;
```

The next two examples use this technique.

Lines, Rectangles, Round Rectangles, Arcs and Ellipses

This example demonstrates several Java 2D shapes from package java.awt.geom, including **Line2D.Double**, **Rectangle2D.Double**, **RoundRectangle2D.Double**, **Arc2D.Double** and **Ellipse2D.Double**. Note the syntax of each class name. Each class represents a shape with dimensions specified as double values. There is a separate version of each represented with float values (e.g., **Ellipse2D.Float**). In each case, Double is a public static nested class of the class specified to the left of the dot (e.g., Ellipse2D). To use the static nested class, we simply qualify its name with the outer class name.

In Figs. 15.29–15.30, we draw Java 2D shapes and modify their drawing characteristics, such as changing line thickness, filling shapes with patterns and drawing dashed lines. These are just a few of the many capabilities provided by Java 2D.

```java
1   // Fig. 15.29: ShapesJPanel.java
2   // Demonstrating some Java 2D shapes.
3   import java.awt.Color;
4   import java.awt.Graphics;
5   import java.awt.BasicStroke;
6   import java.awt.GradientPaint;
7   import java.awt.TexturePaint;
8   import java.awt.Rectangle;
9   import java.awt.Graphics2D;
10  import java.awt.geom.Ellipse2D;
11  import java.awt.geom.Rectangle2D;
12  import java.awt.geom.RoundRectangle2D;
13  import java.awt.geom.Arc2D;
14  import java.awt.geom.Line2D;
15  import java.awt.image.BufferedImage;
16  import javax.swing.JPanel;
17
18  public class ShapesJPanel extends JPanel
19  {
20     // draw shapes with Java 2D API
21     public void paintComponent( Graphics g )
22     {
23        super.paintComponent( g ); // call superclass's paintComponent
24
25        Graphics2D g2d = ( Graphics2D ) g; // cast g to Graphics2D
26
27        // draw 2D ellipse filled with a blue-yellow gradient
28        g2d.setPaint( new GradientPaint( 5, 30, Color.BLUE, 35, 100,
29           Color.YELLOW, true ) );
30        g2d.fill( new Ellipse2D.Double( 5, 30, 65, 100 ) );
31
32        // draw 2D rectangle in red
33        g2d.setPaint( Color.RED );
34        g2d.setStroke( new BasicStroke( 10.0f ) );
35        g2d.draw( new Rectangle2D.Double( 80, 30, 65, 100 ) );
36
37        // draw 2D rounded rectangle with a buffered background
38        BufferedImage buffImage = new BufferedImage( 10, 10,
39           BufferedImage.TYPE_INT_RGB );
40
41        // obtain Graphics2D from buffImage and draw on it
42        Graphics2D gg = buffImage.createGraphics();
43        gg.setColor( Color.YELLOW ); // draw in yellow
44        gg.fillRect( 0, 0, 10, 10 ); // draw a filled rectangle
45        gg.setColor( Color.BLACK );  // draw in black
46        gg.drawRect( 1, 1, 6, 6 ); // draw a rectangle
47        gg.setColor( Color.BLUE ); // draw in blue
```

Fig. 15.29 | Java 2D shapes. (Part 1 of 2.)

```
48          gg.fillRect( 1, 1, 3, 3 ); // draw a filled rectangle
49          gg.setColor( Color.RED ); // draw in red
50          gg.fillRect( 4, 4, 3, 3 ); // draw a filled rectangle
51
52          // paint buffImage onto the JFrame
53          g2d.setPaint( new TexturePaint( buffImage,
54             new Rectangle( 10, 10 ) ) );
55          g2d.fill(
56             new RoundRectangle2D.Double( 155, 30, 75, 100, 50, 50 ) );
57
58          // draw 2D pie-shaped arc in white
59          g2d.setPaint( Color.WHITE );
60          g2d.setStroke( new BasicStroke( 6.0f ) );
61          g2d.draw(
62             new Arc2D.Double( 240, 30, 75, 100, 0, 270, Arc2D.PIE ) );
63
64          // draw 2D lines in green and yellow
65          g2d.setPaint( Color.GREEN );
66          g2d.draw( new Line2D.Double( 395, 30, 320, 150 ) );
67
68          // draw 2D line using stroke
69          float[] dashes = { 10 }; // specify dash pattern
70          g2d.setPaint( Color.YELLOW );
71          g2d.setStroke( new BasicStroke( 4, BasicStroke.CAP_ROUND,
72             BasicStroke.JOIN_ROUND, 10, dashes, 0 ) );
73          g2d.draw( new Line2D.Double( 320, 30, 395, 150 ) );
74       } // end method paintComponent
75    } // end class ShapesJPanel
```

Fig. 15.29 | Java 2D shapes. (Part 2 of 2.)

```
 1   // Fig. 15.30: Shapes.java
 2   // Demonstrating some Java 2D shapes.
 3   import javax.swing.JFrame;
 4
 5   public class Shapes
 6   {
 7      // execute application
 8      public static void main( String[] args )
 9      {
10         // create frame for ShapesJPanel
11         JFrame frame = new JFrame( "Drawing 2D shapes" );
12         frame.setDefaultCloseOperation( JFrame.EXIT_ON_CLOSE );
13
14         // create ShapesJPanel
15         ShapesJPanel shapesJPanel = new ShapesJPanel();
16
17         frame.add( shapesJPanel ); // add shapesJPanel to frame
18         frame.setSize( 425, 200 ); // set frame size
19         frame.setVisible( true ); // display frame
20      } // end main
21   } // end class Shapes
```

Fig. 15.30 | Creating JFrame to display shapes. (Part 1 of 2.)

Fig. 15.30 | Creating JFrame to display shapes. (Part 2 of 2.)

Line 25 of Fig. 15.29 casts the Graphics reference received by paintComponent to a Graphics2D reference and assigns it to g2d to allow access to the Java 2D features.

Ovals, Gradient Fills and Paint Objects

The first shape we draw is an oval filled with gradually changing colors. Lines 28–29 invoke Graphics2D method **setPaint** to set the **Paint** object that determines the color for the shape to display. A Paint object implements interface java.awt.Paint. It can be something as simple as one of the predeclared Color objects introduced in Section 15.3 (class Color implements Paint), or it can be an instance of the Java 2D API's Gradient-Paint, **SystemColor**, TexturePaint, LinearGradientPaint or RadialGradientPaint classes. In this case, we use a GradientPaint object.

Class GradientPaint helps draw a shape in gradually changing colors—called a **gradient**. The GradientPaint constructor used here requires seven arguments. The first two specify the starting coordinate for the gradient. The third specifies the starting Color for the gradient. The fourth and fifth specify the ending coordinate for the gradient. The sixth specifies the ending Color for the gradient. The last argument specifies whether the gradient is **cyclic** (true) or **acyclic** (false). The two sets of coordinates determine the direction of the gradient. Because the second coordinate (35, 100) is down and to the right of the first coordinate (5, 30), the gradient goes down and to the right at an angle. Because this gradient is cyclic (true), the color starts with blue, gradually becomes yellow, then gradually returns to blue. If the gradient is acyclic, the color transitions from the first color specified (e.g., blue) to the second color (e.g., yellow).

Line 30 uses Graphics2D method **fill** to draw a filled **Shape** object—an object that implements interface Shape (package java.awt). In this case, we display an Ellipse2D.Double object. The Ellipse2D.Double constructor receives four arguments specifying the bounding rectangle for the ellipse to display.

Rectangles, Strokes

Next we draw a red rectangle with a thick border. Line 33 invokes setPaint to set the Paint object to Color.RED. Line 34 uses Graphics2D method **setStroke** to set the characteristics of the rectangle's border (or the lines for any other shape). Method setStroke requires as its argument an object that implements interface **Stroke** (package java.awt). In this case, we use an instance of class BasicStroke. Class BasicStroke provides several constructors to specify the width of the line, how the line ends (called the **end caps**), how lines join together (called **line joins**) and the dash attributes of the line (if it's a dashed line). The constructor here specifies that the line should be 10 pixels wide.

Line 35 uses Graphics2D method **draw** to draw a Shape object—in this case, a Rectangle2D.Double. The Rectangle2D.Double constructor receives arguments specifying the rectangle's upper-left x-coordinate, upper-left y-coordinate, width and height.

Rounded Rectangles, BufferedImages and TexturePaint Objects

Next we draw a rounded rectangle filled with a pattern created in a **BufferedImage** (package java.awt.image) object. Lines 38–39 create the BufferedImage object. Class BufferedImage can be used to produce images in color and grayscale. This particular BufferedImage is 10 pixels wide and 10 pixels tall (as specified by the first two arguments of the constructor). The third argument **BufferedImage.TYPE_INT_RGB** indicates that the image is stored in color using the RGB color scheme.

To create the rounded rectangle's fill pattern, we must first draw into the BufferedImage. Line 42 creates a Graphics2D object (by calling BufferedImage method **createGraphics**) that can be used to draw into the BufferedImage. Lines 43–50 use methods setColor, fillRect and drawRect (discussed earlier in this chapter) to create the pattern.

Lines 53–54 set the Paint object to a new TexturePaint (package java.awt) object. A TexturePaint object uses the image stored in its associated BufferedImage (the first constructor argument) as the fill texture for a filled-in shape. The second argument specifies the Rectangle area from the BufferedImage that will be replicated through the texture. In this case, the Rectangle is the same size as the BufferedImage. However, a smaller portion of the BufferedImage can be used.

Lines 55–56 use Graphics2D method fill to draw a filled Shape object—in this case, a RoundRectangle2D.Double. The constructor for class RoundRectangle2D.Double receives six arguments specifying the rectangle dimensions and the arc width and arc height used to determine the rounding of the corners.

Arcs

Next we draw a pie-shaped arc with a thick white line. Line 59 sets the Paint object to Color.WHITE. Line 60 sets the Stroke object to a new BasicStroke for a line 6 pixels wide. Lines 61–62 use Graphics2D method draw to draw a Shape object—in this case, an Arc2D.Double. The Arc2D.Double constructor's first four arguments specify the upper-left x-coordinate, upper-left y-coordinate, width and height of the bounding rectangle for the arc. The fifth argument specifies the start angle. The sixth argument specifies the arc angle. The last argument specifies how the arc is closed. Constant **Arc2D.PIE** indicates that the arc is closed by drawing two lines—one line from the arc's starting point to the center of the bounding rectangle and one line from the center of the bounding rectangle to the ending point. Class Arc2D provides two other static constants for specifying how the arc is closed. Constant **Arc2D.CHORD** draws a line from the starting point to the ending point. Constant **Arc2D.OPEN** specifies that the arc should not be closed.

Lines

Finally, we draw two lines using **Line2D** objects—one solid and one dashed. Line 65 sets the Paint object to Color.GREEN. Line 66 uses Graphics2D method draw to draw a Shape object—in this case, an instance of class Line2D.Double. The Line2D.Double constructor's arguments specify the starting coordinates and ending coordinates of the line.

Line 69 declares a one-element float array containing the value 10. This array describes the dashes in the dashed line. In this case, each dash will be 10 pixels long. To create dashes of different lengths in a pattern, simply provide the length of each dash as an element in the array. Line 70 sets the Paint object to Color.YELLOW. Lines 71–72 set the Stroke object to a new BasicStroke. The line will be 4 pixels wide and will have rounded ends (**BasicStroke.CAP_ROUND**). If lines join together (as in a rectangle at the corners), their joining will be rounded (**BasicStroke.JOIN_ROUND**). The dashes argument specifies the dash lengths for the line. The last argument indicates the starting index in the dashes array for the first dash in the pattern. Line 73 then draws a line with the current Stroke.

Creating Your Own Shapes with General Paths
Next we present a **general path**—a shape constructed from straight lines and complex curves. A general path is represented with an object of class **GeneralPath** (package java.awt.geom). The application of Figs. 15.31 and 15.32 demonstrates drawing a general path in the shape of a five-pointed star.

```
 1   // Fig. 15.31: Shapes2JPanel.java
 2   // Demonstrating a general path.
 3   import java.awt.Color;
 4   import java.awt.Graphics;
 5   import java.awt.Graphics2D;
 6   import java.awt.geom.GeneralPath;
 7   import java.util.Random;
 8   import javax.swing.JPanel;
 9
10   public class Shapes2JPanel extends JPanel
11   {
12      // draw general paths
13      public void paintComponent( Graphics g )
14      {
15         super.paintComponent( g ); // call superclass's paintComponent
16         Random random = new Random(); // get random number generator
17
18         int[] xPoints = { 55, 67, 109, 73, 83, 55, 27, 37, 1, 43 };
19         int[] yPoints = { 0, 36, 36, 54, 96, 72, 96, 54, 36, 36 };
20
21         Graphics2D g2d = ( Graphics2D ) g;
22         GeneralPath star = new GeneralPath(); // create GeneralPath object
23
24         // set the initial coordinate of the General Path
25         star.moveTo( xPoints[ 0 ], yPoints[ 0 ] );
26
27         // create the star--this does not draw the star
28         for ( int count = 1; count < xPoints.length; count++ )
29            star.lineTo( xPoints[ count ], yPoints[ count ] );
30
31         star.closePath(); // close the shape
32
33         g2d.translate( 150, 150 ); // translate the origin to (150, 150)
34
35         // rotate around origin and draw stars in random colors
36         for ( int count = 1; count <= 20; count++ )
37         {
38            g2d.rotate( Math.PI / 10.0 ); // rotate coordinate system
```

Fig. 15.31 | Java 2D general paths. (Part 1 of 2.)

```
39
40            // set random drawing color
41            g2d.setColor( new Color( random.nextInt( 256 ),
42               random.nextInt( 256 ), random.nextInt( 256 ) ) );
43
44            g2d.fill( star ); // draw filled star
45         } // end for
46      } // end method paintComponent
47   } // end class Shapes2JPanel
```

Fig. 15.31 | Java 2D general paths. (Part 2 of 2.)

```
 1   // Fig. 15.32: Shapes2.java
 2   // Demonstrating a general path.
 3   import java.awt.Color;
 4   import javax.swing.JFrame;
 5
 6   public class Shapes2
 7   {
 8      // execute application
 9      public static void main( String[] args )
10      {
11         // create frame for Shapes2JPanel
12         JFrame frame = new JFrame( "Drawing 2D Shapes" );
13         frame.setDefaultCloseOperation( JFrame.EXIT_ON_CLOSE );
14
15         Shapes2JPanel shapes2JPanel = new Shapes2JPanel();
16         frame.add( shapes2JPanel ); // add shapes2JPanel to frame
17         frame.setBackground( Color.WHITE ); // set frame background color
18         frame.setSize( 315, 330 ); // set frame size
19         frame.setVisible( true ); // display frame
20      } // end main
21   } // end class Shapes2
```

Fig. 15.32 | Creating JFrame to display stars.

Lines 18–19 declare two int arrays representing the *x*- and *y*-coordinates of the points in the star. Line 22 creates GeneralPath object star. Line 25 uses GeneralPath method **moveTo** to specify the first point in the star. The for statement in lines 28–29 uses GeneralPath method **lineTo** to draw a line to the next point in the star. Each new call to lineTo draws a line from the previous point to the current point. Line 31 uses General-Path method **closePath** to draw a line from the last point to the point specified in the last call to moveTo. This completes the general path.

Line 33 uses Graphics2D method **translate** to move the drawing origin to location (150, 150). All drawing operations now use location (150, 150) as (0, 0).

The for statement in lines 36–45 draws the star 20 times by rotating it around the new origin point. Line 38 uses Graphics2D method **rotate** to rotate the next displayed shape. The argument specifies the rotation angle in radians (with 360° = 2π radians). Line 44 uses Graphics2D method fill to draw a filled version of the star.

15.9 Wrap-Up

In this chapter, you learned how to use Java's graphics capabilities to produce colorful drawings. You learned how to specify the location of an object using Java's coordinate system, and how to draw on a window using the paintComponent method. You were introduced to class Color, and you learned how to use this class to specify different colors using their RGB components. You used the JColorChooser dialog to allow users to select colors in a program. You then learned how to work with fonts when drawing text on a window. You learned how to create a Font object from a font name, style and size, as well as how to access the metrics of a font. From there, you learned how to draw various shapes on a window, such as rectangles (regular, rounded and 3D), ovals and polygons, as well as lines and arcs. You then used the Java 2D API to create more complex shapes and to fill them with gradients or patterns. The chapter concluded with a discussion of general paths, used to construct shapes from straight lines and complex curves. In the next chapter, we discuss class String and its methods. We also introduce regular expressions for pattern matching in strings and demonstrate how to validate user input with regular expressions.

Summary

Section 15.1 Introduction
- Java's coordinate system is a scheme for identifying every point on the screen.
- A coordinate pair has an *x*-coordinate (horizontal) and a *y*-coordinate (vertical).
- Coordinates are used to indicate where graphics should be displayed on a screen.
- Coordinate units are measured in pixels. A pixel is a display monitor's smallest unit of resolution.

Section 15.2 Graphics Contexts and Graphics Objects
- A Java graphics context enables drawing on the screen.
- Class Graphics contains methods for drawing strings, lines, rectangles and other shapes. Methods are also included for font manipulation and color manipulation.
- A Graphics object manages a graphics context and draws pixels on the screen that represent text and other graphical object (e.g., lines, ellipses, rectangles and other polygons).
- Class Graphics is an abstract class. Each Java implementation has a Graphics subclass that provides drawing capabilities. This implementation is hidden from us by class Graphics, which supplies the interface that enables us to use graphics in a platform-independent manner.
- Method paintComponent can be used to draw graphics in any JComponent component.
- Method paintComponent receives a Graphics object that is passed to the method by the system when a lightweight Swing component needs to be repainted.

- You seldom call method paintComponent directly, because drawing graphics is an event-driven process. When an application executes, the application container calls method paintComponent. For paintComponent to be called again, an event must occur.

- When a JComponent is displayed, its paintComponent method is called.

- Calling method repaint on a component updates the graphics drawn on that component.

Section 15.3 Color Control

- Class Color declares methods and constants for manipulating colors in a Java program.

- Every color is created from a red, a green and a blue component. Together these components are called RGB values. The RGB components specify the amount of red, green and blue in a color, respectively. The larger the RGB value, the greater the amount of that particular color.

- Color methods getRed, getGreen and getBlue return int values from 0 to 255 representing the amount of red, green and blue, respectively.

- Graphics method getColor returns a Color object representing the current drawing color.

- Graphics method setColor sets the current drawing color.

- Graphics method fillRect draws a rectangle filled by the current color of the Graphics object.

- Graphics method drawString draws a String in the current color.

- The JColorChooser GUI component enables application users to select colors.

- JColorChooser static method showDialog creates a JColorChooser object, attaches it to a dialog box and displays the dialog. When it is on the screen, the user can interact only with the dialog. This type of dialog is called a modal dialog.

Section 15.4 Manipulating Fonts

- Class Font contains methods and constants for manipulating fonts.

- Class Font's constructor takes three arguments—the font name, font style and font size.

- A Font's font style can be Font.PLAIN, Font.ITALIC or Font.BOLD (each is a static field of class Font). Font styles can be used in combination (e.g., Font.ITALIC + Font.BOLD).

- The font size is measured in points. A point is 1/72 of an inch.

- Graphics method setFont sets the drawing font in which text will be displayed.

- Font method getStyle returns an integer value representing the current Font's style.

- Font method getSize returns the font size in points.

- Font method getName returns the current font name as a string.

- Font method getFamily returns the name of the font family to which the current font belongs. The name of the font family is platform specific.

- Class FontMetrics contains methods for obtaining font information.

- Font metrics include height, descent and leading.

Section 15.5 Drawing Lines, Rectangles and Ovals

- Graphics methods fillRoundRect and drawRoundRect draw rectangles with rounded corners.

- Graphics methods draw3DRect and fill3DRect draw three-dimensional rectangles.

- Graphics methods drawOval and fillOval draw ovals.

Section 15.6 Drawing Arcs

- An arc is drawn as a portion of an oval.

- Arcs sweep from a starting angle by the number of degrees specified by their arc angle.

- Graphics methods drawArc and fillArc are used for drawing arcs.

Section 15.7 Drawing Polygons and Polylines
- Class `Polygon` contains methods for creating polygons.
- Polygons are closed multisided shapes composed of straight-line segments.
- Polylines are a sequence of connected points.
- `Graphics` method `drawPolyline` displays a series of connected lines.
- `Graphics` methods `drawPolygon` and `fillPolygon` are used to draw polygons.
- `Polygon` method `addPoint` of class `Polygon` adds pairs of *x*- and *y*-coordinates to the `Polygon`.

Section 15.8 Java 2D API
- The Java 2D API provides advanced two-dimensional graphics capabilities.
- Class `Graphics2D`—a subclass of `Graphics`—is used for drawing with the Java 2D API.
- The Java 2D API's classes for drawing shapes include `Line2D.Double`, `Rectangle2D.Double`, `RoundRectangle2D.Double`, `Arc2D.Double` and `Ellipse2D.Double`.
- Class `GradientPaint` helps draw a shape in gradually changing colors—called a gradient.
- `Graphics2D` method `fill` draws a filled object of any type that implements interface `Shape`.
- Class `BasicStroke` helps specify the drawing characteristics of lines.
- `Graphics2D` method `draw` is used to draw a `Shape` object.
- Classes `GradientPaint` and `TexturePaint` help specify the characteristics for filling shapes with colors or patterns.
- A general path is a shape constructed from straight lines and complex curves and is represented with an object of class `GeneralPath`.
- `GeneralPath` method `moveTo` specifies the first point in a general path.
- `GeneralPath` method `lineTo` draws a line to the next point in the path. Each new call to `lineTo` draws a line from the previous point to the current point.
- `GeneralPath` method `closePath` draws a line from the last point to the point specified in the last call to `moveTo`. This completes the general path.
- `Graphics2D` method `translate` is used to move the drawing origin to a new location.
- `Graphics2D` method `rotate` is used to rotate the next displayed shape.

Terminology

acyclic gradient 668
addPoint method of class Polygon 665
arc 660
arc angle 660
Arc2D.Double class 665
ascent of a font 654
BasicStroke class 641
BOLD constant of class Font 651
bounding rectangle 657
brightness 650
BufferedImage class 669
CAP_ROUND constant of class BasicStroke 670
CHORD constant of class Arc2D 669
closePath method of class GeneralPath 672
Color class 641
coordinate system 641

createGraphics method of class BufferedImage 669
cyclic gradient 668
descent of a font 653
draw method of class Graphics2D 669
draw3DRect method of class Graphics 659
drawArc method of class Graphics 660
drawOval method of class Graphics 659
drawPolygon method of class Graphics 665
drawPolyline method of class Graphics 665
drawRoundRect 657
drawRoundRect method of class Graphics 657
drawString method of class Graphics 647
Ellipse2D.Double class 665
Ellipse2D.Float class 665
end caps (of a line) 668

Self-Review Exercises

15.1 Fill in the blanks in each of the following statements:

a) In Java 2D, method _____ of class _____ sets the characteristics of a line used to draw a shape.

b) Class _____ helps specify the fill for a shape such that the fill gradually changes from one color to another.

c) The _____ method of class Graphics draws a line between two points.

d) RGB is short for _____, _____ and _____.

e) Font sizes are measured in units called _____.

f) Class _____ helps specify the fill for a shape using a pattern drawn in a `Buffered-Image`.

15.2 State whether each of the following is *true* or *false*. If *false*, explain why.

a) The first two arguments of `Graphics` method `drawOval` specify the center coordinate of the oval.

b) In the Java coordinate system, *x*-coordinates increase from left to right and *y*-coordinates from top to bottom.

c) `Graphics` method `fillPolygon` draws a filled polygon in the current color.

d) `Graphics` method `drawArc` allows negative angles.

e) `Graphics` method `getSize` returns the size of the current font in centimeters.

f) Pixel coordinate (0, 0) is located at the exact center of the monitor.

15.3 Find the error(s) in each of the following and explain how to correct them. Assume that `g` is a `Graphics` object.

a) `g.setFont( "SansSerif" );`

b) `g.erase( x, y, w, h );    // clear rectangle at (x, y)`

c) `Font f = new Font( "Serif", Font.BOLDITALIC, 12 );`

d) `g.setColor( 255, 255, 0 );  // change color to yellow`

Answers to Self-Review Exercises

15.1 a) `setStroke`, `Graphics2D`. b) `GradientPaint`. c) `drawLine`. d) red, green, blue. e) points. f) `TexturePaint`.

15.2 a) False. The first two arguments specify the upper-left corner of the bounding rectangle.

b) True.

c) True.

d) True.

e) False. Font sizes are measured in points.

f) False. The coordinate (0,0) corresponds to the upper-left corner of a GUI component on which drawing occurs.

15.3 a) The `setFont` method takes a `Font` object as an argument—not a `String`.

b) The `Graphics` class does not have an `erase` method. The `clearRect` method should be used.

c) `Font.BOLDITALIC` is not a valid font style. To get a bold italic font, use `Font.BOLD + Font.ITALIC`.

d) Method `setColor` takes a `Color` object as an argument, not three integers.

Exercises

15.4 *(Concentric Circles Using Method drawArc)* Write an application that draws a series of eight concentric circles. The circles should be separated by 10 pixels. Use `Graphics` method `drawArc`.

15.5 *(Concentric Circles Using Class Ellipse2D.Double)* Modify your solution to Exercise 15.4 to draw the ovals by using class `Ellipse2D.Double` and method `draw` of class `Graphics2D`.

15.6 *(Random Lines Using Class Line2D.Double)* Modify your solution to Exercise 15.5 to draw random lines, in random colors and random line thicknesses. Use class `Line2D.Double` and method `draw` of class `Graphics2D` to draw the lines.

15.7 *(Grid Using Method drawLine)* Write an application that draws an 8-by-8 grid. Use `Graphics` method `drawLine`.

15.8 *(Grid Using Class Line2D.Double)* Modify your solution to Exercise 15.7 to draw the grid using instances of class Line2D.Double and method draw of class Graphics2D.

15.9 *(Grid Using Method drawRect)* Write an application that draws a 10-by-10 grid. Use the Graphics method drawRect.

15.10 *(Grid Using Class Rectangle2D.Double)* Modify your solution to Exercise 15.9 to draw the grid by using class Rectangle2D.Double and method draw of class Graphics2D.

15.11 *(Drawing Cubes)* Write an application that draws a cube. Use class GeneralPath and method draw of class Graphics2D.

15.12 *(Circles Using Class Ellipse2D.Double)* Write an application that asks the user to input the radius of a circle as a floating-point number and draws the circle, as well as the values of the circle's diameter, circumference and area. Use the value 3.14159 for π. [*Note:* You may also use the pre-defined constant Math.PI for the value of π. This constant is more precise than the value 3.14159. Class Math is declared in the java.lang package, so you need not import it.] Use the following formulas (*r* is the radius):

$$diameter = 2r$$
$$circumference = 2\pi r$$
$$area = \pi r^2$$

The user should also be prompted for a set of coordinates in addition to the radius. Then draw the circle, and display its diameter, circumference and area, using an Ellipse2D.Double object to represent the circle and method draw of class Graphics2D to display it.

15.13 *(Screen Saver)* Write an application that simulates a screen saver. The application should randomly draw lines using method drawLine of class Graphics. After drawing 100 lines, the application should clear itself and start drawing lines again. To allow the program to draw continuously, place a call to repaint as the last line in method paintComponent. Do you notice any problems with this on your system?

15.14 *(Screen Saver Using Timer)* Package javax.swing contains a class called Timer that is capable of calling method actionPerformed of interface ActionListener at a fixed time interval (specified in milliseconds). Modify your solution to Exercise 15.13 to remove the call to repaint from method paintComponent. Declare your class to implement ActionListener. (The actionPerformed method should simply call repaint.) Declare an instance variable of type Timer called timer in your class. In the constructor for your class, write the following statements:

```
timer = new Timer( 1000, this );
timer.start();
```

This creates an instance of class Timer that will call this object's actionPerformed method every 1000 milliseconds (i.e., every second).

15.15 *(Turtle Graphics)* Modify your solution to Exercise 7.16—*Turtle Graphics*—to add a graphical user interface using JTextFields and JButtons. Draw lines rather than asterisks (*). When the turtle graphics program specifies a move, translate the number of positions into a number of pixels on the screen by multiplying the number of positions by 10 (or any value you choose). Implement the drawing with Java 2D API features.

15.16 *(Knight's Tour)* Produce a graphical version of the Knight's Tour problem (Exercise 7.17, Exercise 7.18 and Exercise 7.21). As each move is made, the appropriate cell of the chessboard should be updated with the proper move number. If the result of the program is a *full tour* or a *closed tour*, the program should display an appropriate message. If you like, use class Timer (see Exercise 15.14) to help animate the Knight's Tour.

15.17 *(Drawing Spirals)* Write an application that uses Graphics method drawPolyline to draw a spiral similar to the one shown in Fig. 15.33.

Fig. 15.33 | Spiral drawn using method drawPolyline.

15.18 *(Selecting Shapes)* Write an application that allows the user to select a shape from a JComboBox and draws it 20 times with random locations and dimensions in method paintComponent. The first item in the JComboBox should be the default shape that is displayed the first time paintComponent is called.

15.19 *(Random Colors)* Modify Exercise 15.18 to draw each of the 20 randomly sized shapes in a randomly selected color. Use all 13 predefined Color objects in an array of Colors.

15.20 *(JColorChooser Dialog)* Modify Exercise 15.18 to allow the user to select the color in which shapes should be drawn from a JColorChooser dialog.

(Optional) GUI and Graphics Case Study: Adding Java2D

15.21 Java2D introduces many new capabilities for creating unique and impressive graphics. We'll add a small subset of these features to the drawing application you created in Exercise 14.11. In this version, you'll enable the user to specify gradients for filling shapes and to change stroke characteristics for drawing lines and outlines of shapes. The user will be able to choose which colors compose the gradient and set the width and dash length of the stroke.

First, you must update the MyShape hierarchy to support Java2D functionality. Make the following changes in class MyShape:

> a) Change abstract method draw's parameter type from Graphics to Graphics2D.
> b) Change all variables of type Color to type Paint to enable support for gradients. [*Note:* Recall that class Color implements interface Paint.]
> c) Add an instance variable of type Stroke in class MyShape and a Stroke parameter in the constructor to initialize the new instance variable. The default stroke should be an instance of class BasicStroke.

Classes MyLine, MyBoundedShape, MyOval and MyRectangle should each add a Stroke parameter to their constructors. In the draw methods, each shape should set the Paint and the Stroke before drawing or filling a shape. Since Graphics2D is a subclass of Graphics, we can continue to use Graphics methods drawLine, drawOval, fillOval, and so on. to draw the shapes. When these methods are called, they'll draw the appropriate shape using the specified Paint and Stroke settings.

Next, you'll update the DrawPanel to handle the Java2D features. Change all Color variables to Paint variables. Declare an instance variable currentStroke of type Stroke and provide a *set* method for it. Update the calls to the individual shape constructors to include the Paint and

Stroke arguments. In method `paintComponent`, cast the `Graphics` reference to type `Graphics2D` and use the `Graphics2D` reference in each call to `MyShape` method `draw`.

Next, make the new Java2D features accessible from the GUI. Create a `JPanel` of GUI components for setting the Java2D options. Add these components at the top of the `DrawFrame` below the panel that currently contains the standard shape controls (see Fig. 15.34). These GUI components should include:

a) A check box to specify whether to paint using a gradient.

b) Two `JButton`s that each show a `JColorChooser` dialog to allow the user to choose the first and second color in the gradient. (These will replace the `JComboBox` used for choosing the color in Exercise 14.11.)

c) A text field for entering the `Stroke` width.

d) A text field for entering the `Stroke` dash length.

e) A check box for selecting whether to draw a dashed or solid line.

If the user selects to draw with a gradient, set the `Paint` on the `DrawPanel` to be a gradient of the two colors chosen by the user. The expression

```
new GradientPaint( 0, 0, color1, 50, 50, color2, true ) )
```

Fig. 15.34 | Drawing with Java2D.

creates a `GradientPaint` that cycles diagonally from the upper-left to the bottom-right every 50 pixels. Variables `color1` and `color2` represent the colors chosen by the user. If the user does not select to use a gradient, then simply set the `Paint` on the `DrawPanel` to be the first `Color` chosen by the user.

For strokes, if the user chooses a solid line, then create the `Stroke` with the expression

```
new BasicStroke( width, BasicStroke.CAP_ROUND, BasicStroke.JOIN_ROUND )
```

where variable `width` is the width specified by the user in the line-width text field. If the user chooses a dashed line, then create the `Stroke` with the expression

```
new BasicStroke( width, BasicStroke.CAP_ROUND, BasicStroke.JOIN_ROUND,
   10, dashes, 0 )
```

where `width` again is the width in the line-width field, and `dashes` is an array with one element whose value is the length specified in the dash-length field. The `Panel` and `Stroke` objects should be passed to the shape object's constructor when the shape is created in `DrawPanel`.

Making a Difference

15.22 *(Large-Type Displays for People with Low Vision)* The accessibility of computers and the Internet to all people, regardless of disabilities, is becoming more important as these tools play increasing roles in our personal and business lives. According to a recent estimate by the World Health Organization (www.who.int/mediacentre/factsheets/fs282/en/), 124 million people worldwide have low vision. To learn more about low vision, check out the GUI-based low vision simulation at www.webaim.org/simulations/lowvision.php. People with low vision might prefer to choose a font and/or a larger font size when reading electronic documents and web pages. Java has five built-in "logical" fonts that are guaranteed to be available in any Java implementation, including Serif, Sans-serif and Monospaced. Write a GUI application that provides a JTextArea in which the user can type text. Allow the user to select Serif, Sans-serif or Monospaced from a JComboBox. Provide a **Bold** JCheckBox, which, if checked, makes the text bold. Include **Increase Font Size** and **Decrease Font Size** JButtons that allow the user to scale the size of the font up or down, respectively, by one point at a time. Start with a font size of 18 points. For the purposes of this exercise, set the font size on the JComboBox, JButtons and JCheckBox to 20 points so that a person with low vision will be able to read the text on them.

The chief defect of Henry King
Was chewing little bits of string.
—Hilaire Belloc

Vigorous writing is concise. A sentence should contain
no unnecessary words, a paragraph no unnecessary
sentences.
—William Strunk, Jr.

I have made this letter longer than usual, because I
lack the time to make it short.
—Blaise Pascal

Strings, Characters and Regular Expressions

Objectives

In this chapter you'll learn:

- To create and manipulate immutable character-string objects of class `String`.
- To create and manipulate mutable character-string objects of class `StringBuilder`.
- To create and manipulate objects of class `Character`.
- To break a `String` object into tokens using `String` method `split`.
- To use regular expressions to validate `String` data entered into an application.

16.1 Introduction

This chapter introduces Java's string- and character-processing capabilities. The techniques discussed here are appropriate for validating program input, displaying information to users and other text-based manipulations. They are also appropriate for developing text editors, word processors, page-layout software, computerized typesetting systems and other kinds of text-processing software. We've already presented several string-processing capabilities in earlier chapters. This chapter discusses in detail the capabilities of class `String`, and class `StringBuilder` and class `Character` from the `java.lang` package. These classes provide the foundation for string and character manipulation in Java.

The chapter also discusses regular expressions that provide applications with the capability to validate input. The functionality is located in the `String` class along with classes `Matcher` and `Pattern` located in the `java.util.regex` package.

16.2 Fundamentals of Characters and Strings

Characters are the fundamental building blocks of Java source programs. Every program is composed of a sequence of characters that—when grouped together meaningfully—are interpreted by the computer as a series of instructions used to accomplish a task. A program may contain **character literals**. A character literal is an integer value represented as a character in single quotes. For example, `'z'` represents the integer value of z, and `'\n'` represents the integer value of newline. The value of a character literal is the integer value of the character in the **Unicode character set**. Appendix B presents the integer equivalents of the characters in the ASCII character set, which is a subset of Unicode (discussed in Appendix L). For detailed information on Unicode, visit www.unicode.org.

Recall from Section 2.2 that a string is a sequence of characters treated as a single unit. A string may include letters, digits and various **special characters**, such as +, -, *, / and $. A string is an object of class String. **String literals** (stored in memory as String objects) are written as a sequence of characters in double quotation marks, as in:

```
"John Q. Doe"               (a name)
"9999 Main Street"          (a street address)
"Waltham, Massachusetts"    (a city and state)
"(201) 555-1212"            (a telephone number)
```

A string may be assigned to a String reference. The declaration

```
String color = "blue";
```

initializes String variable color to refer to a String object that contains the string "blue".

Performance Tip 16.1

Java treats all string literals with the same contents as a single String object that has many references to it. This conserves memory.

16.3 **Class String**

Class String is used to represent strings in Java. The next several subsections cover many of class String's capabilities.

16.3.1 String Constructors

Class String provides constructors for initializing String objects in a variety of ways. Four of the constructors are demonstrated in the main method of Fig. 16.1.

```
 1   // Fig. 16.1: StringConstructors.java
 2   // String class constructors.
 3
 4   public class StringConstructors
 5   {
 6      public static void main( String[] args )
 7      {
 8         char[] charArray = { 'b', 'i', 'r', 't', 'h', ' ', 'd', 'a', 'y' };
 9         String s = new String( "hello" );
10
11         // use String constructors
12         String s1 = new String();
13         String s2 = new String( s );
14         String s3 = new String( charArray );
15         String s4 = new String( charArray, 6, 3 );
16
17         System.out.printf(
18            "s1 = %s\ns2 = %s\ns3 = %s\ns4 = %s\n",
19            s1, s2, s3, s4 ); // display strings
20      } // end main
21   } // end class StringConstructors
```

Fig. 16.1 | String class constructors. (Part 1 of 2.)

```
s1 =
s2 = hello
s3 = birth day
s4 = day
```

Fig. 16.1 | String class constructors. (Part 2 of 2.)

Line 12 instantiates a new String using class String's no-argument constructor and assigns its reference to s1. The new String object contains no characters (i.e., the **empty string**, which can also be represented as "") and has a length of 0. Line 13 instantiates a new String object using class String's constructor that takes a String object as an argument and assigns its reference to s2. The new String object contains the same sequence of characters as the String object s that is passed as an argument to the constructor.

Software Engineering Observation 16.1

*It's not necessary to copy an existing String object. String objects are **immutable**—their character contents cannot be changed after they are created, because class String does not provide any methods that allow the contents of a String object to be modified.*

Line 14 instantiates a new String object and assigns its reference to s3 using class String's constructor that takes a char array as an argument. The new String object contains a copy of the characters in the array.

Line 15 instantiates a new String object and assigns its reference to s4 using class String's constructor that takes a char array and two integers as arguments. The second argument specifies the starting position (the offset) from which characters in the array are accessed. Remember that the first character is at position 0. The third argument specifies the number of characters (the count) to access in the array. The new String object is formed from the accessed characters. If the offset or the count specified as an argument results in accessing an element outside the bounds of the character array, a StringIndexOutOfBoundsException is thrown.

Common Programming Error 16.1

Accessing a character outside the bounds of a String (i.e., an index less than 0 or an index greater than or equal to the String's length) results in a StringIndexOutOfBounds-Exception.

16.3.2 String Methods length, charAt and getChars

String methods **length**, **charAt** and **getChars** return the length of a String, obtain the character at a specific location in a String and retrieve a set of characters from a String as a char array, respectively. Figure 16.2 demonstrates each of these methods.

```
1   // Fig. 16.2: StringMiscellaneous.java
2   // This application demonstrates the length, charAt and getChars
3   // methods of the String class.
4
5   public class StringMiscellaneous
6   {
```

Fig. 16.2 | String class character-manipulation methods. (Part 1 of 2.)

```
7      public static void main( String[] args )
8      {
9         String s1 = "hello there";
10        char[] charArray = new char[ 5 ];
11
12        System.out.printf( "s1: %s", s1 );
13
14        // test length method
15        System.out.printf( "\nLength of s1: %d", s1.length() );
16
17        // loop through characters in s1 with charAt and display reversed
18        System.out.print( "\nThe string reversed is: " );
19
20        for ( int count = s1.length() - 1; count >= 0; count-- )
21           System.out.printf( "%c ", s1.charAt( count ) );
22
23        // copy characters from string into charArray
24        s1.getChars( 0, 5, charArray, 0 );
25        System.out.print( "\nThe character array is: " );
26
27        for ( char character : charArray )
28           System.out.print( character );
29
30        System.out.println();
31     } // end main
32  } // end class StringMiscellaneous
```

```
s1: hello there
Length of s1: 11
The string reversed is: e r e h t   o l l e h
The character array is: hello
```

Fig. 16.2 | String class character-manipulation methods. (Part 2 of 2.)

Line 15 uses String method length to determine the number of characters in string s1. Like arrays, strings know their own length. However, unlike arrays, you cannot access a String's length via a length field—instead you must call the String's length method.

Lines 20–21 print the characters of the String s1 in reverse order (and separated by spaces). String method charAt (line 21) returns the character at a specific position in the String. Method charAt receives an integer argument that is used as the index and returns the character at that position. Like arrays, the first element of a String is at position 0.

Line 24 uses String method getChars to copy the characters of a String into a character array. The first argument is the starting index in the String from which characters are to be copied. The second argument is the index that is one past the last character to be copied from the String. The third argument is the character array into which the characters are to be copied. The last argument is the starting index where the copied characters are placed in the target character array. Next, lines 27–28 print the char array contents one character at a time.

16.3.3 Comparing Strings

Chapter 19 discusses sorting and searching arrays. Frequently, the information being sorted or searched consists of Strings that must be compared to place them into order or to determine whether a string appears in an array (or other collection). Class `String` provides methods for comparing strings, as are demonstrated in the next two examples.

To understand what it means for one string to be greater than or less than another, consider the process of alphabetizing a series of last names. No doubt, you'd place "Jones" before "Smith" because the first letter of "Jones" comes before the first letter of "Smith" in the alphabet. But the alphabet is more than just a list of 26 letters—it's an ordered set of characters. Each letter occurs in a specific position within the set. Z is more than just a letter of the alphabet—it's specifically the twenty-sixth letter of the alphabet.

How does the computer know that one letter comes before another? All characters are represented in the computer as numeric codes (see Appendix B). When the computer compares strings, it actually compares the numeric codes of the characters in the strings.

Figure 16.3 demonstrates `String` methods `equals`, `equalsIgnoreCase`, `compareTo` and **regionMatches** and using the equality operator `==` to compare `String` objects.

```
 1   // Fig. 16.3: StringCompare.java
 2   // String methods equals, equalsIgnoreCase, compareTo and regionMatches.
 3
 4   public class StringCompare
 5   {
 6      public static void main( String[] args )
 7      {
 8         String s1 = new String( "hello" ); // s1 is a copy of "hello"
 9         String s2 = "goodbye";
10         String s3 = "Happy Birthday";
11         String s4 = "happy birthday";
12
13         System.out.printf(
14            "s1 = %s\ns2 = %s\ns3 = %s\ns4 = %s\n\n", s1, s2, s3, s4 );
15
16         // test for equality
17         if ( s1.equals( "hello" ) )   // true
18            System.out.println( "s1 equals \"hello\"" );
19         else
20            System.out.println( "s1 does not equal \"hello\"" );
21
22         // test for equality with ==
23         if ( s1 == "hello" )   // false; they are not the same object
24            System.out.println( "s1 is the same object as \"hello\"" );
25         else
26            System.out.println( "s1 is not the same object as \"hello\"" );
27
28         // test for equality (ignore case)
29         if ( s3.equalsIgnoreCase( s4 ) )   // true
30            System.out.printf( "%s equals %s with case ignored\n", s3, s4 );
31         else
32            System.out.println( "s3 does not equal s4" );
33
34         // test compareTo
35         System.out.printf(
36            "\ns1.compareTo( s2 ) is %d", s1.compareTo( s2 ) );
```

Fig. 16.3 | String methods `equals`, `equalsIgnoreCase`, `compareTo` and `regionMatches`. (Part 1 of 2.)

```
37          System.out.printf(
38              "\ns2.compareTo( s1 ) is %d", s2.compareTo( s1 ) );
39          System.out.printf(
40              "\ns1.compareTo( s1 ) is %d", s1.compareTo( s1 ) );
41          System.out.printf(
42              "\ns3.compareTo( s4 ) is %d", s3.compareTo( s4 ) );
43          System.out.printf(
44              "\ns4.compareTo( s3 ) is %d\n\n", s4.compareTo( s3 ) );
45
46          // test regionMatches (case sensitive)
47          if ( s3.regionMatches( 0, s4, 0, 5 ) )
48              System.out.println( "First 5 characters of s3 and s4 match" );
49          else
50              System.out.println(
51                  "First 5 characters of s3 and s4 do not match" );
52
53          // test regionMatches (ignore case)
54          if ( s3.regionMatches( true, 0, s4, 0, 5 ) )
55              System.out.println(
56                  "First 5 characters of s3 and s4 match with case ignored" );
57          else
58              System.out.println(
59                  "First 5 characters of s3 and s4 do not match" );
60      } // end main
61  } // end class StringCompare
```

```
s1 = hello
s2 = goodbye
s3 = Happy Birthday
s4 = happy birthday

s1 equals "hello"
s1 is not the same object as "hello"
Happy Birthday equals happy birthday with case ignored

s1.compareTo( s2 ) is 1
s2.compareTo( s1 ) is -1
s1.compareTo( s1 ) is 0
s3.compareTo( s4 ) is -32
s4.compareTo( s3 ) is 32

First 5 characters of s3 and s4 do not match
First 5 characters of s3 and s4 match with case ignored
```

Fig. 16.3 | String methods equals, equalsIgnoreCase, compareTo and regionMatches. (Part 2 of 2.)

The condition at line 17 uses method equals to compare String s1 and the String literal "hello" for equality. Method equals (a method of class Object overridden in String) tests any two objects for equality—the strings contained in the two objects are identical. The method returns true if the contents of the objects are equal, and false otherwise. The preceding condition is true because String s1 was initialized with the string literal "hello". Method equals uses a **lexicographical comparison**—it compares the integer Unicode values (see Appendix L, for more information) that represent each character in each String. Thus, if the String "hello" is compared with the string "HELLO", the result is `false`, because the integer representation of a lowercase letter is different from that of the corresponding uppercase letter.

The condition at line 23 uses the equality operator `==` to compare `String s1` for equality with the `String` literal `"hello"`. When primitive-type values are compared with `==`, the result is `true` if both values are identical. When references are compared with `==`, the result is `true` if both references refer to the same object in memory. To compare the actual contents (or state information) of objects for equality, a method must be invoked. In the case of `Strings`, that method is `equals`. The preceding condition evaluates to `false` at line 23 because the reference `s1` was initialized with the statement

```
s1 = new String( "hello" );
```

which creates a new `String` object with a copy of string literal `"hello"` and assigns the new object to variable `s1`. If `s1` had been initialized with the statement

```
s1 = "hello";
```

which directly assigns the string literal `"hello"` to variable `s1`, the condition would be `true`. Remember that Java treats all string literal objects with the same contents as one `String` object to which there can be many references. Thus, lines 8, 17 and 23 all refer to the same `String` object `"hello"` in memory.

Common Programming Error 16.2

Comparing references with `==` can lead to logic errors, because `==` compares the references to determine whether they refer to the same object, not whether two objects have the same contents. When two identical (but separate) objects are compared with `==`, the result will be `false`. When comparing objects to determine whether they have the same contents, use method `equals`.

If you are sorting `Strings`, you may compare them for equality with method `equalsIgnoreCase`, which ignores whether the letters in each `String` are uppercase or lowercase when performing the comparison. Thus, `"hello"` and `"HELLO"` compare as equal. Line 29 uses `String` method `equalsIgnoreCase` to compare `String s3`—Happy Birthday—for equality with `String s4`—happy birthday. The result of this comparison is `true` because the comparison ignores case sensitivity.

Lines 35–44 use method `compareTo` to compare `Strings`. Method `compareTo` is declared in the `Comparable` interface and implemented in the `String` class. Line 36 compares `String s1` to `String s2`. Method `compareTo` returns 0 if the `Strings` are equal, a negative number if the `String` that invokes `compareTo` is less than the `String` that is passed as an argument and a positive number if the `String` that invokes `compareTo` is greater than the `String` that is passed as an argument. Method `compareTo` uses a lexicographical comparison—it compares the numeric values of corresponding characters in each `String`. (For more information on the exact value returned by the `compareTo` method, see `java.sun.com/javase/6/docs/api/java/lang/String.html`.)

The condition at line 47 uses `String` method `regionMatches` to compare portions of two `Strings` for equality. The first argument is the starting index in the `String` that invokes the method. The second argument is a comparison `String`. The third argument is the starting index in the comparison `String`. The last argument is the number of characters to compare between the two `Strings`. The method returns `true` only if the specified number of characters are lexicographically equal.

Finally, the condition at line 54 uses a five-argument version of String method regionMatches to compare portions of two Strings for equality. When the first argument is true, the method ignores the case of the characters being compared. The remaining arguments are identical to those described for the four-argument regionMatches method.

The next example (Fig. 16.4) demonstrates String methods **startsWith** and **ends-With**. Method main creates array strings containing "started", "starting", "ended"

```
1   // Fig. 16.4: StringStartEnd.java
2   // String methods startsWith and endsWith.
3
4   public class StringStartEnd
5   {
6      public static void main( String[] args )
7      {
8         String[] strings = { "started", "starting", "ended", "ending" };
9
10        // test method startsWith
11        for ( String string : strings )
12        {
13           if ( string.startsWith( "st" ) )
14              System.out.printf( "\"%s\" starts with \"st\"\n", string );
15        } // end for
16
17        System.out.println();
18
19        // test method startsWith starting from position 2 of string
20        for ( String string : strings )
21        {
22           if ( string.startsWith( "art", 2 ) )
23              System.out.printf(
24                 "\"%s\" starts with \"art\" at position 2\n", string );
25        } // end for
26
27        System.out.println();
28
29        // test method endsWith
30        for ( String string : strings )
31        {
32           if ( string.endsWith( "ed" ) )
33              System.out.printf( "\"%s\" ends with \"ed\"\n", string );
34        } // end for
35     } // end main
36  } // end class StringStartEnd
```

```
"started" starts with "st"
"starting" starts with "st"

"started" starts with "art" at position 2
"starting" starts with "art" at position 2

"started" ends with "ed"
"ended" ends with "ed"
```

Fig. 16.4 | String methods startsWith and endsWith.

and "ending". The remainder of method main consists of three for statements that test the elements of the array to determine whether they start with or end with a particular set of characters.

Lines 11–15 use the version of method startsWith that takes a String argument. The condition in the if statement (line 13) determines whether each String in the array starts with the characters "st". If so, the method returns true and the application prints that String. Otherwise, the method returns false and nothing happens.

Lines 20–25 use the startsWith method that takes a String and an integer as arguments. The integer specifies the index at which the comparison should begin in the String. The condition in the if statement (line 22) determines whether each String in the array has the characters "art" beginning with the third character in each String. If so, the method returns true and the application prints the String.

The third for statement (lines 30–34) uses method endsWith, which takes a String argument. The condition at line 32 determines whether each String in the array ends with the characters "ed". If so, the method returns true and the application prints the String.

16.3.4 Locating Characters and Substrings in Strings

Often it's useful to search a string for a character or set of characters. For example, if you are creating your own word processor, you might want to provide a capability for searching through documents. Figure 16.5 demonstrates the many versions of String methods **indexOf** and **lastIndexOf** that search for a specified character or substring in a String.

```
 1   // Fig. 16.5: StringIndexMethods.java
 2   // String searching methods indexOf and lastIndexOf.
 3
 4   public class StringIndexMethods
 5   {
 6      public static void main( String[] args )
 7      {
 8         String letters = "abcdefghijklmabcdefghijklm";
 9
10         // test indexOf to locate a character in a string
11         System.out.printf(
12            "'c' is located at index %d\n", letters.indexOf( 'c' ) );
13         System.out.printf(
14            "'a' is located at index %d\n", letters.indexOf( 'a', 1 ) );
15         System.out.printf(
16            "'$' is located at index %d\n\n", letters.indexOf( '$' ) );
17
18         // test lastIndexOf to find a character in a string
19         System.out.printf( "Last 'c' is located at index %d\n",
20            letters.lastIndexOf( 'c' ) );
21         System.out.printf( "Last 'a' is located at index %d\n",
22            letters.lastIndexOf( 'a', 25 ) );
23         System.out.printf( "Last '$' is located at index %d\n\n",
24            letters.lastIndexOf( '$' ) );
25
26         // test indexOf to locate a substring in a string
27         System.out.printf( "\"def\" is located at index %d\n",
28            letters.indexOf( "def" ) );
```

Fig. 16.5 | String-searching methods indexOf and lastIndexOf. (Part 1 of 2.)

```
29        System.out.printf( "\"def\" is located at index %d\n",
30           letters.indexOf( "def", 7 ) );
31        System.out.printf( "\"hello\" is located at index %d\n\n",
32           letters.indexOf( "hello" ) );
33
34        // test lastIndexOf to find a substring in a string
35        System.out.printf( "Last \"def\" is located at index %d\n",
36           letters.lastIndexOf( "def" ) );
37        System.out.printf( "Last \"def\" is located at index %d\n",
38           letters.lastIndexOf( "def", 25 ) );
39        System.out.printf( "Last \"hello\" is located at index %d\n",
40           letters.lastIndexOf( "hello" ) );
41     } // end main
42  } // end class StringIndexMethods
```

```
'c' is located at index 2
'a' is located at index 13
'$' is located at index -1

Last 'c' is located at index 15
Last 'a' is located at index 13
Last '$' is located at index -1

"def" is located at index 3
"def" is located at index 16
"hello" is located at index -1

Last "def" is located at index 16
Last "def" is located at index 16
Last "hello" is located at index -1
```

Fig. 16.5 | String-searching methods indexOf and lastIndexOf. (Part 2 of 2.)

All the searches in this example are performed on the String letters (initialized with "abcdefghijklmabcdefghijklm"). Lines 11–16 use method indexOf to locate the first occurrence of a character in a String. If the method finds the character, it returns the character's index in the String—otherwise, it returns -1. There are two versions of indexOf that search for characters in a String. The expression in line 12 uses the version of method indexOf that takes an integer representation of the character to find. The expression at line 14 uses another version of method indexOf, which takes two integer arguments—the character and the starting index at which the search of the String should begin.

Lines 19–24 use method lastIndexOf to locate the last occurrence of a character in a String. The method searches from the end of the String toward the beginning. If it finds the character, it returns the character's index in the String—otherwise, it returns –1. There are two versions of lastIndexOf that search for characters in a String. The expression at line 20 uses the version that takes the integer representation of the character. The expression at line 22 uses the version that takes two integer arguments—the integer representation of the character and the index from which to begin searching backward.

Lines 27–40 demonstrate versions of methods indexOf and lastIndexOf that each take a String as the first argument. These versions perform identically to those described earlier except that they search for sequences of characters (or substrings) that are specified by their String arguments. If the substring is found, these methods return the index in the String of the first character in the substring.

16.3.5 Extracting Substrings from Strings

Class String provides two substring methods to enable a new String object to be created by copying part of an existing String object. Each method returns a new String object. Both methods are demonstrated in Fig. 16.6.

```java
 1   // Fig. 16.6: SubString.java
 2   // String class substring methods.
 3
 4   public class SubString
 5   {
 6      public static void main( String[] args )
 7      {
 8         String letters = "abcdefghijklmabcdefghijklm";
 9
10         // test substring methods
11         System.out.printf( "Substring from index 20 to end is \"%s\"\n",
12            letters.substring( 20 ) );
13         System.out.printf( "%s \"%s\"\n",
14            "Substring from index 3 up to, but not including 6 is",
15            letters.substring( 3, 6 ) );
16      } // end main
17   } // end class SubString
```

```
Substring from index 20 to end is "hijklm"
Substring from index 3 up to, but not including 6 is "def"
```

Fig. 16.6 | String class substring methods.

The expression letters.substring(20) at line 12 uses the substring method that takes one integer argument. The argument specifies the starting index in the original String letters from which characters are to be copied. The substring returned contains a copy of the characters from the starting index to the end of the String. Specifying an index outside the bounds of the String causes a **StringIndexOutOfBoundsException**.

Line 15 uses the substring method that takes two integer arguments—the starting index from which to copy characters in the original String and the index one beyond the last character to copy (i.e., copy up to, but not including, that index in the String). The substring returned contains a copy of the specified characters from the original String. An index outside the bounds of the String causes a StringIndexOutOfBoundsException.

16.3.6 Concatenating Strings

String method **concat** (Fig. 16.7) concatenates two String objects and returns a new String object containing the characters from both original Strings. The expression s1.concat(s2) at line 13 forms a String by appending the characters in s2 to the characters in s1. The original Strings to which s1 and s2 refer are not modified.

```java
 1   // Fig. 16.7: StringConcatenation.java
 2   // String method concat.
 3
```

Fig. 16.7 | String method concat. (Part 1 of 2.)

```
4   public class StringConcatenation
5   {
6      public static void main( String[] args )
7      {
8         String s1 = "Happy ";
9         String s2 = "Birthday";
10
11        System.out.printf( "s1 = %s\ns2 = %s\n\n",s1, s2 );
12        System.out.printf(
13           "Result of s1.concat( s2 ) = %s\n", s1.concat( s2 ) );
14        System.out.printf( "s1 after concatenation = %s\n", s1 );
15     } // end main
16  } // end class StringConcatenation
```

```
s1 = Happy
s2 = Birthday

Result of s1.concat( s2 ) = Happy Birthday
s1 after concatenation = Happy
```

Fig. 16.7 | String method concat. (Part 2 of 2.)

16.3.7 Miscellaneous String Methods

Class String provides several methods that return modified copies of Strings or that return character arrays. These methods are demonstrated in the application in Fig. 16.8.

```
1   // Fig. 16.8: StringMiscellaneous2.java
2   // String methods replace, toLowerCase, toUpperCase, trim and toCharArray.
3
4   public class StringMiscellaneous2
5   {
6      public static void main( String[] args )
7      {
8         String s1 = "hello";
9         String s2 = "GOODBYE";
10        String s3 = "   spaces   ";
11
12        System.out.printf( "s1 = %s\ns2 = %s\ns3 = %s\n\n", s1, s2, s3 );
13
14        // test method replace
15        System.out.printf(
16           "Replace 'l' with 'L' in s1: %s\n\n", s1.replace( 'l', 'L' ) );
17
18        // test toLowerCase and toUpperCase
19        System.out.printf( "s1.toUpperCase() = %s\n", s1.toUpperCase() );
20        System.out.printf( "s2.toLowerCase() = %s\n\n", s2.toLowerCase() );
21
22        // test trim method
23        System.out.printf( "s3 after trim = \"%s\"\n\n", s3.trim() );
24
```

Fig. 16.8 | String methods replace, toLowerCase, toUpperCase, trim and toCharArray. (Part 1 of 2.)

```
25          // test toCharArray method
26          char[] charArray = s1.toCharArray();
27          System.out.print( "s1 as a character array = " );
28
29          for ( char character : charArray )
30             System.out.print( character );
31
32          System.out.println();
33       } // end main
34    } // end class StringMiscellaneous2
```

```
s1 = hello
s2 = GOODBYE
s3 =     spaces

Replace 'l' with 'L' in s1: heLLo

s1.toUpperCase() = HELLO
s2.toLowerCase() = goodbye

s3 after trim = "spaces"

s1 as a character array = hello
```

Fig. 16.8 | String methods replace, toLowerCase, toUpperCase, trim and toCharArray. (Part 2 of 2.)

Line 16 uses String method replace to return a new String object in which every occurrence in s1 of character 'l' (lowercase el) is replaced with character 'L'. Method replace leaves the original String unchanged. If there are no occurrences of the first argument in the String, method replace returns the original String. An overloaded version of method replace enables you to replace substrings rather than individual characters.

Line 19 uses String method **toUpperCase** to generate a new String with uppercase letters where corresponding lowercase letters exist in s1. The method returns a new String object containing the converted String and leaves the original String unchanged. If there are no characters to convert, method toUpperCase returns the original String.

Line 20 uses String method **toLowerCase** to return a new String object with lowercase letters where corresponding uppercase letters exist in s2. The original String remains unchanged. If there are no characters in the original String to convert, toLowerCase returns the original String.

Line 23 uses String method **trim** to generate a new String object that removes all whitespace characters that appear at the beginning or end of the String on which trim operates. The method returns a new String object containing the String without leading or trailing whitespace. The original String remains unchanged.

Line 26 uses String method **toCharArray** to create a new character array containing a copy of the characters in s1. Lines 29–30 output each char in the array.

16.3.8 String Method valueOf

As we've seen, every object in Java has a toString method that enables a program to obtain the object's string representation. Unfortunately, this technique cannot be used with primitive types because they do not have methods. Class String provides static methods that take an argument of any type and convert it to a String object. Figure 16.9 demonstrates the String class **valueOf** methods.

```
1    // Fig. 16.9: StringValueOf.java
2    // String valueOf methods.
3
4    public class StringValueOf
5    {
6       public static void main( String[] args )
7       {
8          char[] charArray = { 'a', 'b', 'c', 'd', 'e', 'f' };
9          boolean booleanValue = true;
10         char characterValue = 'Z';
11         int integerValue = 7;
12         long longValue = 10000000000L; // L suffix indicates long
13         float floatValue = 2.5f; // f indicates that 2.5 is a float
14         double doubleValue = 33.333; // no suffix, double is default
15         Object objectRef = "hello"; // assign string to an Object reference
16
17         System.out.printf(
18            "char array = %s\n", String.valueOf( charArray ) );
19         System.out.printf( "part of char array = %s\n",
20            String.valueOf( charArray, 3, 3 ) );
21         System.out.printf(
22            "boolean = %s\n", String.valueOf( booleanValue ) );
23         System.out.printf(
24            "char = %s\n", String.valueOf( characterValue ) );
25         System.out.printf( "int = %s\n", String.valueOf( integerValue ) );
26         System.out.printf( "long = %s\n", String.valueOf( longValue ) );
27         System.out.printf( "float = %s\n", String.valueOf( floatValue ) );
28         System.out.printf(
29            "double = %s\n", String.valueOf( doubleValue ) );
30         System.out.printf( "Object = %s", String.valueOf( objectRef ) );
31      } // end main
32   } // end class StringValueOf
```

```
char array = abcdef
part of char array = def
boolean = true
char = Z
int = 7
long = 10000000000
float = 2.5
double = 33.333
Object = hello
```

Fig. 16.9 | String valueOf methods.

The expression String.valueOf(charArray) at line 18 uses the character array charArray to create a new String object. The expression String.valueOf(charArray, 3, 3) at line 20 uses a portion of the character array charArray to create a new String object. The second argument specifies the starting index from which the characters are used. The third argument specifies the number of characters to be used.

There are seven other versions of method valueOf, which take arguments of type boolean, char, int, long, float, double and Object, respectively. These are demonstrated in lines 21–30. Note that the version of valueOf that takes an Object as an argument can do so because all Objects can be converted to Strings with method toString.

[*Note:* Lines 12–13 use literal values 10000000000L and 2.5f as the initial values of long variable longValue and float variable floatValue, respectively. By default, Java treats integer literals as type int and floating-point literals as type double. Appending the letter L to the literal 10000000000 and appending letter f to the literal 2.5 indicates to the compiler that 10000000000 should be treated as a long and that 2.5 should be treated as a float. An uppercase L or lowercase l can be used to denote a variable of type long and an uppercase F or lowercase f can be used to denote a variable of type float.]

16.4 Class StringBuilder

We now discuss the features of class **StringBuilder** for creating and manipulating dynamic string information—that is, modifiable strings. Every StringBuilder is capable of storing a number of characters specified by its capacity. If the capacity of a StringBuilder is exceeded, the capacity expands to accommodate the additional characters.

Performance Tip 16.2
Java can perform certain optimizations involving String objects (such as referring to one String object from multiple variables) because it knows these objects will not change. Strings (not StringBuilders) should be used if the data will not change.

Performance Tip 16.3
In programs that frequently perform string concatenation, or other string modifications, it's often more efficient to implement the modifications with class StringBuilder.

Software Engineering Observation 16.2
*StringBuilders are not thread safe. If multiple threads require access to the same dynamic string information, use class **StringBuffer** in your code. Classes StringBuilder and StringBuffer provide identical capabilities, but class StringBuffer is thread safe. For more details on threading, see Chapter 26.*

16.4.1 StringBuilder Constructors

Class StringBuilder provides four constructors. We demonstrate three of these in Fig. 16.10. Line 8 uses the no-argument StringBuilder constructor to create a String-Builder with no characters in it and an initial capacity of 16 characters (the default for a StringBuilder). Line 9 uses the StringBuilder constructor that takes an integer argument to create a StringBuilder with no characters in it and the initial capacity specified by the integer argument (i.e., 10). Line 10 uses the StringBuilder constructor that takes a String argument to create a StringBuilder containing the characters in the String argument. The initial capacity is the number of characters in the String argument plus 16.

Lines 12–14 use the method toString of class StringBuilder to output the String-Builders with the printf method. In Section 16.4.4, we discuss how Java uses String-Builder objects to implement the + and += operators for string concatenation.

```
 1   // Fig. 16.10: StringBuilderConstructors.java
 2   // StringBuilder constructors.
 3
 4   public class StringBuilderConstructors
 5   {
 6      public static void main( String[] args )
 7      {
 8         StringBuilder buffer1 = new StringBuilder();
 9         StringBuilder buffer2 = new StringBuilder( 10 );
10         StringBuilder buffer3 = new StringBuilder( "hello" );
11
12         System.out.printf( "buffer1 = \"%s\"\n", buffer1.toString() );
13         System.out.printf( "buffer2 = \"%s\"\n", buffer2.toString() );
14         System.out.printf( "buffer3 = \"%s\"\n", buffer3.toString() );
15      } // end main
16   } // end class StringBuilderConstructors
```

```
buffer1 = ""
buffer2 = ""
buffer3 = "hello"
```

Fig. 16.10 | StringBuilder constructors.

16.4.2 StringBuilder Methods length, capacity, setLength and ensureCapacity

Class StringBuilder provides methods **length** and **capacity** to return the number of characters currently in a StringBuilder and the number of characters that can be stored in a StringBuilder without allocating more memory, respectively. Method **ensure-Capacity** guarantees that a StringBuilder has at least the specified capacity. Method setLength increases or decreases the length of a StringBuilder. Figure 16.11 demonstrates these methods.

```
 1   // Fig. 16.11: StringBuilderCapLen.java
 2   // StringBuilder length, setLength, capacity and ensureCapacity methods.
 3
 4   public class StringBuilderCapLen
 5   {
 6      public static void main( String[] args )
 7      {
 8         StringBuilder buffer = new StringBuilder( "Hello, how are you?" );
 9
10         System.out.printf( "buffer = %s\nlength = %d\ncapacity = %d\n\n",
11            buffer.toString(), buffer.length(), buffer.capacity() );
12
13         buffer.ensureCapacity( 75 );
14         System.out.printf( "New capacity = %d\n\n", buffer.capacity() );
15
16         buffer.setLength( 10 );
```

Fig. 16.11 | StringBuilder length, setLength, capacity and ensureCapacity methods. (Part 1 of 2.)

```
17          System.out.printf( "New length = %d\nbuffer = %s\n",
18             buffer.length(), buffer.toString() );
19      } // end main
20   } // end class StringBuilderCapLen
```

```
buffer = Hello, how are you?
length = 19
capacity = 35

New capacity = 75

New length = 10
buffer = Hello, how
```

Fig. 16.11 | StringBuilder length, setLength, capacity and ensureCapacity methods. (Part 2 of 2.)

The application contains one StringBuilder called buffer. Line 8 uses the String-Builder constructor that takes a String argument to initialize the StringBuilder with "Hello, how are you?". Lines 10–11 print the contents, length and capacity of the StringBuilder. Note in the output window that the capacity of the StringBuilder is initially 35. Recall that the StringBuilder constructor that takes a String argument initializes the capacity to the length of the string passed as an argument plus 16.

Line 13 uses method ensureCapacity to expand the capacity of the StringBuilder to a minimum of 75 characters. Actually, if the original capacity is less than the argument, the method ensures a capacity that is the greater of the number specified as an argument and twice the original capacity plus 2. The StringBuilder's current capacity remains unchanged if it's more than the specified capacity.

Performance Tip 16.4
Dynamically increasing the capacity of a StringBuilder can take a relatively long time. Executing a large number of these operations can degrade the performance of an application. If a StringBuilder is going to increase greatly in size, possibly multiple times, setting its capacity high at the beginning will increase performance.

Line 16 uses method setLength to set the length of the StringBuilder to 10. If the specified length is less than the current number of characters in the StringBuilder, the buffer is truncated to the specified length (i.e., the characters in the StringBuilder after the specified length are discarded). If the specified length is greater than the number of characters currently in the StringBuilder, null characters (characters with the numeric representation 0) are appended until the total number of characters in the StringBuilder is equal to the specified length.

16.4.3 StringBuilder Methods charAt, setCharAt, getChars and reverse

Class StringBuilder provides methods **charAt**, **setCharAt**, **getChars** and **reverse** to manipulate the characters in a StringBuilder (Fig. 16.12). Method charAt (line 12) takes an integer argument and returns the character in the StringBuilder at that index. Method getChars (line 15) copies characters from a StringBuilder into the character array passed as an argument. This method takes four arguments—the starting index from which characters should be copied in the StringBuilder, the index one past the last character to be copied from the StringBuilder, the character array into which the characters are to be copied and the starting location in the character array where the first character should be placed. Method setCharAt (lines 21 and 22) takes an integer and a character argument and sets the character at the specified position in the StringBuilder to the character argument. Method reverse (line 25) reverses the contents of the StringBuilder.

Common Programming Error 16.3

Attempting to access a character that is outside the bounds of a StringBuilder (i.e., with an index less than 0 or greater than or equal to the StringBuilder's length) results in a StringIndexOutOfBoundsException.

```
1   // Fig. 16.12: StringBuilderChars.java
2   // StringBuilder methods charAt, setCharAt, getChars and reverse.
3
4   public class StringBuilderChars
5   {
6      public static void main( String[] args )
7      {
8         StringBuilder buffer = new StringBuilder( "hello there" );
9
10        System.out.printf( "buffer = %s\n", buffer.toString() );
11        System.out.printf( "Character at 0: %s\nCharacter at 4: %s\n\n",
12           buffer.charAt( 0 ), buffer.charAt( 4 ) );
13
14        char[] charArray = new char[ buffer.length() ];
15        buffer.getChars( 0, buffer.length(), charArray, 0 );
16        System.out.print( "The characters are: " );
17
18        for ( char character : charArray )
19           System.out.print( character );
20
21        buffer.setCharAt( 0, 'H' );
22        buffer.setCharAt( 6, 'T' );
23        System.out.printf( "\n\nbuffer = %s", buffer.toString() );
24
25        buffer.reverse();
26        System.out.printf( "\n\nbuffer = %s\n", buffer.toString() );
27     } // end main
28  } // end class StringBuilderChars
```

```
buffer = hello there
Character at 0: h
Character at 4: o

The characters are: hello there

buffer = Hello There

buffer = erehT olleH
```

Fig. 16.12 | StringBuilder methods charAt, setCharAt, getChars and reverse.

16.4.4 StringBuilder append Methods

Class StringBuilder provides overloaded **append** methods (Fig. 16.13) to allow values of various types to be appended to the end of a StringBuilder. Versions are provided for each of the primitive types, and for character arrays, Strings, Objects, and more. (Remember that method toString produces a string representation of any Object.) Each method takes its argument, converts it to a string and appends it to the StringBuilder.

```java
1   // Fig. 16.13: StringBuilderAppend.java
2   // StringBuilder append methods.
3
4   public class StringBuilderAppend
5   {
6      public static void main( String[] args )
7      {
8         Object objectRef = "hello";
9         String string = "goodbye";
10        char[] charArray = { 'a', 'b', 'c', 'd', 'e', 'f' };
11        boolean booleanValue = true;
12        char characterValue = 'Z';
13        int integerValue = 7;
14        long longValue = 10000000000L;
15        float floatValue = 2.5f;
16        double doubleValue = 33.333;
17
18        StringBuilder lastBuffer = new StringBuilder( "last buffer" );
19        StringBuilder buffer = new StringBuilder();
20
21        buffer.append( objectRef );
22        buffer.append( "\n" );
23        buffer.append( string );
24        buffer.append( "\n" );
25        buffer.append( charArray );
26        buffer.append( "\n" );
27        buffer.append( charArray, 0, 3 );
28        buffer.append( "\n" );
29        buffer.append( booleanValue );
30        buffer.append( "\n" );
31        buffer.append( characterValue );
32        buffer.append( "\n" );
33        buffer.append( integerValue );
34        buffer.append( "\n" );
35        buffer.append( longValue );
36        buffer.append( "\n" );
37        buffer.append( floatValue );
38        buffer.append( "\n" );
39        buffer.append( doubleValue );
40        buffer.append( "\n" );
41        buffer.append( lastBuffer );
42
43        System.out.printf( "buffer contains %s\n", buffer.toString() );
44     } // end main
45  } // end StringBuilderAppend
```

Fig. 16.13 | StringBuilder append methods. (Part 1 of 2.)

```
buffer contains hello
goodbye
abcdef
abc
true
Z
7
10000000000
2.5
33.333
last buffer
```

Fig. 16.13 | StringBuilder append methods. (Part 2 of 2.)

Actually, a compiler can use StringBuilder (or StringBuffer) and the append methods to implement the + and += String concatenation operators. For example, assuming the declarations

```
String string1 = "hello";
String string2 = "BC";
int value = 22;
```

the statement

```
String s = string1 + string2 + value;
```

concatenates "hello", "BC" and 22. The concatenation can be performed as follows:

```
String s = new StringBuilder().append( "hello" ).append( "BC" ).
    append( 22 ).toString();
```

First, the preceding statement creates an empty StringBuilder, then appends to it the strings "hello" and "BC" and the integer 22. Next, StringBuilder's toString method converts the StringBuilder to a String object to be assigned to String s. The statement

```
s += "!";
```

can be performed as follows:

```
s = new StringBuilder().append( s ).append( "!" ).toString();
```

First, the preceding statement creates an empty StringBuilder, then it appends to it the current contents of s followed by "!". Next, StringBuilder's method toString converts the StringBuilder to a string representation, and the result is assigned to s.

16.4.5 StringBuilder Insertion and Deletion Methods

Class StringBuilder provides overloaded **insert** methods to insert values of various types at any position in a StringBuilder. Versions are provided for the primitive types and for character arrays, Strings, Objects and CharSequences. Each method takes its second argument, converts it to a String and inserts it at the index specified by the first argument. If the first argument less than 0 or greater than the StringBuilder's length, a String-IndexOutOfBoundsException occurs. Class StringBuilder also provides methods **delete** and **deleteCharAt** to delete characters at any position in a StringBuilder. Method delete takes two arguments—the starting index and the index one past the end of the characters to delete. All characters beginning at the starting index up to but not including the ending index are deleted. Method `deleteCharAt` takes one argument—the index of the character to delete. Invalid indices cause both methods to throw a `StringIndexOutOfBoundsExcep-tion`. Figure 16.14 demonstrates methods `insert`, `delete` and `deleteCharAt`.

```java
1   // Fig. 16.14: StringBuilderInsertDelete.java
2   // StringBuilder methods insert, delete and deleteCharAt.
3
4   public class StringBuilderInsertDelete
5   {
6      public static void main( String[] args )
7      {
8         Object objectRef = "hello";
9         String string = "goodbye";
10        char[] charArray = { 'a', 'b', 'c', 'd', 'e', 'f' };
11        boolean booleanValue = true;
12        char characterValue = 'K';
13        int integerValue = 7;
14        long longValue = 10000000;
15        float floatValue = 2.5f; // f suffix indicates that 2.5 is a float
16        double doubleValue = 33.333;
17
18        StringBuilder buffer = new StringBuilder();
19
20        buffer.insert( 0, objectRef );
21        buffer.insert( 0, "  " ); // each of these contains two spaces
22        buffer.insert( 0, string );
23        buffer.insert( 0, "  " );
24        buffer.insert( 0, charArray );
25        buffer.insert( 0, "  " );
26        buffer.insert( 0, charArray, 3, 3 );
27        buffer.insert( 0, "  " );
28        buffer.insert( 0, booleanValue );
29        buffer.insert( 0, "  " );
30        buffer.insert( 0, characterValue );
31        buffer.insert( 0, "  " );
32        buffer.insert( 0, integerValue );
33        buffer.insert( 0, "  " );
34        buffer.insert( 0, longValue );
35        buffer.insert( 0, "  " );
36        buffer.insert( 0, floatValue );
37        buffer.insert( 0, "  " );
38        buffer.insert( 0, doubleValue );
39
40        System.out.printf(
41           "buffer after inserts:\n%s\n\n", buffer.toString() );
42
43        buffer.deleteCharAt( 10 ); // delete 5 in 2.5
44        buffer.delete( 2, 6 ); // delete .333 in 33.333
45
46        System.out.printf(
47           "buffer after deletes:\n%s\n", buffer.toString() );
48     } // end main
49  } // end class StringBuilderInsertDelete
```

Fig. 16.14 | StringBuilder methods insert, delete and deleteCharAt. (Part 1 of 2.)

```
buffer after inserts:
33.333  2.5  10000000  7  K  true  def  abcdef  goodbye  hello

buffer after deletes:
33  2.  10000000  7  K  true  def  abcdef  goodbye  hello
```

Fig. 16.14 | `StringBuilder` methods `insert`, `delete` and `deleteCharAt`. (Part 2 of 2.)

16.5 Class Character

Java provides eight type-wrapper classes—`Boolean`, `Character`, `Double`, `Float`, `Byte`, `Short`, `Integer` and `Long`—that enable primitive-type values to be treated as objects. In this section, we present class `Character`—the type-wrapper class for primitive type `char`.

Most `Character` methods are `static` methods designed for convenience in processing individual `char` values. These methods take at least a character argument and perform either a test or a manipulation of the character. Class `Character` also contains a constructor that receives a `char` argument to initialize a `Character` object. Most of the methods of class `Character` are presented in the next three examples. For more information on class `Character` (and all the type-wrapper classes), see the `java.lang` package in the Java API documentation.

Figure 16.15 demonstrates `static` methods that test characters to determine whether they are a specific character type and the `static` methods that perform case conversions on characters. You can enter any character and apply the methods to the character.

```java
1   // Fig. 16.15: StaticCharMethods.java
2   // Character static methods for testing characters and converting case.
3   import java.util.Scanner;
4
5   public class StaticCharMethods
6   {
7      public static void main( String[] args )
8      {
9         Scanner scanner = new Scanner( System.in ); // create scanner
10        System.out.println( "Enter a character and press Enter" );
11        String input = scanner.next();
12        char c = input.charAt( 0 ); // get input character
13
14        // display character info
15        System.out.printf( "is defined: %b\n", Character.isDefined( c ) );
16        System.out.printf( "is digit: %b\n", Character.isDigit( c ) );
17        System.out.printf( "is first character in a Java identifier: %b\n",
18           Character.isJavaIdentifierStart( c ) );
19        System.out.printf( "is part of a Java identifier: %b\n",
20           Character.isJavaIdentifierPart( c ) );
21        System.out.printf( "is letter: %b\n", Character.isLetter( c ) );
22        System.out.printf(
23           "is letter or digit: %b\n", Character.isLetterOrDigit( c ) );
24        System.out.printf(
25           "is lower case: %b\n", Character.isLowerCase( c ) );
```

Fig. 16.15 | `Character static` methods for testing characters and converting case. (Part 1 of 2.)

```
26          System.out.printf(
27             "is upper case: %b\n", Character.isUpperCase( c ) );
28          System.out.printf(
29             "to upper case: %s\n", Character.toUpperCase( c ) );
30          System.out.printf(
31             "to lower case: %s\n", Character.toLowerCase( c ) );
32       } // end main
33    } // end class StaticCharMethods
```

```
Enter a character and press Enter
A
is defined: true
is digit: false
is first character in a Java identifier: true
is part of a Java identifier: true
is letter: true
is letter or digit: true
is lower case: false
is upper case: true
to upper case: A
to lower case: a
```

```
Enter a character and press Enter
8
is defined: true
is digit: true
is first character in a Java identifier: false
is part of a Java identifier: true
is letter: false
is letter or digit: true
is lower case: false
is upper case: false
to upper case: 8
to lower case: 8
```

```
Enter a character and press Enter
$
is defined: true
is digit: false
is first character in a Java identifier: true
is part of a Java identifier: true
is letter: false
is letter or digit: false
is lower case: false
is upper case: false
to upper case: $
to lower case: $
```

Fig. 16.15 | Character static methods for testing characters and converting case. (Part 2 of 2.)

Line 15 uses Character method **isDefined** to determine whether character c is defined in the Unicode character set. If so, the method returns true; otherwise, it returns false. Line 16 uses Character method **isDigit** to determine whether character c is a defined Unicode digit. If so, the method returns true, and otherwise, false.

Line 18 uses Character method **isJavaIdentifierStart** to determine whether c is a character that can be the first character of an identifier in Java—that is, a letter, an underscore (_) or a dollar sign ($). If so, the method returns true, and otherwise, false. Line 20 uses Character method **isJavaIdentifierPart** to determine whether character c is a character that can be used in an identifier in Java—that is, a digit, a letter, an underscore (_) or a dollar sign ($). If so, the method returns true, and otherwise, false.

Line 21 uses Character method **isLetter** to determine whether character c is a letter. If so, the method returns true, and otherwise, false. Line 23 uses Character method **isLetterOrDigit** to determine whether character c is a letter or a digit. If so, the method returns true, and otherwise, false.

Line 25 uses Character method **isLowerCase** to determine whether character c is a lowercase letter. If so, the method returns true, and otherwise, false. Line 27 uses Character method **isUpperCase** to determine whether character c is an uppercase letter. If so, the method returns true, and otherwise, false.

Line 29 uses Character method **toUpperCase** to convert the character c to its uppercase equivalent. The method returns the converted character if the character has an uppercase equivalent, and otherwise, the method returns its original argument. Line 31 uses Character method **toLowerCase** to convert the character c to its lowercase equivalent. The method returns the converted character if the character has a lowercase equivalent, and otherwise, the method returns its original argument.

Figure 16.16 demonstrates static Character methods **digit** and **forDigit**, which convert characters to digits and digits to characters, respectively, in different number systems. Common number systems include decimal (base 10), octal (base 8), hexadecimal (base 16) and binary (base 2). The base of a number is also known as its **radix**. For more information on conversions between number systems, see Appendix H.

```java
1   // Fig. 16.16: StaticCharMethods2.java
2   // Character class static conversion methods.
3   import java.util.Scanner;
4
5   public class StaticCharMethods2
6   {
7      // executes application
8      public static void main( String[] args )
9      {
10        Scanner scanner = new Scanner( System.in );
11
12        // get radix
13        System.out.println( "Please enter a radix:" );
14        int radix = scanner.nextInt();
15
16        // get user choice
17        System.out.printf( "Please choose one:\n1 -- %s\n2 -- %s\n",
18           "Convert digit to character", "Convert character to digit" );
19        int choice = scanner.nextInt();
20
21        // process request
22        switch ( choice )
23        {
```

Fig. 16.16 | Character class static conversion methods. (Part 1 of 2.)

```
24              case 1: // convert digit to character
25                  System.out.println( "Enter a digit:" );
26                  int digit = scanner.nextInt();
27                  System.out.printf( "Convert digit to character: %s\n",
28                      Character.forDigit( digit, radix ) );
29                  break;
30
31              case 2: // convert character to digit
32                  System.out.println( "Enter a character:" );
33                  char character = scanner.next().charAt( 0 );
34                  System.out.printf( "Convert character to digit: %s\n",
35                      Character.digit( character, radix ) );
36                  break;
37          } // end switch
38      } // end main
39  } // end class StaticCharMethods2
```

```
Please enter a radix:
16
Please choose one:
1 -- Convert digit to character
2 -- Convert character to digit
2
Enter a character:
A
Convert character to digit: 10
```

```
Please enter a radix:
16
Please choose one:
1 -- Convert digit to character
2 -- Convert character to digit
1
Enter a digit:
13
Convert digit to character: d
```

Fig. 16.16 | Character class static conversion methods. (Part 2 of 2.)

Line 28 uses method forDigit to convert the integer digit into a character in the number system specified by the integer radix (the base of the number). For example, the decimal integer 13 in base 16 (the radix) has the character value 'd'. Lowercase and uppercase letters represent the same value in number systems. Line 35 uses method digit to convert variable character into an integer in the number system specified by the integer radix (the base of the number). For example, the character 'A' is the base 16 (the radix) representation of the base 10 value 10. The radix must be between 2 and 36, inclusive.

Figure 16.17 demonstrates the constructor and several non-static methods of class Character—**charValue**, toString and equals. Lines 7–8 instantiate two Character objects by assigning the character constants 'A' and 'a', respectively, to the Character variables. Java automatically converts these char literals into Character objects—a process known as autoboxing that we discuss in more detail in Section 20.4. Line 11 uses Character method charValue to return the char value stored in Character object c1. Line 11 returns a string representation of Character object c2 using method toString. The condition in line 13 uses method equals to determine whether the object c1 has the same contents as the object c2 (i.e., the characters inside each object are equal).

```
 1   // Fig. 16.17: OtherCharMethods.java
 2   // Character class non-static methods.
 3   public class OtherCharMethods
 4   {
 5      public static void main( String[] args )
 6      {
 7         Character c1 = 'A';
 8         Character c2 = 'a';
 9
10         System.out.printf(
11            "c1 = %s\nc2 = %s\n\n", c1.charValue(), c2.toString() );
12
13         if ( c1.equals( c2 ) )
14            System.out.println( "c1 and c2 are equal\n" );
15         else
16            System.out.println( "c1 and c2 are not equal\n" );
17      } // end main
18   } // end class OtherCharMethods
```

```
c1 = A
c2 = a

c1 and c2 are not equal
```

Fig. 16.17 | Character class non-static methods.

16.6 Tokenizing Strings

When you read a sentence, your mind breaks it into **tokens**—individual words and punctuation marks that convey meaning to you. Compilers also perform tokenization. They break up statements into individual pieces like keywords, identifiers, operators and other programming-language elements. We now study class String's **split** method, which breaks a String into its component tokens. Tokens are separated from one another by **delimiters**, typically white-space characters such as space, tab, newline and carriage return. Other characters can also be used as delimiters to separate tokens. The application in Fig. 16.18 demonstrates String's split method.

```
 1   // Fig. 16.18: TokenTest.java
 2   // StringTokenizer object used to tokenize strings.
 3   import java.util.Scanner;
 4   import java.util.StringTokenizer;
 5
 6   public class TokenTest
 7   {
```

Fig. 16.18 | StringTokenizer object used to tokenize strings. (Part 1 of 2.)

```
8      // execute application
9      public static void main( String[] args )
10     {
11        // get sentence
12        Scanner scanner = new Scanner( System.in );
13        System.out.println( "Enter a sentence and press Enter" );
14        String sentence = scanner.nextLine();
15
16        // process user sentence
17        String[] tokens = sentence.split( " " );
18        System.out.printf( "Number of elements: %d\nThe tokens are:\n",
19           tokens.length );
20
21        for ( String token : tokens )
22           System.out.println( token );
23     } // end main
24  } // end class TokenTest
```

```
Enter a sentence and press Enter
This is a sentence with seven tokens
Number of elements: 7
The tokens are:
This
is
a
sentence
with
seven
tokens
```

Fig. 16.18 | `StringTokenizer` object used to tokenize strings. (Part 2 of 2.)

When the user presses the *Enter* key, the input sentence is stored in variable `sentence`. Line 17 invokes `String` method `split` with the `String` argument `" "`, which returns an array of `String`s. The space character in the argument `String` is the delimiter that method `split` uses to locate the tokens in the `String`. As you'll learn in the next section, the argument to method split can be a regular expression for more complex tokenizing. Line 19 displays the length of the array `tokens`—i.e., the number of tokens in `sentence`. Lines 21–22 output each token on a separate line.

16.7 Regular Expressions, Class Pattern and Class Matcher

A **regular expression** is a specially formatted `String` that describes a search pattern for matching characters in other `String`s. They are useful for validating input and ensuring that data is in a particular format. For example, a ZIP code must consist of five digits, and a last name must contain only letters, spaces, apostrophes and hyphens. One application of regular expressions is to facilitate the construction of a compiler. Often, a large and complex regular expression is used to validate the syntax of a program. If the program code does not match the regular expression, the compiler knows that there is a syntax error within the code.

Class String provides several methods for performing regular-expression operations, the simplest of which is the matching operation. String method **matches** receives a String that specifies the regular expression and matches the contents of the String object on which it's called to the regular expression. The method returns a boolean indicating whether the match succeeded.

A regular expression consists of literal characters and special symbols. Figure 16.19 specifies some **predefined character classes** that can be used with regular expressions. A character class is an escape sequence that represents a group of characters. A digit is any numeric character. A **word character** is any letter (uppercase or lowercase), any digit or the underscore character. A white-space character is a space, a tab, a carriage return, a newline or a form feed. Each character class matches a single character in the String we're attempting to match with the regular expression.

Character	Matches	Character	Matches
\d	any digit	\D	any nondigit
\w	any word character	\W	any nonword character
\s	any white-space character	\S	any nonwhite-space character

Fig. 16.19 | Predefined character classes.

Regular expressions are not limited to these predefined character classes. The expressions employ various operators and other forms of notation to match complex patterns. We examine several of these techniques in the application in Figs. 16.20 and 16.21, which validates user input via regular expressions. [*Note:* This application is not designed to match all possible valid user input.]

```
1   // Fig. 16.20: ValidateInput.java
2   // Validate user information using regular expressions.
3
4   public class ValidateInput
5   {
6      // validate first name
7      public static boolean validateFirstName( String firstName )
8      {
9         return firstName.matches( "[A-Z][a-zA-Z]*" );
10     } // end method validateFirstName
11
12     // validate last name
13     public static boolean validateLastName( String lastName )
14     {
15        return lastName.matches( "[a-zA-z]+([ '-][a-zA-Z]+)*" );
16     } // end method validateLastName
17
18     // validate address
19     public static boolean validateAddress( String address )
20     {
```

Fig. 16.20 | Validating user information using regular expressions. (Part 1 of 2.)

```
21        return address.matches(
22          "\\d+\\s+([a-zA-Z]+|[a-zA-Z]+\\s[a-zA-Z]+)" );
23     } // end method validateAddress
24
25     // validate city
26     public static boolean validateCity( String city )
27     {
28        return city.matches( "([a-zA-Z]+|[a-zA-Z]+\\s[a-zA-Z]+)" );
29     } // end method validateCity
30
31     // validate state
32     public static boolean validateState( String state )
33     {
34        return state.matches( "([a-zA-Z]+|[a-zA-Z]+\\s[a-zA-Z]+)" ) ;
35     } // end method validateState
36
37     // validate zip
38     public static boolean validateZip( String zip )
39     {
40        return zip.matches( "\\d{5}" );
41     } // end method validateZip
42
43     // validate phone
44     public static boolean validatePhone( String phone )
45     {
46        return phone.matches( "[1-9]\\d{2}-[1-9]\\d{2}-\\d{4}" );
47     } // end method validatePhone
48  } // end class ValidateInput
```

Fig. 16.20 | Validating user information using regular expressions. (Part 2 of 2.)

```
1   // Fig. 16.21: Validate.java
2   // Validate user information using regular expressions.
3   import java.util.Scanner;
4
5   public class Validate
6   {
7      public static void main( String[] args )
8      {
9         // get user input
10        Scanner scanner = new Scanner( System.in );
11        System.out.println( "Please enter first name:" );
12        String firstName = scanner.nextLine();
13        System.out.println( "Please enter last name:" );
14        String lastName = scanner.nextLine();
15        System.out.println( "Please enter address:" );
16        String address = scanner.nextLine();
17        System.out.println( "Please enter city:" );
18        String city = scanner.nextLine();
19        System.out.println( "Please enter state:" );
20        String state = scanner.nextLine();
21        System.out.println( "Please enter zip:" );
22        String zip = scanner.nextLine();
```

Fig. 16.21 | Inputs and validates data from user using the ValidateInput class. (Part 1 of 3.)

```
23              System.out.println( "Please enter phone:" );
24              String phone = scanner.nextLine();
25
26              // validate user input and display error message
27              System.out.println( "\nValidate Result:" );
28
29              if ( !ValidateInput.validateFirstName( firstName ) )
30                 System.out.println( "Invalid first name" );
31              else if ( !ValidateInput.validateLastName( lastName ) )
32                 System.out.println( "Invalid last name" );
33              else if ( !ValidateInput.validateAddress( address ) )
34                 System.out.println( "Invalid address" );
35              else if ( !ValidateInput.validateCity( city ) )
36                 System.out.println( "Invalid city" );
37              else if ( !ValidateInput.validateState( state ) )
38                 System.out.println( "Invalid state" );
39              else if ( !ValidateInput.validateZip( zip ) )
40                 System.out.println( "Invalid zip code" );
41              else if ( !ValidateInput.validatePhone( phone ) )
42                 System.out.println( "Invalid phone number" );
43              else
44                 System.out.println( "Valid input.  Thank you." );
45        } // end main
46  } // end class Validate
```

```
Please enter first name:
Jane
Please enter last name:
Doe
Please enter address:
123 Some Street
Please enter city:
Some City
Please enter state:
SS
Please enter zip:
123
Please enter phone:
123-456-7890

Validate Result:
Invalid zip code
```

```
Please enter first name:
Jane
Please enter last name:
Doe
Please enter address:
123 Some Street
Please enter city:
Some City
Please enter state:
SS
```

Fig. 16.21 | Inputs and validates data from user using the ValidateInput class. (Part 2 of 3.)

```
Please enter zip:
12345
Please enter phone:
123-456-7890

Validate Result:
Valid input.  Thank you.
```

Fig. 16.21 | Inputs and validates data from user using the `ValidateInput` class. (Part 3 of 3.)

Figure 16.20 validates user input. Line 9 validates the first name. To match a set of characters that does not have a predefined character class, use square brackets, []. For example, the pattern "[aeiou]" matches a single character that's a vowel. Character ranges are represented by placing a dash (-) between two characters. In the example, "[A-Z]" matches a single uppercase letter. If the first character in the brackets is "^", the expression accepts any character other than those indicated. However, it's important to note that "[^Z]" is not the same as "[A-Y]", which matches uppercase letters A–Y—"[^Z]" matches any character other than capital Z, including lowercase letters and nonletters such as the newline character. Ranges in character classes are determined by the letters' integer values. In this example, "[A-Za-z]" matches all uppercase and lowercase letters. The range "[A-z]" matches all letters and also matches those characters (such as [and \) with an integer value between uppercase Z and lowercase a (for more information on integer values of characters see Appendix B). Like predefined character classes, character classes delimited by square brackets match a single character in the search object.

In line 9, the asterisk after the second character class indicates that any number of letters can be matched. In general, when the regular-expression operator "*" appears in a regular expression, the application attempts to match zero or more occurrences of the subexpression immediately preceding the "*". Operator "+" attempts to match one or more occurrences of the subexpression immediately preceding "+". So both "A*" and "A+" will match "AAA" or "A", but only "A*" will match an empty string.

If method `validateFirstName` returns `true` (line 29 of Fig. 16.21), the application attempts to validate the last name (line 31) by calling `validateLastName` (lines 13–16 of Fig. 16.20). The regular expression to validate the last name matches any number of letters split by spaces, apostrophes or hyphens.

Line 33 of Fig. 16.21 calls method `validateAddress` (lines 19–23 of Fig. 16.20) to validate the address. The first character class matches any digit one or more times (\\d+). Note that two \ characters are used, because \ normally starts an escape sequence in a string. So \\d in a `String` represents the regular expression pattern \d. Then we match one or more white-space characters (\\s+). The character "|" matches the expression to its left or to its right. For example, "Hi (John|Jane)" matches both "Hi John" and "Hi Jane". The parentheses are used to group parts of the regular expression. In this example, the left side of | matches a single word, and the right side matches two words separated by any amount of whitespace. So the address must contain a number followed by one or two words. Therefore, "10 Broadway" and "10 Main Street" are both valid addresses in this example. The city (lines 26–29 of Fig. 16.20) and state (lines 32–35 of Fig. 16.20) methods also match any word of at least one character or, alternatively, any two words of at least one character if the words are separated by a single space, so both `Waltham` and `West Newton` would match.

Quantifiers
The asterisk (*) and plus (+) are formally called **quantifiers**. Figure 16.22 lists all the quantifiers. We've already discussed how the asterisk (*) and plus (+) quantifiers work. All quantifiers affect only the subexpression immediately preceding the quantifier. Quantifier question mark (?) matches zero or one occurrences of the expression that it quantifies. A set of braces containing one number ({*n*}) matches exactly *n* occurrences of the expression it quantifies. We demonstrate this quantifier to validate the zip code in Fig. 16.20 at line 40. Including a comma after the number enclosed in braces matches at least *n* occurrences of the quantified expression. The set of braces containing two numbers ({*n*, *m*}), matches between *n* and *m* occurrences of the expression that it qualifies. Quantifiers may be applied to patterns enclosed in parentheses to create more complex regular expressions.

Quantifier	Matches
*	Matches zero or more occurrences of the pattern.
+	Matches one or more occurrences of the pattern.
?	Matches zero or one occurrences of the pattern.
{*n*}	Matches exactly *n* occurrences.
{*n*,}	Matches at least *n* occurrences.
{*n*, *m*}	Matches between *n* and *m* (inclusive) occurrences.

Fig. 16.22 | Quantifiers used in regular expressions.

All of the quantifiers are **greedy**. This means that they'll match as many occurrences as they can as long as the match is still successful. However, if any of these quantifiers is followed by a question mark (?), the quantifier becomes **reluctant** (sometimes called **lazy**). It then will match as few occurrences as possible as long as the match is still successful.

The zip code (line 40 in Fig. 16.20) matches a digit five times. This regular expression uses the digit character class and a quantifier with the digit 5 between braces. The phone number (line 46 in Fig. 16.20) matches three digits (the first one cannot be zero) followed by a dash followed by three more digits (again the first one cannot be zero) followed by four more digits.

`String` Method `matches` checks whether an entire `String` conforms to a regular expression. For example, we want to accept "Smith" as a last name, but not "9@Smith#". If only a substring matches the regular expression, method `matches` returns `false`.

Replacing Substrings and Splitting Strings
Sometimes it's useful to replace parts of a string or to split a string into pieces. For this purpose, class `String` provides methods **replaceAll**, **replaceFirst** and **split**. These methods are demonstrated in Fig. 16.23.

```
1   // Fig. 16.23: RegexSubstitution.java
2   // String methods replaceFirst, replaceAll and split.
3   import java.util.Arrays;
4
```

Fig. 16.23 | String methods `replaceFirst`, `replaceAll` and `split`. (Part 1 of 2.)

```
 5   public class RegexSubstitution
 6   {
 7      public static void main( String[] args )
 8      {
 9         String firstString = "This sentence ends in 5 stars *****";
10         String secondString = "1, 2, 3, 4, 5, 6, 7, 8";
11
12         System.out.printf( "Original String 1: %s\n", firstString );
13
14         // replace '*' with '^'
15         firstString = firstString.replaceAll( "\\*", "^" );
16
17         System.out.printf( "^ substituted for *: %s\n", firstString );
18
19         // replace 'stars' with 'carets'
20         firstString = firstString.replaceAll( "stars", "carets" );
21
22         System.out.printf(
23            "\"carets\" substituted for \"stars\": %s\n", firstString );
24
25         // replace words with 'word'
26         System.out.printf( "Every word replaced by \"word\": %s\n\n",
27            firstString.replaceAll( "\\w+", "word" ) );
28
29         System.out.printf( "Original String 2: %s\n", secondString );
30
31         // replace first three digits with 'digit'
32         for ( int i = 0; i < 3; i++ )
33            secondString = secondString.replaceFirst( "\\d", "digit" );
34
35         System.out.printf(
36            "First 3 digits replaced by \"digit\" : %s\n", secondString );
37
38         System.out.print( "String split at commas: " );
39         String[] results = secondString.split( ",\\s*" ); // split on commas
40         System.out.println( Arrays.toString( results ) );
41      } // end main
42   } // end class RegexSubstitution
```

```
Original String 1: This sentence ends in 5 stars *****
^ substituted for *: This sentence ends in 5 stars ^^^^^
"carets" substituted for "stars": This sentence ends in 5 carets ^^^^^
Every word replaced by "word": word word word word word word ^^^^^

Original String 2: 1, 2, 3, 4, 5, 6, 7, 8
First 3 digits replaced by "digit" : digit, digit, digit, 4, 5, 6, 7, 8
String split at commas: ["digit", "digit", "digit", "4", "5", "6", "7", "8"]
```

Fig. 16.23 | String methods replaceFirst, replaceAll and split. (Part 2 of 2.)

Method replaceAll replaces text in a String with new text (the second argument) wherever the original String matches a regular expression (the first argument). Line 15 replaces every instance of "*" in firstString with "^". Note that the regular expression ("*") precedes character * with two backslashes. Normally, * is a quantifier indicating that a regular expression should match any number of occurrences of a preceding pattern. However, in line 15, we want to find all occurrences of the literal character *—to do this, we must escape character * with character \. Escaping a special regular-expression character with \ instructs the matching engine to find the actual character. Since the expression is stored in a Java String and \ is a special character in Java Strings, we must include an additional \. So the Java String "*" represents the regular-expression pattern * which matches a single * character in the search string. In line 20, every match for the regular expression "stars" in firstString is replaced with "carets". Line 27 uses replaceAll to replace all words in the string with "word".

Method replaceFirst (line 33) replaces the first occurrence of a pattern match. Java Strings are immutable; therefore, method replaceFirst returns a new String in which the appropriate characters have been replaced. This line takes the original String and replaces it with the String returned by replaceFirst. By iterating three times we replace the first three instances of a digit (\d) in secondString with the text "digit".

Method split divides a String into several substrings. The original is broken in any location that matches a specified regular expression. Method split returns an array of Strings containing the substrings between matches for the regular expression. In line 39, we use method split to tokenize a String of comma-separated integers. The argument is the regular expression that locates the delimiter. In this case, we use the regular expression ",\\s*" to separate the substrings wherever a comma occurs. By matching any white-space characters, we eliminate extra spaces from the resulting substrings. Note that the commas and white-space characters are not returned as part of the substrings. Again, note that the Java String ",\\s*" represents the regular expression ,\s*. Line 40 uses Arrays method toString to display the contents of array results in square brackets and separated by commas.

Classes Pattern and Matcher

In addition to the regular-expression capabilities of class String, Java provides other classes in package java.util.regex that help developers manipulate regular expressions. Class **Pattern** represents a regular expression. Class **Matcher** contains both a regular-expression pattern and a CharSequence in which to search for the pattern.

CharSequence (package java.lang) is an interface that allows read access to a sequence of characters. The interface requires that the methods charAt, length, subSequence and toString be declared. Both String and StringBuilder implement interface CharSequence, so an instance of either of these classes can be used with class Matcher.

Common Programming Error 16.4

A regular expression can be tested against an object of any class that implements interface CharSequence, but the regular expression must be a String. Attempting to create a regular expression as a StringBuilder is an error.

If a regular expression will be used only once, static Pattern method **matches** can be used. This method takes a String that specifies the regular expression and a CharSequence on which to perform the match. This method returns a boolean indicating whether the search object (the second argument) matches the regular expression.

If a regular expression will be used more than once (in a loop for example), it's more efficient to use static Pattern method **compile** to create a specific Pattern object for that regular expression. This method receives a String representing the pattern and returns a new `Pattern` object, which can then be used to call method **matcher**. This method receives a `CharSequence` to search and returns a `Matcher` object.

`Matcher` provides method **matches**, which performs the same task as `Pattern` method matches, but receives no arguments—the search pattern and search object are encapsulated in the `Matcher` object. Class `Matcher` provides other methods, including **find**, **lookingAt**, **replaceFirst** and **replaceAll**.

Figure 16.24 presents a simple example that employs regular expressions. This program matches birthdays against a regular expression. The expression matches only birthdays that do not occur in April and that belong to people whose names begin with "J".

Lines 11–12 create a `Pattern` by invoking static `Pattern` method `compile`. The dot character "." in the regular expression (line 12) matches any single character except a newline character.

```java
1   // Fig. 16.24: RegexMatches.java
2   // Classes Pattern and Matcher.
3   import java.util.regex.Matcher;
4   import java.util.regex.Pattern;
5
6   public class RegexMatches
7   {
8      public static void main( String[] args )
9      {
10        // create regular expression
11        Pattern expression =
12           Pattern.compile( "J.*\\d[0-35-9]-\\d\\d-\\d\\d" );
13
14        String string1 = "Jane's Birthday is 05-12-75\n" +
15           "Dave's Birthday is 11-04-68\n" +
16           "John's Birthday is 04-28-73\n" +
17           "Joe's Birthday is 12-17-77";
18
19        // match regular expression to string and print matches
20        Matcher matcher = expression.matcher( string1 );
21
22        while ( matcher.find() )
23           System.out.println( matcher.group() );
24     } // end main
25  } // end class RegexMatches
```

```
Jane's Birthday is 05-12-75
Joe's Birthday is 12-17-77
```

Fig. 16.24 | Classes `Pattern` and `Matcher`.

Line 20 creates the `Matcher` object for the compiled regular expression and the matching sequence (`string1`). Lines 22–23 use a `while` loop to iterate through the `String`. Line 22 uses `Matcher` method `find` to attempt to match a piece of the search object to the search pattern. Each call to this method starts at the point where the last call ended, so multiple matches can be found. `Matcher` method `lookingAt` performs the same way, except that it always starts from the beginning of the search object and will always find the first match if there is one.

Common Programming Error 16.5

Method matches *(from class* String, Pattern *or* Matcher*) will return* true *only if the entire search object matches the regular expression. Methods* find *and* lookingAt *(from class* Matcher*) will return* true *if a portion of the search object matches the regular expression.*

Line 23 uses Matcher method **group**, which returns the String from the search object that matches the search pattern. The String that is returned is the one that was last matched by a call to find or lookingAt. The output in Fig. 16.24 shows the two matches that were found in string1.

For more information on regular expressions, visit our Regular Expressions Resource Center at www.deitel.com/regularexpressions/.

16.8 Wrap-Up

In this chapter, you learned about more String methods for selecting portions of Strings and manipulating Strings. You learned about the Character class and some of the methods it declares to handle chars. The chapter also discussed the capabilities of the StringBuilder class for creating Strings. The end of the chapter discussed regular expressions, which provide a powerful capability to search and match portions of Strings that fit a particular pattern. In the next chapter, you'll learn about file processing, including how persistent data is stored and and retrieved.

Summary

Section 16.2 Fundamentals of Characters and Strings

- A character literal's value is its integer value in Unicode. Strings can include letters, digits and special characters such as +, -, *, / and $. A string in Java is an object of class String. String literals are often referred to as String objects and are written in a program in double quotes.

Section 16.3 Class **String**

- String objects are immutable—after they are created, their character contents cannot be changed.
- String method length returns the number of characters in a String.
- String method charAt returns the character at a specific position.
- String method equals tests for equality. The method returns true if the contents of the Strings are equal, false otherwise. Method equals uses a lexicographical comparison for Strings.
- When primitive-type values are compared with ==, the result is true if both values are identical. When references are compared with ==, the result is true if both refer to the same object.
- Java treats all string literals with the same contents as a single String object.
- String method equalsIgnoreCase performs a case-insensitive string comparison.
- String method compareTo uses a lexicographical comparison and returns 0 if the Strings are equal, a negative number if the string that calls compareTo is less than the argument String and a positive number if the string that calls compareTo is greater than than the argument String.
- String method regionMatches compares portions of two strings for equality.
- String method startsWith determines whether a string starts with the specified characters. String method endsWith determines whether a string ends with the specified characters.

- String method indexOf locates the first occurrence of a character or a substring in a string. String method lastIndexOf locates the last occurrence of a character or a substring in a string.
- String method substring copies and returns part of an existing string object.
- String method concat concatenates two string objects and returns a new string object.
- String method replace returns a new string object that replaces every occurrence in a String of its first character argument with its second character argument.
- String method toUpperCase returns a new string with uppercase letters in the positions where the original string had lowercase letters. String method toLowerCase returns a new string with lowercase letters in the positions where the original string had uppercase letters.
- String method trim returns a new string object in which all white-space characters (e.g., spaces, newlines and tabs) have been removed from the beginning and end of a string.
- String method toCharArray returns a char array containing a copy of the string's characters.
- String class static method valueOf returns its argument converted to a string.

Section 16.4 Class *StringBuilder*

- Class StringBuilder provides constructors that enable StringBuilders to be initialized with no characters and an initial capacity of 16 characters, with no characters and an initial capacity specified in the integer argument, or with a copy of the characters of the String argument and an initial capacity that is the number of characters in the String argument plus 16.
- StringBuilder method length returns the number of characters currently stored in a String-Builder. StringBuilder method capacity returns the number of characters that can be stored in a StringBuilder without allocating more memory.
- StringBuilder method ensureCapacity ensures that a StringBuilder has at least the specified capacity. StringBuilder method setLength increases or decreases the length of a StringBuilder.
- StringBuilder method charAt returns the character at the specified index. StringBuilder method setCharAt sets the character at the specified position. StringBuilder method getChars copies characters in the StringBuilder into the character array passed as an argument.
- StringBuilder's overloaded append methods add primitive-type, character array, String, Object or CharSequence values to the end of a StringBuilder.
- StringBuilder's overloaded insert methods insert primitive-type, character array, String, Object or CharSequence values at any position in a StringBuilder.

Section 16.5 Class *Character*

- Character method isDefined determines whether a character is in the Unicode character set.
- Character method isDigit determines whether a character is a defined Unicode digit.
- Character method isJavaIdentifierStart determines whether a character can be used as the first character of a Java identifier. Character method isJavaIdentifierPart determines if a character can be used in an identifier.
- Character method isLetter determines if a character is a letter. Character method isLetterOrDigit determines if a character is a letter or a digit.
- Character method isLowerCase determines whether a character is a lowercase letter. Character method isUpperCase determines whether a character is an uppercase letter.
- Character method toUpperCase converts a character to its uppercase equivalent. Character method toLowerCase converts a character to its lowercase equivalent.
- Character method digit converts its character argument into an integer in the number system specified by its integer argument radix. Character method forDigit converts its integer argument digit into a character in the number system specified by its integer argument radix.

- Character method charValue returns the char stored in a Character object. Character method toString returns a String representation of a Character.

Section 16.6 Tokenizing *Strings*
- Class String's split method tokenizes a String based on the delimiter specified as an argument and returns an array of Strings containing the tokens.

Section 16.7 Regular Expressions, Class *Pattern and Class* Matcher
- Regular expressions are sequences of characters and symbols that define a set of strings. They are useful for validating input and ensuring that data is in a particular format.

- String method matches receives a string that specifies the regular expression and matches the contents of the String object on which it's called to the regular expression. The method returns a boolean indicating whether the match succeeded.

- A character class is an escape sequence that represents a group of characters. Each character class matches a single character in the string we are attempting to match with the regular expression.

- A word character (\w) is any letter (uppercase or lowercase), any digit or the underscore character.

- A white-space character (\s) is a space, a tab, a carriage return, a newline or a form feed.

- A digit (\d) is any numeric character.

- To match a set of characters that does not have a predefined character class, use square brackets, []. Ranges can be represented by placing a dash (-) between two characters. If the first character in the brackets is "^", the expression accepts any character other than those indicated.

- When the regular expression operator "*" appears in a regular expression, the program attempts to match zero or more occurrences of the subexpression immediately preceding the "*".

- Operator "+" attempts to match one or more occurrences of the subexpression preceding it.

- The character "|" allows a match of the expression to its left or to its right.

- Parentheses ( ) are used to group parts of the regular expression.

- The asterisk (*) and plus (+) are formally called quantifiers.

- A quantifier affects only the subexpression immediately preceding it.

- Quantifier question mark (?) matches zero or one occurrences of the expression that it quantifies.

- A set of braces containing one number ({*n*}) matches exactly *n* occurrences of the expression it quantifies. Including a comma after the number enclosed in braces matches at least *n* occurrences.

- A set of braces containing two numbers ({*n*,*m*}) matches between *n* and *m* occurrences of the expression that it qualifies.

- Quantifiers are greedy—they'll match as many occurrences as they can as long as the match is successful. If a quantifier is followed by a question mark (?), the quantifier becomes reluctant, matching as few occurrences as possible as long as the match is successful.

- String method replaceAll replaces text in a string with new text (the second argument) wherever the original string matches a regular expression (the first argument).

- Escaping a special regular-expression character with a \ instructs the regular-expression matching engine to find the actual character, as opposed to what it represents in a regular expression.

- String method replaceFirst replaces the first occurrence of a pattern match and returns a new string in which the appropriate characters have been replaced.

- String method split divides a string into substrings at any location that matches a specified regular expression and returns an array of the substrings.

- Class Pattern represents a regular expression.

- Class Matcher contains a regular-expression pattern and a CharSequence in which to search.

- CharSequence is an interface that allows read access to a sequence of characters. Both String and StringBuilder implement this interface, so they can be used with class Matcher.

- If a regular expression will be used only once, static Pattern method matches takes a string that specifies the regular expression and a CharSequence on which to perform the match. This method returns a boolean indicating whether the search object matches the regular expression.

- If a regular expression will be used more than once, it's more efficient to use static Pattern method compile to create a specific Pattern object for that regular expression. This method receives a string representing the pattern and returns a new Pattern object.

- Pattern method matcher receives a CharSequence to search and returns a Matcher object. Matcher method matches performs the same task as Pattern method matches but without arguments.

- Matcher method find attempts to match a piece of the search object to the search pattern. Each call to this method starts at the point where the last call ended, so multiple matches can be found.

- Matcher method lookingAt performs the same as find, except that it always starts from the beginning of the search object and will always find the first match if there is one.

- Matcher method group returns the string from the search object that matches the search pattern. The string returned is the one that was last matched by a call to find or lookingAt.

Terminology

append method of class StringBuilder 700
capacity method of class StringBuilder 697
character literal 682
charAt method of class String 684
charAt method of class StringBuilder 698
CharSequence interface 715
charValue method of class Character 706
compile method of class Pattern 715
delete method of class StringBuilder 701
deleteCharAt method of class StringBuilder 701
delimiter for tokens 707
digit method of class Character 705
empty string 684
endsWith method of class String 689
ensureCapacity method of class StringBuilder 697
find method of class Matcher 716
forDigit method of class Character 705
getChars method of class String 684
getChars method of class StringBuilder 698
greedy quantifier (regular expressions) 713
group method of class Matcher 717
immutable String object 684
indexOf method of class String 690
insert method of class StringBuilder 701
isDefined method of class Character 704
isDigit method of class Character 704
isJavaIdentifierPart method of class Character 705
isJavaIdentifierStart method of class Character 705

isLetter method of class Character 705
isLetterOrDigit method of class Character 705
isLowerCase method of class Character 705
isUpperCase method of class Character 705
lastIndexOf method of class String 690
lazy quantifier (regular expressions) 713
length method of class String 684
length method of class StringBuilder 697
lexicographical comparison 687
lookingAt method of class Matcher 716
Matcher class 715
matcher method of class Pattern 716
matches method of class Matcher 716
matches method of class Pattern 715
matches method of class String 709
Pattern class 715
predefined character class (regular expressions) 709
quantifier in a regular expression 713
radix (base) of a number 705
regionMatches method of class String 686
regular expression 708
reluctant quantifier (regular expressions) 713
replaceAll method of class Matcher 716
replaceAll method of class String 713
replaceFirst method of class Matcher 716
replaceFirst method of class String 713
reverse method of class StringBuilder 698
setCharAt method of class StringBuilder 698
special character 683
split method of class String 713

Self-Review Exercises

16.1   State whether each of the following is *true* or *false*. If *false*, explain why.

a) When String objects are compared using ==, the result is true if the Strings contain the same values.

b) A String can be modified after it's created.

16.2   For each of the following, write a single statement that performs the indicated task:

a) Compare the string in s1 to the string in s2 for equality of contents.

b) Append the string s2 to the string s1, using +=.

c) Determine the length of the string in s1.

Answers to Self-Review Exercises

16.1   a) False. String objects are compared using operator == to determine whether they are the same object in memory.

b) False. String objects are immutable and cannot be modified after they are created. StringBuilder objects can be modified after they are created.

16.2   a) `s1.equals( s2 )`

b) `s1 += s2;`

c) `s1.length()`

Exercises

16.3   *(Comparing Strings)* Write an application that uses String method compareTo to compare two strings input by the user. Output whether the first string is less than, equal to or greater than the second.

16.4   *(Comparing Portions of Strings)* Write an application that uses String method region-Matches to compare two strings input by the user. The application should input the number of characters to be compared and the starting index of the comparison. The application should state whether the strings are equal. Ignore the case of the characters when performing the comparison.

16.5   *(Tokenizing Telephone Numbers)* Write an application that inputs a telephone number as a string in the form (555) 555-5555. The application should String method split to extract the area code as a token, the first three digits of the phone number as a token and the last four digits of the phone number as a token. The seven digits of the phone number should be concatenated into one string. Both the area code and the phone number should be printed. Remember that you'll have to change delimiter characters during the tokenization process.

16.6   *(Displaying a Sentence with Its Words Reversed)* Write an application that inputs a line of text, tokenizes the line with String method split and outputs the tokens in reverse order. Use space characters as delimiters.

16.7   *(Searching Strings)* Write an application that inputs a line of text and a search character and uses String method indexOf to determine the number of occurrences of the character in the text.

16.8 *(Searching Strings)* Write an application based on the application in Exercise 16.7 that inputs a line of text and uses String method indexOf to determine the total number of occurrences of each letter of the alphabet in the text. Uppercase and lowercase letters should be counted together. Store the totals for each letter in an array, and print the values in tabular format after the totals have been determined.

16.9 *(Tokenizing and Comparing Strings)* Write an application that reads a line of text, tokenizes it using space characters as delimiters and outputs only those words ending with the letters "ED".

16.10 *(Converting int Values to Characters)* Write an application that inputs an integer code for a character and displays the corresponding character. Modify this application so that it generates all possible three-digit codes in the range from 000 to 255 and attempts to print the corresponding characters.

16.11 *(Creating Three-Letter Strings from a Five-Letter Word)* Write an application that reads a five-letter word from the user and produces every possible three-letter string that can be derived from the letters of that word. For example, the three-letter words produced from the word "bathe" include "ate," "bat," "bet," "tab," "hat," "the" and "tea."

Special Section: Advanced String-Manipulation Exercises

The preceding exercises are keyed to the text and designed to test your understanding of fundamental string-manipulation concepts. This section includes a collection of intermediate and advanced string-manipulation exercises. You should find these problems challenging, yet entertaining. The problems vary considerably in difficulty. Some require an hour or two of application writing and implementation. Others are useful for lab assignments that might require two or three weeks of study and implementation. Some are challenging term projects.

16.12 *(Text Analysis)* The availability of computers with string-manipulation capabilities has resulted in some rather interesting approaches to analyzing the writings of great authors. Much attention has been focused on whether William Shakespeare ever lived. Some scholars believe there is substantial evidence indicating that Christopher Marlowe actually penned the masterpieces attributed to Shakespeare. Researchers have used computers to find similarities in the writings of these two authors. This exercise examines three methods for analyzing texts with a computer.

    a) Write an application that reads a line of text from the keyboard and prints a table indicating the number of occurrences of each letter of the alphabet in the text. For example, the phrase

```
To be, or not to be: that is the question:
```

       contains one "a," two "b's," no "c's," and so on.

    b) Write an application that reads a line of text and prints a table indicating the number of one-letter words, two-letter words, three-letter words, and so on, appearing in the text. For example, Fig. 16.25 shows the counts for the phrase

```
Whether 'tis nobler in the mind to suffer
```

Word length	Occurrences
1	0
2	2
3	1

Fig. 16.25 | Word-length counts for the string
"Whether 'tis nobler in the mind to suffer". (Part 1 of 2.)

Word length	Occurrences
4	2 (including `'tis`)
5	0
6	2
7	1

Fig. 16.25 | Word-length counts for the string
`"Whether 'tis nobler in the mind to suffer"`. (Part 2 of 2.)

c) Write an application that reads a line of text and prints a table indicating the number of occurrences of each different word in the text. The application should include the words in the table in the same order in which they appear in the text. For example, the lines

```
To be, or not to be: that is the question:
Whether 'tis nobler in the mind to suffer
```

contain the word "to" three times, the word "be" two times, the word "or" once, etc.

16.13 *(Check Protection)* Computers are frequently employed in check-writing systems, such as payroll and accounts payable applications. There are many strange stories about weekly paychecks being printed (by mistake) for amounts in excess of $1 million. Incorrect amounts are printed by computerized check-writing systems because of human error or machine failure. Systems designers build controls into their systems to prevent such erroneous checks from being issued.

Another serious problem is the intentional alteration of a check amount by someone who plans to cash a check fraudulently. To prevent a dollar amount from being altered, some computerized check-writing systems employ a technique called check protection. Checks designed for imprinting by computer contain a fixed number of spaces in which the computer may print an amount. Suppose a paycheck contains eight blank spaces in which the computer is supposed to print the amount of a weekly paycheck. If the amount is large, then all eight of the spaces will be filled. For example,

```
1,230.60 (check amount)
--------
12345678 (position numbers)
```

On the other hand, if the amount is less than $1000, then several of the spaces would ordinarily be left blank. For example,

```
   99.87
--------
12345678
```

contains three blank spaces. If a check is printed with blank spaces, it's easier for someone to alter the amount. To prevent alteration, many check-writing systems insert *leading asterisks* to protect the amount as follows:

```
***99.87
--------
12345678
```

Write an application that inputs a dollar amount to be printed on a check, then prints the amount in check-protected format with leading asterisks if necessary. Assume that nine spaces are available for printing the amount.

16.14 *(Writing the Word Equivalent of a Check Amount)* Continuing the discussion in Exercise 16.13, we reiterate the importance of designing check-writing systems to prevent alteration of check amounts. One common security method requires that the amount be written in numbers and spelled out in words as well. Even if someone is able to alter the numerical amount of the check, it's extremely difficult to change the amount in words. Write an application that inputs a numeric check amount that is less than $1000 and writes the word equivalent of the amount. For example, the amount 112.43 should be written as

```
ONE hundred TWELVE and 43/100
```

16.15 *(Morse Code)* Perhaps the most famous of all coding schemes is the Morse code, developed by Samuel Morse in 1832 for use with the telegraph system. The Morse code assigns a series of dots and dashes to each letter of the alphabet, each digit, and a few special characters (e.g., period, comma, colon, semicolon). In sound-oriented systems, the dot represents a short sound and the dash a long sound. Other representations of dots and dashes are used with light-oriented systems and signal-flag systems. Separation between words is indicated by a space or, simply, the absence of a dot or dash. In a sound-oriented system, a space is indicated by a short time during which no sound is transmitted. The international version of the Morse code appears in Fig. 16.26.

Write an application that reads an English-language phrase and encodes it into Morse code. Also write an application that reads a phrase in Morse code and converts it into the English-language equivalent. Use one blank between each Morse-coded letter and three blanks between each Morse-coded word.

Character	Code	Character	Code
A	.-	T	-
B	-...	U	..-
C	-.-.	V	...-
D	-..	W	.--
E	.	X	-..-
F	..-.	Y	-.--
G	--.	Z	--..
H	....		
I	..	*Digits*	
J	.---	1	.----
K	-.-	2	..---
L	.-..	3	...--
M	--	4	....-
N	-.	5	.....
O	---	6	-....
P	.--.	7	--...
Q	--.-	8	---..
R	.-.	9	----.
S	...	0	-----

Fig. 16.26 | Letters and digits as expressed in international Morse code.

16.16 *(Metric Conversions)* Write an application that will assist the user with metric conversions. Your application should allow the user to specify the names of the units as strings (i.e., centimeters, liters, grams, and so on, for the metric system and inches, quarts, pounds, and so on, for the English system) and should respond to simple questions, such as

```
"How many inches are in 2 meters?"
"How many liters are in 10 quarts?"
```

Your application should recognize invalid conversions. For example, the question

```
"How many feet are in 5 kilograms?"
```

is not meaningful because `"feet"` is a unit of length, whereas `"kilograms"` is a unit of mass.

Special Section: Challenging String-Manipulation Projects

16.17 *(Project: A Spelling Checker)* Many popular word-processing software packages have built-in spell checkers. In this project, you are asked to develop your own spell-checker utility. We make suggestions to help get you started. You should then consider adding more capabilities. Use a computerized dictionary (if you have access to one) as a source of words.

Why do we type so many words with incorrect spellings? In some cases, it's because we simply do not know the correct spelling, so we make a best guess. In some cases, it's because we transpose two letters (e.g., "defualt" instead of "default"). Sometimes we double-type a letter accidentally (e.g., "hanndy" instead of "handy"). Sometimes we type a nearby key instead of the one we intended (e.g., "biryhday" instead of "birthday"), and so on.

Design and implement a spell-checker application in Java. Your application should maintain an array `wordList` of strings. Enable the user to enter these strings. [*Note:* In Chapter 17, we introduce file processing. With this capability, you can obtain the words for the spell checker from a computerized dictionary stored in a file.]

Your application should ask a user to enter a word. The application should then look up that word in the `wordList` array. If the word is in the array, your application should print `"Word is spelled correctly."` If the word is not in the array, your application should print `"Word is not spelled correctly."` Then your application should try to locate other words in `wordList` that might be the word the user intended to type. For example, you can try all possible single transpositions of adjacent letters to discover that the word "default" is a direct match to a word in `wordList`. Of course, this implies that your application will check all other single transpositions, such as "edfault," "dfeault," "deafult," "defalut" and "defautl." When you find a new word that matches one in `wordList`, print it in a message, such as

```
Did you mean "default"?
```

Implement other tests, such as replacing each double letter with a single letter, and any other tests you can develop to improve the value of your spell checker.

Making a Difference

16.18 *(Cooking with Healthier Ingredients)* Obesity in America is increasing at an alarming rate. Check the map from the Centers for Disease Control and Prevention (CDC) at www.cdc.gov/nccdphp/dnpa/Obesity/trend/maps/index.htm, which shows obesity trends in the United States over the last 20 years. As obesity increases, so do occurrences of related problems (e.g., heart disease, high blood pressure, high cholesterol, type 2 diabetes). Write a program that helps users choose healthier ingredients when cooking, and helps those allergic to certain foods (e.g., nuts, gluten) find substitutes. The program should read a recipe from a `JTextArea` and suggest healthier replacements for some of the ingredients. For simplicity, your program should assume the recipe has no abbreviations for measures such as teaspoons, cups, and tablespoons, and uses numerical digits for quantities (e.g., 1 egg, 2 cups) rather than spelling them out (one egg, two cups). Some common substitutions are shown in Fig. 16.27. Your program should display a warning such as, "Always consult your physician before making significant changes to your diet."

Your program should take into consideration that replacements are not always one-for-one. For example, if a cake recipe calls for three eggs, it might reasonably use six egg whites instead. Conversion data for measurements and substitutes can be obtained at websites such as:

```
chinesefood.about.com/od/recipeconversionfaqs/f/usmetricrecipes.htm
www.pioneerthinking.com/eggsub.html
www.gourmetsleuth.com/conversions.htm
```

Your program should consider the user's health concerns, such as high cholesterol, high blood pressure, weight loss, gluten allergy, and so on. For high cholesterol, the program should suggest substitutes for eggs and dairy products; if the user wishes to lose weight, low-calorie substitutes for ingredients such as sugar should be suggested.

Ingredient	Substitution
1 cup sour cream	1 cup yogurt
1 cup milk	1/2 cup evaporated milk and 1/2 cup water
1 teaspoon lemon juice	1/2 teaspoon vinegar
1 cup sugar	1/2 cup honey, 1 cup molasses or 1/4 cup agave nectar
1 cup butter	1 cup margarine or yogurt
1 cup flour	1 cup rye or rice flour
1 cup mayonnaise	1 cup cottage cheese or 1/8 cup mayonnaise and 7/8 cup yogurt
1 egg	2 tablespoons cornstarch, arrowroot flour or potato starch or 2 egg whites or 1/2 of a large banana (mashed)
1 cup milk	1 cup soy milk
1/4 cup oil	1/4 cup applesauce
white bread	whole-grain bread

Fig. 16.27 | Typical ingredient substitutes.

16.19 *(Spam Scanner)* Spam (or junk e-mail) costs U.S. organizations billions of dollars a year in spam-prevention software, equipment, network resources, bandwidth, and lost productivity. Research online some of the most common spam e-mail messages and words, and check your own junk e-mail folder. Create a list of 30 words and phrases commonly found in spam messages. Write an application in which the user enters an e-mail message in a JTextArea. Then, scan the message for each of the 30 keywords or phrases. For each occurrence of one of these within the message, add a point to the message's "spam score." Next, rate the likelihood that the message is spam, based on the number of points it received.

16.20 *(SMS Language)* Short Message Service (SMS) is a communications service that allows sending text messages of 160 or fewer characters between mobile phones. With the proliferation of mobile phone use worldwide, SMS is being used in many developing nations for political purposes (e.g., voicing opinions and opposition), reporting news about natural disasters, and so on. For example, check out comunica.org/radio2.0/archives/87. Since the length of SMS messages is limited, SMS Language—abbreviations of common words and phrases in mobile text messages, e-mails, instant messages, etc.—is often used. For example, "in my opinion" is "imo" in SMS Language. Research SMS Language online. Write a GUI application in which the user can enter a message using SMS Language, then click a button to translate it into English (or your own language). Also provide a mechanism to translate text written in English (or your own language) into SMS Language. One potential problem is that one SMS abbreviation could expand into a variety of phrases. For example, IMO (as used above) could also stand for "International Maritime Organization," "in memory of," etc.

I can only assume that a "Do Not File" document is
filed in a "Do Not File" file.
—Senator Frank Church
Senate Intelligence Subcommittee Hearing, 1975

Consciousness ... does not appear to itself chopped up
in bits. ... A "river" or a "stream" are the metaphors by
which it is most naturally described.
—William James

I read part of it all the way through.
—Samuel Goldwyn

A great memory does not make a philosopher, any more
than a dictionary can be called grammar.
—John Henry, Cardinal Newman

17

Files, Streams and
Object Serialization

Objectives

In this chapter you'll learn:

- What files are and how they are used to retain application data between successive executions.
- To create, read, write and update files.
- To use class `File` to retrieve information about files and directories.
- The Java input/output stream class hierarchy.
- The differences between text files and binary files.
- Sequential-access file processing.
- To use classes `Scanner` and `Formatter` to process text files.
- To use classes `FileInputStream` and `FileOutputStream` to read from and write to files.
- To use classes `ObjectInputStream` and `ObjectOutputStream` to read objects from and write objects to files.
- To use a `JFileChooser` dialog.

17.1 Introduction

Data stored in variables and arrays is temporary—it's lost when a local variable goes out of scope or when the program terminates. For long-term retention of data, even after the programs that create the data terminate, computers use **files**. You use files every day for tasks such as writing an e-mail or creating a spreadsheet. Computers store files on **secondary storage devices** such as hard disks, optical disks, flash drives and magnetic tapes. Data maintained in files is **persistent data** because it exists beyond the duration of program execution. In this chapter, we explain how Java programs create, update and process files.

A programming language must be capable of file processing to support commercial applications, which typically process massive amounts of persistent data. This chapter discusses Java's file-processing and stream input/output features. The term "stream" refers to ordered data that is read from or written to a file. We discuss streams in detail in Section 17.3. File processing is a subset of Java's stream-processing capabilities, which include reading from and writing to memory, files and network connections. In this chapter, we'll introduce file-processing concepts (making you more comfortable with using files programmatically) and provide you with sufficient stream-processing capabilities to support the networking features introduced in Chapter 27, Networking. We discuss two forms of file processing here—text-file processing and object serialization.

We begin by discussing the hierarchy of data contained in files. We then cover Java's architecture for handling files programmatically—we discuss several classes in package `java.io`. Next we explain that data can be stored in text files and binary files—and we cover the differences between them. We demonstrate retrieving information about files and directories using class `File`, then devote several sections to the different mechanisms for writing data to and reading data from files. We demonstrate creating and manipulating sequential-access text files. Working with text files allows the reader to quickly and easily start manipulating files. As you'll learn, however, it's difficult to read data from text files back into object form. Fortunately, many object-oriented languages (including Java) provide ways to write objects to and read objects from files (known as object serialization and deserialization). To demonstrate this, we recreate some of our sequential-access programs that used text files, this time by storing objects in binary files.

17.2 Data Hierarchy

Ultimately, a computer processes data items as combinations of zeros and ones, because it's simple and economical for engineers to build electronic devices that can assume two stable states—one representing 0 and the other representing 1. It's remarkable that the impressive functions performed by computers involve only the most fundamental manipulations of 0s and 1s.

Bits
The smallest data item in a computer can assume the value 0 or the value 1. Such a data item is called a **bit** (short for "binary digit"—a digit that can assume one of two values). Computer circuitry performs various simple bit manipulations, such as examining a bit's value, setting a bit's value and reversing a bit's value (from 1 to 0 or from 0 to 1).

Characters
It's cumbersome for programmers to work with data in the low-level form of bits. Instead, they prefer to work with **decimal digits** (0–9), **letters** (A–Z and a–z), and **special symbols** (e.g., $, @, %, &, *, (,), –, +, ", :, ? and /). Digits, letters and special symbols are known as **characters**. The computer's **character set** is the set of all the characters used to write programs and represent data items. Computers process only 1s and 0s, so a computer's character set represents every character as a pattern of 1s and 0s. Java uses **Unicode** characters that are composed of two **bytes**, each composed of eight bits. Java type **byte** can be used to represent byte data. Unicode contains characters for many of the world's languages. See Appendix L for more information on this character set. See Appendix B, for more information on the **ASCII (American Standard Code for Information Interchange)** character set, a popular subset of Unicode that represents uppercase and lowercase letters, digits and various common special characters.

Fields
Just as characters are composed of bits, **fields** are composed of characters or bytes. A field is a group of characters or bytes that conveys meaning. For example, a field consisting of uppercase and lowercase letters can be used to represent a person's name.

Data items processed by computers form a **data hierarchy** that becomes larger and more complex in structure as we progress from bits to characters to fields, and so on.

Records and Files
Typically, several fields compose a **record** (implemented as a class in Java). In a payroll system, for example, the record for an employee might consist of the following fields (possible types for these fields are shown in parentheses):

- Employee identification number (int)
- Name (String)
- Address (String)
- Hourly pay rate (double)
- Number of exemptions claimed (int)
- Year-to-date earnings (int or double)
- Amount of taxes withheld (int or double)

Thus, a record is a group of related fields. In the preceding example, all the fields belong to the same employee. A company might have many employees and thus have a payroll record for each one. A **file** is a group of related records. [*Note:* More generally, a file contains arbitrary data in arbitrary formats. In some operating systems, a file is viewed as nothing more than a collection of bytes—any organization of the bytes in a file (e.g., organizing the data into records) is a view created by the applications programmer.] A company's payroll file normally contains one record per employee. Thus, a payroll file for a small company might contain only 22 records, whereas one for a large company might contain thousands. It's not unusual for a company to have many files, some containing billions, or even trillions, of characters of information. Figure 17.1 illustrates a portion of the data hierarchy.

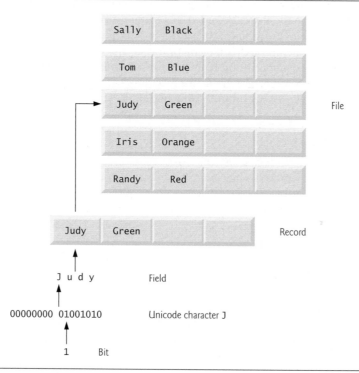

Fig. 17.1 | Data hierarchy.

Record Keys

To facilitate the retrieval of specific records from a file, at least one field in each record is chosen as a **record key**. A record key identifies a record as belonging to a particular person or entity and is unique to each record. This field typically is used to search and sort records. In the payroll record described previously, the employee identification number normally would be chosen as the record key.

Sequential Files

There are many ways to organize records in a file. The most common is called a **sequential file**, in which records are stored in order by the record-key field. For example, a payroll file commonly places records in ascending order by employee identification number.

Databases

Most organizations store data in many different files. Companies might have payroll files, accounts receivable files (listing money due from clients), accounts payable files (listing money due to suppliers), inventory files (listing facts about all the items handled by the business) and many others. Often, a group of related files is called a **database**. A collection of programs designed to create and manage databases is called a **database management system** (**DBMS**). We discuss this topic in Chapter 28, Accessing Databases with JDBC.

17.3 Files and Streams

Java views each file as a sequential **stream of bytes** (Fig. 17.2). Every operating system provides a mechanism to determine the end of a file, such as an **end-of-file marker** or a count of the total bytes in the file that is recorded in a system-maintained administrative data structure. A Java program processing a stream of bytes simply receives an indication from the operating system when it reaches the end of the stream—the program does not need to know how the underlying platform represents files or streams. In some cases, the end-of-file indication occurs as an exception. In other cases, the indication is a return value from a method invoked on a stream-processing object.

Fig. 17.2 | Java's view of a file of *n* bytes.

Byte-Based and Character-Based Streams

File streams can be used to input and output data as bytes or characters. Streams that input and output bytes are known as **byte-based streams**, representing data in its binary format. Streams that input and output characters are known as **character-based streams**, representing data as a sequence of characters. For instance, if the value 5 were being stored using a byte-based stream, it would be stored in the binary format of the numeric value 5, or 101. If the value 5 were being stored using a character-based stream, it would be stored in the binary format of the character 5, or 00000000 00110101 (this is the binary representation for the numeric value 53, which indicates the character 5 in the Unicode character set). The difference between the two forms is that the numeric value can be used as an integer in calculations, whereas the character 5 is simply a character that can be used in a string of text, as in "Sarah Miller is 15 years old". Files that are created using byte-based streams are referred to as **binary files**, while files created using character-based streams are referred to as **text files**. Text files can be read by text editors, while binary files are read by programs that understand the specific content of the file and the ordering of that content.

Standard Input, Standard Output and Standard Error Streams

A Java program **opens** a file by creating an object and associating a stream of bytes or characters with it. The classes used to create these objects are discussed shortly. Java can also associate streams with different devices. In fact, Java creates three stream objects that are associated with devices when a Java program begins executing—System.in, System.out and System.err. System.in (the standard input stream object) normally enables a program to input bytes from the keyboard; object System.out (the standard output stream object) normally enables a program to output character data to the screen; and object System.err (the standard error stream object) normally enables a program to output character-based error messages to the screen. Each of these streams can be redirected. For System.in, this capability enables the program to read bytes from a different source. For System.out and System.err, this capability enables the output to be sent to a different location, such as a file on disk. Class System provides methods **setIn**, **setOut** and **setErr** to **redirect** the standard input, output and error streams, respectively.

The java.io Package

Java programs perform file processing by using classes from package **java.io**. This package includes definitions for stream classes, such as **FileInputStream** (for byte-based input from a file), **FileOutputStream** (for byte-based output to a file), **FileReader** (for character-based input from a file) and **FileWriter** (for character-based output to a file), which inherit from classes InputStream, OutputStream, Reader and Writer, respectively (these classes will be discussed later in this chapter). Thus, the methods of the stream classes can also be applied to file streams. You open a file by creating an object of one these stream classes. The object's constructor interacts with the operating system to open the file.

Java contains classes that enable you to perform input and output of objects or variables of primitive data types. The data will still be stored as bytes or characters behind the scenes, allowing you to read or write data in the form of ints, Strings, or other types without having to worry about the details of converting such values to byte format. To perform such input and output, objects of classes **ObjectInputStream** and **ObjectOutputStream** can be used together with the byte-based file stream classes FileInputStream and FileOutputStream (these classes will be discussed in more detail shortly). The complete hierarchy of classes in package java.io can be viewed in the online documentation at

java.sun.com/javase/6/docs/api/java/io/package-tree.html

Each class is indented under its superclass. For example, class InputStream is a subclass of Object. To view the details of a class, click its name in the hierarchy.

As you can see in the hierarchy, Java offers many classes for performing input/output operations. We use several of these classes in this chapter to implement file-processing programs that create and manipulate sequential-access files. We also include a detailed example on class **File**, which is useful for obtaining information about files and directories. In Chapter 27, we use stream classes extensively to implement networking applications. Several other classes in the java.io package that we do not use in this chapter are discussed briefly in Section 17.7.

In addition to the java.io classes, character-based input and output can be performed with classes Scanner and **Formatter**. Class Scanner is used extensively to input data from the keyboard. This class can also read data from a file. Class Formatter enables formatted data to be output to any text-based stream in a manner similar to method System.out.printf. Appendix G presents the details of formatted output with printf. All these features can be used to format text files as well.

17.4 Class File

This section presents class File, which is particularly useful for retrieving information about files or directories from disk. Objects of class File do not open files or provide any file-processing capabilities. However, File objects are used frequently with objects of other java.io classes to specify files or directories to manipulate.

Creating *File* Objects

Class File provides four constructors. The one with a String argument specifies the name of a file or directory to associate with the File object. The name can contain **path information** as well as a file or directory name. A file or directory's path specifies its location on disk. The path includes some or all of the directories leading to the file or directory. An **absolute path** contains all the directories, starting with the **root directory**, that lead to a specific file or directory. Every file or directory on a particular disk drive has the same root directory in its path. A **relative path** normally starts from the directory in which the application began executing and is therefore "relative" to the current directory. The constructor with two String arguments specifies an absolute or relative path as the first argument and the file or directory to associate with the File object as the second argument. The constructor with File and String arguments uses an existing File object that specifies the parent directory of the file or directory specified by the String argument. The fourth constructor uses a URI object to locate the file. A **Uniform Resource Identifier (URI)** is a more general form of the **Uniform Resource Locators (URLs)** that are used to locate websites. For example, http://www.deitel.com/ is the URL for the Deitel & Associates website. URIs for locating files vary across operating systems. On Windows platforms, the URI

```
file://C:/data.txt
```

identifies the file data.txt stored in the root directory of the C: drive. On UNIX/Linux platforms, the URI

```
file:/home/student/data.txt
```

identifies the file data.txt stored in the home directory of the user student.

Error-Prevention Tip 17.1

*Use File method **isFile** to determine whether a File object represents a file (not a directory) before attempting to open the file.*

Figure 17.3 lists some common File methods. The complete list can be viewed at java.sun.com/javase/6/docs/api/java/io/File.html.

Method	Description
boolean canRead()	Returns true if a file is readable by the current application; false otherwise.
boolean canWrite()	Returns true if a file is writable by the current application; false otherwise.
boolean exists()	Returns true if the file or directory represented by the File object exists; false otherwise.
boolean isFile()	Returns true if the name specified as the argument to the File constructor is a file; false otherwise.

Fig. 17.3 | File methods. (Part 1 of 2.)

Method	Description
boolean isDirectory()	Returns true if the name specified as the argument to the File constructor is a directory; false otherwise.
boolean isAbsolute()	Returns true if the arguments specified to the File constructor indicate an absolute path to a file or directory; false otherwise.
String getAbsolutePath()	Returns a String with the absolute path of the file or directory.
String getName()	Returns a String with the name of the file or directory.
String getPath()	Returns a String with the path of the file or directory.
String getParent()	Returns a String with the parent directory of the file or directory (i.e., the directory in which the file or directory is located).
long length()	Returns the length of the file, in bytes. If the File object represents a directory, an unspecified value is returned.
long lastModified()	Returns a platform-dependent representation of the time at which the file or directory was last modified. The value returned is useful only for comparison with other values returned by this method.
String[] list()	Returns an array of Strings representing a directory's contents. Returns null if the File object does not represent a directory.

Fig. 17.3 | File methods. (Part 2 of 2.)

Demonstrating Class File

Figure 17.4 prompts the user to enter the name of a file or directory, then uses class File to output information about the file or directory.

```
 1  // Fig. 17.4: FileDemonstration.java
 2  // File class used to obtain file and directory information.
 3  import java.io.File;
 4  import java.util.Scanner;
 5
 6  public class FileDemonstration
 7  {
 8     public static void main( String[] args )
 9     {
10        Scanner input = new Scanner( System.in );
11
12        System.out.print( "Enter file or directory name: " );
13        analyzePath( input.nextLine() );
14     } // end main
15
16     // display information about file user specifies
17     public static void analyzePath( String path )
18     {
19        // create File object based on user input
20        File name = new File( path );
21
```

Fig. 17.4 | File class used to obtain file and directory information. (Part 1 of 3.)

```
22          if ( name.exists() ) // if name exists, output information about it
23          {
24             // display file (or directory) information
25             System.out.printf(
26                "%s%s\n%s\n%s\n%s\n%s%s\n%s%s\n%s%s\n%s%s\n%s%s",
27                name.getName(), " exists",
28                ( name.isFile() ? "is a file" : "is not a file" ),
29                ( name.isDirectory() ? "is a directory" :
30                   "is not a directory" ),
31                ( name.isAbsolute() ? "is absolute path" :
32                   "is not absolute path" ), "Last modified: ",
33                name.lastModified(), "Length: ", name.length(),
34                "Path: ", name.getPath(), "Absolute path: ",
35                name.getAbsolutePath(), "Parent: ", name.getParent() );
36
37             if ( name.isDirectory() ) // output directory listing
38             {
39                String[] directory = name.list();
40                System.out.println( "\n\nDirectory contents:\n" );
41
42                for ( String directoryName : directory )
43                   System.out.println( directoryName );
44             } // end if
45          } // end outer if
46          else // not file or directory, output error message
47          {
48             System.out.printf( "%s %s", path, "does not exist." );
49          } // end else
50       } // end method analyzePath
51    } // end class FileDemonstration
```

```
Enter file or directory name: E:\Program Files\Java\jdk1.6.0_11\demo\jfc
jfc exists
is not a file
is a directory
is absolute path
Last modified: 1228404395024
Length: 4096
Path: E:\Program Files\Java\jdk1.6.0_11\demo\jfc
Absolute path: E:\Program Files\Java\jdk1.6.0_11\demo\jfc
Parent: E:\Program Files\Java\jdk1.6.0_11\demo

Directory contents:

CodePointIM
FileChooserDemo
Font2DTest
Java2D
Laffy
Metalworks
Notepad
SampleTree
Stylepad
SwingApplet
SwingSet2
SwingSet3
```

Fig. 17.4 | File class used to obtain file and directory information. (Part 2 of 3.)

```
Enter file or directory name: C:\Program Files\Java\jdk1.6.0_11\demo\jfc
\Java2D\README.txt
README.txt exists
is a file
is not a directory
is absolute path
Last modified: 1228404384270
Length: 7518
Path: E:\Program Files\Java\jdk1.6.0_11\demo\jfc\Java2D\README.txt
Absolute path: E:\Program Files\Java\jdk1.6.0_11\demo\jfc\Java2D\README.txt
Parent: E:\Program Files\Java\jdk1.6.0_11\demo\jfc\Java2D
```

Fig. 17.4 | File class used to obtain file and directory information. (Part 3 of 3.)

The program begins by prompting the user for a file or directory (line 12). Line 13 inputs the file name or directory name and passes it to method analyzePath (lines 17–50). The method creates a new File object (line 20) and assigns its reference to name. Line 22 invokes File method exists to determine whether the name input by the user exists (either as a file or as a directory) on the disk. If the name does not exist, control proceeds to lines 46–49 and displays a message to the screen containing the name the user typed, followed by "does not exist." Otherwise, the if statement (lines 22–45) executes. The program outputs the name of the file or directory (line 27), followed by the results of testing the File object with isFile (line 28), isDirectory (line 29) and isAbsolute (line 31). Next, the program displays the values returned by lastModified (line 33), length (line 33), getPath (line 34), getAbsolutePath (line 35) and getParent (line 35). If the File object represents a directory (line 37), the program obtains a list of the directory's contents as an array of Strings by using File method list (line 39) and displays the list on the screen.

The first output of this program demonstrates a File object associated with the jfc directory from the JDK. The second output demonstrates a File object associated with the README.txt file from the Java 2D example that comes with the JDK. In both cases, we specified an absolute path on our computer.

A **separator character** is used to separate directories and files in the path. On a Windows computer, the separator character is a backslash (\). On a UNIX system, it's a forward slash (/). Java processes both characters identically in a path name. For example, if we were to use the path

```
c:\Program Files\Java\jdk1.6.0_11\demo/jfc
```

which employs each separator character, Java would still process the path properly. When building Strings that represent path information, use File.separator to obtain the local computer's proper separator character rather than explicitly using / or \. This constant returns a String consisting of one character—the proper separator for the system.

Common Programming Error 17.1

Using \ as a directory separator rather than \\ in a string literal is a logic error. A single \ indicates that the \ followed by the next character represents an escape sequence. Use \\ to insert a \ in a string literal.

17.5 Sequential-Access Text Files

Next, we create and manipulate sequential-access files in which records are stored in order by the record-key field. We begin with text files, enabling the reader to quickly create and edit human-readable files. We discuss creating, writing data to, reading data from and updating sequential-access text files. We also include a credit-inquiry program that retrieves specific data from a file.

17.5.1 Creating a Sequential-Access Text File

Java imposes no structure on a file—notions such as records do not exist as part of the Java language. Therefore, you must structure files to meet the requirements of your applications. In the following example, we see how to impose a keyed record structure on a file.

The program in Figs. 17.5, 17.6 and 17.8 creates a simple sequential-access file that might be used in an accounts receivable system to keep track of the amounts owed to a company by its credit clients. For each client, the program obtains from the user an account number and the client's name and balance (i.e., the amount the client owes the company for goods and services received). Each client's data constitutes a "record" for that client. This application uses the account number as the record key—the file will be created and maintained in account-number order. The program assumes that the user enters the records in account-number order. In a comprehensive accounts receivable system (based on sequential-access files), a sorting capability would be provided so that the user could enter the records in any order. The records would then be sorted and written to the file.

Class AccountRecord
Class AccountRecord (Fig. 17.5) encapsulates the client record information used by the examples in this chapter. AccountRecord is declared in package com.deitel.ch17 (line 3), so that it can be imported into several of this chapter's examples for reuse. (Section 8.14 provides information on compiling and using your own packages.) Class AccountRecord contains private instance variables account, firstName, lastName and balance (lines 7–10) and *set* and *get* methods for accessing these fields. Though the *set* methods do not validate the data in this example, they should do so in a industrial-strength system.

```
1   // Fig. 17.5: AccountRecord.java
2   // AccountRecord class maintains information for one account.
3   package com.deitel.ch17; // packaged for reuse
4
5   public class AccountRecord
6   {
7      private int account;
8      private String firstName;
9      private String lastName;
10     private double balance;
11
12     // no-argument constructor calls other constructor with default values
13     public AccountRecord()
14     {
```

Fig. 17.5 | AccountRecord class maintains information for one account. (Part 1 of 3.)

```
15          this( 0, "", "", 0.0 ); // call four-argument constructor
16       } // end no-argument AccountRecord constructor
17
18       // initialize a record
19       public AccountRecord( int acct, String first, String last, double bal )
20       {
21          setAccount( acct );
22          setFirstName( first );
23          setLastName( last );
24          setBalance( bal );
25       } // end four-argument AccountRecord constructor
26
27       // set account number
28       public void setAccount( int acct )
29       {
30          account = acct;
31       } // end method setAccount
32
33       // get account number
34       public int getAccount()
35       {
36          return account;
37       } // end method getAccount
38
39       // set first name
40       public void setFirstName( String first )
41       {
42          firstName = first;
43       } // end method setFirstName
44
45       // get first name
46       public String getFirstName()
47       {
48          return firstName;
49       } // end method getFirstName
50
51       // set last name
52       public void setLastName( String last )
53       {
54          lastName = last;
55       } // end method setLastName
56
57       // get last name
58       public String getLastName()
59       {
60          return lastName;
61       } // end method getLastName
62
63       // set balance
64       public void setBalance( double bal )
65       {
66          balance = bal;
67       } // end method setBalance
68
```

Fig. 17.5 | AccountRecord class maintains information for one account. (Part 2 of 3.)

```
69      // get balance
70      public double getBalance()
71      {
72         return balance;
73      } // end method getBalance
74   } // end class AccountRecord
```

Fig. 17.5 | AccountRecord class maintains information for one account. (Part 3 of 3.)

To compile class AccountRecord, open a command window, change directories to this chapter's fig17_05 directory (which contains AccountRecord.java), then type:

```
javac -d .. AccountRecord.java
```

This places AccountRecord.class in its package directory structure and places the package in the ch17 folder that contains all the examples for this chapter. When you compile class AccountRecord (or any other classes that will be reused in this chapter), you should place them in a common directory. When you compile or execute classes that use class AccountRecord (e.g., CreateTextFile in Fig. 17.6), you must specify the command-line argument -classpath to both javac and java, as in

```
javac -classpath .;c:\examples\ch17 CreateTextFile.java
java -classpath .;c:\examples\ch17 CreateTextFile
```

Note that the current directory (specified with .) is included in the classpath to ensure that the compiler can locate other classes in the same directory as the class being compiled. The path separator used in the preceding commands must be appropriate for your platform—a semicolon (;) on Windows and a colon (:) on UNIX/Linux/Mac OS X. The preceding commands assume that the package containing AccountRecord is located at in the directory C:\examples\ch17 on a Windows computer.

Class *CreateTextFile*

Now let's examine class CreateTextFile (Fig. 17.6). Line 14 declares Formatter variable output. As discussed in Section 17.3, a Formatter object outputs formatted Strings, using the same formatting capabilities as method System.out.printf. A Formatter object can output to various locations, such as the screen or a file, as is done here. The Formatter object is instantiated in line 21 in method openFile (lines 17–34). The constructor used in line 21 takes one argument—a String containing the name of the file, including its path. If a path is not specified, as is the case here, the JVM assumes that the file is in the directory from which the program was executed. For text files, we use the .txt file extension. If the file does not exist, it will be created. If an existing file is opened, its contents are **truncated**—all the data in the file is discarded. At this point the file is open for writing, and the resulting Formatter object can be used to write data to the file.

```
1   // Fig. 17.6: CreateTextFile.java
2   // Writing data to a sequential text file with class Formatter.
3   import java.io.FileNotFoundException;
4   import java.lang.SecurityException;
5   import java.util.Formatter;
```

Fig. 17.6 | Writing data to a sequential text file with class Formatter. (Part 1 of 3.)

```
 6   import java.util.FormatterClosedException;
 7   import java.util.NoSuchElementException;
 8   import java.util.Scanner;
 9
10   import com.deitel.ch17.AccountRecord;
11
12   public class CreateTextFile
13   {
14      private Formatter output; // object used to output text to file
15
16      // enable user to open file
17      public void openFile()
18      {
19         try
20         {
21            output = new Formatter( "clients.txt" ); // open the file
22         } // end try
23         catch ( SecurityException securityException )
24         {
25            System.err.println(
26               "You do not have write access to this file." );
27            System.exit( 1 ); // terminate the program
28         } // end catch
29         catch ( FileNotFoundException fileNotFoundException )
30         {
31            System.err.println( "Error opening or creating file." );
32            System.exit( 1 ); // terminate the program
33         } // end catch
34      } // end method openFile
35
36      // add records to file
37      public void addRecords()
38      {
39         // object to be written to file
40         AccountRecord record = new AccountRecord();
41
42         Scanner input = new Scanner( System.in );
43
44         System.out.printf( "%s\n%s\n%s\n%s\n\n",
45            "To terminate input, type the end-of-file indicator ",
46            "when you are prompted to enter input.",
47            "On UNIX/Linux/Mac OS X type <ctrl> d then press Enter",
48            "On Windows type <ctrl> z then press Enter" );
49
50         System.out.printf( "%s\n%s",
51            "Enter account number (> 0), first name, last name and balance.",
52            "? " );
53
54         while ( input.hasNext() ) // loop until end-of-file indicator
55         {
56            try // output values to file
57            {
58               // retrieve data to be output
59               record.setAccount( input.nextInt() ); // read account number
```

Fig. 17.6 | Writing data to a sequential text file with class Formatter. (Part 2 of 3.)

```
60              record.setFirstName( input.next() ); // read first name
61              record.setLastName( input.next() ); // read last name
62              record.setBalance( input.nextDouble() ); // read balance
63
64              if ( record.getAccount() > 0 )
65              {
66                 // write new record
67                 output.format( "%d %s %s %.2f\n", record.getAccount(),
68                    record.getFirstName(), record.getLastName(),
69                    record.getBalance() );
70              } // end if
71              else
72              {
73                 System.out.println(
74                    "Account number must be greater than 0." );
75              } // end else
76           } // end try
77           catch ( FormatterClosedException formatterClosedException )
78           {
79              System.err.println( "Error writing to file." );
80              return;
81           } // end catch
82           catch ( NoSuchElementException elementException )
83           {
84              System.err.println( "Invalid input. Please try again." );
85              input.nextLine(); // discard input so user can try again
86           } // end catch
87
88           System.out.printf( "%s %s\n%s", "Enter account number (>0),",
89              "first name, last name and balance.", "? " );
90        } // end while
91     } // end method addRecords
92
93     // close file
94     public void closeFile()
95     {
96        if ( output != null )
97           output.close();
98     } // end method closeFile
99  } // end class CreateTextFile
```

Fig. 17.6 | Writing data to a sequential text file with class `Formatter`. (Part 3 of 3.)

Lines 23–28 handle the **SecurityException**, which occurs if the user does not have permission to write data to the file. Lines 29–33 handle the **FileNotFoundException**, which occurs if the file does not exist and a new file cannot be created. This exception may also occur if there is an error opening the file. Note that in both exception handlers we call static method **System.exit** and pass the value 1. This method terminates the application. An argument of 0 to method exit indicates successful program termination. A nonzero value, such as 1 in this example, normally indicates that an error has occurred. This value is passed to the command window that executed the program. The argument is useful if the program is executed from a **batch file** on Windows systems or a **shell script** on UNIX/Linux/Mac OS X systems. Batch files and shell scripts offer a convenient way of executing several programs in sequence. When the first program ends, the next program begins execution. It's possible to use the argument to method `exit` in a batch file or shell script to determine whether other programs should execute. For more information on batch files or shell scripts, see your operating system's documentation.

Method `addRecords` (lines 37–91) prompts the user to enter the various fields for each record or to enter the end-of-file key sequence when data entry is complete. Figure 17.7 lists the key combinations for entering end-of-file for various computer systems.

Operating system	Key combination
UNIX/Linux/Mac OS X	*<Enter> <Ctrl> d*
Windows	*<Ctrl> z*

Fig. 17.7 | End-of-file key combinations.

Line 40 creates an `AccountRecord` object, which will be used to store the values of the current record entered by the user. Line 42 creates a `Scanner` object to read input from the user at the keyboard. Lines 44–48 and 50–52 prompt the user for input.

Line 54 uses `Scanner` method `hasNext` to determine whether the end-of-file key combination has been entered. The loop executes until `hasNext` encounters end-of-file.

Lines 59–62 read data from the user, storing the record information in the `AccountRecord` object. Each statement throws a **NoSuchElementException** (handled in lines 82–86) if the data is in the wrong format (e.g., a `String` when an `int` is expected) or if there is no more data to input. If the account number is greater than 0 (line 64), the record's information is written to `clients.txt` (lines 67–69) using method **format**, which can perform identical formatting to the `System.out.printf` method used extensively in earlier chapters. Method `format` outputs a formatted `String` to the output destination of the `Formatter` object—the file `clients.txt`. The format string `"%d %s %s %.2f\n"` indicates that the current record will be stored as an integer (the account number) followed by a `String` (the first name), another `String` (the last name) and a floating-point value (the balance). Each piece of information is separated from the next by a space, and the double value (the balance) is output with two digits to the right of the decimal point (as indicated by the `.2` in `%.2f`). The data in the text file can be viewed with a text editor or retrieved later by a program designed to read the file (Section 17.5.2).

When lines 67–69 execute, if the `Formatter` object is closed, a **FormatterClosedException** will be thrown. This exception is handled in lines 77–81. [*Note:* You can also output data to a text file using class **java.io.PrintWriter**, which provides `format` and `printf` methods for outputting formatted data.]

Lines 94–98 declare method `closeFile`, which closes the `Formatter` and the underlying output file. Line 97 closes the object by simply calling method **close**. If method `close` is not called explicitly, the operating system normally will close the file when program execution terminates—this is an example of operating-system "housekeeping." However, you should always explicitly close a file when it is no longer needed.

Platform-Specific Line-Separator Characters

Lines 67–69 output a line of text followed by a newline (\n). If you use a text editor to open the `clients.txt` file produced, each record might not display on a separate line. For example, in Notepad (Microsoft Windows), users will see one continuous line of text. This occurs because different platforms use different line-separator characters. On UNIX/ Linux/Mac OS X, the line separator is a newline (\n). On Windows, it is a combination of a carriage return and a line feed—represented as \r\n. You can use the **%n** format specifier in a format control string to output a platform-specific line separator, thus ensuring that the text file can be opened and viewed correctly in a text editor for the platform on which the file was created. Note that the method System.out.println outputs a platform-specific line separator after its argument. Also, note that regardless of the line separator used in a text file, a Java program can still recognize the lines of text and read them.

Class CreateTextFileTest

Figure 17.8 runs the program. Line 8 creates a CreateTextFile object, which is then used to open, add records to and close the file (lines 10–12). The sample data for this application is shown in Fig. 17.9. In the sample execution for this program, the user enters information for five accounts, then enters end-of-file to signal that data entry is complete. The sample execution does not show how the data records actually appear in the file. In the next section, to verify that the file has been created successfully, we present a program that reads the file and prints its contents. Because this is a text file, you can also verify the information by opening the file in a text editor.

```
 1   // Fig. 17.8: CreateTextFileTest.java
 2   // Testing the CreateTextFile class.
 3
 4   public class CreateTextFileTest
 5   {
 6      public static void main( String[] args )
 7      {
 8         CreateTextFile application = new CreateTextFile();
 9
10         application.openFile();
11         application.addRecords();
12         application.closeFile();
13      } // end main
14   } // end class CreateTextFileTest
```

```
To terminate input, type the end-of-file indicator
when you are prompted to enter input.
On UNIX/Linux/Mac OS X type <ctrl> d then press Enter
On Windows type <ctrl> z then press Enter

Enter account number (> 0), first name, last name and balance.
? 100 Bob Jones 24.98
Enter account number (> 0), first name, last name and balance.
? 200 Steve Doe -345.67
Enter account number (> 0), first name, last name and balance.
? 300 Pam White 0.00
Enter account number (> 0), first name, last name and balance.
? 400 Sam Stone -42.16
Enter account number (> 0), first name, last name and balance.
? 500 Sue Rich 224.62
Enter account number (> 0), first name, last name and balance.
? ^Z
```

Fig. 17.8 | Testing the CreateTextFile class.

Sample data			
100	Bob	Jones	24.98
200	Steve	Doe	-345.67
300	Pam	White	0.00
400	Sam	Stone	-42.16
500	Sue	Rich	224.62

Fig. 17.9 | Sample data for the program in Figs. 17.6–17.8.

17.5.2 Reading Data from a Sequential-Access Text File

Data is stored in files so that it may be retrieved for processing when needed. Section 17.5.1 demonstrated how to create a file for sequential access. This section shows how to read data sequentially from a text file. We demonstrate how class Scanner can be used to input data from a file rather than the keyboard.

The application in Figs. 17.10 and 17.11 reads records from the file "clients.txt" created by the application of Section 17.5.1 and displays the record contents. Line 13 of Fig. 17.10 declares a Scanner that will be used to retrieve input from the file.

```
1   // Fig. 17.10: ReadTextFile.java
2   // This program reads a text file and displays each record.
3   import java.io.File;
4   import java.io.FileNotFoundException;
5   import java.lang.IllegalStateException;
6   import java.util.NoSuchElementException;
7   import java.util.Scanner;
8
9   import com.deitel.ch17.AccountRecord;
10
11  public class ReadTextFile
12  {
13     private Scanner input;
14
15     // enable user to open file
16     public void openFile()
17     {
18        try
19        {
20           input = new Scanner( new File( "clients.txt" ) );
21        } // end try
22        catch ( FileNotFoundException fileNotFoundException )
23        {
24           System.err.println( "Error opening file." );
25           System.exit( 1 );
26        } // end catch
27     } // end method openFile
28
29     // read record from file
30     public void readRecords()
31     {
```

Fig. 17.10 | Sequential file reading using a Scanner. (Part 1 of 2.)

```
32            // object to be written to screen
33            AccountRecord record = new AccountRecord();
34
35            System.out.printf( "%-10s%-12s%-12s%10s\n", "Account",
36               "First Name", "Last Name", "Balance" );
37
38            try // read records from file using Scanner object
39            {
40               while ( input.hasNext() )
41               {
42                  record.setAccount( input.nextInt() ); // read account number
43                  record.setFirstName( input.next() ); // read first name
44                  record.setLastName( input.next() ); // read last name
45                  record.setBalance( input.nextDouble() ); // read balance
46
47                  // display record contents
48                  System.out.printf( "%-10d%-12s%-12s%10.2f\n",
49                     record.getAccount(), record.getFirstName(),
50                     record.getLastName(), record.getBalance() );
51               } // end while
52            } // end try
53            catch ( NoSuchElementException elementException )
54            {
55               System.err.println( "File improperly formed." );
56               input.close();
57               System.exit( 1 );
58            } // end catch
59            catch ( IllegalStateException stateException )
60            {
61               System.err.println( "Error reading from file." );
62               System.exit( 1 );
63            } // end catch
64         } // end method readRecords
65
66         // close file and terminate application
67         public void closeFile()
68         {
69            if ( input != null )
70               input.close(); // close file
71         } // end method closeFile
72      } // end class ReadTextFile
```

Fig. 17.10 | Sequential file reading using a Scanner. (Part 2 of 2.)

```
1   // Fig. 17.11: ReadTextFileTest.java
2   // Testing the ReadTextFile class.
3
4   public class ReadTextFileTest
5   {
6      public static void main( String[] args )
7      {
8         ReadTextFile application = new ReadTextFile();
9
```

Fig. 17.11 | Testing the ReadTextFile class. (Part 1 of 2.)

```
10            application.openFile();
11            application.readRecords();
12            application.closeFile();
13       } // end main
14   } // end class ReadTextFileTest
```

```
Account    First Name   Last Name     Balance
100        Bob          Jones           24.98
200        Steve        Doe           -345.67
300        Pam          White            0.00
400        Sam          Stone          -42.16
500        Sue          Rich           224.62
```

Fig. 17.11 | Testing the ReadTextFile class. (Part 2 of 2.)

Method openFile (lines 16–27) opens the file for reading by instantiating a Scanner object in line 20. We pass a File object to the constructor, which specifies that the Scanner object will read from the file "clients.txt" located in the directory from which the application executes. If the file cannot be found, a FileNotFoundException occurs. The exception is handled in lines 22–26.

Method readRecords (lines 30–64) reads and displays records from the file. Line 33 creates AccountRecord object record to store the current record's information. Lines 35–36 display headers for the columns in the application's output. Lines 40–51 read data from the file until the end-of-file marker is reached (in which case, method hasNext will return false at line 40). Lines 42–45 use Scanner methods nextInt, next and nextDouble to input an int (the account number), two Strings (the first and last names) and a double value (the balance). Each record is one line of data in the file. The values are stored in object record. If the information in the file is not properly formed (e.g., there is a last name where there should be a balance), a NoSuchElementException occurs when the record is input. This exception is handled in lines 53–58. If the Scanner was closed before the data was input, an **IllegalStateException** occurs (handled in lines 59–63). If no exceptions occur, the record's information is displayed on the screen (lines 48–50). Note in the format string in line 48 that the account number, first name and last name are left justified, while the balance is right justified and output with two digits of precision. Each iteration of the loop inputs one line of text from the text file, which represents one record.

Lines 67–71 define method closeFile, which closes the Scanner. Method main is defined in Fig. 17.11 in lines 6–13. Line 8 creates a ReadTextFile object, which is then used to open, add records to and close the file (lines 10–12).

17.5.3 Case Study: A Credit-Inquiry Program

To retrieve data sequentially from a file, programs start from the beginning of the file and read all the data consecutively until the desired information is found. It might be necessary to process the file sequentially several times (from the beginning of the file) during the execution of a program. Class Scanner does not allow repositioning to the beginning of the file. If it's necessary to read the file again, the program must close the file and reopen it.

The program in Figs. 17.12–17.14 allows a credit manager to obtain lists of customers with zero balances (i.e., customers who do not owe any money), customers with credit balances (i.e., customers to whom the company owes money) and customers with debit balances (i.e., customers who owe the company money for goods and services received). A credit balance is a negative amount, a debit balance a positive amount.

MenuOption Enumeration

We begin by creating an enum type (Fig. 17.12) to define the different menu options the user will have. The options and their values are listed in lines 7–10. Method getValue (lines 19–22) retrieves the value of a specific enum constant.

```
1   // Fig. 17.12: MenuOption.java
2   // Enumeration for the credit-inquiry program's options.
3
4   public enum MenuOption
5   {
6      // declare contents of enum type
7      ZERO_BALANCE( 1 ),
8      CREDIT_BALANCE( 2 ),
9      DEBIT_BALANCE( 3 ),
10     END( 4 );
11
12     private final int value; // current menu option
13
14     MenuOption( int valueOption )
15     {
16        value = valueOption;
17     } // end MenuOptions enum constructor
18
19     public int getValue()
20     {
21        return value;
22     } // end method getValue
23  } // end enum MenuOption
```

Fig. 17.12 | Enumeration for the credit-inquiry program's menu options.

CreditInquiry Class

Figure 17.13 contains the functionality for the credit-inquiry program, and Fig. 17.14 contains the main method that executes the program. The program displays a text menu and allows the credit manager to enter one of three options to obtain credit information. Option 1 (ZERO_BALANCE) displays accounts with zero balances. Option 2 (CREDIT_BALANCE) displays accounts with credit balances. Option 3 (DEBIT_BALANCE) displays accounts with debit balances. Option 4 (END) terminates program execution.

```
1   // Fig. 17.13: CreditInquiry.java
2   // This program reads a file sequentially and displays the
3   // contents based on the type of account the user requests
4   // (credit balance, debit balance or zero balance).
5   import java.io.File;
6   import java.io.FileNotFoundException;
7   import java.lang.IllegalStateException;
8   import java.util.NoSuchElementException;
```

Fig. 17.13 | Credit-inquiry program. (Part 1 of 4.)

```
 9   import java.util.Scanner;
10
11   import com.deitel.ch17.AccountRecord;
12
13   public class CreditInquiry
14   {
15      private MenuOption accountType;
16      private Scanner input;
17      private final static MenuOption[] choices = { MenuOption.ZERO_BALANCE,
18         MenuOption.CREDIT_BALANCE, MenuOption.DEBIT_BALANCE,
19         MenuOption.END };
20
21      // read records from file and display only records of appropriate type
22      private void readRecords()
23      {
24         // object to store data that will be written to file
25         AccountRecord record = new AccountRecord();
26
27         try // read records
28         {
29            // open file to read from beginning
30            input = new Scanner( new File( "clients.txt" ) );
31
32            while ( input.hasNext() ) // input the values from the file
33            {
34               record.setAccount( input.nextInt() ); // read account number
35               record.setFirstName( input.next() ); // read first name
36               record.setLastName( input.next() ); // read last name
37               record.setBalance( input.nextDouble() ); // read balance
38
39               // if proper acount type, display record
40               if ( shouldDisplay( record.getBalance() ) )
41                  System.out.printf( "%-10d%-12s%-12s%10.2f\n",
42                     record.getAccount(), record.getFirstName(),
43                     record.getLastName(), record.getBalance() );
44            } // end while
45         } // end try
46         catch ( NoSuchElementException elementException )
47         {
48            System.err.println( "File improperly formed." );
49            input.close();
50            System.exit( 1 );
51         } // end catch
52         catch ( IllegalStateException stateException )
53         {
54            System.err.println( "Error reading from file." );
55            System.exit( 1 );
56         } // end catch
57         catch ( FileNotFoundException fileNotFoundException )
58         {
59            System.err.println( "File cannot be found." );
60            System.exit( 1 );
61         } // end catch
```

Fig. 17.13 | Credit-inquiry program. (Part 2 of 4.)

```
62          finally
63          {
64             if ( input != null )
65                input.close(); // close the Scanner and the file
66          } // end finally
67       } // end method readRecords
68
69       // use record type to determine if record should be displayed
70       private boolean shouldDisplay( double balance )
71       {
72          if ( ( accountType == MenuOption.CREDIT_BALANCE )
73             && ( balance < 0 ) )
74             return true;
75
76          else if ( ( accountType == MenuOption.DEBIT_BALANCE )
77             && ( balance > 0 ) )
78             return true;
79
80          else if ( ( accountType == MenuOption.ZERO_BALANCE )
81             && ( balance == 0 ) )
82             return true;
83
84          return false;
85       } // end method shouldDisplay
86
87       // obtain request from user
88       private MenuOption getRequest()
89       {
90          Scanner textIn = new Scanner( System.in );
91          int request = 1;
92
93          // display request options
94          System.out.printf( "\n%s\n%s\n%s\n%s\n%s\n",
95             "Enter request", " 1 - List accounts with zero balances",
96             " 2 - List accounts with credit balances",
97             " 3 - List accounts with debit balances", " 4 - End of run" );
98
99          try // attempt to input menu choice
100         {
101            do // input user request
102            {
103               System.out.print( "\n? " );
104               request = textIn.nextInt();
105            } while ( ( request < 1 ) || ( request > 4 ) );
106         } // end try
107         catch ( NoSuchElementException elementException )
108         {
109            System.err.println( "Invalid input." );
110            System.exit( 1 );
111         } // end catch
112
113         return choices[ request - 1 ]; // return enum value for option
114      } // end method getRequest
115
```

Fig. 17.13 | Credit-inquiry program. (Part 3 of 4.)

```
116    public void processRequests()
117    {
118       // get user's request (e.g., zero, credit or debit balance)
119       accountType = getRequest();
120
121       while ( accountType != MenuOption.END )
122       {
123          switch ( accountType )
124          {
125             case ZERO_BALANCE:
126                System.out.println( "\nAccounts with zero balances:\n" );
127                break;
128             case CREDIT_BALANCE:
129                System.out.println( "\nAccounts with credit balances:\n" );
130                break;
131             case DEBIT_BALANCE:
132                System.out.println( "\nAccounts with debit balances:\n" );
133                break;
134          } // end switch
135
136          readRecords();
137          accountType = getRequest();
138       } // end while
139    } // end method processRequests
140 } // end class CreditInquiry
```

Fig. 17.13 | Credit-inquiry program. (Part 4 of 4.)

```
1    // Fig. 17.14: CreditInquiryTest.java
2    // This program tests class CreditInquiry.
3
4    public class CreditInquiryTest
5    {
6       public static void main( String[] args )
7       {
8          CreditInquiry application = new CreditInquiry();
9          application.processRequests();
10      } // end main
11   } // end class CreditInquiryTest
```

Fig. 17.14 | Testing the CreditInquiry class.

```
Enter request
 1 - List accounts with zero balances
 2 - List accounts with credit balances
 3 - List accounts with debit balances
 4 - End of run

? 1

Accounts with zero balances:

300        Pam        White        0.00
```

Fig. 17.15 | Sample output of the credit-inquiry program in Fig. 17.14. (Part 1 of 2.)

```
Enter request
 1 - List accounts with zero balances
 2 - List accounts with credit balances
 3 - List accounts with debit balances
 4 - End of run

? 2

Accounts with credit balances:
200        Steve      Doe          -345.67
400        Sam        Stone         -42.16

Enter request
 1 - List accounts with zero balances
 2 - List accounts with credit balances
 3 - List accounts with debit balances
 4 - End of run

? 3

Accounts with debit balances:
100        Bob        Jones          24.98
500        Sue        Rich          224.62

? 4
```

Fig. 17.15 | Sample output of the credit-inquiry program in Fig. 17.14. (Part 2 of 2.)

The record information is collected by reading through the file and determining if each record satisfies the criteria for the selected account type. Method processRequests (lines 116–139 of Fig. 17.13) calls method getRequest to display the menu options (line 119), translates the number typed by the user into a MenuOption and stores the result in MenuOption variable accountType. Lines 121–138 loop until the user specifies that the program should terminate. Lines 123–134 display a header for the current set of records to be output to the screen. Line 136 calls method readRecords (lines 22–67), which loops through the file and reads every record.

Line 30 of method readRecords opens the file for reading with a Scanner. Note that the file will be opened for reading with a new Scanner object each time this method is called, so that we can again read from the beginning of the file. Lines 34–37 read a record. Line 40 calls method shouldDisplay (lines 70–85) to determine whether the current record satisfies the account type requested. If shouldDisplay returns true, the program displays the account information. When the end-of-file marker is reached, the loop terminates and line 65 calls the Scanner's close method to close the Scanner and the file. Notice that this occurs in a finally block, which will execute whether or not the file was successfully read. Once all the records have been read, control returns to method processRequests and getRequest is again called (line 137) to retrieve the user's next menu option. Figure 17.14 contains method main, and calls method processRequests in line 9.

17.5.4 Updating Sequential-Access Files

The data in many sequential files cannot be modified without the risk of destroying other data in the file. For example, if the name "White" needed to be changed to "Worthington," the old name cannot simply be overwritten, because the new name requires more space. The record for White was written to the file as

```
300 Pam White 0.00
```

If the record is rewritten beginning at the same location in the file using the new name, the record will be

```
300 Pam Worthington 0.00
```

The new record is larger (has more characters) than the original record. The characters beyond the second "o" in "Worthington" will overwrite the beginning of the next sequential record in the file. The problem here is that fields in a text file—and hence records—can vary in size. For example, 7, 14, –117, 2074 and 27383 are all ints stored in the same number of bytes (4) internally, but they are different-sized fields when displayed on the screen or written to a file as text. Therefore, records in a sequential-access file are not usually updated in place. Instead, the entire file is usually rewritten. To make the preceding name change, the records before 300 Pam White 0.00 would be copied to a new file, the new record (which can be of a different size than the one it replaces) would be written and the records after 300 Pam White 0.00 would be copied to the new file. Rewriting the entire file is uneconomical to update just one record, but reasonable if a substantial number of records need to be updated.

17.6 Object Serialization

In Section 17.5, we demonstrated how to write the individual fields of an AccountRecord object into a file as text, and how to read those fields from a file and place their values into an AccountRecord object in memory. In the examples, AccountRecord was used to aggregate the information for one record. When the instance variables for an AccountRecord were output to a disk file, certain information was lost, such as the type of each value. For instance, if the value "3" is read from a file, there is no way to tell whether it came from an int, a String or a double. We have only data, not type information, on a disk. If the program that is going to read this data "knows" what object type the data corresponds to, then the data is simply read into objects of that type. For example, in Section 17.5.2, we know that we are inputting an int (the account number), followed by two Strings (the first and last name) and a double (the balance). We also know that these values are separated by spaces, with only one record on each line. Sometimes we'll not know exactly how the data is stored in a file. In such cases, we want to read or write an entire object from a file. Java provides such a mechanism, called **object serialization**. A so-called **serialized object** is an object represented as a sequence of bytes that includes the object's data as well as information about the object's type and the types of data stored in the object. After a serialized object has been written into a file, it can be read from the file and **deserialized**—that is, the type information and bytes that represent the object and its data can be used to recreate the object in memory.

Software Engineering Observation 17.1

The serialization mechanism makes exact copies of objects. This makes it a simple way to clone objects without having to override Object method clone.

Classes *ObjectInputStream* and *ObjectOutputStream*

Classes ObjectInputStream and ObjectOutputStream, which respectively implement the **ObjectInput** and **ObjectOutput** interfaces, enable entire objects to be read from or written to a stream (possibly a file). To use serialization with files, we initialize ObjectInputStream and ObjectOutputStream objects with stream objects that read from and write to files—objects of classes FileInputStream and FileOutputStream, respectively. Initializing stream objects with other stream objects in this manner is sometimes called **wrapping**—the new stream object being created wraps the stream object specified as a constructor argument. To wrap a FileInputStream in an ObjectInputStream, for instance, we pass the FileInputStream object to the ObjectInputStream's constructor.

Interfaces *ObjectOutput and ObjectInput*

The ObjectOutput interface contains method **writeObject**, which takes an Objectas an argument and writes its information to an OutputStream. A class that implements interface ObjectOuput (such as ObjectOutputStream) declares this method and ensures that the object being output implements interface Serializable (discussed shortly). Correspondingly, the ObjectInput interface contains method **readObject**, which reads and returns a reference to an Object from an InputStream. After an object has been read, its reference can be cast to the object's actual type. As you'll see in Chapter 27, applications that communicate via a network, such as the Internet, can also transmit entire objects across the network.

17.6.1 Creating a Sequential-Access File Using Object Serialization

This section and Section 17.6.2 create and manipulate sequential-access files using object serialization. The object serialization we show here is performed with byte-based streams, so the sequential files created and manipulated will be binary files. Recall that binary files typically cannot be viewed in standard text editors. For this reason, we write a separate application that knows how to read and display serialized objects. We begin by creating and writing serialized objects to a sequential-access file. The example is similar to the one in Section 17.5, so we focus only on the new features.

Defining Class *AccountRecordSerializable*

Let's begin by modifying our AccountRecord class so that objects of this class can be serialized. Class AccountRecordSerializable (Fig. 17.16) implements interface **Serializable** (line 7), which allows objects of AccountRecordSerializable to be serialized and deserialized with ObjectOutputStreams and ObjectInputStreams, respectively. Interface Serializable is a **tagging interface**. Such an interface does not contain methods. A class that implements Serializable is tagged as being a Serializable object. This is important, because an ObjectOutputStream will not output an object unless it *is a* Serializable object, which is the case for any object of a class that implements Serializable.

```
1   // Fig. 17.16: AccountRecordSerializable.java
2   // AccountRecordSerializable class for serializable objects.
3   package com.deitel.ch17; // packaged for reuse
4
5   import java.io.Serializable;
6
7   public class AccountRecordSerializable implements Serializable
8   {
9      private int account;
10     private String firstName;
11     private String lastName;
```

Fig. 17.16 | AccountRecordSerializable class for serializable objects. (Part 1 of 3.)

```
12      private double balance;
13
14      // no-argument constructor calls other constructor with default values
15      public AccountRecordSerializable()
16      {
17         this( 0, "", "", 0.0 );
18      } // end no-argument AccountRecordSerializable constructor
19
20      // four-argument constructor initializes a record
21      public AccountRecordSerializable(
22         int acct, String first, String last, double bal )
23      {
24         setAccount( acct );
25         setFirstName( first );
26         setLastName( last );
27         setBalance( bal );
28      } // end four-argument AccountRecordSerializable constructor
29
30      // set account number
31      public void setAccount( int acct )
32      {
33         account = acct;
34      } // end method setAccount
35
36      // get account number
37      public int getAccount()
38      {
39         return account;
40      } // end method getAccount
41
42      // set first name
43      public void setFirstName( String first )
44      {
45         firstName = first;
46      } // end method setFirstName
47
48      // get first name
49      public String getFirstName()
50      {
51         return firstName;
52      } // end method getFirstName
53
54      // set last name
55      public void setLastName( String last )
56      {
57         lastName = last;
58      } // end method setLastName
59
60      // get last name
61      public String getLastName()
62      {
63         return lastName;
64      } // end method getLastName
65
```

Fig. 17.16 | AccountRecordSerializable class for serializable objects. (Part 2 of 3.)

```
66      // set balance
67      public void setBalance( double bal )
68      {
69         balance = bal;
70      } // end method setBalance
71
72      // get balance
73      public double getBalance()
74      {
75         return balance;
76      } // end method getBalance
77   } // end class AccountRecordSerializable
```

Fig. 17.16 | `AccountRecordSerializable` class for serializable objects. (Part 3 of 3.)

In a class that implements `Serializable`, the programmer must ensure that every instance variable is a `Serializable` type. Otherwise, it must be declared **transient** to indicate that it's not `Serializable` and should be ignored during the serialization process. By default, all primitive-type variables are serializable. For reference-type variables, you must check the class's documentation (and possibly its superclasses) to ensure that the type is `Serializable`. For example, `Strings` are `Serializable`. By default, arrays are serializable; however, in a reference-type array, the referenced objects may or may not be serializable. Class `AccountRecordSerializable` contains `private` data members account, `firstName`, `lastName` and `balance`—all of which are `Serializable`. This class also provides `public` *get* and *set* methods for accessing the `private` fields.

Writing Serialized Objects to a Sequential-Access File
Now let's discuss the code that creates the sequential-access file (Figs. 17.17–17.18). We concentrate only on new concepts here. As stated in Section 17.3, a program can open a file by creating an object of stream class `FileInputStream` or `FileOutputStream`. In this example, the file is to be opened for output, so the program creates a `FileOutputStream` (line 21 of Fig. 17.17). The `String` argument that is passed to the `FileOutputStream`'s constructor represents the name and path of the file to be opened. Existing files that are opened for output in this manner are truncated. Note that the `.ser` file extension is used—we use this file extension for binary files that contain serialized objects.

```
1    // Fig. 17.17: CreateSequentialFile.java
2    // Writing objects sequentially to a file with class ObjectOutputStream.
3    import java.io.FileOutputStream;
4    import java.io.IOException;
5    import java.io.ObjectOutputStream;
6    import java.util.NoSuchElementException;
7    import java.util.Scanner;
8
9    import com.deitel.ch17.AccountRecordSerializable;
10
11   public class CreateSequentialFile
12   {
13      private ObjectOutputStream output; // outputs data to file
```

Fig. 17.17 | Sequential file created using `ObjectOutputStream`. (Part 1 of 3.)

```
14
15       // allow user to specify file name
16       public void openFile()
17       {
18          try // open file
19          {
20             output = new ObjectOutputStream(
21                new FileOutputStream( "clients.ser" ) );
22          } // end try
23          catch ( IOException ioException )
24          {
25             System.err.println( "Error opening file." );
26          } // end catch
27       } // end method openFile
28
29       // add records to file
30       public void addRecords()
31       {
32          AccountRecordSerializable record; // object to be written to file
33          int accountNumber = 0; // account number for record object
34          String firstName; // first name for record object
35          String lastName; // last name for record object
36          double balance; // balance for record object
37
38          Scanner input = new Scanner( System.in );
39
40          System.out.printf( "%s\n%s\n\n%s\n\n%s\n\n",
41             "To terminate input, type the end-of-file indicator ",
42             "when you are prompted to enter input.",
43             "On UNIX/Linux/Mac OS X type <ctrl> d then press Enter",
44             "On Windows type <ctrl> z then press Enter" );
45
46          System.out.printf( "%s\n%s",
47             "Enter account number (> 0), first name, last name and balance.",
48             "? " );
49
50          while ( input.hasNext() ) // loop until end-of-file indicator
51          {
52             try // output values to file
53             {
54                accountNumber = input.nextInt(); // read account number
55                firstName = input.next(); // read first name
56                lastName = input.next(); // read last name
57                balance = input.nextDouble(); // read balance
58
59                if ( accountNumber > 0 )
60                {
61                   // create new record
62                   record = new AccountRecordSerializable( accountNumber,
63                      firstName, lastName, balance );
64                   output.writeObject( record ); // output record
65                } // end if
66                else
67                {
```

Fig. 17.17 | Sequential file created using `ObjectOutputStream`. (Part 2 of 3.)

```
68                      System.out.println(
69                         "Account number must be greater than 0." );
70                   } // end else
71                } // end try
72                catch ( IOException ioException )
73                {
74                   System.err.println( "Error writing to file." );
75                   return;
76                } // end catch
77                catch ( NoSuchElementException elementException )
78                {
79                   System.err.println( "Invalid input. Please try again." );
80                   input.nextLine(); // discard input so user can try again
81                } // end catch
82
83                System.out.printf( "%s %s\n%s", "Enter account number (>0),",
84                   "first name, last name and balance.", "? " );
85             } // end while
86          } // end method addRecords
87
88          // close file and terminate application
89          public void closeFile()
90          {
91             try // close file
92             {
93                if ( output != null )
94                   output.close();
95             } // end try
96             catch ( IOException ioException )
97             {
98                System.err.println( "Error closing file." );
99                System.exit( 1 );
100            } // end catch
101         } // end method closeFile
102      } // end class CreateSequentialFile
```

Fig. 17.17 | Sequential file created using `ObjectOutputStream`. (Part 3 of 3.)

```
1   // Fig. 17.18: CreateSequentialFileTest.java
2   // Testing class CreateSequentialFile.
3
4   public class CreateSequentialFileTest
5   {
6      public static void main( String[] args )
7      {
8         CreateSequentialFile application = new CreateSequentialFile();
9
10        application.openFile();
11        application.addRecords();
12        application.closeFile();
13     } // end main
14  } // end class CreateSequentialFileTest
```

Fig. 17.18 | Testing class `CreateSequentialFile`. (Part 1 of 2.)

```
To terminate input, type the end-of-file indicator
when you are prompted to enter input.
On UNIX/Linux/Mac OS X type <ctrl> d then press Enter
On Windows type <ctrl> z then press Enter

Enter account number (> 0), first name, last name and balance.
? 100 Bob Jones 24.98
Enter account number (> 0), first name, last name and balance.
? 200 Steve Doe -345.67
Enter account number (> 0), first name, last name and balance.
? 300 Pam White 0.00
Enter account number (> 0), first name, last name and balance.
? 400 Sam Stone -42.16
Enter account number (> 0), first name, last name and balance.
? 500 Sue Rich 224.62
Enter account number (> 0), first name, last name and balance.
? ^Z
```

Fig. 17.18 | Testing class `CreateSequentialFile`. (Part 2 of 2.)

Common Programming Error 17.2

It's a logic error to open an existing file for output when, in fact, you wish to preserve the file. Class `FileOutputStream` provides an overloaded constructor that enables you to open a file and append data to the end of the file. This will preserve the contents of the file.

Class `FileOutputStream` provides methods for writing byte arrays and individual bytes to a file, but we wish to write objects to a file. For this reason, we wrap a `FileOutputStream` in an `ObjectOutputStream` by passing the new `FileOutputStream` object to the `ObjectOutputStream`'s constructor (lines 20–21). The `ObjectOutputStream` object uses the `FileOutputStream` object to write objects into the file. Lines 20–21 may throw an **IOException** if a problem occurs while opening the file (e.g., when a file is opened for writing on a drive with insufficient space or when a read-only file is opened for writing). If so, the program displays an error message (lines 23–26). If no exception occurs, the file is open, and variable `output` can be used to write objects to it.

This program assumes that data is input correctly and in the proper record-number order. Method `addRecords` (lines 30–86) performs the write operation. Lines 62–63 create an `AccountRecordSerializable` object from the data entered by the user. Line 64 calls `ObjectOutputStream` method `writeObject` to write the `record` object to the output file. Note that only one statement is required to write the entire object.

Method `closeFile` (lines 89–101) calls `ObjectOutputStream` method **close** on `output` to close both the `ObjectOutputStream` and its underlying `FileOutputStream` (line 94). Note that the call to method `close` is contained in a `try` block. Method `close` throws an `IOException` if the file cannot be closed properly. In this case, it's important to notify the user that the information in the file might be corrupted. When using wrapped streams, closing the outermost stream also closes the underlying file.

In the sample execution for the program in Fig. 17.18, we entered information for five accounts—the same information shown in Fig. 17.9. The program does not show how the data records actually appear in the file. Remember that now we are using binary files, which are not humanly readable. To verify that the file has been created successfully, the next section presents a program to read the file's contents.

17.6.2 Reading and Deserializing Data from a Sequential-Access File

The preceding section showed how to create a file for sequential access using object serialization. In this section, we discuss how to read serialized data sequentially from a file.

The program in Figs. 17.19–17.20 reads records from a file created by the program in Section 17.6.1 and displays the contents. The program opens the file for input by creating a FileInputStream object (line 21). The name of the file to open is specified as an argument to the FileInputStream constructor. In Fig. 17.17, we wrote objects to the file, using an ObjectOutputStream object. Data must be read from the file in the same format in which it was written. Therefore, we use an ObjectInputStream wrapped around a FileInputStream in this program (lines 20–21). If no exceptions occur when opening the file, variable input can be used to read objects from the file.

```java
1   // Fig. 17.19: ReadSequentialFile.java
2   // Reading a file of objects sequentially with ObjectInputStream
3   // and displaying each record.
4   import java.io.EOFException;
5   import java.io.FileInputStream;
6   import java.io.IOException;
7   import java.io.ObjectInputStream;
8
9   import com.deitel.ch17.AccountRecordSerializable;
10
11  public class ReadSequentialFile
12  {
13     private ObjectInputStream input;
14
15     // enable user to select file to open
16     public void openFile()
17     {
18        try // open file
19        {
20           input = new ObjectInputStream(
21              new FileInputStream( "clients.ser" ) );
22        } // end try
23        catch ( IOException ioException )
24        {
25           System.err.println( "Error opening file." );
26        } // end catch
27     } // end method openFile
28
29     // read record from file
30     public void readRecords()
31     {
32        AccountRecordSerializable record;
33        System.out.printf( "%-10s%-12s%-12s%10s\n", "Account",
34           "First Name", "Last Name", "Balance" );
35
36        try // input the values from the file
37        {
```

Fig. 17.19 | Reading a file of objects sequentially with ObjectInputStream and displaying each record. (Part I of 2.)

```
38              while ( true )
39              {
40                  record = ( AccountRecordSerializable ) input.readObject();
41
42                  // display record contents
43                  System.out.printf( "%-10d%-12s%-12s%10.2f\n",
44                      record.getAccount(), record.getFirstName(),
45                      record.getLastName(), record.getBalance() );
46              } // end while
47          } // end try
48          catch ( EOFException endOfFileException )
49          {
50              return; // end of file was reached
51          } // end catch
52          catch ( ClassNotFoundException classNotFoundException )
53          {
54              System.err.println( "Unable to create object." );
55          } // end catch
56          catch ( IOException ioException )
57          {
58              System.err.println( "Error during read from file." );
59          } // end catch
60      } // end method readRecords
61
62      // close file and terminate application
63      public void closeFile()
64      {
65          try // close file and exit
66          {
67              if ( input != null )
68                  input.close();
69          } // end try
70          catch ( IOException ioException )
71          {
72              System.err.println( "Error closing file." );
73              System.exit( 1 );
74          } // end catch
75      } // end method closeFile
76  } // end class ReadSequentialFile
```

Fig. 17.19 | Reading a file of objects sequentially with ObjectInputStream and displaying each record. (Part 2 of 2.)

The program reads records from the file in method readRecords (lines 30–60). Line 40 calls ObjectInputStream method readObject to read an Object from the file. To use AccountRecordSerializable-specific methods, we downcast the returned Object to type AccountRecordSerializable. Method readObject throws an **EOFException** (processed at lines 48–51) if an attempt is made to read beyond the end of the file. Method readObject throws a ClassNotFoundException if the class for the object being read cannot be located. This may occur if the file is accessed on a computer that does not have the class. Figure 17.20 contains method main (lines 6–13), which opens the file, calls method read-Records and closes the file.

```
 1   // Fig. 17.20: ReadSequentialFileTest.java
 2   // Testing class ReadSequentialFile.
 3
 4   public class ReadSequentialFileTest
 5   {
 6      public static void main( String[] args )
 7      {
 8         ReadSequentialFile application = new ReadSequentialFile();
 9
10         application.openFile();
11         application.readRecords();
12         application.closeFile();
13      } // end main
14   } // end class ReadSequentialFileTest
```

```
Account   First Name   Last Name   Balance
100       Bob          Jones         24.98
200       Steve        Doe         -345.67
300       Pam          White         0.00
400       Sam          Stone       -42.16
500       Sue          Rich        224.62
```

Fig. 17.20 | Testing class `ReadSequentialFile`.

17.7 Additional java.io Classes

This section overviews additional interfaces and classes (from package java.io) for byte-based input and output streams and character-based input and output streams.

17.7.1 Interfaces and Classes for Byte-Based Input and Output

InputStream and **OutputStream** are abstract classes that declare methods for performing byte-based input and output, respectively. We used various concrete subclasses FileInputStream InputStream and OutputStream to manipulate files in this chapter.

Pipe Streams
Pipes are synchronized communication channels between threads. We discuss threads in Chapter 26, Multithreading. Java provides **PipedOutputStream** (a subclass of Output-Stream) and **PipedInputStream** (a subclass of InputStream) to establish pipes between two threads in a program. One thread sends data to another by writing to a PipedOutput-Stream. The target thread reads information from the pipe via a PipedInputStream.

Filter Streams
A **FilterInputStream** filters an InputStream, and a FilterOutputStream filters an Out-putStream. **Filtering** means simply that the filter stream provides additional functionality, such as aggregating data bytes into meaningful primitive-type units. FilterInputStream and FilterOutputStream are typically extended, so some of their filtering capabilities are provided by their subclasses.

A **PrintStream** (a subclass of FilterOutputStream) performs text output to the specified stream. Actually, we've been using PrintStream output throughout the text to this point—System.out and System.err are PrintStream objects.

Data Streams

Reading data as raw bytes is fast, but crude. Usually, programs read data as aggregates of bytes that form ints, floats, doubles and so on. Java programs can use several classes to input and output data in aggregate form.

Interface DataInput describes methods for reading primitive types from an input stream. Classes **DataInputStream** and RandomAccessFile each implement this interface to read sets of bytes and view them as primitive-type values. Interface DataInput includes methods such as readBoolean, readByte, readChar, readDouble, readFloat, readFully (for byte arrays), readInt, readLong, readShort, readUnsignedByte, readUnsigned-Short, readUTF (for reading Unicode characters encoded by Java—we discuss UTF encoding in Appendix L) and skipBytes.

Interface DataOutput describes a set of methods for writing primitive types to an output stream. Classes **DataOutputStream** (a subclass of FilterOutputStream) and RandomAccessFile each implement this interface to write primitive-type values as bytes. Interface DataOutput includes overloaded versions of method write (for a byte or for a byte array) and methods writeBoolean, writeByte, writeBytes, writeChar, writeChars (for Unicode Strings), writeDouble, writeFloat, writeInt, writeLong, writeShort and writeUTF (to output text modified for Unicode).

Buffered Streams

Buffering is an I/O-performance-enhancement technique. With a **BufferedOutputStream** (a subclass of class FilterOutputStream), each output statement does not necessarily result in an actual physical transfer of data to the output device (which is a slow operation compared to processor and main memory speeds). Rather, each output operation is directed to a region in memory called a **buffer** that is large enough to hold the data of many output operations. Then, actual transfer to the output device is performed in one large **physical output operation** each time the buffer fills. The output operations directed to the output buffer in memory are often called **logical output operations**. With a BufferedOutputStream, a partially filled buffer can be forced out to the device at any time by invoking the stream object's **flush** method.

Using buffering can greatly increase the performance of an application. Typical I/O operations are extremely slow compared with the speed of accessing data in computer memory. Buffering reduces the number of I/O operations by first combining smaller outputs together in memory. The number of actual physical I/O operations is small compared with the number of I/O requests issued by the program. Thus, the program that is using buffering is more efficient.

Performance Tip 17.1

Buffered I/O can yield significant performance improvements over unbuffered I/O.

With a **BufferedInputStream** (a subclass of class FilterInputStream), many "logical" chunks of data from a file are read as one large **physical input operation** into a memory buffer. As a program requests each new chunk of data, it's taken from the buffer. (This procedure is sometimes referred to as a **logical input operation**.) When the buffer is empty, the next actual physical input operation from the input device is performed to read in the next group of "logical" chunks of data. Thus, the number of actual physical input operations is small compared with the number of read requests issued by the program.

Memory-Based **byte** Array Steams

Java stream I/O includes capabilities for inputting from byte arrays in memory and out-putting to byte arrays in memory. A ByteArrayInputStream (a subclass of InputStream) reads from a byte array in memory. A ByteArrayOutputStream (a subclass of Output-Stream) outputs to a byte array in memory. One use of byte-array I/O is data validation. A program can input an entire line at a time from the input stream into a byte array. Then a validation routine can scrutinize the contents of the byte array and correct the data if necessary. Finally, the program can proceed to input from the byte array, "knowing" that the input data is in the proper format. Outputting to a byte array is a nice way to take advantage of the powerful output-formatting capabilities of Java streams. For example, data can be stored in a byte array, using the same formatting that will be displayed at a later time, and the byte array can then be output to a file to preserve the formatting.

Sequencing Input from Multiple Streams

A SequenceInputStream (a subclass of InputStream) logically concatenates several Input-Streams—the program sees the group as one continuous InputStream. When the program reaches the end of one input stream, that stream closes, and the next stream in the se-quence opens.

17.7.2 Interfaces and Classes for Character-Based Input and Output

In addition to the byte-based streams, Java provides the **Reader** and **Writer** abstract classes, which are Unicode two-byte, character-based streams. Most of the byte-based streams have corresponding character-based concrete Reader or Writer classes.

Character-Based Buffering Readers and Writers

Classes **BufferedReader** (a subclass of abstract class Reader) and **BufferedWriter** (a subclass of abstract class Writer) enable buffering for character-based streams. Remem-ber that character-based streams use Unicode characters—such streams can process data in any language that the Unicode character set represents.

Memory-Based **char** Array Readers and Writers

Classes **CharArrayReader** and **CharArrayWriter** read and write, respectively, a stream of characters to a char array. A **LineNumberReader** (a subclass of BufferedReader) is a buff-ered character stream that keeps track of the number of lines read—newlines, returns and-carriage-return–line-feed combinations increment the line count. Keeping track of line numbers can be useful if the program needs to inform the reader of an error on a specific line.

Character-Based File, Pipe and String Readers and Writers

An InputStream can be converted to a Reader via class **InputStreamReader**. Similarly, an OuputStream can be converted to a Writer via class **OutputStreamWriter**. Class File-Reader (a subclass of InputStreamReader) and class FileWriter (a subclass of Output-StreamWriter) read characters from and write characters to a file, respectively. Class **PipedReader** and class **PipedWriter** implement piped-character streams for transfering data between threads. Class **StringReader** and **StringWriter** read characters from and write characters to Strings, respectively. A PrintWriter writes characters to a stream.

17.8 Opening Files with JFileChooser

Class **JFileChooser** displays a dialog (known as the JFileChooser dialog) that enables the user to easily select files or directories. To demonstrate the JFileChooser dialog, we enhance the example in Section 17.4, as shown in Figs. 17.21–17.22. The example now contains a graphical user interface, but still displays the same data as before. The constructor calls method analyzePath in line 34. This method then calls method getFile in line 68 to retrieve the File object.

```java
1   // Fig. 17.21: FileDemonstration.java
2   // Demonstrating JFileChooser.
3   import java.awt.BorderLayout;
4   import java.awt.event.ActionEvent;
5   import java.awt.event.ActionListener;
6   import java.io.File;
7   import javax.swing.JFileChooser;
8   import javax.swing.JFrame;
9   import javax.swing.JOptionPane;
10  import javax.swing.JScrollPane;
11  import javax.swing.JTextArea;
12  import javax.swing.JTextField;
13
14  public class FileDemonstration extends JFrame
15  {
16     private JTextArea outputArea; // used for output
17     private JScrollPane scrollPane; // used to provide scrolling to output
18
19     // set up GUI
20     public FileDemonstration()
21     {
22        super( "Testing class File" );
23
24        outputArea = new JTextArea();
25
26        // add outputArea to scrollPane
27        scrollPane = new JScrollPane( outputArea );
28
29        add( scrollPane, BorderLayout.CENTER ); // add scrollPane to GUI
30
31        setSize( 400, 400 ); // set GUI size
32        setVisible( true ); // display GUI
33
34        analyzePath(); // create and analyze File object
35     } // end FileDemonstration constructor
36
37     // allow user to specify file or directory name
38     private File getFileOrDirectory()
39     {
40        // display file dialog, so user can choose file or directory to open
41        JFileChooser fileChooser = new JFileChooser();
42        fileChooser.setFileSelectionMode(
43           JFileChooser.FILES_AND_DIRECTORIES );
```

Fig. 17.21 | Demonstrating JFileChooser. (Part 1 of 3.)

```
44
45          int result = fileChooser.showOpenDialog( this );
46
47          // if user clicked Cancel button on dialog, return
48          if ( result == JFileChooser.CANCEL_OPTION )
49             System.exit( 1 );
50
51          File fileName = fileChooser.getSelectedFile(); // get File
52
53          // display error if invalid
54          if ( ( ( fileName == null ) || ( fileName.getName().equals( "" ) ) ) )
55          {
56             JOptionPane.showMessageDialog( this, "Invalid Name",
57                "Invalid Name", JOptionPane.ERROR_MESSAGE );
58             System.exit( 1 );
59          } // end if
60
61          return fileName;
62       } // end method getFile
63
64       // display information about file or directory user specifies
65       public void analyzePath()
66       {
67          // create File object based on user input
68          File name = getFileOrDirectory();
69
70          if ( name.exists() ) // if name exists, output information about it
71          {
72             // display file (or directory) information
73             outputArea.setText( String.format(
74                "%s%s\n%s\n%s\n%s%s\n%s%s\n%s%s\n%s%s\n%s%s",
75                name.getName(), " exists",
76                ( name.isFile() ? "is a file" : "is not a file" ),
77                ( name.isDirectory() ? "is a directory" :
78                   "is not a directory" ),
79                ( name.isAbsolute() ? "is absolute path" :
80                   "is not absolute path" ), "Last modified: ",
81                name.lastModified(), "Length: ", name.length(),
82                "Path: ", name.getPath(), "Absolute path: ",
83                name.getAbsolutePath(), "Parent: ", name.getParent() ) );
84
85             if ( name.isDirectory() ) // output directory listing
86             {
87                String[] directory = name.list();
88                outputArea.append( "\n\nDirectory contents:\n" );
89
90                for ( String directoryName : directory )
91                   outputArea.append( directoryName + "\n" );
92             } // end else
93          } // end outer if
94          else // not file or directory, output error message
95          {
96             JOptionPane.showMessageDialog( this, name +
97                " does not exist.", "ERROR", JOptionPane.ERROR_MESSAGE );
```

Fig. 17.21 | Demonstrating `JFileChooser`. (Part 2 of 3.)

```
98            } // end else
99         } // end method analyzePath
100    } // end class FileDemonstration
```

Fig. 17.21 | Demonstrating JFileChooser. (Part 3 of 3.)

```
1    // Fig. 17.22: FileDemonstrationTest.java
2    // Testing class FileDemonstration.
3    import javax.swing.JFrame;
4
5    public class FileDemonstrationTest
6    {
7       public static void main( String[] args )
8       {
9          FileDemonstration application = new FileDemonstration();
10         application.setDefaultCloseOperation( JFrame.EXIT_ON_CLOSE );
11      } // end main
12   } // end class FileDemonstrationTest
```

Fig. 17.22 | Testing class FileDemonstration.

Method getFile is defined in lines 38–62 of Fig. 17.21. Line 41 creates a JFile-Chooser and assigns its reference to fileChooser. Lines 42–43 call method **setFile-**

SelectionMode to specify what the user can select from the fileChooser. For this program, we use JFileChooser static constant **FILES_AND_DIRECTORIES** to indicate that files and directories can be selected. Other static constants include **FILES_ONLY** (the default) and **DIRECTORIES_ONLY**.

Line 45 calls method **showOpenDialog** to display the JFileChooser dialog titled **Open**. Argument this specifies the JFileChooser dialog's parent window, which determines the position of the dialog on the screen. If null is passed, the dialog is displayed in the center of the screen—otherwise, the dialog is centered over the application window (specified by the argument this). A JFileChooser dialog is a modal dialog that does not allow the user to interact with any other window in the program until the user closes the JFileChooser by clicking the **Open** or **Cancel** button. The user selects the drive, directory or file name, then clicks **Open**. Method showOpenDialog returns an integer specifying which button (**Open** or **Cancel**) the user clicked to close the dialog. Line 48 tests whether the user clicked **Cancel** by comparing the result with static constant **CANCEL_OPTION**. If they are equal, the program terminates. Line 51 retrieves the file the user selected by calling JFileChooser method **getSelectedFile**. The program then displays information about the selected file or directory.

17.9 Wrap-Up

In this chapter, you learned how to use file processing to manipulate persistent data. You learned that data is stored in computers as 0s and 1s, and that combinations of these values are used to form bytes, fields, records and eventually files. We compared character-based and byte-based streams, and introduced several file-processing classes provided by the java.io package. You used class File to retrieve information about a file or directory. You used sequential-access file processing to manipulate records that are stored in order by the record-key field. You learned the differences between text-file processing and object serialization, and used serialization to store and retrieve entire objects. The chapter concluded with an overview of other classes provided by the java.io package, and a small example of using a JFileChooser dialog to allow users to easily select files from a GUI. In the next chapter, you'll learn the concept of recursion—methods that call themselves. Defining methods in this manner can lead to more intuitive programs.

Summary

Section 17.1 Introduction
- Computers use files for long-term retention of large amounts of persistent data, even after the programs that created the data terminate.
- Computers store files on secondary storage devices such as hard disks.

Section 17.2 Data Hierarchy
- The smallest data item in a computer can assume the value 0 or the value 1 and is called a bit. Ultimately, a computer processes all data items as combinations of zeros and ones.
- The computer's character set is the set of all characters used to write programs and represent data.
- Characters in Java are Unicode characters composed of two bytes, each composed of eight bits.
- A field is a group of characters or bytes that conveys meaning.

- Data items processed by computers form a data hierarchy that becomes larger and more complex in structure as we progress from bits to characters to fields, and so on.
- Typically, several fields compose a record (implemented as a class in Java).
- A record is a group of related fields. A file is a group of related records.
- A record key identifies a record as belonging to a particular person or entity and is unique to each record. Record keys facilitate the retrieval of specific records from a file.
- There are many ways to organize records in a file. The most common is called a sequential file, in which records are stored in order by the record-key field.
- A group of related files is often called a database. A collection of programs designed to create and manage databases is called a database management system (DBMS).

Section 17.3 Files and Streams
- Java views each file as a sequential stream of bytes.
- Every operating system provides a mechanism to determine the end of a file, such as an end-of-file marker or a count of the total bytes in the file.
- Byte-based streams represent data in binary format.
- Character-based streams represent data as sequences of characters.
- Files that are created using byte-based streams are binary files. Files created using character-based streams are text files. Text files can be read by text editors, whereas binary files are read by a program that converts the data to a human-readable format.
- Java also can associate streams with different devices. Three stream objects are associated with devices when a Java program begins executing—System.in, System.out and System.err.
- The java.io package includes stream classes, such as FileInputStream (for byte-based input from a file), FileOutputStream (for byte-based output to a file), FileReader (for character-based input from a file) and FileWriter (for character-based output to a file). Files are opened by creating objects of these stream classes.

Section 17.4 Class File
- Class File is used to obtain information about files and directories.
- Character-based input and output can be performed with classes Scanner and Formatter.
- Class Formatter enables formatted data to be output to the screen or to a file in a manner similar to System.out.printf.
- A file or directory's path specifies its location on disk.
- An absolute path contains all the directories, starting with the root directory, that lead to a specific file or directory. Every file or directory on a disk drive has the same root directory in its path.
- A relative path normally starts from the directory in which the application began executing.
- A separator character is used to separate directories and files in the path.

Section 17.5 Sequential-Access Text Files
- Java imposes no structure on a file. You must structure files to meet your application's needs.
- To retrieve data sequentially from a file, programs normally start from the beginning of the file and read all the data consecutively until the desired information is found.
- Data in many sequential files cannot be modified without the risk of destroying other data in the file. Therefore, records in a sequential-access file are not usually updated in place. Instead, the entire file is usually rewritten.

Section 17.6 Object Serialization

- Java provides a mechanism called object serialization that enables entire objects to be written to or read from a stream.

- A serialized object is represented as a sequence of bytes that includes the object's data as well as information about the object's type and the types of data stored in the object.

- After a serialized object has been written into a file, it can be read from the file and deserialized to recreate the object in memory.

- Classes `ObjectInputStream` and `ObjectOutputStream` enable entire objects to be read from or written to a stream (possibly a file).

- Only classes that implement interface `Serializable` can be serialized and deserialized.

- The `ObjectOutput` interface contains method `writeObject`, which takes an `Object` as an argument and writes its information to an `OutputStream`. A class that implements this interface, such as `ObjectOutputStream`, would ensure that the `Object` is `Serializable`.

- The `ObjectInput` interface contains method `readObject`, which reads and returns a reference to an `Object` from an `InputStream`. After an object has been read, its reference can be cast to the object's actual type.

Section 17.7 Additional `java.io` *Classes*

- `InputStream` and `OutputStream` are abstract classes for performing byte-based input and output.

- Classes `FileInputStream` (a subclass of `InputStream`) and `FileOutputStream` (a subclass of `OutputStream`) manipulate files.

- Pipes are synchronized communication channels between threads. One thread sends data to another by writing to a `PipedOutputStream`. The target thread reads information from the pipe via a `PipedInputStream`.

- A filter stream provides additional functionality, such as aggregating data bytes into meaningful primitive-type units. `FilterInputStream` and `FilterOutputStream` are typically extended, so some of their filtering capabilities are provided by their concrete subclasses.

- A `PrintStream` performs text output. `System.out` and `System.err` are `PrintStream` objects.

- Interface `DataInput` describes methods for reading primitive types from an input stream. Classes `DataInputStream` and `RandomAccessFile` each implement this interface.

- Interface `DataOutput` describes methods for writing primitive types to an output stream. Classes `DataOutputStream` and `RandomAccessFile` each implement this interface.

- Buffering is an I/O-performance-enhancement technique. Typical I/O operations are extremely slow compared with the accessing of data in computer memory. Buffering reduces the number of I/O operations by combining smaller outputs together in memory. The number of physical I/O operations is much smaller than the number of I/O requests issued by the program.

- With a `BufferedOutputStream` each output operation is directed to a buffer large enough to hold the data of many output operations. Actual transfer to the output device is performed in one large physical output operation each time the buffer fills. A partially filled buffer can be forced out to the device at any time by invoking the stream object's `flush` method.

- With a `BufferedInputStream`, many "logical" chunks of data from a file are read as one large physical input operation into a memory buffer. As a program requests data, it's taken from the buffer. When the buffer is empty, the next actual physical input operation is performed.

- A `ByteArrayInputStream` reads from a byte array in memory. A `ByteArrayOutputStream` outputs to a byte array in memory.

- A `SequenceInputStream` concatenates several `InputStream`s. When the program reaches the end of an input stream, that stream closes, and the next stream in the sequence opens.

- The Reader and Writer abstract classes are Unicode character-based streams. Most of the byte-based streams have corresponding character-based concrete Reader or Writer classes.
- Classes BufferedReader and BufferedWriter enable buffering for character-based streams.
- Classes CharArrayReader and CharArrayWriter manipulate a char array in memory.
- A LineNumberReader is a buffered character stream that keeps track of the number of lines read.
- Classes FileReader and FileWriter read characters from and write characters to a file.
- Class PipedReader and class PipedWriter implement piped-character streams for transfering data between threads.
- Class StringReader and StringWriter read characters from and write characters to Strings, respectively. A PrintWriter writes characters to a stream.

Section 17.8 Opening Files with *JFileChooser*
- Class JFileChooser is used to display a dialog that enables users of a program to easily select files or directories from a GUI.

Terminology

absolute path 734
ASCII (American Standard Code for Information Interchange 730
batch file 742
binary digit (bit) 730
binary file 732
buffer 763
buffered I/O 763
BufferedInputStream class 763
BufferedOutputStream class 763
BufferedReader class 764
BufferedWriter class 764
byte 730
byte-based stream 732
byte primitive type 730
CANCEL_OPTION constant of JFileChooser 768
character 730
character-based stream 732
character set 730
CharArrayReader class 764
CharArrayWriter class 764
close method of Formatter 743
close method of ObjectOutputStream 759
data hierarchy 730
database 732
database management system (DBMS) 732
DataInputStream class 763
DataOutputStream class 763
decimal digit 730
deserialize an object 753
DIRECTORIES_ONLY constant of JFileChooser 768
end-of-file marker 732
EndOfFileException class 761

exit method of System 742
field 730
file 729
File class 733
FileInputStream class 733
FileNotFoundException class 742
FileOutputStream class 733
FileReader class 733
FILES_AND_DIRECTORIES constant of JFileChooser 768
FILES_ONLY constant of JFileChooser 768
FileWriter class 733
filter a stream 762
FilterInputStream class 762
flush method of BufferedOutputStream 763
format method of Formatter 743
Formatter class 733
FormatterClosedException class 743
getSelectedFile method of JFileChooser 768
IllegalStateException class 747
InputStream class 762
InputStreamReader class 764
IOException class 759
isFile method of File 734
java.io package 733
JFileChooser class 765
letter 730
LineNumberReader class 764
logical input operations 763
logical output operations 763
%n format specifier (line separator) 744
NoSuchElementException class 743
object serialization 753
ObjectInput interface 753

Self-Review Exercises

17.1 Fill in the blanks in each of the following statements:
a) Ultimately, all data items processed by a computer are reduced to combinations of _____ and _____.
b) The smallest data item a computer can process is called a(n) _____.
c) A(n) _____ can sometimes be viewed as a group of related records.
d) Digits, letters and special symbols are referred to as _____.
e) A database is a group of related _____.
f) Object _____ normally enables a program to output error messages to the screen.

17.2 Determine whether each of the following statements is *true* or *false*. If *false*, explain why.
a) You must explicitly create the stream objects System.in, System.out and System.err.
b) When reading data from a file using class Scanner, if you wish to read data in the file multiple times, the file must be closed and reopened to read from the beginning of the file.
c) Method exists of class File returns true if the name specified as the argument to the File constructor is a file or directory in the specified path.
d) Binary files are human readable in a text editor.
e) An absolute path contains all the directories, starting with the root directory, that lead to a specific file or directory.
f) Class Formatter contains method printf, which enables formatted data to be output to the screen or to a file.

17.3 Complete the following tasks, assuming that each applies to the same program:
a) Write a statement that opens file "oldmast.txt" for input—use Scanner variable in-OldMaster.

b) Write a statement that opens file `"trans.txt"` for input—use `Scanner` variable `in-Transaction`.

c) Write a statement that opens file `"newmast.txt"` for output (and creation)—use `for-matter` variable `outNewMaster`.

d) Write the statements needed to read a record from the file `"oldmast.txt"`. Use the data to create an object of class `AccountRecord`—use `Scanner` variable `inOldMaster`. Assume that class `AccountRecord` is the same as the `AccountRecord` class in Fig. 17.5.

e) Write the statements needed to read a record from the file `"trans.txt"`. The record is an object of class `TransactionRecord`—use `Scanner` variable `inTransaction`. Assume that class `TransactionRecord` contains method `setAccount` (which takes an `int`) to set the account number and method `setAmount` (which takes a `double`) to set the amount of the transaction.

f) Write a statement that outputs a record to the file `"newmast.txt"`. The record is an object of type `AccountRecord`—use `Formatter` variable `outNewMaster`.

17.4 Complete the following tasks, assuming that each applies to the same program:

a) Write a statement that opens file `"oldmast.ser"` for input—use `ObjectInputStream` variable `inOldMaster` to wrap a `FileInputStream` object.

b) Write a statement that opens file `"trans.ser"` for input—use `ObjectInputStream` variable `inTransaction` to wrap a `FileInputStream` object.

c) Write a statement that opens file `"newmast.ser"` for output (and creation)—use `ObjectOutputStream` variable `outNewMaster` to wrap a `FileOutputStream`.

d) Write a statement that reads a record from the file `"oldmast.ser"`. The record is an object of class `AccountRecordSerializable`—use `ObjectInputStream` variable `inOld-Master`. Assume class `AccountRecordSerializable` is the same as the `AccountRecord-Serializable` class in Fig. 17.16

e) Write a statement that reads a record from the file `"trans.ser"`. The record is an object of class `TransactionRecord`—use `ObjectInputStream` variable `inTransaction`.

f) Write a statement that outputs a record of type `AccountRecordSerializable` to the file `"newmast.ser"`—use `ObjectOutputStream` variable `outNewMaster`.

17.5 Find the error in each block of code and show how to correct it.

a) Assume that `account`, `company` and `amount` are declared.

```
ObjectOutputStream outputStream;
outputStream.writeInt( account );
outputStream.writeChars( company );
outputStream.writeDouble( amount );
```

b) The following statements should read a record from the file `"payables.txt"`. The Scanner variable `inPayable` should be used to refer to this file.

```
Scanner inPayable = new Scanner( new File( "payables.txt" ) );
PayablesRecord record = ( PayablesRecord ) inPayable.readObject();
```

Answers to Self-Review Exercises

17.1 a) ones, zeros. b) bit. c) file. d) characters. e) files. f) `System.err`.

17.2 a) False. These three streams are created for you when a Java application begins executing.
b) True.
c) True.
d) False. Text files are human readable in a text editor. Binary files might be human readable, but only if the bytes in the file represent ASCII characters
e) True.
f) False. Class `Formatter` contains method `format`, which enables formatted data to be output to the screen or to a file.

17.3 a) `Scanner inOldMaster = new Scanner( new File ( "oldmast.txt" ) );`

b) `Scanner inTransaction = new Scanner( new File( "trans.txt" ) );`

c) `Formatter outNewMaster = new Formatter( "newmast.txt" );`

d) `AccountRecord account = new AccountRecord();`
`account.setAccount( inOldMaster.nextInt() );`
`account.setFirstName( inOldMaster.next() );`
`account.setLastName( inOldMaster.next() );`
`account.setBalance( inOldMaster.nextDouble() );`

e) `TransactionRecord transaction = new Transaction();`
`transaction.setAccount( inTransaction.nextInt() );`
`transaction.setAmount( inTransaction.nextDouble() );`

f) `outNewMaster.format( "%d %s %s %.2f\n",`
`account.getAccount(), account.getFirstName(),`
`account.getLastName(), account.getBalance() );`

17.4 a) `ObjectInputStream inOldMaster = new ObjectInputStream(`
`new FileInputStream( "oldmast.ser" ) );`

b) `ObjectInputStream inTransaction = new ObjectInputStream(`
`new FileInputStream( "trans.ser" ) );`

c) `ObjectOutputStream outNewMaster = new ObjectOutputStream(`
`new FileOutputStream( "newmast.ser" ) );`

d) `accountRecord = ( AccountRecordSerializable ) inOldMaster.readObject();`

e) `transactionRecord = ( TransactionRecord ) inTransaction.readObject();`

f) `outNewMaster.writeObject( newAccountRecord );`

17.5 a) Error: The file was not opened before the attempt to output data to the stream.
Correction: Open a file for output by creating a new `ObjectOutputStream` object that wraps a `FileOutputStream` object.

b) Error: This example uses text files with a `Scanner`; there is no object serialization. As a result, method `readObject` cannot be used to read that data from the file. Each piece of data must be read separately, then used to create a `PayablesRecord` object.
Correction: Use methods of `inPayable` to read each piece of the `PayablesRecord` object.

Exercises

17.6 Fill in the blanks in each of the following statements:

a) Computers store large amounts of data on secondary storage devices as _____.

b) A(n) _____ is composed of several fields.

c) To facilitate the retrieval of specific records from a file, one field in each record is chosen as a(n) _____.

d) Files that are created using byte-based streams are referred to as _____ files, while files created using character-based streams are referred to as _____ files.

e) The standard stream objects are _____, _____ and _____.

17.7 *(File Matching)* Self-Review Exercise 17.3 asked you to write a series of single statements. Actually, these statements form the core of an important type of file-processing program, namely, a file-matching program. In commercial data processing, it's common to have several files in each application system. In an accounts receivable system, for example, there is generally a master file containing detailed information about each customer, such as the customer's name, address, telephone number, outstanding balance, credit limit, discount terms, contract arrangements and possibly a condensed history of recent purchases and cash payments.

As transactions occur (i.e., sales are made and payments arrive in the mail), information about them is entered into a file. At the end of each business period (a month for some companies, a week for others, and a day in some cases), the file of transactions (called `"trans.txt"`) is applied to the master file (called "oldmast.txt") to update each account's purchase and payment record. During an update, the master file is rewritten as the file "newmast.txt", which is then used at the end of the next business period to begin the updating process again.

File-matching programs must deal with certain problems that do not arise in single-file programs. For example, a match does not always occur. If a customer on the master file has not made any purchases or cash payments in the current business period, no record for this customer will appear on the transaction file. Similarly, a customer who did make some purchases or cash payments could have just moved to this community, and if so, the company may not have had a chance to create a master record for this customer.

Write a complete file-matching accounts receivable program. Use the account number on each file as the record key for matching purposes. Assume that each file is a sequential text file with records stored in increasing account-number order.

a) Define class TransactionRecord. Objects of this class contain an account number and amount for the transaction. Provide methods to modify and retrieve these values.

b) Modify class AccountRecord in Fig. 17.5 to include method combine, which takes a TransactionRecord object and combines the balance of the AccountRecord object and the amount value of the TransactionRecord object.

c) Write a program to create data for testing the program. Use the sample account data in Figs. 17.23 and 17.24. Run the program to create the files trans.txt and oldmast.txt, to be used by your file-matching program.

Master file account number	Name	Balance
100	Alan Jones	348.17
300	Mary Smith	27.19
500	Sam Sharp	0.00
700	Suzy Green	-14.22

Fig. 17.23 | Sample data for master file.

Transaction file account number	Transaction amount
100	27.14
300	62.11
400	100.56
900	82.17

Fig. 17.24 | Sample data for transaction file.

d) Create class FileMatch to perform the file-matching functionality. The class should contain methods that read oldmast.txt and trans.txt. When a match occurs (i.e., records with the same account number appear in both the master file and the transaction file), add the dollar amount in the transaction record to the current balance in the master record, and write the "newmast.txt" record. (Assume that purchases are indicated by positive amounts in the transaction file and payments by negative amounts.) When there is a master record for a particular account, but no corresponding transaction record, merely write the master record to "newmast.txt". When there is a transaction record, but no corresponding master record, print to a log file the message "Unmatched transaction record for account number..." (fill in the account number from the transaction record). The log file should be a text file named "log.txt".

17.8 *(File Matching with Multiple Transactions)* It's possible (and actually common) to have several transaction records with the same record key. This situation occurs, for example, when a customer makes several purchases and cash payments during a business period. Rewrite your accounts receivable file-matching program from Exercise 17.7 to provide for the possibility of handling several transaction records with the same record key. Modify the test data of CreateData.java to include the additional transaction records in Fig. 17.25.

Account number	Dollar amount
300	83.89
700	80.78
700	1.53

Fig. 17.25 | Additional transaction records.

17.9 *(File Matching with Object Serialization)* Recreate your solution for Exercise 17.8 using object serialization. Use the statements from Exercise 17.4 as your basis for this program. You may want to create applications to read the data stored in the .ser files—the code in Section 17.6.2 can be modified for this purpose.

17.10 *(Student Poll)* Figure 7.8 contains an array of survey responses that is hard coded into the program. Suppose we wish to process survey results that are stored in a file. This exercise requires two separate programs. First, create an application that prompts the user for survey responses and outputs each response to a file. Use a Formatter to create a file called numbers.txt. Each integer should be written using method format. Then modify the program in Fig. 7.8 to read the survey responses from numbers.txt. The responses should be read from the file by using a Scanner. Use method nextInt to input one integer at a time from the file. The program should continue to read responses until it reaches the end of the file. The results should be output to the text file "output.txt".

17.11 *(Adding Object Serialization to the MyShape Drawing Application)* Modify Exercise 14.11 to allow the user to save a drawing into a file or load a prior drawing from a file using object serialization. Add buttons **Load** (to read objects from a file) and **Save** (to write objects to a file). Use an ObjectOutputStream to write to the file and an ObjectInputStream to read from the file. Write the array of MyShape objects using method writeObject (class ObjectOutputStream), and read the array using method readObject (ObjectInputStream). Note that the object-serialization mechanism can read or write entire arrays—it's not necessary to manipulate each element of the array of MyShape objects individually. It's simply required that all the shapes be Serializable. For both the **Load** and **Save** buttons, use a JFileChooser to allow the user to select the file in which the shapes will be stored or from which they'll be read. When the user first runs the program, no shapes should be displayed on the screen. The user can display shapes by opening a previously saved file or by drawing new shapes. Once there are shapes on the screen, users can save them to a file using the **Save** button.

Making a Difference

17.12 *(Phishing Scanner)* Phishing is a form of identity theft in which, in an e-mail, a sender posing as a trustworthy source attempts to acquire private information, such as your user names, passwords, credit-card numbers and social security number. Phishing e-mails claiming to be from popular banks, credit-card companies, auction sites, social networks and online payment services may look quite legitimate. These fraudulent messages often provide links to spoofed (fake) websites where you're asked to enter sensitive information.

Visit McAfee® (www.mcafee.com/us/threat_center/anti_phishing/phishing_top10.html), Security Extra (www.securityextra.com/), www.snopes.com and other websites to find lists of the top phishing scams. Also check out the Anti-Phishing Working Group (www.antiphishing.org/), and the FBI's Cyber Investigations website (www.fbi.gov/cyberinvest/cyberhome.htm), where you'll find information about the latest scams and how to protect yourself.

Create a list of 30 words, phrases and company names commonly found in phishing messages. Assign a point value to each based on your estimate of its likeliness to be in a phishing message (e.g., one point if it's somewhat likely, two points if moderately likely, or three points if highly likely). Write an application that scans a file of text for these terms and phrases. For each occurrence of a keyword or phrase within the text file, add the assigned point value to the total points for that word or phrase. For each keyword or phrase found, output one line with the word or phrase, the number of occurrences and the point total. Then show the point total for the entire message. Does your program assign a high point total to some actual phishing e-mails you've received? Does it assign a high point total to some legitimate e-mails you've received?

We must learn to explore all the options and
possibilities that confront us in a complex and rapidly
changing world.
—James William Fulbright

O! thou hast damnable iteration, and art indeed able
to corrupt a saint.
—William Shakespeare

It's a poor sort of memory that only works backwards.
—Lewis Carroll

Life can only be understood backwards; but it must be
lived forwards.
—Soren Kierkegaard

Push on—keep moving.
—Thomas Morton

Recursion

Objectives

In this chapter you'll learn:

- The concept of recursion.

- How to write and use recursive methods.

- How to determine the base case and recursion step in a recursive algorithm.

- How recursive method calls are handled by the system.

- The differences between recursion and iteration, and when it's appropriate to use each.

- What the geometric shapes called fractals are and how to draw them using recursion.

- What recursive backtracking is and why it's an effective problem-solving technique.

18.1 Introduction

The programs we've discussed so far are generally structured as methods that call one another in a hierarchical manner. For some problems, it's useful to have a method call itself. A method that does so is known as a **recursive method**. A recursive method can call itself either directly or indirectly through another method. Recursion is an important topic discussed at length in upper-level computer science courses. In this chapter, we consider recursion conceptually, then present several programs containing recursive methods. Figure 18.1 summarizes the recursion examples and exercises in this book.

Chapter	Recursion examples and exercises in this book
18	Factorial Method (Figs. 18.3 and 18.4)
	Fibonacci Method (Fig. 18.5)
	Towers of Hanoi (Fig. 18.11)
	Fractals (Figs. 18.18 and 18.19)
	What Does This Code Do? (Exercise 18.7 and Exercise 18.11)
	Find the Error in the Following Code (Exercise 18.8)
	Raising an Integer to an Integer Power (Exercise 18.9)
	Greatest Common Divisor (Exercise 18.10)
	Determine Whether a String Is a Palindrome (Exercise 18.12)
	Print an Array (Exercise 18.13)
	Print an Array Backward (Exercise 18.14)
	Minimum Value in an Array (Exercise 18.15)
	Star Fractal (Exercise 18.16)
	Maze Traversal Using Recursive Backtracking (Exercise 18.17)
	Generating Mazes Randomly (Exercise 18.18)
	Mazes of Any Size (Exercise 18.19)
19	Merge Sort (Figs. 19.10 and 19.11)
	Linear Search (Exercise 19.8)
	Binary Search (Exercise 19.9)
	Quicksort (Exercise 19.10)
22	Binary-Tree Insert (Fig. 22.17)
	Preorder Traversal of a Binary Tree (Fig. 22.17)

Fig. 18.1 | Summary of the recursion examples and exercises in this text. (Part 1 of 2.)

Chapter	Recursion examples and exercises in this book
22 (cont.)	Inorder Traversal of a Binary Tree (Fig. 22.17) Postorder Traversal of a Binary Tree (Fig. 22.17) Print a Linked List Backward (Exercise 22.19) Search a Linked List (Exercise 22.20)

Fig. 18.1 | Summary of the recursion examples and exercises in this text. (Part 2 of 2.)

18.2 Recursion Concepts

Recursive problem-solving approaches have a number of elements in common. When a recursive method is called to solve a problem, it actually is capable of solving only the simplest case(s), or **base case(s)**. If the method is called with a base case, it returns a result. If the method is called with a more complex problem, it typically divides the problem into two conceptual pieces—a piece that the method knows how to do and a piece that it does not know how to do. To make recursion feasible, the latter piece must resemble the original problem, but be a slightly simpler or smaller version of it. Because this new problem looks like the original problem, the method calls a fresh copy of itself to work on the smaller problem—this is referred to as a **recursive call** and is also called the **recursion step**. The recursion step normally includes a return statement, because its result will be combined with the portion of the problem the method knew how to solve to form a result that will be passed back to the original caller. This concept of separating the problem into two smaller portions is a form of the divide-and-conquer approach introduced in Chapter 6.

The recursion step executes while the original method call is still active (i.e., it has not finished executing). It can result in many more recursive calls as the method divides each new subproblem into two conceptual pieces. For the recursion to eventually terminate, each time the method calls itself with a simpler version of the original problem, the sequence of smaller and smaller problems must converge on a base case. When the method recognizes the base case, it returns a result to the previous copy of the method. A sequence of returns ensues until the original method call returns the final result to the caller.

A recursive method may call another method, which may in turn make a call back to the recursive method. This is known as an **indirect recursive call** or **indirect recursion**. For example, method A calls method B, which makes a call back to method A. This is still recursion, because the second call to method A is made while the first call to method A is active—that is, the first call to method A has not yet finished executing (because it's waiting on method B to return a result to it) and has not returned to method A's original caller.

To better understand the concept of recursion, let's look at an example that's quite familiar to computer users—the recursive definition of a directory on a computer. A computer normally stores related files in a directory. A directory can be empty, can contain files and/or can contain other directories (usually referred to as subdirectories). Each of these subdirectories, in turn, may also contain both files and directories. If we want to list each file in a directory (including all the files in the directory's subdirectories), we need to create a method that first lists the initial directory's files, then makes recursive calls to list the files in each of that directory's subdirectories. The base case occurs when a directory is reached that does not contain any subdirectories. At this point, all the files in the original directory have been listed and no further recursion is necessary.

18.3 Example Using Recursion: Factorials

Let's write a recursive program to perform a popular mathematical calculation. Consider the factorial of a positive integer n, written $n!$ (pronounced "n factorial"), which is the product

$$n \cdot (n-1) \cdot (n-2) \cdot \ldots \cdot 1$$

with 1! equal to 1 and 0! defined to be 1. For example, 5! is the product $5 \cdot 4 \cdot 3 \cdot 2 \cdot 1$, which is equal to 120.

The factorial of integer number (where number ≥ 0) can be calculated iteratively (non-recursively) using a for statement as follows:

```
factorial = 1;
for ( int counter = number; counter >= 1; counter-- )
    factorial *= counter;
```

A recursive declaration of the factorial method is arrived at by observing the following relationship:

$$n! = n \cdot (n-1)!$$

For example, 5! is clearly equal to $5 \cdot 4!$, as shown by the following equations:

$$5! = 5 \cdot 4 \cdot 3 \cdot 2 \cdot 1$$
$$5! = 5 \cdot (4 \cdot 3 \cdot 2 \cdot 1)$$
$$5! = 5 \cdot (4!)$$

The evaluation of 5! would proceed as shown in Fig. 18.2. Figure 18.2(a) shows how the succession of recursive calls proceeds until 1! (the base case) is evaluated to be 1, which terminates the recursion. Figure 18.2(b) shows the values returned from each recursive call to its caller until the final value is calculated and returned.

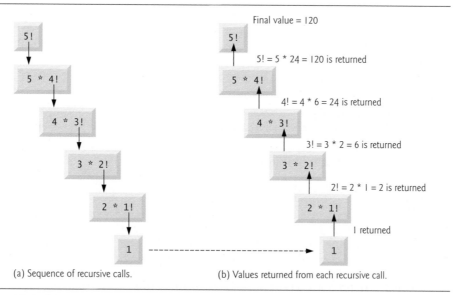

(a) Sequence of recursive calls.　　　　(b) Values returned from each recursive call.

Fig. 18.2 | Recursive evaluation of 5!.

Figure 18.3 uses recursion to calculate and print the factorials of the integers from 0–21. The recursive method `factorial` (lines 7–13) first tests to determine whether a terminating condition (line 9) is true. If `number` is less than or equal to 1 (the base case), `factorial` returns 1, no further recursion is necessary and the method returns. If `number` is greater than 1, line 12 expresses the problem as the product of `number` and a recursive call to `factorial` evaluating the factorial of `number - 1`, which is a slightly smaller problem than the original calculation, `factorial( number )`.

```java
1   // Fig. 18.3: FactorialCalculator.java
2   // Recursive factorial method.
3
4   public class FactorialCalculator
5   {
6      // recursive method factorial (assumes its parameter is >= 0)
7      public long factorial( long number )
8      {
9         if ( number <= 1 ) // test for base case
10           return 1; // base cases: 0! = 1 and 1! = 1
11        else // recursion step
12           return number * factorial( number - 1 );
13     } // end method factorial
14
15     // output factorials for values 0-21
16     public static void main( String[] args )
17     {
18        // calculate the factorials of 0 through 21
19        for ( int counter = 0; counter <= 21; counter++ )
20           System.out.printf( "%d! = %d\n", counter, factorial( counter ) );
21     } // end main
22  } // end class FactorialCalculator
```

```
0! = 1
1! = 1
2! = 2
3! = 6
4! = 24
5! = 120
...
12! = 479001600 ——— 12! causes overflow for int variables
...
20! = 2432902008176640000
21! = -4249290049419214848 ——— 21! causes overflow for long variables
```

Fig. 18.3 | Factorial calculations with a recursive method.

Common Programming Error 18.1

*Either omitting the base case or writing the recursion step incorrectly so that it does not converge on the base case can cause a logic error known as **infinite recursion**, where recursive calls are continuously made until memory is exhausted. This error is analogous to the problem of an infinite loop in an iterative (nonrecursive) solution.*

Method `main` (lines 16–21) displays the factorials of 0–21. The call to the `factorial` method occurs in line 20. Method `factorial` receives a parameter of type `long` and returns a result of type long. The program's output shows that factorial values become large quickly. We use type long (which can represent relatively large integers) so the program can calculate factorials greater than 12!. Unfortunately, the factorial method produces large values so quickly that we exceed the largest long value when we attempt to calculate 21!, as you can see in the last line of the program's output.

Due to the limitations of integral types, float or double variables may ultimately be needed to calculate factorials of larger numbers. This points to a weakness in some programming languages—namely, that they are not easily extended with new types to handle unique application requirements. As we saw in Chapter 9, Java is an extensible language that allows us to create arbitrarily large integers if we wish. In fact, package java.math provides classes **BigInteger** and **BigDecimal** explicitly for arbitrary precision calculations that cannot be performed with primitive types. You can learn more about these classes at java.sun.com/javase/6/docs/api/java/math/BigInteger.html and java.sun.com/javase/6/docs/api/java/math/BigDecimal.html, respectively.

Reimplementing Class FactorialCalculator *Using Class* BigInteger

Figure 18.4 reimplements class FactorialCalculator using BigInteger variables. To demonstrate larger values than what long variables can store, we calculate the factorials of the numbers 0–50. Line 3 imports class BigInteger from package java.math. The new factorial method (lines 8–15) receives a BigInteger as an argument and returns a BigInteger.

Since BigInteger is not a primitive type, we can't use the arithmetic, relational and equality operators with BigIntegers; instead, we must use BigInteger methods to

```
 1   // Fig. 18.4: FactorialCalculator.java
 2   // Recursive factorial method.
 3   import java.math.BigInteger;
 4
 5   public class FactorialCalculator
 6   {
 7      // recursive method factorial (assumes its parameter is >= 0)
 8      public static BigInteger factorial( BigInteger number )
 9      {
10         if ( number.compareTo( BigInteger.ONE ) <= 0 ) // test base case
11            return BigInteger.ONE; // base cases: 0! = 1 and 1! = 1
12         else // recursion step
13            return number.multiply(
14               factorial( number.subtract( BigInteger.ONE ) ) );
15      } // end method factorial
16
17      // output factorials for values 0-50
18      public static void main( String[] args )
19      {
20         // calculate the factorials of 0 through 50
21         for ( int counter = 0; counter <= 50; counter++ )
22            System.out.printf( "%d! = %d\n", counter,
23               factorial( BigInteger.valueOf( counter ) ) );
24      } // end main
25   } // end class FactorialCalculator
```

Fig. 18.4 | Factorial calculations with a recursive method. (Part 1 of 2.)

```
0! = 1
1! = 1
2! = 2
3! = 6
...
21! = 51090942171709440000 ─── 21! and larger values no longer cause overflow
22! = 1124000727777607680000
...
47! = 258623241511168180642964355153611979969197632389120000000000
48! = 1241391559253607267086228904737337503852148635467776000000000
49! = 60828186403426756087225216332129537688755283137921024000000000
50! = 3041409320171337804361260816606476884437764156896051200000000000
```

Fig. 18.4 | Factorial calculations with a recursive method. (Part 2 of 2.)

perform these tasks. Line 10 tests for the base case using `BigInteger` method **compareTo**. This method compares the `BigInteger` that calls the method to the method's `BigInteger` argument. The method returns -1 if the `BigIteger` that calls the method is less than the argument, 0 if they are equal or 1 if the `BigInteger` that calls the method is greater than the argument. Line 10 compares the `BigInteger` number with the `BigInteger` constant **ONE**, which represents the integer value 1. If `compareTo` returns -1 or 0, then number is less than or equal to 1 (the base case) and the method returns the constant `BigInteger.ONE`. Otherwise, lines 13–14 perform the recursion step using `BigInteger` methods **multiply** and **subtract** to implement the calculations required to multiply number by the factorial of number - 1). The program's output shows that `BigInteger` easily handles the large values produced by the factorial calculation.

18.4 Example Using Recursion: Fibonacci Series

The **Fibonacci series**,

> 0, 1, 1, 2, 3, 5, 8, 13, 21, ...

begins with 0 and 1 and has the property that each subsequent Fibonacci number is the sum of the previous two. This series occurs in nature and describes a form of spiral. The ratio of successive Fibonacci numbers converges on a constant value of 1.618..., a number that has been called the **golden ratio** or the **golden mean**. Humans tend to find the golden mean aesthetically pleasing. Architects often design windows, rooms and buildings whose length and width are in the ratio of the golden mean. Postcards are often designed with a golden-mean length-to-width ratio.

The Fibonacci series may be defined recursively as follows:

> fibonacci(0) = 0
> fibonacci(1) = 1
> fibonacci(n) = fibonacci($n - 1$) + fibonacci($n - 2$)

Note that there are *two base cases* for the Fibonacci calculation: `fibonacci(0)` is defined to be 0, and `fibonacci(1)` to be 1. The program in Fig. 18.5 calculates the ith Fibonacci number recursively, using method `fibonacci` (lines 10–18). Method `main` (lines 21–26) tests `fibonacci`, displaying the Fibonacci values of 0–40. The variable `counter` created in the `for` header (line 23) indicates which Fibonacci number to calculate for each iteration of the loop. Fibonacci numbers tend to become large quickly (though not as quickly as factorials). Therefore, we use type `BigInteger` as the parameter type and the return type of method `fibonacci`.

```
1   // Fig. 18.5: FibonacciCalculator.java
2   // Recursive fibonacci method.
3   import java.math.BigInteger;
4
5   public class FibonacciCalculator
6   {
7      private static BigInteger TWO = BigInteger.valueOf( 2 );
8
9      // recursive declaration of method fibonacci
10     public static BigInteger fibonacci( BigInteger number )
11     {
12        if ( number.equals( BigInteger.ZERO ) ||
13           number.equals( BigInteger.ONE ) ) // base cases
14           return number;
15        else // recursion step
16           return fibonacci( number.subtract( BigInteger.ONE ) ).add(
17              fibonacci( number.subtract( TWO ) ) );
18     } // end method fibonacci
19
20     // displays the fibonacci values from 0-40
21     public static void main( String[] args )
22     {
23        for ( int counter = 0; counter <= 40; counter++ )
24           System.out.printf( "Fibonacci of %d is: %d\n", counter,
25              fibonacci( BigInteger.valueOf( counter ) ) );
26     } // end main
27  } // end class FibonacciCalculator
```

```
Fibonacci of 0 is: 0
Fibonacci of 1 is: 1
Fibonacci of 2 is: 1
Fibonacci of 3 is: 2
Fibonacci of 4 is: 3
Fibonacci of 5 is: 5
Fibonacci of 6 is: 8
Fibonacci of 7 is: 13
Fibonacci of 8 is: 21
Fibonacci of 9 is: 34
Fibonacci of 10 is: 55
...
Fibonacci of 37 is: 24157817
Fibonacci of 38 is: 39088169
Fibonacci of 39 is: 63245986
Fibonacci of 40 is: 102334155
```

Fig. 18.5 | Fibonacci numbers generated with a recursive method.

The call to method `fibonacci` (line 25 of Fig. 18.5) from `main` is not a recursive call, but all subsequent calls to `fibonacci` performed from lines 16–17 of Fig. 18.5 are recursive, because at that point the calls are initiated by method `fibonacci` itself. Each time `fibonacci` is called, it immediately tests for the base cases—number equal to 0 or number equal to 1 (Fig. 18.5, lines 12–13). Note that we use `BigInteger` constants **ZERO** and ONE to represent the values 0 and 1, respectively. If the condition in lines 12–13 is true, fibonacci simply returns number, because fibonacci(0) is 0 and fibonacci(1) is 1. Interestingly, if number is greater than 1, the recursion step generates *two* recursive calls (lines 16–17), each for a slightly smaller problem than the original call to fibonacci. Lines 16–17 use BigInteger methods **add** and subtract to help implement the recursive step. We also use a constant of type BigInteger named TWO that we defined at line 7.

Analyzing the Calls to Method **Fibonacci**
Figure 18.6 shows how method fibonacci evaluates fibonacci(3). Note that at the bottom of the figure we are left with the values 1, 0 and 1—the results of evaluating the base cases. The first two return values (from left to right), 1 and 0, are returned as the values for the calls fibonacci(1) and fibonacci(0). The sum 1 plus 0 is returned as the value of fibonacci(2). This is added to the result (1) of the call to fibonacci(1), producing the value 2. This final value is then returned as the value of fibonacci(3).

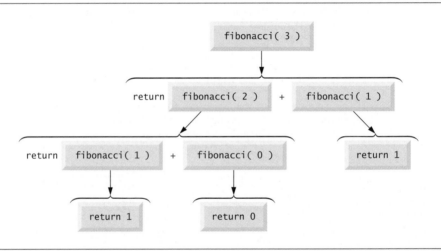

Fig. 18.6 | Set of recursive calls for fibonacci(3).

Figure 18.6 raises some interesting issues about the order in which Java compilers evaluate the operands of operators. This order is different from that in which operators are applied to their operands—namely, the order dictated by the rules of operator precedence. From Figure 18.6, it appears that while fibonacci(3) is being evaluated, two recursive calls will be made—fibonacci(2) and fibonacci(1). But in what order will they be made? The Java language specifies that the order of evaluation of the operands is from left to right. Thus, the call fibonacci(2) is made first and the call fibonacci(1) second.

A word of caution is in order about recursive programs like the one we use here to generate Fibonacci numbers. Each invocation of the fibonacci method that does not match one of the base cases (0 or 1) results in *two more recursive calls* to the fibonacci method. Hence, this set of recursive calls rapidly gets out of hand. Calculating the Fibonacci value of 20 with the program in Fig. 18.5 requires 21,891 calls to the fibonacci method; calculating the Fibonacci value of 30 requires 2,692,537 calls! As you try to calculate larger Fibonacci values, you'll notice that each consecutive Fibonacci number you use the application to calculate results in a substantial increase in calculation time and in the number of calls to the `fibonacci` method. For example, the Fibonacci value of 31 requires 4,356,617 calls, and the Fibonacci value of 32 requires 7,049,155 calls! As you can see, the number of calls to `fibonacci` increases quickly—1,664,080 additional calls between Fibonacci values of 30 and 31 and 2,692,538 additional calls between Fibonacci values of 31 and 32! The difference in the number of calls made between Fibonacci values of 31 and 32 is more than 1.5 times the difference in the number of calls for Fibonacci values between 30 and 31. Problems of this nature can humble even the world's most powerful computers. [*Note:* In the field of complexity theory, computer scientists study how hard algorithms work to complete their tasks. Complexity issues are discussed in detail in the upper-level computer science curriculum course generally called "Algorithms." We introduce various complexity issues in Chapter 19, Searching, Sorting and Big O.] In the exercises, you'll be asked to enhance the Fibonacci program of Fig. 18.5 so that it calculates the approximate amount of time required to perform the calculation. For this purpose, you'll call `static` `System` method `currentTimeMillis`, which takes no arguments and returns the computer's current time in milliseconds.

> **Performance Tip 18.1**
>
> *Avoid Fibonacci-style recursive programs, because they result in an exponential "explosion" of method calls.*

18.5 Recursion and the Method-Call Stack

In Chapter 6, the stack data structure was introduced in the context of understanding how Java performs method calls. We discussed both the method-call stack (also known as the program-execution stack) and activation records. In this section, we'll use these concepts to demonstrate how the program-execution stack handles recursive method calls.

Let's begin by returning to the Fibonacci example—specifically, calling method `fibonacci` with the value 3, as in Fig. 18.6. To show the order in which the method calls' activation records are placed on the stack, we've lettered the method calls in Fig. 18.7.

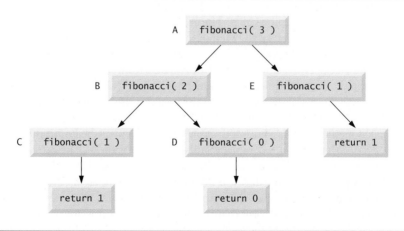

Fig. 18.7 | Method calls made within the call `fibonacci( 3 )`.

When the first method call (A) is made, an activation record containing the value of the local variable number (3, in this case) is pushed onto the program-execution stack. The program-execution stack, including the activation record for method call A, is illustrated in part (a) of Fig. 18.8. [*Note:* We use a simplified stack here. An actual program-execution stack and its activation records would be more complex than in Fig. 18.8, containing such information as where the method call is to return to when it has completed execution.]

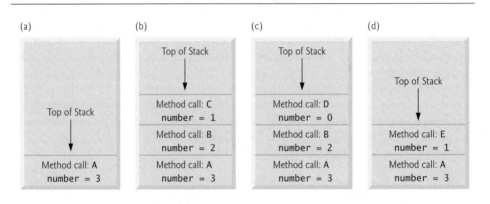

Fig. 18.8 | Method calls on the program-execution stack.

Within method call A, method calls B and E are made. The original method call has not yet completed, so its activation record remains on the stack. The first method call to be made from within A is method call B, so the activation record for method call B is pushed onto the stack on top of the one for method call A. Method call B must execute and complete before method call E is made. Within method call B, method calls C and D will be made. Method call C is made first, and its activation record is pushed onto the stack [part (b) of Fig. 18.8]. Method call B has not yet finished, and its activation record is still on the method-call stack. When method call C executes, it makes no further method calls, but simply returns the value 1. When this method returns, its activation record is popped off the top of the stack. The method call at the top of the stack is now B, which continues to execute by performing method call D. The activation record for method call D is pushed onto the stack [part (c) of Fig. 18.8]. Method call D completes without making any more method calls and returns the value 0. The activation record for this method call is then popped off the stack. Now, both method calls made from within method call B have returned. Method call B continues to execute, returning the value 1. Method call B completes, and its activation record is popped off the stack. At this point, the activation record for method call A is at the top of the stack and the method continues its execution. This method makes method call E, whose activation record is now pushed onto the stack [part (d) of Fig. 18.8]. Method call E completes and returns the value 1. The activation record for this method call is popped off the stack, and once again method call A continues to execute. At this point, method call A will not be making any other method calls and can finish its execution, returning the value 2 to A's caller (fibonacci(3) = 2). A's activation record is popped off the stack. Note that the executing method is always the one whose activation record is at the top of the stack, and the activation record for that method contains the values of its local variables.

18.6 Recursion vs. Iteration

We've studied methods `factorial` and `fibonacci`, which can easily be implemented either recursively or iteratively. In this section, we compare the two approaches and discuss why you might choose one approach over the other in a particular situation.

Both iteration and recursion are based on a control statement: Iteration uses a repetition statement (e.g., `for`, `while` or `do...while`), whereas recursion uses a selection statement (e.g., `if`, `if...else` or `switch`). Both iteration and recursion involve repetition: Iteration explicitly uses a repetition statement, whereas recursion achieves repetition through repeated method calls. Iteration and recursion each involve a termination test: Iteration terminates when the loop-continuation condition fails, whereas recursion terminates when a base case is reached. Iteration with counter-controlled repetition and recursion each gradually approach termination: Iteration keeps modifying a counter until the counter assumes a value that makes the loop-continuation condition fail, whereas recursion keeps producing smaller versions of the original problem until the base case is reached. Both iteration and recursion can occur infinitely: An infinite loop occurs with iteration if the loop-continuation test never becomes false, whereas infinite recursion occurs if the recursion step does not reduce the problem each time in a manner that converges on the base case, or if the base case is not tested.

To illustrate the differences between iteration and recursion, let's examine an iterative solution to the factorial problem (Fig. 18.9). Note that a repetition statement is used (lines 12–13) rather than the selection statement of the recursive solution (lines 9–12 of Fig. 18.3). Note that both solutions use a termination test. In the recursive solution, line 9 tests for the base case. In the iterative solution, line 12 tests the loop-continuation condition—if the test fails, the loop terminates. Finally, note that instead of producing smaller versions of the original problem, the iterative solution uses a counter that is modified until the loop-continuation condition becomes false.

```java
1   // Fig. 18.9: FactorialCalculator.java
2   // Iterative factorial method.
3
4   public class FactorialCalculator
5   {
6      // recursive declaration of method factorial
7      public long factorial( long number )
8      {
9         long result = 1;
10
11         // iterative declaration of method factorial
12         for ( long i = number; i >= 1; i-- )
13            result *= i;
14
15         return result;
16      } // end method factorial
17
18      // output factorials for values 0-10
19      public static void main( String[] args )
20      {
```

Fig. 18.9 | Iterative factorial solution. (Part 1 of 2.)

```
21        // calculate the factorials of 0 through 10
22        for ( int counter = 0; counter <= 10; counter++ )
23            System.out.printf( "%d! = %d\n", counter, factorial( counter ) );
24    } // end main
25 } // end class FactorialCalculator
```

```
 0! = 1
 1! = 1
 2! = 2
 3! = 6
 4! = 24
 5! = 120
 6! = 720
 7! = 5040
 8! = 40320
 9! = 362880
10! = 3628800
```

Fig. 18.9 | Iterative factorial solution. (Part 2 of 2.)

Recursion has many negatives. It repeatedly invokes the mechanism, and consequently the overhead, of method calls. This repetition can be expensive in terms of both processor time and memory space. Each recursive call causes another copy of the method (actually, only the method's variables, stored in the activation record) to be created—this set of copies can consume considerable memory space. Since iteration occurs within a method, repeated method calls and extra memory assignment are avoided. So why choose recursion?

Software Engineering Observation 18.1

Any problem that can be solved recursively can also be solved iteratively (nonrecursively). A recursive approach is normally preferred over an iterative approach when the recursive approach more naturally mirrors the problem and results in a program that is easier to understand and debug. A recursive approach can often be implemented with fewer lines of code. Another reason to choose a recursive approach is that an iterative one might not be apparent.

Performance Tip 18.2

Avoid using recursion in situations requiring high performance. Recursive calls take time and consume additional memory.

Common Programming Error 18.2

Accidentally having a nonrecursive method call itself either directly or indirectly through another method can cause infinite recursion.

18.7 Towers of Hanoi

Earlier in this chapter we studied methods that can be easily implemented both recursively and iteratively. Now, we present a problem whose recursive solution demonstrates the elegance of recursion, and whose iterative solution may not be as apparent.

The **Towers of Hanoi** is one of the classic problems every budding computer scientist must grapple with. Legend has it that in a temple in the Far East, priests are attempting to move a stack of golden disks from one diamond peg to another (Fig. 18.10). The initial stack has 64 disks threaded onto one peg and arranged from bottom to top by decreasing size. The priests are attempting to move the stack from one peg to another under the constraints that exactly one disk is moved at a time and at no time may a larger disk be placed above a smaller disk. Three pegs are provided, one being used for temporarily holding disks. Supposedly, the world will end when the priests complete their task, so there is little incentive for us to facilitate their efforts.

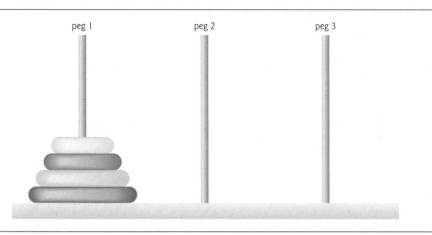

Fig. 18.10 | Towers of Hanoi for the case with four disks.

Let's assume that the priests are attempting to move the disks from peg 1 to peg 3. We wish to develop an algorithm that prints the precise sequence of peg-to-peg disk transfers.

If we try to find an iterative solution, we'll likely find ourselves hopelessly "knotted up" in managing the disks. Instead, attacking this problem recursively quickly yields a solution. Moving n disks can be viewed in terms of moving only $n - 1$ disks (hence the recursion) as follows:

1. Move $n - 1$ disks from peg 1 to peg 2, using peg 3 as a temporary holding area.

2. Move the last disk (the largest) from peg 1 to peg 3.

3. Move $n - 1$ disks from peg 2 to peg 3, using peg 1 as a temporary holding area.

The process ends when the last task involves moving $n = 1$ disk (i.e., the base case). This task is accomplished by moving the disk, without using a temporary holding area.

In Fig. 18.11, method solveTowers (lines 6–25) solves the Towers of Hanoi, given the total number of disks (in this case 3), the starting peg, the ending peg, and the temporary holding peg as parameters. The base case (lines 10–14) occurs when only one disk needs to be moved from the starting peg to the ending peg. In the recursion step (lines 18–24), line 18 moves disks - 1 disks from the first peg (sourcePeg) to the temporary holding peg (tempPeg). When all but one of the disks have been moved to the temporary peg, line 21 moves the largest disk from the start peg to the destination peg. Line 24 finishes the rest of the moves by calling the method solveTowers to recursively move disks - 1 disks from the temporary peg (tempPeg) to the destination peg (destinationPeg), this time using the first peg (sourcePeg) as the temporary peg. Line 35 in main calls the recursive solveTowers method, which outputs the steps to the command prompt.

```
 1   // Fig. 18.11: TowersOfHanoi.java
 2   // Towers of Hanoi solution with a recursive method.
 3   public class TowersOfHanoi
 4   {
 5      // recursively move disks between towers
 6      public static void solveTowers( int disks, int sourcePeg,
 7         int destinationPeg, int tempPeg )
 8      {
 9         // base case -- only one disk to move
10         if ( disks == 1 )
11         {
12            System.out.printf( "\n%d --> %d", sourcePeg, destinationPeg );
13            return;
14         } // end if
15
16         // recursion step -- move (disk - 1) disks from sourcePeg
17         // to tempPeg using destinationPeg
18         solveTowers( disks - 1, sourcePeg, tempPeg, destinationPeg );
19
20         // move last disk from sourcePeg to destinationPeg
21         System.out.printf( "\n%d --> %d", sourcePeg, destinationPeg );
22
23         // move ( disks - 1 ) disks from tempPeg to destinationPeg
24         solveTowers( disks - 1, tempPeg, destinationPeg, sourcePeg );
25      } // end method solveTowers
26
27      public static void main( String[] args )
28      {
29         int startPeg = 1; // value 1 used to indicate startPeg in output
30         int endPeg = 3; // value 3 used to indicate endPeg in output
31         int tempPeg = 2; // value 2 used to indicate tempPeg in output
32         int totalDisks = 3; // number of disks
33
34         // initial nonrecursive call: move all disks.
35         towersOfHanoi.solveTowers( totalDisks, startPeg, endPeg, tempPeg );
36      } // end main
37   } // end class TowersOfHanoi
```

```
1 --> 3
1 --> 2
3 --> 2
1 --> 3
2 --> 1
2 --> 3
1 --> 3
```

Fig. 18.11 | Towers of Hanoi solution with a recursive method.

18.8 Fractals

A **fractal** is a geometric figure that can be generated from a pattern repeated recursively (Fig. 18.12). The figure is modified by applying the pattern to each segment of the original figure. We'll look at a few such approximations in this section. [*Note:* We'll refer to our geometric figures as fractals, even though they're approximations.] Although these figures had been studied before the 20th century, it was the mathematician Benoit Mandelbrot who in the 1970s introduced the term "fractal," along with the specifics of how a fractal is created and the practical applications of fractals. Mandelbrot's fractal geometry provides mathematical models for many complex forms found in nature, such as mountains, clouds and coastlines. Fractals have many uses in mathematics and science. They can be used to better understand systems or patterns that appear in nature (e.g., ecosystems), in the human body (e.g., in the folds of the brain), or in the universe (e.g., galaxy clusters). Not all fractals resemble objects in nature. Drawing fractals has become a popular art form. Fractals have a **self-similar property**—when subdivided into parts, each resembles a reduced-size copy of the whole. Many fractals yield an exact copy of the original when a portion of the fractal is magnified—such a fractal is said to be **strictly self-similar**. See our Recursion Resource Center (www.deitel.com/recursion/) for websites that demonstrate fractals.

As an example, let's look at the strictly self-similar **Koch Curve** fractal (Fig. 18.12). It is formed by removing the middle third of each line in the drawing and replacing it with two lines that form a point, such that if the middle third of the original line remained, an equilateral triangle would be formed. Formulas for creating fractals often involve removing all or part of the previous fractal image. This pattern has already been determined for this fractal—we focus here on how to use those formulas in a recursive solution.

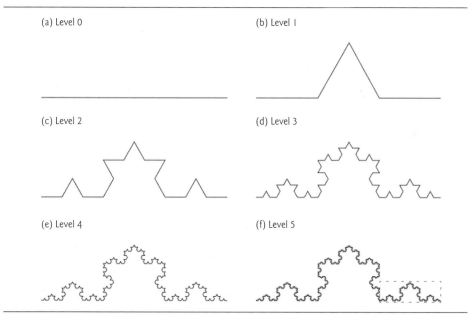

(a) Level 0   (b) Level 1

(c) Level 2   (d) Level 3

(e) Level 4   (f) Level 5

Fig. 18.12 | Koch Curve fractal.

We start with a straight line (Fig. 18.12(a)) and apply the pattern, creating a triangle from the middle third (Fig. 18.12(b)). We then apply the pattern again to each straight line, resulting in Fig. 18.12(c). Each time the pattern is applied, we say that the fractal is at a new **level**, or **depth** (sometimes the term **order** is also used). Fractals can be displayed at many levels—for instance, a fractal at level 3 has had three iterations of the pattern applied (Fig. 18.12(d)). After only a few iterations, this fractal begins to look like a portion of a snowflake (Fig. 18.12(e and f)). Since this is a strictly self-similar fractal, each portion of it contains an exact copy of the fractal. In Fig. 18.12(f), for example, we've highlighted a portion of the fractal with a dashed red box. If the image in this box were increased in size, it would look exactly like the entire fractal of part (f).

A similar fractal, the **Koch Snowflake**, is the same as the Koch Curve but begins with a triangle rather than a line. The same pattern is applied to each side of the triangle, resulting in an image that looks like an enclosed snowflake. For simplicity, we've chosen to focus on the Koch Curve. To learn more about the Koch Curve and Koch Snowflake, see the links in our Recursion Resource Center (www.deitel.com/recursion/).

The "Lo Fractal"

We now demonstrate the use of recursion to draw fractals by writing a program to create a strictly self-similar fractal. We call this the "Lo fractal," named for Sin Han Lo, a Deitel & Associates colleague who created it. The fractal will eventually resemble one-half of a feather (see the outputs in Fig. 18.19). The base case, or fractal level of 0, begins as a line between two points, A and B (Fig. 18.13). To create the next higher level, we find the midpoint (C) of the line. To calculate the location of point C, use the following formula:

```
xC = (xA + xB) / 2;
yC = (yA + yB) / 2;
```

[*Note:* The x and y to the left of each letter refer to the *x*-coordinate and *y*-coordinate of that point, respectively. For instance, xA refers to the *x*-coordinate of point A, while yC refers to the *y*-coordinate of point C. In our diagrams we denote the point by its letter, followed by two numbers representing the *x*- and *y*-coordinates.]

To create this fractal, we also must find a point D that lies left of segment AC and creates an isosceles right triangle ADC. To calculate point D's location, use the following formulas:

```
xD = xA + (xC - xA) / 2 - (yC - yA) / 2;
yD = yA + (yC - yA) / 2 + (xC - xA) / 2;
```

Fig. 18.13 | "Lo fractal" at level 0.

We now move from level 0 to level 1 as follows: First, add points C and D (as in Fig. 18.14). Then, remove the original line and add segments DA, DC and DB. The remaining lines will curve at an angle, causing our fractal to look like a feather. For the next level of the fractal, this algorithm is repeated on each of the three lines in level 1. For each line, the formulas above are applied, where the former point D is now considered to be point A, while the other end of each line is considered to be point B. Figure 18.15 contains the line from level 0 (now a dashed line) and the three added lines from level 1. We've changed point D to be point A, and the original points A, C and B to B1, B2 and B3, respectively. The preceding formulas have been used to find the new points C and D on each line. These points are also numbered 1–3 to keep track of which point is associated with each line. The points C1 and D1, for instance, represent points C and D associated with the line formed from points A to B1. To achieve level 2, the three lines in Fig. 18.15 are removed and replaced with new lines from the C and D points just added. Figure 18.16 shows the new lines (the lines from level 2 are shown as dashed lines for your convenience). Figure 18.17 shows level 2 without the dashed lines from level 1. Once this process has been repeated several times, the fractal created will begin to look like one-half of a feather, as shown in the output of Fig. 18.19. We'll present the code for this application shortly.

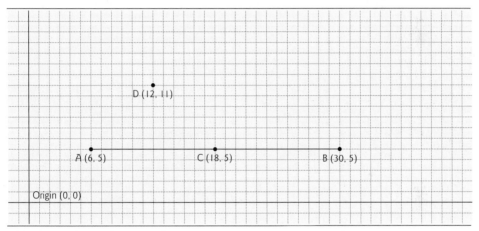

Fig. 18.14 | Determining points C and D for level 1 of the "Lo fractal."

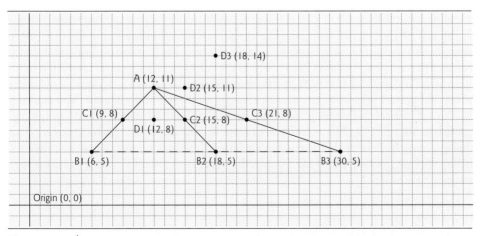

Fig. 18.15 | "Lo fractal" at level 1, with C and D points determined for level 2. [*Note:* The fractal at level 0 is included as a dashed line as a reminder of where the line was located in relation to the current fractal.]

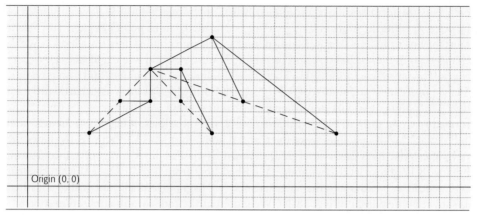

Fig. 18.16 | "Lo fractal" at level 2, with dashed lines from level 1 provided.

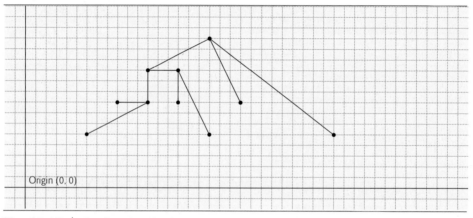

Fig. 18.17 | "Lo fractal" at level 2.

The application in Fig. 18.18 defines the user interface for drawing this fractal (shown at the end of Fig. 18.19). The interface consists of three buttons—one for the user to change the color of the fractal, one to increase the level of recursion and one to decrease the level of recursion. A JLabel keeps track of the current level of recursion, which is modified by calling method setLevel, to be discussed shortly. Lines 15–16 specify constants WIDTH and HEIGHT to be 400 and 480, respectively, for the size of the JFrame. The user triggers an ActionEvent by clicking the **Color** button. The event handler for this button is registered in lines 37–53. The method actionPerformed displays a JColorChooser. This dialog returns the selected Color object or blue (if the user presses **Cancel** or closes the dialog without pressing **OK**). Line 50 calls the setColor method in class FractalJPanel to update the color.

```
1   // Fig. 18.18: Fractal.java
2   // Fractal user interface.
3   import java.awt.Color;
```

Fig. 18.18 | Fractal user interface. (Part 1 of 4.)

```
4   import java.awt.FlowLayout;
5   import java.awt.event.ActionEvent;
6   import java.awt.event.ActionListener;
7   import javax.swing.JFrame;
8   import javax.swing.JButton;
9   import javax.swing.JLabel;
10  import javax.swing.JPanel;
11  import javax.swing.JColorChooser;
12
13  public class Fractal extends JFrame
14  {
15     private static final int WIDTH = 400;  // define width of GUI
16     private static final int HEIGHT = 480; // define height of GUI
17     private static final int MIN_LEVEL = 0, MAX_LEVEL = 15;
18
19     private JButton changeColorJButton, increaseLevelJButton,
20        decreaseLevelJButton;
21     private JLabel levelJLabel;
22     private FractalJPanel drawSpace;
23     private JPanel mainJPanel, controlJPanel;
24
25     // set up GUI
26     public Fractal()
27     {
28        super( "Fractal" );
29
30        // set up control panel
31        controlJPanel = new JPanel();
32        controlJPanel.setLayout( new FlowLayout() );
33
34        // set up color button and register listener
35        changeColorJButton = new JButton( "Color" );
36        controlJPanel.add( changeColorJButton );
37        changeColorJButton.addActionListener(
38           new ActionListener() // anonymous inner class
39           {
40              // process changeColorJButton event
41              public void actionPerformed( ActionEvent event )
42              {
43                 Color color = JColorChooser.showDialog(
44                    Fractal.this, "Choose a color", Color.BLUE );
45
46                 // set default color, if no color is returned
47                 if ( color == null )
48                    color = Color.BLUE;
49
50                 drawSpace.setColor( color );
51              } // end method actionPerformed
52           }  // end anonymous inner class
53        ); // end addActionListener
54
55        // set up decrease level button to add to control panel and
56        // register listener
57        decreaseLevelJButton = new JButton( "Decrease Level" );
```

Fig. 18.18 | Fractal user interface. (Part 2 of 4.)

```
58        controlJPanel.add( decreaseLevelJButton );
59        decreaseLevelJButton.addActionListener(
60           new ActionListener() // anonymous inner class
61           {
62              // process decreaseLevelJButton event
63              public void actionPerformed( ActionEvent event )
64              {
65                 int level = drawSpace.getLevel();
66                 --level; // decrease level by one
67
68                 // modify level if possible
69                 if ( ( level >= MIN_LEVEL ) ) &&
70                    ( level <= MAX_LEVEL ) )
71                 {
72                    levelJLabel.setText( "Level: " + level );
73                    drawSpace.setLevel( level );
74                    repaint();
75                 } // end if
76              } // end method actionPerformed
77           } // end anonymous inner class
78        ); // end addActionListener
79
80        // set up increase level button to add to control panel
81        // and register listener
82        increaseLevelJButton = new JButton( "Increase Level" );
83        controlJPanel.add( increaseLevelJButton );
84        increaseLevelJButton.addActionListener(
85           new ActionListener() // anonymous inner class
86           {
87              // process increaseLevelJButton event
88              public void actionPerformed( ActionEvent event )
89              {
90                 int level = drawSpace.getLevel();
91                 ++level; // increase level by one
92
93                 // modify level if possible
94                 if ( ( level >= MIN_LEVEL ) ) &&
95                    ( level <= MAX_LEVEL ) )
96                 {
97                    levelJLabel.setText( "Level: " + level );
98                    drawSpace.setLevel( level );
99                    repaint();
100                } // end if
101             } // end method actionPerformed
102          } // end anonymous inner class
103       ); // end addActionListener
104
105       // set up levelJLabel to add to controlJPanel
106       levelJLabel = new JLabel( "Level: 0" );
107       controlJPanel.add( levelJLabel );
108
109       drawSpace = new FractalJPanel( 0 );
110
```

Fig. 18.18 | Fractal user interface. (Part 3 of 4.)

```
111        // create mainJPanel to contain controlJPanel and drawSpace
112        mainJPanel = new JPanel();
113        mainJPanel.add( controlJPanel );
114        mainJPanel.add( drawSpace );
115
116        add( mainJPanel ); // add JPanel to JFrame
117
118        setSize( WIDTH, HEIGHT ); // set size of JFrame
119        setVisible( true ); // display JFrame
120     } // end Fractal constructor
121
122     public static void main( String[] args )
123     {
124        Fractal demo = new Fractal();
125        demo.setDefaultCloseOperation( JFrame.EXIT_ON_CLOSE );
126     } // end main
127  } // end class Fractal
```

Fig. 18.18 | Fractal user interface. (Part 4 of 4.)

The **Decrease Level** button's event handler is registered in lines 59–78. Method actionPerformed retrieves the current level of recursion and decrements it by 1 (lines 65–66). Lines 69–70 ensure that the level is greater than or equal to MIN_LEVEL and less than or equal to MAX_LEVEL—the fractal is not defined for recursion levels less than MIN_LEVEL and you can't see the additional detail above MAX_LEVEL. You can go up to any desired level, but around level 10 and higher, the fractal rendering becomes slow due to the details to be drawn. Lines 72–74 reset the level label to reflect the change—the new level is set and the repaint method is called to update the image to show the fractal at the new level.

The **Increase Level** JButton works like the **Decrease Level** JButton, but the level is incremented rather than decremented to show more details of the fractal (lines 90–91). When the application is first executed, the level will be set to 0, which will display a blue line between two points that were specified in the FractalJPanel class.

Class FractalJPanel (Fig. 18.19) specifies the drawing JPanel's dimensions as 400 by 400 (lines 13–14). The FractalJPanel constructor (lines 18–24) takes the current level as a parameter and assigns it to its instance variable level. Instance variable color is set to blue by default. Lines 22–23 change the JPanel's background color to white (so the fractal is easy to see), and set the drawing FractalJPanel's dimensions.

```
1   // Fig. 18.19: FractalJPanel.java
2   // Drawing the "Lo fractal" using recursion.
3   import java.awt.Graphics;
4   import java.awt.Color;
5   import java.awt.Dimension;
6   import javax.swing.JPanel;
7
8   public class FractalJPanel extends JPanel
9   {
10     private Color color; // stores color used to draw fractal
11     private int level;   // stores current level of fractal
```

Fig. 18.19 | Drawing the "Lo fractal" using recursion. (Part 1 of 4.)

```
12
13      private static final int WIDTH = 400;  // defines width of JPanel
14      private static final int HEIGHT = 400; // defines height of JPanel
15
16      // set the initial fractal level to the value specified
17      // and set up JPanel specifications
18      public FractalJPanel( int currentLevel )
19      {
20         color = Color.BLUE;  // initialize drawing color to blue
21         level = currentLevel; // set initial fractal level
22         setBackground( Color.WHITE );
23         setPreferredSize( new Dimension( WIDTH, HEIGHT ) );
24      } // end FractalJPanel constructor
25
26      // draw fractal recursively
27      public void drawFractal( int level, int xA, int yA, int xB,
28         int yB, Graphics g )
29      {
30         // base case: draw a line connecting two given points
31         if ( level == 0 )
32            g.drawLine( xA, yA, xB, yB );
33         else // recursion step: determine new points, draw next level
34         {
35            // calculate midpoint between (xA, yA) and (xB, yB)
36            int xC = ( xA + xB ) / 2;
37            int yC = ( yA + yB ) / 2;
38
39            // calculate the fourth point (xD, yD) which forms an
40            // isosceles right triangle between (xA, yA) and (xC, yC)
41            // where the right angle is at (xD, yD)
42            int xD = xA + ( xC - xA ) / 2 - ( yC - yA ) / 2;
43            int yD = yA + ( yC - yA ) / 2 + ( xC - xA ) / 2;
44
45            // recursively draw the Fractal
46            drawFractal( level - 1, xD, yD, xA, yA, g );
47            drawFractal( level - 1, xD, yD, xC, yC, g );
48            drawFractal( level - 1, xD, yD, xB, yB, g );
49         } // end else
50      } // end method drawFractal
51
52      // start drawing the fractal
53      public void paintComponent( Graphics g )
54      {
55         super.paintComponent( g );
56
57         // draw fractal pattern
58         g.setColor( color );
59         drawFractal( level, 100, 90, 290, 200, g );
60      } // end method paintComponent
61
62      // set the drawing color to c
63      public void setColor( Color c )
64      {
```

Fig. 18.19 | Drawing the "Lo fractal" using recursion. (Part 2 of 4.)

```
65          color = c;
66      } // end method setColor
67
68      // set the new level of recursion
69      public void setLevel( int currentLevel )
70      {
71          level = currentLevel;
72      } // end method setLevel
73
74      // returns level of recursion
75      public int getLevel()
76      {
77          return level;
78      } // end method getLevel
79  } // end class FractalJPanel
```

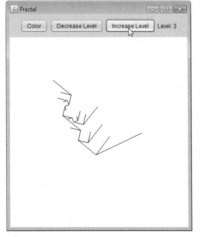

Fig. 18.19 | Drawing the "Lo fractal" using recursion. (Part 3 of 4.)

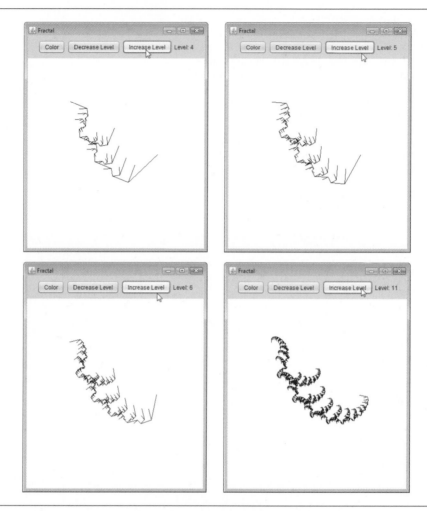

Fig. 18.19 | Drawing the "Lo fractal" using recursion. (Part 4 of 4.)

Lines 27–50 define the recursive method that creates the fractal. This method takes six parameters: the level, four integers that specify the x- and y-coordinates of two points, and the Graphics object g. The base case for this method (line 31) occurs when level equals 0, at which time a line will be drawn between the two points given as parameters. Lines 36–43 calculate (xC, yC), the midpoint between (xA, yA) and (xB, yB), and (xD, yD), the point that creates a right isosceles triangle with (xA, yA) and (xC, yC). Lines 46–48 make three recursive calls on three different sets of points.

In method paintComponent, line 59 makes the first call to method drawFractal to start the drawing. This method call is not recursive, but all subsequent calls to draw-Fractal performed from the body of drawFractal are. Since the lines will not be drawn until the base case is reached, the distance between two points decreases on each recursive call. As the level of recursion increases, the fractal becomes smoother and more detailed. The shape of this fractal stabilizes as the level approaches 11. Fractals will stabilize at different levels based on the shape and size of the fractal.

Figure 18.19 shows the development of the fractal from levels 0 to 6. The last image shows the defining shape of the fractal at level 11. If we focus on one of the arms of this fractal, it will be identical to the whole image. This property defines the fractal to be strictly self-similar. See our Recursion Resource Center at `www.deitel.com/recursion/` for further resources on fractals.

18.9 Recursive Backtracking

Our recursive methods all have a similar architecture—if the base case is reached, return a result; if not, make one or more recursive calls. This section explores a more complex recursive technique that finds a path through a maze, returning true if there is a possible solution to the maze. The solution involves moving through the maze one step at a time, where moves can be made by going down, right, up or left (diagonal moves are not permitted). From the current location in the maze (starting with the entry point), the following steps are taken: For each possible direction, the move is made in that direction and a recursive call is made to solve the remainder of the maze from the new location. When a dead end is reached (i.e., we cannot take any more steps forward without hitting a wall), we back up to the previous location and try to go in a different direction. If no other direction can be taken, we back up again. This process continues until we find a point in the maze where a move *can* be made in another direction. Once such a location is found, we move in the new direction and continue with another recursive call to solve the rest of the maze.

To back up to the previous location in the maze, our recursive method simply returns false, moving up the method-call chain to the previous recursive call (which references the previous location in the maze). Using recursion to return to an earlier decision point is known as **recursive backtracking**. If one set of recursive calls does not result in a solution to the problem, the program backs up to the previous decision point and makes a different decision, often resulting in another set of recursive calls. In this example, the previous decision point is the previous location in the maze, and the decision to be made is the direction that the next move should take. One direction has led to a dead end, so the search continues with a different direction. The recursive backtracking solution to the maze problem uses recursion to return only partway up the method-call chain, then try a different direction. If the backtracking reaches the entry location of the maze and the paths in all directions have been attempted, the maze does not have a solution.

The exercises ask you to implement recursive backtracking solutions to the maze problem (Exercises 18.17–18.19) and the Eight Queens problem (Exercise 18.15), which attempts to find a way to place eight queens on an empty chessboard so that no queen is "attacking" any other (i.e., no two queens are in the same row, in the same column or along the same diagonal). See our Recursion Resource Center at `www.deitel.com/recursion/` for more information on recursive backtracking.

18.10 Wrap-Up

In this chapter, you learned how to create recursive methods—i.e., methods that call themselves. You learned that recursive methods typically divide a problem into two conceptual pieces—a piece that the method knows how to do (the base case) and a piece that the method does not know how to do (the recursion step). The recursion step is a slightly smaller version of the original problem and is performed by a recursive method call. You saw some popular recursion examples, including calculating factorials and producing values in the Fibonacci series. You then learned how recursion works "under the hood," including the order in which recursive method calls are pushed on or popped off the program-execution stack. Next, you compared recursive and iterative (non-recursive) approaches. You learned how to solve more complex problems using recursion—the Towers of Hanoi and displaying fractals. The chapter concluded with an introduction to recursive backtracking, a technique for solving problems that involves backing up through recursive calls to try different possible solutions. In the next chapter, you'll learn numerous techniques for sorting lists of data and searching for an item in a list of data, and you'll explore the circumstances under which each searching and sorting technique should be used.

Summary

Section 18.1 Introduction
- A recursive method calls itself directly or indirectly through another method.

Section 18.2 Recursion Concepts
- When a recursive method is called to solve a problem, the method actually is capable of solving only the simplest case(s), or base case(s). If it's called with a base case, the method returns a result.
- If a recursive method is called with a more complex problem than a base case, it typically divides the problem into two conceptual pieces—a piece that the method knows how to do and a piece that it does not know how to do.
- To make recursion feasible, the piece that the method does not know how to do must resemble the original problem, but be a slightly simpler or smaller version of it. Because this new problem looks like the original problem, the method calls a fresh copy of itself to work on the smaller problem—this is called the recursion step.
- For recursion to eventually terminate, each time a method calls itself with a simpler version of the original problem, the sequence of smaller and smaller problems must converge on a base case. When, the method recognizes the base case, it returns a result to the previous copy of the method.
- A recursive call may be a call to another method, which in turn makes a call back to the original method. Such a process still results in a recursive call to the original method. This is known as an indirect recursive call or indirect recursion.

Section 18.3 Example Using Recursion: Factorials
- Either omitting the base case or writing the recursion step incorrectly so that it does not converge on the base case can cause infinite recursion, eventually exhausting memory. This error is analogous to the problem of an infinite loop in an iterative (nonrecursive) solution.

Section 18.4 Example Using Recursion: Fibonacci Series
- The Fibonacci series begins with 0 and 1 and has the property that each subsequent Fibonacci number is the sum of the preceding two.
- The ratio of successive Fibonacci numbers converges on a constant value of 1.618..., a number that has been called the golden ratio or the golden mean.
- Some recursive solutions, such as Fibonacci, result in an "explosion" of method calls.

Section 18.5 Recursion and the Method-Call Stack
- The executing method is always the one whose activation record is at the top of the stack, and the activation record for that method contains the values of its local variables.

Section 18.6 Recursion vs. Iteration

- Both iteration and recursion are based on a control statement: Iteration uses a repetition statement, recursion a selection statement.

- Both iteration and recursion involve repetition: Iteration explicitly uses a repetition statement, whereas recursion achieves repetition through repeated method calls.

- Iteration and recursion each involve a termination test: Iteration terminates when the loop-continuation condition fails, recursion when a base case is recognized.

- Iteration with counter-controlled repetition and recursion each gradually approach termination: Iteration keeps modifying a counter until the counter assumes a value that makes the loop-continuation condition fail, whereas recursion keeps producing simpler versions of the original problem until the base case is reached.

- Both iteration and recursion can occur infinitely: An infinite loop occurs with iteration if the loop-continuation test never becomes false, whereas infinite recursion occurs if the recursion step does not reduce the problem each time in a manner that converges on the base case.

- Recursion repeatedly invokes the mechanism, and consequently the overhead, of method calls.

- Any problem that can be solved recursively can also be solved iteratively.

- A recursive approach is normally preferred over an iterative approach when it more naturally mirrors the problem and results in a program that is easier to understand and debug.

- A recursive approach can often be implemented with few lines of code, but a corresponding iterative approach might take a large amount of code. Another reason to choose a recursive solution is that an iterative solution might not be apparent.

Section 18.8 Fractals

- A fractal is a geometric figure that is generated from a pattern repeated recursively an infinite number of times.

- Fractals have a self-similar property—subparts are reduced-size copies of the whole.

Section 18.9 Recursive Backtracking

- Using recursion to return to an earlier decision point is known as recursive backtracking. If one set of recursive calls does not result in a solution to the problem, the program backs up to the previous decision point and makes a different decision, often resulting in another set of recursive calls.

Terminology

add method of class `BigInteger` 786
base case 780
`BigDecimal` class 783
`BigInteger` class 783
compareTo method of class `BigInteger` 784
depth of a fractal 793
Fibonacci series 784
fractal 792
golden mean 784
golden ratio 784
indirect recursion 780
indirect recursive call 780
infinite recursion 782
Koch Curve fractal 793

Koch Snowflake fractal 794
level of a fractal 793
multiply method of class `BigInteger` 784
ONE constant of class `BigInteger` 784
order of a fractal 793
recursion step 780
recursive backtracking 803
recursive call 780
recursive method 779
self-similar property of a fractal 793
strictly self-similar fractal 793
subtract method of class `BigInteger` 784
Towers of Hanoi 790
ZERO constant of class `BigInteger` 785

Self-Review Exercises

18.1   State whether each of the following is *true* or *false*. If *false*, explain why.
   a) A method that calls itself indirectly is not an example of recursion.
   b) Recursion can be efficient in computation because of reduced memory-space usage.
   c) When a recursive method is called to solve a problem, it actually is capable of solving only the simplest case(s), or base case(s).
   d) To make recursion feasible, the recursion step in a recursive solution must resemble the original problem, but be a slightly larger version of it.

18.2   A _____ is needed to terminate recursion.
   a) recursion step
   b) break statement
   c) void return type
   d) base case

18.3   The first call to invoke a recursive method is _____.
   a) not recursive
   b) recursive
   c) the recursion step
   d) none of the above

18.4   Each time a fractal's pattern is applied, the fractal is said to be at a new _____.
   a) width
   b) height
   c) level
   d) volume

18.5   Iteration and recursion each involve a _____.
   a) repetition statement
   b) termination test
   c) counter variable
   d) none of the above

18.6   Fill in the blanks in each of the following statements:
   a) The ratio of successive Fibonacci numbers converges on a constant value of 1.618..., a number that has been called the _____ or the _____.
   b) Iteration normally uses a repetition statement, whereas recursion normally uses a(n) _____ statement.
   c) Fractals have a(n) _____ property—when subdivided into parts, each is a reduced-size copy of the whole.

Answers to Self-Review Exercises

18.1   a) False. A method that calls itself in this manner is an example of indirect recursion. b) False. Recursion can be inefficient in computation because of multiple method calls and memory-space usage. c) True. d) False. To make recursion feasible, the recursion step in a recursive solution must resemble the original problem, but be a slightly *smaller* version of it.

18.2   d

18.3   a

18.4   c

18.5   b

18.6   a) golden ratio, golden mean. b) selection. c) self-similar.

Exercises

18.7   What does the following code do?

```
1   public int mystery( int a, int b )
2   {
3      if ( b == 1 )
4         return a;
5      else
6         return a + mystery( a, b - 1 );
7   } // end method mystery
```

18.8   Find the error(s) in the following recursive method, and explain how to correct it (them). This method should find the sum of the values from 0 to n.

```
1   public int sum( int n )
2   {
3      if ( n == 0 )
4         return 0;
5      else
6         return n + sum( n );
7   } // end method sum
```

18.9   *(Recursive power Method)* Write a recursive method power(base, exponent) that, when called, returns

   $base^{\ exponent}$

For example, power(3,4) = 3 * 3 * 3 * 3. Assume that exponent is an integer greater than or equal to 1. [*Hint:* The recursion step should use the relationship

   $base^{\ exponent} = base \cdot base^{\ exponent - 1}$

and the terminating condition occurs when exponent is equal to 1, because

   $base^1 = base$

Incorporate this method into a program that enables the user to enter the base and exponent.]

18.10   *(Greatest Common Divisor)* The greatest common divisor of integers x and y is the largest integer that evenly divides into both x and y. Write a recursive method gcd that returns the greatest common divisor of x and y. The gcd of x and y is defined recursively as follows: If y is equal to 0, then gcd(x, y) is x; otherwise, gcd(x, y) is gcd(y, x % y), where % is the remainder operator. Use this method to replace the one you wrote in the application of Exercise 6.24.

18.11   What does the following program do?

```
1    // Exercise 18.12 Solution: MysteryClass.java
2    public class MysteryClass
3    {
4       public static int mystery( int[] array2, int size )
5       {
6          if ( size == 1 )
7             return array2[ 0 ];
8          else
9             return array2[ size - 1 ] + mystery( array2, size - 1 );
10      } // end method mystery
11
12      public static void main( String[] args )
```

```
13      {
14          int[] array = { 1, 2, 3, 4, 5, 6, 7, 8, 9, 10 };
15
16          int result = mystery( array, array.length );
17          System.out.printf( "Result is: %d\n", result );
18      } // end method main
19   } // end class MysteryClass
```

18.12 *(Palindromes)* A palindrome is a string that is spelled the same way forward and backward. Some examples of palindromes are "radar," "able was i ere i saw elba" and (if spaces are ignored) "a man a plan a canal panama." Write a recursive method `testPalindrome` that returns boolean value `true` if the string stored in the array is a palindrome and `false` otherwise. The method should ignore spaces and punctuation in the string.

18.13 *(Print an Array)* Write a recursive method `printArray` that displays all the elements in an array of integers, separated by spaces.

18.14 *(Print an Array Backward)* Write a recursive method `stringReverse` that takes a character array containing a string as an argument and prints the string backward. [*Hint:* Use `String` method `toCharArray`, which takes no arguments, to get a `char` array containing the characters in the `String`.]

18.15 *(Find the Minimum Value in an Array)* Write a recursive method `recursiveMinimum` that determines the smallest element in an array of integers. The method should return when it receives an array of one element.

18.16 *(Fractals)* Repeat the fractal pattern in Section 18.8 to form a star. Begin with five lines (see Fig. 18.20, instead of one, where each line is a different arm of the star. Apply the "Lo fractal" pattern to each arm of the star.

Fig. 18.20 | Sample outputs for Exercise 18.16.

18.17 *(Maze Traversal Using Recursive Backtracking)* The grid of #s and dots (.) in Fig. 18.21 is a two-dimensional array representation of a maze. The #s represent the walls of the maze, and the dots represent locations in the possible paths through the maze. Moves can be made only to a location in the array that contains a dot.

Fig. 18.21 | Two-dimensional array representation of a maze.

Write a recursive method (mazeTraversal) to walk through mazes like the one in Fig. 18.21. The method should receive as arguments a 12-by-12 character array representing the maze and the current location in the maze (the first time this method is called, the current location should be the entry point of the maze). As mazeTraversal attempts to locate the exit, it should place the character x in each square in the path. There is a simple algorithm for walking through a maze that guarantees finding the exit (assuming there is an exit). If there is no exit, you'll arrive at the starting location again. The algorithm is as follows: From the current location in the maze, try to move one space in any of the possible directions (down, right, up or left). If it's possible to move in at least one direction, call mazeTraversal recursively, passing the new spot on the maze as the current spot. If it's not possible to go in any direction, "back up" to a previous location in the maze and try a new direction for that location. Program the method to display the maze after each move so the user can watch as the maze is solved. The final output of the maze should display only the path needed to solve the maze—if going in a particular direction results in a dead end, the x's going in that direction should not be displayed. [*Hint:* To display only the final path, it may be helpful to mark off spots that result in a dead end with another character (such as '0').]

18.18 *(Generating Mazes Randomly)* Write a method mazeGenerator that takes as an argument a two-dimensional 12-by-12 character array and randomly produces a maze. The method should also provide the starting and ending locations of the maze. Test your method mazeTraversal from Exercise 18.17, using several randomly generated mazes.

18.19 *(Mazes of Any Size)* Generalize methods mazeTraversal and mazeGenerator of Exercise 18.17 and Exercise 18.18 to process mazes of any width and height.

With sobs and tears he sorted out
Those of the largest size ...
—Lewis Carroll

Attempt the end, and never stand to doubt;
Nothing's so hard, but search will find it out.
—Robert Herrick

'Tis in my memory lock'd,
And you yourself shall keep the key of it.
—William Shakespeare

It is an immutable law in business that words are
words, explanations are explanations, promises are
promises — but only performance is reality.
—Harold S. Green

Searching, Sorting and Big O

Objectives

In this chapter you'll learn:

- To search for a given value in an array using linear search and binary search.
- To sort arrays using the iterative selection and insertion sort algorithms.
- To sort arrays using the recursive merge sort algorithm.
- To determine the efficiency of searching and sorting algorithms.

19.1 Introduction

Searching data involves determining whether a value (referred to as the **search key**) is present in the data and, if so, finding its location. Two popular search algorithms are the simple linear search and the faster but more complex binary search. **Sorting** places data in ascending or descending order, based on one or more **sort keys**. A list of names could be sorted alphabetically, bank accounts could be sorted by account number, employee payroll records could be sorted by social security number, and so on. This chapter introduces two simple sorting algorithms, the selection sort and the insertion sort, along with the more efficient but more complex merge sort. Figure 19.1 summarizes the searching and sorting algorithms discussed in the examples and exercises of this book.

Chapter	Algorithm	Location
Searching Algorithms:		
19	Linear search	Section 19.2.1
	Binary search	Section 19.2.2
	Recursive linear search	Exercise 19.8
	Recursive binary search	Exercise 19.9
20	binarySearch method of class Collections	Fig. 20.12
22	Linear search of a List	Exercise 22.20
	Binary tree search	Exercise 22.21
Sorting Algorithms:		
19	Selection sort	Section 19.3.1
	Insertion sort	Section 19.3.2
	Recursive merge sort	Section 19.3.3
	Bubble sort	Exercises 19.5– and 19.6
	Bucket sort	Exercise 19.7
	Recursive quicksort	Exercise 19.10
20	sort method of class Collections	Figs. 20.6–20.9
	SortedSet collection	Fig. 20.17
22	Binary tree sort	Section 22.7

Fig. 19.1 | Searching and sorting algorithms in this text.

19.2 Searching Algorithms

Looking up a phone number, finding a website via a search engine and checking the definition of a word in a dictionary all involve searching large amounts of data. The next two sections discuss two common search algorithms—one that is easy to program yet relatively inefficient and one that is relatively efficient but more complex and difficult to program.

19.2.1 Linear Search

The **linear search algorithm** searches each element in an array sequentially. If the search key does not match an element in the array, the algorithm tests each element, and when the end of the array is reached, informs the user that the search key is not present. If the search key is in the array, the algorithm tests each element until it finds one that matches the search key and returns the index of that element.

As an example, consider an array containing the following values

34	56	2	10	77	51	93	30	5	52

and a program that is searching for 51. Using the linear search algorithm, the program first checks whether 34 matches the search key. It does not, so the algorithm checks whether 56 matches the search key. The program continues moving through the array sequentially, testing 2, then 10, then 77. When the program tests 51, which matches the search key, the program returns the index 5, which is the location of 51 in the array. If, after checking every array element, the program determines that the search key does not match any element in the array, it returns a sentinel value (e.g., -1).

Figure 19.2 declares the `LinearArray` class. This class has two `private` instance variables—an array of `int`s named `data`, and a `static Random` object to fill the array with randomly generated `int`s. When an object of class `LinearArray` is instantiated, the constructor (lines 13–20) creates and initializes the array `data` with random `int`s in the range 10–99. If there are duplicate values in the array, linear search returns the index of the first element in the array that matches the search key.

```java
1  // Fig. 19.2: LinearArray.java
2  // Class that contains an array of random integers and a method
3  // that will search that array sequentially.
4  import java.util.Random;
5  import java.util.Arrays;
6
7  public class LinearArray
8  {
9     private int[] data; // array of values
10    private static final Random generator = new Random();
11
12    // create array of given size and fill with random numbers
13    public LinearArray( int size )
14    {
15       data = new int[ size ]; // create space for array
16
```

Fig. 19.2 | Class that contains an array of random integers and a method that will search that array sequentially. (Part I of 2.)

```
17          // fill array with random ints in range 10-99
18          for ( int i = 0; i < size; i++ )
19              data[ i ] = 10 + generator.nextInt( 90 );
20      } // end LinearArray constructor
21
22      // perform a linear search on the data
23      public int linearSearch( int searchKey )
24      {
25          // loop through array sequentially
26          for ( int index = 0; index < data.length; index++ )
27              if ( data[ index ] == searchKey )
28                  return index; // return index of integer
29
30          return -1; // integer was not found
31      } // end method linearSearch
32
33      // method to output values in array
34      public String toString()
35      {
36          return Arrays.toString( data );
37      } // end method toString
38  } // end class LinearArray
```

Fig. 19.2 | Class that contains an array of random integers and a method that will search that array sequentially. (Part 2 of 2.)

Lines 23–31 perform the linear search. The search key is passed to parameter searchKey. Lines 26–28 loop through the elements in the array. Line 27 compares each with searchKey. If the values are equal, line 28 returns the index of the element. If the loop ends without finding the value, line 30 returns -1. Lines 34–37 declare method toString, which returns a String representation of the array for printing. We use Arrays static method toString to return a String representation of the array.

Figure 19.3 creates a LinearArray object containing an array of 10 ints (line 16) and allows the user to search the array. Lines 20–22 prompt the user for and store the search key. The array holds ints from 10–99 (line 18 of Fig. 19.2). Line 28 calls method linearSearch to determine whether searchInt is in the array. If it's not, linearSearch returns -1 and the program notifies the user (lines 31–32). If searchInt is in the array, linearSearch returns the position of the element, which the program outputs in lines 34–35. Lines 38–40 retrieve the next integer from the user.

```
1   // Fig. 19.3: LinearSearchTest.java
2   // Sequentially searching an array for an item.
3   import java.util.Scanner;
4
5   public class LinearSearchTest
6   {
7       public static void main( String[] args )
8       {
9           // create Scanner object to input data
10          Scanner input = new Scanner( System.in );
```

Fig. 19.3 | Sequentially searching an array for an item. (Part 1 of 2.)

```
11
12        int searchInt; // search key
13        int position; // location of search key in array
14
15        // create array and output it
16        LinearArray searchArray = new LinearArray( 10 );
17        System.out.println( searchArray + "\n" ); // print array
18
19        // get input from user
20        System.out.print(
21           "Please enter an integer value (-1 to quit): " );
22        searchInt = input.nextInt(); // read first int from user
23
24        // repeatedly input an integer; -1 terminates the program
25        while ( searchInt != -1 )
26        {
27           // perform linear search
28           position = searchArray.linearSearch( searchInt );
29
30           if ( position == -1 ) // integer was not found
31              System.out.println( "The integer " + searchInt +
32                 " was not found.\n" );
33           else // integer was found
34              System.out.println( "The integer " + searchInt +
35                 " was found in position " + position + ".\n" );
36
37           // get input from user
38           System.out.print(
39              "Please enter an integer value (-1 to quit): " );
40           searchInt = input.nextInt(); // read next int from user
41        } // end while
42     } // end main
43  } // end class LinearSearchTest
```

```
[59, 97, 34, 90, 79, 56, 24, 51, 30, 69]

Please enter an integer value (-1 to quit): 79
The integer 79 was found in position 4.

Please enter an integer value (-1 to quit): 61
The integer 61 was not found.

Please enter an integer value (-1 to quit): 51
The integer 51 was found in position 7.

Please enter an integer value (-1 to quit): -1
```

Fig. 19.3 | Sequentially searching an array for an item. (Part 2 of 2.)

Efficiency of Linear Search

Searching algorithms all accomplish the same goal—finding an element that matches a given search key, if such an element does, in fact, exist. There are, however, a number of things that differentiate search algorithms from one another. The major difference is the amount of effort they require to complete the search. One way to describe this effort is with **Big O notation**, which indicates the worst-case run time for an algorithm—that is, how hard an algorithm may have to work to solve a problem. For searching and sorting algorithms, this depends particularly on how many data elements there are.

Suppose an algorithm is designed to test whether the first element of an array is equal to the second. If the array has 10 elements, this algorithm requires one comparison. If the array has 1000 elements, it still requires one comparison. In fact, the algorithm is completely independent of the number of elements in the array. This algorithm is said to have a **constant run time**, which is represented in Big O notation as $O(1)$. An algorithm that is $O(1)$ does not necessarily require only one comparison. $O(1)$ just means that the number of comparisons is *constant*—it does not grow as the size of the array increases. An algorithm that tests whether the first element of an array is equal to any of the next three elements is still $O(1)$ even though it requires three comparisons.

An algorithm that tests whether the first array element is equal to *any* of the other array elements will require at most $n - 1$ comparisons, where n is the number of array elements. If the array has 10 elements, this algorithm requires up to nine comparisons. If the array has 1000 elements, it requires up to 999 comparisons. As n grows larger, the n part of the expression "dominates," and subtracting one becomes inconsequential. Big O is designed to highlight these dominant terms and ignore terms that become unimportant as n grows. For this reason, an algorithm that requires a total of $n - 1$ comparisons (such as the one we described earlier) is said to be $O(n)$. An $O(n)$ algorithm is referred to as having a **linear run time**. $O(n)$ is often pronounced "on the order of n" or simply "order n."

Now suppose you have an algorithm that tests whether *any* element of an array is duplicated elsewhere in the array. The first element must be compared with every other element in the array. The second element must be compared with every other element except the first (it was already compared to the first). The third element must be compared with every other element except the first two. In the end, this algorithm will end up making $(n - 1) + (n - 2) + \ldots + 2 + 1$ or $n^2/2 - n/2$ comparisons. As n increases, the n^2 term dominates and the n term becomes inconsequential. Again, Big O notation highlights the n^2 term, leaving $n^2/2$. But, as we'll soon see, constant factors are omitted in Big O notation.

Big O is concerned with how an algorithm's run time grows in relation to the number of items processed. Suppose an algorithm requires n^2 comparisons. With four elements, the algorithm requires 16 comparisons; with eight elements, 64 comparisons. With this algorithm, doubling the number of elements quadruples the number of comparisons. Consider a similar algorithm requiring $n^2/2$ comparisons. With four elements, the algorithm requires eight comparisons; with eight elements, 32 comparisons. Again, doubling the number of elements quadruples the number of comparisons. Both of these algorithms grow as the square of n, so Big O ignores the constant and both algorithms are considered to be $O(n^2)$, which is referred to as **quadratic run time** and pronounced "on the order of n-squared" or more simply "order n-squared."

When n is small, $O(n^2)$ algorithms (running on today's computers) will not noticeably affect performance. But as n grows, you'll start to notice the performance degradation. An $O(n^2)$ algorithm running on a million-element array would require a trillion "operations" (where each could actually require several machine instructions to execute). This could take several hours. A billion-element array would require a quintillion operations, a number so large that the algorithm could take decades! $O(n^2)$ algorithms, unfortunately, are easy to write, as you'll see in this chapter. You'll also see algorithms with more favorable Big O measures. These efficient algorithms often take a bit more cleverness and work to create, but their superior performance can be well worth the extra effort, especially as *n* gets large and as algorithms are combined into larger programs.

The linear search algorithm runs in *O*(*n*) time. The worst case in this algorithm is that every element must be checked to determine whether the search item exists in the array. If the size of the array is doubled, the number of comparisons that the algorithm must perform is also doubled. Note that linear search can provide outstanding performance if the element matching the search key happens to be at or near the front of the array. But we seek algorithms that perform well, on average, across all searches, including those where the element matching the search key is near the end of the array.

Linear search is easy to program, but it can be slow compared to other search algorithms. If a program needs to perform many searches on large arrays, it's better to implement a more efficient algorithm, such as the binary search, which we present next.

Performance Tip 19.1

Sometimes the simplest algorithms perform poorly. Their virtue is that they are easy to program, test and debug. Sometimes more complex algorithms are required to realize maximum performance.

19.2.2 Binary Search

The **binary search algorithm** is more efficient than linear search, but it requires that the array be sorted. The first iteration of this algorithm tests the middle element in the array. If this matches the search key, the algorithm ends. Assuming the array is sorted in ascending order, then if the search key is less than the middle element, it cannot match any element in the second half of the array and the algorithm continues with only the first half of the array (i.e., the first element up to, but not including, the middle element). If the search key is greater than the middle element, it cannot match any element in the first half of the array and the algorithm continues with only the second half (i.e., the element after the middle element through the last element). Each iteration tests the middle value of the remaining portion of the array. If the search key does not match the element, the algorithm eliminates half of the remaining elements. The algorithm ends by either finding an element that matches the search key or reducing the subarray to zero size.

As an example consider the sorted 15-element array

2	3	5	10	27	30	34	51	56	65	77	81	82	93	99

and a search key of 65. A program implementing the binary search algorithm would first check whether 51 is the search key (because 51 is the middle element of the array). The search key (65) is larger than 51, so 51 is discarded along with the first half of the array (all elements smaller than 51) leaving

56	65	77	81	82	93	99

Next, the algorithm checks whether 81 (the middle element of the remainder of the array) matches the search key. The search key (65) is smaller than 81, so 81 is discarded along with the elements larger than 81. After just two tests, the algorithm has narrowed the number of values to check to three (56, 65 and 77). It then checks 65 (which indeed matches the search key) and returns the index of the array element containing 65. This algorithm required just three comparisons to determine whether the search key matched an element of the array. Using a linear search algorithm would have required 10 comparisons. [*Note:* In this example, we've chosen to use an array with 15 elements so that there will always be an obvious middle element in the array. With an even number of elements, the middle of the array lies between two elements. We implement the algorithm to chose the higher of those two elements.]

Binary Search Implementation
Figure 19.4 declares class `BinaryArray`. This class is similar to `LinearArray`—it has two `private` instance variables, a constructor, a search method (`binarySearch`), a remaining-`Elements` method and a `toString` method. Lines 13–22 declare the constructor. After the array has been initialized with random `int`s from 10–99 (lines 18–19), line 21 calls the `Arrays.sort` method on the array `data`. The **sort method** is a `static` method of class `Arrays` that sorts the elements in an array in ascending order by default; an overloaded version of this method allows you to change the sorting order. Recall that the binary search algorithm will work only on a sorted array.

```java
 1  // Fig. 19.4: BinaryArray.java
 2  // Class that contains an array of random integers and a method
 3  // that uses binary search to find an integer.
 4  import java.util.Random;
 5  import java.util.Arrays;
 6
 7  public class BinaryArray
 8  {
 9     private int[] data; // array of values
10     private static final Random generator = new Random();
11
12     // create array of given size and fill with random integers
13     public BinaryArray( int size )
14     {
15        data = new int[ size ]; // create space for array
16
17        // fill array with random ints in range 10-99
18        for ( int i = 0; i < size; i++ )
19           data[ i ] = 10 + generator.nextInt( 90 );
20
21        Arrays.sort( data );
22     } // end BinaryArray constructor
23
24     // perform a binary search on the data
25     public int binarySearch( int searchElement )
26     {
27        int low = 0; // low end of the search area
28        int high = data.length - 1; // high end of the search area
29        int middle = ( low + high + 1 ) / 2; // middle element
30        int location = -1; // return value; -1 if not found
31
32        do // loop to search for element
33        {
34           // print remaining elements of array
35           System.out.print( remainingElements( low, high ) );
```

Fig. 19.4 | Class that contains an array of random integers and a method that uses binary search to find an integer. (Part 1 of 2.)

```
36
37          // output spaces for alignment
38          for ( int i = 0; i < middle; i++ )
39             System.out.print( "   " );
40          System.out.println( " * " ); // indicate current middle
41
42          // if the element is found at the middle
43          if ( searchElement == data[ middle ] )
44             location = middle; // location is the current middle
45
46          // middle element is too high
47          else if ( searchElement < data[ middle ] )
48             high = middle - 1; // eliminate the higher half
49          else  // middle element is too low
50             low = middle + 1; // eliminate the lower half
51
52          middle = ( low + high + 1 ) / 2; // recalculate the middle
53       } while ( ( low <= high ) && ( location == -1 ) );
54
55       return location; // return location of search key
56    } // end method binarySearch
57
58    // method to output certain values in array
59    public String remainingElements( int low, int high )
60    {
61       StringBuilder temporary = new StringBuilder();
62
63       // output spaces for alignment
64       for ( int i = 0; i < low; i++ )
65          temporary.append( "   " );
66
67       // output elements left in array
68       for ( int i = low; i <= high; i++ )
69          temporary.append( data[ i ] + " " );
70
71       temporary.append( "\n" );
72       return temporary.toString();
73    } // end method remainingElements
74
75    // method to output values in array
76    public String toString()
77    {
78       return remainingElements( 0, data.length - 1 );
79    } // end method toString
80 } // end class BinaryArray
```

Fig. 19.4 | Class that contains an array of random integers and a method that uses binary search to find an integer. (Part 2 of 2.)

Lines 25–56 declare method binarySearch. The search key is passed into parameter searchElement (line 25). Lines 27–29 calculate the low end index, high end index and middle index of the portion of the array that the program is currently searching. At the beginning of the method, the low end is 0, the high end is the length of the array minus 1 and the middle is the average of these two values. Line 30 initializes the location of the element to -1—the value that will be returned if the element is not found. Lines 32–53 loop until low is greater than high (this occurs when the element is not found) or location does not equal -1 (indicating that the search key was found). Line 43 tests whether the value in the middle element is equal to searchElement. If this is true, line 44 assigns middle to location. Then the loop terminates and location is returned to the caller. Each iteration of the loop tests a single value (line 43) and eliminates half of the remaining values in the array (line 48 or 50).

Figure 19.5 performs a binary search using the search key the user enters to determine whether it matches an element in the array. The first line of output from this program is the array of ints, in increasing order. When the user instructs the program to search for 23, the program first tests the middle element, which is 42 (as indicated by *). The search key is less than 42, so the program eliminates the second half of the array and tests the middle element from the first half. The search key is smaller than 34, so the program eliminates the second half of the array, leaving only three elements. Finally, the program checks 23 (which matches the search key) and returns the index 1.

```java
1   // Fig. 19.5: BinarySearchTest.java
2   // Use binary search to locate an item in an array.
3   import java.util.Scanner;
4
5   public class BinarySearchTest
6   {
7      public static void main( String[] args )
8      {
9         // create Scanner object to input data
10        Scanner input = new Scanner( System.in );
11
12        int searchInt; // search key
13        int position; // location of search key in array
14
15        // create array and output it
16        BinaryArray searchArray = new BinaryArray( 15 );
17        System.out.println( searchArray );
18
19        // get input from user
20        System.out.print(
21           "Please enter an integer value (-1 to quit): " );
22        searchInt = input.nextInt(); // read an int from user
23        System.out.println();
24
25        // repeatedly input an integer; -1 terminates the program
26        while ( searchInt != -1 )
27        {
28           // use binary search to try to find integer
29           position = searchArray.binarySearch( searchInt );
30
31           // return value of -1 indicates integer was not found
32           if ( position == -1 )
33              System.out.println( "The integer " + searchInt +
34                 " was not found.\n" );
```

Fig. 19.5 | Use binary search to locate an item in an array (* in the output marks the middle element). (Part 1 of 2.)

```
35                else
36                    System.out.println( "The integer " + searchInt +
37                        " was found in position " + position + ".\n" );
38
39                // get input from user
40                System.out.print(
41                    "Please enter an integer value (-1 to quit): " );
42                searchInt = input.nextInt(); // read an int from user
43                System.out.println();
44            } // end while
45        } // end main
46    } // end class BinarySearchTest
```

```
13 23 24 34 35 36 38 42 47 51 68 74 75 85 97

Please enter an integer value (-1 to quit): 23

13 23 24 34 35 36 38 42 47 51 68 74 75 85 97
                              *
13 23 24 34 35 36 38
            *
13 23 24
      *
The integer 23 was found in position 1.

Please enter an integer value (-1 to quit): 75

13 23 24 34 35 36 38 42 47 51 68 74 75 85 97
                  *
                     47 51 68 74 75 85 97
                              *
                              75 85 97
                                 *
                              75
                               *
The integer 75 was found in position 12.

Please enter an integer value (-1 to quit): 52

13 23 24 34 35 36 38 42 47 51 68 74 75 85 97
                  *
                     47 51 68 74 75 85 97
                              *
                     47 51 68
                        *
                           68
                            *
The integer 52 was not found.

Please enter an integer value (-1 to quit): -1
```

Fig. 19.5 | Use binary search to locate an item in an array (* in the output marks the middle element). (Part 2 of 2.)

Efficiency of Binary Search

In the worst-case scenario, searching a sorted array of 1023 elements takes only 10 comparisons when using a binary search. Repeatedly dividing 1023 by 2 (because after each comparison we can eliminate half the array) and rounding down (because we also remove the middle element) yields the values 511, 255, 127, 63, 31, 15, 7, 3, 1 and 0. The number 1023 (2^{10} – 1) is divided by 2 only 10 times to get the value 0, which indicates that there are no more elements to test. Dividing by 2 is equivalent to one comparison in the binary search algorithm. Thus, an array of 1,048,575 (2^{20} – 1) elements takes a maximum of 20 comparisons to find the key, and an array of over one billion elements takes a maximum of 30 comparisons to find the key. This is a tremendous improvement in performance over the linear search. For a one-billion-element array, this is a difference between an average of 500 million comparisons for the linear search and a maximum of only 30 comparisons for the binary search! The maximum number of comparisons needed for the binary search of any sorted array is the exponent of the first power of 2 greater than the number of elements in the array, which is represented as $\log_2 n$. All logarithms grow at roughly the same rate, so in big O notation the base can be omitted. This results in a big O of $O(\log n)$ for a binary search, which is also known as **logarithmic run time**.

19.3 Sorting Algorithms

Sorting data (i.e., placing the data into some particular order, such as ascending or descending) is one of the most important computing applications. A bank sorts all checks by account number so that it can prepare individual bank statements at the end of each month. Telephone companies sort their lists of accounts by last name and, further, by first name to make it easy to find phone numbers. Virtually every organization must sort some data, and often massive amounts of it. Sorting data is an intriguing, computer-intensive problem that has attracted intense research efforts.

An important item to understand about sorting is that the end result—the sorted array—will be the same no matter which algorithm you use to sort the array. The choice of algorithm affects only the run time and memory use of the program. The rest of this chapter introduces three common sorting algorithms. The first two—selection sort and insertion sort—are easy to program but inefficient. The last algorithm—merge sort—is much faster than selection sort and insertion sort but harder to program. We focus on sorting arrays of primitive-type data, namely ints. It's possible to sort arrays of class objects as well. We discuss this in Section 20.7.1.

19.3.1 Selection Sort

Selection sort is a simple, but inefficient, sorting algorithm. Its first iteration selects the smallest element in the array and swaps it with the first element. The second iteration selects the second-smallest item (which is the smallest item of the remaining elements) and swaps it with the second element. The algorithm continues until the last iteration selects the second-largest element and swaps it with the second-to-last index, leaving the largest element in the last index. After the *i*th iteration, the smallest *i* items of the array will be sorted into increasing order in the first *i* elements of the array.

As an example, consider the array

| 34 | 56 | 4 | 10 | 77 | 51 | 93 | 30 | 5 | 52 |

A program that implements selection sort first determines the smallest element (4) of this array, which is contained in index 2. The program swaps 4 with 34, resulting in

| 4 | 56 | 34 | 10 | 77 | 51 | 93 | 30 | 5 | 52 |

The program then determines the smallest value of the remaining elements (all elements except 4), which is 5, contained in index 8. The program swaps 5 with 56, resulting in

| 4 | 5 | 34 | 10 | 77 | 51 | 93 | 30 | 56 | 52 |

On the third iteration, the program determines the next smallest value (10) and swaps it with 34.

| 4 | 5 | 10 | 34 | 77 | 51 | 93 | 30 | 56 | 52 |

The process continues until the array is fully sorted.

| 4 | 5 | 10 | 30 | 34 | 51 | 52 | 56 | 77 | 93 |

Note that after the first iteration, the smallest element is in the first position. After the second iteration, the two smallest elements are in order in the first two positions. After the third iteration, the three smallest elements are in order in the first three positions.

Figure 19.6 declares the SelectionSort class. This class has two private instance variables—an array of ints named data, and a static Random object to generate random integers to fill the array. When an object of class SelectionSort is instantiated, the constructor (lines 13–20) creates and initializes the array data with random ints in the range 10–99.

```
1    // Fig. 19.6: SelectionSort.java
2    // Class that creates an array filled with random integers.
3    // Provides a method to sort the array with selection sort.
4    import java.util.Arrays;
5    import java.util.Random;
6
7    public class SelectionSort
8    {
9       private int[] data; // array of values
10      private static final Random generator = new Random();
11
12      // create array of given size and fill with random integers
13      public SelectionSort( int size )
14      {
15         data = new int[ size ]; // create space for array
16
17         // fill array with random ints in range 10-99
18         for ( int i = 0; i < size; i++ )
19            data[ i ] = 10 + generator.nextInt( 90 );
20      } // end SelectionSort constructor
21
22      // sort array using selection sort
23      public void sort()
24      {
25         int smallest; // index of smallest element
26
27         // loop over data.length - 1 elements
28         for ( int i = 0; i < data.length - 1; i++ )
29         {
30            smallest = i; // first index of remaining array
```

Fig. 19.6 | Class that creates an array filled with random integers. Provides a method to sort the array with selection sort. (Part 1 of 2.)

```
31
32          // loop to find index of smallest element
33          for ( int index = i + 1; index < data.length; index++ )
34             if ( data[ index ] < data[ smallest ] )
35                smallest = index;
36
37          swap( i, smallest ); // swap smallest element into position
38          printPass( i + 1, smallest ); // output pass of algorithm
39       } // end outer for
40    } // end method sort
41
42    // helper method to swap values in two elements
43    public void swap( int first, int second )
44    {
45       int temporary = data[ first ]; // store first in temporary
46       data[ first ] = data[ second ]; // replace first with second
47       data[ second ] = temporary; // put temporary in second
48    } // end method swap
49
50    // print a pass of the algorithm
51    public void printPass( int pass, int index )
52    {
53       System.out.print( String.format( "after pass %2d: ", pass ) );
54
55       // output elements till selected item
56       for ( int i = 0; i < index; i++ )
57          System.out.print( data[ i ] + "  " );
58
59       System.out.print( data[ index ] + "* " ); // indicate swap
60
61       // finish outputting array
62       for ( int i = index + 1; i < data.length; i++ )
63          System.out.print( data[ i ] + "  " );
64
65       System.out.print( "\n               " ); // for alignment
66
67       // indicate amount of array that is sorted
68       for ( int j = 0; j < pass; j++ )
69          System.out.print( "--  " );
70       System.out.println( "\n" ); // add endline
71    } // end method printPass
72
73    // method to output values in array
74    public String toString()
75    {
76       return Arrays.toString( data );
77    } // end method toString
78 } // end class SelectionSort
```

Fig. 19.6 | Class that creates an array filled with random integers. Provides a method to sort the array with selection sort. (Part 2 of 2.)

Lines 23–40 declare the sort method. Line 25 declares the variable smallest, which will store the index of the smallest element in the remaining array. Lines 28–39 loop data.length - 1 times. Line 30 initializes the index of the smallest element to the current item. Lines 33–35 loop over the remaining elements in the array. For each of these elements, line 34 compares its value to the value of the smallest element. If the current element is smaller than the smallest element, line 35 assigns the current element's index to smallest. When this loop finishes, smallest will contain the index of the smallest element in the remaining array. Line 36 calls method swap (lines 43–48) to place the smallest remaining element in the next ordered spot in the array.

Line 9 of Fig. 19.7 creates a SelectionSort object with 10 elements. Line 12 outputs the unsorted object. Line 14 calls method sort (lines 22–39 of Fig. 19.6), which sorts the elements using selection sort. Then lines 16–17 output the sorted object. The output uses dashes (lines 67–68) to indicate the portion of the array that is sorted after each pass. An asterisk is placed next to the position of the element that was swapped with the smallest element on that pass. On each pass, the element next to the asterisk (specified at line 58) and the element above the rightmost set of dashes were swapped.

```java
 1   // Fig. 19.7: SelectionSortTest.java
 2   // Testing the selection sort class.
 3
 4   public class SelectionSortTest
 5   {
 6      public static void main( String[] args )
 7      {
 8         // create object to perform selection sort
 9         SelectionSort sortArray = new SelectionSort( 10 );
10
11         System.out.println( "Unsorted array:" );
12         System.out.println( sortArray + "\n" ); // print unsorted array
13
14         sortArray.sort(); // sort array
15
16         System.out.println( "Sorted array:" );
17         System.out.println( sortArray ); // print sorted array
18      } // end main
19   } // end class SelectionSortTest
```

```
Unsorted array:
[61, 87, 80, 58, 40, 50, 20, 13, 71, 45]

after pass  1: 13  87  80  58  40  50  20  61* 71  45
               --

after pass  2: 13  20  80  58  40  50  87* 61  71  45
               --  --

after pass  3: 13  20  40  58  80* 50  87  61  71  45
               --  --  --

after pass  4: 13  20  40  45  80  50  87  61  71  58*
               --  --  --  --

after pass  5: 13  20  40  45  50  80* 87  61  71  58
               --  --  --  --  --

after pass  6: 13  20  40  45  50  58  87  61  71  80*
               --  --  --  --  --  --
```

Fig. 19.7 | Testing the selection sort class. (Part 1 of 2.)

```
after pass  6: 13  20  40  45  50  58  87  61  71  80*
               --  --  --  --  --  --

after pass  7: 13  20  40  45  50  58  61  87* 71  80
               --  --  --  --  --  --  --

after pass  8: 13  20  40  45  50  58  61  71  87* 80
               --  --  --  --  --  --  --  --

after pass  9: 13  20  40  45  50  58  61  71  80  87*
               --  --  --  --  --  --  --  --  --

Sorted array:
[13, 20, 40, 45, 50, 58, 61, 71, 80, 87]
```

Fig. 19.7 | Testing the selection sort class. (Part 2 of 2.)

Efficiency of Selection Sort

The selection sort algorithm runs in $O(n^2)$ time. The sort method in lines 23–40 of Fig. 19.6, which implements the selection sort algorithm, contains two for loops. The outer for loop (lines 28–39) iterates over the first $n - 1$ elements in the array, swapping the smallest remaining item into its sorted position. The inner for loop (lines 33–35) iterates over each item in the remaining array, searching for the smallest element. This loop executes $n - 1$ times during the first iteration of the outer loop, $n - 2$ times during the second iteration, then $n - 3, \ldots, 3, 2, 1$. This inner loop will iterate a total of $n(n - 1)/2$ or $(n^2 - n)/2$. In Big O notation, smaller terms drop out and constants are ignored, leaving a final Big O of $O(n^2)$.

19.3.2 Insertion Sort

Insertion sort is another simple, but inefficient, sorting algorithm. The first iteration of this algorithm takes the second element in the array and, if it's less than the first element, swaps it with the first element. The second iteration looks at the third element and inserts it into the correct position with respect to the first two, so all three elements are in order. At the ith iteration of this algorithm, the first i elements in the original array will be sorted.

Consider as an example the following array. [*Note:* This array is identical to the one used in the discussions of selection sort and merge sort.]

| 34 | 56 | 4 | 10 | 77 | 51 | 93 | 30 | 5 | 52 |

A program that implements the insertion sort algorithm will first look at the first two elements of the array, 34 and 56. These are already in order, so the program continues. (If they were out of order, the program would swap them.)

In the next iteration, the program looks at the third value, 4. This value is less than 56, so the program stores 4 in a temporary variable and moves 56 one element to the right. The program then checks and determines that 4 is less than 34, so it moves 34 one element to the right. The program has now reached the beginning of the array, so it places 4 in the zeroth element. The array now is

| 4 | 34 | 56 | 10 | 77 | 51 | 93 | 30 | 5 | 52 |

In the next iteration, the program stores 10 in a temporary variable. Then it compares 10 to 56 and moves 56 one element to the right because it's larger than 10. The program then compares 10 to 34, moving 34 right one element. When the program compares 10 to 4, it observes that 10 is larger than 4 and places 10 in element 1. The array now is

4	10	34	56	77	51	93	30	5	52

Using this algorithm, at the ith iteration, the first i elements of the original array are sorted, but they may not be in their final locations—smaller values may be located later in the array.

Figure 19.8 declares the InsertionSort class. Lines 23–47 declare the sort method. Line 25 declares the variable insert, which holds the element you are going to insert while you move the other elements. Lines 28–46 loop over data.length - 1 items in the array. In each iteration, line 31 stores in insert the value of the element that will be inserted into the sorted portion of the array. Line 34 declares and initializes the variable moveItem, which keeps track of where to insert the element. Lines 37–42 loop to locate the correct position where the element should be inserted. The loop will terminate either when the program reaches the front of the array or when it reaches an element that is less than the value to be inserted. Line 40 moves an element to the right, and line 41 decrements the position at which to insert the next element. After the loop ends, line 44 inserts the element into place. Figure 19.9 is the same as Fig. 19.7 except that it creates and uses an InsertionSort object. The output of this program uses dashes to indicate the portion of the array that is sorted after each pass. An asterisk is placed next to the element that was inserted into place on that pass.

```
1   // Fig. 19.8: InsertionSort.java
2   // Class that creates an array filled with random integers.
3   // Provides a method to sort the array with insertion sort.
4   import java.util.Arrays;
5   import java.util.Random;
6
7   public class InsertionSort
8   {
9      private int[] data; // array of values
10     private static final Random generator = new Random();
11
12     // create array of given size and fill with random integers
13     public InsertionSort( int size )
14     {
15        data = new int[ size ]; // create space for array
16
17        // fill array with random ints in range 10-99
18        for ( int i = 0; i < size; i++ )
19           data[ i ] = 10 + generator.nextInt( 90 );
20     } // end InsertionSort constructor
21
22     // sort array using insertion sort
23     public void sort()
24     {
25        int insert; // temporary variable to hold element to insert
```

Fig. 19.8 | Class that creates an array filled with random integers. Provides a method to sort the array with insertion sort. (Part 1 of 2.)

```
26
27          // loop over data.length - 1 elements
28          for ( int next = 1; next < data.length; next++ )
29          {
30             // store value in current element
31             insert = data[ next ];
32
33             // initialize location to place element
34             int moveItem = next;
35
36             // search for place to put current element
37             while ( moveItem > 0 && data[ moveItem - 1 ] > insert )
38             {
39                // shift element right one slot
40                data[ moveItem ] = data[ moveItem - 1 ];
41                moveItem--;
42             } // end while
43
44             data[ moveItem ] = insert; // place inserted element
45             printPass( next, moveItem ); // output pass of algorithm
46          } // end for
47       } // end method sort
48
49       // print a pass of the algorithm
50       public void printPass( int pass, int index )
51       {
52          System.out.print( String.format( "after pass %2d: ", pass ) );
53
54          // output elements till swapped item
55          for ( int i = 0; i < index; i++ )
56             System.out.print( data[ i ] + "  " );
57
58          System.out.print( data[ index ] + "* " ); // indicate swap
59
60          // finish outputting array
61          for ( int i = index + 1; i < data.length; i++ )
62             System.out.print( data[ i ] + "  " );
63
64          System.out.print( "\n              " ); // for alignment
65
66          // indicate amount of array that is sorted
67          for( int i = 0; i <= pass; i++ )
68             System.out.print( "--  " );
69          System.out.println( "\n" ); // add endline
70       } // end method printPass
71
72       // method to output values in array
73       public String toString()
74       {
75          return Arrays.toString( data );
76       } // end method toString
77    } // end class InsertionSort
```

Fig. 19.8 | Class that creates an array filled with random integers. Provides a method to sort the array with insertion sort. (Part 2 of 2.)

```
1   // Fig. 19.9: InsertionSortTest.java
2   // Testing the insertion sort class.
3
4   public class InsertionSortTest
5   {
6      public static void main( String[] args )
7      {
8         // create object to perform insertion sort
9         InsertionSort sortArray = new InsertionSort( 10 );
10
11        System.out.println( "Unsorted array:" );
12        System.out.println( sortArray + "\n" ); // print unsorted array
13
14        sortArray.sort(); // sort array
15
16        System.out.println( "Sorted array:" );
17        System.out.println( sortArray ); // print sorted array
18     } // end main
19  } // end class InsertionSortTest
```

```
Unsorted array:
[40, 17, 45, 82, 62, 32, 30, 44, 93, 10]

after pass  1: 17* 40  45  82  62  32  30  44  93  10
               --  --

after pass  2: 17  40  45* 82  62  32  30  44  93  10
               --  --  --

after pass  3: 17  40  45  82* 62  32  30  44  93  10
               --  --  --  --

after pass  4: 17  40  45  62* 82  32  30  44  93  10
               --  --  --  --  --

after pass  5: 17  32* 40  45  62  82  30  44  93  10
               --  --  --  --  --  --

after pass  6: 17  30* 32  40  45  62  82  44  93  10
               --  --  --  --  --  --  --

after pass  7: 17  30  32  40  44* 45  62  82  93  10
               --  --  --  --  --  --  --  --

after pass  8: 17  30  32  40  44  45  62  82  93* 10
               --  --  --  --  --  --  --  --  --

after pass  9: 10* 17  30  32  40  44  45  62  82  93
               --  --  --  --  --  --  --  --  --  --

Sorted array:
[10, 17, 30, 32, 40, 44, 45, 62, 82, 93]
```

Fig. 19.9 | Testing the insertion sort class.

Efficiency of Insertion Sort

The insertion sort algorithm also runs in $O(n^2)$ time. Like selection sort, the implementation of insertion sort (lines 23–47 of Fig. 19.8) contains two loops. The for loop (lines

28–46) iterates data.length - 1 times, inserting an element into the appropriate position in the elements sorted so far. For the purposes of this application, data.length - 1 is equivalent to $n - 1$ (as data.length is the size of the array). The while loop (lines 37–42) iterates over the preceding elements in the array. In the worst case, this while loop will require $n - 1$ comparisons. Each individual loop runs in $O(n)$ time. In Big O notation, nested loops mean that you must multiply the number of comparisons. For each iteration of an outer loop, there will be a certain number of iterations of the inner loop. In this algorithm, for each $O(n)$ iterations of the outer loop, there will be $O(n)$ iterations of the inner loop. Multiplying these values results in a Big O of $O(n^2)$.

19.3.3 Merge Sort

Merge sort is an efficient sorting algorithm but is conceptually more complex than selection sort and insertion sort. The merge sort algorithm sorts an array by splitting it into two equal-sized subarrays, sorting each subarray, then merging them into one larger array. With an odd number of elements, the algorithm creates the two subarrays such that one has one more element than the other.

The implementation of merge sort in this example is recursive. The base case is an array with one element, which is, of course, sorted, so the merge sort immediately returns in this case. The recursion step splits the array into two approximately equal pieces, recursively sorts them, then merges the two sorted arrays into one larger, sorted array.

Suppose the algorithm has already merged smaller arrays to create sorted arrays A:

4	10	34	56	77

and B:

5	30	51	52	93

Merge sort combines these two arrays into one larger, sorted array. The smallest element in A is 4 (located in the zeroth index of A). The smallest element in B is 5 (located in the zeroth index of B). In order to determine the smallest element in the larger array, the algorithm compares 4 and 5. The value from A is smaller, so 4 becomes the first element in the merged array. The algorithm continues by comparing 10 (the second element in A) to 5 (the first element in B). The value from B is smaller, so 5 becomes the second element in the larger array. The algorithm continues by comparing 10 to 30, with 10 becoming the third element in the array, and so on.

Lines 22–25 of Fig. 19.10 declare the sort method. Line 24 calls method sortArray with 0 and data.length - 1 as the arguments—corresponding to the beginning and ending indices, respectively, of the array to be sorted. These values tell method sortArray to operate on the entire array.

Method sortArray is declared in lines 28–49. Line 31 tests the base case. If the size of the array is 1, the array is already sorted, so the method returns immediately. If the size of the array is greater than 1, the method splits the array in two, recursively calls method sortArray to sort the two subarrays, then merges them. Line 43 recursively calls method sortArray on the first half of the array, and line 44 recursively calls method sortArray on the second half. When these two method calls return, each half of the array has been sorted. Line 47 calls method merge (lines 52–91) on the two halves of the array to combine the two sorted arrays into one larger sorted array.

```
 1   // Fig. 19.10: MergeSort.java
 2   // Class creates an array filled with random integers.
 3   // Provides a method to sort the array with merge sort.
 4   import java.util.Random;
 5
 6   public class MergeSort
 7   {
 8      private int[] data; // array of values
 9      private static final Random generator = new Random();
10
11      // create array of given size and fill with random integers
12      public MergeSort( int size )
13      {
14         data = new int[ size ]; // create space for array
15
16         // fill array with random ints in range 10-99
17         for ( int i = 0; i < size; i++ )
18            data[ i ] = 10 + generator.nextInt( 90 );
19      } // end MergeSort constructor
20
21      // calls recursive split method to begin merge sorting
22      public void sort()
23      {
24         sortArray( 0, data.length - 1 ); // split entire array
25      } // end method sort
26
27      // splits array, sorts subarrays and merges subarrays into sorted array
28      private void sortArray( int low, int high )
29      {
30         // test base case; size of array equals 1
31         if ( ( high - low ) >= 1 ) // if not base case
32         {
33            int middle1 = ( low + high ) / 2; // calculate middle of array
34            int middle2 = middle1 + 1; // calculate next element over
35
36            // output split step
37            System.out.println( "split:   " + subarray( low, high ) );
38            System.out.println( "         " + subarray( low, middle1 ) );
39            System.out.println( "         " + subarray( middle2, high ) );
40            System.out.println();
41
42            // split array in half; sort each half (recursive calls)
43            sortArray( low, middle1 ); // first half of array
44            sortArray( middle2, high ); // second half of array
45
46            // merge two sorted arrays after split calls return
47            merge ( low, middle1, middle2, high );
48         } // end if
49      } // end method sortArray
50
51      // merge two sorted subarrays into one sorted subarray
52      private void merge( int left, int middle1, int middle2, int right )
53      {
```

Fig. 19.10 | Class that creates an array filled with random integers. Provides a method to sort the array with merge sort. (Part 1 of 3.)

```
54      int leftIndex = left; // index into left subarray
55      int rightIndex = middle2; // index into right subarray
56      int combinedIndex = left; // index into temporary working array
57      int[] combined = new int[ data.length ]; // working array
58
59      // output two subarrays before merging
60      System.out.println( "merge:   " + subarray( left, middle1 ) );
61      System.out.println( "              " + subarray( middle2, right ) );
62
63      // merge arrays until reaching end of either
64      while ( leftIndex <= middle1 && rightIndex <= right )
65      {
66          // place smaller of two current elements into result
67          // and move to next space in arrays
68          if ( data[ leftIndex ] <= data[ rightIndex ] )
69              combined[ combinedIndex++ ] = data[ leftIndex++ ];
70          else
71              combined[ combinedIndex++ ] = data[ rightIndex++ ];
72      } // end while
73
74      // if left array is empty
75      if ( leftIndex == middle2 )
76          // copy in rest of right array
77          while ( rightIndex <= right )
78              combined[ combinedIndex++ ] = data[ rightIndex++ ];
79      else // right array is empty
80          // copy in rest of left array
81          while ( leftIndex <= middle1 )
82              combined[ combinedIndex++ ] = data[ leftIndex++ ];
83
84      // copy values back into original array
85      for ( int i = left; i <= right; i++ )
86          data[ i ] = combined[ i ];
87
88      // output merged array
89      System.out.println( "              " + subarray( left, right ) );
90      System.out.println();
91   } // end method merge
92
93   // method to output certain values in array
94   public String subarray( int low, int high )
95   {
96      StringBuilder temporary = new StringBuilder();
97
98      // output spaces for alignment
99      for ( int i = 0; i < low; i++ )
100         temporary.append( "   " );
101
102     // output elements left in array
103     for ( int i = low; i <= high; i++ )
104         temporary.append( " " + data[ i ] );
105
```

Fig. 19.10 | Class that creates an array filled with random integers. Provides a method to sort the array with merge sort. (Part 2 of 3.)

```
106            return temporary.toString();
107        } // end method subarray
108
109        // method to output values in array
110        public String toString()
111        {
112            return subarray( 0, data.length - 1 );
113        } // end method toString
114    } // end class MergeSort
```

Fig. 19.10 | Class that creates an array filled with random integers. Provides a method to sort the array with merge sort. (Part 3 of 3.)

Lines 64–72 in the merge method loop until the program reaches the end of either subarray. Line 68 tests which element at the beginning of the arrays is smaller. If the element in the left array is smaller, line 69 places it in position in the combined array. If the element in the right array is smaller, line 71 places it in position in the combined array. When the while loop has completed (line 72), one entire subarray is placed in the combined array, but the other subarray still contains data. Line 75 tests whether the left array has reached the end. If so, lines 77–78 fill the combined array with the elements of the right array. If the left array has not reached the end, then the right array must have reached the end, and lines 81–82 fill the combined array with the elements of the left array. Finally, lines 85–86 copy the combined array into the original array. Figure 19.11 creates and uses a MergeSort object. The output from this program displays the splits and merges performed by merge sort, showing the progress of the sort at each step of the algorithm. It's well worth your time to step through these outputs to fully understand this elegant sorting algorithm.

```
1   // Figure 16.11: MergeSortTest.java
2   // Testing the merge sort class.
3
4   public class MergeSortTest
5   {
6      public static void main( String[] args )
7      {
8         // create object to perform merge sort
9         MergeSort sortArray = new MergeSort( 10 );
10
11         // print unsorted array
12         System.out.println( "Unsorted:" + sortArray + "\n" );
13
14         sortArray.sort(); // sort array
15
16         // print sorted array
17         System.out.println( "Sorted:   " + sortArray );
18      } // end main
19   } // end class MergeSortTest
```

Fig. 19.11 | Testing the merge sort class. (Part 1 of 3.)

```
Unsorted: 75 56 85 90 49 26 12 48 40 47

split:    75 56 85 90 49 26 12 48 40 47
          75 56 85 90 49
                         26 12 48 40 47

split:    75 56 85 90 49
          75 56 85
                   90 49

split:    75 56 85
          75 56
                85

split:    75 56
          75
             56

merge:    75
             56
          56 75

merge:    56 75
                85
          56 75 85

split:              90 49
                    90
                       49

merge:              90
                       49
                    49 90

merge:    56 75 85
                    49 90
          49 56 75 85 90

split:                   26 12 48 40 47
                         26 12 48
                                  40 47

split:                   26 12 48
                         26 12
                               48

split:                   26 12
                         26
                            12

merge:                   26
                            12
                         12 26

merge:                   12 26
                               48
                         12 26 48

split:                            40 47
                                  40
                                     47
```

Fig. 19.11 | Testing the merge sort class. (Part 2 of 3.)

```
merge:                                40
                                         47
                                      40  47

merge:                    12  26  48
                                      40  47
                          12  26  40  47  48

merge:     49  56  75  85  90
                          12  26  40  47  48
           12  26  40  47  48  49  56  75  85  90

Sorted:    12  26  40  47  48  49  56  75  85  90
```

Fig. 19.11 | Testing the merge sort class. (Part 3 of 3.)

Efficiency of Merge Sort

Merge sort is a far more efficient algorithm than either insertion or selection sort. Consider the first (nonrecursive) call to method sortArray. This results in two recursive calls to method sortArray with subarrays each approximately half the size of the original array, and a single call to method merge. This call to merge requires, at worst, $n - 1$ comparisons to fill the original array, which is $O(n)$. (Recall that each element in the array can be chosen by comparing one element from each of the subarrays.) The two calls to method sortArray result in four more recursive calls to method sortArray, each with a subarray approximately a quarter the size of the original array along with two calls to method merge. These two calls to method merge each require, at worst, $n/2 - 1$ comparisons, for a total number of comparisons of $O(n)$. This process continues, each call to sortArray generating two additional calls to sortArray and a call to merge, until the algorithm has split the array into one-element subarrays. At each level, $O(n)$ comparisons are required to merge the subarrays. Each level splits the size of the arrays in half, so doubling the size of the array requires one more level. Quadrupling the size of the array requires two more levels. This pattern is logarithmic and results in $\log_2 n$ levels. This results in a total efficiency of $O(n \log n)$.

Figure 19.12 summarizes the searching and sorting algorithms covered in this chapter with the Big O for each. Figure 19.13 lists the Big O values we've covered in this chapter along with a number of values for n to highlight the differences in the growth rates.

Algorithm	Location	Big O
Searching Algorithms:		
Linear search	Section 19.2.1	$O(n)$
Binary search	Section 19.2.2	$O(\log n)$
Recursive linear search	Exercise 19.8	$O(n)$
Recursive binary search	Exercise 19.9	$O(\log n)$
Sorting Algorithms:		
Selection sort	Section 19.3.1	$O(n^2)$
Insertion sort	Section 19.3.2	$O(n^2)$
Merge sort	Section 19.3.3	$O(n \log n)$
Bubble sort	Exercise 19.5 and 19.6	$O(n^2)$

Fig. 19.12 | Searching and sorting algorithms with Big O values.

$n =$	$O(\log n)$	$O(n)$	$O(n \log n)$	$O(n^2)$
1	0	1	0	1
2	1	2	2	4
3	1	3	3	9
4	1	4	4	16
5	1	5	5	25
10	1	10	10	100
100	2	100	200	10,000
1000	3	1000	3000	10^6
1,000,000	6	1,000,000	6,000,000	10^{12}
1,000,000,000	9	1,000,000,000	9,000,000,000	10^{18}

Fig. 19.13 | Number of comparisons for common Big O notations.

19.4 Wrap-Up

This chapter introduced searching and sorting. We discussed two searching algorithms—linear search and binary search—and three sorting algorithms—selection sort, insertion sort and merge sort. We introduced Big O notation, which helps you analyze the efficiency of an algorithm. The next three chapters continue our discussion of dynamic data structures that can grow or shrink at execution time. Chapter 20 presents the Java API's built-in algorithms (such as searching and sorting) and generic collections. Chapter 21 demonstrates how to use Java's generics capabilities to implement generic methods and classes. Chapter 22 discusses the details of implementing generic data structures.

Summary

Section 19.1 Introduction
- Searching involves determining if a search key is in the data and, if so, finding its location.
- Sorting involves arranging data into order.

Section 19.2 Searching Algorithms
- The linear search algorithm searches each element in the array sequentially until it finds the correct element, or until it reaches the end of the array without finding the element.
- A major difference among searching algorithms is the amount of effort they require in order to return a result.
- Big O notation describes an algorithm's efficiency in terms of the work required to solve a problem. For searching and sorting algorithms typically it depends on the number of elements in the data.
- An algorithm that is $O(1)$ does not necessarily require only one comparison. It just means that the number of comparisons does not grow as the size of the array increases.
- An $O(n)$ algorithm is referred to as having a linear run time.
- Big O is designed to highlight dominant factors and ignore terms that become unimportant with high n values.
- Big O notation is concerned with the growth rate of algorithm run times, so constants are ignored.
- The linear search algorithm runs in $O(n)$ time.

- The worst case in linear search is that every element must be checked to determine whether the search item exists. This occurs if the search key is the last element in the array or is not present.

- The binary search algorithm is more efficient than the linear search algorithm, but it requires that the array be sorted.

- The first iteration of binary search tests the middle element in the array. If this is the search key, the algorithm returns its location. If the search key is less than the middle element, the search continues with the first half of the array. If the search key is greater than the middle element, the search continues with the second half of the array. Each iteration tests the middle value of the remaining array and, if the element is not found, eliminates half of the remaining elements.

- Binary search is a more efficient searching algorithm than linear search because each comparison eliminates from consideration half of the elements in the array.

- Binary search runs in $O(\log n)$ time because each step removes half of the remaining elements.

- If the array size is doubled, binary search requires only one extra comparison.

Section 19.3 Sorting Algorithms

- Selection sort is a simple, but inefficient, sorting algorithm.

- The first iteration of selection sort selects the smallest item in the array and swaps it with the first element. The second iteration of selection sort selects the second-smallest item (which is the smallest remaining item) and swaps it with the second element. Selection sort continues until the last iteration selects the second-largest element and swaps it with the second-to-last element, leaving the largest element in the last index. At the ith iteration of selection sort, the smallest i items of the whole array are sorted into the first i indices.

- The selection sort algorithm runs in $O(n^2)$ time.

- The first iteration of insertion sort takes the second element in the array and, if it's less than the first element, swaps it with the first element. The second iteration of insertion sort looks at the third element and inserts it in the correct position with respect to the first two elements. After the ith iteration of insertion sort, the first i elements in the original array are sorted.

- The insertion sort algorithm runs in $O(n^2)$ time.

- Merge sort is a sorting algorithm that is faster, but more complex to implement, than selection sort and insertion sort.

- The merge sort algorithm sorts an array by splitting the array into two equal-sized subarrays, sorting each subarray recursively and merging the subarrays into one larger array.

- Merge sort's base case is an array with one element. A one-element array is already sorted, so merge sort immediately returns when it's called with a one-element array. The merge part of merge sort takes two sorted arrays and combines them into one larger sorted array.

- Merge sort performs the merge by looking at the first element in each array, which is also the smallest element in the array. Merge sort takes the smallest of these and places it in the first element of the larger array. If there are still elements in the subarray, merge sort looks at the second of these (which is now the smallest element remaining) and compares it to the first element in the other subarray. Merge sort continues this process until the larger array is filled.

- In the worst case, the first call to merge sort has to make $O(n)$ comparisons to fill the n slots in the final array.

- The merging portion of the merge sort algorithm is performed on two subarrays, each of approximately size $n/2$. Creating each of these subarrays requires $n/2 - 1$ comparisons for each subarray, or $O(n)$ comparisons total. This pattern continues as each level works on twice as many arrays, but each is half the size of the previous array.

- Similar to binary search, this halving results in $\log n$ levels for a total efficiency of $O(n \log n)$.

Terminology

Big O notation 815
binary search algorithm 817
constant run time 816
insertion sort algorithm 826
linear run time 816
linear search algorithm 813
logarithmic run time 822
merge sort 830
$O(1)$ 816
$O(\log n)$ 822

$O(n \log n)$ time 835
$O(n)$ time 816
$O(n^2)$ time 816
quadratic run time 816
search key 812
searching data 812
selection sort 822
sort key 812
sort method of class `Arrays` 818
sorting data 812

Self-Review Exercises

19.1 Fill in the blanks in each of the following statements:
   a) A selection sort application would take approximately _____ times as long to run on a 128-element array as on a 32-element array.
   b) The efficiency of merge sort is _____.

19.2 What key aspect of both the binary search and the merge sort accounts for the logarithmic portion of their respective Big Os?

19.3 In what sense is the insertion sort superior to the merge sort? In what sense is the merge sort superior to the insertion sort?

19.4 In the text, we say that after the merge sort splits the array into two subarrays, it then sorts these two subarrays and merges them. Why might someone be puzzled by our statement that "it then sorts these two subarrays"?

Answers to Self-Review Exercises

19.1 a) 16, because an $O(n^2)$ algorithm takes 16 times as long to sort four times as much information. b) $O(n \log n)$.

19.2 Both of these algorithms incorporate "halving"—somehow reducing something by half. The binary search eliminates from consideration one-half of the array after each comparison. The merge sort splits the array in half each time it's called.

19.3 The insertion sort is easier to understand and to program than the merge sort. The merge sort is far more efficient [$O(n \log n)$] than the insertion sort [$O(n^2)$].

19.4 In a sense, it does not really sort these two subarrays. It simply keeps splitting the original array in half until it provides a one-element subarray, which is, of course, sorted. It then builds up the original two subarrays by merging these one-element arrays to form larger subarrays, which are then merged, and so on.

Exercises

19.5 *(Bubble Sort)* Implement bubble sort—another simple yet inefficient sorting technique. It's called bubble sort or sinking sort because smaller values gradually "bubble" their way to the top of the array (i.e., toward the first element) like air bubbles rising in water, while the larger values sink to the bottom (end) of the array. The technique uses nested loops to make several passes through the array. Each pass compares successive pairs of elements. If a pair is in increasing order (or the values are equal), the bubble sort leaves the values as they are. If a pair is in decreasing order, the bubble sort swaps their values in the array.

The first pass compares the first two elements of the array and swaps their values if necessary. It then compares the second and third elements in the array. The end of this pass compares the last two elements in the array and swaps them if necessary. After one pass, the largest element will be in the last index. After two passes, the largest two elements will be in the last two indices. Explain why bubble sort is an $O(n^2)$ algorithm.

19.6 *(Enhanced Bubble Sort)* Make the following simple modifications to improve the performance of the bubble sort you developed in Exercise 19.5:

a) After the first pass, the largest number is guaranteed to be in the highest-numbered element of the array; after the second pass, the two highest numbers are "in place"; and so on. Instead of making nine comparisons on every pass for a ten element array, modify the bubble sort to make eight comparisons on the second pass, seven on the third pass, and so on.

b) The data in the array may already be in proper or near-proper order, so why make nine passes if fewer will suffice? Modify the sort to check at the end of each pass whether any swaps have been made. If none have been made, the data must already be in the proper order, so the program should terminate. If swaps have been made, at least one more pass is needed.

19.7 *(Bucket Sort)* A bucket sort begins with a one-dimensional array of positive integers to be sorted and a two-dimensional array of integers with rows indexed from 0 to 9 and columns indexed from 0 to $n - 1$, where n is the number of values to be sorted. Each row of the two-dimensional array is referred to as a *bucket*. Write a class named BucketSort containing a method called sort that operates as follows:

a) Place each value of the one-dimensional array into a row of the bucket array, based on the value's "ones" (rightmost) digit. For example, 97 is placed in row 7, 3 is placed in row 3 and 100 is placed in row 0. This procedure is called a *distribution pass*.

b) Loop through the bucket array row by row, and copy the values back to the original array. This procedure is called a *gathering pass*. The new order of the preceding values in the one-dimensional array is 100, 3 and 97.

c) Repeat this process for each subsequent digit position (tens, hundreds, thousands, etc.). On the second (tens digit) pass, 100 is placed in row 0, 3 is placed in row 0 (because 3 has no tens digit) and 97 is placed in row 9. After the gathering pass, the order of the values in the one-dimensional array is 100, 3 and 97. On the third (hundreds digit) pass, 100 is placed in row 1, 3 is placed in row 0 and 97 is placed in row 0 (after the 3). After this last gathering pass, the original array is in sorted order.

Note that the two-dimensional array of buckets is 10 times the length of the integer array being sorted. This sorting technique provides better performance than a bubble sort, but requires much more memory—the bubble sort requires space for only one additional element of data. This comparison is an example of the space/time trade-off: The bucket sort uses more memory than the bubble sort, but performs better. This version of the bucket sort requires copying all the data back to the original array on each pass. Another possibility is to create a second two-dimensional bucket array and repeatedly swap the data between the two bucket arrays.

19.8 *(Recursive Linear Search)* Modify Fig. 19.2 to use recursive method recursiveLinearSearch to perform a linear search of the array. The method should receive the search key and starting index as arguments. If the search key is found, return its index in the array; otherwise, return –1. Each call to the recursive method should check one index in the array.

19.9 *(Recursive Binary Search)* Modify Fig. 19.4 to use recursive method recursiveBinarySearch to perform a binary search of the array. The method should receive the search key, starting index and ending index as arguments. If the search key is found, return its index in the array. If the search key is not found, return –1.

19.10 *(Quicksort)* The recursive sorting technique called quicksort uses the following basic algorithm for a one-dimensional array of values:

a) *Partitioning Step*: Take the first element of the unsorted array and determine its final location in the sorted array (i.e., all values to the left of the element in the array are less than the element, and all values to the right of the element in the array are greater than the element—we show how to do this below). We now have one element in its proper location and two unsorted subarrays.

b) *Recursive Step*: Perform *Step 1* on each unsorted subarray. Each time *Step 1* is performed on a subarray, another element is placed in its final location of the sorted array, and two unsorted subarrays are created. When a subarray consists of one element, that element is in its final location (because a one-element array is already sorted).

The basic algorithm seems simple enough, but how do we determine the final position of the first element of each subarray? As an example, consider the following set of values (the element in bold is the partitioning element—it will be placed in its final location in the sorted array):

> 37 2 6 4 89 8 10 12 68 45

Starting from the rightmost element of the array, compare each element with 37 until an element less than 37 is found; then swap 37 and that element. The first element less than 37 is 12, so 37 and 12 are swapped. The new array is

> *12* 2 6 4 89 8 10 37 68 45

Element 12 is in italics to indicate that it was just swapped with 37.

Starting from the left of the array, but beginning with the element after 12, compare each element with 37 until an element greater than 37 is found—then swap 37 and that element. The first element greater than 37 is 89, so 37 and 89 are swapped. The new array is

> 12 2 6 4 37 8 10 *89* 68 45

Starting from the right, but beginning with the element before 89, compare each element with 37 until an element less than 37 is found—then swap 37 and that element. The first element less than 37 is 10, so 37 and 10 are swapped. The new array is

> 12 2 6 4 *10* 8 37 89 68 45

Starting from the left, but beginning with the element after 10, compare each element with 37 until an element greater than 37 is found—then swap 37 and that element. There are no more elements greater than 37, so when we compare 37 with itself, we know that 37 has been placed in its final location in the sorted array. Every value to the left of 37 is smaller than it, and every value to the right of 37 is larger than it.

Once the partition has been applied on the previous array, there are two unsorted subarrays. The subarray with values less than 37 contains 12, 2, 6, 4, 10 and 8. The subarray with values greater than 37 contains 89, 68 and 45. The sort continues recursively with both subarrays being partitioned in the same manner as the original array.

Based on the preceding discussion, write recursive method `quickSortHelper` to sort a one-dimensional integer array. The method should receive as arguments a starting index and an ending index on the original array being sorted.

I think this is the most extraordinary collection of talent, of human knowledge, that has ever been gathered together at the White House—with the possible exception of when Thomas Jefferson dined alone.
—John F. Kennedy

The shapes a bright container can contain!
—Theodore Roethke

Journey over all the universe in a map.
—Miguel de Cervantes

Not by age but by capacity is wisdom acquired.
—Titus Maccius Plautus

It is a riddle wrapped in a mystery inside an enigma.
—Winston Churchill

Generic Collections

Objectives

In this chapter you'll learn:

- What collections are.
- To use class `Arrays` for array manipulations.
- To form linked data structures using references, self-referential classes and recursion.
- The type-wrapper classes that enable programs to process primitive data values as objects.
- To use the collections framework (prebuilt data structure) implementations.
- To use collections framework methods (such as `search`, `sort` and `fill`) to manipulate collections.
- To use the collections framework interfaces to program with collections polymorphically.
- To use iterators to "walk through" a collection.
- To use persistent hash tables manipulated with objects of class `Properties`.
- To use synchronization and modifiability wrappers.

20.1 Introduction

In this chapter, we consider the Java **collections framework**, which contains prebuilt data structures, interfaces and methods for manipulating those data structures. Some examples of collections are the cards you hold in a card game, your favorite songs stored in your computer, the members of a sports team and the real-estate records in your local registry of deeds (which map book numbers and page numbers to property owners).

With collections, you use existing data structures, without concern for how they're implemented. This is a marvelous example of code reuse. You can code faster and can expect excellent performance, maximizing execution speed and minimizing memory consumption. In this chapter, we discuss the collections framework interfaces that declare the capabilities of each collection type, the implementation classes, the methods that process the collections, and the so-called **iterators** that "walk through" collections. This chapter provides an introduction to the collections framework. For complete details, visit `java.sun.com/javase/6/docs/technotes/guides/collections/index.html`.

The Java collections framework provides ready-to-go, reusable componentry—you do not need to write your own collection classes, but you can if you wish to. The collections are standardized so that applications can share them easily without concern for the details of their implementation. The collections framework encourages even further reusability. As new data structures and methods are developed that fit this framework, a large base of programmers will already be familiar with the interfaces and methods they implement.

20.2 Collections Overview

A **collection** is a data structure—actually, an object—that can hold references to other objects. Usually, collections contain references to objects that are all of the same type. The collections framework interfaces declare the operations to be performed generically on various types of collections. Figure 20.1 lists some of the interfaces of the collections framework. Several implementations of these interfaces are provided within the framework. You may also provide implementations specific to your own requirements.

Interface	Description
Collection	The root interface in the collections hierarchy from which interfaces Set, Queue and List are derived.
Set	A collection that does not contain duplicates.
List	An ordered collection that can contain duplicate elements.
Map	Associates keys to values and cannot contain duplicate keys.
Queue	Typically a first-in, first-out collection that models a waiting line; other orders can be specified.

Fig. 20.1 | Some collections framework interfaces.

The classes and interfaces of the collections framework are members of package java.util. In the next section, we begin our discussion by examining the collections framework capabilities for array manipulation.

In earlier versions of Java, the classes in the collections framework stored and manipulated Object references, enabling you to store *any* object in a collection. One inconvenient aspect of storing Object references occurs when retrieving them from a collection. A program normally needs to process specific types of objects. As a result, the Object references obtained from a collection typically need to be cast to an appropriate type to allow the program to process the objects correctly.

In Java SE 5, the collections framework was enhanced with the generics capabilities we introduced in Chapter 7 when discussing generic ArrayLists. This means that you can specify the exact type that will be stored in a collection. You also receive the benefits of compile-time type checking—the compiler ensures that you are using appropriate types with your collection and, if not, issues compile-time error messages. Also, once you specify the type stored in a collection, any reference you retrieve from the collection will have the specified type. This eliminates the need for explicit type casts that can throw Class-CastExceptions if the referenced object is not of the appropriate type. In addition, the generic collections are backward compatible with Java code that was written before generics were introduced in Java SE 5.

20.3 Type-Wrapper Classes for Primitive Types

Each primitive type (listed in Appendix D, Primitive Types) has a corresponding **type-wrapper class** (in package java.lang). These classes are called **Boolean**, **Byte**, **Character**, **Double**, **Float**, **Integer**, **Long** and **Short**. Each type-wrapper class enables you to manipulate primitive-type values as objects. The data structures that we reuse or develop in Chapters 20–22 manipulate and share objects—they cannot manipulate variables of primitive types. However, they can manipulate objects of the type-wrapper classes, because every class ultimately derives from Object.

Each of the numeric type-wrapper classes—Byte, Short, Integer, Long, Float and Double—extends class Number. Also, the type-wrapper classes are final classes, so you cannot extend them.

Primitive types do not have methods, so the methods related to a primitive type are located in the corresponding type-wrapper class (e.g., method `parseInt`, which converts a `String` to an `int` value, is located in class `Integer`). If you need to manipulate a primitive value in your program, first refer to the documentation for the type-wrapper classes—the method you need might already be declared.

20.4 Autoboxing and Auto-Unboxing

Prior to Java SE 5, if you wanted to insert a primitive value into a data structure, you had to create a new object of the corresponding type-wrapper class, then insert it in the collection. Similarly, if you wanted to retrieve an object of a type-wrapper class from a collection and manipulate its primitive value, you had to invoke a method on the object to obtain its corresponding primitive-type value. For example, suppose you want to add an `int` to an array that stores only references to `Integer` objects. Prior to Java SE 5, you'd be required to "wrap" an `int` value in an `Integer` object before adding the integer to the array and to "unwrap" the `int` value from the `Integer` object to retrieve the value from the array, as in

```
Integer[] integerArray = new Integer[ 5 ]; // create integerArray

// assign Integer 10 to integerArray[ 0 ]
integerArray[ 0 ] = new Integer( 10 );

// get int value of Integer
int value = integerArray[ 0 ].intValue();
```

Notice that the `int` primitive value 10 is used to initialize an `Integer` object. This achieves the desired result but requires extra code and is cumbersome. We then need to invoke method `intValue` of class `Integer` to obtain the `int` value in the `Integer` object.

Java SE 5 introduced two new conversions—the boxing conversion and the unboxing conversion—to simplify converting between primitive-type values and type-wrapper objects with no additional coding on the part of the programmer. A **boxing conversion** converts a value of a primitive type to an object of the corresponding type-wrapper class. An **unboxing conversion** converts an object of a type-wrapper class to a value of the corresponding primitive type. These conversions can be performed automatically (called **autoboxing** and **auto-unboxing**). For example, the previous statements can be rewritten as

```
Integer[] integerArray = new Integer[ 5 ]; // create integerArray
integerArray[ 0 ] = 10; // assign Integer 10 to integerArray[ 0 ]
int value = integerArray[ 0 ]; // get int value of Integer
```

In this case, autoboxing occurs when assigning an `int` value (10) to `integerArray[0]`, because `integerArray` stores references to `Integer` objects, not `int` values. Auto-unboxing occurs when assigning `integerArray[0]` to `int` variable `value`, because variable `value` stores an `int` value, not a reference to an `Integer` object. Boxing conversions also occur in conditions, which can evaluate to primitive `boolean` values or `Boolean` objects. Many of the examples in Chapters 20–22 use these conversions to store primitive values in and to retrieve them from data structures.

20.5 Interface Collection and Class Collections

Interface **Collection** is the root interface in the collection hierarchy from which interfaces `Set`, `Queue` and `List` are derived. Interface **Set** defines a collection that does not contain duplicates. Interface **Queue** defines a collection that represents a waiting line—typically, insertions are made at the back of a queue and deletions are made from the front, though other orders can be specified. We discuss Queue and Set in Sections 20.9–20.10. Interface Collection contains **bulk operations** (i.e., operations performed on an entire collection) for operations such as adding, clearing and comparing objects (or elements) in a collection. A Collection can also be converted to an array. In addition, interface Collection provides a method that returns an **Iterator** object, which allows a program to walk through the collection and remove elements from the collection during the iteration. We discuss class Iterator in Section 20.6.1. Other methods of interface Collection enable a program to determine a collection's size and whether a collection is empty.

Software Engineering Observation 20.1
Collection is used commonly as a parameter type in methods to allow polymorphic processing of all objects that implement interface Collection.

Software Engineering Observation 20.2
Most collection implementations provide a constructor that takes a Collection argument, thereby allowing a new collection to be constructed containing the elements of the specified collection.

Class **Collections** provides static methods that search, sort and perform other operations on collections. Section 20.7 discusses more about the methods that are available in class Collections. We also cover the **wrapper methods** of class Collections that enable you to treat a collection as a synchronized collection (Section 20.13) or an unmodifiable collection (Section 20.14). Such collections are useful when a client of a class needs to view the elements of a collection, but they should not be allowed to modify the collection by adding and removing elements. Synchronized collections are for use with a powerful capability called multithreading (discussed in Chapter 26). Multithreading enables programs to perform operations in parallel. When two or more threads of a program share a collection, there is the potential for problems to occur. As a brief analogy, consider a traffic intersection. We cannot allow all cars access to one intersection at the same time— if we did, accidents would occur. For this reason, traffic lights are provided to control access to the intersection. Similarly, we can synchronize access to a collection to ensure that only one thread manipulates the collection at a time. The synchronization wrapper methods of class Collections return synchronized versions of collections that can be shared among threads in a program.

20.6 Lists

A List (sometimes called a **sequence**) is an ordered Collection that can contain duplicate elements. Like array indices, List indices are zero based (i.e., the first element's index is zero). In addition to the methods inherited from Collection, List provides methods for manipulating elements via their indices, manipulating a specified range of elements, searching for elements and obtaining a **ListIterator** to access the elements.

Interface List is implemented by several classes, including classes **ArrayList**, **LinkedList** and **Vector**. Autoboxing occurs when you add primitive-type values to objects of these classes, because they store only references to objects. Class ArrayList and Vector are resizable-array implementations of List. Inserting an element between existing elements of an `ArrayList` or `Vector` is an inefficient operation—all elements after the new one must be moved out of the way, which could be an expensive operation in a collection with a large number of elements. A `LinkedList` enables efficient insertion (or removal) of elements in the middle of a collection. We discuss the architecture of linked lists in Chapter 22.

Classes `ArrayList` and `Vector` have nearly identical behaviors. The primary difference between them is that `Vector`s are synchronized by default, whereas `ArrayList`s are not. Also, class `Vector` is from Java 1.0, before the collections framework was added to Java. As such, `Vector` has several methods that are not part of interface `List` and are not implemented in class `ArrayList` but perform identical tasks. For example, `Vector` methods `addElement` and `add` both append an element to a `Vector`, but only method `add` is specified in interface `List` and implemented by `ArrayList`. Unsynchronized collections provide better performance than synchronized ones. For this reason, `ArrayList` is typically preferred over `Vector` in programs that do not share a collection among threads. Separately, the Java collections API provides so-called synchronization wrappers (Section 20.13) that can be used to add synchronization to the unsynchronized collections, and several powerful synchronized collections are available in the Java concurrency APIs.

Performance Tip 20.1

`ArrayList`s behave like `Vector`s without synchronization and therefore execute faster than `Vector`s because `ArrayList`s do not have the overhead of thread synchronization.

Software Engineering Observation 20.3

`LinkedList`s can be used to create stacks, queues and deques (double-ended queues, pronounced "decks"). The collections framework provides implementations of some of these data structures.

The following three subsections demonstrate the `List` and `Collection` capabilities with several examples. Section 20.6.1 focuses on removing elements from an `ArrayList` with an `Iterator`. Section 20.6.2 focuses on `ListIterator` and several `List`- and `LinkedList`-specific methods.

20.6.1 ArrayList and Iterator

Figure 20.2 uses an `ArrayList` (introduced in Section 7.14) to demonstrate several capabilities of interface `Collection`. The program places two `Color` arrays in `ArrayList`s and uses an `Iterator` to remove elements in the second `ArrayList` collection from the first `ArrayList` collection.

```
1   // Fig. 20.2: CollectionTest.java
2   // Collection interface demonstrated via an ArrayList object.
3   import java.util.List;
4   import java.util.ArrayList;
5   import java.util.Collection;
6   import java.util.Iterator;
7
8   public class CollectionTest
9   {
```

Fig. 20.2 | `Collection` interface demonstrated via an `ArrayList` object. (Part 1 of 2.)

```
10      public static void main( String[] args )
11      {
12         // add elements in colors array to list
13         String[] colors = { "MAGENTA", "RED", "WHITE", "BLUE", "CYAN" };
14         List< String > list = new ArrayList< String >();
15
16         for ( String color : colors )
17            list.add( color ); // adds color to end of list
18
19         // add elements in removeColors array to removeList
20         String[] removeColors = { "RED", "WHITE", "BLUE" };
21         List< String > removeList = new ArrayList< String >();
22
23         for ( String color : removeColors )
24            removeList.add( color );
25
26         // output list contents
27         System.out.println( "ArrayList: " );
28
29         for ( int count = 0; count < list.size(); count++ )
30            System.out.printf( "%s ", list.get( count ) );
31
32         // remove from list the colors contained in removeList
33         removeColors( list, removeList );
34
35         // output list contents
36         System.out.println( "\n\nArrayList after calling removeColors: " );
37
38         for ( String color : list )
39            System.out.printf( "%s ", color );
40      } // end main
41
42      // remove colors specified in collection2 from collection1
43      private static void removeColors( Collection< String > collection1,
44         Collection< String > collection2 )
45      {
46         // get iterator
47         Iterator< String > iterator = collection1.iterator();
48
49         // loop while collection has items
50         while ( iterator.hasNext() )
51         {
52            if ( collection2.contains( iterator.next() ) )
53               iterator.remove(); // remove current Color
54         } // end while
55      } // end method removeColors
56   } // end class CollectionTest
```

```
ArrayList:
MAGENTA RED WHITE BLUE CYAN

ArrayList after calling removeColors:
MAGENTA CYAN
```

Fig. 20.2 | Collection interface demonstrated via an ArrayList object. (Part 2 of 2.)

Lines 13 and 20 declare and initialize String arrays colors and removeColors. Lines 14 and 21 create ArrayList<String> objects and assign their references to List<String> variables list and removeList, respectively. Recall that ArrayList is a generic class, so we can specify a type argument (String in this case) to indicate the type of the elements in each list. Note that we refer to the ArrayLists in this example via List variables. This makes our code more flexible and easier to modify. If we later decide that LinkedLists would be more appropriate, we'll need to modify only lines 14 and 21 where we created the ArrayList objects.

Lines 16–17 populate list with Strings stored in array colors, and lines 23–24 populate removeList with Strings stored in array removeColors using **List method add**. Lines 29–30 output each element of list. Line 29 calls **List method size** to get the number of elements in the ArrayList. Line 30 uses **List method get** to retrieve individual element values. Note that lines 29–30 also could have used the enhanced for statement (which we'll demonstrate with collections in other examples).

Line 33 calls method removeColors (lines 43–55), passing list and removeList as arguments. Method removeColors deletes the Strings in removeList from the Strings in list. Lines 38–39 print list's elements after removeColors completes its task.

Method removeColors declares two Collection<String> parameters (lines 43–44) that allow any two Collections containing strings to be passed as arguments to this method. The method accesses the elements of the first Collection (collection1) via an Iterator. Line 47 calls **Collection method iterator** to get an Iterator for the Collection. Note that interfaces Collection and Iterator are generic types. The loop-continuation condition (line 50) calls **Iterator method hasNext** to determine whether the Collection contains more elements. Method hasNext returns true if another element exists and false otherwise.

The if condition in line 52 calls **Iterator method next** to obtain a reference to the next element, then uses method **contains** of the second Collection (collection2) to determine whether collection2 contains the element returned by next. If so, line 53 calls **Iterator method remove** to remove the element from the Collection collection1.

Common Programming Error 20.1

If a collection is modified by one of its methods after an iterator is created for that collection, the iterator immediately becomes invalid—operations performed with the iterator after this point throw ConcurrentModificationExceptions. For this reason, iterators are said to be "fail fast."

20.6.2 LinkedList

Figure 20.3 demonstrates various operations on LinkedLists. The program creates two LinkedLists of Strings. The elements of one List are added to the other. Then all the Strings are converted to uppercase, and a range of elements is deleted.

```
1   // Fig. 20.3: ListTest.java
2   // Lists, LinkedLists and ListIterators.
3   import java.util.List;
4   import java.util.LinkedList;
```

Fig. 20.3 | Lists, LinkedLists and ListIterators. (Part 1 of 3.)

```
5    import java.util.ListIterator;
6
7    public class ListTest
8    {
9       public static void main( String[] args )
10      {
11         // add colors elements to list1
12         String[] colors =
13            { "black", "yellow", "green", "blue", "violet", "silver" };
14         List< String > list1 = new LinkedList< String >();
15
16         for ( String color : colors )
17            list1.add( color );
18
19         // add colors2 elements to list2
20         String[] colors2 =
21            { "gold", "white", "brown", "blue", "gray", "silver" };
22         List< String > list2 = new LinkedList< String >();
23
24         for ( String color : colors2 )
25            list2.add( color );
26
27         list1.addAll( list2 ); // concatenate lists
28         list2 = null; // release resources
29         printList( list1 ); // print list1 elements
30
31         convertToUppercaseStrings( list1 ); // convert to uppercase string
32         printList( list1 ); // print list1 elements
33
34         System.out.print( "\nDeleting elements 4 to 6..." );
35         removeItems( list1, 4, 7 ); // remove items 4-6 from list
36         printList( list1 ); // print list1 elements
37         printReversedList( list1 ); // print list in reverse order
38      } // end main
39
40      // output List contents
41      private static void printList( List< String > list )
42      {
43         System.out.println( "\nlist: " );
44
45         for ( String color : list )
46            System.out.printf( "%s ", color );
47
48         System.out.println();
49      } // end method printList
50
51      // locate String objects and convert to uppercase
52      private static void convertToUppercaseStrings( List< String > list )
53      {
54         ListIterator< String > iterator = list.listIterator();
55
56         while ( iterator.hasNext() )
57         {
```

Fig. 20.3 | Lists, LinkedLists and ListIterators. (Part 2 of 3.)

```
58              String color = iterator.next(); // get item
59              iterator.set( color.toUpperCase() ); // convert to upper case
60          } // end while
61      } // end method convertToUppercaseStrings
62
63      // obtain sublist and use clear method to delete sublist items
64      private static void removeItems( List< String > list,
65          int start, int end )
66      {
67          list.subList( start, end ).clear(); // remove items
68      } // end method removeItems
69
70      // print reversed list
71      private static void printReversedList( List< String > list )
72      {
73          ListIterator< String > iterator = list.listIterator( list.size() );
74
75          System.out.println( "\nReversed List:" );
76
77          // print list in reverse order
78          while ( iterator.hasPrevious() )
79              System.out.printf( "%s ", iterator.previous() );
80      } // end method printReversedList
81  } // end class ListTest
```

```
list:
black yellow green blue violet silver gold white brown blue gray silver

list:
BLACK YELLOW GREEN BLUE VIOLET SILVER GOLD WHITE BROWN BLUE GRAY SILVER

Deleting elements 4 to 6...
list:
BLACK YELLOW GREEN BLUE WHITE BROWN BLUE GRAY SILVER

Reversed List:
SILVER GRAY BLUE BROWN WHITE BLUE GREEN YELLOW BLACK
```

Fig. 20.3 | Lists, LinkedLists and ListIterators. (Part 3 of 3.)

Lines 14 and 22 create LinkedLists list1 and list2 of type String. LinkedList is a generic class that has one type parameter for which we specify the type argument String in this example. Lines 16–17 and 24–25 call List method add to append elements from arrays colors and colors2 to the end of list1 and list2, respectively.

Line 27 calls **List method addAll** to append all elements of list2 to the end of list1. Line 28 sets list2 to null, so the LinkedList to which list2 referred can be garbage collected. Line 29 calls method printList (lines 41–49) to output list list1's contents. Line 31 calls method convertToUppercaseStrings (lines 52–61) to convert each String element to uppercase, then line 32 calls printList again to display the modified Strings. Line 35 calls method removeItems (lines 64–68) to remove the elements starting at index 4 up to, but not including, index 7 of the list. Line 37 calls method printReversedList (lines 71–80) to print the list in reverse order.

Method convertToUppercaseStrings

Method convertToUppercaseStrings (lines 52–61) changes lowercase String elements in its List argument to uppercase Strings. Line 54 calls **List method listIterator** to get the List's **bidirectional iterator** (i.e., one that can traverse a List backward or forward). ListIterator is also a generic class. In this example, the ListIterator references String objects, because method listIterator is called on a List of Strings. Line 56 calls method hasNext to determine whether the List contains another element. Line 58 gets the next String in the List. Line 59 calls **String method toUpperCase** to get an uppercase version of the String and calls **ListIterator method set** to replace the current String to which iterator refers with the String returned by method toUpperCase. Like method toUpperCase, **String method toLowerCase** returns a lowercase version of the String.

Method removeItems

Method removeItems (lines 64–68) removes a range of items from the list. Line 67 calls **List method subList** to obtain a portion of the List (called a **sublist**). This is a so-called **range-view method**, which enables the program to view a portion of the list. The sublist is simply a view into the List on which subList is called. Method subList takes as arguments the beginning and ending index for the sublist. The ending index is not part of the range of the sublist. In this example, line 35 passes 4 for the beginning index and 7 for the ending index to subList. The sublist returned is the set of elements with indices 4 through 6. Next, the program calls **List method clear** on the sublist to remove the elements of the sublist from the List. Any changes made to a sublist are also made to the original List.

Method printReversedList

Method printReversedList (lines 71–80) prints the list backward. Line 73 calls List method listIterator with the starting position as an argument (in our case, the last element in the list) to get a bidirectional iterator for the list. **List method size** returns the number of items in the List. The while condition (line 78) calls **ListIterator's hasPrevious method** to determine whether there are more elements while traversing the list backward. Line 79 calls **ListIterator's previous method** to get the previous element from the list and outputs it to the standard output stream.

Views into Collections and Arrays Method asList

An important feature of the collections framework is the ability to manipulate the elements of one collection type (such as a set) through a different collection type (such as a list), regardless of the collection's internal implementation. The set of public methods through which collections are manipulated is called a **view**.

Class Arrays provides static method **asList** to view an array (sometimes called the **backing array**) as a **List** collection. A List view allows you to manipulate the array as if it were a list. This is useful for adding the elements in an array to a collection (e.g., a LinkedList) and for sorting array elements. The next example demonstrates how to create a LinkedList with a List view of an array, because we cannot pass the array to a LinkedList constructor. Sorting array elements with a List view is demonstrated in Fig. 20.7. Any modifications made through the List view change the array, and any modifications made to the array change the List view. The only operation permitted on the view returned by asList is *set*, which changes the value of the view and the backing array. Any other attempts to change the view (such as adding or removing elements) result in an **UnsupportedOperationException**.

Viewing Arrays as Lists and Converting Lists to Arrays

Figure 20.4 uses Arrays method asList to view an array as a List and uses **List method toArray** to get an array from a LinkedList collection. The program calls method asList to create a List view of an array, which is used to initialize a LinkedList object, then adds a series of strings to the LinkedList and calls method toArray to obtain an array containing references to the Strings.

```
 1   // Fig. 20.4: UsingToArray.java
 2   // Viewing arrays as Lists and converting Lists to arrays.
 3   import java.util.LinkedList;
 4   import java.util.Arrays;
 5
 6   public class UsingToArray
 7   {
 8      // creates a LinkedList, adds elements and converts to array
 9      public static void main( String[] args )
10      {
11         String[] colors = { "black", "blue", "yellow" };
12
13         LinkedList< String > links =
14            new LinkedList< String >( Arrays.asList( colors ) );
15
16         links.addLast( "red" ); // add as last item
17         links.add( "pink" ); // add to the end
18         links.add( 3, "green" ); // add at 3rd index
19         links.addFirst( "cyan" ); // add as first item
20
21         // get LinkedList elements as an array
22         colors = links.toArray( new String[ links.size() ] );
23
24         System.out.println( "colors: " );
25
26         for ( String color : colors )
27            System.out.println( color );
28      } // end main
29   } // end class UsingToArray
```

```
colors:
cyan
black
blue
yellow
green
red
pink
```

Fig. 20.4 | Viewing arrays as Lists and converting Lists to arrays.

Lines 13–14 construct a LinkedList of Strings containing the elements of array colors. Line 14 uses Arrays method asList to return a List view of the array, then uses that to initialize the LinkedList with its constructor that receives a Collection as an argument (a List *is a* Collection). Line 16 calls **LinkedList method addLast** to add "red" to the end of links. Lines 17–18 call **LinkedList method add** to add "pink" as the last element and "green" as the element at index 3 (i.e., the fourth element). Method addLast (line 16) functions identically to method add (line 17). Line 19 calls **LinkedList method addFirst** to add "cyan" as the new first item in the LinkedList. The add operations are permitted because they operate on the LinkedList object, not the view returned by asList. [*Note:* When "cyan" is added as the first element, "green" becomes the fifth element in the LinkedList.]

Line 22 calls the List interface's toArray method to get a String array from links. The array is a copy of the list's elements—modifying the array's contents does not modify the list. The array passed to method toArray is of the same type that you'd like method toArray to return. If the number of elements in that array is greater than or equal to the number of elements in the LinkedList, toArray copies the list's elements into its array argument and returns that array. If the LinkedList has more elements than the number of elements in the array passed to toArray, toArray allocates a new array of the same type it receives as an argument, copies the list's elements into the new array and returns the new array.

Common Programming Error 20.2

Passing an array that contains data to toArray can cause logic errors. If the number of elements in the array is smaller than the number of elements in the list on which toArray is called, a new array is allocated to store the list's elements—without preserving the array argument's elements. If the number of elements in the array is greater than the number of elements in the list, the elements of the array (starting at index zero) are overwritten with the list's elements. Array elements that are not overwritten retain their values.

20.7 Collections Methods

Class Collections provides several high-performance algorithms for manipulating collection elements. The algorithms (Fig. 20.5) are implemented as static methods. The methods sort, binarySearch, reverse, shuffle, fill and copy operate on Lists. Methods min, max, addAll, frequency and disjoint operate on Collections.

Method	Description
sort	Sorts the elements of a List.
binarySearch	Locates an object in a List.
reverse	Reverses the elements of a List.
shuffle	Randomly orders a List's elements.
fill	Sets every List element to refer to a specified object.
copy	Copies references from one List into another.
min	Returns the smallest element in a Collection.
max	Returns the largest element in a Collection.
addAll	Appends all elements in an array to a Collection.
frequency	Calculates how many collection elements are equal to the specified element.
disjoint	Determines whether two collections have no elements in common.

Fig. 20.5 | Collections methods.

Software Engineering Observation 20.4

The collections framework methods are polymorphic. That is, each can operate on objects that implement specific interfaces, regardless of the underlying implementations.

20.7.1 Method sort

Method sort sorts the elements of a List, which must implement the **Comparable** interface. The order is determined by the natural order of the elements' type as implemented by a compareTo method. Method compareTo is declared in interface Comparable and is sometimes called the **natural comparison method**. The sort call may specify as a second argument a **Comparator** object that determines an alternative ordering of the elements.

Sorting in Ascending Order
Figure 20.6 uses Collections method sort to order the elements of a List in ascending order (line 17). Recall that List is a generic type and accepts one type argument that specifies the list element type—line 14 creates list as a List of Strings. Note that lines 15 and 20 each use an implicit call to the list's toString method to output the list contents in the format shown on the second and fourth lines of the output.

```
1   // Fig. 20.6: Sort1.java
2   // Collections method sort.
3   import java.util.List;
4   import java.util.Arrays;
5   import java.util.Collections;
6
7   public class Sort1
8   {
9      public static void main( String[] args )
10     {
11        String[] suits = { "Hearts", "Diamonds", "Clubs", "Spades" };
12
13        // Create and display a list containing the suits array elements
14        List< String > list = Arrays.asList( suits ); // create List
15        System.out.printf( "Unsorted array elements: %s\n", list );
16
17        Collections.sort( list ); // sort ArrayList
18
19        // output list
20        System.out.printf( "Sorted array elements: %s\n", list );
21     } // end main
22  } // end class Sort1
```

```
Unsorted array elements: [Hearts, Diamonds, Clubs, Spades]
Sorted array elements: [Clubs, Diamonds, Hearts, Spades]
```

Fig. 20.6 | Collections method sort.

Sorting in Descending Order
Figure 20.7 sorts the same list of strings used in Fig. 20.6 in descending order. The example introduces the Comparator interface, which is used for sorting a Collection's elements in a different order. Line 18 calls Collections's method sort to order the List in de-

scending order. The static **Collections** method **reverseOrder** returns a Comparator object that orders the collection's elements in reverse order.

```
 1   // Fig. 20.7: Sort2.java
 2   // Using a Comparator object with method sort.
 3   import java.util.List;
 4   import java.util.Arrays;
 5   import java.util.Collections;
 6
 7   public class Sort2
 8   {
 9      public static void main( String[] args )
10      {
11         String[] suits = { "Hearts", "Diamonds", "Clubs", "Spades" };
12
13         // Create and display a list containing the suits array elements
14         List< String > list = Arrays.asList( suits ); // create List
15         System.out.printf( "Unsorted array elements: %s\n", list );
16
17         // sort in descending order using a comparator
18         Collections.sort( list, Collections.reverseOrder() );
19
20         // output List elements
21         System.out.printf( "Sorted list elements: %s\n", list );
22      } // end main
23   } // end class Sort2
```

```
Unsorted array elements: [Hearts, Diamonds, Clubs, Spades]
Sorted list elements: [Spades, Hearts, Diamonds, Clubs]
```

Fig. 20.7 | Collections method sort with a Comparator object.

Sorting with a *Comparator*

Figure 20.8 creates a custom Comparator class, named TimeComparator, that implements interface Comparator to compare two Time2 objects. Class Time2, declared in Fig. 8.5, represents times with hours, minutes and seconds.

```
 1   // Fig. 20.8: TimeComparator.java
 2   // Custom Comparator class that compares two Time2 objects.
 3   import java.util.Comparator;
 4
 5   public class TimeComparator implements Comparator< Time2 >
 6   {
 7      public int compare( Time2 time1, Time2 time2 )
 8      {
 9         int hourCompare = time1.getHour() - time2.getHour(); // compare hour
10
11         // test the hour first
12         if ( hourCompare != 0 )
13            return hourCompare;
14
```

Fig. 20.8 | Custom Comparator class that compares two Time2 objects. (Part 1 of 2.)

```
15          int minuteCompare =
16              time1.getMinute() - time2.getMinute(); // compare minute
17
18          // then test the minute
19          if ( minuteCompare != 0 )
20              return minuteCompare;
21
22          int secondCompare =
23              time1.getSecond() - time2.getSecond(); // compare second
24
25          return secondCompare; // return result of comparing seconds
26      } // end method compare
27  } // end class TimeComparator
```

Fig. 20.8 | Custom `Comparator` class that compares two `Time2` objects. (Part 2 of 2.)

Class `TimeComparator` implements interface `Comparator`, a generic type that takes one type argument (in this case `Time2`). A class that implements `Comparator` must declare a `compare` method that receives two arguments and returns a negative integer if the first argument is less than the second, 0 if the arguments are equal or a positive integer if the first argument is greater than the second. Method `compare` (lines 7–26) performs comparisons between `Time2` objects. Line 9 compares the two hours of the `Time2` objects. If the hours are different (line 12), then we return this value. If this value is positive, then the first hour is greater than the second and the first time is greater than the second. If this value is negative, then the first hour is less than the second and the first time is less than the second. If this value is zero, the hours are the same and we must test the minutes (and maybe the seconds) to determine which time is greater.

Figure 20.9 sorts a list using the custom `Comparator` class `TimeComparator`. Line 11 creates an `ArrayList` of `Time2` objects. Recall that both `ArrayList` and `List` are generic types and accept a type argument that specifies the element type of the collection. Lines 13–17 create five `Time2` objects and add them to this list. Line 23 calls method `sort`, passing it an object of our `TimeComparator` class (Fig. 20.8).

```
1   // Fig. 20.9: Sort3.java
2   // Collections method sort with a custom Comparator object.
3   import java.util.List;
4   import java.util.ArrayList;
5   import java.util.Collections;
6
7   public class Sort3
8   {
9       public static void main( String[] args )
10      {
11          List< Time2 > list = new ArrayList< Time2 >(); // create List
12
13          list.add( new Time2(  6, 24, 34 ) );
14          list.add( new Time2( 18, 14, 58 ) );
15          list.add( new Time2(  6, 05, 34 ) );
16          list.add( new Time2( 12, 14, 58 ) );
17          list.add( new Time2(  6, 24, 22 ) );
```

Fig. 20.9 | `Collections` method `sort` with a custom `Comparator` object. (Part 1 of 2.)

```
18
19        // output List elements
20        System.out.printf( "Unsorted array elements:\n%s\n", list );
21
22        // sort in order using a comparator
23        Collections.sort( list, new TimeComparator() );
24
25        // output List elements
26        System.out.printf( "Sorted list elements:\n%s\n", list );
27    } // end main
28 } // end class Sort3
```

```
Unsorted array elements:
[6:24:34 AM, 6:14:58 PM, 6:05:34 AM, 12:14:58 PM, 6:24:22 AM]
Sorted list elements:
[6:05:34 AM, 6:24:22 AM, 6:24:34 AM, 12:14:58 PM, 6:14:58 PM]
```

Fig. 20.9 | Collections method sort with a custom Comparator object. (Part 2 of 2.)

20.7.2 Method shuffle

Method **shuffle** randomly orders a List's elements. In Chapter 7, we presented a card shuffling and dealing simulation that used a loop to shuffle a deck of cards. In Fig. 20.10, we use method shuffle to shuffle a deck of Card objects that might be used in a card-game simulator.

Class Card (lines 8–41) represents a card in a deck of cards. Each Card has a face and a suit. Lines 10–12 declare two enum types—Face and Suit—which represent the face and the suit of the card, respectively. Method toString (lines 37–40) returns a String containing the face and suit of the Card separated by the string " of ". When an enum constant is converted to a string, the constant's identifier is used as the string representation. Normally we would use all uppercase letters for enum constants. In this example, we chose to use capital letters for only the first letter of each enum constant because we want the card to be displayed with initial capital letters for the face and the suit (e.g., "Ace of Spades").

```
1   // Fig. 20.10: DeckOfCards.java
2   // Card shuffling and dealing with Collections method shuffle.
3   import java.util.List;
4   import java.util.Arrays;
5   import java.util.Collections;
6
7   // class to represent a Card in a deck of cards
8   class Card
9   {
10      public static enum Face { Ace, Deuce, Three, Four, Five, Six,
11         Seven, Eight, Nine, Ten, Jack, Queen, King  };
12      public static enum Suit { Clubs, Diamonds, Hearts, Spades };
13
14      private final Face face; // face of card
15      private final Suit suit; // suit of card
16
```

Fig. 20.10 | Card shuffling and dealing with Collections method shuffle. (Part 1 of 3.)

```
17      // two-argument constructor
18      public Card( Face cardFace, Suit cardSuit )
19      {
20          face = cardFace; // initialize face of card
21          suit = cardSuit; // initialize suit of card
22      } // end two-argument Card constructor
23
24      // return face of the card
25      public Face getFace()
26      {
27          return face;
28      } // end method getFace
29
30      // return suit of Card
31      public Suit getSuit()
32      {
33          return suit;
34      } // end method getSuit
35
36      // return String representation of Card
37      public String toString()
38      {
39          return String.format( "%s of %s", face, suit );
40      } // end method toString
41  } // end class Card
42
43  // class DeckOfCards declaration
44  public class DeckOfCards
45  {
46      private List< Card > list; // declare List that will store Cards
47
48      // set up deck of Cards and shuffle
49      public DeckOfCards()
50      {
51          Card[] deck = new Card[ 52 ];
52          int count = 0; // number of cards
53
54          // populate deck with Card objects
55          for ( Card.Suit suit : Card.Suit.values() )
56          {
57              for ( Card.Face face : Card.Face.values() )
58              {
59                  deck[ count ] = new Card( face, suit );
60                  ++count;
61              } // end for
62          } // end for
63
64          list = Arrays.asList( deck ); // get List
65          Collections.shuffle( list );  // shuffle deck
66      } // end DeckOfCards constructor
67
68      // output deck
69      public void printCards()
70      {
```

Fig. 20.10 | Card shuffling and dealing with Collections method shuffle. (Part 2 of 3.)

```
71          // display 52 cards in two columns
72          for ( int i = 0; i < list.size(); i++ )
73             System.out.printf( "%-19s%s", list.get( i ),
74                ( ( i + 1 ) % 4 == 0 ) ? "\n" : "" );
75       } // end method printCards
76
77       public static void main( String[] args )
78       {
79          DeckOfCards cards = new DeckOfCards();
80          cards.printCards();
81       } // end main
82    } // end class DeckOfCards
```

```
Deuce of Clubs        Six of Spades       Nine of Diamonds    Ten of Hearts
Three of Diamonds     Five of Clubs       Deuce of Diamonds   Seven of Clubs
Three of Spades       Six of Diamonds     King of Clubs       Jack of Hearts
Ten of Spades         King of Diamonds    Eight of Spades     Six of Hearts
Nine of Clubs         Ten of Diamonds     Eight of Diamonds   Eight of Hearts
Ten of Clubs          Five of Hearts      Ace of Clubs        Deuce of Hearts
Queen of Diamonds     Ace of Diamonds     Four of Clubs       Nine of Hearts
Ace of Spades         Deuce of Spades     Ace of Hearts       Jack of Diamonds
Seven of Diamonds     Three of Hearts     Four of Spades      Four of Diamonds
Seven of Spades       King of Hearts      Seven of Hearts     Five of Diamonds
Eight of Clubs        Three of Clubs      Queen of Clubs      Queen of Spades
Six of Clubs          Nine of Spades      Four of Hearts      Jack of Clubs
Five of Spades        King of Spades      Jack of Spades      Queen of Hearts
```

Fig. 20.10 | Card shuffling and dealing with `Collections` method `shuffle`. (Part 3 of 3.)

Lines 55–62 populate the deck array with cards that have unique face and suit combinations. Both Face and Suit are public static enum types of class Card. To use these enum types outside of class Card, you must qualify each enum's type name with the name of the class in which it resides (i.e., Card) and a dot (.) separator. Hence, lines 55 and 57 use Card.Suit and Card.Face to declare the control variables of the for statements. Recall that method values of an enum type returns an array that contains all the constants of the enum type. Lines 55–62 use enhanced for statements to construct 52 new Cards.

The shuffling occurs in line 65, which calls static method shuffle of class Collections to shuffle the elements of the array. Method shuffle requires a List argument, so we must obtain a List view of the array before we can shuffle it. Line 64 invokes static method asList of class Arrays to get a List view of the deck array.

Method printCards (lines 69–75) displays the deck of cards in four columns. In each iteration of the loop, lines 73–74 output a card left justified in a 19-character field followed by either a newline or an empty string based on the number of cards output so far. If the number of cards is divisible by 4, a newline is output; otherwise, the empty string is output.

20.7.3 Methods reverse, fill, copy, max and min

Class Collections provides methods for reversing, filling and copying Lists. **Collections method reverse** reverses the order of the elements in a List, and **method fill** overwrites elements in a List with a specified value. The fill operation is useful for reinitializing a List. **Method copy** takes two arguments—a destination List and a source List. Each source List element is copied to the destination List. The destination List must be at least as long as the source List; otherwise, an IndexOutOfBoundsException occurs. If the destination List is longer, the elements not overwritten are unchanged.

Each method we've seen so far operates on Lists. Methods **min** and **max** each operate on any Collection. Method min returns the smallest element in a Collection, and method max returns the largest element in a Collection. Both of these methods can be called with a Comparator object as a second argument to perform custom comparisons of objects, such as the TimeComparator in Fig. 20.9. Figure 20.11 demonstrates methods reverse, fill, copy, min and max.

```java
 1   // Fig. 20.11: Algorithms1.java
 2   // Collections methods reverse, fill, copy, max and min.
 3   import java.util.List;
 4   import java.util.Arrays;
 5   import java.util.Collections;
 6
 7   public class Algorithms1
 8   {
 9      public static void main( String[] args )
10      {
11         // create and display a List< Character >
12         Character[] letters = { 'P', 'C', 'M' };
13         List< Character > list = Arrays.asList( letters ); // get List
14         System.out.println( "list contains: " );
15         output( list );
16
17         // reverse and display the List< Character >
18         Collections.reverse( list ); // reverse order the elements
19         System.out.println( "\nAfter calling reverse, list contains: " );
20         output( list );
21
22         // create copyList from an array of 3 Characters
23         Character[] lettersCopy = new Character[ 3 ];
24         List< Character > copyList = Arrays.asList( lettersCopy );
25
26         // copy the contents of list into copyList
27         Collections.copy( copyList, list );
28         System.out.println( "\nAfter copying, copyList contains: " );
29         output( copyList );
30
31         // fill list with Rs
32         Collections.fill( list, 'R' );
33         System.out.println( "\nAfter calling fill, list contains: " );
34         output( list );
35      } // end main
36
37      // output List information
38      private static void output( List< Character > listRef )
39      {
40         System.out.print( "The list is: " );
41
42         for ( Character element : listRef )
43            System.out.printf( "%s ", element );
```

Fig. 20.11 | Collections methods reverse, fill, copy, max and min. (Part 1 of 2.)

```
44
45          System.out.printf( "\nMax: %s", Collections.max( listRef ) );
46          System.out.printf( "  Min: %s\n", Collections.min( listRef ) );
47       } // end method output
48    } // end class Algorithms1
```

```
list contains:
The list is: P C M
Max: P  Min: C

After calling reverse, list contains:
The list is: M C P
Max: P  Min: C

After copying, copyList contains:
The list is: M C P
Max: P  Min: C

After calling fill, list contains:
The list is: R R R
Max: R  Min: R
```

Fig. 20.11 | Collections methods reverse, fill, copy, max and min. (Part 2 of 2.)

Line 13 creates List<Character> variable list and initializes it with a List view of the Character array letters. Lines 14–15 output the current contents of the List. Line 18 calls Collections method reverse to reverse the order of list. Method reverse takes one List argument. Since list is a List view of array letters, the array's elements are now in reverse order. The reversed contents are output in lines 19–20. Line 27 uses Collections method copy to copy list's elements into copyList. Changes to copyList do not change letters, because copyList is a separate List that is not a List view of the array letters. Method copy requires two List arguments—the destination List and the source List. Line 32 calls Collections method fill to place the character 'R' in each list element. Because list is a List view of the array letters, this operation changes each element in letters to 'R'. Method fill requires a List for the first argument and an Object for the second argument—in this case, the Object is the boxed version of the character 'R'. Lines 45–46 call Collections methods max and min to find the largest and the smallest element of a Collection, respectively. Recall that interface List extends interface Collection, so a List *is a* Collection.

20.7.4 Method binarySearch

In Section 19.2.2, we studied the high-speed binary search algorithm. This algorithm is built into the Java collections framework as a static **Collections method binarySearch**, which locates an object in a List (e.g., a LinkedList or an ArrayList). If the object is found, its index is returned. If the object is not found, binarySearch returns a negative value. Method binarySearch determines this negative value by first calculating the insertion point and making its sign negative. Then, binarySearch subtracts 1 from the insertion point to obtain the return value, which guarantees that method binarySearch returns positive numbers (>= 0) if and only if the object is found. If multiple elements in the list match the search key, there is no guarantee which one will be located first. Figure 20.12 uses method binarySearch to search for a series of strings in an ArrayList.

```
 1    // Fig. 20.12: BinarySearchTest.java
 2    // Collections method binarySearch.
 3    import java.util.List;
 4    import java.util.Arrays;
 5    import java.util.Collections;
 6    import java.util.ArrayList;
 7
 8    public class BinarySearchTest
 9    {
10       public static void main( String[] args )
11       {
12          // create an ArrayList< String > from the contents of colors array
13          String[] colors = { "red", "white", "blue", "black", "yellow",
14             "purple", "tan", "pink" };
15          List< String > list =
16             new ArrayList< String >( Arrays.asList( colors ) );
17
18          Collections.sort( list ); // sort the ArrayList
19          System.out.printf( "Sorted ArrayList: %s\n", list );
20
21          // search list for various values
22          printSearchResults( list, colors[ 3 ] ); // first item
23          printSearchResults( list, colors[ 0 ] ); // middle item
24          printSearchResults( list, colors[ 7 ] ); // last item
25          printSearchResults( list, "aqua" ); // below lowest
26          printSearchResults( list, "gray" ); // does not exist
27          printSearchResults( list, "teal" ); // does not exist
28       } // end main
29
30       // perform search and display result
31       private static void printSearchResults(
32          List< String > list, String key )
33       {
34          int result = 0;
35
36          System.out.printf( "\nSearching for: %s\n", key );
37          result = Collections.binarySearch( list, key );
38
39          if ( result >= 0 )
40             System.out.printf( "Found at index %d\n", result );
41          else
42             System.out.printf( "Not Found (%d)\n",result );
43       } // end method printSearchResults
44    } // end class BinarySearchTest
```

```
Sorted ArrayList: [black, blue, pink, purple, red, tan, white, yellow]

Searching for: black
Found at index 0

Searching for: red
Found at index 4

Searching for: pink
Found at index 2
```

Fig. 20.12 | Collections method binarySearch. (Part 1 of 2.)

```
Searching for: aqua
Not Found (-1)

Searching for: gray
Not Found (-3)

Searching for: teal
Not Found (-7)
```

Fig. 20.12 | Collections method binarySearch. (Part 2 of 2.)

Lines 15–16 initialize list with an ArrayList containing a copy of the elements in array colors. Collections method binarySearch expects its List argument's elements to be sorted in ascending order, so line 18 uses Collections method sort to sort the list. If the List argument's elements are not sorted, the result of using binarySearch is undefined. Line 19 outputs the sorted list. Lines 22–27 call method printSearchResults (lines 31–43) to perform searches and output the results. Line 37 calls Collections method binarySearch to search list for the specified key. Method binarySearch takes a List as the first argument and an Object as the second argument. Lines 39–42 output the results of the search. An overloaded version of binarySearch takes a Comparator object as its third argument, which specifies how binarySearch should compare the search key to the List's elements.

20.7.5 Methods addAll, frequency and disjoint

Class Collections also provides the methods addAll, frequency and disjoint. **Collections method addAll** takes two arguments—a Collection into which to insert the new element(s) and an array that provides elements to be inserted. **Collections method frequency** takes two arguments—a Collection to be searched and an Object to be searched for in the collection. Method frequency returns the number of times that the second argument appears in the collection. **Collections method disjoint** takes two Collections and returns true if they have no elements in common. Figure 20.13 demonstrates the use of methods addAll, frequency and disjoint.

```
 1   // Fig. 20.13: Algorithms2.java
 2   // Collections methods addAll, frequency and disjoint.
 3   import java.util.ArrayList;
 4   import java.util.List;
 5   import java.util.Arrays;
 6   import java.util.Collections;
 7
 8   public class Algorithms2
 9   {
10      public static void main( String[] args )
11      {
12         // initialize list1 and list2
13         String[] colors = { "red", "white", "yellow", "blue" };
14         List< String > list1 = Arrays.asList( colors );
15         ArrayList< String > list2 = new ArrayList< String >();
```

Fig. 20.13 | Collections methods addAll, frequency and disjoint. (Part 1 of 2.)

```
16
17      list2.add( "black" ); // add "black" to the end of list2
18      list2.add( "red" ); // add "red" to the end of list2
19      list2.add( "green" ); // add "green" to the end of list2
20
21      System.out.print( "Before addAll, list2 contains: " );
22
23      // display elements in list2
24      for ( String s : list2 )
25         System.out.printf( "%s ", s );
26
27      Collections.addAll( list2, colors ); // add colors Strings to list2
28
29      System.out.print( "\nAfter addAll, list2 contains: " );
30
31      // display elements in list2
32      for ( String s : list2 )
33         System.out.printf( "%s ", s );
34
35      // get frequency of "red"
36      int frequency = Collections.frequency( list2, "red" );
37      System.out.printf(
38         "\nFrequency of red in list2: %d\n", frequency );
39
40      // check whether list1 and list2 have elements in common
41      boolean disjoint = Collections.disjoint( list1, list2 );
42
43      System.out.printf( "list1 and list2 %s elements in common\n",
44         ( disjoint ? "do not have" : "have" ) );
45   } // end main
46 } // end class Algorithms2
```

```
Before addAll, list2 contains: black red green
After addAll, list2 contains: black red green red white yellow blue
Frequency of red in list2: 2
list1 and list2 have elements in common
```

Fig. 20.13 | Collections methods addAll, frequency and disjoint. (Part 2 of 2.)

Line 14 initializes list1 with elements in array colors, and lines 17–19 add Strings "black", "red" and "green" to list2. Line 27 invokes method addAll to add elements in array colors to list2. Line 36 gets the frequency of String "red" in list2 using method frequency. Line 41 invokes method disjoint to test whether Collections list1 and list2 have elements in common, which they do in this example.

20.8 Stack Class of Package `java.util`

We introduced the concept of a stack in Section 6.6 when we discussed the method-call stack. In Chapter 22, Custom Generic Data Structures, we'll learn how to build data structures, including linked lists, stacks, queues and trees. In a world of software reuse, rather than building data structures as we need them, we can often take advantage of existing data structures. In this section, we investigate class **Stack** in the Java utilities package (java.util).

Class Stack extends class Vector to implement a stack data structure. Because class Stack extends class Vector, the entire public interface of class Vector is available to clients of class Stack. Figure 20.14 demonstrates several Stack methods. For the details of class Stack, visit java.sun.com/javase/6/docs/api/java/util/Stack.html.

Error-Prevention Tip 20.1

Because Stack extends Vector, all public Vector methods can be called on Stack objects, even if the methods do not represent conventional stack operations. For example, Vector method add can be used to insert an element anywhere in a stack—an operation that could "corrupt" the stack. When manipulating a Stack, only methods push and pop should be used to add elements to and remove elements from the Stack, respectively.

```java
1   // Fig. 20.14: StackTest.java
2   // Stack class of package java.util.
3   import java.util.Stack;
4   import java.util.EmptyStackException;
5
6   public class StackTest
7   {
8      public static void main( String[] args )
9      {
10        Stack< Number > stack = new Stack< Number >(); // create a Stack
11
12        // use push method
13        stack.push( 12L ); // push long value 12L
14        System.out.println( "Pushed 12L" );
15        printStack( stack );
16        stack.push( 34567 ); // push int value 34567
17        System.out.println( "Pushed 34567" );
18        printStack( stack );
19        stack.push( 1.0F ); // push float value 1.0F
20        System.out.println( "Pushed 1.0F" );
21        printStack( stack );
22        stack.push( 1234.5678 ); // push double value 1234.5678
23        System.out.println( "Pushed 1234.5678 " );
24        printStack( stack );
25
26        // remove items from stack
27        try
28        {
29           Number removedObject = null;
30
31           // pop elements from stack
32           while ( true )
33           {
34              removedObject = stack.pop(); // use pop method
35              System.out.printf( "Popped %s\n", removedObject );
36              printStack( stack );
37           } // end while
38        } // end try
39        catch ( EmptyStackException emptyStackException )
40        {
```

Fig. 20.14 | Stack class of package java.util. (Part 1 of 2.)

```
41                    emptyStackException.printStackTrace();
42           } // end catch
43      } // end main
44
45      // display Stack contents
46      private static void printStack( Stack< Number > stack )
47      {
48          if ( stack.isEmpty() )
49              System.out.println( "stack is empty\n" ); // the stack is empty
50          else // stack is not empty
51              System.out.printf( "stack contains: %s (top)\n", stack );
52      } // end method printStack
53   } // end class StackTest
```

```
Pushed 12L
stack contains: [12] (top)
Pushed 34567
stack contains: [12, 34567] (top)
Pushed 1.0F
stack contains: [12, 34567, 1.0] (top)
Pushed 1234.5678
stack contains: [12, 34567, 1.0, 1234.5678] (top)
Popped 1234.5678
stack contains: [12, 34567, 1.0] (top)
Popped 1.0
stack contains: [12, 34567] (top)
Popped 34567
stack contains: [12] (top)
Popped 12
stack is empty

java.util.EmptyStackException
        at java.util.Stack.peek(Unknown Source)
        at java.util.Stack.pop(Unknown Source)
        at StackTest.main(StackTest.java:34)
```

Fig. 20.14 | Stack class of package `java.util`. (Part 2 of 2.)

Line 10 creates an empty Stack of Numbers. Class Number (in package java.lang) is the superclass of the type-wrapper classes for the primitive numeric types (e.g., Integer, Double). By creating a Stack of Numbers, objects of any class that extends Number can be pushed onto the Stack. Lines 13, 16, 19 and 22 each call Stack method **push** to add a Number object to the top of the stack. Note the literals 12L (line 13) and 1.0F (line 19). Any integer literal that has the **suffix L** is a long value. An integer literal without a suffix is an int value. Similarly, any floating-point literal that has the **suffix F** is a float value. A floating-point literal without a suffix is a double value. You can learn more about numeric literals in the *Java Language Specification* at java.sun.com/docs/books/jls/third_edition/html/expressions.html#15.8.1.

An infinite loop (lines 32–37) calls **Stack method pop** to remove the top element of the stack. The method returns a Number reference to the removed element. If there are no elements in the Stack, method pop throws an **EmptyStackException**, which terminates the loop. Class Stack also declares **method peek**. This method returns the top element of the stack without popping the element off the stack.

Method printStack (lines 46–52) displays the stack's contents. The current top of the stack (the last value pushed onto the stack) is the first value printed. Line 48 calls **Stack method isEmpty** (inherited by Stack from class Vector) to determine whether the stack is empty. If it's empty, the method returns true; otherwise, false.

20.9 Class PriorityQueue and Interface Queue

Recall that a queue is a collection that represents a waiting line—typically, insertions are made at the back of a queue and deletions are made from the front. In Section 22.6, we'll discuss and implement a queue data structure. In this section, we investigate Java's **Queue** interface and **PriorityQueue** class from package java.util. Interface Queue extends interface Collection and provides additional operations for inserting, removing and inspecting elements in a queue. PriorityQueue, which implements the Queue interface, orders elements by their natural ordering as specified by Comparable elements' compareTo method or by a Comparator object that is supplied to the constructor.

Class PriorityQueue provides functionality that enables insertions in sorted order into the underlying data structure and deletions from the front of the underlying data structure. When adding elements to a PriorityQueue, the elements are inserted in priority order such that the highest-priority element (i.e., the largest value) will be the first element removed from the PriorityQueue.

The common PriorityQueue operations are **offer** to insert an element at the appropriate location based on priority order, **poll** to remove the highest-priority element of the priority queue (i.e., the head of the queue), **peek** to get a reference to the highest-priority element of the priority queue (without removing that element), **clear** to remove all elements in the priority queue and **size** to get the number of elements in the priority queue. Figure 20.15 demonstrates the PriorityQueue class.

```java
1   // Fig. 20.15: PriorityQueueTest.java
2   // PriorityQueue test program.
3   import java.util.PriorityQueue;
4
5   public class PriorityQueueTest
6   {
7      public static void main( String[] args )
8      {
9         // queue of capacity 11
10        PriorityQueue< Double > queue = new PriorityQueue< Double >();
11
12        // insert elements to queue
13        queue.offer( 3.2 );
14        queue.offer( 9.8 );
15        queue.offer( 5.4 );
16
17        System.out.print( "Polling from queue: " );
18
19        // display elements in queue
20        while ( queue.size() > 0 )
21        {
22           System.out.printf( "%.1f ", queue.peek() ); // view top element
```

Fig. 20.15 | PriorityQueue test program. (Part 1 of 2.)

```
23               queue.poll(); // remove top element
24            } // end while
25         } // end main
26      } // end class PriorityQueueTest
```

```
Polling from queue: 3.2 5.4 9.8
```

Fig. 20.15 | PriorityQueue test program. (Part 2 of 2.)

Line 10 creates a PriorityQueue that stores Doubles with an initial capacity of 11 elements and orders the elements according to the object's natural ordering (the defaults for a PriorityQueue). Note that PriorityQueue is a generic class and that line 10 instantiates a PriorityQueue with a type argument Double. Class PriorityQueue provides five additional constructors. One of these takes an int and a Comparator object to create a PriorityQueue with the initial capacity specified by the int and the ordering by the Comparator. Lines 13–15 use method offer to add elements to the priority queue. Method offer throws a NullPointerException if the program attempts to add a null object to the queue. The loop in lines 20–24 uses method size to determine whether the priority queue is empty (line 20). While there are more elements, line 22 uses PriorityQueue method peek to retrieve the highest-priority element in the queue for output (without actually removing the element from the queue). Line 23 removes the highest-priority element in the queue with method poll, which returns the removed element.

20.10 Sets

A **Set** is an unordered Collection of unique elements (i.e., no duplicate elements). The collections framework contains several Set implementations, including **HashSet** and **TreeSet**. HashSet stores its elements in a hash table, and TreeSet stores its elements in a tree. Hash tables are presented in Section 20.11. Trees are discussed in Section 22.7.

Figure 20.16 uses a HashSet to remove duplicate strings from a List. Recall that both List and Collection are generic types, so line 16 creates a List that contains String objects, and line 20 passes a Collection of Strings to method printNonDuplicates.

```
 1   // Fig. 20.16: SetTest.java
 2   // HashSet used to remove duplicate values from array of strings.
 3   import java.util.List;
 4   import java.util.Arrays;
 5   import java.util.HashSet;
 6   import java.util.Set;
 7   import java.util.Collection;
 8
 9   public class SetTest
10   {
11      public static void main( String[] args )
12      {
13         // create and display a List< String >
14         String[] colors = { "red", "white", "blue", "green", "gray",
15            "orange", "tan", "white", "cyan", "peach", "gray", "orange" };
```

Fig. 20.16 | HashSet used to remove duplicate values from an array of strings. (Part 1 of 2.)

```
16          List< String > list = Arrays.asList( colors );
17          System.out.printf( "List: %s\n", list );
18
19          // eliminate duplicates then print the unique values
20          printNonDuplicates( list );
21       } // end main
22
23       // create a Set from a Collection to eliminate duplicates
24       private static void printNonDuplicates( Collection< String > values )
25       {
26          // create a HashSet
27          Set< String > set = new HashSet< String >( values );
28
29          System.out.print( "\nNonduplicates are: " );
30
31          for ( String value : set )
32             System.out.printf( "%s ", value );
33
34          System.out.println();
35       } // end method printNonDuplicates
36    } // end class SetTest
```

```
List: [red, white, blue, green, gray, orange, tan, white, cyan, peach, gray,
orange]

Nonduplicates are: orange green white peach gray cyan red blue tan
```

Fig. 20.16 | HashSet used to remove duplicate values from an array of strings. (Part 2 of 2.)

Method printNonDuplicates (lines 24–35) takes a Collection argument. Line 27 constructs a HashSet<String> from the Collection<String> argument. By definition, Sets do not contain duplicates, so when the HashSet is constructed, it removes any duplicates in the Collection. Lines 31–32 output elements in the Set.

Sorted Sets
The collections framework also includes the **SortedSet** interface (which extends Set) for sets that maintain their elements in sorted order—either the elements' natural order (e.g., numbers are in ascending order) or an order specified by a Comparator. Class TreeSet implements SortedSet. The program in Fig. 20.17 places strings into a TreeSet. The strings are sorted as they are added to the TreeSet. This example also demonstrates range-view methods, which enable a program to view a portion of a collection.

```
1    // Fig. 20.17: SortedSetTest.java
2    // Using SortedSets and TreeSets.
3    import java.util.Arrays;
4    import java.util.SortedSet;
5    import java.util.TreeSet;
6
7    public class SortedSetTest
8    {
```

Fig. 20.17 | Using SortedSets and TreeSets. (Part 1 of 2.)

```
 9      public static void main( String[] args )
10      {
11         // create TreeSet from array colors
12         String[] colors = { "yellow", "green", "black", "tan", "grey",
13            "white", "orange", "red", "green" };
14         SortedSet< String > tree =
15            new TreeSet< String >( Arrays.asList( colors ) );
16
17         System.out.print( "sorted set: " );
18         printSet( tree ); // output contents of tree
19
20         // get headSet based on "orange"
21         System.out.print( "headSet (\"orange\"):   " );
22         printSet( tree.headSet( "orange" ) );
23
24         // get tailSet based upon "orange"
25         System.out.print( "tailSet (\"orange\"):   " );
26         printSet( tree.tailSet( "orange" ) );
27
28         // get first and last elements
29         System.out.printf( "first: %s\n", tree.first() );
30         System.out.printf( "last : %s\n", tree.last() );
31      } // end main
32
33      // output SortedSet using enhanced for statement
34      private static void printSet( SortedSet< String > set )
35      {
36         for ( String s : set )
37            System.out.printf( "%s ", s );
38
39         System.out.println();
40      } // end method printSet
41   } // end class SortedSetTest
```

```
sorted set: black green grey orange red tan white yellow
headSet ("orange"):   black green grey
tailSet ("orange"):   orange red tan white yellow
first: black
last : yellow
```

Fig. 20.17 | Using SortedSets and TreeSets. (Part 2 of 2.)

Lines 14–15 of create a TreeSet<String> that contains the elements of array colors, then assigns the new TreeSet<String> to SortedSet<String> variable tree. Line 18 outputs the initial set of strings using method printSet (lines 34–40), which we discuss momentarily. Line 22 calls **TreeSet method headSet** to get a subset of the TreeSet in which every element is less than "orange". The view returned from headSet is then output with printSet. If any changes are made to the subset, they'll also be made to the original TreeSet, because the subset returned by headSet is a view of the TreeSet.

Line 26 calls **TreeSet method tailSet** to get a subset in which each element is greater than or equal to "orange", then outputs the result. Any changes made through the tailSet view are made to the original TreeSet. Lines 29–30 call **SortedSet methods first** and **last** to get the smallest and largest elements of the set, respectively.

Method printSet (lines 34–40) accepts a SortedSet as an argument and prints it. Lines 36–37 print each element of the SortedSet using the enhanced for statement.

20.11 Maps

Maps associate keys to values. The keys in a Map must be unique, but the associated values need not be. If a Map contains both unique keys and unique values, it is said to implement a **one-to-one mapping**. If only the keys are unique, the Map is said to implement a **many-to-one mapping**—many keys can map to one value.

Maps differ from Sets in that Maps contain keys and values, whereas Sets contain only values. Three of the several classes that implement interface Map are **Hashtable**, **HashMap** and **TreeMap**. Hashtables and HashMaps store elements in hash tables, and TreeMaps store elements in trees. This section discusses hash tables and provides an example that uses a HashMap to store key/value pairs. **Interface SortedMap** extends Map and maintains its keys in sorted order—either the elements' natural order or an order specified by a Comparator. Class TreeMap implements SortedMap.

Map *Implementation with Hash Tables*
Object-oriented programming languages facilitate creating new types. When a program creates objects of new or existing types, it may need to store and retrieve them efficiently. Storing and retrieving information with arrays is efficient if some aspect of your data directly matches a numerical key value and if the keys are unique and tightly packed. If you have 100 employees with nine-digit social security numbers and you want to store and retrieve employee data by using the social security number as a key, the task will require an array with over 700 million elements because nine-digit Social Security numbers must begin with 001–733 as per the Social Security Administration's website

```
www.socialsecurity.gov/employer/stateweb.htm
```

This is impractical for virtually all applications that use social security numbers as keys. A program having an array that large could achieve high performance for both storing and retrieving employee records by simply using the social security number as the array index.

Numerous applications have this problem—namely, that either the keys are of the wrong type (e.g., not positive integers that correspond to array subscripts) or they are of the right type, but sparsely spread over a huge range. What is needed is a high-speed scheme for converting keys such as social security numbers, inventory part numbers and the like into unique array indices. Then, when an application needs to store something, the scheme could convert the application's key rapidly into an index, and the record could be stored at that slot in the array. Retrieval is accomplished the same way: Once the application has a key for which it wants to retrieve a data record, the application simply applies the conversion to the key—this produces the array index where the data is stored and retrieved.

The scheme we describe here is the basis of a technique called **hashing**. Why the name? When we convert a key into an array index, we literally scramble the bits, forming a kind of "mishmashed," or hashed, number. The number actually has no real significance beyond its usefulness in storing and retrieving a particular data record.

A glitch in the scheme is called a **collision**—this occurs when two different keys "hash into" the same cell (or element) in the array. We cannot store two values in the same space, so we need to find an alternative home for all values beyond the first that hash to a particular array index. There are many schemes for doing this. One is to "hash again" (i.e., to apply another hashing transformation to the key to provide a next candidate cell in the array). The hashing process is designed to distribute the values throughout the table, so the assumption is that an available cell will be found with just a few hashes.

Another scheme uses one hash to locate the first candidate cell. If that cell is occupied, successive cells are searched in order until an available cell is found. Retrieval works the same way: The key is hashed once to determine the initial location and check whether it contains the desired data. If it does, the search is finished. If it does not, successive cells are searched linearly until the desired data is found.

The most popular solution to hash-table collisions is to have each cell of the table be a hash "bucket," typically a linked list of all the key/value pairs that hash to that cell. This is the solution that Java's Hashtable and HashMap classes (from package java.util) implement. Both Hashtable and HashMap implement the Map interface. The primary differences between them are that HashMap is unsynchronized (multiple threads should not modify a HashMap concurrently) and allows null keys and null values.

A hash table's **load factor** affects the performance of hashing schemes. The load factor is the ratio of the number of occupied cells in the hash table to the total number of cells in the hash table. The closer this ratio gets to 1.0, the greater the chance of collisions.

Performance Tip 20.2

The load factor in a hash table is a classic example of a memory-space/execution-time trade-off: By increasing the load factor, we get better memory utilization, but the program runs slower, due to increased hashing collisions. By decreasing the load factor, we get better program speed, because of reduced hashing collisions, but we get poorer memory utilization, because a larger portion of the hash table remains empty.

Hash tables are complex to program. Computer science students study hashing schemes in courses called "Data Structures" and "Algorithms." Classes Hashtable and HashMap enable you to use hashing without having to implement hash-table mechanisms. This concept is profoundly important in our study of object-oriented programming. As discussed in earlier chapters, classes encapsulate and hide complexity (i.e., implementation details) and offer user-friendly interfaces. Properly crafting classes to exhibit such behavior is one of the most valued skills in the field of object-oriented programming. Figure 20.18 uses a HashMap to count the number of occurrences of each word in a string.

```
1   // Fig. 20.18: WordTypeCount.java
2   // Program counts the number of occurrences of each word in a String.
3   import java.util.Map;
4   import java.util.HashMap;
5   import java.util.Set;
6   import java.util.TreeSet;
7   import java.util.Scanner;
8
9   public class WordTypeCount
10  {
11     public static void main( String[] args )
12     {
13        // create HashMap to store String keys and Integer values
14        Map< String, Integer > myMap = new HashMap< String, Integer >();
```

Fig. 20.18 | Program counts the number of occurrences of each word in a String. (Part 1 of 3.)

```
15
16          createMap( myMap ); // create map based on user input
17          displayMap( myMap ); // display map content
18       } // end main
19
20       // create map from user input
21       private static void createMap( Map< String, Integer > map )
22       {
23          Scanner scanner = new Scanner( System.in ); // create scanner
24          System.out.println( "Enter a string:" ); // prompt for user input
25          String input = scanner.nextLine();
26
27          // tokenize the input
28          String[] tokens = input.split( " " );
29
30          // processing input text
31          for ( String token : tokens )
32          {
33             String word = token.toLowerCase(); // get lowercase word
34
35             // if the map contains the word
36             if ( map.containsKey( word ) ) // is word in map
37             {
38                int count = map.get( word ); // get current count
39                map.put( word, count + 1 ); // increment count
40             } // end if
41             else
42                map.put( word, 1 ); // add new word with a count of 1 to map
43          } // end for
44       } // end method createMap
45
46       // display map content
47       private static void displayMap( Map< String, Integer > map )
48       {
49          Set< String > keys = map.keySet(); // get keys
50
51          // sort keys
52          TreeSet< String > sortedKeys = new TreeSet< String >( keys );
53
54          System.out.println( "\nMap contains:\nKey\t\tValue" );
55
56          // generate output for each key in map
57          for ( String key : sortedKeys )
58             System.out.printf( "%-10s%10s\n", key, map.get( key ) );
59
60          System.out.printf(
61             "\nsize: %d\nisEmpty: %b\n", map.size(), map.isEmpty() );
62       } // end method displayMap
63    } // end class WordTypeCount
```

```
Enter a string:
this is a sample sentence with several words this is another sample
sentence with several different words
```

Fig. 20.18 | Program counts the number of occurrences of each word in a String. (Part 2 of 3.)

```
Map contains:
Key             Value
a                 1
another           1
different         1
is                2
sample            2
sentence          2
several           2
this              2
with              2
words             2

size: 10
isEmpty: false
```

Fig. 20.18 | Program counts the number of occurrences of each word in a `String`. (Part 3 of 3.)

Line 14 creates an empty `HashMap` with a default initial capacity (16 elements) and a default load factor (0.75)—these defaults are built into the implementation of `HashMap`. When the number of occupied slots in the `HashMap` becomes greater than the capacity times the load factor, the capacity is doubled automatically. Note that `HashMap` is a generic class that takes two type arguments—the type of key (i.e., `String`) and the type of value (i.e., `Integer`). Recall that the type arguments passed to a generic class must be reference types, hence the second type argument is `Integer`, not `int`.

Line 16 calls method `createMap` (lines 21–44), which uses a map to store the number of occurrences of each word in the sentence. Line 25 obtains the user input, and line 28 tokenizes it. The loop in lines 31–43 converts the next token to lowercase letters (line 33), then calls **Map method `containsKey`** (line 36) to determine whether the word is in the map (and thus has occurred previously in the string). If the `Map` does not contain a mapping for the word, line 42 uses **Map method `put`** to create a new entry in the map, with the word as the key and an `Integer` object containing 1 as the value. Autoboxing occurs when the program passes integer 1 to method `put`, because the map stores the number of occurrences of the word as an `Integer`. If the word does exist in the map, line 38 uses **Map method `get`** to obtain the key's associated value (the count) in the map. Line 39 increments that value and uses put to replace the key's associated value in the map. Method put returns the key's prior associated value, or `null` if the key was not in the map.

Method `displayMap` (lines 47–62) displays all the entries in the map. It uses **HashMap method `keySet`** (line 49) to get a set of the keys. The keys have type `String` in the map, so method keySet returns a generic type Set with type parameter specified to be `String`. Line 52 creates a `TreeSet` of the keys, in which the keys are sorted. The loop in lines 57–58 accesses each key and its value in the map. Line 58 displays each key and its value using format specifier %-10s to left justify each key and format specifier %10s to right justify each value. Note that the keys are displayed in ascending order. Line 61 calls **Map method `size`** to get the number of key/value pairs in the Map. Line 61 also calls **Map method `isEmpty`**, which returns a `boolean` indicating whether the Map is empty.

20.12 Properties Class

A **Properties** object is a persistent `Hashtable` that normally stores key/value pairs of strings—assuming that you use methods **setProperty** and **getProperty** to manipulate the table rather than inherited `Hashtable` methods `put` and `get`. By "persistent," we mean that the `Properties` object can be written to an output stream (possibly a file) and read back in through an input stream. A common use of `Properties` objects in prior versions of Java was to maintain application-configuration data or user preferences for applications. [*Note:* The **Preferences API** (package **java.util.prefs**) is meant to replace this particular use of class `Properties` but is beyond the scope of this book. To learn more, visit `java.sun.com/javase/6/docs/technotes/guides/preferences/index.html`.]

Class `Properties` extends class `Hashtable`. Figure 20.19 demonstrates several methods of class `Properties`.

```java
1   // Fig. 20.19: PropertiesTest.java
2   // Demonstrates class Properties of the java.util package.
3   import java.io.FileOutputStream;
4   import java.io.FileInputStream;
5   import java.io.IOException;
6   import java.util.Properties;
7   import java.util.Set;
8
9   public class PropertiesTest
10  {
11     public static void main( String[] args )
12     {
13        Properties table = new Properties(); // create Properties table
14
15        // set properties
16        table.setProperty( "color", "blue" );
17        table.setProperty( "width", "200" );
18
19        System.out.println( "After setting properties" );
20        listProperties( table ); // display property values
21
22        // replace property value
23        table.setProperty( "color", "red" );
24
25        System.out.println( "After replacing properties" );
26        listProperties( table ); // display property values
27
28        saveProperties( table ); // save properties
29
30        table.clear(); // empty table
31
32        System.out.println( "After clearing properties" );
33        listProperties( table ); // display property values
34
35        loadProperties( table ); // load properties
36
37        // get value of property color
38        Object value = table.getProperty( "color" );
39
40        // check if value is in table
41        if ( value != null )
42           System.out.printf( "Property color's value is %s\n", value );
```

Fig. 20.19 | Properties class of package `java.util`. (Part 1 of 3.)

```
43            else
44               System.out.println( "Property color is not in table" );
45      } // end main
46
47      // save properties to a file
48      private static void saveProperties( Properties props )
49      {
50         // save contents of table
51         try
52         {
53            FileOutputStream output = new FileOutputStream( "props.dat" );
54            props.store( output, "Sample Properties" ); // save properties
55            output.close();
56            System.out.println( "After saving properties" );
57            listProperties( props ); // display property values
58         } // end try
59         catch ( IOException ioException )
60         {
61            ioException.printStackTrace();
62         } // end catch
63      } // end method saveProperties
64
65      // load properties from a file
66      private static void loadProperties( Properties props )
67      {
68         // load contents of table
69         try
70         {
71            FileInputStream input = new FileInputStream( "props.dat" );
72            props.load( input ); // load properties
73            input.close();
74            System.out.println( "After loading properties" );
75            listProperties( props ); // display property values
76         } // end try
77         catch ( IOException ioException )
78         {
79            ioException.printStackTrace();
80         } // end catch
81      } // end method loadProperties
82
83      // output property values
84      private static void listProperties( Properties props )
85      {
86         Set< Object > keys = props.keySet(); // get property names
87
88         // output name/value pairs
89         for ( Object key : keys )
90            System.out.printf(
91               "%s\t%s\n", key, props.getProperty( ( String ) key ) );
92
93         System.out.println();
94      } // end method listProperties
95   } // end class PropertiesTest
```

Fig. 20.19 | Properties class of package `java.util`. (Part 2 of 3.)

```
After setting properties
color    blue
width    200

After replacing properties
color    red
width    200

After saving properties
color    red
width    200

After clearing properties

After loading properties
color    red
width    200

Property color's value is red
```

Fig. 20.19 | `Properties` class of package `java.util`. (Part 3 of 3.)

Line 13 uses the no-argument constructor to create an empty `Properties` table with no default properties. Class `Properties` also provides an overloaded constructor that receives a reference to a `Properties` object containing default property values. Lines 16 and 17 each call `Properties` method `setProperty` to store a value for the specified key. If the key does not exist in the `table`, `setProperty` returns `null`; otherwise, it returns the previous value for that key.

Line 38 calls `Properties` method `getProperty` to locate the value associated with the specified key. If the key is not found in this `Properties` object, `getProperty` returns `null`. An overloaded version of this method receives a second argument that specifies the default value to return if `getProperty` cannot locate the key.

Line 54 calls **`Properties` method `store`** to save the `Properties` object's contents to the `OutputStream` specified as the first argument (in this case, a `FileOutputStream`). The second argument, a `String`, is a description written into the file. **`Properties` method `list`**, which takes a `PrintStream` argument, is useful for displaying the list of properties.

Line 72 calls **`Properties` method `load`** to restore the contents of the `Properties` object from the `InputStream` specified as the first argument (in this case, a `FileInput-Stream`). Line 86 calls `Properties` method `keySet` to obtain a `Set` of the property names. Line 91 obtains the value of a property by passing a key to method `getProperty`.

20.13 Synchronized Collections

In Chapter 26, we discuss multithreading. Except for `Vector` and `Hashtable`, the collections in the collections framework are unsynchronized by default, so they can operate efficiently when multithreading is not required. Because they are unsynchronized, however, concurrent access to a `Collection` by multiple threads could cause indeterminate results or fatal errors. To prevent potential threading problems, **synchronization wrappers** are used for collections that might be accessed by multiple threads. A **wrapper** object receives method calls, adds thread synchronization (to prevent concurrent access to the collection) and delegates the calls to the wrapped collection object. The `Collections` API provides a set of `static` methods for wrapping collections as synchronized versions. Method headers for the synchronization wrappers are listed in Fig. 20.20. Details about these methods are available at java.sun.com/javase/6/docs/api/java/util/Collections.html. All these methods take a generic type and return a synchronized view of the generic type. For example, the following code creates a synchronized List (list2) that stores String objects:

```
List< String > list1 = new ArrayList< String >();
List< String > list2 = Collections.synchronizedList( list1 );
```

public static method headers

```
< T > Collection< T > synchronizedCollection( Collection< T > c )
< T > List< T > synchronizedList( List< T > aList )
< T > Set< T > synchronizedSet( Set< T > s )
< T > SortedSet< T > synchronizedSortedSet( SortedSet< T > s )
< K, V > Map< K, V > synchronizedMap( Map< K, V > m )
< K, V > SortedMap< K, V > synchronizedSortedMap( SortedMap< K, V > m )
```

Fig. 20.20 | Synchronization wrapper methods.

20.14 **Unmodifiable Collections**

The Collections class provides a set of static methods that create **unmodifiable wrappers** for collections. Unmodifiable wrappers throw UnsupportedOperationExceptions if attempts are made to modify the collection. Headers for these methods are listed in Fig. 20.21. Details about these methods are available at java.sun.com/javase/6/docs/api/java/util/Collections.html. All these methods take a generic type and return an unmodifiable view of the generic type. For example, the following code creates an unmodifiable List (list2) that stores String objects:

```
List< String > list1 = new ArrayList< String >();
List< String > list2 = Collections.unmodifiableList( list1 );
```

public static method headers

```
< T > Collection< T > unmodifiableCollection( Collection< T > c )
< T > List< T > unmodifiableList( List< T > aList )
< T > Set< T > unmodifiableSet( Set< T > s )
< T > SortedSet< T > unmodifiableSortedSet( SortedSet< T > s )
< K, V > Map< K, V > unmodifiableMap( Map< K, V > m )
< K, V > SortedMap< K, V > unmodifiableSortedMap( SortedMap< K, V > m )
```

Fig. 20.21 | Unmodifiable wrapper methods.

Software Engineering Observation 20.5

You can use an unmodifiable wrapper to create a collection that offers read-only access to others, while allowing read/write access to yourself. You do this simply by giving others a reference to the unmodifiable wrapper while retaining for yourself a reference to the original collection.

20.15 **Abstract Implementations**

The collections framework provides various abstract implementations of Collection interfaces from which you can quickly "flesh out" complete customized implementations. These abstract implementations include a thin Collection implementation called an **AbstractCollection**, a List implementation that allows random access to its elements called an **AbstractList**, a Map implementation called an **AbstractMap**, a List implementation that allows sequential access to its elements called an **AbstractSequentialList**, a Set implementation called an **AbstractSet** and a Queue implementation called **AbstractQueue**. You can learn more about these classes at java.sun.com/javase/6/docs/api/ java/util/package-summary.html.

To write a custom implementation, you can extend the abstract implementation that best meets your needs, and implement each of the class's abstract methods. Then, if your collection is to be modifiable, override any concrete methods that prevent modification.

20.16 **Wrap-Up**

This chapter introduced the Java collections framework. You learned the collection hierarchy and how to use the collections framework interfaces to program with collections polymorphically. You used classes ArrayList and LinkedList, which both implement the List interface. We presented Java's built-in interfaces and classes for manipulating stacks and queues. You used several predefined methods for manipulating collections. Next, you learned how to use the Set interface and class HashSet to manipulate an unordered collection of unique values. We continued our presentation of sets with the SortedSet interface and class TreeSet for manipulating a sorted collection of unique values. You then learned about Java's interfaces and classes for manipulating key/value pairs—Map, SortedMap, Hashtable, HashMap and TreeMap. We then discussed the specialized Properties class for manipulating key/value pairs of Strings that can be stored to a file and retrieved from a file. Finally, we discussed the Collections class's static methods for obtaining unmodifiable and synchronized views of collections. Chapter 21 demonstrates how to use Java's generics capabilities to implement your own generic methods and classes.

Summary

Section 20.1 Introduction
- The Java collections framework gives you access to prebuilt data structures as well as to methods for manipulating them.

Section 20.2 Collections Overview
- A collection is an object that can hold references to other objects.
- The classes and interfaces of the collections framework are in package java.util.

Section 20.3 Type-Wrapper Classes for Primitive Types
- Type-wrapper classes (e.g., Integer, Double, Boolean) enable programmers to manipulate primitive-type values as objects. Objects of these classes can be used in collections.

Section 20.4 Autoboxing and Auto-Unboxing

- Boxing converts a primitive value to an object of the corresponding type-wrapper class. Unboxing converts a type-wrapper object to the corresponding primitive value.

- Java performs boxing conversions and unboxing conversions automatically.

Section 20.5 Interface `Collection` *and Class* `Collections`

- Interface `Collection` is the root interface in the collection hierarchy. Interfaces `Set` and `List` extend `Collection`. Interface `Collection` contains operations for adding, clearing, comparing and retaining objects in a collection, and method `iterator` to obtain a collection's `Iterator`.

- Class `Collections` provides `static` methods for manipulating collections.

Section 20.6 Lists

- A `List` is an ordered `Collection` that can contain duplicate elements.

- Interface `List` is implemented by classes `ArrayList`, `LinkedList` and `Vector`. `ArrayList` is a resizable-array implementation of a `List`. `LinkedList` is a linked list implementation of a `List`.

- `Iterator` method `hasNext` determines whether a `Collection` contains another element. Method `next` returns a reference to the next object in the `Collection` and advances the `Iterator`.

- Method `subList` returns a view into a `List`. Changes made to this view are also made to the `List`.

- Method `clear` removes elements from a `List`.

- Method `toArray` returns the contents of a collection as an array.

Section 20.7 Collections Methods

- Algorithms `sort`, `binarySearch`, `reverse`, `shuffle`, `fill`, `copy`, `addAll`, `frequency` and `disjoint` operate on `List`s. Algorithms `min` and `max` operate on `Collection`s.

- Algorithm `addAll` appends all the elements in an array to a collection, `frequency` calculates how many elements in the collection are equal to the specified element, and `disjoint` determines whether two collections have elements in common.

- Algorithms `min` and `max` find the smallest and largest items in a collection.

- The `Comparator` interface provides a means of sorting a `Collection`'s elements in an order other than their natural order.

- `Collections` method `reverseOrder` returns a `Comparator` object that can be used with `sort` to sort a collection's elements in reverse order.

- Algorithm `shuffle` randomly orders the elements of a `List`.

- Algorithm `binarySearch` locates an `Object` in a sorted `List`.

Section 20.8 **Stack** *Class of Package* `java.util`

- Class `Stack` extends `Vector`. `Stack` method `push` adds its argument to the top of the stack. Method `pop` removes the top element of the stack. Method `peek` returns a reference to the top element without removing it. `Stack` method `isEmpty` determines whether the stack is empty.

Section 20.9 Class **PriorityQueue** *and Interface* **Queue**

- Interface `Queue` extends interface `Collection` and provides additional operations for inserting, removing and inspecting elements in a queue.

- `PriorityQueue` implements interface `Queue` and orders elements by their natural ordering or by a `Comparator` object that is supplied to the constructor.

- `PriorityQueue` method `offer` inserts an element at the appropriate location based on priority order. Method `poll` removes the highest-priority element of the priority queue. Method `peek` gets a reference to the highest-priority element of the priority queue. Method clear removes all elements in the priority queue. Method size gets the number of elements in the priority queue.

Section 20.10 Sets

- A Set is an unordered Collection that contains no duplicate elements. HashSet stores its elements in a hash table. TreeSet stores its elements in a tree.
- Interface SortedSet extends Set and represents a set that maintains its elements in sorted order. Class TreeSet implements SortedSet.
- TreeSet method headSet gets a TreeSet view containing elements that are less than a specified element. Method tailSet gets a TreeSet view containing elements that are greater than or equal to a specified element. Any changes made to these views are made to the original TreeSet.

Section 20.11 Maps

- Maps store key/value pairs and cannot contain duplicate keys. HashMaps and Hashtables store elements in a hash table, and TreeMaps store elements in a tree.
- HashMap takes two type arguments—the type of key and the type of value.
- HashMap method put adds a key and a value into a HashMap. Method get locates the value associated with the specified key. Method isEmpty determines whether the map is empty.
- HashMap method keySet returns a set of the keys. Map method size returns the number of key/value pairs in the Map.
- Interface SortedMap extends Map and represents a map that maintains its keys in sorted order. Class TreeMap implements SortedMap.

Section 20.12 *Properties Class*

- A Properties object is a persistent Hashtable object. Class Properties extends Hashtable.
- The Properties no-argument constructor creates an empty Properties table. An overloaded constructor receives a Properties object containing default property values.
- Properties method setProperty specifies the value associated with its key argument. Method getProperty locates the value of the key specified as an argument. Method store saves the contents of a Properties object to specified OutputStream. Method load restores the contents of a Properties object from the specified InputStream.

Section 20.13 Synchronized Collections

- Collections from the collections framework are unsynchronized. Synchronization wrappers are provided for collections that can be accessed by multiple threads simultaneously.

Section 20.14 Unmodifiable Collections

- Class Collections provides a set of public static methods for converting collections to unmodifiable versions. Unmodifiable wrappers throw UnsupportedOperationExceptions if attempts are made to modify the collection.

Section 20.15 Abstract Implementations

- The collections framework provides various abstract implementations of collection interfaces from which you can quickly flesh out complete customized implementations.

Terminology

AbstractCollection class 879
AbstractList class 879
AbstractMap class 879

AbstractQueue class 879
AbstractSequentialList class 879
AbstractSet class 879

Self-Review Exercises

20.1 Fill in the blanks in each of the following statements:
- a) A(n) _____ is used to iterate through a collection and can remove elements from the collection during the iteration.
- b) An element in a List can be accessed by using the element's _____.
- c) Assuming that myArray contains references to Double objects, _____ occurs when the statement "myArray[0] = 1.25;" executes.
- d) Java classes _____ and _____ provide the capabilities of arraylike data structures that can resize themselves dynamically.
- e) If you do not specify a capacity increment, the system will _____ the size of the Vector each time additional capacity is needed.
- f) You can use a(n) _____ to create a collection that offers only read-only access to others while allowing read/write access to yourself.
- g) Assuming that myArray contains references to Double objects, _____ occurs when the statement "double number = myArray[0];" executes.
- h) Algorithm _____ of Collections determines whether two collections have elements in common.

20.2 Determine whether each statement is *true* or *false*. If *false*, explain why.
- a) Values of primitive types may be stored directly in a collection.
- b) A Set can contain duplicate values.
- c) A Map can contain duplicate keys.
- d) A LinkedList can contain duplicate values.
- e) Collections is an interface.
- f) Iterators can remove elements.
- g) With hashing, as the load factor increases, the chance of collisions decreases.
- h) A PriorityQueue permits null elements.

Answers to Self-Review Exercises

20.1 a) Iterator. b) index. c) autoboxing. d) ArrayList, Vector. e) double. f) unmodifiable wrapper. g) auto-unboxing. h) disjoint.

20.2
- a) False. Autoboxing occurs when adding a primitive type to a collection, which means the primitive type is converted to its corresponding type-wrapper class.
- b) False. A Set cannot contain duplicate values.
- c) False. A Map cannot contain duplicate keys.
- d) True.
- e) False. Collections is a class; Collection is an interface.
- f) True.
- g) False. As the load factor increases, fewer slots are available relative to the total number of slots, so the chance of a collision increases.
- h) False. Attempting to insert a null element causes a NullPointerException.

Execises

20.3   Explain briefly the operation of each of the following methods of class `Vector`:
   a) `add`
   b) `set`
   c) `remove`
   d) `removeAllElements`
   e) `removeElementAt`
   f) `firstElement`
   g) `lastElement`
   h) `contains`
   i) `indexOf`
   j) `size`
   k) `capacity`

20.4   Explain why inserting additional elements into a `Vector` object whose current size is less than its capacity is a relatively fast operation and why inserting additional elements into a `Vector` object whose current size is at capacity is a relatively slow operation.

20.5   Briefly answer the following questions:
   a) What is the primary difference between a `Set` and a `Map`?
   b) What happens when you add a primitive type (e.g., `double`) value to a collection?
   c) Can you print all the elements in a collection without using an `Iterator`? If yes, how?

20.6   Explain briefly the operation of each of the following `Iterator`-related methods:
   a) `iterator`
   b) `hasNext`
   c) `next`

20.7   Explain briefly the operation of each of the following methods of class `HashMap`:
   a) `put`
   b) `get`
   c) `isEmpty`
   d) `containsKey`
   e) `keySet`

20.8   Explain the operation of each of the following methods of the `Properties` class:
   a) `load`
   b) `store`
   c) `getProperty`
   d) `list`

20.9   Rewrite lines 16–25 in Fig. 20.3 to be more concise by using the `asList` method and the `LinkedList` constructor that takes a `Collection` argument.

20.10   *(Counting Letters)* Modify the program of Fig. 20.18 to count the number of occurrences of each letter rather than of each word. For example, the string `"HELLO THERE"` contains two `H`s, three `E`s, two `L`s, one `O`, one `T` and one `R`. Display the results.

20.11   *(Counting Duplicate Words)* Write a program that determines and prints the number of duplicate words in a sentence. Treat uppercase and lowercase letters the same. Ignore punctuation.

20.12   *(Inserting Elements in a **LinkedList** in Sorted Order)* Write a program that inserts 25 random integers from 0 to 100 in order into a `LinkedList` object. The program should sort the elements, then calculate the sum of the elements and the floating-point average of the elements.

20.13 *(Copying and Reversing LinkedLists)* Write a program that creates a LinkedList object of 10 characters, then creates a second LinkedList object containing a copy of the first list, but in reverse order.

20.14 *(Prime Numbers and Prime Factors)* Write a program that takes a whole number input from a user and determines whether it's prime. If the number is not prime, display its unique prime factors. Remember that a prime number's factors are only 1 and the prime number itself. Every number that is not prime has a unique prime factorization. For example, consider the number 54. The prime factors of 54 are 2, 3, 3 and 3. When the values are multiplied together, the result is 54. For the number 54, the prime factors output should be 2 and 3. Use Sets as part of your solution.

20.15 *(Sorting Words with a TreeSet)* Write a program that uses a String method split to tokenize a line of text input by the user and places each token in a TreeSet. Print the elements of the TreeSet. [*Note:* This should cause the elements to be printed in ascending sorted order.]

20.16 *(Changing a PriorityQueue's Sort Order)* The output of Fig. 20.15 (PriorityQueueTest) shows that PriorityQueue orders Double elements in ascending order. Rewrite Fig. 20.15 so that it orders Double elements in descending order (i.e., 9.8 should be the highest-priority element rather than 3.2).

Every man of genius sees the world at a different angle from his fellows.
—Havelock Ellis

…our special individuality, as distinguished from our generic humanity.
—Oliver Wendell Holmes, Sr.

Born under one law, to another bound.
—Lord Brooke

You deal in the raw material of opinion, and, if my convictions have any validity, opinion ultimately governs the world.
—Woodrow Wilson

Generic Classes and Methods

Objectives

In this chapter you'll learn:

- To create generic methods that perform identical tasks on arguments of different types.
- To create a generic **Stack** class that can be used to store objects of any class or interface type.
- To understand how to overload generic methods with nongeneric methods or with other generic methods.
- To understand raw types and how they help achieve backward compatibility.
- To use wildcards when precise type information about a parameter is not required in the method body.
- The relationship between generics and inheritance.

21.1 Introduction

You've used existing generic methods and classes in Chapters 7 and 20. In this chapter, you'll learn how to write your own. You'll also learn the relationships between generics and other Java features, such as overloading and inheritance.

It would be nice if we could write a single sort method to sort the elements in an Integer array, a String array or an array of any type that supports ordering (i.e., its elements can be compared). It would also be nice if we could write a single Stack class that could be used as a Stack of integers, a Stack of floating-point numbers, a Stack of Strings or a Stack of any other type. It would be even nicer if we could detect type mismatches at compile time—known as **compile-time type safety**. For example, if a Stack stores only integers, attempting to push a String onto that Stack should issue a *compile-time* error.

This chapter discusses **generics**, which provide the means to create the general models mentioned above. **Generic methods** and **generic classes** (and interfaces) enable you to specify, with a single method declaration, a set of related methods, or with a single class declaration, a set of related types, respectively. Generics also provide compile-time type safety that allows you to catch invalid types at compile time.

We might write a generic method for sorting an array of objects, then invoke the generic method with Integer arrays, Double arrays, String arrays and so on, to sort the array elements. The compiler could perform type checking to ensure that the array passed to the sorting method contains the same type elements. We might write a single generic Stack class that manipulates a stack of objects, then instantiate Stack objects for a stack of Integers, a stack of Doubles, a stack of Strings and so on. The compiler could perform type checking to ensure that the Stack stores elements of the same type.

> **Software Engineering Observation 21.1**
> *Generic methods and classes are among Java's most powerful capabilities for software reuse with compile-time type safety.*

21.2 Motivation for Generic Methods

Overloaded methods are often used to perform similar operations on different types of data. To motivate generic methods, let's begin with an example (Fig. 21.1) containing overloaded printArray methods (lines 21–28, lines 31–38 and lines 41–48) that print the String representations of the elements of an Integer array, a Double array and a Character array, respectively. We could have used arrays of primitive types int, double and char. We are using arrays of the type-wrapper classes to set up our generic method example, because only reference types can be used with generic methods and classes.

```java
1   // Fig. 21.1: OverloadedMethods.java
2   // Printing array elements using overloaded methods.
3   public class OverloadedMethods
4   {
5      public static void main( String[] args )
6      {
7         // create arrays of Integer, Double and Character
8         Integer[] integerArray = { 1, 2, 3, 4, 5, 6 };
9         Double[] doubleArray = { 1.1, 2.2, 3.3, 4.4, 5.5, 6.6, 7.7 };
10        Character[] characterArray = { 'H', 'E', 'L', 'L', 'O' };
11
12        System.out.println( "Array integerArray contains:" );
13        printArray( integerArray ); // pass an Integer array
14        System.out.println( "\nArray doubleArray contains:" );
15        printArray( doubleArray ); // pass a Double array
16        System.out.println( "\nArray characterArray contains:" );
17        printArray( characterArray ); // pass a Character array
18     } // end main
19
20     // method printArray to print Integer array
21     public static void printArray( Integer[] inputArray )
22     {
23        // display array elements
24        for ( Integer element : inputArray )
25           System.out.printf( "%s ", element );
26
27        System.out.println();
28     } // end method printArray
29
30     // method printArray to print Double array
31     public static void printArray( Double[] inputArray )
32     {
33        // display array elements
34        for ( Double element : inputArray )
35           System.out.printf( "%s ", element );
36
37        System.out.println();
38     } // end method printArray
39
40     // method printArray to print Character array
41     public static void printArray( Character[] inputArray )
42     {
43        // display array elements
44        for ( Character element : inputArray )
45           System.out.printf( "%s ", element );
46
47        System.out.println();
48     } // end method printArray
49  } // end class OverloadedMethods
```

Fig. 21.1 | Printing array elements using overloaded methods. (Part 1 of 2.)

```
Array integerArray contains:
1 2 3 4 5 6

Array doubleArray contains:
1.1 2.2 3.3 4.4 5.5 6.6 7.7

Array characterArray contains:
H E L L O
```

Fig. 21.1 | Printing array elements using overloaded methods. (Part 2 of 2.)

The program begins by declaring and initializing three arrays—six-element Integer array integerArray (line 8), seven-element Double array doubleArray (line 9) and five-element Character array characterArray (line 10). Then, lines 12–17 display the contents of each array.

When the compiler encounters a method call, it attempts to locate a method declaration with the same name and parameters that match the argument types in the call. In this example, each printArray call matches one of the printArray method declarations. For example, line 13 calls printArray with integerArray as its argument. The compiler determines the argument's type (i.e., Integer[]) and attempts to locate a printArray method that specifies an Integer[] parameter (lines 21–28), then sets up a call to that method. Similarly, when the compiler encounters the call at line 15, it determines the argument's type (i.e., Double[]), then attempts to locate a printArray method that specifies a Double[] parameter (lines 31–38), then sets up a call to that method. Finally, when the compiler encounters the call at line 17, it determines the argument's type (i.e., Character[]), then attempts to locate a printArray method that specifies a Character[] parameter (lines 41–48), then sets up a call to that method.

Study each printArray method. Note that the type array element type appears in each method's header (lines 21, 31 and 41) and for-statement header (lines 24, 34 and 44). If we were to replace the element types in each method with a generic name—T by convention—then all three methods would look like the one in Fig. 21.2. It appears that if we can replace the array element type in each of the three methods with a single generic type, then we should be able to declare one printArray method that can display the String representations of the elements of any array that contains objects. The method in Fig. 21.2 is similar to the generic printArray method declaration we discuss in Section 21.3.

```
1   public static void printArray( T[] inputArray )
2   {
3      // display array elements
4      for ( T element : inputArray )
5         System.out.printf( "%s ", element );
6
7      System.out.println();
8   } // end method printArray
```

Fig. 21.2 | printArray method in which actual type names are replaced by convention with the generic name T.

21.3 Generic Methods: Implementation and Compile-Time Translation

If the operations performed by several overloaded methods are identical for each argument type, the overloaded methods can be more compactly and conveniently coded using a generic method. You can write a single generic method declaration that can be called with arguments of different types. Based on the types of the arguments passed to the generic method, the compiler handles each method call appropriately.

Figure 21.3 reimplements the application of Fig. 21.1 using a generic printArray method (lines 22–29). Note that the printArray method calls in lines 14, 16 and 18 are identical to those of Fig. 21.1 (lines 14, 16 and 18) and that the outputs of the two applications are identical. This dramatically demonstrates the expressive power of generics.

```java
1   // Fig. 21.3: GenericMethodTest.java
2   // Printing array elements using generic method printArray.
3
4   public class GenericMethodTest
5   {
6      public static void main( String[] args )
7      {
8         // create arrays of Integer, Double and Character
9         Integer[] intArray = { 1, 2, 3, 4, 5 };
10        Double[] doubleArray = { 1.1, 2.2, 3.3, 4.4, 5.5, 6.6, 7.7 };
11        Character[] charArray = { 'H', 'E', 'L', 'L', 'O' };
12
13        System.out.println( "Array integerArray contains:" );
14        printArray( integerArray ); // pass an Integer array
15        System.out.println( "\nArray doubleArray contains:" );
16        printArray( doubleArray ); // pass a Double array
17        System.out.println( "\nArray characterArray contains:" );
18        printArray( characterArray ); // pass a Character array
19     } // end main
20
21     // generic method printArray
22     public static < T > void printArray( T[] inputArray )
23     {
24        // display array elements
25        for ( T element : inputArray )
26           System.out.printf( "%s ", element );
27
28        System.out.println();
29     } // end method printArray
30  } // end class GenericMethodTest
```

```
Array integerArray contains:
1 2 3 4 5 6

Array doubleArray contains:
1.1 2.2 3.3 4.4 5.5 6.6 7.7

Array characterArray contains:
H E L L O
```

Fig. 21.3 | Printing array elements using generic method printArray.

Line 22 begins method printArray's declaration. All generic method declarations have a **type-parameter section** delimited by **angle brackets** (< and >) that precedes the method's return type (< T > in this example). Each type-parameter section contains one or more **type parameters** (also called **formal type parameters**), separated by commas. A type parameter, also known as a **type variable**, is an identifier that specifies a generic type name. The type parameters can be used to declare the return type, parameter types and local variable types in a generic method declaration, and they act as placeholders for the types of the arguments passed to the generic method, which are known as **actual type arguments**. A generic method's body is declared like that of any other method. Note that type parameters can represent only reference types—not primitive types (like int, double and char). Note, too, that the type-parameter names throughout the method declaration must match those declared in the type-parameter section. For example, line 25 declares element as type T, which matches the type parameter (T) declared in line 22. Also, a type parameter can be declared only once in the type-parameter section but can appear more than once in the method's parameter list. For example, the type-parameter name T appears twice in the following method's parameter list:

```
public static < T > void printTwoArrays( T[] array1, T[] array2 )
```

Type-parameter names need not be unique among different generic methods.

Common Programming Error 21.1
When declaring a generic method, failing to place a type-parameter section before the return type of a method is a syntax error—the compiler will not understand the type-parameter names when they're encountered in the method.

Method printArray's type-parameter section declares type parameter T as the placeholder for the array element type that printArray will output. Note that T appears in the parameter list as the array element type (line 22). The for-statement header (line 25) also uses T as the element type. These are the same two locations where the overloaded print-Array methods of Fig. 21.1 specified Integer, Double or Character as the array element type. The remainder of printArray is identical to the versions presented in Fig. 21.1.

Good Programming Practice 21.1
It's recommended that type parameters be specified as individual capital letters. Typically, a type parameter that represents an array element's type (or other collection) is named T.

As in Fig. 21.1, the program begins by declaring and initializing six-element Integer array integerArray (line 9), seven-element Double array doubleArray (line 10) and five-element Character array characterArray (line 11). Then the program outputs each array by calling printArray (lines 14, 16 and 18)—once with argument integerArray, once with argument doubleArray and once with argument characterArray.

When the compiler encounters line 14, it first determines argument integerArray's type (i.e., Integer[]) and attempts to locate a method named printArray that specifies a single Integer[] parameter. There is no such method in this example. Next, the compiler determines whether there is a generic method named printArray that specifies a single array parameter and uses a type parameter to represent the array element type. The compiler determines that printArray (lines 22–29) is a match and sets up a call to the method. The same process is repeated for the calls to method printArray at lines 16 and 18.

Common Programming Error 21.2

If the compiler cannot match a method call to a nongeneric or a generic method declaration, a compilation error occurs.

Common Programming Error 21.3

If the compiler does not find a method declaration that matches a method call exactly, but does find two or more generic methods that can satisfy the method call, a compilation error occurs.

In addition to setting up the method calls, the compiler also determines whether the operations in the method body can be applied to elements of the type stored in the array argument. The only operation performed on the array elements in this example is to output their String representation. Line 26 performs an implicit toString call on every element. To work with generics, every element of the array must be an object of a class or interface type. Since all objects have a toString method, the compiler is satisfied that line 26 performs a valid operation for any object in printArray's array argument. The toString methods of classes Integer, Double and Character return the String representation of the underlying int, double or char value, respectively.

Erasure at Compilation Time

When the compiler translates generic method printArray into Java bytecodes, it removes the type-parameter section and replaces the type parameters with actual types. This process is known as **erasure**. By default all generic types are replaced with type Object. So the compiled version of method printArray appears as shown in Fig. 21.4—there is only one copy of this code, which is used for all printArray calls in the example. This is quite different from other, similar mechanisms, such as C++'s templates, in which a separate copy of the source code is generated and compiled for every type passed as an argument to the method. As you'll see in Section 21.4, the translation and compilation of generics is a bit more involved than what we've discussed in this section.

By declaring printArray as a generic method in Fig. 21.3, we eliminated the need for the overloaded methods of Fig. 21.1, saving 19 lines of code and creating a reusable method that can output the String representations of the elements in any array that contains objects. However, this particular example could have simply declared the printArray method as shown in Fig. 21.4, using an Object array as the parameter. This would have yielded the same results, because any Object can be output as a String. In a generic method, the benefits become apparent when the method also uses a type parameter as the method's return type, as we demonstrate in the next section.

```
1   public static void printArray( Object[] inputArray )
2   {
3      // display array elements
4      for ( Object element : inputArray )
5         System.out.printf( "%s ", element );
6
7      System.out.println();
8   } // end method printArray
```

Fig. 21.4 | Generic method printArray after erasure is performed by the compiler.

21.4 Additional Compile-Time Translation Issues: Methods That Use a Type Parameter as the Return Type

Let's consider a generic method example in which type parameters are used in the return type and in the parameter list (Fig. 21.5). The application uses a generic method `maximum` to determine and return the largest of its three arguments of the same type. Unfortunately, the relational operator > cannot be used with reference types. However, it's possible to compare two objects of the same class if that class implements the generic **interface Comparable\<T>** (package java.lang). All the type-wrapper classes for primitive types implement this interface. Like generic classes, **generic interfaces** enable you to specify, with a single interface declaration, a set of related types. Comparable\<T> objects have a **compareTo** method. For example, if we have two Integer objects, integer1 and integer2, they can be compared with the expression:

```
integer1.compareTo( integer2 )
```

It's your responsibility when you declare a class that implements Comparable\<T> to declare method compareTo such that it compares the contents of two objects of that class and returns the comparison results. The method must return 0 if the objects are equal, a negative integer if object1 is less than object2 or a positive integer if object1 is greater than object2. For example, class Integer's compareTo method compares the int values stored in two Integer objects. A benefit of implementing interface Comparable\<T> is that Comparable\<T> objects can be used with the sorting and searching methods of class Collections (package java.util). We discussed those methods in Chapter 20, Generic Collections. In this example, we'll use method compareTo in method maximum to help determine the largest value.

```java
1   // Fig. 21.5: MaximumTest.java
2   // Generic method maximum returns the largest of three objects.
3
4   public class MaximumTest
5   {
6      public static void main( String[] args )
7      {
8         System.out.printf( "Maximum of %d, %d and %d is %d\n\n", 3, 4, 5,
9            maximum( 3, 4, 5 ) );
10        System.out.printf( "Maximum of %.1f, %.1f and %.1f is %.1f\n\n",
11           6.6, 8.8, 7.7, maximum( 6.6, 8.8, 7.7 ) );
12        System.out.printf( "Maximum of %s, %s and %s is %s\n", "pear",
13           "apple", "orange", maximum( "pear", "apple", "orange" ) );
14     } // end main
15
16     // determines the largest of three Comparable objects
17     public static < T extends Comparable< T > > T maximum( T x, T y, T z )
18     {
19        T max = x; // assume x is initially the largest
20
21        if ( y.compareTo( max ) > 0 )
22           max = y; // y is the largest so far
23
```

Fig. 21.5 | Generic method `maximum` with an upper bound on its type parameter. (Part 1 of 2.)

```
24          if ( z.compareTo( max ) > 0 )
25             max = z; // z is the largest
26
27          return max; // returns the largest object
28       } // end method maximum
29    } // end class MaximumTest
```

```
Maximum of 3, 4 and 5 is 5

Maximum of 6.6, 8.8 and 7.7 is 8.8

Maximum of pear, apple and orange is pear
```

Fig. 21.5 | Generic method maximum with an upper bound on its type parameter. (Part 2 of 2.)

Generic Method maximum
Generic method maximum (lines 17–28) uses type parameter T as the return type of the method (line 17), as the type of method parameters x, y and z (line 17), and as the type of local variable max (line 19). The type-parameter section specifies that T extends Comparable<T>—only objects of classes that implement interface Comparable<T> can be used with this method. In this case, Comparable is known as the **upper bound** of the type parameter. By default, Object is the upper bound. Note that type-parameter declarations that bound the parameter always use keyword extends regardless of whether the type parameter extends a class or implements an interface. This type parameter is more restrictive than the one specified for printArray in Fig. 21.3, which was able to output arrays containing any type of object. The restriction of using Comparable<T> objects is important, because not all objects can be compared. However, Comparable<T> objects are guaranteed to have a compareTo method.

Method maximum uses the same algorithm that we used in Section 6.4 to determine the largest of its three arguments. The method assumes that its first argument (x) is the largest and assigns it to local variable max (line 19). Next, the if statement at lines 21–22 determines whether y is greater than max. The condition invokes y's compareTo method with the expression y.compareTo(max), which returns a negative integer , 0 or a positive integer, to determine y's relationship to max. If the return value of the compareTo is greater than 0, then y is greater and is assigned to variable max. Similarly, the if statement at lines 24–25 determines whether z is greater than max. If so, line 25 assigns z to max. Then line 27 returns max to the caller.

Calling Method maximum
In main (lines 6–14), line 9 calls maximum with the integers 3, 4 and 5. When the compiler encounters this call, it first looks for a maximum method that takes three arguments of type int. There is no such method, so the compiler looks for a generic method that can be used and finds generic method maximum. However, recall that the arguments to a generic method must be of a reference type. So the compiler autoboxes the three int values as Integer objects and specifies that the three Integer objects will be passed to maximum. Note that class Integer (package java.lang) implements the Comparable<Integer> interface such that method compareTo compares the int values in two Integer objects. Therefore, Integers are valid arguments to method maximum. When the Integer representing the max-

imum is returned, we attempt to output it with the %d format specifier, which outputs an int primitive-type value. So maximum's return value is output as an int value.

A similar process occurs for the three double arguments passed to maximum in line 11. Each double is autoboxed as a Double object and passed to maximum. Again, this is allowed because class Double (package java.lang) implements the Comparable<Double> interface. The Double returned by maximum is output with the format specifier %.1f, which outputs a double primitive-type value. So maximum's return value is auto-unboxed and output as a double. The call to maximum in line 13 receives three Strings, which are also Comparable<String> objects. Note that we intentionally placed the largest value in a different position in each method call (lines 9, 11 and 13) to show that the generic method always finds the maximum value, regardless of its position in the argument list.

Upper Bound of a Type Parameter

When the compiler translates generic method maximum into Java bytecodes, it uses erasure (introduced in Section 21.3) to replace the type parameters with actual types. In Fig. 21.3, all generic types were replaced with type Object. Actually, all type parameters are replaced with the so-called upper bound of the type parameter, which is specified in the type-parameter section. To indicate the upper bound, follow the type parameter's name with the keyword extends and the class or interface name that represents the upper bound, or a comma-separated list of the types that represent the upper bound. The list may contain zero or one class and zero or more interfaces. For example, in method maximum's type-parameter section (Fig. 21.5), we specified the upper bound of the type parameter T as type Comparable<T> as follows:

```
T extends Comparable< T >
```

Thus, only Comparable<T> objects can be passed as arguments to maximum—anything that is not a Comparable<T> will result in compilation errors. Unless specified otherwise, Object is the default upper bound. Figure 21.6 simulates the erasure of method maximum's types by showing the method's source code after the type-parameter section is removed and type parameter T is replaced with the upper bound, Comparable, throughout the method declaration. Note that the erasure of Comparable<T> is simply Comparable.

```
 1   public static Comparable maximum(Comparable x, Comparable y, Comparable z)
 2   {
 3      Comparable max = x; // assume x is initially the largest
 4
 5      if ( y.compareTo( max ) > 0 )
 6         max = y; // y is the largest so far
 7
 8      if ( z.compareTo( max ) > 0 )
 9         max = z; // z is the largest
10
11      return max; // returns the largest object
12   } // end method maximum
```

Fig. 21.6 | Generic method maximum after erasure is performed by the compiler.

After erasure, the compiled version of method maximum specifies that it returns type Comparable. However, the calling method does not expect to receive a Comparable. It expects to receive an object of the same type that was passed to maximum as an argument—Integer, Double or String in this example. When the compiler replaces the type-parameter information with the upper-bound type in the method declaration, it also inserts explicit cast operations in front of each method call to ensure that the returned value is of the type expected by the caller. Thus, the call to maximum in line 9 (Fig. 21.5) is preceded by an Integer cast, as in

```
(Integer) maximum( 3, 4, 5 )
```

the call to maximum in line 11 is preceded by a Double cast, as in

```
(Double) maximum( 6.6, 8.8, 7.7 )
```

and the call to maximum in line 13 is preceded by a String cast, as in

```
(String) maximum( "pear", "apple", "orange" )
```

In each case, the type of the cast for the return value is inferred from the types of the method arguments in the particular method call, because, according to the method declaration, the return type and the argument types match.

Possible *ClassCastExceptions*

In this example, you cannot use a method that accepts Objects, because class Object provides only an equality comparison. Also, without generics, you'd be responsible for implementing the cast operation. Using generics ensures that the inserted cast will never throw a ClassCastException, assuming that generics are used throughout your code (i.e., you do not mix old code with new generics code).

21.5 Overloading Generic Methods

A generic method may be overloaded. A class can provide two or more generic methods that specify the same method name but different method parameters. For example, generic method printArray of Fig. 21.3 could be overloaded with another printArray generic method with the additional parameters lowSubscript and highSubscript to specify the portion of the array to output (see Exercise 21.4).

A generic method can also be overloaded by nongeneric methods. When the compiler encounters a method call, it searches for the method declaration that most precisely matches the method name and the argument types specified in the call. For example, generic method printArray of Fig. 21.3 could be overloaded with a version that is specific to Strings, which outputs the Strings in neat, tabular format.

When the compiler encounters a method call, it performs a matching process to determine which method to invoke. The compiler tries to find and use a precise match in which the method name and argument types of the method call match those of a specific method declaration. If there is no such method, the compiler attempts to find a method with compatible types or a matching generic method.

21.6 Generic Classes

The concept of a data structure, such as a stack, can be understood independently of the element type it manipulates. Generic classes provide a means for describing the concept of a stack (or any other class) in a type-independent manner. We can then instantiate type-specific objects of the generic class. This capability provides a wonderful opportunity for software reusability.

As you saw in Chapter 20, once you have a generic class, you can use a simple, concise notation to indicate the actual type(s) that should be used in place of the class's type parameter(s). At compilation time, the Java compiler ensures the type safety of your code and uses the erasure techniques described in Sections 21.3–21.4 to enable your client code to interact with the generic class.

One generic Stack class, for example, could be the basis for creating many logical Stack classes (e.g., "Stack of Double," "Stack of Integer," "Stack of Character," "Stack of Employee"). These classes are known as **parameterized classes** or **parameterized types** because they accept one or more type parameters. Recall that type parameters represent only reference types, which means the Stack generic class cannot be instantiated with primitive types. However, we can instantiate a Stack that stores objects of Java's type-wrapper classes and allow Java to use autoboxing to convert the primitive values into objects. Recall that autoboxing occurs when a value of a primitive type (e.g., int) is pushed onto a Stack that contains wrapper-class objects (e.g., Integer). Auto-unboxing occurs when an object of the wrapper class is popped off the Stack and assigned to a primitive-type variable.

Implementing a Generic *Stack Class*

Figure 21.7 presents a generic Stack class declaration. A generic class declaration looks like a nongeneric one, but the class name is followed by a type-parameter section (line 5). In this case, type parameter T represents the element type the Stack will manipulate. As with generic methods, the type-parameter section of a generic class can have one or more type parameters separated by commas. (You'll create a generic class with two type parameters in Exercise 21.6.) Type parameter T is used throughout the Stack class declaration to represent the element type. [*Note:* This example implements a Stack as an ArrayList.]

```
1   // Fig. 21.7: Stack.java
2   // Stack generic class declaration.
3   import java.util.ArrayList;
4
5   public class Stack< T >
6   {
7      private ArrayList< T > elements; // ArrayList stores stack elements
8
9      // no-argument constructor creates a stack of the default size
10     public Stack()
11     {
12        this( 10 ); // default stack size
13     } // end no-argument Stack constructor
14
15     // constructor creates a stack of the specified number of elements
16     public Stack( int capacity )
17     {
18        int initCapacity = capacity > 0 ? capacity : 10; // validate
19        elements = new ArrayList< T >( initCapacity ); // create ArrayList
20     } // end one-argument Stack constructor
21
```

Fig. 21.7 | Stack generic class declaration. (Part I of 2.)

```
22      // push element onto stack
23      public void push( T pushValue )
24      {
25          elements.add( pushValue ); // place pushValue on Stack
26      } // end method push
27
28      // return the top element if not empty; else throw EmptyStackException
29      public T pop()
30      {
31          if ( elements.isEmpty() ) // if stack is empty
32              throw new EmptyStackException( "Stack is empty, cannot pop" );
33
34          // remove and return top element of Stack
35          return elements.remove( elements.size() - 1 );
36      } // end method pop
37  } // end class Stack< T >
```

Fig. 21.7 | Stack generic class declaration. (Part 2 of 2.)

Class Stack declares variable elements as an ArrayList<T> (line 7). This ArrayList will store the Stack's elements. As you know, an ArrayList can grow dynamically, so objects of our Stack class can also grow dynamically. The Stack class's no-argument constructor (lines 10–13) invokes the one-argument constructor (lines 16–20) to create a Stack in which the underlying ArrayList has a capacity of 10 elements. The one-argument constructor can also be called directly to create a Stack with a specified initial capacity. Line 18 validates the constructor's argument. Line 19 creates the ArrayList of the specified capacity (or 10 if the capacity was invalid).

Method push (lines 23–26) uses ArrayList method add to append the pushed item to the end of the ArrayList elements. The last element in the ArrayList represents the top of the stack.

Method pop (lines 29–36) first determines whether an attempt is being made to pop an element from an empty Stack. If so, line 32 throws an EmptyStackException (declared in Fig. 21.8). Otherwise, line 35 returns the top element of the Stack by removing the last element in the underlying ArrayList.

Class EmptyStackException (Fig. 21.8) provides a no-argument constructor and a one-argument constructor. The no-argument constructor sets the default error message, and the one-argument constructor sets a custom error message.

```
1   // Fig. 21.8: EmptyStackException.java
2   // EmptyStackException class declaration.
3   public class EmptyStackException extends RuntimeException
4   {
5       // no-argument constructor
6       public EmptyStackException()
7       {
8           this( "Stack is empty" );
9       } // end no-argument EmptyStackException constructor
10
```

Fig. 21.8 | EmptyStackException class declaration. (Part 1 of 2.)

```
11      // one-argument constructor
12      public EmptyStackException( String message )
13      {
14         super( message );
15      } // end one-argument EmptyStackException constructor
16  } // end class EmptyStackException
```

Fig. 21.8 | EmptyStackException class declaration. (Part 2 of 2.)

As with generic methods, when a generic class is compiled, the compiler performs erasure on the class's type parameters and replaces them with their upper bounds. For class Stack (Fig. 21.7), no upper bound is specified, so the default upper bound, Object, is used. The scope of a generic class's type parameter is the entire class. However, type parameters cannot be used in a class's static variable declarations.

Testing the Generic *Stack* Class of Fig. 21.7

Now, let's consider the application (Fig. 21.9) that uses the Stack generic class (Fig. 21.7). Lines 12–13 create and initialize variables of type Stack<Double> (pronounced "Stack of Double") and Stack<Integer> (pronounced "Stack of Integer"). The types Double and Integer are known as the Stack's **type arguments**. They are used by the compiler to replace the type parameters so that the compiler can perform type checking and insert cast operations as necessary. We'll discuss the cast operations in more detail shortly. Lines 12–13 instantiate doubleStack with a capacity of 5 and integerStack with a capacity of 10 (the default). Lines 16–17 and 20–21 call methods testPushDouble (lines 25–36), testPopDouble (lines 39–59), testPushInteger (lines 62–73) and testPopInteger (lines 76–96), respectively, to demonstrate the two Stacks in this example.

```
1   // Fig. 21.9: StackTest.java
2   // Stack generic class test program.
3
4   public class StackTest
5   {
6      public static void main( String[] args )
7      {
8         double[] doubleElements = { 1.1, 2.2, 3.3, 4.4, 5.5 };
9         int[] integerElements = { 1, 2, 3, 4, 5, 6, 7, 8, 9, 10 };
10
11         // Create a Stack< Double > and a Stack< Integer >
12         Stack< Double > doubleStack = new Stack< Double >( 5 );
13         Stack< Integer > integerStack = new Stack< Integer >();
14
15         // push elements of doubleElements onto doubleStack
16         testPushDouble( doubleStack, doubleElements );
17         testPopDouble( doubleStack ); // pop from doubleStack
18
19         // push elements of integerElements onto integerStack
20         testPushInteger( integerStack, integerElements );
21         testPopInteger( integerStack ); // pop from integerStack
22      } // end main
```

Fig. 21.9 | Stack generic class test program. (Part 1 of 3.)

```
23
24     // test push method with double stack
25     private static void testPushDouble(
26        Stack< Double > stack, double[] values )
27     {
28        System.out.println( "\nPushing elements onto doubleStack" );
29
30        // push elements to Stack
31        for ( double value : values )
32        {
33           System.out.printf( "%.1f ", value );
34           stack.push( value ); // push onto doubleStack
35        } // end for
36     } // end method testPushDouble
37
38     // test pop method with double stack
39     private static void testPopDouble( Stack< Double > stack )
40     {
41        // pop elements from stack
42        try
43        {
44           System.out.println( "\nPopping elements from doubleStack" );
45           double popValue; // store element removed from stack
46
47           // remove all elements from Stack
48           while ( true )
49           {
50              popValue = stack.pop(); // pop from doubleStack
51              System.out.printf( "%.1f ", popValue );
52           } // end while
53        } // end try
54        catch( EmptyStackException emptyStackException )
55        {
56           System.err.println();
57           emptyStackException.printStackTrace();
58        } // end catch EmptyStackException
59     } // end method testPopDouble
60
61     // test push method with integer stack
62     private static void testPushInteger(
63        Stack< Integer > stack, int[] values )
64     {
65        System.out.println( "\nPushing elements onto integerStack" );
66
67        // push elements to Stack
68        for ( int value : values )
69        {
70           System.out.printf( "%d ", value );
71           stack.push( value ); // push onto integerStack
72        } // end for
73     } // end method testPushInteger
74
```

Fig. 21.9 | Stack generic class test program. (Part 2 of 3.)

```
75      // test pop method with integer stack
76      private static void testPopInteger( Stack< Integer > stack )
77      {
78         // pop elements from stack
79         try
80         {
81            System.out.println( "\nPopping elements from integerStack" );
82            int popValue; // store element removed from stack
83
84            // remove all elements from Stack
85            while ( true )
86            {
87               popValue = stack.pop(); // pop from intStack
88               System.out.printf( "%d ", popValue );
89            } // end while
90         } // end try
91         catch( EmptyStackException emptyStackException )
92         {
93            System.err.println();
94            emptyStackException.printStackTrace();
95         } // end catch EmptyStackException
96      } // end method testPopInteger
97   } // end class StackTest
```

```
Pushing elements onto doubleStack
1.1 2.2 3.3 4.4 5.5
Popping elements from doubleStack
5.5 4.4 3.3 2.2 1.1
EmptyStackException: Stack is empty, cannot pop
        at Stack.pop(Stack.java:32)
        at StackTest.testPopDouble(StackTest.java:50)
        at StackTest.main(StackTest.java:17)

Pushing elements onto integerStack
1 2 3 4 5 6 7 8 9 10
Popping elements from integerStack
10 9 8 7 6 5 4 3 2 1
EmptyStackException: Stack is empty, cannot pop
        at Stack.pop(Stack.java:32)
        at StackTest.testPopInteger(StackTest.java:87)
        at StackTest.main(StackTest.java:21)
```

Fig. 21.9 | Stack generic class test program. (Part 3 of 3.)

Methods **testPushDouble** *and* **testPopDouble**

Method testPushDouble (lines 25–36) invokes method push (line 34) to place the double values 1.1, 2.2, 3.3, 4.4 and 5.5 from array doubleElements onto doubleStack. Note that autoboxing occurs in line 34 when the program tries to push a primitive double value onto the doubleStack, which stores only references to Double objects.

Method testPopDouble (lines 39–59) invokes Stack method pop (line 50) in an infinite while loop (lines 48–52) to remove all the values from the stack. Note in the output that the values indeed pop off in last-in, first-out order (the defining characteristic of stacks). When the loop attempts to pop a sixth value, the doubleStack is empty, so the pop throws an EmptyStackException, which causes the program to proceed to the catch block (lines 54–58) to handle the exception. The stack trace indicates the exception that occurred and shows that Stack method pop generated the exception at line 32 of the file Stack.java (Fig. 21.7). The trace also shows that method pop was called by StackTest method testPopDouble at line 50 of StackTest.java and that method testPopDouble was called from method main at line 17 of StackTest.java. This information enables you to determine the methods that were on the method-call stack at the time that the exception occurred. Because the program catches the exception, the exception is considered to have been handled and the program can continue executing.

Auto-unboxing occurs in line 50 when the program assigns the Double object popped from the stack to a double primitive variable. Recall from Section 21.4 that the compiler inserts casts to ensure that the proper types are returned from generic methods. After erasure, Stack method pop returns type Object, but the client code in testPopDouble expects to receive a double when method pop returns. So the compiler inserts a Double cast, as in

```
popValue = ( Double ) stack.pop();
```

The value assigned to popValue will be unboxed from the Double object returned by pop.

Methods *testPushInteger* and *testPopInteger*
Method testPushInteger (lines 62–73) invokes Stack method push to place values onto integerStack until it's full. Method testPopInteger (lines 76–96) invokes Stack method pop to remove values from integerStack. Once again, note that the values are popped in last-in, first-out order. During the erasure process, the compiler recognizes that the client code in method testPopInteger expects to receive an int when method pop returns. So the compiler inserts an Integer cast, as in

```
popValue = ( Integer ) stack.pop();
```

The value assigned to popValue will be unboxed from the Integer object returned by pop.

Creating Generic Methods to Test Class *Stack<T>*
Note that the code in methods testPushDouble and testPushInteger is almost identical for pushing values onto a Stack<Double> or a Stack<Integer>, respectively, and the code in methods testPopDouble and testPopInteger is almost identical for popping values from a Stack<Double> or a Stack<Integer>, respectively. This presents another opportunity to use generic methods. Figure 21.10 declares generic method testPush (lines 24–35) to perform the same tasks as testPushDouble and testPushInteger in Fig. 21.9—that is, push values onto a Stack<T>. Similarly, generic method testPop (lines 38–58) performs the same tasks as testPopDouble and testPopInteger in Fig. 21.9—that is, pop values off a Stack<T>. Note that the output of Fig. 21.10 precisely matches that of Fig. 21.9.

```
1   // Fig. 21.10: StackTest2.java
2   // Passing generic Stack objects to generic methods.
3   public class StackTest2
4   {
5      public static void main( String[] args )
6      {
```

Fig. 21.10 | Passing generic Stack objects to generic methods. (Part 1 of 3.)

```
7          Double[] doubleElements = { 1.1, 2.2, 3.3, 4.4, 5.5 };
8          Integer[] integerElements = { 1, 2, 3, 4, 5, 6, 7, 8, 9, 10 };
9
10         // Create a Stack< Double > and a Stack< Integer >
11         Stack< Double > doubleStack = new Stack< Double >( 5 );
12         Stack< Integer > integerStack = new Stack< Integer >();
13
14         // push elements of doubleElements onto doubleStack
15         testPush( "doubleStack", doubleStack, doubleElements );
16         testPop( "doubleStack", doubleStack ); // pop from doubleStack
17
18         // push elements of integerElements onto integerStack
19         testPush( "integerStack", integerStack, integerElements );
20         testPop( "integerStack", integerStack ); // pop from integerStack
21      } // end main
22
23      // generic method testPush pushes elements onto a Stack
24      public static < T > void testPush( String name , Stack< T > stack,
25         T[] elements )
26      {
27         System.out.printf( "\nPushing elements onto %s\n", name );
28
29         // push elements onto Stack
30         for ( T element : elements )
31         {
32            System.out.printf( "%s ", element );
33            stack.push( element ); // push element onto stack
34         } // end for
35      } // end method testPush
36
37      // generic method testPop pops elements from a Stack
38      public static < T > void testPop( String name, Stack< T > stack )
39      {
40         // pop elements from stack
41         try
42         {
43            System.out.printf( "\nPopping elements from %s\n", name );
44            T popValue; // store element removed from stack
45
46            // remove all elements from Stack
47            while ( true )
48            {
49               popValue = stack.pop();
50               System.out.printf( "%s ", popValue );
51            } // end while
52         } // end try
53         catch( EmptyStackException emptyStackException )
54         {
55            System.out.println();
56            emptyStackException.printStackTrace();
57         } // end catch EmptyStackException
58      } // end method testPop
59   } // end class StackTest2
```

Fig. 21.10 | Passing generic Stack objects to generic methods. (Part 2 of 3.)

```
Pushing elements onto doubleStack
1.1 2.2 3.3 4.4 5.5
Popping elements from doubleStack
5.5 4.4 3.3 2.2 1.1
EmptyStackException: Stack is empty, cannot pop
        at Stack.pop(Stack.java:32)
        at StackTest2.testPop(StackTest2.java:50)
        at StackTest2.main(StackTest2.java:17)

Pushing elements onto integerStack
1 2 3 4 5 6 7 8 9 10
Popping elements from integerStack
10 9 8 7 6 5 4 3 2 1
EmptyStackException: Stack is empty, cannot pop
        at Stack.pop(Stack.java:32)
        at StackTest2.testPop(StackTest2.java:50)
        at StackTest2.main(StackTest2.java:21
```

Fig. 21.10 | Passing generic `Stack` objects to generic methods. (Part 3 of 3.)

Lines 11–12 create the `Stack<Double>` and `Stack<Integer>` objects, respectively. Lines 15–16 and 19–20 invoke generic methods `testPush` and `testPop` to test the `Stack` objects. Recall that type parameters can represent only reference types. Therefore, to be able to pass arrays `doubleElements` and `integerElements` to generic method `testPush`, the arrays declared in lines 7–8 must be declared with the wrapper types `Double` and `Integer`. When these arrays are initialized with primitive values, the compiler autoboxes each primitive value.

Generic method `testPush` (lines 24–35) uses type parameter `T` (specified at line 24) to represent the data type stored in the `Stack<T>`. The generic method takes three arguments—a `String` that represents the name of the `Stack<T>` object for output purposes, a reference to an object of type `Stack<T>` and an array of type `T`—the type of elements that will be pushed onto `Stack<T>`. Note that the compiler enforces consistency between the type of the `Stack` and the elements that will be pushed onto the `Stack` when `push` is invoked, which is the real value of the generic method call. Generic method `testPop` (lines 38–58) takes two arguments—a `String` that represents the name of the `Stack<T>` object for output purposes and a reference to an object of type `Stack<T>`.

21.7 Raw Types

The test programs for generic class `Stack` in Section 21.6 instantiate `Stack`s with type arguments `Double` and `Integer`. It's also possible to instantiate generic class `Stack` without specifying a type argument, as follows:

```
Stack objectStack = new Stack( 5 ); // no type-argument specified
```

In this case, the `objectStack` is said to have a **raw type**, which means that the compiler implicitly uses type `Object` throughout the generic class for each type argument. Thus the preceding statement creates a `Stack` that can store objects of any type. This is important for backward compatibility with prior versions of Java. For example, the data structures of the Java Collections Framework (see Chapter 20, Generic Collections) all stored references to `Object`s, but are now implemented as generic types.

A raw-type Stack variable can be assigned a Stack that specifies a type argument, such as a Stack<Double> object, as follows:

```
Stack rawTypeStack2 = new Stack< Double >( 5 );
```

because type Double is a subclass of Object. This assignment is allowed because the elements in a Stack<Double> (i.e., Double objects) are certainly objects—class Double is an indirect subclass of Object.

Similarly, a Stack variable that specifies a type argument in its declaration can be assigned a raw-type Stack object, as in:

```
Stack< Integer > integerStack = new Stack( 10 );
```

Although this assignment is permitted, it's unsafe because a Stack of raw type might store types other than Integer. In this case, the compiler issues a warning message which indicates the unsafe assignment.

Using Raw Types with Generic Class Stack

The test program of Fig. 21.11 uses the notion of raw type. Line 11 instantiates generic class Stack with raw type, which indicates that rawTypeStack1 can hold objects of any type. Line 14 assigns a Stack<Double> to variable rawTypeStack2, which is declared as a Stack of raw type. Line 17 assigns a Stack of raw type to Stack<Integer> variable, which is legal but causes the compiler to issue a warning message (Fig. 21.12) indicating a potentially unsafe assignment—again, this occurs because a Stack of raw type might store types other than Integer. Also, the calls to generic methods testPush and testPop in lines 19–22 results in compiler warning messages (Fig. 21.12). These occur because rawTypeStack1 and rawTypeStack2 are declared as Stacks of raw type, but methods testPush and testPop each expect a second argument that is a Stack with a specific type argument. The warnings indicate that the compiler cannot guarantee that the types manipulated by the stacks are the correct types, since we did not supply a variable declared with a type argument. Methods testPush (lines 28–39) and testPop (lines 42–62) are the same as in Fig. 21.10.

```java
1   // Fig. 21.11: RawTypeTest.java
2   // Raw type test program.
3   public class RawTypeTest
4   {
5      public static void main( String[] args )
6      {
7         Double[] doubleElements = { 1.1, 2.2, 3.3, 4.4, 5.5 };
8         Integer[] integerElements = {  1, 2, 3, 4, 5, 6, 7, 8, 9, 10 };
9
10        // Stack of raw types assigned to Stack of raw types variable
11        Stack rawTypeStack1 = new Stack( 5 );
12
13        // Stack< Double > assigned to Stack of raw types variable
14        Stack rawTypeStack2 = new Stack< Double >( 5 );
15
16        // Stack of raw types assigned to Stack< Integer > variable
17        Stack< Integer > integerStack = new Stack( 10 );
18
```

Fig. 21.11 | Raw-type test program. (Part 1 of 3.)

```
19          testPush( "rawTypeStack1", rawTypeStack1, doubleElements );
20          testPop( "rawTypeStack1", rawTypeStack1 );
21          testPush( "rawTypeStack2", rawTypeStack2, doubleElements );
22          testPop( "rawTypeStack2", rawTypeStack2 );
23          testPush( "integerStack", integerStack, integerElements );
24          testPop( "integerStack", integerStack );
25       } // end main
26
27       // generic method pushes elements onto stack
28       public static < T > void testPush( String name, Stack< T > stack,
29          T[] elements )
30       {
31          System.out.printf( "\nPushing elements onto %s\n", name );
32
33          // push elements onto Stack
34          for ( T element : elements )
35          {
36             System.out.printf( "%s ", element );
37             stack.push( element ); // push element onto stack
38          } // end for
39       } // end method testPush
40
41       // generic method testPop pops elements from stack
42       public static < T > void testPop( String name, Stack< T > stack )
43       {
44          // pop elements from stack
45          try
46          {
47             System.out.printf( "\nPopping elements from %s\n", name );
48             T popValue; // store element removed from stack
49
50             // remove elements from Stack
51             while ( true )
52             {
53                popValue = stack.pop(); // pop from stack
54                System.out.printf( "%s ", popValue );
55             } // end while
56          } // end try
57          catch( EmptyStackException emptyStackException )
58          {
59             System.out.println();
60             emptyStackException.printStackTrace();
61          } // end catch EmptyStackException
62       } // end method testPop
63    } // end class RawTypeTest
```

```
Pushing elements onto rawTypeStack1
1.1 2.2 3.3 4.4 5.5
Popping elements from rawTypeStack1
5.5 4.4 3.3 2.2 1.1
EmptyStackException: Stack is empty, cannot pop
        at Stack.pop(Stack.java:32)
        at RawTypeTest.testPop(RawTypeTest.java:53)
        at RawTypeTest.main(RawTypeTest.java:20)
```

Fig. 21.11 | Raw-type test program. (Part 2 of 3.)

```
Pushing elements onto rawTypeStack2
1.1 2.2 3.3 4.4 5.5
Popping elements from rawTypeStack2
5.5 4.4 3.3 2.2 1.1
EmptyStackException: Stack is empty, cannot pop
        at Stack.pop(Stack.java:32)
        at RawTypeTest.testPop(RawTypeTest.java:53)
        at RawTypeTest.main(RawTypeTest.java:22)

Pushing elements onto integerStack
1 2 3 4 5 6 7 8 9 10
Popping elements from integerStack
10 9 8 7 6 5 4 3 2 1
EmptyStackException: Stack is empty, cannot pop
        at Stack.pop(Stack.java:32)
        at RawTypeTest.testPop(RawTypeTest.java:53)
        at RawTypeTest.main(RawTypeTest.java:24)
```

Fig. 21.11 | Raw-type test program. (Part 3 of 3.)

Figure 21.12 shows the warning messages generated by the compiler when the file RawTypeTest.java (Fig. 21.11) is compiled with the -Xlint:unchecked option, which provides more information about potentially unsafe operations in code that uses generics. The first warning is generated for line 17, which assigned a raw-type Stack to a Stack<Integer> variable—the compiler cannot ensure that all objects in the Stack will be Integer objects. The next warning occurs at line 19. The compiler determines method testPush's type argument from the Double array passed as the third argument, because the second method argument is a raw-type Stack variable. In this case, Double is the type argument, so the compiler expects a Stack<Double> as the second argument. The warning occurs because the compiler cannot ensure that a raw-type Stack contains only Doubles. The warning at line 21 occurs for the same reason, even though the actual Stack that rawTypeStack2 references is a Stack<Double>. The compiler cannot guarantee that the variable will always refer to the same Stack object, so it must use the variable's declared type to perform all type checking. Lines 20 and 22 each generate warnings because method testPop expects as an argument a Stack for which a type argument has been specified. However, in each call to testPop, we pass a raw-type Stack variable. Thus, the compiler indicates a warning because it cannot check the types used in the body of the method.

```
RawTypeTest.java:17: warning: [unchecked] unchecked conversion
found    : Stack
required: Stack<java.lang.Integer>
      Stack< Integer > integerStack = new Stack( 10 );
                                      ^

RawTypeTest.java:19: warning: [unchecked] unchecked conversion
found    : Stack
required: Stack<java.lang.Double>
      testPush( "rawTypeStack1", rawTypeStack1, doubleElements );
                ^
```

Fig. 21.12 | Warning messages from the compiler. (Part 1 of 2.)

```
RawTypeTest.java:19: warning: [unchecked] unchecked method invocation:
<T>testPush(java.lang.String,Stack<T>,T[]) in RawTypeTest is applied to
(java.lang.String,Stack,java.lang.Double[])
      testPush( "rawTypeStack1", rawTypeStack1, doubleElements );
           ^
RawTypeTest.java:20: warning: [unchecked] unchecked conversion
found    : Stack
required: Stack<T>
      testPop( "rawTypeStack1", rawTypeStack1 );
                               ^
RawTypeTest.java:20: warning: [unchecked] unchecked method invocation:
<T>testPop(java.lang.String,Stack<T>) in RawTypeTest is applied to
(java.lang.String,Stack)
      testPop( "rawTypeStack1", rawTypeStack1 );
          ^
RawTypeTest.java:21: warning: [unchecked] unchecked conversion
found    : Stack
required: Stack<java.lang.Double>
      testPush( "rawTypeStack2", rawTypeStack2, doubleElements );
                               ^
RawTypeTest.java:21: warning: [unchecked] unchecked method invocation:
<T>testPush(java.lang.String,Stack<T>,T[]) in RawTypeTest is applied to
(java.lang.String,Stack,java.lang.Double[])
      testPush( "rawTypeStack2", rawTypeStack2, doubleElements );
           ^
RawTypeTest.java:22: warning: [unchecked] unchecked conversion
found    : Stack
required: Stack<T>
      testPop( "rawTypeStack2", rawTypeStack2 );
                               ^
RawTypeTest.java:22: warning: [unchecked] unchecked method invocation:
<T>testPop(java.lang.String,Stack<T>) in RawTypeTest is applied to
(java.lang.String,Stack)
      testPop( "rawTypeStack2", rawTypeStack2 );
          ^
9 warnings
```

Fig. 21.12 | Warning messages from the compiler. (Part 2 of 2.)

21.8 Wildcards in Methods That Accept Type Parameters

In this section, we introduce a powerful generics concept known as **wildcards**. For this purpose, we'll also introduce a new data structure from package java.util. In Chapter 20, we discussed the Java Collections Framework, which provides many generic data structures and algorithms that manipulate the elements of those data structures. Perhaps the simplest of these data structures is class ArrayList—a dynamically resizable, arraylike data structure. As part of this discussion, you'll learn how to create an ArrayList, add elements to it and traverse those elements using an enhanced for statement.

Before we introduce wildcards, let's consider an example that helps us motivate their use. Suppose that you'd like to implement a generic method sum that totals the numbers in a collection, such as an ArrayList. You'd begin by inserting the numbers in the collection. As you know, generic classes can be used only with class or interface types, so the numbers would be autoboxed as objects of the type-wrapper classes. For example, any int value would be autoboxed as an `Integer` object, and any `double` value would be autoboxed as a `Double` object. We'd like to be able to total all the numbers in the `ArrayList` regardless of their type. For this reason, we'll declare the `ArrayList` with the type argument `Number`, which is the superclass of both `Integer` and `Double`. In addition, method `sum` will receive a parameter of type `ArrayList<Number>` and total its elements. Figure 21.13 demonstrates totaling the elements of an `ArrayList` of `Number`s.

```java
1   // Fig. 21.13: TotalNumbers.java
2   // Totaling the numbers in an ArrayList<Number>.
3   import java.util.ArrayList;
4
5   public class TotalNumbers
6   {
7      public static void main( String[] args )
8      {
9         // create, initialize and output ArrayList of Numbers containing
10        // both Integers and Doubles, then display total of the elements
11        Number[] numbers = { 1, 2.4, 3, 4.1 }; // Integers and Doubles
12        ArrayList< Number > numberList = new ArrayList< Number >();
13
14        for ( Number element : numbers )
15           numberList.add( element ); // place each number in numberList
16
17        System.out.printf( "numberList contains: %s\n", numberList );
18        System.out.printf( "Total of the elements in numberList: %.1f\n",
19           sum( numberList ) );
20     } // end main
21
22     // calculate total of ArrayList elements
23     public static double sum( ArrayList< Number > list )
24     {
25        double total = 0; // initialize total
26
27        // calculate sum
28        for ( Number element : list )
29           total += element.doubleValue();
30
31        return total;
32     } // end method sum
33  } // end class TotalNumbers
```

```
numberList contains: [1, 2.4, 3, 4.1]
Total of the elements in numberList: 10.5
```

Fig. 21.13 | Totaling the numbers in an `ArrayList<Number>`.

Line 11 declares and initializes an array of `Number`s. Because the initializers are primitive values, Java autoboxes each primitive value as an object of its corresponding wrapper type. The `int` values 1 and 3 are autoboxed as `Integer` objects, and the `double` values 2.4 and 4.1 are autoboxed as `Double` objects. Line 12 declares and creates an `ArrayList` object that stores `Number`s and assigns it to variable `numberList`. Note that we do not have to specify the size of the `ArrayList` because it will grow automatically as we insert objects.

Lines 14–15 traverse array numbers and place each element in numberList. Line 17 outputs the contents of the ArrayList as a String. This statement implicitly invokes the ArrayList's toString method, which returns a String of the form "[*elements*]" in which *elements* is a comma-separated list of the elements' String representations. Lines 18–19 display the sum of the elements that is returned by the call to method sum.

Method sum (lines 23–32) receives an ArrayList of Numbers and calculates the total of the Numbers in the collection. The method uses double values to perform the calculations and returns the result as a double. Lines 28–29 use the enhanced for statement, which is designed to work with both arrays and the collections of the Collections Framework, to total the elements of the ArrayList. The for statement assigns each Number in the ArrayList to variable element, then uses **Number method doubleValue** to obtain the Number's underlying primitive value as a double value. The result is added to total. When the loop terminates, the method returns the total.

*Implementing Method **sum** With a Wildcard Type Argument in Its Parameter*

Recall that the purpose of method sum in Fig. 21.13 was to total any type of Numbers stored in an ArrayList. We created an ArrayList of Numbers that contained both Integer and Double objects. The output of Fig. 21.13 demonstrates that method sum worked properly. Given that method sum can total the elements of an ArrayList of Numbers, you might expect that the method would also work for ArrayLists that contain elements of only one numeric type, such as ArrayList<Integer>. So we modified class TotalNumbers to create an ArrayList of Integers and pass it to method sum. When we compile the program, the compiler issues the following error message:

```
sum(java.util.ArrayList<java.lang.Number>) in TotalNumbersErrors
cannot be applied to (java.util.ArrayList<java.lang.Integer>)
```

Although Number is the superclass of Integer, the compiler does not consider the parameterized type ArrayList<Number> to be a superclass of ArrayList<Integer>. If it were, then every operation we could perform on ArrayList<Number> would also work on an ArrayList<Integer>. Consider the fact that you can add a Double object to an ArrayList<Number> because a Double *is a* Number, but you cannot add a Double object to an ArrayList<Integer> because a Double *is not an* Integer. Thus, the subtype relationship does not hold.

How do we create a more flexible version of the sum method that can total the elements of any ArrayList containing elements of any subclass of Number? This is where **wildcard-type arguments** are important. Wildcards enable you to specify method parameters, return values, variables or fields, and so on, that act as supertypes or subtypes of parameterized types. In Fig. 21.14, method sum's parameter is declared in line 50 with the type:

```
ArrayList< ? extends Number >
```

A wildcard-type argument is denoted by a question mark (**?**), which by itself represents an "unknown type." In this case, the wildcard extends class Number, which means that the wildcard has an upper bound of Number. Thus, the unknown-type argument must be either Number or a subclass of Number. With the parameter type shown here, method sum can receive an ArrayList argument that contains any type of Number, such as ArrayList<Integer> (line 20), ArrayList<Double> (line 33) or ArrayList<Number> (line 46).

```
 1    // Fig. 21.14: WildcardTest.java
 2    // Wildcard test program.
 3    import java.util.ArrayList;
 4
 5    public class WildcardTest
 6    {
 7       public static void main( String[] args )
 8       {
 9          // create, initialize and output ArrayList of Integers, then
10          // display total of the elements
11          Integer[] integers = { 1, 2, 3, 4, 5 };
12          ArrayList< Integer > integerList = new ArrayList< Integer >();
13
14          // insert elements in integerList
15          for ( Integer element : integers )
16             integerList.add( element );
17
18          System.out.printf( "integerList contains: %s\n", integerList );
19          System.out.printf( "Total of the elements in integerList: %.0f\n\n",
20             sum( integerList ) );
21
22          // create, initialize and output ArrayList of Doubles, then
23          // display total of the elements
24          Double[] doubles = { 1.1, 3.3, 5.5 };
25          ArrayList< Double > doubleList = new ArrayList< Double >();
26
27          // insert elements in doubleList
28          for ( Double element : doubles )
29             doubleList.add( element );
30
31          System.out.printf( "doubleList contains: %s\n", doubleList );
32          System.out.printf( "Total of the elements in doubleList: %.1f\n\n",
33             sum( doubleList ) );
34
35          // create, initialize and output ArrayList of Numbers containing
36          // both Integers and Doubles, then display total of the elements
37          Number[] numbers = { 1, 2.4, 3, 4.1 }; // Integers and Doubles
38          ArrayList< Number > numberList = new ArrayList< Number >();
39
40          // insert elements in numberList
41          for ( Number element : numbers )
42             numberList.add( element );
43
44          System.out.printf( "numberList contains: %s\n", numberList );
45          System.out.printf( "Total of the elements in numberList: %.1f\n",
46             sum( numberList ) );
47       } // end main
48
49       // total the elements; using a wildcard in the ArrayList parameter
50       public static double sum( ArrayList< ? extends Number > list )
51       {
52          double total = 0; // initialize total
53
```

Fig. 21.14 | Generic wildcard test program. (Part 1 of 2.)

```
54            // calculate sum
55            for ( Number element : list )
56                total += element.doubleValue();
57
58            return total;
59        } // end method sum
60    } // end class WildcardTest
```

```
integerList contains: [1, 2, 3, 4, 5]
Total of the elements in integerList: 15

doubleList contains: [1.1, 3.3, 5.5]
Total of the elements in doubleList: 9.9

numberList contains: [1, 2.4, 3, 4.1]
Total of the elements in numberList: 10.5
```

Fig. 21.14 | Generic wildcard test program. (Part 2 of 2.)

Lines 11–20 create and initialize an `ArrayList<Integer>`, output its elements and total its elements by calling method sum (line 20). Lines 24–33 perform the same operations for an `ArrayList<Double>`. Lines 37–46 perform the same operations for an `Array-List<Number>` that contains `Integer`s and `Double`s.

In method sum (lines 50–59), although the `ArrayList` argument's element types are not directly known by the method, they are known to be at least of type `Number`, because the wildcard was specified with the upper bound `Number`. For this reason line 56 is allowed, because all `Number` objects have a `doubleValue` method.

Although wildcards provide flexibility when passing parameterized types to a method, they also have some disadvantages. Because the wildcard (?) in the method's header (line 50) does not specify a type-parameter name, you cannot use it as a type name throughout the method's body (i.e., you cannot replace `Number` with ? in line 55). You could, however, declare method sum as follows:

```
public static <T extends Number> double sum( ArrayList< T > list )
```

which allows the method to receive an `ArrayList` that contains elements of any `Number` subclass. You could then use the type parameter `T` throughout the method body.

If the wildcard is specified without an upper bound, then only the methods of type `Object` can be invoked on values of the wildcard type. Also, methods that use wildcards in their parameter's type arguments cannot be used to add elements to a collection referenced by the parameter.

Common Programming Error 21.4

Using a wildcard in a method's type-parameter section or using a wildcard as an explicit type of a variable in the method body is a syntax error.

21.9 Generics and Inheritance: Notes

Generics can be used with inheritance in several ways:

- A generic class can be derived from a nongeneric class. For example, the `Object` class is a direct or indirect superclass of every generic class.

- A generic class can be derived from another generic class. For example, generic class Stack (in package java.util) is a subclass of generic class Vector (in package java.util). We discussed these classes in Chapter 20.

- A nongeneric class can be derived from a generic class. For example, nongeneric class Properties (in package java.util) is a subclass of generic class Hashtable (in package java.util). We also discussed these classes in Chapter 20.

- Finally, a generic method in a subclass can override a generic method in a superclass if both methods have the same signatures.

21.10 Wrap-Up

This chapter introduced generics. You learned how to declare generic methods and classes. We discussed how backward compatibility is achieved via raw types. You also learned how to use wildcards in a generic method or a generic class. In Chapter 22, you'll learn how to implement your own custom dynamic data structures that can grow or shrink at execution time. In particular, you'll implement these data structures using the generics capabilities you learned in this chapter. For more information on generics, please visit our Java Resource Center at www.deitel.com/Java/ and click the topic **Java Generics** under the heading **Resource Center Contents**.

Summary

Section 21.1 Introduction
- Generic methods enable you to specify, with one method declaration, a set of related methods.
- Generic classes and interfaces enable you to specify sets of related types.

Section 21.2 Motivation for Generic Methods
- Overloaded methods are often used to perform similar operations on different types of data.
- When the compiler encounters a method call, it attempts to locate a method declaration that has the same method name and parameters that are compatible with the argument types in the method call.

Section 21.3 Generic Methods: Implementation and Compile-Time Translation
- If the operations performed by several overloaded methods are identical for each argument type, they can be more compactly and conveniently coded using a generic method. A single generic method declaration can be called with arguments of different data types. Based on the types of the arguments passed to a generic method, the compiler handles each method call appropriately.
- All generic method declarations have a type-parameter section delimited by angle brackets (< and >) that precedes the method's return type.
- A type-parameter section contains one or more type parameters separated by commas.
- A type parameter is an identifier that specifies a generic type name. Type parameters can be used as the return type, parameter types and local variable types in a generic method declaration, and they act as placeholders for the types of the arguments passed to the generic method, which are known as actual type arguments. Type parameters can represent only reference types.
- Type-parameter names used throughout a method declaration must match those declared in the type-parameter section. A type-parameter name can be declared only once in the type-parameter section but can appear more than once in the method's parameter list.

- When the compiler encounters a method call, it determines the argument types and attempts to locate a method with the same name and parameters that match the argument types. If there is no such method, the compiler searches for methods with the same name and compatible parameters and for matching generic methods.

- Objects of a class that implements generic interface `Comparable` can be compared with method `compareTo`, which returns 0 if the objects are equal, a negative integer if the first object is less than the second or a positive integer if the first object is greater than the second.

- All the type-wrapper classes for primitive types implement `Comparable`.

- `Comparable` objects can be used with the sorting and searching methods of class `Collections`.

- When a generic method is compiled, the compiler removes the type-parameter section and replaces the type parameters with actual types. This process is known as erasure. By default each type parameter is replaced with its upper bound, which is `Object` unless specified otherwise.

Section 21.4 Additional Compile-Time Translation Issues: Methods That Use a Type Parameter as the Return Type

- When erasure is performed on a method that returns a type variable, explicit casts are inserted in front of each method call to ensure that the returned value has the type expected by the caller.

Section 21.5 Overloading Generic Methods

- A generic method may be overloaded with other generic methods or with nongeneric methods.

Section 21.6 Generic Classes

- Generic classes provide a means for describing a class in a type-independent manner. We can then instantiate type-specific objects of the generic class.

- A generic class declaration looks like a nongeneric class declaration, except that the class name is followed by a type-parameter section. The type-parameter section of a generic class can have one or more type parameters separated by commas.

- When a generic class is compiled, the compiler performs erasure on the class's type parameters and replaces them with their upper bounds.

- Type parameters cannot be used in a class's `static` declarations.

- When instantiating an object of a generic class, the types specified in angle brackets after the class name are known as type arguments. The compiler uses them to replace the type parameters so that it can perform type checking and insert cast operations as necessary.

Section 21.7 Raw Types

- It's possible to instantiate a generic class without specifying a type argument. In this case, the new object of the class is said to have a raw type—the compiler implicitly uses type `Object` (or the type parameter's upper bound) throughout the generic class for each type argument.

Section 21.8 Wildcards in Methods That Accept Type Parameters

- Class `Number` is the superclass of both `Integer` and `Double`.

- `Number` method `doubleValue` obtains the `Number`'s underlying primitive value as a `double` value.

- Wildcard-type arguments enable you to specify method parameters, return values, variables, and so on. that act as supertypes of parameterized types. A wildcard-type argument is denoted by the question mark (?), which represents an "unknown type." A wildcard can also have an upper bound.

- Because a wildcard (?) is not a type-parameter name, you cannot use it as a type name throughout a method's body.

- If a wildcard is specified without an upper bound, then only the methods of type Object can be invoked on values of the wildcard type.
- Methods that use wildcards as type arguments cannot be used to add elements to a collection referenced by the parameter.

Section 21.9 Generics and Inheritance: Notes
- A generic class can be derived from a nongeneric class. For example, Object is a direct or indirect superclass of every generic class.
- A generic class can be derived from another generic class.
- A nongeneric class can be derived from a generic class.
- A generic method in a subclass can override a generic method in a superclass if both methods have the same signatures.

Terminology

? (wildcard type argument) 910
actual type arguments 891
angle brackets (< and >) 891
Comparable<T> interface 893
compareTo method of Comparable<T> 893
compile-time type safety 887
doubleValue method of Number 910
erasure 892
formal type parameter 891
generic classes 887
generic interface 893
generic method 887

generics 887
parameterized class 897
parameterized type 897
raw type 904
type argument 899
type parameter 891
type parameter section 891
type variable 891
upper bound of a type parameter 894
wildcard in a generic type parameter 908
wildcard type argument 910

Self-Review Exercises

21.1 State whether each of the following is *true* or *false*. If *false*, explain why.
  a) A generic method cannot have the same method name as a nongeneric method.
  b) All generic method declarations have a type-parameter section that immediately precedes the method name.
  c) A generic method can be overloaded by another generic method with the same method name but different method parameters.
  d) A type parameter can be declared only once in the type-parameter section but can appear more than once in the method's parameter list.
  e) Type-parameter names among different generic methods must be unique.
  f) The scope of a generic class's type parameter is the entire class except its static members.

21.2 Fill in the blanks in each of the following:
  a) _____ and _____ enable you to specify, with a single method declaration, a set of related methods, or with a single class declaration, a set of related types, respectively.
  b) A type-parameter section is delimited by _____.
  c) A generic method's _____ can be used to specify the method's argument types, to specify the method's return type and to declare variables within the method.
  d) The statement "Stack objectStack = new Stack();" indicates that objectStack stores _____.
  e) In a generic class declaration, the class name is followed by a(n) _____.
  f) The syntax _____ specifies that the upper bound of a wildcard is type T.

Answers to Self-Review Exercises

21.1   a) False. Generic and nongeneric methods can have the same method name. A generic method can overload another generic method with the same method name but different method parameters. A generic method also can be overloaded by providing nongeneric methods with the same method name and number of arguments. b) False. All generic method declarations have a type-parameter section that immediately precedes the method's return type. c) True. d) True. e) False. Type-parameter names among different generic methods need not be unique. f) True.

21.2   a) Generic methods, generic classes. b) angle brackets (< and >). c) type parameters. d) a raw type. e) type-parameter section. f) ? extends T.

Exercises

21.3   Write a generic method selectionSort based on the sort program of Figs. 19.6–19.7. Write a test program that inputs, sorts and outputs an Integer array and a Float array. [*Hint:* Use <T extends Comparable<T> > in the type-parameter section for method selectionSort, so that you can use method compareTo to compare the objects of the type that T represents.]

21.4   Overload generic method printArray of Fig. 21.3 so that it takes two additional integer arguments, lowSubscript and highSubscript. A call to this method prints only the designated portion of the array. Validate lowSubscript and highSubscript. If either is out of range, the overloaded printArray method should throw an InvalidSubscriptException; otherwise, printArray should return the number of elements printed. Then modify main to exercise both versions of printArray on arrays integerArray, doubleArray and characterArray. Test all capabilities of both versions of printArray.

21.5   Write a simple generic version of method isEqualTo that compares its two arguments with the equals method and returns true if they are equal and false otherwise. Use this generic method in a program that calls isEqualTo with a variety of built-in types, such as Object or Integer. What result do you get when you attempt to run this program?

21.6   Write a generic class Pair which has two type parameters—F and S—each representing the type of the first and second element of the pair, respectively. Add *get* and *set* methods for the first and second elements of the pair. [*Hint:* The class header should be public class Pair<F, S>.]

21.7   How can generic methods be overloaded?

21.8   Explain why a Java program might use the statement

```
ArrayList< Employee > workerList = new ArrayList< Employee >();
```

Much that I bound, I could not free;
Much that I freed returned to me.
—Lee Wilson Dodd

'Will you walk a little faster?' said a whiting to a snail,
'There's a porpoise close behind us, and he's treading on
my tail.'
—Lewis Carroll

There is always room at the top.
—Daniel Webster

Push on—keep moving.
—Thomas Morton

I'll turn over a new leaf.
—Miguel de Cervantes

Custom Generic
Data Structures

Objectives

In this chapter you'll learn:

- To form linked data structures using references, self-referential classes, recursion and generics.

- To create and manipulate dynamic data structures, such as linked lists, queues, stacks and binary trees.

- Various important applications of linked data structures.

- How to create reusable data structures with classes, inheritance and composition.

22.1 Introduction

This chapter shows how to build **dynamic data structures** that grow and shrink at execution time. **Linked lists** are collections of data items "linked up in a chain"; insertions and deletions can be made anywhere in a linked list. **Stacks** are important in compilers and operating systems; insertions and deletions are made only at one end of a stack—its **top**. **Queues** represent waiting lines; insertions are made at the back (also referred to as the **tail**) of a queue and deletions are made from the front (also referred to as the **head**). **Binary trees** facilitate high-speed searching and sorting of data, eliminating duplicate data items efficiently, representing file-system directories, compiling expressions into machine language and many other interesting applications.

We discuss each of these major data-structure types and implement programs that create and manipulate them. We use classes, inheritance and composition to create and package them for reusability and maintainability. In general, you'd use one of the predefined collection classes that we discussed in Chapter 20. However, the techniques we present here can be used if you ever need to build your own custom collections.

For simplicity, this chapter's examples manipulate primitive values. However, the data-structure implementations in this chapter can store objects of most types. (The binary tree example requires objects that implement the `Comparable<T>` interface.)

If you feel ambitious, you might want to attempt the major project described in the special section entitled Building Your Own Compiler, which we've posted online at `www.deitel.com/books/jhtp8/`. You've been using a Java compiler to translate your Java programs to bytecodes so that you could execute these programs. In this project, you'll actually build your own compiler. It will read statements written in a simple, yet powerful high-level language similar to early versions of the popular language BASIC and translate these statements into Simpletron Machine Language (SML) instructions—SML is the language you learned in the Chapter 7 special section, Building Your Own Computer. Your Simpletron Simulator program will then execute the SML program produced by your compiler! Implementing this project by using an object-oriented approach will give you a wonderful opportunity to exercise most of what you've learned in this book. The special section carefully walks you through the specifications of the high-level language and describes the algorithms you'll need to convert each high-level language statement into machine-language instructions. If you enjoy being challenged, you might attempt the many enhancements to both the compiler and the Simpletron Simulator suggested in the exercises.

22.2 Self-Referential Classes

A **self-referential class** contains an instance variable that refers to another object of the same class type. For example, the generic class declaration

```
class Node< T >
{
   private T data;
   private Node< T > nextNode; // reference to next linked node

   public Node( T data ) { /* constructor body */ }
   public void setData( T data ) { /* method body */ }
   public T getData() { /* method body */ }
   public void setNext( Node< T > next ) { /* method body */ }
   public Node< T > getNext() { /* method body */ }
} // end class Node< T >
```

declares class Node, which has two private instance variables—data (of the generic type T) and Node<T> variable nextNode. Variable nextNode references a Node<T> object, an object of the same class being declared here—hence, the term "self-referential class." Field nextNode is a **link**—it "links" an object of type Node<T> to another object of the same type. Type Node<T> also has five methods: a constructor that receives a value to initialize data, a setData method to set the value of data, a getData method to return the value of data, a setNext method to set the value of nextNode and a getNext method to return a reference to the next node.

Programs can link self-referential objects together to form such useful data structures as lists, queues, stacks and trees. Figure 22.1 illustrates two self-referential objects linked together to form a list. A backslash—representing a null reference—is placed in the link member of the second self-referential object to indicate that the link does not refer to another object. Note that the backslash is illustrative; it does not correspond to the backslash character in Java. We use the null reference to indicate the end of a data structure.

Fig. 22.1 | Self-referential-class objects linked together.

22.3 **Dynamic Memory Allocation**

Creating and maintaining dynamic data structures requires **dynamic memory allocation**—allowing a program to obtain more memory space at execution time to hold new nodes and to release space no longer needed. Remember that Java programs do not explicitly release dynamically allocated memory. Rather, Java performs automatic garbage collection of objects that are no longer referenced in a program.

The limit for dynamic memory allocation can be as large as the amount of available physical memory in the computer or the amount of available disk space in a virtual-memory system. Often the limits are much smaller, because the computer's available memory must be shared among many applications.

The declaration and class-instance-creation expression

```
// 10 is nodeToAdd's data
Node< Integer > nodeToAdd = new Node< Integer >( 10 );
```

allocates the memory to store a Node<Integer> object and returns a reference to the object, which is assigned to nodeToAdd. If insufficient memory is available, the expression throws an OutOfMemoryError.

The following sections discuss lists, stacks, queues and trees that all use dynamic memory allocation and self-referential classes to create dynamic data structures.

22.4 Linked Lists

A linked list is a linear collection (i.e., a sequence) of self-referential-class objects, called **nodes**, connected by reference links—hence, the term "linked" list. Typically, a program accesses a linked list via a reference to its first node. The program accesses each subsequent node via the link reference stored in the previous node. By convention, the link reference in the last node of the list is set to null. Data is stored in a linked list dynamically—the program creates each node as necessary. Stacks and queues are also linear data structures and, as we'll see, are constrained versions of linked lists. Trees are nonlinear data structures.

Lists of data can be stored in arrays, but linked lists provide several advantages. A linked list is appropriate when the number of data elements to be represented in the data structure is unpredictable. Linked lists are dynamic, so the length of a list can increase or decrease as necessary, whereas the size of a "conventional" Java array cannot be altered—it is fixed when the program creates the array. "Conventional" arrays can become full. Linked lists become full only when the system has insufficient memory to satisfy dynamic storage allocation requests. Package java.util contains class LinkedList (discussed in Chapter 20) for implementing and manipulating linked lists that grow and shrink during program execution.

Performance Tip 22.1

An array can be declared to contain more elements than the number of items expected, but this wastes memory. In these situations, linked lists provide better memory utilization allowing the program to adapt to storage needs at runtime.

Performance Tip 22.2

Insertion into a linked list is fast—only two references have to be modified (after locating the insertion point). All existing node objects remain at their current locations in memory.

Linked lists can be maintained in sorted order simply by inserting each new element at the proper point in the list. (It does, of course, take time to locate the proper insertion point.) Existing list elements do not need to be moved.

Performance Tip 22.3

Insertion and deletion in a sorted array can be time consuming—all the elements following the inserted or deleted element must be shifted appropriately.

Singly Linked Lists

Linked list nodes normally are not stored contiguously in memory. Rather, they are logically contiguous. Figure 22.2 illustrates a linked list with several nodes. This diagram presents a **singly linked list**—each node contains one reference to the next node in the list. Often, linked lists are implemented as doubly linked lists—each node contains a reference to the next node in the list and a reference to the proceding one. Java's LinkedList class is a doubly linked list implementation.

Fig. 22.2 | Linked-list graphical representation.

Performance Tip 22.4
Normally, the elements of an array are contiguous in memory. This allows immediate access to any array element, because its address can be calculated directly as its offset from the beginning of the array. Linked lists do not afford such immediate access—an element can be accessed only by traversing the list from the front (or from the back in a doubly linked list).

Implementing a Generic **List** Class

The program of Figs. 22.3–22.5 uses an object of our generic List class to manipulate a list of miscellaneous objects. The program consists of four classes—ListNode (Fig. 22.3, lines 6–37), List (Fig. 22.3, lines 40–147), EmptyListException (Fig. 22.4) and List-Test (Fig. 22.5). The List, ListNode and EmptyListException classes are placed in package com.deitel.ch22, so they can be reused throughout this chapter. Encapsulated in each List object is a linked list of ListNode objects. [*Note:* Many of the classes in this chapter are declared in the package com.deitel.ch22. Each such class should be compiled with the -d command-line option to javac. When compiling the classes that are not in this package and when running the programs, be sure to use the option -classpath with javac and java, respectively.]

```java
1   // Fig. 22.3: List.java
2   // ListNode and List class declarations.
3   package com.deitel.ch22;
4
5   // class to represent one node in a list
6   class ListNode< T >
7   {
8      // package access members; List can access these directly
9      T data; // data for this node
10     ListNode< T > nextNode; // reference to the next node in the list
11
12     // constructor creates a ListNode that refers to object
13     ListNode( T object )
14     {
15        this( object, null );
16     } // end ListNode one-argument constructor
17
```

Fig. 22.3 | ListNode and List class declarations. (Part 1 of 4.)

```
18      // constructor creates ListNode that refers to the specified
19      // object and to the next ListNode
20      ListNode( T object, ListNode< T > node )
21      {
22         data = object;
23         nextNode = node;
24      } // end ListNode two-argument constructor
25
26      // return reference to data in node
27      T getData()
28      {
29         return data; // return item in this node
30      } // end method getData
31
32      // return reference to next node in list
33      ListNode< T > getNext()
34      {
35         return nextNode; // get next node
36      } // end method getNext
37   } // end class ListNode< T >
38
39   // class List definition
40   public class List< T >
41   {
42      private ListNode< T > firstNode;
43      private ListNode< T > lastNode;
44      private String name; // string like "list" used in printing
45
46      // constructor creates empty List with "list" as the name
47      public List()
48      {
49         this( "list" );
50      } // end List no-argument constructor
51
52      // constructor creates an empty List with a name
53      public List( String listName )
54      {
55         name = listName;
56         firstNode = lastNode = null;
57      } // end List one-argument constructor
58
59      // insert item at front of List
60      public void insertAtFront( T insertItem )
61      {
62         if ( isEmpty() ) // firstNode and lastNode refer to same object
63            firstNode = lastNode = new ListNode< T >( insertItem );
64         else // firstNode refers to new node
65            firstNode = new ListNode< T >( insertItem, firstNode );
66      } // end method insertAtFront
67
68      // insert item at end of List
69      public void insertAtBack( T insertItem )
70      {
```

Fig. 22.3 | ListNode and List class declarations. (Part 2 of 4.)

```
71          if ( isEmpty() ) // firstNode and lastNode refer to same object
72              firstNode = lastNode = new ListNode< T >( insertItem );
73          else // lastNode's nextNode refers to new node
74              lastNode = lastNode.nextNode = new ListNode< T >( insertItem );
75      } // end method insertAtBack
76
77      // remove first node from List
78      public T removeFromFront() throws EmptyListException
79      {
80          if ( isEmpty() ) // throw exception if List is empty
81              throw new EmptyListException( name );
82
83          T removedItem = firstNode.data; // retrieve data being removed
84
85          // update references firstNode and lastNode
86          if ( firstNode == lastNode )
87              firstNode = lastNode = null;
88          else
89              firstNode = firstNode.nextNode;
90
91          return removedItem; // return removed node data
92      } // end method removeFromFront
93
94      // remove last node from List
95      public T removeFromBack() throws EmptyListException
96      {
97          if ( isEmpty() ) // throw exception if List is empty
98              throw new EmptyListException( name );
99
100         T removedItem = lastNode.data; // retrieve data being removed
101
102         // update references firstNode and lastNode
103         if ( firstNode == lastNode )
104             firstNode = lastNode = null;
105         else // locate new last node
106         {
107             ListNode< T > current = firstNode;
108
109             // loop while current node does not refer to lastNode
110             while ( current.nextNode != lastNode )
111                 current = current.nextNode;
112
113             lastNode = current; // current is new lastNode
114             current.nextNode = null;
115         } // end else
116
117         return removedItem; // return removed node data
118     } // end method removeFromBack
119
120     // determine whether list is empty
121     public boolean isEmpty()
122     {
123         return firstNode == null; // return true if list is empty
124     } // end method isEmpty
```

Fig. 22.3 | ListNode and List class declarations. (Part 3 of 4.)

```
125
126        // output list contents
127        public void print()
128        {
129            if ( isEmpty() )
130            {
131                System.out.printf( "Empty %s\n", name );
132                return;
133            } // end if
134
135            System.out.printf( "The %s is: ", name );
136            ListNode< T > current = firstNode;
137
138            // while not at end of list, output current node's data
139            while ( current != null )
140            {
141                System.out.printf( "%s ", current.data );
142                current = current.nextNode;
143            } // end while
144
145            System.out.println( "\n" );
146        } // end method print
147    } // end class List< T >
```

Fig. 22.3 | ListNode and List class declarations. (Part 4 of 4.)

```
1    // Fig. 22.4: EmptyListException.java
2    // Class EmptyListException declaration.
3    package com.deitel.ch22;
4
5    public class EmptyListException extends RuntimeException
6    {
7        // no-argument constructor
8        public EmptyListException()
9        {
10           this( "List" ); // call other EmptyListException constructor
11       } // end EmptyListException no-argument constructor
12
13       // one-argument constructor
14       public EmptyListException( String name )
15       {
16           super( name + " is empty" ); // call superclass constructor
17       } // end EmptyListException one-argument constructor
18   } // end class EmptyListException
```

Fig. 22.4 | EmptyListException class declaration.

```
1    // Fig. 22.5: ListTest.java
2    // ListTest class to demonstrate List capabilities.
3    import com.deitel.ch22.List;
4    import com.deitel.ch22.EmptyListException;
5
```

Fig. 22.5 | ListTest class to demonstrate List capabilities. (Part 1 of 3.)

```
6   public class ListTest
7   {
8      public static void main( String[] args )
9      {
10         List< Integer > list = new List< Integer >(); // create a List
11
12         // insert integers in list
13         list.insertAtFront( -1 );
14         list.print();
15         list.insertAtFront( 0 );
16         list.print();
17         list.insertAtBack( 1 );
18         list.print();
19         list.insertAtBack( 5 );
20         list.print();
21
22         // remove objects from list; print after each removal
23         try
24         {
25            int removedItem = list.removeFromFront();
26            System.out.printf( "\n%d removed\n", removedItem );
27            list.print();
28
29            removedItem = list.removeFromFront();
30            System.out.printf( "\n%d removed\n", removedItem );
31            list.print();
32
33            removedItem = list.removeFromBack();
34            System.out.printf( "\n%d removed\n", removedItem );
35            list.print();
36
37            removedItem = list.removeFromBack();
38            System.out.printf( "\n%d removed\n", removedItem );
39            list.print();
40         } // end try
41         catch ( EmptyListException emptyListException )
42         {
43            emptyListException.printStackTrace();
44         } // end catch
45      } // end main
46   } // end class ListTest
```

```
The list is: -1
The list is: 0 -1
The list is: 0 -1 1
The list is: 0 -1 1 5

0 removed
The list is: -1 1 5

-1 removed
The list is: 1 5                                        (continued...)
```

Fig. 22.5 | ListTest class to demonstrate List capabilities. (Part 2 of 3.)

```
5 removed
The list is: 1

1 removed
Empty list
```

Fig. 22.5 | ListTest class to demonstrate List capabilities. (Part 3 of 3.)

Generic Classes *ListNode and List*

Generic class ListNode (Fig. 22.3, lines 6–37) declares package-access fields data and nextNode. The data field is a reference of type T, so its type will be determined when the client code creates the corresponding List object. Variable nextNode stores a reference to the next ListNode object in the linked list (or null if the node is the last one in the list).

Lines 42–43 of class List (Fig. 22.3, lines 40–47) declare references to the first and last ListNodes in a List (firstNode and lastNode, respectively). The constructors (lines 47–50 and 53–57) initialize both references to null. The most important methods of class List are insertAtFront (lines 60–66), insertAtBack (lines 69–75), removeFromFront (lines 78–92) and removeFromBack (lines 95–118). Method isEmpty (lines 121–124) is a *predicate method* that determines whether the list is empty (i.e., the reference to the first node of the list is null). Predicate methods typically test a condition and do not modify the object on which they are called. If the list is empty, method isEmpty returns true; otherwise, it returns false. Method print (lines 127–146) displays the list's contents. We discuss class List's methods in more detail after we discuss class ListTest.

Class *ListTest*

Method main of class ListTest (Fig. 22.5) creates a List<Integer> object (line 10), then inserts objects at the beginning of the list using method insertAtFront, inserts objects at the end of the list using method insertAtBack, deletes objects from the front of the list using method removeFromFront and deletes objects from the end of the list using method removeFromBack. After each insert and remove operation, ListTest calls List method print to display the current list contents. If an attempt is made to remove an item from an empty list, an EmptyListException (Fig. 22.4) is thrown, so the method calls to removeFromFront and removeFromBack are placed in a try block that is followed by an appropriate exception handler. Notice in lines 13, 15, 17 and 19 that the application passes literal primitive int values to methods insertAtFront and insertAtBack. Each of these methods was declared with a parameter of the generic type T (Fig. 22.3, lines 60 and 69). Since this example manipulates a List<Integer>, the type T represents the type-wrapper class Integer. In this case, the JVM autoboxes each literal value in an Integer object, and that object is actually inserted into the list.

List *Method insertAtFront*

Now we discuss each method of class List (Fig. 22.3) in detail and provide diagrams showing the reference manipulations performed by methods insertAtFront, insertAtBack, removeFromFront and removeFromBack. Method insertAtFront (lines 60–66 of Fig. 22.3) places a new node at the front of the list. The steps are:

1. Call isEmpty to determine whether the list is empty (line 62).

2. If the list is empty, assign to firstNode and lastNode the new ListNode that was initialized with insertItem (line 63). (Recall that assignment operators evaluate

right to left.) The ListNode constructor at lines 13–16 calls the ListNode constructor at lines 20–24 to set instance variable data to refer to the insertItem passed as an argument and to set reference nextNode to null, because this is the first and last node in the list.

3. If the list is not empty, the new node is "linked" into the list by setting firstNode to a new ListNode object and initializing that object with insertItem and firstNode (line 65). When the ListNode constructor (lines 20–24) executes, it sets instance variable data to refer to the insertItem passed as an argument and performs the insertion by setting the nextNode reference of the new node to the ListNode passed as an argument, which previously was the first node.

In Fig. 22.6, part (a) shows a list and a new node during the insertAtFront operation and before the program links the new node into the list. The dotted arrows in part (b) illustrate *Step 3* of the insertAtFront operation that enables the node containing 12 to become the new first node in the list.

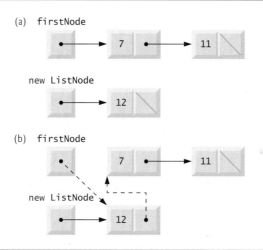

Fig. 22.6 | Graphical representation of operation insertAtFront.

List *Method* *insertAtBack*

Method insertAtBack (lines 69–75 of Fig. 22.3) places a new node at the back of the list. The steps are:

1. Call isEmpty to determine whether the list is empty (line 71).

2. If the list is empty, assign to firstNode and lastNode the new ListNode that was initialized with insertItem (line 72). The ListNode constructor at lines 13–16 calls the constructor at lines 20–24 to set instance variable data to refer to the insertItem passed as an argument and to set reference nextNode to null.

3. If the list is not empty, line 74 links the new node into the list by assigning to lastNode and lastNode.nextNode the reference to the new ListNode that was initialized with insertItem. ListNode's constructor (lines 13–16) sets instance variable data to refer to the insertItem passed as an argument and sets reference nextNode to null, because this is the last node in the list.

In Fig. 22.7, part (a) shows a list and a new node during the `insertAtBack` operation and before linking the new node into the list. The dotted arrows in part (b) illustrate *Step 3* of method `insertAtBack`, which adds the new node to the end of a list that is not empty.

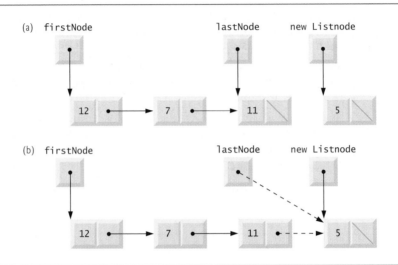

Fig. 22.7 | Graphical representation of operation `insertAtBack`.

List *Method* *removeFromFront*

Method `removeFromFront` (lines 78–92 of Fig. 22.3) removes the first node of the list and returns a reference to the removed data. If the list is empty when the program calls this method, the method throws an `EmptyListException` (lines 80–81). Otherwise, the method returns a reference to the removed data. The steps are:

1. Assign `firstNode.data` (the data being removed) to `removedItem` (line 83).

2. If `firstNode` and `lastNode` refer to the same object (line 86), the list has only one element at this time. So, the method sets `firstNode` and `lastNode` to `null` (line 87) to remove the node from the list (leaving the list empty).

3. If the list has more than one node, then the method leaves reference `lastNode` as is and assigns the value of `firstNode.nextNode` to `firstNode` (line 89). Thus, `firstNode` references the node that was previously the second node in the list.

4. Return the `removedItem` reference (line 91).

In Fig. 22.8, part (a) illustrates the list before the removal operation. The dashed lines and arrows in part (b) show the reference manipulations.

List *Method* *removeFromBack*

Method `removeFromBack` (lines 95–118 of Fig. 22.3) removes the last node of a list and returns a reference to the removed data. The method throws an `EmptyListException` (lines 97–98) if the list is empty when the program calls this method. The steps are:

1. Assign `lastNode.data` (the data being removed from the list) to `removedItem` (line 100).

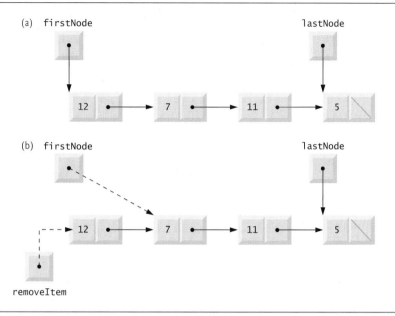

Fig. 22.8 | Graphical representation of operation removeFromFront.

2. If the firstNode and lastNode refer to the same object (line 103), the list has only one element at this time. So, line 104 sets firstNode and lastNode to null to remove that node from the list (leaving the list empty).

3. If the list has more than one node, create the ListNode reference current and assign it firstNode (line 107).

4. Now "walk the list" with current until it references the node before the last node. The while loop (lines 110–111) assigns current.nextNode to current as long as current.nextNode (the next node in the list) is not lastNode.

5. After locating the second-to-last node, assign current to lastNode (line 113) to update which node is last in the list.

6. Set the current.nextNode to null (line 114) to remove the last node from the list and terminate the list at the current node.

7. Return the removedItem reference (line 117).

In Fig. 22.9, part (a) illustrates the list before the removal operation. The dashed lines and arrows in part (b) show the reference manipulations.

List Method **print**

Method print (lines 127–146) first determines whether the list is empty (lines 129–133). If so, print displays a message indicating that the list is empty and returns control to the calling method. Otherwise, print outputs the list's data. Line 136 creates ListNode current and initializes it with firstNode. While current is not null, there are more items in the list. Therefore, line 141 outputs a string representation of current.data. Line 142 moves to the next node in the list by assigning the value of reference current.nextNode to current. This printing algorithm is identical for linked lists, stacks and queues.

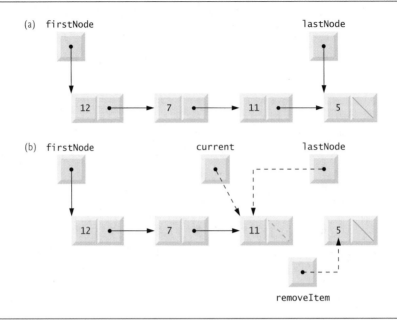

Fig. 22.9 | Graphical representation of operation removeFromBack.

22.5 Stacks

A stack is a constrained version of a list—new nodes can be added to and removed from a stack only at the top. For this reason, a stack is referred to as a **last-in, first-out (LIFO)** data structure. The link member in the bottom node is set to null to indicate the bottom of the stack. Note that a stack is not required to be implemented as a linked list—it can also be implemented using an array.

The primary methods for manipulating a stack are **push** and **pop**, which add a new node to the top of the stack and remove a node from the top of the stack, respectively. Method pop also returns the data from the popped node.

Stacks have many interesting applications. For example, when a program calls a method, the called method must know how to return to its caller, so the return address of the calling method is pushed onto the program-execution stack (discussed in Section 6.6). If a series of method calls occurs, the successive return addresses are pushed onto the stack in last-in, first-out order so that each method can return to its caller. Stacks support recursive method calls in the same manner as they do conventional nonrecursive method calls.

The program-execution stack also contains the memory for local variables on each invocation of a method during a program's execution. When the method returns to its caller, the memory for that method's local variables is popped off the stack, and those variables are no longer known to the program. If the local variable is a reference and the object to which it referred has no other variables referring to it, the object can be garbage collected.

Compilers use stacks to evaluate arithmetic expressions and generate machine-language code to process them. The exercises in this chapter explore several applications of stacks, including using them to develop a complete working compiler. Also, package java.util contains class Stack (see Chapter 20) for implementing and manipulating stacks that can grow and shrink during program execution.

In this section, we take advantage of the close relationship between lists and stacks to implement a stack class by reusing the List<T> class of Fig. 22.3. We demonstrate two different forms of reusability. First, we implement the stack class by extending class List. Then we implement an identically performing stack class through composition by including a reference to a List object as a private instance variable. The list, stack and queue data structures in this chapter are implemented to store references to objects of any type to encourage further reusability.

Stack Class That Inherits from *List<T>*

Figures 22.10 and 22.11 create and manipulate a stack class that extends the List<T> class of Fig. 22.3. We want the stack to have methods push, pop, isEmpty and print. Essentially, these are the List<T> methods insertAtFront, removeFromFront, isEmpty and print. Of course, class List<T> contains other methods (such as insertAtBack and removeFrom-Back) that we would rather not make accessible through the public interface to the stack class. It's important to remember that all methods in List<T>'s public interface class also are public methods of the subclass StackInheritance<T> (Fig. 22.10). Each method of StackInheritance<T> calls the appropriate List<T> method—for example, method push calls insertAtFront and method pop calls removeFromFront. StackInheritance<T> clients can call methods isEmpty and print because they are inherited from List<T>. Class StackInheritance<T> is declared in package com.deitel.ch22 (line 3) for reuse. Note that StackInheritance<T> does not import List<T>—the classes are in the same package.

```
1   // Fig. 22.10: StackInheritance.java
2   // StackInheritance extends class List.
3   package com.deitel.ch22;
4
5   public class StackInheritance< T > extends List< T >
6   {
7      // no-argument constructor
8      public StackInheritance()
9      {
10        super( "stack" );
11     } // end StackInheritance no-argument constructor
12
13     // add object to stack
14     public void push( T object )
15     {
16        insertAtFront( object );
17     } // end method push
18
19     // remove object from stack
20     public T pop() throws EmptyListException
21     {
22        return removeFromFront();
23     } // end method pop
24  } // end class StackInheritance
```

Fig. 22.10 | StackInheritance extends class List.

Class `StackInheritanceTest`'s method `main` (Fig. 22.11) creates an object of class `StackInheritance<T>` called `stack` (lines 10–11). The program pushes integers onto the stack (lines 14, 16, 18 and 20). Autoboxing is used here to insert `Integer` objects into the data structure. Lines 28–33 pop the objects from the stack in an infinite `while` loop. If method `pop` is invoked on an empty stack, the method throws an `EmptyListException`. In this case, the program displays the exception's stack trace, which shows the methods on the program-execution stack at the time the exception occurred. Note that the program uses method `print` (inherited from `List`) to output the contents of the stack.

```java
1   // Fig. 22.11: StackInheritanceTest.java
2   // Stack manipulation program.
3   import com.deitel.ch22.StackInheritance;
4   import com.deitel.ch22.EmptyListException;
5
6   public class StackInheritanceTest
7   {
8      public static void main( String[] args )
9      {
10        StackInheritance< Integer > stack =
11           new StackInheritance< Integer >();
12
13        // use push method
14        stack.push( -1 );
15        stack.print();
16        stack.push( 0 );
17        stack.print();
18        stack.push( 1 );
19        stack.print();
20        stack.push( 5 );
21        stack.print();
22
23        // remove items from stack
24        try
25        {
26           int removedItem;
27
28           while ( true )
29           {
30              removedItem = stack.pop(); // use pop method
31              System.out.printf( "\n%d popped\n", removedItem );
32              stack.print();
33           } // end while
34        } // end try
35        catch ( EmptyListException emptyListException )
36        {
37           emptyListException.printStackTrace();
38        } // end catch
39     } // end main
40  } // end class StackInheritanceTest
```

```
The stack is: -1
The stack is: 0 -1                                    (continued...)
```

Fig. 22.11 | Stack manipulation program. (Part 1 of 2.)

```
The stack is: 1  0 -1
The stack is: 5  1  0 -1

5 popped
The stack is: 1 0 -1

1 popped
The stack is: 0 -1

0 popped
The stack is: -1

-1 popped
Empty stack
com.deitel.ch22.EmptyListException: stack is empty
        at com.deitel.ch22.List.removeFromFront(List.java:81)
        at com.deitel.ch22.StackInheritance.pop(StackInheritance.java:22)
        at StackInheritanceTest.main(StackInheritanceTest.java:30)
```

Fig. 22.11 | Stack manipulation program. (Part 2 of 2.)

Stack Class That Contains a Reference to a List

You can also implement a class by reusing a list class through composition. Figure 22.12 uses a private List<T> (line 7) in class StackComposition<T>'s declaration. Composition enables us to hide the List<T> methods that should not be in our stack's public interface. We provide public interface methods that use only the required List<T> methods. Implementing each stack method as a call to a List<T> method is called **delegation**—the stack method invoked delegates the call to the appropriate List<T> method. In particular, StackComposition<T> delegates calls to List<T> methods insertAtFront, removeFrom-Front, isEmpty and print. In this example, we do not show class StackCompositionTest, because the only difference is that we change the type of the stack from StackInheritance to StackComposition (lines 3 and 10–11 of Fig. 22.11).

```
 1   // Fig. 22.12: StackComposition.java
 2   // StackComposition uses a composed List object.
 3   package com.deitel.ch22;
 4
 5   public class StackComposition< T >
 6   {
 7      private List< T > stackList;
 8
 9      // no-argument constructor
10      public StackComposition()
11      {
12         stackList = new List< T >( "stack" );
13      } // end StackComposition no-argument constructor
14
15      // add object to stack
16      public void push( T object )
17      {
```

Fig. 22.12 | StackComposition uses a composed List object. (Part 1 of 2.)

```
18          stackList.insertAtFront( object );
19       } // end method push
20
21       // remove object from stack
22       public T pop() throws EmptyListException
23       {
24          return stackList.removeFromFront();
25       } // end method pop
26
27       // determine if stack is empty
28       public boolean isEmpty()
29       {
30          return stackList.isEmpty();
31       } // end method isEmpty
32
33       // output stack contents
34       public void print()
35       {
36          stackList.print();
37       } // end method print
38    } // end class StackComposition
```

Fig. 22.12 | StackComposition uses a composed List object. (Part 2 of 2.)

22.6 Queues

Another commonly used data structure is the queue. A queue is similar to a checkout line in a supermarket—the cashier services the person at the beginning of the line first. Other customers enter the line only at the end and wait for service. Queue nodes are removed only from the head (or front) of the queue and are inserted only at the tail (or end). For this reason, a queue is a **first-in, first-out** (**FIFO**) data structure. The insert and remove operations are known as **enqueue** and **dequeue**.

Queues have many uses in computer systems. Each CPU in a computer can service only one application at a time. Each application requiring processor time is placed in a queue. The application at the front of the queue is the next to receive service. Each application gradually advances to the front as the applications before it receive service.

Queues are also used to support **print spooling**. For example, a single printer might be shared by all users of a network. Many users can send print jobs to the printer, even when the printer is already busy. These print jobs are placed in a queue until the printer becomes available. A program called a **spooler** manages the queue to ensure that, as each print job completes, the next print job is sent to the printer.

Information packets also wait in queues in computer networks. Each time a packet arrives at a network node, it must be routed to the next node along the path to the packet's final destination. The routing node routes one packet at a time, so additional packets are enqueued until the router can route them.

A file server in a computer network handles file-access requests from many clients throughout the network. Servers have a limited capacity to service requests from clients. When that capacity is exceeded, client requests wait in queues.

Figure 22.13 creates a Queue<T> class that contains a List<T> (Fig. 22.3) object and provides methods enqueue, dequeue, isEmpty and print. Class List<T> contains some methods (e.g., insertAtFront and removeFromBack) that we'd rather not make accessible through Queue<T>'s public interface. Using composition enables us to hide class List<T>'s other public methods from clients of class Queue<T>. Each Queue<T> method calls an appropriate List<T> method—method enqueue calls List<T> method insertAt-Back, method dequeue calls List<T> method removeFromFront, method isEmpty calls List<T> method isEmpty and method print calls List<T> method print. For reuse, class Queue<T> is declared in package com.deitel.ch22.

```java
1   // Fig. 22.13: Queue.java
2   // Queue uses class List.
3   package com.deitel.ch22;
4
5   public class Queue
6   {
7      private List< T > queueList;
8
9      // no-argument constructor
10     public Queue()
11     {
12        queueList = new List< T >( "queue" );
13     } // end Queue no-argument constructor
14
15     // add object to queue
16     public void enqueue( T object )
17     {
18        queueList.insertAtBack( object );
19     } // end method enqueue
20
21     // remove object from queue
22     public T dequeue() throws EmptyListException
23     {
24        return queueList.removeFromFront();
25     } // end method dequeue
26
27     // determine if queue is empty
28     public boolean isEmpty()
29     {
30        return queueList.isEmpty();
31     } // end method isEmpty
32
33     // output queue contents
34     public void print()
35     {
36        queueList.print();
37     } // end method print
38  } // end class Queue
```

Fig. 22.13 | Queue uses class List.

Class QueueTest's (Fig. 22.14) main method creates and initializes Queue<T> variable queue (line 10). Lines 13, 15, 17 and 19 enqueue four integers, taking advantage of auto-boxing to insert Integer objects into the queue. Lines 27–32 use an infinite loop to dequeue the objects in first-in, first-out order. When the queue is empty, method dequeue throws an EmptyListException, and the program displays the exception's stack trace.

```
1   // Fig. 22.14: QueueTest.java
2   // Class QueueTest.
3   import com.deitel.ch22.Queue;
4   import com.deitel.ch22.EmptyListException;
5
6   public class QueueTest
7   {
8      public static void main( String[] args )
9      {
10         Queue< Integer > queue = new Queue< Integer >();
11
12         // use enqueue method
13         queue.enqueue( -1 );
14         queue.print();
15         queue.enqueue( 0 );
16         queue.print();
17         queue.enqueue( 1 );
18         queue.print();
19         queue.enqueue( 5 );
20         queue.print();
21
22         // remove objects from queue
23         try
24         {
25            int removedItem;
26
27            while ( true )
28            {
29               removedItem = queue.dequeue(); // use dequeue method
30               System.out.printf( "\n%d dequeued\n", removedItem );
31               queue.print();
32            } // end while
33         } // end try
34         catch ( EmptyListException emptyListException )
35         {
36            emptyListException.printStackTrace();
37         } // end catch
38      } // end main
39   } // end class QueueTest
```

```
The queue is: -1
The queue is: -1 0
The queue is: -1 0 1
The queue is: -1 0 1 5

-1 dequeued
The queue is: 0 1 5

0 dequeued
The queue is: 1 5

1 dequeued
The queue is: 5                                          (continued...)
```

Fig. 22.14 | Queue processing program. (Part 1 of 2.)

```
5 dequeued
Empty queue
com.deitel.ch22.EmptyListException: queue is empty
        at com.deitel.ch22.List.removeFromFront(List.java:81)
        at com.deitel.ch22.Queue.dequeue(Queue.java:24)
        at QueueTest.main(QueueTest.java:29)
```

Fig. 22.14 | Queue processing program. (Part 2 of 2.)

22.7 **Trees**

Lists, stacks and queues are **linear data structures** (i.e., **sequences**). A tree is a nonlinear, two-dimensional data structure with special properties. Tree nodes contain two or more links. This section discusses binary trees (Fig. 22.15)—trees whose nodes each contain two links (one or both of which may be null). The **root node** is the first node in a tree. Each link in the root node refers to a **child**. The **left child** is the first node in the **left subtree** (also known as the root node of the left subtree), and the **right child** is the first node in the **right subtree** (also known as the root node of the right subtree). The children of a specific node are called **siblings**. A node with no children is called a **leaf node**. Computer scientists normally draw trees from the root node down—the opposite of the way most trees grow in nature.

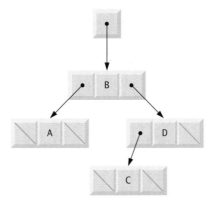

Fig. 22.15 | Binary tree graphical representation.

In our example, we create a special binary tree called a **binary search tree**. A binary search tree (with no duplicate node values) has the characteristic that the values in any left subtree are less than the value in that subtree's parent node, and the values in any right subtree are greater than the value in that subtree's parent node. Figure 22.16 illustrates a binary search tree with 12 integer values. Note that the shape of the binary search tree that corresponds to a set of data can vary, depending on the order in which the values are inserted into the tree.

Figures 22.17 and 22.18 create a generic binary search tree class and use it to manipulate a tree of integers. The application in Fig. 22.18 traverses the tree (i.e., walks through all its nodes) three ways—using recursive **inorder, preorder** and **postorder traversals.** The program generates 10 random numbers and inserts each into the tree. Class Tree<T> is declared in package com.deitel.ch22 for reuse.

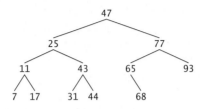

Fig. 22.16 | Binary search tree containing 12 values.

```
1   // Fig. 22.17: Tree.java
2   // TreeNode and Tree class declarations for a binary search tree.
3   package com.deitel.ch22;
4
5   // class TreeNode definition
6   class TreeNode< T extends Comparable< T > >
7   {
8      // package access members
9      TreeNode< T > leftNode; // left node
10     T data; // node value
11     TreeNode< T > rightNode; // right node
12
13     // constructor initializes data and makes this a leaf node
14     public TreeNode( T nodeData )
15     {
16        data = nodeData;
17        leftNode = rightNode = null; // node has no children
18     } // end TreeNode constructor
19
20     // locate insertion point and insert new node; ignore duplicate values
21     public void insert( T insertValue )
22     {
23        // insert in left subtree
24        if ( insertValue.compareTo( data ) < 0 )
25        {
26           // insert new TreeNode
27           if ( leftNode == null )
28              leftNode = new TreeNode< T >( insertValue );
29           else // continue traversing left subtree recursively
30              leftNode.insert( insertValue );
31        } // end if
32        // insert in right subtree
33        else if ( insertValue.compareTo( data ) > 0 )
34        {
35           // insert new TreeNode
36           if ( rightNode == null )
37              rightNode = new TreeNode< T >( insertValue );
```

Fig. 22.17 | TreeNode and Tree class declarations for a binary search tree. (Part 1 of 3.)

```
38              else // continue traversing right subtree recursively
39                  rightNode.insert( insertValue );
40          } // end else if
41      } // end method insert
42  } // end class TreeNode
43
44  // class Tree definition
45  public class Tree< T extends Comparable< T > >
46  {
47      private TreeNode< T > root;
48
49      // constructor initializes an empty Tree of integers
50      public Tree()
51      {
52          root = null;
53      } // end Tree no-argument constructor
54
55      // insert a new node in the binary search tree
56      public void insertNode( T insertValue )
57      {
58          if ( root == null )
59              root = new TreeNode< T >( insertValue ); // create root node
60          else
61              root.insert( insertValue ); // call the insert method
62      } // end method insertNode
63
64      // begin preorder traversal
65      public void preorderTraversal()
66      {
67          preorderHelper( root );
68      } // end method preorderTraversal
69
70      // recursive method to perform preorder traversal
71      private void preorderHelper( TreeNode< T > node )
72      {
73          if ( node == null )
74              return;
75
76          System.out.printf( "%s ", node.data ); // output node data
77          preorderHelper( node.leftNode );       // traverse left subtree
78          preorderHelper( node.rightNode );      // traverse right subtree
79      } // end method preorderHelper
80
81      // begin inorder traversal
82      public void inorderTraversal()
83      {
84          inorderHelper( root );
85      } // end method inorderTraversal
86
87      // recursive method to perform inorder traversal
88      private void inorderHelper( TreeNode< T > node )
89      {
90          if ( node == null )
91              return;
```

Fig. 22.17 | TreeNode and Tree class declarations for a binary search tree. (Part 2 of 3.)

```
92
93         inorderHelper( node.leftNode );        // traverse left subtree
94         System.out.printf( "%s ", node.data ); // output node data
95         inorderHelper( node.rightNode );       // traverse right subtree
96      } // end method inorderHelper
97
98      // begin postorder traversal
99      public void postorderTraversal()
100     {
101        postorderHelper( root );
102     } // end method postorderTraversal
103
104     // recursive method to perform postorder traversal
105     private void postorderHelper( TreeNode< T > node )
106     {
107        if ( node == null )
108           return;
109
110        postorderHelper( node.leftNode );      // traverse left subtree
111        postorderHelper( node.rightNode );     // traverse right subtree
112        System.out.printf( "%s ", node.data ); // output node data
113     } // end method postorderHelper
114  } // end class Tree
```

Fig. 22.17 | TreeNode and Tree class declarations for a binary search tree. (Part 3 of 3.)

```
1    // Fig. 22.18: TreeTest.java
2    // Binary tree test program.
3    import java.util.Random;
4    import com.deitel.ch22.Tree;
5
6    public class TreeTest
7    {
8       public static void main( String[] args )
9       {
10         Tree< Integer > tree = new Tree< Integer >();
11         int value;
12         Random randomNumber = new Random();
13
14         System.out.println( "Inserting the following values: " );
15
16         // insert 10 random integers from 0-99 in tree
17         for ( int i = 1; i <= 10; i++ )
18         {
19            value = randomNumber.nextInt( 100 );
20            System.out.printf( "%d ", value );
21            tree.insertNode( value );
22         } // end for
23
24         System.out.println ( "\n\nPreorder traversal" );
25         tree.preorderTraversal(); // perform preorder traversal of tree
26
27         System.out.println ( "\n\nInorder traversal" );
```

Fig. 22.18 | Binary tree test program. (Part 1 of 2.)

```
28            tree.inorderTraversal(); // perform inorder traversal of tree
29
30            System.out.println ( "\n\nPostorder traversal" );
31            tree.postorderTraversal(); // perform postorder traversal of tree
32            System.out.println();
33        } // end main
34    } // end class TreeTest
```

```
Inserting the following values:
49 64 14 34 85 64 46 14 37 55

Preorder traversal
49 14 34 46 37 64 55 85

Inorder traversal
14 34 37 46 49 55 64 85

Postorder traversal
37 46 34 14 55 85 64 49
```

Fig. 22.18 | Binary tree test program. (Part 2 of 2.)

Let's walk through the binary tree program. Method `main` of class `TreeTest` (Fig. 22.18) begins by instantiating an empty `Tree<T>` object and assigning its reference to variable `tree` (line 10). Lines 17–22 randomly generate 10 integers, each of which is inserted into the binary tree by calling method `insertNode` (line 21). The program then performs preorder, inorder and postorder traversals (these will be explained shortly) of `tree` (lines 25, 28 and 31, respectively).

Overview of Class *Tree*
Class `Tree` (Fig. 22.17, lines 45–114) requires its type argument to implement interface `Comparable`, so that each value inserted in the tree can be compared with the existing values to determine the insertion point. The class has `private` field `root` (line 47)—a `TreeNode` reference to the root node of the tree. `Tree`'s constructor (lines 50–53) initializes `root` to `null` to indicate that the tree is empty. The class contains method `insertNode` (lines 56–62) to insert a new node in the tree and methods `preorderTraversal` (lines 65–68), `inorderTraversal` (lines 82–85) and `postorderTraversal` (lines 99–102) to begin traversals of the tree. Each of these methods calls a recursive utility method to perform the traversal operations on the internal representation of the tree. (We discussed recursion in Chapter 18.)

Tree *Method* insertNode
Class `Tree`'s method `insertNode` (lines 56–62) first determines whether the tree is empty. If so, line 59 allocates a new `TreeNode`, initializes the node with the value being inserted in the tree and assigns the new node to reference `root`. If the tree is not empty, line 61 calls `TreeNode` method `insert` (lines 21–41). This method uses recursion to determine the location for the new node in the tree and inserts the node at that location. A node can be inserted only as a leaf node in a binary search tree.

TreeNode *Method* insert
`TreeNode` method `insert` compares the value to insert with the `data` value in the root node. If the insert value is less than the root node data (line 24), the program determines

if the left subtree is empty (line 27). If so, line 28 allocates a new TreeNode, initializes it with the value being inserted and assigns the new node to reference leftNode. Otherwise, line 30 recursively calls insert for the left subtree to insert the value into the left subtree. If the insert value is greater than the root node data (line 33), the program determines if the right subtree is empty (line 36). If so, line 37 allocates a new TreeNode, initializes it with the value being inserted and assigns the new node to reference rightNode. Otherwise, line 39 recursively calls insert for the right subtree to insert the value in the right subtree. If the insertValue is already in the tree, it's simply ignored.

Tree *Methods* inorderTraversal, preorderTraversal *and* postorderTraversal

Methods inorderTraversal, preorderTraversal and postorderTraversal call Tree helper methods inorderHelper (lines 88–96), preorderHelper (lines 71–79) and post-orderHelper (lines 105–113), respectively, to traverse the tree and print the node values. The helper methods in class Tree enable you to start a traversal without having to pass the root node to the method. Reference root is an implementation detail that a programmer should not be able to access. Methods inorderTraversal, preorderTraversal and postorderTraversal simply take the private root reference and pass it to the appropriate helper method to initiate a traversal of the tree. The base case for each helper method determines whether the reference it receives is null and, if so, returns immediately.

Method inorderHelper (lines 88–96) defines the steps for an inorder traversal:

1. Traverse the left subtree with a call to inorderHelper (line 93).

2. Process the value in the node (line 94).

3. Traverse the right subtree with a call to inorderHelper (line 95).

The inorder traversal does not process the value in a node until the values in that node's left subtree are processed. The inorder traversal of the tree in Fig. 22.19 is

```
6 13 17 27 33 42 48
```

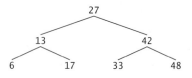

Fig. 22.19 | Binary search tree with seven values.

Note that the inorder traversal of a binary search tree prints the node values in ascending order. The process of creating a binary search tree actually sorts the data; thus, it's called the **binary tree sort**.

Method preorderHelper (lines 71–79) defines the steps for a preorder traversal:

1. Process the value in the node (line 76).

2. Traverse the left subtree with a call to preorderHelper (line 77).

3. Traverse the right subtree with a call to preorderHelper (line 78).

The preorder traversal processes the value in each node as the node is visited. After processing the value in a particular node, the preorder traversal processes the values in the left subtree, then processes the values in the right subtree. The preorder traversal of the tree in Fig. 22.19 is

```
27 13 6 17 42 33 48
```

Method `postorderHelper` (lines 105–113) defines the steps for a postorder traversal:

1. Traverse the left subtree with a call to `postorderHelper` (line 110).
2. Traverse the right subtree with a call to `postorderHelper` (line 111).
3. Process the value in the node (line 112).

The postorder traversal processes the value in each node after the values of all that node's children are processed. The `postorderTraversal` of the tree in Fig. 22.19 is

```
6 17 13 33 48 42 27
```

The binary search tree facilitates **duplicate elimination**. While building a tree, the insertion operation recognizes attempts to insert a duplicate value, because a duplicate follows the same "go left" or "go right" decisions on each comparison as the original value did. Thus, the insertion operation eventually compares the duplicate with a node containing the same value. At this point, the insertion operation can decide to discard the duplicate value (as we do in this example).

Searching a binary tree for a value that matches a key value is fast, especially for **tightly packed (or balanced) trees**. In a tightly packed tree, each level contains about twice as many elements as the previous level. Figure 22.19 is a tightly packed binary tree. A tightly packed binary search tree with n elements has $\log_2 n$ levels. Thus, at most $\log_2 n$ comparisons are required either to find a match or to determine that no match exists. Searching a (tightly packed) 1000-element binary search tree requires at most 10 comparisons, because $2^{10} > 1000$. Searching a (tightly packed) 1,000,000-element binary search tree requires at most 20 comparisons, because $2^{20} > 1,000,000$.

The chapter exercises present algorithms for several other binary tree operations, such as deleting an item from a binary tree, printing a binary tree in a two-dimensional tree format and performing a **level-order traversal of a binary tree**. The level-order traversal visits the nodes of the tree row by row, starting at the root node level. On each level of the tree, a level-order traversal visits the nodes from left to right. Other binary tree exercises include allowing a binary search tree to contain duplicate values, inserting string values in a binary tree and determining how many levels are contained in a binary tree.

22.8 Wrap-Up

This chapter completes our presentation of data structures. We began in Chapter 20 with an introduction to the built-in collections of the Java Collections Framework and continued in Chapter 21 by showing you how to implement generic methods and collections. In this chapter, you learned to build generic dynamic data structures that grow and shrink at execution time. You learned that linked lists are collections of data items that are "linked up in a chain." You also saw that an application can perform insertions and deletions at the beginning and end of a linked list. You learned that the stack and queue data structures are constrained versions of lists. For stacks, you saw that insertions and deletions are made only at the top. For queues that represent waiting lines, you saw that insertions are made at the tail and deletions are made from the head. You also learned the binary tree data structure. You saw a binary search tree that facilitated high-speed searching and sorting of data and eliminating duplicate data items efficiently. Throughout the chapter, you learned how to create and package these data structures for reusability and maintainability.

Next, we introduce Java applets—Java programs that typically execute in a browser. We overview the JDK's sample applets, then show you how to write and execute your own applets. We then introduce the Java Web Start capabilities for launching an applet and installing a desktop shortcut to relaunch the applet in the future without having to revisit the applet's website.

Summary

Section 22.1 Introduction
- Dynamic data structures can grow and shrink at execution time.
- Linked lists are collections of data items "linked up in a chain"—insertions and deletions can be made anywhere in a linked list.
- Stacks are important in compilers and operating systems—insertions and deletions are made only at the top of a stack.
- In a queue, insertions are made at the tail and deletions are made from the head.
- Binary trees facilitate high-speed searching and sorting of data, eliminating duplicate data items efficiently, representing file-system directories and compiling expressions into machine language.

Section 22.2 Self-Referential Classes
- A self-referential class contains a reference that refers to another object of the same class type. Self-referential objects can be linked together to form dynamic data structures.

Section 22.3 Dynamic Memory Allocation
- The limit for dynamic memory allocation can be as large as the available physical memory in the computer or the available disk space in a virtual-memory system. Often the limits are much smaller, because the computer's available memory must be shared among many users.
- If no memory is available, an `OutOfMemoryError` is thrown.

Section 22.4 Linked Lists
- A linked list is accessed via a reference to the first node of the list. Each subsequent node is accessed via the link-reference member stored in the previous node.
- By convention, the link reference in the last node of a list is set to `null` to mark the end of the list.
- A node can contain data of any type, including objects of other classes.
- A linked list is appropriate when the number of data elements to be stored is unpredictable. Linked lists are dynamic, so the length of a list can increase or decrease as necessary.
- The size of a "conventional" Java array cannot be altered—it's fixed at creation time.
- List nodes normally are not stored in contiguous memory. Rather, they are logically contiguous.

Section 22.5 Stacks
- A stack is a last-in, first-out (LIFO) data structure. The primary methods used to manipulate a stack are `push` and `pop`, which add a new node to the top of the stack and remove a node from the top of the stack, respectively. Method `pop` returns the removed node's data.
- When a method call is made, the called method must know how to return to its caller, so the return address is pushed onto the program-execution stack. If a series of method calls occurs, the successive return values are pushed onto the stack in last-in, first-out order so that each method can return to its caller.

- The program-execution stack contains the space created for local variables on each invocation of a method. When the method returns to its caller, the space for that method's local variables is popped off the stack, and those variables are no longer available to the program.

- Stacks are used by compilers to evaluate arithmetic expressions and generate machine-language code to process the expressions.

- The technique of implementing each stack method as a call to a List method is called delegation—the stack method invoked delegates the call to the appropriate List method.

Section 22.6 Queues

- A queue is similar to a checkout line in a supermarket—the first person in line is serviced first, and other customers enter the line only at the end and wait to be serviced.

- Queue nodes are removed only from the head of the queue and are inserted only at the tail. For this reason, a queue is referred to as a first-in, first-out (FIFO) data structure.

- The insert and remove operations for a queue are known as enqueue and dequeue.

- Queues have many uses in computer systems. Most computers have only a single processor, so only one application at a time can be serviced. Entries for the other applications are placed in a queue. The entry at the front of the queue is the next to receive service. Each entry gradually advances to the front of the queue as applications receive service.

Section 22.7 Trees

- A tree is a nonlinear, two-dimensional data structure. Tree nodes contain two or more links.

- A binary tree is a tree whose nodes all contain two links. The root node is the first node in a tree.

- Each link in the root node refers to a child. The left child is the first node in the left subtree, and the right child is the first node in the right subtree.

- The children of a node are called siblings. A node with no children is called a leaf node.

- In a binary search tree with no duplicate values, the values in any left subtree are less than the value in the subtree's parent node, and the values in any right subtree are greater than the value in the subtree's parent node. A node can be inserted only as a leaf node in a binary search tree.

- An inorder traversal of a binary search tree processes the node values in ascending order.

- In a preorder traversal, the value in each node is processed as the node is visited. Then the values in the left subtree are processed, then the values in the right subtree.

- In a postorder traversal, the value in each node is processed after the values of its children.

- The binary search tree facilitates duplicate elimination. As the tree is created, attempts to insert a duplicate value are recognized, because a duplicate follows the same "go left" or "go right" decisions on each comparison as the original value did. Thus, the duplicate eventually is compared with a node containing the same value. The duplicate value can be discarded at this point.

- In a tightly packed tree, each level contains about twice as many elements as the previous one. So a tightly packed binary search tree with n elements has $\log_2 n$ levels, and thus at most $\log_2 n$ comparisons would have to be made either to find a match or to determine that no match exists. Searching a (tightly packed) 1000-element binary search tree requires at most 10 comparisons, because $2^{10} > 1000$. Searching a (tightly packed) 1,000,000-element binary search tree requires at most 20 comparisons, because $2^{20} > 1,000,000$.

Terminology

Self-Review Exercises

22.1 Fill in the blanks in each of the following statements:

a) A self-_____ class is used to form dynamic data structures that can grow and shrink at execution time.

b) A(n) _____ is a constrained version of a linked list in which nodes can be inserted and deleted only from the start of the list.

c) A method that does not alter a linked list, but simply looks at it to determine whether it's empty, is referred to as a(n) _____ method.

d) A queue is referred to as a(n) _____ data structure because the first nodes inserted are the first ones removed.

e) The reference to the next node in a linked list is referred to as a(n) _____.

f) Automatically reclaiming dynamically allocated memory in Java is called _____.

g) A(n) _____ is a constrained version of a linked list in which nodes can be inserted only at the end of the list and deleted only from the start of the list.

h) A(n) _____ is a nonlinear, two-dimensional data structure that contains nodes with two or more links.

i) A stack is referred to as a(n) _____ data structure because the last node inserted is the first node removed.

j) The nodes of a(n) _____ tree contain two link members.

k) The first node of a tree is the _____ node.

l) Each link in a tree node refers to a(n) _____ or _____ of that node.

m) A tree node that has no children is called a(n) _____ node.

n) The three traversal algorithms we mentioned in the text for binary search trees are _____, _____ and _____.

22.2 What are the differences between a linked list and a stack?

22.3 What are the differences between a stack and a queue?

22.4 Perhaps a more appropriate title for this chapter would have been Reusable Data Structures. Comment on how each of the following entities or concepts contributes to the reusability of data structures:

a) classes

b) inheritance

c) composition

22.5 Manually provide the inorder, preorder and postorder traversals of the binary search tree of Fig. 22.20.

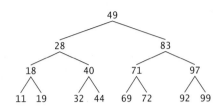

Fig. 22.20 | Binary search tree with 15 nodes.

Answers to Self-Review Exercises

22.1 a) referential. b) stack. c) predicate. d) first-in, first-out (FIFO). e) link. f) garbage collection. g) queue. h) tree i) last-in, first-out (LIFO). j) binary. k) root. l) child or subtree. m) leaf. n) inorder, preorder, postorder.

22.2 It's possible to insert a node anywhere in a linked list and remove a node from anywhere in a linked list. Nodes in a stack may be inserted only at the top of the stack and removed only from the top.

22.3 A queue is a FIFO data structure that has references to both its head and its tail, so that nodes may be inserted at the tail and deleted from the head. A stack is a LIFO data structure that has a single reference to the stack's top, where both insertion and deletion of nodes are performed.

22.4 a) Classes allow us to instantiate as many data structure objects of a certain type (i.e., class) as we wish.
   b) Inheritance enables a subclass to reuse the functionality from a superclass. Public and protected methods of a superclass can be accessed through a subclass to eliminate duplicate logic.
   c) Composition enables a class to reuse code by storing a reference to an instance of another class in a field. Public methods of the instance can be called by methods in the class that contains the reference.

22.5 The inorder traversal is

   11 18 19 28 32 40 44 49 69 71 72 83 92 97 99

The preorder traversal is

   49 28 18 11 19 40 32 44 83 71 69 72 97 92 99

The postorder traversal is

   11 19 18 32 44 40 28 69 72 71 92 99 97 83 49

Exercises

22.6 *(Concatenating Lists)* Write a program that concatenates two linked list objects of characters. Class ListConcatenate should include a static method concatenate that takes references to both list objects as arguments and concatenates the second list to the first list.

22.7 *(Inserting into an Ordered List)* Write a program that inserts 25 random integers from 0 to 100 in order into a linked-list object. For this exercise, you'll need to modify the List<T> class (Fig. 22.3) to maintain an ordered list. Name the new version of the class SortedList.

22.8 *(Merging Ordered Lists)* Modify the SortedList class from Exercise 22.7 to include a merge method that can merge the SortedList it receives as an argument with the SortedList that calls the method. Write an application to test method merge.

22.9 *(Copying a List Backwards)* Write a static method reverseCopy that receives a List<T> as an argument and returns a copy of that List<T> with its elements reversed. Test this method in an application.

22.10 *(Printing a Sentence in Reverse Using a Stack)* Write a program that inputs a line of text and uses a stack to display the words of the line in reverse order.

22.11 *(Palindrome Tester)* Write a program that uses a stack to determine whether a string is a palindrome (i.e., the string is spelled identically backward and forward). The program should ignore spaces and punctuation.

22.12 *(Infix-to-Postfix Converter)* Stacks are used by compilers to help in the process of evaluating expressions and generating machine-language code. In this and the next exercise, we investigate how compilers evaluate arithmetic expressions consisting only of constants, operators and parentheses.

Humans generally write expressions like 3 + 4 and 7 / 9 in which the operator (+ or / here) is written between its operands—this is called *infix notation*. Computers "prefer" *postfix notation*, in which the operator is written to the right of its two operands. The preceding infix expressions would appear in postfix notation as 3 4 + and 7 9 /, respectively.

To evaluate a complex infix expression, a compiler would first convert the expression to postfix notation and evaluate the postfix version. Each of these algorithms requires only a single left-to-right pass of the expression. Each algorithm uses a stack object in support of its operation, but each uses the stack for a different purpose.

In this exercise, you'll write a Java version of the infix-to-postfix conversion algorithm. In the next exercise, you'll write a Java version of the postfix expression evaluation algorithm. In a later exercise, you'll discover that code you write in this exercise can help you implement a complete working compiler.

Write class InfixToPostfixConverter to convert an ordinary infix arithmetic expression (assume a valid expression is entered) with single-digit integers such as

    (6 + 2) * 5 - 8 / 4

to a postfix expression. The postfix version of the preceding infix expression is (note that no parentheses are needed)

    6 2 + 5 * 8 4 / -

The program should read the expression into StringBuffer infix and use one of the stack classes implemented in this chapter to help create the postfix expression in StringBuffer postfix. The algorithm for creating a postfix expression is as follows:

a) Push a left parenthesis '(' on the stack.

b) Append a right parenthesis ')' to the end of infix.

c) While the stack is not empty, read infix from left to right and do the following:
     If the current character in infix is a digit, append it to postfix.
     If the current character in infix is a left parenthesis, push it onto the stack.
     If the current character in infix is an operator:
          Pop operators (if there are any) at the top of the stack while they have equal or higher precedence than the current operator, and append the popped operators to postfix.
          Push the current character in infix onto the stack.
     If the current character in infix is a right parenthesis:
          Pop operators from the top of the stack and append them to postfix until a left parenthesis is at the top of the stack.
          Pop (and discard) the left parenthesis from the stack.

The following arithmetic operations are allowed in an expression:

+   addition

-   subtraction

*   multiplication

/   division

∧   exponentiation

%   remainder

The stack should be maintained with stack nodes that each contain an instance variable and a reference to the next stack node. Some of the methods you may want to provide are as follows:

a)   Method `convertToPostfix`, which converts the infix expression to postfix notation.

b)   Method `isOperator`, which determines whether c is an operator.

c)   Method `precedence`, which determines whether the precedence of `operator1` (from the infix expression) is less than, equal to or greater than that of `operator2` (from the stack). The method returns `true` if `operator1` has lower precedence than `operator2`. Otherwise, `false` is returned.

d)   Method `peek` (this should be added to the stack class), which returns the top value of the stack without popping the stack.

22.13   *(Postfix Evaluator)* Write class `PostfixEvaluator` that evaluates a postfix expression such as

```
6 2 + 5 * 8 4 / -
```

The program should read a postfix expression consisting of digits and operators into a `StringBuffer`. Using modified versions of the stack methods implemented earlier in this chapter, the program should scan the expression and evaluate it (assume it's valid). The algorithm is as follows:

a)   Append a right parenthesis `')'` to the end of the postfix expression. When the right-parenthesis character is encountered, no further processing is necessary.

b)   When the right-parenthesis character has not been encountered, read the expression from left to right.

If the current character is a digit, do the following:

Push its integer value on the stack (the integer value of a digit character is its value in the Unicode character set minus the value of `'0'` in Unicode).

Otherwise, if the current character is an *operator*:

Pop the two top elements of the stack into variables x and y.

Calculate y *operator* x.

Push the result of the calculation onto the stack.

c)   When the right parenthesis is encountered in the expression, pop the top value of the stack. This is the result of the postfix expression.

[*Note:* In b) above (based on the sample expression at the beginning of this exercise), if the operator is `'/'`, the top of the stack is 4 and the next element in the stack is 40, then pop 4 into x, pop 40 into y, evaluate 40 / 4 and push the result, 10, back on the stack. This note also applies to operator `'-'`.] The arithmetic operations allowed in an expression are:

+   addition

-   subtraction

*   multiplication

/   division

∧   exponentiation

%   remainder

The stack should be maintained with one of the stack classes introduced in this chapter. You may want to provide the following methods:

a)   Method `evaluatePostfixExpression`, which evaluates the postfix expression.

b)   Method `calculate`, which evaluates the expression op1 operator op2.

22.14 *(Postfix Evaluator Modification)* Modify the postfix evaluator program of Exercise 22.13 so that it can process integer operands larger than 9.

22.15 *(Allowing Duplicates in a Binary Tree)* Modify Figs. 22.17 and 22.18 to allow the binary tree to contain duplicates.

22.16 *(Processing a Binary Search Tree of Strings)* Write a program based on the program of Figs. 22.17 and 22.18 that inputs a line of text, tokenizes the sentence into separate words, inserts the words in a binary search tree and prints the inorder, preorder and postorder traversals of the tree.

22.17 *(Duplicate Elimination)* In this chapter, we saw that duplicate elimination is straightforward when creating a binary search tree. Describe how you'd perform duplicate elimination when using only a one-dimensional array. Compare the performance of array-based duplicate elimination with the performance of binary-search-tree-based duplicate elimination.

22.18 *(Depth of a Binary Tree)* Modify Figs. 22.17 and 22.18 so the Tree class provides a method getDepth that determines how many levels are in the tree. Test the method in an application that inserts 20 random integers in a Tree.

22.19 *(Recursively Print a List Backward)* Modify the List<T> class of Fig. 22.3 to include method printListBackward that recursively outputs the items in a linked-list object in reverse order. Write a test program that creates a list of integers and prints the list in reverse order.

22.20 *(Recursively Search a List)* Modify the List<T> class of Fig. 22.3 to include method search that recursively searches a linked-list object for a specified value. The method should return a reference to the value if it's found; otherwise, it should return null. Use your method in a test program that creates a list of integers. The program should prompt the user for a value to locate in the list.

22.21 *(Binary Tree Search)* Modify class Tree of Fig. 22.17 to include method contains, which attempts to locate a specified value in a binary-search-tree object. The method should take as an argument a search key to locate. If the node containing the search key is found, the method should return a reference to that node's data; otherwise, it should return null.

22.22 *(Level-Order Binary Tree Traversal)* The program of Figs. 22.17 and 22.18 illustrated three recursive methods of traversing a binary tree—inorder, preorder and postorder traversals. This exercise presents the *level-order traversal* of a binary tree, in which the node values are printed level by level, starting at the root node level. The nodes on each level are printed from left to right. The level-order traversal is not a recursive algorithm. It uses a queue object to control the output of the nodes. The algorithm is as follows:

    a) Insert the root node in the queue.
    b) While there are nodes left in the queue, do the following:
        Get the next node in the queue.
        Print the node's value.
        If the reference to the left child of the node is not null:
            Insert the left child node in the queue.
        If the reference to the right child of the node is not null:
            Insert the right child node in the queue.

Write method levelOrder to perform a level-order traversal of a binary tree object. Modify the program of Figs. 22.17 and 22.18 to use this method. [*Note:* You'll also need to use the queue-processing methods of Fig. 22.13 in this program.]

22.23 *(Printing Trees)* Modify class Tree of Fig. 22.17 to include a recursive outputTree method to display a binary tree object. The method should output the tree row by row, with the top of the tree at the left of the screen and the bottom of the tree toward the right. Each row is output vertically. For example, the binary tree illustrated in Fig. 22.20 is output as shown in Fig. 22.21.

Fig. 22.21 | Sample output of recursive method `outputTree`.

The rightmost leaf node appears at the top of the output in the rightmost column and the root node appears at the left of the output. Each column starts five spaces to the right of the preceding column. Method `outputTree` should receive an argument `totalSpaces` representing the number of spaces preceding the value to be output. (This variable should start at zero so that the root node is output at the left of the screen.) The method uses a modified inorder traversal to output the tree—it starts at the rightmost node in the tree and works back to the left. The algorithm is as follows:

> While the reference to the current node is not null, perform the following:
> Recursively call `outputTree` with the right subtree of the current node and `totalSpaces + 5`.
> Use a `for` statement to count from 1 to `totalSpaces` and output spaces.
> Output the value in the current node.
> Set the reference to the current node to refer to the left subtree of the current node.
> Increment `totalSpaces` by 5.

22.24 *(Insert/Delete Anywhere in a Linked List)* Our linked list class allowed insertions and deletions at only the front and the back of the linked list. These capabilities were convenient for us when we used inheritance or composition to produce a stack class and a queue class with a minimal amount of code simply by reusing the list class. Linked lists are normally more general than those we provided. Modify the linked list class we developed in this chapter to handle insertions and deletions anywhere in the list.

22.25 *(Lists and Queues without Tail References)* Our implementation of a linked list (Fig. 22.3) used both a `firstNode` and a `lastNode`. The `lastNode` was useful for the `insertAtBack` and `removeFromBack` methods of the `List` class. The `insertAtBack` method corresponds to the `enqueue` method of the `Queue` class.

Rewrite the `List` class so that it does not use a `lastNode`. Thus, any operations on the tail of a list must begin searching the list from the front. Does this affect our implementation of the `Queue` class (Fig. 22.13)?

22.26 *(Performance of Binary Tree Sorting and Searching)* One problem with the binary tree sort is that the order in which the data is inserted affects the shape of the tree—for the same collection of data, different orderings can yield binary trees of dramatically different shapes. The performance of the binary tree sorting and searching algorithms is sensitive to the shape of the binary tree. What shape would a binary tree have if its data were inserted in increasing order? in decreasing order? What shape should the tree have to achieve maximal searching performance?

22.27 *(Indexed Lists)* As presented in the text, linked lists must be searched sequentially. For large lists, this can result in poor performance. A common technique for improving list-searching performance is to create and maintain an index to the list. An index is a set of references to key places in the list. For example, an application that searches a large list of names could improve performance by creating an index with 26 entries—one for each letter of the alphabet. A search operation for a last name beginning with 'Y' would then first search the index to determine where the 'Y' entries began, then "jump into" the list at that point and search linearly until the desired name was found. This would be much faster than searching the linked list from the beginning. Use the List class of Fig. 22.3 as the basis of an IndexedList class.

Write a program that demonstrates the operation of indexed lists. Be sure to include methods insertInIndexedList, searchIndexedList and deleteFromIndexedList.

22.28 *(Queue Class that Inherits from a List class)* In Section 22.5, we created a stack class from class List with inheritance (Fig. 22.10) and with composition (Fig. 22.12). In Section 22.6 we created a queue class from class List with composition (Fig. 22.13). Create a queue class by inheriting from class List. What are the differences between this class and the one we created with composition?

Special Section: Building Your Own Compiler

In Exercises 7.30–7.32, we introduced Simpletron Machine Language (SML), and you implemented a Simpletron computer simulator to execute SML programs. In Exercises 22.29–22.33, we build a compiler that converts programs written in a high-level programming language to SML. This section "ties" together the entire programming process. You'll write programs in this new high-level language, compile them on the compiler you build and run them on the simulator you built in Exercise 7.31. You should make every effort to implement your compiler in an object-oriented manner. [*Note:* Due to the size of the descriptions for Exercises 22.29–22.33, we've posted them in a PDF document located at www.deitel.com/books/jhtp8/.]

*Observe due measure, for right timing is in all things
the most important factor.*
—Hesiod

*Painting is only a bridge linking the painter's mind
with that of the viewer.*
—Eugene Delacroix

*The direction in which education starts a man will
determine his future in life.*
—Plato

Applets and Java Web Start

Objectives

In this chapter you'll learn:

- What applets are and how they are used in web pages.
- To observe some of Java's exciting capabilities through the JDK's demonstration applets.
- To write simple applets.
- To write a simple Extensible HyperText Markup Language (XHTML) document to load an applet into an applet container and execute the applet.
- Five methods that are called automatically by an applet container during an applet's life cycle.
- What the sandbox security model is and how it enables you to run downloaded code safely.
- What Java Web Start is and how to use it to download, install and run applets outside of the web browser.

23.1 **Introduction**

[*Note:* This chapter is intentionally small and simple for readers who wish to study applets after reading only the book's first few chapters. We present more complex applets in Chapter 24, Multimedia: Applets and Applications, and Chapter 27, Networking. Also, the examples in this chapter require some knowledge of XHTML to create a web page that loads an applet. With each example we supply sample XHTML documents that you can modify for your own purposes. To learn more about XHTML, visit the **XMTML Tutorials** link in our XHTML Resource Center (www.deitel.com/xhtml/).]

This chapter introduces **applets**—Java programs that are typically embedded in **XHTML (Extensible HyperText Markup Language) documents**—also called web pages. When a Java-enabled web browser loads a web page containing an applet, the applet downloads into the browser and executes.

Applet Containers

The application in which an applet executes is known as the **applet container**. It is the applet container's responsibility to load the applet's class(es), create an instance of the applet and manage its life cycle (which we discuss in more detail in Section 23.4). The Java Development Kit (JDK) includes one called the **appletviewer** for testing applets as you develop them and before you embed them in web pages. We demonstrate applets using both the appletviewer and web browsers, which execute Java applets via the **Java Plug-In**. Some browsers don't come with the plug-in by default. You can visit java.com to determine whether your browser is ready to execute Java applets. If not, you can click the **Free Java Download** button to install Java for your browser. Several popular browsers are supported. We tested our applets in Mozilla's Firefox 3, Microsoft's Internet Explorer 7, Google's Chrome, Opera 9 and Apple's Safari 3.

Java Web Start and the Java Network Launch Protocol (JNLP)

This chapter concludes with an introduction to Java Web Start and the Java Network Launch Protocol (JNLP). Together, these enable you to package your applets and applications so that they can be installed onto the user's desktop. As you'll learn in Chapter 24, Java Web Start also enables you to give the user control over whether an applet or application downloaded from the web can have limited access to resources on the local file system. For example, if you create a downloadable text-editor program in Java, users would probably want to store their documents on their own computers.

23.2 Sample Applets Provided with the JDK

Before we discuss our own applets, let's consider several demonstration applets provided with the JDK. Each sample applet comes with its source code. Some programmers find it interesting to read this source code to learn exciting Java features.

The demonstration programs provided with the JDK are located in a directory called demo. For Windows, the default location of the JDK 6.0's demo directory is

```
C:\Program Files\Java\jdk1.6.0_##\demo
```

where _## represents the JDK update number. On UNIX/Linux, the default location is the directory in which you install the JDK followed by jdk1.6.0_##/demo—for example,

```
/usr/local/jdk1.6.0_##/demo
```

For other platforms, there will be a similar directory (or folder) structure. This chapter assumes that the JDK is installed in C:\Program Files\Java\jdk1.6.0_11 on Windows or in your home directory in ~/jdk1.6.0_11 on UNIX/Linux. You may need to update the locations specified here to reflect your chosen installation directory and disk drive, or a different version of the JDK.

If you are using a Java development tool that does not come with the Sun Java demos, you can download the current JDK from java.sun.com/javase/downloads/index.jsp. Mac OS X users should visit developer.apple.com/java for information about Java on the Mac, or use virtualization software to run the Windows or Linux versions of Java in a virtual machine.

Overview of the Demonstration Applets
Open a command window and use the cd command to change directories to the JDK's demo directory. The demo directory contains several subdirectories. You can list them by issuing the dir command on Windows or the ls command on UNIX/Linux/Max OS X. We discuss sample programs in the applets and jfc subdirectories. The applets directory contains demonstration applets. The jfc (Java Foundation Classes) directory contains applets and applications that demonstrate Java's powerful graphics and GUI capabilities.

Change to the applets directory and list its contents to see the directory names for the demonstration applets. Figure 23.1 provides a brief description of each. If your browser supports Java, you can test an applet by opening the XHTML document for it in the applet's directory. We'll demonstrate three of these applets by using the appletviewer command in a command window.

Example	Description
Animator	Performs one of four separate animations.
ArcTest	Demonstrates drawing arcs. You can interact with the applet to change attributes of the arc that is displayed.
BarChart	Draws a simple bar chart.

Fig. 23.1 | The examples from the applets directory. (Part 1 of 2.)

Example	Description
Blink	Displays blinking text in different colors.
CardTest	Demonstrates several GUI components and layouts.
Clock	Draws a clock with rotating hands, the current date and the current time. The clock updates once per second.
DitherTest	Demonstrates drawing with a graphics technique known as dithering that allows gradual transformation from one color to another.
DrawTest	Allows the user mouse to draw lines and points in different colors by dragging the mouse.
Fractal	Draws a fractal. Fractals typically require complex calculations to determine how they are displayed. We discuss fractals in Section 18.8.
GraphicsTest	Draws shapes to illustrate graphics capabilities.
GraphLayout	Draws a graph consisting of many nodes (represented as rectangles) connected by lines. Drag a node to see the other nodes in the graph adjust on the screen and demonstrate complex graphical interactions.
ImageMap	Demonstrates an image with hot spots. Positioning the mouse pointer over certain areas of the image highlights the area and displays a message in the lower-left corner of the applet container window. Position over the mouth in the image to hear the applet say "hi."
JumpingBox	Moves a rectangle randomly around the screen. Try to catch it by clicking it with the mouse!
MoleculeViewer	Presents a three-dimensional view of several chemical molecules. Drag the mouse to view the molecule from different angles.
NervousText	Draws text that jumps around the applet.
SimpleGraph	Draws a complex curve.
SortDemo	Compares three sorting techniques. Sorting (described in Chapter 19) arranges information in order—like alphabetizing words. When you execute this example with the appletviewer, three windows appear. When you execute it in a browser, the three demos appear side by side. Click in each demo to start the sort. Note that the sorts all operate at different speeds.
SpreadSheet	Demonstrates a simple spreadsheet of rows and columns.
TicTacToe	Allows the user to play Tic-Tac-Toe against the computer.
WireFrame	Draws a three-dimensional shape as a wire frame. Drag the mouse to view the shape from different angles.

Fig. 23.1 | The examples from the applets directory. (Part 2 of 2.)

TicTacToe *Applet*

This TicTacToe demonstration applet allows you to play Tic-Tac-Toe against the computer. Change directories to subdirectory TicTacToe, where you'll find the file example1.html that loads the applet. In the command window, type the command

```
appletviewer example1.html
```

and press *Enter*. This executes the appletviewer applet container, which loads the XHT-ML document example1.html specified as its command-line argument. The appletviewer determines from the document which applet to load and executes it. Figure 23.2 shows several screen captures of playing Tic-Tac-Toe with this applet. You can open the XHTML document in your browser to execute the applet in the browser.

Fig. 23.2 | `TicTacToe` applet sample execution.

You are player **X**. To interact with the applet, point the mouse at the square where you want to place an **X** and click the mouse button. The applet plays a sound and places an **X** in the square if it is open. If the square is occupied, this is an invalid move, and the applet plays a different sound, indicating that you cannot make the specified move. After you make a valid move, the applet responds by making its own move.

To play again, click the `appletviewer`'s **Applet** menu and select the **Reload** menu item (Fig. 23.3), or click the applet again when the game is over. To terminate the `appletviewer`, click the `appletviewer`'s **Applet** menu and select the **Quit** menu item.

Fig. 23.3 | **Applet** menu in the `appletviewer`.

DrawTest *Applet*

The `DrawTest` applet allows you to draw lines and points in different colors. In the command window, change directories to directory `applets`, then to subdirectory `DrawTest`. You can move up the directory tree incrementally toward `demo` by issuing the command "`cd ..`" in the command window. The `DrawTest` directory contains the `example1.html` document that is used to execute the applet. In the command window, type the command

```
appletviewer example1.html
```

and press *Enter*. The appletviewer loads example1.html, determines from the document which applet to load and executes it. Figure 23.4 shows a screen capture after some lines and points have been drawn.

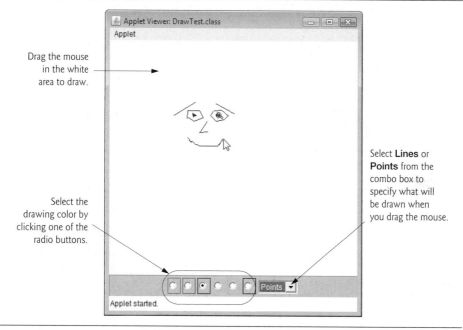

Drag the mouse in the white area to draw.

Select **Lines** or **Points** from the combo box to specify what will be drawn when you drag the mouse.

Select the drawing color by clicking one of the radio buttons.

Fig. 23.4 | DrawTest applet sample execution.

By default the applet allows you to draw black lines by dragging the mouse across the applet. When you drag the mouse, note that the line's start point always remains in the same place and its endpoint follows the mouse pointer around the applet. The line is not permanent until you release the mouse button.

Select a color by clicking one of the radio buttons at the bottom of the applet. You can select from red, green, blue, pink, orange and black. Change the shape to draw from **Lines** to **Points** by selecting **Points** from the combo box. To start a new drawing, select **Reload** from the appletviewer's **Applet** menu.

Java2D Applet

The Java2D applet demonstrates many features of the Java 2D API (which we introduced in Chapter 15). Change directories to the jfc directory in the JDK's demo directory, then change to the Java2D directory. In the command window, type the command

```
appletviewer Java2Demo.html
```

and press *Enter*. The appletviewer loads Java2Demo.html, determines from the document which applet to load and executes it. Figure 23.5 shows a screen capture of one of this applet's many demonstrations of Java's two-dimensional graphics capabilities.

At the top of the applet are tabs that look like file folders in a filing cabinet. This demo provides 12 tabs, each demonstrating Java 2D API features. To change to a different part of the demo, simply click a different tab. Also, try changing the options in the upper-right

Click a tab to select a
two-dimensional graphics demo.

Try changing the options to see
their effect on the demonstration.

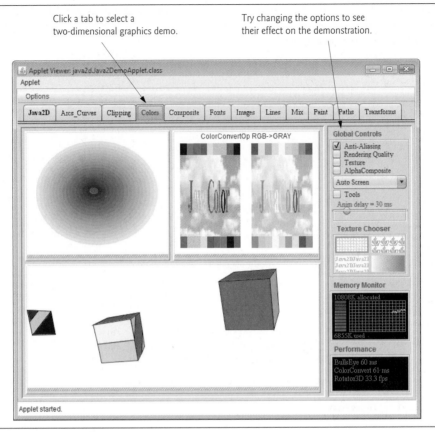

Fig. 23.5 | `Java2D` applet sample execution.

corner of the applet. Some of these affect the speed with which the applet draws the graphics. For example, click the checkbox to the left of the word **Anti-Aliasing** to turn off antialiasing (a graphics technique for producing smoother on-screen graphics in which the edges are blurred). Shapes that are not antialiased are less complex to draw. Accordingly, when the antialiasing feature is turned off, the animation speed increases for the animated shapes at the bottom of the demo (Fig. 23.5).

23.3 Simple Java Applet: Drawing a String

Every Java applet is a graphical user interface on which you can place GUI components using the techniques introduced in Chapter 14 or draw using the techniques demonstrated in Chapter 15. In this chapter, we'll demonstrate drawing on an applet. Examples in Chapters 24 and 27 demonstrate building an applet's graphical user interface.

Now let's build an applet of our own. We begin with a simple applet (Fig. 23.6) that draws "Welcome to Java Programming!" on the applet. We show this applet executing in two applet containers—the `appletviewer` and the Mozilla Firefox web browser. At the end of this section, you'll learn how to execute the applet in a web browser.

```
 1    // Fig. 23.6: WelcomeApplet.java
 2    // Applet that draws a String.
 3    import java.awt.Graphics;   // program uses class Graphics
 4    import javax.swing.JApplet; // program uses class JApplet
 5
 6    public class WelcomeApplet extends JApplet
 7    {
 8       // draw text on applet's background
 9       public void paint( Graphics g )
10       {
11          // call superclass version of method paint
12          super.paint( g );
13
14          // draw a String at x-coordinate 25 and y-coordinate 25
15          g.drawString( "Welcome to Java Programming!", 25, 25 );
16       } // end method paint
17    } // end class WelcomeApplet
```

WelcomeApplet executing in the `appletviewer`

Upper-left corner of drawing area is location *(0, 0)*. Drawing area extends from below the **Applet** menu to above the status bar. *x*-coordinates increase from left to right. *y*-coordinates increase from top to bottom.

Pixel coordinate *(25, 25)* at which the string is displayed

Applet menu

Status bar mimics what would be displayed in the browser's status bar as the applet loads and begins executing.

WelcomeApplet executing in Mozilla Firefox

Upper-left corner of drawing area

Pixel coordinate *(25, 25)*

Fig. 23.6 | Applet that draws a `String`.

Creating the Applet Class

Line 3 imports class `Graphics` to enable the applet to draw graphics, such as lines, rectangles, ovals and strings of characters. Class **`JApplet`** (imported at line 4) from package `javax.swing` is used to create applets. As with applications, every Java applet contains at least one `public` class declaration. An applet container can create only objects of classes that are `public` and extend `JApplet` (or its superclass `Applet`). For this reason, class `WelcomeApplet` (lines 6–17) extends `JApplet`.

An applet container expects every Java applet to have methods named **`init`**, **`start`**, **`paint`**, **`stop`** and **`destroy`**, each of which is declared in class `JApplet`. Each new applet class you create inherits default implementations of these methods from class `JApplet`. These methods can be overridden (redefined) to perform tasks that are specific to your applet. Section 23.4 discusses each of these methods in more detail.

When an applet container loads class WelcomeApplet, the container creates a Welcome-Applet object, then calls its methods init, start and paint in sequence. If you do not declare these methods in your applet, the applet container calls the inherited versions. The superclass methods init and start have empty bodies, so they do not perform any tasks. The superclass method paint does not draw anything on the applet.

You might wonder why it's necessary to inherit methods init, start and paint if their default implementations do not perform tasks. Some applets do not use all three of these methods. However, the applet container does not know that. Thus, it expects every applet to have these methods, so that it can provide a consistent start-up sequence. This is similar to applications' always starting execution with main. Inheriting the "default" versions of these methods guarantees that the applet container can execute each applet uniformly. Also, inheriting default implementations of these methods allows the programmer to concentrate on defining only the methods required for a particular applet.

Overriding Method **paint** *for Drawing*

To enable our applet to draw, class WelcomeApplet overrides method paint (lines 9–16) by placing statements in the body of paint that draw a message on the screen. Method paint receives a parameter of type Graphics (called g by convention), which is used to draw graphics on the applet. You do not call method paint explicitly in an applet. Rather, the applet container calls paint to tell the applet when to draw, and the applet container is responsible for passing a Graphics object as an argument.

Line 12 calls the superclass version of method paint that was inherited from JApplet. This should be the first statement in every applet's paint method. Omitting it can cause subtle drawing errors in applets that combine drawing and GUI components.

Line 15 uses Graphics method drawString to draw Welcome to Java Programming! on the applet. The method receives as arguments the String to draw and the *x-y* coordinates at which the bottom-left corner of the String should appear in the drawing area. When line 15 executes, it draws the String on the applet at the coordinates 25 and 25.

23.3.1 Executing WelcomeApplet in the appletviewer

After creating class WelcomeApplet and saving it in the file WelcomeApplet.java, open a command window, change to the directory in which you saved the applet class declaration and compile class WelcomeApplet.

Recall that applets are embedded in web pages for execution in an applet container (appletviewer or a browser). Before you can execute the applet, you must create an XHTML document that specifies which applet to execute in the applet container. Typically, an XHTML document ends with an **.html** or **.htm** file-name extension. Figure 23.7 shows a simple XHTML document—WelcomeApplet.html—that loads the applet defined in Fig. 23.6 into an applet container.

Most XHTML elements are delimited by pairs of **tags**—e.g., lines 1 and 6 delimit the XHTML document's beginning and end, respectively. Each tag is enclosed in angle brackets (< and >). Lines 2–5 specify the **body element** element of the document—this represents the elements that will be displayed in the web page. Lines 3–4 specify an **applet element** that tells the applet container to load a specific applet and defines the size of its display area (its width and height in pixels) in the applet container.

```
1   <html>
2   <body>
3   <applet code = "WelcomeApplet.class" width = "300" height = "45">
4   </applet>
5   </body>
6   </html>
```

Fig. 23.7 | `WelcomeApplet.html` loads `WelcomeApplet` (Fig. 23.6) into an applet container.

The applet and its corresponding XHTML document are normally stored in the same directory on disk. Typically, a browser loads an XHTML document from a computer (other than your own) connected to the Internet. However, XHTML documents also can reside on your computer (as in Section 23.2). When an applet container encounters an `applet` element in an XHTML document, it loads the applet's `.class` file (or files) from the same location that contains the XHTML document.

The `applet` element has several **attributes**. The first attribute in line 3, `code = "WelcomeApplet.class"`, indicates that the file `WelcomeApplet.class` contains the compiled applet class. The second and third attributes in line 3 indicate the **width** (300) and the **height** (45) of the applet in pixels. The `</applet>` tag (line 4) terminates the `applet` element that began at line 2. The `</html>` tag (line 6) terminates the XHTML document.

Look-and-Feel Observation 23.1

An applet should generally be less than 1024 pixels wide and 768 pixels tall—dimensions supported by most computer screens.

Common Programming Error 23.1

Forgetting the ending `</applet>` tag prevents the applet from executing in some applet containers. The `appletviewer` terminates without indicating an error. Some web browsers simply ignore the incomplete `applet` element.

Error-Prevention Tip 23.1

If you receive a `MissingResourceException` error message when loading an applet into the `appletviewer` or a browser, check the `<applet>` tag in the XHTML document carefully for syntax errors, such as commas (`,`) between the attributes.

The `appletviewer` understands only the `<applet>` and `</applet>` XHTML tags and ignores all other tags in the document. The `appletviewer` is an ideal place to test an applet and ensure that it executes properly. Once the applet's execution is verified, you can add its XHTML tags to a web page that others can view in their web browsers.

To execute `WelcomeApplet` in the `appletviewer`, open a command window, change to the directory containing your applet and XHTML document, then type

```
appletviewer WelcomeApplet.html
```

Error-Prevention Tip 23.2

Test your applets in the `appletviewer` before executing them in a web browser. Browsers often save a copy of an applet in memory until all the browser's windows are closed. If you change an applet, recompile it, then reload it in your browser, the browser may still execute the original version of the applet.

Error-Prevention Tip 23.3

Test your applets in every web browser in which they'll execute to ensure that they operate correctly.

23.3.2 Executing an Applet in a Web Browser

The sample program executions in Fig. 23.6 demonstrate WelcomeApplet executing in the appletviewer and in the Mozilla Firefox web browser. To execute an applet in Firefox, perform the following steps:

1. Select **Open File...** from the **File** menu.

2. In the dialog box that appears, locate the directory containing the XHTML document for the applet you wish to execute.

3. Select the XHTML document.

4. Click the **Open** button.

The steps for executing applets in other web browsers are similar. In most browsers, you can simply type *Ctrl + O* to open a dialog that enables you to select an XHTML document from your local hard disk.

Error-Prevention Tip 23.4

*If your applet executes in the appletviewer, but does not execute in your web browser, Java may not be installed and configured for your browser. In this case, visit the website java.com and click the **Free Java Download** button to install Java for your browser.*

23.4 Applet Life-Cycle Methods

Now that you've created an applet, let's consider the five applet methods that are called by the applet container from the time the applet is loaded into the browser to the time it's terminated by the browser. These methods correspond to various aspects of an applet's life cycle. Figure 23.8 lists these methods, which are inherited into your applet classes from class JApplet. The table specifies when each method gets called and explains its purpose. Other than method paint, these methods have empty bodies by default. If you'd like to declare any of them in your applets and have the applet container call them, you must use the method headers shown in Fig. 23.8.

Method	Description
public void init()	
	Called once by the applet container when an applet is loaded for execution. This method initializes an applet. Typical actions performed here are initializing fields, creating GUI components, loading sounds to play, loading images to display (see Chapter 24) and creating threads (see Chapter 26).

Fig. 23.8 | JApplet life-cycle methods that are called by an applet container during an applet's execution. (Part 1 of 2.)

Method	Description
public void start()	Called by the applet container after method init completes execution. In addition, if the user browses to another website and later returns to the applet's XHTML page, method start is called again. The method performs any tasks that must be completed when the applet is loaded for the first time and that must be performed every time the applet's XHTML page is revisited. Actions performed here might include starting an animation or starting other threads of execution.
public void paint(Graphics g)	Called by the applet container after methods init and start. Method paint is also called when the applet needs to be repainted. For example, if the user covers the applet with another open window on the screen and later uncovers it, the paint method is called. Typical actions performed here involve drawing with the Graphics object g that is passed to the paint method by the applet container.
public void stop()	This method is called by the applet container when the user leaves the applet's web page by browsing to another web page. Since it's possible that the user might return to the web page containing the applet, method stop performs tasks that might be required to suspend the applet's execution, so that the applet does not use computer processing time when it's not displayed on the screen. Typical actions performed here would stop the execution of animations and threads.
public void destroy()	This method is called by the applet container when the applet is being removed from memory. This occurs when the user exits the browsing session by closing all the browser windows and may also occur at the browser's discretion when the user has browsed to other web pages. The method performs any tasks that are required to clean up resources allocated to the applet.

Fig. 23.8 | JApplet life-cycle methods that are called by an applet container during an applet's execution. (Part 2 of 2.)

Common Programming Error 23.2

Declaring methods init, start, paint, stop or destroy with method headers that differ from those shown in Fig. 23.8 results in methods that will not be called by the applet container. The code specified in your versions of the methods will not execute. The @Override annotation can be applied to each method to prevent this problem.

23.5 Initializing an Instance Variable with Method init

Our next applet (Fig. 23.9) computes the sum of two values entered into input dialogs by the user and displays the result by drawing a String inside a rectangle on the applet. The sum is stored in an instance variable of the AdditionApplet class, so it can be used in both the init method and the paint method. The XHTML document that you can use to load this applet into an applet container (i.e., the appletviewer or a web browser) is shown in Fig. 23.10.

```
1   // Fig. 23.9: AdditionApplet.java
2   // Applet that adds two double values entered via input dialogs.
3   import java.awt.Graphics;     // program uses class Graphics
4   import javax.swing.JApplet;   // program uses class JApplet
5   import javax.swing.JOptionPane; // program uses class JOptionPane
6
7   public class AdditionApplet extends JApplet
8   {
9      private double sum; // sum of values entered by user
10
11     // initialize applet by obtaining values from user
12     public void init()
13     {
14        // obtain first number from user
15        String firstNumber = JOptionPane.showInputDialog(
16           "Enter first floating-point value" );
17
18        // obtain second number from user
19        String secondNumber = JOptionPane.showInputDialog(
20           "Enter second floating-point value" );
21
22        // convert numbers from type String to type double
23        double number1 = Double.parseDouble( firstNumber );
24        double number2 = Double.parseDouble( secondNumber );
25
26        sum = number1 + number2; // add numbers
27     } // end method init
28
29     // draw results in a rectangle on applet's background
30     public void paint( Graphics g )
31     {
32        super.paint( g ); // call superclass version of method paint
33
34        // draw rectangle starting from (15, 10) that is 270
35        // pixels wide and 20 pixels tall
36        g.drawRect( 15, 10, 270, 20 );
37
38        // draw results as a String at (25, 25)
39        g.drawString( "The sum is " + sum, 25, 25 );
40     } // end method paint
41  } // end class AdditionApplet
```

Fig. 23.9 | Applet that adds two **double** values entered via input dialogs.

```
1    <html>
2    <body>
3    <applet code = "AdditionApplet.class" width = "300" height = "50">
4    </applet>
5    </body>
6    </html>
```

Fig. 23.10 | `AdditionApplet.html` loads class `AdditionApplet` of Fig. 23.9 into an applet container.

The applet requests that the user enter two floating-point numbers. In Fig. 23.9, line 9 declares instance variable `sum` of type `double`. The applet contains two methods—`init` (lines 12–27) and `paint` (lines 30–40). When an applet container loads this applet, the container creates an instance of class `AdditionApplet` and calls its `init` method—this occurs only once during an applet's execution. Method `init` normally initializes the applet's fields (if they need to be initialized to values other than their defaults) and performs other tasks that should occur only once when the applet begins execution. The first line of `init` always appears as shown in line 12, which indicates that `init` is a `public` method that receives no arguments and returns no information when it completes.

Lines 15–24 declare variables to store the values entered by the user, obtain the user input and convert the `String`s entered by the user to `double` values. Line 26 adds the values stored in variables `number1` and `number2`, and assigns the result to instance variable `sum`. At this point, the applet's `init` method returns program control to the applet container, which then calls the applet's `start` method. We did not declare `start` in this applet, so the one inherited from class `JApplet` is called here.

Next, the applet container calls the applet's `paint` method, which draws a rectangle (line 36) where the addition result will appear. Line 39 calls the `Graphics` object's `draw-String` method to display the results. The statement concatenates the value of instance variable `sum` to the `String` `"The sum is "` and displays the concatenated `String`.

Software Engineering Observation 23.1
The only statements that should be placed in an applet's init *method are those that should execute only once when the applet is initialized.*

23.6 Sandbox Security Model

For security reasons, it's generally considered dangerous to allow applets or any other program that you execute from a web browser to access your local computer. So, you must decide whether *you trust the source*. For example, if you choose to download a new version of the Firefox web browser from Mozilla's `firefox.com` website, you must decide whether you trust Mozilla. After all, their installer program is going to modify your system and place the files to execute Firefox on your computer. Once it's installed, Firefox will be able to access files and other local resources. Most of what you do with your web browsers—such as shopping, browsing the web and downloading software—requires you to trust the sites you visit and to trust the organizations that maintain those sites. If you are not careful, a malicious downloaded program could gain control of your computer, access personal information stored there, corrupt your data and possibly even be used to attack other computers on the Internet—as so often happens with computer viruses today.

Preventing Malicious Applets

Applets are typically downloaded from the Internet. What would happen if you downloaded a malicious applet? Consider the fact that a browser downloads and executes a Java applet automatically—the user *is not asked for approval*. In fact, an applet typically downloads *without the user's knowledge*—it's just another element of the web page the user happens to be visiting.

The designers of Java considered this issue thoroughly, since Java was intended for use in networked environments. To combat malicious code, the Java platform uses a so-called **sandbox security model** that provides a mechanism for executing downloaded code safely. Such code executes in the "sandbox" and is not allowed to "play outside the sandbox." By default, downloaded code cannot access local system resources, and an applet can interact only with the server from which the applet was downloaded.

Digitally Signed Applets

Unfortunately, executing in a sandbox makes it difficult for applets to perform useful tasks. It's possible, however, for an organization that wishes to create applets with access to the local system to obtain a security certificate (also called a digital certificate) from one of several certificate authorities (see en.wikipedia.org/wiki/Certificate_Authority for a list of authorities and more information about certificate authorities). The organization can then use tools provided with the JDK to "digitally sign" an applet that requires access to local system resources. When a user downloads a digitally signed applet, a dialog prompts the user asking whether he or she trusts the applet's source. In that dialog, the user can view the organization's security certificate and see which certificate authority issued it. If the user indicates that he/she trusts the source, only then will the applet be able to access to the local computer's resources.

In the next section, we introduce Java Web Start and the Java Network Launch Protocol (JNLP). These technologies enable applets or applications to interact with the user to request access to specific local system resources. With the user's permission, this enables Java programmers to extend the sandbox, but it does not give their programs access to all of the user's local resources—so the sandbox principles are still in effect. For example, it would be useful for a downloadable text editor program to store the user's files in a folder on the user's computer. The text editor can prompt the user to ask for permission to do this. If the user grants permission for a specific directory on disk, the program can then access only that local directory and its subdirectories.

For more information on digitally signed applets, visit java.sun.com/developer/onlineTraining/Programming/JDCBook/signed.html. For information on the Java Platform security model, visit java.sun.com/javase/6/docs/technotes/guides/security/.

23.7 Java Web Start and the Java Network Launch Protocol (JNLP)

Java Web Start is a framework for running downloaded applets and applications outside the browser. Typically, such programs are stored on a web server for access via the Internet, but they can also be stored on an organization's network for internal distribution, or even on CDs, DVDs or other media. As you'll learn in Chapter 24, Java Web Start enables you to ask the user if a downloaded program can have access to the resources of the user's computer.

Java Web Start Features

Some key Java Web Start features include:

- *Desktop integration:* Users can launch robust applets and applications by clicking a hyperlink in a web page, and can quickly and easily install the programs on their computers. Java Web Start can be configured to ask the user if a desktop icon should be created so the user can launch the program directly from the desktop. Downloaded programs can also have an "offline mode" for execution when the computer is not connected to the Internet.

- *Automatic updating:* When you execute a program via Java Web Start, the program is downloaded and cached (stored) on the user's computer. The next time the user executes that program, Java Web Start launches it from the cache. If the program has been updated since it was last launched, Java Web Start can automatically download the updates, so a user always has the most up-to-date version. This makes installation and updating software simple and seamless to the user.

- *Draggable applets:* This is a new feature as of Java SE 6 Update 10. With a small change to the `applet` element that invokes an applet from an XHTML document, you can allow users to execute an applet in its own window by holding the *Alt* key and dragging the applet out of the web browser. The applet continues to execute even after the web browser closes.

Java Network Launch Protocol (JNLP)

A **Java Network Launch Protocol (JNLP)** document provides the information that Java Web Start needs in order to download and run a program. Also, you must package your program in one or more Java archive (JAR) files that contain the program's code and resources (e.g., images, media files, text files).

By default, programs launched via Java Web Start execute using the sandbox security model. If the user gives permission, such programs can access the local file system, the clipboard and other services via the JNLP APIs of package `javax.jnlp`. We discuss some of these features in Chapter 24. Digitally signed programs can gain greater access to the local system if the user trusts the source.

23.7.1 Packaging the DrawTest Applet for Use with Java Web Start

Let's package the JDK's `DrawTest` demonstration applet (discussed in Section 23.2) so that you can execute it via Java Web Start. To do so, you must first wrap the applet's `.class` files and the resources it uses (if any) into a Java archive (JAR) file. In a command window, change to the `DrawTest` directory, as you did in Section 23.2. Once in that folder, execute the following command:

```
jar cvf DrawTest.jar *.class
```

which creates a JAR file in the current directory named `DrawTest.jar` containing the applet's `.class` files—`DrawControls.class`, `DrawPanel.class` and `DrawTest.class`. If the program had other resources, you'd simply add the file names or the folder names in which those resources are stored to the end of the preceding command. The letters `cvf` are command-line options to the **jar command**. The **c option** indicates that the command should create a new JAR file. The **v option** indicates that the command should produce verbose output so you can see the list of files and directories being included in the JAR file. The **f**

option indicates that the next argument in the command line (`DrawTest.jar`) is the new JAR file's name. Figure 23.11 shows the preceding command's verbose output, which shows the files that were placed into the JAR.

```
added manifest
adding: DrawControls.class(in = 2611) (out= 1488)(deflated 43%)
adding: DrawPanel.class(in = 2703) (out= 1406)(deflated 47%)
adding: DrawTest.class(in = 1170) (out= 706)(deflated 39%)
```

Fig. 23.11 | Output of the `jar` command.

23.7.2 JNLP Document for the DrawTest Applet

Next, you must create a JNLP document that describes the contents of the JAR file and specifies which file in the JAR is the so-called **main-class** that begins the program's execution. For an applet, the `main-class` is the one that extends `JApplet` (i.e., `DrawTest` in this example). For an application, the `main-class` is the one that contains the `main` method. A basic JNLP document for the `DrawTest` applet is shown in Fig. 23.12. We describe this document's elements momentarily.

```
 1   <?xml version="1.0" encoding="UTF-8"?>
 2   <jnlp
 3       codebase=PathToJNLPFile
 4       href="DrawTest.jnlp">
 5
 6       <information>
 7           <title>DrawTest Applet</title>
 8           <vendor>Sun Microsystems, Inc.</vendor>
 9           <shortcut>
10               <desktop/>
11           </shortcut>
12           <offline-allowed/>
13       </information>
14
15       <resources>
16           <java version="1.6+"/>
17           <jar href="DrawTest.jar" main="true"/>
18       </resources>
19
20       <applet-desc
21           name="DrawTest"
22           main-class="DrawTest"
23           width="400"
24           height="400">
25       </applet-desc>
26   </jnlp>
```

Fig. 23.12 | `DrawTest.jnlp` document for launching the `DrawTest` applet.

Overview of XML

JNLP documents are written in **Extensible Markup Language (XML)**—a widely supported standard for describing data. XML is commonly used to exchange data between applications over the Internet, and many applications now use XML to specify configuration information as well—as is the case with JNLP documents for Java Web Start. XML permits you to create markup for virtually any type of information. This enables you to create entirely new markup languages for describing any type of data, such as mathematical formulas, software-configuration instructions, chemical molecular structures, music, news, recipes and financial reports. XML describes data in a way that both humans and computers can understand. JNLP is a so-called XML vocabulary that describes the information Java Web Start needs to launch a program.

XML documents contain **elements** that specify the document's structure, such as `title` (line 7), and text that represents content (i.e., data), such as `DrawTest Applet` (line 7). XML documents delimit elements with **start tags** and **end tags**. A start tag consists of the element name in **angle brackets** (e.g., `<title>` and `<vendor>` in lines 7 and 8). Start tags may also contain attributes of the form *name=value*—for example, the `jnlp` start tag contains the attribute `href="DrawTest.jnlp"`. An end tag consists of the element name preceded by a **forward slash** (/) in angle brackets (e.g., `</title>` and `</vendor>` in lines 7 and 8). An element's start and end tags enclose text that represents a piece of data (e.g., the vendor of the program—`Sun Microsystems, Inc.`—in line 8, which is enclosed by the `<vendor>` start tag and `</vendor>` end tag) or other elements (e.g., the `title`, `vendor`, `shortcut` and `offline-allowed` elements in the `information` element of lines 6–13). Every XML document must have exactly one **root element** that contains all the other elements. In Fig. 23.12, the **jnlp element** (lines 2–26) is the root element.

JNLP Document: `jnlp` Element

The `jnlp` element's start tag (lines 2–4) has two attributes—`codebase` and `href`. The `codebase` attribute's value is a URL that specifies the path where the JNLP document and the JAR file are stored—this is specified in Fig. 23.12 as *PathToJNLPFile*, since this value depends on the location from which the applet is loaded. The `href` attribute specifies the JNLP file that launches the program. We saved the JNLP file and the JAR file in the `Draw-Test` demonstration applet's directory within the JDK's directory structure. We used the following local file system URL as the `codebase`:

```
file:.
```

which indicates that the code is in the current directory (.). Typically, the `codebase` references a directory on a web server with an `http://` URL. If you'd like to serve your applet or application from a web server so users can access it online, you'll need to configure your web server correctly, as described at `java.sun.com/javase/6/docs/technotes/guides/javaws/developersguide/setup.html`.

JNLP Document: `information` Element

The **information element** (lines 6–13) provides details about the program. The **title** element specifies a title for the program. The **vendor element** specifies who created the program. The values of these elements appear in Java Web Start's security warnings and errors that are presented to the user. The `title`'s value also appears in the title bar of the window in which the program executes.

The **desktop element** that is nested in the **shortcut element** (lines 9–11) tells Java Web Start to ask whether the user wishes to install a desktop shortcut. If the user accepts, an icon will appear on the desktop. The user can then launch the program in its own window by double-clicking the desktop icon. Note the syntax of the `<desktop/>` element—a so-called empty XML element. When nothing appears between an element's start and end tags, the element can be written using one tag that ends with />.

The **offline-allowed element** (line 12) indicates that once the program is installed on the user's computer, it can be launched via Java Web Start—even when the computer is not connected to the Internet. This is particularly useful for any program that can be used with files stored on the user's computer.

JNLP Document: **resources** *Element*
The **resources element** (lines 15–18) contains two nested elements. The **java element** lists the minimum version of Java required to execute the program (line 16) and the **jar element** (line 17) specifies the location of the JAR file that contains the program and whether that JAR file contains the class that launches the program. There can be multiple jar elements, as you'll see in the next chapter.

JNLP Document: **applet-desc** *Element*
The **applet-desc element** (lines 20–25) is similar to the applet element in XHTML. The name attribute specifies the applet's name. The main-class attribute specifies the main applet class (the one that extends JApplet). The width and height attributes specify the width and height in pixels, respectively, of the window in which the applet will execute. Chapter 24 discusses a similar element for applications—application-desc.

Launching the Applet with Java Web Start
You're now ready to launch the applet via Java Web Start. There are several ways to do this. You can use the **javaws command** in a command window from the folder that contains the JNLP document, as in

```
javaws DrawTest.jnlp
```

You can also use your operating system's file manager to locate the JNLP on your computer and double click its file name. Normally, the JNLP file is referenced from a web page via a hyperlink. The DrawTestWebPage.html document in Fig. 23.13 (which was saved in the same directory as the JNLP file) contains an anchor (a) element (line 4), which links to the DrawTest.jnlp file. Clicking this hyperlink in the web page downloads the JNLP file (in this case, it's loaded from the local file system) and executes the corresponding applet.

```
1   <html>
2      <head><title>DrawTest Launcher Page</title></head>
3      <body>
4         <a href="DrawTest.jnlp">Launch DrawTest via Java Web Start</a>
5      </body>
6   </html>
```

hyperlink to
DrawTest.jnlp

Fig. 23.13 | XHTML document that launches the DrawTest applet when the user clicks the link.

When you run the applet via Java Web Start the first time, you'll be presented with the dialog in Fig. 23.14. This dialog enables the user to decide if a desktop icon will be installed. If the user clicks **OK**, a new icon labeled with the title specified in the JNLP document appears on the user's desktop. The applet is also cached for future use. After the user clicks **OK** or **Skip** in this dialog, the program executes (Fig. 23.15).

Fig. 23.14 | Dialog asking whether the user wishes to install a desktop shortcut.

Fig. 23.15 | `DrawTest` applet running with Java Web Start.

Viewing the Installed Java Web Start Programs
You can view the installed Java Web Start programs in the **Java Cache Viewer** by typing the following command in a command window:

```
javaws -viewer
```

This displays the window in Fig. 23.16. The **Java Cache Viewer** enables you to manage the Java Web Start programs on your system. You can run a selected program, create a desktop shortcut for a program (if there is not one already), delete installed programs, and more.

For more information on Java Web Start, visit `java.sun.com/javase/6/docs/tech-notes/guides/javaws/`. This site provides an overview of Java Web Start and includes links to the Developer's Guide, an FAQ, the JNLP Specification and the API documentation for the `javax.jnlp` package.

Fig. 23.16 | Viewing installed Java Web Start programs in the **Java Cache Viewer**.

23.8 Wrap-Up

In this chapter, you learned the fundamentals of Java applets and Java Web Start. You leaned basic XHTML concepts for embedding an applet in a web page and executing it in an applet container such as the appletviewer or a web browser. In addition, we discussed the five methods that are called automatically by the applet container during an applet's life cycle. We discussed Java's sandbox security model for executing downloaded code. Then we introduced Java Web Start and the Java Network Launch Protocol (JNLP). You learned how to package a program into a JAR file so that it could be executed via Java Web Start. We also discussed the basic elements of a JNLP document. In the next chapter, you'll see several additional applets as we present basic multimedia capabilities. You'll also learn more features of Java Web Start and JNLP. In Chapter 27, we demonstrate how to customize an applet via parameters that are specified in an applet XHTML element.

Summary

Section 23.1 Introduction
- Applets are Java programs that are typically embedded in XHTML (Extensible HyperText Markup Language) documents—also called web pages. When a Java-enabled web browser loads a web page containing an applet, the applet downloads into the browser and executes.
- The application in which an applet executes is known as the applet container. It is the applet container's responsibility to load the applet's class(es), create an instance of the applet and manage its life cycle. The JDK includes an applet container called the appletviewer for testing applets as you develop them and before you embed them in web pages.
- Web browsers execute Java applets via the Java Plug-In.

Section 23.2 Sample Applets Provided with the JDK
- To re-execute an applet in the appletviewer, click the appletviewer's **Applet** menu and select the **Reload** menu item.
- To terminate the appletviewer, select **Quit** from the appletviewer's **Applet** menu.

Section 23.3 Simple Java Applet: Drawing a String

- Every Java applet is a graphical user interface on which you can place GUI components or draw.

- Class JApplet from package javax.swing is used to create applets.

- An applet container can create only objects of classes that are public and extend JApplet (or the Applet class from early versions of Java).

- An applet container expects every Java applet to have methods named init, start, paint, stop and destroy, each of which is declared in class JApplet. Each new applet class you create inherits default implementations of these methods from class JApplet.

- When an applet container loads an applet, it creates an object of the applet's type, then calls the applet's init, start and paint methods. If you do not declare these methods in your applet, the applet container calls the inherited versions.

- The superclass methods init and start have empty bodies, so they do not perform any tasks. The superclass method paint does not draw anything on the applet.

- To enable an applet to draw, override its method paint. You do not call method paint explicitly in an applet. Rather, the applet container calls paint to tell the applet when to draw, and the container is responsible for passing a Graphics object as an argument.

- The first statement in method paint should be a call to the superclass method paint. Omitting this can cause subtle drawing errors in applets that combine drawing and GUI components.

- Before you can execute an applet, you must create an XHTML (Extensible HyperText Markup Language) document that specifies which applet to execute in the applet container. Typically, an XHTML document ends with an ".html" or ".htm" file-name extension.

- Most XHTML elements are delimited by pairs of tags. All XHTML tags begin with a left angle bracket, <, and end with a right angle bracket, >.

- An applet element tells the applet container to load a specific applet and defines the size of its display area (its width and height in pixels) in the applet container.

- Normally, an applet and its corresponding XHTML document are stored in the same directory.

- When an applet container encounters an XHTML document that contains an applet, the container automatically loads the applet's .class file(s) from the same directory on the computer in which the XHTML document resides.

- The appletviewer understands only the <applet> and </applet> XHTML tags and ignores all other tags in the document.

Section 23.4 Applet Life-Cycle Methods

- Five applet life-cycle methods are called by the applet container from the time the applet is loaded into the browser to the time it is terminated by the browser.

- Method init is called once by the applet container to initialize an applet when it's loaded.

- Method start is called by the applet container after method init completes execution. In addition, if the user browses to another website and later returns to the applet's XHTML page, method start is called again.

- Method paint is called by the applet container after methods init and start. Method paint is also called when the applet needs to be repainted.

- Method stop is called by the applet container when the user leaves the applet's web page by browsing to another web page.

- Method destroy is called by the applet container when the applet is being removed from memory. This occurs when the user exits the browsing session by closing all the browser windows and may also occur at the browser's discretion when the user has browsed to other web pages.

Section 23.5 Initializing an Instance Variable with Method `init`
- `Graphics` method `drawString` draws a `String` at a specified location.

- `Graphics` method `drawRect` draws a rectangle at the specified upper-left corner, width and height.

Section 23.6 Sandbox Security Model
- It's considered dangerous to allow applets or other programs that you execute from a web browser to access your local computer. You must decide whether *you trust the source*.

- A browser downloads an applet *without the user's knowledge*—it's just another element of the web page the user happens to be visiting.

- To combat malicious code, the Java platform uses a sandbox security model that provides a mechanism for executing downloaded code safely. Downloaded code cannot access local system resources, and an applet can interact only with the server from which it was downloaded.

- You can "digitally sign" an applet that requires access to local system resources. If the user indicates that he/she trusts the applet's source, only then will the applet be able to access the local computer's resources.

Section 23.7 Java Web Start and the Java Network Launch Protocol (JNLP)
- Java Web Start is a framework for running downloaded programs outside of the browser. Typically, such programs are stored on a web server, but they can also be stored on an organization's network for internal distribution, or even on CDs, DVDs or other media.

- Users can launch robust applets and applications by clicking a hyperlink in a web page, and can quickly and easily install the programs on their computers.

- Java Web Start can be configured to ask the user if a desktop icon should be created so the user can launch the program directly from the desktop. Downloaded programs can also have an "offline mode" for execution when the computer is not connected to the Internet.

- When you execute a program via Java Web Start, the program is downloaded and cached (stored) on the user's computer. The next time the user executes that program, Java Web Start launches it from the cache.

- If the program has been updated since it was last lauched, Java Web Start can automatically download the new version, so a user always has the most up-to-date version.

- A Java Network Launch Protocol (JNLP) document provides the information that Java Web Start needs to download and run a program.

- Programs launched via Java Web Start execute using the sandbox security model. The user can permit access to the local file system, the clipboard and other services via the JNLP APIs.

Section 23.7.1 Packaging the **DrawTest** Applet for Use with Java Web Start
- The `jar` command is used to create JAR files. Option `c` indicates that the command should create a new JAR file. Option `v` indicates that the command should produce verbose output. Option `f` indicates that the next argument in the command line is the new JAR file's name.

Section 23.7.2 JNLP Document for the **DrawTest** Applet
- A JNLP document describes the contents of the JAR file and specifies which file in the JAR is the so-called `main-class` that begins the program's execution.

- JNLP documents are written in Extensible Markup Language (XML)—a widely supported standard for describing data.

- JNLP is a so-called XML vocabulary that describes the information Java Web Start needs to launch a program.

- XML documents contain elements that specify the document's structure. XML documents delimit elements with start tags and end tags. A start tag consists of the element name in angle brackets. Start tags may also contain attributes of the form *name=value*. An end tag consists of the element name preceded by a forward slash (/) in angle brackets.

- An element's start and end tags enclose text that represents a piece of data or other elements.

- Every XML document must have exactly one root element that contains all the other elements.

- The jnlp element's codebase attribute specifies the path where the JNLP document and the JAR file are stored. The href attribute specifies the JNLP file that launches the program.

- Typically, the codebase references a directory on a web server with an http:// URL.

- The information element provides details about the program.

- The title element specifies a title for the program.

- The vendor element specifies who created the program.

- The desktop element nested in the shortcut element tells Java Web Start to ask users whether they wish to install a desktop shortcut.

- The offline-allowed element indicates that a program can be launched via Java Web Start even when the computer is not connected to the Internet.

- The resources element contains a java element that lists the minimum version of Java required to execute the program and a jar element that specifies the location of the JAR file.

- The applet-desc element's name attribute specifies the applet's name. The main-class attribute specifies the main applet class. The width and height attributes specify the width and height in pixels, respectively, of the window in which the applet will execute.

- To launch the applet via Java Web Start you can use the javaws command. You can also use your operating system's file manager to locate the JNLP on your computer and double click its file name. Normally, a JNLP file is referenced from a web page via a hyperlink.

- When you run an applet via Java Web Start the first time and the JNLP document specifies that a desktop icon should be installed, you'll be presented with a dialog that enables you to decide whether to install the desktop icon. If you click **OK**, a new icon labeled with the title specified in the JNLP document appears on the desktop.

- You can view the installed Java Web Start programs in the **Java Cache Viewer** by typing the command javaws -viewer in a command window:

- The **Java Cache Viewer** enables you to manage the installed Java Web Start programs. You can run a selected program, create a desktop shortcut, delete installed programs, and more.

Terminology

Java Plug-In 955
Java Web Start 968
javaws command 972
jnlp element of a JNLP document 971
main-class specified in an JNLP document 970
offline-allowed element of a JNLP document 972
paint method of class JApplet 961
resources element of a JNLP document 972
root element (XML) 971
sandbox security model 968

shortcut element of a JNLP document 971
start method of class JApplet 961
start tag 971
stop method of class JApplet 961
tag (in an XHTML document) 962
title element of a JNLP document 971
v option of the jar command 969
vendor element of a JNLP document 971
width of an applet in pixels 963
XHTML (Extensible HyperText Markup Language) document 955

Self-Review Exercise

23.1 Fill in the blanks in each of the following:
a) Java applets begin execution with a series of three method calls: _____, _____ and _____.
b) The _____ method is invoked for an applet each time a browser's user leaves an XHTML page on which the applet resides.
c) Every applet should extend class _____.
d) The _____ or a browser can be used to execute a Java applet.
e) The _____ method is called each time the user of a browser revisits the XHTML page on which an applet resides.
f) To load an applet into a browser, you must first define a(n) _____ file.
g) Method _____ is called once when an applet begins execution.
h) Method _____ is invoked to draw on an applet.
i) Method _____ is invoked for an applet when the browser removes it from memory.
j) The _____ and _____ XHTML tags specify that an applet should be loaded into an applet container and executed.
k) _____ is a framework for running downloaded programs outside the browser.
l) A(n) _____ document provides the information that Java Web Start needs to download and run a program.
m) The _____ enables you to manage the Java Web Start programs on your system.

Answers to Self-Review Exercise

23.1 a) init, start, paint. b) stop. c) JApplet (or Applet). d) appletviewer. e) start. f) XHTML. g) init. h) paint. i) destroy. j) <applet>, </applet>. k) Java Web Start. l) Java Network Launch Protocol (JNLP). m) **Java Cache Viewer**.

Exercises

23.2 Write an applet that asks the user to enter two floating-point numbers, obtains the numbers from the user and displays the two numbers, then displays the larger number followed by the words "is larger" as a string on the applet. If the numbers are equal, the applet should print the message "These numbers are equal." Use the techniques shown in Fig. 23.9.

23.3 Write an applet that asks the user to input the radius of a circle as a floating-point number and draws the circle's diameter, circumference and area. Use the value 3.14159 for π. Use the techniques shown in Fig. 23.9. [*Note:* You may also use the predefined constant Math.PI for the value of π. This constant is more precise than the value 3.14159. Class Math is defined in the java.lang package, so you do not need to import it.] Use the following formulas (r is the radius):

$$diameter = 2r$$
$$circumference = 2\pi r$$
$$area = \pi r^2$$

23.4 Write an applet that draws a checkerboard pattern as follows:

```
*  *  *  *  *  *  *  *
 *  *  *  *  *  *  *  *
*  *  *  *  *  *  *  *
 *  *  *  *  *  *  *  *
*  *  *  *  *  *  *  *
 *  *  *  *  *  *  *  *
*  *  *  *  *  *  *  *
 *  *  *  *  *  *  *  *
```

23.5 Write an applet that allows the user to input values for the arguments required by method drawRect, then draws a rectangle using the four input values.

23.6 Class Graphics contains method drawOval, which takes as arguments the same four arguments as method drawRect. The arguments for method drawOval specify the "bounding box" for the oval—the sides of the bounding box are the boundaries of the oval. Write a Java applet that draws an oval and a rectangle with the same four arguments. The oval will touch the rectangle at the center of each side.

23.7 Modify the solution to Exercise 23.6 to output ovals of different shapes and sizes.

23.8 Write an applet that allows the user to input the four arguments required by method drawOval, then draws an oval using the four input values.

23.9 Package the TicTacToe demonstration applet from the JDK (discussed in Section 23.2) for use with Java Web Start, then copy the JNLP document in Fig. 23.12 and modify it so that it launches the TicTacToe applet.

The wheel that squeaks the loudest … gets the grease.
—John Billings (Henry Wheeler Shaw)

We'll use a signal I have tried and found far-reaching and easy to yell. Waa-hoo!
—Zane Grey

There is a natural hootchy-kootchy motion to a goldfish.
—Walt Disney

Between the motion and the act falls the shadow.
—Thomas Stearns Eliot

Multimedia: Applets and Applications

Objectives

In this chapter you'll learn:

- How to get, display and scale images.
- How to create animations from sequences of images.
- How to create image maps.
- How to get, play, loop and stop sounds using an `AudioClip`.
- How to play video using interface `Player`.

24.1 Introduction

Multimedia—using sound, images, graphics, animation and video—makes applications "come alive." Although most multimedia in Java applications is two-dimensional, you can use the **Java 3D API** to create 3D graphics applications (java.sun.com/javase/technologies/desktop/java3d/).

Most new computers sold today are "multimedia ready," with DVD drives, audio and video capabilities. Economical desktop and laptop computers are so powerful that they can store and play DVD-quality (and often, HD-quality) sound and video.

Among users who want graphics, many now want three-dimensional, high-resolution, color graphics. True three-dimensional imaging is already available. We expect high-resolution, "theater-in-the-round," three-dimensional television to eventually become common. Sporting and entertainment events will seem to take place on your living room floor! Medical students worldwide will see operations being performed thousands of miles away, as if they were occurring in the same room. People will learn how to drive with incredibly realistic driving simulators in their homes before they get behind the wheel. The possibilities are endless and exciting.

Multimedia demands extraordinary computing power. Until recently, affordable computers with that kind of power were not widely available. Today's ultrapowerful processors make effective multimedia economical. Users are eager to own faster processors, larger memories and wider communications channels that support demanding multimedia applications. Ironically,these enhanced capabilities may not cost more—fierce competition keeps driving prices down.

The Java APIs provide multimedia facilities that enable you to start developing powerful multimedia applications immediately. This chapter presents several examples, including:

1. the basics of manipulating images.

2. creating smooth animations.

3. playing audio files with the AudioClip interface.

4. creating image maps that can sense when the cursor is over them, even without a mouse click.

5. playing video files using the Player interface.

The chapter also introduces additional JNLP features that, with the user's permission, enable an applet or application to access files on the user's local computer. The exercises suggest dozens of challenging and interesting projects. When we were writing these, the ideas just kept flowing. Multimedia leverages creativity in ways that we did not experience with "conventional" computer capabilities. [*Note:* Java's multimedia capabilities go far beyond those presented in this chapter. They include the **Java Media Framework (JMF) API** (for adding audio and video media to an application), **Java Sound API** (for playing, recording and modifying audio), Java 3D API (for creating and modifying 3D graphics), **Java Advanced Imaging API** (for image-processing capabilities, such as cropping and scaling), **Java Speech API** (for inputting voice commands from the user or outputting voice commands to the user), Java 2D API (for creating and modifying 2D graphics, covered in Chapter 15) and **Java Image I/O API** (for reading images from and outputting images to files). Section 24.8 provides web links for these APIs.]

24.2 Loading, Displaying and Scaling Images

We begin our discussion with images. We'll use several different images in this chapter. You can create your own images with software such as Adobe® Photoshop®, Corel® Paint Shop Pro®, Microsoft® Paint and G.I.M.P. (gimp.org).

The applet of Fig. 24.1 uses Java Web Start and the JNLP **FileOpenService** (package javax.jnlp) to allow the user to select an image, then displays that image and allows the user to scale it. After the user selects an image, the applet gets the bytes from the file, then passes them to the ImageIcon (package javax.swing) constructor to create the image that will be displayed. Class ImageIcon's constructors can receive arguments of several different formats, including a byte array containing the bytes of an image, an **Image** (package java.awt) already loaded in memory, or a String or a URL representing the image's location. Java supports various image formats, including **Graphics Interchange Format (GIF)**, **Joint Photographic Experts Group (JPEG)** and **Portable Network Graphics (PNG)**. File names for these types typically end with **.gif**, **.jpg** (or **.jpeg**) and **.png**, respectively.

```java
1   // Fig. 24.1: LoadImageAndScale.java
2   // Loading, displaying and scaling an image in an applet
3   import java.awt.BorderLayout;
4   import java.awt.Graphics;
5   import java.awt.event.ActionEvent;
6   import java.awt.event.ActionListener;
7   import javax.jnlp.FileContents;
8   import javax.jnlp.FileOpenService;
9   import javax.jnlp.ServiceManager;
10  import javax.swing.ImageIcon;
11  import javax.swing.JApplet;
12  import javax.swing.JButton;
13  import javax.swing.JFrame;
14  import javax.swing.JLabel;
15  import javax.swing.JOptionPane;
16  import javax.swing.JPanel;
17  import javax.swing.JTextField;
18
19  public class LoadImageAndScale extends JApplet
20  {
21     private ImageIcon image; // references image to display
22     private JPanel scaleJPanel; // JPanel containing the scale-selector
```

Fig. 24.1 | Loading, displaying and scaling an image in an applet. (Part 1 of 4.)

```
23      private JLabel percentJLabel; // label for JTextField
24      private JTextField scaleInputJTextField; // obtains user's input
25      private JButton scaleChangeJButton; // initiates scaling of image
26      private double scaleValue = 1.0;  //scale percentage for image
27
28      // load image when applet is loaded
29      public void init()
30      {
31         scaleJPanel = new JPanel();
32         percentJLabel = new JLabel( "scale percent:" );
33         scaleInputJTextField = new JTextField( "100" );
34         scaleChangeJButton = new JButton( "Set Scale" );
35
36         // add components and place scaleJPanel in applet's NORTH region
37         scaleJPanel.add( percentJLabel );
38         scaleJPanel.add( scaleInputJTextField );
39         scaleJPanel.add( scaleChangeJButton );
40         add( scaleJPanel, BorderLayout.NORTH );
41
42         // register event handler for scaleChangeJButton
43         scaleChangeJButton.addActionListener(
44            new ActionListener()
45            {
46               // when the JButton is pressed, set scaleValue and repaint
47               public void actionPerformed( ActionEvent e )
48               {
49                  scaleValue = Double.parseDouble(
50                     scaleInputJTextField.getText() ) / 100.0;
51                  repaint(); // causes image to be redisplyed at new scale
52               } // end method actionPerformed
53            } // end anonymous inner class
54         ); // end call to addActionListener
55
56         // use JNLP services to open an image file that the user selects
57         try
58         {
59            // get a reference to the FileOpenService
60            FileOpenService fileOpenService =
61               (FileOpenService) ServiceManager.lookup(
62                  "javax.jnlp.FileOpenService" );
63
64            // get file's contents from the FileOpenService
65            FileContents contents =
66               fileOpenService.openFileDialog( null, null );
67
68            // byte array to store image's data
69            byte[] imageData = new byte[ (int) contents.getLength() ];
70            contents.getInputStream().read( imageData ); // read image bytes
71            image = new ImageIcon( imageData ); // create the image
72
73            // if image successfully loaded, create and add DrawJPanel
74            add( new DrawJPanel(), BorderLayout.CENTER );
75         } // end try
```

Fig. 24.1 | Loading, displaying and scaling an image in an applet. (Part 2 of 4.)

```
76          catch( Exception e )
77          {
78              e.printStackTrace();
79          } // end catch
80      } // end method init
81
82      // DrawJPanel used to display loaded image
83      private class DrawJPanel extends JPanel
84      {
85          // display image
86          public void paintComponent( Graphics g )
87          {
88              super.paintComponent( g );
89
90              // the following values are used to center the image
91              double spareWidth =
92                  getWidth() - scaleValue * image.getIconWidth();
93              double spareHeight =
94                  getHeight() - scaleValue * image.getIconHeight();
95
96              // draw image with scaled width and height
97              g.drawImage( image.getImage(),
98                  (int) ( spareWidth ) / 2, (int) ( spareHeight ) / 2,
99                  (int) ( image.getIconWidth() * scaleValue ),
100                 (int) ( image.getIconHeight() * scaleValue ), this );
101         } // end method paint
102     } // end class DrawJPanel
103 } // end class LoadImageAndScale
```

(a) Java Web Start security dialog that appears because this applet is requesting access to a file on the local computer.

(b) **Open** dialog that appears if the user clicks **OK** in the security dialog.

Fig. 24.1 | Loading, displaying and scaling an image in an applet. (Part 3 of 4.)

(c) Scaling the image.

Fig. 24.1 | Loading, displaying and scaling an image in an applet. (Part 4 of 4.)

Configuring the GUI and the `JButton's` Event Handler

The applet's `init` method (lines 29–80) configures the GUI and an event handler. It also uses JNLP services to enable the user to select an image to display from the local computer. Line 31 creates the `JPanel` that will contain the `JLabel`, `JTextField` and `JButton` created in lines 32–34. Lines 37–39 add these components to the `JPanel`'s default `FlowLayout`. Line 40 places this `JPanel` in the `NORTH` region of the `JApplet`'s default `BorderLayout`.

Lines 43–54 create the event handler for the `scaleChangeJButton`. When the user clicks this `JButton`, lines 49–50 obtain the user's input from the `scaleInputJTextField`, divide it by `100.0` to calculate the scale percentage and assign the result to `scaleValue`. This value will be used in later calculations to scale the image. For example, if the user enters 50, the scale value will be `0.5` and the image will be displayed at half its original size. Line 51 then repaints the applet to display the image at its new scale.

Opening the Image File Using JNLP's `FileOpenService`

As we mentioned in Section 23.7, with the user's permission, Java Web Start programs can access the local file system via the JNLP APIs of package `javax.jnlp`. In this example, we'd like the user to select an image from the local computer to display in the applet. (We've provided two images in this example's directory with the source code.) You can use JNLP's `FileOpenService` to request limited access to the local file system.

Lines 7–9 import the interfaces and class we need to use the `FileOpenService`. Lines 60–62 use the JNLP **ServiceManager** class's static **lookup** method to obtain a reference to the `FileOpenService`. JNLP provides several services, so this method returns an `Object` reference, which you must cast to the appropriate type. Next, lines 65–66 use the `FileOpenService`'s **openFileDialog** method to display a file-selection dialog. Java Web Start prompts the user (Fig. 24.1(a)) to approve the applet's request for local file-system access. If the user gives permission, the **Open** dialog (Fig. 24.1(b)) is displayed. The open-`FileDialog` method has two parameters—a `String` to suggest a directory to open and a `String` array of acceptable file extensions (such as `"png"` and `"jpg"`). For simplicity, this program does not make use of either parameter, instead passing `null` values, which displays an open dialog open to the user's default directory and allows any file type to be selected.

When the user selects an image file and clicks the **Open** button in the dialog, method openFileDialog returns a FileContents object, which for security reasons does not give the program access to the file's exact location on disk. Instead, the program can get an InputStream and read the file's bytes. Line 69 creates a byte array in which the image's data will be stored. FileContents method **getLength** returns the number of bytes (as a long) in the file. Line 70 obtains the InputStream, then invokes its **read** method to fill the imageData byte array. Line 71 creates an ImageIcon using the byte array as the source of the image's data. Finally, line 74 adds a new DrawJPanel to the CENTER of the applet's BorderLayout. When the applet is displayed, its components' paintComponent methods are called, which causes the DrawJPanel to display the image. You can learn more about the JNLP APIs at java.sun.com/javase/6/docs/jre/api/javaws/jnlp.

*Displaying the Image with Class **DrawJPanel**'s **paintComponent** Method*
To separate the GUI from the area in which the image is displayed, we use a subclass of JPanel named DrawJPanel (lines 83–102). Its paintComponent method (lines 86–101) displays the image. We'd like to center the image in the DrawJPanel, so lines 91–94 calculate the difference between the width of the DrawJPanel and that of the scaled image, then the height of the DrawJPanel and that of the scaled image. DrawJPanel's **getWidth** and **getHeight** methods (inherited indirectly from class Component) return the DrawJPanel's width and height, respectively. The ImageIcon's **getIconWidth** and **getIconHeight** methods return the image's width and height, respectively. The scaleValue is set to 1.0 by default (line 26), and is changed when the user clicks the **Set Scale** JButton.

Lines 97–100 use one of class Graphics's overloaded **drawImage** methods to display a scaled version of the ImageIcon. The first argument invokes the ImageIcon's **getImage** method to obtain the Image to draw. The second and third arguments represent the upper-left corner coordinates of the Image with respect to the DrawJPanel's upper-left corner. The fourth and fifth arguments specify the Image's scaled width and height, respectively. Line 99 scales the image's width by invoking the ImageIcon's getIconWidth method and multiplying its return value by scaleValue. Similarly, line 100 scales the image's height by invoking class ImageIcon's getIconHeight method and multiplying its return value by scaleValue. The last argument is a reference to an **ImageObserver**—an interface implemented by class Component. Since class DrawJPanel indirectly extends Component, a DrawJPanel *is an* ImageObserver. This argument is important when displaying large images that require a long time to load (or download from the Internet). It's possible that a program will attempt to display the image before it has completely loaded (or downloaded). As the Image loads, the ImageObserver receives notifications and updates the image on the screen as necessary. In this example, the images are being loaded from the user's computer, so it's likely that entire image will be displayed immediately.

Compiling the Applet
Compiling and running this applet requires the jnlp.jar file that contains the JNLP APIs. This file can be found in your JDK installation directory under the directories

```
sample
    jnlp
        servlet
```

To compile the applet, use the following command:

```
javac -classpath PathToJnlpJarFile LoadImageAndScale.java
```

where *PathToJnlpJarFile* includes both the path and the file name `jnlp.jar`. For example, on our Windows Vista computer, the *PathToJnlpJarFile* is

```
"C:\Program Files\Java\jdk1.6.0_11\sample\jnlp\servlet\jnlp.jar"
```

Packaging the Applet for Use with Java Web Start

To package the applet for use with Java Web Start, you must create a JAR file that contains the applet's code and the `jnlp.jar` file. To do so, use the command

```
jar cvf LoadImageAndScale.jar *.class PathToJnlpJarFile
```

where *PathToJnlpJarFile* includes both the path and the file name `jnlp.jar`. This will place all the `.class` files for the applet and a copy of the `jnlp.jar` file in the new JAR file `LoadImageAndScale.jar`.

JNLP Document for **LoadImageAndScale** Applet

The JNLP document in Fig. 24.2 is similar to the one introduced in Fig. 23.12. The only new feature in this document is that the `resources` element (lines 10–14) contains a second `jar` element (line 13) that references the `jnlp.jar` file, which is embedded in the file `LoadImageAndScale.jar`.

```
 1  <?xml version="1.0" encoding="UTF-8"?>
 2  <jnlp codebase="file:." href="LoadImageAndScale.jnlp">
 3
 4     <information>
 5        <title>LoadImageAndScale Applet</title>
 6        <vendor>Deitel</vendor>
 7        <offline-allowed/>
 8     </information>
 9
10     <resources>
11        <java version="1.6+"/>
12        <jar href="LoadImageAndScale.jar" main="true"/>
13        <jar href="jnlp.jar"/>
14     </resources>
15
16     <applet-desc
17        name="LoadImageAndScale"
18        main-class="LoadImageAndScale"
19        width="400"
20        height="300">
21     </applet-desc>
22  </jnlp>
```

Fig. 24.2 | JNLP document for the `LoadImageAndScale` applet.

Making the Applet Draggable Outside the Browser Window

The XHTML document in Fig. 24.3 loads the applet into a web browser. In this example, we use an `applet` element to specify the applet's class and provide two `param` elements between the `applet` element's tags. The first (line 4) specifies that this applet should be **draggable**. That is, the user can hold the *Alt* key and use the mouse to drag the applet outside the browser window. The applet will then continue executing, even if the browser is closed. Clicking the close box on the applet when it is executing outside the browser causes the applet to move back into the browser window if it is still open, or to terminate otherwise. The second `param` element shows an alternate way to specify the JNLP file that launches an applet. We discuss applet parameters in more detail in Section 27.2.

```
1   <html>
2   <body>
3   <applet code="LoadImageAndScale.class" width="400" height="300">
4       <param name="draggable" value="true">
5       <param name="jnlp_href" value="LoadImageAndScale.jnlp">
6   </applet>
7   </body>
8   </html>
```

Fig. 24.3 | XHTML document to load the `LoadImageAndScale` applet and make it draggable outside the browser window.

24.3 Animating a Series of Images

Next, we animate a series of images that are stored in an array of `ImageIcons`. In this example, we use the JNLP `FileOpenService` to enable the user to choose a group of images that will be animated by displaying one image at a time at 50-millisecond intervals. The animation presented in Figs. 24.4–24.5 is implemented using a subclass of `JPanel` called `LogoAnimatorJPanel` (Fig. 24.4) that can be attached to an application window or a `JApplet`. Class `LogoAnimator` (Fig. 24.5) declares a `main` method (lines 8–20 of Fig. 24.5) to execute the animation as an application. Method `main` declares an instance of class `JFrame` and attaches a `LogoAnimatorJPanel` object to the `JFrame` to display the animation.

```
1   // Fig. 24.4: LogoAnimatorJPanel.java
2   // Animating a series of images.
3   import java.awt.Dimension;
4   import java.awt.event.ActionEvent;
5   import java.awt.event.ActionListener;
6   import java.awt.Graphics;
7   import javax.jnlp.FileContents;
8   import javax.jnlp.FileOpenService;
9   import javax.jnlp.ServiceManager;
10  import javax.swing.ImageIcon;
11  import javax.swing.JPanel;
12  import javax.swing.Timer;
13
14  public class LogoAnimatorJPanel extends JPanel
15  {
16     protected ImageIcon images[]; // array of images
17     private int currentImage = 0; // current image index
18     private final int ANIMATION_DELAY = 50; // millisecond delay
19     private int width; // image width
20     private int height; // image height
21
22     private Timer animationTimer; // Timer drives animation
23
```

Fig. 24.4 | Animating a series of images. (Part 1 of 3.)

```
24      // constructor initializes LogoAnimatorJPanel by loading images
25      public LogoAnimatorJPanel()
26      {
27         try
28         {
29            // get reference to FileOpenService
30            FileOpenService fileOpenService =
31               (FileOpenService) ServiceManager.lookup(
32                  "javax.jnlp.FileOpenService" );
33
34            // display dialog that allows user to select multiple files
35            FileContents[] contents =
36               fileOpenService.openMultiFileDialog( null, null );
37
38            // create array to store ImageIcon references
39            images = new ImageIcon[ contents.length ];
40
41            // load the selected images
42            for ( int count = 0; count < images.length; count++ )
43            {
44               // create byte array to store an image's data
45               byte[] imageData =
46                  new byte[ (int) contents[ count ].getLength() ];
47
48               // get image's data and create image
49               contents[ count ].getInputStream().read( imageData );
50               images[ count ] = new ImageIcon( imageData );
51            } // end for
52
53            // this example assumes all images have the same width and height
54            width = images[ 0 ].getIconWidth();   // get icon width
55            height = images[ 0 ].getIconHeight(); // get icon height
56         } // end try
57         catch( Exception e )
58         {
59            e.printStackTrace();
60         } // end catch
61      } // end LogoAnimatorJPanel constructor
62
63      // display current image
64      public void paintComponent( Graphics g )
65      {
66         super.paintComponent( g ); // call superclass paintComponent
67
68         images[ currentImage ].paintIcon( this, g, 0, 0 );
69
70         // set next image to be drawn only if Timer is running
71         if ( animationTimer.isRunning() )
72            currentImage = ( currentImage + 1 ) % images.length;
73      } // end method paintComponent
74
75      // start animation, or restart if window is redisplayed
76      public void startAnimation()
77      {
```

Fig. 24.4 | Animating a series of images. (Part 2 of 3.)

```
78            if ( animationTimer == null )
79            {
80               currentImage = 0; // display first image
81
82               // create timer
83               animationTimer =
84                  new Timer( ANIMATION_DELAY, new TimerHandler() );
85
86               animationTimer.start(); // start Timer
87            } // end if
88            else // animationTimer already exists, restart animation
89            {
90               if ( ! animationTimer.isRunning() )
91                  animationTimer.restart();
92            } // end else
93         } // end method startAnimation
94
95         // stop animation Timer
96         public void stopAnimation()
97         {
98            animationTimer.stop();
99         } // end method stopAnimation
100
101        // return minimum size of animation
102        public Dimension getMinimumSize()
103        {
104           return getPreferredSize();
105        } // end method getMinimumSize
106
107        // return preferred size of animation
108        public Dimension getPreferredSize()
109        {
110           return new Dimension( width, height );
111        } // end method getPreferredSize
112
113        // inner class to handle action events from Timer
114        private class TimerHandler implements ActionListener
115        {
116           // respond to Timer's event
117           public void actionPerformed( ActionEvent actionEvent )
118           {
119              repaint(); // repaint animator
120           } // end method actionPerformed
121        } // end class TimerHandler
122     } // end class LogoAnimatorJPanel
```

Fig. 24.4 | Animating a series of images. (Part 3 of 3.)

```
1    // Fig. 24.5: LogoAnimator.java
2    // Displaying animated images on a JFrame.
3    import javax.swing.JFrame;
4
```

Fig. 24.5 | Displaying animated images on a JFrame. (Part 1 of 2.)

```
 5   public class LogoAnimator
 6   {
 7      // execute animation in a JFrame
 8      public static void main( String args[] )
 9      {
10         LogoAnimatorJPanel animation = new LogoAnimatorJPanel();
11
12         JFrame window = new JFrame( "Animator test" ); // set up window
13         window.setDefaultCloseOperation( JFrame.EXIT_ON_CLOSE );
14         window.add( animation ); // add panel to frame
15
16         window.pack();   // make window just large enough for its GUI
17         window.setVisible( true );   // display window
18
19         animation.startAnimation();  // begin animation
20      } // end main
21   } // end class LogoAnimator
```

Fig. 24.5 | Displaying animated images on a JFrame. (Part 2 of 2.)

*Class **LogoAnimatorPanel***

Class LogoAnimatorJPanel (Fig. 24.4) maintains an array of ImageIcons (declared at line 16) that are loaded in the constructor (lines 25–61). The constructor begins by using the JNLP FileOpenService's **openMultiFileDialog** method to display a file-selection dialog that allows the user to select multiple files at once. We named our sample images such that they all have the same base name ("deitel") followed by a two-digit number from 00–29. This ensures that our images are in the proper order for the animation. As in this chapter's first example, first the user is prompted to give permission, then the **Open** dialog appears if permission is granted. FileOpenService method openMultiFileDialog takes the same arguments as method openFileDialog but returns an array of FileContents objects representing the set of files selected by the user. When you run this application, navigate to a folder containing the images you wish to use and select the images. If you wish, you can use the 30 images we provide in this example's subdirectory named images.

Line 39 creates the array of ImageIcons, then lines 42–51 populate the array by creating a byte array (lines 45–46) for the current image's data, reading the bytes of the image into the array (line 49) and creating an ImageIcon object from the byte array. Lines 54–55 determine the width and height of the animation from the size of the first image in array images—we assume that all the images have the same width and height.

*Method **startAnimation***

After the LogoAnimatorJPanel constructor loads the images, method main of Fig. 24.5 sets up the window in which the animation will appear (lines 12–17), and line 19 calls the LogoAnimatorJPanel's startAnimation method (declared at lines 76–93 of Fig. 24.4). This method starts the program's animation for the first time or restarts the animation that the program stopped previously. The animation is driven by an instance of class **Timer** (from package `javax.swing`).

When the program is first run, method `startAnimation` is called to begin the animation. Although we provide the functionality for this method to restart the animation if it has been stopped, the example does not call the method for this purpose. We've added the functionality, however, should the reader choose to add GUI components that enable the user to start and stop the animation.

A `Timer` generates `ActionEvents` at a fixed interval in milliseconds (normally specified as an argument to the `Timer`'s constructor) and notifies all its `ActionListeners` each time an `ActionEvent` occurs. Line 78 determines whether the `Timer` reference `animationTimer` is `null`. If it is, method `startAnimation` is being called for the first time, and a `Timer` needs to be created so that the animation can begin. Line 80 sets `currentImage` to 0, which indicates that the animation should begin with the first element of array `images`. Lines 83–84 assign a new `Timer` object to `animationTimer`. The `Timer` constructor receives two arguments—the delay in milliseconds (`ANIMATION_DELAY` is 50, as specified in line 18) and the `ActionListener` that will respond to the `Timer`'s `ActionEvents`. For the second argument, an object of class `TimerHandler` is created. This class, which implements `Action-Listener`, is declared in lines 114–121. Line 86 calls the `Timer` object's **start** method to start the `Timer`. Once started, `animationTimer` will generate an `ActionEvent` every 50 milliseconds and call the `Timer`'s event handler `actionPerformed` (lines 117–120). Line 119 calls `LogoAnimatorJPanel`'s `repaint` method to schedule a call to `LogoAnimatorJPanel`'s `paintComponent` method (lines 64–73). Remember that any subclass of `JComponent` that draws should do so in its `paintComponent` method. Recall that the first statement in any `paintComponent` method should be a call to the superclass's `paintComponent` method, to ensure that Swing components are displayed correctly.

If the animation started earlier, then our `Timer` was created and the condition in line 78 evaluates to `false`. The program continues with lines 90–91, which restarts the animation that the program stopped previously. The `if` condition at line 90 uses `Timer` method **isRunning** to determine whether the `Timer` is running (i.e., generating events). If it's not running, line 91 calls `Timer` method **restart** to indicate that the `Timer` should start generating events again. Once this occurs, method `actionPerformed` (the `Timer`'s event handler) is again called at regular intervals.

Method *paintComponent*

Line 68 calls the `ImageIcon`'s **paintIcon** method to display the image stored at element `currentImage` in the array. The arguments represent the `Component` on which to draw (`this`), the `Graphics` object that performs the drawing (`g`) and the coordinates of the image's upper-left corner. Lines 71–72 determine whether the `animationTimer` is running and, if so, prepare for the next image to be displayed by incrementing `currentImage` by 1. The remainder calculation ensures that the value of `currentImage` is set to 0 (to repeat the animation sequence) when it's incremented past the last element index in the array. The `if` statement ensures that the same image will be displayed if `paintComponent` is called while the `Timer` is stopped. This can be useful if a GUI is provided that enables the user to start and stop the animation. For example, if the animation is stopped and the user covers it with another window, then uncovers it, method `paintComponent` will be called. In this case, we do not want the animation to show the next image (because the animation has been stopped). We simply want the window to display the same image until the animation is restarted.

Method `stopAnimation`

Method `stopAnimation` (lines 96–99) stops the animation by calling `Timer` method **stop** to indicate that the `Timer` should stop generating events. This prevents `actionPerformed` from calling `repaint` to initiate the painting of the next image in the array. Just as with restarting the animation, this example defines but does not use method `stopAnimation`. We've provided this method for demonstration purposes, or to allow the user to modify this example to stop and restart the animation.

Software Engineering Observation 24.1

When creating an animation for use in an applet, provide a mechanism for disabling the animation when the user browses a new web page different from the one on which the animation applet resides.

Methods `getPreferredSize` *and* `getMinimumSize`

By extending class `JPanel`, we're creating a new GUI component. So, we must ensure that it works like other components for layout purposes. Layout managers often use a component's **getPreferredSize** method (inherited from class `java.awt.Component`) to determine the component's preferred width and height. If a new component has a preferred width and height, it should override method `getPreferredSize` (lines 108–111) to return that width and height as an object of class **Dimension** (package `java.awt`). The `Dimension` class represents the width and height of a GUI component. In this example, the images we provide are 160 pixels wide and 80 pixels tall, so method `getPreferredSize` would return a `Dimension` object containing the numbers 160 and 80 (if you use these images).

Look-and-Feel Observation 24.1

The default size of a `JPanel` *object is 10 pixels wide and 10 pixels tall.*

Look-and-Feel Observation 24.2

When subclassing `JPanel` *(or any other* `JComponent`*), override method* `getPreferredSize` *if the new component is to have a specific preferred width and height.*

Lines 102–105 override method **getMinimumSize**. This method determines the minimum width and height of the component. As with method `getPreferredSize`, new components should override method `getMinimumSize` (also inherited from class `Component`). Method `getMinimumSize` simply calls `getPreferredSize` (a common programming practice) to indicate that the minimum size and preferred size are the same. Some layout managers ignore the dimensions specified by these methods. For example, a `BorderLayout`'s NORTH and SOUTH regions use only the component's preferred height.

Look-and-Feel Observation 24.3

If a new GUI component has a minimum width and height (i.e., smaller dimensions would render the component ineffective on the display), override method `getMinimumSize` *to return the minimum width and height as an instance of class* `Dimension`.

Look-and-Feel Observation 24.4

For many GUI components, method `getMinimumSize` *is implemented to return the result of a call to the component's* `getPreferredSize` *method.*

Compiling the Application

Compiling and running this application requires the jnlp.jar file that contains the JNLP APIs. To compile the application use the following command:

> javac -classpath *PathToJnlpJarFile* *.java

where *PathToJnlpJarFile* includes both the path and the file name jnlp.jar.

Packaging the Application for Use with Java Web Start

To package the application for use with Java Web Start, you must create a JAR file that contains the applet's code and the jnlp.jar file. To do so, use the command

> jar cvf LogoAnimator.jar *.class *PathToJnlpJarFile*

where *PathToJnlpJarFile* includes both the path and the file name jnlp.jar.

*JNLP Document for **LoadImageAndScale** Applet*

The JNLP document in Fig. 24.6 is similar to the one in Fig. 24.2. The only new feature in this document is the application-desc element (lines 16–19), which specifies the name of the application and its main class. To run this application, use the command

> javaws LogoAnimator.jnlp

Recall that you can also run Java Web Start applications via a link in a web page, as we showed in Fig. 23.13.

```
1   <?xml version="1.0" encoding="UTF-8"?>
2   <jnlp codebase="file:." href="LogoAnimator.jnlp">
3
4       <information>
5           <title>LogoAnimator</title>
6           <vendor>Deitel</vendor>
7           <offline-allowed/>
8       </information>
9
10      <resources>
11          <java version="1.6+"/>
12          <jar href="LogoAnimator.jar" main="true"/>
13          <jar href="jnlp.jar"/>
14      </resources>
15
16      <application-desc
17          name="LogoAnimator"
18          main-class="LogoAnimator">
19      </application-desc>
20  </jnlp>
```

Fig. 24.6 | JNLP document for the LoadImageAndScale applet.

24.4 Image Maps

Image maps are commonly used to create interactive web pages. An image map is an image with **hot areas** that the user can click to accomplish a task, such as loading a different web page into a browser. When the user positions the mouse pointer over a hot area, normally a descriptive message appears in the status area of the browser or in a tool tip.

Figure 24.7 loads an image containing several of the programming-tip icons used in this book. The program allows the user to position the mouse pointer over an icon to display a descriptive message associated with it. Event handler mouseMoved (lines 39–43) takes the mouse coordinates and passes them to method translateLocation (lines 58–69). Method translateLocation tests the coordinates to determine the icon over which the mouse was positioned when the mouseMoved event occurred—the method then returns a message indicating what the icon represents. This message is displayed in the applet container's status bar using method **showStatus** of class Applet.

```
1   // Fig. 24.7: ImageMap.java
2   // Image map.
3   import java.awt.event.MouseAdapter;
4   import java.awt.event.MouseEvent;
5   import java.awt.event.MouseMotionAdapter;
6   import java.awt.Graphics;
7   import javax.swing.ImageIcon;
8   import javax.swing.JApplet;
9
10  public class ImageMap extends JApplet
11  {
12     private ImageIcon mapImage;
13
14     private static final String captions[] = { "Common Programming Error",
15        "Good Programming Practice", "Look-and-Feel Observation",
16        "Performance Tip", "Portability Tip",
17        "Software Engineering Observation", "Error-Prevention Tip" };
18
19     // sets up mouse listeners
20     public void init()
21     {
22        addMouseListener(
23
24           new MouseAdapter() // anonymous inner class
25           {
26              // indicate when mouse pointer exits applet area
27              public void mouseExited( MouseEvent event )
28              {
29                 showStatus( "Pointer outside applet" );
30              } // end method mouseExited
31           } // end anonymous inner class
32        ); // end call to addMouseListener
33
34        addMouseMotionListener(
35
36           new MouseMotionAdapter() // anonymous inner class
37           {
38              // determine icon over which mouse appears
39              public void mouseMoved( MouseEvent event )
40              {
```

Fig. 24.7 | Image map. (Part 1 of 3.)

```
41                     showStatus( translateLocation(
42                 event.getX(), event.getY() ) );
43          } // end method mouseMoved
44       } // end anonymous inner class
45     ); // end call to addMouseMotionListener
46
47     mapImage = new ImageIcon( "icons.png" ); // get image
48   } // end method init
49
50   // display mapImage
51   public void paint( Graphics g )
52   {
53      super.paint( g );
54      mapImage.paintIcon( this, g, 0, 0 );
55   } // end method paint
56
57   // return tip caption based on mouse coordinates
58   public String translateLocation( int x, int y )
59   {
60      // if coordinates outside image, return immediately
61      if ( x >= mapImage.getIconWidth() || y >= mapImage.getIconHeight() )
62         return "";
63
64      // determine icon number (0 - 6)
65      double iconWidth = ( double ) mapImage.getIconWidth() / 7.0;
66      int iconNumber = ( int )( ( double ) x / iconWidth );
67
68      return captions[ iconNumber ]; // return appropriate icon caption
69   } // end method translateLocation
70 } // end class ImageMap
```

Fig. 24.7 | Image map. (Part 2 of 3.)

Fig. 24.7 | Image map. (Part 3 of 3.)

Clicking in the applet of Fig. 24.7 will not cause any action. In Chapter 27, Networking, we discuss the techniques for loading another web page into a browser via URLs and the AppletContext interface. Using those techniques, this applet could associate each icon with a URL that the browser would display when the user clicks the icon.

24.5 Loading and Playing Audio Clips

Java programs can manipulate and play **audio clips**. Users can capture their own audio clips, and many clips are available in software products and over the Internet. Your system needs to be equipped with audio hardware (speakers and a sound card) to be able to play the audio clips.

Java provides several mechanisms for playing sounds in an applet. The two simplest are the Applet's **play** method and the **play** method of the **AudioClip** interface. Additional audio capabilities are available in the Java Media Framework and Java Sound APIs. If you'd like to play a sound once in a program, the `Applet` method `play` loads the sound and plays it once, then the sound can be garbage collected. The `Applet` method `play` has two versions:

```
public void play( URL location, String soundFileName );
public void play( URL soundURL );
```

The first version loads the audio clip stored in file `soundFileName` from `location` and plays the sound. The first argument is normally a call to the applet's `getDocumentBase` or **getCodeBase** method. Method `getDocumentBase` returns the location of the HTML file that loaded the applet. (If the applet is in a package, the method returns the location of the package or the JAR file containing the package.) Method `getCodeBase` indicates the location of the applet's `.class` file. The second version of method `play` takes a URL that contains the location and the file name of the audio clip. The statement

```
play( getDocumentBase(), "hi.au" );
```

loads the audio clip in file `hi.au` and plays the clip once.

The **sound engine** that plays the audio clips supports several audio file formats, including **Sun Audio file format** (**.au** extension), **Windows Wave file format** (**.wav** extension), **Macintosh AIFF file format** (**.aif** or **.aiff** extensions) and **Musical Instrument Digital Interface (MIDI) file format** (**.mid** or **.rmi** extensions). The Java Media Framework (JMF) and Java Sound APIs support additional formats.

The program of Fig. 24.8 demonstrates loading and playing an `AudioClip` (package `java.applet`). This technique is more flexible than `Applet` method `play`. An applet can use an `AudioClip` to store audio for repeated use throughout a program's execution. `Applet` method **getAudioClip** has two forms that take the same arguments as method `play` described previously. Method `getAudioClip` returns a reference to an `AudioClip`. An `AudioClip` has three methods—`play`, `loop` and `stop`. As mentioned earlier, method `play` plays the audio clip once. Method **loop** continuously loops through the audio clip in the background. Method **stop** terminates an audio clip that is currently playing. In the program, each of these methods is associated with a button on the applet.

```
1   // Fig. 24.8: LoadAudioAndPlay.java
2   // Loading and playing an AudioClip.
3   import java.applet.AudioClip;
4   import java.awt.event.ItemListener;
5   import java.awt.event.ItemEvent;
6   import java.awt.event.ActionListener;
7   import java.awt.event.ActionEvent;
8   import java.awt.FlowLayout;
9   import javax.swing.JApplet;
10  import javax.swing.JButton;
11  import javax.swing.JComboBox;
12
13  public class LoadAudioAndPlay extends JApplet
14  {
15     private AudioClip sound1, sound2, currentSound;
16     private JButton playJButton, loopJButton, stopJButton;
17     private JComboBox soundJComboBox;
```

Fig. 24.8 | Loading and playing an `AudioClip`. (Part 1 of 3.)

```
18
19      // load the audio when the applet begins executing
20      public void init()
21      {
22         setLayout( new FlowLayout() );
23
24         String choices[] = { "Welcome", "Hi" };
25         soundJComboBox = new JComboBox( choices ); // create JComboBox
26
27         soundJComboBox.addItemListener(
28
29            new ItemListener() // anonymous inner class
30            {
31               // stop sound and change sound to user's selection
32               public void itemStateChanged( ItemEvent e )
33               {
34                  currentSound.stop();
35                  currentSound = soundJComboBox.getSelectedIndex() == 0 ?
36                     sound1 : sound2;
37               } // end method itemStateChanged
38            } // end anonymous inner class
39         ); // end addItemListener method call
40
41         add( soundJComboBox ); // add JComboBox to applet
42
43         // set up button event handler and buttons
44         ButtonHandler handler = new ButtonHandler();
45
46         // create Play JButton
47         playJButton = new JButton( "Play" );
48         playJButton.addActionListener( handler );
49         add( playJButton );
50
51         // create Loop JButton
52         loopJButton = new JButton( "Loop" );
53         loopJButton.addActionListener( handler );
54         add( loopJButton );
55
56         // create Stop JButton
57         stopJButton = new JButton( "Stop" );
58         stopJButton.addActionListener( handler );
59         add( stopJButton );
60
61         // load sounds and set currentSound
62         sound1 = getAudioClip( getDocumentBase(), "welcome.wav" );
63         sound2 = getAudioClip( getDocumentBase(), "hi.au" );
64         currentSound = sound1;
65      } // end method init
66
67      // stop the sound when the user switches web pages
68      public void stop()
69      {
70         currentSound.stop(); // stop AudioClip
71      } // end method stop
```

Fig. 24.8 | Loading and playing an `AudioClip`. (Part 2 of 3.)

```
72
73     // private inner class to handle button events
74     private class ButtonHandler implements ActionListener
75     {
76        // process play, loop and stop button events
77        public void actionPerformed( ActionEvent actionEvent )
78        {
79           if ( actionEvent.getSource() == playJButton )
80              currentSound.play(); // play AudioClip once
81           else if ( actionEvent.getSource() == loopJButton )
82              currentSound.loop(); // play AudioClip continuously
83           else if ( actionEvent.getSource() == stopJButton )
84              currentSound.stop(); // stop AudioClip
85        } // end method actionPerformed
86     } // end class ButtonHandler
87  } // end class LoadAudioAndPlay
```

Fig. 24.8 | Loading and playing an `AudioClip`. (Part 3 of 3.)

Lines 62–63 in the applet's `init` method use `getAudioClip` to load two audio files—a Windows Wave file (`welcome.wav`) and a Sun Audio file (`hi.au`). The user can select which audio clip to play from the `JComboBox soundJComboBox`. Note that the applet's `stop` method is overridden at lines 68–71. When the user switches web pages, the applet container calls the applet's `stop` method. This enables the applet to stop playing the audio clip. Otherwise, it continues to play in the background—even if the applet is not displayed in the browser. This is not necessarily a problem, but it can be annoying to the user if the audio clip is looping. The `stop` method is provided here as a convenience to the user.

Look-and-Feel Observation 24.5
When playing audio clips in an applet or application, provide a mechanism for the user to disable the audio.

24.6 Playing Video and Other Media with Java Media Framework

A simple video can concisely and effectively convey a great deal of information. Recognizing the value of bringing extensible multimedia capabilities to Java, Sun Microsystems, Intel and Silicon Graphics worked together to produce the Java Media Framework (JMF). Using the JMF API, programmers can create Java applications that play, edit, stream and capture many popular media types. The features of JMF are quite extensive. This section briefly introduces some popular media formats and demonstrates playing video using the JMF API.

IBM and Sun developed the latest JMF specification—version 2.0. Sun also provides a reference implementation of the JMF specification—JMF 2.1.1e—that supports media file types such as **Microsoft Audio/Video Interleave** (**.avi**), **Macromedia Flash movies** (**.swf**), **Future Splash** (**.spl**), **MPEG Layer 3 Audio** (**.mp3**), Musical Instrument Digital Interface (MIDI; .mid or .rmi extensions), **MPEG-1 videos** (**.mpeg**, **.mpg**), **QuickTime** (**.mov**), Sun Audio file format (.au extension), and Macintosh AIFF file format (.aif or .aiff extensions). You've already seen some of these file types.

Currently, JMF is available as an extension separate from the Java 2 Software Development Kit. The most recent JMF implementation (2.1.1e) can be downloaded from:

```
java.sun.com/javase/technologies/desktop/media/jmf/2.1.1/
    download.html
```

[*Note:* Keep track of where you install the Java Media Framework on your computer. To compile and run this application, you must include in the class path the jmf.jar file that is installed with the Java Media Framework. Recall that you can specify the class path with both the javac and java commands via the -classpath command-line option.]

The JMF website provides versions of the JMF that take advantage of the performance features of certain platforms. For example, the JMF Windows Performance Pack provides extensive media and device support for Java programs running on Microsoft Windows platforms. The JMF's website (java.sun.com/javase/technologies/desktop/media/jmf/) provides information and resources for JMF programmers.

Creating a Simple Media Player
The JMF offers several mechanisms for playing media. The simplest is using objects that implement interface **Player** declared in package **javax.media**. Package javax.media and its subpackages contain the classes that compose the Java Media Framework. To play a media clip, you must first create a URL object that refers to it. Then pass the URL as an argument to static method **createRealizedPlayer** of class Manager to obtain a Player for the media clip. Class **Manager** declares utility methods for accessing system resources to play and to manipulate media. Figure 24.9 declares a JPanel that demonstrates some of these methods.

```
1   // Fig. 24.9: MediaPanel.java
2   // JPanel that plays a media file from a URL.
3   import java.awt.BorderLayout;
4   import java.awt.Component;
5   import java.io.IOException;
6   import java.net.URL;
7   import javax.media.CannotRealizeException;
8   import javax.media.Manager;
9   import javax.media.NoPlayerException;
10  import javax.media.Player;
11  import javax.swing.JPanel;
12
13  public class MediaPanel extends JPanel
14  {
15     public MediaPanel( URL mediaURL )
16     {
17        setLayout( new BorderLayout() ); // use a BorderLayout
18
```

Fig. 24.9 | JPanel that plays a media file from a URL. (Part 1 of 2.)

```
19          // Use lightweight components for Swing compatibility
20          Manager.setHint( Manager.LIGHTWEIGHT_RENDERER, true );
21
22          try
23          {
24              // create a player to play the media specified in the URL
25              Player mediaPlayer = Manager.createRealizedPlayer( mediaURL );
26
27              // get the components for the video and the playback controls
28              Component video = mediaPlayer.getVisualComponent();
29              Component controls = mediaPlayer.getControlPanelComponent();
30
31              if ( video != null )
32                  add( video, BorderLayout.CENTER ); // add video component
33
34              if ( controls != null )
35                  add( controls, BorderLayout.SOUTH ); // add controls
36
37              mediaPlayer.start(); // start playing the media clip
38          } // end try
39          catch ( NoPlayerException noPlayerException )
40          {
41              System.err.println( "No media player found" );
42          } // end catch
43          catch ( CannotRealizeException cannotRealizeException )
44          {
45              System.err.println( "Could not realize media player" );
46          } // end catch
47          catch ( IOException iOException )
48          {
49              System.err.println( "Error reading from the source" );
50          } // end catch
51      } // end MediaPanel constructor
52  } // end class MediaPanel
```

Fig. 24.9 | JPanel that plays a media file from a URL. (Part 2 of 2.)

The constructor (lines 15–51) sets up the JPanel to play the media file specified by the constructor's URL parameter. MediaPanel uses a BorderLayout (line 17). Line 20 invokes static method **setHint** to set the flag **Manager.LIGHTWEIGHT_RENDERER** to true. This instructs the Manager to use a lightweight renderer that is compatible with lightweight Swing components, as opposed to the default heavyweight renderer. Inside the try block (lines 22–38), line 25 invokes static method createRealizedPlayer of class Manager to create and realize a Player that plays the media file. When a Player realizes, it identifies the system resources it needs to play the media. Depending on the file, realizing can be a resource-consuming and time-consuming process. Method createRealizedPlayer throws three checked exceptions, **NoPlayerException**, **CannotRealizeException** and IOException. A NoPlayerException indicates that the system could not find a player that can play the file format. A CannotRealizeException indicates that the system could not properly identify the resources a media file needs. An IOException indicates that there was an error while reading the file. These exceptions are handled in the catch block in lines 39–50.

Line 28 invokes method **getVisualComponent** of Player to get a Component that displays the visual (generally video) aspect of the media file. Line 29 invokes method **getControlPanelComponent** of Player to get a Component that provides playback and media controls. These components are assigned to local variables video and controls, respectively. The if statements in lines 31–32 and lines 34–35 add the video and the controls if they exist. The video Component is added to the CENTER region (line 32), so it fills any available space on the JPanel. The controls Component, which is added to the SOUTH region, typically provides the following controls:

1. A positioning slider to jump to certain points in the media clip.

2. A pause button.

3. A volume button that provides volume control by right clicking and a mute function by left clicking.

4. A media properties button that provides detailed media information by left clicking and frame-rate control by right clicking.

Line 37 calls Player method **start** to begin playing the media file. Lines 39–50 handle the various exceptions that createRealizedPlayer throws.

The application in Fig. 24.10 displays a JFileChooser dialog for the user to choose a media file. It then creates a MediaPanel that plays the selected file and creates a JFrame to display the MediaPanel.

```java
1   // Fig. 24.10: MediaTest.java
2   // Test application that creates a MediaPanel from a user-selected file.
3   import java.io.File;
4   import java.net.MalformedURLException;
5   import java.net.URL;
6   import javax.swing.JFileChooser;
7   import javax.swing.JFrame;
8
9   public class MediaTest
10  {
11     // launch the application
12     public static void main( String args[] )
13     {
14        // create a file chooser
15        JFileChooser fileChooser = new JFileChooser();
16
17        // show open file dialog
18        int result = fileChooser.showOpenDialog( null );
19
20        if ( result == JFileChooser.APPROVE_OPTION ) // user chose a file
21        {
22           URL mediaURL = null;
23
24           try
25           {
26              // get the file as URL
27              mediaURL = fileChooser.getSelectedFile().toURI().toURL();
28           } // end try
```

Fig. 24.10 | Test application that creates a MediaPanel from a user-selected file. (Part 1 of 2.)

```
29              catch ( MalformedURLException malformedURLException )
30              {
31                 System.err.println( "Could not create URL for the file" );
32              } // end catch
33
34              if ( mediaURL != null ) // only display if there is a valid URL
35              {
36                 JFrame mediaTest = new JFrame( "Media Tester" );
37                 mediaTest.setDefaultCloseOperation( JFrame.EXIT_ON_CLOSE );
38
39                 MediaPanel mediaPanel = new MediaPanel( mediaURL );
40                 mediaTest.add( mediaPanel );
41
42                 mediaTest.setSize( 300, 300 );
43                 mediaTest.setVisible( true );
44              } // end inner if
45           } // end outer if
46        } // end main
47  } // end class MediaTest
```

Fig. 24.10 | Test application that creates a MediaPanel from a user-selected file. (Part 2 of 2.)

Method main (lines 12–46) assigns a new JFileChooser to local variable fileChooser (line 15), shows an open-file dialog (line 18) and assigns the return value to result. Line 20 checks result to determine whether the user chose a file. To create a Player to play the selected media file, you must convert the File object returned by JFileChooser to a URL object. Method **toURI** of class File returns a URI that points to the File on the system. We then invoke method **toURL** of class URI to get the file's URL. The try statement (lines 24–32) creates a URL for the selected file and assigns it to mediaURL. The if statement in lines 34–44 checks that mediaURL is not null and creates the GUI components to play the media.

24.7 Wrap-Up

In this chapter, you learned how to make applications more exciting by including sound, images, graphics and video. We introduced Java's multimedia capabilities, including the Java Media Framework API and Java Sound API. You used class ImageIcon to display and manipulate images stored in files, and you learned about the different image formats supported by Java. You used the JNLP FileOpenService to enable the user of a Java Web Start application to select files from the local file system, then used streams to load the contents of those files for use in your programs. You created animation by displaying a series of images in a specific order. You used image maps to make an application more interactive. You then learned how to load audio clips and how to play them either once or in a continuous loop. The chapter concluded with a demonstration of loading and playing video. In the next chapter, you'll continue your study of GUI concepts, building on the techniques you learned in Chapter 14.

24.8 Web Resources

www.nasa.gov/multimedia/highlights/index.html
The *NASA Multimedia Gallery* contains a wide variety of images, audio clips and video clips that you can download and use to test your Java multimedia programs.

commons.wikimedia.org/wiki/Main_Page
The *Wikimedia Commons* site provides access to millions of media files.

www.anbg.gov.au/anbg/index.html
The *Australian National Botanic Gardens* website provides links to the sounds of many animals. Try, for example, the *Common Birds* link under the "Animals in the Gardens" section.

www.thefreesite.com
This site has links to free sounds and clip art.

www.soundcentral.com
SoundCentral provides audio clips in WAV, AU, AIFF and MIDI formats.

www.animationfactory.com
The *Animation Factory* provides thousands of free GIF animations for personal use.

www.clipart.com
This site is a subscription-based service for images and sounds.

java.sun.com/developer/techDocs/hi/repository/
The *Java look-and-feel Graphics Repository* provides images designed for use in a Swing GUI, including toolbar button images.

www.freebyte.com/graphicprograms/
This guide contains links to several free graphics software programs. The software can be used to modify images and draw graphics.

`graphicssoft.about.com/od/pixelbasedfreewin/`
This site provides links to free graphics programs designed for use on Windows machines.

Java Multimedia API References

`java.sun.com/javase/technologies/desktop/media/`
The online home of the Java Media APIs.

`java.sun.com/products/java-media/sound/`
The *Java Sound API* home page. Java Sound provides capabilities for playing and recording audio.

`java3d.dev.java.net/`
The *Java 3D API* home page. This API can be used to produce three-dimensional images typical of today's video games.

`java.sun.com/products/java-media/speech/`
The *Java Speech API* enables programs to perform speech synthesis and speech recognition.

`freetts.sourceforge.net/docs/index.php`
FreeTTS is an implementation of the Java Speech API.

Summary

Section 24.2 Loading, Displaying and Scaling Images

- Class `ImageIcon`'s constructors can receive arguments of several different formats, including a byte array containing the bytes of an image, an `Image` (package `java.awt`) already loaded in memory, or a `String` or a URL representing the image's location.

- Java supports several image formats, including Graphics Interchange Format (GIF), Joint Photographic Experts Group (JPEG) and Portable Network Graphics (PNG). The file names for these types typically end with `.gif`, `.jpg` (or `.jpeg`) and `.png`, respectively.

- Java Web Start programs can access the local file system via the JNLP APIs of package `javax.jnlp`. You can use JNLP's `FileOpenService` to request limited access to the local file system.

- The JNLP `ServiceManager` class's `static lookup` method obtains a reference to the `FileOpen-Service`. Since other services are provided by JNLP, this method returns an `Object` reference, which you must cast to the appropriate type.

- `FileOpenService` method `openFileDialog` method displays a file-selection dialog. This causes Java Web Start to prompt the user to approve the program's request local file-system access. If the user gives permission, the **Open** dialog is displayed. The `openFileDialog` method has two parameters—a `String` to suggest a directory to open and a `String` array of acceptable file extensions.

- When the user selects an image file and clicks the `Open` button in the dialog, method `openFile-Dialog` returns a `FileContents` object, which for security reasons does not give the program access to the file's exact location on disk. Instead, the program can get an `InputStream` and read the file's bytes.

- `FileContents` method `getLength` returns the number of bytes in the file.

- `Component` methods `getWidth` and `getHeight` return the width and height of a `Component`, respectively.

- `ImageIcon` methods `getIconWidth` and `getIconHeight` return the width and height of an image, respectively.

- Class `Graphics` provides overloaded `drawImage` methods, one of which displays a scaled version of an `Image`. The first argument is the `Image` to draw. The second and third arguments represent the upper-left corner coordinates of the `Image`. The fourth and fifth arguments specify the `Image`'s scaled width and height, respectively. The last argument is a reference to an `ImageObserver`—an interface implemented by class `Component`.

- It's possible that a program will attempt to display an image before it has completely loaded (or downloaded). As an Image loads, the ImageObserver receives notifications and updates the image on the screen as necessary.

- A draggable applet can be dragged outside the browser window by holding the *Alt* key and dragging the applet with the mouse. The applet will then continue executing, even if the browser is closed. Clicking the close box on the applet when it is executing outside the browser causes the applet to move back into the browser window if it is still open, or to terminate otherwise.

Section 24.3 Animating a Series of Images

- The FileOpenService's openMultiFileDialog method displays a file-selection dialog that allows the user to select multiple files at once. FileOpenService method openMultiFileDialog takes the same arguments as method openFileDialog, but returns an array of FileContents objects representing the set of files selected by the user.

- Timer objects generate ActionEvents at fixed millisecond intervals. The Timer constructor receives a delay in milliseconds and an ActionListener. Timer method start starts the Timer. Method stop indicates that the Timer should stop generating events. Method restart indicates that the Timer should start generating events again.

- ImageIcon method paintIcon displays the ImageIcon's image. The method requires four arguments—a reference to the Component on which the image will be displayed, a reference to the Graphics object used to render the image, the *x*-coordinate of the upper-left corner of the image and the *y*-coordinate of the upper-left corner of the image.

Section 24.4 Image Maps

- An image map is an image that has hot areas that the user can click to accomplish a task, such as loading a different web page into a browser.

Section 24.5 Loading and Playing Audio Clips

- Applet method play has two forms:

```
public void play( URL location, String soundFileName );
public void play( URL soundURL );
```

One version loads the audio clip stored in file soundFileName from location and plays the sound. The other version takes a URL that contains the location and the file name of the audio clip.

- Applet method getDocumentBase indicates the location of the HTML file that loaded the applet. Method getCodeBase indicates where the .class file for an applet is located.

- The sound engine that plays audio clips supports several audio file formats, including Sun Audio file format (.au extension), Windows Wave file format (.wav extension), Macintosh AIFF file format (.aif or .aiff extensions) and Musical Instrument Digital Interface (MIDI) file format (.mid or .rmi extensions). The Java Media Framework (JMF) supports additional formats.

- Applet method getAudioClip has two forms that take the same arguments as the play method. Method getAudioClip returns a reference to an AudioClip. AudioClips have three methods—play, loop and stop. Method play plays the audio clip once. Method loop continuously loops the audio clip. Method stop terminates an audio clip that is currently playing.

Section 24.6 Playing Video and Other Media with Java Media Framework

- Sun Microsystems, Intel and Silicon Graphics worked together to produce the Java Media Framework (JMF).

- Package javax.media and its subpackages contain the Java Media Framework classes.

- Class Manager declares methods for accessing system resources to play and to manipulate media.

- Method toURI of class File returns a URI that points to the File on the system.

Terminology

Self-Review Exercises

24.1 Fill in the blanks in each of the following statements:
a) `Graphics` method _____ displays an image on an applet.
b) Java provides two mechanisms for playing sounds in an applet—the `Applet`'s `play` method and the `play` method of the _____ interface.
c) A(n) _____ is an image that has hot areas that the user can click to accomplish a task such as loading a web page.
d) Method _____ of class `ImageIcon` displays the `ImageIcon`'s image.
e) Java supports several image formats, including _____, _____ and _____.
f) The JNLP _____ class's `static` `lookup` method obtains a reference to the `FileOpenService`.

24.2 Determine whether each of the following statements is *true* or *false*. If *false*, explain why.
a) A sound is marked for garbage collection after it plays via the play method of class `Applet`.
b) Class `ImageIcon` provides constructors that allow an `ImageIcon` object to be initialized only with an image from the local computer.
c) Method `play` of class `AudioClip` continuously loops an audio clip.
d) The Java Image I/O API is used for adding 3D graphics to a Java application.
e) `Applet` method `getDocumentBase` returns, as an object of class `URL`, the location on the Internet of the HTML file that invoked the applet.
f) `FileOpenService` methods `openFileDialog` and `openMultiFileDialog` return a `FileContents` object and an array of `FileContents` objects, respectively.

Answers to Self-Review Exercises

24.1 a) `drawImage`. b) `AudioClip`. c) image map. d) `paintIcon`. e) Graphics Interchange Format (GIF), Joint Photographic Experts Group (JPEG), Portable Network Graphics (PNG). f) `ServiceManager`.

24.2 a) True. b) False. `ImageIcon` can load images from the Internet as well. c) False. Method `play` of class `AudioClip` plays an audio clip once. Method `loop` of class `AudioClip` continuously loops an audio clip. d) False. The Java 3D API is used for creating and modifying 3D graphics. The Java Image I/O API is used for reading from and outputting images to files. e) True. f) True.

Exercises

24.3 Describe the Java methods for playing and manipulating audio clips.

24.4 *(Randomly Erasing an Image)* Suppose an image is displayed in a rectangular screen area. One way to erase the image is simply to set every pixel to the same color immediately, but the visual effect is dull. Write a Java program that displays an image, then erases it by using random-number generation to select individual pixels to erase. After most of the image is erased, erase all the remaining pixels at once. You can draw individual pixels as a line that starts and ends at the same coordinates. You might try several variants of this problem. For example, you might display lines randomly or display shapes randomly to erase regions of the screen.

24.5 *(Image Flasher)* Create a Java program that repeatedly flashes an image on the screen. Do this by alternating the image with a plain background-color image.

24.6 *(Digital Clock)* Implement a program that displays a digital clock on the screen.

24.7 *(Image Zooming)* Create a program that enables you to zoom in on or out from an image.

24.8 *(**LoadImageAndScale** Modification)* Modify applet `LoadImageAndScale` (Fig. 24.1) to provide a second button that enables the user to choose a new image. The button's event handler should use the JNLP `FileOpenService` to display an **Open** dialog, so that the user can select a new image.

Special Section: Challenging Multimedia Projects

The preceding exercises are keyed to the text and designed to test your understanding of fundamental multimedia concepts. This section includes a collection of advanced multimedia projects. You should find these problems challenging, yet entertaining. The problems vary in difficulty. Some require an hour or two of program writing and implementation. Others are useful for lab assignments that might require two or three weeks of study and implementation. Some are challenging term projects. [*Note to Instructors:* Solutions are *not* provided for these exercises.]

24.9   *(Animation)* Create a general-purpose Java animation program. It should allow the user to specify the sequence of frames to be displayed, the speed at which the images are displayed, audios to be played while the animation is running and so on.

24.10   *(Random Interimage Transition)* This provides a nice visual effect. If you're displaying one image in a given area on the screen and you'd like to transition to another image in the same area, store the new screen image in an off-screen buffer and randomly copy pixels from it to the display area, overlaying the pixels already at those locations. When the vast majority of the pixels have been copied, copy the entire new image to the display area to be sure you are displaying the complete new image. To implement this program, you may need to use the `PixelGrabber` and `MemoryImageSource` classes (see the Java API documentation for descriptions of these classes). You might try several variants of this problem. For example, select all the pixels in a randomly chosen straight line or shape in the new image and overlay them above the corresponding positions of the old image.

24.11   *(Scrolling Marquee Sign)* Create a program that scrolls dotted characters from right to left (or from left to right if that is appropriate for your language) across a marquee-like display sign. As an option, display the text in a continuous loop, so that after the text disappears at one end, it reappears at the other.

24.12   *(Analog Clock)* Create a program that displays an analog clock with hour, minute and second hands that move appropriately as the time changes.

24.13   *(Automatic Jigsaw Puzzle Generator)* Create a jigsaw puzzle generator and manipulator. The user specifies an image. Your program loads and displays the image, then breaks it into randomly selected shapes and shuffles them. The user then uses the mouse to move the pieces around to solve the puzzle. Add appropriate audio sounds as the pieces are moved around and snapped back into place. You might keep tabs on each piece and where it really belongs—then use audio effects to help the user get the pieces into the correct positions.

24.14   *(One-Armed Bandit)* Develop a multimedia simulation of a "one-armed bandit." Have three spinning wheels. Place symbols and images of various fruits on each wheel. Use random-number generation to simulate the spinning of each wheel and the stopping of each wheel on a symbol.

24.15   *(Shuffleboard)* Develop a multimedia-based simulation of the game of shuffleboard. Use appropriate audio and visual effects.

24.16   *(Artist)* Design an art program that will give an artist a great variety of capabilities to draw, use images and use animations to create a dynamic multimedia art display.

24.17   *(Floor Planner)* Develop a program that will help someone arrange furniture in a home. Add features that enable the person to achieve the best possible arrangement.

24.18   *(15 Puzzle)* Write a multimedia-based program that enables the user to play the game of 15. The game is played on a 4-by-4 board having a total of 16 slots. One slot is empty, the others are occupied by 15 tiles numbered 1 through 15. The user can move any tile next to the currently empty slot into that slot by clicking on the tile. Your program should create the board with the tiles in random order. The goal is to arrange the tiles into sequential order, row by row.

24.19   *(Calendar/Tickler File)* Using both audio and images, create a general-purpose calendar and "tickler" file. For example, the program should sing "Happy Birthday" when you use it on your birthday. Have the program display images and play audios associated with important events. Also, have it remind you in advance of these important events. It would be nice, for example, to have the program give you a week's notice so you can pick up an appropriate greeting card for that special person.

24.20 *(Rotating Images)* Create a program that lets you rotate an image through some number of degrees (out of a maximum of 360 degrees). The program should let you specify that you want to spin the image continuously. It should let you adjust the spin speed dynamically.

24.21 *(Coloring Black-and-White Photographs and Images)* Create a program that lets you paint a black-and-white photograph with color. Provide a color palette for selecting colors. Your program should let you apply different colors to different regions of the image.

24.22 *(Multimedia-Based Simpletron Simulator)* Modify the Simpletron simulator that you developed in the exercises in earlier chapters (Exercises 7.30–7.32) to include multimedia features. Add computer-like sounds to indicate that the Simpletron is executing instructions. Add a breaking-glass sound when a fatal error occurs. Use flashing lights to indicate which cells of memory or which registers are currently being manipulated. Use other multimedia techniques, as appropriate, to make your Simpletron simulator more valuable to its users as an educational tool.

Making a Difference

24.23 *(Accessibility Project: Speech Synthesis)* Computers can help people who are blind or have low vision by speaking web pages, e-mails and other documents using text-to-speech (TTS) or speech-synthesis "engines." Similarly, to help people who have difficulty interacting with a computer via the mouse and keyboard, speech-recognition engines enable computers to recognize spoken commands. With speech synthesis and speech recognition, users can "talk" with computers. In this exercise, you'll research and explore speech synthesis with the Java Speech API (`java.sun.com/products/java-media/speech/`). Download and install the open-source FreeTTS speech synthesizer (`freetts.sourceforge.net/docs/index.php`). Explore the FreeTTS documentation, then implement an application in which the user can enter text in a `JTextArea`. When the user clicks a **Speak** `JButton`, the program should use FreeTTS to speak the text aloud.

24.24 *(Accessibility Project: Speech Recognition)* In this exercise, you'll research and explore speech recognition with the Java Speech API. Download and install the open-source Sphinx-4 speech-recognition engine (`cmusphinx.sourceforge.net/sphinx4/`). Write a program that enables a user to speak to the computer. Use the speech-recognition capabilities to display what the user says in a `JTextArea`. Enable the user to save the contents of the `JTextArea` to a file on disk by speaking the command "save".

24.25 *(Project: Simbad Robotics Simulator)* Robotics holds tremendous promise for handling jobs that are dangerous for humans, such as mining coal; mining and farming the depths of the ocean and exploring deep space. Simbad (`simbad.sourceforge.net`) is an open-source Java-based 3D robotics simulator. According to the project's web page, it supports single- and multi-robot simulations; vision, range and contact sensors; and more. You can download Simbad from `simbad.sourceforge.net/index.php#download`. You'll also need to download and install Java 3D — instructions are provided on this site for Mac OS X, Windows and Linux.

Once you've downloaded Simbad and installed Java 3D, you can try the simple example provided at `simbad.sourceforge.net/example1.php`. After getting this running, read the Simbad Programming Guide at `simbad.sourceforge.net/guide.php` and try modifying the simple example to perform some different tasks. If you're interested in exploring robotics further, study the API documentation at `simbad.sourceforge.net/doc/` and create your own robot simulation program using Simbad. For example, create a simulation of a robot vacuum cleaner that travels in the direction it's facing until it encounters an obstacle, then randomly chooses another direction.

25

GUI Components: Part 2

Objectives

In this chapter you'll learn:

- To create and manipulate sliders, menus, pop-up menus and windows.

- To programatically change the look-and-feel of a GUI, using Swing's pluggable look-and-feel.

- To create a multiple-document interface with `JDesktopPane` and `JInternalFrame`.

- To use additional layout managers.

25.1 Introduction

In this chapter, we continue our study of GUIs. We discuss additional components and layout managers and lay the groundwork for building more complex GUIs.

We begin our discussion with sliders that enable you to select from a range of integer values. Next, we discuss some additional details of windows. You'll learn to use menus that enable the user to effectively perform tasks in the program. The look-and-feel of a Swing GUI can be uniform across all platforms on which a Java program executes, or the GUI can be customized by using Swing's **pluggable look-and-feel** (**PLAF**). We provide an example that illustrates how to change between Swing's default metal look-and-feel (which looks and behaves the same across platforms), the new Nimbus look-and-feel (introduced in Chapter 14), a look-and-feel that simulates **Motif** (a popular UNIX look-and-feel) and one that simulates Microsoft's Windows look-and-feel.

Many of today's applications use a multiple-document interface (MDI)—a main window (often called the parent window) containing other windows (often called child windows) to manage several open documents in parallel. For example, many e-mail programs allow you to have several e-mail windows open at the same time so that you can compose or read multiple e-mail messages. We demonstrate Swing's classes for creating multiple-document interfaces. The chapter finishes with a series of examples discussing additional layout managers for organizing graphical user interfaces.

Swing is a large and complex topic. There are many more GUI components and capabilities than can be presented here. Several more Swing GUI components are introduced in the remaining chapters of this book as they are needed.

25.2 `JSlider`

JSliders enable a user to select from a range of integer values. Class `JSlider` inherits from `JComponent`. Figure 25.1 shows a horizontal `JSlider` with **tick marks** and the **thumb** that allows a user to select a value. `JSliders` can be customized to display major tick marks, minor tick marks and labels for the tick marks. They also support **snap-to ticks**, which cause the thumb, when positioned between two tick marks, to snap to the closest one.

Thumb ⟶   ⟵ Tick mark

Fig. 25.1 | `JSlider` component with horizontal orientation.

Most Swing GUI components support user interactions through the mouse and the keyboard. For example, if a JSlider has the focus (i.e., it's the currently selected GUI component in the user interface), the left arrow key and right arrow key cause the thumb of the JSlider to decrease or increase by 1, respectively. The down arrow key and up arrow key also cause the thumb of the JSlider to decrease or increase by 1 tick, respectively. The *PgDn* (page down) *key* and *PgUp* (page up) *key* cause the thumb of the JSlider to decrease or increase by **block increments** of one-tenth of the range of values, respectively. The *Home key* moves the thumb to the minimum value of the JSlider, and the *End key* moves the thumb to the maximum value of the JSlider.

JSliders have either a horizontal orientation or a vertical orientation. For a horizontal JSlider, the minimum value is at the left end of the JSlider and the maximum is at the right end. For a vertical JSlider, the minimum value is at the bottom and the maximum is at the top. The minimum and maximum value positions on a JSlider can be reversed by invoking JSlider method **setInverted** with boolean argument true. The relative position of the thumb indicates the current value of the JSlider.

The program in Figs. 25.2–25.4 allows the user to size a circle drawn on a subclass of JPanel called OvalPanel (Fig. 25.2). The user specifies the circle's diameter with a horizontal JSlider. Class OvalPanel knows how to draw a circle on itself, using its own instance variable diameter to determine the diameter of the circle—the diameter is used as the width and height of the bounding box in which the circle is displayed. The diameter value is set when the user interacts with the JSlider. The event handler calls method setDiameter in class OvalPanel to set the diameter and calls repaint to draw the new circle. The repaint call results in a call to OvalPanel's paintComponent method.

```java
 1   // Fig. 25.2: OvalPanel.java
 2   // A customized JPanel class.
 3   import java.awt.Graphics;
 4   import java.awt.Dimension;
 5   import javax.swing.JPanel;
 6
 7   public class OvalPanel extends JPanel
 8   {
 9      private int diameter = 10; // default diameter of 10
10
11      // draw an oval of the specified diameter
12      public void paintComponent( Graphics g )
13      {
14         super.paintComponent( g );
15
16         g.fillOval( 10, 10, diameter, diameter ); // draw circle
17      } // end method paintComponent
18
19      // validate and set diameter, then repaint
20      public void setDiameter( int newDiameter )
21      {
22         // if diameter invalid, default to 10
23         diameter = ( newDiameter >= 0 ? newDiameter : 10 );
24         repaint(); // repaint panel
25      } // end method setDiameter
```

Fig. 25.2 | JPanel subclass for drawing circles of a specified diameter. (Part 1 of 2.)

```
26
27    // used by layout manager to determine preferred size
28    public Dimension getPreferredSize()
29    {
30       return new Dimension( 200, 200 );
31    } // end method getPreferredSize
32
33    // used by layout manager to determine minimum size
34    public Dimension getMinimumSize()
35    {
36       return getPreferredSize();
37    } // end method getMinimumSize
38 } // end class OvalPanel
```

Fig. 25.2 | JPanel subclass for drawing circles of a specified diameter. (Part 2 of 2.)

```
1    // Fig. 25.3: SliderFrame.java
2    // Using JSliders to size an oval.
3    import java.awt.BorderLayout;
4    import java.awt.Color;
5    import javax.swing.JFrame;
6    import javax.swing.JSlider;
7    import javax.swing.SwingConstants;
8    import javax.swing.event.ChangeListener;
9    import javax.swing.event.ChangeEvent;
10
11   public class SliderFrame extends JFrame
12   {
13      private JSlider diameterJSlider; // slider to select diameter
14      private OvalPanel myPanel; // panel to draw circle
15
16      // no-argument constructor
17      public SliderFrame()
18      {
19         super( "Slider Demo" );
20
21         myPanel = new OvalPanel(); // create panel to draw circle
22         myPanel.setBackground( Color.YELLOW ); // set background to yellow
23
24         // set up JSlider to control diameter value
25         diameterJSlider =
26            new JSlider( SwingConstants.HORIZONTAL, 0, 200, 10 );
27         diameterJSlider.setMajorTickSpacing( 10 ); // create tick every 10
28         diameterJSlider.setPaintTicks( true ); // paint ticks on slider
29
30         // register JSlider event listener
31         diameterJSlider.addChangeListener(
32
33            new ChangeListener() // anonymous inner class
34            {
35               // handle change in slider value
36               public void stateChanged( ChangeEvent e )
37               {
```

Fig. 25.3 | JSlider value used to determine the diameter of a circle. (Part 1 of 2.)

```
38                  myPanel.setDiameter( diameterJSlider.getValue() );
39              } // end method stateChanged
40          } // end anonymous inner class
41      ); // end call to addChangeListener
42
43      add( diameterJSlider, BorderLayout.SOUTH ); // add slider to frame
44      add( myPanel, BorderLayout.CENTER ); // add panel to frame
45   } // end SliderFrame constructor
46 } // end class SliderFrame
```

Fig. 25.3 | JSlider value used to determine the diameter of a circle. (Part 2 of 2.)

```
1  // Fig. 25.4: SliderDemo.java
2  // Testing SliderFrame.
3  import javax.swing.JFrame;
4
5  public class SliderDemo
6  {
7     public static void main( String[] args )
8     {
9        SliderFrame sliderFrame = new SliderFrame();
10       sliderFrame.setDefaultCloseOperation( JFrame.EXIT_ON_CLOSE );
11       sliderFrame.setSize( 220, 270 ); // set frame size
12       sliderFrame.setVisible( true ); // display frame
13    } // end main
14 } // end class SliderDemo
```

Fig. 25.4 | Test class for SliderFrame.

Class OvalPanel (Fig. 25.2) contains a paintComponent method (lines 12–17) that draws a filled oval (a circle in this example), a setDiameter method (lines 20–25) that changes the circle's diameter and repaints the OvalPanel, a getPreferredSize method (lines 28–31) that returns the preferred width and height of an OvalPanel and a getMinimumSize method (lines 34–37) that returns an OvalPanel's minimum width and height. Section 24.3 introduced getPreferredSize and getMinimumSize, which are used by some layout managers to determine the size of a component.

Class SliderFrame (Fig. 25.3) creates the JSlider that controls the diameter of the circle. Class SliderFrame's constructor (lines 17–45) creates OvalPanel object myPanel (line 21) and sets its background color (line 22). Lines 25–26 create JSlider object diameterSlider to control the diameter of the circle drawn on the OvalPanel. The JSlider constructor takes four arguments. The first argument specifies the orientation of diameterSlider, which is HORIZONTAL (a constant in interface SwingConstants). The second and third arguments indicate the minimum and maximum integer values in the range of values for this JSlider. The last argument indicates that the initial value of the JSlider (i.e., where the thumb is displayed) should be 10.

Lines 27–28 customize the appearance of the JSlider. Method **setMajorTick-Spacing** indicates that each major tick mark represents 10 values in the range of values supported by the JSlider. Method **setPaintTicks** with a true argument indicates that the tick marks should be displayed (they are not displayed by default). For other methods that are used to customize a JSlider's appearance, see the JSlider on-line documentation (java.sun.com/javase/6/docs/api/javax/swing/JSlider.html).

JSliders generate **ChangeEvents** (package javax.swing.event) in response to user interactions. An object of a class that implements interface **ChangeListener** (package javax.swing.event) and declares method **stateChanged** can respond to ChangeEvents. Lines 31–41 register a ChangeListener to handle diameterSlider's events. When method stateChanged (lines 36–39) is called in response to a user interaction, line 38 calls myPanel's setDiameter method and passes the current value of the JSlider as an argument. JSlider method **getValue** returns the current thumb position.

25.3 Windows: Additional Notes

A JFrame is a **window** with a **title bar** and a **border**. Class JFrame is a subclass of Frame (package java.awt), which is a subclass of Window (package java.awt). As such, JFrame is one of the heavyweight Swing GUI components. When you display a window from a Java program, the window is provided by the local platform's windowing toolkit, and therefore the window will look like every other window displayed on that platform. When a Java application executes on a Macintosh and displays a window, the window's title bar and borders will look like those of other Macintosh applications. When a Java application executes on a Microsoft Windows system and displays a window, the window's title bar and borders will look like those of other Microsoft Windows applications. And when a Java application executes on a UNIX platform and displays a window, the window's title bar and borders will look like other UNIX applications on that platform.

By default, when the user closes a JFrame window, it is hidden (i.e., removed from the screen), but you can control this with JFrame method **setDefaultCloseOperation**. Interface **WindowConstants** (package javax.swing), which class JFrame implements, declares three constants—DISPOSE_ON_CLOSE, DO_NOTHING_ON_CLOSE and HIDE_ON_CLOSE (the default)—for use with this method. Some platforms allow only a limited number of windows to be displayed on the screen. Thus, a window is a valuable resource that should be given back to the system when it's no longer needed. Class Window (an indirect superclass of JFrame) declares method **dispose** for this purpose. When a Window is no longer needed in an application, you should explicitly dispose of it. This can be done by calling the Window's dispose method or by calling method setDefaultCloseOperation with the argument WindowConstants.DISPOSE_ON_CLOSE. Terminating an application also returns window resources to the system. Using DO_NOTHING_ON_CLOSE indicates that the program will determine what to do when the user attempts to close the window. For example, the program might want to ask whether to save a file's changes before closing a window.

Performance Tip 25.1

A window is an expensive system resource. Return it to the system by calling its `dispose` method when the window is no longer needed.

By default, a window is not displayed on the screen until the program invokes the window's `setVisible` method (inherited from class `java.awt.Component`) with a `true` argument. A window's size should be set with a call to method `setSize` (inherited from class `java.awt.Component`). The position of a window when it appears on the screen is specified with method **`setLocation`** (inherited from class `java.awt.Component`).

Common Programming Error 25.1

Forgetting to call method `setVisible` on a window is a runtime logic error—the window is not displayed.

Common Programming Error 25.2

Forgetting to call the `setSize` method on a window is a runtime logic error—only the title bar appears.

When the user manipulates the window, this action generates **window events**. Event listeners are registered for window events with `Window` method **`addWindowListener`**. Interface **`WindowListener`** provides seven window-event-handling methods—**`windowActivated`** (called when the user makes a window the active window), **`windowClosed`** (called after the window is closed), **`windowClosing`** (called when the user initiates closing of the window), **`windowDeactivated`** (called when the user makes another window the active window), **`windowDeiconified`** (called when the user restores a window from being minimized), **`windowIconified`** (called when the user minimizes a window) and **`windowOpened`** (called when a program first displays a window on the screen).

25.4 Using Menus with Frames

Menus are an integral part of GUIs. They allow the user to perform actions without unnecessarily cluttering a GUI with extra components. In Swing GUIs, menus can be attached only to objects of the classes that provide method **`setJMenuBar`**. Two such classes are `JFrame` and `JApplet`. The classes used to declare menus are `JMenuBar`, `JMenu`, `JMenuItem`, `JCheckBoxMenuItem` and class `JRadioButtonMenuItem`.

Look-and-Feel Observation 25.1

Menus simplify GUIs because components can be hidden within them. These components will be visible only when the user looks for them by selecting the menu.

Overview of Several Menu-Related Components

Class **`JMenuBar`** (a subclass of `JComponent`) contains the methods necessary to manage a **menu bar**, which is a container for menus. Class **`JMenu`** (a subclass of `javax.swing.JMenuItem`) contains the methods necessary for managing menus. Menus contain menu items and are added to menu bars or to other menus as submenus. When a menu is clicked, it expands to show its list of menu items.

Class **`JMenuItem`** (a subclass of `javax.swing.AbstractButton`) contains the methods necessary to manage **menu items**. A menu item is a GUI component inside a menu that, when selected, causes an action event. A menu item can be used to initiate an action, or it can be a **submenu** that provides more menu items from which the user can select. Submenus are useful for grouping related menu items in a menu.

Class **JCheckBoxMenuItem** (a subclass of javax.swing.JMenuItem) contains the methods necessary to manage menu items that can be toggled on or off. When a JCheckBoxMenuItem is selected, a check appears to the left of the menu item. When the JCheckBoxMenuItem is selected again, the check is removed.

Class **JRadioButtonMenuItem** (a subclass of javax.swing.JMenuItem) contains the methods necessary to manage menu items that can be toggled on or off like JCheckBoxMenuItems. When multiple JRadioButtonMenuItems are maintained as part of a ButtonGroup, only one item in the group can be selected at a given time. When a JRadioButtonMenuItem is selected, a filled circle appears to the left of the menu item. When another JRadioButtonMenuItem is selected, the filled circle of the previously selected menu item is removed.

Using Menus in an Application

Figures 25.5–25.6 demonstrate various menu items and how to specify special characters called **mnemonics** that can provide quick access to a menu or menu item from the keyboard. Mnemonics can be used with all subclasses of javax.swing.AbstractButton. Class MenuFrame (Fig. 25.5) creates the GUI and handles the menu-item events. Most of the code in this application appears in the class's constructor (lines 34–151).

```
 1   // Fig. 25.5: MenuFrame.java
 2   // Demonstrating menus.
 3   import java.awt.Color;
 4   import java.awt.Font;
 5   import java.awt.BorderLayout;
 6   import java.awt.event.ActionListener;
 7   import java.awt.event.ActionEvent;
 8   import java.awt.event.ItemListener;
 9   import java.awt.event.ItemEvent;
10   import javax.swing.JFrame;
11   import javax.swing.JRadioButtonMenuItem;
12   import javax.swing.JCheckBoxMenuItem;
13   import javax.swing.JOptionPane;
14   import javax.swing.JLabel;
15   import javax.swing.SwingConstants;
16   import javax.swing.ButtonGroup;
17   import javax.swing.JMenu;
18   import javax.swing.JMenuItem;
19   import javax.swing.JMenuBar;
20
21   public class MenuFrame extends JFrame
22   {
23      private final Color[] colorValues =
24         { Color.BLACK, Color.BLUE, Color.RED, Color.GREEN };
25      private JRadioButtonMenuItem[] colorItems; // color menu items
26      private JRadioButtonMenuItem[] fonts; // font menu items
27      private JCheckBoxMenuItem[] styleItems; // font style menu items
28      private JLabel displayJLabel; // displays sample text
```

Fig. 25.5 | JMenus and mnemonics. (Part 1 of 5.)

```
29      private ButtonGroup fontButtonGroup; // manages font menu items
30      private ButtonGroup colorButtonGroup; // manages color menu items
31      private int style; // used to create style for font
32
33      // no-argument constructor set up GUI
34      public MenuFrame()
35      {
36         super( "Using JMenus" );
37
38         JMenu fileMenu = new JMenu( "File" ); // create file menu
39         fileMenu.setMnemonic( 'F' ); // set mnemonic to F
40
41         // create About... menu item
42         JMenuItem aboutItem = new JMenuItem( "About..." );
43         aboutItem.setMnemonic( 'A' ); // set mnemonic to A
44         fileMenu.add( aboutItem ); // add about item to file menu
45         aboutItem.addActionListener(
46
47            new ActionListener() // anonymous inner class
48            {
49               // display message dialog when user selects About...
50               public void actionPerformed( ActionEvent event )
51               {
52                  JOptionPane.showMessageDialog( MenuFrame.this,
53                     "This is an example\nof using menus",
54                     "About", JOptionPane.PLAIN_MESSAGE );
55               } // end method actionPerformed
56            } // end anonymous inner class
57         ); // end call to addActionListener
58
59         JMenuItem exitItem = new JMenuItem( "Exit" ); // create exit item
60         exitItem.setMnemonic( 'x' ); // set mnemonic to x
61         fileMenu.add( exitItem ); // add exit item to file menu
62         exitItem.addActionListener(
63
64            new ActionListener() // anonymous inner class
65            {
66               // terminate application when user clicks exitItem
67               public void actionPerformed( ActionEvent event )
68               {
69                  System.exit( 0 ); // exit application
70               } // end method actionPerformed
71            } // end anonymous inner class
72         ); // end call to addActionListener
73
74         JMenuBar bar = new JMenuBar(); // create menu bar
75         setJMenuBar( bar ); // add menu bar to application
76         bar.add( fileMenu ); // add file menu to menu bar
77
78         JMenu formatMenu = new JMenu( "Format" ); // create format menu
79         formatMenu.setMnemonic( 'r' ); // set mnemonic to r
80
81         // array listing string colors
82         String[] colors = { "Black", "Blue", "Red", "Green" };
```

Fig. 25.5 | JMenus and mnemonics. (Part 2 of 5.)

```
83
84     JMenu colorMenu = new JMenu( "Color" ); // create color menu
85     colorMenu.setMnemonic( 'C' ); // set mnemonic to C
86
87     // create radio button menu items for colors
88     colorItems = new JRadioButtonMenuItem[ colors.length ];
89     colorButtonGroup = new ButtonGroup(); // manages colors
90     ItemHandler itemHandler = new ItemHandler(); // handler for colors
91
92     // create color radio button menu items
93     for ( int count = 0; count < colors.length; count++ )
94     {
95        colorItems[ count ] =
96           new JRadioButtonMenuItem( colors[ count ] ); // create item
97        colorMenu.add( colorItems[ count ] ); // add item to color menu
98        colorButtonGroup.add( colorItems[ count ] ); // add to group
99        colorItems[ count ].addActionListener( itemHandler );
100    } // end for
101
102    colorItems[ 0 ].setSelected( true ); // select first Color item
103
104    formatMenu.add( colorMenu ); // add color menu to format menu
105    formatMenu.addSeparator(); // add separator in menu
106
107    // array listing font names
108    String[] fontNames = { "Serif", "Monospaced", "SansSerif" };
109    JMenu fontMenu = new JMenu( "Font" ); // create font menu
110    fontMenu.setMnemonic( 'n' ); // set mnemonic to n
111
112    // create radio button menu items for font names
113    fonts = new JRadioButtonMenuItem[ fontNames.length ];
114    fontButtonGroup = new ButtonGroup(); // manages font names
115
116    // create Font radio button menu items
117    for ( int count = 0; count < fonts.length; count++ )
118    {
119       fonts[ count ] = new JRadioButtonMenuItem( fontNames[ count ] );
120       fontMenu.add( fonts[ count ] ); // add font to font menu
121       fontButtonGroup.add( fonts[ count ] ); // add to button group
122       fonts[ count ].addActionListener( itemHandler ); // add handler
123    } // end for
124
125    fonts[ 0 ].setSelected( true ); // select first Font menu item
126    fontMenu.addSeparator(); // add separator bar to font menu
127
128    String[] styleNames = { "Bold", "Italic" }; // names of styles
129    styleItems = new JCheckBoxMenuItem[ styleNames.length ];
130    StyleHandler styleHandler = new StyleHandler(); // style handler
131
132    // create style checkbox menu items
133    for ( int count = 0; count < styleNames.length; count++ )
134    {
135       styleItems[ count ] =
136          new JCheckBoxMenuItem( styleNames[ count ] ); // for style
```

Fig. 25.5 | JMenus and mnemonics. (Part 3 of 5.)

```
137              fontMenu.add( styleItems[ count ] ); // add to font menu
138              styleItems[ count ].addItemListener( styleHandler ); // handler
139          } // end for
140
141          formatMenu.add( fontMenu ); // add Font menu to Format menu
142          bar.add( formatMenu ); // add Format menu to menu bar
143
144          // set up label to display text
145          displayJLabel = new JLabel( "Sample Text", SwingConstants.CENTER );
146          displayJLabel.setForeground( colorValues[ 0 ] );
147          displayJLabel.setFont( new Font( "Serif", Font.PLAIN, 72 ) );
148
149          getContentPane().setBackground( Color.CYAN ); // set background
150          add( displayJLabel, BorderLayout.CENTER ); // add displayJLabel
151      } // end MenuFrame constructor
152
153      // inner class to handle action events from menu items
154      private class ItemHandler implements ActionListener
155      {
156          // process color and font selections
157          public void actionPerformed( ActionEvent event )
158          {
159              // process color selection
160              for ( int count = 0; count < colorItems.length; count++ )
161              {
162                  if ( colorItems[ count ].isSelected() )
163                  {
164                      displayJLabel.setForeground( colorValues[ count ] );
165                      break;
166                  } // end if
167              } // end for
168
169              // process font selection
170              for ( int count = 0; count < fonts.length; count++ )
171              {
172                  if ( event.getSource() == fonts[ count ] )
173                  {
174                      displayJLabel.setFont(
175                          new Font( fonts[ count ].getText(), style, 72 ) );
176                  } // end if
177              } // end for
178
179              repaint(); // redraw application
180          } // end method actionPerformed
181      } // end class ItemHandler
182
183      // inner class to handle item events from checkbox menu items
184      private class StyleHandler implements ItemListener
185      {
186          // process font style selections
187          public void itemStateChanged( ItemEvent e )
188          {
189              String name = displayJLabel.getFont().getName(); // current Font
190              Font font; // new font based on user selections
```

Fig. 25.5 | JMenus and mnemonics. (Part 4 of 5.)

```
191
192          // determine which items are checked and create Font
193          if ( styleItems[ 0 ].isSelected() &&
194              styleItems[ 1 ].isSelected() )
195            font = new Font( name, Font.BOLD + Font.ITALIC, 72 );
196          else if ( styleItems[ 0 ].isSelected() )
197            font = new Font( name, Font.BOLD, 72 );
198          else if ( styleItems[ 1 ].isSelected() )
199            font = new Font( name, Font.ITALIC, 72 );
200          else
201            font = new Font( name, Font.PLAIN, 72 );
202
203          displayJLabel.setFont( font );
204          repaint(); // redraw application
205       } // end method itemStateChanged
206    } // end class StyleHandler
207 } // end class MenuFrame
```

Fig. 25.5 | JMenus and mnemonics. (Part 5 of 5.)

```
1   // Fig. 25.6: MenuTest.java
2   // Testing MenuFrame.
3   import javax.swing.JFrame;
4
5   public class MenuTest
6   {
7      public static void main( String[] args )
8      {
9         MenuFrame menuFrame = new MenuFrame(); // create MenuFrame
10        menuFrame.setDefaultCloseOperation( JFrame.EXIT_ON_CLOSE );
11        menuFrame.setSize( 500, 200 ); // set frame size
12        menuFrame.setVisible( true ); // display frame
13     } // end main
14  } // end class MenuTest
```

Fig. 25.6 | Test class for MenuFrame.

Setting Up the File Menu

Lines 38–76 set up the **File** menu and attach it to the menu bar. The **File** menu contains an **About...** menu item that displays a message dialog when the menu item is selected and an **Exit** menu item that can be selected to terminate the application.

Line 38 creates a JMenu and passes to the constructor the string "File" as the name of the menu. Line 39 uses JMenu method **setMnemonic** (inherited from class Abstract-Button) to indicate that F is the mnemonic for this menu. Pressing the *Alt* key and the letter *F* opens the menu, just as clicking the menu name with the mouse would. In the GUI, the mnemonic character in the menu's name is displayed with an underline. (See the screen captures in Fig. 25.6.)

Look-and-Feel Observation 25.2

Mnemonics provide quick access to menu commands and button commands through the keyboard.

Look-and-Feel Observation 25.3

Different mnemonics should be used for each button or menu item. Normally, the first letter in the label on the menu item or button is used as the mnemonic. If several buttons or menu items start with the same letter, choose the next most prominent letter in the name (e.g., x is commonly chosen for an **Exit** *button or menu item). Mnemonics are case insensitive.*

Lines 42–43 create JMenuItem aboutItem with the text "About..." and set its mnemonic to the letter A. This menu item is added to fileMenu at line 44 with JMenu method **add**. To access the **About...** menu item through the keyboard, press the *Alt* key and letter *F* to open the **File** menu, then press *A* to select the **About...** menu item. Lines 47–56 create an ActionListener to process aboutItem's action event. Lines 52–54 display a message dialog box. In most prior uses of showMessageDialog, the first argument was null. The purpose of the first argument is to specify the **parent window** that helps determine where the dialog box will be displayed. If the parent window is specified as null, the dialog box appears in the center of the screen. Otherwise, it appears centered over the specified parent window. In this example, the program specifies the parent window with Menu-Frame.this—the this reference of the MenuFrame object. When using the this reference in an inner class, specifying this by itself refers to the inner-class object. To reference the outer-class object's this reference, qualify this with the outer-class name and a dot (.).

Dialog boxes are typically modal. A modal dialog box does not allow any other window in the application to be accessed until the dialog box is dismissed. The dialogs displayed with class JOptionPane are modal dialogs. Class **JDialog** can be used to create your own modal or nonmodal dialogs.

Lines 59–72 create menu item exitItem, set its mnemonic to x, add it to fileMenu and register an ActionListener that terminates the program when the user selects exit-Item.

Lines 74–76 create the JMenuBar, attach it to the window with JFrame method set-JMenuBar and use JMenuBar method **add** to attach the fileMenu to the JMenuBar.

Common Programming Error 25.3

Forgetting to set the menu bar with JFrame method setJMenuBar prevents the menu bar from displaying in the JFrame.

Look-and-Feel Observation 25.4

Menus appear left to right in the order that they are added to a JMenuBar.

Setting Up the Format Menu

Lines 78–79 create menu formatMenu and set its mnemonic to r. (F is not used because that is the **File** menu's mnemonic.)

Lines 84–85 create menu colorMenu (this will be a submenu in the **Format** menu) and set its mnemonic to C. Line 88 creates JRadioButtonMenuItem array colorItems, which refers to the menu items in colorMenu. Line 89 creates ButtonGroup colorButtonGroup, which will ensure that only one of the menu items in the **Color** submenu is selected at a time. Line 90 creates an instance of inner class ItemHandler (declared at lines 154–181) that responds to selections from the **Color** and **Font** submenus (discussed shortly). The for statement at lines 93–100 creates each JRadioButtonMenuItem in array colorItems, adds each menu item to colorMenu and to colorButtonGroup and registers the ActionListener for each menu item.

Line 102 invokes AbstractButton method **setSelected** to select the first element in array colorItems. Line 104 adds colorMenu as a submenu of formatMenu. Line 105 invokes JMenu method **addSeparator** to add a horizontal **separator** line to the menu.

Look-and-Feel Observation 25.5

A submenu is created by adding a menu as a menu item in another menu. When the mouse is positioned over a submenu (or the submenu's mnemonic is pressed), the submenu expands to show its menu items.

Look-and-Feel Observation 25.6

Separators can be added to a menu to group menu items logically.

Look-and-Feel Observation 25.7

Any lightweight GUI component (i.e., a component that is a subclass of JComponent) can be added to a JMenu or to a JMenuBar.

Lines 108–126 create the **Font** submenu and several JRadioButtonMenuItems and select the first element of JRadioButtonMenuItem array fonts. Line 129 creates a JCheckBoxMenuItem array to represent the menu items for specifying bold and italic styles for the fonts. Line 130 creates an instance of inner class StyleHandler (declared at lines 184–206) to respond to the JCheckBoxMenuItem events. The for statement at lines 133–139 creates each JCheckBoxMenuItem, adds each menu item to fontMenu and registers the ItemListener for each menu item. Line 141 adds fontMenu as a submenu of formatMenu. Line 142 adds the formatMenu to bar (the menu bar).

Creating the Rest of the GUI and Defining the Event Handlers

Lines 145–147 create a JLabel for which the **Format** menu items control the font, font color and font style. The initial foreground color is set to the first element of array colorValues (Color.BLACK) by invoking JComponent method **setForeground**. The initial font is set to Serif with PLAIN style and 72-point size. Line 149 sets the background color of the window's content pane to cyan, and line 150 attaches the JLabel to the CENTER of the content pane's BorderLayout.

ItemHandler method actionPerformed (lines 157–180) uses two for statements to determine which font or color menu item generated the event and sets the font or color of the JLabel displayLabel, respectively. The if condition at line 162 uses Abstract-Button method **isSelected** to determine the selected JRadioButtonMenuItem. The if condition at line 172 invokes the event object's getSource method to get a reference to the JRadioButtonMenuItem that generated the event. Line 175 invokes AbstractButton method getText to obtain the name of the font from the menu item.

StyleHandler method itemStateChanged (lines 187–205) is called if the user selects a JCheckBoxMenuItem in the fontMenu. Lines 193–201 determine which JCheckBoxMenu-Items are selected and use their combined state to determine the new font style.

25.5 JPopupMenu

Many of today's computer applications provide so-called **context-sensitive pop-up menus**. In Swing, such menus are created with class **JPopupMenu** (a subclass of JCompo-nent). These menus provide options that are specific to the component for which the **pop-up trigger event** was generated. On most systems, the pop-up trigger event occurs when the user presses and releases the right mouse button.

Look-and-Feel Observation 25.8
The pop-up trigger event is platform specific. On most platforms that use a mouse with multiple buttons, the pop-up trigger event occurs when the user clicks the right mouse button on a component that supports a pop-up menu.

The application in Figs. 25.7–25.8 creates a JPopupMenu that allows the user to select one of three colors and change the background color of the window. When the user clicks the right mouse button on the PopupFrame window's background, a JPopupMenu containing colors appears. If the user clicks a JRadioButtonMenuItem for a color, ItemHandler method actionPerformed changes the background color of the window's content pane.

Line 25 of the PopupFrame constructor (Fig. 25.7, lines 21–69) creates an instance of class ItemHandler (declared in lines 72–87) that will process the item events from the menu items in the pop-up menu. Line 29 creates the JPopupMenu. The for statement (lines 33–39) creates a JRadioButtonMenuItem object (line 35), adds it to popupMenu (line 36), adds it to ButtonGroup colorGroup (line 37) to maintain one selected JRadioButtonMenuItem at a time and registers its ActionListener (line 38). Line 41 sets the initial background to white by invoking method setBackground.

```
1   // Fig. 25.7: PopupFrame.java
2   // Demonstrating JPopupMenus.
3   import java.awt.Color;
4   import java.awt.event.MouseAdapter;
5   import java.awt.event.MouseEvent;
6   import java.awt.event.ActionListener;
7   import java.awt.event.ActionEvent;
8   import javax.swing.JFrame;
```

Fig. 25.7 | JPopupMenu for selecting colors. (Part 1 of 3.)

```
 9  import javax.swing.JRadioButtonMenuItem;
10  import javax.swing.JPopupMenu;
11  import javax.swing.ButtonGroup;
12
13  public class PopupFrame extends JFrame
14  {
15     private JRadioButtonMenuItem[] items; // holds items for colors
16     private final Color[] colorValues =
17        { Color.BLUE, Color.YELLOW, Color.RED }; // colors to be used
18     private JPopupMenu popupMenu; // allows user to select color
19
20     // no-argument constructor sets up GUI
21     public PopupFrame()
22     {
23        super( "Using JPopupMenus" );
24
25        ItemHandler handler = new ItemHandler(); // handler for menu items
26        String[] colors = { "Blue", "Yellow", "Red" }; // array of colors
27
28        ButtonGroup colorGroup = new ButtonGroup(); // manages color items
29        popupMenu = new JPopupMenu(); // create pop-up menu
30        items = new JRadioButtonMenuItem[ colors.length ]; // color items
31
32        // construct menu item, add to pop-up menu, enable event handling
33        for ( int count = 0; count < items.length; count++ )
34        {
35           items[ count ] = new JRadioButtonMenuItem( colors[ count ] );
36           popupMenu.add( items[ count ] ); // add item to pop-up menu
37           colorGroup.add( items[ count ] ); // add item to button group
38           items[ count ].addActionListener( handler ); // add handler
39        } // end for
40
41        setBackground( Color.WHITE ); // set background to white
42
43        // declare a MouseListener for the window to display pop-up menu
44        addMouseListener(
45
46           new MouseAdapter() // anonymous inner class
47           {
48              // handle mouse press event
49              public void mousePressed( MouseEvent event )
50              {
51                 checkForTriggerEvent( event ); // check for trigger
52              } // end method mousePressed
53
54              // handle mouse release event
55              public void mouseReleased( MouseEvent event )
56              {
57                 checkForTriggerEvent( event ); // check for trigger
58              } // end method mouseReleased
59
60              // determine whether event should trigger pop-up menu
61              private void checkForTriggerEvent( MouseEvent event )
62              {
```

Fig. 25.7 | JPopupMenu for selecting colors. (Part 2 of 3.)

```
63                    if ( event.isPopupTrigger() )
64                       popupMenu.show(
65                          event.getComponent(), event.getX(), event.getY() );
66                } // end method checkForTriggerEvent
67             } // end anonymous inner class
68          ); // end call to addMouseListener
69       } // end PopupFrame constructor
70
71       // private inner class to handle menu item events
72       private class ItemHandler implements ActionListener
73       {
74          // process menu item selections
75          public void actionPerformed( ActionEvent event )
76          {
77             // determine which menu item was selected
78             for ( int i = 0; i < items.length; i++ )
79             {
80                if ( event.getSource() == items[ i ] )
81                {
82                   getContentPane().setBackground( colorValues[ i ] );
83                   return;
84                } // end if
85             } // end for
86          } // end method actionPerformed
87       } // end private inner class ItemHandler
88    } // end class PopupFrame
```

Fig. 25.7 | JPopupMenu for selecting colors. (Part 3 of 3.)

```
 1   // Fig. 25.8: PopupTest.java
 2   // Testing PopupFrame.
 3   import javax.swing.JFrame;
 4
 5   public class PopupTest
 6   {
 7      public static void main( String[] args )
 8      {
 9         PopupFrame popupFrame = new PopupFrame(); // create PopupFrame
10         popupFrame.setDefaultCloseOperation( JFrame.EXIT_ON_CLOSE );
11         popupFrame.setSize( 300, 200 ); // set frame size
12         popupFrame.setVisible( true ); // display frame
13      } // end main
14   } // end class PopupTest
```

Fig. 25.8 | Test class for PopupFrame.

Lines 44–68 register a MouseListener to handle the mouse events of the application window. Methods mousePressed (lines 49–52) and mouseReleased (lines 55–58) check for the pop-up trigger event. Each method calls private utility method checkForTrigger-Event (lines 61–66) to determine whether the pop-up trigger event occurred. If it did, MouseEvent method **isPopupTrigger** returns true, and JPopupMenu method **show** displays the JPopupMenu. The first argument to method show specifies the **origin component**, whose position helps determine where the JPopupMenu will appear on the screen. The last two arguments are the *x-y* coordinates (measured from the origin component's upper-left corner) at which the JPopupMenu is to appear.

Look-and-Feel Observation 25.9

Displaying a JPopupMenu for the pop-up trigger event of multiple GUI components re-quires registering mouse-event handlers for each of those GUI components.

When the user selects a menu item from the pop-up menu, class ItemHandler's method actionPerformed (lines 75–86) determines which JRadioButtonMenuItem the user selected and sets the background color of the window's content pane.

25.6 Pluggable Look-and-Feel

A program that uses Java's AWT GUI components (package java.awt) takes on the look-and-feel of the platform on which the program executes. A Java application running on a Mac OS X looks like other Mac OS X applications. One running on Microsoft Windows looks like other Windows applications. One running on a UNIX platform looks like other applications on that UNIX platform. This is sometimes desirable, because it allows users of the application on each platform to use GUI components with which they are already familiar. However, it also introduces interesting portability issues.

Portability Tip 25.1

GUI components look different on different platforms and may require different amounts of space to display. This could change their layout and alignments.

Portability Tip 25.2

GUI components on different platforms have different default functionality (e.g., some platforms allow a button with the focus to be "pressed" with the space bar, and some don't).

Swing's lightweight GUI components eliminate many of these issues by providing uniform functionality across platforms and by defining a uniform cross-platform look-and-feel. As of Java SE 6 Update 10, this is the Nimbus look-and-feel that we discussed in Section 14.2. Earlier versions of Java used the **metal look-and-feel**, which is still the default. Swing also provides the flexibility to customize the look-and-feel to appear as a Microsoft Windows-style look-and-feel (only on Window systems), a Motif-style (UNIX) look-and-feel (across all platforms) or a Macintosh look-and-feel (only on Mac systems). Figures 25.9–25.10 demonstrate a way to change the look-and-feel of a Swing GUI. It creates several GUI components, so you can see the change in their look-and-feel at the same time. The output windows show the Metal, Nimbus, CDE/Motif, Windows and Windows Classic look-and-feels that are available on Windows systems. The installed look-and-feels will vary by platform.

```
1   // Fig. 25.9: LookAndFeelFrame.java
2   // Changing the look-and-feel.
3   import java.awt.GridLayout;
4   import java.awt.BorderLayout;
5   import java.awt.event.ItemListener;
6   import java.awt.event.ItemEvent;
7   import javax.swing.JFrame;
8   import javax.swing.UIManager;
9   import javax.swing.JRadioButton;
10  import javax.swing.ButtonGroup;
11  import javax.swing.JButton;
12  import javax.swing.JLabel;
13  import javax.swing.JComboBox;
14  import javax.swing.JPanel;
15  import javax.swing.SwingConstants;
16  import javax.swing.SwingUtilities;
17
18  public class LookAndFeelFrame extends JFrame
19  {
20     private UIManager.LookAndFeelInfo[] looks; // look and feels
21     private String[] lookNames; // names of look and feels
22     private JRadioButton[] radio; // radio buttons to select look-and-feel
23     private ButtonGroup group; // group for radio buttons
24     private JButton button; // displays look of button
25     private JLabel label; // displays look of label
26     private JComboBox comboBox; // displays look of combo box
27
28     // set up GUI
29     public LookAndFeelFrame()
30     {
31        super( "Look and Feel Demo" );
32
33        // get installed look-and-feel information
34        looks = UIManager.getInstalledLookAndFeels();
35        lookNames = new String[ looks.length ];
36
37        // get names of installed look-and-feels
38        for ( int i = 0; i < looks.length; i++ )
39           lookNames[ i ] = looks[ i ].getName();
40
41        JPanel northPanel = new JPanel(); // create north panel
42        northPanel.setLayout( new GridLayout( 3, 1, 0, 5 ) );
43
44        label = new JLabel( "This is a " + lookNames[0] + " look-and-feel",
45           SwingConstants.CENTER ); // create label
46        northPanel.add( label ); // add label to panel
47
48        button = new JButton( "JButton" ); // create button
49        northPanel.add( button ); // add button to panel
50
51        comboBox = new JComboBox( lookNames ); // create combobox
52        northPanel.add( comboBox ); // add combobox to panel
53
```

Fig. 25.9 | Look-and-feel of a Swing-based GUI. (Part 1 of 3.)

```
54          // create array for radio buttons
55          radio = new JRadioButton[ looks.length ];
56
57          JPanel southPanel = new JPanel(); // create south panel
58
59          // use a GridLayout with 3 buttons in each row
60          int rows = (int) Math.ceil( radio.length / 3.0 );
61          southPanel.setLayout( new GridLayout( rows, 3 ) );
62
63          group = new ButtonGroup(); // button group for looks-and-feels
64          ItemHandler handler = new ItemHandler(); // look-and-feel handler
65
66          for ( int count = 0; count < radio.length; count++ )
67          {
68             radio[ count ] = new JRadioButton( lookNames[ count ] );
69             radio[ count ].addItemListener( handler ); // add handler
70             group.add( radio[ count ] ); // add radio button to group
71             southPanel.add( radio[ count ] ); // add radio button to panel
72          } // end for
73
74          add( northPanel, BorderLayout.NORTH ); // add north panel
75          add( southPanel, BorderLayout.SOUTH ); // add south panel
76
77          radio[ 0 ].setSelected( true ); // set default selection
78       } // end LookAndFeelFrame constructor
79
80       // use UIManager to change look-and-feel of GUI
81       private void changeTheLookAndFeel( int value )
82       {
83          try // change look-and-feel
84          {
85             // set look-and-feel for this application
86             UIManager.setLookAndFeel( looks[ value ].getClassName() );
87
88             // update components in this application
89             SwingUtilities.updateComponentTreeUI( this );
90          } // end try
91          catch ( Exception exception )
92          {
93             exception.printStackTrace();
94          } // end catch
95       } // end method changeTheLookAndFeel
96
97       // private inner class to handle radio button events
98       private class ItemHandler implements ItemListener
99       {
100         // process user's look-and-feel selection
101         public void itemStateChanged( ItemEvent event )
102         {
103            for ( int count = 0; count < radio.length; count++ )
104            {
105               if ( radio[ count ].isSelected() )
106               {
```

Fig. 25.9 | Look-and-feel of a Swing-based GUI. (Part 2 of 3.)

```
107                     label.setText( String.format(
108                        "This is a %s look-and-feel", lookNames[ count ] ) );
109                     comboBox.setSelectedIndex( count ); // set combobox index
110                     changeTheLookAndFeel( count ); // change look-and-feel
111                  } // end if
112               } // end for
113            } // end method itemStateChanged
114         } // end private inner class ItemHandler
115   } // end class LookAndFeelFrame
```

Fig. 25.9 | Look-and-feel of a Swing-based GUI. (Part 3 of 3.)

```
 1   // Fig. 25.10: LookAndFeelDemo.java
 2   // Changing the look-and-feel.
 3   import javax.swing.JFrame;
 4
 5   public class LookAndFeelDemo
 6   {
 7      public static void main( String[] args )
 8      {
 9         LookAndFeelFrame lookAndFeelFrame = new LookAndFeelFrame();
10         lookAndFeelFrame.setDefaultCloseOperation( JFrame.EXIT_ON_CLOSE );
11         lookAndFeelFrame.setSize( 400, 220 ); // set frame size
12         lookAndFeelFrame.setVisible( true ); // display frame
13      } // end main
14   } // end class LookAndFeelDemo
```

Fig. 25.10 | Test class for LookAndFeelFrame.

We've covered the GUI components and event-handling concepts in this example previously, so we focus here on the mechanism for changing the look-and-feel. Class **UIManager** (package javax.swing) contains nested class **LookAndFeelInfo** (a public static class) that maintains information about a look-and-feel. Line 20 declares an array of type UIManager.LookAndFeelInfo (note the syntax used to identify the static inner class LookAndFeelInfo). Line 34 uses UIManager static method **getInstalledLookAndFeels** to get the array of UIManager.LookAndFeelInfo objects that describe each look-and-feel available on your system.

> **Performance Tip 25.2**
> *Each look-and-feel is represented by a Java class. UIManager method getInstalled-LookAndFeels does not load each class. Rather, it provides the names of the available look-and-feel classes so that a choice can be made (presumably once at program start-up). This reduces the overhead of having to load all the look-and-feel classes even if the program will not use some of them.*

Our utility method changeTheLookAndFeel (lines 81–95) is called by the event handler for the JRadioButtons at the bottom of the user interface. The event handler (declared in private inner class ItemHandler at lines 98–114) passes an integer representing the element in array looks that should be used to change the look-and-feel. Line 86 invokes static method **setLookAndFeel** of UIManager to change the look-and-feel. Method **getClassName** of class UIManager.LookAndFeelInfo determines the name of the look-and-feel class that corresponds to the UIManager.LookAndFeelInfo object. If the look-and-feel class is not already loaded, it will be loaded as part of the call to setLookAndFeel. Line 89 invokes static method **updateComponentTreeUI** of class **SwingUtilities** (package javax.swing) to change the look-and-feel of every GUI component attached to its argument (this instance of our application class LookAndFeelFrame) to the new look-and-feel.

25.7 JDesktopPane and JInternalFrame

Many of today's applications use a **multiple-document interface** (MDI)—a main window (called the **parent window**) containing other windows (called **child windows**), to manage several open documents that are being processed in parallel. For example, many e-mail programs allow you to have several windows open at the same time, so you can compose or read multiple e-mail messages simultaneously. Similarly, many word processors allow the user to open multiple documents in separate windows within a main window, making it possible to switch between them without having to close one to open another. The application in Figs. 25.11–25.12 demonstrates Swing's **JDesktopPane** and **JInternalFrame** classes for implementing multiple-document interfaces.

```
1    // Fig. 25.11: DesktopFrame.java
2    // Demonstrating JDesktopPane.
3    import java.awt.BorderLayout;
4    import java.awt.Dimension;
5    import java.awt.Graphics;
6    import java.awt.event.ActionListener;
7    import java.awt.event.ActionEvent;
```

Fig. 25.11 | Multiple-document interface. (Part 1 of 3.)

```
 8   import java.util.Random;
 9   import javax.swing.JFrame;
10   import javax.swing.JDesktopPane;
11   import javax.swing.JMenuBar;
12   import javax.swing.JMenu;
13   import javax.swing.JMenuItem;
14   import javax.swing.JInternalFrame;
15   import javax.swing.JPanel;
16   import javax.swing.ImageIcon;
17
18   public class DesktopFrame extends JFrame
19   {
20      private JDesktopPane theDesktop;
21
22      // set up GUI
23      public DesktopFrame()
24      {
25         super( "Using a JDesktopPane" );
26
27         JMenuBar bar = new JMenuBar(); // create menu bar
28         JMenu addMenu = new JMenu( "Add" ); // create Add menu
29         JMenuItem newFrame = new JMenuItem( "Internal Frame" );
30
31         addMenu.add( newFrame ); // add new frame item to Add menu
32         bar.add( addMenu ); // add Add menu to menu bar
33         setJMenuBar( bar ); // set menu bar for this application
34
35         theDesktop = new JDesktopPane(); // create desktop pane
36         add( theDesktop ); // add desktop pane to frame
37
38         // set up listener for newFrame menu item
39         newFrame.addActionListener(
40
41            new ActionListener() // anonymous inner class
42            {
43               // display new internal window
44               public void actionPerformed( ActionEvent event )
45               {
46                  // create internal frame
47                  JInternalFrame frame = new JInternalFrame(
48                     "Internal Frame", true, true, true, true );
49
50                  MyJPanel panel = new MyJPanel(); // create new panel
51                  frame.add( panel, BorderLayout.CENTER ); // add panel
52                  frame.pack(); // set internal frame to size of contents
53
54                  theDesktop.add( frame ); // attach internal frame
55                  frame.setVisible( true ); // show internal frame
56               } // end method actionPerformed
57            } // end anonymous inner class
58         ); // end call to addActionListener
59      } // end DesktopFrame constructor
60   } // end class DesktopFrame
61
```

Fig. 25.11 | Multiple-document interface. (Part 2 of 3.)

```
62    // class to display an ImageIcon on a panel
63    class MyJPanel extends JPanel
64    {
65       private static Random generator = new Random();
66       private ImageIcon picture; // image to be displayed
67       private final static String[] images = { "yellowflowers.png",
68          "purpleflowers.png", "redflowers.png", "redflowers2.png",
69          "lavenderflowers.png" };
70
71       // load image
72       public MyJPanel()
73       {
74          int randomNumber = generator.nextInt( images.length );
75          picture = new ImageIcon( images[ randomNumber ] ); // set icon
76       } // end MyJPanel constructor
77
78       // display imageIcon on panel
79       public void paintComponent( Graphics g )
80       {
81          super.paintComponent( g );
82          picture.paintIcon( this, g, 0, 0 ); // display icon
83       } // end method paintComponent
84
85       // return image dimensions
86       public Dimension getPreferredSize()
87       {
88          return new Dimension( picture.getIconWidth(),
89             picture.getIconHeight() );
90       } // end method getPreferredSize
91    } // end class MyJPanel
```

Fig. 25.11 | Multiple-document interface. (Part 3 of 3.)

Lines 27–33 create a JMenuBar, a JMenu and a JMenuItem, add the JMenuItem to the JMenu, add the JMenu to the JMenuBar and set the JMenuBar for the application window. When the user selects the JMenuItem newFrame, the application creates and displays a new JInternalFrame object containing an image.

Line 35 assigns JDesktopPane (package javax.swing) variable theDesktop a new JDesktopPane object that will be used to manage the JInternalFrame child windows. Line 36 adds the JDesktopPane to the JFrame. By default, the JDesktopPane is added to the center of the content pane's BorderLayout, so the JDesktopPane expands to fill the entire application window.

Lines 39–58 register an ActionListener to handle the event when the user selects the newFrame menu item. When the event occurs, method actionPerformed (lines 44–56) creates a JInternalFrame object in lines 47–48. The JInternalFrame constructor used here takes five arguments—a String for the title bar of the internal window, a boolean indicating whether the internal frame can be resized by the user, a boolean indicating whether the internal frame can be closed by the user, a boolean indicating whether the internal frame can be maximized by the user and a boolean indicating whether the internal frame can be minimized by the user. For each of the boolean arguments, a true value indicates that the operation should be allowed (as is the case here).

```
 1   // Fig. 25.12: DesktopTest.java
 2   // Demonstrating JDesktopPane.
 3   import javax.swing.JFrame;
 4
 5   public class DesktopTest
 6   {
 7      public static void main( String[] args )
 8      {
 9         DesktopFrame desktopFrame = new DesktopFrame();
10         desktopFrame.setDefaultCloseOperation( JFrame.EXIT_ON_CLOSE );
11         desktopFrame.setSize( 600, 480 ); // set frame size
12         desktopFrame.setVisible( true ); // display frame
13      } // end main
14   } // end class DesktopTest
```

Internal frames   Minimize   Maximize   Close

Minimized internal frames

Position the mouse over any corner of a child window to resize the window (if resizing is allowed).

Maximized internal frame

Fig. 25.12 | Test class for DeskTopFrame.

As with JFrames and JApplets, a JInternalFrame has a content pane to which GUI components can be attached. Line 50 (Fig. 25.11) creates an instance of our class MyJPanel (declared at lines 63–91) that is added to the JInternalFrame at line 51.

Line 52 uses JInternalFrame method **pack** to set the size of the child window. Method pack uses the preferred sizes of the components to determine the window's size. Class MyJPanel declares method getPreferredSize (lines 86–90) to specify the panel's preferred size for use by the pack method. Line 54 adds the JInternalFrame to the JDesktopPane, and line 55 displays the JInternalFrame.

Classes JInternalFrame and JDesktopPane provide many methods for managing child windows. See the JInternalFrame and JDesktopPane online API documentation for complete lists of these methods:

```
java.sun.com/javase/6/docs/api/javax/swing/JInternalFrame.html
java.sun.com/javase/6/docs/api/javax/swing/JDesktopPane.html
```

25.8 JTabbedPane

A **JTabbedPane** arranges GUI components into layers, of which only one is visible at a time. Users access each layer via a tab—similar to folders in a file cabinet. When the user clicks a tab, the appropriate layer is displayed. The tabs appear at the top by default but also can be positioned at the left, right or bottom of the JTabbedPane. Any component can be placed on a tab. If the component is a container, such as a panel, it can use any layout manager to lay out several components on the tab. Class JTabbedPane is a subclass of JComponent. The application in Figs. 25.13–25.14 creates one tabbed pane with three tabs. Each tab displays one of the JPanels—panel1, panel2 or panel3.

```java
 1  // Fig. 25.13: JTabbedPaneFrame.java
 2  // Demonstrating JTabbedPane.
 3  import java.awt.BorderLayout;
 4  import java.awt.Color;
 5  import javax.swing.JFrame;
 6  import javax.swing.JTabbedPane;
 7  import javax.swing.JLabel;
 8  import javax.swing.JPanel;
 9  import javax.swing.JButton;
10  import javax.swing.SwingConstants;
11
12  public class JTabbedPaneFrame extends JFrame
13  {
14     // set up GUI
15     public JTabbedPaneFrame()
16     {
17        super( "JTabbedPane Demo " );
18
19        JTabbedPane tabbedPane = new JTabbedPane(); // create JTabbedPane
20
21        // set up panel1 and add it to JTabbedPane
22        JLabel label1 = new JLabel( "panel one", SwingConstants.CENTER );
23        JPanel panel1 = new JPanel(); // create first panel
24        panel1.add( label1 ); // add label to panel
```

Fig. 25.13 | JTabbedPane used to organize GUI components. (Part 1 of 2.)

```
25        tabbedPane.addTab( "Tab One", null, panel1, "First Panel" );
26
27        // set up panel2 and add it to JTabbedPane
28        JLabel label2 = new JLabel( "panel two", SwingConstants.CENTER );
29        JPanel panel2 = new JPanel(); // create second panel
30        panel2.setBackground( Color.YELLOW ); // set background to yellow
31        panel2.add( label2 ); // add label to panel
32        tabbedPane.addTab( "Tab Two", null, panel2, "Second Panel" );
33
34        // set up panel3 and add it to JTabbedPane
35        JLabel label3 = new JLabel( "panel three" );
36        JPanel panel3 = new JPanel(); // create third panel
37        panel3.setLayout( new BorderLayout() ); // use borderlayout
38        panel3.add( new JButton( "North" ), BorderLayout.NORTH );
39        panel3.add( new JButton( "West" ), BorderLayout.WEST );
40        panel3.add( new JButton( "East" ), BorderLayout.EAST );
41        panel3.add( new JButton( "South" ), BorderLayout.SOUTH );
42        panel3.add( label3, BorderLayout.CENTER );
43        tabbedPane.addTab( "Tab Three", null, panel3, "Third Panel" );
44
45        add( tabbedPane ); // add JTabbedPane to frame
46    } // end JTabbedPaneFrame constructor
47 } // end class JTabbedPaneFrame
```

Fig. 25.13 | JTabbedPane used to organize GUI components. (Part 2 of 2.)

```
1  // Fig. 25.14: JTabbedPaneDemo.java
2  // Demonstrating JTabbedPane.
3  import javax.swing.JFrame;
4
5  public class JTabbedPaneDemo
6  {
7     public static void main( String[] args )
8     {
9        JTabbedPaneFrame tabbedPaneFrame = new JTabbedPaneFrame();
10       tabbedPaneFrame.setDefaultCloseOperation( JFrame.EXIT_ON_CLOSE );
11       tabbedPaneFrame.setSize( 250, 200 ); // set frame size
12       tabbedPaneFrame.setVisible( true ); // display frame
13    } // end main
14 } // end class JTabbedPaneDemo
```

Fig. 25.14 | Test class for JTabbedPaneFrame.

The constructor (lines 15–46) builds the GUI. Line 19 creates an empty JTabbedPane with default settings—that is, tabs across the top. If the tabs do not fit on one line, they'll wrap to form additional lines of tabs. Next the constructor creates the JPanels panel1, panel2 and panel3 and their GUI components. As we set up each panel, we add it to tabbedPane, using JTabbedPane method **addTab** with four arguments. The first argument is a String that specifies the title of the tab. The second argument is an Icon reference that specifies an icon to display on the tab. If the Icon is a null reference, no image is displayed. The third argument is a Component reference that represents the GUI component to display when the user clicks the tab. The last argument is a String that specifies the tool tip for the tab. For example, line 25 adds JPanel panel1 to tabbedPane with title "Tab One" and the tool tip "First Panel". JPanels panel2 and panel3 are added to tabbedPane at lines 32 and 43. To view a tab, click it with the mouse or use the arrow keys to cycle through the tabs.

25.9 Layout Managers: BoxLayout and GridBagLayout

In Chapter 14, we introduced three layout managers—FlowLayout, BorderLayout and GridLayout. This section presents two additional layout managers (summarized in Fig. 25.15). We discuss these layout managers in the examples that follow.

Layout manager	Description
BoxLayout	A layout manager that allows GUI components to be arranged left-to-right or top-to-bottom in a container. Class Box declares a container with BoxLayout as its default layout manager and provides static methods to create a Box with a horizontal or vertical BoxLayout.
GridBagLayout	A layout manager similar to GridLayout, but the components can vary in size and can be added in any order.

Fig. 25.15 | Additional layout managers.

BoxLayout Layout Manager

The BoxLayout layout manager (in package javax.swing) arranges GUI components horizontally along a container's *x*-axis or vertically along its *y*-axis. The application in Figs. 25.16–25.17 demonstrates BoxLayout and the container class Box that uses BoxLayout as its default layout manager.

```
1   // Fig. 25.16: BoxLayoutFrame.java
2   // Demonstrating BoxLayout.
3   import java.awt.Dimension;
4   import javax.swing.JFrame;
5   import javax.swing.Box;
6   import javax.swing.JButton;
7   import javax.swing.BoxLayout;
8   import javax.swing.JPanel;
9   import javax.swing.JTabbedPane;
10
```

Fig. 25.16 | BoxLayout layout manager. (Part 1 of 3.)

```
11   public class BoxLayoutFrame extends JFrame
12   {
13      // set up GUI
14      public BoxLayoutFrame()
15      {
16         super( "Demonstrating BoxLayout" );
17
18         // create Box containers with BoxLayout
19         Box horizontal1 = Box.createHorizontalBox();
20         Box vertical1 = Box.createVerticalBox();
21         Box horizontal2 = Box.createHorizontalBox();
22         Box vertical2 = Box.createVerticalBox();
23
24         final int SIZE = 3; // number of buttons on each Box
25
26         // add buttons to Box horizontal1
27         for ( int count = 0; count < SIZE; count++ )
28            horizontal1.add( new JButton( "Button " + count ) );
29
30         // create strut and add buttons to Box vertical1
31         for ( int count = 0; count < SIZE; count++ )
32         {
33            vertical1.add( Box.createVerticalStrut( 25 ) );
34            vertical1.add( new JButton( "Button " + count ) );
35         } // end for
36
37         // create horizontal glue and add buttons to Box horizontal2
38         for ( int count = 0; count < SIZE; count++ )
39         {
40            horizontal2.add( Box.createHorizontalGlue() );
41            horizontal2.add( new JButton( "Button " + count ) );
42         } // end for
43
44         // create rigid area and add buttons to Box vertical2
45         for ( int count = 0; count < SIZE; count++ )
46         {
47            vertical2.add( Box.createRigidArea( new Dimension( 12, 8 ) ) );
48            vertical2.add( new JButton( "Button " + count ) );
49         } // end for
50
51         // create vertical glue and add buttons to panel
52         JPanel panel = new JPanel();
53         panel.setLayout( new BoxLayout( panel, BoxLayout.Y_AXIS ) );
54
55         for ( int count = 0; count < SIZE; count++ )
56         {
57            panel.add( Box.createGlue() );
58            panel.add( new JButton( "Button " + count ) );
59         } // end for
60
61         // create a JTabbedPane
62         JTabbedPane tabs = new JTabbedPane(
63            JTabbedPane.TOP, JTabbedPane.SCROLL_TAB_LAYOUT );
64
```

Fig. 25.16 | BoxLayout layout manager. (Part 2 of 3.)

```
65        // place each container on tabbed pane
66        tabs.addTab( "Horizontal Box", horizontal1 );
67        tabs.addTab( "Vertical Box with Struts", vertical1 );
68        tabs.addTab( "Horizontal Box with Glue", horizontal2 );
69        tabs.addTab( "Vertical Box with Rigid Areas", vertical2 );
70        tabs.addTab( "Vertical Box with Glue", panel );
71
72        add( tabs ); // place tabbed pane on frame
73     } // end BoxLayoutFrame constructor
74  } // end class BoxLayoutFrame
```

Fig. 25.16 | BoxLayout layout manager. (Part 3 of 3.)

```
1   // Fig. 25.17: BoxLayoutDemo.java
2   // Demonstrating BoxLayout.
3   import javax.swing.JFrame;
4
5   public class BoxLayoutDemo
6   {
7      public static void main( String[] args )
8      {
9         BoxLayoutFrame boxLayoutFrame = new BoxLayoutFrame();
10        boxLayoutFrame.setDefaultCloseOperation( JFrame.EXIT_ON_CLOSE );
11        boxLayoutFrame.setSize( 400, 220 ); // set frame size
12        boxLayoutFrame.setVisible( true ); // display frame
13     } // end main
14  } // end class BoxLayoutDemo
```

Arrows for cycling through tabs

Fig. 25.17 | Test class for BoxLayoutFrame.

Lines 19–22 create Box containers. References horizontal1 and horizontal2 are initialized with static Box method createHorizontalBox, which returns a Box container with a horizontal BoxLayout in which GUI components are arranged left-to-right. Variables vertical1 and vertical2 are initialized with static Box method **createVerticalBox**, which returns references to Box containers with a vertical BoxLayout in which GUI components are arranged top-to-bottom.

The loop at lines 27–28 adds three JButtons to horizontal1. The for statement at lines 31–35 adds three JButtons to vertical1. Before adding each button, line 33 adds a **vertical strut** to the container with static Box method **createVerticalStrut**. A vertical strut is an invisible GUI component that has a fixed pixel height and is used to guarantee a fixed amount of space between GUI components. The int argument to method createVerticalStrut determines the height of the strut in pixels. When the container is resized, the distance between GUI components separated by struts does not change. Class Box also declares method **createHorizontalStrut** for horizontal BoxLayouts.

The for statement at lines 38–42 adds three JButtons to horizontal2. Before adding each button, line 40 adds **horizontal glue** to the container with static Box method **createHorizontalGlue**. Horizontal glue is an invisible GUI component that can be used between fixed-size GUI components to occupy additional space. Normally, extra space appears to the right of the last horizontal GUI component or below the last vertical one in a BoxLayout. Glue allows the extra space to be placed between GUI components. When the container is resized, components separated by glue components remain the same size, but the glue stretches or contracts to occupy the space between them. Class Box also declares method **createVerticalGlue** for vertical BoxLayouts.

The for statement at lines 45–49 adds three JButtons to vertical2. Before each button is added, line 47 adds a **rigid area** to the container with static Box method **createRigidArea**. A rigid area is an invisible GUI component that always has a fixed pixel width and height. The argument to method createRigidArea is a Dimension object that specifies the area's width and height.

Lines 52–53 create a JPanel object and set its layout to a BoxLayout in the conventional manner, using Container method setLayout. The BoxLayout constructor receives a reference to the container for which it controls the layout and a constant indicating whether the layout is horizontal (**BoxLayout.X_AXIS**) or vertical (**BoxLayout.Y_AXIS**).

The for statement at lines 55–59 adds three JButtons to panel. Before adding each button, line 57 adds a glue component to the container with static Box method **createGlue**. This component expands or contracts based on the size of the Box.

Lines 62–63 create a JTabbedPane to display the five containers in this program. The argument **JTabbedPane.TOP** sent to the constructor indicates that the tabs should appear at the top of the JTabbedPane. The argument **JTabbedPane.SCROLL_TAB_LAYOUT** specifies that the tabs should wrap to a new line if there are too many to fit on one line.

The Box containers and the JPanel are attached to the JTabbedPane at lines 66–70. Try executing the application. When the window appears, resize the window to see how the glue components, strut components and rigid area affect the layout on each tab.

GridBagLayout Layout Manager
One of the most powerful predefined layout managers is **GridBagLayout** (in package java.awt). This layout is similar to GridLayout in that it arranges components in a grid. However, GridBagLayout is more flexible. The components can vary in size (i.e., they can occupy multiple rows and columns) and can be added in any order.

The first step in using GridBagLayout is determining the appearance of the GUI. For this step you need only a piece of paper. Draw the GUI, then draw a grid over it, dividing the components into rows and columns. The initial row and column numbers should be 0, so that the GridBagLayout layout manager can use the row and column numbers to properly place the components in the grid. Figure 25.18 demonstrates drawing the lines for the rows and columns over a GUI.

Fig. 25.18 | Designing a GUI that will use GridBagLayout.

A **GridBagConstraints** object describes how a component is placed in a GridBagLayout. Several GridBagConstraints fields are summarized in Fig. 25.19.

Field	Description
anchor	Specifies the relative position (NORTH, NORTHEAST, EAST, SOUTHEAST, SOUTH, SOUTHWEST, WEST, NORTHWEST, CENTER) of the component in an area that it does not fill.
fill	Resizes the component in the specified direction (NONE, HORIZONTAL, VERTICAL, BOTH) when the display area is larger than the component.
gridx	The column in which the component will be placed.
gridy	The row in which the component will be placed.
gridwidth	The number of columns the component occupies.
gridheight	The number of rows the component occupies.
weightx	The amount of extra space to allocate horizontally. The grid slot can become wider when extra space is available.
weighty	The amount of extra space to allocate vertically. The grid slot can become taller when extra space is available.

Fig. 25.19 | GridBagConstraints fields.

GridBagConstraints field **anchor** specifies the relative position of the component in an area that it does not fill. The variable anchor is assigned one of the following GridBagConstraints constants: **NORTH, NORTHEAST, EAST, SOUTHEAST, SOUTH, SOUTHWEST, WEST, NORTHWEST** or **CENTER**. The default value is CENTER.

GridBagConstraints field fill defines how the component grows if the area in which it can be displayed is larger than the component. The variable fill is assigned one of the following GridBagConstraints constants: **NONE**, **VERTICAL**, **HORIZONTAL** or **BOTH**. The default value is NONE, which indicates that the component will not grow in either direction. VERTICAL indicates that it will grow vertically. HORIZONTAL indicates that it will grow horizontally. BOTH indicates that it will grow in both directions.

Variables **gridx** and **gridy** specify where the upper-left corner of the component is placed in the grid. Variable gridx corresponds to the column, and variable gridy corresponds to the row. In Fig. 25.18, the JComboBox (displaying "Iron") has a gridx value of 1 and a gridy value of 2.

Variable **gridwidth** specifies the number of columns a component occupies. The JComboBox occupies two columns. Variable **gridheight** specifies the number of rows a component occupies. The JTextArea on the left side of Fig. 25.18 occupies three rows.

Variable **weightx** specifies how to distribute extra horizontal space to grid slots in a GridBagLayout when the container is resized. A zero value indicates that the grid slot does not grow horizontally on its own. However, if the component spans a column containing a component with nonzero weightx value, the component with zero weightx value will grow horizontally in the same proportion as the other component(s) in that column. This is because each component must be maintained in the same row and column in which it was originally placed.

Variable **weighty** specifies how to distribute extra vertical space to grid slots in a GridBagLayout when the container is resized. A zero value indicates that the grid slot does not grow vertically on its own. However, if the component spans a row containing a component with nonzero weighty value, the component with zero weighty value grows vertically in the same proportion as the other component(s) in the same row.

In Fig. 25.18, the effects of weighty and weightx cannot easily be seen until the container is resized and additional space becomes available. Components with larger weight values occupy more of the additional space than those with smaller weight values.

Components should be given nonzero positive weight values—otherwise they'll "huddle" together in the middle of the container. Figure 25.20 shows the GUI of Fig. 25.18 with all weights set to zero.

Fig. 25.20 | GridBagLayout with the weights set to zero.

The application in Figs. 25.21–25.22 uses the GridBagLayout layout manager to arrange the components of the GUI in Fig. 25.18. The application does nothing except demonstrate how to use GridBagLayout.

```java
1   // Fig. 25.21: GridBagFrame.java
2   // Demonstrating GridBagLayout.
3   import java.awt.GridBagLayout;
4   import java.awt.GridBagConstraints;
5   import java.awt.Component;
6   import javax.swing.JFrame;
7   import javax.swing.JTextArea;
8   import javax.swing.JTextField;
9   import javax.swing.JButton;
10  import javax.swing.JComboBox;
11
12  public class GridBagFrame extends JFrame
13  {
14     private GridBagLayout layout; // layout of this frame
15     private GridBagConstraints constraints; // constraints of this layout
16
17     // set up GUI
18     public GridBagFrame()
19     {
20        super( "GridBagLayout" );
21        layout = new GridBagLayout();
22        setLayout( layout ); // set frame layout
23        constraints = new GridBagConstraints(); // instantiate constraints
24
25        // create GUI components
26        JTextArea textArea1 = new JTextArea( "TextArea1", 5, 10 );
27        JTextArea textArea2 = new JTextArea( "TextArea2", 2, 2 );
28
29        String[] names = { "Iron", "Steel", "Brass" };
30        JComboBox comboBox = new JComboBox( names );
31
32        JTextField textField = new JTextField( "TextField" );
33        JButton button1 = new JButton( "Button 1" );
34        JButton button2 = new JButton( "Button 2" );
35        JButton button3 = new JButton( "Button 3" );
36
37        // weightx and weighty for textArea1 are both 0: the default
38        // anchor for all components is CENTER: the default
39        constraints.fill = GridBagConstraints.BOTH;
40        addComponent( textArea1, 0, 0, 1, 3 );
41
42        // weightx and weighty for button1 are both 0: the default
43        constraints.fill = GridBagConstraints.HORIZONTAL;
44        addComponent( button1, 0, 1, 2, 1 );
45
46        // weightx and weighty for comboBox are both 0: the default
47        // fill is HORIZONTAL
48        addComponent( comboBox, 2, 1, 2, 1 );
49
50        // button2
51        constraints.weightx = 1000;  // can grow wider
52        constraints.weighty = 1;     // can grow taller
53        constraints.fill = GridBagConstraints.BOTH;
54        addComponent( button2, 1, 1, 1, 1 );
```

Fig. 25.21 | GridBagLayout layout manager. (Part 1 of 2.)

```
55
56          // fill is BOTH for button3
57          constraints.weightx = 0;
58          constraints.weighty = 0;
59          addComponent( button3, 1, 2, 1, 1 );
60
61          // weightx and weighty for textField are both 0, fill is BOTH
62          addComponent( textField, 3, 0, 2, 1 );
63
64          // weightx and weighty for textArea2 are both 0, fill is BOTH
65          addComponent( textArea2, 3, 2, 1, 1 );
66       } // end GridBagFrame constructor
67
68       // method to set constraints on
69       private void addComponent( Component component,
70          int row, int column, int width, int height )
71       {
72          constraints.gridx = column; // set gridx
73          constraints.gridy = row; // set gridy
74          constraints.gridwidth = width; // set gridwidth
75          constraints.gridheight = height; // set gridheight
76          layout.setConstraints( component, constraints ); // set constraints
77          add( component ); // add component
78       } // end method addComponent
79    } // end class GridBagFrame
```

Fig. 25.21 | GridBagLayout layout manager. (Part 2 of 2.)

```
1    // Fig. 25.22: GridBagDemo.java
2    // Demonstrating GridBagLayout.
3    import javax.swing.JFrame;
4
5    public class GridBagDemo
6    {
7       public static void main( String[] args )
8       {
9          GridBagFrame gridBagFrame = new GridBagFrame();
10         gridBagFrame.setDefaultCloseOperation( JFrame.EXIT_ON_CLOSE );
11         gridBagFrame.setSize( 300, 150 ); // set frame size
12         gridBagFrame.setVisible( true ); // display frame
13      } // end main
14   } // end class GridBagDemo
```

Fig. 25.22 | Test class for GridBagFrame. (Part 1 of 2.)

Fig. 25.22 | Test class for `GridBagFrame`. (Part 2 of 2.)

The GUI contains three `JButton`s, two `JTextArea`s, a `JComboBox` and a `JTextField`. The layout manager is `GridBagLayout`. Lines 21–22 create the `GridBagLayout` object and set the layout manager for the `JFrame` to layout. Line 23 creates the `GridBagConstraints` object used to determine the location and size of each component in the grid. Lines 26–35 create each GUI component that will be added to the content pane.

Lines 39–40 configure `JTextArea textArea1` and add it to the content pane. The values for `weightx` and `weighty` values are not specified in `constraints`, so each has the value zero by default. Thus, the `JTextArea` will not resize itself even if space is available. However, it spans multiple rows, so the vertical size is subject to the `weighty` values of `JButton`s `button2` and `button3`. When either button is resized vertically based on its `weighty` value, the `JTextArea` is also resized.

Line 39 sets variable `fill` in `constraints` to `GridBagConstraints.BOTH`, causing the `JTextArea` to always fill its entire allocated area in the grid. An anchor value is not specified in `constraints`, so the default `CENTER` is used. We do not use variable anchor in this application, so all the components will use the default. Line 40 calls our utility method `addComponent` (declared at lines 69–78). The `JTextArea` object, the row, the column, the number of columns to span and the number of rows to span are passed as arguments.

`JButton button1` is the next component added (lines 43–44). By default, the `weightx` and `weighty` values are still zero. The `fill` variable is set to `HORIZONTAL`—the component will always fill its area in the horizontal direction. The vertical direction is not filled. The `weighty` value is zero, so the button will become taller only if another component in the same row has a nonzero `weighty` value. `JButton button1` is located at row 0, column 1. One row and two columns are occupied.

`JComboBox comboBox` is the next component added (line 48). By default, the `weightx` and `weighty` values are zero, and the `fill` variable is set to `HORIZONTAL`. The `JComboBox` button will grow only in the horizontal direction. Note that the `weightx`, `weighty` and `fill` variables retain the values set in `constraints` until they are changed. The `JComboBox` button is placed at row 2, column 1. One row and two columns are occupied.

`JButton button2` is the next component added (lines 51–54). It's given a `weightx` value of 1000 and a `weighty` value of 1. The area occupied by the button is capable of growing in the vertical and horizontal directions. The `fill` variable is set to `BOTH`, which specifies that the button will always fill the entire area. When the window is resized, `button2` will grow. The button is placed at row 1, column 1. One row and one column are occupied.

JButton button3 is added next (lines 57–59). Both the weightx value and weighty value are set to zero, and the value of fill is BOTH. JButton button3 will grow if the window is resized—it's affected by the weight values of button2. Note that the weightx value for button2 is much larger than that for button3. When resizing occurs, button2 will occupy a larger percentage of the new space. The button is placed at row 1, column 2. One row and one column are occupied.

Both the JTextField textField (line 62) and JTextArea textArea2 (line 65) have a weightx value of 0 and a weighty value of 0. The value of fill is BOTH. The JTextField is placed at row 3, column 0, and the JTextArea at row 3, column 2. The JTextField occupies one row and two columns, the JTextArea one row and one column.

Method addComponent's parameters are a Component reference component and integers row, column, width and height. Lines 72–73 set the GridBagConstraints variables gridx and gridy. The gridx variable is assigned the column in which the Component will be placed, and the gridy value is assigned the row in which the Component will be placed. Lines 74–75 set the GridBagConstraints variables gridwidth and gridheight. The gridwidth variable specifies the number of columns the Component will span in the grid, and the gridheight variable specifies the number of rows the Component will span in the grid. Line 76 sets the GridBagConstraints for a component in the GridBagLayout. Method **setConstraints** of class GridBagLayout takes a Component argument and a GridBagConstraints argument. Line 77 adds the component to the JFrame.

When you execute this application, try resizing the window to see how the constraints for each GUI component affect its position and size in the window.

GridBagConstraints *Constants* RELATIVE *and* REMAINDER

Instead of gridx and gridy, a variation of GridBagLayout uses GridBagConstraints constants **RELATIVE** and **REMAINDER**. RELATIVE specifies that the next-to-last component in a particular row should be placed to the right of the previous component in the row. REMAINDER specifies that a component is the last component in a row. Any component that is not the second-to-last or last component on a row must specify values for GridBagConstraints variables gridwidth and gridheight. The application in Figs. 25.23–25.24 arranges components in GridBagLayout, using these constants.

```
1   // Fig. 25.23: GridBagFrame2.java
2   // Demonstrating GridBagLayout constants.
3   import java.awt.GridBagLayout;
4   import java.awt.GridBagConstraints;
5   import java.awt.Component;
6   import javax.swing.JFrame;
7   import javax.swing.JComboBox;
8   import javax.swing.JTextField;
9   import javax.swing.JList;
10  import javax.swing.JButton;
11
12  public class GridBagFrame2 extends JFrame
13  {
14     private GridBagLayout layout; // layout of this frame
15     private GridBagConstraints constraints; // constraints of this layout
16
```

Fig. 25.23 | GridBagConstraints constants RELATIVE and REMAINDER. (Part 1 of 3.)

```
17      // set up GUI
18      public GridBagFrame2()
19      {
20          super( "GridBagLayout" );
21          layout = new GridBagLayout();
22          setLayout( layout ); // set frame layout
23          constraints = new GridBagConstraints(); // instantiate constraints
24
25          // create GUI components
26          String[] metals = { "Copper", "Aluminum", "Silver" };
27          JComboBox comboBox = new JComboBox( metals );
28
29          JTextField textField = new JTextField( "TextField" );
30
31          String[] fonts = { "Serif", "Monospaced" };
32          JList list = new JList( fonts );
33
34          String[] names = { "zero", "one", "two", "three", "four" };
35          JButton[] buttons = new JButton[ names.length ];
36
37          for ( int count = 0; count < buttons.length; count++ )
38              buttons[ count ] = new JButton( names[ count ] );
39
40          // define GUI component constraints for textField
41          constraints.weightx = 1;
42          constraints.weighty = 1;
43          constraints.fill = GridBagConstraints.BOTH;
44          constraints.gridwidth = GridBagConstraints.REMAINDER;
45          addComponent( textField );
46
47          // buttons[0] -- weightx and weighty are 1: fill is BOTH
48          constraints.gridwidth = 1;
49          addComponent( buttons[ 0 ] );
50
51          // buttons[1] -- weightx and weighty are 1: fill is BOTH
52          constraints.gridwidth = GridBagConstraints.RELATIVE;
53          addComponent( buttons[ 1 ] );
54
55          // buttons[2] -- weightx and weighty are 1: fill is BOTH
56          constraints.gridwidth = GridBagConstraints.REMAINDER;
57          addComponent( buttons[ 2 ] );
58
59          // comboBox -- weightx is 1: fill is BOTH
60          constraints.weighty = 0;
61          constraints.gridwidth = GridBagConstraints.REMAINDER;
62          addComponent( comboBox );
63
64          // buttons[3] -- weightx is 1: fill is BOTH
65          constraints.weighty = 1;
66          constraints.gridwidth = GridBagConstraints.REMAINDER;
67          addComponent( buttons[ 3 ] );
68
69          // buttons[4] -- weightx and weighty are 1: fill is BOTH
70          constraints.gridwidth = GridBagConstraints.RELATIVE;
```

Fig. 25.23 | GridBagConstraints constants RELATIVE and REMAINDER. (Part 2 of 3.)

```
71          addComponent( buttons[ 4 ] );
72
73          // list -- weightx and weighty are 1: fill is BOTH
74          constraints.gridwidth = GridBagConstraints.REMAINDER;
75          addComponent( list );
76       } // end GridBagFrame2 constructor
77
78       // add a component to the container
79       private void addComponent( Component component )
80       {
81          layout.setConstraints( component, constraints );
82          add( component ); // add component
83       } // end method addComponent
84    } // end class GridBagFrame2
```

Fig. 25.23 | GridBagConstraints constants RELATIVE and REMAINDER. (Part 3 of 3.)

```
1    // Fig. 25.24: GridBagDemo2.java
2    // Demonstrating GridBagLayout constants.
3    import javax.swing.JFrame;
4
5    public class GridBagDemo2
6    {
7       public static void main( String[] args )
8       {
9          GridBagFrame2 gridBagFrame = new GridBagFrame2();
10         gridBagFrame.setDefaultCloseOperation( JFrame.EXIT_ON_CLOSE );
11         gridBagFrame.setSize( 300, 200 ); // set frame size
12         gridBagFrame.setVisible( true ); // display frame
13      } // end main
14   } // end class GridBagDemo2
```

Fig. 25.24 | Test class for GridBagDemo2.

Lines 21–22 create a GridBagLayout and use it to set the JFrame's layout manager. The components that are placed in GridBagLayout are created in lines 27–38—they are a JComboBox, a JTextField, a JList and five JButtons.

The JTextField is added first (lines 41–45). The weightx and weighty values are set to 1. The fill variable is set to BOTH. Line 44 specifies that the JTextField is the last component on the line. The JTextField is added to the content pane with a call to our utility method addComponent (declared at lines 79–83). Method addComponent takes a Component argument and uses GridBagLayout method setConstraints to set the constraints for the Component. Method add attaches the component to the content pane.

JButton buttons[0] (lines 48–49) has weightx and weighty values of 1. The fill variable is BOTH. Because buttons[0] is not one of the last two components on the row, it's given a gridwidth of 1 and so will occupy one column. The JButton is added to the content pane with a call to utility method addComponent.

JButton buttons[1] (lines 52–53) has weightx and weighty values of 1. The fill variable is BOTH. Line 52 specifies that the JButton is to be placed relative to the previous component. The Button is added to the JFrame with a call to addComponent.

JButton buttons[2] (lines 56–57) has weightx and weighty values of 1. The fill variable is BOTH. This JButton is the last component on the line, so REMAINDER is used. The JButton is added to the content pane with a call to addComponent.

The JComboBox (lines 60–62) has a weightx of 1 and a weighty of 0. The JComboBox will not grow vertically. The JComboBox is the only component on the line, so REMAINDER is used. The JComboBox is added to the content pane with a call to addComponent.

JButton buttons[3] (lines 65–67) has weightx and weighty values of 1. The fill variable is BOTH. This JButton is the only component on the line, so REMAINDER is used. The JButton is added to the content pane with a call to addComponent.

JButton buttons[4] (lines 70–71) has weightx and weighty values of 1. The fill variable is BOTH. This JButton is the next-to-last component on the line, so RELATIVE is used. The JButton is added to the content pane with a call to addComponent.

The JList (lines 74–75) has weightx and weighty values of 1. The fill variable is BOTH. The JList is added to the content pane with a call to addComponent.

25.10 Wrap-Up

This chapter completes our introduction to GUIs. In this chapter, we discussed additional GUI topics, such as menus, sliders, pop-up menus, multiple-document interfaces, tabbed panes and Java's pluggable look-and-feel. All these components can be added to existing applications to make them easier to use and understand. We also presented additional layout managers for organizing and sizing GUI components. In the next chapter, you'll learn about multithreading, a powerful capability that allows applications to use threads to perform multiple tasks at once.

Summary

Section 25.2 JSlider

- JSliders enable the user to select from a range of integer values. JSliders can display major tick marks, minor tick marks and labels for the tick marks. They also support snap-to ticks, where positioning the thumb between two tick marks causes the thumb to snap to the closest tick mark.

- If a JSlider has the focus, the left and right arrow keys cause the thumb of the JSlider to decrease or increase by 1. The down and up arrow keys also cause the thumb of the JSlider to decrease or increase by 1, respectively. The *PgDn* (page down) *key* and *PgUp* (page up) *key* cause the thumb to decrease or increase by block increments of one-tenth of the range of values, respectively. The *Home key* moves the thumb to the minimum value, and the *End key* moves it to the maximum value.

- JSliders have either horizontal or vertical orientation. For a horizontal JSlider, the minimum value is at the extreme left and the maximum value at the extreme right. For a vertical JSlider, the minimum value is at the extreme bottom and the maximum value at the extreme top. The position of the thumb indicates the current value of the JSlider. Method getValue of class J-Slider returns the current thumb position.

- JSlider method setMajorTickSpacing sets the spacing for tick marks on a JSlider. Method setPaintTicks with a true argument indicates that the tick marks should be displayed.

- JSliders generate ChangeEvents when the user interacts with a JSlider. A ChangeListener declares method stateChanged that can respond to ChangeEvents.

Section 25.3 Windows: Additional Notes

- Every window generates window events when the user manipulates it. Interface WindowListener provides seven window-event-handling methods—windowActivated, windowClosed, windowClosing, windowDeactivated, windowDeiconified, windowIconified and windowOpened.

Section 25.4 Using Menus with Frames

- Menus are an integral part of GUIs that allow users to perform actions without unnecessarily cluttering a GUI with extra components. In Swing GUIs, menus can be attached only to objects of classes with method setJMenuBar (e.g., JFrame and JApplet).

- Classes used to build menus are JMenuBar, JMenuItem, JMenu, JCheckBoxMenuItem and JRadioButtonMenuItem.

- A JMenuBar is a container for menus. A JMenuItem appears in a menu that, when selected, causes an action to be performed. A JMenu contains menu items and can be added to a JMenuBar or to other JMenus as submenus.

- When a menu is clicked, it expands to show its list of menu items. JMenu method addSeparator adds a separator line to a menu.

- When a JCheckBoxMenuItem is selected, a check appears to the left of the menu item. When the JCheckBoxMenuItem is selected again, the check is removed.

- When multiple JRadioButtonMenuItems are maintained as part of a ButtonGroup, only one can be selected at a time. When one is selected, a filled circle appears to its left. When another is selected, the filled circle to the left of the previously selected item is removed.

- AbstractButton method setMnemonic specifies the mnemonic for an AbstractButton. Mnemonic characters are normally displayed with an underline.

- A modal dialog box does not allow access to any other window in the application until the dialog is dismissed. The dialogs displayed with class JOptionPane are modal dialogs. Class JDialog can be used to create your own modal or nonmodal dialogs.

Section 25.5 JPopupMenu

- Context-sensitive pop-up menus are created with class JPopupMenu. The pop-up trigger event occurs normally when the user presses and releases the right mouse button. MouseEvent method isPopupTrigger returns true if the pop-up trigger event occurred.

- JPopupMenu method show displays a JPopupMenu. The first argument specifies the origin component, which helps determine where the JPopupMenu will appear. The last two arguments are the coordinates from the origin component's upper-left corner, at which the JPopupMenu appears.

Section 25.6 Pluggable Look-and-Feel

- Class UIManager.LookAndFeelInfo maintains information about a look-and-feel.

- UIManager static method getInstalledLookAndFeels returns an array of UIManager.LookAndFeelInfo objects that describe the available look-and-feels.

- UIManager static method setLookAndFeel changes the look-and-feel. SwingUtilities static method updateComponentTreeUI changes the look-and-feel of every component attached to its Component argument to the new look-and-feel.

Section 25.7 *JDesktopPane and JInternalFrame*

- Many of today's applications use a multiple-document interface (MDI) to manage several open documents that are being processed in parallel. Swing's JDesktopPane and JInternalFrame classes provide support for creating multiple-document interfaces.

Section 25.8 *JTabbedPane*

- A JTabbedPane arranges GUI components into layers, of which only one is visible at a time. Users access each layer by clicking its tab.

Section 25.9 *Layout Managers: BoxLayout and GridBagLayout*

- BoxLayout arranges GUI components left-to-right or top-to-bottom in a container.

- Class Box represents a container with BoxLayout as its default layout manager and provides static methods to create a Box with a horizontal or vertical BoxLayout.

- GridBagLayout is similar to GridLayout, but each component size can vary and components can be added in any order.

- A GridBagConstraints object specifies how a component is placed in a GridBagLayout. GridBagLayout method setConstraints takes a Component argument and a GridBagConstraints argument and sets the constraints of the Component.

Terminology

Self-Review Exercises

25.1   Fill in the blanks in each of the following statements:

a) The _____ class is used to create a menu object.

b) The _____ method of class JMenu places a separator bar in a menu.

c) JSlider events are handled by the _____ method of interface _____.

d) The GridBagConstraints instance variable _____ is set to CENTER by default.

25.2   State whether each of the following is *true* or *false*. If *false*, explain why.
  a) When the programmer creates a JFrame, a minimum of one menu must be created and added to the JFrame.
  b) The variable fill belongs to the GridBagLayout class.
  c) Drawing on a GUI component is performed with respect to the (0, 0) upper-left corner coordinate of the component.
  d) The default layout for a Box is BoxLayout.

25.3   Find the error(s) in each of the following and explain how to correct the error(s).
  a) JMenubar b;
  b) mySlider = JSlider(1000, 222, 100, 450);
  c) gbc.fill = GridBagConstraints.NORTHWEST;   // set fill
  d) // override to paint on a customized Swing component
```
public void paintcomponent( Graphics g )
{
    g.drawString( "HELLO", 50, 50 );
} // end method paintComponent
```
  e) // create a JFrame and display it
```
JFrame f = new JFrame( "A Window" );
f.setVisible( true );
```

Answers to Self-Review Exercises

25.1   a) JMenu. b) addSeparator. c) stateChanged, ChangeListener. d) anchor.

25.2   a) False. A JFrame does not require any menus.
  b) False. The variable fill belongs to the GridBagConstraints class.
  c) True.
  d) True.

25.3   a) JMenubar should be JMenuBar.
  b) The first argument to the constructor should be either SwingConstants.HORIZONTAL or SwingConstants.VERTICAL, and the keyword new must be used after the = operator. Also, the minimum value should be less than the maximum and the initial value should be in range.
  c) The constant should be either BOTH, HORIZONTAL, VERTICAL or NONE.
  d) paintcomponent should be paintComponent, and the method should call super.paintComponent(g) as its first statement.
  e) The JFrame's setSize method must also be called to establish the size of the window.

Exercises

25.4   State whether each of the following is *true* or *false*. If *false*, explain why.
  a) Menus require a JMenuBar object so they can be attached to a JFrame.
  b) BoxLayout is the default layout manager for a JFrame.
  c) JApplets can contain menus.

25.5   Write a program that displays a circle of random size and calculates and displays the area, radius, diameter and circumference. Use the following equations: *diameter* = 2 × *radius*, *area* = π × *radius*², *circumference* = 2 × π × *radius*. Use the constant Math.PI for pi (π). All drawing should be done on a subclass of JPanel, and the results of the calculations should be displayed in a read-only JTextArea.

25.6   Explore the effects of varying the weightx and weighty values of the program in Fig. 25.21. What happens when a slot has a nonzero weight but is not allowed to fill the whole area (i.e., the fill value is not BOTH)?

25.7 Declare a subclass of JPanel called MyColorChooser that provides three JSlider objects and three JTextField objects. Each JSlider represents the values from 0 to 255 for the red, green and blue parts of a color. Use these values as the arguments to the Color constructor to create a new Color object. Display the current value of each JSlider in the corresponding JTextField. When the user changes the value of the JSlider, the JTextField should be changed accordingly. Use your new GUI component as part of an application that displays the current Color value by drawing a filled rectangle.

25.8 Modify the MyColorChooser class of Exercise 25.7 to allow the user to enter an integer value into a JTextField to set the red, green or blue value. When the user presses *Enter* in the JTextField, the corresponding JSlider should be set to the appropriate value.

25.9 Modify the application in Exercise 25.8 to draw the current color as a rectangle on an instance of a subclass of JPanel which provides its own paintComponent method to draw the rectangle and provides *set* methods to set the red, green and blue values for the current color. When any *set* method is invoked, the drawing panel should automatically repaint itself.

25.10 Modify the application in Exercise 25.9 to allow the user to drag the mouse across the drawing panel (a subclass of JPanel) to draw a shape in the current color. Enable the user to choose what shape to draw.

25.11 Modify the application in Exercise 25.10 to provide the user with the ability to terminate the application by clicking the close box on the window that is displayed and by selecting Exit from a File menu. Use the techniques shown in Fig. 25.5.

25.12 *(Complete Drawing Application)* Using the techniques developed in this chapter and Chapter 14, create a complete drawing application. The program should use the GUI components from Chapter 14 and Chapter 25 to enable the user to select the shape, color and fill characteristics. Each shape should be stored in an array of MyShape objects, where MyShape is the superclass in your hierarchy of shape classes. Use a JDesktopPane and JInternalFrames to allow the user to create multiple separate drawings in separate child windows. Create the user interface as a separate child window containing all the GUI components that allow the user to determine the characteristics of the shape to be drawn. The user can then click in any JInternalFrame to draw the shape.

The most general definition of beauty...Multeity in Unity.
—Samuel Taylor Coleridge

Do not block the way of inquiry.
—Charles Sanders Peirce

A person with one watch knows what time it is; a person with two watches is never sure.
—Proverb

Learn to labor and to wait.
—Henry Wadsworth Longfellow

The world is moving so fast these days that the man who says it can't be done is generally interrupted by someone doing it.
—Elbert Hubbard

Multithreading

Objectives

In this chapter you'll learn:

- What threads are and why they are useful.
- How threads enable you to manage concurrent activities.
- The life cycle of a thread.
- Thread priorities and scheduling.
- To create and execute `Runnable`s.
- Thread synchronization.
- What producer/consumer relationships are and how they are implemented with multithreading.
- To enable multiple threads to update Swing GUI components in a thread-safe manner.
- About interfaces `Callable` and `Future`, which you can use with threading to execute tasks that return results.

26.1 **Introduction**

It would be nice if we could focus our attention on performing only one action at a time and performing it well, but that is usually difficult to do. The human body performs a great variety of operations **in parallel**—or, as we'll say throughout this chapter, **concurrently**. Respiration, blood circulation, digestion, thinking and walking, for example, can occur concurrently. All the senses—sight, touch, smell, taste and hearing—can be employed at once. Computers, too, can perform operations concurrently. It's common for personal computers to compile a program, send a file to a printer and receive electronic mail messages over a network concurrently. Only computers that have multiple processors can truly execute multiple instructions concurrently. Operating systems on single-processor computers create the illusion of concurrent execution by rapidly switching between activities, but on such computers only a single instruction can execute at once.

Most programming languages do not enable you to specify concurrent activities. Rather, the languages provide sequential control statements which enable you to specify that only one action at a time should be performed, with execution proceeding to the next action after the previous one has finished. Historically, concurrency has been implemented with operating-system primitives available only to experienced systems programmers.

The Ada programming language, developed by the United States Department of Defense, made concurrency primitives widely available to defense contractors building military command-and-control systems. However, Ada has not been widely used in academia and industry.

Java Concurrency

Java makes concurrency available to you through the language and APIs. You specify that an application contains separate **threads of execution**, where each thread has its own method-call stack and program counter, allowing it to execute concurrently with other threads while sharing applicationwide resources such as memory with them. This capability, called **multithreading**, is *not* available in the core C and C++ languages, but there are libraries available that provide this functionality.

Performance Tip 26.1

A problem with single-threaded applications that can lead to poor responsiveness is that lengthy activities must complete before others can begin. In a multithreaded application, threads can be distributed across multiple processors (if available) so that multiple tasks execute truly concurrently and the application can operate more efficiently. Multithreading can also increase performance on single-processor systems that simulate concurrency—when one thread cannot proceed (because, for example, it's waiting for the result of an I/O operation), another can use the processor.

Unlike languages that do not have built-in multithreading capabilities and must therefore make nonportable calls to operating-system multithreading primitives, Java includes multithreading primitives as part of the language itself and as part of its libraries. This facilitates manipulating threads in a portable manner across platforms.

Concurrent Programming Uses

We'll discuss many applications of **concurrent programming**. For example, when downloading a large file (e.g., an image, an audio clip or a video clip) over the Internet, the user may not want to wait until the entire clip downloads before starting the playback. To solve this problem, we can put multiple threads to work—one to download the clip, and another to play it. These activities proceed concurrently. To avoid choppy playback, we **synchronize** (coordinate the actions of) the threads so that the player thread doesn't begin until there is a sufficient amount of the clip in memory to keep the player thread busy.

The Java Virtual Machine (JVM) uses threads as well. It creates threads to run programs, and threads to perform housekeeping tasks such as garbage collection.

Concurrent Programming Is Difficult

Writing multithreaded programs can be tricky. Although the human mind can perform functions concurrently, people find it difficult to jump between parallel trains of thought. To see why multithreaded programs can be difficult to write and understand, try the following experiment: Open three books to page 1, and try reading the books concurrently. Read a few words from the first book, then a few from the second, then a few from the third, then loop back and read the next few words from the first book, and so on. After this experiment, you'll appreciate many of the challenges of multithreading—switching between the books, reading briefly, remembering your place in each book, moving the book you're reading closer so that you can see it and pushing the books you are not reading aside—and, amid all this chaos, trying to comprehend the content of the books!

Use the Prebuilt Concurrency APIs Whenever Possible

Programming concurrent applications is difficult and error prone. If you must use synchronization in a program, you should follow some simple guidelines. *Use existing classes from the Java API* (such as the `ArrayBlockingQueue` class we discuss in Section 26.7) *that manage synchronization for you.* The Java API's classes are written by experts, have been fully tested and debugged, operate efficiently and help you avoid common traps and pitfalls. If you need even more complex capabilities, use interfaces `Lock` and `Condition` that are introduced in Section 26.10.

Interfaces Lock and Condition should be used only by advanced programmers who are familiar with concurrent programming's common traps and pitfalls. We explain these topics in this chapter for several reasons—they provide a solid basis for understanding how concurrent applications synchronize access to shared memory; the concepts are important to understand, even if an application does not use these tools explicitly; and by showing you the complexity involved in using these low-level features, we hope to impress upon you the importance of using prebuilt concurrency capabilities whenever possible.

26.2 Thread States: Life Cycle of a Thread

At any time, a thread is said to be in one of several **thread states**—illustrated in the UML state diagram in Fig. 26.1. Several of the terms in the diagram are defined in later sections.

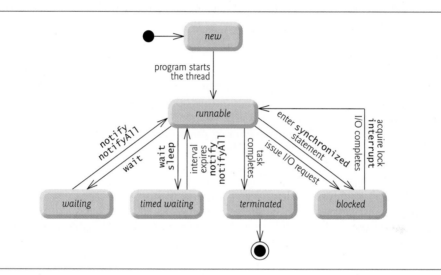

Fig. 26.1 | Thread life-cycle UML state diagram.

New *and* Runnable *States*

A new thread begins its life cycle in the *new* state. It remains in this state until the program starts the thread, which places it in the *runnable* state. A thread in the *runnable* state is considered to be executing its task.

Waiting *State*

Sometimes a *runnable* thread transitions to the *waiting* state while it waits for another thread to perform a task. A *waiting* thread transitions back to the *runnable* state only when another thread notifies it to continue executing.

TimedWaiting *State*

A *runnable* thread can enter the *timed waiting* state for a specified interval of time. It transitions back to the *runnable* state when that time interval expires or when the event it's waiting for occurs. *Timed waiting* and *waiting* threads cannot use a processor, even if one is available. A *runnable* thread can transition to the *timed waiting* state if it provides an optional wait interval when it's waiting for another thread to perform a task. Such a thread returns to the *runnable* state when it's notified by another thread or when the timed interval expires—whichever comes first. Another way to place a thread in the *timed waiting* state is to put a *runnable* thread to sleep. A **sleeping thread** remains in the *timed waiting* state for a designated period of time (called a **sleep interval**), after which it returns to the *runnable* state. Threads sleep when they momentarily do not have work to perform. For example, a word processor may contain a thread that periodically backs up (i.e., writes a copy of) the current document to disk for recovery purposes. If the thread did not sleep between successive backups, it would require a loop in which it continually tested whether it should write a copy of the document to disk. This loop would consume processor time without performing productive work, thus reducing system performance. In this case, it's more efficient for the thread to specify a sleep interval (equal to the period between successive backups) and enter the *timed waiting* state. This thread is returned to the *runnable* state when its sleep interval expires, at which point it writes a copy of the document to disk and reenters the *timed waiting* state.

Blocked *State*

A *runnable* thread transitions to the ***blocked*** state when it attempts to perform a task that cannot be completed immediately and it must temporarily wait until that task completes. For example, when a thread issues an input/output request, the operating system blocks the thread from executing until that I/O request completes—at that point, the *blocked* thread transitions to the *runnable* state, so it can resume execution. A *blocked* thread cannot use a processor, even if one is available.

Terminated *State*

A *runnable* thread enters the ***terminated*** state (sometimes called the ***dead*** state) when it successfully completes its task or otherwise terminates (perhaps due to an error). In the UML state diagram of Fig. 26.1, the *terminated* state is followed by the UML final state (the bull's-eye symbol) to indicate the end of the state transitions.

Operating-System View of the Runnable *State*

At the operating-system level, Java's *runnable* state typically encompasses two separate states (Fig. 26.2). The operating system hides these states from the Java Virtual Machine (JVM), which sees only the *runnable* state. When a thread first transitions to the *runnable* state from the *new* state, it is in the **ready** state. A *ready* thread enters the **running** state (i.e., begins executing) when the operating system assigns it to a processor—also known as **dispatching the thread**. In most operating systems, each thread is given a small amount of processor time—called a **quantum** or **timeslice**—with which to perform its task. Deciding how large the quantum should be is a key topic in operating-systems courses. When its quantum expires, the thread returns to the *ready* state, and the operating system assigns

Fig. 26.2 | Operating system's internal view of Java's *runnable* state.

another thread to the processor (see Section 26.3). Transitions between the *ready* and *running* states are handled solely by the operating system. The JVM does not "see" the transitions—it simply views the thread as being *runnable* and leaves it up to the operating system to transition the thread between *ready* and *running*. The process that an operating system uses to determine which thread to dispatch is called **thread scheduling** and is dependent on thread priorities (discussed in the next section).

26.3 Thread Priorities and Thread Scheduling

Every Java thread has a **thread priority** that helps determine the order in which threads are scheduled. Java priorities range between MIN_PRIORITY (a constant of 1) and MAX_PRIORITY (a constant of 10). By default, every thread is given priority NORM_PRIORITY (a constant of 5). Each new thread inherits the priority of the thread that created it. Informally, higher-priority threads are more important to a program and should be allocated processor time before lower-priority threads. However, thread priorities cannot guarantee the order in which threads execute.

[*Note:* The constants MAX_PRIORITY, MIN_PRIORITY and NORM_PRIORITY are declared in the **Thread** class. It's recommended that you do not explicitly create and use Thread objects to implement concurrency, but rather use the Executor interface (which is described in Section 26.4.2). The Thread class contains some useful static methods, which we discuss later in the chapter.]

Most operating systems support timeslicing, which enables threads of equal priority to share a processor. Without timeslicing, each thread in a set of equal-priority threads runs to completion (unless it leaves the *runnable* state and enters the *waiting* or *timed waiting* state, or gets interrupted by a higher-priority thread) before other threads of equal priority get a chance to execute. With timeslicing, even if a thread has not finished executing when its quantum expires, the processor is taken away from the thread and given to the next thread of equal priority, if one is available.

An operating system's **thread scheduler** determines which thread runs next. One simple thread-scheduler implementation keeps the highest-priority thread *running* at all times and, if there is more than one highest-priority thread, ensures that all such threads execute for a quantum each in **round-robin** fashion. Figure 26.3 illustrates a **multilevel priority queue** for threads. In the figure, assuming a single-processor computer, threads A and B each execute for a quantum in round-robin fashion until both threads complete execution. This means that A gets a quantum of time to run. Then B gets a quantum. Then A gets another quantum. Then B gets another quantum. This continues until one thread completes. The processor then devotes all its power to the thread that remains (unless another priority-10 thread becomes ready). Next, thread C runs to completion (assuming that no higher- or equal-priority threads arrive). Threads D, E and F each execute for a quantum in round-robin fashion until they all complete execution (again assuming that no higher- or equal-priority threads arrive). This process continues until all threads run to completion.

When a higher-priority thread enters the *ready* state, the operating system generally preempts the currently *running* thread (an operation known as **preemptive scheduling**). Depending on the operating system, higher-priority threads could postpone—possibly indefinitely—the execution of lower-priority threads. Such **indefinite postponement** is sometimes referred to more colorfully as **starvation**.

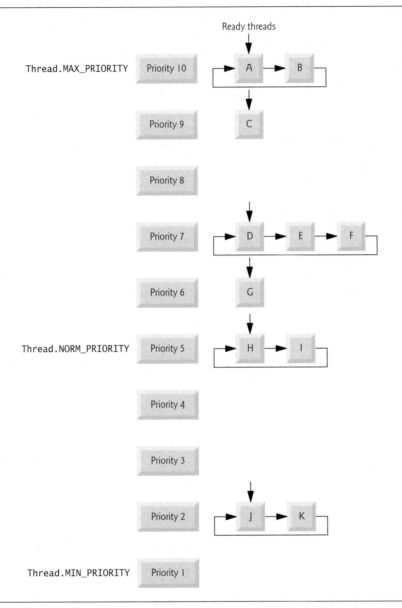

Fig. 26.3 | Thread-priority scheduling.

Java provides higher-level concurrency utilities to hide some of this complexity and make multithreaded programs less error prone. Thread priorities are used behind the scenes to interact with the operating system, but most programmers who use Java multithreading will not be concerned with setting and adjusting thread priorities.

Portability Tip 26.1
Thread scheduling is platform dependent—the behavior of a multithreaded program could vary across different Java implementations.

Portability Tip 26.2

When designing multithreaded programs, consider the threading capabilities of all the platforms on which the programs will execute. Using priorities other than the default will make your programs' behavior platform specific. If portability is your goal, don't adjust thread priorities.

26.4 Creating and Executing Threads

The preferred means of creating multithreaded Java applications is by implementing the **Runnable** interface (of package java.lang). A Runnable object represents a "task" that can execute concurrently with other tasks. The Runnable interface declares the single method **run**, which contains the code that defines the task that a Runnable object should perform. When a thread executing a Runnable is created and started, the thread calls the Runnable object's run method, which executes in the new thread.

26.4.1 Runnables and the Thread Class

Class PrintTask (Fig. 26.4) implements Runnable (line 5), so that multiple PrintTasks can execute concurrently. Variable sleepTime (line 7) stores a random integer value from 0 to 5 seconds created in the PrintTask constructor (line 16). Each thread running a PrintTask sleeps for the amount of time specified by sleepTime, then outputs its task's name and a message indicating that it's done sleeping.

```java
1   // Fig. 26.4: PrintTask.java
2   // PrintTask class sleeps for a random time from 0 to 5 seconds
3   import java.util.Random;
4
5   public class PrintTask implements Runnable
6   {
7      private final int sleepTime; // random sleep time for thread
8      private final String taskName; // name of task
9      private final static Random generator = new Random();
10
11     public PrintTask( String name )
12     {
13        taskName = name; // set task name
14
15        // pick random sleep time between 0 and 5 seconds
16        sleepTime = generator.nextInt( 5000 ); // milliseconds
17     } // end PrintTask constructor
18
19     // method run contains the code that a thread will execute
20     public void run()
21     {
22        try // put thread to sleep for sleepTime amount of time
23        {
24           System.out.printf( "%s going to sleep for %d milliseconds.\n",
25              taskName, sleepTime );
26           Thread.sleep( sleepTime ); // put thread to sleep
27        } // end try
```

Fig. 26.4 | PrintTask class sleeps for a random time from 0 to 5 seconds. (Part 1 of 2.)

```
28          catch ( InterruptedException exception )
29          {
30             System.out.printf( "%s %s\n", taskName,
31                "terminated prematurely due to interruption" );
32          } // end catch
33
34          // print task name
35          System.out.printf( "%s done sleeping\n", taskName );
36       } // end method run
37    } // end class PrintTask
```

Fig. 26.4 | PrintTask class sleeps for a random time from 0 to 5 seconds. (Part 2 of 2.)

A PrintTask executes when a thread calls the PrintTask's run method. Lines 24–25 display a message indicating the name of the currently executing task and that the task is going to sleep for sleepTime milliseconds. Line 26 invokes static method **sleep** of class Thread to place the thread in the *timed waiting* state for the specified amount of time. At this point, the thread loses the processor, and the system allows another thread to execute. When the thread awakens, it reenters the *runnable* state. When the PrintTask is assigned to a processor again, line 35 outputs a message indicating that the task is done sleeping, then method run terminates. Note that the catch at lines 28–32 is required because method sleep might throw a checked exception of type **InterruptedException** if the sleeping thread's **interrupt** method is called.

Figure 26.5 creates Thread objects to execute PrintTasks. Lines 12–14 create three threads, each specifying a new PrintTask to execute. Lines 19–21 call Thread method start on each of the threads, placing each into the *runnable* state and setting up a call to the corresponding Runnable's run method to execute the task. Line 23 outputs a message indicating that all of the threads' tasks have been started and that the main method is finished executing.

```
 1    // Fig. 26.5: ThreadCreator.java
 2    // Creating and starting three threads to execute Runnables.
 3    import java.lang.Thread;
 4
 5    public class ThreadCreator
 6    {
 7       public static void main( String[] args )
 8       {
 9          System.out.println( "Creating threads" );
10
11          // create each thread with a new targeted runnable
12          Thread thread1 = new Thread( new PrintTask( "task1" ) );
13          Thread thread2 = new Thread( new PrintTask( "task2" ) );
14          Thread thread3 = new Thread( new PrintTask( "task3" ) );
15
16          System.out.println( "Threads created, starting tasks." );
17
18          // start threads and place in runnable state
19          thread1.start(); // invokes task1's run method
```

Fig. 26.5 | Creating and starting three threads to execute Runnables. (Part 1 of 2.)

```
20          thread2.start(); // invokes task2's run method
21          thread3.start(); // invokes task3's run method
22
23          System.out.println( "Tasks started, main ends.\n" );
24      } // end main
25  } // end class ThreadCreator
```

```
Creating threads
Threads created, starting tasks
Tasks started, main ends

task3 going to sleep for 491 milliseconds
task2 going to sleep for 71 milliseconds
task1 going to sleep for 3549 milliseconds
task2 done sleeping
task3 done sleeping
task1 done sleeping
```

```
Creating threads
Threads created, starting tasks
task1 going to sleep for 4666 milliseconds
task2 going to sleep for 48 milliseconds
task3 going to sleep for 3924 milliseconds
Tasks started, main ends

task2 done sleeping
task3 done sleeping
task1 done sleeping
```

Fig. 26.5 | Creating and starting three threads to execute `Runnable`s. (Part 2 of 2.)

The code in main executes in the **main thread**, a thread created by the JVM. The code in the run method of PrintTask (lines 20–36 of Fig. 26.4) executes in the threads created in lines 12–14 of Fig. 26.5. When method main terminates, the program itself continues running because there are still threads that are alive (i.e., any of the three threads we created that have not yet reached the *terminated* state). The program will not terminate until its last thread completes execution.

The sample outputs for this program show each task's name and sleep time as the thread goes to sleep. The thread with the shortest sleep time normally awakens first, indicates that it's done sleeping and terminates. In Section 26.9, we discuss multithreading issues that could prevent the thread with the shortest sleep time from awakening first. In the first output, the main thread terminates before any of the other threads output their names and sleep times. This shows that the main thread runs to completion before any of the other threads get a chance to run. In the second output, all of the threads output their names and sleep times before the main thread terminates. This shows that other threads executed before the main thread terminated. This is an example of the round-robin scheduling we discussed in Section 26.3. Also notice that in the first example output, task3 goes to sleep first and task1 last, even though we started task1's thread first. This illustrates the fact that we cannot predict the order in which threads will be scheduled, even if we know the order in which they were created and started.

26.4.2 Thread Management with the Executor Framework

Though it's possible to create threads explicitly, as in Figure 26.5, it's recommended that you use the Executor interface to manage the execution of Runnable objects for you. An **Executor** object typically creates and manages a group of threads called a **thread pool** to execute Runnables. Using an Executor has many advantages over creating threads yourself. Executors can reuse existing threads to eliminate the overhead of creating a new thread for each task and can improve performance by optimizing the number of threads to ensure that the processor stays busy, without creating so many threads that the application runs out of resources.

The Executor interface declares a single method named **execute** which accepts a Runnable as an argument. The Executor assigns every Runnable passed to its execute method to one of the available threads in the thread pool. If there are no available threads, the Executor creates a new thread or waits for a thread to become available and assigns that thread the Runnable that was passed to method execute.

The **ExecutorService interface** (of package java.util.concurrent) extends Executor and declares a number of other methods for managing the life cycle of an Executor. An object that implements the ExecutorService interface can be created using static methods declared in class **Executors** (of package java.util.concurrent). We use interface ExecutorService and a method of class Executors in the next application, which executes three tasks.

Figure 26.6 uses an ExecutorService object to manage threads that execute Print-Tasks. Method main (lines 8–29) creates and names three PrintTask objects (lines 11–13). Line 18 uses Executors method **newCachedThreadPool** to obtain an ExecutorService that creates new threads as they're needed by the application. These threads are used by threadExecutor to execute the Runnables.

```
1   // Fig. 26.6: TaskExecutor.java
2   // Using an ExecutorService to execute Runnables.
3   import java.util.concurrent.Executors;
4   import java.util.concurrent.ExecutorService;
5
6   public class TaskExecutor
7   {
8      public static void main( String[] args )
9      {
10        // create and name each runnable
11        PrintTask task1 = new PrintTask( "task1" );
12        PrintTask task2 = new PrintTask( "task2" );
13        PrintTask task3 = new PrintTask( "task3" );
14
15        System.out.println( "Starting Executor" );
16
17        // create ExecutorService to manage threads
18        ExecutorService threadExecutor = Executors.newCachedThreadPool();
19
20        // start threads and place in runnable state
21        threadExecutor.execute( task1 ); // start task1
22        threadExecutor.execute( task2 ); // start task2
23        threadExecutor.execute( task3 ); // start task3
```

Fig. 26.6 | Using an ExecutorService to execute Runnables. (Part 1 of 2.)

```
24
25          // shut down worker threads when their tasks complete
26          threadExecutor.shutdown();
27
28          System.out.println( "Tasks started, main ends.\n" );
29      } // end main
30  } // end class TaskExecutor
```

```
Starting Executor
Tasks started, main ends

task1 going to sleep for 4806 milliseconds
task2 going to sleep for 2513 milliseconds
task3 going to sleep for 1132 milliseconds
task3 done sleeping
task2 done sleeping
task1 done sleeping
```

```
Starting Executor
task1 going to sleep for 1342 milliseconds
task2 going to sleep for 277 milliseconds
task3 going to sleep for 2737 milliseconds
Tasks started, main ends

task2 done sleeping
task1 done sleeping
task3 done sleeping
```

Fig. 26.6 | Using an ExecutorService to execute Runnables. (Part 2 of 2.)

Lines 21–23 each invoke the ExecutorService's execute method. This method executes the Runnable passed to it as an argument (in this case a PrintTask) some time in the future. The specified task may execute in one of the threads in the ExecutorService's thread pool, in a new thread created to execute it, or in the thread that called the execute method; the ExecutorService manages these details. Method execute returns immediately from each invocation—the program does not wait for each PrintTask to finish. Line 26 calls ExecutorService method **shutdown**, which notifies the ExecutorService to stop accepting new tasks, but continues executing tasks that have already been submitted. Once all of the previously submitted Runnables have completed, the threadExecutor terminates. Line 28 outputs a message indicating that the tasks were started and the main thread is finishing its execution. The sample outputs for this program are similar to those of the previous program and again demonstrate the nondeterminism of thread scheduling.

26.5 Thread Synchronization

When multiple threads share an object and it is modified by one or more of them, indeterminate results may occur (as we'll see in the examples) unless access to the shared object is managed properly. If one thread is in the process of updating a shared object and another thread also tries to update it, it's unclear which thread's update takes effect. When this happens, the program's behavior cannot be trusted—sometimes the program will produce the correct results, and sometimes it won't. In either case, there'll be no indication that the shared object was manipulated incorrectly.

The problem can be solved by giving only one thread at a time *exclusive access* to code that manipulates the shared object. During that time, other threads desiring to manipulate the object are kept waiting. When the thread with exclusive access to the object finishes manipulating it, one of the threads that was waiting is allowed to proceed. This process, called **thread synchronization**, coordinates access to shared data by multiple concurrent threads. By synchronizing threads in this manner, you can ensure that each thread accessing a shared object excludes all other threads from doing so simultaneously—this is called **mutual exclusion**.

Monitors

A common way to perform synchronization is to use Java's built-in **monitors**. Every object has a monitor and a **monitor lock** (or **intrinsic lock**). The monitor ensures that its object's monitor lock is held by a maximum of only one thread at any time. Monitors and monitor locks can thus be used to enforce mutual exclusion. If an operation requires the executing thread to hold a lock while the operation is performed, a thread must acquire the lock before proceeding with the operation. Other threads attempting to perform an operation that requires the same lock will be *blocked* until the first thread releases the lock, at which point the *blocked* threads may attempt to acquire the lock and proceed with the operation.

To specify that a thread must hold a monitor lock to execute a block of code, the code should be placed in a **synchronized statement**. Such code is said to be **guarded** by the monitor lock; a thread must **acquire the lock** to execute the synchronized statements. The monitor allows only one thread at a time to execute statements within synchronized blocks that lock on the same object, as only one thread at a time can hold the monitor lock. The synchronized statements are declared using the **synchronized** keyword:

```
synchronized ( object )
{
    statements
} // end synchronized statement
```

where *object* is the object whose monitor lock will be acquired; *object* is normally this if it's the object in which the synchronized statement appears. If several synchronized statements are trying to execute on an object at the same time, only one of them may be active on the object—all the other threads attempting to enter a synchronized statement on the same object are placed in the *blocked* state.

When a synchronized statement finishes executing, the object's monitor lock is released and one of the *blocked* threads attempting to enter a synchronized statement can be allowed to acquire the lock to proceed. Java also allows **synchronized** methods. Before executing, a non-static synchronized method must acquire the lock on the object that is used to call the method. Similary, a static synchronized method must acquire the lock on the class that is used to call the method.

26.5.1 Unsynchronized Data Sharing

An example here will illustrate the dangers of sharing an object across threads without proper synchronization. In this example, two Runnables maintain references to a single integer array. Each Runnable writes five values to the array, then terminates. This may seem harmless, but it can result in errors if the array is manipulated without synchronization.

Class SimpleArray

A SimpleArray object (Fig. 26.7) will be shared across multiple threads. SimpleArray will enable those threads to place int values into array (declared at line 8). Line 9 initializes variable writeIndex, which will be used to determine the array element that should be written to next. The constructor (lines 13–16) creates an integer array of the desired size.

```java
 1   // Fig. 26.7: SimpleArray.java
 2   // Class that manages an integer array to be shared by multiple threads.
 3   import java.util.Arrays;
 4   import java.util.Random;
 5
 6   public class SimpleArray // CAUTION: NOT THREAD SAFE!
 7   {
 8      private final int[] array; // the shared integer array
 9      private int writeIndex = 0; // index of next element to be written
10      private final static Random generator = new Random();
11
12      // construct a SimpleArray of a given size
13      public SimpleArray( int size )
14      {
15         array = new int[ size ];
16      } // end constructor
17
18      // add a value to the shared array
19      public void add( int value )
20      {
21         int position = writeIndex; // store the write index
22
23         try
24         {
25            // put thread to sleep for 0-499 milliseconds
26            Thread.sleep( generator.nextInt( 500 ) );
27         } // end try
28         catch ( InterruptedException ex )
29         {
30            ex.printStackTrace();
31         } // end catch
32
33         // put value in the appropriate element
34         array[ position ] = value;
35         System.out.printf( "%s wrote %2d to element %d.\n",
36            Thread.currentThread().getName(), value, position );
37
38         ++writeIndex; // increment index of element to be written next
39         System.out.printf( "Next write index: %d\n", writeIndex );
40      } // end method add
41
42      // used for outputting the contents of the shared integer array
43      public String toString()
44      {
45         return "\nContents of SimpleArray:\n" + Arrays.toString( array );
46      } // end method toString
47   } // end class SimpleArray
```

Fig. 26.7 | Class that manages an integer array to be shared by multiple threads.

Method add (lines 19–40) allows new values to be inserted at the end of the array. Line 21 stores the current writeIndex value. Line 26 puts the thread that invokes add to sleep for a random interval from 0 to 499 milliseconds. This is done to make the problems associated with unsynchronized access to shared data more obvious. After the thread is done sleeping, line 34 inserts the value passed to add into the array at the element specified by position. Lines 35–36 output a message indicating the executing thread's name, the value that was inserted in the array and where it was inserted. The expression Thread.currentThread.getName() (line 36) first obtains a reference to the currently executing Thread, then uses that Thread's getName method to obtain its name. Line 38 increments writeIndex so that the next call to add will insert a value in the array's next element. Lines 43–46 override method toString to create a String representation of the array's contents.

Class *ArrayWriter*

Class ArrayWriter (Fig. 26.8) implements the interface Runnable to define a task for inserting values in a SimpleArray object. The constructor (lines 10–14) takes two arguments—an integer value, which is the first value this task will insert in the SimpleArray object, and a reference to the SimpleArray object. Line 20 invokes method add on the SimpleArray object. The task completes after three consecutive integers beginning with startValue are added to the SimpleArray object.

```
1    // Fig. 26.8: ArrayWriter.java
2    // Adds integers to an array shared with other Runnables
3    import java.lang.Runnable;
4
5    public class ArrayWriter implements Runnable
6    {
7       private final SimpleArray sharedSimpleArray;
8       private final int startValue;
9
10      public ArrayWriter( int value, SimpleArray array )
11      {
12         startValue = value;
13         sharedSimpleArray = array;
14      } // end constructor
15
16      public void run()
17      {
18         for ( int i = startValue; i < startValue + 3; i++ )
19         {
20            sharedSimpleArray.add( i ); // add an element to the shared array
21         } // end for
22      } // end method run
23   } // end class ArrayWriter
```

Fig. 26.8 | Adds integers to an array shared with other Runnables.

Class *SharedArrayTest*

Class SharedArrayTest (Fig. 26.9) executes two ArrayWriter tasks that add values to a single SimpleArray object. Line 12 constructs a six-element SimpleArray object. Lines 15–16 create two new ArrayWriter tasks, one that places the values 1–3 in the Simple-Array object, and one that places the values 11–13. Lines 19–21 create an ExecutorService and execute the two ArrayWriters. Line 23 invokes the ExecutorService's shutDown method to prevent additional tasks from starting and to enable the application to terminate when the currently executing tasks complete execution.

Recall that ExecutorService method shutdown returns immediately. Thus any code that appears after the call to ExecutorService method shutdown in line 23 will continue executing as long as the main thread is still assigned to a processor. We'd like to output the SimpleArray object to show you the results *after* the threads complete their tasks. So, we need the program to wait for the threads to complete before main outputs the SimpleArray object's contents. Interface ExecutorService provides the **awaitTermination** method for this purpose. This method returns control to its caller either when all tasks executing in the ExecutorService complete or when the specified timeout elapses. If all tasks are completed before awaitTermination times out, this method returns true; otherwise it returns false. The two arguments to awaitTermination represent a timeout value and a unit of measure specified with a constant from class TimeUnit (in this case, TimeUnit.MINUTES). In this example, if both tasks complete before awaitTermination times out, line 32 displays the SimpleArray object's contents. Otherwise, lines 34–35 print a message indicating that the tasks did not finish executing before awaitTermination timed out.

```java
1   // Fig 26.9: SharedArrayTest.java
2   // Executes two Runnables to add elements to a shared SimpleArray.
3   import java.util.concurrent.Executors;
4   import java.util.concurrent.ExecutorService;
5   import java.util.concurrent.TimeUnit;
6
7   public class SharedArrayTest
8   {
9      public static void main( String[] arg )
10     {
11        // construct the shared object
12        SimpleArray sharedSimpleArray = new SimpleArray( 6 );
13
14        // create two tasks to write to the shared SimpleArray
15        ArrayWriter writer1 = new ArrayWriter( 1, sharedSimpleArray );
16        ArrayWriter writer2 = new ArrayWriter( 11, sharedSimpleArray );
17
18        // execute the tasks with an ExecutorService
19        ExecutorService executor = Executors.newCachedThreadPool();
20        executor.execute( writer1 );
21        executor.execute( writer2 );
22
23        executor.shutdown();
24
25        try
26        {
27           // wait 1 minute for both writers to finish executing
28           boolean tasksEnded = executor.awaitTermination(
29              1, TimeUnit.MINUTES );
30
31           if ( tasksEnded )
32              System.out.println( sharedSimpleArray ); // print contents
```

Fig. 26.9 | Executes two Runnables to insert values in a shared array. (Part 1 of 2.)

```
33              else
34                  System.out.println(
35                      "Timed out while waiting for tasks to finish." );
36          } // end try
37          catch ( InterruptedException ex )
38          {
39              System.out.println(
40                  "Interrupted while waiting for tasks to finish." );
41          } // end catch
42      } // end main
43  } // end class SharedArrayTest
```

```
pool-1-thread-1 wrote  1 to element 0.
Next write index: 1
pool-1-thread-1 wrote  2 to element 1.
Next write index: 2
pool-1-thread-1 wrote  3 to element 2.
Next write index: 3
pool-1-thread-2 wrote 11 to element 0.
Next write index: 4
pool-1-thread-2 wrote 12 to element 4.
Next write index: 5
pool-1-thread-2 wrote 13 to element 5.
Next write index: 6

Contents of SimpleArray:
[11, 2, 3, 0, 12, 13]
```

First `pool-1-thread-1` wrote the value 1 to element 0. Later `pool-1-thread-2` wrote the value 11 to element 0, thus overwriting the previously stored value.

Fig. 26.9 | Executes two `Runnable`s to insert values in a shared array. (Part 2 of 2.)

The output in Fig. 26.9 demonstrates the problems (highlighted in the output) that can be caused by failure to synchronize access to shared data. The value 1 was written to element 0, then overwritten later by the value 11. Also, when `writeIndex` was incremented to 3, nothing was written to that element, as indicated by the 0 in that element of the printed array.

Recall that we added calls to `Thread` method `sleep` between operations on the shared data to emphasize the unpredictability of thread scheduling and increase the likelihood of producing erroneous output. It's important to note that even if these operations were allowed to proceed at their normal pace, you could still see errors in the program's output. However, modern processors can handle the simple operations of the `SimpleArray` method `add` so quickly that you might not see the errors caused by the two threads executing this method concurrently, even if you tested the program dozens of times. One of the challenges of multithreaded programming is spotting the errors—they may occur so infrequently that a broken program does not produce incorrect results during testing, creating the illusion that the program is correct.

26.5.2 Synchronized Data Sharing—Making Operations Atomic

The output errors of Fig. 26.9 can be attributed to the fact that the shared object, `SimpleArray`, is not **thread safe**—`SimpleArray` is susceptible to errors if it's accessed concurrently by multiple threads. The problem lies in method `add`, which stores the value of `writeIndex`, places a new value in that element, then increments `writeIndex`. Such a method would present no problem in a single-threaded program. However, if one thread obtains the value of `writeIndex`, there is no guarantee that another thread cannot come along and increment `writeIndex` before the first thread has had a chance to place a value in the array. If this happens, the first thread will be writing to the array based on a **stale value** of `writeIndex`—a value that is no longer valid. Another possibility is that one thread might obtain the value of `writeIndex` after another thread adds an element to the array but before `writeIndex` is incremented. In this case, too, the first thread would write to the array based on an invalid value for `writeIndex`.

`SimpleArray` is not thread safe because it allows any number of threads to read and modify shared data concurrently, which can cause errors. To make `SimpleArray` thread safe, we must ensure that no two threads can access it at the same time. We also must ensure that while one thread is in the process of storing `writeIndex`, adding a value to the array, and incrementing `writeIndex`, no other thread may read or change the value of `writeIndex` or modify the contents of the array at any point during these three operations. In other words, we want these three operations—storing `writeIndex`, writing to the array, incrementing `writeIndex`—to be an **atomic operation**, which cannot be divided into smaller suboperations. We can simulate atomicity by ensuring that only one thread carries out the three operations at a time. Any other threads that need to perform the operation must wait until the first thread has finished the `add` operation in its entirety.

Atomicity can be achieved using the `synchronized` keyword. By placing our three suboperations in a `synchronized` statement or `synchronized` method, we allow only one thread at a time to acquire the lock and perform the operations. When that thread has completed all of the operations in the `synchronized` block and releases the lock, another thread may acquire the lock and begin executing the operations. This ensures that a thread executing the operations will see the actual values of the shared data and that these values will not change unexpectedly in the middle of the operations as a result of another thread's modifying them.

Software Engineering Observation 26.1
Place all accesses to mutable data that may be shared by multiple threads inside `synchronized` statements or `synchronized` methods that synchronize on the same lock. When performing multiple operations on shared data, hold the lock for the entirety of the operation to ensure that the operation is effectively atomic.

Class *SimpleArray with Synchronization*
Figure 26.10 displays class `SimpleArray` with the proper synchronization. Notice that it's identical to the `SimpleArray` class of Fig. 26.7, except that `add` is now a `synchronized` method (line 20). So, only one thread at a time can execute this method. We reuse classes `ArrayWriter` (Fig. 26.8) and `SharedArrayTest` (Fig. 26.9) from the previous example.

```
1   // Fig. 26.10: SimpleArray.java
2   // Class that manages an integer array to be shared by multiple threads
3   // threads with synchronization.
4   import java.util.Arrays;
5   import java.util.Random;
```

Fig. 26.10 | Class that manages an integer array to be shared by multiple threads with synchronization. (Part 1 of 3.)

```
6
7   public class SimpleArray
8   {
9       private final int[] array; // the shared integer array
10      private int writeIndex = 0; // index of next element to be written
11      private final static Random generator = new Random();
12
13      // construct a SimpleArray of a given size
14      public SimpleArray( int size )
15      {
16          array = new int[ size ];
17      } // end constructor
18
19      // add a value to the shared array
20      public synchronized void add( int value )
21      {
22          int position = writeIndex; // store the write index
23
24          try
25          {
26              // put thread to sleep for 0-499 milliseconds
27              Thread.sleep( generator.nextInt( 500 ) );
28          } // end try
29          catch ( InterruptedException ex )
30          {
31              ex.printStackTrace();
32          } // end catch
33
34          // put value in the appropriate element
35          array[ position ] = value;
36          System.out.printf( "%s wrote %2d to element %d.\n",
37              Thread.currentThread().getName(), value, position );
38
39          ++writeIndex; // increment index of element to be written next
40          System.out.printf( "Next write index: %d\n", writeIndex );
41      } // end method add
42
43      // used for outputting the contents of the shared integer array
44      public String toString()
45      {
46          return "\nContents of SimpleArray:\n" + Arrays.toString( array );
47      } // end method toString
48  } // end class SimpleArray
```

```
pool-1-thread-1 wrote  1 to element 0.
Next write index: 1
pool-1-thread-2 wrote 11 to element 1.
Next write index: 2
pool-1-thread-2 wrote 12 to element 2.
Next write index: 3
pool-1-thread-2 wrote 13 to element 3.
Next write index: 4                                    (continued...)
```

Fig. 26.10 | Class that manages an integer array to be shared by multiple threads with synchronization. (Part 2 of 3.)

```
pool-1-thread-1 wrote  2 to element 4.
Next write index: 5
pool-1-thread-1 wrote  3 to element 5.
Next write index: 6

Contents of SimpleArray:
1 11 12 13 2 3
```

Fig. 26.10 | Class that manages an integer array to be shared by multiple threads with synchronization. (Part 3 of 3.)

Line 20 declares method as synchronized, making all of the operations in this method behave as a single, atomic operation. Line 22 performs the first suboperation—storing the value of writeIndex. Line 35 defines the second suboperation, writing an element to the element at the index position. Line 39 increments writeIndex. When the method finishes executing at line 41, the executing thread releases the SimpleArray lock, making it possible for another thread to begin executing the add method.

In the synchronized add method, we print messages to the console indicating the progress of threads as they execute this method, in addition to performing the actual operations required to insert a value in the array. We do this so that the messages will be printed in the correct order, allowing us to see whether the method is properly synchronized by comparing these outputs with those of the previous, unsynchronized example. We continue to output messages from synchronized blocks in later examples for demonstration purposes; typically, however, I/O *should not* be performed in synchronized blocks, because it's important to minimize the amount of time that an object is "locked." Also, line 27 in this example calls Thread method sleep to emphasize the unpredictability of thread scheduling. You should *never* call sleep while holding a lock in a real application.

Performance Tip 26.2

Keep the duration of synchronized statements as short as possible while maintaining the needed synchronization. This minimizes the wait time for blocked threads. Avoid performing I/O, lengthy calculations and operations that do not require synchronization while holding a lock.

Another note on thread safety: We've said that it's necessary to synchronize access to all data that may be shared across multiple threads. Actually, this synchronization is necessary only for **mutable data**, or data that may change in its lifetime. If the shared data will not change in a multithreaded program, then it's not possible for a thread to see old or incorrect values as a result of another thread's manipulating that data.

When you share immutable data across threads, declare the corresponding data fields final to indicate that the values of the variables will not change after they're initialized. This prevents accidental modification of the shared data later in a program, which could compromise thread safety. Labeling object references as final indicates that the reference will not change, but it does not guarantee that the object itself is immutable—this depends entirely on the object's properties. However, it's still good practice to mark references that will not change as final, as doing so forces the object's constructor to be atomic—the object will be fully constructed with all its fields initialized before the program accesses it.

Good Programming Practice 26.1

Always declare data fields that you do not expect to change as final. Primitive variables that are declared as final can safely be shared across threads. An object reference that is declared as final ensures that the object it refers to will be fully constructed and initialized before it's used by the program, and prevents the reference from pointing to another object.

26.6 Producer/Consumer Relationship without Synchronization

In a **producer/consumer relationship**, the **producer** portion of an application generates data and stores it in a shared object, and the **consumer** portion of the application reads data from the shared object. The producer/consumer relationship separates the task of identifying work to be done from the tasks involved in actually carrying out the work. One example of a common producer/consumer relationship is **print spooling**. Although a printer might not be available when you want to print from an application (i.e., the producer), you can still "complete" the print task, as the data is temporarily placed on disk until the printer becomes available. Similarly, when the printer (i.e., a consumer) is available, it doesn't have to wait until a current user wants to print. The spooled print jobs can be printed as soon as the printer becomes available. Another example of the producer/consumer relationship is an application that copies data onto CDs by placing data in a fixed-size buffer, which is emptied as the CD-RW drive "burns" the data onto the CD.

In a multithreaded producer/consumer relationship, a **producer thread** generates data and places it in a shared object called a **buffer**. A **consumer thread** reads data from the buffer. This relationship requires synchronization to ensure that values are produced and consumed properly. All operations on mutable data that is shared by multiple threads (e.g., the data in the buffer) must be guarded with a lock to prevent corruption, as discussed in Section 26.5. Operations on the buffer data shared by a producer and consumer thread are also **state dependent**—the operations should proceed only if the buffer is in the correct state. If the buffer is in a not-full state, the producer may produce; if the buffer is in a not-empty state, the consumer may consume. All operations that access the buffer must use synchronization to ensure that data is written to the buffer or read from the buffer only if the buffer is in the proper state. If the producer attempting to put the next data into the buffer determines that it's full, the producer thread should wait until there's space to write a new value. If a consumer thread finds the buffer empty or finds that the previous data has already been read, the consumer must also wait for new data to become available.

Consider how logic errors can arise if we do not synchronize access among multiple threads manipulating shared data. Our next example (Fig. 26.11–Fig. 26.15) implements a producer/consumer relationship without the proper synchronization. A producer thread writes the numbers 1 through 10 into a shared buffer—a single memory location shared between two threads (a single int variable called buffer in line 6 of Fig. 26.14 in this example). The consumer thread reads this data from the shared buffer and displays the data. The program's output shows the values that the producer writes (produces) into the shared buffer and the values that the consumer reads (consumes) from the shared buffer.

Each value the producer thread writes to the shared buffer must be consumed exactly once by the consumer thread. However, the threads in this example erroneously are not synchronized. Therefore, data can be lost or garbled if the producer places new data into the shared buffer before the consumer reads the previous data. Also, data can be incorrectly duplicated if the consumer consumes data again before the producer produces the next value. To show these possibilities, the consumer thread in the following example keeps a total of all the values it reads. The producer thread produces values from 1 through 10. If the consumer reads each value produced once and only once, the total will be 55. However, if you execute this program several times, you'll see that the total is not always 55 (as shown in the outputs in Fig. 26.15). To emphasize the point, the producer and consumer threads in the example each sleep for random intervals of up to three seconds between performing their tasks. Thus, we do not know when the producer thread will attempt to write a new value, or when the consumer thread will attempt to read a value.

Implementing the Producer/Consumer Relationship
The program consists of interface `Buffer` (Fig. 26.11) and classes `Producer` (Fig. 26.12), `Consumer` (Fig. 26.13), `UnsynchronizedBuffer` (Fig. 26.14) and `SharedBufferTest` (Fig. 26.15). Interface `Buffer` (Fig. 26.11) declares methods `set` (line 6) and `get` (line 9) that a `Buffer` (such as `UnsynchronizedBuffer`) must implement to enable the `Producer` thread to place a value in the `Buffer` and the `Consumer` thread to retrieve a value from the `Buffer`, respectively. In subsequent examples, methods `set` and `get` will call methods that throw `InterruptedExceptions`. We declare each method with a `throws` clause here so that we don't have to modify this interface for the later examples.

```
1   // Fig. 26.11: Buffer.java
2   // Buffer interface specifies methods called by Producer and Consumer.
3   public interface Buffer
4   {
5      // place int value into Buffer
6      public void set( int value ) throws InterruptedException;
7
8      // return int value from Buffer
9      public int get() throws InterruptedException;
10  } // end interface Buffer
```

Fig. 26.11 | Buffer interface specifies methods called by `Producer` and `Consumer`.

Class `Producer` (Fig. 26.12) implements the `Runnable` interface, allowing it to be executed as a task in a separate thread. The constructor (lines 11–14) initializes the `Buffer` reference `sharedLocation` with an object created in `main` (line 14 of Fig. 26.15) and passed to the constructor. As we'll see, this is an `UnsynchronizedBuffer` object that implements interface `Buffer` without synchronizing access to the shared object. The `Producer` thread in this program executes the tasks specified in the method `run` (lines 17–39). Each iteration of the loop (lines 21–35) invokes `Thread` method `sleep` (line 25) to place the `Producer` thread into the *timed waiting* state for a random time interval between 0 and 3 seconds. When the thread awakens, line 26 passes the value of control variable `count` to the `Buffer` object's `set` method to set the shared buffer's value. Lines 27–28 keep a total of all the values produced so far and output that value. When the loop completes, lines 37–38 display a message indicating that the `Producer` has finished producing data and is terminating. Next, method `run` terminates, which indicates that the `Producer` completed its task. Note that any method called from a `Runnable`'s `run` method (e.g., `Buffer` method `set`) executes as part of that task's thread of execution. This fact becomes important in Section 26.7 when we add synchronization to the producer/consumer relationship.

```
1    // Fig. 26.12: Producer.java
2    // Producer with a run method that inserts the values 1 to 10 in buffer.
3    import java.util.Random;
4
5    public class Producer implements Runnable
6    {
7       private final static Random generator = new Random();
8       private final Buffer sharedLocation; // reference to shared object
9
10      // constructor
11      public Producer( Buffer shared )
12      {
13         sharedLocation = shared;
14      } // end Producer constructor
15
16      // store values from 1 to 10 in sharedLocation
17      public void run()
18      {
19         int sum = 0;
20
21         for ( int count = 1; count <= 10; count++ )
22         {
23            try // sleep 0 to 3 seconds, then place value in Buffer
24            {
25               Thread.sleep( generator.nextInt( 3000 ) ); // random sleep
26               sharedLocation.set( count ); // set value in buffer
27               sum += count; // increment sum of values
28               System.out.printf( "\t%2d\n", sum );
29            } // end try
30            // if lines 25 or 26 get interrupted, print stack trace
31            catch ( InterruptedException exception )
32            {
33               exception.printStackTrace();
34            } // end catch
35         } // end for
36
37         System.out.println(
38            "Producer done producing\nTerminating Producer" );
39      } // end method run
40   } // end class Producer
```

Fig. 26.12 | Producer with a run method that inserts the values 1 to 10 in buffer.

Class Consumer (Fig. 26.13) also implements interface Runnable, allowing the Consumer to execute concurrently with the Producer. Lines 11–14 initialize Buffer reference sharedLocation with an object that implements the Buffer interface (created in main, Fig. 26.15) and passed to the constructor as the parameter shared. As we'll see, this is the same UnsynchronizedBuffer object that is used to initialize the Producer object—thus, the two threads share the same object. The Consumer thread in this program performs the tasks specified in method run (lines 17–39). Lines 21–35 iterate 10 times. Each iteration invokes Thread method sleep (line 26) to put the Consumer thread into the *timed waiting* state for up to 3 seconds. Next, line 27 uses the Buffer's get method to retrieve the value in the shared buffer, then adds the value to variable sum. Line 28 displays the total of all the values consumed so far. When the loop completes, lines 37–38 display a line indicating the sum of the consumed values. Then method run terminates, which indicates that the Consumer completed its task. Once both threads enter the *terminated* state, the program ends.

```java
1   // Fig. 26.13: Consumer.java
2   // Consumer with a run method that loops, reading 10 values from buffer.
3   import java.util.Random;
4
5   public class Consumer implements Runnable
6   {
7      private final static Random generator = new Random();
8      private final Buffer sharedLocation; // reference to shared object
9
10     // constructor
11     public Consumer( Buffer shared )
12     {
13        sharedLocation = shared;
14     } // end Consumer constructor
15
16     // read sharedLocation's value 10 times and sum the values
17     public void run()
18     {
19        int sum = 0;
20
21        for ( int count = 1; count <= 10; count++ )
22        {
23           // sleep 0 to 3 seconds, read value from buffer and add to sum
24           try
25           {
26              Thread.sleep( generator.nextInt( 3000 ) );
27              sum += sharedLocation.get();
28              System.out.printf( "\t\t\t%2d\n", sum );
29           } // end try
30           // if lines 26 or 27 get interrupted, print stack trace
31           catch ( InterruptedException exception )
32           {
33              exception.printStackTrace();
34           } // end catch
35        } // end for
36
37        System.out.printf( "\n%s %d\n%s\n",
38           "Consumer read values totaling", sum, "Terminating Consumer" );
39     } // end method run
40  } // end class Consumer
```

Fig. 26.13 | Consumer with a run method that loops, reading 10 values from buffer.

[*Note:* We call method sleep in method run of the Producer and Consumer classes to emphasize the fact that, in multithreaded applications, it's unpredictable when each thread will perform its task and for how long it will perform the task when it has a processor. Normally, these thread scheduling issues are beyond the control of the Java developer. In this program, our thread's tasks are quite simple—the Producer writes the values 1 to 10 to the buffer, and the Consumer reads 10 values from the buffer and adds each value to variable sum. Without the sleep method call, and if the Producer executes first, given today's phenomenally fast processors, the Producer would likely complete its task before the Consumer got a chance to execute. If the Consumer executed first, it would likely consume garbage data ten times, then terminate before the Producer could produce the first real value.]

Class UnsynchronizedBuffer (Fig. 26.14) implements interface Buffer (line 4). An object of this class is shared between the Producer and the Consumer. Line 6 declares instance variable buffer and initializes it with the value –1. This value is used to demonstrate the case in which the Consumer attempts to consume a value before the Producer ever places a value in buffer. Methods set (lines 9–13) and get (lines 16–20) do not synchronize access to the field buffer. Method set simply assigns its argument to buffer (line 12), and method get simply returns the value of buffer (line 19).

```
1   // Fig. 26.14: UnsynchronizedBuffer.java
2   // UnsynchronizedBuffer maintains the shared integer that is accessed by
3   // a producer thread and a consumer thread via methods set and get.
4   public class UnsynchronizedBuffer implements Buffer
5   {
6      private int buffer = -1; // shared by producer and consumer threads
7
8      // place value into buffer
9      public void set( int value ) throws InterruptedException
10     {
11        System.out.printf( "Producer writes\t%2d", value );
12        buffer = value;
13     } // end method set
14
15     // return value from buffer
16     public int get() throws InterruptedException
17     {
18        System.out.printf( "Consumer reads\t%2d", buffer );
19        return buffer;
20     } // end method get
21  } // end class UnsynchronizedBuffer
```

Fig. 26.14 | UnsynchronizedBuffer maintains the shared integer that is accessed by a producer thread and a consumer thread via methods set and get.

In class SharedBufferTest (Fig. 26.15), line 11 creates an ExecutorService to execute the Producer and Consumer Runnables. Line 14 creates an UnsynchronizedBuffer object and assigns it to Buffer variable sharedLocation. This object stores the data that the Producer and Consumer threads will share. Lines 23–24 create and execute the Producer and Consumer. Note that the Producer and Consumer constructors are each passed the same Buffer object (sharedLocation), so each object is initialized with a reference to the same Buffer. These lines also implicitly launch the threads and call each Runnable's run method. Finally, line 26 calls method shutdown so that the application can terminate when the threads executing the Producer and Consumer complete their tasks. When main terminates (line 27), the main thread of execution enters the *terminated* state.

```
1   // Fig. 26.15: SharedBufferTest.java
2   // Application with two threads manipulating an unsynchronized buffer.
3   import java.util.concurrent.ExecutorService;
```

Fig. 26.15 | Application with two threads manipulating an unsynchronized buffer. (Part 1 of 3.)

```
4   import java.util.concurrent.Executors;
5
6   public class SharedBufferTest
7   {
8      public static void main( String[] args )
9      {
10         // create new thread pool with two threads
11         ExecutorService application = Executors.newCachedThreadPool();
12
13         // create UnsynchronizedBuffer to store ints
14         Buffer sharedLocation = new UnsynchronizedBuffer();
15
16         System.out.println(
17            "Action\t\tValue\tSum of Produced\tSum of Consumed" );
18         System.out.println(
19            "------\t\t-----\t---------------\t--------------\n" );
20
21         // execute the Producer and Consumer, giving each of them access
22         // to sharedLocation
23         application.execute( new Producer( sharedLocation ) );
24         application.execute( new Consumer( sharedLocation ) );
25
26         application.shutdown(); // terminate application when tasks complete
27      } // end main
28   } // end class SharedBufferTest
```

Action	Value	Sum of Produced	Sum of Consumed	
Producer writes	1	1		
Producer writes	2	3		—— 1 is lost
Producer writes	3	6		—— 2 is lost
Consumer reads	3		3	
Producer writes	4	10		
Consumer reads	4		7	
Producer writes	5	15		
Producer writes	6	21		—— 5 is lost
Producer writes	7	28		—— 6 is lost
Consumer reads	7		14	
Consumer reads	7		21	—— 7 read again
Producer writes	8	36		
Consumer reads	8		29	
Consumer reads	8		37	—— 8 read again
Producer writes	9	45		
Producer writes	10	55		—— 9 is lost
Producer done producing				
Terminating Producer				
Consumer reads	10		47	
Consumer reads	10		57	—— 10 read again
Consumer reads	10		67	—— 10 read again
Consumer reads	10		77	—— 10 read again
Consumer read values totaling 77				
Terminating Consumer				

Fig. 26.15 | Application with two threads manipulating an unsynchronized buffer. (Part 2 of 3.)

```
Action            Value   Sum of Produced  Sum of Consumed
------            -----   ---------------  ---------------

Consumer reads    -1                               -1 ——— reads -1 bad data
Producer writes    1        1
Consumer reads     1                                0
Consumer reads     1                                1 ——— I read again
Consumer reads     1                                2 ——— I read again
Consumer reads     1                                3 ——— I read again
Consumer reads     1                                4 ——— I read again
Producer writes    2        3
Consumer reads     2                                6
Producer writes    3        6
Consumer reads     3                                9
Producer writes    4       10
Consumer reads     4                               13
Producer writes    5       15
Producer writes    6       21                         ——— 5 is lost
Consumer reads     6                               19

Consumer read values totaling 19
Terminating Consumer
Producer writes    7       28                         ——— 7 never read
Producer writes    8       36                         ——— 8 never read
Producer writes    9       45                         ——— 9 never read
Producer writes   10       55                         ——— 10 never read

Producer done producing
Terminating Producer
```

Fig. 26.15 | Application with two threads manipulating an unsynchronized buffer. (Part 3 of 3.)

Recall from the overview of this example that we would like the Producer to execute first and every value produced by the Producer to be consumed exactly once by the Consumer. However, when we study the first output of Fig. 26.15, we see that the Producer writes the values 1, 2 and 3 before the Consumer reads its first value (3). Therefore, the values 1 and 2 are lost. Later, the values 5, 6 and 9 are lost, while 7 and 8 are read twice and 10 is read four times. So the first output produces an incorrect total of 77, instead of the correct total of 55. In the second output, the Consumer reads the value -1 before the Producer ever writes a value. The Consumer reads the value 1 five times before the Producer writes the value 2. Meanwhile, the values 5, 7, 8, 9 and 10 are all lost—the last four because the Consumer terminates before the Producer. An incorrect consumer total of 19 is displayed. (Lines in the output where the Producer or Consumer has acted out of order are highlighted.)

Error-Prevention Tip 26.1

Access to a shared object by concurrent threads must be controlled carefully or a program may produce incorrect results.

To solve the problems of lost and duplicated data, Section 26.7 presents an example in which we use an ArrayBlockingQueue (from package java.util.concurrent) to synchronize access to the shared object, guaranteeing that each and every value will be processed once and only once.

26.7 Producer/Consumer Relationship: ArrayBlockingQueue

One way to synchronize producer and consumer threads is to use classes from Java's concurrency package that encapsulate the synchronization for you. Java includes the class **ArrayBlockingQueue** (from package java.util.concurrent)—a fully implemented, thread-safe buffer class that implements interface **BlockingQueue**. This interface extends the Queue interface discussed in Chapter 20 and declares methods **put** and **take**, the blocking equivalents of Queue methods offer and poll, respectively. Method put places an element at the end of the BlockingQueue, waiting if the queue is full. Method take removes an element from the head of the BlockingQueue, waiting if the queue is empty. These methods make class ArrayBlockingQueue a good choice for implementing a shared buffer. Because method put blocks until there is room in the buffer to write data, and method take blocks until there is new data to read, the producer must produce a value first, the consumer correctly consumes only after the producer writes a value and the producer correctly produces the next value (after the first) only after the consumer reads the previous (or first) value. ArrayBlockingQueue stores the shared data in an array. The array's size is specified as an argument to the ArrayBlockingQueue constructor. Once created, an ArrayBlockingQueue is fixed in size and will not expand to accommodate extra elements.

Figures 26.16–26.17 demonstrates a Producer and a Consumer accessing an ArrayBlockingQueue. Class BlockingBuffer (Fig. 26.16) uses an ArrayBlockingQueue object that stores an Integer (line 7). Line 11 creates the ArrayBlockingQueue and passes 1 to the constructor so that the object holds a single value, as we did with the UnsynchronizedBuffer of Fig. 26.14. Note that lines 7 and 11 use generics, which we discussed in Chapters 20–21. We discuss multiple-element buffers in Section 26.9. Because our BlockingBuffer class uses the thread-safe ArrayBlockingQueue class to manage access to the shared buffer, BlockingBuffer is itself thread safe, even though we have not implemented the synchronization ourselves.

```
 1    // Fig. 26.16: BlockingBuffer.java
 2    // Creating a synchronized buffer using an ArrayBlockingQueue.
 3    import java.util.concurrent.ArrayBlockingQueue;
 4
 5    public class BlockingBuffer implements Buffer
 6    {
 7       private final ArrayBlockingQueue<Integer> buffer; // shared buffer
 8
 9       public BlockingBuffer()
10       {
11          buffer = new ArrayBlockingQueue<Integer>( 1 );
12       } // end BlockingBuffer constructor
13
14       // place value into buffer
15       public void set( int value ) throws InterruptedException
16       {
17          buffer.put( value ); // place value in buffer
```

Fig. 26.16 | Creating a synchronized buffer using an `ArrayBlockingQueue`. (Part 1 of 2.)

```
18              System.out.printf( "%s%2d\t%s%d\n", "Producer writes ", value,
19                  "Buffer cells occupied: ", buffer.size() );
20          } // end method set
21
22          // return value from buffer
23          public int get() throws InterruptedException
24          {
25              int readValue = buffer.take(); // remove value from buffer
26              System.out.printf( "%s %2d\t%s%d\n", "Consumer reads ",
27                  readValue, "Buffer cells occupied: ", buffer.size() );
28
29              return readValue;
30          } // end method get
31      } // end class BlockingBuffer
```

Fig. 26.16 | Creating a synchronized buffer using an `ArrayBlockingQueue`. (Part 2 of 2.)

BlockingBuffer implements interface Buffer (Fig. 26.11) and use classes Producer (Fig. 26.12 modified to remove line 28) and Consumer (Fig. 26.13 modified to remove line 28) from the example in Section 26.6. This approach demonstrates that the threads accessing the shared object are unaware that their buffer accesses are now synchronized. The synchronization is handled entirely in the set and get methods of BlockingBuffer by calling the synchronized ArrayBlockingQueue methods put and take, respectively. Thus, the Producer and Consumer Runnables are properly synchronized simply by calling the shared object's set and get methods.

Line 17 in method set (Fig. 26.16, lines 15–20) calls the ArrayBlockingQueue object's put method. This method call blocks if necessary until there is room in the buffer to place the value. Method get (lines 23–30) calls the ArrayBlockingQueue object's take method (line 25). This method call blocks if necessary until there is an element in the buffer to remove. Lines 18–19 and 26–27 use the ArrayBlockingQueue object's **size** method to display the total number of elements currently in the ArrayBlockingQueue.

Class BlockingBufferTest (Fig. 26.17) contains the main method that launches the application. Line 12 creates an ExecutorService, and line 15 creates a BlockingBuffer object and assigns its reference to the Buffer variable sharedLocation. Lines 17–18 execute the Producer and Consumer Runnables. Line 19 calls method shutdown to end the application when the threads finish executing the Producer and Consumer tasks.

```
1   // Fig. 26.17: BlockingBufferTest.java
2   // Two threads manipulating a blocking buffer that properly
3   // implements the producer/consumer relationship.
4   import java.util.concurrent.ExecutorService;
5   import java.util.concurrent.Executors;
6
7   public class BlockingBufferTest
8   {
9       public static void main( String[] args )
10      {
```

Fig. 26.17 | Two threads manipulating a blocking buffer that properly implements the producer/consumer relationship. (Part 1 of 2.)

```
11          // create new thread pool with two threads
12          ExecutorService application = Executors.newCachedThreadPool();
13
14          // create BlockingBuffer to store ints
15          Buffer sharedLocation = new BlockingBuffer();
16
17          application.execute( new Producer( sharedLocation ) );
18          application.execute( new Consumer( sharedLocation ) );
19
20          application.shutdown();
21      } // end main
22  } // end class BlockingBufferTest
```

```
Producer writes  1      Buffer cells occupied: 1
Consumer reads   1      Buffer cells occupied: 0
Producer writes  2      Buffer cells occupied: 1
Consumer reads   2      Buffer cells occupied: 0
Producer writes  3      Buffer cells occupied: 1
Consumer reads   3      Buffer cells occupied: 0
Producer writes  4      Buffer cells occupied: 1
Consumer reads   4      Buffer cells occupied: 0
Producer writes  5      Buffer cells occupied: 1
Consumer reads   5      Buffer cells occupied: 0
Producer writes  6      Buffer cells occupied: 1
Consumer reads   6      Buffer cells occupied: 0
Producer writes  7      Buffer cells occupied: 1
Consumer reads   7      Buffer cells occupied: 0
Producer writes  8      Buffer cells occupied: 1
Consumer reads   8      Buffer cells occupied: 0
Producer writes  9      Buffer cells occupied: 1
Consumer reads   9      Buffer cells occupied: 0
Producer writes 10      Buffer cells occupied: 1

Producer done producing
Terminating Producer
Consumer reads  10      Buffer cells occupied: 0

Consumer read values totaling 55
Terminating Consumer
```

Fig. 26.17 | Two threads manipulating a blocking buffer that properly implements the producer/consumer relationship. (Part 2 of 2.)

Note that while methods `put` and `take` of `ArrayBlockingQueue` are properly synchronized, `BlockingBuffer` methods `set` and `get` (Fig. 26.16) are not declared to be synchronized. Thus, the statements performed in method `set`—the `put` operation (line 17) and the output (lines 18–19)—are not atomic; nor are the statements in method `get`—the `take` operation (line 25) and the output (lines 26–27). So there is no guarantee that each output will occur immediately after the corresponding `put` or `take` operation, and the outputs may appear out of order. Even if they do, the `ArrayBlockingQueue` object is properly synchronizing access to the data, as evidenced by the fact that the sum of values read by the consumer is always correct.

26.8 Producer/Consumer Relationship with Synchronization

The previous example showed how multiple threads can share a single-element buffer in a thread-safe manner by using the `ArrayBlockingQueue` class that encapsulates the synchronization necessary to protect the shared data. For educational purposes, we now explain how you can implement a shared buffer yourself using the `synchronized` keyword and methods of class `Object`. Using an `ArrayBlockingQueue` will result in more-maintainable and better-performing code.

The first step in synchronizing access to the buffer is to implement methods `get` and `set` as synchronized methods. This requires that a thread obtain the monitor lock on the `Buffer` object before attempting to access the buffer data, but it does not automatically ensure that threads proceed with an operation only if the buffer is in the proper state. We need a way to allow our threads to wait, depending on whether certain conditions are true. In the case of placing a new item in the buffer, the condition that allows the operation to proceed is that the buffer is not full. In the case of fetching an item from the buffer, the condition that allows the operation to proceed is that the buffer is not empty. If the condition in question is true, the operation may proceed; if it's false, the thread must wait until it becomes true. When a thread is waiting on a condition, it's removed from contention for the processor and placed into the *waiting*, state and the lock it holds is released.

Methods `wait`, `notify` and `notifyAll`

`Object` methods `wait`, `notify` and `notifyAll`, which are inherited by all other classes, can be used with conditions to make threads wait when they cannot perform their tasks. If a thread obtains the monitor lock on an object, then determines that it cannot continue with its task on that object until some condition is satisfied, the thread can call `Object` method **wait** on the synchronized object; this releases the monitor lock on the object, and the thread waits in the *waiting* state while the other threads try to enter the object's synchronized statement(s) or method(s). When a thread executing a synchronized statement (or method) completes or satisfies the condition on which another thread may be waiting, it can call `Object` method **notify** on the synchronized object to allow a waiting thread to transition to the *runnable* state again. At this point, the thread that was transitioned from the *waiting* state to the *runnable* state can attempt to reacquire the monitor lock on the object. Even if the thread is able to reacquire the monitor lock, it still might not be able to perform its task at this time—in which case the thread will reenter the *waiting* state and implicitly release the monitor lock. If a thread calls **notifyAll** on the synchronized object, then all the threads waiting for the monitor lock become eligible to reacquire the lock (that is, they all transition to the *runnable* state). Remember that only one thread at a time can obtain the monitor lock on the object—other threads that attempt to acquire the same monitor lock will be *blocked* until the monitor lock becomes available again (i.e., until no other thread is executing in a synchronized statement on that object).

Common Programming Error 26.1

It's an error if a thread issues a `wait`*, a* `notify` *or a* `notifyAll` *on an object without having acquired a lock for it. This causes an* **IllegalMonitorStateException***.*

Error-Prevention Tip 26.2

It's a good practice to use `notifyAll` to notify waiting threads to become runnable. Doing so avoids the possibility that your program would forget about waiting threads, which would otherwise starve.

The application in Fig. 26.18 and Fig. 26.19 demonstrates a Producer and a Consumer accessing a shared buffer with synchronization. In this case, the Producer always produces a value first, the Consumer correctly consumes only after the Producer produces a value and the Producer correctly produces the next value only after the Consumer consumes the previous (or first) value. We reuse interface Buffer and classes Producer and Consumer from the example in Section 26.6, except that line 28 is removed from class Producer and class Consumer. The synchronization is handled in the set and get methods of class SynchronizedBuffer (Fig. 26.18), which implements interface Buffer (line 4). Thus, the Producer's and Consumer's run methods simply call the shared object's synchronized set and get methods.

```java
1   // Fig. 26.18: SynchronizedBuffer.java
2   // Synchronizing access to shared data using Object
3   // methods wait and notifyAll.
4   public class SynchronizedBuffer implements Buffer
5   {
6      private int buffer = -1; // shared by producer and consumer threads
7      private boolean occupied = false; // whether the buffer is occupied
8
9      // place value into buffer
10     public synchronized void set( int value ) throws InterruptedException
11     {
12        // while there are no empty locations, place thread in waiting state
13        while ( occupied )
14        {
15           // output thread information and buffer information, then wait
16           System.out.println( "Producer tries to write." );
17           displayState( "Buffer full. Producer waits." );
18           wait();
19        } // end while
20
21        buffer = value; // set new buffer value
22
23        // indicate producer cannot store another value
24        // until consumer retrieves current buffer value
25        occupied = true;
26
27        displayState( "Producer writes " + buffer );
28
29        notifyAll(); // tell waiting thread(s) to enter runnable state
30     } // end method set; releases lock on SynchronizedBuffer
31
32     // return value from buffer
33     public synchronized int get() throws InterruptedException
34     {
```

Fig. 26.18 | Synchronizing access to shared data using Object methods wait and notifyAll. (Part 1 of 2.)

```
35          // while no data to read, place thread in waiting state
36          while ( !occupied )
37          {
38             // output thread information and buffer information, then wait
39             System.out.println( "Consumer tries to read." );
40             displayState( "Buffer empty. Consumer waits." );
41             wait();
42          } // end while
43
44          // indicate that producer can store another value
45          // because consumer just retrieved buffer value
46          occupied = false;
47
48          displayState( "Consumer reads " + buffer );
49
50          notifyAll(); // tell waiting thread(s) to enter runnable state
51
52          return buffer;
53       } // end method get; releases lock on SynchronizedBuffer
54
55       // display current operation and buffer state
56       public void displayState( String operation )
57       {
58          System.out.printf( "%-40s%d\t\t%b\n\n", operation, buffer,
59             occupied );
60       } // end method displayState
61    } // end class SynchronizedBuffer
```

Fig. 26.18 | Synchronizing access to shared data using `Object` methods `wait` and `notifyAll`. (Part 2 of 2.)

Fields and Methods of Class *SynchronizedBuffer*

Class `SynchronizedBuffer` contains fields `buffer` (line 6) and `occupied` (line 7). Methods `set` (lines 10–30) and `get` (lines 33–53) are declared as synchronized—only one thread can call either of these methods at a time on a particular `SynchronizedBuffer` object. Field `occupied` is used to determine whether it's the `Producer`'s or the `Consumer`'s turn to perform a task. This field is used in conditional expressions in both the `set` and `get` methods. If `occupied` is `false`, then `buffer` is empty, so the `Consumer` cannot read the value of `buffer`, but the `Producer` can place a value into `buffer`. If `occupied` is `true`, the `Consumer` can read a value from `buffer`, but the `Producer` cannot place a value into `buffer`.

Method *set* and the *Producer Thread*

When the `Producer` thread's `run` method invokes synchronized method `set`, the thread implicitly attempts to acquire the `SynchronizedBuffer` object's monitor lock. If the monitor lock is available, the `Producer` thread implicitly acquires the lock. Then the loop at lines 13–19 first determines whether `occupied` is `true`. If so, `buffer` is full, so line 16 outputs a message indicating that the `Producer` thread is trying to write a value, and line 17 invokes method `displayState` (lines 56–60) to output another message indicating that `buffer` is full and that the `Producer` thread is waiting until there is space. Line 18 invokes method `wait` (inherited from `Object` by `SynchronizedBuffer`) to place the thread that called method `set` (i.e., the `Producer` thread) in the *waiting* state for the Synchronized-

Buffer object. The call to wait causes the calling thread to implicitly release the lock on the SynchronizedBuffer object. This is important because the thread cannot currently perform its task and because other threads (in this case, the Consumer) should be allowed to access the object to allow the condition (occupied) to change. Now another thread can attempt to acquire the SynchronizedBuffer object's lock and invoke the object's set or get method.

The Producer thread remains in the *waiting* state until another thread notifies the Producer that it may proceed—at which point the Producer returns to the *runnable* state and attempts to implicitly reacquire the lock on the SynchronizedBuffer object. If the lock is available, the Producer thread reacquires it, and method set continues executing with the next statement after the wait call. Because wait is called in a loop, the loop-continuation condition is tested again to determine whether the thread can proceed. If not, then wait is invoked again—otherwise, method set continues with the next statement after the loop.

Line 21 in method set assigns the value to the buffer. Line 25 sets occupied to true to indicate that the buffer now contains a value (i.e., a consumer can read the value, but a Producer cannot yet put another value there). Line 27 invokes method displayState to output a message indicating that the Producer is writing a new value into the buffer. Line 29 invokes method notifyAll (inherited from Object). If any threads are waiting on the SynchronizedBuffer object's monitor lock, those threads enter the *runnable* state and can now attempt to reacquire the lock. Method notifyAll returns immediately, and method set then returns to the caller (i.e., the Producer's run method). When method set returns, it implicitly releases the monitor lock on the SynchronizedBuffer object.

Method get and the Consumer Thread

Methods get and set are implemented similarly. When the Consumer thread's run method invokes synchronized method get, the thread attempts to acquire the monitor lock on the SynchronizedBuffer object. If the lock is available, the Consumer thread acquires it. Then the while loop at lines 36–42 determines whether occupied is false. If so, the buffer is empty, so line 39 outputs a message indicating that the Consumer thread is trying to read a value, and line 40 invokes method displayState to output a message indicating that the buffer is empty and that the Consumer thread is waiting. Line 41 invokes method wait to place the thread that called method get (i.e., the Consumer) in the *waiting* state for the SynchronizedBuffer object. Again, the call to wait causes the calling thread to implicitly release the lock on the SynchronizedBuffer object, so another thread can attempt to acquire the SynchronizedBuffer object's lock and invoke the object's set or get method. If the lock on the SynchronizedBuffer is not available (e.g., if the Producer has not yet returned from method set), the Consumer is blocked until the lock becomes available.

The Consumer thread remains in the *waiting* state until it's notified by another thread that it may proceed—at which point the Consumer thread returns to the *runnable* state and attempts to implicitly reacquire the lock on the SynchronizedBuffer object. If the lock is available, the Consumer reacquires it, and method get continues executing with the next statement after wait. Because wait is called in a loop, the loop-continuation condition is tested again to determine whether the thread can proceed with its execution. If not, wait is invoked again—otherwise, method get continues with the next statement after the loop. Line 46 sets occupied to false to indicate that buffer is now empty (i.e., a Consumer cannot read the value, but a Producer can place another value in buffer), line 48 calls method `displayState` to indicate that the consumer is reading and line 50 invokes method `notifyAll`. If any threads are in the *waiting* state for the lock on this SynchronizedBuffer object, they enter the *runnable* state and can now attempt to reacquire the lock. Method `notifyAll` returns immediately, then method `get` returns the value of `buffer` to its caller. When method `get` returns, the lock on the SynchronizedBuffer object is implicitly released.

> **Error-Prevention Tip 26.3**
>
> *Always invoke method* `wait` *in a loop that tests the condition the task is waiting on. It's possible that a thread will reenter the* runnable *state (via a timed wait or another thread calling* `notifyAll`*) before the condition is satisfied. Testing the condition again ensures that the thread will not erroneously execute if it was notified early.*

Testing Class *SynchronizedBuffer*

Class SharedBufferTest2 (Fig. 26.19) is similar to class SharedBufferTest (Fig. 26.15). SharedBufferTest2 contains method main (lines 8–24), which launches the application. Line 11 creates an ExecutorService to run the Producer and Consumer tasks. Line 14 creates a SynchronizedBuffer object and assigns its reference to Buffer variable sharedLocation. This object stores the data that will be shared between the Producer and Consumer. Lines 16–17 display the column heads for the output. Lines 20–21 execute a Producer and a Consumer. Finally, line 23 calls method shutdown to end the application when the Producer and Consumer complete their tasks. When method main ends (line 24), the main thread of execution terminates.

```java
1   // Fig. 26.19: SharedBufferTest2.java
2   // Two threads correctly manipulating a synchronized buffer.
3   import java.util.concurrent.ExecutorService;
4   import java.util.concurrent.Executors;
5
6   public class SharedBufferTest2
7   {
8      public static void main( String[] args )
9      {
10        // create a newCachedThreadPool
11        ExecutorService application = Executors.newCachedThreadPool();
12
13        // create SynchronizedBuffer to store ints
14        Buffer sharedLocation = new SynchronizedBuffer();
15
16        System.out.printf( "%-40s%s\t\t%s\n%-40s%s\n\n", "Operation",
17           "Buffer", "Occupied", "---------", "------\t\t--------" );
18
19        // execute the Producer and Consumer tasks
20        application.execute( new Producer( sharedLocation ) );
21        application.execute( new Consumer( sharedLocation ) );
22
23        application.shutdown();
24     } // end main
25  } // end class SharedBufferTest2
```

Fig. 26.19 | Two threads correctly manipulating a synchronized buffer. (Part 1 of 3.)

```
Operation                              Buffer      Occupied
---------                              ------      --------

Consumer tries to read.
Buffer empty. Consumer waits.          -1          false

Producer writes 1                      1           true

Consumer reads 1                       1           false

Consumer tries to read.
Buffer empty. Consumer waits.          1           false

Producer writes 2                      2           true

Consumer reads 2                       2           false

Producer writes 3                      3           true

Consumer reads 3                       3           false

Producer writes 4                      4           true

Producer tries to write.
Buffer full. Producer waits.           4           true

Consumer reads 4                       4           false

Producer writes 5                      5           true

Consumer reads 5                       5           false

Producer writes 6                      6           true

Producer tries to write.
Buffer full. Producer waits.           6           true

Consumer reads 6                       6           false

Producer writes 7                      7           true

Producer tries to write.
Buffer full. Producer waits.           7           true

Consumer reads 7                       7           false

Producer writes 8                      8           true

Consumer reads 8                       8           false

Consumer tries to read.
Buffer empty. Consumer waits.          8           false

Producer writes 9                      9           true

Consumer reads 9                       9           false
```

Fig. 26.19 | Two threads correctly manipulating a synchronized buffer. (Part 2 of 3.)

```
Consumer tries to read.
Buffer empty. Consumer waits.            9              false

Producer writes 10                      10              true

Consumer reads 10                       10              false


Producer done producing
Terminating Producer

Consumer read values totaling 55
Terminating Consumer
```

Fig. 26.19 | Two threads correctly manipulating a synchronized buffer. (Part 3 of 3.)

Study the outputs in Fig. 26.19. Observe that every integer produced is consumed exactly once—no values are lost, and no values are consumed more than once. The synchronization ensures that the Producer produces a value only when the buffer is empty and the Consumer consumes only when the buffer is full. The Producer always goes first, the Consumer waits if the Producer has not produced since the Consumer last consumed, and the Producer waits if the Consumer has not yet consumed the value that the Producer most recently produced. Execute this program several times to confirm that every integer produced is consumed exactly once. In the sample output, note the highlighted lines indicating when the Producer and Consumer must wait to perform their respective tasks.

26.9 Producer/Consumer Relationship: Bounded Buffers

The program in Section 26.8 uses thread synchronization to guarantee that two threads manipulate data in a shared buffer correctly. However, the application may not perform optimally. If the two threads operate at different speeds, one them will spend more (or most) of its time waiting. For example, in the program in Section 26.8 we shared a single integer variable between the two threads. If the Producer thread produces values faster than the Consumer can consume them, then the Producer thread waits for the Consumer, because there are no other locations in the buffer in which to place the next value. Similarly, if the Consumer consumes values faster than the Producer produces them, the Consumer waits until the Producer places the next value in the shared buffer. Even when we have threads that operate at the same relative speeds, those threads may occasionally become "out of sync" over a period of time, causing one of them to wait for the other. *We cannot make assumptions about the relative speeds of concurrent threads*—interactions that occur with the operating system, the network, the user and other components can cause the threads to operate at different speeds. When this happens, threads wait. When threads wait excessively, programs become less efficient, interactive programs become less responsive and applications suffer longer delays.

Bounded Buffers
To minimize the amount of waiting time for threads that share resources and operate at the same average speeds, we can implement a **bounded buffer** that provides a fixed number of buffer cells into which the Producer can place values, and from which the Consumer can retrieve those values. (In fact, we've already done this with the ArrayBlockingQueue class in Section 26.7.) If the Producer temporarily produces values faster than the Consumer can

consume them, the Producer can write additional values into the extra buffer cells, if any are available. This capability enables the Producer to perform its task even though the Consumer is not ready to retrieve the current value being produced. Similarly, if the Consumer consumes faster than the Producer produces new values, the Consumer can read additional values (if there are any) from the buffer. This enables the Consumer to keep busy even though the Producer is not ready to produce additional values.

Even a bounded buffer is inappropriate if the Producer and the Consumer operate consistently at different speeds. If the Consumer always executes faster than the Producer, then a buffer containing one location is enough. Additional locations would simply waste memory. If the Producer always executes faster, only a buffer with an "infinite" number of locations would be able to absorb the extra production. However, if the Producer and Consumer execute at about the same average speed, a bounded buffer helps to smooth the effects of any occasional speeding up or slowing down in either thread's execution.

The key to using a bounded buffer with a Producer and Consumer that operate at about the same speed is to provide the buffer with enough locations to handle the anticipated "extra" production. If, over a period of time, we determine that the Producer often produces as many as three more values than the Consumer can consume, we can provide a buffer of at least three cells to handle the extra production. Making the buffer too small would cause threads to wait longer; making the buffer too large would waste memory.

Performance Tip 26.3
Even when using a bounded buffer, it's possible that a producer thread could fill the buffer, which would force the producer to wait until a consumer consumed a value to free an element in the buffer. Similarly, if the buffer is empty at any given time, a consumer thread must wait until the producer produces another value. The key to using a bounded buffer is to optimize the buffer size to minimize the amount of thread wait time, while not wasting space.

Bounded Buffers Using *ArrayBlockingQueue*

The simplest way to implement a bounded buffer is to use an ArrayBlockingQueue for the buffer so that *all of the synchronization details are handled for you*. This can be done by reusing the example from Section 26.7 and simply passing the desired size for the bounded buffer into the ArrayBlockingQueue constructor. Rather than repeat our previous ArrayBlockingQueue example with a different size, we instead present an example that illustrates how you can build a bounded buffer yourself. Again, note that using an ArrayBlockingQueue will result in more-maintainable and better-performing code. In Exercise 26.8, we ask you to reimplement this section's example, using the Java Concurrency API techniques presented in Section 26.10.

Implementing Your Own Bounded Buffer as a Circular Buffer

The program in Fig. 26.20 and Fig. 26.21 demonstrates a Producer and a Consumer accessing a bounded buffer with synchronization. Again, we reuse interface Buffer and classes Producer and Consumer from the example in Section 26.6, except that line 28 is removed from class Producer and class Consumer. We implement the bounded buffer in class CircularBuffer (Fig. 26.20) as a **circular buffer** that uses a shared array of three elements. A circular buffer writes into and reads from the array elements in order, beginning at the first cell and moving toward the last. When a Producer or Consumer reaches the last element, it returns to the first and begins writing or reading, respectively, from there. In this version of the producer/consumer relationship, the Consumer consumes a value only when the array is not empty and the Producer produces a value only when the array is not full. The statements that created and started the thread objects in the main method of class SharedBufferTest2 (Fig. 26.19) now appear in class CircularBufferTest (Fig. 26.21).

```java
 1   // Fig. 26.20: CircularBuffer.java
 2   // Synchronizing access to a shared three-element bounded buffer.
 3   public class CircularBuffer implements Buffer
 4   {
 5      private final int[] buffer = { -1, -1, -1 }; // shared buffer
 6
 7      private int occupiedCells = 0; // count number of buffers used
 8      private int writeIndex = 0; // index of next element to write to
 9      private int readIndex = 0; // index of next element to read
10
11      // place value into buffer
12      public synchronized void set( int value ) throws InterruptedException
13      {
14         // wait until buffer has space avaialble, then write value;
15         // while no empty locations, place thread in blocked state
16         while ( occupiedCells == buffer.length )
17         {
18            System.out.printf( "Buffer is full. Producer waits.\n" );
19            wait(); // wait until a buffer cell is free
20         } // end while
21
22         buffer[ writeIndex ] = value; // set new buffer value
23
24         // update circular write index
25         writeIndex = ( writeIndex + 1 ) % buffer.length;
26
27         ++occupiedCells; // one more buffer cell is full
28         displayState( "Producer writes " + value );
29         notifyAll(); // notify threads waiting to read from buffer
30      } // end method set
31
32      // return value from buffer
33      public synchronized int get() throws InterruptedException
34      {
35         // wait until buffer has data, then read value;
36         // while no data to read, place thread in waiting state
37         while ( occupiedCells == 0 )
38         {
39            System.out.printf( "Buffer is empty. Consumer waits.\n" );
40            wait(); // wait until a buffer cell is filled
41         } // end while
42
43         int readValue = buffer[ readIndex ]; // read value from buffer
44
45         // update circular read index
46         readIndex = ( readIndex + 1 ) % buffer.length;
47
48         --occupiedCells; // one fewer buffer cells are occupied
```

Fig. 26.20 | Synchronizing access to a shared three-element bounded buffer. (Part 1 of 2.)

```
49              displayState( "Consumer reads " + readValue );
50              notifyAll(); // notify threads waiting to write to buffer
51
52              return readValue;
53          } // end method get
54
55          // display current operation and buffer state
56          public void displayState( String operation )
57          {
58              // output operation and number of occupied buffer cells
59              System.out.printf( "%s%s%d)\n%s", operation,
60                  " (buffer cells occupied: ", occupiedCells, "buffer cells:   " );
61
62              for ( int value : buffer )
63                  System.out.printf( " %2d  ", value ); // output values in buffer
64
65              System.out.print( "\n                " );
66
67              for ( int i = 0; i < buffer.length; i++ )
68                  System.out.print( "---- " );
69
70              System.out.print( "\n                " );
71
72              for ( int i = 0; i < buffer.length; i++ )
73              {
74                  if ( i == writeIndex && i == readIndex )
75                      System.out.print( " WR" ); // both write and read index
76                  else if ( i == writeIndex )
77                      System.out.print( " W   " ); // just write index
78                  else if ( i == readIndex )
79                      System.out.print( "  R   " ); // just read index
80                  else
81                      System.out.print( "      " ); // neither index
82              } // end for
83
84              System.out.println( "\n" );
85          } // end method displayState
86      } // end class CircularBuffer
```

Fig. 26.20 | Synchronizing access to a shared three-element bounded buffer. (Part 2 of 2.)

Line 5 initializes array buffer as a three-element int array that represents the circular buffer. Variable occupiedCells (line 7) counts the number of elements in buffer that contain data to be read. When occupiedBuffers is 0, there is no data in the circular buffer and the Consumer must wait—when occupiedCells is 3 (the size of the circular buffer), the circular buffer is full and the Producer must wait. Variable writeIndex (line 8) indicates the next location in which a value can be placed by a Producer. Variable readIndex (line 9) indicates the position from which the next value can be read by a Consumer.

CircularBuffer Method set
CircularBuffer method set (lines 12–30) performs the same tasks as in Fig. 26.18, with a few modifications. The loop at lines 16–20 determines whether the Producer must wait (i.e., all buffer cells are full). If so, line 18 indicates that the Producer is waiting to perform

its task. Then line 19 invokes method wait, causing the Producer thread to release the CircularBuffer's lock and wait until there is space for a new value to be written into the buffer. When execution continues at line 22 after the while loop, the value written by the Producer is placed in the circular buffer at location writeIndex. Then line 25 updates writeIndex for the next call to CircularBuffer method set. This line is the key to the buffer's "circularity." When writeIndex is incremented past the end of the buffer, the line sets it to 0. Line 27 increments occupiedCells, because there is now one more value in the buffer that the Consumer can read. Next, line 28 invokes method displayState (lines 56–85) to update the output with the value produced, the number of occupied buffer cells, the contents of the buffer cells and the current writeIndex and readIndex. Line 29 invokes method notifyAll to transition *waiting* threads to the runnable state, so that a waiting Consumer thread (if there is one) can now try again to read a value from the buffer.

CircularBuffer *Method* get

CircularBuffer method get (lines 33–53) also performs the same tasks as it did in Fig. 26.18, with a few minor modifications. The loop at lines 37–41 determines whether the Consumer must wait (i.e., all buffer cells are empty). If the Consumer must wait, line 39 updates the output to indicate that the Consumer is waiting to perform its task. Then line 40 invokes method wait, causing the current thread to release the lock on the Circular-Buffer and wait until data is available to read. When execution eventually continues at line 43 after a notifyAll call from the Producer, readValue is assigned the value at location readIndex in the circular buffer. Then line 46 updates readIndex for the next call to CircularBuffer method get. This line and line 25 implement the "circularity" of the buffer. Line 48 decrements occupiedCells, because there is now one more position in the buffer in which the Producer thread can place a value. Line 49 invokes method display-State to update the output with the consumed value, the number of occupied buffer cells, the contents of the buffer cells and the current writeIndex and readIndex. Line 50 invokes method notifyAll to allow any Producer threads waiting to write into the Circular-Buffer object to attempt to write again. Then line 52 returns the consumed value to the caller.

CircularBuffer *Method* displayState

Method displayState (lines 56–85) outputs the application's state. Lines 62–63 output the values of the buffer cells. Line 63 uses method printf with a "%2d" format specifier to print the contents of each buffer with a leading space if it's a single digit. Lines 70–82 output the current writeIndex and readIndex with the letters W and R, respectively.

Testing Class *CircularBuffer*

Class CircularBufferTest (Fig. 26.21) contains the main method that launches the application. Line 11 creates the ExecutorService, and line 14 creates a CircularBuffer object and assigns its reference to CircularBuffer variable sharedLocation. Line 17 invokes the CircularBuffer's displayState method to show the initial state of the buffer. Lines 20–21 execute the Producer and Consumer tasks. Line 23 calls method shutdown to end the application when the threads complete the Producer and Consumer tasks.

Each time the Producer writes a value or the Consumer reads a value, the program outputs a message indicating the action performed (a read or a write), the contents of buffer, and the location of writeIndex and readIndex. In the output of Fig. 26.21, the Producer first writes the value 1. The buffer then contains the value 1 in the first cell and the value

–1 (the default value that we use for output purposes) in the other two cells. The write index is updated to the second cell, while the read index stays at the first cell. Next, the Consumer reads 1. The buffer contains the same values, but the read index has been updated to the second cell. The Consumer then tries to read again, but the buffer is empty and the Consumer is forced to wait. Note that only once in this execution of the program was it necessary for either thread to wait.

```
1   // Fig. 26.21: CircularBufferTest.java
2   // Producer and Consumer threads manipulating a circular buffer.
3   import java.util.concurrent.ExecutorService;
4   import java.util.concurrent.Executors;
5
6   public class CircularBufferTest
7   {
8      public static void main( String[] args )
9      {
10        // create new thread pool with two threads
11        ExecutorService application = Executors.newCachedThreadPool();
12
13        // create CircularBuffer to store ints
14        CircularBuffer sharedLocation = new CircularBuffer();
15
16        // display the initial state of the CircularBuffer
17        sharedLocation.displayState( "Initial State" );
18
19        // execute the Producer and Consumer tasks
20        application.execute( new Producer( sharedLocation ) );
21        application.execute( new Consumer( sharedLocation ) );
22
23        application.shutdown();
24     } // end main
25  } // end class CircularBufferTest
```

```
Initial State (buffer cells occupied: 0)
buffer cells:    -1    -1    -1
                ----  ----  ----
                 WR

Producer writes 1 (buffer cells occupied: 1)
buffer cells:     1    -1    -1
                ----  ----  ----
                  R     W

Consumer reads 1 (buffer cells occupied: 0)
buffer cells:     1    -1    -1
                ----  ----  ----
                        WR

Buffer is empty. Consumer waits.
Producer writes 2 (buffer cells occupied: 1)
buffer cells:     1     2    -1
                ----  ----  ----
                        R     W
```

Fig. 26.21 | Producer and Consumer threads manipulating a circular buffer. (Part 1 of 3.)

```
Consumer reads 2 (buffer cells occupied: 0)
buffer cells:    1    2   -1
                ---- ---- ----
                          WR

Producer writes 3 (buffer cells occupied: 1)
buffer cells:    1    2    3
                ---- ---- ----
                 W         R

Consumer reads 3 (buffer cells occupied: 0)
buffer cells:    1    2    3
                ---- ---- ----
                WR

Producer writes 4 (buffer cells occupied: 1)
buffer cells:    4    2    3
                ---- ---- ----
                 R    W

Producer writes 5 (buffer cells occupied: 2)
buffer cells:    4    5    3
                ---- ---- ----
                 R         W

Consumer reads 4 (buffer cells occupied: 1)
buffer cells:    4    5    3
                ---- ---- ----
                      R    W

Producer writes 6 (buffer cells occupied: 2)
buffer cells:    4    5    6
                ---- ---- ----
                 W    R

Producer writes 7 (buffer cells occupied: 3)
buffer cells:    7    5    6
                ---- ---- ----
                      WR

Consumer reads 5 (buffer cells occupied: 2)
buffer cells:    7    5    6
                ---- ---- ----
                      W    R

Producer writes 8 (buffer cells occupied: 3)
buffer cells:    7    8    6
                ---- ---- ----
                          WR

Consumer reads 6 (buffer cells occupied: 2)
buffer cells:    7    8    6
                ---- ---- ----
                 R         W

Consumer reads 7 (buffer cells occupied: 1)
buffer cells:    7    8    6
                ---- ---- ----
                      R    W
```

Fig. 26.21 | Producer and Consumer threads manipulating a circular buffer. (Part 2 of 3.)

```
Producer writes 9 (buffer cells occupied: 2)
buffer cells:    7    8    9
                ---- ---- ----
                 W    R

Consumer reads 8 (buffer cells occupied: 1)
buffer cells:    7    8    9
                ---- ---- ----
                 W         R

Consumer reads 9 (buffer cells occupied: 0)
buffer cells:    7    8    9
                ---- ---- ----
                 WR

Producer writes 10 (buffer cells occupied: 1)
buffer cells:    10   8    9
                ---- ---- ----
                 R    W


Producer done producing
Terminating Producer
Consumer reads 10 (buffer cells occupied: 0)
buffer cells:    10   8    9
                ---- ---- ----
                      WR


Consumer read values totaling: 55
Terminating Consumer
```

Fig. 26.21 | Producer and Consumer threads manipulating a circular buffer. (Part 3 of 3.)

26.10 Producer/Consumer Relationship: The Lock and Condition Interfaces

Though the synchronized keyword provides for most basic thread-synchronization needs, Java provides other tools to assist in developing concurrent programs. In this section, we discuss the Lock and Condition interfaces, which were introduced in Java SE 5. These interfaces give you more precise control over thread synchronization, but are more complicated to use.

Interface Lock and Class ReentrantLock

Any object can contain a reference to an object that implements the **Lock** interface (of package java.util.concurrent.locks). A thread calls the Lock's **lock** method to acquire the lock. Once a Lock has been obtained by one thread, the Lock object will not allow another thread to obtain the Lock until the first thread releases the Lock (by calling the Lock's **unlock** method). If several threads are trying to call method lock on the same Lock object at the same time, only one of these threads can obtain the lock—all the others are placed in the *waiting* state for that lock. When a thread calls method unlock, the lock on the object is released and a waiting thread attempting to lock the object proceeds.

Class **ReentrantLock** (of package java.util.concurrent.locks) is a basic implementation of the Lock interface. The constructor for a ReentrantLock takes a boolean argument that specifies whether the lock has a **fairness policy**. If the argument is true, the ReentrantLock's fairness policy is "the longest-waiting thread will acquire the lock when it's available." Such a fairness policy guarantees that indefinite postponement (also called starvation) cannot occur. If the fairness policy argument is set to false, there is no guarantee as to which waiting thread will acquire the lock when it's available.

Software Engineering Observation 26.2

Using a ReentrantLock with a fairness policy avoids indefinite postponement.

Performance Tip 26.4

Using a ReentrantLock with a fairness policy can decrease program performance significantly.

Condition Objects and Interface `Condition`

If a thread that owns a Lock determines that it cannot continue with its task until some condition is satisfied, the thread can wait on a **condition object.** Using Lock objects allows you to explicitly declare the condition objects on which a thread may need to wait. For example, in the producer/consumer relationship, producers can wait on one object and consumers can wait on another. This is not possible when using the synchronized keywords and an object's built-in monitor lock. Condition objects are associated with a specific Lock and are created by calling a Lock's **newCondition** method, which returns an object that implements the **Condition** interface (of package java.util.concurrent.locks). To wait on a condition object, the thread can call the Condition's **await** method. This immediately releases the associated Lock and places the thread in the *waiting* state for that Condition. Other threads can then try to obtain the Lock. When a *runnable* thread completes a task and determines that the *waiting* thread can now continue, the *runnable* thread can call Condition method **signal** to allow a thread in that Condition's *waiting* state to return to the *runnable* state. At this point, the thread that transitioned from the *waiting* state to the *runnable* state can attempt to reacquire the Lock. Even if it's able to reacquire the Lock, the thread still might not be able to perform its task at this time—in which case the thread can call the Condition's await method to release the Lock and reenter the *waiting* state. If multiple threads are in a Condition's *waiting* state when signal is called, the default implementation of Condition signals the longest-waiting thread to transition to the *runnable* state. If a thread calls Condition method **signalAll**, then all the threads waiting for that condition transition to the *runnable* state and become eligible to reacquire the Lock. Only one of those threads can obtain the Lock on the object—the others will wait until the Lock becomes available again. If the Lock has a fairness policy, the longest-waiting thread acquires the Lock. When a thread is finished with a shared object, it must call method unlock to release the Lock.

Common Programming Error 26.2

Deadlock occurs when a waiting thread (let's call this thread1) cannot proceed because it's waiting (either directly or indirectly) for another thread (let's call this thread2) to proceed, while simultaneously thread2 cannot proceed because it's waiting (either directly or indirectly) for thread1 to proceed. The two threads are waiting for each other, so the actions that would enable each thread to continue execution can never occur.

Error-Prevention Tip 26.4

When multiple threads manipulate a shared object using locks, ensure that if one thread calls method await *to enter the* waiting *state for a condition object, a separate thread eventually will call* Condition *method* signal *to transition the thread waiting on the condition object back to the* runnable *state. If multiple threads may be waiting on the condition object, a separate thread can call* Condition *method* signalAll *as a safeguard to ensure that all the waiting threads have another opportunity to perform their tasks. If this is not done, starvation might occur.*

Common Programming Error 26.3

An IllegalMonitorStateException *occurs if a thread issues an* await*, a* signal*, or a* signalAll *on a* Condition *object that was created from a* ReentrantLock *without having acquired the lock for that* Condition *object.*

Lock *and* Condition *vs. the* synchronized *Keyword*

In some applications, using Lock and Condition objects may be preferable to using the synchronized keyword. Locks allow you to interrupt waiting threads or to specify a time-out for waiting to acquire a lock, which is not possible using the synchronized keyword. Also, a Lock is not constrained to be acquired and released in the same block of code, which is the case with the synchronized keyword. Condition objects allow you to specify multiple conditions on which threads may wait. Thus, it's possible to indicate to waiting threads that a specific condition object is now true by calling signal or signalAll on that Condition object. With the synchronized keyword, there is no way to explicitly state the condition on which threads are waiting, and thus there is no way to notify threads waiting on one condition that they may proceed without also signaling threads waiting on any other conditions. There are other possible advantages to using Lock and Condition objects, but note that generally it's best to use the synchronized keyword unless your application requires advanced synchronization capabilities.

Error-Prevention Tip 26.5

Using interfaces Lock *and* Condition *is error prone—*unlock *is not guaranteed to be called, whereas the monitor in a* synchronized *statement will always be released when the statement completes execution.*

Using Locks *and* Conditions *to Implement Synchronization*

To illustrate how to use the Lock and Condition interfaces, we now implement the producer/consumer relationship using Lock and Condition objects to coordinate access to a shared single-element buffer (Fig. 26.22 and Fig. 26.23). In this case, each produced value is correctly consumed exactly once. Again, we reuse interface Buffer and classes Producer and Consumer from the example in Section 26.6, except that line 28 is removed from class Producer and class Consumer.

Class SynchronizedBuffer (Fig. 26.22) contains five fields. Line 11 creates a new object of type ReentrantLock and assigns its reference to Lock variable accessLock. The ReentrantLock is created without the fairness policy because at any time only a single Producer or Consumer will be waiting to acquire the Lock in this example. Lines 14–15 create two Conditions using Lock method newCondition. Condition canWrite contains a queue for a Producer thread waiting while the buffer is full (i.e., there is data in the buffer that the Consumer has not read yet). If the buffer is full, the Producer calls method await on this Condition. When the Consumer reads data from a full buffer, it calls method signal on this Condition. Condition canRead contains a queue for a Consumer thread waiting while the buffer is empty (i.e., there is no data in the buffer for the Consumer to read). If the buffer is empty, the Consumer calls method await on this Condition. When the Producer writes to the empty buffer, it calls method signal on this Condition. The int variable buffer (line 17) holds the shared data. The boolean variable occupied (line 18) keeps track of whether the buffer currently holds data (that the Consumer should read).

```
1   // Fig. 26.22: SynchronizedBuffer.java
2   // Synchronizing access to a shared integer using the Lock and Condition
3   // interfaces
4   import java.util.concurrent.locks.Lock;
5   import java.util.concurrent.locks.ReentrantLock;
6   import java.util.concurrent.locks.Condition;
7
8   public class SynchronizedBuffer implements Buffer
9   {
10     // Lock to control synchronization with this buffer
11     private final Lock accessLock = new ReentrantLock();
12
13     // conditions to control reading and writing
14     private final Condition canWrite = accessLock.newCondition();
15     private final Condition canRead = accessLock.newCondition();
16
17     private int buffer = -1; // shared by producer and consumer threads
18     private boolean occupied = false; // whether buffer is occupied
19
20     // place int value into buffer
21     public void set( int value ) throws InterruptedException
22     {
23        accessLock.lock(); // lock this object
24
25        // output thread information and buffer information, then wait
26        try
27        {
28           // while buffer is not empty, place thread in waiting state
29           while ( occupied )
30           {
31              System.out.println( "Producer tries to write." );
32              displayState( "Buffer full. Producer waits." );
33              canWrite.await(); // wait until buffer is empty
34           } // end while
35
36           buffer = value; // set new buffer value
37
38           // indicate producer cannot store another value
39           // until consumer retrieves current buffer value
40           occupied = true;
41
42           displayState( "Producer writes " + buffer );
```

Fig. 26.22 | Synchronizing access to a shared integer using the Lock and Condition interfaces. (Part 1 of 2.)

```
43
44                // signal thread waiting to read from buffer
45                canRead.signal();
46            } // end try
47            finally
48            {
49                accessLock.unlock(); // unlock this object
50            } // end finally
51        } // end method set
52
53        // return value from buffer
54        public int get() throws InterruptedException
55        {
56            int readValue = 0; // initialize value read from buffer
57            accessLock.lock(); // lock this object
58
59            // output thread information and buffer information, then wait
60            try
61            {
62                // if there is no data to read, place thread in waiting state
63                while ( !occupied )
64                {
65                    System.out.println( "Consumer tries to read." );
66                    displayState( "Buffer empty. Consumer waits." );
67                    canRead.await(); // wait until buffer is full
68                } // end while
69
70                // indicate that producer can store another value
71                // because consumer just retrieved buffer value
72                occupied = false;
73
74                readValue = buffer; // retrieve value from buffer
75                displayState( "Consumer reads " + readValue );
76
77                // signal thread waiting for buffer to be empty
78                canWrite.signal();
79            } // end try
80            finally
81            {
82                accessLock.unlock(); // unlock this object
83            } // end finally
84
85            return readValue;
86        } // end method get
87
88        // display current operation and buffer state
89        public void displayState( String operation )
90        {
91            System.out.printf( "%-40s%d\t\t%b\n\n", operation, buffer,
92                occupied );
93        } // end method displayState
94    } // end class SynchronizedBuffer
```

Fig. 26.22 | Synchronizing access to a shared integer using the Lock and Condition interfaces. (Part 2 of 2.)

Line 23 in method set calls method lock on the SynchronizedBuffer's accessLock. If the lock is available (i.e., no other thread has acquired it), this thread now owns the lock and the thread continues. If the lock is unavailable (i.e., it's held by another thread), method lock waits until the lock is released. After the lock is acquired, lines 26–46 execute. Line 29 tests occupied to determine whether buffer is full. If it is, lines 31–32 display a message indicating that the thread will wait. Line 33 calls Condition method await on the canWrite condition object, which temporarily releases the SynchronizedBuffer's Lock and waits for a signal from the Consumer that buffer is available for writing. When buffer is available, the method proceeds, writing to buffer (line 36), setting occupied to true (line 40) and displaying a message indicating that the producer wrote a value (line 42). Line 45 calls Condition method signal on condition object canRead to notify the waiting Consumer (if there is one) that the buffer has new data to be read. Line 49 calls method unlock from a finally block to release the lock and allow the Consumer to proceed.

Error-Prevention Tip 26.6

Place calls to Lock method unlock in a finally block. If an exception is thrown, unlock must still be called or deadlock could occur.

Line 57 of method get (lines 54–86) calls method lock to acquire the Lock. This method waits until the Lock is available. Once the Lock is acquired, line 63 tests whether occupied is false, indicating that the buffer is empty. If so, line 67 calls method await on condition object canRead. Recall that method signal is called on variable canRead in the set method (line 45). When the Condition object is signaled, the get method continues. Line 72–74 set occupied to false, store the value of buffer in readValue and output the readValue. Then line 78 signals the condition object canWrite. This awakens the Producer if it's indeed waiting for the buffer to be emptied. Line 82 calls method unlock from a finally block to release the lock, and line 85 returns readValue to the caller.

Common Programming Error 26.4

Forgetting to signal a waiting thread is a logic error. The thread will remain in the waiting state, which will prevent it from proceeding. Such waiting can lead to indefinite postponement or deadlock.

Class SharedBufferTest2 (Fig. 26.23) is identical to that of Fig. 26.19. Study the outputs in Fig. 26.23. Observe that every integer produced is consumed exactly once—no values are lost, and no values are consumed more than once. The Lock and Condition objects ensure that the Producer and Consumer cannot perform their tasks unless it's their turn. The Producer must go first, the Consumer must wait if the Producer has not produced since the Consumer last consumed and the Producer must wait if the Consumer has not yet consumed the value that the Producer most recently produced. Execute this program several times to confirm that every integer produced is consumed exactly once. In the sample output, note the highlighted lines indicating when the Producer and Consumer must wait to perform their respective tasks.

```
1   // Fig. 26.23: SharedBufferTest2.java
2   // Two threads manipulating a synchronized buffer.
3   import java.util.concurrent.ExecutorService;
```

Fig. 26.23 | Two threads manipulating a synchronized buffer. (Part 1 of 3.)

```
 4    import java.util.concurrent.Executors;
 5
 6    public class SharedBufferTest2
 7    {
 8       public static void main( String[] args )
 9       {
10          // create new thread pool with two threads
11          ExecutorService application = Executors.newCachedThreadPool();
12
13          // create SynchronizedBuffer to store ints
14          Buffer sharedLocation = new SynchronizedBuffer();
15
16          System.out.printf( "%-40s%s\t\t%s\n%-40s%s\n\n", "Operation",
17             "Buffer", "Occupied", "---------", "------\t\t--------" );
18
19          // execute the Producer and Consumer tasks
20          application.execute( new Producer( sharedLocation ) );
21          application.execute( new Consumer( sharedLocation ) );
22
23          application.shutdown();
24       } // end main
25    } // end class SharedBufferTest2
```

Operation	Buffer	Occupied
Producer writes 1	1	true
Producer tries to write. Buffer full. Producer waits.	1	true
Consumer reads 1	1	false
Producer writes 2	2	true
Producer tries to write. Buffer full. Producer waits.	2	true
Consumer reads 2	2	false
Producer writes 3	3	true
Consumer reads 3	3	false
Producer writes 4	4	true
Consumer reads 4	4	false
Consumer tries to read. Buffer empty. Consumer waits.	4	false
Producer writes 5	5	true
Consumer reads 5	5	false
Consumer tries to read. Buffer empty. Consumer waits.	5	false
Producer writes 6	6	true

Fig. 26.23 | Two threads manipulating a synchronized buffer. (Part 2 of 3.)

Consumer reads 6	6	false
Producer writes 7	7	true
Consumer reads 7	7	false
Producer writes 8	8	true
Consumer reads 8	8	false
Producer writes 9	9	true
Consumer reads 9	9	false
Producer writes 10	10	true
Producer done producing		
Terminating Producer		
Consumer reads 10	10	false
Consumer read values totaling 55		
Terminating Consumer		

Fig. 26.23 | Two threads manipulating a synchronized buffer. (Part 3 of 3.)

26.11 Multithreading with GUI

Swing applications present a unique set of challenges for multithreaded programming. All Swing applications have a single thread, called the **event dispatch thread**, to handle interactions with the application's GUI components. Typical interactions include updating GUI components or processing user actions such as mouse clicks. All tasks that require interaction with an application's GUI are placed in an event queue and are executed sequentially by the event dispatch thread.

Swing GUI components are not thread safe—they cannot be manipulated by multiple threads without the risk of incorrect results. Unlike the other examples presented in this chapter, thread safety in GUI applications is achieved not by synchronizing thread actions, but by ensuring that Swing components are accessed from only a single thread—the event dispatch thread. This technique is called **thread confinement**. Allowing just one thread to access non-thread-safe objects eliminates the possibility of corruption due to multiple threads accessing these objects concurrently.

Usually it's sufficient to perform simple calculations on the event dispatch thread in sequence with GUI component manipulations. If an application must perform a lengthy computation in response to a user interface interaction, the event dispatch thread cannot attend to other tasks in the event queue while the thread is tied up in that computation. This causes the GUI components to become unresponsive. It's preferable to handle a long-running computation in a separate thread, freeing the event dispatch thread to continue managing other GUI interactions. Of course, to update the GUI based on the computation's results, you must update the GUI from the event dispatch thread, rather than from the worker thread that performed the computation.

Class *SwingWorker*

Java SE 6 provides class **SwingWorker** (in package javax.swing) to perform long-running computations in a worker thread and to update Swing components from the event dispatch thread based on the computations' results. SwingWorker implements the Runnable interface, meaning that a SwingWorker object can be scheduled to execute in a separate thread. The SwingWorker class provides several methods to simplify performing computations in a worker thread and making the results available for display in a GUI. Some common SwingWorker methods are described in Fig. 26.24.

Method	Description
doInBackground	Defines a long computation and is called in a worker thread.
done	Executes on the event dispatch thread when doInBackground returns.
execute	Schedules the SwingWorker object to be executed in a worker thread.
get	Waits for the computation to complete, then returns the result of the computation (i.e., the return value of doInBackground).
publish	Sends intermediate results from the doInBackground method to the process method for processing on the event dispatch thread.
process	Receives intermediate results from the publish method and processes these results on the event dispatch thread.
setProgress	Sets the progress property to notify any property change listeners on the event dispatch thread of progress bar updates.

Fig. 26.24 | Commonly used SwingWorker methods.

26.11.1 Performing Computations in a Worker Thread

In the next example, the user enters a number *n* and the program gets the *n*th Fibonacci number, which we calculate using the recursive algorithm discussed in Section 18.4. Since the algorithm is time consuming for large values, we use a SwingWorker object to perform the calculation in a worker thread. The GUI also provides a separate set of components that get the next Fibonacci number in the sequence with each click of a button, beginning with fibonacci(1). This set of components performs its short computation directly in the event dispatch thread. Note that this program is capable of producing up to the 92nd Fibonacci number—subsequent values are outside the range that can be represented by a long. Recall that you can use class BigInteger to represent arbitrarily large integer values.

Class BackgroundCalculator (Fig. 26.25) performs the recursive Fibonacci calculation in a worker thread. This class extends SwingWorker (line 8), overriding the methods doInBackground and done. Method doInBackground (lines 21–25) computes the *n*th Fibonacci number in a worker thread and returns the result. Method done (lines 28–44) displays the result in a JLabel.

```
1   // Fig. 26.25: BackgroundCalculator.java
2   // SwingWorker subclass for calculating Fibonacci numbers
3   // in a background thread.
```

Fig. 26.25 | SwingWorker subclass for calculating Fibonacci numbers in a background thread. (Part 1 of 2.)

```
4    import javax.swing.SwingWorker;
5    import javax.swing.JLabel;
6    import java.util.concurrent.ExecutionException;
7
8    public class BackgroundCalculator extends SwingWorker< Long, Object >
9    {
10      private final int n; // Fibonacci number to calculate
11      private final JLabel resultJLabel; // JLabel to display the result
12
13      // constructor
14      public BackgroundCalculator( int number, JLabel label )
15      {
16         n = number;
17         resultJLabel = label;
18      } // end BackgroundCalculator constructor
19
20      // long-running code to be run in a worker thread
21      public Long doInBackground()
22      {
23         long nthFib = fibonacci( n );
24         return String.valueOf( nthFib );
25      } // end method doInBackground
26
27      // code to run on the event dispatch thread when doInBackground returns
28      protected void done()
29      {
30         try
31         {
32            // get the result of doInBackground and display it
33            resultJLabel.setText( get().toString() );
34         } // end try
35         catch ( InterruptedException ex )
36         {
37            resultJLabel.setText( "Interrupted while waiting for results." );
38         } // end catch
39         catch ( ExecutionException ex )
40         {
41            resultJLabel.setText(
42               "Error encountered while performing calculation." );
43         } // end catch
44      } // end method done
45
46      // recursive method fibonacci; calculates nth Fibonacci number
47      public long fibonacci( long number )
48      {
49         if ( number == 0 || number == 1 )
50            return number;
51         else
52            return fibonacci( number - 1 ) + fibonacci( number - 2 );
53      } // end method fibonacci
54   } // end class BackgroundCalculator
```

Fig. 26.25 | SwingWorker subclass for calculating Fibonacci numbers in a background thread. (Part 2 of 2.)

Note that SwingWorker is a generic class. In line 8, the first type parameter is Long and the second is Object. The first type parameter indicates the type returned by the doIn-Background method; the second indicates the type that is passed between the publish and process methods to handle intermediate results. Since we do not use publish and process in this example, we simply use Object as the second type parameter. We discuss publish and process in Section 26.11.2.

A BackgroundCalculator object can be instantiated from a class that controls a GUI. A BackgroundCalculator maintains instance variables for an integer that represents the Fibonacci number to be calculated and a JLabel that displays the results of the calculation (lines 10–11). The BackgroundCalculator constructor (lines 14–18) initializes these instance variables with the arguments that are passed to the constructor.

Software Engineering Observation 26.3

Any GUI components that will be manipulated by SwingWorker methods, such as components that will be updated from methods process or done, should be passed to the SwingWorker subclass's constructor and stored in the subclass object. This gives these methods access to the GUI components they'll manipulate.

When method execute is called on a BackgroundCalculator object, the object is scheduled for execution in a worker thread. Method doInBackground is called from the worker thread and invokes the fibonacci method (lines 47–53), passing instance variable n as an argument (line 23). Method fibonacci uses recursion to compute the Fibonacci of n. When fibonacci returns, method doInBackground returns the result.

After doInBackground returns, method done is called from the event dispatch thread. This method attempts to set the result JLabel to the return value of doInBackground by calling method get to retrieve this return value (line 33). Method get waits for the result to be ready if necessary, but since we call it from method done, the computation will be complete before get is called. Lines 35–38 catch InterruptedException if the current thread is interrupted while waiting for get to return. This exception will not occur in this example since the calculation will have already completed by the time get is called. Lines 39–43 catch ExecutionException, which is thrown if an exception occurs during the computation.

Class FibonacciNumbers

Class FibonacciNumbers (Fig. 26.26) displays a window containing two sets of GUI components—one set to compute a Fibonacci number in a worker thread and another to get the next Fibonacci number in response to the user's clicking a JButton. The constructor (lines 38–109) places these components in separate titled JPanels. Lines 46–47 and 78–79 add two JLabels, a JTextField and a JButton to the workerJPanel to allow the user to enter an integer whose Fibonacci number will be calculated by the BackgroundWorker. Lines 84–85 and 103 add two JLabels and a JButton to the event dispatch thread panel to allow the user to get the next Fibonacci number in the sequence. Instance variables n1 and n2 contain the previous two Fibonacci numbers in the sequence and are initialized to 0 and 1, respectively (lines 29–30). Instance variable count stores the most recently computed sequence number and is initialized to 1 (line 31). The two JLabels display count and n2 initially, so that the user will see the text Fibonacci of 1: 1 in the eventThread-JPanel when the GUI starts.

```
1   // Fig. 26.26: FibonacciNumbers.java
2   // Using SwingWorker to perform a long calculation with
3   // results displayed in a GUI.
4   import java.awt.GridLayout;
5   import java.awt.event.ActionEvent;
6   import java.awt.event.ActionListener;
7   import javax.swing.JButton;
8   import javax.swing.JFrame;
9   import javax.swing.JPanel;
10  import javax.swing.JLabel;
11  import javax.swing.JTextField;
12  import javax.swing.border.TitledBorder;
13  import javax.swing.border.LineBorder;
14  import java.awt.Color;
15  import java.util.concurrent.ExecutionException;
16
17  public class FibonacciNumbers extends JFrame
18  {
19     // components for calculating the Fibonacci of a user-entered number
20     private final JPanel workerJPanel =
21        new JPanel( new GridLayout( 2, 2, 5, 5 ) );
22     private final JTextField numberJTextField = new JTextField();
23     private final JButton goJButton = new JButton( "Go" );
24     private final JLabel fibonacciJLabel = new JLabel();
25
26     // components and variables for getting the next Fibonacci number
27     private final JPanel eventThreadJPanel =
28        new JPanel( new GridLayout( 2, 2, 5, 5 ) );
29     private long n1 = 0; // initialize with first Fibonacci number
30     private long n2 = 1; // initialize with second Fibonacci number
31     private int count = 1; // current Fibonacci number to display
32     private final JLabel nJLabel = new JLabel( "Fibonacci of 1: " );
33     private final JLabel nFibonacciJLabel =
34        new JLabel( String.valueOf( n2 ) );
35     private final JButton nextNumberJButton = new JButton( "Next Number" );
36
37     // constructor
38     public FibonacciNumbers()
39     {
40        super( "Fibonacci Numbers" );
41        setLayout( new GridLayout( 2, 1, 10, 10 ) );
42
43        // add GUI components to the SwingWorker panel
44        workerJPanel.setBorder( new TitledBorder(
45           new LineBorder( Color.BLACK ), "With SwingWorker" ) );
46        workerJPanel.add( new JLabel( "Get Fibonacci of:" ) );
47        workerJPanel.add( numberJTextField );
48        goJButton.addActionListener(
49           new ActionListener()
50           {
51              public void actionPerformed( ActionEvent event )
52              {
```

Fig. 26.26 | Using SwingWorker to perform a long calculation with results displayed in a GUI. (Part 1 of 3.)

```
53                      int n;
54
55                      try
56                      {
57                         // retrieve user's input as an integer
58                         n = Integer.parseInt( numberJTextField.getText() );
59                      } // end try
60                      catch( NumberFormatException ex )
61                      {
62                         // display an error message if the user did not
63                         // enter an integer
64                         fibonacciJLabel.setText( "Enter an integer." );
65                         return;
66                      } // end catch
67
68                      // indicate that the calculation has begun
69                      fibonacciJLabel.setText( "Calculating..." );
70
71                      // create a task to perform calculation in background
72                      BackgroundCalculator task =
73                         new BackgroundCalculator( n, fibonacciJLabel );
74                      task.execute(); // execute the task
75                   } // end method actionPerformed
76                } // end anonymous inner class
77             ); // end call to addActionListener
78             workerJPanel.add( goJButton );
79             workerJPanel.add( fibonacciJLabel );
80
81             // add GUI components to the event-dispatching thread panel
82             eventThreadJPanel.setBorder( new TitledBorder(
83                new LineBorder( Color.BLACK ), "Without SwingWorker" ) );
84             eventThreadJPanel.add( nJLabel );
85             eventThreadJPanel.add( nFibonacciJLabel );
86             nextNumberJButton.addActionListener(
87                new ActionListener()
88                {
89                   public void actionPerformed( ActionEvent event )
90                   {
91                      // calculate the Fibonacci number after n2
92                      long temp = n1 + n2;
93                      n1 = n2;
94                      n2 = temp;
95                      ++count;
96
97                      // display the next Fibonacci number
98                      nJLabel.setText( "Fibonacci of " + count + ": " );
99                      nFibonacciJLabel.setText( String.valueOf( n2 ) );
100                  } // end method actionPerformed
101               } // end anonymous inner class
102            ); // end call to addActionListener
103            eventThreadJPanel.add( nextNumberJButton );
104
```

Fig. 26.26 | Using SwingWorker to perform a long calculation with results displayed in a GUI. (Part 2 of 3.)

```
105        add( workerJPanel );
106        add( eventThreadJPanel );
107        setSize( 275, 200 );
108        setVisible( true );
109     } // end constructor
110
111     // main method begins program execution
112     public static void main( String[] args )
113     {
114        FibonacciNumbers application = new FibonacciNumbers();
115        application.setDefaultCloseOperation( EXIT_ON_CLOSE );
116     } // end main
117  } // end class FibonacciNumbers
```

a) Begin calculating Fibonacci of 40 in the background.

b) Calculating other Fibonacci values while Fibonacci of 40 continues calculating.

c) Fibonacci of 40 calculation finishes.

Fig. 26.26 | Using SwingWorker to perform a long calculation with results displayed in a GUI. (Part 3 of 3.)

Lines 48–77 register the event handler for the goJButton. If the user clicks this JButton, line 58 gets the value entered in the numberJTextField and attempts to parse it as an integer. Lines 72–73 create a new BackgroundCalculator object, passing in the user-entered value and the fibonacciJLabel that is used to display the calculation's results. Line 74 calls method execute on the BackgroundCalculator, scheduling it for execution in a separate worker thread. Method execute does not wait for the BackgroundCalculator to finish executing. It returns immediately, allowing the GUI to continue processing other events while the computation is performed.

If the user clicks the nextNumberJButton in the eventThreadJPanel, the event handler registered in lines 86–102 executes. Lines 92–95 add the previous two Fibonacci numbers stored in n1 and n2 to determine the next number in the sequence, update n1 and n2 to their new values and increment count. Then lines 98–99 update the GUI to display the next number. The code for these calculations is in method `actionPerformed`, so they are performed on the event dispatch thread. Handling such short computations in the event dispatch thread does not cause the GUI to become unresponsive, as with the recursive algorithm for calculating the Fibonacci of a large number. Because the longer Fibonacci computation is performed in a separate worker thread using the `SwingWorker`, it's possible to get the next Fibonacci number while the recursive computation is still in progress.

26.11.2 Processing Intermediate Results with SwingWorker

We've presented an example that uses the `SwingWorker` class to execute a long process in a background thread and update the GUI when the process is finished. We now present an example of updating the GUI with intermediate results before the long process completes. Figure 26.27 presents class `PrimeCalculator`, which extends `SwingWorker` to compute the first *n* prime numbers in a worker thread. In addition to the `doInBackground` and `done` methods used in the previous example, this class uses `SwingWorker` methods `publish`, `process` and `setProgress`. In this example, method `publish` sends prime numbers to method `process` as they're found, method `process` displays these primes in a GUI component and method `setProgress` updates the progress property. We later show how to use this property to update a `JProgressBar`.

```java
1   // Fig. 26.27: PrimeCalculator.java
2   // Calculates the first n primes, displaying them as they are found.
3   import javax.swing.JTextArea;
4   import javax.swing.JLabel;
5   import javax.swing.JButton;
6   import javax.swing.SwingWorker;
7   import java.util.Random;
8   import java.util.List;
9   import java.util.concurrent.CancellationException;
10  import java.util.concurrent.ExecutionException;
11
12  public class PrimeCalculator extends SwingWorker< Integer, Integer >
13  {
14     private final Random generator = new Random();
15     private final JTextArea intermediateJTextArea; // displays found primes
16     private final JButton getPrimesJButton;
17     private final JButton cancelJButton;
18     private final JLabel statusJLabel; // displays status of calculation
19     private final boolean[] primes; // boolean array for finding primes
20
21     // constructor
22     public PrimeCalculator( int max, JTextArea intermediate, JLabel status,
23        JButton getPrimes, JButton cancel )
24     {
25        intermediateJTextArea = intermediate;
26        statusJLabel = status;
27        getPrimesJButton = getPrimes;
28        cancelJButton = cancel;
```

Fig. 26.27 | Calculates the first *n* primes, displaying them as they are found. (Part 1 of 3.)

```
29              primes = new boolean[ max ];
30
31              // initialize all prime array values to true
32              for ( int i = 0; i < max; i ++ )
33                 primes[ i ] = true;
34          } // end constructor
35
36          // finds all primes up to max using the Sieve of Eratosthenes
37          public Integer doInBackground()
38          {
39              int count = 0; // the number of primes found
40
41              // starting at the third value, cycle through the array and put
42              // false as the value of any greater number that is a multiple
43              for ( int i = 2; i < primes.length; i++ )
44              {
45                 if ( isCancelled() ) // if calculation has been canceled
46                    return count;
47                 else
48                 {
49                    setProgress( 100 * ( i + 1 ) / primes.length );
50
51                    try
52                    {
53                       Thread.sleep( generator.nextInt( 5 ) );
54                    } // end try
55                    catch ( InterruptedException ex )
56                    {
57                       statusJLabel.setText( "Worker thread interrupted" );
58                       return count;
59                    } // end catch
60
61                    if ( primes[ i ] ) // i is prime
62                    {
63                       publish( i ); // make i available for display in prime list
64                       ++count;
65
66                       for ( int j = i + i; j < primes.length; j += i )
67                          primes[ j ] = false; // i is not prime
68                    } // end if
69                 } // end else
70              } // end for
71
72              return count;
73          } // end method doInBackground
74
75          // displays published values in primes list
76          protected void process( List< Integer > publishedVals )
77          {
78              for ( int i = 0; i < publishedVals.size(); i++ )
79                 intermediateJTextArea.append( publishedVals.get( i ) + "\n" );
80          } // end method process
81
```

Fig. 26.27 | Calculates the first *n* primes, displaying them as they are found. (Part 2 of 3.)

```
82          // code to execute when doInBackground completes
83          protected void done()
84          {
85              getPrimesJButton.setEnabled( true ); // enable Get Primes button
86              cancelJButton.setEnabled( false ); // disable Cancel button
87
88              int numPrimes;
89
90              try
91              {
92                  numPrimes = get(); // retrieve doInBackground return value
93              } // end try
94              catch ( InterruptedException ex )
95              {
96                  statusJLabel.setText( "Interrupted while waiting for results." );
97                  return;
98              } // end catch
99              catch ( ExecutionException ex )
100             {
101                 statusJLabel.setText( "Error performing computation." );
102                 return;
103             } // end catch
104             catch ( CancellationException ex )
105             {
106                 statusJLabel.setText( "Cancelled." );
107                 return;
108             } // end catch
109
110             statusJLabel.setText( "Found " + numPrimes + " primes." );
111         } // end method done
112 } // end class PrimeCalculator
```

Fig. 26.27 | Calculates the first *n* primes, displaying them as they are found. (Part 3 of 3.)

Class `PrimeCalculator` extends `SwingWorker` (line 12), with the first type parameter indicating the return type of method `doInBackground` and the second indicating the type of intermediate results passed between methods `publish` and `process`. In this case, both type parameters are `Integers`. The constructor (lines 22–34) takes as arguments an integer that indicates the upper limit of the prime numbers to locate, a `JTextArea` used to display primes in the GUI, one `JButton` for initiating a calculation and one for canceling it, and a `JLabel` used to display the status of the calculation.

Sieve of Eratosthenes

Lines 32–33 initialize the elements of the `boolean` array `primes` to `true`. `PrimeCalculator` uses this array and the **Sieve of Eratosthenes** algorithm (described in Exercise 7.22) to find all primes less than `max`. The Sieve of Eratosthenes takes a list of integers and, beginning with the first prime number, filters out all multiples of that prime. It then moves to the next prime, which will be the next number that is not yet filtered out, and eliminates all of its multiples. It continues until the end of the list is reached and all nonprimes have been filtered out. Algorithmically, we begin with element 2 of the `boolean` array and set the cells corresponding to all values that are multiples of 2 to `false` to indicate that they're divisible by 2 and thus not prime. We then move to the next array element, check whether it's true, and if so set all of its multiples to false to indicate that they're divisible by the current index. When the whole array has been traversed in this way, all indices that contain true are prime, as they have no divisors.

Method *doInBackground*

In method doInBackground (lines 37–73), the control variable i for the loop (lines 43–70) controls the current index for implementing the Sieve of Eratosthenes. Line 45 calls the inherited SwingWorker method **isCancelled** to determine whether the user has clicked the **Cancel** button. If isCancelled returns true, method doInBackground returns the number of primes found so far (line 46) without finishing the computation.

If the calculation isn't canceled, line 49 calls setProgress to update the percentage of the array that has been traversed so far. Line 53 puts the currently executing thread to sleep for up to 4 milliseconds. We discuss the reason for this shortly. Line 61 tests whether the element of array primes at the current index is true (and thus prime). If so, line 63 passes the index to method publish so that it can be displayed as an intermediate result in the GUI and line 64 increments the number of primes found. Lines 66–67 set all multiples of the current index to false to indicate that they're not prime. When the entire array has been traversed, line 72 returns the number of primes found.

Method *process*

Lines 76–80 declare method process, which executes in the event dispatch thread and receives its argument publishedVals from method publish. The passing of values between publish in the worker thread and process in the event dispatch thread is asynchronous; process might not be invoked for every call to publish. All Integers published since the last call to process are received as a List by method process. Lines 78–79 iterate through this list and display the published values in a JTextArea. Because the computation in method doInBackground progresses quickly, publishing values often, updates to the JTextArea can pile up on the event dispatch thread, causing the GUI to become sluggish. In fact, when searching for a large number of primes, the event dispatch thread may receive so many requests in quick succession to update the JTextArea that it runs out of memory in its event queue. This is why we put the worker thread to sleep for a few milliseconds between calls to publish. The calculation is slowed just enough to allow the event dispatch thread to keep up with requests to update the JTextArea with new primes, enabling the GUI to update smoothly and remain responsive.

Method *done*

Lines 83–111 define method done. When the calculation is finished or canceled, method done enables the **Get Primes** button and disables the **Cancel** button (lines 85–86). Line 92 gets the return value—the number of primes found—from method doInBackground. Lines 94–108 catch the exceptions thrown by method get and display an appropriate message in the statusJLabel. If no exceptions occur, line 110 sets the statusJLabel to indicate the number of primes found.

Class *FindPrimes*

Class FindPrimes (Fig. 26.28) displays a JTextField that allows the user to enter a number, a JButton to begin finding all primes less than that number and a JTextArea to display the primes. A JButton allows the user to cancel the calculation, and a JProgressBar indicates the calculation's progress. The FindPrimes constructor (lines 32–125) initializes these components and displays them in a JFrame using BorderLayout.

Lines 42–94 register the event handler for the getPrimesJButton. When the user clicks this JButton, lines 47–49 reset the JProgressBar and clear the displayPrimes-JTextArea and the statusJLabel. Lines 53–63 parse the value in the JTextField and display an error message if the value is not an integer. Lines 66–68 construct a new PrimeCalculator object, passing as arguments the integer the user entered, the display-PrimesJTextArea for displaying the primes, the statusJLabel and the two JButtons.

```
1   // Fig 26.28: FindPrimes.java
2   // Using a SwingWorker to display prime numbers and update a JProgressBar
3   // while the prime numbers are being calculated.
4   import javax.swing.JFrame;
5   import javax.swing.JTextField;
6   import javax.swing.JTextArea;
7   import javax.swing.JButton;
8   import javax.swing.JProgressBar;
9   import javax.swing.JLabel;
10  import javax.swing.JPanel;
11  import javax.swing.JScrollPane;
12  import javax.swing.ScrollPaneConstants;
13  import java.awt.BorderLayout;
14  import java.awt.GridLayout;
15  import java.awt.event.ActionListener;
16  import java.awt.event.ActionEvent;
17  import java.util.concurrent.ExecutionException;
18  import java.beans.PropertyChangeListener;
19  import java.beans.PropertyChangeEvent;
20
21  public class FindPrimes extends JFrame
22  {
23     private final JTextField highestPrimeJTextField = new JTextField();
24     private final JButton getPrimesJButton = new JButton( "Get Primes" );
25     private final JTextArea displayPrimesJTextArea = new JTextArea();
26     private final JButton cancelJButton = new JButton( "Cancel" );
27     private final JProgressBar progressJProgressBar = new JProgressBar();
28     private final JLabel statusJLabel = new JLabel();
29     private PrimeCalculator calculator;
30
31     // constructor
32     public FindPrimes()
33     {
34        super( "Finding Primes with SwingWorker" );
35        setLayout( new BorderLayout() );
36
37        // initialize panel to get a number from the user
38        JPanel northJPanel = new JPanel();
39        northJPanel.add( new JLabel( "Find primes less than: " ) );
40        highestPrimeJTextField.setColumns( 5 );
41        northJPanel.add( highestPrimeJTextField );
42        getPrimesJButton.addActionListener(
43           new ActionListener()
44           {
```

Fig. 26.28 | Using a SwingWorker to display prime numbers and update a JProgressBar while the prime numbers are being calculated. (Part 1 of 3.)

```
45              public void actionPerformed( ActionEvent e )
46              {
47                 progressJProgressBar.setValue( 0 ); // reset JProgressBar
48                 displayPrimesJTextArea.setText( "" ); // clear JTextArea
49                 statusJLabel.setText( "" ); // clear JLabel
50
51                 int number; // search for primes up through this value
52
53                 try
54                 {
55                    // get user input
56                    number = Integer.parseInt(
57                       highestPrimeJTextField.getText() );
58                 } // end try
59                 catch ( NumberFormatException ex )
60                 {
61                    statusJLabel.setText( "Enter an integer." );
62                    return;
63                 } // end catch
64
65                 // construct a new PrimeCalculator object
66                 calculator = new PrimeCalculator( number,
67                    displayPrimesJTextArea, statusJLabel, getPrimesJButton,
68                    cancelJButton );
69
70                 // listen for progress bar property changes
71                 calculator.addPropertyChangeListener(
72                    new PropertyChangeListener()
73                    {
74                       public void propertyChange( PropertyChangeEvent e )
75                       {
76                          // if the changed property is progress,
77                          // update the progress bar
78                          if ( e.getPropertyName().equals( "progress" ) )
79                          {
80                             int newValue = ( Integer ) e.getNewValue();
81                             progressJProgressBar.setValue( newValue );
82                          } // end if
83                       } // end method propertyChange
84                    } // end anonymous inner class
85                 ); // end call to addPropertyChangeListener
86
87                 // disable Get Primes button and enable Cancel button
88                 getPrimesJButton.setEnabled( false );
89                 cancelJButton.setEnabled( true );
90
91                 calculator.execute(); // execute the PrimeCalculator object
92              } // end method ActionPerformed
93           } // end anonymous inner class
94        ); // end call to addActionListener
95        northJPanel.add( getPrimesJButton );
96
```

Fig. 26.28 | Using a SwingWorker to display prime numbers and update a JProgressBar while the prime numbers are being calculated. (Part 2 of 3.)

```
97          // add a scrollable JList to display results of calculation
98          displayPrimesJTextArea.setEditable( false );
99          add( new JScrollPane( displayPrimesJTextArea,
100            ScrollPaneConstants.VERTICAL_SCROLLBAR_ALWAYS,
101            ScrollPaneConstants.HORIZONTAL_SCROLLBAR_NEVER ) );
102
103         // initialize a panel to display cancelJButton,
104         // progressJProgressBar, and statusJLabel
105         JPanel southJPanel = new JPanel( new GridLayout( 1, 3, 10, 10 ) );
106         cancelJButton.setEnabled( false );
107         cancelJButton.addActionListener(
108            new ActionListener()
109            {
110               public void actionPerformed( ActionEvent e )
111               {
112                  calculator.cancel( true ); // cancel the calculation
113               } // end method ActionPerformed
114            } // end anonymous inner class
115         ); // end call to addActionListener
116         southJPanel.add( cancelJButton );
117         progressJProgressBar.setStringPainted( true );
118         southJPanel.add( progressJProgressBar );
119         southJPanel.add( statusJLabel );
120
121         add( northJPanel, BorderLayout.NORTH );
122         add( southJPanel, BorderLayout.SOUTH );
123         setSize( 350, 300 );
124         setVisible( true );
125      } // end constructor
126
127      // main method begins program execution
128      public static void main( String[] args )
129      {
130         FindPrimes application = new FindPrimes();
131         application.setDefaultCloseOperation( EXIT_ON_CLOSE );
132      } // end main
133   } // end class FindPrimes
```

Fig. 26.28 | Using a `SwingWorker` to display prime numbers and update a `JProgressBar` while the prime numbers are being calculated. (Part 3 of 3.)

Lines 71–85 register a PropertyChangeListener for the PrimeCalculator object. **PropertyChangeListener** is an interface from package java.beans that defines a single method, propertyChange. Every time method setProgress is invoked on a PrimeCalculator, the PrimeCalculator generates a PropertyChangeEvent to indicate that the progress property has changed. Method propertyChange listens for these events. Line 78 tests whether a given PropertyChangeEvent indicates a change to the progress property. If so, line 80 gets the new value of the property and line 81 updates the JProgressBar with the new progress property value.

The **Get Primes** JButton is disabled (line 88) so that only one calculation that updates the GUI can execute at a time, and the **Cancel** JButton is enabled (line 89) to allow the user to stop the computation before it completes. Line 91 executes the PrimesCalculator to begin finding primes. If the user clicks the cancelJButton, the event handler registered at lines 107–115 calls PrimeCalculator's method **cancel** (line 112), which is inherited from class SwingWorker, and the calculation returns early. The argument true to method cancel indicates that the thread performing the task should be interrupted in an attempt to cancel the task.

26.12 Interfaces Callable and Future

Interface Runnable provides only the most basic functionality for multithreaded programming. In fact, this interface has several limitations. Suppose a Runnable encounters a problem and tries to throw a checked exception. The run method is not declared to throw any exceptions, so the problem must be handled within the Runnable—the exception cannot be passed to the calling thread. Now suppose a Runnable is performing a long calculation and the application wants to retrieve the result of that calculation. The run method cannot return a value, so the application must use shared data to pass the value back to the calling thread. This also involves the overhead of synchronizing access to the data. The developers of the concurrency APIs introduced in Java SE 5 recognized these limitations and created a new interface to fix them. The **Callable** interface (of package java.util.concurrent) declares a single method named **call**. This interface is designed to be similar to the Runnable interface—allowing an action to be performed concurrently in a separate thread— but the call method allows the thread to return a value or to throw a checked exception.

An application that creates a Callable likely wants to run it concurrently with other Runnables and Callables. The ExecutorService interface provides method **submit**, which will execute a Callable passed in as its argument. The submit method returns an object of type **Future** (of package java.util.concurrent), which is an interface that represents the executing Callable. The Future interface declares method **get** to return the result of the Callable and provides other methods to manage a Callable's execution.

26.13 Wrap-Up

In this chapter, you learned that concurrency has historically been implemented with operating-system primitives available only to experienced systems programmers, but that Java makes concurrency available to you through the language and APIs. You also learned that the JVM itself creates threads to run a program, and that it also can create threads to perform housekeeping tasks such as garbage collection.

We discussed the life cycle of a thread and the states that a thread may occupy during its lifetime. We also discussed Java's thread priorities, which help the system schedule threads for execution. You learned that you should avoid manipulating Java thread priorities directly and you learned about problems associated with thread priorities, such as indefinite postponement (sometimes called starvation).

Next, we presented the interface Runnable, which is used to specify a task that can execute concurrently with other tasks. This interface's run method is invoked by the thread executing the task. We showed how to execute a Runnable object by associating it with an object of class Thread. Then we showed how to use the Executor interface to manage the execution of Runnable objects via thread pools, which can reuse existing threads to eliminate the overhead of creating a new thread for each task and can improve performance by optimizing the number of threads to ensure that the processor stays busy.

You learned that when multiple threads share an object and one or more of them modify that object, indeterminate results may occur unless access to the shared object is managed properly. We showed you how to solve this problem via thread synchronization, which coordinates access to shared data by multiple concurrent threads. You learned several techniques for performing synchronization—first with the built-in class ArrayBlockingQueue (which handles all the synchronization details for you), then with Java's built-in monitors and the synchronized keyword, and finally with interfaces Lock and Condition.

We discussed the fact that Swing GUIs are not thread safe, so all interactions with and modifications to the GUI must be performed in the event dispatch thread. We also discussed the problems associated with performing long-running calculations in the event dispatch thread. Then we showed how you can use Java SE 6's SwingWorker class to perform long-running calculations in worker threads. You learned how to display the results of a SwingWorker in a GUI when the calculation completed and how to display intermediate results while the calculation was still in process.

Finally, we discussed the Callable and Future interfaces, which enable you to execute tasks that return results and to obtain those results, respectively. We use the multithreading techniques introduced here again in Chapter 27, Networking, to help build multithreaded servers that can interact with multiple clients concurrently.

Summary

Section 26.1 Introduction
- Historically, concurrency has been implemented with operating-system primitives available only to experienced systems programmers.
- The Ada programming language made concurrency primitives widely available.
- Java makes concurrency available to you through the language and APIs.
- The JVM creates threads to run a program and for housekeeping tasks such as garbage collection.

Section 26.2 Thread States: Life Cycle of a Thread
- A new thread begins its life cycle in the *new* state. When the program starts the thread, it's placed in the *runnable* state. A thread in the *runnable* state is considered to be executing its task.
- A *runnable* thread transitions to the *waiting* state to wait for another thread to perform a task. A *waiting* thread transitions to *runnable* when another thread notifies it to continue executing.
- A *runnable* thread can enter the *timed waiting* state for a specified interval of time, transitioning back to *runnable* when that time interval expires or when the event it's waiting for occurs.

- A *runnable* thread can transition to the *timed waiting* state if it provides an optional wait interval when it's waiting for another thread to perform a task. Such a thread will return to the *runnable* state when it's notified by another thread or when the timed interval expires.

- A sleeping thread remains in the *timed waiting* state for a designated period of time, after which it returns to the *runnable* state.

- A *runnable* thread transitions to the *blocked* state when it attempts to perform a task that cannot be completed immediately and the thread must temporarily wait until that task completes. At that point, the *blocked* thread transitions to the *runnable* state, so it can resume execution.

- A *runnable* thread enters the *terminated* state when it successfully completes its task or otherwise terminates (perhaps due to an error).

- At the operating-system level, the *runnable* state typically encompasses two separate states. When a thread first transitions to the *runnable* state from the *new* state, it is in the *ready* state. A *ready* thread enters the *running* state when the operating system dispatches it.

- Most operating systems allot a quantum or timeslice in which a thread performs its task. When this expires, the thread returns to the *ready* state and another thread is assigned to the processor.

- Thread scheduling determines which thread to dispatch based on thread priorities.

Section 26.3 Thread Priorities and Thread Scheduling

- Every Java thread has a thread priority (from MIN_PRIORITY to MAX_PRIORITY) that helps the operating system determine the order in which threads are scheduled.

- By default, every thread is given priority NORM_PRIORITY (a constant of 5). Each new thread inherits the priority of the thread that created it.

- The job of an operating system's thread scheduler is to determine which thread runs next.

- When a higher-priority thread enters the *ready* state, the operating system generally preempts the currently *running* thread (an operation known as preemptive scheduling).

- Depending on the operating system, higher-priority threads could postpone—possibly indefinitely—the execution of lower-priority threads.

Section 26.4 Creating and Executing Threads

- A Runnable object represents a "task" that can execute concurrently with other tasks.

- Interface Runnable declares method run in which you place the code that defines the task to perform. The thread executing a Runnable calls method run to perform the task.

- A program will not terminate until its last thread completes execution.

- You cannot predict the order in which threads will be scheduled, even if you know the order in which they were created and started.

- It's recommended that you use the Executor interface to manage the execution of Runnable objects. An Executor object typically creates and manages a group of threads—called a thread pool.

- Executors can reuse existing threads (to eliminate the overhead of creating new threads) and can improve performance by optimizing the number of threads to ensure that the processor stays busy.

- Executor method execute receives a Runnable and assigns it to an available thread in a thread pool. If there are none, the Executor creates a new thread or waits for one to become available.

- Interface ExecutorService (of package java.util.concurrent) extends interface Executor and declares other methods for managing the life cycle of an Executor.

- An object that implements the ExecutorService interface can be created using static methods declared in class Executors (of package java.util.concurrent).

- Executors method newCachedThreadPool returns an ExecutorService that creates new threads as they're needed by the application.

- `ExecutorService` method `execute` executes its `Runnable` sometime in the future. The method returns immediately from each invocation—the program does not wait for each task to finish.

- `ExecutorService` method `shutdown` notifies the `ExecutorService` to stop accepting new tasks, but continues executing existing tasks and terminates when those tasks complete execution.

Section 26.5 Thread Synchronization

- Thread synchronization coordinates access to shared data by multiple concurrent threads.

- By synchronizing threads, you can ensure that each thread accessing a shared object excludes all other threads from doing so simultaneously—this is called mutual exclusion.

- A common way to perform synchronization is to use Java's built-in monitors. Every object has a monitor and a monitor lock. The monitor ensures that its object's monitor lock is held by a maximum of only one thread at any time, and thus can be used to enforce mutual exclusion.

- If an operation requires the executing thread to hold a lock while the operation is performed, a thread must acquire the lock before it can proceed with the operation. Any other threads attempting to perform an operation that requires the same lock will be *blocked* until the first thread releases the lock, at which point the *blocked* threads may attempt to acquire the lock.

- To specify that a thread must hold a monitor lock to execute a block of code, the code should be placed in a `synchronized` statement. Such code is said to be guarded by the monitor lock.

- The `synchronized` statements are declared using the `synchronized` keyword:

```
synchronized ( object )
{
    statements
} // end synchronized statement
```

  where *object* is the object whose monitor lock will be acquired; *object* is normally `this` if it's the object in which the `synchronized` statement appears.

- Java also allows `synchronized` methods. Before executing, a non-`static` `synchronized` method must acquire the lock on the object that is used to call the method. Similarly, a `static` synchronized method must acquire the lock on the class that is used to call the method.

- `ExecutorService` method `awaitTermination` forces a program to wait for threads to terminate. It returns control to its caller either when all tasks executing in the `ExecutorService` complete or when the specified timeout elapses. If all tasks complete before the timeout elapses, the method returns `true`; otherwise, it returns `false`.

- You can simulate atomicity by ensuring that only one thread performs a set of operations at a time. Atomicity can be achieved with `synchronized` statements or `synchronized` methods.

- When you share immutable data across threads, you should declare the corresponding data fields `final` to indicate that variables' values will not change after they're initialized.

Section 26.6 Producer/Consumer Relationship without Synchronization

- In a multithreaded producer/consumer relationship, a producer thread generates data and places it in a shared object called a buffer. A consumer thread reads data from the buffer.

- Operations on a buffer data shared by a producer and a consumer should proceed only if the buffer is in the correct state. If the buffer is not full, the producer may produce; if the buffer is not empty, the consumer may consume. If the buffer is full when the producer attempts to write into it, the producer must wait until there is space. If the buffer is empty or the previous value was already read, the consumer must wait for new data to become available.

Section 26.7 Producer/Consumer Relationship: **ArrayBlockingQueue**

- `ArrayBlockingQueue` is a fully implemented buffer class from package `java.util.concurrent` that implements the `BlockingQueue` interface.

- An `ArrayBlockingQueue` can implement a shared buffer in a producer/consumer relationship. Method `put` places an element at the end of the `BlockingQueue`, waiting if the queue is full. Method `take` removes an element from the head of the `BlockingQueue`, waiting if the queue is empty.

- `ArrayBlockingQueue` stores shared data in an array that is sized with an argument passed to the constructor. Once created, an `ArrayBlockingQueue` is fixed in size.

Section 26.8 Producer/Consumer Relationship with Synchronization

- You can implement a shared buffer yourself using the `synchronized` keyword and `Object` methods `wait`, `notify` and `notifyAll`.

- A thread can call `Object` method `wait` to release an object's monitor lock, and wait in the *waiting* state while the other threads try to enter the object's `synchronized` statement(s) or method(s).

- When a thread executing a `synchronized` statement (or method) completes or satisfies the condition on which another thread may be waiting, it can call `Object` method `notify` to allow a waiting thread to transition to the *runnable* state again. At this point, the thread that was transitioned from the *wait* state to the *runnable* state can attempt to reacquire the monitor lock on the object.

- If a thread calls `notifyAll`, then all the threads waiting for the monitor lock become eligible to reacquire the lock (that is, they all transition to the *runnable* state).

Section 26.9 Producer/Consumer Relationship: Bounded Buffers

- You cannot make assumptions about the relative speeds of concurrent threads.

- A bounded buffer can be used to minimize the amount of waiting time for threads that share resources and operate at the same average speeds. If the producer temporarily produces values faster than the consumer can consume them, the producer can write additional values into the extra buffer space (if any are available). If the consumer consumes faster than the producer produces new values, the consumer can read additional values (if there are any) from the buffer.

- The key to using a bounded buffer with a producer and consumer that operate at about the same speed is to provide the buffer with enough locations to handle the anticipated "extra" production.

- The simplest way to implement a bounded buffer is to use an `ArrayBlockingQueue` for the buffer so that all of the synchronization details are handled for you.

Section 26.10 Producer/Consumer Relationship: The **Lock** and **Condition** Interfaces

- The `Lock` and `Condition` interfaces, which were introduced in Java SE 5, give programmers more precise control over thread synchronization, but are more complicated to use.

- Any object can contain a reference to an object that implements the `Lock` interface (of package `java.util.concurrent.locks`). A thread calls the `Lock`'s `lock` method to acquire the lock. Once a `Lock` has been obtained by one thread, the `Lock` object will not allow another thread to obtain the `Lock` until the first thread releases the `Lock` (by calling the `Lock`'s `unlock` method).

- If several threads are trying to call method `lock` on the same `Lock` object at the same time, only one thread can obtain the lock—the others are placed in the *waiting* state. When a thread calls `unlock`, the object's lock is released and a waiting thread attempting to lock the object proceeds.

- Class `ReentrantLock` is a basic implementation of the `Lock` interface.

- The `ReentrantLock` constructor takes a `boolean` that specifies whether the lock has a fairness policy. If `true`, the `ReentrantLock`'s fairness policy is "the longest-waiting thread will acquire the lock when it's available"—this prevents indefinite postponement. If the argument is set to `false`, there is no guarantee as to which waiting thread will acquire the lock when it's available.

- If a thread that owns a `Lock` determines that it cannot continue with its task until some condition is satisfied, the thread can wait on a condition object. Using `Lock` objects allows you to explicitly declare the condition objects on which a thread may need to wait.

- Condition objects are associated with a specific Lock and are created by calling Lock method new-Condition, which returns a Condition object. To wait on a Condition, the thread can call the Condition's await method. This immediately releases the associated Lock and places the thread in the *waiting* state for that Condition. Other threads can then try to obtain the Lock.

- When a *runnable* thread completes a task and determines that a *waiting* thread can now continue, the *runnable* thread can call Condition method signal to allow a thread in that Condition's *waiting* state to return to the *runnable* state. At this point, the thread that transitioned from the *waiting* state to the *runnable* state can attempt to reacquire the Lock.

- If multiple threads are in a Condition's *waiting* state when signal is called, the default implementation of Condition signals the longest-waiting thread to transition to the *runnable* state.

- If a thread calls Condition method signalAll, then all the threads waiting for that condition transition to the *runnable* state and become eligible to reacquire the Lock.

- When a thread is finished with a shared object, it must call method unlock to release the Lock.

- Locks allow you to interrupt waiting threads or to specify a timeout for waiting to acquire a lock—not possible with synchronized. Also, a Lock object is not constrained to be acquired and released in the same block of code, which is the case with the synchronized keyword.

- Condition objects allow you to specify multiple conditions on which threads may wait. Thus, it's possible to indicate to waiting threads that a specific condition object is now true by calling that Condition object's signal or signallAll methods. With synchronized, there is no way to explicitly state the condition on which threads are waiting.

Section 26.11 Multithreading with GUI

- The event dispatch thread handles interactions with the application's GUI components. All tasks that interact with the GUI are placed in an event queue and executed sequentially by this thread.

- Swing GUI components are not thread safe. Thread safety is achieved by ensuring that Swing components are accessed from only the event dispatch thread.

- Performing a lengthy computation in response to a user interface interaction ties up the event dispatch thread, preventing it from attending to other tasks and causing the GUI components to become unresponsive. Long-running computations should be handled in separate threads.

- You can extend generic class SwingWorker (package javax.swing), which implements Runnable, to perform long-running computations in a worker thread and to update Swing components from the event dispatch thread based on the computations' results. You override its doInBackground and done methods. Method doInBackground performs the computation and returns the result. Method done displays the results in the GUI.

- Class SwingWorker's first type parameter indicates the type returned by the doInBackground method; the second indicates the type that is passed between the publish and process methods to handle intermediate results.

- Method doInBackground is called from a worker thread. After doInBackground returns, method done is called from the event dispatch thread to display the results.

- An ExecutionException is thrown if an exception occurs during the computation.

- SwingWorker method publish repeatedly sends intermediate results to method process, which displays the results in a GUI component. Method setProgress updates the progress property.

- Method process executes in the event dispatch thread and receives data from method publish. The passing of values between publish in the worker thread and process in the event dispatch thread is asynchronous; process is not necessarily invoked for every call to publish.

- PropertyChangeListener is an interface from package java.beans that defines a single method, propertyChange. Every time method setProgress is invoked, a PropertyChangeEvent is generated to indicate that the progress property has changed.

Section 26.12 Interfaces *Callable* and *Future*

- The Callable interface (of package java.util.concurrent) declares a single method named call. The interface is similar to Runnable—allowing an action to be performed concurrently in a separate thread—but call allows the thread to return a value or to throw a checked exception.

- ExecutorService method submit executes a Callable passed in as its argument.

- Method submit returns an object of type Future (of package java.util.concurrent) that represents the executing Callable. Interface Future declares method get to return the result of the Callable and provides other methods to manage a Callable's execution.

Terminology

Self-Review Exercises

26.1   Fill in the blanks in each of the following statements:
   a) C and C++ are _____-threaded languages, whereas Java is a(n) _____-threaded language.
   b) A thread enters the *terminated* state when _____.
   c) To pause for a designated number of milliseconds and resume execution, a thread should call method _____ of class _____.
   d) Method _____ of class `Condition` moves a single thread in an object's *waiting* state to the *runnable* state.
   e) Method _____ of class `Condition` moves every thread in an object's *waiting* state to the *runnable* state.
   f) A(n) _____ thread enters the _____ state when it completes its task or otherwise terminates.
   g) A *runnable* thread can enter the _____ state for a specified interval of time.
   h) At the operating-system level, the *runnable* state actually encompasses two separate states, _____ and _____.
   i) `Runnable`s are executed using a class that implements the _____ interface.
   j) `ExecutorService` method _____ ends each thread in an `ExecutorService` as soon as it finishes executing its current `Runnable`, if any.
   k) A thread can call method _____ on a `Condition` object to release the associated `Lock` and place that thread in the _____ state.
   l) In a(n) _____ relationship, the _____ generates data and stores it in a shared object, and the _____ reads data from the shared object.
   m) Class _____ implements the `BlockingQueue` interface using an array.
   n) Keyword _____ indicates that only one thread at a time should execute on an object.

26.2   State whether each of the following is *true* or *false*. If *false*, explain why.
   a) A thread is not *runnable* if it has terminated.
   b) Some operating systems use timeslicing with threads. Therefore, they can enable threads to preempt threads of the same priority.
   c) When the thread's quantum expires, the thread returns to the *running* state as the operating system assigns it to a processor.
   d) On a single-processor system without timeslicing, each thread in a set of equal-priority threads (with no other threads present) runs to completion before other threads of equal priority get a chance to execute.

Answers to Self-Review Exercises

26.1   a) single, multi. b) its run method ends. c) `sleep`, `Thread`. d) `signal`. e) `signalAll`.
f) *runnable, terminated*. g) *timed waiting*. h) *ready, running*. i) `Executor`. j) `shutdown`. k) `await`,
waiting. l) producer/consumer, producer, consumer. m) `ArrayBlockingQueue`. n) `synchronized`.

26.2 a) True. b) False. Timeslicing allows a thread to execute until its timeslice (or quantum) expires. Then other threads of equal priority can execute. c) False. When a thread's quantum expires, the thread returns to the *ready* state and the operating system assigns to the processor another thread. d) True.

Exercises

26.3 Define each of the following terms.
a) thread
b) multithreading
c) *runnable* state
d) *timed waiting* state
e) preemptive scheduling
f) Runnable interface
g) notifyAll method
h) producer/consumer relationship
i) quantum

26.4 Discuss each of the following terms in the context of Java's threading mechanisms:
a) synchronized
b) producer
c) consumer
d) wait
e) notify
f) Lock
g) Condition

26.5 *(Bouncing Ball)* Write a program that bounces a blue ball inside a JPanel. The ball should begin moving with a mousePressed event. When the ball hits the edge of the JPanel, it should bounce off the edge and continue in the opposite direction. The ball should be updated using a Runnable.

26.6 *(Bouncing Balls)* Modify the program in Exercise 26.5 to add a new ball each time the user clicks the mouse. Provide for a minimum of 20 balls. Randomly choose the color for each new ball.

26.7 *(Bouncing Balls with Shadows)* Modify the program in Exercise 26.6 to add shadows. As a ball moves, draw a solid black oval at the bottom of the JPanel. You may consider adding a 3-D effect by increasing or decreasing the size of each ball when it hits the edge of the JPanel.

26.8 *(Circular Buffer with Locks and Conditions)* Reimplement the example in Section 26.9 so using the Lock and Condition concepts presented in Section 26.10.

If the presence of electricity can be made visible in any part of a circuit, I see no reason why intelligence may not be transmitted instantaneously by electricity.
—Samuel F. B. Morse

Protocol is everything.
—Francois Giuliani

What networks of railroads, highways and canals were in another age, the networks of telecommunications, information and computerization ... are today.
—Bruno Kreisky

The port is near, the bells I hear, the people all exulting.
—Walt Whitman

Networking

Objectives

In this chapter you'll learn:

- To understand Java networking with URLs, sockets and datagrams.
- To implement Java networking applications by using sockets and datagrams.
- To understand how to implement Java clients and servers that communicate with one another.
- To understand how to implement network-based collaborative applications.
- To construct a multithreaded server.

27.1 Introduction

There is much excitement about the Internet and the World Wide Web. The Internet ties the information world together. The World Wide Web makes the Internet easy to use and gives it the flair and sizzle of multimedia. Organizations see the Internet and the web as crucial to their information-systems strategies. Java provides a number of built-in networking capabilities that make it easy to develop Internet-based and web-based applications. Java can enable programs to search the world for information and to collaborate with programs running on other computers internationally, nationally or just within an organization. Java can enable applets and applications to communicate with one another (subject to security constraints).

Java's fundamental networking capabilities are declared by the classes and interfaces of package **java.net**, through which Java offers **stream-based communications** that enable applications to view networking as streams of data. The classes and interfaces of package java.net also offer **packet-based communications** for transmitting individual **packets** of information—commonly used to transmit data images, audio and video over the Internet. In this chapter, we show how to create and manipulate sockets and how to communicate with packets and streams of data.

We focus on both sides of the **client/server relationship**. The **client** requests that some action be performed, and the **server** performs the action and responds to the client. A common implementation of the request-response model is between web browsers and web servers. When a user selects a website to browse through a browser (the client application), a request is sent to the appropriate web server (the server application). The server normally responds to the client by sending an appropriate web page.

We introduce Java's **socket-based communications**, which enable applications to view networking as if it were file I/O—a program can read from a **socket** or write to a socket as simply as reading from a file or writing to a file. The socket is simply a software construct that represents one endpoint of a connection. We show how to create and manipulate stream sockets and datagram sockets.

With **stream sockets**, a process establishes a **connection** to another process. While the connection is in place, data flows between the processes in continuous **streams**. Stream sockets are said to provide a **connection-oriented service**. The protocol used for transmission is the popular **TCP** (**Transmission Control Protocol**).

With **datagram sockets**, individual **packets** of information are transmitted. This is not appropriate for everyday programmers, because the protocol used—**UDP**, the **User Datagram Protocol**—is a **connectionless service**, and thus does not guarantee that packets arrive in any particular order. With UDP, packets can even be lost or duplicated. Significant extra programming is required on your part to deal with these problems (if you choose to do so). UDP is most appropriate for network applications that do not require the error checking and reliability of TCP. Stream sockets and the TCP protocol will be more desirable for the vast majority of Java programmers.

Performance Tip 27.1

Connectionless services generally offer greater performance but less reliability than connection-oriented services.

Portability Tip 27.1

TCP, UDP and related protocols enable heterogeneous computer systems (i.e., computer systems with different processors and different operating systems) to intercommunicate.

We present a case study that implements a client/server chat application similar to the instant-messaging services popular on the web today. This case study is provided as a web bonus at www.deitel.com/books/jhtp8/. The application incorporates many networking techniques introduced in this chapter. It also introduces **multicasting**, in which a server can publish information and many clients can subscribe to it. Each time the server publishes more information, all subscribers receive it. Throughout the examples of this chapter, we'll see that many of the networking details are handled by the Java APIs.

27.2 Manipulating URLs

[*Note:* The example in this section requires some knowledge of XHTML. To learn more about XHTML, visit our XHTML Resource Center at www.deitel.com/xhtml/. You might also be interested in the web page formatting capability known as Cascading Style Sheets (CSS). For more information, visit our CSS Resource Center at www.deitel.com/css21/.]

The Internet offers many protocols. The **HyperText Transfer Protocol (HTTP)**, which forms the basis of the World Wide Web, uses **URIs (Uniform Resource Identifiers)** to identify data on the Internet. URIs that specify the locations of documents are called **URLs (Uniform Resource Locators)**. Common URLs refer to files or directories and can reference objects that perform complex tasks, such as database lookups and Internet searches. If you know the URL of a publicly available web page, you can access it through HTTP.

Java makes it easy to manipulate URLs. When you use a URL that refers to the exact location of a resource (e.g., a web page) as an argument to the **showDocument** method of interface **AppletContext**, the browser in which the applet is executing will access and display that resource. The applet in Figs. 27.1–27.2 demonstrates simple networking capabilities. It enables the user to select a web page from a JList and causes the browser to display the corresponding page. In this example, the networking is performed by the browser.

```
 1   <html>
 2   <head>
 3      <title>Site Selector</title>
 4   </head>
 5   <body>
 6      <applet code = "SiteSelector.class" width = "300" height = "75">
 7         <param name = "title0" value = "Java Home Page">
 8         <param name = "location0" value = "http://java.sun.com/">
 9         <param name = "title1" value = "Deitel">
10         <param name = "location1" value = "http://www.deitel.com/">
11         <param name = "title2" value = "JGuru">
12         <param name = "location2" value = "http://www.jGuru.com/">
13         <param name = "title3" value = "JavaWorld">
14         <param name = "location3" value = "http://www.javaworld.com/">
15      </applet>
16   </body>
17   </html>
```

Fig. 27.1 | XHTML document to load SiteSelector applet.

```
 1   // Fig. 27.2: SiteSelector.java
 2   // Loading a document from a URL into a browser.
 3   import java.net.MalformedURLException;
 4   import java.net.URL;
 5   import java.util.HashMap;
 6   import java.util.ArrayList;
 7   import java.awt.BorderLayout;
 8   import java.applet.AppletContext;
 9   import javax.swing.JApplet;
10   import javax.swing.JLabel;
11   import javax.swing.JList;
12   import javax.swing.JScrollPane;
13   import javax.swing.event.ListSelectionEvent;
14   import javax.swing.event.ListSelectionListener;
15
16   public class SiteSelector extends JApplet
17   {
18      private HashMap< String, URL > sites; // site names and URLs
19      private ArrayList< String > siteNames; // site names
20      private JList siteChooser; // list of sites to choose from
21
22      // read parameters and set up GUI
23      public void init()
24      {
25         sites = new HashMap< String, URL >(); // create HashMap
26         siteNames = new ArrayList< String >(); // create ArrayList
27
28         // obtain parameters from XHTML document
29         getSitesFromHTMLParameters();
30
31         // create GUI components and lay out interface
32         add( new JLabel( "Choose a site to browse" ), BorderLayout.NORTH );
33
```

Fig. 27.2 | Loading a document from a URL into a browser. (Part 1 of 3.)

```
34             siteChooser = new JList( siteNames.toArray() ); // populate JList
35             siteChooser.addListSelectionListener(
36                new ListSelectionListener() // anonymous inner class
37                {
38                   // go to site user selected
39                   public void valueChanged( ListSelectionEvent event )
40                   {
41                      // get selected site name
42                      Object object = siteChooser.getSelectedValue();
43
44                      // use site name to locate corresponding URL
45                      URL newDocument = sites.get( object );
46
47                      // get applet container
48                      AppletContext browser = getAppletContext();
49
50                      // tell applet container to change pages
51                      browser.showDocument( newDocument );
52                   } // end method valueChanged
53                } // end anonymous inner class
54             ); // end call to addListSelectionListener
55
56             add( new JScrollPane( siteChooser ), BorderLayout.CENTER );
57       } // end method init
58
59       // obtain parameters from XHTML document
60       private void getSitesFromHTMLParameters()
61       {
62          String title; // site title
63          String location; // location of site
64          URL url; // URL of location
65          int counter = 0; // count number of sites
66
67          title = getParameter( "title" + counter ); // get first site title
68
69          // loop until no more parameters in XHTML document
70          while ( title != null )
71          {
72             // obtain site location
73             location = getParameter( "location" + counter );
74
75             try // place title/URL in HashMap and title in ArrayList
76             {
77                url = new URL( location ); // convert location to URL
78                sites.put( title, url ); // put title/URL in HashMap
79                siteNames.add( title ); // put title in ArrayList
80             } // end try
81             catch ( MalformedURLException urlException )
82             {
83                urlException.printStackTrace();
84             } // end catch
85
86             ++counter;
```

Fig. 27.2 | Loading a document from a URL into a browser. (Part 2 of 3.)

```
87                  title = getParameter( "title" + counter ); // get next site title
88          } // end while
89      } // end method getSitesFromHTMLParameters
90  } // end class SiteSelector
```

Fig. 27.2 | Loading a document from a URL into a browser. (Part 3 of 3.)

Processing Applet Parameters

This applet takes advantage of **applet parameters** specified in the XHTML document that invokes the applet. When browsing the World Wide Web, you'll often come across applets that are in the public domain—you can use them free of charge on your own web pages (normally in exchange for crediting the applet's creator). Many applets can be customized via parameters supplied from the XHTML file that invokes the applet. For example, Fig. 27.1 contains the XHTML that invokes the applet SiteSelector in Fig. 27.2.

The XHTML document contains eight parameters specified with the **param** element—these lines must appear between the starting and ending applet tags. The applet can read these values and use them to customize itself. Any number of param elements can appear between the starting and ending applet tags. Each parameter has a unique **name** and a **value**. Applet method **getParameter** returns the value associated with a specific parameter name as a String. The argument passed to getParameter is a String containing the name of the parameter in the param element. In this example, parameters represent the title and location of each website the user can select. Parameters specified for this applet are named title#, where the value of # starts at 0 and increments by 1 for each new title. Each title should have a corresponding location parameter of the form location#, where the value of # starts at 0 and increments by 1 for each new location. The statement

```
String title = getParameter( "title0" );
```

gets the value associated with parameter "title0" and assigns it to reference title. If there is no param tag containing the specified parameter, getParameter returns null.

Storing the Website Names and URLs

The applet (Fig. 27.2) obtains from the XHTML document (Fig. 27.1) the choices that will be displayed in the applet's JList. Class SiteSelector uses a HashMap (package java.util) to store the website names and URLs. In this example, the *key* is the String in the JList that represents the website name, and the *value* is a URL object that stores the location of the website to display in the browser.

Class SiteSelector also contains an ArrayList (package java.util) in which the site names are placed so that they can be used to initialize the JList (one version of the JList constructor receives an array of Objects which is returned by ArrayList's toArray method). An ArrayList is a dynamically resizable array of references. Class ArrayList provides method add to add a new element to the end of the ArrayList. (ArrayList and HashMap were discussed in Chapter 20.)

Lines 25–26 in the applet's init method (lines 23–57) create a HashMap object and an ArrayList object. Line 29 calls our utility method getSitesFromHTMLParameters (declared at lines 60–89) to obtain the XHTML parameters from the XHTML document that invoked the applet.

Method getSitesFromHTMLParameters uses Applet method getParameter (line 67) to obtain a website title. If the title is not null, lines 73–87 execute. Line 73 uses Applet method getParameter to obtain the website location. Line 77 uses the location as the value of a new URL object. The URL constructor determines whether its argument represents a valid URL. If not, the URL constructor throws a **MalformedURLException**. Note that the URL constructor must be called in a try block. If the URL constructor generates a MalformedURLException, the call to printStackTrace (line 83) causes the program to output a stack trace to the Java console. On Windows machines, the Java console can be viewed by right clicking the Java icon in the notification area of the taskbar. On other platforms, this is typically accessible through a desktop icon. Then the program attempts to obtain the next website title. The program does not add the site for the invalid URL to the HashMap, so the title will not be displayed in the JList.

For a proper URL, line 78 places the title and URL into the HashMap, and line 79 adds the title to the ArrayList. Line 87 gets the next title from the XHTML document. When the call to getParameter at line 87 returns null, the loop terminates.

Building the Applet's GUI

When method getSitesFromHTMLParameters returns to init, lines 32–56 construct the applet's GUI. Line 32 adds the JLabel "Choose a site to browse" to the NORTH of the JApplet's BorderLayout. Line 34 creates JList siteChooser to allow the user to select web page to view. Lines 35–54 register a ListSelectionListener to handle the JList's events. Line 56 adds siteChooser to the CENTER of the JFrame's BorderLayout.

Processing a User Selection

When the user selects one of the websites listed in siteChooser, the program calls method valueChanged (lines 39–52). Line 42 obtains the selected site name from the JList. Line 45 passes the selected site name (the *key*) to HashMap method get, which locates and returns a reference to the corresponding URL object (the *value*) that is assigned to reference newDocument.

Line 48 uses Applet method **getAppletContext** to get a reference to an AppletContext object that represents the applet container. Line 51 uses the AppletContext reference browser to invoke method showDocument, which receives a URL object as an argument and passes it to the `AppletContext` (i.e., the browser). The browser displays in the current browser window the resource associated with that URL. In this example, all the resources are XHTML documents.

Specifying the Target Frame for Method **showDocument**

A second version of `AppletContext` method `showDocument` enables an applet to specify the so-called **target frame** in which to display the web resource. This second version takes two arguments—a URL object specifying the resource to display and a String representing the target frame. There are some special target frames that can be used as the second argument. The target frame **_blank** results in a new web browser window to display the content from the specified URL. The target frame **_self** specifies that the content from the specified URL should be displayed in the same frame as the applet (the applet's XHTML page is replaced in this case). The target frame **_top** specifies that the browser should remove the current frames in the browser window, then display the content from the specified URL in the current window.

> **Error-Prevention Tip 27.1**
>
> *The applet in Fig. 27.2 must be run from a web browser, such as Mozilla Firefox or Microsoft Internet Explorer, to see the results of displaying another web page. The* appletviewer *is capable only of executing applets—it ignores all other XHTML tags. If the websites in the program contained Java applets, only those applets would appear in the* appletviewer *when the user selected a website. Each applet would execute in a separate* appletviewer *window.*

27.3 Reading a File on a Web Server

Our next example once again hides the networking details from us. The application in Fig. 27.3 uses Swing GUI component **JEditorPane** (from package `javax.swing`) to display the contents of a file on a web server. The user enters a URL in the JTextField at the top of the window, and the application displays the corresponding document (if it exists) in the JEditorPane. Class JEditorPane is able to render both plain text and XHTML-formatted text, as illustrated in the two screen captures (Fig. 27.4), so this application acts as a simple web browser. The application also demonstrates how to process **Hyperlink-Events** when the user clicks a hyperlink in the XHTML document. The techniques shown in this example can also be used in applets. However, an applet is allowed to read files only on the server from which it was downloaded. [*Note:* This program might not work if your web browser must access the web through a proxy server. If you create a JNLP document for this program and use Java Web Start to launch it, Java Web Start will use the proxy server settings from your default web browser.]

```
1   // Fig. 27.3: ReadServerFile.java
2   // Reading a file by opening a connection through a URL.
3   import java.awt.BorderLayout;
4   import java.awt.event.ActionEvent;
5   import java.awt.event.ActionListener;
6   import java.io.IOException;
7   import javax.swing.JEditorPane;
```

Fig. 27.3 | Reading a file by opening a connection through a URL. (Part 1 of 3.)

```java
 8   import javax.swing.JFrame;
 9   import javax.swing.JOptionPane;
10   import javax.swing.JScrollPane;
11   import javax.swing.JTextField;
12   import javax.swing.event.HyperlinkEvent;
13   import javax.swing.event.HyperlinkListener;
14
15   public class ReadServerFile extends JFrame
16   {
17      private JTextField enterField; // JTextField to enter site name
18      private JEditorPane contentsArea; // to display website
19
20      // set up GUI
21      public ReadServerFile()
22      {
23         super( "Simple Web Browser" );
24
25         // create enterField and register its listener
26         enterField = new JTextField( "Enter file URL here" );
27         enterField.addActionListener(
28            new ActionListener()
29            {
30               // get document specified by user
31               public void actionPerformed( ActionEvent event )
32               {
33                  getThePage( event.getActionCommand() );
34               } // end method actionPerformed
35            } // end inner class
36         ); // end call to addActionListener
37
38         add( enterField, BorderLayout.NORTH );
39
40         contentsArea = new JEditorPane(); // create contentsArea
41         contentsArea.setEditable( false );
42         contentsArea.addHyperlinkListener(
43            new HyperlinkListener()
44            {
45               // if user clicked hyperlink, go to specified page
46               public void hyperlinkUpdate( HyperlinkEvent event )
47               {
48                  if ( event.getEventType() ==
49                     HyperlinkEvent.EventType.ACTIVATED )
50                     getThePage( event.getURL().toString() );
51               } // end method hyperlinkUpdate
52            } // end inner class
53         ); // end call to addHyperlinkListener
54
55         add( new JScrollPane( contentsArea ), BorderLayout.CENTER );
56         setSize( 400, 300 ); // set size of window
57         setVisible( true ); // show window
58      } // end ReadServerFile constructor
59
```

Fig. 27.3 | Reading a file by opening a connection through a URL. (Part 2 of 3.)

```
60    // load document
61    private void getThePage( String location )
62    {
63       try // load document and display location
64       {
65          contentsArea.setPage( location ); // set the page
66          enterField.setText( location ); // set the text
67       } // end try
68       catch ( IOException ioException )
69       {
70          JOptionPane.showMessageDialog( this,
71             "Error retrieving specified URL", "Bad URL",
72             JOptionPane.ERROR_MESSAGE );
73       } // end catch
74    } // end method getThePage
75 } // end class ReadServerFile
```

Fig. 27.3 | Reading a file by opening a connection through a URL. (Part 3 of 3.)

```
1    // Fig. 27.4: ReadServerFileTest.java
2    // Create and start a ReadServerFile.
3    import javax.swing.JFrame;
4
5    public class ReadServerFileTest
6    {
7       public static void main( String[] args )
8       {
9          ReadServerFile application = new ReadServerFile();
10         application.setDefaultCloseOperation( JFrame.EXIT_ON_CLOSE );
11      } // end main
12   } // end class ReadServerFileTest
```

Fig. 27.4 | Test class for ReadServerFile.

The application class ReadServerFile contains JTextField enterField, in which the user enters the URL of the file to read and JEditorPane contentsArea to display the contents of the file. When the user presses the *Enter* key in enterField, the application calls method actionPerformed (lines 31–34). Line 33 uses ActionEvent method getActionCommand to get the String the user input in the JTextField and passes the String to utility method getThePage (lines 61–74).

Line 65 invokes JEditorPane method **setPage** to download the document specified by location and display it in the JEditorPane. If there is an error downloading the document, method setPage throws an IOException. Also, if an invalid URL is specified, a MalformedURLException (a subclass of IOException) occurs. If the document loads successfully, line 66 displays the current location in enterField.

Typically, an XHTML document contains **hyperlinks** that, when clicked, provide quick access to another document on the web. If a JEditorPane contains an XHTML document and the user clicks a hyperlink, the JEditorPane generates a **HyperlinkEvent** (package javax.swing.event) and notifies all registered **HyperlinkListeners** (package javax.swing.event) of that event. Lines 42–53 register a HyperlinkListener to handle HyperlinkEvents. When a HyperlinkEvent occurs, the program calls method **hyperlinkUpdate** (lines 46–51). Lines 48–49 use HyperlinkEvent method **getEventType** to determine the type of the HyperlinkEvent. Class HyperlinkEvent contains a public nested class called **EventType** that declares three static EventType objects, which represent the hyperlink event types. **ACTIVATED** indicates that the user clicked a hyperlink to change web pages, **ENTERED** indicates that the user moved the mouse over a hyperlink and **EXITED** indicates that the user moved the mouse away from a hyperlink. If a hyperlink was ACTIVATED, line 50 uses HyperlinkEvent method **getURL** to obtain the URL represented by the hyperlink. Method toString converts the returned URL to a String that can be passed to utility method getThePage.

Look-and-Feel Observation 27.1

A JEditorPane generates HyperlinkEvents only if it's uneditable.

27.4 **Establishing a Simple Server Using Stream Sockets**

The two examples discussed so far use high-level Java networking capabilities to communicate between applications. In the examples, it was not your responsibility to establish the connection between a client and a server. The first program relied on the web browser to communicate with a web server. The second program relied on a JEditorPane to perform the connection. This section begins our discussion of creating your own applications that can communicate with one another.

*Step 1: Create a **ServerSocket***
Establishing a simple server in Java requires five steps. *Step 1* is to create a **ServerSocket** object. A call to the ServerSocket constructor, such as

```
ServerSocket server = new ServerSocket( portNumber, queueLength );
```

registers an available TCP **port number** and specifies the maximum number of clients that can wait to connect to the server (i.e., the **queue length**). The port number is used by clients to locate the server application on the server computer. This is often called the **handshake point**. If the queue is full, the server refuses client connections. The constructor establishes the port where the server waits for connections from clients—a process known as **binding the server to the port**. Each client will ask to connect to the server on this **port**. Only one application at a time can be bound to a specific port on the server.

Software Engineering Observation 27.1

Port numbers can be between 0 and 65,535. Most operating systems reserve port numbers below 1024 for system services (e.g., e-mail and World Wide Web servers). Generally, these ports should not be specified as connection ports in user programs. In fact, some operating systems require special access privileges to bind to port numbers below 1024.

Step 2: Wait for a Connection

Programs manage each client connection with a **Socket** object. In *Step 2*, the server listens indefinitely (or **blocks**) for an attempt by a client to connect. To listen for a client connection, the program calls ServerSocket method **accept**, as in

```
Socket connection = server.accept();
```

which returns a Socket when a connection with a client is established. The Socket allows the server to interact with the client. The interactions with the client actually occur at a different server port from the handshake point. This allows the port specified in *Step 1* to be used again in a multithreaded server to accept another client connection. We demonstrate this concept in Section 27.8.

Step 3: Get the Socket's I/O Streams

Step 3 is to get the OutputStream and InputStream objects that enable the server to communicate with the client by sending and receiving bytes. The server sends information to the client via an OutputStream and receives information from the client via an Input-Stream. The server invokes method **getOutputStream** on the Socket to get a reference to the Socket's OutputStream and invokes method **getInputStream** on the Socket to get a reference to the Socket's InputStream.

The stream objects can be used to send or receive individual bytes or sequences of bytes with the OutputStream's method write and the InputStream's method read, respectively. Often it's useful to send or receive values of primitive types (e.g., int and double) or Serializable objects (e.g., Strings or other serializable types) rather than sending bytes. In this case, we can use the techniques discussed in Chapter 17 to wrap other stream types (e.g., ObjectOutputStream and ObjectInputStream) around the Out-putStream and InputStream associated with the Socket. For example,

```
ObjectInputStream input =
    new ObjectInputStream( connection.getInputStream() );
ObjectOutputStream output =
    new ObjectOutputStream( connection.getOutputStream() );
```

The beauty of establishing these relationships is that whatever the server writes to the ObjectOutputStream is sent via the OutputStream and is available at the client's InputStream, and whatever the client writes to its OutputStream (with a corresponding ObjectOutputStream) is available via the server's InputStream. The transmission of the data over the network is seamless and is handled completely by Java.

Step 4: Perform the Processing

Step 4 is the *processing* phase, in which the server and the client communicate via the Out-putStream and InputStream objects.

Step 5: Close the Connection
In *Step 5*, when the transmission is complete, the server closes the connection by invoking the **close** method on the streams and on the Socket.

> **Software Engineering Observation 27.2**
> *With sockets, network I/O appears to Java programs to be similar to sequential file I/O. Sockets hide much of the complexity of network programming from you.*

> **Software Engineering Observation 27.3**
> *A multithreaded server can take the Socket returned by each call to accept and create a new thread that manages network I/O across that Socket. Alternatively, a multithreaded server can maintain a pool of threads (a set of already existing threads) ready to manage network I/O across the new Sockets as they are created. These techniques enable multithreaded servers to manage many simultaneous client connections.*

> **Performance Tip 27.2**
> *In high-performance systems in which memory is abundant, a multithreaded server can create a pool of threads that can be assigned quickly to handle network I/O for new Sockets as they're created. Thus, when the server receives a connection, it need not incur thread creation overhead. When the connection is closed, the thread is returned to the pool for reuse.*

27.5 Establishing a Simple Client Using Stream Sockets

Establishing a simple client in Java requires four steps.

Step 1: Create a **Socket** to Connect to the sServer
In *Step 1*, we create a Socket to connect to the server. The Socket constructor establishes the connection. For example, the statement

```
Socket connection = new Socket( serverAddress, port );
```

uses the Socket constructor with two arguments—the server's address (*serverAddress*) and the *port* number. If the connection attempt is successful, this statement returns a Socket. A connection attempt that fails throws an instance of a subclass of IOException, so many programs simply catch IOException. An **UnknownHostException** occurs specifically when the system is unable to resolve the server name specified in the call to the Socket constructor to a corresponding IP address.

Step 2: Get the **Socket's** I/O Streams
In *Step 2*, the client uses Socket methods getInputStream and getOutputStream to obtain references to the Socket's InputStream and OutputStream. As we mentioned in the preceding section, we can use the techniques of Chapter 17 to wrap other stream types around the InputStream and OutputStream associated with the Socket. If the server is sending information in the form of actual types, the client should receive the information in the same format. Thus, if the server sends values with an ObjectOutputStream, the client should read those values with an ObjectInputStream.

Step 3: Perform the Processing
Step 3 is the processing phase in which the client and the server communicate via the InputStream and OutputStream objects.

Step 5: Close the Connection
In *Step 4*, the client closes the connection when the transmission is complete by invoking the close method on the streams and on the Socket. The client must determine when the server is finished sending information so that it can call close to close the Socket connection. For example, the InputStream method read returns the value −1 when it detects end-of-stream (also called EOF—end-of-file). If an ObjectInputStream reads information from the server, an EOFException occurs when the client attempts to read a value from a stream on which end-of-stream is detected.

27.6 Client/Server Interaction with Stream Socket Connections

Figures 27.5 and 27.7 use stream sockets, ObjectInputStream and ObjectOutputStream to demonstrate a simple **client/server chat application**. The server waits for a client connection attempt. When a client connects to the server, the server application sends the client a String object (recall that Strings are Serializable objects) indicating that the connection was successful. Then the client displays the message. The client and server applications each provide text fields that allow the user to type a message and send it to the other application. When the client or the server sends the String "TERMINATE", the connection terminates. Then the server waits for the next client to connect. The declaration of class Server appears in Fig. 27.5. The declaration of class Client appears in Fig. 27.7. The screen captures showing the execution between the client and the server are shown in Fig. 27.8.

Server Class
Server's constructor (Fig. 27.5, lines 30–55) creates the server's GUI, which contains a JTextField and a JTextArea. Server displays its output in the JTextArea. When the main method (lines 6–11 of Fig. 27.6) executes, it creates a Server object, specifies the window's default close operation and calls method runServer (Fig. 27.5, lines 57–86).

```
 1   // Fig. 27.5: Server.java
 2   // Server portion of a client/server stream-socket connection.
 3   import java.io.EOFException;
 4   import java.io.IOException;
 5   import java.io.ObjectInputStream;
 6   import java.io.ObjectOutputStream;
 7   import java.net.ServerSocket;
 8   import java.net.Socket;
 9   import java.awt.BorderLayout;
10   import java.awt.event.ActionEvent;
11   import java.awt.event.ActionListener;
12   import javax.swing.JFrame;
13   import javax.swing.JScrollPane;
14   import javax.swing.JTextArea;
15   import javax.swing.JTextField;
16   import javax.swing.SwingUtilities;
```

Fig. 27.5 | Server portion of a client/server stream-socket connection. (Part 1 of 5.)

```
17
18    public class Server extends JFrame
19    {
20       private JTextField enterField; // inputs message from user
21       private JTextArea displayArea; // display information to user
22       private ObjectOutputStream output; // output stream to client
23       private ObjectInputStream input; // input stream from client
24       private ServerSocket server; // server socket
25       private Socket connection; // connection to client
26       private int counter = 1; // counter of number of connections
27
28       // set up GUI
29       public Server()
30       {
31          super( "Server" );
32
33          enterField = new JTextField(); // create enterField
34          enterField.setEditable( false );
35          enterField.addActionListener(
36             new ActionListener()
37             {
38                // send message to client
39                public void actionPerformed( ActionEvent event )
40                {
41                   sendData( event.getActionCommand() );
42                   enterField.setText( "" );
43                } // end method actionPerformed
44             } // end anonymous inner class
45          ); // end call to addActionListener
46
47          add( enterField, BorderLayout.NORTH );
48
49          displayArea = new JTextArea(); // create displayArea
50          add( new JScrollPane( displayArea ), BorderLayout.CENTER );
51
52          setSize( 300, 150 ); // set size of window
53          setVisible( true ); // show window
54       } // end Server constructor
55
56       // set up and run server
57       public void runServer()
58       {
59          try // set up server to receive connections; process connections
60          {
61             server = new ServerSocket( 12345, 100 ); // create ServerSocket
62
63             while ( true )
64             {
65                try
66                {
67                   waitForConnection(); // wait for a connection
68                   getStreams(); // get input & output streams
69                   processConnection(); // process connection
70                } // end try
```

Fig. 27.5 | Server portion of a client/server stream-socket connection. (Part 2 of 5.)

```
71                  catch ( EOFException eofException )
72                  {
73                     displayMessage( "\nServer terminated connection" );
74                  } // end catch
75                  finally
76                  {
77                     closeConnection(); // close connection
78                     ++counter;
79                  } // end finally
80              } // end while
81          } // end try
82          catch ( IOException ioException )
83          {
84              ioException.printStackTrace();
85          } // end catch
86      } // end method runServer
87
88      // wait for connection to arrive, then display connection info
89      private void waitForConnection() throws IOException
90      {
91          displayMessage( "Waiting for connection\n" );
92          connection = server.accept(); // allow server to accept connection
93          displayMessage( "Connection " + counter + " received from: " +
94              connection.getInetAddress().getHostName() );
95      } // end method waitForConnection
96
97      // get streams to send and receive data
98      private void getStreams() throws IOException
99      {
100         // set up output stream for objects
101         output = new ObjectOutputStream( connection.getOutputStream() );
102         output.flush(); // flush output buffer to send header information
103
104         // set up input stream for objects
105         input = new ObjectInputStream( connection.getInputStream() );
106
107         displayMessage( "\nGot I/O streams\n" );
108     } // end method getStreams
109
110     // process connection with client
111     private void processConnection() throws IOException
112     {
113         String message = "Connection successful";
114         sendData( message ); // send connection successful message
115
116         // enable enterField so server user can send messages
117         setTextFieldEditable( true );
118
119         do // process messages sent from client
120         {
121             try // read message and display it
122             {
123                 message = ( String ) input.readObject(); // read new message
```

Fig. 27.5 | Server portion of a client/server stream-socket connection. (Part 3 of 5.)

```
124            displayMessage( "\n" + message ); // display message
125         } // end try
126         catch ( ClassNotFoundException classNotFoundException )
127         {
128            displayMessage( "\nUnknown object type received" );
129         } // end catch
130
131      } while ( !message.equals( "CLIENT>>> TERMINATE" ) );
132   } // end method processConnection
133
134   // close streams and socket
135   private void closeConnection()
136   {
137      displayMessage( "\nTerminating connection\n" );
138      setTextFieldEditable( false ); // disable enterField
139
140      try
141      {
142         output.close(); // close output stream
143         input.close(); // close input stream
144         connection.close(); // close socket
145      } // end try
146      catch ( IOException ioException )
147      {
148         ioException.printStackTrace();
149      } // end catch
150   } // end method closeConnection
151
152   // send message to client
153   private void sendData( String message )
154   {
155      try // send object to client
156      {
157         output.writeObject( "SERVER>>> " + message );
158         output.flush(); // flush output to client
159         displayMessage( "\nSERVER>>> " + message );
160      } // end try
161      catch ( IOException ioException )
162      {
163         displayArea.append( "\nError writing object" );
164      } // end catch
165   } // end method sendData
166
167   // manipulates displayArea in the event-dispatch thread
168   private void displayMessage( final String messageToDisplay )
169   {
170      SwingUtilities.invokeLater(
171         new Runnable()
172         {
173            public void run() // updates displayArea
174            {
175               displayArea.append( messageToDisplay ); // append message
176            } // end method run
```

Fig. 27.5 | Server portion of a client/server stream-socket connection. (Part 4 of 5.)

```
177              } // end anonymous inner class
178          ); // end call to SwingUtilities.invokeLater
179      } // end method displayMessage
180
181      // manipulates enterField in the event-dispatch thread
182      private void setTextFieldEditable( final boolean editable )
183      {
184          SwingUtilities.invokeLater(
185              new Runnable()
186              {
187                  public void run() // sets enterField's editability
188                  {
189                      enterField.setEditable( editable );
190                  } // end method run
191              } // end inner class
192          ); // end call to SwingUtilities.invokeLater
193      } // end method setTextFieldEditable
194  } // end class Server
```

Fig. 27.5 | Server portion of a client/server stream-socket connection. (Part 5 of 5.)

```
1   // Fig. 27.6: ServerTest.java
2   // Test the Server application.
3   import javax.swing.JFrame;
4
5   public class ServerTest
6   {
7       public static void main( String[] args )
8       {
9           Server application = new Server(); // create server
10          application.setDefaultCloseOperation( JFrame.EXIT_ON_CLOSE );
11          application.runServer(); // run server application
12      } // end main
13  } // end class ServerTest
```

Fig. 27.6 | Test class for Server.

Method *runServer*

Method runServer (Fig. 27.5, lines 57–86) sets up the server to receive a connection and processes one connection at a time. Line 61 creates a ServerSocket called server to wait for connections. The ServerSocket listens for a connection from a client at port 12345. The second argument to the constructor is the number of connections that can wait in a queue to connect to the server (100 in this example). If the queue is full when a client attempts to connect, the server refuses the connection.

Common Programming Error 27.1

*Specifying a port that is already in use or specifying an invalid port number when creating a ServerSocket results in a **BindException**.*

Line 67 calls method waitForConnection (declared at lines 89–95) to wait for a client connection. After the connection is established, line 68 calls method getStreams (declared at lines 98–108) to obtain references to the connection's streams. Line 69 calls method processConnection (declared at lines 111–132) to send the initial connection message to the client and to process all messages received from the client. The finally block (lines 75–79) terminates the client connection by calling method closeConnection (lines 135–150), even if an exception occurs. These methods call displayMessage (lines 168–179), which uses the event-dispatch thread to display messages in the application's JTextArea. **SwingUtilities** method **invokeLater** receives a Runnable object as its argument and places it into the event-dispatch thread for execution. This ensures that we don't modify a GUI component from a thread other than the event-dispatch thread, which is important since Swing GUI components are not thread safe. We use a similar technique in method setTextFieldEditable (lines 182–193), to set the editability of enterField. For more information on interface Runnable, see Chapter 26.

Method waitForConnection
Method waitForConnection (lines 89–95) uses ServerSocket method accept (line 92) to wait for a connection from a client. When a connection occurs, the resulting Socket is assigned to connection. Method accept blocks until a connection is received (i.e., the thread in which accept is called stops executing until a client connects). Lines 93–94 output the host name of the computer that made the connection. Socket method **getInet-Address** returns an **InetAddress** (package java.net) containing information about the client computer. InetAddress method **getHostName** returns the host name of the client computer. For example, a special IP address (**127.0.0.1**) and host name (**localhost**) are useful for testing networking applications on your local computer (this is also known as the **loopback address**). If getHostName is called on an InetAddress containing 127.0.0.1, the corresponding host name returned by the method will be localhost.

Method getStreams
Method getStreams (lines 98–108) obtains the Socket's streams and uses them to initialize an ObjectOutputStream (line 101) and an ObjectInputStream (line 105), respectively. Note the call to ObjectOutputStream method **flush** at line 102. This statement causes the ObjectOutputStream on the server to send a **stream header** to the corresponding client's ObjectInputStream. The stream header contains such information as the version of object serialization being used to send objects. This information is required by the Object-InputStream so that it can prepare to receive those objects correctly.

Software Engineering Observation 27.4
When using ObjectOutputStream and ObjectInputStream to send and receive data over a network connection, always create the ObjectOutputStream first and flush the stream so that the client's ObjectInputStream can prepare to receive the data. This is required for networking applications that communicate using ObjectOutputStream and ObjectInputStream.

Performance Tip 27.3
A computer's I/O components are typically much slower than its memory. Output buffers are used to increase the efficiency of an application by sending larger amounts of data fewer times, reducing the number of times an application accesses the computer's I/O components.

Method **processConnection**

Line 114 of method processConnection (lines 111–132) calls method sendData to send "SERVER>>> Connection successful" as a String to the client. The loop at lines 119–131 executes until the server receives the message "CLIENT>>> TERMINATE". Line 123 uses ObjectInputStream method readObject to read a String from the client. Line 124 invokes method displayMessage to append the message to the JTextArea.

Method **closeConnection**

When the transmission is complete, method processConnection returns, and the program calls method closeConnection (lines 135–150) to close the streams associated with the Socket and close the Socket. Then the server waits for the next connection attempt from a client by continuing with line 67 at the beginning of the while loop.

  Note that Server receives a connection, processes it, closes it and waits for the next connection. A more likely scenario would be a Server that receives a connection, sets it up to be processed as a separate thread of execution, then immediately waits for new connections. The separate threads that process existing connections can continue to execute while the Server concentrates on new connection requests. This makes the server more efficient, because multiple client requests can be processed concurrently. We demonstrate a multithreaded server in Section 27.8.

Processing User Interactions

When the user of the server application enters a String in the text field and presses the *Enter* key, the program calls method actionPerformed (lines 39–43), which reads the String from the text field and calls utility method sendData (lines 153–165) to send the String to the client. Method sendData writes the object, flushes the output buffer and appends the same String to the text area in the server window. It's not necessary to invoke displayMessage to modify the text area here, because method sendData is called from an event handler—thus, sendData executes as part of the event-dispatch thread.

Client Class

Like class Server, class Client's constructor (Fig. 27.7, lines 29–56) creates the GUI of the application (a JTextField and a JTextArea). Client displays its output in the text area. When method main (lines 7–19 of Fig. 27.8) executes, it creates an instance of class Client, specifies the window's default close operation and calls method runClient (Fig. 27.7, lines 59–79). In this example, you can execute the client from any computer on the Internet and specify the IP address or host name of the server computer as a command-line argument to the program. For example, the command

```
java Client 192.168.1.15
```

attempts to connect to the Server on the computer with IP address 192.168.1.15.

```
1   // Fig. 27.7: Client.java
2   // Client portion of a stream-socket connection between client and server.
3   import java.io.EOFException;
4   import java.io.IOException;
5   import java.io.ObjectInputStream;
6   import java.io.ObjectOutputStream;
```

Fig. 27.7 | Client portion of a stream-socket connection between client and server. (Part 1 of 5.)

```
7    import java.net.InetAddress;
8    import java.net.Socket;
9    import java.awt.BorderLayout;
10   import java.awt.event.ActionEvent;
11   import java.awt.event.ActionListener;
12   import javax.swing.JFrame;
13   import javax.swing.JScrollPane;
14   import javax.swing.JTextArea;
15   import javax.swing.JTextField;
16   import javax.swing.SwingUtilities;
17
18   public class Client extends JFrame
19   {
20      private JTextField enterField; // enters information from user
21      private JTextArea displayArea; // display information to user
22      private ObjectOutputStream output; // output stream to server
23      private ObjectInputStream input; // input stream from server
24      private String message = ""; // message from server
25      private String chatServer; // host server for this application
26      private Socket client; // socket to communicate with server
27
28      // initialize chatServer and set up GUI
29      public Client( String host )
30      {
31         super( "Client" );
32
33         chatServer = host; // set server to which this client connects
34
35         enterField = new JTextField(); // create enterField
36         enterField.setEditable( false );
37         enterField.addActionListener(
38            new ActionListener()
39            {
40               // send message to server
41               public void actionPerformed( ActionEvent event )
42               {
43                  sendData( event.getActionCommand() );
44                  enterField.setText( "" );
45               } // end method actionPerformed
46            } // end anonymous inner class
47         ); // end call to addActionListener
48
49         add( enterField, BorderLayout.NORTH );
50
51         displayArea = new JTextArea(); // create displayArea
52         add( new JScrollPane( displayArea ), BorderLayout.CENTER );
53
54         setSize( 300, 150 ); // set size of window
55         setVisible( true ); // show window
56      } // end Client constructor
57
58      // connect to server and process messages from server
59      public void runClient()
60      {
```

Fig. 27.7 | Client portion of a stream-socket connection between client and server. (Part 2 of 5.)

```
61          try // connect to server, get streams, process connection
62          {
63             connectToServer(); // create a Socket to make connection
64             getStreams(); // get the input and output streams
65             processConnection(); // process connection
66          } // end try
67          catch ( EOFException eofException )
68          {
69             displayMessage( "\nClient terminated connection" );
70          } // end catch
71          catch ( IOException ioException )
72          {
73             ioException.printStackTrace();
74          } // end catch
75          finally
76          {
77             closeConnection(); // close connection
78          } // end finally
79       } // end method runClient
80
81       // connect to server
82       private void connectToServer() throws IOException
83       {
84          displayMessage( "Attempting connection\n" );
85
86          // create Socket to make connection to server
87          client = new Socket( InetAddress.getByName( chatServer ), 12345 );
88
89          // display connection information
90          displayMessage( "Connected to: " +
91             client.getInetAddress().getHostName() );
92       } // end method connectToServer
93
94       // get streams to send and receive data
95       private void getStreams() throws IOException
96       {
97          // set up output stream for objects
98          output = new ObjectOutputStream( client.getOutputStream() );
99          output.flush(); // flush output buffer to send header information
100
101         // set up input stream for objects
102         input = new ObjectInputStream( client.getInputStream() );
103
104         displayMessage( "\nGot I/O streams\n" );
105      } // end method getStreams
106
107      // process connection with server
108      private void processConnection() throws IOException
109      {
110         // enable enterField so client user can send messages
111         setTextFieldEditable( true );
112
113         do // process messages sent from server
114         {
```

Fig. 27.7 | Client portion of a stream-socket connection between client and server. (Part 3 of 5.)

```
115              try // read message and display it
116              {
117                 message = ( String ) input.readObject(); // read new message
118                 displayMessage( "\n" + message ); // display message
119              } // end try
120              catch ( ClassNotFoundException classNotFoundException )
121              {
122                 displayMessage( "\nUnknown object type received" );
123              } // end catch
124
125          } while ( !message.equals( "SERVER>>> TERMINATE" ) );
126      } // end method processConnection
127
128      // close streams and socket
129      private void closeConnection()
130      {
131          displayMessage( "\nClosing connection" );
132          setTextFieldEditable( false ); // disable enterField
133
134          try
135          {
136              output.close(); // close output stream
137              input.close(); // close input stream   1
138              client.close(); // close socket
139          } // end try
140          catch ( IOException ioException )
141          {
142              ioException.printStackTrace();
143          } // end catch
144      } // end method closeConnection
145
146      // send message to server
147      private void sendData( String message )
148      {
149          try // send object to server
150          {
151              output.writeObject( "CLIENT>>> " + message );
152              output.flush(); // flush data to output
153              displayMessage( "\nCLIENT>>> " + message );
154          } // end try
155          catch ( IOException ioException )
156          {
157              displayArea.append( "\nError writing object" );
158          } // end catch
159      } // end method sendData
160
161      // manipulates displayArea in the event-dispatch thread
162      private void displayMessage( final String messageToDisplay )
163      {
164          SwingUtilities.invokeLater(
165              new Runnable()
166              {
167                  public void run() // updates displayArea
168                  {
```

Fig. 27.7 | Client portion of a stream-socket connection between client and server. (Part 4 of 5.)

```
169                    displayArea.append( messageToDisplay );
170             } // end method run
171          } // end anonymous inner class
172       ); // end call to SwingUtilities.invokeLater
173    } // end method displayMessage
174
175    // manipulates enterField in the event-dispatch thread
176    private void setTextFieldEditable( final boolean editable )
177    {
178       SwingUtilities.invokeLater(
179          new Runnable()
180          {
181             public void run() // sets enterField's editability
182             {
183                enterField.setEditable( editable );
184             } // end method run
185          } // end anonymous inner class
186       ); // end call to SwingUtilities.invokeLater
187    } // end method setTextFieldEditable
188 } // end class Client
```

Fig. 27.7 | Client portion of a stream-socket connection between client and server. (Part 5 of 5.)

```
1  // Fig. 27.8: ClientTest.java
2  // Class that tests the Client.
3  import javax.swing.JFrame;
4
5  public class ClientTest
6  {
7     public static void main( String[] args )
8     {
9        Client application; // declare client application
10
11       // if no command line args
12       if ( args.length == 0 )
13          application = new Client( "127.0.0.1" ); // connect to localhost
14       else
15          application = new Client( args[ 0 ] ); // use args to connect
16
17       application.setDefaultCloseOperation( JFrame.EXIT_ON_CLOSE );
18       application.runClient(); // run client application
19    } // end main
20 } // end class ClientTest
```

Fig. 27.8 | Class that tests the Client.

Method runClient

Client method runClient (Fig. 27.7, lines 59–79) sets up the connection to the server, processes messages received from the server and closes the connection when communication is complete. Line 63 calls method connectToServer (declared at lines 82–92) to perform the connection. After connecting, line 64 calls method getStreams (declared at lines 95–105) to obtain references to the Socket's stream objects. Then line 65 calls method processConnection (declared at lines 108–126) to receive and display messages sent from the server. The finally block (lines 75–78) calls closeConnection (lines 129–144) to close the streams and the Socket even if an exception has occurred. Method displayMessage (lines 162–173) is called from these methods to use the event-dispatch thread to display messages in the application's text area.

Method connectToServer

Method connectToServer (lines 82–92) creates a Socket called client (line 87) to establish a connection. The method passes two arguments to the Socket constructor—the IP address of the server computer and the port number (12345) where the server application is awaiting client connections. In the first argument, InetAddress static method **get-ByName** returns an InetAddress object containing the IP address specified as a command-line argument to the application (or 127.0.0.1 if no command-line arguments are specified). Method getByName can receive a String containing either the actual IP address or the host name of the server. The first argument also could have been written other ways. For the localhost address 127.0.0.1, the first argument could be specified with either of the following expressions:

```
InetAddress.getByName( "localhost" )
InetAddress.getLocalHost()
```

Also, there are versions of the Socket constructor that receive the IP address or host name as a String. The first argument could have been specified as the IP address "127.0.0.1" or the host name "localhost". We chose to demonstrate the client/server relationship by connecting between applications on the same computer (localhost). Normally, this first argument would be the IP address of another computer. The InetAddress object for another computer can be obtained by specifying the computer's IP address or host name as the argument to InetAddress method getByName. The Socket constructor's second argument is the server port number. This must match the port number at which the server is waiting for connections (called the handshake point). Once the connection is made, lines 90–91 display a message in the text area indicating the name of the server computer to which the client has connected.

The Client uses an ObjectOutputStream to send data to the server and an Object-InputStream to receive data from the server. Method getStreams (lines 95–105) creates the ObjectOutputStream and ObjectInputStream objects that use the streams associated with the client socket.

Methods processConnection and closeConnection

Method processConnection (lines 108–126) contains a loop that executes until the client receives the message "SERVER>>> TERMINATE". Line 117 reads a String object from the server. Line 118 invokes displayMessage to append the message to the text area. When the transmission is complete, method closeConnection (lines 129–144) closes the streams and the Socket.

Processing User Interactions
When the client application user enters a String in the text field and presses *Enter*, the program calls method actionPerformed (lines 41–45) to read the String, then invokes utility method sendData (147–159) to send the String to the server. Method sendData writes the object, flushes the output buffer and appends the same String to the client window's JTextArea. Once again, it's not necessary to invoke utility method displayMessage to modify the text area here, because method sendData is called from an event handler.

27.7 Connectionless Client/Server Interaction with Datagrams

We've been discussing connection-oriented, streams-based transmission. Now we consider **connectionless transmission with datagrams**.

Connection-oriented transmission is like the telephone system in which you dial and are given a connection to the telephone of the person with whom you wish to communicate. The connection is maintained for your phone call, even when you're not talking.

Connectionless transmission with datagrams is more like the way mail is carried via the postal service. If a large message will not fit in one envelope, you break it into separate pieces that you place in sequentially numbered envelopes. All of the letters are then mailed at once. The letters could arrive in order, out of order or not at all (the last case is rare). The person at the receiving end reassembles the pieces into sequential order before attempting to make sense of the message.

If your message is small enough to fit in one envelope, you need not worry about the "out-of-sequence" problem, but it's still possible that your message might not arrive. One advantage of datagrams over postal mail is that duplicates of datagrams can arrive at the receiving computer.

Figures 27.9–27.12 use datagrams to send packets of information via the User Datagram Protocol (UDP) between a client application and a server application. In the Client application (Fig. 27.11), the user types a message into a text field and presses *Enter*. The program converts the message into a byte array and places it in a datagram packet that is sent to the server. The Server (Figs. 27.9–27.10) receives the packet and displays the information in it, then **echoes** the packet back to the client. Upon receiving the packet, the client displays the information it contains.

Server Class
Class Server (Fig. 27.9) declares two **DatagramPackets** that the server uses to send and receive information and one **DatagramSocket** that sends and receives the packets. The constructor (lines 19–37), which is called from main (Fig. 27.10, lines 7–12), creates the GUI in which the packets of information will be displayed. Line 30 creates the Datagram-Socket in a try block. Line 30 in Fig. 27.9 uses the DatagramSocket constructor that takes an integer port-number argument (5000 in this example) to bind the server to a port where it can receive packets from clients. Clients sending packets to this Server specify the same port number in the packets they send. A **SocketException** is thrown if the DatagramSocket constructor fails to bind the DatagramSocket to the specified port.

Common Programming Error 27.2
Specifying a port that is already in use or specifying an invalid port number when creating a DatagramSocket results in a SocketException.

```
1    // Fig. 27.9: Server.java
2    // Server side of connectionless client/server computing with datagrams.
3    import java.io.IOException;
4    import java.net.DatagramPacket;
5    import java.net.DatagramSocket;
6    import java.net.SocketException;
7    import java.awt.BorderLayout;
8    import javax.swing.JFrame;
9    import javax.swing.JScrollPane;
10   import javax.swing.JTextArea;
11   import javax.swing.SwingUtilities;
12
13   public class Server extends JFrame
14   {
15      private JTextArea displayArea; // displays packets received
16      private DatagramSocket socket; // socket to connect to client
17
18      // set up GUI and DatagramSocket
19      public Server()
20      {
21         super( "Server" );
22
23         displayArea = new JTextArea(); // create displayArea
24         add( new JScrollPane( displayArea ), BorderLayout.CENTER );
25         setSize( 400, 300 ); // set size of window
26         setVisible( true ); // show window
27
28         try // create DatagramSocket for sending and receiving packets
29         {
30            socket = new DatagramSocket( 5000 );
31         } // end try
32         catch ( SocketException socketException )
33         {
34            socketException.printStackTrace();
35            System.exit( 1 );
36         } // end catch
37      } // end Server constructor
38
39      // wait for packets to arrive, display data and echo packet to client
40      public void waitForPackets()
41      {
42         while ( true )
43         {
44            try // receive packet, display contents, return copy to client
45            {
46               byte[] data = new byte[ 100 ]; // set up packet
47               DatagramPacket receivePacket =
48                  new DatagramPacket( data, data.length );
49
50               socket.receive( receivePacket ); // wait to receive packet
51
52               // display information from received packet
53               displayMessage( "\nPacket received:" +
54                  "\nFrom host: " + receivePacket.getAddress() +
```

Fig. 27.9 | Server side of connectionless client/server computing with datagrams. (Part 1 of 2.)

```
55                "\nHost port: " + receivePacket.getPort() +
56                "\nLength: " + receivePacket.getLength() +
57                "\nContaining:\n\t" + new String( receivePacket.getData(),
58                   0, receivePacket.getLength() ) );
59
60             sendPacketToClient( receivePacket ); // send packet to client
61          } // end try
62          catch ( IOException ioException )
63          {
64             displayMessage( ioException + "\n" );
65             ioException.printStackTrace();
66          } // end catch
67       } // end while
68    } // end method waitForPackets
69
70    // echo packet to client
71    private void sendPacketToClient( DatagramPacket receivePacket )
72       throws IOException
73    {
74       displayMessage( "\n\nEcho data to client..." );
75
76       // create packet to send
77       DatagramPacket sendPacket = new DatagramPacket(
78          receivePacket.getData(), receivePacket.getLength(),
79          receivePacket.getAddress(), receivePacket.getPort() );
80
81       socket.send( sendPacket ); // send packet to client
82       displayMessage( "Packet sent\n" );
83    } // end method sendPacketToClient
84
85    // manipulates displayArea in the event-dispatch thread
86    private void displayMessage( final String messageToDisplay )
87    {
88       SwingUtilities.invokeLater(
89          new Runnable()
90          {
91             public void run() // updates displayArea
92             {
93                displayArea.append( messageToDisplay ); // display message
94             } // end method run
95          } // end anonymous inner class
96       ); // end call to SwingUtilities.invokeLater
97    } // end method displayMessage
98 } // end class Server
```

Fig. 27.9 | Server side of connectionless client\server computing with datagrams. (Part 2 of 2.)

```
1  // Fig. 27.10: ServerTest.java
2  // Class that tests the Server.
3  import javax.swing.JFrame;
4
5  public class ServerTest
6  {
```

Fig. 27.10 | Class that tests the Server. (Part 1 of 2.)

```
 7     public static void main( String[] args )
 8     {
 9        Server application = new Server(); // create server
10        application.setDefaultCloseOperation( JFrame.EXIT_ON_CLOSE );
11        application.waitForPackets(); // run server application
12     } // end main
13  } // end class ServerTest
```

Server window after packet
of data is received from Client

Fig. 27.10 | Class that tests the Server. (Part 2 of 2.)

Method *waitForPackets*

Server method waitForPackets (Fig. 27.9, lines 40–68) uses an infinite loop to wait for packets to arrive at the Server. Lines 47–48 create a DatagramPacket in which a received packet of information can be stored. The DatagramPacket constructor for this purpose receives two arguments—a byte array in which the data will be stored and the length of the array. Line 50 uses DatagramSocket method **receive** to wait for a packet to arrive at the Server. Method receive blocks until a packet arrives, then stores the packet in its DatagramPacket argument. The method throws an IOException if an error occurs while receiving a packet.

Method *displayMessage*

When a packet arrives, lines 53–58 call method displayMessage (declared at lines 86–97) to append the packet's contents to the text area. DatagramPacket method **getAddress** (line 54) returns an InetAddress object containing the IP address of the computer from which the packet was sent. Method **getPort** (line 55) returns an integer specifying the port number through which the client computer sent the packet. Method **getLength** (line 56) returns an integer representing the number of bytes of data received. Method **getData** (line 57) returns a byte array containing the data. Lines 57–58 initialize a String object using a three-argument constructor that takes a byte array, the offset and the length. This String is then appended to the text to display.

Method *sendPacketToClient*

After displaying a packet, line 60 calls method sendPacketToClient (declared at lines 71–83) to create a new packet and send it to the client. Lines 77–79 create a DatagramPacket and pass four arguments to its constructor. The first argument specifies the byte array to send. The second argument specifies the number of bytes to send. The third argument specifies the client computer's IP address, to which the packet will be sent. The fourth argument specifies the port where the client is waiting to receive packets. Line 81 sends the packet over the network. Method **send** of DatagramSocket throws an IOException if an error occurs while sending a packet.

Client Class

The Client (Figs. 27.11–27.12) works similarly to class Server, except that the Client sends packets only when the user types a message in a text field and presses the *Enter* key. When this occurs, the program calls method actionPerformed (Fig. 27.11, lines 32–57), which converts the String the user entered into a byte array (line 41). Lines 44–45 create a DatagramPacket and initialize it with the byte array, the length of the String that was entered by the user, the IP address to which the packet is to be sent (InetAddress.getLocalHost() in this example) and the port number at which the Server is waiting for packets (5000 in this example). Line 47 sends the packet. Note that the client in this example must know that the server is receiving packets at port 5000—otherwise, the server will not receive the packets.

```java
1    // Fig. 27.11: Client.java
2    // Client side of connectionless client/server computing with datagrams.
3    import java.io.IOException;
4    import java.net.DatagramPacket;
5    import java.net.DatagramSocket;
6    import java.net.InetAddress;
7    import java.net.SocketException;
8    import java.awt.BorderLayout;
9    import java.awt.event.ActionEvent;
10   import java.awt.event.ActionListener;
11   import javax.swing.JFrame;
12   import javax.swing.JScrollPane;
13   import javax.swing.JTextArea;
14   import javax.swing.JTextField;
15   import javax.swing.SwingUtilities;
16
17   public class Client extends JFrame
18   {
19      private JTextField enterField; // for entering messages
20      private JTextArea displayArea; // for displaying messages
21      private DatagramSocket socket; // socket to connect to server
22
23      // set up GUI and DatagramSocket
24      public Client()
25      {
26         super( "Client" );
27
28         enterField = new JTextField( "Type message here" );
29         enterField.addActionListener(
30            new ActionListener()
31            {
32               public void actionPerformed( ActionEvent event )
33               {
34                  try // create and send packet
35                  {
```

Fig. 27.11 | Client side of connectionless client/server computing with datagrams. (Part 1 of 3.)

```
36                          // get message from textfield
37                          String message = event.getActionCommand();
38                          displayArea.append( "\nSending packet containing: " +
39                             message + "\n" );
40
41                          byte[] data = message.getBytes(); // convert to bytes
42
43                          // create sendPacket
44                          DatagramPacket sendPacket = new DatagramPacket( data,
45                             data.length, InetAddress.getLocalHost(), 5000 );
46
47                          socket.send( sendPacket ); // send packet
48                          displayArea.append( "Packet sent\n" );
49                          displayArea.setCaretPosition(
50                             displayArea.getText().length() );
51                       } // end try
52                       catch ( IOException ioException )
53                       {
54                          displayMessage( ioException + "\n" );
55                          ioException.printStackTrace();
56                       } // end catch
57                    } // end actionPerformed
58                 } // end inner class
59              ); // end call to addActionListener
60
61           add( enterField, BorderLayout.NORTH );
62
63           displayArea = new JTextArea();
64           add( new JScrollPane( displayArea ), BorderLayout.CENTER );
65
66           setSize( 400, 300 ); // set window size
67           setVisible( true ); // show window
68
69           try // create DatagramSocket for sending and receiving packets
70           {
71              socket = new DatagramSocket();
72           } // end try
73           catch ( SocketException socketException )
74           {
75              socketException.printStackTrace();
76              System.exit( 1 );
77           } // end catch
78        } // end Client constructor
79
80        // wait for packets to arrive from Server, display packet contents
81        public void waitForPackets()
82        {
83           while ( true )
84           {
85              try // receive packet and display contents
86              {
87                 byte[] data = new byte[ 100 ]; // set up packet
```

Fig. 27.11 | Client side of connectionless client/server computing with datagrams. (Part 2 of 3.)

```
88            DatagramPacket receivePacket = new DatagramPacket(
89               data, data.length );
90
91            socket.receive( receivePacket ); // wait for packet
92
93            // display packet contents
94            displayMessage( "\nPacket received:" +
95               "\nFrom host: " + receivePacket.getAddress() +
96               "\nHost port: " + receivePacket.getPort() +
97               "\nLength: " + receivePacket.getLength() +
98               "\nContaining:\n\t" + new String( receivePacket.getData(),
99                  0, receivePacket.getLength() ) );
100        } // end try
101        catch ( IOException exception )
102        {
103           displayMessage( exception + "\n" );
104           exception.printStackTrace();
105        } // end catch
106     } // end while
107  } // end method waitForPackets
108
109  // manipulates displayArea in the event-dispatch thread
110  private void displayMessage( final String messageToDisplay )
111  {
112     SwingUtilities.invokeLater(
113        new Runnable()
114        {
115           public void run() // updates displayArea
116           {
117              displayArea.append( messageToDisplay );
118           } // end method run
119        } // end inner class
120     ); // end call to SwingUtilities.invokeLater
121  } // end method displayMessage
122 } // end class Client
```

Fig. 27.11 | Client side of connectionless client/server computing with datagrams. (Part 3 of 3.)

```
1  // Fig. 27.12: ClientTest.java
2  // Tests the Client class.
3  import javax.swing.JFrame;
4
5  public class ClientTest
6  {
7     public static void main( String[] args )
8     {
9        Client application = new Client(); // create client
10       application.setDefaultCloseOperation( JFrame.EXIT_ON_CLOSE );
11       application.waitForPackets(); // run client application
12    } // end main
13 } // end class ClientTest
```

Fig. 27.12 | Class that tests the Client. (Part 1 of 2.)

Client window after sending packet to Server and receiving packet back from Server

Fig. 27.12 | Class that tests the Client. (Part 2 of 2.)

Note that the DatagramSocket constructor call (Fig. 27.11, line 71) in this application does not specify any arguments. This no-argument constructor allows the computer to select the next available port number for the DatagramSocket. The client does not need a specific port number, because the server receives the client's port number as part of each DatagramPacket sent by the client. Thus, the server can send packets back to the same computer and port number from which it receives a packet of information.

Method *waitForPackets*
Client method waitForPackets (lines 81–107) uses an infinite loop to wait for packets from the server. Line 91 blocks until a packet arrives. This does not prevent the user from sending a packet, because the GUI events are handled in the event-dispatch thread. It only prevents the while loop from continuing until a packet arrives at the Client. When a packet arrives, line 91 stores it in receivePacket, and lines 94–99 call method displayMessage (declared at lines 110–121) to display the packet's contents in the text area.

27.8 Client/Server Tic-Tac-Toe Using a Multithreaded Server

This section presents the popular game Tic-Tac-Toe implemented by using client/server techniques with stream sockets. The program consists of a TicTacToeServer application (Figs. 27.13–27.14) that allows two TicTacToeClient applications (Figs. 27.15–27.16) to connect to the server and play Tic-Tac-Toe. Sample outputs are shown in Fig. 27.17.

TicTacToeServer Class
As the TicTacToeServer receives each client connection, it creates an instance of inner-class Player (Fig. 27.13, lines 182–304) to process the client in a separate thread. These threads enable the clients to play the game independently. The first client to connect to the server is player X and the second is player O. Player X makes the first move. The server maintains the information about the board so it can determine if a player's move is valid.

```
1    // Fig. 27.13: TicTacToeServer.java
2    // Server side of client/server Tic-Tac-Toe program.
3    import java.awt.BorderLayout;
4    import java.net.ServerSocket;
5    import java.net.Socket;
6    import java.io.IOException;
7    import java.util.Formatter;
8    import java.util.Scanner;
9    import java.util.concurrent.ExecutorService;
10   import java.util.concurrent.Executors;
11   import java.util.concurrent.locks.Lock;
12   import java.util.concurrent.locks.ReentrantLock;
13   import java.util.concurrent.locks.Condition;
14   import javax.swing.JFrame;
15   import javax.swing.JTextArea;
16   import javax.swing.SwingUtilities;
17
18   public class TicTacToeServer extends JFrame
19   {
20      private String[] board = new String[ 9 ]; // tic-tac-toe board
21      private JTextArea outputArea; // for outputting moves
22      private Player[] players; // array of Players
23      private ServerSocket server; // server socket to connect with clients
24      private int currentPlayer; // keeps track of player with current move
25      private final static int PLAYER_X = 0; // constant for first player
26      private final static int PLAYER_O = 1; // constant for second player
27      private final static String[] MARKS = { "X", "O" }; // array of marks
28      private ExecutorService runGame; // will run players
29      private Lock gameLock; // to lock game for synchronization
30      private Condition otherPlayerConnected; // to wait for other player
31      private Condition otherPlayerTurn; // to wait for other player's turn
32
33      // set up tic-tac-toe server and GUI that displays messages
34      public TicTacToeServer()
35      {
36         super( "Tic-Tac-Toe Server" ); // set title of window
37
38         // create ExecutorService with a thread for each player
39         runGame = Executors.newFixedThreadPool( 2 );
40         gameLock = new ReentrantLock(); // create lock for game
41
42         // condition variable for both players being connected
43         otherPlayerConnected = gameLock.newCondition();
44
45         // condition variable for the other player's turn
46         otherPlayerTurn = gameLock.newCondition();
47
48         for ( int i = 0; i < 9; i++ )
49            board[ i ] = new String( "" ); // create tic-tac-toe board
50         players = new Player[ 2 ]; // create array of players
51         currentPlayer = PLAYER_X; // set current player to first player
52
```

Fig. 27.13 | Server side of client/server Tic-Tac-Toe program. (Part 1 of 6.)

```
53          try
54          {
55             server = new ServerSocket( 12345, 2 ); // set up ServerSocket
56          } // end try
57          catch ( IOException ioException )
58          {
59             ioException.printStackTrace();
60             System.exit( 1 );
61          } // end catch
62
63          outputArea = new JTextArea(); // create JTextArea for output
64          add( outputArea, BorderLayout.CENTER );
65          outputArea.setText( "Server awaiting connections\n" );
66
67          setSize( 300, 300 ); // set size of window
68          setVisible( true ); // show window
69       } // end TicTacToeServer constructor
70
71       // wait for two connections so game can be played
72       public void execute()
73       {
74          // wait for each client to connect
75          for ( int i = 0; i < players.length; i++ )
76          {
77             try // wait for connection, create Player, start runnable
78             {
79                players[ i ] = new Player( server.accept(), i );
80                runGame.execute( players[ i ] ); // execute player runnable
81             } // end try
82             catch ( IOException ioException )
83             {
84                ioException.printStackTrace();
85                System.exit( 1 );
86             } // end catch
87          } // end for
88
89          gameLock.lock(); // lock game to signal player X's thread
90
91          try
92          {
93             players[ PLAYER_X ].setSuspended( false ); // resume player X
94             otherPlayerConnected.signal(); // wake up player X's thread
95          } // end try
96          finally
97          {
98             gameLock.unlock(); // unlock game after signalling player X
99          } // end finally
100      } // end method execute
101
102      // display message in outputArea
103      private void displayMessage( final String messageToDisplay )
104      {
```

Fig. 27.13 | Server side of client/server Tic-Tac-Toe program. (Part 2 of 6.)

```
105          // display message from event-dispatch thread of execution
106          SwingUtilities.invokeLater(
107             new Runnable()
108             {
109                public void run() // updates outputArea
110                {
111                   outputArea.append( messageToDisplay ); // add message
112                } // end  method run
113             } // end inner class
114          ); // end call to SwingUtilities.invokeLater
115       } // end method displayMessage
116
117       // determine if move is valid
118       public boolean validateAndMove( int location, int player )
119       {
120          // while not current player, must wait for turn
121          while ( player != currentPlayer )
122          {
123             gameLock.lock(); // lock game to wait for other player to go
124
125             try
126             {
127                otherPlayerTurn.await(); // wait for player's turn
128             } // end try
129             catch ( InterruptedException exception )
130             {
131                exception.printStackTrace();
132             } // end catch
133             finally
134             {
135                gameLock.unlock(); // unlock game after waiting
136             } // end finally
137          } // end while
138
139          // if location not occupied, make move
140          if ( !isOccupied( location ) )
141          {
142             board[ location ] = MARKS[ currentPlayer ]; // set move on board
143             currentPlayer = ( currentPlayer + 1 ) % 2; // change player
144
145             // let new current player know that move occurred
146             players[ currentPlayer ].otherPlayerMoved( location );
147
148             gameLock.lock(); // lock game to signal other player to go
149
150             try
151             {
152                otherPlayerTurn.signal(); // signal other player to continue
153             } // end try
154             finally
155             {
156                gameLock.unlock(); // unlock game after signaling
157             } // end finally
158
```

Fig. 27.13 | Server side of client/server Tic-Tac-Toe program. (Part 3 of 6.)

```
159            return true; // notify player that move was valid
160         } // end if
161         else // move was not valid
162            return false; // notify player that move was invalid
163      } // end method validateAndMove
164
165      // determine whether location is occupied
166      public boolean isOccupied( int location )
167      {
168         if ( board[ location ].equals( MARKS[ PLAYER_X ] ) ||
169            board [ location ].equals( MARKS[ PLAYER_O ] ) )
170            return true; // location is occupied
171         else
172            return false; // location is not occupied
173      } // end method isOccupied
174
175      // place code in this method to determine whether game over
176      public boolean isGameOver()
177      {
178         return false; // this is left as an exercise
179      } // end method isGameOver
180
181      // private inner class Player manages each Player as a runnable
182      private class Player implements Runnable
183      {
184         private Socket connection; // connection to client
185         private Scanner input; // input from client
186         private Formatter output; // output to client
187         private int playerNumber; // tracks which player this is
188         private String mark; // mark for this player
189         private boolean suspended = true; // whether thread is suspended
190
191         // set up Player thread
192         public Player( Socket socket, int number )
193         {
194            playerNumber = number; // store this player's number
195            mark = MARKS[ playerNumber ]; // specify player's mark
196            connection = socket; // store socket for client
197
198            try // obtain streams from Socket
199            {
200               input = new Scanner( connection.getInputStream() );
201               output = new Formatter( connection.getOutputStream() );
202            } // end try
203            catch ( IOException ioException )
204            {
205               ioException.printStackTrace();
206               System.exit( 1 );
207            } // end catch
208         } // end Player constructor
209
210         // send message that other player moved
211         public void otherPlayerMoved( int location )
212         {
```

Fig. 27.13 | Server side of client/server Tic-Tac-Toe program. (Part 4 of 6.)

```
213            output.format( "Opponent moved\n" );
214            output.format( "%d\n", location ); // send location of move
215            output.flush(); // flush output
216        } // end method otherPlayerMoved
217
218        // control thread's execution
219        public void run()
220        {
221            // send client its mark (X or O), process messages from client
222            try
223            {
224                displayMessage( "Player " + mark + " connected\n" );
225                output.format( "%s\n", mark ); // send player's mark
226                output.flush(); // flush output
227
228                // if player X, wait for another player to arrive
229                if ( playerNumber == PLAYER_X )
230                {
231                    output.format( "%s\n%s", "Player X connected",
232                        "Waiting for another player\n" );
233                    output.flush(); // flush output
234
235                    gameLock.lock(); // lock game to  wait for second player
236
237                    try
238                    {
239                        while( suspended )
240                        {
241                            otherPlayerConnected.await(); // wait for player O
242                        } // end while
243                    } // end try
244                    catch ( InterruptedException exception )
245                    {
246                        exception.printStackTrace();
247                    } // end catch
248                    finally
249                    {
250                        gameLock.unlock(); // unlock game after second player
251                    } // end finally
252
253                    // send message that other player connected
254                    output.format( "Other player connected. Your move.\n" );
255                    output.flush(); // flush output
256                } // end if
257                else
258                {
259                    output.format( "Player O connected, please wait\n" );
260                    output.flush(); // flush output
261                } // end else
262
263                // while game not over
264                while ( !isGameOver() )
265                {
```

Fig. 27.13 | Server side of client/server Tic-Tac-Toe program. (Part 5 of 6.)

```
266                    int location = 0; // initialize move location
267
268                    if ( input.hasNext() )
269                        location = input.nextInt(); // get move location
270
271                    // check for valid move
272                    if ( validateAndMove( location, playerNumber ) )
273                    {
274                        displayMessage( "\nlocation: " + location );
275                        output.format( "Valid move.\n" ); // notify client
276                        output.flush(); // flush output
277                    } // end if
278                    else // move was invalid
279                    {
280                        output.format( "Invalid move, try again\n" );
281                        output.flush(); // flush output
282                    } // end else
283                } // end while
284            } // end try
285            finally
286            {
287                try
288                {
289                    connection.close(); // close connection to client
290                } // end try
291                catch ( IOException ioException )
292                {
293                    ioException.printStackTrace();
294                    System.exit( 1 );
295                } // end catch
296            } // end finally
297        } // end method run
298
299        // set whether or not thread is suspended
300        public void setSuspended( boolean status )
301        {
302            suspended = status; // set value of suspended
303        } // end method setSuspended
304    } // end class Player
305 } // end class TicTacToeServer
```

Fig. 27.13 | Server side of client/server Tic-Tac-Toe program. (Part 6 of 6.)

```
1   // Fig. 27.14: TicTacToeServerTest.java
2   // Class that tests Tic-Tac-Toe server.
3   import javax.swing.JFrame;
4
5   public class TicTacToeServerTest
6   {
7       public static void main( String[] args )
8       {
9           TicTacToeServer application = new TicTacToeServer();
```

Fig. 27.14 | Class that tests Tic-Tac-Toe server. (Part 1 of 2.)

```
10              application.setDefaultCloseOperation( JFrame.EXIT_ON_CLOSE );
11              application.execute();
12        } // end main
13    } // end class TicTacToeServerTest
```

Fig. 27.14 | Class that tests Tic-Tac-Toe server. (Part 2 of 2.)

We begin with a discussion of the server side of the Tic-Tac-Toe game. When the TicTacToeServer application executes, the main method (lines 7–12 of Fig. 27.14) creates a TicTacToeServer object called application. The constructor (Fig. 27.13, lines 34–69) attempts to set up a ServerSocket. If successful, the program displays the server window, then main invokes the TicTacToeServer method execute (lines 72–100). Method execute loops twice, blocking at line 79 each time while waiting for a client connection. When a client connects, line 79 creates a new Player object to manage the connection as a separate thread, and line 80 executes the Player in the runGame thread pool.

When the TicTacToeServer creates a Player, the Player constructor (lines 192–208) receives the Socket object representing the connection to the client and gets the associated input and output streams. Line 201 creates a Formatter (see Chapter 17) by wrapping it around the output stream of the socket. The Player's run method (lines 219–297) controls the information that is sent to and received from the client. First, it passes to the client the character that the client will place on the board when a move is made (line 225). Line 226 calls Formatter method **flush** to force this output to the client. Line 241 suspends player X's thread as it starts executing, because player X can move only after player O connects.

When player O connects, the game can be played, and the run method begins executing its while statement (lines 264–283). Each iteration of this loop reads an integer (line 269) representing the location where the client wants to place a mark (blocking to wait for input, if necessary), and line 272 invokes the TicTacToeServer method validateAndMove (declared at lines 118–163) to check the move. If the move is valid, line 275 sends a message to the client to this effect. If not, line 280 sends a message indicating that the move was invalid. The program maintains board locations as numbers from 0 to 8 (0 through 2 for the first row, 3 through 5 for the second row and 6 through 8 for the third row).

Method validateAndMove (lines 118–163 in class TicTacToeServer) allows only one player at a time to move, thereby preventing them from modifying the state information of the game simultaneously. If the Player attempting to validate a move is not the current player (i.e., the one allowed to make a move), it's placed in a *wait* state until its turn to move. If the position for the move being validated is already occupied on the board, validMove returns false. Otherwise, the server places a mark for the player in its local representation of the board (line 142), notifies the other Player object (line 146) that a move has been made (so that the client can be sent a message), invokes method signal (line 152) so that the waiting Player (if there is one) can validate a move and returns true (line 159) to indicate that the move is valid.

TicTacToeClient *Class*

Each TicTacToeClient application (Figs. 27.15–27.16; sample outputs in Fig. 27.17) maintains its own GUI version of the Tic-Tac-Toe board on which it displays the state of the game. The clients can place a mark only in an empty square on the board. Inner class Square (Fig. 27.15, lines 205–261) implements each of the nine squares on the board. When a TicTacToeClient begins execution, it creates a JTextArea in which messages from the server and a representation of the board using nine Square objects are displayed. The startClient method (lines 80–100) opens a connection to the server and gets the associated input and output streams from the Socket object. Lines 85–86 make a connection to the server. Class TicTacToeClient implements interface Runnable so that a separate thread can read messages from the server. This approach enables the user to interact with the board (in the event-dispatch thread) while waiting for messages from the server. After establishing the connection to the server, line 99 executes the client with the worker ExecutorService. The run method (lines 103–126) controls the separate thread of execution. The method first reads the mark character (X or O) from the server (line 105), then loops continuously (lines 121–125) and reads messages from the server (line 124). Each message is passed to the processMessage method (lines 129–156) for processing.

```
 1   // Fig. 27.15: TicTacToeClient.java
 2   // Client side of client/server Tic-Tac-Toe program.
 3   import java.awt.BorderLayout;
 4   import java.awt.Dimension;
 5   import java.awt.Graphics;
 6   import java.awt.GridLayout;
 7   import java.awt.event.MouseAdapter;
 8   import java.awt.event.MouseEvent;
 9   import java.net.Socket;
10   import java.net.InetAddress;
11   import java.io.IOException;
12   import javax.swing.JFrame;
13   import javax.swing.JPanel;
14   import javax.swing.JScrollPane;
15   import javax.swing.JTextArea;
16   import javax.swing.JTextField;
17   import javax.swing.SwingUtilities;
18   import java.util.Formatter;
19   import java.util.Scanner;
20   import java.util.concurrent.Executors;
21   import java.util.concurrent.ExecutorService;
22
```

Fig. 27.15 | Client side of client/server Tic-Tac-Toe program. (Part 1 of 6.)

```
23    public class TicTacToeClient extends JFrame implements Runnable
24    {
25       private JTextField idField; // textfield to display player's mark
26       private JTextArea displayArea; // JTextArea to display output
27       private JPanel boardPanel; // panel for tic-tac-toe board
28       private JPanel panel2; // panel to hold board
29       private Square[][] board; // tic-tac-toe board
30       private Square currentSquare; // current square
31       private Socket connection; // connection to server
32       private Scanner input; // input from server
33       private Formatter output; // output to server
34       private String ticTacToeHost; // host name for server
35       private String myMark; // this client's mark
36       private boolean myTurn; // determines which client's turn it is
37       private final String X_MARK = "X"; // mark for first client
38       private final String O_MARK = "O"; // mark for second client
39
40       // set up user-interface and board
41       public TicTacToeClient( String host )
42       {
43          ticTacToeHost = host; // set name of server
44          displayArea = new JTextArea( 4, 30 ); // set up JTextArea
45          displayArea.setEditable( false );
46          add( new JScrollPane( displayArea ), BorderLayout.SOUTH );
47
48          boardPanel = new JPanel(); // set up panel for squares in board
49          boardPanel.setLayout( new GridLayout( 3, 3, 0, 0 ) );
50
51          board = new Square[ 3 ][ 3 ]; // create board
52
53          // loop over the rows in the board
54          for ( int row = 0; row < board.length; row++ )
55          {
56             // loop over the columns in the board
57             for ( int column = 0; column < board[ row ].length; column++ )
58             {
59                // create square
60                board[ row ][ column ] = new Square( ' ', row * 3 + column );
61                boardPanel.add( board[ row ][ column ] ); // add square
62             } // end inner for
63          } // end outer for
64
65          idField = new JTextField(); // set up textfield
66          idField.setEditable( false );
67          add( idField, BorderLayout.NORTH );
68
69          panel2 = new JPanel(); // set up panel to contain boardPanel
70          panel2.add( boardPanel, BorderLayout.CENTER ); // add board panel
71          add( panel2, BorderLayout.CENTER ); // add container panel
72
73          setSize( 300, 225 ); // set size of window
74          setVisible( true ); // show window
75
76          startClient();
```

Fig. 27.15 | Client side of client/server Tic-Tac-Toe program. (Part 2 of 6.)

```
 77       } // end TicTacToeClient constructor
 78
 79       // start the client thread
 80       public void startClient()
 81       {
 82          try // connect to server and get streams
 83          {
 84             // make connection to server
 85             connection = new Socket(
 86                InetAddress.getByName( ticTacToeHost ), 12345 );
 87
 88             // get streams for input and output
 89             input = new Scanner( connection.getInputStream() );
 90             output = new Formatter( connection.getOutputStream() );
 91          } // end try
 92          catch ( IOException ioException )
 93          {
 94             ioException.printStackTrace();
 95          } // end catch
 96
 97          // create and start worker thread for this client
 98          ExecutorService worker = Executors.newFixedThreadPool( 1 );
 99          worker.execute( this ); // execute client
100       } // end method startClient
101
102       // control thread that allows continuous update of displayArea
103       public void run()
104       {
105          myMark = input.nextLine(); // get player's mark (X or O)
106
107          SwingUtilities.invokeLater(
108             new Runnable()
109             {
110                public void run()
111                {
112                   // display player's mark
113                   idField.setText( "You are player \"" + myMark + "\"" );
114                } // end method run
115             } // end anonymous inner class
116          ); // end call to SwingUtilities.invokeLater
117
118          myTurn = ( myMark.equals( X_MARK ) ); // determine if client's turn
119
120          // receive messages sent to client and output them
121          while ( true )
122          {
123             if ( input.hasNextLine() )
124                processMessage( input.nextLine() );
125          } // end while
126       } // end method run
127
128       // process messages received by client
129       private void processMessage( String message )
130       {
```

Fig. 27.15 | Client side of client/server Tic-Tac-Toe program. (Part 3 of 6.)

```
131          // valid move occurred
132          if ( message.equals( "Valid move." ) )
133          {
134             displayMessage( "Valid move, please wait.\n" );
135             setMark( currentSquare, myMark ); // set mark in square
136          } // end if
137          else if ( message.equals( "Invalid move, try again" ) )
138          {
139             displayMessage( message + "\n" ); // display invalid move
140             myTurn = true; // still this client's turn
141          } // end else if
142          else if ( message.equals( "Opponent moved" ) )
143          {
144             int location = input.nextInt(); // get move location
145             input.nextLine(); // skip newline after int location
146             int row = location / 3; // calculate row
147             int column = location % 3; // calculate column
148
149             setMark( board[ row ][ column ],
150                ( myMark.equals( X_MARK ) ? O_MARK : X_MARK ) ); // mark move
151             displayMessage( "Opponent moved. Your turn.\n" );
152             myTurn = true; // now this client's turn
153          } // end else if
154          else
155             displayMessage( message + "\n" ); // display the message
156       } // end method processMessage
157
158       // manipulate displayArea in event-dispatch thread
159       private void displayMessage( final String messageToDisplay )
160       {
161          SwingUtilities.invokeLater(
162             new Runnable()
163             {
164                public void run()
165                {
166                   displayArea.append( messageToDisplay ); // updates output
167                } // end method run
168             } // end inner class
169          ); // end call to SwingUtilities.invokeLater
170       } // end method displayMessage
171
172       // utility method to set mark on board in event-dispatch thread
173       private void setMark( final Square squareToMark, final String mark )
174       {
175          SwingUtilities.invokeLater(
176             new Runnable()
177             {
178                public void run()
179                {
180                   squareToMark.setMark( mark ); // set mark in square
181                } // end method run
182             } // end anonymous inner class
183          ); // end call to SwingUtilities.invokeLater
184       } // end method setMark
```

Fig. 27.15 | Client side of client/server Tic-Tac-Toe program. (Part 4 of 6.)

```
185
186       // send message to server indicating clicked square
187       public void sendClickedSquare( int location )
188       {
189          // if it is my turn
190          if ( myTurn )
191          {
192             output.format( "%d\n", location ); // send location to server
193             output.flush();
194             myTurn = false; // not my turn any more
195          } // end if
196       } // end method sendClickedSquare
197
198       // set current Square
199       public void setCurrentSquare( Square square )
200       {
201          currentSquare = square; // set current square to argument
202       } // end method setCurrentSquare
203
204       // private inner class for the squares on the board
205       private class Square extends JPanel
206       {
207          private String mark; // mark to be drawn in this square
208          private int location; // location of square
209
210          public Square( String squareMark, int squareLocation )
211          {
212             mark = squareMark; // set mark for this square
213             location = squareLocation; // set location of this square
214
215             addMouseListener(
216                new MouseAdapter()
217                {
218                   public void mouseReleased( MouseEvent e )
219                   {
220                      setCurrentSquare( Square.this ); // set current square
221
222                      // send location of this square
223                      sendClickedSquare( getSquareLocation() );
224                   } // end method mouseReleased
225                } // end anonymous inner class
226             ); // end call to addMouseListener
227          } // end Square constructor
228
229          // return preferred size of Square
230          public Dimension getPreferredSize()
231          {
232             return new Dimension( 30, 30 ); // return preferred size
233          } // end method getPreferredSize
234
235          // return minimum size of Square
236          public Dimension getMinimumSize()
237          {
```

Fig. 27.15 | Client side of client/server Tic-Tac-Toe program. (Part 5 of 6.)

```
238              return getPreferredSize(); // return preferred size
239           } // end method getMinimumSize
240
241           // set mark for Square
242           public void setMark( String newMark )
243           {
244              mark = newMark; // set mark of square
245              repaint(); // repaint square
246           } // end method setMark
247
248           // return Square location
249           public int getSquareLocation()
250           {
251              return location; // return location of square
252           } // end method getSquareLocation
253
254           // draw Square
255           public void paintComponent( Graphics g )
256           {
257              super.paintComponent( g );
258
259              g.drawRect( 0, 0, 29, 29 ); // draw square
260              g.drawString( mark, 11, 20 ); // draw mark
261           } // end method paintComponent
262        } // end inner-class Square
263     } // end class TicTacToeClient
```

Fig. 27.15 | Client side of client/server Tic-Tac-Toe program. (Part 6 of 6.)

```
1     // Fig. 27.16: TicTacToeClientTest.java
2     // Test class for Tic-Tac-Toe client.
3     import javax.swing.JFrame;
4
5     public class TicTacToeClientTest
6     {
7        public static void main( String[] args )
8        {
9           TicTacToeClient application; // declare client application
10
11          // if no command line args
12          if ( args.length == 0 )
13             application = new TicTacToeClient( "127.0.0.1" ); // localhost
14          else
15             application = new TicTacToeClient( args[ 0 ] ); // use args
16
17          application.setDefaultCloseOperation( JFrame.EXIT_ON_CLOSE );
18       } // end main
19    } // end class TicTacToeClientTest
```

Fig. 27.16 | Test class for Tic-Tac-Toe client.

If the message received is "Valid move.", lines 134–135 display the message "Valid move, please wait." and call method setMark (lines 173–184) to set the client's mark in the current square (the one in which the user clicked), using SwingUtilities method invokeLater to ensure that the GUI updates occur in the event-dispatch thread. If the message received is "Invalid move, try again.", line 139 displays the message so that the user can click a different square. If the message received is "Opponent moved.", line 144 reads an integer from the server indicating where the opponent moved, and lines 149–150 place a mark in that square of the board (again using SwingUtilities method invoke-Later to ensure that the GUI updates occur in the event-dispatch thread). If any other message is received, line 155 simply displays the message.

Fig. 27.17 | Sample outputs from the client/server Tic-Tac-Toe program.

27.9 [Web Bonus] Case Study: DeitelMessenger Server and Client

[*Note:* This case study is available at www.deitel.com/books/jhtp8/.] Chat rooms are common on the Internet. They provide a central location where users can chat with each other via short text messages. Each participant can see all the messages that the other users post, and each user can post messages. This case study integrates many of the Java networking, multithreading and Swing GUI features you've learned thus far to build an online chat system. We also introduce **multicasting**, which enables an application to send DatagramPackets to groups of clients.

The DeitelMessenger case study is a significant application that uses many intermediate Java features, such as networking with Sockets, DatagramPackets and MulticastSockets, multithreading and Swing GUI. The case study also demonstrates good software engineering practices by separating interface from implementation, enabling developers to support different network protocols and provide different user interfaces. After reading this case study, you'll be able to build more significant networking applications.

27.10 Wrap-Up

In this chapter, you learned the basics of network programming in Java. We began with a simple applet and application in which Java performed the networking for you. You then learned two different methods of sending data over a network—streams-based networking using TCP/IP and datagrams-based networking using UDP. We showed how to build simple client/server chat programs using both streams-based and datagram-based networking. You then saw a client/server Tic-Tac-Toe game that enables two clients to play by interacting with a multithreaded server that maintains the game's state and logic. In the next chapter, you'll learn basic database concepts, how to interact with data in a database using SQL and how to use JDBC to allow Java applications to manipulate database data.

Summary

Section 27.1 Introduction

- Java provides stream sockets and datagram sockets. With stream sockets, a process establishes a connection to another process. While the connection is in place, data flows between the processes in streams. Stream sockets are said to provide a connection-oriented service. The protocol used for transmission is the popular TCP (Transmission Control Protocol).

- With datagram sockets, individual packets of information are transmitted. UDP (User Datagram Protocol) is a connectionless service that does not guarantee that packets will not be lost, duplicated or arrive out of sequence.

Section 27.2 Manipulating URLs

- The HTTP protocol (Hypertext Transfer Protocol) that forms the basis of the web uses URIs (Uniform Resource Identifiers) to locate data on the Internet. Common URIs represent files or directories and can represent complex tasks such as database lookups and Internet searches. A URI that represents a document is called a URL (Uniform Resource Locator).

- Applet method getAppletContext returns an AppletContext that represents the browser in which the applet is executing. AppletContext method showDocument receives a URL and passes it to the AppletContext, which displays the corresponding web resource. A second version of show-Document enables an applet to specify the target frame in which to display a web resource.

Section 27.3 Reading a File on a Web Server
- JEditorPane method setPage downloads the document specified by its argument and displays it.
- Typically, an XHTML document contains hyperlinks that, when clicked, link other documents on the web. If an XHTML document is displayed in an uneditable JEditorPane and the user clicks a hyperlink, the JEditorPane generates a HyperlinkEvent and notifies its HyperlinkListeners.
- HyperlinkEvent method getEventType determines the event type. HyperlinkEvent contains nested class EventType, which declares three hyperlink event types: ACTIVATED (hyperlink clicked), ENTERED (mouse over a hyperlink) and EXITED (mouse moved away from a hyperlink). HyperlinkEvent method getURL obtains the URL represented by the hyperlink.

Section 27.4 Establishing a Simple Server Using Stream Sockets
- Stream-based connections are managed with Socket objects.
- A ServerSocket object establishes the port where a server waits for connections from clients. The second argument to the ServerSocket constructor is the number of connections that can wait in a queue to connect to the server. If the queue of clients is full, client connections are refused. The ServerSocket method accept waits indefinitely (i.e., blocks) for a connection from a client and returns a Socket object when a connection is established.
- Socket methods getOutputStream and getInputStream get references to a Socket's OutputStream and InputStream, respectively. Socket method close terminates a connection.

Section 27.5 Establishing a Simple Client Using Stream Sockets
- A server name and port number are specified when creating a Socket object to enable it to connect a client to the server. A failed connection attempt throws an IOException.
- InetAddress method getByName returns an InetAddress object containing the IP address of the specified computer. InetAddress method getLocalHost returns an InetAddress object containing the IP address of the local computer executing the program.

Section 27.7 Connectionless Client/Server Interaction with Datagrams
- Connection-oriented transmission is like the telephone system—you dial and are given a connection to the telephone of the person with whom you wish to communicate. The connection is maintained for the duration of your phone call, even when you are not talking.
- Connectionless transmission with datagrams is similar to mail carried via the postal service. A large message that will not fit in one envelope can be broken into separate message pieces that are placed in separate, sequentially numbered envelopes. All the letters are then mailed at once. They could arrive in order, out of order or not at all.
- DatagramPacket objects store packets of data that are to be sent or that are received by an application. DatagramSockets send and receive DatagramPackets.
- The DatagramSocket constructor that takes no arguments binds the DatagramSocket to a port chosen by the computer executing the program. The one that takes an integer port-number argument binds the DatagramSocket to the specified port. If a DatagramSocket constructor fails to bind the DatagramSocket to a port, a SocketException occurs. DatagramSocket method receive blocks (waits) until a packet arrives, then stores the packet in its argument.
- DatagramPacket method getAddress returns an InetAddress object containing information about the computer from which or to which the packet was sent. Method getPort returns an integer specifying the port number through which the DatagramPacket was sent or received. Method getLength returns an integer representing the number of bytes of data in a DatagramPacket. Method getData returns a byte array containing the data in a DatagramPacket.

- The `DatagramPacket` constructor for a packet to be sent takes four arguments—the byte array to be sent, the number of bytes to be sent, the client address to which the packet will be sent and the port number where the client is waiting to receive packets.

- `DatagramSocket` method send sends a `DatagramPacket` out over the network.

- If an error occurs when receiving or sending a `DatagramPacket`, an `IOException` occurs.

Terminology

127.0.0.1 (localhost) 1149
accept method of class `ServerSocket` 1142
`ACTIVATED` constant of nested class `EventType` 1141
`AppletContext` interface 1133
`BindException` class 1148
binding the server to the port 1142
_blank target frame 1138
block 1142
client 1132
client-server relationship 1132
client/server chat 1144
close method of class `Socket` 1143
connection 1132
connection-oriented service 1132
connectionless service 1133
connectionless transmission 1156
datagram packet 1133
datagram socket 1133
`DatagramPacket` class 1156
`DatagramSocket` class 1156
echoes a packet back to the client 1156
`ENTERED` constant of nested class `EventType` 1141
`EventType` nested class of `HyperlinkEvent` 1141
`EXITED` constant of nested class `EventType` 1141
flush method of class `Formatter` 1170
flush method of class `ObjectOutputStream` 1149
getAddress method of class `DatagramPacket` 1159
getAppletContext method of class `Applet` 1137
getByName method of class `InetAddress` 1155
getData method of class `DatagramPacket` 1159
getEventType method of class `HyperlinkEvent` 1141
getHostName method of class `InetAddress` 1149
getInetAddress method of class `Socket` 1149
getInputStream method of class `Socket` 1142
getLength method of class `DatagramPacket` 1159
getLocalHost method of class `InetAddress` 1155
getOutputStream method of class `Socket` 1142

getParameter method of class `Applet` 1136
getPort method of class `DatagramPacket` 1159
getURL method of class `HyperlinkEvent` 1141
handshake point 1141
hyperlink 1141
`HyperlinkEvent` class 1138, 1141
`HyperlinkListener` interface 1141
hyperlinkUpdate method of interface `HyperlinkListener` 1141
HyperText Transfer Protocol (HTTP) 1133
`InetAddress` class 1149
invokeLater method of class `SwingUtilities` 1149
java.net package 1132
`JEditorPane` class 1138
localhost (127.0.0.1) address 1149
loopback address 1149
`MalformedURLException` class 1137
multicast 1133
packet 1132
packet-based communications 1132
param element 1136
port 1142
port number 1141
queue length 1141
receive method of class `DatagramSocket` 1159
register a port 1141
_self target frame 1138
send method of class `DatagramSocket` 1160
server 1132
`ServerSocket` class 1141
setPage method of class `JEditorPane` 1141
showDocument method of interface `AppletContext` 1133
socket 1132
socket-based communication 1132
`Socket` class 1142
`SocketException` class 1156
stream-based communications 1132
stream header 1149
stream socket 1132
streams 1132
`SwingUtilities` class 1149
target frame 1138

TCP (Transmission Control Protocol) 1132
_top target frame 1138
UDP (User Datagram Protocol) 1133

UnknownHostException class 1143
URI (Uniform Resource Identifier) 1133
URL (Uniform Resource Locator) 1133

Self-Review Exercises

27.1   Fill in the blanks in each of the following statements:

a)   Exception _____ occurs when an input/output error occurs when closing a socket.

b)   Exception _____ occurs when a hostname indicated by a client cannot be resolved to an address.

c)   If a DatagramSocket constructor fails to set up a DatagramSocket properly, an exception of type _____ occurs.

d)   Many of Java's networking classes are contained in package _____.

e)   Class _____ binds the application to a port for datagram transmission.

f)   An object of class _____ contains an IP address.

g)   The two types of sockets we discussed in this chapter are _____ and _____.

h)   The acronym URL stands for _____.

i)   The acronym URI stands for _____.

j)   The key protocol that forms the basis of the World Wide Web is _____.

k)   AppletContext method _____ receives a URL object as an argument and displays in a browser the World Wide Web resource associated with that URL.

l)   Method getLocalHost returns a(n) _____ object containing the local IP address of the computer on which the program is executing.

m)   The URL constructor determines whether its String argument is a valid URL. If so, the URL object is initialized with that location. If not, a(n) _____ exception occurs.

27.2   State whether each of the following is *true or false*. If *false*, explain why.

a)   UDP is a connection-oriented protocol.

b)   With stream sockets a process establishes a connection to another process.

c)   A server waits at a port for connections from a client.

d)   Datagram packet transmission over a network is reliable—packets are guaranteed to arrive in sequence.

Answers to Self-Review Exercises

27.1   a) IOException. b) UnknownHostException. c) SocketException. d) java.net. e) DatagramSocket. f) InetAddress. g) stream sockets, datagram sockets. h) Uniform Resource Locator. i) Uniform Resource Identifier. j) HTTP. k) showDocument. l) InetAddress. m) MalformedURLException.

27.2   a)   False; UDP is a connectionless protocol and TCP is a connection-oriented protocol. b) True. c) True. d) False; packets can be lost, arrive out of order or be duplicated.

Exercises

27.3   How does a client determine the hostname of the client computer?

27.4   How can a client get a line of text from a server?

27.5   Describe how a client connects to a server.

27.6   Describe how a server sends data to a client.

27.7   How does a server listen for streams-based socket connections at a port?

27.8   As described in the text, what reasons might cause a server to refuse a connection request from a client?

27.9   Multithreaded servers are quite popular today, especially because of the increasing use of multiprocessing servers. Modify the simple server application presented in Section 27.6 to be a multithreaded server. Then use several client applications and have each of them connect to the server simultaneously. Use an `ArrayList` to store the client threads. `ArrayList` provides several methods to use in this exercise. Method `size` determines the number of elements in an `ArrayList`. Method `get` returns the element in the location specified by its argument. Method `add` places its argument at the end of the `ArrayList`. Method `remove` deletes its argument from the `ArrayList`.

27.10   *(Blackjack Game)* Develop a blackjack card game program in which the server application deals cards to each of the clients. The server should deal additional cards (per the rules of the game) to each player as requested.

27.11   *(Poker Game)* Develop a poker card game in which the server application deals cards to each of the clients. The server should deal additional cards (per the rules of the game) to each player as requested.

27.12   *(Modifications to the Multithreaded Tic-Tac-Toe Program)* The programs in Figs. 27.13 and 27.15 implemented a multithreaded, client/server version of the game of Tic-Tac-Toe. Our goal in developing this game was to demonstrate a multithreaded server that could process multiple connections from clients at the same time. The server in the example is really a mediator between the two client applets—it makes sure that each move is valid and that each client moves in the proper order. The server does not determine who won or lost or whether there was a draw. Also, there is no capability to allow a new game to be played or to terminate an existing game.

The following is a list of suggested modifications to Figs. 27.13 and 27.15:

    a) Modify the `TicTacToeServer` class to test for a win, loss or draw after each move. Send a message to each client that indicates the result of the game when the game is over.

    b) Modify the `TicTacToeClient` class to display a button that when clicked allows the client to play another game. The button should be enabled only when a game completes. Note that both class `TicTacToeClient` and class `TicTacToeServer` must be modified to reset the board and all state information. Also, the other `TicTacToeClient` should be notified that a new game is about to begin so that its board and state can be reset.

    c) Modify the `TicTacToeClient` class to provide a button that allows a client to terminate the program at any time. When the user clicks the button, the server and the other client should be notified. The server should then wait for a connection from another client so that a new game can begin.

    d) Modify the `TicTacToeClient` class and the `TicTacToeServer` class so that the winner of a game can choose game piece X or O for the next game. Remember: X always goes first.

    e) If you'd like to be ambitious, allow a client to play against the server while the server waits for a connection from another client.

27.13   *(Networked Morse Code)* Perhaps the most famous of all coding schemes is the Morse code, developed by Samuel Morse in 1832 for use with the telegraph system. The Morse code assigns a series of dots and dashes to each letter of the alphabet, each digit, and a few special characters (e.g., period, comma, colon and semicolon). In sound-oriented systems, the dot represents a short sound and the dash a long sound. Other representations of dots and dashes are used with light-oriented systems and signal-flag systems. Separation between words is indicated by a space or, simply, the absence of a dot or dash. In a sound-oriented system, a space is indicated by a short time during which no sound is transmitted. The international version of the Morse code appears in Fig. 27.18.

Character	Code	Character	Code	Character	Code
A	.–	N	–.	*Digits*	
B	–...	O	–––	1	.––––
C	–.–.	P	.––.	2	..–––
D	–..	Q	––.–	3	...––
E	.	R	.–.	4	....–
F	..–.	S	...	5	.....
G	––.	T	–	6	–....
H	....	U	..–	7	––...
I	..	V	...–	8	–––..
J	.–––	W	.––	9	––––.
K	–.–	X	–..–	0	–––––
L	.–..	Y	–.––		
M	––	Z	––..		

Fig. 27.18 | Letters and digits in international Morse code.

Write a client/server application in which two clients can send Morse-code messages to each other through a multithreaded server application. The client application should allow the user to type English-language phrases in a JTextArea. When the user sends the message, the client application encodes the text into Morse code and sends the coded message through the server to the other client. Use one blank between each Morse-coded letter and three blanks between each Morse-coded word. When messages are received, they should be decoded and displayed as normal characters and as Morse code. The client should have one JTextField for typing and one JTextArea for displaying the other client's messages.

It is a capital mistake to theorize before one has data.
—Arthur Conan Doyle

Now go, write it before them in a table, and note it in a book, that it may be for the time to come for ever and ever.
—The Holy Bible, Isaiah 30:8

Get your facts first, and then you can distort them as much as you please.
—Mark Twain

I like two kinds of men: domestic and foreign.
—Mae West

Accessing Databases with JDBC

Objectives

In this Chapter you'll learn:

- Relational database concepts.
- To use Structured Query Language (SQL) to retrieve data from and manipulate data in a database.
- To use the JDBC™ API of package `java.sql` to access databases.
- To use the `RowSet` interface from package `javax.sql` to manipulate databases.
- To use JDBC 4.0's automatic JDBC driver discovery.
- To use `PreparedStatement`s to create precompiled SQL statements with parameters.
- How transaction processing makes database applications more robust.

28.1 Introduction

A **database** is an organized collection of data. There are many different strategies for organizing data to facilitate easy access and manipulation. A **database management system (DBMS)** provides mechanisms for storing, organizing, retrieving and modifying data for many users. Database management systems allow for the access and storage of data without concern for the internal representation of data.

Today's most popular database systems are relational databases, where the data is stored without consideration of its physical structure (Section 28.2). A language called **SQL**—pronounced "sequel," or as its individual letters—is the international standard language used almost universally with relational databases to perform **queries** (i.e., to request information that satisfies given criteria) and to manipulate data. [*Note:* As you learn about SQL, you'll see some authors writing "a SQL statement" (which assumes the pronunciation "sequel") and others writing "an SQL statement" (which assumes that the individual letters are pronounced). In this book we pronounce SQL as "sequel."]

Some popular **relational database management systems (RDBMSs)** are Microsoft SQL Server, Oracle, Sybase, IBM DB2, Informix, PostgreSQL and MySQL. The JDK now comes with a pure-Java RDBMS called Java DB—Sun's version of Apache Derby. In this chapter, we present examples using MySQL and Java DB.

Java programs communicate with databases and manipulate their data using the **Java Database Connectivity (JDBC™) API**. A **JDBC driver** enables Java applications to connect to a database in a particular DBMS and allows you to manipulate that database using the JDBC API.

Software Engineering Observation 28.1

Using the JDBC API enables developers to change the underlying DBMS without modifying the Java code that accesses the database.

Most popular database management systems now provide JDBC drivers. There are also many third-party JDBC drivers available. In this chapter, we introduce JDBC and use it to manipulate MySQL and Java DB databases. The techniques demonstrated here can also be used to manipulate other databases that have JDBC drivers. Check your DBMS's documentation to determine whether your DBMS comes with a JDBC driver. If not, third-party vendors provide JDBC drivers for many DBMSs.

> **Software Engineering Observation 28.2**
>
> *Most major database vendors provide their own JDBC database drivers, and many third-party vendors provide JDBC drivers as well. For more information visit devapp.sun.com/product/jdbc/drivers.*

For more information on JDBC, visit

```
java.sun.com/javase/technologies/database/index.jsp
```

which contains JDBC information including the JDBC specification, FAQs, a learning resource center and software downloads to search for JDBC drivers for your DBMS, and

```
developers.sun.com/product/jdbc/drivers/
```

which provides a search engine to help you locate drivers appropriate for your DBMS.

28.2 Relational Databases

A **relational database** is a logical representation of data that allows the data to be accessed without consideration of its physical structure. A relational database stores data in **tables**. Figure 28.1 illustrates a sample table that might be used in a personnel system. The table name is Employee, and its primary purpose is to store the attributes of an employee. Tables are composed of **rows**, and rows are composed of **columns** in which values are stored. This table consists of six rows. The Number column of each row is the table's **primary key**—a column (or group of columns) with a unique value that cannot be duplicated in other rows. This guarantees that each row can be identified by its primary key. Good examples of primary key columns are a social security number, an employee ID number and a part number in an inventory system, as values in each of these columns are guaranteed to be unique. The rows in Fig. 28.1 are displayed in order by primary key. In this case, the rows are listed in increasing order, but we could also use decreasing order.

	Number	Name	Department	Salary	Location
	23603	Jones	413	1100	New Jersey
	24568	Kerwin	413	2000	New Jersey
Row	34589	Larson	642	1800	Los Angeles
	35761	Myers	611	1400	Orlando
	47132	Neumann	413	9000	New Jersey
	78321	Stephens	611	8500	Orlando
	Primary key		Column		

Fig. 28.1 | Employee table sample data.

Rows in tables are not guaranteed to be stored in any particular order. As we'll demonstrate in an upcoming example, programs can specify ordering criteria when requesting data from a database.

Each column represents a different data attribute. Rows are normally unique (by primary key) within a table, but particular column values may be duplicated between rows. For example, three different rows in the Employee table's Department column contain number 413.

Different users of a database are often interested in different data and different relationships among the data. Most users require only subsets of the rows and columns. To obtain these subsets, you use queries to specify which data to select from a table. You use SQL to define complex queries. For example, you might select data from the Employee table to create a result that shows where each department is located, presenting the data sorted in increasing order by department number. This result is shown in Fig. 28.2. SQL queries are discussed in Section 28.4.

Department	Location
413	New Jersey
611	Orlando
642	Los Angeles

Fig. 28.2 | Result of selecting distinct Department and Location data from table Employee.

28.3 Relational Database Overview: The books Database

We now overview relational databases in the context of a sample books database we created for this chapter. Before we discuss SQL, we discuss the tables of the books database. We use this database to introduce various database concepts, including how to use SQL to obtain information from the database and to manipulate the data. We provide a script to create the database. You can find the script in the examples directory for this chapter. Section 28.7 explains how to use this script.

The database consists of three tables: Authors, AuthorISBN and Titles. The Authors table (described in Fig. 28.3) consists of three columns that maintain each author's unique ID number, first name and last name. Figure 28.4 contains sample data from the Authors table of the books database.

Column	Description
AuthorID	Author's ID number in the database. In the books database, this integer column is defined as **autoincremented**—for each row inserted in this table, the AuthorID value is increased by 1 automatically to ensure that each row has a unique AuthorID. This column represents the table's primary key.
FirstName	Author's first name (a string).
LastName	Author's last name (a string).

Fig. 28.3 | Authors table from the books database.

AuthorID	FirstName	LastName
1	Harvey	Deitel
2	Paul	Deitel
3	Andrew	Goldberg
4	David	Choffnes

Fig. 28.4 | Sample data from the Authors table.

The AuthorISBN table (described in Fig. 28.5) consists of two columns that maintain each ISBN and the corresponding author's ID number. This table associates authors with their books. Both columns are foreign keys that represent the relationship between the tables Authors and Titles—one row in table Authors may be associated with many rows in table Titles, and vice versa. The combined columns of the AuthorISBN table represent the table's primary key—thus, each row in this table must be a unique combination of an AuthorID and an ISBN. Figure 28.6 contains sample data from the AuthorISBN table of the books database. [*Note:* To save space, we have split the contents of this table into two columns, each containing the AuthorID and ISBN columns.] The AuthorID column is a **foreign key**—a column in this table that matches the primary key column in another table (i.e., AuthorID in the Authors table). Foreign keys are specified when creating a table. The foreign key helps maintain the **Rule of Referential Integrity**—every foreign-key value must appear as another table's primary-key value. This enables the DBMS to determine whether the AuthorID value for a particular book is valid. Foreign keys also allow related data in multiple tables to be selected from those tables for analytic purposes—this is known as **joining** the data.

Column	Description
AuthorID	The author's ID number, a foreign key to the Authors table.
ISBN	The ISBN for a book, a foreign key to the Titles table.

Fig. 28.5 | AuthorISBN table from the books database.

AuthorID	ISBN	AuthorID	ISBN
1	0131869000	2	0131450913
2	0131869000	1	0131828274
1	0132222205	2	0131828274
2	0132222205	3	0131450913
1	0131450913	4	0131828274

Fig. 28.6 | Sample data from the AuthorISBN table of books.

The Titles table described in Fig. 28.7 consists of four columns that stand for the ISBN, the title, the edition number and the copyright year. The table is in Fig. 28.8.

Column	Description
ISBN	ISBN of the book (a string). The table's primary key. ISBN is an abbreviation for "International Standard Book Number"—a numbering scheme that publishers use to give every book a unique identification number.
Title	Title of the book (a string).
EditionNumber	Edition number of the book (an integer).
Copyright	Copyright year of the book (a string).

Fig. 28.7 | Titles table from the books database.

ISBN	Title	EditionNumber	Copyright
0131869000	Visual Basic 2005 How to Program	3	2006
0131525239	Visual C# 2005 How to Program	2	2006
0132222205	Java How to Program	7	2007
0131857576	C++ How to Program	5	2005
0132404168	C How to Program	5	2007
0131450913	Internet & World Wide Web How to Program	3	2004
0131828274	Operating Systems	3	2004

Fig. 28.8 | Sample data from the Titles table of the books database .

There is a one-to-many relationship between a primary key and a corresponding foreign key (e.g., one publisher can publish many books). A foreign key can appear many times in its own table, but can appear only once (as the primary key) in another table. Figure 28.9 is an **entity-relationship** (**ER**) **diagram** for the books database. This diagram shows the database tables and the relationships among them. The first compartment in each box contains the table's name and the remaining compartments contain the table's columns. The names in italic are primary keys. A table's primary key uniquely identifies each row in the table. Every row must have a primary-key value, and that value must be unique in the table. This is known as the **Rule of Entity Integrity**. Again, for the Author-ISBN table, the primary key is the combination of both columns.

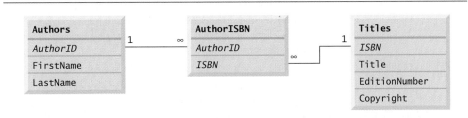

Fig. 28.9 | Table relationships in the books database.

Common Programming Error 28.1

Not providing a value for every column in a primary key breaks the Rule of Entity Integrity and causes the DBMS to report an error.

Common Programming Error 28.2

Providing the same primary-key value in multiple rows causes the DBMS to report an error.

The lines connecting the tables (Fig. 28.9) represent the relationships between the tables. Consider the line between the AuthorISBN and Authors tables. On the Authors end of the line is a 1, and on the AuthorISBN end is an infinity symbol (∞), indicating a **one-to-many relationship** in which every author in the Authors table can have an arbitrary number of books in the AuthorISBN table. The relationship line links the AuthorID column in Authors (i.e., its primary key) to the AuthorID column in AuthorISBN (i.e., its foreign key). The AuthorID column in the AuthorISBN table is a foreign key.

Common Programming Error 28.3

Providing a foreign-key value that does not appear as a primary-key value in another table breaks the Rule of Referential Integrity and causes the DBMS to report an error.

The line between Titles and AuthorISBN illustrates another one-to-many relationship; a title can be written by any number of authors. In fact, the sole purpose of the AuthorISBN table is to provide a many-to-many relationship between Authors and Titles—an author can write many books and a book can have many authors.

28.4 SQL

We now provide an overview of SQL in the context of our books database. You'll be able to use the SQL discussed here in the examples later in the chapter and in examples in Chapters 30–31.

The next several subsections discuss the SQL keywords listed in Fig. 28.10 in the context of SQL queries and statements. Other SQL keywords are beyond this text's scope. To learn other keywords, refer to the SQL reference guide supplied by the vendor of the RDBMS you are using. [*Note:* For more information on SQL, refer to the web resources in Section 28.15.]

SQL keyword	Description
SELECT	Retrieves data from one or more tables.
FROM	Tables involved in the query. Required in every SELECT.
WHERE	Criteria for selection that determine the rows to be retrieved, deleted or updated. Optional in a SQL query or a SQL statement.
GROUP BY	Criteria for grouping rows. Optional in a SELECT query.
ORDER BY	Criteria for ordering rows. Optional in a SELECT query.

Fig. 28.10 | SQL query keywords. (Part 1 of 2.)

SQL keyword	Description
INNER JOIN	Merge rows from multiple tables.
INSERT	Insert rows into a specified table.
UPDATE	Update rows in a specified table.
DELETE	Delete rows from a specified table.

Fig. 28.10 | SQL query keywords. (Part 2 of 2.)

28.4.1 Basic SELECT Query

Let us consider several SQL queries that extract information from database books. A SQL query "selects" rows and columns from one or more tables in a database. Such selections are performed by queries with the **SELECT** keyword. The basic form of a SELECT query is

SELECT * FROM *tableName*

in which the **asterisk** (*) wildcard character indicates that all columns from the *tableName* table should be retrieved. For example, to retrieve all the data in the Authors table, use

SELECT * FROM Authors

Most programs do not require all the data in a table. To retrieve only specific columns, replace the asterisk (*) with a comma-separated list of the column names. For example, to retrieve only the columns AuthorID and LastName for all rows in the Authors table, use the query

SELECT AuthorID, LastName FROM Authors

This query returns the data listed in Fig. 28.11.

AuthorID	LastName
1	Deitel
2	Deitel
3	Goldberg
4	Choffnes

Fig. 28.11 | Sample AuthorID and LastName data from the Authors table.

Software Engineering Observation 28.3

For most queries, the asterisk (*) should not be used to specify column names. In general, you process results by knowing in advance the order of the columns in the result—for example, selecting AuthorID and LastName from table Authors ensures that the columns will appear in the result with AuthorID as the first column and LastName as the second column. Programs typically process result columns by specifying the column number in the result (starting from number 1 for the first column). Selecting columns by name also avoids returning unneeded columns and protects against changes in the actual order of the columns in the table(s) by returning the columns in the exact order specified.

Common Programming Error 28.4

If you assume that the columns are always returned in the same order from a query that uses the asterisk (*), the program may process the results incorrectly. If the column order in the table(s) changes or if additional columns are added at a later time, the order of the columns in the result will change accordingly.

28.4.2 WHERE Clause

In most cases, it is necessary to locate rows in a database that satisfy certain **selection criteria**. Only rows that satisfy the selection criteria (formally called **predicates**) are selected. SQL uses the optional **WHERE clause** in a query to specify the selection criteria for the query. The basic form of a query with selection criteria is

> SELECT *columnName1*, *columnName2*, ... FROM *tableName* WHERE *criteria*

For example, to select the `Title`, `EditionNumber` and `Copyright` columns from table `Titles` for which the `Copyright` date is greater than 2005, use the query

```
SELECT Title, EditionNumber, Copyright
    FROM Titles
    WHERE Copyright > '2005'
```

Notice that strings in SQL are delimited by single (') rather than double (") quotes.

Figure 28.12 shows the result of the preceding query. The `WHERE` clause criteria can contain the operators <, >, <=, >=, =, <> and `LIKE`. Operator **LIKE** is used for **pattern matching** with wildcard characters **percent (%)** and **underscore (_)**. Pattern matching allows SQL to search for strings that match a given pattern.

Title	EditionNumber	Copyright
Visual C# 2005 How to Program	2	2006
Visual Basic 2005 How to Program	3	2006
Java How to Program	7	2007
C How to Program	5	2007

Fig. 28.12 | Sampling of titles with copyrights after 2005 from table `Titles`.

A pattern that contains a percent character (%) searches for strings that have zero or more characters at the percent character's position in the pattern. For example, the next query locates the rows of all the authors whose last name starts with the letter D:

```
SELECT AuthorID, FirstName, LastName
    FROM Authors
    WHERE LastName LIKE 'D%'
```

This query selects the two rows shown in Fig. 28.13—two of the four authors have a last name starting with the letter D (followed by zero or more characters). The % symbol in the `WHERE` clause's `LIKE` pattern indicates that any number of characters can appear after the letter D in the `LastName`. Note that the pattern string is surrounded by single-quote characters.

AuthorID	FirstName	LastName
1	Harvey	Deitel
2	Paul	Deitel

Fig. 28.13 | Authors whose last name starts with D from the Authors table.

Portability Tip 28.1

See the documentation for your database system to determine whether SQL is case sensitive on your system and to determine the syntax for SQL keywords (i.e., should they be all uppercase letters, all lowercase letters or some combination of the two?).

Portability Tip 28.2

Read your database system's documentation carefully to determine whether it supports the LIKE operator as discussed here. The SQL we discuss is supported by most RDBMSs, but it is always a good idea to check the features of SQL that are supported by your RDBMS.

An underscore (_) in the pattern string indicates a single wildcard character at that position in the pattern. For example, the following query locates the rows of all the authors whose last names start with any character (specified by _), followed by the letter o, followed by any number of additional characters (specified by %):

```
SELECT AuthorID, FirstName, LastName
   FROM Authors
   WHERE LastName LIKE '_o%'
```

The preceding query produces the row shown in Fig. 28.14, because only one author in our database has a last name that contains the letter o as its second letter.

AuthorID	FirstName	LastName
3	Andrew	Goldberg

Fig. 28.14 | The only author from the Authors table whose last name contains o as the second letter.

28.4.3 ORDER BY Clause

The rows in the result of a query can be sorted into ascending or descending order by using the optional **ORDER BY clause**. The basic form of a query with an ORDER BY clause is

```
SELECT columnName1, columnName2, ... FROM tableName ORDER BY column ASC
SELECT columnName1, columnName2, ... FROM tableName ORDER BY column DESC
```

where ASC specifies ascending order (lowest to highest), DESC specifies descending order (highest to lowest) and *column* specifies the column on which the sort is based. For example, to obtain the list of authors in ascending order by last name (Fig. 28.15), use the query

```
SELECT AuthorID, FirstName, LastName
   FROM Authors
   ORDER BY LastName ASC
```

AuthorID	FirstName	LastName
4	David	Choffnes
1	Harvey	Deitel
2	Paul	Deitel
3	Andrew	Goldberg

Fig. 28.15 | Sample data from table `Authors` in ascending order by `LastName`.

Note that the default sorting order is ascending, so ASC is optional. To obtain the same list of authors in descending order by last name (Fig. 28.16), use the query

```
SELECT AuthorID, FirstName, LastName
   FROM Authors
   ORDER BY LastName DESC
```

AuthorID	FirstName	LastName
3	Andrew	Goldberg
1	Harvey	Deitel
2	Paul	Deitel
4	David	Choffnes

Fig. 28.16 | Sample data from table `Authors` in descending order by `LastName`.

Multiple columns can be used for sorting with an ORDER BY clause of the form

```
ORDER BY column1 sortingOrder, column2 sortingOrder, ...
```

where *sortingOrder* is either ASC or DESC. Note that the *sortingOrder* does not have to be identical for each column. The query

```
SELECT AuthorID, FirstName, LastName
   FROM Authors
   ORDER BY LastName, FirstName
```

sorts all the rows in ascending order by last name, then by first name. If any rows have the same last-name value, they are returned sorted by first name (Fig. 28.17).

AuthorID	FirstName	LastName
4	David	Choffnes
1	Harvey	Deitel
2	Paul	Deitel
3	Andrew	Goldberg

Fig. 28.17 | Sample data from `Authors` in ascending order by `LastName` and `FirstName`.

The WHERE and ORDER BY clauses can be combined in one query, as in

```
SELECT ISBN, Title, EditionNumber, Copyright
    FROM Titles
    WHERE Title LIKE '%How to Program'
    ORDER BY Title ASC
```

which returns the ISBN, Title, EditionNumber and Copyright of each book in the Titles table that has a Title ending with "How to Program" and sorts them in ascending order by Title. The query results are shown in Fig. 28.18.

ISBN	Title	Edition- Number	Copy- right
0132404168	C How to Program	5	2007
0131857576	C++ How to Program	5	2005
0131450913	Internet and World Wide Web How to Program	3	2004
0132222205	Java How to Program	7	2007
0131869000	Visual Basic 2005 How to Program	3	2006
013152539	Visual C# 2005 How to Program	2	2006

Fig. 28.18 | Sampling of books from table Titles whose titles end with How to Program in ascending order by Title.

28.4.4 Merging Data from Multiple Tables: INNER JOIN

Database designers often split related data into separate tables to ensure that a database does not store data redundantly. For example, the books database has tables Authors and Titles. We use an AuthorISBN table to store the relationship data between authors and their corresponding titles. If we did not separate this information into individual tables, we would need to include author information with each entry in the Titles table. This would result in the database's storing duplicate author information for authors who wrote multiple books. Often, it is necessary to merge data from multiple tables into a single result. Referred to as joining the tables, this is specified by an **INNER JOIN** operator in the query. An INNER JOIN merges rows from two tables by matching values in columns that are common to the tables. The basic form of an INNER JOIN is:

```
SELECT columnName1, columnName2, ...
FROM table1
INNER JOIN table2
    ON table1.columnName = table2.columnName
```

The **ON clause** of the INNER JOIN specifies the columns from each table that are compared to determine which rows are merged. For example, the following query produces a list of authors accompanied by the ISBNs for books written by each author:

```
SELECT FirstName, LastName, ISBN
FROM Authors
INNER JOIN AuthorISBN
    ON Authors.AuthorID = AuthorISBN.AuthorID
ORDER BY LastName, FirstName
```

The query merges the FirstName and LastName columns from table Authors with the ISBN column from table AuthorISBN, sorting the result in ascending order by LastName and FirstName. Note the use of the syntax *tableName.columnName* in the ON clause. This syntax, called a **qualified name**, specifies the columns from each table that should be compared to join the tables. The "*tableName.*" syntax is required if the columns have the same name in both tables. The same syntax can be used in any SQL statement to distinguish columns in different tables that have the same name. In some systems, table names qualified with the database name can be used to perform cross-database queries. As always, the query can contain an ORDER BY clause. Figure 28.19 shows the results of the preceding query, ordered by LastName and FirstName. [*Note:* To save space, we split the result of the query into two columns, each containing the FirstName, LastName and ISBN columns.]

FirstName	LastName	ISBN	FirstName	LastName	ISBN
David	Choffnes	0131828274	Paul	Deitel	0131869000
Harvey	Deitel	0131869000	Paul	Deitel	0131525239
Harvey	Deitel	0131525239	Paul	Deitel	0132222205
Harvey	Deitel	0132222205	Paul	Deitel	0131857576
Harvey	Deitel	0131857576	Paul	Deitel	0132404168
Harvey	Deitel	0132404168	Paul	Deitel	0131450913
Harvey	Deitel	0131450913	Paul	Deitel	0131828274
Harvey	Deitel	0131828274	Andrew	Goldberg	0131450913

Fig. 28.19 | Sampling of authors and ISBNs for the books they have written in ascending order by LastName and FirstName.

Software Engineering Observation 28.4

If a SQL statement includes columns with the same name from multiple tables, the statement must precede those column names with their table names and a dot (e.g., Authors.AuthorID).

Common Programming Error 28.5

Failure to qualify names for columns that have the same name in two or more tables is an error.

28.4.5 INSERT Statement

The **INSERT** statement inserts a row into a table. The basic form of this statement is

```
INSERT INTO tableName ( columnName1, columnName2, ..., columnNameN )
    VALUES ( value1, value2, ..., valueN )
```

where *tableName* is the table in which to insert the row. The *tableName* is followed by a comma-separated list of column names in parentheses (this list is not required if the INSERT operation specifies a value for every column of the table in the correct order). The list of column names is followed by the SQL keyword **VALUES** and a comma-separated list of values in parentheses. The values specified here must match the columns specified after the table name in both order and type (e.g., if *columnName1* is supposed to be the FirstName column, then *value1* should be a string in single quotes representing the first name). Always explicitly list the columns when inserting rows. If the table's column order changes or a new column is added, using only VALUES may cause an error. The INSERT statement

```
INSERT INTO Authors ( FirstName, LastName )
   VALUES ( 'Sue', 'Smith' )
```

inserts a row into the Authors table. The statement indicates that values are provided for the FirstName and LastName columns. The corresponding values are 'Sue' and 'Smith'. We do not specify an AuthorID in this example because AuthorID is an autoincremented column in the Authors table. For every row added to this table, the DBMS assigns a unique AuthorID value that is the next value in the autoincremented sequence (i.e., 1, 2, 3 and so on). In this case, Sue Smith would be assigned AuthorID number 5. Figure 28.20 shows the Authors table after the INSERT operation. [*Note:* Not every database management system supports autoincremented columns. Check the documentation for your DBMS for alternatives to autoincremented columns.]

AuthorID	FirstName	LastName
1	Harvey	Deitel
2	Paul	Deitel
3	Andrew	Goldberg
4	David	Choffnes
5	Sue	Smith

Fig. 28.20 | Sample data from table Authors after an INSERT operation.

Common Programming Error 28.6
It is normally an error to specify a value for an autoincrement column.

Common Programming Error 28.7
SQL delimits strings with single quotes ('). A string containing a single quote (e.g., O'Malley) must have two single quotes in the position where the single quote appears (e.g., 'O''Malley'). The first acts as an escape character for the second. Not escaping single-quote characters in a string that is part of a SQL statement is a SQL syntax error.

28.4.6 UPDATE Statement

An **UPDATE** statement modifies data in a table. Its basic form is

```
UPDATE tableName
   SET columnName1 = value1, columnName2 = value2, ..., columnNameN = valueN
   WHERE criteria
```

where *tableName* is the table to update. The *tableName* is followed by keyword **SET** and a comma-separated list of column name/value pairs in the format *columnName = value*. The optional WHERE clause provides criteria that determine which rows to update. Though not required, the WHERE clause is typically used, unless a change is to be made to every row. The UPDATE statement

```
UPDATE Authors
   SET LastName = 'Jones'
   WHERE LastName = 'Smith' AND FirstName = 'Sue'
```

updates a row in the Authors table. The statement indicates that LastName will be assigned the value Jones for the row in which LastName is equal to Smith and FirstName is equal to Sue. [*Note:* If there are multiple rows with the first name "Sue" and the last name "Smith," this statement will modify all such rows to have the last name "Jones."] If we know the AuthorID in advance of the UPDATE operation (possibly because we searched for it previously), the WHERE clause can be simplified as follows:

```
WHERE AuthorID = 5
```

Figure 28.21 shows the Authors table after the UPDATE operation has taken place.

AuthorID	FirstName	LastName
1	Harvey	Deitel
2	Paul	Deitel
3	Andrew	Goldberg
4	David	Choffnes
5	Sue	Jones

Fig. 28.21 | Sample data from table Authors after an UPDATE operation.

28.4.7 DELETE Statement

A SQL **DELETE** statement removes rows from a table. Its basic form is

```
DELETE FROM tableName WHERE criteria
```

where *tableName* is the table from which to delete. The optional WHERE clause specifies the criteria used to determine which rows to delete. If this clause is omitted, all the table's rows are deleted. The DELETE statement

```
DELETE FROM Authors
   WHERE LastName = 'Jones' AND FirstName = 'Sue'
```

deletes the row for Sue Jones in the Authors table. If we know the AuthorID in advance of the DELETE operation, the WHERE clause can be simplified as follows:

```
WHERE AuthorID = 5
```

Figure 28.22 shows the Authors table after the DELETE operation has taken place.

AuthorID	FirstName	LastName
1	Harvey	Deitel
2	Paul	Deitel
3	Andrew	Goldberg
4	David	Choffnes

Fig. 28.22 | Sample data from table Authors after a DELETE operation.

28.5 Instructions for Installing MySQL and MySQL Connector/J

MySQL 5.0 Community Edition is an open-source database management system that executes on many platforms, including Windows, Solaris, Linux, and Macintosh. Complete information about MySQL is available from `www.mysql.com`. The examples in Sections 28.8–28.9 manipulate MySQL databases.

Installing MySQL
To install MySQL Community Edition:

1. To learn about the installation requirements for your platform, visit the site `dev.mysql.com/doc/refman/5.0/en/installing-cs.html`.

2. Visit `dev.mysql.com/downloads/mysql/5.0.html` and download the installer for your platform. For the MySQL examples in this chapter, you need only the Windows Essentials package on Microsoft Windows, or the Standard package on most other platforms. [*Note:* For these instructions, we assume you are running Microsoft Windows. Complete installation instructions for other platforms are available at `dev.mysql.com/doc/refman/5.0/en/installing.html`.]

3. Double click `mysql-essential-5.0.67-win32.msi` to start the installer. [*Note:* This name may differ based on the current version of MySQL 5.0.] Click **Next >**.

4. Choose **Typical** for the **Setup Type** and click **Next >**. Then click **Install**.

When the installation completes, click **Next >** twice, then **Finish** to begin configuring the server. To configure the server:

1. Click **Next >**, then select **Standard Configuration** and click **Next >** again.

2. You have the option of installing MySQL as a Windows service, which enables the MySQL server to begin executing automatically each time your system starts. For our examples, this is unnecessary, so uncheck **Install as a Windows Service**, then check **Include Bin Directory in Windows PATH**. This will enable you to use the MySQL commands in the Windows Command Prompt.

3. Click **Next >**, then click **Execute** to perform the server configuration.

4. Click **Finish** to close the wizard.

Installing MySQL Connector/J
To use MySQL with JDBC, you also need to install **MySQL Connector/J** (the J stands for Java)—a JDBC driver that allows programs to use JDBC to interact with MySQL. MySQL Connector/J can be downloaded from

```
dev.mysql.com/downloads/connector/j/5.1.html
```

The documentation for Connector/J is located at `dev.mysql.com/doc/connector/j/en/connector-j.html`. At the time of this writing, the current generally available release of MySQL Connector/J is 5.1.7. To install MySQL Connector/J:

1. Download `mysql-connector-java-5.1.7.tar.gz`.

2. Open `mysql-connector-java-5.1.7.tar.gz` with a file extractor, such as Win-Zip (`www.winzip.com`). Extract its contents to the `C:\` drive. This will create a directory named `mysql-connector-java-5.1.7`. This folder's docs subdirectory

contains the MySQL Connector/J documentation (connector-j.pdf). You can also view it online at dev.mysql.com/doc/connector/j/en/connector-j.html.

28.6 Instructions for Setting Up a MySQL User Account

For the MySQL examples to execute correctly, you need to set up a user account that allows users to create, delete and modify a database. After MySQL is installed, follow the steps below to set up a user account (these steps assume MySQL is installed in its default installation directory):

1. Open a Command Prompt and start the database server by executing the command mysqld-nt.exe. Note that this command has no output—it simply starts the MySQL server. Do not close this window—doing so terminates the server.

2. Next, you'll start the MySQL monitor so you can set up a user account, open another Command Prompt and execute the command

   ```
   mysql -h localhost -u root
   ```

   The -h option indicates the host (i.e., computer) on which the MySQL server is running—in this case your local computer (localhost). The -u option indicates the user account that will be used to log in to the server—root is the default user account that is created during installation to allow you to configure the server. Once you've logged in, you'll see a mysql> prompt at which you can type commands to interact with the MySQL server.

3. At the mysql> prompt, type

   ```
   USE mysql;
   ```

   to select the built-in database named mysql, which stores server information, such as user accounts and their privileges for interacting with the server. Note that each command must end with a semicolon. To confirm the command, MySQL issues the message "Database changed."

4. Next, you'll add the deitel user account to the mysql built-in database. The mysql database contains a table called user with columns that represent the user's name, password and various privileges. To create the deitel user account with the password deitel, execute the following commands from the mysql> prompt:

   ```
   create user 'deitel'@'localhost' identified by 'deitel';
   grant select, insert, update, delete, create, drop, references,
       execute on *.* to 'deitel'@'localhost';
   ```

   This creates the deitel user with the privileges needed to create the databases used in this chapter and manipulate them.

5. Type the command

   ```
   exit;
   ```

   to terminate the MySQL monitor.

28.7 Creating Database books in MySQL

For each MySQL database we discuss, we provide a SQL script in a .sql file that sets up the database and its tables. You can execute these scripts in the MySQL monitor. In this chapter's examples directory, you'll find the script `books.sql` to create the `books` database. For the following steps, we assume that the MySQL server (`mysqld-nt.exe`) is still running. To execute the `books.sql` script:

1. Open a Command Prompt and use the `cd` command to change directories to the location that contains the `books.sql` script.

2. Start the MySQL monitor by typing

   ```
   mysql -h localhost -u deitel -p
   ```

   The `-p` option prompts you for the password for the `deitel` user account. When prompted, enter the password `deitel`.

3. Execute the script by typing

   ```
   source books.sql;
   ```

   This creates a new directory named `books` in the server's `data` directory—located by default on Windows at `C:\Program Files\MySQL\MySQL Server 5.0\data`. This new directory contains the `books` database.

4. Type the command

   ```
   exit;
   ```

   to terminate the MySQL monitor. You are now ready to proceed to the first JDBC example.

28.8 Manipulating Databases with JDBC

In this section, we present two examples. The first introduces how to connect to a database and query the database. The second demonstrates how to display the result of the query in a `JTable`.

28.8.1 Connecting to and Querying a Database

The example of Fig. 28.23 performs a simple query on the `books` database that retrieves the entire `Authors` table and displays the data. The program illustrates connecting to the database, querying the database and processing the result. The discussion that follows presents the key JDBC aspects of the program. [*Note:* Sections 28.5–28.7 demonstrate how to start the MySQL server, configure a user account and create the `books` database. These steps *must* be performed before executing the program of Fig. 28.23.]

```
 1   // Fig. 28.23: DisplayAuthors.java
 2   // Displaying the contents of the Authors table.
 3   import java.sql.Connection;
 4   import java.sql.Statement;
 5   import java.sql.DriverManager;
 6   import java.sql.ResultSet;
 7   import java.sql.ResultSetMetaData;
 8   import java.sql.SQLException;
 9
```

Fig. 28.23 | Displaying the contents of the `Authors` table. (Part 1 of 3.)

```
10   public class DisplayAuthors
11   {
12      // database URL
13      static final String DATABASE_URL = "jdbc:mysql://localhost/books";
14
15      // launch the application
16      public static void main( String args[] )
17      {
18         Connection connection = null; // manages connection
19         Statement statement = null; // query statement
20         ResultSet resultSet = null; // manages results
21
22         // connect to database books and query database
23         try
24         {
25            // establish connection to database
26            connection = DriverManager.getConnection(
27               DATABASE_URL, "deitel", "deitel" );
28
29            // create Statement for querying database
30            statement = connection.createStatement();
31
32            // query database
33            resultSet = statement.executeQuery(
34               "SELECT AuthorID, FirstName, LastName FROM Authors" );
35
36            // process query results
37            ResultSetMetaData metaData = resultSet.getMetaData();
38            int numberOfColumns = metaData.getColumnCount();
39            System.out.println( "Authors Table of Books Database:\n" );
40
41            for ( int i = 1; i <= numberOfColumns; i++ )
42               System.out.printf( "%-8s\t", metaData.getColumnName( i ) );
43            System.out.println();
44
45            while ( resultSet.next() )
46            {
47               for ( int i = 1; i <= numberOfColumns; i++ )
48                  System.out.printf( "%-8s\t", resultSet.getObject( i ) );
49               System.out.println();
50            } // end while
51         } // end try
52         catch ( SQLException sqlException )
53         {
54            sqlException.printStackTrace();
55         } // end catch
56         finally // ensure resultSet, statement and connection are closed
57         {
58            try
59            {
60               resultSet.close();
61               statement.close();
62               connection.close();
63            } // end try
```

Fig. 28.23 | Displaying the contents of the Authors table. (Part 2 of 3.)

```
64              catch ( Exception exception )
65              {
66                 exception.printStackTrace();
67              } // end catch
68          } // end finally
69      } // end main
70  } // end class DisplayAuthors
```

```
Authors Table of Books Database:

AuthorID       FirstName     LastName
1              Harvey        Deitel
2              Paul          Deitel
3              Andrew        Goldberg
4              David         Choffnes
```

Fig. 28.23 | Displaying the contents of the Authors table. (Part 3 of 3.)

Lines 3–8 import the JDBC interfaces and classes from package java.sql used in this program. Line 13 declares a string constant for the database URL. This identifies the name of the database to connect to, as well as information about the protocol used by the JDBC driver (discussed shortly). Method main (lines 16–69) connects to the books database, queries the database, displays the result of the query and closes the database connection.

In past versions of Java, programs were required to load an appropriate database driver before connecting to a database. JDBC 4.0, part of Java SE 6, supports **automatic driver discovery**—you are no longer required to load the database driver in advance. To ensure that the program can locate the database driver class, you must include the class's location in the program's classpath when you execute the program. For MySQL, you include the file mysql-connector-java-5.1.7-bin.jar (in the C:\mysql-connector-java-5.1.7 directory) in your program's classpath, as in:

```
java -classpath
    .;c:\mysql-connector-java-5.1.7\mysql-connector-java-5.1.7-bin.jar
    DisplayAuthors
```

Notice the period (.) at the beginning of the classpath information. If it is missing, the JVM will not look for classes in the current directory and thus will not find the Display-Authors class file. You may also copy the mysql-connector-java-5.1.7-bin.jar file to your JDK's \jre\lib\ext folder. After doing so, you can run the application simply using the command

```
java DisplayAuthors
```

Lines 26–27 of Fig. 28.23 create a **Connection** object (package java.sql) referenced by connection. An object that implements interface Connection manages the connection between the Java program and the database. Connection objects enable programs to create SQL statements that manipulate databases. The program initializes connection with the result of a call to static method **getConnection** of class **DriverManager** (package java.sql), which attempts to connect to the database specified by its URL. Method get-Connection takes three arguments—a String that specifies the database URL, a String that specifies the username and a String that specifies the password. The username and password are set in Section 28.6. If you used a different username and password, you need to replace the username (second argument) and password (third argument) passed to method `getConnection` in line 27. The URL locates the database (possibly on a network or in the local file system of the computer). The URL `jdbc:mysql://localhost/books` specifies the protocol for communication (`jdbc`), the **subprotocol** for communication (`mysql`) and the location of the database (`//localhost/books`, where `localhost` is the host running the MySQL server and `books` is the database name). The subprotocol `mysql` indicates that the program uses a MySQL-specific subprotocol to connect to the MySQL database. If the `DriverManager` cannot connect to the database, method `getConnection` throws a **SQLException** (package `java.sql`). Figure 28.24 lists the JDBC driver names and database URL formats of several popular RDBMSs.

RDBMS	Database URL format
MySQL	`jdbc:mysql://`*hostname*:*portNumber/databaseName*
ORACLE	`jdbc:oracle:thin:@`*hostname*:*portNumber*:*databaseName*
DB2	`jdbc:db2:`*hostname*:*portNumber/databaseName*
Java DB/Apache Derby	`jdbc:derby:`*dataBaseName* (embedded) `jdbc:derby://`*hostname*:*portNumber/databaseName* (network)
Microsoft SQL Server	`jdbc:sqlserver://`*hostname*:*portNumber*;`databaseName=`*dataBaseName*
Sybase	`jdbc:sybase:Tds:`*hostname*:*portNumber/databaseName*

Fig. 28.24 | Popular JDBC database URL formats.

Software Engineering Observation 28.5

Most database management systems require the user to log in before accessing the database contents. `DriverManager` method `getConnection` is overloaded with versions that enable the program to supply the user name and password to gain access.

Line 30 invokes `Connection` method **createStatement** to obtain an object that implements interface `Statement` (package `java.sql`). The program uses the **Statement** object to submit SQL statements to the database.

Lines 33–34 use the `Statement` object's **executeQuery** method to submit a query that selects all the author information from table `Authors`. This method returns an object that implements interface **ResultSet** and contains the query results. The `ResultSet` methods enable the program to manipulate the query result.

Lines 37–50 process the `ResultSet`. Line 37 obtains the metadata for the `ResultSet` as a **ResultSetMetaData** (package `java.sql`) object. The **metadata** describes the `ResultSet`'s contents. Programs can use metadata programmatically to obtain information about the `ResultSet`'s column names and types. Line 38 uses `ResultSetMetaData` method **getColumnCount** to retrieve the number of columns in the `ResultSet`. Lines 41–42 display the column names.

Software Engineering Observation 28.6

Metadata enables programs to process `ResultSet` contents dynamically when detailed information about the `ResultSet` is not known in advance.

Lines 45–50 display the data in each ResultSet row. First, the program positions the ResultSet cursor (which points to the row being processed) to the first row in the ResultSet with method **next** (line 45). Method next returns boolean value true if it is able to position to the next row; otherwise, the method returns false.

Common Programming Error 28.8

Initially, a ResultSet cursor is positioned before the first row. A SQLException occurs if you attempt to access a ResultSet's contents before positioning the ResultSet cursor to the first row with method next.

If there are rows in the ResultSet, lines 47–48 extract and display the contents of each column in the current row. When a ResultSet is processed, each column can be extracted as a specific Java type. In fact, ResultSetMetaData method **getColumnType** returns a constant integer from class **Types** (package java.sql) indicating the type of a specified column. Programs can use these values in a switch statement to invoke ResultSet methods that return the column values as appropriate Java types. If the type of a column is Types.INTEGER, ResultSet method **getInt** returns the column value as an int. ResultSet *get* methods typically receive as an argument either a column number (as an int) or a column name (as a String) indicating which column's value to obtain. Visit

```
java.sun.com/javase/6/docs/technotes/guides/jdbc/getstart/
    GettingStartedTOC.fm.html
```

for detailed mappings of SQL data types to Java types and to determine the appropriate ResultSet method to call for each SQL data type.

Performance Tip 28.1

If a query specifies the exact columns to select from the database, the ResultSet contains the columns in the specified order. In this case, using the column number to obtain the column's value is more efficient than using the column name. The column number provides direct access to the specified column. Using the column name requires a search of the column names to locate the appropriate column.

Error-Prevention Tip 28.1

Using column names to obtain values from a ResultSet produces code that is less error prone than obtaining values by column number—you don't need to remember the column order. Also, if the column order changes, your code does not have to change.

For simplicity, this example treats each value as an Object. The program retrieves each column value with ResultSet method **getObject** (line 48) and prints the String representation of the Object. Note that, unlike array indices, which start at 0, ResultSet column numbers start at 1. The finally block (lines 56–68) closes the ResultSet (line 60), the Statement (line 61) and the database Connection (line 62). [*Note:* Lines 60–62 will throw NullPointerExceptions if the ResultSet, Statement or Connection objects were not created properly. For code used in industry, you should check the variables that refer to these objects to see if they are null before you call close.]

Common Programming Error 28.9

Specifying column number 0 when obtaining values from a ResultSet causes a SQL-Exception.

Common Programming Error 28.10

A SQLException occurs if you attempt to manipulate a ResultSet after closing the Statement that created it. The ResultSet is discarded when the corresponding Statement is closed.

Software Engineering Observation 28.7

Each Statement object can open only one ResultSet object at a time. When a Statement returns a new ResultSet, the Statement closes the prior ResultSet. To use multiple ResultSets in parallel, separate Statement objects must return the ResultSets.

28.8.2 Querying the books Database

The next example (Fig. 28.25 and Fig. 28.28) allows the user to enter any query into the program. The example displays the result of a query in a **JTable**, using a **TableModel** object to provide the ResultSet data to the JTable. A JTable is a swing GUI component that can be bound to a database to display the results of a query. Class ResultSetTableModel (Fig. 28.25) performs the connection to the database via a TableModel and maintains the ResultSet. Class DisplayQueryResults (Fig. 28.28) creates the GUI and specifies an instance of class ResultSetTableModel to provide data for the JTable.

ResultSetTableModel Class

Class ResultSetTableModel (Fig. 28.25) extends class **AbstractTableModel** (package javax.swing.table), which implements interface TableModel. ResultSetTableModel overrides TableModel methods **getColumnClass**, **getColumnCount**, **getColumnName**, **getRowCount** and **getValueAt**. The default implementations of TableModel methods isCellEditable and setValueAt (provided by AbstractTableModel) are not overridden, because this example does not support editing the JTable cells. The default implementations of TableModel methods **addTableModelListener** and **removeTableModelListener** (provided by AbstractTableModel) are not overridden, because the implementations of these methods in AbstractTableModel properly add and remove event listeners.

```
 1   // Fig. 28.25: ResultSetTableModel.java
 2   // A TableModel that supplies ResultSet data to a JTable.
 3   import java.sql.Connection;
 4   import java.sql.Statement;
 5   import java.sql.DriverManager;
 6   import java.sql.ResultSet;
 7   import java.sql.ResultSetMetaData;
 8   import java.sql.SQLException;
 9   import javax.swing.table.AbstractTableModel;
10
11   // ResultSet rows and columns are counted from 1 and JTable
12   // rows and columns are counted from 0. When processing
13   // ResultSet rows or columns for use in a JTable, it is
14   // necessary to add 1 to the row or column number to manipulate
15   // the appropriate ResultSet column (i.e., JTable column 0 is
16   // ResultSet column 1 and JTable row 0 is ResultSet row 1).
17   public class ResultSetTableModel extends AbstractTableModel
18   {
```

Fig. 28.25 | A TableModel that supplies ResultSet data to a JTable. (Part 1 of 5.)

```
19      private Connection connection;
20      private Statement statement;
21      private ResultSet resultSet;
22      private ResultSetMetaData metaData;
23      private int numberOfRows;
24
25      // keep track of database connection status
26      private boolean connectedToDatabase = false;
27
28      // constructor initializes resultSet and obtains its meta data object;
29      // determines number of rows
30      public ResultSetTableModel( String url, String username,
31         String password, String query ) throws SQLException
32      {
33         // connect to database
34         connection = DriverManager.getConnection( url, username, password );
35
36         // create Statement to query database
37         statement = connection.createStatement(
38            ResultSet.TYPE_SCROLL_INSENSITIVE,
39            ResultSet.CONCUR_READ_ONLY );
40
41         // update database connection status
42         connectedToDatabase = true;
43
44         // set query and execute it
45         setQuery( query );
46      } // end constructor ResultSetTableModel
47
48      // get class that represents column type
49      public Class getColumnClass( int column ) throws IllegalStateException
50      {
51         // ensure database connection is available
52         if ( !connectedToDatabase )
53            throw new IllegalStateException( "Not Connected to Database" );
54
55         // determine Java class of column
56         try
57         {
58            String className = metaData.getColumnClassName( column + 1 );
59
60            // return Class object that represents className
61            return Class.forName( className );
62         } // end try
63         catch ( Exception exception )
64         {
65            exception.printStackTrace();
66         } // end catch
67
68         return Object.class; // if problems occur above, assume type Object
69      } // end method getColumnClass
70
```

Fig. 28.25 | A `TableModel` that supplies `ResultSet` data to a `JTable`. (Part 2 of 5.)

```
71      // get number of columns in ResultSet
72      public int getColumnCount() throws IllegalStateException
73      {
74         // ensure database connection is available
75         if ( !connectedToDatabase )
76            throw new IllegalStateException( "Not Connected to Database" );
77
78         // determine number of columns
79         try
80         {
81            return metaData.getColumnCount();
82         } // end try
83         catch ( SQLException sqlException )
84         {
85            sqlException.printStackTrace();
86         } // end catch
87
88         return 0; // if problems occur above, return 0 for number of columns
89      } // end method getColumnCount
90
91      // get name of a particular column in ResultSet
92      public String getColumnName( int column ) throws IllegalStateException
93      {
94         // ensure database connection is available
95         if ( !connectedToDatabase )
96            throw new IllegalStateException( "Not Connected to Database" );
97
98         // determine column name
99         try
100        {
101           return metaData.getColumnName( column + 1 );
102        } // end try
103        catch ( SQLException sqlException )
104        {
105           sqlException.printStackTrace();
106        } // end catch
107
108        return ""; // if problems, return empty string for column name
109     } // end method getColumnName
110
111     // return number of rows in ResultSet
112     public int getRowCount() throws IllegalStateException
113     {
114        // ensure database connection is available
115        if ( !connectedToDatabase )
116           throw new IllegalStateException( "Not Connected to Database" );
117
118        return numberOfRows;
119     } // end method getRowCount
120
121     // obtain value in particular row and column
122     public Object getValueAt( int row, int column )
123        throws IllegalStateException
124     {
```

Fig. 28.25 | A TableModel that supplies ResultSet data to a JTable. (Part 3 of 5.)

```
125          // ensure database connection is available
126          if ( !connectedToDatabase )
127             throw new IllegalStateException( "Not Connected to Database" );
128
129          // obtain a value at specified ResultSet row and column
130          try
131          {
132             resultSet.absolute( row + 1 );
133             return resultSet.getObject( column + 1 );
134          } // end try
135          catch ( SQLException sqlException )
136          {
137             sqlException.printStackTrace();
138          } // end catch
139
140          return ""; // if problems, return empty string object
141       } // end method getValueAt
142
143       // set new database query string
144       public void setQuery( String query )
145          throws SQLException, IllegalStateException
146       {
147          // ensure database connection is available
148          if ( !connectedToDatabase )
149             throw new IllegalStateException( "Not Connected to Database" );
150
151          // specify query and execute it
152          resultSet = statement.executeQuery( query );
153
154          // obtain meta data for ResultSet
155          metaData = resultSet.getMetaData();
156
157          // determine number of rows in ResultSet
158          resultSet.last(); // move to last row
159          numberOfRows = resultSet.getRow(); // get row number
160
161          // notify JTable that model has changed
162          fireTableStructureChanged();
163       } // end method setQuery
164
165       // close Statement and Connection
166       public void disconnectFromDatabase()
167       {
168          if ( connectedToDatabase )
169          {
170             // close Statement and Connection
171             try
172             {
173                resultSet.close();
174                statement.close();
175                connection.close();
176             } // end try
177             catch ( SQLException sqlException )
178             {
```

Fig. 28.25 | A TableModel that supplies ResultSet data to a JTable. (Part 4 of 5.)

```
179                sqlException.printStackTrace();
180          } // end catch
181          finally  // update database connection status
182          {
183             connectedToDatabase = false;
184          } // end finally
185       } // end if
186    } // end method disconnectFromDatabase
187 }  // end class ResultSetTableModel
```

Fig. 28.25 | A `TableModel` that supplies `ResultSet` data to a `JTable`. (Part 5 of 5.)

The `ResultSetTableModel` constructor (lines 30–46) accepts four `String` arguments—the URL of the database, the username, the password and the default query to perform. The constructor throws any exceptions that occur in its body back to the application that created the `ResultSetTableModel` object, so that the application can determine how to handle the exception (e.g., report an error and terminate the application). Line 34 establishes a connection to the database. Lines 37–39 invoke `Connection` method `createStatement` to create a `Statement` object. This example uses a version of method `createStatement` that takes two arguments—the result set type and the result set concurrency. The **result set type** (Fig. 28.26) specifies whether the `ResultSet`'s cursor is able to scroll in both directions or forward only and whether the `ResultSet` is sensitive to changes made to the underlying data.

ResultSet constant	Description
TYPE_FORWARD_ONLY	Specifies that a `ResultSet`'s cursor can move only in the forward direction (i.e., from the first to the last row in the `ResultSet`).
TYPE_SCROLL_INSENSITIVE	Specifies that a `ResultSet`'s cursor can scroll in either direction and that the changes made to the underlying data during `ResultSet` processing are not reflected in the `ResultSet` unless the program queries the database again.
TYPE_SCROLL_SENSITIVE	Specifies that a `ResultSet`'s cursor can scroll in either direction and that the changes made to the underlying data during `ResultSet` processing are reflected immediately in the `ResultSet`.

Fig. 28.26 | `ResultSet` constants for specifying `ResultSet` type.

Portability Tip 28.3

Some JDBC drivers do not support scrollable `ResultSets`. In such cases, the driver typically returns a `ResultSet` in which the cursor can move only forward. For more information, see your database driver documentation.

Common Programming Error 28.11

Attempting to move the cursor backward through a `ResultSet` when the database driver does not support backward scrolling causes a `SQLFeatureNotSupportedException`.

`ResultSet`s that are sensitive to changes reflect those changes immediately after they are made with methods of interface `ResultSet`. If a `ResultSet` is insensitive to changes, the query that produced the ResultSet must be executed again to reflect any changes made. The **result set concurrency** (Fig. 28.27) specifies whether the ResultSet can be updated with ResultSet's update methods.

ResultSet static concurrency constant	Description
CONCUR_READ_ONLY	Specifies that a ResultSet cannot be updated (i.e., changes to the ResultSet contents cannot be reflected in the database with ResultSet's update methods).
CONCUR_UPDATABLE	Specifies that a ResultSet can be updated (i.e., changes to the ResultSet contents can be reflected in the database with ResultSet's update methods).

Fig. 28.27 | ResultSet constants for specifying result properties.

 Portability Tip 28.4
Some JDBC drivers do not support updatable ResultSets. In such cases, the driver typically returns a read-only ResultSet. For more information, see your database driver documentation.

 Common Programming Error 28.12
Attempting to update a ResultSet when the database driver does not support updatable ResultSets causes SQLFeatureNotSupportedExceptions.

This example uses a ResultSet that is scrollable, insensitive to changes and read only. Line 45 invokes our method setQuery (lines 144–163) to perform the default query.

Method getColumnClass (lines 49–69) returns a Class object that represents the superclass of all objects in a particular column. The JTable uses this information to configure the default cell renderer and cell editor for that column in the JTable. Line 58 uses ResultSetMetaData method **getColumnClassName** to obtain the fully qualified class name for the specified column. Line 61 loads the class and returns the corresponding Class object. If an exception occurs, the catch in lines 63–66 prints a stack trace and line 68 returns Object.class—the Class instance that represents class Object—as the default type. [*Note:* Line 58 uses the argument column + 1. Like arrays, JTable row and column numbers are counted from 0. However, ResultSet row and column numbers are counted from 1. Thus, when processing ResultSet rows or columns for use in a JTable, it is necessary to add 1 to the row or column number to manipulate the appropriate ResultSet row or column.]

Method getColumnCount (lines 72–89) returns the number of columns in the model's underlying ResultSet. Line 81 uses ResultSetMetaData method **getColumnCount** to obtain the number of columns in the ResultSet. If an exception occurs, the catch in lines 83–86 prints a stack trace and line 88 returns 0 as the default number of columns.

Method getColumnName (lines 92–109) returns the name of the column in the model's underlying ResultSet. Line 101 uses ResultSetMetaData method **getColumn-Name** to obtain the column name from the ResultSet. If an exception occurs, the catch in lines 103–106 prints a stack trace and line 108 returns the empty string as the default column name.

Method getRowCount (lines 112–119) returns the number of rows in the model's underlying ResultSet. When method setQuery (lines 144–163) performs a query, it stores the number of rows in variable numberOfRows.

Method getValueAt (lines 122–141) returns the Object in a particular row and column of the model's underlying ResultSet. Line 132 uses ResultSet method **absolute** to position the ResultSet cursor at a specific row. Line 133 uses ResultSet method get-Object to obtain the Object in a specific column of the current row. If an exception occurs, the catch in lines 135–138 prints a stack trace and line 140 returns an empty string as the default value.

Method setQuery (lines 144–163) executes the query it receives as an argument to obtain a new ResultSet (line 152). Line 155 gets the ResultSetMetaData for the new ResultSet. Line 158 uses ResultSet method **last** to position the ResultSet cursor at the last row in the ResultSet. [*Note:* This can be slow if the table contains many rows.] Line 159 uses ResultSet method **getRow** to obtain the row number for the current row in the ResultSet. Line 162 invokes method **fireTableStructureChanged** (inherited from class AbstractTableModel) to notify any JTable using this ResultSetTableModel object as its model that the structure of the model has changed. This causes the JTable to repopulate its rows and columns with the new ResultSet data. Method setQuery throws any exceptions that occur in its body back to the application that invoked setQuery.

Method disconnectFromDatabase (lines 166–186) implements an appropriate termination method for class ResultSetTableModel. A class designer should provide a public method that clients of the class must invoke explicitly to free resources that an object has used. In this case, method disconnectFromDatabase closes the ResultSet, Statement and Connection (lines 173–175), which are considered limited resources. Clients of the ResultSetTableModel class should always invoke this method when the instance of this class is no longer needed. Before releasing resources, line 168 verifies whether the connection is already terminated. If not, the method proceeds. Note that the other methods in class ResultSetTableModel each throw an IllegalStateException if connectedToDatabase is false. Method disconnectFromDatabase sets connectedTo-Database to false (line 183) to ensure that clients do not use an instance of ResultSet-TableModel after that instance has already been terminated. IllegalStateException is an exception from the Java libraries that is appropriate for indicating this error condition.

DisplayQueryResults *Class*
Class DisplayQueryResults (Fig. 28.28) implements the application's GUI and interacts with the ResultSetTableModel via a JTable object. This application also demonstrates the JTable sorting and filtering capabilities introduced in Java SE 6.

```
1   // Fig. 28.28: DisplayQueryResults.java
2   // Display the contents of the Authors table in the books database.
3   import java.awt.BorderLayout;
4   import java.awt.event.ActionListener;
5   import java.awt.event.ActionEvent;
6   import java.awt.event.WindowAdapter;
7   import java.awt.event.WindowEvent;
8   import java.sql.SQLException;
9   import java.util.regex.PatternSyntaxException;
```

Fig. 28.28 | Displays contents of the database books. (Part 1 of 6.)

```java
10   import javax.swing.JFrame;
11   import javax.swing.JTextArea;
12   import javax.swing.JScrollPane;
13   import javax.swing.ScrollPaneConstants;
14   import javax.swing.JTable;
15   import javax.swing.JOptionPane;
16   import javax.swing.JButton;
17   import javax.swing.Box;
18   import javax.swing.JLabel;
19   import javax.swing.JTextField;
20   import javax.swing.RowFilter;
21   import javax.swing.table.TableRowSorter;
22   import javax.swing.table.TableModel;
23
24   public class DisplayQueryResults extends JFrame
25   {
26      // database URL, username and password
27      static final String DATABASE_URL = "jdbc:mysql://localhost/books";
28      static final String USERNAME = "deitel";
29      static final String PASSWORD = "deitel";
30
31      // default query retrieves all data from Authors table
32      static final String DEFAULT_QUERY = "SELECT * FROM Authors";
33
34      private ResultSetTableModel tableModel;
35      private JTextArea queryArea;
36
37      // create ResultSetTableModel and GUI
38      public DisplayQueryResults()
39      {
40         super( "Displaying Query Results" );
41
42         // create ResultSetTableModel and display database table
43         try
44         {
45            // create TableModel for results of query SELECT * FROM Authors
46            tableModel = new ResultSetTableModel( DATABASE_URL,
47               USERNAME, PASSWORD, DEFAULT_QUERY );
48
49            // set up JTextArea in which user types queries
50            queryArea = new JTextArea( DEFAULT_QUERY, 3, 100 );
51            queryArea.setWrapStyleWord( true );
52            queryArea.setLineWrap( true );
53
54            JScrollPane scrollPane = new JScrollPane( queryArea,
55               ScrollPaneConstants.VERTICAL_SCROLLBAR_AS_NEEDED,
56               ScrollPaneConstants.HORIZONTAL_SCROLLBAR_NEVER );
57
58            // set up JButton for submitting queries
59            JButton submitButton = new JButton( "Submit Query" );
60
61            // create Box to manage placement of queryArea and
62            // submitButton in GUI
63            Box boxNorth = Box.createHorizontalBox();
```

Fig. 28.28 | Displays contents of the database **books**. (Part 2 of 6.)

```
64          boxNorth.add( scrollPane );
65          boxNorth.add( submitButton );
66
67          // create JTable based on the tableModel
68          JTable resultTable = new JTable( tableModel );
69
70          JLabel filterLabel = new JLabel( "Filter:" );
71          final JTextField filterText = new JTextField();
72          JButton filterButton = new JButton( "Apply Filter" );
73          Box boxSouth = Box.createHorizontalBox();
74
75          boxSouth.add( filterLabel );
76          boxSouth.add( filterText );
77          boxSouth.add( filterButton );
78
79          // place GUI components on content pane
80          add( boxNorth, BorderLayout.NORTH );
81          add( new JScrollPane( resultTable ), BorderLayout.CENTER );
82          add( boxSouth, BorderLayout.SOUTH );
83
84          // create event listener for submitButton
85          submitButton.addActionListener(
86
87             new ActionListener()
88             {
89                // pass query to table model
90                public void actionPerformed( ActionEvent event )
91                {
92                   // perform a new query
93                   try
94                   {
95                      tableModel.setQuery( queryArea.getText() );
96                   } // end try
97                   catch ( SQLException sqlException )
98                   {
99                      JOptionPane.showMessageDialog( null,
100                        sqlException.getMessage(), "Database error",
101                        JOptionPane.ERROR_MESSAGE );
102
103                     // try to recover from invalid user query
104                     // by executing default query
105                     try
106                     {
107                        tableModel.setQuery( DEFAULT_QUERY );
108                        queryArea.setText( DEFAULT_QUERY );
109                     } // end try
110                     catch ( SQLException sqlException2 )
111                     {
112                        JOptionPane.showMessageDialog( null,
113                          sqlException2.getMessage(), "Database error",
114                          JOptionPane.ERROR_MESSAGE );
115
116                        // ensure database connection is closed
117                        tableModel.disconnectFromDatabase();
```

Fig. 28.28 | Displays contents of the database books. (Part 3 of 6.)

```
118
119                       System.exit( 1 ); // terminate application
120                    } // end inner catch
121                 } // end outer catch
122              } // end actionPerformed
123           }  // end ActionListener inner class
124        ); // end call to addActionListener
125
126        final TableRowSorter< TableModel > sorter =
127           new TableRowSorter< TableModel >( tableModel );
128        resultTable.setRowSorter( sorter );
129        setSize( 500, 250 ); // set window size
130        setVisible( true ); // display window
131
132        // create listener for filterButton
133        filterButton.addActionListener(
134           new ActionListener()
135           {
136              // pass filter text to listener
137              public void actionPerformed( ActionEvent e )
138              {
139                 String text = filterText.getText();
140
141                 if ( text.length() == 0 )
142                    sorter.setRowFilter( null );
143                 else
144                 {
145                    try
146                    {
147                       sorter.setRowFilter(
148                          RowFilter.regexFilter( text ) );
149                    } // end try
150                    catch ( PatternSyntaxException pse )
151                    {
152                       JOptionPane.showMessageDialog( null,
153                          "Bad regex pattern", "Bad regex pattern",
154                          JOptionPane.ERROR_MESSAGE );
155                    } // end catch
156                 } // end else
157              } // end method actionPerfomed
158           } // end annonymous inner class
159        ); // end call to addActionLister
160     } // end try
161     catch ( SQLException sqlException )
162     {
163        JOptionPane.showMessageDialog( null, sqlException.getMessage(),
164           "Database error", JOptionPane.ERROR_MESSAGE );
165
166        // ensure database connection is closed
167        tableModel.disconnectFromDatabase();
168
169        System.exit( 1 ); // terminate application
170     } // end catch
171
```

Fig. 28.28 | Displays contents of the database books. (Part 4 of 6.)

```
172        // dispose of window when user quits application (this overrides
173        // the default of HIDE_ON_CLOSE)
174        setDefaultCloseOperation( DISPOSE_ON_CLOSE );
175
176        // ensure database connection is closed when user quits application
177        addWindowListener(
178
179           new WindowAdapter()
180           {
181              // disconnect from database and exit when window has closed
182              public void windowClosed( WindowEvent event )
183              {
184                 tableModel.disconnectFromDatabase();
185                 System.exit( 0 );
186              } // end method windowClosed
187           } // end WindowAdapter inner class
188        ); // end call to addWindowListener
189     } // end DisplayQueryResults constructor
190
191     // execute application
192     public static void main( String args[] )
193     {
194        new DisplayQueryResults();
195     } // end main
196  } // end class DisplayQueryResults
```

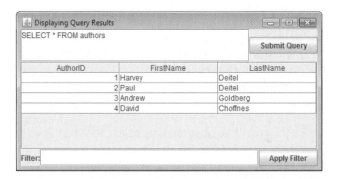

Fig. 28.28 | Displays contents of the database books. (Part 5 of 6.)

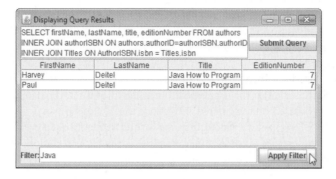

Fig. 28.28 | Displays contents of the database books. (Part 6 of 6.)

Lines 27–29 and 32 declare the URL, username, password and default query that are passed to the ResultSetTableModel constructor to make the initial connection to the database and perform the default query. The DisplayQueryResults constructor (lines 38–189) creates a ResultSetTableModel object and the GUI for the application. Line 68 creates the JTable object and passes a ResultSetTableModel object to the JTable constructor, which then registers the JTable as a listener for TableModelEvents generated by the ResultSetTableModel.

Note that the local variables filterText (line 71) and sorter (lines 126–127) are declared final. These are both used from an event handler that is implemented as an anonymous inner class (lines 134–158). Any local variable that will be used in an anonymous inner class *must* be declared final; otherwise, a compilation error occurs.

Lines 85–124 register an event handler for the submitButton that the user clicks to submit a query to the database. When the user clicks the button, method actionPerformed (lines 90–122) invokes method setQuery from the class ResultSetTableModel to execute the new query (line 95). If the user's query fails (e.g., because of a syntax error in the user's input), lines 107–108 execute the default query. If the default query also fails, there could be a more serious error, so line 117 ensures that the database connection is closed and line 119 exits the program. The screen captures in Fig. 28.28 show the results of two queries. The first screen capture shows the default query that retrieves all the data from table Authors of database books. The second screen capture shows a query that selects each author's first name and last name from the Authors table and combines that information with the title and edition number from the Titles table. Try entering your own queries in the text area and clicking the **Submit Query** button to execute the query.

As of Java SE 6, JTables now allow users to sort rows by the data in a specific column. Lines 126–127 use the **TableRowSorter** class (from package **javax.swing.table**) to create an object that uses our ResultSetTableModel to sort rows in the JTable that displays query results. When the user clicks the title of a particular JTable column, the TableRowSorter interacts with the underlying TableModel to reorder the rows based on the data in that column. Line 128 uses JTable method **setRowSorter** to specify the TableRowSorter for resultTable.

JTables can now show subsets of the data from the underlying TableModel. This is known as filtering the data. Lines 133–159 register an event handler for the filterButton that the user clicks to filter the data. In method actionPerformed (lines 137–157), line

139 obtains the filter text. If the user did not specify filter text, line 142 uses JTable method **setRowFilter** to remove any prior filter by setting the filter to null. Otherwise, lines 147–148 use setRowFilter to specify a **RowFilter** (from package javax.swing) based on the user's input. Class RowFilter provides several methods for creating filters. The static method **regexFilter** receives a String containing a regular expression pattern as its argument and an optional set of indices that specify which columns to filter. If no indices are specified, then all the columns are searched. In this example, the regular expression pattern is the text the user typed. Once the filter is set, the data displayed in the JTable is updated based on the filtered TableModel.

Lines 177–188 register a **WindowListener** for the **windowClosed** event, which occurs when the user closes the window. Since WindowListeners can handle several window events, we extend class **WindowAdapter** and override only the windowClosed event handler.

28.9 RowSet Interface

In the previous examples, you learned how to query a database by explicitly establishing a Connection to the database, preparing a Statement for querying the database and executing the query. In this section, we demonstrate the **RowSet interface**, which configures the database connection and prepares query statements automatically. The interface RowSet provides several *set* methods that allow you to specify the properties needed to establish a connection (such as the database URL, user name and password of the database) and create a Statement (such as a query). RowSet also provides several *get* methods that return these properties.

There are two types of RowSet objects—connected and disconnected. A **connected RowSet** object connects to the database once and remains connected while the object is in use. A **disconnected RowSet** object connects to the database, executes a query to retrieve the data from the database and then closes the connection. A program may change the data in a disconnected RowSet while it is disconnected. Modified data can be updated in the database after a disconnected RowSet reestablishes the connection with the database.

Package **javax.sql.rowset** contains two subinterfaces of RowSet—JdbcRowSet and CachedRowSet. **JdbcRowSet**, a connected RowSet, acts as a wrapper around a ResultSet object and allows you to scroll through and update the rows in the ResultSet. Recall that by default, a ResultSet object is nonscrollable and read only—you must explicitly set the result set type constant to TYPE_SCROLL_INSENSITIVE and set the result set concurrency constant to CONCUR_UPDATABLE to make a ResultSet object scrollable and updatable. A JdbcRowSet object is scrollable and updatable by default. **CachedRowSet**, a disconnected RowSet, caches the data of a ResultSet in memory and disconnects from the database. Like JdbcRowSet, a CachedRowSet object is scrollable and updatable by default. A Cached-RowSet object is also serializable, so it can be passed between Java applications through a network, such as the Internet. However, CachedRowSet has a limitation—the amount of data that can be stored in memory is limited. Package javax.sql.rowset contains three other subinterfaces of RowSet. For details of these interfaces, visit java.sun.com/javase/6/docs/technotes/guides/jdbc/getstart/rowsetImpl.html.

Portability Tip 28.5

A RowSet can provide scrolling capability for drivers that do not support scrollable ResultSets.

Figure 28.29 reimplements the example of Fig. 28.23 using a RowSet. Rather than establish the connection and create a Statement explicitly, Fig. 28.29 uses a JdbcRowSet object to create a Connection and a Statement automatically.

```
1   // Fig. 28.29: JdbcRowSetTest.java
2   // Displaying the contents of the Authors table using JdbcRowSet.
3   import java.sql.ResultSetMetaData;
4   import java.sql.SQLException;
5   import javax.sql.rowset.JdbcRowSet;
6   import com.sun.rowset.JdbcRowSetImpl; // Sun's JdbcRowSet implementation
7
8   public class JdbcRowSetTest
9   {
10     // JDBC driver name and database URL
11     static final String DATABASE_URL = "jdbc:mysql://localhost/books";
12     static final String USERNAME = "deitel";
13     static final String PASSWORD = "deitel";
14
15     // constructor connects to database, queries database, processes
16     // results and displays results in window
17     public JdbcRowSetTest()
18     {
19        // connect to database books and query database
20        try
21        {
22           // specify properties of JdbcRowSet
23           JdbcRowSet rowSet = new JdbcRowSetImpl();
24           rowSet.setUrl( DATABASE_URL ); // set database URL
25           rowSet.setUsername( USERNAME ); // set username
26           rowSet.setPassword( PASSWORD ); // set password
27           rowSet.setCommand( "SELECT * FROM Authors" ); // set query
28           rowSet.execute(); // execute query
29
30           // process query results
31           ResultSetMetaData metaData = rowSet.getMetaData();
32           int numberOfColumns = metaData.getColumnCount();
33           System.out.println( "Authors Table of Books Database:\n" );
34
35           // display rowset header
36           for ( int i = 1; i <= numberOfColumns; i++ )
37              System.out.printf( "%-8s\t", metaData.getColumnName( i ) );
38           System.out.println();
39
40           // display each row
41           while ( rowSet.next() )
42           {
43              for ( int i = 1; i <= numberOfColumns; i++ )
44                 System.out.printf( "%-8s\t", rowSet.getObject( i ) );
45              System.out.println();
46           } // end while
47
48           // close the underlying ResultSet, Statement and Connection
49           rowSet.close();
50        } // end try
```

Fig. 28.29 | Displaying the Authors table using JdbcRowSet. (Part 1 of 2.)

```
51              catch ( SQLException sqlException )
52              {
53                 sqlException.printStackTrace();
54                 System.exit( 1 );
55              } // end catch
56           } // end DisplayAuthors constructor
57
58           // launch the application
59           public static void main( String args[] )
60           {
61              JdbcRowSetTest application = new JdbcRowSetTest();
62           } // end main
63        } // end class JdbcRowSetTest
```

```
Authors Table of Books Database:

AuthorID        FirstName       LastName
1               Harvey          Deitel
2               Paul            Deitel
3               Andrew          Goldberg
4               David           Choffnes
```

Fig. 28.29 | Displaying the Authors table using JdbcRowSet. (Part 2 of 2.)

The package **com.sun.rowset** provides Sun's reference implementations of the interfaces in package javax.sql.rowset. Line 23 uses Sun's reference implementation of the JdbcRowSet interface—**JdbcRowSetImpl**—to create a JdbcRowSet object. We used class JdbcRowSetImpl here to demonstrate the capability of the JdbcRowSet interface. Other databases may provide their own RowSet implementations.

Lines 24–26 set the RowSet properties that the DriverManager uses to establish a database connection. Line 24 invokes JdbcRowSet method **setUrl** to specify the database URL. Line 25 invokes JdbcRowSet method **setUsername** to specify the username. Line 26 invokes JdbcRowSet method **setPassword** to specify the password. Line 27 invokes Jdbc-RowSet method **setCommand** to specify the SQL query that will be used to populate the RowSet. Line 28 invokes JdbcRowSet method **execute** to execute the SQL query. Method execute performs four actions—it establishes a Connection to the database, prepares the query Statement, executes the query and stores the ResultSet returned by query. The Connection, Statement and ResultSet are encapsulated in the JdbcRowSet object.

The remaining code is almost identical to Fig. 28.23, except that line 31 obtains a ResultSetMetaData object from the JdbcRowSet, line 41 uses the JdbcRowSet's next method to get the next row of the result and line 44 uses the JdbcRowSet's getObject method to obtain a column's value. Line 49 invokes JdbcRowSet method **close**, which closes the RowSet's encapsulated ResultSet, Statement and Connection. In a Cached-RowSet, invoking close also releases the resources held by that RowSet. Note that the output of this application is the same as that of Fig. 28.23.

28.10 Java DB/Apache Derby

As of JDK 6, Sun Microsystems now bundles the open-source, pure Java database **Java DB** (the Sun branded version of Apache Derby) with the JDK. In Section 28.11, we use Java

DB to demonstrate `PreparedStatements`. Before you can execute the application in the next section, you must set up the `AddressBook` database in Java DB. Section 28.11 uses the embedded version of Java DB. There is also a network version that executes similarly to the MySQL DBMS introduced earlier in the chapter. For the purpose of the following steps, we assume you are running Microsoft Windows with Java installed in its default location. [*Note:* Mac OS X users may need to download and install Apache Derby (db.apache.org/derby/) if Java DB is not installed by default. Linux users should visit developers.sun.com/javadb/reference/docs/ and read "Getting Started with Java DB" for installation and configuration instructions.]

1. Java DB comes with several batch files to configure and run it. Before executing these batch files from a command prompt, you must set the environment variable `JAVA_HOME` to refer to the JDK's `C:\Program Files\Java\jdk1.6.0_11` installation directory. [*Note:* You may need to change this based on the version of the JDK installed on your computer.]

2. Open the batch file `setEmbeddedCP.bat` (located in `C:\Program Files\Sun\JavaDB\bin`) in a text editor such as Notepad. Locate the line

   ```
   @rem set DERBY_INSTALL=
   ```

   and change it to

   ```
   @set DERBY_INSTALL=C:\Program Files\Sun\JavaDB
   ```

   Save your changes and close this file.

3. Open a Command Prompt and change directories to `C:\Program Files\Sun\JavaDB\bin`. Then, type `setEmbeddedCP.bat` and press *Enter* to set the environment variables required by Java DB.

4. An embedded Java DB database must reside in the same location as the application that manipulates the database. For this reason, change to the directory that contains the code for Figs. 28.30–28.32. This directory contains a SQL script `address.sql` that builds the `AddressBook` database.

5. Execute the command

   ```
   "C:\Program Files\Sun\JavaDB\bin\ij"
   ```

   to start the command-line tool for interacting with Java DB. The double quotes are necessary because the path contains a space. This will display the `ij>` prompt.

6. At the `ij>` prompt type

   ```
   connect 'jdbc:derby:AddressBook;create=true;user=deitel;
       password=deitel';
   ```

   to create the `AddressBook` database in the current directory. This command also creates the user `deitel` with the password `deitel` for accessing the database.

7. To create the database table and insert sample data in the database, type

   ```
   run 'address.sql';
   ```

8. To terminate the Java DB command-line tool, type

   ```
   exit;
   ```

You are now ready to execute the AddressBook application in Section 28.11. Note that MySQL (or any other database that supports JDBC PreparedStatements) could also be used in Section 28.11.

28.11 PreparedStatements

Interface **PreparedStatement** enables you to create compiled SQL statements that execute more efficiently than Statement objects. PreparedStatements also can specify parameters, making them more flexible than Statements. Programs can execute the same query repeatedly with different parameter values. For example, in the books database, you might want to locate all book titles for an author with a specific last name and first name, and you might want to execute that query for several authors. With a PreparedStatement, that query is defined as follows:

```
PreparedStatement authorBooks = connection.prepareStatement(
   "SELECT LastName, FirstName, Title " +
   "FROM Authors INNER JOIN AuthorISBN " +
      "ON Authors.AuthorID=AuthorISBN.AuthorID " +
   "INNER JOIN Titles " +
      "ON AuthorISBN.ISBN=Titles.ISBN " +
   "WHERE LastName = ? AND FirstName = ?" );
```

The two question marks (?) in the the preceding SQL statement's last line are placeholders for values that will be passed as part of the query to the database. Before executing a PreparedStatement, the program must specify the parameter values by using the PreparedStatement interface's *set* methods.

For the preceding query, both parameters are strings that can be set with PreparedStatement method **setString** as follows:

```
authorBooks.setString( 1, "Deitel" );
authorBooks.setString( 2, "Paul" );
```

Method setString's first argument represents the parameter number being set, and the second argument is that parameter's value. Parameter numbers are counted from 1, starting with the first question mark (?). When the program executes the preceding PreparedStatement with the parameter values shown here, the SQL passed to the database is

```
SELECT LastName, FirstName, Title
FROM Authors INNER JOIN AuthorISBN
   ON Authors.AuthorID=AuthorISBN.AuthorID
INNER JOIN Titles
   ON AuthorISBN.ISBN=Titles.ISBN
WHERE LastName = 'Deitel' AND FirstName = 'Paul'
```

Method setString automatically escapes String parameter values as necessary. For example, if the last name is O'Brien, the statement

```
authorBooks.setString( 1, "O'Brien" );
```

escapes the ' character in O'Brien by replacing it with two single-quote characters.

Performance Tip 28.2

PreparedStatements are more efficient than Statements when executing SQL statements multiple times and with different parameter values.

> **Error-Prevention Tip 28.2**
>
> *Use PreparedStatements with parameters for queries that receive String values as arguments to ensure that the Strings are quoted properly in the SQL statement.*

Interface PreparedStatement provides *set* methods for each supported SQL type. It is important to use the *set* method that is appropriate for the parameter's SQL type in the database—SQLExceptions occur when a program attempts to convert a parameter value to an incorrect type. For a complete list of interface PreparedStatement's *set* methods, see java.sun.com/javase/6/docs/api/java/sql/PreparedStatement.html.

Address Book Application that Uses PreparedStatements

We now present an address book application that enables you to browse existing entries, add new entries and search for entries with a specific last name. Our AddressBook Java DB database contains an Addresses table with the columns addressID, FirstName, LastName, Email and PhoneNumber. The column addressID is a so-called identity column. This is the SQL standard way to represent an autoincremented column. The SQL script we provide for this database uses the SQL **IDENTITY** keyword to mark the addressID column as an identity column. For more information on using the IDENTITY keyword and creating databases, see the Java DB Developer's Guide at developers.sun.com/docs/javadb/10.4.2.0/devguide/derbydev.pdf.

Our address book application consists of three classes—Person (Fig. 28.30), Person-Queries (Fig. 28.31) and AddressBookDisplay (Fig. 28.32). Class Person is a simple class that represents one person in the address book. The class contains fields for the address ID, first name, last name, email address and phone number, as well as *set* and *get* methods for manipulating these fields.

```
1   // Fig. 28.30: Person.java
2   // Person class that represents an entry in an address book.
3   public class Person
4   {
5      private int addressID;
6      private String firstName;
7      private String lastName;
8      private String email;
9      private String phoneNumber;
10
11     // no-argument constructor
12     public Person()
13     {
14     } // end no-argument Person constructor
15
16     // constructor
17     public Person( int id, String first, String last,
18        String emailAddress, String phone )
19     {
20        setAddressID( id );
21        setFirstName( first );
22        setLastName( last );
23        setEmail( emailAddress );
```

Fig. 28.30 | Person class that represents an entry in an AddressBook. (Part 1 of 3.)

```
24          setPhoneNumber( phone );
25      } // end five-argument Person constructor
26
27      // sets the addressID
28      public void setAddressID( int id )
29      {
30          addressID = id;
31      } // end method setAddressID
32
33      // returns the addressID
34      public int getAddressID()
35      {
36          return addressID;
37      } // end method getAddressID
38
39      // sets the firstName
40      public void setFirstName( String first )
41      {
42          firstName = first;
43      } // end method setFirstName
44
45      // returns the first name
46      public String getFirstName()
47      {
48          return firstName;
49      } // end method getFirstName
50
51      // sets the lastName
52      public void setLastName( String last )
53      {
54          lastName = last;
55      } // end method setLastName
56
57      // returns the last name
58      public String getLastName()
59      {
60          return lastName;
61      } // end method getLastName
62
63      // sets the email address
64      public void setEmail( String emailAddress )
65      {
66          email = emailAddress;
67      } // end method setEmail
68
69      // returns the email address
70      public String getEmail()
71      {
72          return email;
73      } // end method getEmail
74
75      // sets the phone number
76      public void setPhoneNumber( String phone )
77      {
```

Fig. 28.30 | Person class that represents an entry in an AddressBook. (Part 2 of 3.)

```
78          phoneNumber = phone;
79       } // end method setPhoneNumber
80
81       // returns the phone number
82       public String getPhoneNumber()
83       {
84          return phoneNumber;
85       } // end method getPhoneNumber
86    } // end class Person
```

Fig. 28.30 | Person class that represents an entry in an AddressBook. (Part 3 of 3.)

Class *PersonQueries*

Class PersonQueries (Fig. 28.31) manages the address book application's database connection and creates the PreparedStatements that the application uses to interact with the database. Lines 18–20 declare three PreparedStatement variables. The constructor (lines 23–49) connects to the database at lines 27–28.

Lines 31–32 invoke Connection method **prepareStatement** to create the PreparedStatement named selectAllPeople that selects all the rows in the Addresses table. Lines 35–36 create the PreparedStatement named selectPeopleByLastName with a parameter. This statement selects all the rows in the Addresses table that match a particular last name. Notice the ? character that is used to specify the last-name parameter. Lines 39–42 create the PreparedStatement named insertNewPerson with four parameters that represent the first name, last name, email address and phone number for a new entry. Again, notice the ? characters used to represent these parameters.

```
 1    // Fig. 28.31: PersonQueries.java
 2    // PreparedStatements used by the Address Book application.
 3    import java.sql.Connection;
 4    import java.sql.DriverManager;
 5    import java.sql.PreparedStatement;
 6    import java.sql.ResultSet;
 7    import java.sql.SQLException;
 8    import java.util.List;
 9    import java.util.ArrayList;
10
11    public class PersonQueries
12    {
13       private static final String URL = "jdbc:derby:AddressBook";
14       private static final String USERNAME = "deitel";
15       private static final String PASSWORD = "deitel";
16
17       private Connection connection = null; // manages connection
18       private PreparedStatement selectAllPeople = null;
19       private PreparedStatement selectPeopleByLastName = null;
20       private PreparedStatement insertNewPerson = null;
21
22       // constructor
23       public PersonQueries()
24       {
```

Fig. 28.31 | PreparedStatements used by the Address Book application. (Part 1 of 4.)

```
25      try
26      {
27         connection =
28            DriverManager.getConnection( URL, USERNAME, PASSWORD );
29
30         // create query that selects all entries in the AddressBook
31         selectAllPeople =
32            connection.prepareStatement( "SELECT * FROM Addresses" );
33
34         // create query that selects entries with a specific last name
35         selectPeopleByLastName = connection.prepareStatement(
36            "SELECT * FROM Addresses WHERE LastName = ?" );
37
38         // create insert that adds a new entry into the database
39         insertNewPerson = connection.prepareStatement(
40            "INSERT INTO Addresses " +
41            "( FirstName, LastName, Email, PhoneNumber ) " +
42            "VALUES ( ?, ?, ?, ? )" );
43      } // end try
44      catch ( SQLException sqlException )
45      {
46         sqlException.printStackTrace();
47         System.exit( 1 );
48      } // end catch
49   } // end PersonQueries constructor
50
51   // select all of the addresses in the database
52   public List< Person > getAllPeople()
53   {
54      List< Person > results = null;
55      ResultSet resultSet = null;
56
57      try
58      {
59         // executeQuery returns ResultSet containing matching entries
60         resultSet = selectAllPeople.executeQuery();
61         results = new ArrayList< Person >();
62
63         while ( resultSet.next() )
64         {
65            results.add( new Person(
66               resultSet.getInt( "addressID" ),
67               resultSet.getString( "FirstName" ),
68               resultSet.getString( "LastName" ),
69               resultSet.getString( "Email" ),
70               resultSet.getString( "PhoneNumber" ) ) );
71         } // end while
72      } // end try
73      catch ( SQLException sqlException )
74      {
75         sqlException.printStackTrace();
76      } // end catch
77      finally
78      {
```

Fig. 28.31 | PreparedStatements used by the Address Book application. (Part 2 of 4.)

```
79          try
80          {
81              resultSet.close();
82          } // end try
83          catch ( SQLException sqlException )
84          {
85              sqlException.printStackTrace();
86              close();
87          } // end catch
88       } // end finally
89
90       return results;
91    } // end method getAllPeople
92
93    // select person by last name
94    public List< Person > getPeopleByLastName( String name )
95    {
96       List< Person > results = null;
97       ResultSet resultSet = null;
98
99       try
100      {
101          selectPeopleByLastName.setString( 1, name ); // specify last name
102
103          // executeQuery returns ResultSet containing matching entries
104          resultSet = selectPeopleByLastName.executeQuery();
105
106          results = new ArrayList< Person >();
107
108          while ( resultSet.next() )
109          {
110             results.add( new Person( resultSet.getInt( "addressID" ),
111                resultSet.getString( "FirstName" ),
112                resultSet.getString( "LastName" ),
113                resultSet.getString( "Email" ),
114                resultSet.getString( "PhoneNumber" ) ) );
115          } // end while
116       } // end try
117       catch ( SQLException sqlException )
118       {
119          sqlException.printStackTrace();
120       } // end catch
121       finally
122       {
123          try
124          {
125             resultSet.close();
126          } // end try
127          catch ( SQLException sqlException )
128          {
129             sqlException.printStackTrace();
130             close();
131          } // end catch
132       } // end finally
```

Fig. 28.31 | PreparedStatements used by the Address Book application. (Part 3 of 4.)

```
133
134        return results;
135     } // end method getPeopleByName
136
137     // add an entry
138     public int addPerson(
139        String fname, String lname, String email, String num )
140     {
141        int result = 0;
142
143        // set parameters, then execute insertNewPerson
144        try
145        {
146           insertNewPerson.setString( 1, fname );
147           insertNewPerson.setString( 2, lname );
148           insertNewPerson.setString( 3, email );
149           insertNewPerson.setString( 4, num );
150
151           // insert the new entry; returns # of rows updated
152           result = insertNewPerson.executeUpdate();
153        } // end try
154        catch ( SQLException sqlException )
155        {
156           sqlException.printStackTrace();
157           close();
158        } // end catch
159
160        return result;
161     } // end method addPerson
162
163     // close the database connection
164     public void close()
165     {
166        try
167        {
168           connection.close();
169        } // end try
170        catch ( SQLException sqlException )
171        {
172           sqlException.printStackTrace();
173        } // end catch
174     } // end method close
175  } // end class PersonQueries
```

Fig. 28.31 | PreparedStatements used by the Address Book application. (Part 4 of 4.)

Method getAllPeople (lines 52–91) executes PreparedStatement selectAllPeople (line 60) by calling method **executeQuery**, which returns a ResultSet containing the rows that match the query (in this case, all the rows in the Addresses table). Lines 61–71 place the query results in an ArrayList of Person objects, which is returned to the caller at line 90. Method getPeopleByLastName (lines 94–135) uses PreparedStatement method set-String to set the parameter to selectPeopleByLastName (line 101). Then, line 104 executes the query and lines 106–115 place the query results in an ArrayList of Person objects. Line 134 returns the ArrayList to the caller.

Method addPerson (lines 138–161) uses PreparedStatement method setString (lines 146–149) to set the parameters for the insertNewPerson PreparedStatement. Line 152 uses PreparedStatement method **executeUpdate** to insert the new record. This method returns an integer indicating the number of rows that were updated (or inserted) in the database. Method close (lines 164–174) simply closes the database connection.

Class AddressBookDisplay

The AddressBookDisplay (Fig. 28.32) application uses a PersonQueries object to interact with the database. Line 59 creates the PersonQueries object. When the user presses the **Browse All Entries** JButton, the browseButtonActionPerformed handler (lines 309–335) is called. Line 313 calls the method getAllPeople on the PersonQueries object to obtain all the entries in the database. The user can then scroll through the entries using the **Previous** and **Next** JButtons. When the user presses the **Find** JButton, the queryButtonActionPerformed handler (lines 265–287) is called. Lines 267–268 call method getPeopleByLastName on the PersonQueries object to obtain the entries in the database that match the specified last name. If there are several such entries, the user can then scroll through them using the **Previous** and **Next** JButtons.

```java
1   // Fig. 28.32: AddressBookDisplay.java
2   // A simple address book
3   import java.awt.event.ActionEvent;
4   import java.awt.event.ActionListener;
5   import java.awt.event.WindowAdapter;
6   import java.awt.event.WindowEvent;
7   import java.awt.FlowLayout;
8   import java.awt.GridLayout;
9   import java.util.List;
10  import javax.swing.JButton;
11  import javax.swing.Box;
12  import javax.swing.JFrame;
13  import javax.swing.JLabel;
14  import javax.swing.JPanel;
15  import javax.swing.JTextField;
16  import javax.swing.WindowConstants;
17  import javax.swing.BoxLayout;
18  import javax.swing.BorderFactory;
19  import javax.swing.JOptionPane;
20
21  public class AddressBookDisplay extends JFrame
22  {
23     private Person currentEntry;
24     private PersonQueries personQueries;
25     private List< Person > results;
26     private int numberOfEntries = 0;
27     private int currentEntryIndex;
28
29     private JButton browseButton;
30     private JLabel emailLabel;
31     private JTextField emailTextField;
32     private JLabel firstNameLabel;
33     private JTextField firstNameTextField;
```

Fig. 28.32 | A simple address book. (Part 1 of 8.)

```
34      private JLabel idLabel;
35      private JTextField idTextField;
36      private JTextField indexTextField;
37      private JLabel lastNameLabel;
38      private JTextField lastNameTextField;
39      private JTextField maxTextField;
40      private JButton nextButton;
41      private JLabel ofLabel;
42      private JLabel phoneLabel;
43      private JTextField phoneTextField;
44      private JButton previousButton;
45      private JButton queryButton;
46      private JLabel queryLabel;
47      private JPanel queryPanel;
48      private JPanel navigatePanel;
49      private JPanel displayPanel;
50      private JTextField queryTextField;
51      private JButton insertButton;
52
53      // no-argument constructor
54      public AddressBookDisplay()
55      {
56         super( "Address Book" );
57
58         // establish database connection and set up PreparedStatements
59         personQueries = new PersonQueries();
60
61         // create GUI
62         navigatePanel = new JPanel();
63         previousButton = new JButton();
64         indexTextField = new JTextField( 2 );
65         ofLabel = new JLabel();
66         maxTextField = new JTextField( 2 );
67         nextButton = new JButton();
68         displayPanel = new JPanel();
69         idLabel = new JLabel();
70         idTextField = new JTextField( 10 );
71         firstNameLabel = new JLabel();
72         firstNameTextField = new JTextField( 10 );
73         lastNameLabel = new JLabel();
74         lastNameTextField = new JTextField( 10 );
75         emailLabel = new JLabel();
76         emailTextField = new JTextField( 10 );
77         phoneLabel = new JLabel();
78         phoneTextField = new JTextField( 10 );
79         queryPanel = new JPanel();
80         queryLabel = new JLabel();
81         queryTextField = new JTextField( 10 );
82         queryButton = new JButton();
83         browseButton = new JButton();
84         insertButton = new JButton();
85
86         setLayout( new FlowLayout( FlowLayout.CENTER, 10, 10 ) );
87         setSize( 400, 300 );
```

Fig. 28.32 | A simple address book. (Part 2 of 8.)

```
88          setResizable( false );
89
90          navigatePanel.setLayout(
91             new BoxLayout( navigatePanel, BoxLayout.X_AXIS ) );
92
93          previousButton.setText( "Previous" );
94          previousButton.setEnabled( false );
95          previousButton.addActionListener(
96             new ActionListener()
97             {
98                public void actionPerformed( ActionEvent evt )
99                {
100                  previousButtonActionPerformed( evt );
101               } // end method actionPerformed
102            } // end anonymous inner class
103         ); // end call to addActionListener
104
105         navigatePanel.add( previousButton );
106         navigatePanel.add( Box.createHorizontalStrut( 10 ) );
107
108         indexTextField.setHorizontalAlignment(
109            JTextField.CENTER );
110         indexTextField.addActionListener(
111            new ActionListener()
112            {
113               public void actionPerformed( ActionEvent evt )
114               {
115                  indexTextFieldActionPerformed( evt );
116               } // end method actionPerformed
117            } // end anonymous inner class
118         ); // end call to addActionListener
119
120         navigatePanel.add( indexTextField );
121         navigatePanel.add( Box.createHorizontalStrut( 10 ) );
122
123         ofLabel.setText( "of" );
124         navigatePanel.add( ofLabel );
125         navigatePanel.add( Box.createHorizontalStrut( 10 ) );
126
127         maxTextField.setHorizontalAlignment(
128            JTextField.CENTER );
129         maxTextField.setEditable( false );
130         navigatePanel.add( maxTextField );
131         navigatePanel.add( Box.createHorizontalStrut( 10 ) );
132
133         nextButton.setText( "Next" );
134         nextButton.setEnabled( false );
135         nextButton.addActionListener(
136            new ActionListener()
137            {
138               public void actionPerformed( ActionEvent evt )
139               {
140                  nextButtonActionPerformed( evt );
141               } // end method actionPerformed
```

Fig. 28.32 | A simple address book. (Part 3 of 8.)

```
142            } // end anonymous inner class
143         ); // end call to addActionListener
144
145         navigatePanel.add( nextButton );
146         add( navigatePanel );
147
148         displayPanel.setLayout( new GridLayout( 5, 2, 4, 4 ) );
149
150            idLabel.setText( "Address ID:" );
151            displayPanel.add( idLabel );
152
153            idTextField.setEditable( false );
154            displayPanel.add( idTextField );
155
156            firstNameLabel.setText( "First Name:" );
157            displayPanel.add( firstNameLabel );
158            displayPanel.add( firstNameTextField );
159
160            lastNameLabel.setText( "Last Name:" );
161            displayPanel.add( lastNameLabel );
162            displayPanel.add( lastNameTextField );
163
164            emailLabel.setText( "Email:" );
165            displayPanel.add( emailLabel );
166            displayPanel.add( emailTextField );
167
168            phoneLabel.setText( "Phone Number:" );
169            displayPanel.add( phoneLabel );
170            displayPanel.add( phoneTextField );
171            add( displayPanel );
172
173         queryPanel.setLayout(
174            new BoxLayout( queryPanel, BoxLayout.X_AXIS) );
175
176         queryPanel.setBorder( BorderFactory.createTitledBorder(
177            "Find an entry by last name" ) );
178         queryLabel.setText( "Last Name:" );
179         queryPanel.add( Box.createHorizontalStrut( 5 ) );
180         queryPanel.add( queryLabel );
181         queryPanel.add( Box.createHorizontalStrut( 10 ) );
182         queryPanel.add( queryTextField );
183         queryPanel.add( Box.createHorizontalStrut( 10 ) );
184
185         queryButton.setText( "Find" );
186         queryButton.addActionListener(
187            new ActionListener()
188            {
189               public void actionPerformed( ActionEvent evt )
190               {
191                  queryButtonActionPerformed( evt );
192               } // end method actionPerformed
193            } // end anonymous inner class
194         ); // end call to addActionListener
195
```

Fig. 28.32 | A simple address book. (Part 4 of 8.)

```
196        queryPanel.add( queryButton );
197        queryPanel.add( Box.createHorizontalStrut( 5 ) );
198        add( queryPanel );
199
200        browseButton.setText( "Browse All Entries" );
201        browseButton.addActionListener(
202           new ActionListener()
203           {
204              public void actionPerformed( ActionEvent evt )
205              {
206                 browseButtonActionPerformed( evt );
207              } // end method actionPerformed
208           } // end anonymous inner class
209        ); // end call to addActionListener
210
211        add( browseButton );
212
213        insertButton.setText( "Insert New Entry" );
214        insertButton.addActionListener(
215           new ActionListener()
216           {
217              public void actionPerformed( ActionEvent evt )
218              {
219                 insertButtonActionPerformed( evt );
220              } // end method actionPerformed
221           } // end anonymous inner class
222        ); // end call to addActionListener
223
224        add( insertButton );
225
226        addWindowListener(
227           new WindowAdapter()
228           {
229              public void windowClosing( WindowEvent evt )
230              {
231                 personQueries.close(); // close database connection
232                 System.exit( 0 );
233              } // end method windowClosing
234           } // end anonymous inner class
235        ); // end call to addWindowListener
236
237        setVisible( true );
238     } // end no-argument constructor
239
240     // handles call when previousButton is clicked
241     private void previousButtonActionPerformed( ActionEvent evt )
242     {
243        currentEntryIndex--;
244
245        if ( currentEntryIndex < 0 )
246           currentEntryIndex = numberOfEntries - 1;
247
248        indexTextField.setText( "" + ( currentEntryIndex + 1 ) );
```

Fig. 28.32 | A simple address book. (Part 5 of 8.)

```
249          indexTextFieldActionPerformed( evt );
250       } // end method previousButtonActionPerformed
251
252       // handles call when nextButton is clicked
253       private void nextButtonActionPerformed( ActionEvent evt )
254       {
255          currentEntryIndex++;
256
257          if ( currentEntryIndex >= numberOfEntries )
258             currentEntryIndex = 0;
259
260          indexTextField.setText( "" + ( currentEntryIndex + 1 ) );
261          indexTextFieldActionPerformed( evt );
262       } // end method nextButtonActionPerformed
263
264       // handles call when queryButton is clicked
265       private void queryButtonActionPerformed( ActionEvent evt )
266       {
267          results =
268             personQueries.getPeopleByLastName( queryTextField.getText() );
269          numberOfEntries = results.size();
270
271          if ( numberOfEntries != 0 )
272          {
273             currentEntryIndex = 0;
274             currentEntry = results.get( currentEntryIndex );
275             idTextField.setText( "" + currentEntry.getAddressID() );
276             firstNameTextField.setText( currentEntry.getFirstName() );
277             lastNameTextField.setText( currentEntry.getLastName() );
278             emailTextField.setText( currentEntry.getEmail() );
279             phoneTextField.setText( currentEntry.getPhoneNumber() );
280             maxTextField.setText( "" + numberOfEntries );
281             indexTextField.setText( "" + ( currentEntryIndex + 1 ) );
282             nextButton.setEnabled( true );
283             previousButton.setEnabled( true );
284          } // end if
285          else
286             browseButtonActionPerformed( evt );
287       } // end method queryButtonActionPerformed
288
289       // handles call when a new value is entered in indexTextField
290       private void indexTextFieldActionPerformed( ActionEvent evt )
291       {
292          currentEntryIndex =
293             ( Integer.parseInt( indexTextField.getText() ) - 1 );
294
295          if ( numberOfEntries != 0 && currentEntryIndex < numberOfEntries )
296          {
297             currentEntry = results.get( currentEntryIndex );
298             idTextField.setText("" + currentEntry.getAddressID() );
299             firstNameTextField.setText( currentEntry.getFirstName() );
300             lastNameTextField.setText( currentEntry.getLastName() );
301             emailTextField.setText( currentEntry.getEmail() );
302             phoneTextField.setText( currentEntry.getPhoneNumber() );
```

Fig. 28.32 | A simple address book. (Part 6 of 8.)

```
303          maxTextField.setText( "" + numberOfEntries );
304          indexTextField.setText( "" + ( currentEntryIndex + 1 ) );
305       } // end if
306    } // end method indexTextFieldActionPerformed
307
308    // handles call when browseButton is clicked
309    private void browseButtonActionPerformed( ActionEvent evt )
310    {
311       try
312       {
313          results = personQueries.getAllPeople();
314          numberOfEntries = results.size();
315
316          if ( numberOfEntries != 0 )
317          {
318             currentEntryIndex = 0;
319             currentEntry = results.get( currentEntryIndex );
320             idTextField.setText( "" + currentEntry.getAddressID() );
321             firstNameTextField.setText( currentEntry.getFirstName() );
322             lastNameTextField.setText( currentEntry.getLastName() );
323             emailTextField.setText( currentEntry.getEmail() );
324             phoneTextField.setText( currentEntry.getPhoneNumber() );
325             maxTextField.setText( "" + numberOfEntries );
326             indexTextField.setText( "" + ( currentEntryIndex + 1 ) );
327             nextButton.setEnabled( true );
328             previousButton.setEnabled( true );
329          } // end if
330       } // end try
331       catch ( Exception e )
332       {
333          e.printStackTrace();
334       } // end catch
335    } // end method browseButtonActionPerformed
336
337    // handles call when insertButton is clicked
338    private void insertButtonActionPerformed( ActionEvent evt )
339    {
340       int result = personQueries.addPerson( firstNameTextField.getText(),
341          lastNameTextField.getText(), emailTextField.getText(),
342          phoneTextField.getText() );
343
344       if ( result == 1 )
345          JOptionPane.showMessageDialog( this, "Person added!",
346             "Person added", JOptionPane.PLAIN_MESSAGE );
347       else
348          JOptionPane.showMessageDialog( this, "Person not added!",
349             "Error", JOptionPane.PLAIN_MESSAGE );
350
351       browseButtonActionPerformed( evt );
352    } // end method insertButtonActionPerformed
353
354    // main method
355    public static void main( String args[] )
356    {
```

Fig. 28.32 | A simple address book. (Part 7 of 8.)

```
357          new AddressBookDisplay();
358       } // end method main
359    } // end class AddressBookDisplay
```

Fig. 28.32 | A simple address book. (Part 8 of 8.)

To add a new entry into the AddressBook database, the user can enter the first name, last name, email and phone number (the AddressID will autoincrement) in the JText-Fields and press the **Insert New Entry** JButton. When the user presses **Insert New Entry**, the insertButtonActionPerformed handler (lines 338–352) is called. Lines 340–342 call the method addPerson on the PersonQueries object to add a new entry to the database. Line

351 calls `browseButtonActionPerformed` to obtain the updated set of people in the address book and update the GUI accordingly.

The user can then view different entries by pressing the **Previous** `JButton` or **Next** `JButton`, which results in calls to methods `previousButtonActionPerformed` (lines 241–250) or `nextButtonActionPerformed` (lines 253–262), respectively. Alternatively, the user can enter a number in the `indexTextField` and press *Enter* to view a particular entry. This results in a call to method `indexTextFieldActionPerformed` (lines 290–306) to display the specified record.

28.12 **Stored Procedures**

Many database management systems can store individual SQL statements or sets of SQL statements in a database, so that programs accessing that database can invoke them. Such named collections of SQL statements are called **stored procedures**. JDBC enables programs to invoke stored procedures using objects that implement the interface **CallableStatement**. `CallableStatements` can receive arguments specified with the methods inherited from interface `PreparedStatement`. In addition, `CallableStatements` can specify **output parameters** in which a stored procedure can place return values. Interface `CallableStatement` includes methods to specify which parameters in a stored procedure are output parameters. The interface also includes methods to obtain the values of output parameters returned from a stored procedure. To learn more about `CallableStatements`, visit

    java.sun.com/javase/6/docs/technotes/guides/jdbc/getstart/
    callablestatement.html#999652

Portability Tip 28.6

Although the syntax for creating stored procedures differs across database management systems, the interface CallableStatement provides a uniform interface for specifying input and output parameters for stored procedures and for invoking stored procedures.

Portability Tip 28.7

According to the Java API documentation for interface CallableStatement, for maximum portability between database systems, programs should process the update counts (which indicate how many rows were updated) or ResultSets returned from a CallableStatement before obtaining the values of any output parameters.

28.13 **Transaction Processing**

Many database applications require guarantees that a series of database insertions, updates and deletions executes properly before the applications continue processing the next database operation. For example, when you transfer money electronically between bank accounts, several factors determine if the transaction is successful. You begin by specifying the source account and the amount you wish to transfer from that account to a destination account. Next, you specify the destination account. The bank checks the source account to determine whether its funds are sufficient to complete the transfer. If so, the bank withdraws the specified amount and, if all goes well, deposits it into the destination account to complete the transfer. What happens if the transfer fails after the bank withdraws the money from the source account? In a proper banking system, the bank redeposits the money in the source account. How would you feel if the money was subtracted from your source account and the bank *did not* deposit the money in the destination account?

Transaction processing enables a program that interacts with a database to treat a database operation (or set of operations) as a single operation. Such an operation also is known as an **atomic operation** or a **transaction**. At the end of a transaction, a decision can be made either to **commit the transaction** or **roll back the transaction**. Committing the transaction finalizes the database operation(s); all insertions, updates and deletions performed as part of the transaction cannot be reversed without performing a new database operation. Rolling back the transaction leaves the database in its state prior to the database operation. This is useful when a portion of a transaction fails to complete properly. In our bank-account-transfer discussion, the transaction would be rolled back if the deposit could not be made into the destination account.

Java provides transaction processing via methods of interface `Connection`. Method `setAutoCommit` specifies whether each SQL statement commits after it completes (a `true` argument) or whether several SQL statements should be grouped as a transaction (a `false` argument). If the argument to `setAutoCommit` is `false`, the program must follow the last SQL statement in the transaction with a call to `Connection` method `commit` (to commit the changes to the database) or `Connection` method `rollback` (to return the database to its state prior to the transaction). Interface `Connection` also provides method `getAutoCommit` to determine the autocommit state for the `Connection`.

28.14 Wrap-Up

In this chapter, you learned basic database concepts, how to interact with data in a database using SQL and how to use JDBC to allow Java applications to manipulate MySQL and Java DB databases. You learned about the SQL commands `SELECT`, `INSERT`, `UPDATE` and `DELETE`, as well as clauses such as `WHERE`, `ORDER BY` and `INNER JOIN`. You learned the explicit steps for obtaining a `Connection` to the database, creating a `Statement` to interact with the database's data, executing the statement and processing the results. Then you used a `RowSet` to simplify the process of connecting to a database and creating statements. You used `PreparedStatements` to create precompiled SQL statements. You also learned how to create and configure databases in both MySQL and Java DB by using predefined SQL scripts. We also provided overviews of `CallableStatements` and transaction processing. In the next chapter, you'll learn about web application development with JavaServer Faces.

28.15 Web Resources

`java.sun.com/javase/technologies/database/index.jsp`
Sun Microsystems, Java SE database technologies home page.

`java.sun.com/docs/books/tutorial/jdbc/index.html`
The Java Tutorial's JDBC track.

`developers.sun.com/product/jdbc/drivers`
Sun Microsystems search engine for locating JDBC drivers.

`www.sql.org`
This SQL portal provides links to many resources, including SQL syntax, tips, tutorials, books, magazines, discussion groups, companies with SQL services, SQL consultants and free software.

`www.datadirect.com/developer/jdbc/topics/perfoptjdbc/index.ssp`
White paper that discusses designing a good JDBC application.

`java.sun.com/javase/6/docs/technotes/guides/jdbc/index.html`
Sun Microsystems JDBC API documentation.

`www.mysql.com`
This site is the MySQL database home page. You can download the latest versions of MySQL and MySQL Connector/J and access their online documentation.

`dev.mysql.com/doc/refman/5.0/en/index.html`
MySQL reference manual.

`java.sun.com/javase/6/docs/technotes/guides/jdbc/getstart/rowsetImpl.html`
Overviews the `RowSet` interface and its subinterfaces. This site also discusses the reference implementations of these interfaces from Sun and their usage.

`java.sun.com/developer/Books/JDBCTutorial/chapter5.html`
Chapter 5 (RowSet Tutorial) of the book *The JDBC 2.0 API Tutorial and Reference, Second Edition*.

Summary

Section 28.1 Introduction

- A database is an integrated collection of data. A database management system (DBMS) provides mechanisms for storing, organizing, retrieving and modifying data for many users.
- Today's most popular database management systems are relational database systems.
- SQL is the international standard language used to query and manipulate relational data.
- Programs connect to, and interact with, relational databases via an interface—software that facilitates communications between a database management system and a program.
- A JDBC driver enables Java applications to connect to a database in a particular DBMS and allows you to retrieve and manipulate database data.

Section 28.2 Relational Databases

- A relational database stores data in tables. Tables are composed of rows, and rows are composed of columns in which values are stored.
- A primary key provides a unique value that cannot be duplicated in other rows of the same table.
- Each column of a table represents a different attribute.
- The primary key can be composed of more than one column.
- Every column in a primary key must have a value, and the value of the primary key must be unique. This is known as the Rule of Entity Integrity.
- A one-to-many relationship between tables indicates that a row in one table can have many related rows in a separate table.
- A foreign key is a column in a table that must match the primary-key column in another table. This is known as the Rule of Referential Integrity.
- Foreign keys enable information from multiple tables to be joined together. There is a one-to-many relationship between a primary key and its corresponding foreign key.

Section 28.4.1 Basic SELECT Query

- The basic form of a query is

      SELECT * FROM *tableName*

  where the asterisk (*) indicates that all columns from *tableName* should be selected, and *tableName* specifies the table in the database from which rows will be retrieved.
- To retrieve specific columns, replace the * with a comma-separated list of column names.

Section 28.4.2 WHERE Clause

- The optional WHERE clause in a query specifies the selection criteria for the query. The basic form of a query with selection criteria is

    SELECT *columnName1*, *columnName2*, ... FROM *tableName* WHERE *criteria*

- The WHERE clause can contain operators <, >, <=, >=, =, <> and LIKE. Operator LIKE is used for string pattern matching with wildcard characters percent (%) and underscore (_).

- A percent character (%) in a pattern indicates that a string matching the pattern can have zero or more characters at the percent character's location in the pattern.

- An underscore (_) in the pattern string indicates a single character at that position in the pattern.

Section 28.4.3 ORDER BY Clause

- A query's result can be sorted with the ORDER BY clause. The simplest form of an ORDER BY clause is

    SELECT *columnName1*, *columnName2*, ... FROM *tableName* ORDER BY *column* ASC
    SELECT *columnName1*, *columnName2*, ... FROM *tableName* ORDER BY *column* DESC

    where ASC specifies ascending order, DESC specifies descending order and *column* specifies the column on which the sort is based. The default sorting order is ascending, so ASC is optional.

- Multiple columns can be used for ordering purposes with an ORDER BY clause of the form

    ORDER BY *column1 sortingOrder*, *column2 sortingOrder*, ...

- The WHERE and ORDER BY clauses can be combined in one query. If used, ORDER BY must be the last clause in the query.

Section 28.4.4 Merging Data from Multiple Tables: INNER JOIN

- An INNER JOIN merges rows from two tables by matching values in columns that are common to the tables. The basic form for the INNER JOIN operator is:

    SELECT *columnName1, columnName2, ...*
    FROM *table1*
    INNER JOIN *table2*
        ON *table1.columnName* = *table2.columnName*

    The ON clause specifies the columns from each table that are compared to determine which rows are joined. If a SQL statement uses columns with the same name from multiple tables, the column names must be fully qualified by prefixing them with their table names and a dot (.).

Section 28.4.5 INSERT Statement

- An INSERT statement inserts a new row into a table. The basic form of this statement is

    INSERT INTO *tableName* (*columnName1*, *columnName2*, ..., *columnNameN*)
        VALUES (*value1*, *value2*, ..., *valueN*)

    where *tableName* is the table in which to insert the row. The *tableName* is followed by a comma-separated list of column names in parentheses. The list of column names is followed by the SQL keyword VALUES and a comma-separated list of values in parentheses.

- SQL uses single quotes (') to delimit strings. To specify a string containing a single quote in SQL, escape the single quote with another single quote (i.e., '').

Section 28.4.6 UPDATE Statement

- An UPDATE statement modifies data in a table. The basic form of an UPDATE statement is

    UPDATE *tableName*
        SET *columnName1* = *value1*, *columnName2* = *value2*, ..., *columnNameN* = *valueN*
        WHERE *criteria*

where *tableName* is the table in which to update data. The *tableName* is followed by keyword SET and a comma-separated list of *columnName* = *value* pairs. The optional WHERE clause *criteria* determines which rows to update.

Section 28.4.7 *DELETE Statement*

- A DELETE statement removes rows from a table. The simplest form for a DELETE statement is

    DELETE FROM *tableName* WHERE *criteria*

    where *tableName* is the table from which to delete a row (or rows). The optional WHERE *criteria* determines which rows to delete. If this clause is omitted, all the table's rows are deleted.

Section 28.8.1 *Connecting to and Querying a Database*

- Package java.sql contains classes and interfaces for accessing relational databases in Java.

- A Connection object manages the connection between a Java program and a database. Connection objects enable programs to create SQL statements that access data.

- DriverManager method getConnection attempts to connect to a database at a URL that specifies the protocol for communication, the subprotocol for communication and the database name.

- Connection method createStatement creates a Statement object, which can be used to submit SQL statements to the database.

- Statement method executeQuery executes a query and returns a ResultSet object containing the query result. ResultSet methods enable a program to manipulate query results.

- A ResultSetMetaData object describes a ResultSet's contents. Programs can use metadata programmatically to obtain information about the ResultSet column names and types.

- ResultSetMetaData method getColumnCount retrieves the number of ResultSet columns.

- ResultSet method next positions the ResultSet cursor to the next row and returns true if the row exists; otherwise, it returns false. This method must be called to begin processing a ResultSet because the cursor is intially positioned before the first row.

- It's possible to extract each ResultSet column as a specific Java type. ResultSetMetaData method getColumnType returns a Types constant (package java.sql) indicating the column's type.

- ResultSet *get* methods typically receive as an argument either a column number (as an int) or a column name (as a String) indicating which column's value to obtain.

- ResultSet row and column numbers start at 1.

- Each Statement object can open only one ResultSet at a time. When a Statement returns a new ResultSet, the Statement closes the prior ResultSet.

- Connection method createStatement has an overloaded version that receives the result type and the result concurrency. The result type specifies whether the ResultSet's cursor is able to scroll in both directions or forward only and whether the ResultSet is sensitive to changes. The result concurrency specifies whether the ResultSet can be updated with ResultSet's update methods.

- Some JDBC drivers do not support scrollable or updatable ResultSets.

Section 28.8.2 *Querying the **books** Database*

- TableModel method getColumnClass returns a Class object that represents the superclass of all objects in a particular column. A JTable uses this information to set up the default cell renderer and cell editor for that column in a JTable.

- ResultSetMetaData method getColumnClassName obtains a column's fully qualified class name.

- TableModel method getColumnCount returns the number of columns in the underlying ResultSet.

- TableModel method getColumnName returns the column name in the underlying ResultSet.

- ResultSetMetaData method getColumnName obtains the column name from the ResultSet.

- `TableModel` method `getRowCount` returns the number of rows in the model's `ResultSet`.

- `TableModel` method `getValueAt` returns the `Object` at a particular row and column of the model's underlying `ResultSet`.

- `ResultSet` method `absolute` positions the `ResultSet` cursor at a specific row.

- `AbstractTableModel` method `fireTableStructureChanged` notifies any `JTable` using a particular `TableModel` object as its model that the data in the model has changed.

Section 28.9 *RowSet Interface*
- Interface `RowSet` configures a database connection and executes a query automatically.

- A connected `RowSet` remains connected to the database while the object is in use. A disconnected `RowSet` connects, executes a query, then closes the connection.

- `JdbcRowSet`, a connected `RowSet`, wraps a `ResultSet` object and allows you to scroll and update its rows. Unlike a `ResultSet` object, a `JdbcRowSet` object is scrollable and updatable by default.

- `CachedRowSet`, a disconnected `RowSet`, caches a `ResultSet`'s data in memory. A `CachedRowSet` is scrollable and updatable. A `CachedRowSet` is also serializable.

Section 28.10 *Java DB/Apache Derby*
- As of JDK 6, Sun Microsystems bundles the open-source, pure Java database Java DB (the Sun branded version of Apache Derby) with the JDK.

- Java DB has both an embedded version and a network version.

Section 28.11 *PreparedStatements*
- `PreparedStatements` are compiled, so they execute more efficiently than `Statements`.

- `PreparedStatements` can have parameters, so the same query can execute with different arguments.

- A parameter is specified with a question mark (?) in the SQL statement. Before executing a `PreparedStatement`, you must use `PreparedStatement`'s *set* methods to specify the arguments.

- `PreparedStatement` method `setString`'s first argument represents the parameter number being set and the second argument is that parameter's value.

- Parameter numbers are counted from 1, starting with the first question mark (?).

- Method `setString` automatically escapes `String` parameter values as necessary.

- Interface `PreparedStatement` provides set methods for each supported SQL type.

- An identity column is the SQL standard way to represent an autoincremented column. The SQL `IDENTITY` keyword marks a column as an identity column.

Section 28.12 *Stored Procedures*
- JDBC enables programs to invoke stored procedures using `CallableStatement` objects.

- `CallableStatement` can specify input parameters. `CallableStatement` can specify output parameters in which a stored procedure can place return values.

Section 28.13 *Transaction Processing*
- Transaction processing enables a program that interacts with a database to treat a database operation (or set of operations) as a single operation—known as an atomic operation or a transaction.

- At the end of a transaction, a decision can be made to either commit or roll back the transaction.

- Committing a transaction finalizes the database operation(s)—inserts, updates and deletes cannot be reversed without performing a new database operation.

- Rolling back a transaction leaves the database in its state prior to the database operation.

- Java provides transaction processing via methods of interface `Connection`.

- Method `setAutoCommit` specifies whether each SQL statement commits after it completes (a `true` argument) or whether several SQL statements should be grouped as a transaction.
- When autocommit is disabled, the program must follow the last SQL statement in the transaction with a call to `Connection` method `commit` (to commit the changes to the database) or `Connection` method `rollback` (to return the database to its state prior to the transaction).
- Method `getAutoCommit` determines the autocommit state for the `Connection`.

Terminology

Self-Review Exercise

28.1 Fill in the blanks in each of the following statements:

a) The international standard database language is _____.

b) A table in a database consists of _____ and _____.

c) Statement objects return SQL query results as _____ objects.

d) The _____ uniquely identifies each row in a table.

e) SQL keyword _____ is followed by the selection criteria that specify the rows to select in a query.

f) SQL keywords _____ specify the order in which rows are sorted in a query.

g) Merging rows from multiple database tables is called _____ the tables.

h) A(n) _____ is an organized collection of data.

i) A(n) _____ is a set of columns whose values match the primary-key values of another table.

j) _____ method _____ is used to obtain a Connection to a database.

k) Interface _____ helps manage the connection between a Java program and a database.

l) A(n) _____ object is used to submit a query to a database.

m) Unlike a ResultSet object, _____ and _____ objects are scrollable and updatable by default.

n) _____, a disconnected RowSet, caches the data of a ResultSet in memory.

Answers to Self-Review Exercise

28.1 a) SQL. b) rows, columns. c) ResultSet. d) primary key. e) WHERE. f) ORDER BY. g) joining. h) database. i) foreign key. j) DriverManager, getConnection. k) Connection. l) Statement. m) JdbcRowSet, CachedRowSet n) CachedRowSet.

Exercises

28.2 *(Query Application for the **books** Database)* Using the techniques shown in this chapter, define a complete query application for the books database. Provide the following predefined queries:

  a) Select all authors from the Authors table.
  b) Select a specific author and list all books for that author. Include each book's title, year and ISBN. Order the information alphabetically by the author's last then first name.
  c) Select a specific publisher and list all books published by that publisher. Include the title, year and ISBN. Order the information alphabetically by title.
  d) Provide any other queries you feel are appropriate.

Display a JComboBox with appropriate names for each predefined query. Also allow users to supply their own queries.

28.3 *(Employee Database)* In Section 10.7, we introduced an employee-payroll hierarchy to calculate each employee's payroll. In this exercise, we provide a database of employees that corresponds to the employee-payroll hierarchy. (A SQL script to create the employees database is provided with the examples for this chapter.) Write an application that allows the user to:

  a) Add employees to the employee table.
  b) Add payroll information to the appropriate table for each new employee. For example, for a salaried employee add the payroll information to the salariedEmployees table.

Figure 28.33 is the entity-relationship diagram for the employees database.

28.4 *(Employee Database Query Application)* Modify Exercise 28.3 to provide a JComboBox and a JTextArea to allow the user to perform a query that is either selected from the JComboBox or defined in the JTextArea. Sample predefined queries are:

  a) Select all employees working in Department SALES.
  b) Select hourly employees working over 30 hours.
  c) Select all commission employees in descending order of the commission rate.

28.5 *(Employee Database Data Manipulation Application)* Modify Exercise 28.4 to perform the following tasks:

  a) Increase base salary by 10% for all base-plus-commission employees.
  b) If the employee's birthday is in the current month, add a $100 bonus.
  c) For all commission employees with gross sales over $10,000, add a $100 bonus.

28.6 *(AddressBook Modification: Update an Existing Entry)* Modify the program in Figs. 28.30–28.32 to provide a JButton that allows the user to call a method named updatePerson in PersonQueries class to update the current entry in the AddressBook database.

28.7 *(AddressBook Modification: Delete an Existing Entry)* Modify the program of Exercise 28.6 to provide a JButton that allows the user to call a method named deletePerson in PersonQueries class to delete the current entry in the AddressBook database.

28.8 *(ATM Case Study with a Database)* Modify the ATM Case Study (Chapters 12–13) to use an actual database to store the account information. We provide a SQL script to create the BankDatabase, which has a single table consisting of four columns—AccountNumber (an int), PIN (an int), AvailableBalance (a double) and TotalBalance (a double).

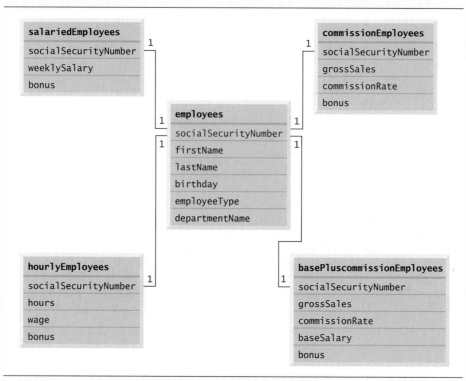

Fig. 28.33 | Table relationships in the employees database.

If any man will draw up his case, and put his name at
the foot of the first page, I will give him an immediate
reply. Where he compels me to turn over the sheet, he
must wait my leisure.
—Lord Sandwich

Rule One: Our client is always right.
Rule Two: If you think our client is wrong, see Rule
One.
—Anonymous

A fair question should be followed by a deed in silence.
—Dante Alighieri

You will come here and get books that will open your
eyes, and your ears, and your curiosity, and turn you
inside out or outside in.
—Ralph Waldo Emerson

JavaServer™ Faces
Web Applications

Objectives

In this Chapter you'll learn:

- Web application development using Java Technologies and NetBeans.
- To create JavaServer Pages with JavaServer Faces components.
- To create web applications consisting of multiple pages.
- To validate user input on a web page.
- To maintain user-specific state information throughout a web application with session tracking and cookies.

29.1 Introduction

In this chapter, we introduce web application development in Java. Web-based applications create content for web browser clients. This content includes Extensible HyperText Markup Language (XHTML), client-side scripting, images and binary data. If you are not familiar with XHTML, visit our XHTML Resource Center at www.deitel.com/XHTML/ for introductions, tutorials and other resources that will help you learn XHTML. For a complete list of our Resource Centers, visit www.deitel.com/ResourceCenters.html.

This chapter begins with an overview of multitier application architecture and Java's web technologies for implementing multitier applications. We then present several web application examples. The first example introduces you to Java web development. In the second example, we build a web application that simply shows the look-and-feel of several web application GUI components. Next, we show how to use validation components and custom validation methods to ensure that user input is valid before it is submitted for processing on the server. The chapter finishes with two examples of maintaining user-specific information in a web application. Chapter 30 continues our discussion of Java web application development with more advanced concepts.

Throughout this chapter and Chapter 30, we use the **NetBeans 6.5** IDE and the **GlassFish v2 UR2** open source application server. To implement the examples presented in this chapter, you must install these software products. NetBeans is available from

```
www.netbeans.org/downloads/index.html
```

Download and execute the **Java** or **All** version of the installer—the installer you choose must include **Java Web and EE** and **Glassfish V2 UR2**. Both versions install the NetBeans IDE and the GlassFish server. We assume you use the default installation options. Once you've installed NetBeans, run it. Then, use the **Help** menu's **Check for Updates** option to make sure you have the most up-to-date components.

Much of the code that we present in this chapter is generated by the NetBeans IDE. We've reformatted this code and deleted the Javadoc comments that the IDE generates to match our coding conventions used throughout this book and to save space. We sometimes show only a portion of the code. In such cases, we provide comments indicating where code was removed, and all line numbers match the complete example source code.

29.2 Simple HTTP Transactions

Consider what occurs behind the scenes when a user requests a web page in a browser. In its simplest form, a web page is nothing more than an XHTML document that describes to a browser how to display and format the document's information. XHTML documents normally contain hyperlinks that link to different pages or to other parts of the same page. When the user clicks a hyperlink, the requested web page loads into the user's web browser. Similarly, the user can type the address of a page into the browser's address field.

URIs

The HTTP protocol allows clients and servers to interact and exchange information in a uniform and reliable manner. HTTP uses URIs (Uniform Resource Identifiers) to identify data on the Internet. URIs that specify document locations are called URLs (Uniform Resource Locators). Common URLs refer to files, directories or objects that perform complex tasks, such as database lookups and Internet searches. If you know the URL of a publicly available resource or file anywhere on the web, you can access it through HTTP.

Parts of a URL

A URL contains information that directs a browser to the resource that the user wishes to access. Computers that run **web-server** software make such resources available. Let's examine the components of the URL

```
http://www.deitel.com/books/downloads.html
```

The `http://` indicates that the resource is to be obtained using the HTTP protocol. The middle portion, `www.deitel.com`, is the server's fully qualified **hostname**—the name of the server on which the resource resides. The computer that houses and maintains resources is usually is referred to as the **host**. The hostname `www.deitel.com` is translated into an **IP address**—a unique numerical value that identifies the server, much as a telephone number uniquely defines a particular phone line. This translation is performed by a **domain-name system (DNS) server**—a computer that maintains a database of host-names and their corresponding IP addresses—and the process is called a **DNS lookup**. To test web applications, you'll often use your computer as the host. This host is referred to using the reserved domain name `localhost`, which translates to the IP address `127.0.0.1`. (See `en.wikipedia.org/wiki/IP_address` for more information on IP addresses.) The fully qualified hostname can be followed by a colon (`:`) and a port number. Web servers await requests on port 80 by default; however, many development web servers use a different port number, such as 8080—as you'll see in Section 29.5.4.

The remainder of the URL (i.e., `/books/downloads.html`) specifies both the name of the requested resource (the XHTML document `downloads.html`) and its path, or location (`/books`), on the web server. The path could specify the location of an actual directory on the web server's file system. For security reasons, however, the path normally specifies the location of a **virtual directory**. The server translates the virtual directory into a real location on the server (or on another computer on the server's network), thus hiding the true location of the resource. Some resources are created dynamically using other information stored on the server computer, such as a database. The hostname in the URL for such a resource specifies the correct server; the path and resource information identify the resource with which to interact to respond to the client's request.

Making a Request and Receiving a Response

When given a URL, a web browser performs an HTTP transaction to retrieve and display the web page at that address. Figure 29.1 illustrates the transaction, showing the interaction between the web browser (the client) and the web server application (the server).

In Fig. 29.1, the web browser sends an HTTP request to the server. The request (in its simplest form) is

```
GET /books/downloads.html HTTP/1.1
```

The word **GET** is an **HTTP method** indicating that the client wishes to obtain a resource from the server. The remainder of the request provides the path name of the resource (e.g., an XHTML document) and the protocol's name and version number (HTTP/1.1). The client's request also contains some required and optional headers, such as Host (which identifies the target computer) or User-Agent (which identifies the browser type and version).

Fig. 29.1 | Client interacting with web server. *Step 1:* The GET request.

Any server that understands HTTP (version 1.1) can translate this request and respond appropriately. Figure 29.2 depicts the server responding to a request.

Fig. 29.2 | Client interacting with web server. *Step 2:* The HTTP response.

The server first responds by sending a line of text that indicates the HTTP version, followed by a numeric code and a phrase describing the status of the transaction. For example,

```
HTTP/1.1 200 OK
```

indicates success, whereas

```
HTTP/1.1 404 Not found
```

informs the client that the web server could not locate the requested resource. On a successful request, the server appends the requested document to the HTTP response. A complete list of numeric codes indicating the status of an HTTP transaction can be found at www.w3.org/Protocols/rfc2616/rfc2616-sec10.html.

HTTP Headers

The server then sends one or more **HTTP headers**, which provide additional information about the data that will be sent. In this case, the server is sending an XHTML text document, so one HTTP header for this example would read:

```
Content-type: text/html
```

The information provided in this header specifies the **Multipurpose Internet Mail Extensions (MIME)** type of the content that the server is transmitting to the browser. MIME is an Internet standard that specifies data formats so that programs can interpret data correctly. For example, the MIME type text/plain indicates that the sent information is text that can be displayed directly, without any interpretation of the content as XHTML markup. Similarly, the MIME type image/jpeg indicates that the content is a JPEG image. When the browser receives this MIME type, it attempts to display the image. For a list of available MIME types, visit www.w3schools.com/media/media_mimeref.asp.

The header or set of headers is followed by a blank line, which indicates to the client browser that the server is finished sending HTTP headers. The server then sends the contents of the requested XHTML document (downloads.html). The client-side browser parses the XHTML markup it receives and **renders** (or displays) the results. The server normally keeps the connection open to process other requests from the client.

HTTP GET and POST Requests

The two most common **HTTP request types** (also known as **request methods**) are GET and POST. A GET request typically asks for a specific resource on a server. Common uses of GET requests are to retrieve an XHTML document or an image or to fetch search results based on a user-submitted search term. A POST request typically posts (or sends) data to a server. Common uses of POST requests are to send form data or documents to a server.

An HTTP request often posts data to a **server-side form handler** that processes the data. For example, when a user performs a search or participates in a web-based survey, the web server receives the information specified in the XHTML form as part of the request. GET requests and POST requests can both be used to send form data to a web server, yet each request type sends the information differently.

A GET request sends information to the server in the URL, e.g., www.google.com/search?q=deitel. In this case, search is the name of Google's server-side form handler, q is the name of a variable in Google's search form and deitel is the search term. A ? separates the **query string** from the rest of the URL in a request. A *name/value* pair is passed to the server with the *name* and the *value* separated by an equals sign (=). If more than one *name/value* pair is submitted, each is separated from the next by an ampersand (&). The server uses data passed in a query string to retrieve an appropriate resource from the server. The server then sends a **response** to the client. A GET request may be initiated by submitting an XHTML form whose `method` attribute is set to `"get"`, by typing the URL (possibly containing a query string) directly into the browser's address bar or through a hyperlink.

A `POST` request sends form data as part of the HTTP message, not as part of the URL. A `GET` request typically limits the query string (i.e., everything to the right of the ?) to a specific number of characters (2083 in Internet Explorer; more in other browsers), so it is often necessary to send large pieces of information using the `POST` method. The `POST` method is also sometimes preferred because it hides the submitted data from the user by embedding it in an HTTP message.

Software Engineering Observation 29.1

The data sent in a POST request is not part of the URL, and the user can't see the data by default. However, there are tools available that expose this data, so you should not assume that the data is secure just because a POST request is used.

Client-Side Caching

Browsers often **cache** (save on disk) web pages for quick reloading. If there are no changes between the version stored in the cache and the current version on the web, this speeds up your browsing experience. An HTTP response can indicate the length of time for which the content remains "fresh." If this amount of time has not been reached, the browser can avoid another request to the server. Otherwise, the browser requests the document from the server. Thus, the browser minimizes the amount of data that must be downloaded for you to view a web page. Browsers typically do not cache the server's response to a `POST` request, because the next `POST` might not return the same result. For example, in a survey, many users could visit the same web page and answer a question. The survey results could then be displayed for the user. Each new answer changes the overall results of the survey.

When you use a web-based search engine, the browser normally supplies the information you specify in an XHTML form to the search engine with a `GET` request. The search engine performs the search, then returns the results to you as a web page. Such pages are sometimes cached by the browser in case you perform the same search again.

29.3 Multitier Application Architecture

Web-based applications are **multitier applications** (sometimes referred to as *n*-**tier applications**). Multitier applications divide functionality into separate **tiers** (i.e., logical groupings of functionality). Although tiers can be located on the same computer, the tiers of web-based applications typically reside on separate computers. Figure 29.3 presents the basic structure of a three-tier web-based application.

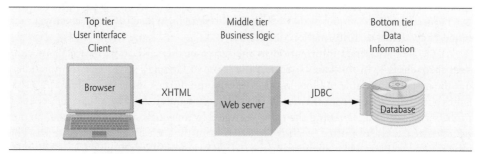

Fig. 29.3 | Three-tier architecture.

The **information tier** (also called the **data tier** or the **bottom tier**) maintains data pertaining to the application. This tier typically stores data in a relational database management system (RDBMS). We discussed RDBMSs in Chapter 28. For example, a retail store might have a database for storing product information, such as descriptions, prices and quantities in stock. The same database also might contain customer information, such as user names, billing addresses and credit card numbers. This tier can contain multiple databases, which together comprise the data needed for our application.

The **middle tier** implements **business logic**, **controller logic** and **presentation logic** to control interactions between the application's clients and the application's data. The middle tier acts as an intermediary between data in the information tier and the application's clients. The middle-tier controller logic processes client requests (such as requests to view a product catalog) and retrieves data from the database. The middle-tier presentation logic then processes data from the information tier and presents the content to the client. Web applications typically present data to clients as XHTML documents.

Business logic in the middle tier enforces **business rules** and ensures that data is reliable before the server application updates the database or presents the data to users. Business rules dictate how clients can and cannot access application data, and how applications process data. For example, a business rule in the middle tier of a retail store's web-based application might ensure that all product quantities remain positive. A client request to set a negative quantity in the bottom tier's product-information database would be rejected by the middle tier's business logic.

The **client tier**, or **top tier**, is the application's user interface, which gathers input and displays output. Users interact directly with the application through the user interface (typically viewed in a web browser), keyboard and mouse. In response to user actions (e.g., clicking a hyperlink), the client tier interacts with the middle tier to make requests and to retrieve data from the information tier. The client tier then displays the data retrieved from the middle tier to the user. The client tier never directly interacts with the information tier.

29.4 Java Web Technologies

Java web technologies continually evolve to provide developers with higher levels of abstraction and greater separation of the application's tiers, which makes web applications more maintainable and extensible. It also allows for an effective division of labor. A graphic designer can build the application's user interface without concern for the underlying page logic, which will be handled by a programmer. Meanwhile, you are free to focus on the application's business logic, leaving the details of building an attractive and easy-to-use application to the designer. NetBeans allows you to develop a web application's GUI in a drag-and-drop design tool, while handling the business logic in separate Java classes.

Java multitier applications are typically implemented using the features of Java Enterprise Edition (Java EE). The technologies we use to develop web applications in Chapters 29–30 are part of Java EE 5 (java.sun.com/javaee).

29.4.1 Servlets

Servlets are the lowest-level view of web development technologies in Java that we'll discuss in this chapter. They use the HTTP request/response model of communication between client and server.

Servlets extend a server's functionality by allowing it to generate dynamic content. For instance, servlets can dynamically generate custom XHTML documents, help provide secure access to a website, interact with databases on behalf of a client and maintain unique session information for each client. A web server component called the **servlet container** executes and interacts with servlets. Packages `javax.servlet` and `javax.servlet.http` provide the classes and interfaces to define servlets. The servlet container receives HTTP requests from a client and directs each request to the appropriate servlet. The servlet processes the request and returns an appropriate response to the client—usually in the form of an XHTML or XML (Extensible Markup Language) document to display in the browser. XML is a language used to exchange structured data on the web.

Architecturally, all servlets must implement the `Servlet` interface of package `javax.servlet`, which ensures that each servlet can execute in the framework provided by the servlet container. Interface `Servlet` declares methods used by the servlet container to manage the servlet's life cycle. A servlet's life cycle begins when the servlet container loads it into memory—usually in response to the first request for the servlet. Before the servlet can handle that request, the container invokes the servlet's `init` method, which is called only once during a servlet's life cycle to initialize the servlet. After `init` completes execution, the servlet is ready to respond to its first request. All requests are handled by a servlet's **service method**, which is the key method in defining a servlet's functionality. The `service` method receives the request, processes it and sends a response to the client. During a servlet's life cycle, `service` is called once per request. Each new request is typically handled in a separate thread of execution (managed by the servlet container), so each servlet must be thread safe. When the servlet container terminates the servlet (e.g. when the servlet container needs more memory or when it is shut down), the servlet's `destroy` method is called to release any resources held by the servlet.

29.4.2 JavaServer Pages

JavaServer Pages (JSP) technology is an extension of servlet technology. Each JSP is a document that is translated by the JSP container into a servlet. Unlike servlets, JSPs help you separate presentation from content. JavaServer Pages enable web application programmers to create dynamic content by reusing predefined components and by interacting with components using server-side scripting. JSP programmers can use special software components called JavaBeans and custom tag libraries that encapsulate complex, dynamic functionality. A **JavaBean** is a reusable component that follows certain conventions for class design and that can be manipulated visually in a builder tool such as NetBeans or Eclipse. JavaBeans classes that allow reading and writing of instance variables must provide appropriate *get* and *set* methods—together, these define properties of JavaBeans classes. The complete set of class design conventions is discussed in the JavaBeans specification (`java.sun.com/javase/technologies/desktop/javabeans/glasgow/index.html`).

Custom Tag Libraries

Recall from Chapter 23 that XHTML and XML documents typically consist of elements that are delimited by tags. **Custom tag libraries** are a powerful feature of JSP that allows Java developers to hide code for database access and other complex operations in **custom tags**. To use such capabilities, you simply add the custom tags to the page. This simplicity enables web-page designers who are not familiar with Java to enhance web pages with powerful dynamic content and dynamic processing capabilities. The JSP classes and interfaces are located in the packages `javax.servlet.jsp` and `javax.servlet.jsp.tagext`.

JSP Components

There are four key components to JSPs—directives, actions, scripting elements and tag libraries. **Directives** are messages to the **JSP container**—the web server component that executes JSPs. Directives enable you to specify page settings, to include content from other resources and to specify custom tag libraries for use in JSPs. **Actions** encapsulate functionality in predefined tags that programmers can embed in JSPs. Actions are often performed based on the information sent to the server as part of a particular client request. They can also create Java objects for use in JSPs. **Scripting elements** enable you to insert Java code that interacts with components in a JSP (and possibly other web application components) to perform request processing. **Tag libraries** are part of the **tag extension mechanism** that enables programmers to create custom tags. Such tags enable web-page designers to manipulate JSP content without prior Java knowledge. The **JavaServer Pages Standard Tag Library** (**JSTL**) provides the functionality for many common web application tasks, such as iterating over a collection of objects and executing SQL statements.

Static Content

JSPs can contain other static content. For example, JSPs normally include XHTML or XML markup. Such markup is known as **fixed-template data** or **fixed-template text**. Any literal text or XHTML markup in a JSP is translated to a `String` in the servlet representation of the JSP.

Processing a JSP Request

When a JSP-enabled server receives the first request for a JSP, the JSP container translates the JSP into a servlet that handles the current request and future requests to the JSP. JSPs thus rely on the same request/response mechanism as servlets to process requests from and send responses to clients.

Performance Tip 29.1

Some JSP containers translate JSPs into servlets at the JSP's deployment time (i.e., when the application is placed on a web server). This eliminates the translation overhead for the first client that requests each JSP, as the JSP will be translated before it is ever requested by a client.

29.4.3 JavaServer Faces

JavaServer Faces (**JSF**)—supported by Java Enterprise Edition 5 (Java EE 5) compliant servers, like GlassFish v2 UR2—is a web application framework that simplifies the design of an application's user interface and further separates a web application's presentation from its business logic. A **framework** provides libraries and sometimes software tools to help you organize and build your applications. Though the JSF framework can use many technologies to define the pages in web applications, this chapter focuses on JSF applications that use JavaServer Pages. JSF provides a set of user interface components, or **JSF components**, that simplify web-page design. These components are similar to the Swing components used to build GUI applications. JSF provides two JSP custom tag libraries for adding these components to a JSP page. JSF also includes APIs for handling component events (such as processing component state changes and validating user input), navigating between web application pages and more. You design the look-and-feel of a page with JSF by adding elements to a JSP document and manipulating their attributes. You define the page's behavior separately in related Java source-code files.

Though the standard JSF components are sufficient for most basic web applications, you can also write custom component libraries. Additional component libraries are available through various open source projects and from third parties. For example, Oracle provides almost 100 components in its ADF Faces library. [*Note:* There are many other popular web application frameworks, including Spring, Struts and Hibernate—each of which is also supported in NetBeans. We've chosen to demonstrate only JavaServer Faces.]

29.4.4 Web Technologies in NetBeans

NetBeans web applications that use the JavaServer Faces framework consist of one or more JSP web pages. These JSP files have the filename extension **.jsp** and contain the web pages' GUI elements. The JSPs can also contain JavaScript to add functionality to the page. JSPs can be customized in NetBeans by adding JSF components, including labels, text fields, images, buttons and other GUI components. The IDE allows you to design pages visually by dragging and dropping these components onto a page; you can also customize a web page by editing the .jsp file manually.

Every JSP file created in NetBeans represents a web page and has a corresponding JavaBean class called the **page bean**. A JavaBean class must have a default (or no-argument) constructor, and *get* and *set* methods for all of the bean's properties (i.e., instance variables). The page bean defines properties for each of the page's elements that you wish to interact with programmatically. The page bean also contains event handlers and page life-cycle methods for managing tasks such as page initialization and rendering, and other supporting code for the web application.

Every NetBeans JSF web application defines three more JavaBeans. The **RequestBean** object is maintained in **request scope**—it exists only for an HTTP request's duration. A **SessionBean** object has **session scope**—it exists throughout a user's browsing session or until the session times out. There is a unique SessionBean object for each user. Finally, the **ApplicationBean** object has **application scope**—it is shared by all instances of an application and exists as long as the application remains deployed on a web server. This object is used for application-wide data storage or processing; only one instance exists for the application, regardless of the number of open sessions.

29.5 Creating and Running a Simple Application in NetBeans

Our first example displays the web server's time of day in a browser window. When run, this program displays the text "Current time on the web server:", followed by the web server's time. The application contains a single web page and, as mentioned previously, consists of two related files—a JSP document (Fig. 29.4) and a supporting page bean file (Fig. 29.6). The application also has the three scoped data beans for request, session and application scopes that are not used in this example. We first discuss the markup in the JSP document, the application output and the code in the page bean file, then we provide step-by-step instructions for creating this web application. [*Note:* The markup in Fig. 29.4 and other JSP file listings in this chapter is the same as the markup that appears in Net-Beans, but we've reformatted these listings for presentation purposes.]

```
 I  <?xml version="1.0" encoding="UTF-8"?>
 2
 3  <!-- Fig. 29.4 Time.jsp -->
 4  <!-- JSP document generated by NetBeans that displays -->
 5  <!-- the current time on the web server -->
 6  <jsp:root version="2.1" xmlns:f="http://java.sun.com/jsf/core"
 7     xmlns:h="http://java.sun.com/jsf/html"
 8     xmlns:jsp="http://java.sun.com/JSP/Page"
 9     xmlns:webuijsf="http://www.sun.com/webui/webuijsf">
10     <jsp:directive.page contentType="text/html;charset=UTF-8"
11        pageEncoding="UTF-8"/>
12     <f:view>
13        <webuijsf:page id="page1">
14           <webuijsf:html id="html1">
15              <webuijsf:head id="head1" title="Web Time: A Simple Example">
16                 <webuijsf:link id="link1" url="/resources/stylesheet.css"/>
17                 <webuijsf:meta content="60" httpEquiv="refresh"/>
18              </webuijsf:head>
19              <webuijsf:body id="body1" style="-rave-layout: grid">
20                 <webuijsf:form id="form1">
21                    <webuijsf:staticText id="timeHeader"
22                       style="font-size: 18px; left: 24px; top: 24px;
23                       position: absolute"
24                       text="Current time on the web server:"/>
25                    <webuijsf:staticText binding="#{Time.clockText}"
26                       id="clockText" style="background-color: black;
27                       color: yellow; font-size: 18px; left: 24px;
28                       top: 48px; position: absolute"/>
29                 </webuijsf:form>
30              </webuijsf:body>
31           </webuijsf:html>
32        </webuijsf:page>
33     </f:view>
34  </jsp:root>
```

Fig. 29.4 | JSP document generated by NetBeans that displays the current time on the web server.

NetBeans generates most of the markup shown in Fig. 29.4 when you set the web page's title, drag two **Static Text** components onto the page and set the properties of the **Static Text** components. **Static Text** components display text that cannot be edited by the user. We show these steps shortly.

29.5.1 Examining a JSP Document

The JSP documents in this and the following examples are generated almost entirely by NetBeans, which provides a visual editor that allows you to build a page's GUI by dragging and dropping components onto a design area. The IDE generates a JSP file in response to your interactions. Line 1 of Fig. 29.4 is the XML declaration, indicating the fact that the JSP is expressed in XML syntax and the version of XML that is used. Lines 3–5 are comments that we added to the JSP to indicate its figure number, filename and purpose.

Line 6 begins the JSP's root element. All JSPs must have this **jsp:root** element, which has a version attribute to indicate the JSP version being used (line 6) and one or more xmlns attributes (lines 6–9). Each **xmlns attribute** specifies a prefix and a URL for a tag library, allowing the page to use elements from that library. For example, line 8 allows the page to use the standard JSP elements, but each element's tag must be preceded by the jsp prefix. All JSPs generated by NetBeans include the tag libraries specified in lines 6–9 (the JSF core components library, the JSF HTML components library, the JSP standard components library and the JSF user interface components library).

Lines 10–11 are the **jsp:directive.page** element. Its contentType attribute specifies the MIME type (text/html) and the character set (UTF-8) the page uses. The pageEncoding attribute specifies the character encoding used by the page source. These attributes help the client (typically a web browser) determine how to render the content.

All pages containing JSF components are represented in a **component tree** (similar to the one shown in Fig. 29.5) with the root JSF element **f:view**, which is of type **UIViewRoot**. This component tree structure is represented in a JSP by nesting all JSF component tags inside the f:view element (lines 12–33 in this example).

Lines 13–18 begin the JSP's definition with the **webuijsf:page**, **webuijsf:html** and **webuijsf::head** elements, all from the webuijsf (JSF user interface components) tag library. The webuijsf:head element (lines 15–18) has a title attribute that specifies the page's title. This element also contains a **webuijsf:link** element (line 16) that specifies the CSS stylesheet used by the page, and a **webuijsf:meta** element (line 17) that causes the page to refresh every 60 seconds. The **webuijsf:body** element (lines 19–30) contains a **webuijsf:form** element (lines 20–29), which contains two **webuijsf:staticText** components (lines 21–24 and 25–28) that display the page's text. The timeHeader component (lines 21–24) has a text attribute (line 24) that specifies the text to display (i.e., "Current time on the web server"). The clockText component (lines 25–28) does not specify a text attribute because this component's text will be set programmatically.

The webuijsf:staticText element at lines 25–28 has the attribute binding = "#{Time.clockText}" (line 25). This attribute uses **JSF Expression Language** notation (i.e., #{Time.clockText}) to reference the clockText property in the Time class that represents the page bean (you'll see this class in Fig. 29.6). You can bind an attribute of a JSP element to the value of a property in any of the web application's JavaBeans. For instance, the text attribute of a webuijsf:staticText component can be bound to an int property in the application's SessionBean (as you'll see in Section 29.7.2).

All the JSP's elements are mapped by the application server to a combination of XHTML elements and JavaScript code that enables the browser to render the page. JavaScript is a scripting language that is interpreted in all of today's popular web browsers. It can be used to perform tasks that manipulate web-page elements in a web browser and provide interactivity with the user. You can learn more about JavaScript in our JavaScript Resource Center at www.deitel.com/JavaScript/.

The same web component can map to different XHTML elements and JavaScript code, depending on the client browser and the component's property settings. The

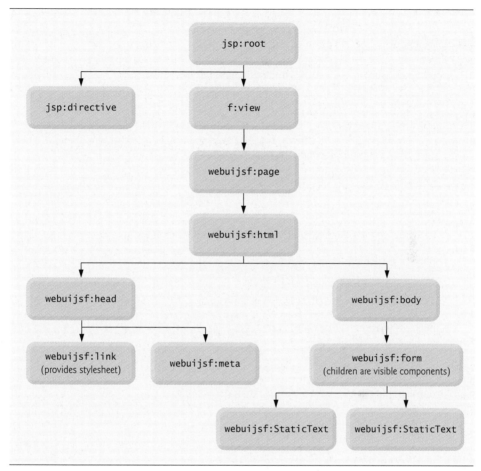

Fig. 29.5 | Sample JSF component tree within a JSP document.

webuijsf:staticText components (lines 21–24, 25–28) typically map to XHTML **span** elements. A span element contains text that is displayed on a web page and is typically used to control the formatting of the text. The style attributes of a JSP's webuijsf:static-Text element are mapped to the corresponding span element's style attribute, which the browser then uses to control the element's appearance.

29.5.2 Examining a Page Bean File

Figure 29.6 presents the autogenerated page bean file. Line 11 begins class Time's declaration and indicates that it inherits from class **AbstractPageBean** (from the package **com.sun.rave.web.ui.appbase**). All page bean classes that support JSP documents with JSF components must inherit from the abstract class AbstractPageBean, which provides page life-cycle methods. Note that the IDE makes the class name match the page name. Package **com.sun.webui.jsf.component** provides classes for many of the basic JSF user interface components, including the StaticText component.

```
1    // Fig. 29.6: Time.java
2    // Page bean file that sets clockText to the time on the web server
3    package webtime;
4
5    import com.sun.rave.web.ui.appbase.AbstractPageBean;
6    import com.sun.webui.jsf.component.StaticText;
7    import javax.faces.FacesException;
8    import java.text.DateFormat;
9    import java.util.Date;
10
11   public class Time extends AbstractPageBean
12   {
13      private void _init() throws Exception
14      {
15      } // end method _init
16
17      private StaticText clockText = new StaticText();
18
19      public StaticText getClockText()
20      {
21         return clockText;
22      } // end method getClockText
23
24      public void setClockText( StaticText st )
25      {
26         this.clockText = st;
27      } // end method setClockText
28
29      public Time()
30      {
31      } // end constructor
32
33      @Override
34      public void init()
35      {
36         super.init();
37
38         try
39         {
40            _init();
41         } // end try
42         catch ( Exception e )
43         {
44            log( "Page1 Initialization Failure" , e );
45            throw e instanceof FacesException ? ( FacesException ) e :
46               new FacesException( e );
47         } // end catch
48      } // end method init
49
50      // method called when a postback occurs
51      @Override
52      public void preprocess()
53      {
54      } // end method preprocess
```

Fig. 29.6 | Page bean file that sets `clockText` to the time on the web server. (Part 1 of 2.)

```
55
56       // method called before the page is rendered
57       @Override
58       public void prerender()
59       {
60          clockText.setValue( DateFormat.getTimeInstance(
61             DateFormat.LONG ).format( new Date() ) );
62       } // end method prerender
63
64       // method called after rendering completes, if init was called
65       @Override
66       public void destroy()
67       {
68       } // end method
69
70       // returns a reference to the session bean
71       protected SessionBean1 getSessionBean1()
72       {
73          return ( SessionBean1 ) getBean( "SessionBean1" );
74       } // end method
75
76       // returns a reference to the request bean
77       protected RequestBean1 getRequestBean1()
78       {
79          return ( RequestBean1 ) getBean( "RequestBean1" );
80       } // end method
81
82       // returns a reference to the application bean
83       protected ApplicationBean1 getApplicationBean1()
84       {
85          return ( ApplicationBean1 ) getBean( "ApplicationBean1" );
86       } // end method
87    } // end class Time
```

Fig. 29.6 | Page bean file that sets clockText to the time on the web server. (Part 2 of 2.)

This page bean file defines a variable (line 17) for programmatically interacting with the clockText element of the JSP document of Fig. 29.4. The IDE also autogenerates *get* and *set* methods (lines 19–27) for this variable, as you'll see in Section 29.5.4, *Step 9*. The clockText variable is of type StaticText.

The only logic required in this page is to set the clockText component's text to the current time on the server. We do this in the prerender method (lines 58–62). The meaning of this and other page bean methods is discussed in Section 29.5.3. Lines 60–61 fetch and format the time on the server and set the value of clockText to that time.

29.5.3 Event-Processing Life Cycle

Several methods in the page bean tie into the JSF **event-processing life cycle's** four major stages—initialization, preprocessing, prerendering and destruction. Each corresponds to a method in the page bean class—init, preprocess, prerender and destroy, respectively. NetBeans creates these overridden methods, so you can customize them to handle life-cycle processing tasks, such as rendering an element on a page only if a user clicks a button.

The **init method** (Fig. 29.6, lines 34–48) is called by the JSP container the first time the page is requested and on postbacks. A **postback** occurs when form data is submitted, and the page and its contents are sent to the server to be processed. Method init invokes its superclass version (line 36) then tries to call the method _init (declared in lines 13–15). The _init method is also automatically generated and handles component initialization tasks (if there are any), such as setting the options for a group of radio buttons.

The **preprocess method** (lines 52–54) is called after init, but only if the page is processing a postback. The **prerender method** (lines 58–62) is called just before a page is rendered (i.e., displayed) by the browser. This method should be used to set component properties; properties that are set sooner (such as in method init) may be overwritten before the page is actually rendered by the browser. For this reason, we set the value of clockText in the prerender method.

Finally, the **destroy method** (lines 66–68) is called after the page has been rendered, but only if the init method was called. This method handles tasks such as freeing resources used to render the page.

29.5.4 Building a Web Application in NetBeans

Now that we have presented the JSP file, the page bean file and the resulting XHTML web page sent to the web browser, we discuss the steps to create this application. To build the WebTime application, perform the following steps in NetBeans:

Step 1: Creating the Web Application Project
Select **File > New Project...** to display the **New Project** dialog. Select **Java Web** in the **Categories** pane, **Web Application** in the **Projects** pane and click **Next >**. Change the project name to WebTime. In the **Project Location** field, specify where you'd like to store the project. These settings will create a WebTime directory to store the project's files in the parent directory you specified. Keep the other default settings and click **Next >**. Keep the default options for **Server and Settings** and click **Next >**. Select **Visual Web JavaServer Faces** as the framework to use in this web application, then click **Finish** to create the web application project.

Step 2: Examining the Visual Editor Window of the New Project
The next several figures describe important NetBeans features, beginning with the **visual editor** window (Fig. 29.7). NetBeans creates a single web page named Page1 for each new project. This page is open by default in the visual editor in **Design** mode when the project first loads. As you drag and drop new components onto the page, **Design** mode allows you to see how the browser will render your page. The JSP file for this page, named Page1.jsp, can be viewed by clicking the **JSP** button at the top of the visual editor or by right clicking anywhere in the visual editor and selecting **Edit JSP Source**. As mentioned previously, each web page is supported by a page bean file. NetBeans creates a file named Page1.java when a new project is created. To open it, click the **Java** button at the top of the visual editor or right click anywhere in the visual editor and select **Edit Java Source**.

The **Preview in Browser** button at the top of the visual editor window allows you to view your pages in a browser without having to build and run the entire application. The **Refresh** button redraws the page in the visual editor. The **Show Virtual Forms** button allows you to see which form elements participate in virtual forms (discussed in Chapter 30). The **Target Browser Size** drop-down list lets you specify the optimal browser resolution for viewing the page and lets you see what the page will look like in different screen resolutions.

Preview in Browser...   Refresh   Show Virtual Forms   Target Browser Size

Design mode

View JSP file

View Java page
bean file

Fig. 29.7 | Visual editor window in **Design** mode.

Step 3: Examining the Palette in NetBeans

Figure 29.8 shows the **Palette** displayed in the IDE when the project loads. Part (a) displays the **Woodstock Basic** list of web components, and part (b) displays the **Woodstock Layout** components. Woodstock is a set of user interface components for JavaServer Faces applications. You can learn more about these components at woodstock.dev.java.net. We discuss specific components in Fig. 29.8 as they are used throughout the chapter.

(a) **Woodstock Basic** category of the **Palette**   (b) **Woodstock Layout** category of the **Palette** and other collapsed categories

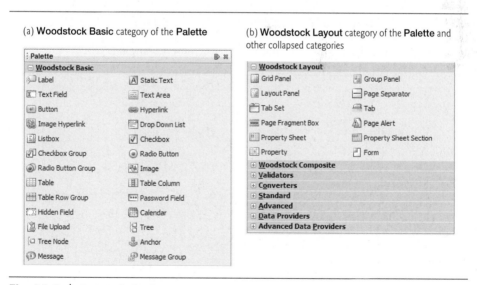

Fig. 29.8 | **Palette** in NetBeans.

Step 4: Examining the Projects Window

Figure 29.9 displays the **Projects** window, which appears in the upper-left corner of the IDE. This window displays the hierarchy of all files included in the project. The JSP files for each page are listed under the **Web Pages** node. This node also includes the **resources** folder, which contains the CSS stylesheet for the project and any other files the pages may need to display properly, such as image files. The Java source code, including the page bean file for each web page and the application, session and request scope beans, can be found under the **Source Packages** node.

Fig. 29.9 | **Projects** window for the WebTime project.

Step 5: Examining the JSP and Java Files in the IDE

Figure 29.10 displays Page1.jsp—the JSP document generated by NetBeans for Page1. [*Note:* We reformatted the code to match our coding conventions.] Click the **JSP** button at the top of the visual editor to view this file. When this file is first created, it contains elements for setting up the page, including linking to the page's style sheet and declaring the JSF libraries that will be used. By default, NetBeans does not show line numbers in the source-code editor. To view the line numbers, select **View > Show Line Numbers**.

```
 1  <?xml version="1.0" encoding="UTF-8"?>
 2  <jsp:root version="2.1" xmlns:f="http://java.sun.com/jsf/core"
 3     xmlns:h="http://java.sun.com/jsf/html"
 4     xmlns:jsp="http://java.sun.com/JSP/Page"
 5     xmlns:webuijsf="http://www.sun.com/webui/webuijsf">
 6     <jsp:directive.page contentType="text/html;charset=UTF-8"
 7        pageEncoding="UTF-8"/>
 8     <f:view>
 9        <webuijsf:page id="page1">
10           <webuijsf:html id="html1">
11              <webuijsf:head id="head1">
12                 <webuijsf:link id="link1" url="/resources/stylesheet.css"/>
13              </webuijsf:head>
14              <webuijsf:body id="body1" style="-rave-layout: grid">
15                 <webuijsf:form id="form1">
16                 </webuijsf:form>
17              </webuijsf:body>
18           </webuijsf:html>
19        </webuijsf:page>
20     </f:view>
21  </jsp:root>
```

Fig. 29.10 | JSP document generated for Page1 by NetBeans.

Figure 29.11 displays part of `Page1.java`—the page bean file generated by NetBeans for `Page1`. Click the **Java** button at the top of the visual editor to open the page bean file. This file contains a Java class with the same name as the page (i.e., `Page1`), which extends the `AbstractPageBean` class. As previously mentioned, `AbstractPageBean` has several methods that manage the page's life cycle. Four of these methods—`init`, `preprocess`, `prerender` and `destroy`—are overridden by `Page1.java`. Other than method `init`, these methods are initially empty. They serve as placeholders for you to customize the behavior of your web application.

Click this plus (+) sign to display the collapsed generated code

Fig. 29.11 | Page bean file for `Page1.jsp` generated by NetBeans.

Step 6: Renaming the JSP and Java Files

Typically, you'll want to rename the JSP and Java files, so that their names are relevant to your application. Right click `Page1.jsp` in the **Projects** window and select **Refactor > Rename...** to display the **Rename Page1** dialog. Enter the new name, `Time`, and check the **Apply Rename on Comments** checkbox. To make the changes immediately, click the **Refactor** button. If you wish to preview the changes before they're applied, click the **Preview** button to display the **Refactoring** window at the bottom of the IDE. **Refactoring** is the process of modifying source code to improve its readability and reusability without changing its behavior—for example, by renaming methods or variables, or breaking long methods into shorter ones. NetBeans has built-in refactoring tools that automate some refactoring tasks. Using these tools to rename the project files updates the name of the JSP file to `Time.jsp` and its corresponding page bean file to `Time.java`. The refactoring tool also changes the class name in the page bean file and all of the attribute bindings in the JSP document to reflect the new class name. If you choose to preview the refactoring changes, none of the changes will be made until you click the **Do Refactoring** button in the **Refactoring** window.

Step 7: Changing the Title of the Page

Before designing the content of the web page, we give it the title "Web Time: A Simple Example". By default, the page does not have a title when it is generated by the IDE. To add a title, open the JSP file in **Design** mode. In the **Properties** window, enter the new title next to the **Title** property and press *Enter*. View the JSP to see that the attribute title="Web Time: A Simple Example" was automatically added to the webuijsf:head tag. The page's title will appear in the browser's title bar when the page is rendered.

Step 8: Designing the Page

Designing a web page is simple in NetBeans. To add components to the page in **Design** mode, drag and drop them from the **Palette** onto the page. Each component is an object that has properties, methods and events. You can set these properties and events visually using the **Properties** window or programmatically in the page bean file.

The IDE generates the JSP tags for the components you drag and drop using a grid layout, as specified in the webuijsf:body tag. The components are rendered using **absolute positioning**—they appear exactly where they are dropped on the page. As you add components, the style attribute in each component's JSP element will include the number of pixels from the top and left margins of the page at which the component is positioned.

This example uses two **Static Text** components. To add the first one, drag and drop it from the **Palette**'s **Woodstock Basic** components list to the page. Edit the component's text by typing "Current time on the web server:" directly into the component. The text can also be edited by changing the component's text property in the **Properties** window. NetBeans is a WYSIWYG (What You See Is What You Get) editor—when you make a change to a page in **Design** mode, the IDE creates the markup (visible in **JSP** mode) necessary to achieve the desired visual effects seen in **Design** mode and might also add Java code to the page bean's .java file. After adding the text to the web page, switch to **JSP** mode. You should see that the IDE nested a webuijsf:staticText element (with the text attribute that contains the text you just entered) in the webuijsf:form element inside the webuijsf:body element. The **Static Text** component is bound to the object staticText1 in the page bean file. Back in **Design** mode, click the **Static Text** component to select it. In the **Properties** window, click the ellipsis button (⬚) next to the style property to open a dialog box to edit the text's style. Select **18 px** for the font size and click **OK**. Again in the **Properties** window, change the id property to timeHeader. Setting the id property also changes the name of the component's corresponding variable name in the page bean and updates its binding attribute in the JSP accordingly. The IDE should now appear as in Fig. 29.12. You can view the JSP file to see that font-size: 18 px has been added to the style attribute and the id attribute has been changed to timeHeader in the component's tag.

Drop a second **Static Text** component onto the page and set its id to clockText. Edit its style property so that the font size is **18 px**, the text color is yellow, and the background color is black. Do not edit the component's text, as this will be set programmatically in the page bean file. The component will display with the text *Static Text* in the IDE, but will not display any text at runtime unless the text is set programmatically. Figure 29.13 shows the IDE after the second component is added.

Step 9: Adding Page Logic

After designing the user interface, you can modify the page bean file to set the text of the clockText element. To interact with a JSF component programmatically, you must first

Fig. 29.12 | `Time.jsp` after inserting the first **Static Text** component.

Fig. 29.13 | `Time.jsp` after adding the second `StaticText` component.

right click the control in **Design** mode and select **Add Binding Attribute**. In the page bean file, this creates a variable that you can use to interact with the component as well as *set* and *get* methods for accessing the component.

In this example, we add a statement to method `prerender` (lines 58–62 of Fig. 29.6) in **Java** mode. Recall that we use method `prerender` to ensure that `clockText` will be updated each time the page is refreshed. Lines 60–61 of Fig. 29.6 programmatically set the text of `clockText` to the current time on the server. For this statement to work, you'll also need the two `import`s shown in lines 8–9 of Fig. 29.6. The IDE can insert these `import` statements for you. Simply right click in the code editor window and select **Fix Imports** from the pop-up menu that appears

We'd like this page to refresh once per minute to display an up-to-date time. To accomplish this, add `<webuijsf:meta content = "60" httpEquiv = "refresh" />` to the JSP document, as the last element nested in the `webuijsf:head` element. This element tells the browser to reload the page automatically every 60 seconds. You can also add this tag by dragging a **Meta** component from the **Advanced** section of the **Palette** to your page, then setting the component's `content` attribute to 60 and its `httpEquiv` attribute to `refresh`. If you do this, the **Meta** component will show up in the **Navigator** window.

Step 10: Examining the Navigator Window

Figure 29.14 displays the NetBeans **Navigator** window. We expanded the **Time** node, which represents the page bean file and shows the contents of the component tree. The request, session and application scope beans are collapsed, as we have not added any properties to these beans in this example. Clicking an item in the page's component tree selects the item in the visual editor.

Fig. 29.14 | **Navigator** window in NetBeans.

Step 11: Running the Application

After creating the web page, you can view it several ways. First, you can select **Run > Build Project**, and after the build completes, select **Run > Run Project**, to run the application in a browser window. You can also run a project that has already been built by pressing the **Run Project** icon (▷) in the toolbar at the top of the IDE or by pressing *F6*. Note that if changes are made to a project, the project must be rebuilt before they'll be reflected when the application is viewed in a browser—this will happen automatically if you run the project without explicitly rebuilding. Because this application was built on the local file system, the URL displayed in the address bar of the browser when the application is run will be `http://localhost:8080/WebTime/` (Fig. 29.4), where 8080 is the port number on which the test server—GlassFish v2 UR2—runs by default.

Alternatively, you can press *Ctrl + F5* to build the application, then run it in debug mode—the NetBeans built-in debugger can help you troubleshoot applications. (Visit `www.deitel.com/books/jhtp8/` for a video that introduces the NetBeans debugger.) If you press *F6*, the program executes without debugging enabled.

Error-Prevention Tip 29.1

If you have trouble building your project due to errors in the NetBeans-generated XML files used for building, try cleaning the project and building again. You can do this by selecting **Run > Clean and Build Project** *or by pressing* Shift + F11.

Error-Prevention Tip 29.2

If you attempt to clean and rebuild your project and receive an error message indicating that one or more files could not be deleted, stop the GlassFish server, then attempt the clean and rebuild process again. To stop the server, click the **Services** *tab in NetBeans, expand the* **Servers** *node, right click* **GlassFish v2** *and select* **Stop**. *Once the server has stopped running, select* **Run > Clean and Build Project** *or press* Shift + F11 *to clean and rebuild the project.*

Finally, you can run your built application by opening a browser window and typing the web page's URL in the **Address** field. Since your application resides on the local file system, you must first start the GlassFish application server. If you have previously run the application using one of the methods above, the server will already be started. Otherwise, you can start the server from the IDE by opening the **Services** tab (located in the same panel as the **Projects**), expanding the **Servers** node, right clicking **GlassFish v2** and selecting **Start**. Then you can type the URL (including the port number for the application server, 8080) in the browser to execute the application. For this example it is not necessary to type the entire URL, `http://localhost:8080/WebTime/faces/Time.jsp`. The path to the file `Time.jsp` (i.e., `faces/Time.jsp`) can be omitted, because this file was set by default as the project's start page. For projects with multiple pages, you can change the start page by right clicking the desired page in the **Projects** window and selecting **Set As Start Page**. The start page is indicated by an icon with a green play button symbol ( ) next to the page's name in the **Projects** window.

29.6 JSF Components

This section introduces some of the JSF components featured in the **Palette** (Fig. 29.8). Figure 29.15 summarizes some of the JSF components used in the chapter examples.

JSF component	Description
Label	Displays text that can be associated with an input element.
Static Text	Displays text that the user cannot edit.
Text Field	Gathers user input and displays text.
Button	Triggers an event when clicked.
Hyperlink	Displays a hyperlink.
Drop Down List	Displays a drop-down list of choices.
Radio Button Group	Groups radio buttons.
Image	Displays images (e.g., GIF and JPG).

Fig. 29.15 | Commonly used JSF components.

29.6.1 Text and Graphics Components

Figure 29.16 displays a simple form for gathering user input. This example uses most of the components in Fig. 29.15. All the code in Fig. 29.16 was generated by NetBeans in response to actions performed in **Design** mode. To create this application from scratch, review the steps in Section 29.5.4. This example does not perform a task when the user clicks **Register**. Later, we demonstrate how to add functionality to many of these components.

```
 1    <?xml version="1.0" encoding="UTF-8"?>
 2
 3    <!-- Fig.29.16: WebComponents.jsp -->
 4    <!-- Registration form that demonstrates JSF components -->
 5    <jsp:root version="2.1" xmlns:f="http://java.sun.com/jsf/core"
 6       xmlns:h="http://java.sun.com/jsf/html"
 7       xmlns:jsp="http://java.sun.com/JSP/Page"
 8       xmlns:webuijsf="http://www.sun.com/webui/webuijsf">
 9       <jsp:directive.page contentType="text/html;charset=UTF-8"
10          pageEncoding="UTF-8"/>
11       <f:view>
12          <webuijsf:page id="page1">
13             <webuijsf:html id="html1">
14                <webuijsf:head id="head1">
15                   <webuijsf:link id="link1" url="/resources/stylesheet.css"/>
16                </webuijsf:head>
17                <webuijsf:body id="body1" style="-rave-layout: grid">
18                   <webuijsf:form id="form1">
19                      <webuijsf:staticText id="headerText"
20                         style="font-size: 18px; left: 24px; top: 24px;
21                            position: absolute"
22                         text="This is a sample registration form"/>
23                      <webuijsf:staticText id="instructionText"
24                         style="font-style: italic; left: 24px; top: 48px;
25                            position: absolute"
26                         text="Please fill in all fields and click Register"/>
27                      <webuijsf:image id="userImage" style="left: 24px;
28                         top: 72px; position: absolute"
29                         url="/resources/user.png"/>
30                      <h:panelGrid columns="4" id="gridPanel"
31                         style="height: 96px; left: 24px; top: 96px;
32                            position: absolute" width="456">
33                         <webuijsf:image id="firstNameImage"
34                            url="/resources/fname.png"/>
35                         <webuijsf:textField id="firstNameTextField"/>
36                         <webuijsf:image id="lastNameImage"
37                            url="/resources/lname.png"/>
38                         <webuijsf:textField id="lastNameTextField"/>
39                         <webuijsf:image id="emailImage"
40                            url="/resources/email.png"/>
41                         <webuijsf:textField id="emailTextField"/>
42                         <webuijsf:image id="phoneImage"
43                            url="/resources/phone.png"/>
44                         <webuijsf:textField id="phoneTextField"/>
45                      </h:panelGrid>
46                      <webuijsf:image id="publicationsImage"
47                         style="position: absolute; left: 24px; top: 216px"
48                         url="/resources/publications.png"/>
49                      <webuijsf:staticText id="publicationText"
50                         style="left: 216px; top: 216px; position: absolute"
51                         text="Which book would you like information about?"/>
52                      <webuijsf:dropDown id="booksDropDown" items=
53                         "#{WebComponents.booksDropDownDefaultOptions.
54                            options}"
```

Fig. 29.16 | Registration form that demonstrates JSF components. (Part 1 of 2.)

```
55                      style="position: absolute; left: 24px; top: 240px"/>
56                   <webuijsf:hyperlink id="deitelHyperlink"
57                      style="position: absolute; left: 24px; top: 264px"
58                      text="Click here to learn more about our books"
59                      url="http://www.deitel.com"/>
60                   <webuijsf:image id="osImage" style="left: 24px;
61                      top: 312px; position: absolute"
62                      url="/resources/os.png"/>
63                   <webuijsf:radioButtonGroup id="osRadioButtonGroup"
64                      items="#{WebComponents.
65                         osRadioButtonGroupDefaultOptions.options}"
66                      style="left: 24px; top: 336px; position: absolute"/>
67                   <webuijsf:button id="registerButton" style="left: 359px;
68                      top: 456px; position: absolute; width: 96px"
69                      text="Register"/>
70                </webuijsf:form>
71             </webuijsf:body>
72          </webuijsf:html>
73       </webuijsf:page>
74    </f:view>
75 </jsp:root>
```

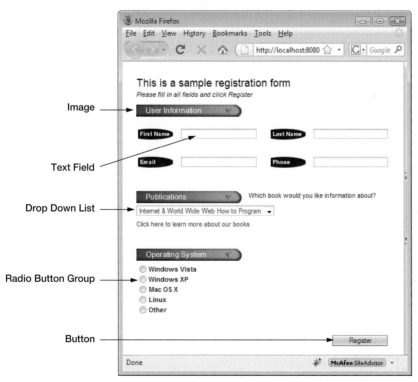

Fig. 29.16 | Registration form that demonstrates JSF components. (Part 2 of 2.)

Recall that NetBeans uses absolute positioning by default, so components are rendered wherever they were dropped in the visual editor. In this example, in addition to absolute positioning, we use a **Grid Panel** component (lines 30–45) from the **Palette's**

Woodstock Layout component group. The h: prefix indicates that it can be found in the JSF HTML tag library. This component—an object of class `HtmlPanelGrid` in package `javax.faces.component.html`—controls the positioning of the components it contains. The **Grid Panel** component allows the designer to specify the number of columns the grid should contain. Components may then be dropped inside the panel, and they will automatically be repositioned into evenly spaced columns in the order in which they are dropped. When the number of components exceeds the number of columns, the panel moves the additional components to a new row. The **Grid Panel** behaves like an XHTML table and is in fact rendered as an XHTML table in the browser. In this example, we use the **Grid Panel** to control the positions of the **Image** and **Text Field** components in the user information section of the page.

Adding a Formatting Component to a Web Page

To create the layout for the **User Information** section of the form shown in Fig. 29.16, drag a **Grid Panel** component onto the page. In the **Properties** window, change the component's id to `gridPanel` and set the component's `columns` property to 4. The component also has properties to control the cell padding, cell spacing and other elements of the component's appearance. In this case, accept the defaults for these properties. Now you can simply drag the **Image**s and **Text Field**s for user information into the **Grid Panel**. The **Grid Panel** will manage their spacing and their organization into rows and columns.

Examining Web Components on a Sample Registration Form

Here we focus on the new user interface elements in the example. Lines 27–29 of Fig. 29.16 define an **Image**, an object of class `ImageComponent` which inserts an image into a web page. The images in this example are located in the ch29\images directory. Images to be displayed on a web page must be placed in the project's `resources` folder. To add images to the project, drop an **Image** component onto the page and click the ellipsis button (🔲) next to the **url** property in the **Properties** window. This opens a dialog in which you can select the image to display. Since no images have been added to the `resources` folder yet, click the **Add File** button, locate the image ch29\images directory and click the **Add File** button to copy the file you selected into the project's `resources` folder in the Web Pages folder. Now you can select the image and click **OK** to insert it into the page.

Lines 30–45 contain an h:panelGrid element representing the **Grid Panel** component. Within this element, there are eight **Image** and **Text Field** components. **Text Field**s allow you to obtain text input from the user. For example, line 35 defines a **Text Field** control used to obtain the first name. You can label a **Text Field** by setting its `label` property, which places text to the left of the **Text Field**. Alternatively, you can label a **Text Field** by dragging and dropping a **Label** component onto the page, which allows you to customize the **Label**'s position and style. In this example, we're using images to indicate the purpose of each **Text Field**.

The order in which **Text Field**s are dragged to the page is the order in which their JSP elements are added to the JSP document. By default, when a user presses the *Tab* key to navigate between input fields, the focus shifts from component to component in the order the JSP elements occur in the JSP document. To specify the navigation order, you can drag components onto the page in the appropriate order, or you can set each input field's `tabIndex` property in the **Properties** window to explicitly set the tab order. A component with a tab index of 1 will be the first in the tab sequence.

Lines 52–55 define a **Drop Down List**. When a user clicks the drop-down list, it expands and displays a list from which the user can make a selection. This component is an object of class DropDown and is bound to the object booksDropDownDefaultOptions, a SingleSelectOptionsList object that manages the list of options. This object can be configured automatically by right clicking the drop-down list in **Design** mode and selecting **Configure Default Options...**, which opens the **Options Customizer** dialog box so you can add options to the list. Each option consists of a display String that the user will see in the browser and a value String that is returned when you programmatically retrieve the user's selection from the drop-down list. NetBeans constructs the SingleSelectOptionsList object in the page bean file based on the display-value pairs entered in the **Options Customizer** dialog box. To view the code that constructs the object, close the dialog box by clicking **OK**, open the page bean file, and expand the **Managed Component Definition** node that follows the class definition's opening curly brace. The object is constructed in the _init method, which is called by method init the first time the page loads.

The **Hyperlink** component (lines 56–59) of class Hyperlink adds a hyperlink to a web page. The url property of this component specifies the resource (http://www.deitel.com in this case) that is requested when a user clicks the hyperlink. By default, **Hyperlink** components cause pages to open in the same browser window, but you can set the component's target property to change this behavior.

Lines 63–66 define a **Radio Button Group** component of class RadioButtonGroup, which provides a series of radio buttons from which the user can select only one. Like a **Drop Down List**, a **Radio Button Group** is bound to a SingleSelectOptionList object. The options can be edited by right clicking the component and selecting **Configure Default Options....** Also like the drop-down list, the SingleSelectOptionsList is automatically generated by the IDE and placed in the _init method of the page bean class.

Lines 67–69 define a **Button** component of class Button that triggers an action when clicked. A **Button** component typically maps to an input XHTML element with attribute type set to submit. As stated earlier, clicking the **Register** button in this example does not do anything.

29.6.2 Validation Using Validator Components and Custom Validators

Validating user input is an important step in collecting information from users. Form **validation** helps prevent processing errors due to incomplete or improperly formatted user input. For example, you may perform validation to ensure that all required fields contain data or that a zip-code field has the correct number of digits. NetBeans provides three validator components. A **Length Validator** determines whether a field contains an acceptable number of characters. **Double Range Validator**s and **Long Range Validator**s determine whether numeric input falls within acceptable ranges. Package **javax.faces.validators** contains the classes for these validators. NetBeans also allows custom validation with validator methods in the page bean file. The following example demonstrates validation using both a validator component and custom validation.

Validating Form Data in a Web Application

The example in this section prompts the user to enter a name, e-mail address and phone number. After the user enters any data, but before the data is sent to the web server, validation ensures that the user entered a value in each field, that the entered name does not exceed 30 characters, and that the e-mail address and phone-number values are in an acceptable format. If the client does not have JavaScript enabled, then the validation is performed on the server. In this example, (555) 123-4567, 555-123-4567 and 123-4567 are all considered valid phone numbers. Once the data is submitted, the web server responds by displaying an appropriate message and a **Grid Panel** component repeating the submitted information. Note that a real business application would typically store the submitted data in a database or in a file on the server. We simply send the data back to the page to demonstrate that the server received the data.

Building the Web Page

[*Note:* To create this application from scratch, review the steps in Section 29.5.4.] This web application introduces the **Label** and **Message** JSF components from the **Woodstock Basic** section of the **Palette**. Each of the page's three text fields should have its own label and message. **Label** components describe other components and can be associated with user input fields by setting their for property. **Message** components display error messages when validation fails. This page requires three **Text Fields**, three **Labels** and three **Messages**, as well as a submit **Button**. To associate the **Label** components and **Message** components with their corresponding **Text Field** components, hold the *Ctrl* and *Shift* keys, then drag the label or message to the appropriate **Text Field**. In the **Properties** window, notice that each **Label** and **Message** component's for property is set to the appropriate **Text Field**.

You should also add a **Static Text** component to display a validation success message at the bottom of the page. Set the text to "Thank you for your submission.
We received the following information:" and change the component's id to resultText. In the **Properties** window, unset the component's rendered and escape properties. The **rendered** property controls whether the component will be displayed the first time the page loads. Setting **escape** to false (i.e., unchecked) enables the browser to recognize the XHTML <br/> tag so it can start a new line of text rather than display the characters "<br/>" in the web page.

> **Look-and-Feel Observation 29.1**
>
> *When you set a component's rendered property to false (unchecked), the component no longer appears in the visual editor. To select such a control so you can manipulate its properties, use the **Navigator** window in **Design** mode (as shown in Fig. 29.12).*

Add a **Grid Panel** component below the resultText component. The panel should have two columns, one for displaying **Static Text** components that label the user's validated data (named nameText, emailText and phoneText, respectively), and one for displaying **Static Text** components that display that data (named nameValueText, emailValueText and phoneValueText, respectively). The panel's rendered property should be set to false so that it is not initially displayed.

Adding Binding Attributes for Programmatically Interacting with Components

Recall that for each control you plan to interact with programmatically, you must right click the control in **Design** mode and select **Add Binding Attribute** to add a property for the control to the page bean file. In this example, you should do this for each of the **Text Field** components (so you can obtain their values), for the resultText **Static Text** component (so you can display it), for the **Grid Panel** component (so you can display it) and for the **Static Text** components nameValueText, emailValueText and phoneValueText in the **Grid Panel** (so you can set their text).

Reviewing the JSP Document

The JSP file for this page is displayed in Fig. 29.17. Lines 31–35, 42–46 and 54–58 define **webuijsf:textFields** for retrieving the user's name, e-mail address and phone number, respectively. Lines 28–30, 39–41 and 51–53 define **webuijsf:labels** for each of these text fields. Lines 36–38, 47–50 and 59–62 define the text fields' **webuijsf:message** elements. Lines 63–66 define a **Submit** webuijsf:button. Lines 67–71 create a webuijsf:static-Text named resultText that displays text when the user successfully submits the form, and lines 72–91 define a h:panelGrid that contains components for displaying the validated user input in the browser.

```
I    <?xml version="1.0" encoding="UTF-8"?>
2
3    <!-- Fig. 29.17 Validation.jsp -->
4    <!-- JSP that demonstrates validation of user input. -->
5    <jsp:root version="2.1" xmlns:f="http://java.sun.com/jsf/core"
6       xmlns:h="http://java.sun.com/jsf/html"
7       xmlns:jsp="http://java.sun.com/JSP/Page"
8       xmlns:webuijsf="http://www.sun.com/webui/webuijsf">
9       <jsp:directive.page contentType="text/html;charset=UTF-8"
10         pageEncoding="UTF-8"/>
11      <f:view>
12         <webuijsf:page id="page1">
13            <webuijsf:html id="html1">
14               <webuijsf:head id="head1">
15                  <webuijsf:link id="link1" url="/resources/stylesheet.css"/>
16               </webuijsf:head>
17               <webuijsf:body id="body1" style="-rave-layout: grid">
18                  <webuijsf:form id="form1">
19                     <webuijsf:staticText id="headerText"
20                        style="font-size: 18px; left: 24px; top: 24px;
21                           position: absolute"
22                        text="Please fill out the following form:"/>
23                     <webuijsf:staticText id="instructionText"
24                        style="font-style: italic; left: 24px; top: 48px;
25                           position: absolute"
26                        text="All fields are required and must contain
27                           valid information."/>
28                     <webuijsf:label for="nameTextField" id="nameLabel"
29                        style="left: 24px; top: 72px; position: absolute"
30                        text="Name:"/>
31                     <webuijsf:textField binding="#{Page1.nameTextField}"
32                        columns="30" id="nameTextField" required="true"
33                        style="position: absolute; left: 96px; top: 72px"
34                        validatorExpression=
35                           "#{Page1.nameLengthValidator.validate}"/>
36                     <webuijsf:message for="nameTextField" id="nameMessage"
37                        showDetail="false" showSummary="true"
38                        style="left: 312px; top: 72px; position: absolute"/>
39                     <webuijsf:label for="emailTextField" id="emailLabel"
40                        style="left: 24px; top: 96px; position: absolute"
41                        text="E-Mail:"/>
```

Fig. 29.17 | JSP that demonstrates validation of user input. (Part 1 of 4.)

```
42              <webuijsf:textField binding="#{Page1.emailTextField}"
43                 columns="30" id="emailTextField" required="true"
44                 style="left: 96px; top: 96px; position: absolute"
45                 validatorExpression=
46                   "#{Page1.emailTextField_validate}"/>
47              <webuijsf:message for="emailTextField"
48                 id="emailMessage" showDetail="false"
49                 showSummary="true"
50                 style="left: 312px; top: 96px; position: absolute"
51              <webuijsf:label for="phoneTextField" id="phoneLabel"
52                 style="left: 24px; top: 120px; position: absolute"
53                 text="Phone:"/>
54              <webuijsf:textField binding="#{Page1.phoneTextField}"
55                 columns="30" id="phoneTextField" required="true"
56                 style="left: 96px; top: 120px; position: absolute"
57                 validatorExpression=
58                   "#{Page1.phoneTextField_validate}"/>
59              <webuijsf:message for="phoneTextField"
60                 id="phoneMessage" showDetail="false"
61                 showSummary="true" style="left: 312px; top: 120px;
62                   position: absolute"/>
63              <webuijsf:button actionExpression=
64                 "#{Page1.submitButton_action}" id="submitButton"
65                 style="position: absolute; left: 24px; top: 144px"
66                 text="Submit"/>
67              <webuijsf:staticText binding="#{Page1.resultText}"
68                 escape="false" id="resultText" rendered="false"
69                 style="left: 24px; top: 168px; position: absolute"
70                 text="Thank you for your submission.&lt;br/&gt;We
71                   received the following information:"/>
72              <h:panelGrid binding="#{Page1.gridPanel}"
73                 columns="2" id="gridPanel" rendered="false"
74                 style="border-width: 1px; border-style: solid;
75                   background-color: #ffff99; height: 96px;
76                   left: 24px; top: 216px; position: absolute"
77                 width="264">
78                 <webuijsf:staticText id="nameText" text="Name:"/>
79                 <webuijsf:staticText
80                   binding="#{Page1.nameValueText}"
81                   id="nameValueText"/>
82                 <webuijsf:staticText id="emailText"
83                   text="E-Mail:"/>
84                 <webuijsf:staticText
85                   binding="#{Page1.emailValueText}"
86                   id="emailValueText"/>
87                 <webuijsf:staticText id="phoneText" text="Phone:"/>
88                 <webuijsf:staticText
89                   binding="#{Page1.phoneValueText}"
90                   id="phoneValueText"/>
91              </h:panelGrid>
92            </webuijsf:form>
93          </webuijsf:body>
94        </webuijsf:html>
```

Fig. 29.17 | JSP that demonstrates validation of user input. (Part 2 of 4.)

```
95              </webuijsf:page>
96          </f:view>
97      </jsp:root>
```

(a) Submitting the form before entering any information

(b) Error messages displayed after submitting the empty form

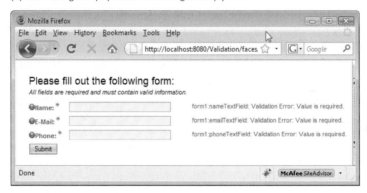

(c) Error messages displayed after submitting invalid information

Fig. 29.17 | JSP that demonstrates validation of user input. (Part 3 of 4.)

(d) Successfully submitted form

Fig. 29.17 | JSP that demonstrates validation of user input. (Part 4 of 4.)

*Setting the **Required** Property of an Input Component*
Ensuring that the user has made a selection or entered some text in a required input element is a basic type of validation. This is accomplished by checking the **required** box in the element's **Properties** window. If you add a validator component or custom validator method to an input field, the field's `required` property must be set to `true` (checked) for validation to occur. Each of the three input `webuijsf:textFields` in this example has its `required` property set to `true`. Also note in the visual editor that the label for a required field is automatically marked by a red asterisk. If a user submits this form with empty text fields, the default error message for a required field will be displayed in the empty field's associated `webuijsf:message` component. To customize the error message, you must provide a custom validator.

*Using the **LengthValidator** Component*
In this example, we use the **Length Validator** component (found in the **Validators** section of the **Palette**) to ensure that the length of the user's name does not exceed 30 characters. This might be useful to ensure that a value will fit in a particular database field.

To add a **Length Validator** to a component, simply drag the validator from the **Palette** and drop it onto the field to validate. A **lengthValidator1** node will appear in the **Outline** window. To edit the validation component's properties, click this node and set the `maximum` and `minimum` properties to the desired number of characters in the **Properties** window. Here, we set only the `maximum` property to 30. We also changed the component's `id` to `nameLengthValidator`. Notice that the `nameTextField`'s `validatorExpression` property has been bound to the `nameLengthValidator`'s `validate` method in the page bean file (lines 34–35). Remember that most client-side validation can be circumvented, so important validation should always be performed on the server.

This validator allows users to type as much text in the field as they wish, and if they exceed the limit, the default length validation error message will be displayed in the field's `webuijsf:message` component after the user clicks the **Submit** button. It is possible to limit the length of user input without using validation. By setting a **Text Field**'s maxLength property, the **Text Field**'s cursor will not advance beyond the maximum allowable number of characters, so the user cannot submit data that exceeds the length limit.

Using Regular Expressions to Perform Custom Validation

Some of the most common validation tasks involve validating user input. For instance, it may be necessary to check user-entered e-mail addresses and telephone numbers to ensure that they conform to the standard formatting for valid e-mail addresses and phone numbers. Matching user input against a regular expression is an effective way to ensure that the input is properly formatted. This is frequently done on the client side before data is submitted to the server so the user is notified immediately if they supply invalid input. Servers typically revalidate the data as well for security purposes. NetBeans does not provide components for validation using regular expressions, so we'll add our own custom validator methods to the page bean file. To add a custom validator to an input component, right click the component and select **Edit Event Handler > validate**. This creates a validation method for the component with an empty body in the page bean file. We'll add code to this method shortly. Note that both emailTextField and phoneTextField's validator-Expression attributes are bound to their respective custom validation methods in the page bean file (lines 45–46 and 57–58).

Examining the Page Bean File for a Form That Receives User Input

Figure 29.18 contains the page bean file for the JSP file in Fig. 29.17. Line 21 sets the maximum length for the nameLengthValidator, which is a property of this page bean. Recall that the name text field was bound to this property in the JSP document. Methods emailTextField_validate (lines 189–200) and phoneTextField_validate (lines 204–216) are the custom validator methods that verify the user-entered e-mail address and phone number, respectively. The submitButton_action method (lines 219–230) echoes the data back to the user if validation succeeds. The validator methods are called before the event handler, so if validation fails, submitButton_action will not be called and the user input will not be echoed.

```
1   // Fig. 29.18: Validation.java
2   // Validating user input.
3   package validation;
4
5   import com.sun.rave.web.ui.appbase.AbstractPageBean;
6   import com.sun.webui.jsf.component.StaticText;
7   import com.sun.webui.jsf.component.TextField;
8   import javax.faces.FacesException;
9   import javax.faces.application.FacesMessage;
10  import javax.faces.component.UIComponent;
11  import javax.faces.component.html.HtmlPanelGrid;
12  import javax.faces.context.FacesContext;
13  import javax.faces.validator.LengthValidator;
14  import javax.faces.validator.ValidatorException;
15
16  public class Validation extends AbstractPageBean
17  {
```

Fig. 29.18 | Page bean for validating user input and redisplaying that input if valid. (Part 1 of 2.)

```
18      // Managed Component Definition
19      private void _init() throws Exception
20      {
21          nameLengthValidator.setMaximum( 30 );
22      } // end method _init
23
24      // To save space, we omitted the code in lines 24-186. The complete
25      // source code is provided with this chapter's examples.
26
187     // validates entered e-mail address against the regular expression
188     // that represents the form of a valid e-mail address
189     public void emailTextField_validate( FacesContext context,
190         UIComponent component, Object value )
191     {
192         String email = String.valueOf( value );
193
194         // if entered e-mail address is not in a valid format
195         if ( !email.matches(
196             "\\w+([-+.']\\w+)*@\\w+([-.]\\w+)*\\.\\w+([-.]\\w+)*" ) ) {
197             throw new ValidatorException( new FacesMessage(
198                 "Enter a valid e-mail address, e.g. user@domain.com" ) )
199         } // end if
200     } // end method emailTextField_validate
201
202     // validates entered phone number against the regular expression
203     // that represents the form of a valid phone number
204     public void phoneTextField_validate( FacesContext context,
205         UIComponent component, Object value )
206     {
207         String phone = String.valueOf( value );
208
209         // if entered phone number is not in a valid format
210         if ( !phone.matches(
211             "((\\(\\d{3}\\) ?)|(\\d{3}-))?\\d{3}-\\d{4}" ) )
212         {
213             throw new ValidatorException( new FacesMessage(
214                 "Enter a valid phone number, e.g. (555) 555-1234" ) );
215         } // end if
216     } // end method phoneTextField_validate
217
218     // displays the values the user entered and submitted
219     public String submitButton_action()
220     {
221         String name = String.valueOf( nameTextField.getValue() );
222         String email = String.valueOf( emailTextField.getValue() );
223         String phone = String.valueOf( phoneTextField.getValue() );
224         nameValueText.setValue( name );
225         emailValueText.setValue( email );
226         phoneValueText.setValue( phone );
227         gridPanel.setRendered( true );
228         resultText.setRendered( true );
229         return null;
230     } // end method submitButton_action
231 } // end class Validation
```

Fig. 29.18 | Page bean for validating user input and redisplaying that input if valid. (Part 2 of 2.)

The two custom validator methods in this page bean file validate a text field's contents against a regular expression using the `String` method `matches`, which takes a regular expression as an argument and returns `true` if the `String` conforms to the specified format.

For the `emailTextField_validate` method, we use the validation expression

```
\w+([-+.']\w+)*@\w+([-.]\w+)*\.\w+([-.]\w+)*
```

Note that each backslash in the regular expression `String` (line 196) must be escaped with another backslash (as in `\\`), because the backslash character normally represents the beginning of an escape sequence in Java. This regular expression indicates that an e-mail address is valid if the part before the `@` symbol contains one or more word characters (i.e., alphanumeric characters or underscores), followed by zero or more `String`s comprised of a hyphen, plus sign, period or apostrophe and additional word characters. After the `@` symbol, a valid e-mail address must contain one or more groups of word characters potentially separated by hyphens or periods, followed by a required period and another group of one or more word characters potentially separated by hyphens or periods. For example, the e-mail addresses `bob's-personal.email@white.email.com`, `bob-white@my-email.com` and `bob.white@email.com` are all valid. If the user enters text in `emailTextField` that does not have the correct format and attempts to submit the form, lines 197–198 throw a `ValidatorException`. The `Message` component catches this exception and displays the message in red.

The regular expression in `phoneTextField_validate` ensures that the `phoneTextField`contains a valid phone number before the form is submitted. The user input is matched against the regular expression

```
((\(\d{3}\) ?)|(\d{3}-))?\d{3}-\d{4}
```

(Again, each backslash is escaped in the regular expression `String` in line 211.) This expression indicates that a phone number can contain a three-digit area code either in parentheses and followed by an optional space or without parentheses and followed by a required hyphen. After an optional area code, a phone number must contain three digits, a hyphen and another four digits. For example, `(555) 123-4567`, `555-123-4567` and `123-4567` are all valid phone numbers. If a user enters an invalid phone number, lines 213–214 throw a `ValidatorException` The `Message` component catches this exception and displays the error message in red.

If all six validators are successful (i.e., each `TextField` contains data, the name is less than 30 characters and the e-mail address and phone number are valid), clicking the **Submit** button sends the form's data to the server. As shown in Fig. 29.17(d), the `submitButton_action` method displays the submitted data in the Grid Panel component `gridPanel` (lines 221–227) and displays the `resultsText` **Static Text** component (line 228).

29.7 Session Tracking

In the early days of the Internet, e-businesses could not provide the kind of customized service typically experienced in "brick-and-mortar" stores. To address this problem, e-businesses began to establish mechanisms by which they could personalize users' browsing experiences, tailoring content to individual users while enabling them to bypass irrelevant information. Businesses achieve this level of service by tracking each customer's movement through their websites and combining the collected data with information provided by the consumer, including billing information, personal preferences, interests and hobbies.

Personalization

Personalization makes it possible for e-businesses to communicate effectively with their customers and also improves the user's ability to locate desired products and services. Companies that provide content of particular interest to users can establish relationships with customers and build on those relationships over time. Furthermore, by targeting consumers with personal offers, recommendations, advertisements, promotions and services, e-businesses create customer loyalty. Websites can use sophisticated technology to allow visitors to customize home pages to suit their individual needs and preferences. Similarly, online shopping sites often store personal information for customers, tailoring notifications and special offers to their interests. Such services encourage customers to visit sites and make purchases more frequently.

Privacy

A trade-off exists, however, between personalized e-business service and protection of privacy. Some consumers embrace the idea of tailored content, but others fear the possible adverse consequences if the info they provide to e-businesses is released or collected by tracking technologies. Consumers and privacy advocates ask: What if the e-business to which we give personal data sells or gives that information to another organization without our knowledge? What if we do not want our actions on the Internet—a supposedly anonymous medium—to be tracked and recorded by unknown parties? What if unauthorized parties gain access to sensitive private data, such as credit card numbers or medical history? All of these are questions that must be debated and addressed by programmers, consumers, e-businesses and lawmakers alike.

Recognizing Clients

To provide personalized services to consumers, e-businesses must be able to recognize clients when they request information from a site. As we have discussed, the request/response system on which the web operates is facilitated by HTTP. Unfortunately, HTTP is a **stateless protocol**—it does not support persistent connections that would enable web servers to maintain state information regarding particular clients. So, web servers cannot determine whether a request comes from a particular client or whether a series of requests comes from one or several clients. To circumvent this problem, sites can provide mechanisms to identify individual clients. A session represents a unique client on a website. If the client leaves a site and then returns later, the client will still be recognized as the same user. To help the server distinguish among clients, each client must identify itself to the server.

Tracking individual clients, known as **session tracking**, can be achieved in a number of ways in JSPs. One popular technique uses cookies (Section 29.7.1); another uses the `SessionBean` object (Section 29.7.2). Additional session-tracking techniques include using `input` `form` elements of type `"hidden"` and URL rewriting. With `"hidden"` form elements, a Web Form can write session-tracking data into a `form` in the web page that it returns to the client in response to a prior request. When the user submits the form in the new web page, all the form data, including the `"hidden"` fields, is sent to the form handler on the web server. With URL rewriting, the web server embeds session-tracking information directly in the URLs of hyperlinks that the user clicks to send subsequent requests to the web server.

29.7.1 Cookies

Cookies provide web developers with a tool for personalizing web pages. A cookie is a piece of data typically stored in a text file on the user's computer. A cookie maintains information about the client during and between browser sessions. The first time a user visits the website, the user's computer might receive a cookie; this cookie is then reactivated each time the user revisits that site. The aim is to create an anonymous record containing data that is used to personalize the user's future visits to the site. For example, cookies in a shopping application might store unique identifiers for users. When a user adds items to an online shopping cart or performs another task resulting in a request to the web server, the server receives a cookie from the client containing the user's unique identifier. The server then uses the unique identifier to locate the shopping cart and perform any necessary processing.

In addition to identifying users, cookies also can indicate clients' shopping preferences. When a web server receives a request from a client, the server can examine the cookie(s) it sent to the client during previous communications, identify the client's preferences and immediately display products of interest to the client.

Every HTTP-based interaction between a client and a server includes a header containing information either about the request (when the communication is from the client to the server) or about the response (when the communication is from the server to the client). When a page receives a request, the header includes information such as the request type (e.g., GET or POST) and any cookies that have been sent previously from the server to be stored on the client machine. When the server formulates its response, the header information contains any cookies the server wants to store on the client computer and other information, such as the MIME type of the response.

The **expiration date** of a cookie determines how long the cookie remains on the client's computer. If you do not set an expiration date for a cookie, the web browser maintains the cookie for the duration of the browsing session. Otherwise, the web browser maintains the cookie until the expiration date occurs. When the browser requests a resource from a web server, cookies previously sent to the client by that web server are returned to the web server as part of the request formulated by the browser. Cookies are deleted when they expire.

> **Portability Tip 29.1**
> *Clients may disable cookies in their web browsers for more privacy. When such clients use web applications that depend on cookies to maintain state information, the applications will not execute correctly.*

Using Cookies to Provide Book Recommendations

The next web application shows how to use cookies. The example contains two pages. In the Options.jsp page (Figs. 29.19 and 29.21), users select a favorite programming language from a group of radio buttons and submit the form to the web server for processing. The web server responds by creating a cookie that stores the selected language and the ISBN number for a recommended book on that topic. The server then renders different components in the browser that allow the user either to view the options and select another favorite programming language or to view the Recommendations.jsp page in our application (Figs. 29.22–29.23), which lists recommended books pertaining to the programming language(s) that the user selected. Because we'll be programmatically hiding and showing the components in the Options.jsp file, each component in the page requires a binding attribute. When the user clicks the hyperlink to view the recommended books, the cookies previously stored on the client are sent to the server, read by the application and used to form the recommended books list.

The Options.jsp file in Fig. 29.19 contains a **Radio Button Group** (lines 24–28) with the options **Java, C++, Visual Basic 2008, Visual C# 2008** and **Internet & Web**. Recall that you can set the display and value Strings of radio buttons by right clicking the **Radio Button Group** and selecting **Configure Default Options....** The code for these options is shown in lines 22–34 of Fig. 29.21. The user selects a programming language by clicking a radio button, then pressing **Submit** to send the selection to the server. This makes an HTTP POST request to the web application on the server, which obtains the user's selection, creates a cookie containing the selection and adds it to the HTTP response header that is sent to the client as part of the response. The browser then stores the cookie on the client computer.

```
 1   <?xml version="1.0" encoding="UTF-8"?>
 2
 3   <!-- Fig. 29.19: Options.jsp -->
 4   <!-- JSP file that allows the user to select a programming language -->
 5   <jsp:root version="2.1" xmlns:f="http://java.sun.com/jsf/core"
 6      xmlns:h="http://java.sun.com/jsf/html"
 7      xmlns:jsp="http://java.sun.com/JSP/Page"
 8      xmlns:webuijsf="http://www.sun.com/webui/webuijsf">
 9      <jsp:directive.page contentType="text/html;charset=UTF-8"
10         pageEncoding="UTF-8"/>
11      <f:view>
12         <webuijsf:page id="page1">
13            <webuijsf:html id="html1">
14               <webuijsf:head id="head1">
15                  <webuijsf:link id="link1" url="/resources/stylesheet.css"/>
16               </webuijsf:head>
17               <webuijsf:body id="body1" style="-rave-layout: grid">
18                  <webuijsf:form id="form1">
19                     <webuijsf:staticText
20                        binding="#{Options.instructionText}"
21                        id="instructionText" style="font-size: 18px;
22                           left: 24px; top: 24px; position: absolute"
23                        text="Select a programming language:"/>
24                     <webuijsf:radioButtonGroup
25                        binding="#{Options.languageRadioButtonGroup}"
26                        id="languageRadioButtonGroup" items="#{Options.
27                           languageRadioButtonGroupDefaultOptions.options}"
28                        style="left: 24px; top: 48px; position: absolute"/>
29                     <webuijsf:button
30                        actionExpression="#{Options.submitButton_action}"
31                        binding="#{Options.submitButton}" id="submitButton"
32                        style="left: 23px; top: 168px; position: absolute"
33                        text="Submit"/>
34                     <webuijsf:staticText binding="#{Options.responseText}"
35                        id="responseText" rendered="false"
36                        style="font-size: 18px; left: 24px; top: 24px;
37                           position: absolute"/>
```

Fig. 29.19 | JSP file that allows the user to select a programming language. (Part 1 of 3.)

```
38                          <webuijsf:hyperlink
39                              actionExpression="#{Options.languagesLink_action}"
40                              binding="#{Options.languagesLink}" id="languagesLink"
41                              rendered="false" style="left: 24px; top: 72px;
42                                  position: absolute"
43                              text="Click here to choose another language."/>
44                          <webuijsf:hyperlink
45                              binding="#{Options.recommendationsLink}"
46                              id="recommendationsLink" rendered="false"
47                              style="left: 24px; top: 96px; position: absolute"
48                              text="Click here to get book recommendations."
49                              url="/faces/Recommendations.jsp"/>
50                      </webuijsf:form>
51                  </webuijsf:body>
52              </webuijsf:html>
53          </webuijsf:page>
54      </f:view>
55  </jsp:root>
```

(a) User selects a programming language and clicks **Submit** to rerequest Options.jsp.

(b) Options.jsp displays a welcome message and provides links allowing the user to select another language or view book recommendations. User chooses to select another language, which rerequests Options.jsp.

Fig. 29.19 | JSP file that allows the user to select a programming language. (Part 2 of 3.)

(c) User selects a programming language and clicks **Submit** to rerequest `Options.jsp`.

(d) `Options.jsp` displays a welcome message and provides links allowing the user to select another language or view book recommendations. User chooses to view book recommendations.

Fig. 29.19 | JSP file that allows the user to select a programming language. (Part 3 of 3.)

When the user clicks **Submit**, the `webuijsf:staticText`, `webuijsf:radioButton-Group` and `webuijsf:button` elements used to select a language are hidden, and a `webuijsf:staticText` and two `webuijsf:hyperlink` elements are displayed. One `webuijsf:staticText` and both `webuijsf:hyperlinks` initially have their rendered properties set to `false` (lines 35, 41, and 46). This indicates that these components are not visible when the page loads, as we want the user's first view of the page to include only the components for selecting a programming language and submitting the selection.

The first hyperlink (lines 38–43) requests this page, and the second (lines 44–49) requests `Recommendations.jsp`. The `url` property is not set for the first link; we discuss this momentarily. The second link's `url` property is set to `/faces/Recommendations.jsp`. Recall that earlier in the chapter, we set a `url` property to a remote website (`http://www.deitel.com`). To set this property to a page within the current application, you can click the ellipsis button (⬜) next to the `url` property in the **Properties** window to open a dialog containing a list of the application's pages, then select an existing page as the link's destination.

Adding and Linking to a New Web Page

To set the url property to a destination page (i.e., Recommendations.jsp) in the current application, the destination page must already exist. To create Recommendations.jsp, right click the **Web Pages** node in the **Projects** window and select **New > Visual Web JSF Page...** from the menu that appears. In the **New Visual Web JSF Page** dialog, change the name of the page to Recommendations and click **Finish** to create the files Recommendations.jsp and Recommendations.java. (We discuss the contents of these files shortly.) You can now select Recommendations.jsp as the url value for recommendationsLink. You can see the url's value in line 49.

Hiding and Showing Elements of a Page and Rerequesting the Page

When the user clicks the languagesLink, we'd like to rerequest Options.jsp and display the list of options so the user can make another choice. Rather than setting the languagesLink's url property, we'll add an action handler for this component to the page bean. You can do this by right clicking languagesLink in the **Navigator** window (while in **Design** mode) and selecting **Edit action Event Handler**. The action handler will enable us to show and hide components of the page without redirecting the user to another page. Specifying a destination url would override the component's action handler and redirect the user to the specified page. So it is important that we do not set the url property in this case, because we want to hide some elements of the page and show others. Since we use the languagesLink to reload the current page, we simply return null from its action handler, which causes Options.jsp to reload.

Adding an Action Handler to a Hyperlink and Redirecting to Another Page

If you need to add an action handler to a hyperlink that should also direct the user to another page, you must add a rule to the **Page Navigation** file (Fig. 29.20). [*Note:* This is not required for the current example.] To edit this file, right click anywhere in the visual designer and select **Page Navigation**. Click the plus (⊞) icon for Options.jsp in the navigation designer to display its components that might cause the page to request another page. Locate the link whose navigation rule you would like to set (e.g., recommendationsLink) and drag it to the destination page (e.g., Recommendations.jsp). Now the link can direct the user to a new page (Recommendations.jsp) and you can also place code in the **Hyperlink** component's action handler that will execute when the user clicks the link. Editing the **Page Navigation** file is also useful when you would like action elements that cannot specify a url property, such as buttons, to direct users to another page.

Fig. 29.20 | Editing the **Page Navigation** file.

Page Bean File for **Options.jsp**

Figure 29.21 contains the code that writes a cookie to the client machine when the user selects a programming language. The file also determines which components appear on the page, displaying either the components for choosing a language or the hyperlinks for navigating through the application, depending on the user's actions.

```java
 1   // Fig. 29.21: Options.java
 2   // Page bean that stores user's language selection
 3   // as a cookie on the client.
 4   package cookies;
 5
 6   import com.sun.rave.web.ui.appbase.AbstractPageBean;
 7   import com.sun.webui.jsf.component.Button;
 8   import com.sun.webui.jsf.component.Hyperlink;
 9   import com.sun.webui.jsf.component.RadioButtonGroup;
10   import com.sun.webui.jsf.component.StaticText;
11   import com.sun.webui.jsf.model.SingleSelectOptionsList;
12   import java.util.HashMap;
13   import javax.faces.FacesException;
14   import javax.servlet.http.Cookie;
15   import javax.servlet.http.HttpServletResponse;
16
17   public class Options extends AbstractPageBean
18   {
19      // Managed Component Definition
20      private void _init() throws Exception
21      {
22         languageRadioButtonGroupDefaultOptions.setOptions(
23            new com.sun.webui.jsf.model.Option[]
24            {
25               new com.sun.webui.jsf.model.Option( "Java", "Java" ),
26               new com.sun.webui.jsf.model.Option( "C++", "C++" ),
27               new com.sun.webui.jsf.model.Option( "Visual-Basic-2008",
28                  "Visual Basic 2008" ),
29               new com.sun.webui.jsf.model.Option( "Visual-C#-2008",
30                  "Visual C# 2008" ),
31               new com.sun.webui.jsf.model.Option( "Internet-&-Web",
32                  "Internet & Web" )
33            } // end array initializer
34         ); // end call to setOptions
35      } // end method _init
36
37      private SingleSelectOptionsList languageRadioButtonGroupDefaultOptions =
38         new SingleSelectOptionsList();
39
40      // To save space, we omitted the code in lines 40-121. The complete
41      // source code is provided with this chapter's examples.
42
122      private HashMap<String, String> books = new HashMap<String, String>();
123
124      // Construct a new page bean instance and initialize the properties
125      // that map languages to ISBN numbers of recommended books.
```

Fig. 29.21 | Page bean that stores the user's language selection in a client cookie. (Part 1 of 3.)

```
126      public Options()
127      {
128         // initialize HashMap object of values to be stored as cookies.
129         books.put( "Java", "0132222205" );
130         books.put( "C++", "0136152503" );
131         books.put( "Visual-Basic-2008", "013605305X" );
132         books.put( "Visual-C#-2008", "013605322X" );
133         books.put( "Internet-&-Web", "0131752421" );
134      } // end Options constructor
135
136      // To save space, we omitted the code in lines 136-185. The complete
137      // source code is provided with this chapter's examples.
138
186      // Action handler for the Submit button. Checks whether a language
187      // was selected and, if so, creates a cookie for that language and
188      // sets the responseText to indicate the chosen language.
189      public String submitButton_action()
190      {
191         String message = "Welcome to Cookies! You ";
192
193         // if the user made a selection
194         if ( languageRadioButtonGroup.getSelected() != null )
195         {
196            String language =
197               languageRadioButtonGroup.getSelected().toString();
198            message += "selected " + language.replace( '-', ' ' ) + ".";
199
200            // get ISBN number of book for the given language
201            String ISBN = books.get( language );
202
203            // create cookie using language-ISBN name-value pair
204            Cookie cookie = new Cookie( language, ISBN );
205
206            // add cookie to response header to place it on user's machine
207            HttpServletResponse response =
208               ( HttpServletResponse ) getExternalContext().getResponse();
209            response.addCookie( cookie );
210         } // end if
211         else
212         {
213            message += "did not select a language.";
214         } // end else
215
216         responseText.setValue( message );
217         languageRadioButtonGroup.setRendered( false ); // hide
218         instructionText.setRendered( false ); // hide
219         submitButton.setRendered( false ); // hide
220         responseText.setRendered( true ); // show
221         languagesLink.setRendered( true ); // show
222         recommendationsLink.setRendered( true ); // show
223         return null; // reloads the page
224      } // end method submitButton_action
225
```

Fig. 29.21 | Page bean that stores the user's language selection in a client cookie. (Part 2 of 3.)

```
226      // redisplay the components for selecting a language
227      public String languagesLink_action()
228      {
229         responseText.setRendered( false ); // hide
230         languagesLink.setRendered( false ); // hide
231         recommendationsLink.setRendered( false ); // hide
232         languageRadioButtonGroup.setRendered( true ); // show
233         instructionText.setRendered( true ); // show
234         submitButton.setRendered( true ); // show
235         return null; // reloads the page
236      } // end method languagesLink_action
237   } // end class Options
```

Fig. 29.21 | Page bean that stores the user's language selection in a client cookie. (Part 3 of 3.)

As mentioned previously, the _init method handles component initialization. Since this page contains a RadioButtonGroup object that requires initialization, method _init (lines 20–35) constructs an array of Option objects to be displayed by the buttons.

Lines 129–133 in the constructor initialize a HashMap object (defined at line 122)—a data structure that stores key/value pairs. In this case, the keys and values are Strings. The application uses the key to store and retrieve the associated value in the HashMap object. In this example, the keys contain the programming language names, and the values contain the ISBN numbers for the recommended books. Class HashMap provides method put, which takes as arguments a key and a value. A value that is added via method put is placed in the HashMap at a location determined by the key. The value for a specific HashMap entry can be determined by invoking the method get on the HashMap object with that value's key as an argument.

Note that NetBeans can automatically import any missing packages your Java file needs. For example, after adding the HashMap object to Options.java, you can right click in the Java editor window and select **Fix Imports** to import java.util.HashMap. This option can also remove unused import declarations.

Clicking **Submit** invokes the event handler submitButton_action (lines 189–224), which displays a message indicating the selected language in the responseText element and adds a new cookie to the response. If a language was selected (line 194), the selected item is retrieved (lines 196–197). Line 198 adds the selected language to the message string.

Line 201 retrieves the ISBN for the selected language from the books HashMap object. Then line 204 creates a new Cookie object (in package javax.servlet.http), using the selected language as the cookie's name and a corresponding ISBN as the cookie's value. This cookie is added to the HTTP response header in lines 207–209. An object of class HttpServletResponse (from package javax.servlet.http) represents the response. This object can be accessed by invoking the inherited method getExternalContext on the page bean, then invoking getResponse on the resulting object. If a language was not selected, line 213 sets the results message to indicate that no selection was made. [*Note:* Cookie names cannot contain whitespace. For this reason, we hyphenated the multiword names that represent the cookie names (i.e., the programming language names in this example) in lines 27, 29, 31 and 131–133. We use String method replace to replace the hyphens with spaces when we display the language name.]

Lines 216–222 control the appearance of the page after the user clicks **Submit**. Line 216 sets the responseText to display the String message. Since the user has just submitted a language selection, the components used to collect the selection are hidden (lines 217–219), and responseText and the links used to navigate the application are displayed (lines 220–222). The action handler returns null at line 223, which reloads Options.jsp.

Lines 227–236 contain the languagesLink's event handler. When the user clicks this link, responseText and the two links are hidden (lines 229–231), and the components that allow the user to select a language are redisplayed (lines 232–234). The method returns null at line 235, causing Options.jsp to reload.

Displaying Book Recommendations Based on Cookie Values
After clicking **Submit**, the user may request a book recommendation. The book recommendations hyperlink forwards the user to Recommendations.jsp (Fig. 29.22) to display recommendations based on the user's language selections.

```
1   <?xml version="1.0" encoding="UTF-8"?>
2
3   <!-- Fig. 29.22 Recommendations.jsp -->
4   <!-- Displays book recommendations using cookies -->
5   <jsp:root version="2.1" xmlns:f="http://java.sun.com/jsf/core"
6      xmlns:h="http://java.sun.com/jsf/html"
7      xmlns:jsp="http://java.sun.com/JSP/Page"
8      xmlns:webuijsf="http://www.sun.com/webui/webuijsf">
9      <jsp:directive.page contentType="text/html;charset=UTF-8"
10         pageEncoding="UTF-8"/>
11     <f:view>
12        <webuijsf:page id="page1">
13           <webuijsf:html id="html1">
14              <webuijsf:head id="head1">
15                 <webuijsf:link id="link1" url="/resources/stylesheet.css"/>
16              </webuijsf:head>
17              <webuijsf:body id="body1" style="-rave-layout: grid">
18                 <webuijsf:form id="form1">
19                    <webuijsf:label for="recommendationsTextArea"
20                       id="recommendationsLabel" style="font-size: 14px;
21                          left: 24px; top: 24px; position: absolute"
22                       text="Recommendations"/>
23                    <webuijsf:textArea
24                       binding="#{Recommendations.recommendationsTextArea}"
25                       columns="60" id="recommendationsTextArea" rows="6"
26                       style="left: 24px; top: 48px; position: absolute"/>
27                    <webuijsf:hyperlink id="optionsLink"
28                       style="left: 24px; top: 168px; position: absolute"
29                       text="Click here to choose another language."
30                       url="/faces/Options.jsp"/>
31                 </webuijsf:form>
32              </webuijsf:body>
33           </webuijsf:html>
34        </webuijsf:page>
35     </f:view>
36  </jsp:root>
```

Fig. 29.22 | JSP file that displays book recommendations based on cookies. (Part 1 of 2.)

Fig. 29.22 | JSP file that displays book recommendations based on cookies. (Part 2 of 2.)

Recommendations.jsp contains a **Label** (lines 19–22), a **Text Area** (lines 23–26) and a **Hyperlink** (lines 27–30). The **Label** displays the text Recommendations at the top of the page. A **Text Area** component can display multiple lines of text. The **Text Area** in this example displays the recommendations created by the Recommendations.java page bean (Fig. 29.23), or the text "No Recommendations. Please select a language." The **Hyperlink** allows the user to return to Options.jsp (specified by the link's url) to select additional languages.

Page Bean That Creates Book Recommendations from Cookies
In Recommendations.java (Fig. 29.23), method prerender (lines 65–96) retrieves the cookies from the client, using the request object's getCookies method (lines 68–70). An object of class HttpServletRequest (from package javax.servlet.http) represents the request. This object can be obtained by invoking method getExternalContext on the page bean, then invoking getRequest on the resulting object. The call to getCookies returns an array of the cookies previously written to the client. Cookies can be read by an application only if they were created by a server in the domain in which the application is running—for security reasons, a web server cannot access cookies created by servers in other domains. For example, a cookie created by a web server in the deitel.com domain cannot be read by a web server in any other domain.

```
1   // Fig. 29.23: Recommendations.java
2   // Displays book recommendations based on cookies that
3   // contain the user's selected programming languages.
4   package cookies;
5
6   import com.sun.rave.web.ui.appbase.AbstractPageBean;
7   import com.sun.webui.jsf.component.TextArea;
8   import javax.faces.FacesException;
9   import javax.servlet.http.Cookie;
10  import javax.servlet.http.HttpServletRequest;
11
```

Fig. 29.23 | Page bean that displays book recommendations based on cookies storing user's selected languages. (Part 1 of 2.)

```
12  public class Recommendations extends AbstractPageBean
13  {
14     // To save space, we omitted the code in lines 14-62. The complete
15     // source code is provided with this chapter's examples.
16
63     // process and display user's selections
64     @Override
65     public void prerender()
66     {
67        // retrieve cookies
68        HttpServletRequest request =
69           ( HttpServletRequest ) getExternalContext().getRequest();
70        Cookie[] cookies = request.getCookies();
71
72        // if there are cookies, store the corresponding
73        // books and ISBN numbers in a String
74        String recommendations = "";
75
76        if ( cookies.length > 1 )
77        {
78           for ( int i = 0; i < cookies.length - 1; i++ )
79           {
80              String language = cookies[ i ].getName().replace( '-', ' ' );
81
82              // ignore cookie created when user returns to
83              // Options.jsp from Recommendations.jsp
84              if ( !language.equals( "/Recommendations.jsp" ) )
85                 recommendations += language + " How to Program.  ISBN#: " +
86                    cookies[ i ].getValue() + "\n";
87           } // end for
88        } // end if
89        else
90        {
91           recommendations =
92              "No recommendations. Please select a language.";
93        } // end else
94
95        recommendationsTextArea.setText( recommendations );
96     } // end method prerender
97
98     // To save space, we omitted the code in lines 98-116. The complete
99     // source code is provided with this chapter's examples.
117 } // end class Recommendations
```

Fig. 29.23 | Page bean that displays book recommendations based on cookies storing user's selected languages. (Part 2 of 2.)

Line 76 determines whether at least two cookies exist. Lines 78–87 add the information in the cookie(s) to the string recommendations, provided that the cookie's name is not "/Recommendations.jsp"—a cookie by this name is added when the user returns from Recommendations.jsp to Options.jsp. The loop retrieves the name and value of each cookie, using the control variable to determine the current value in the cookie array. If no language was selected, lines 91–92 assign recommendations a message instructing the user to select a language. Line 95 sets `recommendationsTextArea` to display the resulting recommendations string. We summarize commonly used `Cookie` methods in Fig. 29.24.

Method	Description
getDomain	Returns a `String` containing the cookie's domain (i.e., the domain from which the cookie was written). This determines which web servers can receive the cookie. By default, cookies are sent to the web server that originally sent the cookie to the client. Changing the `Domain` property causes the cookie to be returned to a web server other than the one that originally wrote it.
getMaxAge	Returns an `int` indicating how many seconds the cookie will persist on the browser. This is −1 by default, meaning the cookie will persist until the browser is shut down.
getName	Returns a `String` containing the cookie's name.
getPath	Returns a `String` containing the path to a directory on the server to which the cookie applies. Cookies can be "targeted" to specific directories on the web server. By default, a cookie is returned only to applications operating in the same directory as the application that sent the cookie or a subdirectory of that directory. Changing the `Path` property causes the cookie to be returned to a directory other than the one from which it was originally written.
getSecure	Returns a `boolean` value indicating whether the cookie should be transmitted through a secure protocol. The value `true` causes a secure protocol to be used.
getValue	Returns a `String` containing the cookie's value.

Fig. 29.24 | `javax.servlet.http.Cookie` methods.

29.7.2 Session Tracking with Session Beans

You can also perform session tracking with the subclass of **AbstractSessionBean** that is provided in each web application. By default, the subclass is named `SessionBean1`. When a user requests a page in the web application, a `SessionBean1` object is created on the server. Properties of this object can be accessed throughout a browser session by invoking page bean method `getSessionBean1`. To demonstrate session-tracking techniques using the `SessionBean1`, we modified the page bean files in Figs. 29.21 and 29.23 so that they use the `SessionBean1` object to store the user's language selections. We begin with the updated `Options.jsp` file (Fig. 29.25). Figure 29.27 presents the `SessionBean1.java` file, and Fig. 29.28 presents the modified page bean file for `Options.jsp`.

The `Options.jsp` file in Fig. 29.25 is similar to the one from Fig. 29.19. Lines 38–47 define two additional `webuijsf:staticText` elements. The first displays the text `"Number of selections so far:"`. The second's `text` attribute is bound to property numberOfSelections in the `SessionBean1` object (line 47). We discuss how to bind the `text` attribute to a session bean property momentarily.

```
1   <?xml version="1.0" encoding="UTF-8"?>
2
3   <!-- Fig. 29.25 Options.jsp -->
```

Fig. 29.25 | JSP file that allows the user to select a programming language. (Part 1 of 4.)

```
 4    <!-- JSP file that allows the user to select a programming language -->
 5    <jsp:root version="2.1" xmlns:f="http://java.sun.com/jsf/core"
 6       xmlns:h="http://java.sun.com/jsf/html"
 7       xmlns:jsp="http://java.sun.com/JSP/Page"
 8       xmlns:webuijsf="http://www.sun.com/webui/webuijsf">
 9       <jsp:directive.page contentType="text/html;charset=UTF-8"
10          pageEncoding="UTF-8"/>
11       <f:view>
12          <webuijsf:page id="page1">
13             <webuijsf:html id="html1">
14                <webuijsf:head id="head1">
15                   <webuijsf:link id="link1" url="/resources/stylesheet.css"/>
16                </webuijsf:head>
17                <webuijsf:body id="body1" style="-rave-layout: grid">
18                   <webuijsf:form id="form1">
19                      <webuijsf:staticText
20                         binding="#{Options.instructionText}"
21                         id="instructionText" style="font-size: 18px;
22                            left: 24px; top: 24px; position: absolute"
23                         text="Select a programming language:"/>
24                      <webuijsf:radioButtonGroup
25                         binding="#{Options.languageRadioButtonGroup}"
26                         id="languageRadioButtonGroup" items="#{Options.
27                            languageRadioButtonGroupDefaultOptions.options}"
28                         style="left: 24px; top: 48px; position: absolute"/>
29                      <webuijsf:button
30                         actionExpression="#{Options.submitButton_action}"
31                         binding="#{Options.submitButton}" id="submitButton"
32                         style="left: 23px; top: 168px; position: absolute"
33                         text="Submit"/>
34                      <webuijsf:staticText binding="#{Options.responseText}"
35                         id="responseText" rendered="false"
36                         style="font-size: 18px; left: 24px; top: 24px;
37                            position: absolute"/>
38                      <webuijsf:staticText
39                         binding="#{Options.selectionsText}"
40                         id="selectionsText" rendered="false"
41                         style="left: 24px; top: 72px; position: absolute"
42                         text="Number of selections so far:"/>
43                      <webuijsf:staticText
44                         binding="#{Options.selectionsValueText}"
45                         id="selectionsValueText" rendered="false"
46                         style="left: 168px; top: 72px; position: absolute"
47                         text="#{SessionBean1.numberOfSelections}"/>
48                      <webuijsf:hyperlink
49                         actionExpression="#{Options.languagesLink_action}"
50                         binding="#{Options.languagesLink}" id="languagesLink"
51                         rendered="false" style="left: 24px; top: 96px;
52                            position: absolute"
53                         text="Click here to choose another language."/>
54                      <webuijsf:hyperlink
55                         binding="#{Options.recommendationsLink}"
56                         id="recommendationsLink" rendered="false"
57                         style="left: 24px; top: 120px; position: absolute"
```

Fig. 29.25 | JSP file that allows the user to select a programming language. (Part 2 of 4.)

```
58                          text="Click here to get book recommendations."
59                          url="/faces/Recommendations.jsp"/>
60                      </webuijsf:form>
61                  </webuijsf:body>
62              </webuijsf:html>
63          </webuijsf:page>
64      </f:view>
65  </jsp:root>
```

(a) User selects a programming language and clicks **Submit** to rerequest `Options.jsp`.

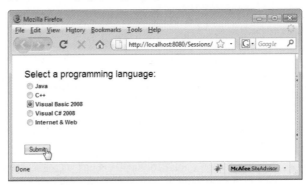

(b) `Options.jsp` displays a welcome message and provides links allowing the user to select another language or view book recommendations. User chooses to select another language, which rerequests `Options.jsp`.

(c) User selects a programming language and clicks **Submit** to rerequest `Options.jsp`.

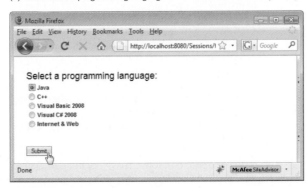

Fig. 29.25 | JSP file that allows the user to select a programming language. (Part 3 of 4.)

(d) `Options.jsp` displays a welcome message and provides links allowing the user to select another language or view book recommendations. User chooses to view book recommendations.

Fig. 29.25 | JSP file that allows the user to select a programming language. (Part 4 of 4.)

*Adding Properties to the **SessionBean***
This example uses session tracking to store the user's selected languages and the number of selections the user makes. To store session information, we add properties to the `SessionBean1` class.

Begin by double clicking the `SessionBean1` node in the **Navigator** window to open `SessionBean1.java` in the editor. Declare a `numberOfSelections` instance variable of type `int` to store the number of selections the user makes. Next, right click the variable in the editor and select **Refactor > Encapsulate Fields...** In the dialog that appears, keep the default options and click the **Refactor** button. This creates *get* and *set* methods for instance variable `numberOfSelections` at the bottom of the source-code file. Together, the instance variable and its *get* and *set* methods represent the bean's `numberOfSelections` property.

As you'll see, we manipulate property `numberOfSelections` in the page bean file to keep track of the number of languages the user selects. You can see in Fig. 29.25(b) and (d) that we display this value in the page each time the user makes another selection. To display the value in the `selectionsValueText` element, change to **Design** mode, right click the element in the **Navigator** window or the visual editor and select **Bind to Data...** In the **Bind to Data** dialog (Fig. 29.26), click the **Bind to an Object** tab, select property `numberOfSelections` in the `SessionBean1` node and click **OK**. The `selectionsValueText` element is now bound to the value of `SessionBean1`'s `numberOfSelections` property. When the property's value changes, the text in the page changes accordingly—you need not programmatically set the text in the page bean file.

Now that we've added a property to class `SessionBean1` to store the number of selections, let's add another property to store the selections themselves. We'd like to store selections as key/value pairs of the selected language and the ISBN number of a related book, similar to the way selections were stored using cookies. To do this, add a `HashMap` instance variable named `selections` to class `SessionBean1`, then refactor the code to create the *get* and *set* methods as you did for `numberOfSelections`. The two properties we added are shown in the `SessionBean1.java` file (Fig. 29.27).

Fig. 29.26 | **Bind to Data** dialog.

```
1   // Fig. 29.27: SessionBean1.java
2   // SessionBean file for storing language selections.
3   package sessions;
4
5   import com.sun.rave.web.ui.appbase.AbstractSessionBean;
6   import java.util.HashMap;
7   import javax.faces.FacesException;
8
9   public class SessionBean1 extends AbstractSessionBean
10  {
11     private int numberOfSelections; // stores number of languages selected
12
13     // stores HashMap containing user's selections
14     private HashMap<String, String> selections =
15       new HashMap<String, String>();
16
17     // To save space, we omitted the code in lines 17-69. The complete
18     // source code is provided with this chapter's examples.
19
70     public int getNumberOfSelections()
71     {
72        return numberOfSelections;
73     } // end method getNumberOfSelections
74
75     public void setNumberOfSelections( int numberOfSelections )
76     {
77        this.numberOfSelections = numberOfSelections;
78     } // end method setNumberOfSelections
```

Fig. 29.27 | SessionBean file for storing language selections. (Part 1 of 2.)

```
79
80     public HashMap<String, String> getSelectedLanguages()
81     {
82        return selections;
83     } // end method getSelectedLanguages
84
85     public void setSelectedLanguages( HashMap<String, String> selections )
86     {
87        this.selections = selections;
88     } // end method setSelectedLanguages
89  } // end class SessionBean1
```

Fig. 29.27 | SessionBean file for storing language selections. (Part 2 of 2.)

Line 11 declares the numberOfSelections instance variable, and lines 70–73 and 75–78 define its *get* and *set* methods, respectively, to complete the numberOfSelections property. Lines 14–15 define the HashMap object selections that will store user selections. Lines 80–83 and 85–88 are the *get* and *set* methods for this property. Recall that the IDE generated the *get* and *set* methods when we right clicked each instance variable, selected **Refactor > Encapsulate Fields...** and clicked the **Refactor** button.

Manipulating Session Bean Properties in a Page Bean File

The page bean file for the Options.jsp page is displayed in Fig. 29.28. Because much of this example is identical to the preceding one, we discuss only the new features. Since we are not using cookies in this example, we don't need to hyphenate the programming language names that were previously used as cookie names (lines 24, 26, 28 and 151–153).

```
1   // Fig. 29.28: Options.java
2   // Page bean that stores user's language selection in a SessionBean.
3   package sessions;
4
5   import com.sun.rave.web.ui.appbase.AbstractPageBean;
6   import com.sun.webui.jsf.component.Button;
7   import com.sun.webui.jsf.component.Hyperlink;
8   import com.sun.webui.jsf.component.RadioButtonGroup;
9   import com.sun.webui.jsf.component.StaticText;
10  import com.sun.webui.jsf.model.SingleSelectOptionsList;
11  import java.util.HashMap;
12  import javax.faces.FacesException;
13
14  public class Options extends AbstractPageBean
15  {
16     // Managed Component Definition"
17     private void _init() throws Exception
18     {
19        languageRadioButtonGroupDefaultOptions.setOptions(
20           new com.sun.webui.jsf.model.Option[]
21           {
22              new com.sun.webui.jsf.model.Option( "Java", "Java" ),
23              new com.sun.webui.jsf.model.Option( "C++", "C++" ),
```

Fig. 29.28 | Page bean that stores language selections in a SessionBean property. (Part 1 of 3.)

```
24              new com.sun.webui.jsf.model.Option( "Visual Basic 2008",
25                 "Visual Basic 2008" ),
26              new com.sun.webui.jsf.model.Option( "Visual C# 2008",
27                 "Visual C# 2008" ),
28              new com.sun.webui.jsf.model.Option( "Internet & Web",
29                 "Internet & Web" )
30           } // end array initializer
31        ); // end call to setOptions
32     } // end method _init
33
34     private SingleSelectOptionsList languageRadioButtonGroupDefaultOptions =
35        new SingleSelectOptionsList();
36
37     // To save space, we omitted the code in lines 36-141. The complete
38     // source code is provided with this chapter's examples.
39
142    private HashMap<String, String> books = new HashMap<String, String>();
143
144    // Construct a new page bean instance and initialize the properties
145    // that map languages to ISBN numbers of recommended books.
146    public Options()
147    {
148       // initialize HashMap object of values to be stored in the session.
149       books.put( "Java", "0132222205" );
150       books.put( "C++", "0136152503" );
151       books.put( "Visual Basic 2008", "013605305X" );
152       books.put( "Visual C# 2008", "013605322X" );
153       books.put( "Internet & Web", "0131752421" );
154    } // end Options constructor
155
156    // To save space, we omitted the code in lines 156-205. The complete
157    // source code is provided with this chapter's examples.
158
206    // Action handler for the Submit button. Checks whether a language
207    // was selected and, if so, creates an entry for that language and
208    // sets the responseText to indicate the chosen language.
209    public String submitButton_action()
210    {
211       String message = "Welcome to Sessions! You ";
212
213       // if the user made a selection
214       if ( languageRadioButtonGroup.getSelected() != null )
215       {
216          String language =
217             languageRadioButtonGroup.getSelected().toString();
218          message += "selected " + language + ".";
219
220          // get ISBN number of book for the given language
221          String ISBN = books.get( language );
222
223          // add the selection to the SessionBean's Properties object
224          HashMap<String, String> selections =
225             getSessionBean1().getSelectedLanguages();
226          String result = selections.put( language, ISBN );
```

Fig. 29.28 | Page bean that stores language selections in a `SessionBean` property. (Part 2 of 3.)

```
227
228            // increment numbeOfSelections in the SessionBean
229            // if user has not made this selection before
230            if ( result == null )
231            {
232                int selected = getSessionBean1().getNumberOfSelections();
233                getSessionBean1().setNumberOfSelections( ++selected );
234            } // end if
235        } // end if
236        else
237        {
238            message += "did not select a language.";
239        } // end else
240
241        responseText.setValue( message );
242        languageRadioButtonGroup.setRendered( false ); // hide
243        instructionText.setRendered( false ); // hide
244        submitButton.setRendered( false ); // hide
245        responseText.setRendered( true ); // show
246        selectionsText.setRendered( true ); // show
247        selectionsValueText.setRendered( true ); // show
248        languagesLink.setRendered( true ); // show
249        recommendationsLink.setRendered( true ); // show
250        return null; // reloads the page
251    } // end method submitButton_action
252
253    // redisplay the components for selecting a language
254    public String languagesLink_action()
255    {
256        responseText.setRendered( false ); // hide
257        selectionsText.setRendered( false ); // hide
258        selectionsValueText.setRendered( false ); // hide
259        languagesLink.setRendered( false ); // hide
260        recommendationsLink.setRendered( false ); // hide
261        languageRadioButtonGroup.setRendered( true ); // show
262        instructionText.setRendered( true ); // show
263        submitButton.setRendered( true ); // show
264        return null; // reloads the page
265    } // end method languagesLink_action
266 } // end class Options
```

Fig. 29.28 | Page bean that stores language selections in a `SessionBean` property. (Part 3 of 3.)

The `submitButton`'s action handler (lines 209–251) stores the user's selections in `SessionBean1` and increments the number of selections made, if necessary. Lines 224–225 retrieve from `SessionBean1` the `HashMap` object that contains the user's selections. Line 226 adds the current selection to the `HashMap`. Method `put` returns the value previously associated with the new key, or `null` if this key was not already stored in the `HashMap` object. If adding the new property returns `null`, then the user has made a new selection. In this case, lines 232–233 increment `SessionBean1`'s `numberOfSelections` property. Lines 242–249 and the `languaguesLink` action handler (lines 254–265) control the components that are displayed, just as in the cookies examples.

> **Software Engineering Observation 29.2**
>
> *A benefit of using session bean properties (rather than cookies) is that they can store any type of object (not just Strings) as attribute values. This provides you with increased flexibility and power in maintaining client-state information.*

Displaying Recommendations Based on Session Values

As in the cookies example, this application provides a link to Recommendations.jsp, which displays a list of book recommendations based on the user's language selections. Since this JSP is identical to the version in Fig. 29.22, we show only the sample output of this page in Fig. 29.29.

*Page Bean That Creates Book Recommendations from a **SessionBean** Property*

Figure 29.30 presents the page bean for Recommendations.jsp. Again, much of it is similar to the page bean used in the cookies example. We discuss only the new features.

Lines 67–68 retrieve the HashMap object containing the user's selections from the session bean, and line 69 retrieves the number of selections made. If any selections were made, lines 78–82 append book recommendations to the string recommendations. Line 78 uses the HashMap's keySet method to obtain a Set of the keys in the HashMap, and line 81 uses each key to obtain the ISBN of the corresponding book.

Fig. 29.29 | JSP file that displays book recommendations based on language selections stored in session scope.

```
1   // Fig. 29.30: Recommendations.java
2   // Displays book recommendations based on a HashMap property in the
3   // session bean that contains the user's selected programming languages.
4   package sessions;
5
6   import com.sun.rave.web.ui.appbase.AbstractPageBean;
7   import com.sun.webui.jsf.component.TextArea;
8   import java.util.HashMap;
9   import javax.faces.FacesException;
```

Fig. 29.30 | Displays book recommendations based on a **SessionBean** property. (Part 1 of 2.)

```
10
11   public class Recommendations extends AbstractPageBean
12   {
13      // To save space, we omitted the code in lines 13-61. The complete
14      // source code is provided with this chapter's examples.
15
62      // process and display user's selections
63      @Override
64      public void prerender()
65      {
66         // retrieve user's selections and number of selections made
67         HashMap<String, String> languages =
68            getSessionBean1().getSelectedLanguages();
69         int numberSelected = getSessionBean1().getNumberOfSelections();
70
71         // if there are selections, store the corresponding
72         // books and ISBN numbers in a String
73         String recommendations = "";
74
75         // if at least one selection was made
76         if ( numberSelected > 0 )
77         {
78            for ( String language : languages.keySet() )
79            {
80               recommendations += language + " How to Program.  ISBN#: " +
81                  languages.get( language ) + "\n";
82            } // end for
83         } // end if
84         else
85         {
86            recommendations =
87               "No recommendations. Please select a language.";
88         } // end else
89
90         recommendationsTextArea.setText( recommendations );
91      } // end method prerender
92
93      // To save space, we omitted the code in lines 92-111. The complete
94      // source code is provided with this chapter's examples.
112  } // end class Recommendations
```

Fig. 29.30 | Displays book recommendations based on a `SessionBean` property. (Part 2 of 2.)

29.8 Wrap-Up

In this chapter, we introduced web application development using JavaServer Pages and JavaServer Faces in NetBeans. We began by discussing the simple HTTP transactions that take place when you request and receive a web page through a web browser. We then discussed the three tiers (i.e., the client or top tier, the business logic or middle tier and the information or bottom tier) that comprise most web applications.

You learned the role of JSP files and page bean files, and the relationship between them. You learned how to use NetBeans to visually build web applications using Net-Beans's drag-and-drop capabilities, then you compiled and executed them.

We demonstrated several common JSF components used for displaying text and images on web pages. We also discussed validation components and custom validator methods, which allow you to ensure that user input satisfies the requirements of your application.

We discussed the benefits of maintaining user information across multiple pages of a website. We then demonstrated how you can include such functionality in a web application using either cookies or properties of the session bean class that is included in each web application.

In Chapter 30, we continue our discussion of Java web application development with more advanced concepts. You'll learn how to access a database from a JSF web application, how to use AJAX-enabled JSF components and how to use virtual forms. AJAX helps web-based applications provide the interactivity and responsiveness that users typically expect of desktop applications.

Summary

Section 29.1 Introduction

- Web-based applications create content, such as Extensible HyperText Markup Language (XHTML), client-side scripting, images and binary data, for web browser clients.

Section 29.2 Simple HTTP Transactions

- In its simplest form, a web page is nothing more than an XHTML document that describes to a web browser how to display and format the document's information.

- XHTML documents normally contain hyperlinks that link to different pages or to other parts of the same page. When the user clicks a hyperlink, the requested web page loads into the browser.

- The HTTP protocol allows clients and servers to interact and exchange information.

- HTTP uses URIs (Uniform Resource Identifiers) to identify data on the Internet. URIs that specify document locations are called URLs (Uniform Resource Locators).

- A URL contains information that directs a browser to the resource that the user wishes to access. Computers that run web-server software make such resources available.

- The computer that houses and maintains resources is usually referred to as the host.

- Host names are translated into IP addresses by domain-name system (DNS) servers.

- When given a URL, a web browser performs an HTTP transaction to retrieve and display the web page at that address.

- HTTP headers provide additional information about the data that will be sent.

- Multipurpose Internet Mail Extensions (MIME) is an Internet standard that specifies data formats so that programs can interpret data correctly.

- The two most common HTTP request types are GET and POST. A GET request typically asks for a specific resource on a server. A POST request typically posts (or sends) data to a server.

- GET requests and POST requests can both be used to send form data to a web server, yet each request type sends the information differently. A GET request sends information to the server in the URL. A POST request sends form data as part of the HTTP message.

- Browsers often cache web pages for quick reloading. If there are no changes between the version stored in the cache and the current version on the web, this speeds up your browsing experience.

- An HTTP response can indicate the length of time for which the content remains "fresh." If this amount of time has not been reached, the browser can avoid another request to the server.

- Browsers typically do not cache the server's response to a POST request, because the next POST might not return the same result.

Section 29.3 Multitier Application Architecture

- Web-based applications are multitier (*n*-tier) applications that divide functionality into separate tiers (i.e., logical groupings of functionality). Although tiers can be located on the same computer, the tiers of web-based applications typically reside on separate computers.
- The information tier maintains data pertaining to the application.
- The middle tier implements business logic, controller logic and presentation logic to control interactions between the application's clients and the application's data. Business logic in the middle tier enforces business rules and ensures that data is reliable before the server application updates the database or presents the data to users. Business rules dictate how clients can and cannot access application data, and how applications process data.
- The client tier is the application's user interface, which gathers input and displays output. Users interact directly with the application through the user interface. In response to user actions (e.g., clicking a hyperlink), the client tier interacts with the middle tier to make requests and to retrieve data from the information tier.

Section 29.4 Java Web Technologies

- Java multitier applications are implemented using the features of Java Enterprise Edition.

Section 29.4.1 Servlets

- Servlets use the HTTP request/response model of communication between client and server.
- Servlets extend a server's functionality by allowing it to generate dynamic content.
- A web server component called the servlet container executes and interacts with servlets. The servlet container receives HTTP requests from a client and directs each request to the appropriate servlet. The servlet processes the request and returns an appropriate response to the client.
- All servlets must implement the Servlet interface of package javax.servlet, which ensures that each servlet can execute in the framework provided by the servlet container.
- Interface Servlet declares servlet lifecycle methods. The container invokes the servlet's init method only once during a servlet's life cycle to initialize the servlet. After init completes execution, the servlet is ready to respond to its first request. Each request is handled by a servlet's service method, which receives the request, processes it and sends a response to the client.
- When the servlet container terminates the servlet, the servlet's destroy method is called to release any resources held by the servlet.

Section 29.4.2 JavaServer Pages

- JavaServer Pages (JSP) technology is an extension of servlet technology. Each JSP is translated by the JSP container into a servlet.
- JSPs help you separate presentation from content. JSPs enable you to create dynamic content by reusing predefined components and by interacting with components using server-side scripting.
- A JavaBean is a reusable component that follows certain conventions for class design and that can be manipulated visually in a builder tool such as NetBeans or Eclipse. JavaBeans classes that allow reading and writing of instance variables must provide appropriate *get* and *set* methods—together, these define properties of JavaBeans classes.
- Custom tag libraries allow you to hide code for database access and other complex operations in custom tags. To use such capabilities, you simply add the custom tags to the page. This simplicity enables web-page designers who are not familiar with Java to enhance web pages with powerful dynamic content and dynamic processing capabilities.

- There are four key components to JSPs—directives, actions, scripting elements and tag libraries. Directives are messages to the JSP container that enable you to specify page settings, to include content from other resources and to specify custom tag libraries for use in JSPs. Actions encapsulate functionality in predefined tags that programmers can embed in JSPs. Scripting elements enable you to insert Java code that interacts with components in a JSP to perform request processing. Tag libraries are part of the tag extension mechanism that enables programmers to create custom tags. The JavaServer Pages Standard Tag Library (JSTL) provides the functionality for many common web application tasks.

- JSPs can contain static content, such as XHTML or XML markup. Such markup is known as fixed-template data or fixed-template text.

- When a JSP-enabled server receives the first request for a JSP, the JSP container translates the JSP into a servlet that handles the current request and future requests to the JSP.

Section 29.4.3 JavaServer Faces
- JavaServer Faces (JSF) is a web application framework that simplifies the design of an application's user interface and further separates a web application's presentation from its business logic.

- JSF components simplify web-page design. JSF provides two JSP custom tag libraries for adding these components to a JSP page. JSF also includes APIs for handling component events, navigating between web application pages and more.

- You design the look-and-feel of a page with JSF by adding elements to a JSP document and manipulating their attributes. You define the page's behavior separately in related Java files.

Section 29.4.4 Web Technologies in NetBeans
- NetBeans web applications that use the JavaServer Faces framework consist of one or more JSP web pages. These JSPs have the filename extension .jsp and contain the web pages' GUI elements. JSPs can be customized in NetBeans by adding JSF components.

- Every JSP file created in NetBeans represents a web page and has a corresponding JavaBean class called the page bean. A JavaBean class must have a default (or no-argument) constructor, and *get* and *set* methods for all of the bean's properties (i.e., instance variables). The page bean defines properties for each of the page's elements that you wish to interact with programmatically. The page bean also contains event handlers and page life-cycle methods for managing tasks such as page initialization and rendering, and other supporting code for the web application.

- Every NetBeans JSF web application defines three more JavaBeans. The RequestBean object is maintained in request scope—it exists only for an HTTP request's duration. A SessionBean object has session scope—it exists throughout a user's browsing session or until the session times out. There is a unique SessionBean object for each user. Finally, the ApplicationBean object has application scope—it is shared by all instances of an application and exists as long as the application remains deployed on a web server. This object is used for applicationwide data storage or processing; only one instance exists for the application, regardless of the number of open sessions.

Section 29.5.1 Examining a JSP Document
- All JSPs must have a jsp:root element, which has a version attribute to indicate the JSP version being used and one or more xmlns attributes. Each xmlns attribute specifies a prefix and a URL for a tag library, allowing the page to use elements from that library.

- The jsp:directive.page element's contentType attribute specifies the MIME type (text/html) and the character set (UTF-8) the page uses. Its pageEncoding attribute specifies the character encoding used by the page source. These attributes help the browser render the content.

- All pages containing JSF components are represented in a component tree with the root JSF element f:view in which other JSF component tags are nested.

- The webuijsf:head element has a title attribute that specifies the page's title.

- The webuijsf:body element contains a webuijsf:form element in which the JSF components of the user interface are defined.
- A webuijsf:staticText displays text on the page.
- JSF Expression Language enables you to bind an attribute of a JSP element to the value of a property in any of the web application's JavaBeans.
- JSP elements are mapped by the application server to a combination of XHTML elements and JavaScript code that enables the browser to render the page.
- JavaScript is a scripting language that is interpreted in all of today's popular web browsers. It can be used to manipulate web-page elements in a browser and provide interactivity with the user.
- The same web component can map to different XHTML elements and JavaScript code, depending on the client browser and the component's property settings.

Section 29.5.2 Examining a Page Bean File
- Page bean classes extend class AbstractPageBean (from package com.sun.rave.web.ui.appbase), which provides page life-cycle methods.
- Package com.sun.webui.jsf.component provides many of the basic JSF GUI components.

Section 29.5.3 Event-Processing Life Cycle
- Several methods in the page bean tie into the JSF event-processing life cycle's four major stages—initialization, preprocessing, prerendering and destruction. Each corresponds to a method in the page bean class—init, preprocess, prerender and destroy, respectively.
- The JSP container calls init the first time the page is requested and on postbacks. A postback occurs when form data is submitted to the server for processing.
- The preprocess method is called after init, but only if the page is processing a postback. The prerender method sets component properties just before a page is rendered by the browser.
- The destroy method is called after the page has been rendered, but only if the init method was called. This method handles tasks such as freeing resources used to render the page.

Section 29.5.4 Building a Web Application in NetBeans
- To create a web application project, select **File > New Project...** to display the **New Project** dialog. Select **Java Web** in the **Categories** pane, **Web Application** in the **Projects** pane and click **Next >**. Name the project and, in the **Project Location** field, specify where you'd like to store the project. Keep the other default settings and click **Next >**. Keep the default options for **Server** and **Settings** and click **Next >**. Select **Visual Web JavaServer Faces** as the framework to use in this web application, then click **Finish** to create the web application project.
- The **Palette** displayed in the IDE shows the Woodstock components. Woodstock is a set of user interface components for JavaServer Faces applications.
- The **Projects** window displays the hierarchy of all files included in the project. The JSP files for each page are listed under the **Web Pages** node. The Java code is in the **Source Packages** node.
- Refactoring is the process of modifying source code to improve its readability and reusability without changing its behavior. NetBeans has built-in refactoring tools.
- To add components to the page in **Design** mode, drag and drop them from the **Palette** onto the page. Each component is an object that has properties, methods and events. You can manipulate these visually using the **Properties** window or programmatically in the page bean file.
- NetBeans is a WYSIWYG (What You See Is What You Get) editor—when you make a change to a page in **Design** mode, the IDE creates the markup (visible in **JSP** mode) necessary to achieve the desired visual effects seen in **Design** mode and might add code to the page bean's .java file.

- In the **Properties** window, you can click the ellipsis button (⊡) next to the `style` property of a component to open a dialog box to edit the component's style.

- To interact with a JSF component programmatically, you must first right click the control in **Design** mode and select **Add Binding Attribute**. This creates a variable in the page bean that you can use to interact with the component and *set* and *get* methods for accessing the component.

- You can run your project by selecting **Run > Build Project**, then **Run > Run Project**. You can also run a project that has already been built by pressing the **Run Project** icon (▷) in the toolbar at the top of the IDE or by pressing *F6*.

- You can press *Ctrl + F5* to build the application, then run it in debug mode. If you press *F6*, the program executes without debugging enabled.

- For projects with multiple pages, you can change the start page by right clicking the desired page in the **Projects** window and selecting **Set As Start Page**. The start page is indicated by an icon with a green play button symbol (⊡▸) next to the page's name in the **Projects** window.

Section 29.6.1 Text and Graphics Components

- NetBeans uses absolute positioning by default, so components are rendered wherever they were dropped in the visual editor.

- A **Grid Panel** allows the designer to specify the number of columns the grid should contain. Components are positioned in evenly spaced columns in the order in which they are added.

- To add an image, drop an **Image** component onto the page and click the ellipsis button (⊡) next to its **url** property in the **Properties** window, then select the image to display.

- You can label a **Text Field** by setting its `label` property, which places text to the left of the **Text Field**. Alternatively, you can label a **Text Field** by dragging and dropping a **Label** component onto the page, which allows you to customize the **Label**'s position and style.

- The order in which components are dragged to the page is the order in which their JSP elements are added to the JSP document.

- By default, when a user presses the *Tab* key to navigate between input fields, the focus shifts from component to component in the order the JSP elements occur in the JSP document. To specify the navigation order, you can drag components onto the page in the appropriate order, or you can set each input field's `tabIndex` property in the **Properties** window.

- A **Drop Down List** displays a list of options from which the user can make a selection. A `SingleSelectOptionsList` object manages the list of options. This object can be configured by right clicking the drop-down list in **Design** mode and selecting **Configure Default Options...**, which opens the **Options Customizer** dialog box so you can add options to the list.

- The **Hyperlink** component adds a hyperlink to a web page. Its **url** property specifies the resource to request when a user clicks the hyperlink.

- A **Radio Button Group** provides radio buttons from which the user can select only one. A **Radio Button Group** is bound to a `SingleSelectOptionList` object. The options can be edited by right clicking the component and selecting **Configure Default Options...**.

- A **Button** component triggers an action when clicked and typically maps to an `input` XHTML element with attribute `type` set to `submit`.

Section 29.6.2 Validation Using Validator Components and Custom Validators

- Form validation helps prevent processing errors due to incomplete or improperly formatted user input. A **Length Validator** determines whether a field contains an acceptable number of characters. **Double Range Validator**s and **Long Range Validator**s determine whether numeric input falls within acceptable ranges. You can also create custom validator methods in the page bean file.

- **Message** components display error messages when validation fails.

- To associate the **Label** and **Message** components with a corresponding **Text Field**, hold the *Ctrl* and *Shift* keys, then drag the **Label** or **Message** to the **Text Field**. In the **Properties** window, notice that each **Label** and **Message** component's for property is set to the appropriate **Text Field**.

- To ensure that the user made a selection or entered some text in a required input element check the required box in the element's **Properties** window. A component's required property must be set to true (checked) for validation to occur.

- To add a **Length Validator** to a component, drag the validator from the **Palette** and drop it onto the field to validate. Set the **Length Validator**'s maximum and minimum properties to the desired number of characters in the **Properties** window.

- Client-side validation can be circumvented. Perform important validation on the server.

- It's possible to limit the length of user input by setting a **Text Field**'s maxLength property.

- Matching user input against a regular expression is an effective way to ensure that the input is properly formatted. This can be done with custom validators.

Section 29.7 Session Tracking
- Personalization makes it possible for e-businesses to communicate effectively with their customers and also improves the user's ability to locate desired products and services.

- A trade-off exists between personalized e-business service and protection of privacy. Some consumers embrace the idea of tailored content, but others fear the possible adverse consequences if the information they provide to e-businesses is released or collected by tracking technologies.

- HTTP is a stateless protocol—it does not support persistent connections that would enable web servers to maintain state information regarding particular clients. So, web servers cannot determine whether a request comes from a particular client or whether a series of requests comes from one or several clients.

- To help the server distinguish among clients, each client must identify itself to the server. Tracking individual clients, known as session tracking, can be achieved in a number of ways. One popular technique uses cookies; another uses the SessionBean object.

- With "hidden" form elements, a web form can write session-tracking data into a form in the web page that it returns to the client in response to a prior request. When the user submits the form in the new web page, all the form data, including the "hidden" fields, is sent to the form handler on the web server. With URL rewriting, the web server embeds session-tracking information directly in the URLs of hyperlinks that the user clicks to send subsequent requests.

Section 29.7.1 Cookies
- A cookie is a piece of data typically stored in a text file on the user's computer. A cookie maintains information about the client during and between browser sessions.

- The first time a user visits the website, the user's computer might receive a cookie; this cookie is then reactivated each time the user revisits that site. The collected information is intended to be an anonymous record containing data that is used to personalize the user's future visits to the site.

- Every HTTP-based interaction between a client and a server includes a header containing information either about the request (when the communication is from the client to the server) or about the response (when the communication is from the server to the client).

- When a page receives a request, the header includes information such as the request type and any cookies that have been sent previously from the server to be stored on the client machine. When the server formulates its response, the header information contains any cookies the server wants to store on the client computer and other information, such as the MIME type of the response.

- A cookie's expiration date determines how long the cookie remains on the client's computer. If you do not set a cookie's expiration date, the web browser maintains the cookie for the browsing session's duration. Otherwise, it maintains the cookie until the expiration date.

- Setting the action handler for a **Hyperlink** enables you to respond to a click without redirecting the user to another page.

- To add an action handler to a **Hyperlink** that should also direct the user to another page, you must add a rule to the **Page Navigation** file. To edit this file, right click in the Visual Designer and select **Page Navigation...**, then drag the appropriate **Hyperlink** to the destination page.

- A cookie object is an instance of class `Cookie` in package `javax.servlet.http`.

- An object of class `HttpServletResponse` (from package `javax.servlet.http`) represents the response. This object can be accessed by invoking the method `getExternalContext` on the page bean, then invoking `getResponse` on the resulting object.

- An object of class `HttpServletRequest` (from package `javax.servlet.http`) represents the request. This object can be obtained by invoking method `getExternalContext` on the page bean, then invoking `getRequest` on the resulting object.

- `HttpServletRespone` method `addCookie` adds a cookie to the HTTP response.

- `HttpServletRequest` method `getCookies` returns the cookies previously written to the client.

- A web server cannot access cookies created by servers in other domains.

Section 29.7.2 Session Tracking with Session Beans

- You can perform session tracking with the `AbstractSessionBean` subclass provided in each NetBeans web application. By default, the subclass is named `SessionBean1`. Properties of this object can be accessed throughout a browser session by invoking the method `getSessionBean1` on the page bean, then invoking the appropriate methods to access the session bean's properties.

- To store session information, you add properties to the session bean. To do so, declare a variable of the appropriate type in the session bean, then right click the variable name and select **Refactor > Encapsulate Fields...** to create the appropriate *get* and *set* methods.

Terminology

absolute positioning 1266
`AbstractPageBean` class 1259
`AbstractSessionBean` class 1294
action 1255
application scope 1256
`ApplicationBean` 1256
bottom tier 1253
business logic 1253
business rule 1253
Button JSF component 1273
cache 1252
client tier 1253
`com.sun.rave.web.ui.appbase` package 1259
`com.sun.webui.jsf.component` package 1259
component tree 1258
controller logic 1253
cookie 1283
custom tag libraries 1254
custom tags 1254
data tier 1253
Design mode in NetBeans 1262
destroy method of the page bean 1262
directive 1255

DNS (domain name system) server 1249
DNS lookup 1249
Double Range Validator JSF component 1273
Drop Down List JSF component 1273
escape property of a **Static Text** component 1274
event processing life cycle 1261
expiration date of a cookie 1283
`f:view` element 1258
fixed-template data 1255
fixed-template text 1255
framework 1255
GET HTTP request 1250
GlassFish v2 UR2 application server 1248
Grid Panel JSF component 1271
host 1249
hostname 1249
HTTP (Hypertext Transfer Protocol) header 1251
HTTP (Hypertext Transfer Protocol) method 1250
HTTP (Hypertext Transfer Protocol) request type 1251

Self-Review Exercises

29.1   State whether each of the following is *true* or *false*. If *false*, explain why.
   a)   Every JSP web page created in NetBeans has its own `ApplicationBean`, `SessionBean`, and `RequestBean` files.
   b)   Event-processing life-cycle method `init` is invoked every time a page loads.
   c)   Every component on a JSP web page is bound to a property in the Java page bean file.
   d)   A single JSF component may have multiple validation components placed on it.
   e)   If no expiration date is set for a cookie, that cookie will be destroyed at the end of the browser session.
   f)   Each JSF component maps to exactly one corresponding XHTML element.

    g) Expressions in the JSF Expression Language syntax are delimited by `<!--` and `-->`.

    h) The `SessionBean` can store only primitive properties and properties of type `String`.

29.2 Fill in the blanks in each of the following statements:

    a) Web applications contain three basic tiers: _____, _____, and _____.

    b) The _____ JSF component is used to display error messages if validation fails.

    c) A component that checks the input in another component before submitting that input to the server is called a(n) _____.

    d) Every page bean class inherits from class _____.

    e) When a page loads the first time, the _____ event occurs first, followed by the _____ event.

    f) The _____ file contains the functionality for a JSP.

    g) A(n) _____ can be used in a custom validator method to validate the format of user input.

    h) The array of `Cookie` objects stored on the client can be obtained by calling `getCookies` on the _____ object.

    i) In a multitier application, the _____ tier controls interactions between the application's clients and the application's data.

Answers to Self-Review Exercises

29.1 a) False. If an application contains multiple JSPs, those JSPs will share the scoped data beans. b) False. `init` is invoked the first time the page is requested, but not on page refreshes. c) False. You must manually add a binding attribute for the JSF component so that it will have a property in the page bean file. d) True. e) True. f) False. A web component can map to a group of XHTML elements—JSPs can generate complex XHTML markup from simple components. g) False. `#{` and `}` delimit JSF Expression Language statements. h) False. The scoped data beans may store any type of property.

29.2 a) bottom (data/information), middle (business logic), top (client/user interface). b) **Message**. c) validator. d) `AbstractPageBean`. e) `init`, `prerender`. f) page bean. g) regular expression. h) Request (`HttpServletRequest`). i) middle.

Exercises

29.3 *(Registration Form Modification)* Modify the `WebComponents` application to add functionality to the **Register** button. When the user clicks **Submit**, validate all input fields to make sure the user has filled out the form completely and entered a valid email address and phone number. Then, direct the user to another page that displays a message indicating successful registration and echoes back the user's registration information.

29.4 *(Page Hit Counter with `ApplicationBean`)* Create a JSP that uses the `ApplicationBean` to keep track of how many times a page has been visited. [*Note:* if you were to deploy this page on the web, it would count the number of times that any computer requested the page, unlike in the previous exercise.] Display the number of page hits (i.e., the value of an `int` property in the `ApplicationBean`) every time the page loads.

Whatever is in any way beautiful hath its source of
beauty in itself, and is complete in itself; praise forms
no part of it.
—Marcus Aurelius Antoninus

There is something in a face, An air, and a peculiar
grace, Which boldest painters cannot trace.
—William Somerville

Cato said the best way to keep good acts in memory was
to refresh them with new.
—Francis Bacon

I never forget a face, but in your case I'll make an
exception.
—Groucho Marx

Ajax-Enabled JavaServer™ Faces Web Applications

Objectives

In this Chapter you'll learn:

- To use data providers to access databases from web applications built in NetBeans.
- The basic principles and advantages of Ajax technology.
- To use Ajax-enabled JSF components in a NetBeans web application project.
- To configure virtual forms that enable subsets of a form's input components to be submitted to the server.

30.1 Introduction

This chapter continues our discussion of web application development with several advanced concepts. We discuss accessing, updating and searching databases in a web application, adding virtual forms to web pages to enable subsets of a form's input components to be submitted to the server, and using so-called Ajax-enabled component libraries to improve application performance and component responsiveness.

We present a single address book application developed in three stages to illustrate these concepts. The application is backed by a Java DB database for storing the contact names and their addresses.

The address book application presents a form that allows the user to enter a new name and address to store in the address book, and it displays the contents of the address book in table format. It also provides a search form that allows the user to search for a contact and, if found, display the contact's address. The first version of this application demonstrates how to add contacts to the database and how to display the list of contacts in a JSF **Table** component. In the second version, we add an Ajax-enabled Autocomplete **Text Field** component and enable it to suggest a list of contact names as the user types. When the user selects a contact, the contact's information is displayed.

This chapter's examples, like those in Chapter 29, were developed in NetBeans. Some of the Woodstock components that come with NetBeans, such as the **Text Field** component, are Ajax enabled. These components use the Dojo Toolkit on the client side in the web browser. Dojo is a cross-browser, cross-platform JavaScript library for creating rich client-side user interfaces and performing Ajax interactions with web servers. For more information on this toolkit, see our Dojo Resource Center at www.deitel.com/dojo/. [*Note:* In the future, the Woodstock components will be replaced with IceFaces. For information on IceFaces, visit icefaces.org. The IceFaces website provides a document on migrating from Woodstock to IceFaces at www.icefaces.org/main/product/woodstock-migration.iface.]

30.2 Accessing Databases in Web Applications

Many web applications access databases to store and retrieve persistent data. In this section, we build a web application that uses a Java DB database to store contacts in the address book and display contacts from the address book on a web page.

The web page enables the user to enter new contacts in a form. This form consists of **Text Field** components for the contact's first name, last name, street address, city, state and zip code. The form also has a **Submit** button to send the data to the server and a **Clear** button to reset the form's fields. The application stores the address book information in a database named AddressBook, which has a single table named Addresses. (We provide this database in the examples directory for this chapter.) This example also introduces the **Table** JSF component, which displays the addresses from the database in tabular format.

30.2.1 Building a Web Application That Displays Data from a Database

We now explain how to build the AddressBook application's GUI and set up a data binding that allows the **Table** component to display information from the database. We present the generated JSP file later in the section, and we discuss the related page bean file in Section 30.2.2. To build the AddressBook application, perform the following steps:

Step 1: Creating the Project
In NetBeans, create a new **Web Application** project named AddressBook. Be sure to select **Visual Web JavaServer Faces** as the framework, as you did in Chapter 29. Rename the JSP and page bean files from Page1 to AddressBook using the refactoring tools.

Step 2: Creating the Form for User Input
In **Design** mode, create the form shown in Fig. 30.1. Add a **Static Text** component containing "Add a contact to the address book:". Use the component's style property to set the font size to 18px. Add six pairs of **Label** and **Text Field** components to the page. Rename the **Text Field**s firstNameTextField, lastNameTextField, streetTextField, cityTextField, stateTextField and zipTextField. Set each **Text Field**'s required property to true (checked) by selecting the **Text Field**, then clicking the required property's checkbox. Associate each **Label** with its corresponding **Text Field** by holding the *Ctrl* and *Shift* keys, then dragging the label to the appropriate **Text Field**. Add a binding attribute to the page bean for each **Text Field** (right click the component and select **Add Binding Attribute**). Finally, add **Submit** and **Clear** buttons and set them to fixed widths in pixels. Set the **Submit** button's **primary** property to true (checked) to make it more prominent on the page than the **Clear** button and to allow the user to submit a new contact by pressing *Enter* rather than by clicking the button. Set the **Clear** button's **reset** property to true

Fig. 30.1 | AddressBook application form for adding a contact.

(checked) to prevent validation when the user clicks the button—since we're clearing the fields, we don't need to ensure that they contain information. We discuss the **Submit** button's action handler when we present the page bean file. The **Clear** button does not need an action-handler method—setting reset to true automatically configures the button to reset all of the page's input fields.

Step 3: Adding a Table Component to the Page

Drag a **Table** component from the **Basic** section of the **Palette** to the page and place it just below the two **Button** components. Name it addressesTable. The **Table** component formats and displays data from database tables. In the **Properties** window, change the **Table**'s title property to Contacts. We show how to configure the **Table** to interact with the AddressBook database shortly.

Step 4: Creating a Java DB Database

This example uses a database called AddressBook to store the address information. To create this database, perform the following steps:

1. In the NetBeans **Services** tab (to the right of the **Projects** and **Files** tabs), expand the **Databases** node, then right click **Java DB** and select **Create Database....**

2. Enter the name of the database to create (AddressBook), a username (test) and a password (test).

3. If you wish to change the location where the database is stored on your system, click the **Properties...** button and specify the new location.

4. Click **OK** to create the database.

In the **Services** tab, the preceding steps create a new entry in the **Databases** node showing the URL of the database (jdbc:derby://localhost:1527/AddressBook). The new Java DB database resides on the local machine and accepts connections on port 1527.

Step 5: Adding a Table and Data to the AddressBook Database

You can use the **Services** tab to create tables and to execute SQL statements that populate the database with data:

1. In the **Services** tab, expand the **Databases** node.

2. NetBeans must be connected to the database to execute SQL statements. If NetBeans is already connected to the database, the icon ▣ is displayed next to the database's URL (jdbc:derby://localhost:1527/AddressBook). In this case, proceed to *Step 3.* If NetBeans is not connected to the database, the icon ▣ appears next to the database's URL. In this case, right click the icon and select **Connect....** Once connected, the icon changes to ▣.

3. Expand the node for the AddressBook database, right click the **Tables** node and select **Execute Command...** to open a **SQL Command** editor in NetBeans. We provided the file AddressBook.sql in this chapter's examples folder. Open that file in a text editor, copy the SQL statements and paste them into the **SQL Command** editor in NetBeans. Then highlight all the SQL commands, right click inside the **SQL Command** editor and select **Run Selection**. This will create the Addresses table with the sample data shown in Fig. 30.2. [*Note:* The SQL script attempts to connect to the database if it already exists. If it does not exist, you'll receive an

error message, but the database will still be created properly.] You may need to refresh (right click it and select **Refresh**) and expand the **Tables** node to see the new table. You can view the data in the table by expanding the **Tables** node, right clicking **ADDRESSES** and selecting **View Data**....

FirstName	LastName	Street	City	State	Zip
Bob	Green	5 Bay St.	San Francisco	CA	94133
Liz	White	100 5th Ave.	New York	NY	10011
Mike	Brown	3600 Delmar Blvd.	St. Louis	MO	63108
Mary	Green	300 Massachusetts Ave.	Boston	MA	02115
John	Gray	500 South St.	Philadelphia	PA	19147
Meg	Gold	1200 Stout St.	Denver	CO	80204
James	Blue	1000 Harbor Ave.	Seattle	WA	98116
Sue	Black	1000 Michigan Ave.	Chicago	IL	60605

Fig. 30.2 | Addresses table data.

Step 6: Binding the Table Component to the Addresses Table of the AddressBook Database

Now that we've configured the **AddressBook** database and created the Addresses table, let's configure the **Table** component to display the AddressBook data. Drag the database table from the **Services** tab and drop it on the **Table** component to create the binding.

To select specific columns to display, right click the **Table** component and select **Bind to Data** to display the **Bind to Data** dialog containing the list of the columns in the Addresses database table (Fig. 30.3). The items under the **Selected** heading will be displayed in the **Table**. To remove a column, select it and click the **<** button. We'd like to display all the columns in this example, so you should simply click **OK** to exit the dialog.

Fig. 30.3 | Dialog for binding to the Addresses table.

By default, the **Table** uses the database table's column names in all uppercase letters as headings. To change these headings, select a column and edit its headerText property in the **Properties** window. To select a column, click the column's name in the **Design** mode. We also changed the id property of each column to make the variable names in the code more readable. In **Design** mode, your **Table**'s column heads should appear as in Fig. 30.4. If any of the column heads wrap to two lines, you can increase the width of the table.

Fig. 30.4 | Table component after binding it to a database table and editing its column names for display purposes.

An address book might contain many contacts, so we'd like to display only a few at a time. Setting the table's **paginationControls** property to true (checked) in the **Properties** window configures this **Table** for automatic pagination. This adds buttons to the bottom of the **Table** for moving forward and backward between groups of contacts. You may use the **Table Layout** dialog's **Options** tab to select the number of rows to display at a time. To do so, right click the **Table**'s header, select **Table Layout...**, then click the **Options** tab. For this example, we set the **Page Size** property to 5. Click the **OK** button to apply the changes.

Next, set the addressesTable's **internalVirtualForm** property to true (checked). Virtual forms allow subsets of a form's input components to be submitted to the server. Setting this property prevents the pagination control buttons on the **Table** from submitting the **Text Field**s on the form every time the user wishes to view the next group of contacts. Virtual forms are discussed in Section 30.4.1.

Binding the **Table** component to a data provider added the addressesDataProvider object (an instance of class CachedRowSetDataProvider) to the **AddressBook** node in the **Navigator** window. A **CachedRowSetDataProvider** provides a scrollable RowSet that can be bound to a **Table** component to display the RowSet's data. This data provider is a wrapper for a CachedRowSet object. If you click the **addressesDataProvider** node in the **Navigator** window, you can see in the **Properties** window that its CachedRowSet property is set to addressesRowSet, a session bean property that implements interface CachedRowSet.

Step 7: Modifying addressesRowSet's SQL Statement

The CachedRowSet object wrapped by our addressesDataProvider is configured by default to execute a SQL query that selects all the data in the Addresses table of the AddressBook database. You can edit this SQL query. To do so, ensure that you are in **Design** mode for the page bean, then expand the SessionBean1 node in the **Navigator** window and double click the addressesRowSet element to open the query editor window (Fig. 30.5). We'd like to edit the SQL statement so that records with duplicate last names are sorted by last name, then by first name. To do this, click the **Sort Type** column next to the **LASTNAME** row and select **Ascending**. Then repeat this for the **FIRSTNAME** row. Notice that the expression

```
ORDER BY TEST.ADDRESSES.LASTNAME ASC, TEST.ADDRESSES.FIRSTNAME ASC
```

was added to the end of the SQL statement at the bottom of the editor. Save your application (**File > Save All**), then close the query editor tab.

Fig. 30.5 | Editing addressesRowSet's SQL statement.

Step 8: Adding Validation

It is important to validate the form data on this page to ensure that the data can be successfully inserted into the AddressBook database. All of the database's columns are of type varchar and have length restrictions. For this reason, you should either add a **Length Validator** to each **Text Field** component or set each **Text Field** component's maxLength property. We chose to do the latter. The first name, last name, street, city, state and zip code **Text Field** components may not exceed 30, 30, 150, 30, 2 and 5 characters, respectively.

Finally, drag a **Message Group** component onto your page to the right of the **Text Fields**. This component displays system messages. We use it to display an error message when an attempt to add a contact to the database fails. Set the **Message Group**'s show-GlobalOnly property to true (checked) to prevent component-level validation error messages from being displayed here.

Reviewing the JSP Document for a Web Page That Interacts with a Database

The JSP file for the application is shown in Fig. 30.6. This file contains a large amount of generated markup for components you learned in Chapter 29. We discuss the markup for only the components that are new in this example.

```
1   <?xml version="1.0" encoding="UTF-8"?>
2   <!-- Fig. 30.6: AddressBook.jsp -->
3   <!-- AddressBook JSP with an add form and a Table JSF component. -->
4   <jsp:root version="2.1" xmlns:f="http://java.sun.com/jsf/core"
5       xmlns:h="http://java.sun.com/jsf/html"
6       xmlns:jsp="http://java.sun.com/JSP/Page"
7       xmlns:webuijsf="http://www.sun.com/webui/webuijsf">
8       <jsp:directive.page contentType="text/html;charset=UTF-8"
9           pageEncoding="UTF-8"/>
```

Fig. 30.6 | AddressBook JSP with an add form and a **Table** JSF component. (Part 1 of 4.)

```
10      <f:view>
11        <webuijsf:page id="page1">
12          <webuijsf:html id="html1">
13            <webuijsf:head id="head1">
14              <webuijsf:link id="link1" url="/resources/stylesheet.css"/>
15            </webuijsf:head>
16            <webuijsf:body id="body1" style="-rave-layout: grid">
17              <webuijsf:form id="form1">
18                <webuijsf:staticText id="instructionText"
19                  style="font-size: 18px; left: 24px; top: 24px;
20                    position: absolute"
21                  text="Add a contact to the address book:"/>
22                <webuijsf:label for="firstNameTextField"
23                  id="firstNameLabel" style="left: 24px; top: 72px;
24                    position: absolute" text="First name:"/>
25                <webuijsf:textField
26                  binding="#{AddressBook.firstNameTextField}"
27                  id="firstNameTextField" maxLength="30"
28                  required="true" style="left: 120px; top: 72px;
29                    position: absolute"/>
30                <webuijsf:label for="lastNameTextField"
31                  id="lastNameLabel" style="left: 25px; top: 96px;
32                    position: absolute" text="Last name:"/>
33                <webuijsf:textField
34                  binding="#{AddressBook.lastNameTextField}"
35                  id="lastNameTextField" maxLength="30" required="true"
36                  style="left: 120px; top: 96px; position: absolute"/>
37                <webuijsf:label for="streetTextField" id="streetLabel"
38                  style="left: 49px; top: 120px; position: absolute"
39                  text="Street:"/>
40                <webuijsf:textField
41                  binding="#{AddressBook.streetTextField}"
42                  id="streetTextField" maxLength="150" required="true"
43                  style="left: 120px; top: 120px; position: absolute"/>
44                <webuijsf:label for="cityTextField" id="cityLabel"
45                  style="left: 62px; top: 144px; position: absolute"
46                  text="City:"/>
47                <webuijsf:textField
48                  binding="#{AddressBook.cityTextField}"
49                  id="cityTextField" maxLength="30" required="true"
50                  style="left: 120px; top: 144px; position: absolute"/>
51                <webuijsf:label for="stateTextField" id="stateLabel"
52                  style="left: 55px; top: 168px; position: absolute"
53                  text="State:"/>
54                <webuijsf:textField
55                  binding="#{AddressBook.stateTextField}"
56                  id="stateTextField" maxLength="2" required="true"
57                  style="left: 120px; top: 168px; position: absolute"/>
58                <webuijsf:label for="zipTextField" id="zipLabel"
59                  style="left: 66px; top: 192px; position: absolute"
60                  text="Zip:"/>
61                <webuijsf:textField
62                  binding="#{AddressBook.zipTextField}"
63                  id="zipTextField" maxLength="5" required="true"
```

Fig. 30.6 | AddressBook JSP with an add form and a **Table** JSF component. (Part 2 of 4.)

```
64                      style="left: 120px; top: 192px; position: absolute"/>
65                  <webuijsf:button
66                      actionExpression="#{AddressBook.submitButton_action}"
67                      id="submitButton" primary="true" style="left: 47px;
68                          top: 240px; position: absolute; width: 95px"
69                      text="Submit"/>
70                  <webuijsf:button id="clearButton" reset="true"
71                      style="left: 150px; top: 240px; position: absolute;
72                          width: 96px" text="Clear"/>
73                  <webuijsf:table augmentTitle="false"
74                      binding="#{AddressBook.addressesTable}"
75                      id="addressesTable" paginateButton="true"
76                      paginationControls="true" style="left: 24px;
77                          top: 288px; position: absolute" 
78                      title="Contacts" width="744">
79                      <webuijsf:tableRowGroup id="tableRowGroup1" rows="5"
80                          sourceData="#{AddressBook.addressesDataProvider}"
81                          sourceVar="currentRow">
82                          <webuijsf:tableColumn headerText="First name"
83                              id="firstNameColumn"
84                              sort="ADDRESSES.FIRSTNAME">
85                              <webuijsf:staticText id="staticText1"
86                                  text="#{currentRow.value[
87                                      'ADDRESSES.FIRSTNAME']}"/>
88                          </webuijsf:tableColumn>
89                          <webuijsf:tableColumn headerText="Last name"
90                              id="lastNameColumn" sort="ADDRESSES.LASTNAME">
91                              <webuijsf:staticText id="staticText2"
92                                  text="#{currentRow.value[
93                                      'ADDRESSES.LASTNAME']}"/>
94                          </webuijsf:tableColumn>
95                          <webuijsf:tableColumn headerText="Street"
96                              id="streetColumn" sort="ADDRESSES.STREET">
97                              <webuijsf:staticText id="staticText3"
98                                  text="#{currentRow.value[
99                                      'ADDRESSES.STREET']}"/>
100                         </webuijsf:tableColumn>
101                         <webuijsf:tableColumn headerText="City"
102                             id="cityColumn" sort="ADDRESSES.CITY">
103                             <webuijsf:staticText id="staticText4"
104                                 text="#{currentRow.value[
105                                     'ADDRESSES.CITY']}"/>
106                         </webuijsf:tableColumn>
107                         <webuijsf:tableColumn headerText="State"
108                             id="stateColumn" sort="ADDRESSES.STATE">
109                             <webuijsf:staticText id="staticText5"
110                                 text="#{currentRow.value[
111                                     'ADDRESSES.STATE']}"/>
112                         </webuijsf:tableColumn>
113                         <webuijsf:tableColumn headerText="zip"
114                             id="zipColumn" sort="ADDRESSES.ZIP">
115                             <webuijsf:staticText id="staticText6"
116                                 text="#{currentRow.value[
117                                     'ADDRESSES.ZIP']}"/>
```

Fig. 30.6 | AddressBook JSP with an add form and a **Table** JSF component. (Part 3 of 4.)

```
118                          </webuijsf:tableColumn>
119                       </webuijsf:tableRowGroup>
120                    </webuijsf:table>
121                    <webuijsf:messageGroup id="messageGroup1"
122                       showGlobalOnly="true"
123                       style="left: 264px; top: 72px; position: absolute"/>
124                 </webuijsf:form>
125              </webuijsf:body>
126           </webuijsf:html>
127        </webuijsf:page>
128     </f:view>
129  </jsp:root>
```

(a) Adding a new contact to the database

(b) Page 2 of the **Table** showing the new database entry

Fig. 30.6 | AddressBook JSP with an add form and a **Table** JSF component. (Part 4 of 4.)

Lines 18–72 contain the JSF components for the form that gathers user input. Lines 73–120 define the **Table** element (webuijsf:table) that displays address information from the database. **Table**s may have multiple groups of rows displaying different data. This **Table** has a single webuijsf:tableRowGroup with a start tag in lines 79–81. The row group's sourceData attribute is bound to our addressesDataProvider in the page bean and given the variable name currentRow. The row group also defines the **Table**'s columns. Each webuijsf:tableColumn element (e.g., lines 82–88) contains a webuijsf:static-Text element with its text attribute bound to a column in the data provider currentRow. These webuijsf:staticText elements enable the **Table** to display each row's data.

Session Bean for the *AddressBook* Application

Figure 30.7 displays the SessionBean1.java file generated by NetBeans for the Address-Book application. The CachedRowSet that the **Table** component's data provider uses to access the AddressBook database is a property of this class (lines 31–41). The _init method (lines 13–29) configures addressesRowSet to interact with the AddressBook database. Lines 15–16 connect the row set to the database. Lines 17–27 set addressesRowSet's SQL command to the query configured in Fig. 30.5. Line 28 sets the RowSet's table name.

```
1   // Fig. 30.7: SessionBean1.java
2   // Session bean initializes the data source for the
3   // AddressBook database.
4   package addressbook;
5
6   import com.sun.rave.web.ui.appbase.AbstractSessionBean;
7   import com.sun.sql.rowset.CachedRowSetXImpl;
8   import javax.faces.FacesException;
9
10  public class SessionBean1 extends AbstractSessionBean
11  {
12      // Managed Component Definition
13      private void _init() throws Exception
14      {
15          addressesRowSet.setDataSourceName(
16              "java:comp/env/jdbc/TEST_ApacheDerby" );
17          addressesRowSet.setCommand(
18              "SELECT ALL " +
19              "TEST.ADDRESSES.FIRSTNAME, " +
20              "TEST.ADDRESSES.LASTNAME, " +
21              "TEST.ADDRESSES.STREET, " +
22              "TEST.ADDRESSES.CITY, " +
23              "TEST.ADDRESSES.STATE, " +
24              "TEST.ADDRESSES.ZIP " +
25              "FROM TEST.ADDRESSES " +
26              "ORDER BY TEST.ADDRESSES.LASTNAME ASC, " +
27              "TEST.ADDRESSES.FIRSTNAME ASC" );
28          addressesRowSet.setTableName( "ADDRESSES" );
29      } // end method _init
30
31      private CachedRowSetXImpl addressesRowSet = new CachedRowSetXImpl();
32
```

Fig. 30.7 | Session bean initializes the data source for the **AddressBook** database. (Part 1 of 2.)

```
33    public CachedRowSetXImpl getAddressesRowSet()
34    {
35       return addressesRowSet;
36    } // end method getAddressesRowSet
37
38    public void setAddressesRowSet( CachedRowSetXImpl crsxi )
39    {
40       this.addressesRowSet = crsxi;
41    } // end method setAddressesRowSet
42
43    // To save space, we omitted the code in lines 42-88. The complete
44    // source code is provided with this chapter's examples.
89 } // end class SessionBean1
```

Fig. 30.7 | Session bean initializes the data source for the **AddressBook** database. (Part 2 of 2.)

30.2.2 Modifying the Page Bean File for the AddressBook Application

After building the web page and configuring the components used in this example, double click the **Submit** button to create its action event handler (submitButton_action, lines 179–223) in the page bean file (Fig. 30.8). The code to insert a contact into the database is placed in this method. Figure 30.8 shows the page bean with the completed event handler.

```
 1  // Fig. 30.8: AddressBook.java
 2  // Page bean for adding a contact to the address book.
 3  package addressbook;
 4
 5  import com.sun.data.provider.RowKey;
 6  import com.sun.data.provider.impl.CachedRowSetDataProvider;
 7  import com.sun.rave.web.ui.appbase.AbstractPageBean;
 8  import com.sun.webui.jsf.component.Table;
 9  import com.sun.webui.jsf.component.TextField;
10  import javax.faces.FacesException;
11
12  public class AddressBook extends AbstractPageBean
13  {
14     // Managed Component Definition
15     private void _init() throws Exception
16     {
17        addressesTable.setInternalVirtualForm( true );
18        addressesDataProvider.setCachedRowSet(
19           ( javax.sql.rowset.CachedRowSet ) getValue(
20              "#{SessionBean1.addressesRowSet}" ) );
21     } // end method _init
22
23     private Table addressesTable = new Table();
24
25     public Table getAddressesTable()
26     {
27        return addressesTable;
28     } // end method getAddressesTable
29
```

Fig. 30.8 | Page bean for adding a contact to the address book. (Part 1 of 3.)

```
30      public void setAddressesTable( Table t )
31      {
32         this.addressesTable = t;
33      } // end method setAddressesTable
34
35      private CachedRowSetDataProvider addressesDataProvider =
36         new CachedRowSetDataProvider();
37
38      public CachedRowSetDataProvider getAddressesDataProvider()
39      {
40         return addressesDataProvider;
41      } // end method getAddressesDataProvider
42
43      public void setAddressesDataProvider( CachedRowSetDataProvider crsdp )
44      {
45         this.addressesDataProvider = crsdp;
46      } // end method setAddressesDataProvider
47
48      // To save space, we omitted the code in lines 48-149. The complete
49      // source code is provided with this chapter's examples.
50
150     @Override
151     public void prerender()
152     {
153        addressesDataProvider.refresh();
154     } // end method prerender
155
156     @Override
157     public void destroy()
158     {
159        addressesDataProvider.close();
160     } // end method destroy
161
162     // To save space, we omitted the code in lines 162-176. The complete
163     // source code is provided with this chapter's examples.
164
177     // action handler that adds a contact to the AddressBook
178     // database when the user clicks submit
179     public String submitButton_action()
180     {
181        // check whether a row can be appended
182        if ( addressesDataProvider.canAppendRow() )
183        {
184           try
185           {
186              // append new row and move cursor to that row
187              RowKey rk = addressesDataProvider.appendRow();
188              addressesDataProvider.setCursorRow( rk );
189
190              // set values for the new row's columns
191              addressesDataProvider.setValue( "ADDRESSES.FIRSTNAME",
192                 firstNameTextField.getValue() );
193              addressesDataProvider.setValue( "ADDRESSES.LASTNAME",
194                 lastNameTextField.getValue() );
```

Fig. 30.8 | Page bean for adding a contact to the address book. (Part 2 of 3.)

```
195              addressesDataProvider.setValue( "ADDRESSES.STREET",
196                 streetTextField.getValue() );
197              addressesDataProvider.setValue( "ADDRESSES.CITY",
198                 cityTextField.getValue() );
199              addressesDataProvider.setValue( "ADDRESSES.STATE",
200                 stateTextField.getValue() );
201              addressesDataProvider.setValue( "ADDRESSES.ZIP",
202                 zipTextField.getValue() );
203
204              // commit the changes to the database
205              addressesDataProvider.commitChanges();
206
207              // reset text fields
208              firstNameTextField.setValue( "" );
209              lastNameTextField.setValue( "" );
210              streetTextField.setValue( "" );
211              cityTextField.setValue( "" );
212              stateTextField.setValue( "" );
213              zipTextField.setValue( "" );
214           } // end try
215           catch ( Exception ex )
216           {
217              error( "The address book was not updated. " +
218                 ex.getMessage() );
219           } // end catch
220        } // end if
221
222        return null;
223     } // end method submitButton_action
224  } // end class AddressBook
```

Fig. 30.8 | Page bean for adding a contact to the address book. (Part 3 of 3.)

Line 17 in method _init sets the **Table** component's internalVirtualForm property to true. This prevents the pagination control buttons on the **Table** from submitting the form's **Text Field**s every time the user wishes to view the next group of contacts. Lines 18–20 set the addressesDataProvider's CachedRowSet so the table rows can be populated with the contents of the database. The CachedRowSet is obtained from the session bean.

Lines 179–223 contain the event-handling code for the **Submit** button. Line 182 determines whether a new row can be appended to the data provider. If so, we append a new row (line 187). Every row in a CachedRowSetDataProvider has its own key; method **appendRow** returns the key for the new row as a RowKey object. Line 188 sets the data provider's cursor to the new row, so that any changes we make to the data provider affect that row. Lines 191–202 set each of the row's columns to the values the user entered in the corresponding **Text Field**s. Line 205 stores the new contact by calling method **commitChanges** of class CachedRowSetDataProvider to insert the new row into the AddressBook database.

Lines 208–213 clear the form's **Text Field**s. If these lines are omitted, the fields will retain their current values after the database is updated and the page reloads. Also, the **Clear** button will not work properly if the **Text Field**s are not cleared. Rather than emptying the **Text Field**s, it resets them to the values they held the last time the form was submitted.

Lines 215–219 catch any exceptions that might occur while updating the Address-Book database. If an exception occurs, lines 217–218 display a message in the page's MessageGroup component indicating that the database was not updated and showing the exception's error message.

In method prerender, we added line 153 which calls CachedRowSetDataProvider method **refresh** to reexecute the wrapped CachedRowSet's SQL statement and re-sort the **Table**'s rows so that the new row is displayed in the proper order. If you do not call refresh, the new address is displayed at the end of the **Table** (since we appended the new row to the end of the data provider). The IDE automatically generated code to free resources used by the data provider (line 159) in the destroy method. Run the application to test its functionality.

30.3 Ajax-Enabled JSF Components

The term **Ajax**—short for **Asynchronous JavaScript and XML**—was coined by Jesse James Garrett of Adaptive Path, Inc., in February 2005 to describe a range of technologies for developing highly responsive, dynamic web applications. Ajax applications include Google Maps, Yahoo's FlickR and many more. Ajax separates the user interaction portion of an application from its server interaction, enabling both to proceed in parallel. This enables Ajax web-based applications to perform at speeds approaching those of desktop applications, reducing or even eliminating the performance advantage that desktop applications have traditionally had over web-based applications. This has huge ramifications for the desktop applications industry—the applications platform of choice is starting to shift from the desktop to the web. Many people believe that the web—especially in the context of abundant open-source software, inexpensive computers and exploding Internet bandwidth—will create the next major growth phase for Internet companies.

Ajax makes asynchronous calls to the server to exchange small amounts of data with each call. Where normally the entire page would be submitted and reloaded with every user interaction on a web page, Ajax allows only the necessary portions of the page to reload, saving time and resources.

Ajax applications typically make use of client-side scripting technologies such as JavaScript to interact with page elements. They use the browser's **XMLHttpRequest object** to perform the asynchronous exchanges with the web server that make Ajax applications so responsive. This object can be used by most scripting languages to pass XML data from the client to the server and to process XML data sent from the server back to the client.

Using Ajax technologies in web applications can dramatically improve performance, but programming in Ajax is complex and error prone. It requires page designers to know both scripting and markup languages. **Ajax libraries**—such as the Dojo Toolkit used by JSF—make it possible to reap Ajax's benefits without the labor of writing "raw" Ajax. These libraries provide Ajax-enabled page elements that can be included in web pages simply by adding library-defined tags to the page's markup. We limit our discussion of building Ajax applications to using the JSF Woodstock components in NetBeans.

Traditional Web Applications

Figure 30.9 presents the typical interactions between the client and the server in a traditional web application, such as one that uses a user registration form. The user first fills in the form's fields, then submits the form (Fig. 30.9, *Step 1*). The browser generates a request to the server, which receives the request and processes it (*Step 2*). The server generates and sends a response containing the exact page that the browser will render (*Step 3*), which causes the browser to load the new page (*Step 4*) and temporarily makes the browser window blank. Note that the client *waits* for the server to respond and *reloads the entire page* with the data from the response (*Step 4*). While such a **synchronous request** is being processed on the server, the user cannot interact with the client web page. Frequent long periods of waiting, due perhaps to Internet congestion, have led some users to refer to the World Wide Web as the "World Wide Wait." If the user interacts with and submits another form, the process begins again (*Steps 5–8*).

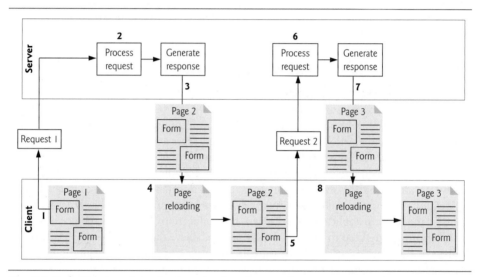

Fig. 30.9 | Classic web application reloading the page for every user interaction.

This model was originally designed for a web of hypertext documents—what some people call the "brochure web." As the web evolved into a full-scale applications platform, the model shown in Fig. 30.9 yielded "choppy" application performance. Every full-page refresh required users to reestablish their understanding of the full-page contents. Users began to demand a model that would yield the responsive feel of desktop applications.

Ajax Web Applications

Ajax applications add a layer between the client and the server to manage communication between the two (Fig. 30.10). When the user interacts with the page, the client creates an XMLHttpRequest object to manage a request (*Step 1*). The XMLHttpRequest object sends the request to the server (*Step 2*) and awaits the response. The requests are **asynchronous**, so the user can continue interacting with the application on the client side while the server processes the earlier request concurrently. Other user interactions could result in additional requests to the server (*Steps 3* and *4*). Once the server responds to the original request (*Step 5*), the XMLHttpRequest object that issued the request calls a client-side function to process the data returned by the server. This function—known as a **callback function**—uses **partial page updates** (*Step 6*) to display the data in the existing web page *without reloading the entire page*. At the same time, the server may be responding to the second request (*Step 7*) and the client side may be starting to do another partial page update (*Step 8*). The callback function updates only a designated part of the page. Such partial page updates help make web applications more responsive, making them feel more like desktop applications. The web application does not load a new page while the user interacts with it.

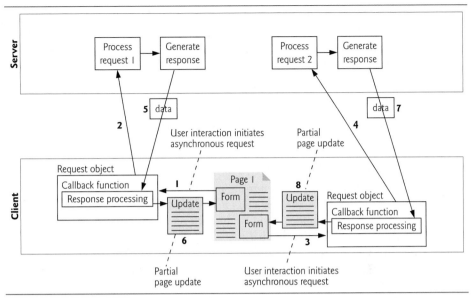

Fig. 30.10 | Ajax-enabled web application interacting with the server asynchronously.

30.4 Creating an Autocomplete Text Field and Using Virtual Forms

We now modify the AddressBook application to provide a search form that enables the user to locate a contact and display the contact's information. We take advantage of the **Text Field** component's built-in Ajax capabilities to provide autocomplete functionality—the **Text Field** provides a list of suggestions as the user types. It obtains the suggestions from a data source, such as a database or web service. Eventually, the updated application will allow users to search the address book by last name. If the user selects a contact, the application will display the contact's information in a **Text Area** component.

Adding Search Components to the AddressBook.jsp Page
Using the AddressBook application from Section 30.2, drop a **Static Text** component named searchText below addressesTable. Change its text to "Search the address book by last name:" and change its font size to 18px. Now drag a **Text Field** component to the page and name it lastNameSearchTextField. Set this field's required and autoComplete properties to true. Add a **Label** named lastNameSearchLabel containing the text "Last name:" to the left of the **Text Field** and associate it with the **Text Field**. Add a button called searchButton with the text Find to the right of the **Text Field** and a **Text Area** named searchTextArea to the right of the button. Double click the button to create its event handler. Also, add binding attributes to the page bean for the **Text Field** and the **Text Area** (right click each component and select **Add Binding Attribute**).

30.4.1 Configuring Virtual Forms

Virtual forms are used when you would like a button to submit a subset of the page's input fields to the server. Recall that we previously enabled the **Table**'s internal virtual forms so that clicking the pagination buttons would not submit the data in the **Text Field**s used to add a contact to the AddressBook database. Virtual forms are particularly useful for displaying multiple forms on the same page. They allow you to specify a **submitter** component and one or more **participant** components for a form. When the virtual form's submitter component is clicked, only the values of its participant components will be submitted to the server. We use virtual forms in our AddressBook application to separate the form for adding a contact from the form for searching the database.

To add virtual forms to the page, right click the **Submit** button on the upper form and select **Configure Virtual Forms...** to display the **Configure Virtual Forms** dialog. Click **New** to add a virtual form, then click in the **Name** column and change the new form's name to addForm. Double click the cell under the **Submit** column and change the option to **Yes** to indicate that this button should be used to submit the addForm virtual form. Click **OK** to exit the dialog. Next, hold the *Ctrl* key and click each of the **Text Field**s used to enter a contact's information in the upper form. Right click one of the selected **Text Field**s and choose **Configure Virtual Forms....** Double click the cell under the addForm's **Participate** column to change the option to **Yes**, indicating that the values in these **Text Field**s should be submitted to the server when the form is submitted. Click **OK** to exit.

Repeat the process described above to create a second virtual form named searchForm for the lower form. The **Find Button** should submit the searchForm, and lastName-SearchTextField and searchTextArea should participate in the searchForm. Figure 30.11 shows the **Configure Virtual Forms** dialog after both virtual forms have been added.

Fig. 30.11 | **Configure Virtual Forms** dialog.

Next, return to **Design** mode and click the **Show Virtual Forms** button (🖳) at the top of the Visual Designer panel to display a legend of the virtual forms on the page. Your virtual forms should be configured as in Fig. 30.12. The **Text Field**s outlined in blue participate in the virtual form addForm. Those outlined in green participate in the virtual form searchForm. The components outlined with a dashed line submit their respective forms. A color key is provided at the bottom right of the **Design** area so that you know which components belong to each virtual form.

Fig. 30.12 | Virtual forms legend.

30.4.2 JSP File with Virtual Forms and an Autocomplete Text Field

Figure 30.13 presents the JSP file generated by NetBeans for this stage of the AddressBook application. We focus only on the new features of this JSP. To enable Ajax capabilities, you must add the attribute webuiJsfx="true" to the webuijsf:head element's start tag (as shown in line 13).

```
 I   <?xml version="1.0" encoding="UTF-8"?>
 2   <!-- Fig. 30.13: AddressBook.jsp -->
 3   <!-- AddressBook JSP with an add form and a Table JSF component. -->
 4   <jsp:root version="2.1" xmlns:f="http://java.sun.com/jsf/core"
 5      xmlns:h="http://java.sun.com/jsf/html"
 6      xmlns:jsp="http://java.sun.com/JSP/Page"
 7      xmlns:webuijsf="http://www.sun.com/webui/webuijsf">
 8   <jsp:directive.page contentType="text/html;charset=UTF-8"
 9      pageEncoding="UTF-8"/>
10      <f:view>
11         <webuijsf:page id="page1">
12            <webuijsf:html id="html1">
13               <webuijsf:head id="head1" webuiJsfx="true">
14                  <webuijsf:link id="link1" url="/resources/stylesheet.css"/>
15               </webuijsf:head>
16               <webuijsf:body id="body1" style="-rave-layout: grid">
```

Fig. 30.13 | AddressBook JSP with an **AutoComplete Text Field** component. (Part 1 of 4.)

```
17              <webuijsf:form id="form1" virtualFormsConfig=
18              "addForm | firstNameTextField lastNameTextField
19              streetTextField cityTextField stateTextField
20              zipTextField | submitButton ,
21              SearchForm | lastNameSearchTextField searchTextArea |
22              searchButton">
23                  <webuijsf:staticText id="instructionText"
24                      style="font-size: 18px; left: 24px; top: 24px;
25                          position: absolute"
26                      text="Add a contact to the address book:"/>
27                  <webuijsf:label for="firstNameTextField"
28                      id="firstNameLabel" style="left: 24px; top: 72px;
29                          position: absolute" text="First name:"/>
30                  <webuijsf:textField
31                      binding="#{AddressBook.firstNameTextField}"
32                      id="firstNameTextField" maxLength="30"
33                      required="true" style="left: 120px; top: 72px;
34                          position: absolute"/>
35                  <webuijsf:label for="lastNameTextField"
36                      id="lastNameLabel" style="left: 25px; top: 96px;
37                          position: absolute" text="Last name:"/>
38                  <webuijsf:textField
39                      binding="#{AddressBook.lastNameTextField}"
40                      id="lastNameTextField" maxLength="30" required="true"
41                      style="left: 120px; top: 96px; position: absolute"/>
42                  <webuijsf:label for="streetTextField" id="streetLabel"
43                      style="left: 49px; top: 120px; position: absolute"
44                      text="Street:"/>
45                  <webuijsf:textField
46                      binding="#{AddressBook.streetTextField}"
47                      id="streetTextField" maxLength="150" required="true"
48                      style="left: 120px; top: 120px; position: absolute"/>
49                  <webuijsf:label for="cityTextField" id="cityLabel"
50                      style="left: 62px; top: 144px; position: absolute"
51                      text="City:"/>
52                  <webuijsf:textField
53                      binding="#{AddressBook.cityTextField}"
54                      id="cityTextField" maxLength="30" required="true"
55                      style="left: 120px; top: 144px; position: absolute"/>
56                  <webuijsf:label for="stateTextField" id="stateLabel"
57                      style="left: 55px; top: 168px; position: absolute"
58                      text="State:"/>
59                  <webuijsf:textField
60                      binding="#{AddressBook.stateTextField}"
61                      id="stateTextField" maxLength="2" required="true"
62                      style="left: 120px; top: 168px; position: absolute"/>
63                  <webuijsf:label for="zipTextField" id="zipLabel"
64                      style="left: 66px; top: 192px; position: absolute"
65                      text="Zip:"/>
66                  <webuijsf:textField
67                      binding="#{AddressBook.zipTextField}"
68                      id="zipTextField" maxLength="5" required="true"
69                      style="left: 120px; top: 192px; position: absolute"/>
```

Fig. 30.13 | AddressBook JSP with an **AutoComplete Text Field** component. (Part 2 of 4.)

```
70                          <webuijsf:button
71                             actionExpression="#{AddressBook.submitButton_action}"
72                             id="submitButton" primary="true" style="left: 47px;
73                                top: 240px; position: absolute; width: 95px"
74                             text="Submit"/>
75                          <webuijsf:button id="clearButton" reset="true"
76                             style="left: 150px; top: 240px; position: absolute;
77                                width: 96px" text="Clear"/>
78                          <webuijsf:table augmentTitle="false"
79                             binding="#{AddressBook.addressesTable}"
80                             id="addressesTable" paginateButton="true"
81                             paginationControls="true" style="left: 24px;
82                                top: 288px; position: absolute"
83                             title="Contacts" width="744">
84                             <webuijsf:tableRowGroup id="tableRowGroup1" rows="5"
85                                sourceData="#{AddressBook.addressesDataProvider}"
86                                sourceVar="currentRow">
87                                <webuijsf:tableColumn headerText="First name"
88                                   id="firstNameColumn"
89                                   sort="ADDRESSES.FIRSTNAME">
90                                   <webuijsf:staticText id="staticText1"
91                                      text="#{currentRow.value[
92                                         'ADDRESSES.FIRSTNAME']}"/>
93                                </webuijsf:tableColumn>
94                                <webuijsf:tableColumn headerText="Last name"
95                                   id="lastNameColumn" sort="ADDRESSES.LASTNAME">
96                                   <webuijsf:staticText id="staticText2"
97                                      text="#{currentRow.value[
98                                         'ADDRESSES.LASTNAME']}"/>
99                                </webuijsf:tableColumn>
100                               <webuijsf:tableColumn headerText="Street"
101                                  id="streetColumn" sort="ADDRESSES.STREET">
102                                  <webuijsf:staticText id="staticText3"
103                                     text="#{currentRow.value[
104                                        'ADDRESSES.STREET']}"/>
105                               </webuijsf:tableColumn>
106                               <webuijsf:tableColumn headerText="City"
107                                  id="cityColumn" sort="ADDRESSES.CITY">
108                                  <webuijsf:staticText id="staticText4"
109                                     text="#{currentRow.value[
110                                        'ADDRESSES.CITY']}"/>
111                               </webuijsf:tableColumn>
112                               <webuijsf:tableColumn headerText="State"
113                                  id="stateColumn" sort="ADDRESSES.STATE">
114                                  <webuijsf:staticText id="staticText5"
115                                     text="#{currentRow.value[
116                                        'ADDRESSES.STATE']}"/>
117                               </webuijsf:tableColumn>
118                               <webuijsf:tableColumn headerText="zip"
119                                  id="zipColumn" sort="ADDRESSES.ZIP">
120                                  <webuijsf:staticText id="staticText6"
121                                     text="#{currentRow.value[
122                                        'ADDRESSES.ZIP']}"/>
123                               </webuijsf:tableColumn>
```

Fig. 30.13 | AddressBook JSP with an **AutoComplete Text Field** component. (Part 3 of 4.)

```
124                              </webuijsf:tableRowGroup>
125                          </webuijsf:table>
126                          <webuijsf:messageGroup id="messageGroup1"
127                              showGlobalOnly="true"
128                              style="left: 264px; top: 72px; position: absolute"/>
129                          <webuijsf:staticText id="searchText"
130                              style="font-size: 18px; left: 24px; top: 516px;
131                                  position: absolute"
132                              text="Search the address book by last name:"/>
133                          <webuijsf:label for="lastNameSearchTextField"
134                              id="lastNameSearchLabel"
135                              style="left: 24px; top: 552px; position: absolute"
136                              text="Last name:"/>
137                          <webuijsf:textField autoComplete="true"
138                              autoCompleteExpression="#{SessionBean1.getOptions}"
139                              binding="#{AddressBook.lastNameSearchTextField}"
140                              id="lastNameSearchTextField" required="true"
141                              style="left: 120px; top: 552px; position: absolute"/>
142                          <webuijsf:button
143                              actionExpression="#{AddressBook.searchButton_action}"
144                              id="searchButton" style="left: 263px; top: 552px;
145                                  position: absolute; width: 38px" text="Find"/>
146                          <webuijsf:textArea
147                              binding="#{AddressBook.searchTextArea}" columns="50"
148                              id="searchTextArea" rows="4" style="left: 336px;
149                                  top: 552px; position: absolute; z-index: 500"/>
150                      </webuijsf:form>
151                  </webuijsf:body>
152              </webuijsf:html>
153          </webuijsf:page>
154      </f:view>
155  </jsp:root>
```

(a) User begins typing in the **Text Field**, and a list of last names that start with the **Text Field**'s contents is displayed.

(b) User selects a name, which is then displayed in the **Text Field**.

(c) User clicks **Find** to locate the contact's data, which is then displayed in the **Text Area**.

Fig. 30.13 | AddressBook JSP with an **AutoComplete Text Field** component. (Part 4 of 4.)

Lines 17–22 configure the virtual forms for this page. Lines 137–141 define the **Text Field** component with the autocomplete functionality. Notice that the **Text Field**'s **auto-Complete** attribute is set to "true", which enables the component to submit Ajax requests to the server. The **Text Field**'s **autoCompleteExpression** attribute is bound to the method that will be called (SessionBean1.getOptions) to provide the list of options the **Text Field** component should suggest. You can set this binding by selecting the **Text Field** and setting the autoCompleteExpression to #{SessionBean1.getOptions} in the **Properties** window. We discuss how to implement the getOptions method in Section 30.4.3.

30.4.3 Providing Suggestions for an Autocomplete Text Field

Figure 30.14 displays the application's session bean file. It includes the **getOptions** method, which provides the suggestions for the autocomplete **Text Field**. Much of the code in this file is identical to Fig. 30.7, so we discuss only the new features here.

```
1   // Fig. 30.14: SessionBean1.java
2   // Session bean initializes the data source for the AddressBook
3   // database and provides Options for the autocomplete capability.
4   package addressbook;
5
6   import com.sun.data.provider.impl.CachedRowSetDataProvider;
7   import com.sun.rave.web.ui.appbase.AbstractSessionBean;
8   import com.sun.sql.rowset.CachedRowSetXImpl;
9   import com.sun.webui.jsf.model.AutoComplete;
10  import javax.faces.FacesException;
11  import com.sun.webui.jsf.model.Option;
12  import java.util.ArrayList;
13
14  public class SessionBean1 extends AbstractSessionBean
15     implements AutoComplete
16  {
17     // To save space, we omitted the code in lines 17-85. The complete
18     // source code is provided with this chapter's examples.
19
86     // search for last names that match the specified filter string
87     public Option[] getOptions( String filter )
88     {
89        // create ArrayList to store matching names as Options
90        ArrayList< Option > list = new ArrayList< Option >();
91
92        // get AddressBook page bean's addressesDataProvider
93        AddressBook addressBook = (AddressBook) getBean( "AddressBook" );
94        CachedRowSetDataProvider addressesDataProvider =
95           addressBook.getAddressesDataProvider();
96
97        try
98        {
99           // move to first row in database
100          boolean hasNext = addressesDataProvider.cursorFirst();
101
102          // while there are records
103          while ( hasNext )
104          {
```

Fig. 30.14 | Session bean initializes the data source for the AddressBook database and provides Options for the autocomplete capability. (Part 1 of 2.)

```
105                // get a name from the database
106                String name =
107                    (String) addressesDataProvider.getValue(
108                    "ADDRESSES.LASTNAME" ) + ", " +
109                    (String) addressesDataProvider.getValue(
110                    "ADDRESSES.FIRSTNAME" );
111
112                // if the name in the database starts with the prefix,
113                // add it to the list of suggestions
114                if ( name.toLowerCase().startsWith( filter.toLowerCase() ) )
115                {
116                    list.add( new Option( name, name ) );
117                } // end if
118                else
119                {
120                    // terminate the loop if the filter prefix is
121                    // alphabetically less than the remaining names
122                    if ( filter.compareTo( name ) < 0 )
123                    {
124                        break;
125                    } // end if
126                } // end else
127
128                // move cursor to next row of database
129                hasNext = addressesDataProvider.cursorNext();
130            } // end while
131        } // end try
132        catch ( Exception ex )
133        {
134            list.add( new Option( ex.getClass().getName(),
135                "Exception getting matching names." ) );
136        } // end catch
137
138        return list.toArray( new Option[ list.size() ] ); // return Options
139    } // end method getOptions
140 } // end class SessionBean1
```

Fig. 30.14 | Session bean initializes the data source for the `AddressBook` database and provides `Option`s for the autocomplete capability. (Part 2 of 2.)

Method `getOptions` (lines 87–139) is invoked after every keystroke in the autocomplete **Text Field** to update the list of suggestions based on what the user typed. The class in which you define `getOptions` must implement the interface `AutoComplete` (package `com.sun.webui.jsf.model`), which declares a `getOptions` method that receives a string (`filter`) containing the text the user has entered and returns an array of `Option`s (package `com.sun.webui.jsf.model`) to be displayed by an autocomplete **Text Field**. The method iterates through the `addressesDataProvider`, retrieves the name from each row, checks whether the name begins with the letters typed so far and, if so, adds the name to `list` (an `ArrayList` of `Option`s created at line 90). Lines 93–95 get the `AddressBook` bean and use it to obtain the `addressesDataProvider`. Line 100 sets the cursor to the first row in the data provider. Line 103 determines whether there are more rows in the data provider. If so, lines 106–110 retrieve the last and first names from the current row and create a `String` in the format *last name, first name*. Line 114 compares the lowercase versions of name and filter to determine whether the name starts with the characters in filter (i.e, the characters typed so far). If so, the name is a match, and line 116 adds it to list.

Recall that the data provider wraps a CachedRowSet object containing a SQL query which returns the rows in the database sorted by last name, then first name. This allows us to stop iterating through the data provider once we reach a row whose name comes alphabetically after the text entered by the user—names in the rows beyond this will all be alphabetically greater and thus are not potential matches. If the name does not match the text entered so far, line 122 tests whether the current name is alphabetically greater than the filter. If so, line 124 terminates the loop.

Performance Tip 30.1

*When using database columns to provide suggestions in an autocomplete **Text Field**, sorting the columns eliminates the need to check every row in the database for potential matches. This significantly improves autocomplete performance when dealing with a large database.*

If the name is neither a match nor alphabetically greater than filter, line 129 moves the cursor to the next row in the data provider. While there are more rows, the loop checks whether the name in the next row matches the filter and should be added to list.

Lines 132–136 catch any exceptions generated while searching the database. Lines 134–135 add text to the suggestion box indicating the error to the user.

Once the loop terminates, line 138 converts the ArrayList of Options to an array of Options and returns the array. The data in the array is sent to the client web browser as the response to the initial Ajax request, then used to display a drop-down list of the matching database entries. This is handled by the Dojo JavaScript code that JSF outputs to render the **Text Field** component on the client. The user can click one of the displayed entries to select it, then press the **Find** button to display the selected contact's information. We discuss the **Find** button's event handler next.

30.4.4 Displaying the Contact's Information

Figure 30.15 displays the page bean file for the JSP in Fig. 30.13. The event-handling method searchButton_action displays the selected contact's information. Much of the code in this file is identical to Fig. 30.8, so we show only the new features here.

```
 1   // Fig. 30.15: AddressBook.java
 2   // Page bean for adding a contact to the address book
 3   // and displaying a contact's information
 4   package addressbook;
 5
 6   import com.sun.data.provider.RowKey;
 7   import com.sun.data.provider.impl.CachedRowSetDataProvider;
 8   import com.sun.rave.web.ui.appbase.AbstractPageBean;
 9   import com.sun.webui.jsf.component.Table;
10   import com.sun.webui.jsf.component.TextArea;
11   import com.sun.webui.jsf.component.TextField;
12   import javax.faces.FacesException;
13
```

Fig. 30.15 | Page bean that suggests names in the **AutoComplete Text Field**. (Part 1 of 3.)

```
14    public class AddressBook extends AbstractPageBean
15    {
16        // To save space, we omitted the code in lines 16-121. The complete
17        // source code is provided with this chapter's examples.
18
122       private TextField lastNameSearchTextField = new TextField();
123
124       public TextField getLastNameSearchTextField()
125       {
126           return lastNameSearchTextField;
127       }
128
129       public void setLastNameSearchTextField( TextField tf )
130       {
131           this.lastNameSearchTextField = tf;
132       }
133
134       private TextArea searchTextArea = new TextArea();
135
136       public TextArea getSearchTextArea()
137       {
138           return searchTextArea;
139       }
140
141       public void setSearchTextArea( TextArea ta )
142       {
143           this.searchTextArea = ta;
144       }
145
146       // To save space, we omitted the code in lines 146-250. The complete
147       // source code is provided with this chapter's examples.
148
251       // locate and display the selected contact's information
252       public String searchButton_action()
253       {
254           // get selected name and split into tokens
255           String name = lastNameSearchTextField.getText().toString();
256           String[] names = name.split( ", " );
257
258           // locate the RowKey for the row in database containing this name
259           RowKey row = addressesDataProvider.findFirst(
260               new String[] { "ADDRESSES.LASTNAME", "ADDRESSES.FIRSTNAME" },
261               new String[] { names[0], names[1] } );
262
263           // move to the row in the database
264           addressesDataProvider.setCursorRow( row );
265
266           // obtain contact information
267           String result = name + "\n" +
268               addressesDataProvider.getValue( "ADDRESSES.STREET" ) + "\n" +
269               addressesDataProvider.getValue( "ADDRESSES.CITY" ) + ", " +
270               addressesDataProvider.getValue( "ADDRESSES.STATE" ) + " " +
271               addressesDataProvider.getValue( "ADDRESSES.ZIP" ) + "\n";
272
```

Fig. 30.15 | Page bean that suggests names in the **AutoComplete Text Field**. (Part 2 of 3.)

```
273            searchTextArea.setText( result ); // display the contact information
274            return null;
275         } // end method searchButton_action
276      } // end class AddressBook
```

Fig. 30.15 | Page bean that suggests names in the **AutoComplete Text Field**. (Part 3 of 3.)

Lines 252–275 define method searchButton_action. Line 255 obtains the text from the lastNameSearchTextField, then line 256 parses the name into a last name and a first name. Note that the getText method (line 255) returns an Object, so we must invoke toString on that Object to get its String representation. Lines 259–261 use the address-DataProvider's findFirst method to find the first entry in the database with the specified last name and first name. This method returns a RowKey that uniquely identifies that row in the database table. Line 264 moves the cursor to that row. Lines 267–271 obtain the remaining data for the contact and build a result string, which is then displayed in the **Text Area** (line 273).

30.5 Wrap-Up

In this chapter, we presented a case study on building a web application that interacts with a database and provides rich user interaction using an Ajax-enabled JSF component. We first built an AddressBook application that allowed a user to add and browse contacts. You learned how to insert user input into a Java DB database and how to display the contents of a database on a web page using a **Table** JSF component. You also learned that some of the Woodstock JSF components are Ajax enabled. We extended the AddressBook application to include an autocomplete **Text Field** component. We showed how to use a database to display suggestions as the user types in the **Text Field**. You also learned how to use virtual forms to submit subsets of a form's input components to the server for processing. In Chapter 31, you'll use NetBeans to create web services and consume them from desktop and web applications.

Summary

Section 30.2 Accessing Databases in Web Applications
- Setting a **Button**'s primary property to true (checked) makes it more prominent on the page and allows the user to submit a form by pressing *Enter* rather than by clicking the button.
- Setting a **Button**'s reset property to true (checked) prevents validation when the user clicks the button and automatically configures the button to reset all of the page's input fields.
- The **Table** component formats and displays data from database tables.
- To create a Java DB database, in the NetBeans **Services** tab, expand the **Databases** node, then right click **Java DB** and select **Create Database...**. After you create a database, the **Services** tab will have a new entry in the **Databases** node showing the URL of the database.
- You can use the **Services** tab to create database tables and to execute SQL statements that manipulate the database. NetBeans must be connected to the database to execute SQL statements. If NetBeans is connected to the database, the icon ▦ appears next to the database's URL; otherwise, the icon ▦ appears—in this case, right click the icon and select **Connect...**.
- You can view the data in the table by expanding the **Tables** node, right clicking the table and selecting **View Data...**.

- To bind a database table to a **Table** component, drag the database table from the **Services** tab and drop it on the **Table** component.

- To select specific columns to display, right click the **Table** component and select **Bind to Data** to display the **Bind to Data** dialog containing the list of the columns in the database table.

- By default, the **Table** uses the database table's column names in all uppercase letters as headings. To change these headings, select a column in **Design** mode and edit its headerText property in the **Properties** window.

- Setting a **Table**'s paginationControls property to true configures this **Table** for automatic pagination and provides buttons for moving forward and backward between records.

- Setting a **Table**'s internalVirtualForm property to true prevents the **Table**'s pagination buttons from submitting the entire form when the user is navigating through pages of records.

- A CachedRowSetDataProvider provides a scrollable RowSet that can be bound to a **Table** component to display the RowSet's data. This data provider is a wrapper for a CachedRowSet object.

- A **Message Group** component displays system messages, such as error messages when an attempt to manipulate a database fails. Set the **Message Group**'s showGlobalOnly property to true to prevent component-level validation error messages from being displayed here.

- Every row in a CachedRowSetDataProvider has its own key; method appendRow returns the key for the new row.

- Calling method commitChanges of class CachedRowSetDataProvider updates the database based on the changes to the CachedRowSetDataProvider.

- CachedRowSetDataProvider method refresh reexecutes the CachedRowSet's SQL statement.

Section 30.3 Ajax-Enabled JSF Components
- The term Ajax—short for Asynchronous JavaScript and XML—was coined by Jesse James Garrett of Adaptive Path, Inc., in February 2005 to describe a range of technologies for developing highly responsive, dynamic web applications.

- Ajax separates the user interaction portion of an application from its server interaction, enabling both to proceed asynchronously in parallel. This enables Ajax web-based applications to perform at speeds approaching those of desktop applications.

- Ajax makes asynchronous calls to the server to exchange small amounts of data with each call. Where normally the entire page would be submitted and reloaded with every user interaction on a web page, Ajax reloads only the necessary portions of the page, saving time and resources.

- Ajax applications typically make use of client-side scripting technologies such as JavaScript to interact with page elements. They use the browser's XMLHttpRequest object to perform the asynchronous exchanges with the web server that make Ajax applications so responsive.

- Ajax libraries—such as the Dojo Toolkit used by JSF—make it possible to reap Ajax's benefits without the labor of writing "raw" Ajax.

- In a traditional web application, the user fills in a form's fields, then submits the form. The browser generates a request to the server, which receives the request and processes it. The server generates and sends a response containing the exact page that the browser will render. The browser loads the new page, temporarily making the browser window blank. The client *waits* for the server to respond and *reloads the entire page* with the data from the response. While such a synchronous request is being processed on the server, the user cannot interact with the web page. This model yields "choppy" application performance.

- In an Ajax application, when the user interacts with the page, the client creates an XMLHttpRequest object to manage a request. This object sends the request to the server and awaits the response. The requests are asynchronous, so the user can interact with the application on the client side while the server processes the earlier request concurrently. Other user interactions could result in additional requests to the server. Once the server responds to the original request, the XML-HttpRequest object that issued the request calls a client-side function to process the data returned by the server. This callback function uses partial page updates to display the data in the existing web page *without reloading the entire page*. At the same time, the server may be responding to the second request and the client side may be starting to do another partial page update.

• Partial page updates help make web applications more responsive, making them feel more like desktop applications.

Section 30.4 Creating an AutoComplete Text Field and Using Virtual Forms

• Virtual forms are used when you would like a button to submit a subset of the page's input fields to the server and for displaying multiple forms on the same page. You specify a submitter component and one or more participant components for a form. When the submitter component is clicked, only the values of its participant components will be submitted to the server.

• To add virtual forms to the page, right click a **Button** on the page and select **Configure Virtual Forms...** to display the **Configure Virtual Forms** dialog. Click **New** to add a virtual form, then click in the **Name** column and change the new form's name. Double click the cell under the **Submit** column and change the option to **Yes** to indicate that this button should submit the virtual form. Click **OK** to exit the dialog. Next, hold the *Ctrl* key and click each component that should be submitted as part of the virtual form. Right click one of the selected components and choose **Configure Virtual Forms....** Double click the cell under the virtual form's **Participate** column to change the option to **Yes**, indicating that the values in these components should be submitted to the server when the form is submitted. Click **OK** to exit.

• In **Design** mode, click the **Show Virtual Forms** button ( ) to display a legend of the virtual forms on the page. The components outlined with a dashed line submit their respective forms. A color key at the bottom right of the **Design** area shows which components belong to each virtual form.

• Set a **Text Field**'s autoComplete attribute to "true" to enable the component to submit Ajax requests to the server. The **Text Field**'s autoCompleteExpression attribute is bound to the method that will be called to provide the list of options the **Text Field** component should suggest.

• Method getOptions is invoked after every keystroke in the autocomplete **Text Field** to update the list of suggestions based on what the user typed. The class in which you define getOptions must implement interface AutoComplete (package com.sun.webui.jsf.model), which declares method getOptions, receives a string containing the text the user has entered and returns an array of Options (package com.sun.webui.jsf.model) to be displayed by an autocomplete **Text Field**.

Terminology

Self-Review Exercises

30.1 State whether each of the following is *true* or *false*. If *false*, explain why.
  a) The **Table** JSF component allows you to lay out other components and text in tabular format.
  b) Virtual forms allow multiple forms, each with its own **Submit** button, to be displayed on the same web page.
  c) A CachedRowSetDataProvider is stored in the SessionBean and executes SQL queries to provide Table components with data to display.
  d) The XMLHttpRequest object provides access to a page's request object.
  e) You set a **Text Field**'s autoComplete attribute to "true" to enable the component to submit Ajax requests to the server.
  f) A data provider automatically reexecutes its SQL command to provide updated database information at every page refresh.

30.2 Fill in the blanks in each of the following statements.
  a) Ajax is an acronym for _____.
  b) Method _____ of class _____ updates a database to reflect any changes made in the database's data provider.
  c) A virtual form specifies that certain JSF components are _____ whose data will be submitted when the submitter component is clicked.

Answers to Self-Review Exercises

30.1 a) False. Table components are used to display data from databases. b) True. c) False. The CachedRowSetDataProvider is a property of the page bean. It wraps a CachedRowSet, which is stored in the SessionBean and executes SQL queries. d) False. The XMLHttpRequest object is an object that allows asynchronous exchanges with a web server. e) True. f) False. You must call method refresh on the data provider to reexecute the SQL command.

30.2 a) Asynchronous JavaScript and XML. b) commitChanges, CachedRowSetDataProvider. c) participants.

Exercises

30.3 *(Guestbook Application)* Create a JSF web page that allows users to sign and view a guestbook. Use the Guestbook database to store guestbook entries. [*Note:* A SQL script to create the Guestbook database is provided in the examples directory for this chapter.] The Guestbook database has a single table, Messages, which has four columns: Date, Name, Email and Message. The database already contains a few sample entries. On the web page, provide **Text Fields** for the user's name and email address and a **Text Area** for the message. Add a **Submit Button** and a **Table** component and configure the **Table** to display guestbook entries. Use the **Submit Button**'s action-handler method to insert a new row containing the user's input and today's date into the Guestbook database.

A client is to me a mere unit, a factor in a problem.
—Sir Arthur Conan Doyle

They also serve who only stand and wait.
—John Milton

...if the simplest things of nature have a message that you understand, rejoice, for your soul is alive.
—Eleonora Duse

Protocol is everything.
—Francoise Giuliani

Web Services

Objectives

In this chapter you will learn:

- What a web service is.
- How to publish and consume web services in NetBeans.
- How XML, JSON, XML-Based Simple Object Access Protocol (SOAP) and Representational State Transfer (REST) Architecture enable Java web services.
- The elements that comprise services.
- How to create client desktop and web applications that consume web services.
- How to use session tracking in web services to maintain client state information.
- How to connect to databases from web services.
- How to pass objects of user-defined types to and return them from a web service.

31.1 Introduction

This chapter introduces web services, which promote software portability and reusability in applications that operate over the Internet. A **web service** is a software component stored on one computer that can be accessed by an application (or other software component) on another computer over a network. Web services communicate using such technologies as XML, JSON and HTTP. In this chapter, we use two Java APIs that facilitate web services. The first, **JAX-WS**, is based on the **Simple Object Access Protocol (SOAP)**—an XML-based protocol that allows web services and clients to communicate, even if the client and the web service are written in different languages. The second, **JAX-RS**, uses **Representational State Transfer (REST)**—a network architecture that uses the web's traditional request/response mechanisms such as GET and POST requests. For more information on SOAP-based and REST-based web services, visit our Web Services Resource Centers:

```
www.deitel.com/WebServices/
www.deitel.com/RESTWebServices/
```

These Resource Centers include information about designing and implementing web services in many languages and about web services offered by companies such as Google, Amazon and eBay. You'll also find many additional tools for publishing and consuming web services. For more information about REST-based Java web services, check out the Jersey project:

```
jersey.dev.java.net/
```

The XML used in this chapter is created and manipulated for you by the APIs, so you need not know the details of XML to use it here. If you wish to learn more about XML, read the following tutorials:

```
www.deitel.com/articles/xml_tutorials/20060401/XMLBasics/
www.deitel.com/articles/xml_tutorials/20060401/XMLStructuringData/
```

and visit our XML Resource Center:

```
www.deitel.com/XML/
```

Business-to-Business Transactions

Rather than relying on proprietary applications, businesses can conduct transactions via standardized, widely available web services. This has important implications for **business-to-business (B2B) transactions**. Web services are platform and language independent, enabling companies to collaborate without worrying about the compatibility of their hardware, software and communications technologies. Companies such as Amazon, Google, eBay, PayPal and many others are benefiting by making their server-side applications available to partners via web services.

By purchasing some web services and using other free ones that are relevant to their businesses, companies can spend less time developing applications and can create new ones that are more innovative. E-businesses for example, can provide their customers with enhanced shopping experiences. Consider an online music store. The store's website links to information about various CDs, enabling users to purchase them, to learn about the artists, to find more titles by those artists, to find other artists' music they may enjoy, and more. The store's website may also link to the site of a company that sells concert tickets and provides a web service that displays upcoming concert dates for various artists, allowing users to buy tickets. By consuming the concert-ticket web service on its site, the online music store can provide an additional service to its customers, increase its site traffic and perhaps earn a commission on concert-ticket sales. The company that sells concert tickets also benefits from the business relationship by selling more tickets and possibly by receiving revenue from the online music store for the use of the web service.

Any Java programmer with a knowledge of web services can write applications that "consume" web services. The resulting applications would invoke web services running on servers that could be thousands of miles away.

NetBeans

NetBeans is one of the many tools that enable you to "publish" and/or "consume" web services. We demonstrate how to use NetBeans to implement web services using the JAX-

WS and JAX-RS APIs and how to invoke them from client applications. For each example, we provide the web service's code, then present a client application that uses the web service. Our first examples build simple web services and client applications in NetBeans. Then we demonstrate web services that use more sophisticated features, such as manipulating databases with JDBC and manipulating class objects. For information on downloading and installing the NetBeans and the GlassFish v2 UR2 server, see Section 29.1.

31.2 Web Service Basics

The machine on which a web service resides is referred to as a **web service host**. The client application sends a request over a network to the web service host, which processes the request and returns a response over the network to the application. This kind of distributed computing benefits systems in various ways. For example, an application without direct access to data on another system might be able to retrieve the data via a web service. Similarly, an application lacking the processing power to perform specific computations could use a web service to take advantage of another system's superior resources.

In Java, a web service is implemented as a class. In previous chapters, all the pieces of an application resided on one machine. The class that represents the web service resides on a server—it's not part of the client application. Making a web service available to receive client requests is known as **publishing a web service**; using a web service from a client application is known as **consuming a web service**.

31.3 Simple Object Access Protocol (SOAP)

The Simple Object Access Protocol (SOAP) is a platform-independent protocol that uses XML to make remote procedure calls, typically over HTTP. You can view the SOAP specification at www.w3.org/TR/soap/. Each request and response is packaged in a **SOAP message**—XML markup containing the information that a web service requires to process the message. SOAP messages are written in XML so that they are computer readable, human readable and platform independent. Most **firewalls**—security barriers that restrict communication among networks—allow HTTP traffic to pass through, so that clients can browse the web by sending requests to and receiving responses from web servers. Thus, SOAP-based services can send and receive SOAP messages over HTTP connections with few limitations.

SOAP supports an extensive set of types. The **wire format** used to transmit requests and responses must support all types passed between the applications. SOAP types include the primitive types (e.g., `int`), as well as `DateTime`, `XmlNode` and others. SOAP can also transmit arrays of these types.

When a program invokes a method of a SOAP web service, the request and all relevant information are packaged in a SOAP message enclosed in a **SOAP envelope** and sent to the server on which the web service resides. When the web service receives this SOAP message, it parses the XML representing the message, then processes the message's contents. The message specifies the method that the client wishes to execute and the arguments the client passed to that method. Next, the web service calls the method with the specified arguments (if any) and sends the response back to the client in another SOAP message. The client parses the response to retrieve the method's result. In Section 31.6, you'll build and consume a basic SOAP web service.

31.4 Representational State Transfer (REST)

Representational State Transfer (REST) refers to an architectural style for implementing web services. Such web services are often called **RESTful web services**. Though REST itself is not a standard, RESTful web services are implemented using web standards. Each method in a RESTful web service is identified by a unique URL. Thus, when the server receives a request, it immediately knows what operation to perform. Such web services can be used in a program or directly from a web browser. The results of a particular operation may be cached locally by the browser when the service is invoked with a GET request. This can make subsequent requests for the same operation faster by loading the result directly from the browser's cache. Amazon's web services (aws.amazon.com) are RESTful, as are many others.

RESTful web services are alternatives to those implemented with SOAP. Unlike SOAP-based web services, the request and response of REST services are not wrapped in envelopes. REST is also not limited to returning data in XML format. It can use a variety of formats, such as XML, JSON, HTML, plain text and media files. In Sections 31.7–31.8, you'll build and consume basic RESTful web services.

31.5 JavaScript Object Notation (JSON)

JavaScript Object Notation (JSON) is an alternative to XML for representing data. JSON is a text-based data-interchange format used to represent objects in JavaScript as collections of name/value pairs represented as Strings. It is commonly used in Ajax applications. JSON is a simple format that makes objects easy to read, create and parse and, because it is much less verbose than XML, allows programs to transmit data efficiently across the Internet . Each JSON object is represented as a list of property names and values contained in curly braces, in the following format:

{ *propertyName1* : *value1*, *propertyName2* : *value2* }

Arrays are represented in JSON with square brackets in the following format:

[*value1*, *value2*, *value3*]

Each value in an array can be a string, a number, a JSON object, true, false or null. To appreciate the simplicity of JSON data, examine this representation of an array of address-book entries:

```
[ { first: 'Cheryl', last: 'Black' },
  { first: 'James', last: 'Blue' },
  { first: 'Mike', last: 'Brown' },
  { first: 'Meg', last: 'Gold' } ]
```

Many programming languages now support the JSON data format. An extensive list of JSON libraries sorted by language can be found at www.json.org.

31.6 Publishing and Consuming SOAP-Based Web Services

This section presents our first example of publishing (enabling for client access) and consuming (using) a web service. We begin with a SOAP-based web service.

31.6.1 Creating a Web Application Project and Adding a Web Service Class in NetBeans

When you create a web service in NetBeans, you focus on its logic and let the IDE handle its infrastructure. To create a web service in NetBeans, you first create a **Web Application project**. NetBeans uses this project type for web services that are invoked by other applications.

Creating a Web Application Project in NetBeans
To create a web application, perform the following steps:

1. Select **File > New Project...** to open the **New Project** dialog.

2. Select **Java Web** from the dialog's **Categories** list, then select **Web Application** from the **Projects** list. Click **Next >**.

3. Specify the name of your project (WelcomeSOAP) in the **Project Name** field and specify where you'd like to store the project in the **Project Location** field. You can click the **Browse** button to select the location. Click **Next >**.

4. Select **GlassFish v2** from the **Server** drop-down list and **Java EE 5** from the **Java EE Version** drop-down list.

5. Click **Finish** to dismiss the **New Project** dialog.

This creates a web application that will run in a web browser, similar to the projects used in Chapters 29 and 30.

Adding a Web Service Class to a Web Application Project
Perform the following steps to add a web service class to the project:

1. In the **Projects** tab in NetBeans, right click the **WelcomeSOAP** project's node and select **New > Web Service...** to open the **New Web Service** dialog.

2. Specify WelcomeSOAP in the **Web Service Name** field.

3. Specify com.deitel.welcomesoap in the **Package** field.

4. Click **Finish** to dismiss the **New Web Service** dialog.

The IDE generates a sample web service class with the name you specified in *Step 2*. You can find this class in the **Projects** tab under the project's **Web Services** node. In this class, you'll define the methods that your web service makes available to client applications. When you eventually build your application, the IDE will generate other supporting files (which we'll discuss shortly) for your web service.

31.6.2 Defining the WelcomeSOAP Web Service in NetBeans

Figure 31.1 contains the WelcomeSOAP web service's code. You can implement this code yourself in the WelcomeSOAP.java file created in Section 31.6.1, or you can simply replace the code in WelcomeSOAP.java with a copy of our code from this example's folder. You can find this file in the project's src\java\com\deitel\welcomesoap folder. The book's examples can be downloaded from www.deitel.com/books/jhtp8/.

Lines 5–7 import the annotations used in this example. By default, each new web service class created with the JAX-WS APIs is a **POJO (plain old Java object)**, meaning that—unlike prior web services APIs—you do not need to extend a class or implement an

```
 1   // Fig. 31.1: WelcomeSOAP.java
 2   // Web service that returns a welcome message via SOAP.
 3   package com.deitel.welcomesoap;
 4
 5   import javax.jws.WebService; // program uses the annotation @WebService
 6   import javax.jws.WebMethod; // program uses the annotation @WebMethod
 7   import javax.jws.WebParam; // program uses the annotation @WebParam
 8
 9   @WebService( // annotates the class as a web service
10      name = "WelcomeSOAP", // sets service endpoint interface name
11      serviceName = "WelcomeSOAPService" ) // sets the service name
12   public class WelcomeSOAP
13   {
14      // WebMethod that returns welcome message
15      @WebMethod( operationName = "welcome" )
16      public String welcome( @WebParam( name = "name" ) String name )
17      {
18         return "Welcome to JAX-WS web services with SOAP, " + name + "!";
19      } // end method welcome
20   } // end class WelcomeSOAP
```

Fig. 31.1 | Web service that returns a welcome message via SOAP.

interface to create a web service. When you deploy a web application containing a class that uses the @WebService annotation, the server (GlassFish in our case) recognizes that the class implements a web service and creates all the **server-side artifacts** that support the web service—that is, the framework that allows the web service to wait for client requests and respond to those requests once it is deployed on an application server. Some popular open-source application servers that support Java web services include GlassFish (glassfish.dev.java.net), Apache Tomcat (tomcat.apache.org) and JBoss Application Server (www.jboss.com/products/platforms/application).

Lines 9–11 contain a @WebService annotation (imported at line 5) with properties name and serviceName. The **@WebService annotation** indicates that class WelcomeSOAP implements a web service. The annotation is followed by parentheses containing optional annotation attributes. The **name attribute** (line 10) specifies the name of the service endpoint interface class that will be generated for the client. A **service endpoint interface** (SEI) class (sometimes called a **proxy class**) is used to interact with the web service—a client application consumes the web service by invoking methods on the service endpoint interface object. The **serviceName attribute** (line 11) specifies the service name, which is also the name of the class that the client uses to obtain a service endpoint interface object. If the serviceName attribute is not specified, the web service's name is assumed to be the java class name followed by the word Service. NetBeans places the @WebService annotation at the beginning of each new web service class you create. You can then add the name and serviceName properties in the parentheses following the annotation.

The WelcomeSOAP service has only one method, welcome (lines 15–19), which takes the user's name as a String and returns a String containing a welcome message. This method is tagged with the **@WebMethod annotation** to indicate that it can be called remotely. Any methods that are not tagged with @WebMethod are not accessible to clients that consume the web service. Such methods are typically utility methods within the web service class. Note that the @WebMethod annotation uses the **operationName** attribute to specify the method name that is exposed to the web service's client. If the `operationName` is not specified, it is set to the actual Java method's name.

Common Programming Error 31.1

Failing to expose a method as a web method by declaring it with the @WebMethod annotation prevents clients of the web service from accessing the method. There is one exception—if none of the class's methods are declared with the @WebMethod annotation, then all the `public` methods of the class will be exposed as web methods.

Common Programming Error 31.2

Methods with the @WebMethod annotation cannot be static. An object of the web service class must exist for a client to access the service's web methods.

The `name` parameter to `welcome` is annotated with the **@WebParam annotation** (line 16). The optional @WebParam attribute **name** indicates the parameter name that is exposed to the web service's clients. If you don't specify the name, the actual parameter name is used.

31.6.3 Publishing the WelcomeSOAP Web Service from NetBeans

Now that we've created the `WelcomeSOAP` web service class, we'll use NetBeans to build and publish (i.e., deploy) the web service so that clients can consume its services. NetBeans handles all the details of building and deploying a web service for you. This includes creating the framework required to support the web service. Right click the project name (`WelcomeSOAP`) in the NetBeans **Projects** tab to display the pop-up menu in Fig. 31.2. To determine if there are any compilation errors in your project, select **Build**. When the project compiles successfully, you can select **Deploy** to deploy it to the server you selected when you set up the web application in Section 31.6.1. If the code in the project has changed since the last build, selecting **Deploy** also builds the project. Selecting **Run** executes the web application. If the web application was not previously built or deployed, this option performs these tasks first. Note that both the **Deploy** and **Run** options also start the application server (in our case GlassFish) if it is not already running. To ensure that all source-code

Fig. 31.2 | A portion of the pop-up menu that appears when you right click a project name in the NetBeans **Projects** tab.

files in a project are recompiled during the next build operation, you can use the **Clean** or **Clean and Build** options. If you have not already done so, select **Deploy** now. [*Note:* You can also publish a web service using a standard Java SE 6 application. For more information, see the article today.java.net/pub/a/today/2007/07/03/jax-ws-web-services-without-ee-containers.html.]

31.6.4 Testing the WelcomeSOAP Web Service with GlassFish Application Server's Tester Web Page

The next step is to test the WelcomeSOAP web service. We previously selected the GlassFish application server to execute this web application. This server can dynamically create a web page for testing a web service's methods from a web browser. To use this capability:

1. Expand the project's **Web Services** in the NetBeans **Projects** tab.

2. Right click the web service class name (WelcomeSOAP) and select **Test Web Service**.

The GlassFish application server builds the Tester web page and loads it into your web browser. Figure 31.3 shows the Tester web page for the WelcomeSOAP web service.

Fig. 31.3 | Tester web page created by GlassFish for the WelcomeSOAP web service.

Once you've deployed the web service, you can also type the URL

http://localhost:8080/WelcomeSOAP/WelcomeSOAPService?Tester

in your web browser to view the Tester web page. Note that WelcomeSOAPService is the name (specified in line 11 of Fig. 31.1) that clients use to access the web service.

To test WelcomeSOAP's web method, type your name in the text field to the right of the **welcome** button, then click the button to invoke the method and see the result. Figure 31.4 shows the results of invoking WelcomeSOAP's welcome method with the value John.

Note that you can access the web service only when the application server is running. If NetBeans launches the application server for you, it will automatically shut it down when you close NetBeans. To keep the application server up and running, you can launch it independently of NetBeans before you deploy or run web applications in NetBeans. See the GlassFish Quick Start Guide at glassfish.dev.java.net/downloads/quickstart/index.html for information on starting and stopping the server manually.

(a) Invoking the `WelcomeSOAP` web service's `welcome` method

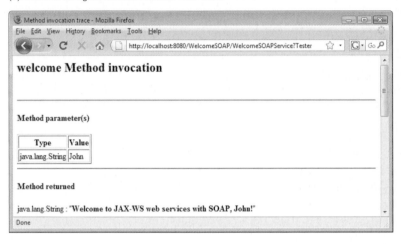

(b) Results of calling the `welcome` method with `"John"`

Fig. 31.4 | Testing `WelcomeSOAP`'s `welcome` method.

Testing the *WelcomeSOAP* Web Service from Another Computer

If your computer is connected to a network and allows HTTP requests, then you can test the web service from another computer on the network by typing the following URL (where *host* is the hostname or IP address of the computer on which the web service is deployed) into a browser on another computer:

```
http://host:8080/WelcomeSOAP/WelcomeSOAPService?Tester
```

Note to *Windows XP and Windows Vista Users*

For security reasons, computers running Windows XP or Windows Vista do not allow HTTP requests from other computers by default. To allow other computers to connect to your computer using HTTP, perform the following steps on Windows XP:

1. Select **Start > Control Panel** to open your system's **Control Panel** window, then double click **Windows Firewall** to view the **Windows Firewall** settings dialog.

2. In the **Windows Firewall** dialog, click the **Exceptions** tab, then click **Add Port...** and add port 8080 with the name GlassFish.

3. Click **OK** to dismiss the **Windows Firewall** settings dialog.

To allow other computers to connect to your Windows Vista computer using HTTP, perform the following steps:

1. Open the **Control Panel**, switch to **Classic View** and double click **Windows Firewall** to open the **Windows Firewall** dialog.

2. In the **Windows Firewall** dialog click the **Change Settings...** link.

3. In the **Windows Firewall** dialog, click the **Exceptions** tab, then click **Add Port...** and add port 8080 with the name GlassFish.

4. Click **OK** to dismiss the **Windows Firewall** settings dialog.

You may also be asked to unblock java.exe the first time you run the GlassFish server.

31.6.5 Describing a Web Service with the Web Service Description Language (WSDL)

To consume a web service, a client must determine its functionality and how to use it. For this purpose, web services normally contain a **service description**. This is an XML document that conforms to the **Web Service Description Language** (WSDL)—an XML vocabulary that defines the methods a web service makes available and how clients interact with them. The WSDL document also specifies lower-level information that clients might need, such as the required formats for requests and responses.

WSDL documents help applications determine how to interact with the web services described in the documents. You do not need to understand WSDL to take advantage of it—the GlassFish application server generates a web service's WSDL dynamically for you, and client tools can parse the WSDL to help create the client-side service endpoint interface class that a client uses to access the web service. Since GlassFish (and most other servers) generate the WSDL dynamically, clients always receive a deployed web service's most up-to-date description. To view the WSDL for the WelcomeSOAP web service, enter the following URL in your browser:

```
http://localhost:8080/WelcomeSOAP/WelcomeSOAPService?WSDL
```

or click the **WSDL File** link in the Tester web page (shown in Fig. 31.3).

Accessing the WelcomeSOAP Web Service's WSDL from Another Computer
Eventually, you'll want clients on other computers to use your web service. Such clients need access to the web service's WSDL, which they would access with the following URL:

```
http://host:8080/WelcomeSOAP/WelcomeSOAPService?WSDL
```

where *host* is the hostname or IP address of the server that hosts the web service. As we discussed in Section 31.6.4, this works only if your computer allows HTTP connections from other computers—as is the case for publicly accessible web and application servers.

31.6.6 Creating a Client to Consume the WelcomeSOAP Web Service

Now that you've defined and deployed the web service, let's consume it from a client application. A web service client can be any type of application or even another web service. You enable a Java-based client application to consume a web service by **adding a web service reference** to the client application. This process defines the service endpoint interface class that allows the client to access the web service.

An application that consumes a web service consists of an object of a service endpoint interface (SEI) class (sometimes called a proxy class) that's used to interact with the web service and a client application that consumes the web service by invoking methods on the service endpoint interface object. The client code invokes methods on the service endpoint interface object, which handles the details of passing method arguments to and receiving return values from the web service on the client's behalf. This communication can occur over a local network, over the Internet or even with a web service on the same computer. The web service performs the corresponding task and returns the results to the service endpoint interface object, which then returns the results to the client code. Figure 31.5 depicts the interactions among the client code, the SEI object and the web service. As you'll soon see, NetBeans creates these service endpoint interface classes for you.

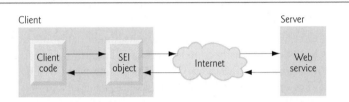

Fig. 31.5 | Interaction between a web service client and a web service.

Requests to and responses from web services created with **JAX-WS** (one of many different web service frameworks) are typically transmitted via SOAP. Any client capable of generating and processing SOAP messages can interact with a web service, regardless of the language in which the web service is written.

We now use NetBeans to create a client Java desktop GUI application. Then you'll add a web service reference to the project so the client can access the web service. When you add the reference, the IDE creates and compiles the **client-side artifacts**—the framework of Java code that supports the client-side service endpoint interface class. The client then calls methods on an object of the service endpoint interface class, which uses the rest of the artifacts to interact with the web service.

Step 1: Creating a Desktop Application Project in NetBeans

Before performing the steps in this section, ensure that the WelcomeSOAP web service has been deployed and that the GlassFish application server is running (see Section 31.6.3). Perform the following steps to create a client Java desktop application in NetBeans:

1. Select **File > New Project...** to open the **New Project** dialog.

2. Select **Java** from the **Categories** list and **Java Application** from the **Projects** list, then click **Next >**.

3. Specify the name WelcomeSOAPClient in the **Project Name** field and uncheck the **Create Main Class** checkbox. Later, you'll add a subclass of JFrame that contains a main method.

4. Click **Finish** to create the project.

Step 2: Adding a Web Service Reference to an Application

Next, you'll add a web service reference to your application so that it can interact with the WelcomeSOAP web service. To add a web service reference, perform the following steps.

1. Right click the project name (`WelcomeSOAPClient`) in the NetBeans **Projects** tab and select **New > Web Service Client…** from the pop-up menu to display the **New Web Service Client** dialog (Fig. 31.6).

Fig. 31.6 | **New Web Service Client** dialog.

2. In the **WSDL URL** field, specify the URL `http://localhost:8080/WelcomeSOAP/WelcomeSOAPService?WSDL` (Fig. 31.6). This URL tells the IDE where to find the web service's WSDL description. [*Note:* If the GlassFish application server is located on a different computer, replace `localhost` with the hostname or IP address of that computer.] The IDE uses this WSDL description to generate the client-side artifacts that compose and support the service endpoint interface. Note that the **New Web Service Client** dialog enables you to search for web services in several locations. Many companies simply distribute the exact WSDL URLs for their web services, which you can place in the **WSDL URL** field.

3. Click **Finish** to create the web service reference and dismiss the **New Web Service Client** dialog.

In the NetBeans **Projects** tab, the `WelcomeSOAPClient` project now contains a **Web Service References** folder with the `WelcomeSOAP` web service's service endpoint interface (Fig. 31.7). Note that the service endpoint interface's name is listed as `WelcomeSOAPService`, as we specified in line 11 of Fig. 31.1.

Folder created when you add a web service client to your project in NetBeans

Fig. 31.7 | NetBeans **Project** tab after adding a web service reference to the project.

When you specify the web service you want to consume, NetBeans accesses and copies its WSDL information to a file in your project (named `WelcomeSOAPService.wsdl` in this example). You can view this file by double clicking the `WelcomeSOAPService` node in the project's **Web Service References** folder. If the web service changes, the client-side artifacts and the client's copy of the WSDL file can be regenerated by right clicking the `Welcome-SOAPService` node shown in Fig. 31.7 and selecting **Refresh Client**.

You can view the IDE-generated client-side artifacts by selecting the NetBeans **Files** tab and expanding the `WelcomeSOAPClient` project's **build** folder, as shown in Fig. 31.8.

Client-side artifacts generated by NetBeans to support the service endpoint interface object

Fig. 31.8 | The `WelcomeSOAP` web service's client-side artifacts generated by NetBeans.

31.6.7 Consuming the `WelcomeSOAP` Web Service

For this example, we use a GUI application to interact with the `WelcomeSOAP` web service. To build the client application's GUI, you must first add a subclass of `JFrame` to the project. To do so, perform the following steps:

1. Right click the project name (`WelcomeSOAPClient`) in the NetBeans **Project** tab and select **New > JFrame Form...** to display the **New JFrame Form** dialog.

2. Specify `WelcomeSOAPClientJFrame` in the **Class Name** field.

3. Specify `com.deitel.welcomesoapclient` in the **Package** field.

4. Click **Finish** to close the **New JFrame Form** dialog.

Next, use the NetBeans GUI design tools to build the GUI shown in the sample screen captures at the end of Fig. 31.9. The GUI consists of a label, a text field and a button.

The application in Fig. 31.9 uses the `WelcomeSOAP` web service to display a welcome message to the user. To save space, we do not show the NetBeans autogenerated `initComponents` method, which contains the code that creates the GUI components, positions them and registers their event handlers. To view the complete source code, open the `WelcomeSOAPClientJFrame.java` file in this example's folder under `src\java\com\deitel\welcomesoapclient`. NetBeans places the GUI component instance-variable declarations at the end of the class (lines 113–115). Java allows instance variables to be declared anywhere in a class's body as long as they are placed outside the class's methods. We continue to declare our own instance variables at the top of the class.

```
 I    // Fig. 31.9: WelcomeSOAPClientJFrame.java
 2    // Client desktop application for the WelcomeSOAP web service.
 3    package com.deitel.welcomesoapclient;
 4
 5    import com.deitel.welcomesoap.WelcomeSOAP;
 6    import com.deitel.welcomesoap.WelcomeSOAPService;
 7    import javax.swing.JOptionPane;
 8
 9    public class WelcomeSOAPClientJFrame extends javax.swing.JFrame
10    {
11       // references the service endpoint interface object (i.e., the proxy)
12       private WelcomeSOAP welcomeSOAPProxy;
13
14       // no-argument constructor
15       public WelcomeSOAPClientJFrame()
16       {
17          initComponents();
18
19          try
20          {
21             // create the objects for accessing the WelcomeSOAP web service
22             WelcomeSOAPService service = new WelcomeSOAPService();
23             welcomeSOAPProxy = service.getWelcomeSOAPPort();
24          } // end try
25          catch ( Exception exception )
26          {
27             exception.printStackTrace();
28             System.exit( 1 );
29          } // end catch
30       } // end WelcomeSOAPClientJFrame constructor
31
32       // The initComponents method is autogenerated by NetBeans and is called
33       // from the constructor to initialize the GUI. This method is not shown
34       // here to save space. Open WelcomeSOAPClientJFrame.java in this
35       // example's folder to view the complete generated code.
36
86       // call the web service with the supplied name and display the message
87       private void submitJButtonActionPerformed(
88          java.awt.event.ActionEvent evt )
89       {
90          String name = nameJTextField.getText(); // get name from JTextField
91
92          // retrieve the welcome string from the web service
93          String message = welcomeSOAPProxy.welcome( name );
94          JOptionPane.showMessageDialog( this, message,
95             "Welcome", JOptionPane.INFORMATION_MESSAGE );
96       } // end method submitJButtonActionPerformed
97
98       // main method begins execution
99       public static void main( String args[] )
100      {
101         java.awt.EventQueue.invokeLater(
102            new Runnable()
103            {
```

Fig. 31.9 | Client desktop application for the WelcomeSOAP web service. (Part I of 2.)

```
104                public void run()
105                {
106                    new WelcomeSOAPClientJFrame().setVisible( true );
107                } // end method run
108            } // end anonymous inner class
109        ); // end call to java.awt.EventQueue.invokeLater
110    } // end main
111
112    // Variables declaration - do not modify
113    private javax.swing.JLabel nameJLabel;
114    private javax.swing.JTextField nameJTextField;
115    private javax.swing.JButton submitJButton;
116    // End of variables declaration
117 } // end class WelcomeSOAPClientJFrame
```

Fig. 31.9 | Client desktop application for the WelcomeSOAP web service. (Part 2 of 2.)

Lines 5–6 import the classes WelcomeSOAP and WelcomeSOAPService that enable the client application to interact with the web service. Notice that we do not have import declarations for most of the GUI components used in this example. When you create a GUI in NetBeans, it uses fully qualified class names (such as javax.swing.JFrame in line 9), so import declarations are unnecessary.

Line 12 declares a variable of type WelcomeSOAP that will refer to the service endpoint interface object. Line 22 in the constructor creates an object of type WelcomeSOAPService. Line 23 uses this object's getWelcomeSOAPPort method to obtain the WelcomeSOAP service endpoint interface object that the application uses to invoke the web service's methods.

The event handler for the **Submit** button (lines 87–96) first retrieves the name the user entered from nameJTextField. It then calls the welcome method on the service endpoint interface object (line 93) to retrieve the welcome message from the web service. This object communicates with the web service on the client's behalf. Once the message has been retrieved, lines 94–95 display it in a message box by calling JOptionPane's showMessage-Dialog method.

31.7 Publishing and Consuming REST-Based XML Web Services

The previous section used a service endpoint interface (proxy) object to pass data to and from a Java web service using the SOAP protocol. Now, we access a Java web service using the REST architecture. We recreate the WelcomeSOAP example to return data in plain XML format. You can create a **Web Application** project as you did in Section 31.6 to begin.

31.7.1 Creating a REST-Based XML Web Service

The **RESTful Web Services** plug-in for NetBeans provides various templates for creating RESTful web services, including ones that can interact with databases on the client's behalf. In this chapter, we focus on simple RESTful web services. To create a RESTful web service:

1. Right-click the **WelcomeRESTXML** node in the **Projects** tab, and select **New > Other...** to display the **New File** dialog.

2. Select **Web Services** under **Categories**, then select **RESTful Web Services from Patterns** and click **Next >**.

3. Under **Select Pattern**, ensure **Singleton** is selected, and click **Next >**.

4. Set the **Resource Package** to com.deitel.welcomerestxml, the **Path** to welcome and the **Class Name** to WelcomeRESTXMLResource. Leave the **MIME Type** and **Representation Class** set to application/xml and java.lang.String, respectively. The correct configuration is shown in Fig. 31.10.

5. Click **Finish** to create the web service.

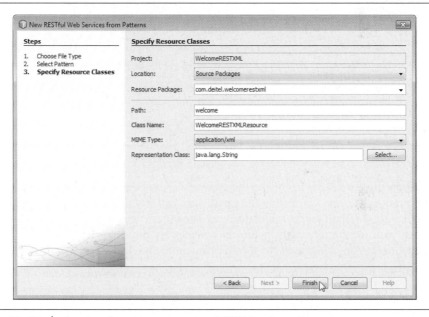

Fig. 31.10 | Creating the WelcomeRESTXML RESTful web service.

NetBeans generates the class and sets up the proper annotations. The class is placed in the project's **RESTful Web Services** folder. The code for the completed service is shown in Fig. 31.11. You'll notice that the completed code does not include some of the code generated by NetBeans. We removed the pieces that were unnecessary for this simple web service. The autogenerated putXml method is not necessary, because this example does not modify state on the server. The UriInfo instance variable is not needed, because we do not use HTTP query parameters or any other advanced processing on the request URI. We also removed the autogenerated constructor, because we have no code to place in it.

Lines 6–9 contain the imports for the JAX-RS annotations that help define the RESTful web service. The **@Path annotation** on the WelcomeRESTXMLResource class (line 12) indicates the URI for accessing the web service. This URI is appended to the web

```
 1   // Fig. 31.11: WelcomeRESTXMLResource.java
 2   // REST web service that returns a welcome message as XML.
 3   package com.deitel.welcomerestxml;
 4
 5   import java.io.StringWriter;
 6   import javax.ws.rs.GET; // annotation to indicate method uses HTTP GET
 7   import javax.ws.rs.Path; // annotation to specify path of resource
 8   import javax.ws.rs.PathParam; // annotation to get parameters from URI
 9   import javax.ws.rs.Produces; // annotation to specify type of data
10   import javax.xml.bind.JAXB; // utility class for common JAXB operations
11
12   @Path( "welcome" ) // URI used to access the resource
13   public class WelcomeRESTXMLResource
14   {
15      // retrieve welcome message
16      @GET // handles HTTP GET requests
17      @Path( "{name}" ) // URI component containing parameter
18      @Produces( "application/xml" ) // response formatted as XML
19      public String getXml( @PathParam( "name" ) String name )
20      {
21         String message = "Welcome to JAX-RS web services with REST and " +
22            "XML, " + name + "!"; // our welcome message
23         StringWriter writer = new StringWriter();
24         JAXB.marshal( message, writer ); // marshal String as XML
25         return writer.toString(); // return XML as String
26      } // end method getXml
27   } // end class WelcomeRESTXMLResource
```

Fig. 31.11 | REST web service that returns a welcome message as XML.

application project's URL to invoke the service. Methods of the class can also use the @Path annotation (line 17). Parts of the path specified in curly braces indicate parameters—they are placeholders for values that are passed to the web service as part of the path. The base path for the service is the project's resources directory. For example, to get a welcome message for someone named John, the complete URL is

```
http://localhost:8080/WelcomeRESTXML/resources/welcome/John
```

Arguments in a URL can be used as arguments to a web service method. To do so, you bind the parameters specified in the @Path specification to parameters of the web service method with the **@PathParam annotation**, as shown in line 19. When the request is received, the server passes the argument(s) in the URL to the appropriate parameter(s) in the web service method.

The **@GET annotation** denotes that this method is accessed via an HTTP GET request. Note that the putXml method the IDE created for us had an @PUT annotation, which indicates that the method is accessed using the HTTP PUT method. Similar annotations exist for HTTP POST, DELETE and HEAD requests.

The **@Produces annotation** denotes the content type returned to the client. It is possible to have multiple methods with the same HTTP method and path but different @Produces annotations, and JAX-RS will call the method matching the content type requested by the client. Standard Java method overloading rules apply, so such methods must have different names. The **@Consumes annotation** for the autogenerated putXml method (which we deleted) restricts the content type that the web service will accept from a PUT operation.

Line 10 imports the **JAXB class** from package javax.xml.bind. **JAXB (Java Architecture for XML Binding)** is a set of classes for converting POJOs to and from XML. There are many related classes in the same package that implement the serializations we perform, but the JAXB class contains easy-to-use wrappers for common operations. After creating the welcome message (lines 21–22), we create a StringWriter (line 23) to which JAXB will output the XML. Line 24 calls the JAXB class's static method **marshal** to convert the String containing our message to XML format. Line 25 calls StringWriter's toString method to retrieve the XML text to return to the client.

Testing RESTful Web Services
Section 31.6.4 demonstrated testing a SOAP service using GlassFish's Tester page. Glass-Fish does not provide a testing facility for RESTful services, but NetBeans automatically generates a test page that can be accessed by right clicking the **WelcomeRESTXML** node in the **Projects** tab and selecting **Test RESTful Web Services**. This will compile and deploy the web service, if you have not yet done so, then open the test page. Your browser will probably require you to acknowledge a potential security issue before allowing the test page to perform its tasks. The test page is loaded from your computer's local file system, *not* the GlassFish server. Browsers consider the local file system and GlassFish as two different servers, even though they are both on the local computer. For security reasons, browsers do not allow so-called cross-site scripting in which a web page tries to interact with a server other than the one that served the page.

On the test page (Fig. 31.12), expand the **welcome** element in the left column and select {name}. The form on the right side of the page displays a form that allows you to choose the MIME type of the data (application/xml by default) and lets you enter the name parameter's value. Click the **Test** button to invoke the web service and display the returned XML.

Fig. 31.12 | Test page for the WelcomeRESTXML web service.

The test page shows several tabs containing the results and various other information. The **Raw Text** tab shows the actual XML response. The **Headers** tab shows the HTTP headers returned by the server. The **Http Monitor** tab shows a log of the HTTP transactions that took place to complete the request and response.

The test page provides its functionality by reading a WADL file from the server—you can see the URL of the WADL file in the upper-left corner of the test page. **WADL (Web Application Description Language)** has similar design goals to WSDL, but describes RESTful services instead of SOAP services.

31.7.2 Consuming a REST-Based XML Web Service

As we did with SOAP, we create a Java application that retrieves the welcome message from the web service and displays it to the user. First, create a Java application with the name `WelcomeRESTXMLClient`. RESTful web services do not require web service references, so you can begin building the GUI immediately by creating a `JFrame` form called `WelcomeRESTXMLClientJFrame` and placing it in the `com.deitel.welcomerestxmlclient` package. The GUI is identical to the one in Fig. 31.9, including the names of the GUI elements. To create the GUI quickly, you can simply copy and paste the GUI from the **Design** view of the `WelcomeSOAPClientJFrame` class and paste it into the **Design** view of the `WelcomeRESTXMLClientJFrame` class. Figure 31.13 contains the completed code.

```
1   // Fig. 31.13: WelcomeRESTXMLClientJFrame.java
2   // Client that consumes the WelcomeRESTXML service.
3   package com.deitel.welcomerestxmlclient;
4
5   import javax.swing.JOptionPane;
6   import javax.xml.bind.JAXB; // utility class for common JAXB operations
7
8   public class WelcomeRESTXMLClientJFrame extends javax.swing.JFrame
9   {
10      // no-argument constructor
11      public WelcomeRESTXMLClientJFrame()
12      {
13         initComponents();
14      } // end constructor
15
16      // The initComponents method is autogenerated by NetBeans and is called
17      // from the constructor to initialize the GUI. This method is not shown
18      // here to save space. Open WelcomeRESTXMLClientJFrame.java in this
19      // example's folder to view the complete generated code.
20
72      // call the web service with the supplied name and display the message
73      private void submitJButtonActionPerformed(
74         java.awt.event.ActionEvent evt)
75      {
76         String name = nameJTextField.getText(); // get name from JTextField
77
78         // the URL for the REST service
79         String url =
80            "http://localhost:8080/WelcomeRESTXML/resources/welcome/" + name;
```

Fig. 31.13 | Client that consumes the `WelcomeRESTXML` service. (Part 1 of 2.)

```
81
82        // read from URL and convert from XML to Java String
83        String message = JAXB.unmarshal( url, String.class );
84
85        // display the message to the user
86        JOptionPane.showMessageDialog( this, message,
87           "Welcome", JOptionPane.INFORMATION_MESSAGE );
88     } // end method submitJButtonActionPerformed
89
90     // main method begins execution
91     public static void main( String args[] )
92     {
93        java.awt.EventQueue.invokeLater(
94           new Runnable()
95           {
96              public void run()
97              {
98                 new WelcomeRESTXMLClientJFrame().setVisible( true );
99              } // end method run
100           } // end anonymous inner class
101        ); // end call to java.awt.EventQueue.invokeLater
102     } // end main
103
104     // Variables declaration - do not modify
105     private javax.swing.JLabel nameJLabel;
106     private javax.swing.JTextField nameJTextField;
107     private javax.swing.JButton submitJButton;
108     // End of variables declaration
109  } // end class WelcomeRESTXMLClientJFrame
```

Fig. 31.13 | Client that consumes the WelcomeRESTXML service. (Part 2 of 2.)

You can access a RESTful web service with classes from Java API. As in the RESTful XML web service, we use the JAXB library. The JAXB class (imported on line 6) has a static **unmarshal** method that takes as arguments a file name or URL as a String, and a Class<T> object indicating the Java class to which the XML will be converted (line 83). In this example, the XML contains a String object, so we use the Java compiler shortcut String.class to create the Class<String> object we need as the second argument. The String returned from the call to the unmarshal method is then displayed to the user via JOptionPane's showMessageDialog method (lines 86–87), as it was with the SOAP service. Note that the URL used in this example to extract data from the web service matches the URL used by the test page.

31.8 Publishing and Consuming REST-Based JSON Web Services

While XML was designed primarily as a document interchange format, JSON is designed as a *data* exchange format. Data structures in most programming languages do not map directly to XML constructs—for example, the distinction between elements and attributes is not present in programming-language data structures. JSON is a subset of the JavaScript programming language, and its components—objects, arrays, strings, numbers—can be easily mapped to constructs in Java and other programming languages.

The standard Java libraries do not currently provide capabilities for working with JSON, but there are many open-source JSON libraries for Java and other languages; you can find a list of them at json.org. We chose the Gson library from code.google.com/p/google-gson/, which provides a simple way to convert POJOs to and from JSON.

31.8.1 Creating a REST-Based JSON Web Service

To begin, create a WelcomeRESTJSON web application, then create the web service by following the steps in Section 31.7.1. In *Step 4*, change the **Resource Package** to com.deitel.welcomerestjson, the **Class Name** to WelcomeRESTJSONResource and the **MIME Type** to application/json. Additionally, you must download the Gson library's JAR file, then add it to the project as a library. To do so, right click your project's **Libraries** folder, select **Add JAR/Folder...** locate the downloaded Gson JAR file and click **Open**. The complete code for the service can be found in Fig. 31.14.

```java
 1   // Fig. 31.14: WelcomeRESTJSONResource.java
 2   // REST web service that returns a welcome message as JSON.
 3   package com.deitel.welcomerestjson;
 4
 5   import com.google.gson.Gson; // converts POJO to JSON and back again
 6   import javax.ws.rs.GET; // annotation to indicate method uses HTTP GET
 7   import javax.ws.rs.Path; // annotation to specify path of resource
 8   import javax.ws.rs.PathParam; // annotation to get parameters from URI
 9   import javax.ws.rs.Produces; // annotation to specify type of data
10
11   @Path( "welcome" ) // path used to access the resource
12   public class WelcomeRESTJSONResource
13   {
14      // retrieve welcome message
15      @GET // handles HTTP GET requests
16      @Path( "{name}" ) // takes name as a path parameter
17      @Produces( "application/json" ) // response formatted as JSON
18      public String getJson( @PathParam( "name" ) String name )
19      {
20         // add welcome message to field of TextMessage object
21         TextMessage message = new TextMessage(); // create wrapper object
22         message.setMessage( String.format( "%s, %s!",
23            "Welcome to JAX-RS web services with REST and JSON", name ) );
24
25         return new Gson().toJson( message ); // return JSON-wrapped message
26      } // end method getJson
27   } // end class WelcomeRESTJSONResource
28
29   // private class that contains the message we wish to send
30   class TextMessage
31   {
32      private String message; // message we're sending
33
34      // returns the message
35      public String getMessage()
36      {
```

Fig. 31.14 | REST web service that returns a welcome message as JSON. (Part 1 of 2.)

```
37        return message;
38      } // end method getMessage
39
40      // sets the message
41      public void setMessage( String value )
42      {
43          message = value;
44      } // end method setMessage
45  } // end class TextMessage
```

Fig. 31.14 | REST web service that returns a welcome message as JSON. (Part 2 of 2.)

All the annotations and the basic structure of the WelcomeRESTJSONResource class are the same as REST XML example. Note that the argument to the @Produces attribute (line 19) is "application/json". The TextMessage class (lines 30–45) addresses a difference between JSON and XML. JSON does not permit strings or numbers to stand on their own—they must be encapsulated in a composite data type. So, we created class TextMessage to encapsulate the String representing the message.

When a client invokes this web service, line 21 creates the TextMessage object, then lines 22–23 set its contained message. Next, line 25 creates a **Gson** object (from package com.google.gson.Gson) and calls its **toJson** method to convert the TextMessage into its JSON String representation. We return this String, which is then sent back to the client in the web service's response. There are multiple overloads of the toJson method, such as one that sends its output to a Writer instead of returning a String.

RESTful services returning JSON can be tested in the same way as those returning XML. Follow the procedure outlined in Section 31.7.1, but be sure to change the MIME type to application/json in the test web page; otherwise, the web service will return an error stating that it cannot produce the desired response.

31.8.2 Consuming a REST-Based JSON Web Service

We now create a Java application that retrieves the welcome message from the web service and displays it to the user. First, create a Java application with the name WelcomeREST-JSONClient. Then, create a JFrame form called WelcomeRESTXMLClientJFrame and place it in the com.deitel.welcomerestjsonclient package. The GUI is identical to the one in Fig. 31.9. To create the GUI quickly, copy it from the **Design** view of the WelcomeSOAP-ClientJFrame class and paste it into the **Design** view of the WelcomeRESTJSONClient-JFrame class. Figure 31.13 contains the completed code.

```
1  // Fig. 31.15: WelcomeRESTJSONClientJFrame.java
2  // Client that consumes the WelcomeRESTJSON service.
3  package com.deitel.welcomerestjsonclient;
4
5  import com.google.gson.Gson; // converts POJO to JSON and back again
6  import java.io.InputStreamReader;
7  import java.net.URL;
8  import javax.swing.JOptionPane;
9
```

Fig. 31.15 | Client that consumes the WelcomeRESTJSON service. (Part 1 of 3.)

```
10   public class WelcomeRESTJSONClientJFrame extends javax.swing.JFrame
11   {
12      // no-argument constructor
13      public WelcomeRESTJSONClientJFrame()
14      {
15         initComponents();
16      } // end constructor
17
18      // The initComponents method is autogenerated by NetBeans and is called
19      // from the constructor to initialize the GUI. This method is not shown
20      // here to save space. Open WelcomeRESTJSONClientJFrame.java in this
21      // example's folder to view the complete generated code.
22
74      // call the web service with the supplied name and display the message
75      private void submitJButtonActionPerformed(
76         java.awt.event.ActionEvent evt )
77      {
78         String name = nameJTextField.getText(); // get name from JTextField
79
80         // retrieve the welcome string from the web service
81         try
82         {
83            // the URL of the web service
84            String url = "http://localhost:8080/WelcomeRESTJSON/" +
85               "resources/welcome/" + name;
86
87            // open URL, using a Reader to convert bytes to chars
88            InputStreamReader reader =
89               new InputStreamReader( new URL( url ).openStream() );
90
91            // parse the JSON back into a TextMessage
92            TextMessage message =
93               new Gson().fromJson( reader, TextMessage.class );
94
95            // display message to the user
96            JOptionPane.showMessageDialog( this, message.getMessage(),
97               "Welcome", JOptionPane.INFORMATION_MESSAGE );
98         } // end try
99         catch( Exception exception )
100        {
101           exception.printStackTrace(); // show exception details
102        } // end catch
103     } // end method submitJButtonActionPerformed
104
105     // main method begin execution
106     public static void main( String args[] )
107     {
108        java.awt.EventQueue.invokeLater(
109           new Runnable()
110           {
111              public void run()
112              {
113                 new WelcomeRESTJSONClientJFrame().setVisible( true );
114              } // end method run
```

Fig. 31.15 | Client that consumes the WelcomeRESTJSON service. (Part 2 of 3.)

```
115              } // end anonymous inner class
116          ); // end call to java.awt.EventQueue.invokeLater
117      } // end main
118
119      // Variables declaration - do not modify
120      private javax.swing.JLabel nameJLabel;
121      private javax.swing.JTextField nameJTextField;
122      private javax.swing.JButton submitJButton;
123      // End of variables declaration
124  } // end class WelcomeRESTJSONClientJFrame
125
126  // private class that contains the message we are receiving
127  class TextMessage
128  {
129      private String message; // message we're receiving
130
131      // returns the message
132      public String getMessage()
133      {
134          return message;
135      } // end method getMessage
136
137      // sets the message
138      public void setMessage( String value )
139      {
140          message = value;
141      } // end method setMessage
142  } // end class TextMessage
```

Fig. 31.15 | Client that consumes the `WelcomeRESTJSON` service. (Part 3 of 3.)

Lines 84–85 create the URL `String` that is used to invoke the web service. Lines 88–89 create a URL object using this `String`, then call the URL's **openStream** method to invoke the web service and obtain an `InputStream` from which the client can read the response. The `InputStream` is wrapped in an `InputStreamReader` so it can be passed as the first argument to the Gson class's **fromJson** method. This method is overloaded. The version we use takes as arguments a `Reader` from which to read a JSON `String` and a `Class<T>` object indicating the Java class to which the JSON `String` will be converted (line 93). In this example, the JSON `String` contains a `TextMessage` object, so we use the Java compiler shortcut `TextMessage.class` to create the `Class<TextMessage>` object we need as the second argument. Lines 96–97 display the message in the `TextMessage` object.

Note that the `TextMessage` classes in the web service and client are unrelated. Technically, the client can be written in any programming language, so the manner in which a response is processed can vary greatly. Since our client is written in Java, we duplicated the `TextMessage` class in the client so we could easily convert the JSON object back to Java.

31.9 Session Tracking in a SOAP-Based Web Service

Section 29.7 described the advantages of using session tracking to maintain client-state information so you can personalize the users' browsing experiences. Now we'll incorporate session tracking into a web service. Suppose a client application needs to call several methods from the same web service, possibly several times each. In such a case, it can be beneficial for the web service to maintain state information for the client, thus eliminating the need for client information to be passed between the client and the web service multiple times. For example, a web service that provides local restaurant reviews could store the client user's street address during the initial request, then use it to return personalized, localized results in subsequent requests. Storing session information also enables a web service to distinguish between clients.

31.9.1 Creating a Blackjack Web Service

Our next example is a web service that assists you in developing a blackjack card game. The Blackjack web service (Fig. 31.16) provides web methods to shuffle a deck of cards, deal a card from the deck and evaluate a hand of cards. After presenting the web service, we use it to serve as the dealer for a game of blackjack (Fig. 31.17). The Blackjack web service uses an HttpSession object to maintain a unique deck of cards for each client application. Several clients can use the service at the same time, but web method calls made by a specific client use only the deck of cards stored in that client's session. Our example uses the following blackjack rules:

> *Two cards each are dealt to the dealer and the player. The player's cards are dealt face up. Only the first of the dealer's cards is dealt face up. Each card has a value. A card numbered 2 through 10 is worth its face value. Jacks, queens and kings each count as 10. Aces can count as 1 or 11—whichever value is more beneficial to the player (as we'll soon see). If the sum of the player's two initial cards is 21 (i.e., the player was dealt a card valued at 10 and an ace, which counts as 11 in this situation), the player has "blackjack" and immediately wins the game—if the dealer does not also have blackjack (which would result in a "push"—i.e., a tie). Otherwise, the player can begin taking additional cards one at a time. These cards are dealt face up, and the player decides when to stop taking cards. If the player "busts" (i.e., the sum of the player's cards exceeds 21), the game is over, and the player loses. When the player is satisfied with the current set of cards, the player "stands" (i.e., stops taking cards), and the dealer's hidden card is revealed. If the dealer's total is 16 or less, the dealer must take another card; otherwise, the dealer must stand. The dealer must continue taking cards until the sum of the dealer's cards is greater than or equal to 17. If the dealer exceeds 21, the player wins. Otherwise, the hand with the higher point total wins. If the dealer and the player have the same point total, the game is a "push," and no one wins. Note that the value of an ace for a dealer depends on the dealer's other card(s) and the casino's house rules. A dealer typically must hit for totals of 16 or less and must stand for totals of 17 or more. However, for a "soft 17"—a hand with a total of 17 with one ace counted as 11—some casinos require the dealer to hit and some require the dealer to stand (we require the dealer to stand). Such a hand is known as a "soft 17" because taking another card cannot bust the hand.*

The web service (Fig. 31.16) stores each card as a String consisting of a number, 1–13, representing the card's face (ace through king, respectively), followed by a space and a digit, 0–3, representing the card's suit (hearts, diamonds, clubs or spades, respectively). For example, the jack of clubs is represented as "11 2" and the two of hearts as "2 0". To create and deploy this web service, follow the steps that we presented in Sections 31.6.2–31.6.3 for the WelcomeSOAP service.

```java
 1  // Fig. 31.16: Blackjack.java
 2  // Blackjack web service that deals cards and evaluates hands
 3  package com.deitel.java.blackjack;
 4
 5  import java.util.ArrayList;
 6  import java.util.Random;
 7  import javax.annotation.Resource;
 8  import javax.jws.WebMethod;
 9  import javax.jws.WebParam;
10  import javax.jws.WebService;
11  import javax.servlet.http.HttpServletRequest;
12  import javax.servlet.http.HttpSession;
13  import javax.xml.ws.WebServiceContext;
14  import javax.xml.ws.handler.MessageContext;
15
16  @WebService( name = "Blackjack", serviceName = "BlackjackService" )
17  public class Blackjack
18  {
19     // use @Resource to create a WebServiceContext for session tracking
20     private @Resource WebServiceContext webServiceContext;
21     private MessageContext messageContext; // used in session tracking
22     private HttpSession session; // stores attributes of the session
23
24     // deal one card
25     @WebMethod( operationName = "dealCard" )
26     public String dealCard()
27     {
28        String card = "";
29
30        ArrayList< String > deck =
31           ( ArrayList< String > ) session.getAttribute( "deck" );
32
33        card = deck.get( 0 ); // get top card of deck
34        deck.remove( 0 ); // remove top card of deck
35
36        return card;
37     } // end WebMethod dealCard
38
39     // shuffle the deck
40     @WebMethod( operationName = "shuffle" )
41     public void shuffle()
42     {
43        // obtain the HttpSession object to store deck for current client
44        messageContext = webServiceContext.getMessageContext();
45        session = ( ( HttpServletRequest ) messageContext.get(
46           MessageContext.SERVLET_REQUEST ) ).getSession();
47
48        // populate deck of cards
49        ArrayList< String > deck = new ArrayList< String >();
50
51        for ( int face = 1; face <= 13; face++ ) // loop through faces
52           for ( int suit = 0; suit <= 3; suit++ ) // loop through suits
53              deck.add( face + " " + suit ); // add each card to deck
```

Fig. 31.16 | Blackjack web service that deals cards and evaluates hands. (Part 1 of 3.)

```
54
55          String tempCard; // holds card temporarily during swapping
56          Random randomObject = new Random(); // generates random numbers
57          int index; // index of randomly selected card
58
59          for ( int i = 0; i < deck.size() ; i++ ) // shuffle
60          {
61             index = randomObject.nextInt( deck.size() - 1 );
62
63             // swap card at position i with randomly selected card
64             tempCard = deck.get( i );
65             deck.set( i, deck.get( index ) );
66             deck.set( index, tempCard );
67          } // end for
68
69          // add this deck to user's session
70          session.setAttribute( "deck", deck );
71       } // end WebMethod shuffle
72
73       // determine a hand's value
74       @WebMethod( operationName = "getHandValue" )
75       public int getHandValue( @WebParam( name = "hand" ) String hand )
76       {
77          // split hand into cards
78          String[] cards = hand.split( "\t" );
79          int total = 0; // total value of cards in hand
80          int face; // face of current card
81          int aceCount = 0; // number of aces in hand
82
83          for ( int i = 0; i < cards.length; i++ )
84          {
85             // parse string and get first int in String
86             face = Integer.parseInt(
87                cards[ i ].substring( 0, cards[ i ].indexOf( " " ) ) );
88
89             switch ( face )
90             {
91                case 1: // if ace, increment aceCount
92                   ++aceCount;
93                   break;
94                case 11: // jack
95                case 12: // queen
96                case 13: // king
97                   total += 10;
98                   break;
99                default: // otherwise, add face
100                  total += face;
101                  break;
102            } // end switch
103         } // end for
104
105         // calculate optimal use of aces
106         if ( aceCount > 0 )
107         {
```

Fig. 31.16 | Blackjack web service that deals cards and evaluates hands. (Part 2 of 3.)

```
108              // if possible, count one ace as 11
109              if ( total + 11 + aceCount - 1 <= 21 )
110                 total += 11 + aceCount - 1;
111              else // otherwise, count all aces as 1
112                 total += aceCount;
113           } // end if
114
115           return total;
116        } // end WebMethod getHandValue
117     } // end class Blackjack
```

Fig. 31.16 | Blackjack web service that deals cards and evaluates hands. (Part 3 of 3.)

Session Tracking in Web Services

A client first calls the Blackjack web service's shuffle method (lines 40–71) to shuffle the deck of cards and place it into an HttpSession object that is specific to that client. To use session tracking in a web service, you must include code for the resources that maintain the session-state information. In the past, you had to write the sometimes tedious code to create these resources. This is handled for you via the **@Resource annotation**. This annotation enables tools like NetBeans to "inject" support objects into your class, thus allowing you to focus on your business logic rather than the support code. The server is responsible for initializing the support objects. The concept of using annotations to add code that supports your classes is known as **dependency injection**. Annotations such as @WebService, @WebMethod and @WebParam also perform dependency injection.

Line 20 injects a **WebServiceContext** object into your class. This object enables a web service to access and maintain information, such as session state for a specific request. As you look through the code in Fig. 31.16, you'll notice that we never explicitly create the WebServiceContext object—that code is injected into the class by the application server as a result of the @Resource annotation. Line 21 declares a variable of interface type **MessageContext** that the web service will use to obtain an HttpSession object for the current client. Line 22 declares the HttpSession variable that the web service will use to manipulate the session-state information.

Line 44 in method shuffle uses the WebServiceContext object that was injected in line 20 to obtain a MessageContext object. Lines 45–46 then use the MessageContext object's get method to obtain the HttpSession object for the current client. Method get receives a constant indicating what to get from the MessageContext. In this case, the constant MessageContext.SERVLET_REQUEST indicates that we'd like to get the HttpServlet-Request object for the current client. We then call the HttpServletRequest method **getSession** to obtain the HttpSession object.

Lines 49–70 generate an ArrayList representing a deck of cards, shuffle the deck and store it in the client's session object. Lines 51–53 generate Strings in the form "*face suit*" to represent each possible card in the deck. Lines 59–67 shuffle the deck by swapping each card with another one selected at random. Line 70 uses HttpSession method **setAttribute** to insert the ArrayList in the session object to maintain the deck between method calls from a particular client.

Lines 25–37 define method dealCard as a web method. Lines 30–31 use the session object to obtain the "deck" session attribute that was stored in line 70 of method shuffle. Method **getAttribute** takes as a parameter a String that identifies the Object to obtain from the session state. The HttpSession can store many Objects, provided that each has a unique identifier. Note that method `shuffle` must be called before method `dealCard` is called the first time for a client—otherwise, an exception occurs at line 33, because `get-Attribute` returns `null` at lines 30–31. After obtaining the user's deck, `dealCard` gets the top card from the deck (line 33), removes it from the deck (line 34) and returns the card's value as a `String` (line 36). Without using session tracking, the deck of cards would need to be passed back and forth with each method call. Session tracking makes the `dealCard` method easy to call (it requires no arguments) and eliminates the overhead of sending the deck over the network multiple times.

Method `getHandValue` (lines 74–116) determines the total value of the cards in a hand by trying to attain the highest score possible without going over 21. Recall that an ace can be counted as either 1 or 11, and all face cards count as 10. This method does not use the `session` object, because the deck of cards is not used in this method.

As you'll soon see, the client application maintains a hand of cards as a `String` in which each card is separated by a tab character. Line 78 tokenizes the hand of cards (represented by `hand`) into individual cards by calling `String` method `split` and passing to it a `String` containing the delimiter characters (in this case, just a tab). Method `split` uses the delimiter characters to separate tokens in the `String`. Lines 83–103 count the value of each card. Lines 86–87 retrieve the first integer—the face—and use that value in the `switch` statement (lines 89–102). If the card is an ace, the method increments variable `aceCount`. We discuss how this variable is used shortly. If the card is an 11, 12 or 13 (jack, queen or king), the method adds 10 to the total value of the hand (line 97). If the card is anything else, the method increases the total by that value (line 100).

Because an ace can have either of two values, additional logic is required to process aces. Lines 106–113 of method `getHandValue` process the aces after all the other cards. If a hand contains several aces, only one ace can be counted as 11. The condition in line 109 determines whether counting one ace as 11 and the rest as 1 will result in a total that does not exceed 21. If this is possible, line 110 adjusts the total accordingly. Otherwise, line 112 adjusts the total, counting each ace as 1.

Method `getHandValue` maximizes the value of the current cards without exceeding 21. Imagine, for example, that the dealer has a 7 and receives an ace. The new total could be either 8 or 18. However, `getHandValue` always maximizes the value of the cards without going over 21, so the new total is 18.

31.9.2 Consuming the Blackjack Web Service

The blackjack application in Fig. 31.17 keeps track of the player's and dealer's cards, and the web service tracks the cards that have been dealt. The constructor (lines 34–83) sets up the GUI (line 36), changes the window's background color (line 40) and creates the `Blackjack` web service's service endpoint interface object (lines 46–47). In the GUI, each player has 11 `JLabel`s—the maximum number of cards that can be dealt without automatically exceeding 21 (i.e., four aces, four twos and three threes). These `JLabel`s are placed in an `ArrayList` of `JLabel`s (lines 59–82), so we can index the `ArrayList` during the game to determine the `JLabel` that will display a particular card image.

```
 1   // Fig. 31.17: BlackjackGameJFrame.java
 2   // Blackjack game that uses the Blackjack Web Service.
```

Fig. 31.17 | Blackjack game that uses the `Blackjack` web service. (Part 1 of 11.)

```
 3   package com.deitel.java.blackjackclient;
 4
 5   import com.deitel.java.blackjack.Blackjack;
 6   import com.deitel.java.blackjack.BlackjackService;
 7   import java.awt.Color;
 8   import java.util.ArrayList;
 9   import javax.swing.ImageIcon;
10   import javax.swing.JLabel;
11   import javax.swing.JOptionPane;
12   import javax.xml.ws.BindingProvider;
13
14   public class BlackjackGameJFrame extends javax.swing.JFrame
15   {
16      private String playerCards;
17      private String dealerCards;
18      private ArrayList<JLabel> cardboxes; // list of card image JLabels
19      private int currentPlayerCard; // player's current card number
20      private int currentDealerCard; // blackjackProxy's current card number
21      private BlackjackService blackjackService; // used to obtain proxy
22      private Blackjack blackjackProxy; // used to access the web service
23
24      // enumeration of game states
25      private enum GameStatus
26      {
27         PUSH, // game ends in a tie
28         LOSE, // player loses
29         WIN, // player wins
30         BLACKJACK // player has blackjack
31      } // end enum GameStatus
32
33      // no-argument constructor
34      public BlackjackGameJFrame()
35      {
36         initComponents();
37
38         // due to a bug in NetBeans, we must change the JFrame's background
39         // color here rather than in the designer
40         getContentPane().setBackground( new Color( 0, 180, 0 ) );
41
42         // initialize the blackjack proxy
43         try
44         {
45            // create the objects for accessing the Blackjack web service
46            blackjackService = new BlackjackService();
47            blackjackProxy = blackjackService.getBlackjackPort();
48
49            // enable session tracking
50            ( (BindingProvider) blackjackProxy ).getRequestContext().put(
51               BindingProvider.SESSION_MAINTAIN_PROPERTY, true );
52         } // end try
53         catch ( Exception e )
54         {
55            e.printStackTrace();
56         } // end catch
```

Fig. 31.17 | Blackjack game that uses the Blackjack web service. (Part 2 of 11.)

```
57
58        // add JLabels to cardBoxes ArrayList for programmatic manipulation
59        cardboxes = new ArrayList<JLabel>();
60
61        cardboxes.add( dealerCard1JLabel );
62        cardboxes.add( dealerCard2JLabel );
63        cardboxes.add( dealerCard3JLabel );
64        cardboxes.add( dealerCard4JLabel );
65        cardboxes.add( dealerCard5JLabel );
66        cardboxes.add( dealerCard6JLabel );
67        cardboxes.add( dealerCard7JLabel );
68        cardboxes.add( dealerCard8JLabel );
69        cardboxes.add( dealerCard9JLabel );
70        cardboxes.add( dealerCard10JLabel );
71        cardboxes.add( dealerCard11JLabel );
72        cardboxes.add( playerCard1JLabel );
73        cardboxes.add( playerCard2JLabel );
74        cardboxes.add( playerCard3JLabel );
75        cardboxes.add( playerCard4JLabel );
76        cardboxes.add( playerCard5JLabel );
77        cardboxes.add( playerCard6JLabel );
78        cardboxes.add( playerCard7JLabel );
79        cardboxes.add( playerCard8JLabel );
80        cardboxes.add( playerCard9JLabel );
81        cardboxes.add( playerCard10JLabel );
82        cardboxes.add( playerCard11JLabel );
83     } // end constructor
84
85     // play the dealer's hand
86     private void dealerPlay()
87     {
88        try
89        {
90           // while the value of the dealers's hand is below 17
91           // the dealer must continue to take cards
92           String[] cards = dealerCards.split( "\t" );
93
94           // display dealer's cards
95           for ( int i = 0; i < cards.length; i++ )
96           {
97              displayCard( i, cards[i] );
98           }
99
100          while ( blackjackProxy.getHandValue( dealerCards ) < 17 )
101          {
102             String newCard = blackjackProxy.dealCard(); // deal new card
103             dealerCards += "\t" + newCard; // deal new card
104             displayCard( currentDealerCard, newCard );
105             ++currentDealerCard;
106             JOptionPane.showMessageDialog( this, "Dealer takes a card",
107                "Dealer's turn", JOptionPane.PLAIN_MESSAGE );
108          } // end while
109
110          int dealersTotal = blackjackProxy.getHandValue( dealerCards );
```

Fig. 31.17 | Blackjack game that uses the Blackjack web service. (Part 3 of 11.)

```
111            int playersTotal = blackjackProxy.getHandValue( playerCards );
112
113         // if dealer busted, player wins
114         if ( dealersTotal > 21 )
115         {
116            gameOver( GameStatus.WIN );
117            return;
118         } // end if
119
120         // if dealer and player are below 21
121         // higher score wins, equal scores is a push
122         if ( dealersTotal > playersTotal )
123         {
124            gameOver( GameStatus.LOSE );
125         }
126         else if ( dealersTotal < playersTotal )
127         {
128            gameOver( GameStatus.WIN );
129         }
130         else
131         {
132            gameOver( GameStatus.PUSH );
133         }
134      } // end try
135      catch ( Exception e )
136      {
137         e.printStackTrace();
138      } // end catch
139   } // end method dealerPlay
140
141   // displays the card represented by cardValue in specified JLabel
142   private void displayCard( int card, String cardValue )
143   {
144      try
145      {
146         // retrieve correct JLabel from cardBoxes
147         JLabel displayLabel = cardboxes.get( card );
148
149         // if string representing card is empty, display back of card
150         if ( cardValue.equals( "" ) )
151         {
152            displayLabel.setIcon( new ImageIcon( getClass().getResource(
153               "/com/deitel/java/blackjackclient/" +
154               "blackjack_images/cardback.png" ) ) );
155            return;
156         } // end if
157
158         // retrieve the face value of the card
159         String face = cardValue.substring( 0, cardValue.indexOf( " " ) );
160
161         // retrieve the suit of the card
162         String suit =
163            cardValue.substring( cardValue.indexOf( " " ) + 1 );
164
```

Fig. 31.17 | Blackjack game that uses the Blackjack web service. (Part 4 of 11.)

```
165              char suitLetter; // suit letter used to form image file
166
167              switch ( Integer.parseInt( suit ) )
168              {
169                 case 0: // hearts
170                    suitLetter = 'h';
171                    break;
172                 case 1: // diamonds
173                    suitLetter = 'd';
174                    break;
175                 case 2: // clubs
176                    suitLetter = 'c';
177                    break;
178                 default: // spades
179                    suitLetter = 's';
180                    break;
181              } // end switch
182
183              // set image for displayLabel
184              displayLabel.setIcon( new ImageIcon( getClass().getResource(
185                 "/com/deitel/java/blackjackclient/blackjack_images/" +
186                 face + suitLetter + ".png" ) ) );
187           } // end try
188           catch ( Exception e )
189           {
190              e.printStackTrace();
191           } // end catch
192        } // end method displayCard
193
194        // displays all player cards and shows appropriate message
195        private void gameOver( GameStatus winner )
196        {
197           String[] cards = dealerCards.split( "\t" );
198
199           // display blackjackProxy's cards
200           for ( int i = 0; i < cards.length; i++ )
201           {
202              displayCard( i, cards[i] );
203           }
204
205           // display appropriate status image
206           if ( winner == GameStatus.WIN )
207           {
208              statusJLabel.setText( "You win!" );
209           }
210           else if ( winner == GameStatus.LOSE )
211           {
212              statusJLabel.setText( "You lose." );
213           }
214           else if ( winner == GameStatus.PUSH )
215           {
216              statusJLabel.setText( "It's a push." );
217           }
218           else // blackjack
```

Fig. 31.17 | Blackjack game that uses the Blackjack web service. (Part 5 of 11.)

```
219          {
220             statusJLabel.setText( "Blackjack!" );
221          }
222
223          // display final scores
224          int dealersTotal = blackjackProxy.getHandValue( dealerCards );
225          int playersTotal = blackjackProxy.getHandValue( playerCards );
226          dealerTotalJLabel.setText( "Dealer: " + dealersTotal );
227          playerTotalJLabel.setText( "Player: " + playersTotal );
228
229          // reset for new game
230          standJButton.setEnabled( false );
231          hitJButton.setEnabled( false );
232          dealJButton.setEnabled( true );
233       } // end method gameOver
234
235       // The initComponents method is autogenerated by NetBeans and is called
236       // from the constructor to initialize the GUI. This method is not shown
237       // here to save space. Open BlackjackGameJFrame.java in this
238       // example's folder to view the complete generated code (lines 235-541)
239
542       // handles dealJButton click
543       private void dealJButtonActionPerformed(
544          java.awt.event.ActionEvent evt )
545       {
546          String card; // stores a card temporarily until it's added to a hand
547
548          // clear card images
549          for ( int i = 0; i < cardboxes.size(); i++ )
550          {
551             cardboxes.get( i ).setIcon( null );
552          }
553
554          statusJLabel.setText( "" );
555          dealerTotalJLabel.setText( "" );
556          playerTotalJLabel.setText( "" );
557
558          // create a new, shuffled deck on remote machine
559          blackjackProxy.shuffle();
560
561          // deal two cards to player
562          playerCards = blackjackProxy.dealCard(); // add first card to hand
563          displayCard( 11, playerCards ); // display first card
564          card = blackjackProxy.dealCard(); // deal second card
565          displayCard( 12, card ); // display second card
566          playerCards += "\t" + card; // add second card to hand
567
568          // deal two cards to blackjackProxy, but only show first
569          dealerCards = blackjackProxy.dealCard(); // add first card to hand
570          displayCard( 0, dealerCards ); // display first card
571          card = blackjackProxy.dealCard(); // deal second card
572          displayCard( 1, "" ); // display back of card
573          dealerCards += "\t" + card; // add second card to hand
574
```

Fig. 31.17 | Blackjack game that uses the Blackjack web service. (Part 6 of 11.)

```
575          standJButton.setEnabled( true );
576          hitJButton.setEnabled( true );
577          dealJButton.setEnabled( false );
578
579          // determine the value of the two hands
580          int dealersTotal = blackjackProxy.getHandValue( dealerCards );
581          int playersTotal = blackjackProxy.getHandValue( playerCards );
582
583          // if hands both equal 21, it is a push
584          if ( playersTotal == dealersTotal && playersTotal == 21 )
585          {
586             gameOver( GameStatus.PUSH );
587          }
588          else if ( dealersTotal == 21 ) // blackjackProxy has blackjack
589          {
590             gameOver( GameStatus.LOSE );
591          }
592          else if ( playersTotal == 21 ) // blackjack
593          {
594             gameOver( GameStatus.BLACKJACK );
595          }
596
597          // next card for blackjackProxy has index 2
598          currentDealerCard = 2;
599
600          // next card for player has index 13
601          currentPlayerCard = 13;
602       } // end method dealJButtonActionPerformed
603
604       // handles standJButton click
605       private void hitJButtonActionPerformed(
606          java.awt.event.ActionEvent evt )
607       {
608          // get player another card
609          String card = blackjackProxy.dealCard(); // deal new card
610          playerCards += "\t" + card; // add card to hand
611
612          // update GUI to display new card
613          displayCard( currentPlayerCard, card );
614          ++currentPlayerCard;
615
616          // determine new value of player's hand
617          int total = blackjackProxy.getHandValue( playerCards );
618
619          if ( total > 21 ) // player busts
620          {
621             gameOver( GameStatus.LOSE );
622          }
623          else if ( total == 21 ) // player cannot take any more cards
624          {
625             hitJButton.setEnabled( false );
626             dealerPlay();
627          } // end if
628       } // end method hitJButtonActionPerformed
```

Fig. 31.17 | Blackjack game that uses the Blackjack web service. (Part 7 of 11.)

```
629
630     // handles standJButton click
631     private void standJButtonActionPerformed(
632        java.awt.event.ActionEvent evt )
633     {
634        standJButton.setEnabled( false );
635        hitJButton.setEnabled( false );
636        dealJButton.setEnabled( true );
637        dealerPlay();
638     } // end method standJButtonActionPerformed
639
640     // begins application execution
641     public static void main( String args[] )
642     {
643        java.awt.EventQueue.invokeLater(
644           new Runnable()
645           {
646              public void run()
647              {
648                 new BlackjackGameJFrame().setVisible( true );
649              }
650           }
651        ); // end call to java.awt.EventQueue.invokeLater
652     } // end main
653
654     // Variables declaration - do not modify
655     private javax.swing.JButton dealJButton;
656     private javax.swing.JLabel dealerCard10JLabel;
657     private javax.swing.JLabel dealerCard11JLabel;
658     private javax.swing.JLabel dealerCard1JLabel;
659     private javax.swing.JLabel dealerCard2JLabel;
660     private javax.swing.JLabel dealerCard3JLabel;
661     private javax.swing.JLabel dealerCard4JLabel;
662     private javax.swing.JLabel dealerCard5JLabel;
663     private javax.swing.JLabel dealerCard6JLabel;
664     private javax.swing.JLabel dealerCard7JLabel;
665     private javax.swing.JLabel dealerCard8JLabel;
666     private javax.swing.JLabel dealerCard9JLabel;
667     private javax.swing.JLabel dealerJLabel;
668     private javax.swing.JLabel dealerTotalJLabel;
669     private javax.swing.JButton hitJButton;
670     private javax.swing.JLabel playerCard10JLabel;
671     private javax.swing.JLabel playerCard11JLabel;
672     private javax.swing.JLabel playerCard1JLabel;
673     private javax.swing.JLabel playerCard2JLabel;
674     private javax.swing.JLabel playerCard3JLabel;
675     private javax.swing.JLabel playerCard4JLabel;
676     private javax.swing.JLabel playerCard5JLabel;
677     private javax.swing.JLabel playerCard6JLabel;
678     private javax.swing.JLabel playerCard7JLabel;
679     private javax.swing.JLabel playerCard8JLabel;
680     private javax.swing.JLabel playerCard9JLabel;
681     private javax.swing.JLabel playerJLabel;
682     private javax.swing.JLabel playerTotalJLabel;
```

Fig. 31.17 | Blackjack game that uses the Blackjack web service. (Part 8 of 11.)

```
683    private javax.swing.JButton standJButton;
684    private javax.swing.JLabel statusJLabel;
685    // End of variables declaration
686 } // end class BlackjackGameJFrame
```

a) Dealer and player hands after the user clicks the **Deal** JButton.

b) Dealer and player hands after the user clicks **Hit** twice, then clicks **Stand**. In this case, the result is a push.

Fig. 31.17 | Blackjack game that uses the **Blackjack** web service. (Part 9 of 11.)

c) Dealer and player hands after the user clicks **Stand** based on the initial hand. In this case, the player wins.

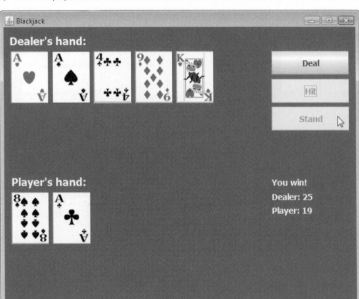

d) Dealer and player hands after the user is dealt blackjack.

Fig. 31.17 | Blackjack game that uses the `Blackjack` web service. (Part 10 of 11.)

e) Dealer and player hands after the dealer is dealt blackjack.

Fig. 31.17 | Blackjack game that uses the `Blackjack` web service. (Part 11 of 11.)

With JAX-WS, the client application must indicate whether it wants to allow the web service to maintain session information. Lines 50–51 in the constructor perform this task. We first cast the service endpoint interface object to interface type `BindingProvider`. A **BindingProvider** enables the client to manipulate the request information that will be sent to the server. This information is stored in an object that implements interface **RequestContext**. The `BindingProvider` and `RequestContext` are part of the framework that is created by the IDE when you add a web service client to the application. Next, we invoke the `BindingProvider`'s **getRequestContext method** to obtain the `RequestContext` object. Then we call the `RequestContext`'s **put method** to set the property

```
BindingProvider.SESSION_MAINTAIN_PROPERTY
```

to `true`. This enables the client side of the session-tracking mechanism, so that the web service knows which client is invoking the service's web methods.

Method `gameOver` (lines 195–233) displays all the dealer's cards, shows the appropriate message in `statusJLabel` and displays the final point totals of both the dealer and the player. Method `gameOver` receives as an argument a member of the `GameStatus` enumeration (defined in lines 25–31). The enumeration represents whether the player tied, lost or won the game; its four members are PUSH, LOSE, WIN and BLACKJACK.

When the player clicks the **Deal** JButton, method `dealJButtonActionPerformed` (lines 543–602) clears all of the JLabels that display cards or game status information. Next, the deck is shuffled (line 559), and the player and dealer receive two cards each (lines 562–573). Lines 580–581 then total each hand. If the player and the dealer both obtain scores of 21, the program calls method `gameOver`, passing `GameStatus.PUSH` (line 586). If only the dealer has 21, the program passes `GameStatus.LOSE` to method `gameOver` (line

590). If only the player has 21 after the first two cards are dealt, the program passes GameStatus.BLACKJACK to method gameOver (line 594).

If dealJButtonActionPerformed does not call gameOver, the player can take more cards by clicking the **Hit** JButton, which calls hitJButtonActionPerformed in lines 605–628. Each time a player clicks **Hit**, the program deals the player one more card (line 609) and displays it in the GUI (line 613). If the player exceeds 21, the game is over and the player loses (line 621). If the player has exactly 21, the player is not allowed to take any more cards (line 625), and method dealerPlay is called (line 626).

Method dealerPlay (lines 86–139) displays the dealer's cards, then deals cards to the dealer until the dealer's hand has a value of 17 or more (lines 100–108). If the dealer exceeds 21, the player wins (line 116); otherwise, the values of the hands are compared, and gameOver is called with the appropriate argument (lines 122–133).

Clicking the **Stand** JButton indicates that a player does not want to be dealt another card. Method standJButtonActionPerformed (lines 631–638) disables the **Hit** and **Stand** buttons, enables the **Deal** button, then calls method dealerPlay.

Method displayCard (lines 142–192) updates the GUI to display a newly dealt card. The method takes as arguments an integer index for the JLabel in the ArrayList that must have its image set and a String representing the card. An empty String indicates that we wish to display the card face down. If method displayCard receives a String that's not empty, the program extracts the face and suit from the String and uses this information to display the correct image. The switch statement (lines 167–181) converts the number representing the suit to an integer and assigns the appropriate character to variable suitLetter (h for hearts, d for diamonds, c for clubs and s for spades). The character in suitLetter is used to complete the image's file name (lines 184–186). *You must add the folder blackjack_images to your project so that lines 152–154 and 184–186 can access the images properly.* To do so, copy the folder blackjack_images from this chapter's examples folder and paste it into the project's src\com\deitel\java\blackjackclient folder.

You just learned how to set up a web service to support session handling so that you could track each client's session state. You also learned how to enable a desktop client application to take part in session tracking. You'll now learn how to access a database from a web service and how to consume a web service from a client web application.

31.10 Consuming a Database-Driven SOAP-Based Web Service

Our prior examples accessed web services from desktop applications created in NetBeans. However, we can just as easily use them in web applications created with NetBeans. In fact, because web-based businesses are becoming increasingly prevalent, it is common for web applications to consume web services. In this section, we present an airline reservation web service that receives information regarding the type of seat a customer wishes to reserve and makes a reservation if such a seat is available. Later in the section, we present a web application that allows a customer to specify a reservation request, then uses the airline reservation web service to attempt to execute the request.

31.10.1 Creating the Reservation Database

In this example, our web service uses a Reservation database containing a single table named Seats to locate a seat matching a client's request. To build the Reservation database, review the steps presented in Section 30.2.1 for building the AddressBook database. This chapter's examples directory contains the Seats.sql SQL script to build the seats table and populate it with sample data. The sample data is shown in Fig. 31.18.

number	location	class	taken
1	Aisle	Economy	0
2	Aisle	Economy	0
3	Aisle	First	0
4	Middle	Economy	0
5	Middle	Economy	0
6	Middle	First	0
7	Window	Economy	0
8	Window	Economy	0
9	Window	First	0
10	Window	First	0

Fig. 31.18 | Data from the seats table.

Creating the Reservation Web Service
You can now create a web service that uses the Reservation database (Fig. 31.19). The airline reservation web service has a single web method—reserve (lines 26–78)—which searches the Seats table to locate a seat matching a user's request. The method takes two arguments—a String representing the desired seat type (i.e., "Window", "Middle" or "Aisle") and a String representing the desired class type (i.e., "Economy" or "First"). If it finds an appropriate seat, method reserve updates the database to make the reservation and returns true; otherwise, no reservation is made, and the method returns false. Note that the statements at lines 34–39 and lines 45–48 that query and update the database use objects of JDBC types ResultSet and PreparedStatement.

Software Engineering Observation 31.1
Using PreparedStatements to create SQL statements is highly recommended to secure against so-called SQL injection attacks in which executable code is inserted into SQL code. The site www.owasp.org/index.php/Preventing_SQL_Injection_in_Java provides a summary of SQL injection attacks and ways to mitigate against them.

```
1   // Fig. 31.19: Reservation.java
2   // Airline reservation web service.
3   package com.deitel.java.reservation;
4
5   import java.sql.Connection;
6   import java.sql.DriverManager;
7   import java.sql.PreparedStatement;
8   import java.sql.ResultSet;
9   import java.sql.SQLException;
10  import javax.jws.WebMethod;
11  import javax.jws.WebParam;
12  import javax.jws.WebService;
```

Fig. 31.19 | Airline reservation web service. (Part 1 of 3.)

```
13
14   @WebService( name = "Reservation", serviceName = "ReservationService" )
15   public class Reservation
16   {
17      private static final String DATABASE_URL =
18         "jdbc:derby://localhost:1527/Reservation";
19      private static final String USERNAME = "test";
20      private static final String PASSWORD = "test";
21      private Connection connection;
22      private PreparedStatement lookupSeat;
23      private PreparedStatement reserveSeat;
24
25      // a WebMethod that can reserve a seat
26      @WebMethod( operationName = "reserve" )
27      public boolean reserve( @WebParam( name = "seatType" ) String seatType,
28         @WebParam( name = "classType" ) String classType )
29      {
30         try
31         {
32            connection = DriverManager.getConnection(
33               DATABASE_URL, USERNAME, PASSWORD );
34            lookupSeat = connection.prepareStatement(
35               "SELECT \"number\" FROM \"seats\" WHERE (\"taken\" = 0) " +
36               "AND (\"location\" = ?) AND (\"class\" = ?)" );
37            lookupSeat.setString( 1, seatType );
38            lookupSeat.setString( 2, classType );
39            ResultSet resultSet = lookupSeat.executeQuery();
40
41            // if requested seat is available, reserve it
42            if ( resultSet.next() )
43            {
44               int seat = resultSet.getInt( 1 );
45               reserveSeat = connection.prepareStatement(
46                  "UPDATE \"seats\" SET \"taken\"=1 WHERE \"number\"=?" );
47               reserveSeat.setInt( 1, seat );
48               reserveSeat.executeUpdate();
49               return true;
50            } // end if
51
52            return false;
53         } // end try
54         catch ( SQLException e )
55         {
56            e.printStackTrace();
57            return false;
58         } // end catch
59         catch ( Exception e )
60         {
61            e.printStackTrace();
62            return false;
63         } // end catch
64         finally
65         {
```

Fig. 31.19 | Airline reservation web service. (Part 2 of 3.)

```
66              try
67              {
68                  lookupSeat.close();
69                  reserveSeat.close();
70                  connection.close();
71              } // end try
72              catch ( Exception e )
73              {
74                  e.printStackTrace();
75                  return false;
76              } // end catch
77          } // end finally
78      } // end WebMethod reserve
79  } // end class Reservation
```

Fig. 31.19 | Airline reservation web service. (Part 3 of 3.)

Our database contains four columns—the seat number (i.e., 1–10), the seat type (i.e., Window, Middle or Aisle), the class type (i.e., Economy or First) and a column containing either 1 (true) or 0 (false) to indicate whether the seat is taken. Lines 34–39 retrieve the seat numbers of any available seats matching the requested seat and class type. This statement fills the resultSet with the results of the query

```
SELECT "number"
FROM "seats"
WHERE ("taken" = 0) AND ("type" = type) AND ("class" = class)
```

The parameters *type* and *class* in the query are replaced with values of method reserve's seatType and classType parameters. When you use the NetBeans tools to create a database table and its columns, the NetBeans tools automatically place the table and column names in double quotes. For this reason, you must place the table and column names in double quotes in the SQL statements that interact with the Reservation database.

If resultSet is not empty (i.e., at least one seat is available that matches the selected criteria), the condition in line 42 is true and the web service reserves the first matching seat number. Recall that ResultSet method next returns true if a nonempty row exists, and positions the cursor on that row. We obtain the seat number (line 44) by accessing resultSet's first column (i.e., resultSet.getInt(1)—the first column in the row). Then lines 45–48 configure a PreparedStatement and execute the SQL:

```
UPDATE "seats"
SET "taken" = 1
WHERE ("number" = number)
```

which marks the seat as taken in the database. The parameter *number* is replaced with the value of seat. Method reserve returns true (line 49) to indicate that the reservation was successful. If there are no matching seats, or if an exception occurred, method reserve returns false (lines 52, 57, 62 and 75) to indicate that no seats matched the user's request.

31.10.2 Creating a Web Application to Interact with the Reservation Service

This section presents a ReservationClient web application that consumes the Reservation web service. The application allows users to select seats based on class ("Economy" or

"First") and location ("Aisle", "Middle" or "Window"), then submit their requests to the airline reservation web service. If the database request is not successful, the application instructs the user to modify the request and try again. The application presented here was built using the techniques presented in Chapters 6–30. We assume that you've already read those chapters and thus know how to build a web application's GUI, create event handlers and add properties to a web application's session bean (Section 29.7.2).

Reserve.jsp

Reserve.jsp (Fig. 31.20) defines two DropDownLists and a Button. The seatTypeDrop-Down (lines 23–28) displays all the seat types from which users can select. The classType-DropDownList (lines 29–35) provides choices for the class type. When the user makes a selection from each of these, corresponding event handlers store the selected values in the session bean. We added seatType and classType properties to the session bean for this purpose. Users click the reserveButton (lines 36–40) to submit requests after making selections from the DropDownLists. The page also defines three Labels—instructionLabel (lines 18–22) to display instructions, successLabel (lines 41–44) to indicate a successful reservation and errorLabel (lines 45–49) to display a message if there are no seats that match the user's selection. The page bean file (Fig. 31.21) contains the event handlers for seatTypeDropDown, classTypeDropDown and reserveButton.

```
1   <?xml version="1.0" encoding="UTF-8"?>
2   <!-- Fig. 31.20 Reserve.jsp -->
3   <!-- JSP that allows a user to select a seat -->
4   <jsp:root version="2.1" xmlns:f="http://java.sun.com/jsf/core"
5      xmlns:h="http://java.sun.com/jsf/html"
6      xmlns:jsp="http://java.sun.com/JSP/Page"
7      xmlns:webuijsf="http://www.sun.com/webui/webuijsf">
8      <jsp:directive.page contentType="text/html;charset=UTF-8"
9         pageEncoding="UTF-8"/>
10     <f:view>
11        <webuijsf:page id="page1">
12           <webuijsf:html id="html1">
13              <webuijsf:head id="head1">
14                 <webuijsf:link id="link1" url="/resources/stylesheet.css"/>
15              </webuijsf:head>
16              <webuijsf:body id="body1" style="-rave-layout: grid">
17                 <webuijsf:form id="form1">
18                    <webuijsf:label binding="#{Reserve.instructionLabel}"
19                       id="instructionLabel"
20                       style="left: 24px; top: 24px; position: absolute"
21                       text="Please select the seat type and class to
22                          reserve:"/>
23                    <webuijsf:dropDown binding="#{Reserve.seatTypeDropDown}"
24                       id="seatTypeDropDown" items="#{Reserve.
25                          seatTypeDropDownDefaultOptions.options}"
26                       style="left: 24px; top: 48px; position: absolute"
27                       valueChangeListenerExpression=
28                          "#{Reserve.seatTypeDropDown_processValueChange}"/>
29                    <webuijsf:dropDown
30                       binding="#{Reserve.classTypeDropDown}"
```

Fig. 31.20 | JSP that allows a user to select a seat. (Part 1 of 3.)

```
31                          id="classTypeDropDown" items="#{Reserve.
32                            classTypeDropDownDefaultOptions.options}"
33                          style="left: 96px; top: 48px; position: absolute"
34                          valueChangeListenerExpression="#{Reserve.
35                            classTypeDropDown_processValueChange}"/>
36                      <webuijsf:button
37                          actionExpression="#{Reserve.reserveButton_action}"
38                          binding="#{Reserve.reserveButton}" id="reserveButton"
39                          style="left: 191px; top: 48px; position: absolute"
40                          text="Reserve"/>
41                      <webuijsf:label binding=v
42                          id="successLabel" rendered="false" style="left: 24px;
43                            top: 24px; position: absolute"
44                          text="Your reservation has been made. Thank you!"/>
45                      <webuijsf:label binding="#{Reserve.errorLabel}"
46                          id="errorLabel" rendered="false" style="color: red;
47                            left: 24px; top: 96px; position: absolute"
48                          text="This type of seat is not available. Please
49                            modify your request and try again."/>
50                  </webuijsf:form>
51              </webuijsf:body>
52          </webuijsf:html>
53      </webuijsf:page>
54    </f:view>
55  </jsp:root>
```

a) Selecting a seat

b) Seat reserved successfully

c) Attempting to reserve another window seat in economy when there are no such seats available

Fig. 31.20 | JSP that allows a user to select a seat. (Part 2 of 3.)

d) No seats
match the
requested seat
type and class

Fig. 31.20 | JSP that allows a user to select a seat. (Part 3 of 3.)

Reserve.java

Figure 31.21 contains the page bean code that provides the logic for Reserve.jsp. As discussed in Section 29.5.2, the class that represents the page's bean extends AbstractPage-Bean. When the user selects a value in one of the DropDownLists, the corresponding event handler—seatTypeDropDown_processValueChange (lines 199–204) or classTypeDrop-Down_processValueChange (lines 207–212)—is called to set the session properties seat-Type and classType, which we added to the web application's session bean. The values of these properties are used as the arguments in the call to the web service's reserve method. When the user clicks **Reserve** in the JSP, the event handler reserveButton_action (lines 215–248) executes. Lines 219–221 use the service endpoint interface object (created in lines 40–41) to invoke the web service's reserve method, passing the selected seat type and class type as arguments. If reserve returns true, lines 225–230 hide the GUI components in the JSP and display the successLabel (line 229) to thank the user for making a reservation; otherwise, lines 234–239 ensure that the GUI components remain displayed, display the errorLabel (line 239) to notify the user that the requested seat type is not available and instruct the user to try again.

```
 1   // Fig. 31.21: Reserve.java
 2   // Page bean for seat reservation client.
 3   package reservationclient;
 4
 5   import com.deitel.java.reservation.Reservation;
 6   import com.deitel.java.reservation.ReservationService;
 7   import com.sun.rave.web.ui.appbase.AbstractPageBean;
 8   import com.sun.webui.jsf.component.Button;
 9   import com.sun.webui.jsf.component.DropDown;
10   import com.sun.webui.jsf.component.Label;
11   import com.sun.webui.jsf.model.SingleSelectOptionsList;
12   import javax.faces.FacesException;
13   import javax.faces.event.ValueChangeEvent;
14
15   public class Reserve extends AbstractPageBean
16   {
17      // references the service endpoint interface object (i.e., the proxy)
18      private Reservation reservationServiceProxy; // reference to proxy
19
```

Fig. 31.21 | Page bean for seat reservation client. (Part 1 of 3.)

```
20     // Managed Component Definition"
21     private void _init() throws Exception
22     {
23        seatTypeDropDownDefaultOptions.setOptions(
24           new com.sun.webui.jsf.model.Option[]
25           {
26              new com.sun.webui.jsf.model.Option( "Aisle", "Aisle" ),
27              new com.sun.webui.jsf.model.Option( "Middle", "Middle" ),
28              new com.sun.webui.jsf.model.Option( "Window", "Window" )
29           }
30        );
31        classTypeDropDownDefaultOptions.setOptions(
32           new com.sun.webui.jsf.model.Option[]
33           {
34              new com.sun.webui.jsf.model.Option( "Economy", "Economy" ),
35              new com.sun.webui.jsf.model.Option( "First", "First" )
36           }
37        );
38
39        // get service endpoint interface
40        ReservationService reservationService = new ReservationService();
41        reservationServiceProxy = reservationService.getReservationPort();
42     } // end method _init
43
44     // Lines 44-197 of the autogenerated code have been removed to save
45     // space. The complete code is available in this example's folder.
46
198    // store selected seat type in session bean
199    public void seatTypeDropDown_processValueChange(
200       ValueChangeEvent event )
201    {
202       getSessionBean1().setSeatType(
203          ( String ) seatTypeDropDown.getSelected() );
204    } // end method seatTypeDropDown_processValueChange
205
206    // store selected class in session bean
207    public void classTypeDropDown_processValueChange(
208       ValueChangeEvent event )
209    {
210       getSessionBean1().setClassType(
211          ( String ) classTypeDropDown.getSelected() );
212    } // end method classTypeDropDown_processValueChange
213
214    // invoke the web service when the user clicks Reserve button
215    public String reserveButton_action()
216    {
217       try
218       {
219          boolean reserved = reservationServiceProxy.reserve(
220             getSessionBean1().getSeatType(),
221             getSessionBean1().getClassType() );
222
223          if ( reserved ) // display successLabel; hide all others
224          {
```

Fig. 31.21 | Page bean for seat reservation client. (Part 2 of 3.)

```
225                instructionLabel.setRendered( false );
226                seatTypeDropDown.setRendered( false );
227                classTypeDropDown.setRendered( false );
228                reserveButton.setRendered( false );
229                successLabel.setRendered( true );
230                errorLabel.setRendered( false );
231           } // end if
232           else // display all but successLabel
233           {
234                instructionLabel.setRendered( true );
235                seatTypeDropDown.setRendered( true );
236                classTypeDropDown.setRendered( true );
237                reserveButton.setRendered( true );
238                successLabel.setRendered( false );
239                errorLabel.setRendered( true );
240           } // end else
241        } // end try
242        catch ( Exception e )
243        {
244           e.printStackTrace();
245        } // end catch
246
247        return null;
248     } // end method reserveButton_action
249 } // end class Reserve
```

Fig. 31.21 | Page bean for seat reservation client. (Part 3 of 3.)

31.11 Equation Generator: Returning User-Defined Types

Most of the web services we've demonstrated received and returned primitive-type instances. It's also possible to process instances of class types in a web service. These types can be passed to or returned from web service methods.

This section presents a RESTful EquationGenerator web service that generates random arithmetic equations of type Equation. The client is a math-tutoring application that accepts information about the mathematical question that the user wishes to attempt (addition, subtraction or multiplication) and the skill level of the user (1 specifies equations using numbers from 1 through 9, 2 specifies equations involving numbers from 10 through 99, and 3 specifies equations containing numbers from 100 through 999). The web service then generates an equation consisting of random numbers in the proper range. The client application receives the Equation and displays the sample question to the user.

Defining Class Equation
We define class Equation in Fig. 31.22. All the programs in this section have a copy of this class in their corresponding package. Except for the package name, the class is identical in each project, so we show it only once. Note that, like the TextMessage class used earlier, the server-side and client-side copies of class Equation are unrelated to each other. The only requirement for serialization and deserialization to work with the JAXB and Gson classes is that class Equation must have the same public properties on both the server and the client. Such properties can be public instance variables or private instance variables that have corresponding *set* and *get* methods.

```
1    // Fig. 31.22: Equation.java
2    // Equation class that contains information about an equation.
3    package com.deitel.equationgeneratorxml;
4
5    public class Equation
6    {
7       private int leftOperand;
8       private int rightOperand;
9       private int result;
10      private String operationType;
11
12      // required no-argument constructor
13      public Equation()
14      {
15         this( 0, 0, "add" );
16      } // end no-argument constructor
17
18      // constructor that receives the operands and operation type
19      public Equation( int leftValue, int rightValue, String type )
20      {
21         leftOperand = leftValue;
22         rightOperand = rightValue;
23
24         // determine result
25         if ( type.equals( "add" ) ) // addition
26         {
27            result = leftOperand + rightOperand;
28            operationType = "+";
29         } // end if
30         else if ( type.equals( "subtract" ) ) // subtraction
31         {
32            result = leftOperand - rightOperand;
33            operationType = "-";
34         } // end if
35         else // multiplication
36         {
37            result = leftOperand * rightOperand;
38            operationType = "*";
39         } // end else
40      } // end three argument constructor
41
42      // gets the leftOperand
43      public int getLeftOperand()
44      {
45         return leftOperand;
46      } // end method getLeftOperand
47
48      // required setter
49      public void setLeftOperand( int value )
50      {
51         leftOperand = value;
52      } // end method setLeftOperand
53
```

Fig. 31.22 | Equation class that contains information about an equation. (Part 1 of 2.)

```
54    // gets the rightOperand
55    public int getRightOperand()
56    {
57       return rightOperand;
58    } // end method getRightOperand
59
60    // required setter
61    public void setRightOperand( int value )
62    {
63       rightOperand = value;
64    } // end method setRightOperand
65
66    // gets the resultValue
67    public int getResult()
68    {
69       return result;
70    } // end method getResult
71
72    // required setter
73    public void setResult( int value )
74    {
75       result = value;
76    } // end method setResult
77
78    // gets the operationType
79    public String getOperationType()
80    {
81       return operationType;
82    } // end method getOperationType
83
84    // required setter
85    public void setOperationType( String value )
86    {
87       operationType = value;
88    } // end method setOperationType
89
90    // returns the left hand side of the equation as a String
91    public String getLeftHandSide()
92    {
93       return leftOperand + " " + operationType + " " + rightOperand;
94    } // end method getLeftHandSide
95
96    // returns the right hand side of the equation as a String
97    public String getRightHandSide()
98    {
99       return "" + result;
100   } // end method getRightHandSide
101
102   // returns a String representation of an Equation
103   public String toString()
104   {
105      return getLeftHandSide() + " = " + getRightHandSide();
106   } // end method toString
107 } // end class Equation
```

Fig. 31.22 | Equation class that contains information about an equation. (Part 2 of 2.)

Lines 19–40 define a constructor that takes two `int`s representing the left and right operands, and a `String` representing the arithmetic operation. The constructor stores this information, then calculates the result. The parameterless constructor (lines 13–16) calls the three-argument constructor (lines 19–40) and passes default values.

Class `Equation` defines *get* and *set* methods for instance variables `leftOperand` (lines 43–52), `rightOperand` (lines 55–64), `result` (line 67–76) and `operationType` (lines 79–88). It also provides *get* methods for the left-hand and right-hand sides of the equation and a `toString` method that returns the entire equation as a `String`. An instance variable can be serialized only if it has both a *get* and a *set* method. Because the different sides of the equation and the result of `toString` can be generated from the other instance variables, there is no need to send them across the wire. The client in this case study does not use the `getRightHandSide` method, but we included it in case future clients choose to use it.

31.11.1 Creating the REST-Based XML EquationGenerator Web Service

Figure 31.23 presents the `EquationGeneratorXML` web service's class for creating randomly generated `Equation`s. Method `getXml` (lines 19–38) takes two parameters—a `String` representing the mathematical operation (`"add"`, `"subtract"` or `"multiply"`) and an `int` representing the difficulty level. JAX-RS automatically converts the arguments to the correct type and will return a "not found" error to the client if the argument cannot be converted from a `String` to the destination type. Supported types for conversion include integer types, floating-point types, `boolean` and the corresponding type-wrapper classes.

```java
 1   // Fig. 31.23: EquationGeneratorXMLResource.java
 2   // RESTful equation generator that returns XML.
 3   package com.deitel.equationgeneratorxml;
 4
 5   import java.io.StringWriter;
 6   import java.util.Random;
 7   import javax.ws.rs.GET;
 8   import javax.ws.rs.Path;
 9   import javax.ws.rs.PathParam;
10   import javax.ws.rs.Produces;
11   import javax.xml.bind.JAXB; // utility class for common JAXB operations
12
13   @Path( "equation" )
14   public class EquationGeneratorXMLResource
15   {
16      static Random randomObject = new Random(); // random number generator
17
18      // retrieve an equation formatted as XML
19      @GET
20      @Path( "{operation}/{level}" )
21      @Produces( "application/xml" )
22      public String getXml( @PathParam( "operation" ) String operation,
23         @PathParam( "level" ) int level )
24      {
25         // compute minimum and maximum values for the numbers
26         int minimum = ( int ) Math.pow( 10, level - 1 );
```

Fig. 31.23 | A REST equation generator that returns XML. (Part 1 of 2.)

```
27        int maximum = ( int ) Math.pow( 10, level );
28
29        // create the numbers on the left-hand side of the equation
30        int first = randomObject.nextInt( maximum - minimum ) + minimum;
31        int second = randomObject.nextInt( maximum - minimum ) + minimum;
32
33        // create Equation object and marshal it into XML
34        Equation equation = new Equation( first, second, operation );
35        StringWriter writer = new StringWriter(); // XML output here
36        JAXB.marshal( equation, writer ); // write Equation to StringWriter
37        return writer.toString(); // return XML string
38     } // end method getXml
39  } // end class EquationGeneratorXMLResource
```

Fig. 31.23 | A REST equation generator that returns XML. (Part 2 of 2.)

The getXml method first determines the minimum (inclusive) and maximum (exclusive) values for the numbers in the equation it will return (lines 26–27). It then uses a static member of the Random class (line 16) to generate two random numbers in that range (lines 30–31). Line 34 creates an Equation object, passing these two numbers and the requested operation to the constructor. The getXml method then uses JAXB to convert the Equation object to XML (line 36), which is output to the StringWriter created on line 35. Finally, it retrieves the data that was written to the StringWriter and returns it to the client. [*Note:* We'll reimplement this web service with JSON in Section 31.11.3.]

31.11.2 Consuming the REST-Based XML EquationGenerator Web Service

The EquationGeneratorXMLClient application (Fig. 31.24) retrieves an Equation object formatted as XML from the EquationGeneratorXML web service. The client application then displays the left-hand side of the Equation and waits for user to evaluate the expression and enter the result.

```
1   // Fig. 31.24: EquationGeneratorXMLClientJFrame.java
2   // Math tutoring program using REST and XML to generate equations.
3   package com.deitel.equationgeneratorxmlclient;
4
5   import javax.swing.JOptionPane;
6   import javax.xml.bind.JAXB; // utility class for common JAXB operations
7
8   public class EquationGeneratorXMLClientJFrame extends javax.swing.JFrame
9   {
10     private String operation = "add"; // operation user is tested on
11     private int difficulty = 1; // 1, 2, or 3 digits in each number
12     private int answer; // correct answer to the question
13
14     // no-argument constructor
15     public EquationGeneratorXMLClientJFrame()
16     {
17        initComponents();
18     } // end no-argument constructor
```

Fig. 31.24 | Math-tutoring program using REST and XML to generate equations. (Part 1 of 4.)

```
19
20      // The initComponents method is autogenerated by NetBeans and is called
21      // from the constructor to initialize the GUI. This method is not shown
22      // here to save space. Open EquationGeneratorXMLClientJFrame.java in
23      // this example's folder to view the complete generated code.
24
143     // determine if the user answered correctly
144     private void checkAnswerJButtonActionPerformed(
145        java.awt.event.ActionEvent evt)
146     {
147        if ( answerJTextField.getText().equals( "" ) )
148        {
149           JOptionPane.showMessageDialog(
150              this, "Please enter your answer." );
151        } // end if
152
153        int userAnswer = Integer.parseInt( answerJTextField.getText() );
154
155        if ( userAnswer == answer )
156        {
157           equationJLabel.setText( "" ); // clear label
158           answerJTextField.setText( "" ); // clear text field
159           checkAnswerJButton.setEnabled( false );
160           JOptionPane.showMessageDialog( this, "Correct! Good Job!",
161              "Correct", JOptionPane.PLAIN_MESSAGE );
162        } // end if
163        else
164        {
165           JOptionPane.showMessageDialog( this, "Incorrect. Try again.",
166              "Incorrect", JOptionPane.PLAIN_MESSAGE );
167        } // end else
168     } // end method checkAnswerJButtonActionPerformed
169
170     // retrieve equation from web service and display left side to user
171     private void generateJButtonActionPerformed(
172        java.awt.event.ActionEvent evt)
173     {
174        try
175        {
176           String url = String.format( "http://localhost:8080/" +
177              "EquationGeneratorXML/resources/equation/%s/%d",
178              operation, difficulty );
179
180           // convert XML back to an Equation object
181           Equation equation = JAXB.unmarshal( url, Equation.class );
182
183           answer = equation.getResult();
184           equationJLabel.setText( equation.getLeftHandSide() + " =" );
185           checkAnswerJButton.setEnabled( true );
186        } // end try
187        catch ( Exception exception )
188        {
189           exception.printStackTrace();
190        } // end catch
```

Fig. 31.24 | Math-tutoring program using REST and XML to generate equations. (Part 2 of 4.)

```
191      } // end method generateJButtonActionPerformed
192
193      // obtains the mathematical operation selected by the user
194      private void operationJComboBoxItemStateChanged(
195         java.awt.event.ItemEvent evt)
196      {
197         String item = ( String ) operationJComboBox.getSelectedItem();
198
199         if ( item.equals( "Addition" ) )
200            operation = "add"; // user selected addition
201         else if ( item.equals( "Subtraction" ) )
202            operation = "subtract"; // user selected subtraction
203         else
204            operation = "multiply"; // user selected multiplication
205      } // end method operationJComboBoxItemStateChanged
206
207      // obtains the difficulty level selected by the user
208      private void levelJComboBoxItemStateChanged(
209         java.awt.event.ItemEvent evt)
210      {
211         // indices start at 0, so add 1 to get the difficulty level
212         difficulty = levelJComboBox.getSelectedIndex() + 1;
213      } // end method levelJComboBoxItemStateChanged
214
215      // main method begins execution
216      public static void main(String args[])
217      {
218         java.awt.EventQueue.invokeLater(
219            new Runnable()
220            {
221               public void run()
222               {
223                  new EquationGeneratorXMLClientJFrame().setVisible( true );
224               } // end method run
225            } // end anonymous inner class
226         ); // end call to java.awt.EventQueue.invokeLater
227      } // end main
228
229      // Variables declaration - do not modify
230      private javax.swing.JLabel answerJLabel;
231      private javax.swing.JTextField answerJTextField;
232      private javax.swing.JButton checkAnswerJButton;
233      private javax.swing.JLabel equationJLabel;
234      private javax.swing.JButton generateJButton;
235      private javax.swing.JComboBox levelJComboBox;
236      private javax.swing.JLabel levelJLabel;
237      private javax.swing.JComboBox operationJComboBox;
238      private javax.swing.JLabel operationJLabel;
239      private javax.swing.JLabel questionJLabel;
240      // End of variables declaration
241 } // end class EquationGeneratorXMLClientJFrame
```

Fig. 31.24 | Math-tutoring program using REST and XML to generate equations. (Part 3 of 4.)

a) Generating a
simple equation.

b) Answering a
more complicated
subtraction
equation.

Fig. 31.24 | Math-tutoring program using REST and XML to generate equations. (Part 4 of 4.)

The default setting for the difficulty level is 1, but the user can change this by choosing a level from the **Choose level** JComboBox. Changing the selected value invokes the level-JComboBoxItemStateChanged event handler (lines 208–213), which sets the difficulty instance variable to the level selected by the user. Although the default setting for the question type is **Addition**, the user also can change this by choosing from the **Choose operation** JComboBox. This invokes the operationJComboBoxItemStateChanged event handler in lines 194–205, which assigns to instance variable operation the String corresponding to the user's selection.

The event handler for generateJButton (lines 171–191) constructs the URL to invoke the web service, then passes this URL to the unmarshal method, along with an instance of Class<Equation>, so that JAXB can convert the XML into an Equation object (line 181). Once the XML has been converted back into an Equation, lines 183–184 retrieve the correct answer and display the left-hand side of the equation. The **Check Answer** button is then enabled (line 185), and the user must solve the problem and enter the answer.

When the user enters a value and clicks **Check Answer**, the checkAnswerJButtonActionPerformed event handler (lines 144–168) retrieves the user's answer from the dialog box (line 153) and compares it to the correct answer that was stored earlier (line 155). If they match, lines 157–161 reset the GUI elements so the user can generate another equation and tell the user that the answer was correct. If they do not match, a message box asking the user to try again is displayed (lines 165–166).

31.11.3 Creating the REST-Based JSON EquationGenerator Web Service

As you saw in Section 31.8, RESTful web services can return data formatted as JSON as well. Figure 31.25 is a reimplementation of the EquationGeneratorXML service that returns an Equation in JSON format.

```
1   // Fig. 31.25: EquationGeneratorJSONResource.java
2   // RESTful equation generator that returns JSON.
3   package com.deitel.equationgeneratorjson;
4
5   import com.google.gson.Gson; // converts POJO to JSON and back again
```

Fig. 31.25 | RESTful equation generator that returns JSON. (Part 1 of 2.)

```
 6   import java.util.Random;
 7   import javax.ws.rs.GET;
 8   import javax.ws.rs.Path;
 9   import javax.ws.rs.PathParam;
10   import javax.ws.rs.Produces;
11
12   @Path( "equation" )
13   public class EquationGeneratorJSONResource
14   {
15      static Random randomObject = new Random(); // random number generator
16
17      // retrieve an equation formatted as JSON
18      @GET
19      @Path( "{operation}/{level}" )
20      @Produces( "application/json" )
21      public String getJson( @PathParam( "operation" ) String operation,
22         @PathParam( "level" ) int level )
23      {
24         // compute minimum and maximum values for the numbers
25         int minimum = ( int ) Math.pow( 10, level - 1 );
26         int maximum = ( int ) Math.pow( 10, level );
27
28         // create the numbers on the left-hand side of the equation
29         int first = randomObject.nextInt( maximum - minimum ) + minimum;
30         int second = randomObject.nextInt( maximum - minimum ) + minimum;
31
32         // create Equation object and return result
33         Equation equation = new Equation( first, second, operation );
34         return new Gson().toJson( equation ); // convert to JSON and return
35      } // end method getJson
36   } // end class EquationGeneratorJSONResource
```

Fig. 31.25 | RESTful equation generator that returns JSON. (Part 2 of 2.)

The logic implemented here is the same as the XML version except for the last line (line 34), which uses Gson to convert the Equation object into JSON instead of using JAXB to convert it into XML. Note that the @Produces annotation (line 20) has also changed to reflect the JSON data format.

31.11.4 Consuming the REST-Based JSON EquationGenerator Web Service

The program in Fig. 31.26 consumes the EquationGeneratorJSON service and performs the same function as EquationGeneratorXMLClient—the only difference is in how the Equation object is retrieved from the web service. Lines 181–183 construct the URL that is used to invoke the EquationGeneratorJSON service. As in the WelcomeRESTJSONClient example, we use the URL class and an InputStreamReader to invoke the web service and read the response (lines 186–187). The retrieved JSON is deserialized using Gson (line 191) and converted back into an Equation object. As before, we use the getResult method (line 194) of the deserialized object to obtain the answer and the getLeftHandSide method (line 195) to display the left side of the equation.

```
 1   // Fig. 31.26: EquationGeneratorJSONClientJFrame.java
 2   // Math tutoring program using REST and JSON to generate equations.
 3   package com.deitel.equationgeneratorjsonclient;
 4
 5   import com.google.gson.Gson; // converts POJO to JSON and back again
 6   import java.io.InputStreamReader;
 7   import java.net.URL;
 8   import javax.swing.JOptionPane;
 9
10   public class EquationGeneratorJSONClientJFrame extends javax.swing.JFrame
11   {
12      private String operation = "add"; // operation user is tested on
13      private int difficulty = 1; // 1, 2, or 3 digits in each number
14      private int answer; // correct answer to the question
15
16      // no-argument constructor
17      public EquationGeneratorJSONClientJFrame()
18      {
19         initComponents();
20      } // end no-argument constructor
21
22      // The initComponents method is autogenerated by NetBeans and is called
23      // from the constructor to initialize the GUI. This method is not shown
24      // here to save space. Open EquationGeneratorJSONClientJFrame.java in
25      // this example's folder to view the complete generated code.
26
147      // determine if the user answered correctly
148      private void checkAnswerJButtonActionPerformed(
149         java.awt.event.ActionEvent evt)
150      {
151         if ( answerJTextField.getText().equals( "" ) )
152         {
153            JOptionPane.showMessageDialog(
154               this, "Please enter your answer." );
155         } // end if
156
157         int userAnswer = Integer.parseInt( answerJTextField.getText() );
158
159         if ( userAnswer == answer )
160         {
161            equationJLabel.setText( "" ); // clear label
162            answerJTextField.setText( "" ); // clear text field
163            checkAnswerJButton.setEnabled( false );
164            JOptionPane.showMessageDialog( this, "Correct! Good Job!",
165               "Correct", JOptionPane.PLAIN_MESSAGE );
166         } // end if
167         else
168         {
169            JOptionPane.showMessageDialog( this, "Incorrect. Try again.",
170               "Incorrect", JOptionPane.PLAIN_MESSAGE );
171         } // end else
172      } // end method checkAnswerJButtonActionPerformed
173
```

Fig. 31.26 | Math-tutoring program using REST and JSON to generate equations. (Part 1 of 3.)

```
174     // retrieve equation from web service and display left side to user
175     private void generateJButtonActionPerformed(
176        java.awt.event.ActionEvent evt)
177     {
178        try
179        {
180           // URL of the EquationGeneratorJSON service, with parameters
181           String url = String.format( "http://localhost:8080/" +
182              "EquationGeneratorJSON/resources/equation/%s/%d",
183              operation, difficulty );
184
185           // open URL and create a Reader to read the data
186           InputStreamReader reader =
187              new InputStreamReader( new URL( url ).openStream() );
188
189           // convert the JSON back into an Equation object
190           Equation equation =
191              new Gson().fromJson( reader, Equation.class );
192
193           // update the internal state and GUI to reflect the equation
194           answer = equation.getResult();
195           equationJLabel.setText( equation.getLeftHandSide() + " =" );
196           checkAnswerJButton.setEnabled( true );
197        } // end try
198        catch ( Exception exception )
199        {
200           exception.printStackTrace();
201        } // end catch
202     } // end method generateJButtonActionPerformed
203
204     // obtains the mathematical operation selected by the user
205     private void operationJComboBoxItemStateChanged(
206        java.awt.event.ItemEvent evt)
207     {
208        String item = ( String ) operationJComboBox.getSelectedItem();
209
210        if ( item.equals( "Addition" ) )
211           operation = "add"; // user selected addition
212        else if ( item.equals( "Subtraction" ) )
213           operation = "subtract"; // user selected subtraction
214        else
215           operation = "multiply"; // user selected multiplication
216     } // end method operationJComboBoxItemStateChanged
217
218     // obtains the difficulty level selected by the user
219     private void levelJComboBoxItemStateChanged(
220        java.awt.event.ItemEvent evt)
221     {
222        // indices start at 0, so add 1 to get the difficulty level
223        difficulty = levelJComboBox.getSelectedIndex() + 1;
224     } // end method levelJComboBoxItemStateChanged
225
```

Fig. 31.26 | Math-tutoring program using REST and JSON to generate equations. (Part 2 of 3.)

```
226    // main method begins execution
227    public static void main( String args[] )
228    {
229       java.awt.EventQueue.invokeLater(
230          new Runnable()
231          {
232             public void run()
233             {
234                new EquationGeneratorJSONClientJFrame().setVisible( true );
235             } // end method run
236          } // end anonymous inner class
237       ); // end call to java.awt.EventQueue.invokeLater
238    } // end main
239
240    // Variables declaration - do not modify
241    private javax.swing.JLabel answerJLabel;
242    private javax.swing.JTextField answerJTextField;
243    private javax.swing.JButton checkAnswerJButton;
244    private javax.swing.JLabel equationJLabel;
245    private javax.swing.JButton generateJButton;
246    private javax.swing.JComboBox levelJComboBox;
247    private javax.swing.JLabel levelJLabel;
248    private javax.swing.JComboBox operationJComboBox;
249    private javax.swing.JLabel operationJLabel;
250    private javax.swing.JLabel questionJLabel;
251    // End of variables declaration
252 } // end class EquationGeneratorJSONClientJFrame
```

Fig. 31.26 | Math-tutoring program using REST and JSON to generate equations. (Part 3 of 3.)

31.12 Wrap-Up

This chapter introduced web services—a set of technologies for building distributed systems in which system components communicate with one another over networks. In particular, we presented JAX-WS SOAP-based web services and JAX-RS REST-based web services. You learned that a web service is a class that allows client software to call the web service's methods remotely via common data formats and protocols, such as XML, JSON, HTTP, SOAP and REST. We also discussed several benefits of distributed computing with web services.

We explained how NetBeans and the JAX-WS and JAX-RS APIs facilitate publishing and consuming web services. You learned how to define web services and methods using both SOAP protocol and REST architecture, and how to return data in both XML and JSON formats. You consumed SOAP-based web services using proxy classes to call the web service's methods. You also consumed REST-based web services by using class URL to invoke the services and open InputStreams from which the clients could read the services' responses. You learned how to define web services and web methods, as well as how to consume them both from Java desktop applications and from web applications. After explaining the mechanics of web services through our Welcome examples, we demonstrated more sophisticated web services that use session tracking, database access and user-defined types. We also explained XML and JSON serialization and showed how to retrieve objects of user-defined types from web services.

Summary

Section 31.1 Introduction
- A web service is a software component stored on one computer that can be accessed by an application (or other software component) on another computer over a network.
- Web services communicate using such technologies as XML, JSON and HTTP.
- JAX-WS is based on the Simple Object Access Protocol (SOAP)—an XML-based protocol that allows web services and clients to communicate.
- JAX-RS uses Representational State Transfer (REST)—a network architecture that uses the web's traditional request/response mechanisms such as GET and POST requests.
- Web services enable businesses to conduct transactions via standardized, widely available web services rather than relying on proprietary applications.
- Web services are platform and language independent, so companies can collaborate via web services without hardware, software and communications compatibility issues.
- NetBeans is one of the many tools that enable you to "publish" and/or "consume" web services.

Section 31.2 Web Service Basics
- The machine on which a web service resides is referred to as a web service host.
- A client application that accesses the web service sends a method call over a network to the web service host, which processes the call and returns a response over the network to the application.
- In Java, a web service is implemented as a class. The class that represents the web service resides on a server—it's not part of the client application.
- Making a web service available to receive client requests is known as publishing a web service; using a web service from a client application is known as consuming a web service.

Section 31.3 Simple Object Access Protocol (SOAP)
- SOAP is a platform-independent protocol that uses XML to make remote procedure calls, typically over HTTP. Each request and response is packaged in a SOAP message—an XML message containing the information that a web service requires to process the message.
- SOAP messages are written in XML so that they are computer readable, human readable and platform independent.
- SOAP supports an extensive set of types—the primitive types, as well as DateTime, XmlNode and others. SOAP can also transmit arrays of these types.
- When a program invokes a method of a SOAP web service, the request and all relevant information are packaged in a SOAP message, enclosed in a SOAP envelope and sent to the server on which the web service resides.
- When a web service receives a SOAP message, it parses the XML representing the message, then processes the message's contents. The message specifies the method that the client wishes to execute and the arguments the client passed to that method.
- After a web service parses a SOAP message, it calls the appropriate method with the specified arguments (if any) and sends the response back to the client in another SOAP message. The client parses the response to retrieve the method's result.

Section 31.4 Representational State Transfer (REST)
- Representational State Transfer (REST) refers to an architectural style for implementing web services. Such web services are often called RESTful web services. Though REST itself is not a standard, RESTful web services are implemented using web standards.
- Each operation in a RESTful web service is identified by a unique URL.
- REST can return data in many formats, including XML and JSON.

Section 31.5 JavaScript Object Notation (JSON)

- JavaScript Object Notation (JSON) is an alternative to XML for representing data.
- JSON is a text-based data-interchange format used to represent objects in JavaScript as collections of name/value pairs represented as `Strings`.
- JSON is a simple format that makes objects easy to read, create and parse and allows programs to transmit data efficiently across the Internet, because it is much less verbose than XML.
- Each value in a JSON array can be a string, a number, a JSON object, `true`, `false` or `null`.

Section 31.6.1 Creating a Web Application Project and Adding a Web Service Class in NetBeans

- When you create a web service in NetBeans, you focus on the web service's logic and let the IDE handle the web service's infrastructure.
- To create a web service in NetBeans, you first create a **Web Application** project.

Section 31.6.2 Defining the `WelcomeSOAP` Web Service in NetBeans

- By default, each new web service class created with the JAX-WS APIs is a POJO (plain old Java object)—you do not need to extend a class or implement an interface to create a web service.
- When you deploy a web application containing a JAX-WS web service, the server creates the server-side artifacts that support the web service.
- The `@WebService` annotation indicates that a class represents a web service. The optional `name` element specifies the service endpoint interface (SEI) class's name. The optional `serviceName` element specifies the name of the class that the client uses to obtain an SEI object.
- NetBeans places the `@WebService` annotation at the beginning of each new web service class you create. You can add the optional `name` and `serviceName` elements in the annotation's parentheses.
- Methods that are tagged with the `@WebMethod` annotation can be called remotely.
- Methods that are not tagged with `@WebMethod` are not accessible to clients that consume the web service. Such methods are typically utility methods within the web service class.
- The `@WebMethod` annotation's optional `operationName` element specifies the method name that is exposed to the web service's clients.
- Web method parameters are annotated with the `@WebParam` annotation. The optional element `name` indicates the parameter name that is exposed to the web service's clients.

Section 31.6.3 Publishing the `WelcomeSOAP` Web Service from NetBeans

- NetBeans handles all the details of building and deploying a web service for you. This includes creating the framework required to support the web service.
- To determine if there are any compilation errors in your project, right click the project name in the NetBeans **Projects** tab, then select the **Build** option.
- When the project compiles successfully, you can select **Deploy** to deploy it to the server you selected during application setup.
- If the code in the project has changed since the last build, selecting **Deploy** also builds the project.
- Selecting **Run** executes the web application.
- The **Deploy** and **Run** options also build the project if it has changed and start the application server if it is not already running.
- To ensure that all source-code files in a project are recompiled during the next build operation, you can use the **Clean** or **Clean and Build** options.

Section 31.6.4 Testing the `WelcomeSOAP` *Web Service with GlassFish Application Server's* `Tester` *Web Page*

- GlassFish can dynamically create a web page for testing a web service's methods from a web browser. To open the test page, expand the project's **Web Services** node in the NetBeans **Projects** tab, then right click the web service class name and select **Test Web Service**.

- A client can access a web service only when the application server is running. If NetBeans launches the application server for you, the server will shut down when you close NetBeans. To keep the application server up and running, you can launch it independently of NetBeans.

Section 31.6.5 Describing a Web Service with the Web Service Description Language (WSDL)

- To consume a web service, a client must know where to find it and must be provided with the web service's description.

- JAX-WS uses the Web Service Description Language (WSDL)—a standard XML vocabulary for describing web services in a platform-independent manner.

- The server generates a web service's WSDL dynamically for you, and client tools can parse the WSDL to help create the client-side proxy class that a client uses to access the web service.

- To view the WSDL for a web service, type its URL in the browser's address field followed by `?WSDL` or click the **WSDL File** link in the service's `Tester` web page.

Section 31.6.6 Creating a Client to Consume the `WelcomeSOAP` *Web Service*

- A web service client can be any type of application or even another web service.

- You enable a Java-based client application to consume a web service by adding a web service reference, which defines the service endpoint interface class so the client can access the web service.

- An application that consumes a SOAP-based web service invokes methods on a service endpoint interface (SEI) object that interact with the web service on the client's behalf.

- The service endpoint interface object handles the details of passing method arguments to and receiving return values from the web service. This communication can occur over a local network, over the Internet or even with a web service on the same computer.

- NetBeans creates these service endpoint interface classes for you.

- When you add the web service reference, the IDE creates and compiles the client-side artifacts— the framework of Java code that supports the client-side service endpoint interface class. The service endpoint interface class uses the rest of the artifacts to interact with the web service.

- A web service reference is added by giving NetBeans the URL of the web service's WSDL file.

Section 31.6.7 Consuming the `WelcomeSOAP` *Web Service*

- When you create a GUI in NetBeans, it uses fully qualified class names, so `import` declarations are unnecessary.

- To consume a JAX-WS web service, you must obtain an SEI object by calling the `getWelcomeSOAPPort` method on the class that was specified with the `@WebService` annotation's `serviceName` element. This method returns an SEI object of the class that was specified with the `@WebService` annotation's `name` element. You then invoke the services methods through the SEI object.

Section 31.7.1 Creating a REST-Based XML Web Service

- The **RESTful Web Services** plug-in for NetBeans provides various templates for creating RESTful web services, including ones that can interact with databases on the client's behalf.

- The `@Path` annotation on a JAX-RS web service class indicates the URI for accessing the web service. This is appended to the web application project's URL to invoke the service. Methods of the class can also use the `@Path` annotation.

- Parts of the path specified in curly braces indicate parameters—they are placeholders for arguments that are passed to the web service as part of the path. The base path for the service is the project's resources directory.

- Arguments in a URL can be used as arguments to a web service method. To do so, you bind the parameters specified in the @Path specification to parameters of a web service method with the @PathParam annotation. When the request is received, the server passes the argument(s) in the URL to the appropriate parameter(s) in the web service method.

- The @GET annotation denotes that a method is accessed via an HTTP GET request. Similar annotations exist for HTTP PUT, POST, DELETE and HEAD requests.

- The @Produces annotation denotes the content type returned to the client. It's possible to have multiple methods with the same HTTP method and path but different @Produces annotations, and JAX-RS will call the method matching the content type requested by the client.

- The @Consumes annotation restricts the content type that a web service accepts from a PUT request.

- JAXB (Java Architecture for XML Binding) is a set of classes for converting POJOs to and from XML. Class JAXB (package javax.xml.bind) contains static methods for common operations.

- Class JAXB's static method marshal converts a Java object to XML format.

- GlassFish does not provide test pages for RESTful services, but NetBeans generates a test page that can be accessed by right clicking the project's node in the **Projects** tab and selecting **Test RESTful Web Services**.

- On the test page, select a method element in the left column. The right side of the page displays a form that allows you to choose the MIME type of the data and lets you enter the method's arguments. Click the **Test** button to invoke the web service and display the returned data.

- WADL (Web Application Description Language) has similar design goals to WSDL, but describes RESTful services instead of SOAP services.

Section 31.7.2 Consuming a REST-Based XML Web Service
- Clients of RESTful web services do not require web service references.

- The JAXB class has a static unmarshal method that takes as arguments a file name or URL as a String, and a Class<T> object indicating the Java class to which the XML will be converted.

Section 31.8 Publishing and Consuming REST-Based JSON Web Services
- JSON components—objects, arrays, strings, numbers—can be easily mapped to constructs in Java and other programming languages.

- There are many open-source JSON libraries for Java and other languages. The Gson library from code.google.com/p/google-gson/ provides a simple way to convert POJOs to and from JSON.

Section 31.8.1 Creating a REST-Based JSON Web Service
- To add a JAR file as a library in NetBeans, right click your project's **Libraries** folder, select **Add JAR/Folder...**, locate the JAR file and click **Open**.

- For a web service method that returns JSON text, the argument to the @Produces attribute must be "application/json".

- In JSON, all data must be encapsulated in a composite data type.

- Create a Gson object (from package com.google.gson) and call its toJson method to convert an object into its JSON String representation.

Section 31.8.2 Consuming a REST-Based JSON Web Service
- To read JSON data from a URL, create a URL object and call its openStream method. This invokes the web service and returns an InputStream from which the client can read the response.

Wrap the `InputStream` in an `InputStreamReader` so it can be passed as the first argument to the `Gson` class's `fromJson` method.

Section 31.9 Session Tracking in a SOAP-Based Web Service

- It can be beneficial for a web service to maintain client state information, thus eliminating the need to pass client information between the client and the web service multiple times. Storing session information also enables a web service to distinguish between clients.

Section 31.9.1 Creating a **Blackjack** Web Service

- To use session tracking in a web service, you must include code for the resources that maintain the session state information. JAX-WS handles this for you via the `@Resource` annotation. This annotation "injects" complex support code into your class, thus allowing you to focus on your business logic rather than the support code.

- Using annotations to add code that supports your classes is known as dependency injection. Annotations like `@WebService`, `@WebMethod` and `@WebParam` also perform dependency injection.

- A `WebServiceContext` object enables a web service to access and maintain information for a specific request. The code that creates a `WebServiceContext` object is injected into the class by an `@Resource` annotation.

- The `WebServiceContext` object is used to obtain a `MessageContext` object. A web service uses a `MessageContext` to obtain an `HttpSession` object for the current client.

- The `MessageContext` object's get method obtains the `HttpSession` object for the current client. Method `get` receives a constant indicating what to get from the `MessageContext`. The constant `MessageContext.SERVLET_REQUEST` indicates that we'd like to get the `HttpServletRequest` object for the current client. We then call method `getSession` to get the `HttpSession` object from the `HttpServletRequest` object.

- `HttpSession` method `getAttribute` receives a `String` that identifies the `Object` to obtain from the session state.

Section 31.9.2 Consuming the **Blackjack** Web Service

- In the JAX-WS framework, the client must indicate whether it wants to allow the web service to maintain session information. To do this, first cast the proxy object to interface type `BindingProvider`. A `BindingProvider` enables the client to manipulate the request information that will be sent to the server. This information is stored in an object that implements interface `RequestContext`. The `BindingProvider` and `RequestContext` are part of the framework that is created by the IDE when you add a web service client to the application.

- Next, invoke the `BindingProvider`'s `getRequestContext` method to obtain the `RequestContext` object. Then call the `RequestContext`'s `put` method to set the property `BindingProvider.SESSION_MAINTAIN_PROPERTY` to true, which enables session tracking from the client side so that the web service knows which client is invoking the service's web methods.

Section 31.11 Equation Generator: Returning User-Defined Types

- It's also possible to process instances of class types in a web service. These types can be passed to or returned from web service methods.

- An instance variable can be serialized only if it is `public` or has both a *get* and a *set* method.

- Properties that can be generated from the values of other properties should not be serialized to prevent redundancy.

- JAX-RS automatically converts arguments from an `@Path` annotation to the correct type, and it will return a "not found" error to the client if the argument cannot be converted from the `String` passed as part of the URL to the destination type. Supported types for conversion include integer types, floating-point types, `boolean` and the corresponding type-wrapper classes.

Terminology

adding a web service reference to an application 1353

`BindingProvider` interface 1382

business-to-business (B2B) transactions 1345

client-side artifacts 1354

`@Consumes` annotation 1360

consuming a web service 1346, 1403

dependency injection 1371

firewall 1346

`fromJson` method of class `Gson` 1367

`@GET` annotation 1360

`getAttribute` method of interface `HttpSession` 1371

`getRequestContext` method of interface `BindingProvider` 1382

`getSession` method of interface `HttpSession` 1371

JAXB (Java Architecture for XML Binding) 1361

`JAXB` class 1361

JAX-WS 1344

JSON (JavaScript Object Notation) 1347

`marshal` method of class `JAXB` 1361

`MessageContext` interface 1371

name attribute of `@WebService` annotation 1349

name element of `@WebParam` annotation 1350

`openStream` method of class `URL` 1367

`operationName` attribute of the `@WebMethod` annotation 1349

`@Path` annotation 1359

`@PathParam` annotation 1360

POJO (Plain Old Java Object) 1348

`@Produces` annotation 1360

proxy class for a web service 1349

publishing a web service 1346, 1403

put method of interface `RequestContext` 1382

`RequestContext` interface 1382

`@Resource` annotation 1371

REST (Representational State Transfer) 1344

RESTful web services 1347

server-side artifacts 1349

service description for a web service 1353

service endpoint interface (SEI) 1349

`serviceName` attribute of `@WebService` annotation 1349

`setAttribute` method of interface `HttpSession` 1371

SOAP (Simple Object Access Protocol) 1344

SOAP message 1346

`StringWriter` class 1361

WADL (Web Application Description Language) 1362

Web Application project 1348

web service 1344

`@WebMethod` annotation 1349

`@WebParam` annotation 1350

`@WebService` annotation 1349

`WebServiceContext` interface 1371

WSDL (Web Service Description Language) 1353

Self-Review Exercises

31.1 State whether each of the following is *true* or *false*. If *false*, explain why.

a) All methods of a web service class can be invoked by clients of that web service.

b) When consuming a web service in a client application created in NetBeans, you must create the proxy class that enables the client to communicate with the web service.

c) A proxy class communicating with a web service normally uses SOAP to send and receive messages.

d) Session tracking is automatically enabled in a client of a web service.

e) Web methods cannot be declared `static`.

f) A user-defined type used in a web service must define both *get* and *set* methods for any property that will be serialized.

g) Operations in a REST web service are defined by their own unique URLs.

h) A SOAP-based web service can return data in JSON format.

31.2 Fill in the blanks for each of the following statements:

a) A key difference between SOAP and REST is that SOAP messages have data wrapped in a(n) _____.

b) A web service in Java is a(n) _____—it does not need to implement any interfaces or extend any classes.

  c) Web service requests are typically transported over the Internet via the _____ protocol.

  d) To set the exposed name of a web method, use the _____ element of the @WebMethod annotation.

  e) _____ transforms an object into a format that can be sent between a web service and a client.

  f) To return data in JSON format from a method of a REST-based web service, the @Produces annotation is set to _____.

  g) To return data in XML format from a method of a REST-based web service, the @Produces annotation is set to _____.

Answers to Self-Review Exercises

31.1 a) False. Only methods declared with the @WebMethod annotation can be invoked by a web service's clients. b) False. The proxy class is created by NetBeans when you add a web service client to the application. c) True. d) False. In the JAX-WS framework, the client must indicate whether it wants to allow the web service to maintain session information. First, you must cast the proxy object to interface type BindingProvider, then use the BindingProvider's getRequestContext method to obtain the RequestContext object. Finally, you must use the RequestContext's put method to set the property BindingProvider.SESSION_MAINTAIN_PROPERTY to true. e) True. f) True. g) True. h) False. A SOAP web service implicitly returns data in XML format.

31.2 a) SOAP message or SOAP envelope. b) POJO (plain old Java object) c) HTTP. d) operationName. e) serialization. f) "application/json". g) "application/xml".

Exercises

31.3 *(Phone Book Web Service)* Create a RESTful web service that stores phone book entries in the database PhoneBookDB and a web client application that consumes this service. The web service should output XML. Use the steps in Section 30.2.1 to create the PhoneBook database using the PhoneBookDB.sql script provided in the examples folder. The database contains one table—PhoneBook—with three columns—LastName, FirstName and PhoneNumber. The LastName and FirstName columns store up to 30 characters. The PhoneNumber column supports phone numbers of the form (800) 555-1212 that contain 14 characters.

  Give the client user the capability to enter a new contact (web method addEntry) and to find contacts by last name (web method getEntries). Pass only Strings as arguments to the web service. The getEntries web method should return an array of Strings that contains the matching phone book entries. Each String in the array should consist of the last name, first name and phone number for one phone book entry. These values should be separated by commas.

  The SELECT query that will find a PhoneBook entry by last name should be:

```
SELECT LastName, FirstName, PhoneNumber
FROM PhoneBook
WHERE (LastName = LastName)
```

The INSERT statement that inserts a new entry into the PhoneBook database should be:

```
INSERT INTO PhoneBook (LastName, FirstName, PhoneNumber)
VALUES (LastName, FirstName, PhoneNumber)
```

31.4 *(Phone Book Web Service Modification)* Modify Exercise 31.3 so that it uses a class named PhoneBookEntry to represent a row in the database. The web service should return objects of type PhoneBookEntry in XML format for the getEntries method, and the client application should use the JAXB method unmarshal to retrieve the PhoneBookEntry objects.

31.5 *(Blackjack Web Service Modification)* Modify the Blackjack web service example in Section 31.9 to include class Card. Modify web method dealCard so that it returns an object of type Card and modify web method getHandValue so that it receives an array of Card objects from the client. Also modify the client application to keep track of what cards have been dealt by using ArrayLists of Card objects. The proxy class created by NetBeans will treat a web method's array parameter as a List, so you can pass these ArrayLists of Card objects directly to the getHandValue method. Your Card class should include *set* and *get* methods for the face and suit of the card.

31.6 *(Airline Reservation Web-Service Modification)* Modify the airline reservation web service in Section 31.10 so that it contains two separate methods—one that allows users to view all available seats, and another that allows users to reserve a particular seat that is currently available. Use an object of type Ticket to pass information to and from the web service. The web service must be able to handle cases in which two users view available seats, one reserves a seat and the second user tries to reserve the same seat, not knowing that it is now taken. The names of the methods that execute should be reserve and getAllAvailableSeats.

31.7 *(Morse Code Web Service)* In Exercise 16.15, you learned about Morse Code and wrote applications that could translate English phrases into Morse Code and vice versa. Create a SOAP-based web service that provides two methods—one that translates an English phrase into Morse Code and one that translates Morse Code into English. Next, build a Morse Code translator GUI application that invokes the web service to perform these translations.

Making a Difference

31.8 *(Spam Scanner Web Service)* In Exercise 16.19, you created a Spam scanner application that scanned an e-mail and gave it a point rating based on the occurrence of certain words and phrases that commonly appear in Spam e-mails and how many times the words and phrases occurred in the e-mail. Create a SOAP-based Spam scanner web service. Next, modify the GUI application you created in Exercise 16.19 to use the web service to scan an e-mail. Then display the point rating returned by the web service.

31.9 *(SMS Web Service)* In Exercise 16.20, you created an SMS message-translator application. Create a SOAP-based web service with three methods:
    a) one that receives an SMS abbreviation and returns the corresponding English word or phrase,
    b) one that receives an entire SMS message and returns the corresponding English text, and
    c) one that translates English text into an SMS message.
Use the web service from a GUI application that displays the web service's responses.

31.10 *(Gender-Neutrality Web Service)* In Exercise 1.12, you researched eliminating sexism in all forms of communication. You then described the algorithm you'd use to read through a paragraph of text and replace gender-specific words with gender-neutral equivalents. Create a SOAP-based web service that receives a paragraph of text, then replaces gender-specific words with gender-neutral ones. Use the web service from a GUI application that displays the resulting gender-neutral text.

Operator Precedence Chart

A

Operators are shown in decreasing order of precedence from top to bottom (Fig. A.1).

Operator	Description	Associativity
++ --	unary postfix increment unary postfix decrement	right to left
++ -- + - ! ~ (*type*)	unary prefix increment unary prefix decrement unary plus unary minus unary logical negation unary bitwise complement unary cast	right to left
* / %	multiplication division remainder	left to right
+ -	addition or string concatenation subtraction	left to right
<< >> >>>	left shift signed right shift unsigned right shift	left to right
< <= > >= instanceof	less than less than or equal to greater than greater than or equal to type comparison	left to right

Fig. A.1 | Operator precedence chart. (Part 1 of 2.)

Operator	Description	Associativity
== !=	is equal to is not equal to	left to right
&	bitwise AND boolean logical AND	left to right
^	bitwise exclusive OR boolean logical exclusive OR	left to right
|	bitwise inclusive OR boolean logical inclusive OR	left to right
&&	conditional AND	left to right
||	conditional OR	left to right
?:	conditional	right to left
= += -= *= /= %= &= ^= |= <<= >>= >>>=	assignment addition assignment subtraction assignment multiplication assignment division assignment remainder assignment bitwise AND assignment bitwise exclusive OR assignment bitwise inclusive OR assignment bitwise left-shift assignment bitwise signed-right-shift assignment bitwise unsigned-right-shift assignment	right to left

Fig. A.1 | Operator precedence chart. (Part 2 of 2.)

ASCII Character Set

	0	1	2	3	4	5	6	7	8	9
0	nul	soh	stx	etx	eot	enq	ack	bel	bs	ht
1	nl	vt	ff	cr	so	si	dle	dc1	dc2	dc3
2	dc4	nak	syn	etb	can	em	sub	esc	fs	gs
3	rs	us	sp	!	"	#	$	%	&	'
4	(	)	*	+	,	-	.	/	0	1
5	2	3	4	5	6	7	8	9	:	;
6	<	=	>	?	@	A	B	C	D	E
7	F	G	H	I	J	K	L	M	N	O
8	P	Q	R	S	T	U	V	W	X	Y
9	Z	[	\	]	^	_	'	a	b	c
10	d	e	f	g	h	i	j	k	l	m
11	n	o	p	q	r	s	t	u	v	w
12	x	y	z	{			}	~	del		

Fig. B.1 | ASCII character set.

The digits at the left of the table are the left digits of the decimal equivalents (0–127) of the character codes, and the digits at the top of the table are the right digits of the character codes. For example, the character code for "F" is 70, and the character code for "&" is 38.

Most users of this book are interested in the ASCII character set used to represent English characters on many computers. The ASCII character set is a subset of the Unicode character set used by Java to represent characters from most of the world's languages. For more information on the Unicode character set, see the web bonus Appendix L.

C
Keywords and Reserved Words

Java Keywords				
abstract	assert	boolean	break	byte
case	catch	char	class	continue
default	do	double	else	enum
extends	final	finally	float	for
if	implements	import	instanceof	int
interface	long	native	new	package
private	protected	public	return	short
static	strictfp	super	switch	synchronized
this	throw	throws	transient	try
void	volatile	while		
Keywords that are not currently used				
const	goto			

Fig. C.1 | Java keywords.

Java also contains the reserved words true and false, which are boolean literals, and null, which is the literal that represents a reference to nothing. Like keywords, these reserved words cannot be used as identifiers.

Primitive Types

Type	Size in bits	Values	Standard
boolean		true or false	
[*Note:* A **boolean**'s representation is specific to the Java Virtual Machine on each platform.]			
char	16	'\u0000' to '\uFFFF' (0 to 65535)	(ISO Unicode character set)
byte	8	-128 to $+127$ (-2^7 to $2^7 - 1$)	
short	16	$-32{,}768$ to $+32{,}767$ (-2^{15} to $2^{15} - 1$)	
int	32	$-2{,}147{,}483{,}648$ to $+2{,}147{,}483{,}647$ (-2^{31} to $2^{31} - 1$)	
long	64	$-9{,}223{,}372{,}036{,}854{,}775{,}808$ to $+9{,}223{,}372{,}036{,}854{,}775{,}807$ (-2^{63} to $2^{63} - 1$)	
float	32	*Negative range:* $-3.4028234663852886E{+}38$ to $-1.40129846432481707e{-}45$ *Positive range:* $1.40129846432481707e{-}45$ to $3.4028234663852886E{+}38$	(IEEE 754 floating point)
double	64	*Negative range:* $-1.7976931348623157E{+}308$ to $-4.94065645841246544e{-}324$ *Positive range:* $4.94065645841246544e{-}324$ to $1.7976931348623157E{+}308$	(IEEE 754 floating point)

Fig. D.1 | Java primitive types.

For more information on IEEE 754 visit `grouper.ieee.org/groups/754/`. For more information on Unicode, see Appendix L, Unicode®.

E

Using the Java API Documentation

E.1 Introduction

The Java class library contains thousands of predefined classes and interfaces that programmers can use to write their own applications. These classes are grouped into packages based on their functionality. For example, the classes and interfaces used for file processing are grouped into the java.io package, and the classes and interfaces for networking applications are grouped into the java.net package. The **Java API documentation** lists the public and protected members of each class and the public members of each interface in the Java class library. The documentation overviews all the classes and interfaces, summarizes their members (i.e., the fields, constructors and methods of classes, and the fields and methods of interfaces) and provides detailed descriptions of each member. Most Java programmers rely on this documentation when writing programs. Normally, programmers would search the API to find the following:

1. The package that contains a particular class or interface.

2. Relationships between a particular class or interface and other classes and interfaces.

3. Class or interface constants—normally declared as public static final fields.

4. Constructors to determine how an object of the class can be initialized.

5. The methods of a class to determine whether they are static or non-static, the number and types of the arguments you need to pass, the return types and any exceptions that might be thrown from the method.

In addition, programmers often rely on the documentation to discover classes and interfaces that they have not used before. For this reason, we demonstrate the documentation with classes you know and classes you may not have studied yet. We show how to use the documentation to locate the information you need to use a class or interface effectively.

E.2 Navigating the Java API

The Java API documentation can be downloaded to your local hard disk or viewed online. To download the Java API documentation, go to java.sun.com/javase/downloads/ scroll down to the **Additional Resources** section and click the **Download** button to the right of **Java SE 6 Documentation**. You'll be asked to accept a license agreement. To do this, click **Accept**, then click **Continue**. Check the checkbox next to **Java SE Development Kit Documentation 6** then click the jdk-6u10-docs.zip link just below the checkbox. After downloading the file, you can use a program such as WinZip (www.winzip.com) to extract the files. If you are using Windows, extract the contents to your JDK's installation directory. To view the API documentation on your local hard disk in Microsoft Windows, open C:\Program Files\Java*YourJDKVersion*\docs\api\index.html page in your browser. To view the API documentation online, go to java.sun.com/javase/6/docs/api/ index.html (Fig. E.1).

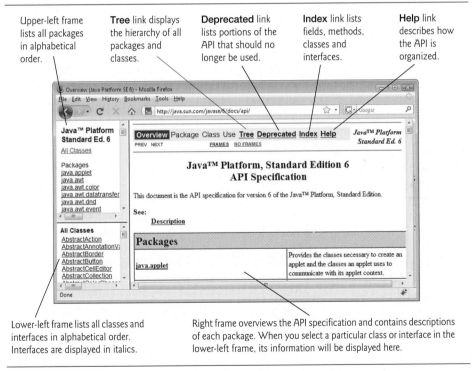

Upper-left frame lists all packages in alphabetical order.

Tree link displays the hierarchy of all packages and classes.

Deprecated link lists portions of the API that should no longer be used.

Index link lists fields, methods, classes and interfaces.

Help link describes how the API is organized.

Lower-left frame lists all classes and interfaces in alphabetical order. Interfaces are displayed in italics.

Right frame overviews the API specification and contains descriptions of each package. When you select a particular class or interface in the lower-left frame, its information will be displayed here.

Fig. E.1 | Java API overview. (Courtesy of Sun Microsystems, Inc.)

Frames in the API Documentation's index.html Page

The API documentation is divided into three frames (see Fig. E.1). The upper-left frame lists all of the Java API's packages in alphabetical order. The lower-left frame initially lists the Java API's classes and interfaces in alphabetical order. Interface names are displayed in italic. When you click a specific package in the upper-left frame, the lower-left frame lists the classes and interfaces of the selected package. The right frame initially provides a brief description of each package of the Java API specification—read this overview to become familiar wth the general capabilities of the Java APIs. If you select a class or interface in the lower-left frame, the right frame displays information about that class or interface.

Important Links in the `index.html` *Page*
At the top of the right frame (Fig. E.1), there are four links—**Tree**, **Deprecated**, **Index** and **Help**. The **Tree** link displays the hierarchy of all packages, classes and interfaces in a tree structure. The **Deprecated** link displays interfaces, classes, exceptions, fields, constructors and methods that should no longer be used. The **Index** link displays classes, interfaces, fields, constructors and methods in alphabetical order. The **Help** link describes how the API documentation is organized. You should probably begin by reading the **Help** page.

Viewing the **Index** *Page*
If you do not know the name of the class you are looking for, but you do know the name of a method or field, you can use the documentation's index to locate the class. The **Index** link is located near the upper-right corner of the right frame. The index page (Fig. E.2) displays fields, constructors, methods, interfaces and classes in alphabetical order. For example, if you are looking for `Scanner` method `hasNextInt`, but do not know the class name, you can click the **H** link to go to the alphabetical listing of all items in the Java API that begin with "h". Scroll to method `hasNextInt` (Fig. E.3). Once there, each method named `hasNextInt` is listed with the package name and class to which the method belongs. From there, you can click the class name to view the class's complete details, or you can click the method name to view the method's details.

Viewing a Specific Package
When you click the package name in the upper-left frame, all classes and interfaces from that package are displayed in the lower-left frame and are divided into five subsections—

Classes, interfaces and their members are listed in alphabetical order. Click a letter to view all fields, constructors, methods, interfaces and classes that start with that letter.

Click the **Index** link to display the documentation's index.

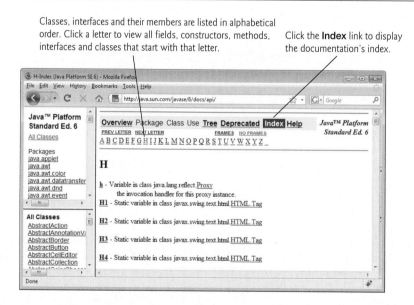

Fig. E.2 | Viewing the **Index** page. (Courtesy of Sun Microsystems, Inc.)

Click the method name to
view the method's details.

Click the class name to view
the class's complete details.

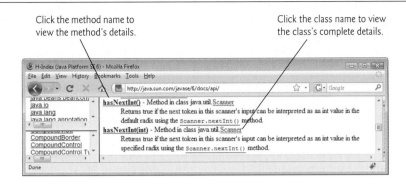

Fig. E.3 | Scroll to method `hasNextInt`. (Courtesy of Sun Microsystems, Inc.)

Interfaces, Classes, Enums, Exceptions and **Errors**—each listed alphabetically. For example, the contents of package `javax.swing` are displayed in the lower-left frame (Fig. E.4) when you click `javax.swing` in the upper-left frame. You can click the package name in the lower-left frame to get an overview of the package. If you think that a package contains several classes that could be useful in your application, the package overview can be especially helpful.

Click a package name in the upper-
left frame to view all classes and
interfaces defined in the package.

Click the package name in the lower-
left frame to display a summary of
that package in the right frame.

Contents of package `javax.swing`
are displayed in the lower-left frame.

Fig. E.4 | Clicking a package name in the upper-left frame to view all classes and interfaces declared in this package. (Courtesy of Sun Microsystems, Inc.)

Viewing the Details of a Class

When you click a class name or interface name in the lower-left frame, the right frame displays the details of that class or interface. First you'll see the class's package name followed by a hierarchy that shows the class's relationship to other classes. You'll also see a list of the interfaces implemented by the class and the class's known subclasses. Figure E.5 shows the beginning of the documentation page for class JButton from the javax.swing package. The page first shows the package name in which the class appears. This is followed by the class hierarchy that leads to class JButton, the interfaces class JButton implements and the subclasses of class JButton. The bottom of the right frame shows the beginning of class JButton's description. Note that when you look at the documentation for an interface, the right frame does not display a hierarchy for that interface. Instead, the right frame lists the interface's superinterfaces, known subinterfaces and known implementing classes.

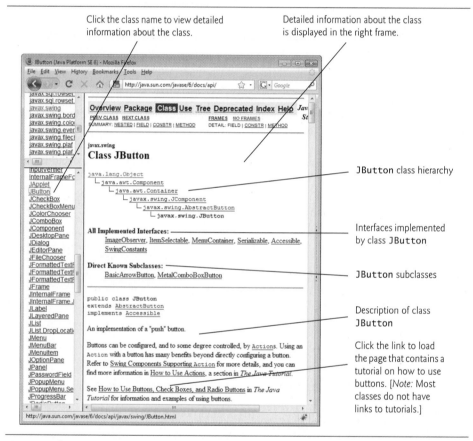

Fig. E.5 | Clicking a class name to view detailed information about the class. (Courtesy of Sun Microsystems, Inc.)

Summary Sections in a Class's Documentation Page

Other parts of each API page are listed below. Each part is presented only if the class contains or inherits the items specified. Class members shown in the summary sections are public unless they are explicitly marked as protected. A class's private members are not shown in the documentation, because they cannot be used directly in your programs.

1. The **Nested Class Summary** section summarizes the class's public and protected nested classes—i.e., classes that are defined inside the class. Unless explicitly specified, these classes are public and non-static.

2. The **Field Summary** section summarizes the class's public and protected fields. Unless explicitly specified, these fields are public and non-static. Figure E.6 shows the **Field Summary** section of class Color.

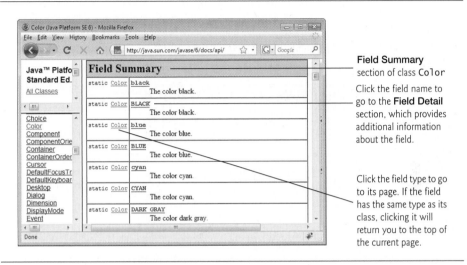

Field Summary section of class Color

Click the field name to go to the **Field Detail** section, which provides additional information about the field.

Click the field type to go to its page. If the field has the same type as its class, clicking it will return you to the top of the current page.

Fig. E.6 | **Field Summary** section of class Color. (Courtesy of Sun Microsystems, Inc.)

3. The **Constructor Summary** section summarizes the class's constructors. Constructors are not inherited, so this section appears in the documentation for a class only if the class declares one or more constructors. Figure E.7 shows the **Constructor Summary** section of class JButton.

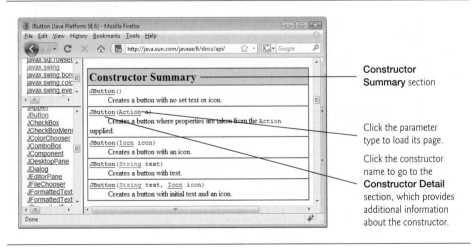

Constructor Summary section

Click the parameter type to load its page.

Click the constructor name to go to the **Constructor Detail** section, which provides additional information about the constructor.

Fig. E.7 | **Constructor Summary** section of class JButton. (Courtesy of Sun Microsystems, Inc.)

4. The **Method Summary** section summarizes the class's `public` and `protected` methods. Unless explicitly specified, these methods are `public` and non-`static`. Figure E.8 shows the **Method Summary** section of class `BufferedInputStream`.

Note that the summary sections typically provide only a one-sentence description of a class member. Additional details are presented in the detail sections discussed next.

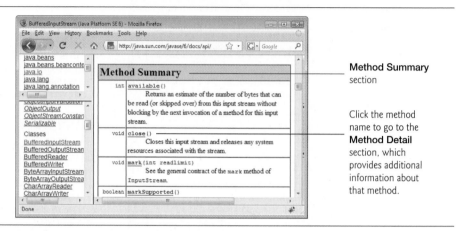

Fig. E.8 | **Method Summary** section of class `BufferedInputStream`. (Courtesy of Sun Microsystems, Inc.)

Detail Sections in a Class's Documentation Page
After the summary sections are detail sections that normally provide more discussion of particular class members. There is not a detail section for nested classes. When you click the link in the **Nested Class Summary** for a particular nested class, a documentation page describing that nested class is displayed. The detail sections are described below.

1. The **Field Detail** section provides the declaration of each field. It also discusses each field, including the field's modifiers and meaning. Figure E.9 shows the **Field Detail** section of class `Color`.

Fig. E.9 | **Field Detail** section of class `Color`. (Courtesy of Sun Microsystems, Inc.)

2. The **Constructor Detail** section provides the first line of each constructor's declaration and discusses the constructors. The discussion includes the modifiers of each constructor, a description of each constructor, each constructor's parameters and any exceptions thrown by each constructor. Figure E.10 shows the **Constructor Detail** section of class `JButton`.

Constructor Detail section describes each constructor.

Fig. E.10 | **Constructor Detail** section of class `JButton`. (Courtesy of Sun Microsystems, Inc.)

3. The **Method Detail** section provides the first line of each method. The discussion of each method includes its modifiers, a more complete method description, the method's parameters, the method's return type and any exceptions thrown by the method. Figure E.11 shows class `BufferedInputStream`'s **Method Detail** section.

Method **read** throws `IOException`. Click `IOException` to load the `IOException` class information page and learn more about the exception type (e.g., why such an exception might be thrown).

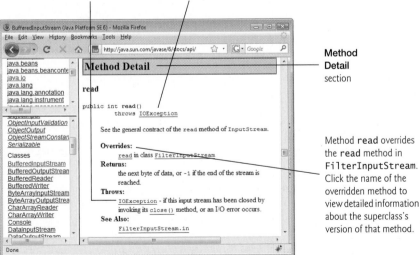

Method Detail section

Method **read** overrides the **read** method in `FilterInputStream`. Click the name of the overridden method to view detailed information about the superclass's version of that method.

Fig. E.11 | **Method Detail** section of class `BufferedInputStream`. (Courtesy of Sun Microsystems, Inc.)

The method details show you other methods that might be of interest (labeled as **See Also**). If the method overrides a method of the superclass, the name of the superclass method and the name of the superclass are provided so you can link to the method or superclass for more information.

As you look through the documentation, you'll notice that there are often links to other fields, methods, nested-classes and top-level classes. These links enable you to jump from the class you are looking at to another relevant portion of the documentation.

And so shall I catch the fly.
—William Shakespeare

We are built to make mistakes, coded for error.
—Lewis Thomas

*What we anticipate seldom occurs; what we least
expect generally happens.*
—Benjamin Disraeli

He can run but he can't hide.
—Joe Louis

*It is one thing to show a man that he is in error, and
another to put him in possession of truth.*
—John Locke

Using the Debugger

Objectives

In this appendix you'll learn:

- To set breakpoints to debug applications.
- To use the `run` command to run an application through the debugger.
- To use the `stop` command to set a breakpoint.
- To use the `cont` command to continue execution.
- To use the `print` command to evaluate expressions.
- To use the `set` command to change variable values during program execution.
- To use the `step`, `step up` and `next` commands to control execution.
- To use the `watch` command to see how a field is modified during program execution.
- To use the `clear` command to list breakpoints or remove a breakpoint.

F.1 Introduction

In Chapter 2, you learned that there are two types of errors—syntax errors and logic errors—and you learned how to eliminate syntax errors from your code. Logic errors do not prevent the application from compiling successfully, but they do cause an application to produce erroneous results when it runs. The JDK includes software called a **debugger** that allows you to monitor the execution of your applications so you can locate and remove logic errors. The debugger will be one of your most important application development tools. Many IDEs provide their own debuggers similar to the one included in the JDK or provide a graphical user interface to the JDK's debugger.

This appendix demonstrates key features of the JDK's debugger using command-line applications that receive no input from the user. The same debugger features discussed here can be used to debug applications that take user input, but debugging such applications requires a slightly more complex setup. To focus on the debugger features, we've opted to demonstrate the debugger with simple command-line applications involving no user input. You can also find more information on the Java debugger at java.sun.com/javase/6/docs/technotes/tools/windows/jdb.html.

F.2 Breakpoints and the run, stop, cont and print Commands

We begin our study of the debugger by investigating **breakpoints**, which are markers that can be set at any executable line of code. When application execution reaches a breakpoint, execution pauses, allowing you to examine the values of variables to help determine whether logic errors exist. For example, you can examine the value of a variable that stores the result of a calculation to determine whether the calculation was performed correctly. Note that setting a breakpoint at a line of code that is not executable (such as a comment) causes the debugger to display an error message.

To illustrate the features of the debugger, we use application AccountTest (Fig. F.1), which creates and manipulates an object of class Account (Fig. 3.13). Execution of AccountTest begins in main (lines 7–24). Line 9 creates an Account object with an initial balance of $50.00. Recall that Account's constructor accepts one argument, which specifies the Account's initial balance. Lines 12–13 output the initial account balance using Account method getBalance. Line 15 declares and initializes a local variable deposit-Amount. Lines 17–19 then print depositAmount and add it to the Account's balance using its credit method. Finally, lines 22–23 display the new balance. [*Note:* The Appendix F examples directory contains a copy of Account.java identical to the one in Fig. 3.13.]

```
 1   // Fig. F.1: AccountTest.java
 2   // Create and manipulate an Account object.
 3
 4   public class AccountTest
 5   {
 6      // main method begins execution
 7      public static void main( String[] args )
 8      {
 9         Account account = new Account( 50.00 ); // create Account object
10
11         // display initial balance of Account object
12         System.out.printf( "initial account balance: $%.2f\n",
13            account.getBalance() );
14
15         double depositAmount = 25.0; // deposit amount
16
17         System.out.printf( "\nadding %.2f to account balance\n\n",
18            depositAmount );
19         account.credit( depositAmount ); // add to account balance
20
21         // display new balance
22         System.out.printf( "new account balance: $%.2f\n",
23            account.getBalance() );
24      } // end main
25
26   } // end class AccountTest
```

```
initial account balance: $50.00

adding 25.00 to account balance

new account balance: $75.00
```

Fig. F.1 | AccountTest class creates and manipulates an Account object.

In the following steps, you'll use breakpoints and various debugger commands to examine the value of the variable depositAmount declared in AccountTest (Fig. F.1).

1. *Opening the* Command Prompt *window and changing directories.* Open the Command Prompt window by selecting **Start > Programs > Accessories > Command Prompt**. Change to the directory containing the Appendix F examples by typing cd C:\examples\debugger [*Note:* If your examples are in a different directory, use that directory here.]

2. *Compiling the application for debugging.* The Java debugger works only with .class files that were compiled with the **-g** compiler option, which generates information that is used by the debugger to help you debug your applications. Compile the application with the -g command-line option by typing javac -g AccountTest.java Account.java. Recall from Chapter 3 that this command compiles both AccountTest.java and Account.java. The command java -g *.java compiles all of the working directory's .java files for debugging.

3. *Starting the debugger.* In the **Command Prompt**, type **jdb** (Fig. F.2). This command will start the Java debugger and enable you to use its features. [*Note:* We modified the colors of our **Command Prompt** window for readability.]

Fig. F.2 | Starting the Java debugger.

4. *Running an application in the debugger.* Run the AccountTest application through the debugger by typing **run** AccountTest (Fig. F.3). If you do not set any breakpoints before running your application in the debugger, the application will run just as it would using the java command.

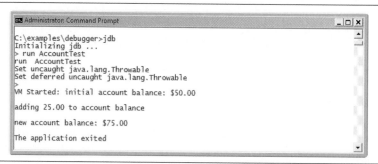

Fig. F.3 | Running the AccountTest application through the debugger.

5. *Restarting the debugger.* To make proper use of the debugger, you must set at least one breakpoint before running the application. Restart the debugger by typing jdb.

6. *Inserting breakpoints in Java.* You set a breakpoint at a specific line of code in your application. The line numbers used in these steps are from the source code in Fig. F.1. Set a breakpoint at line 12 in the source code by typing stop at AccountTest:12 (Fig. F.4). The **stop command** inserts a breakpoint at the line number specified after the command. You can set as many breakpoints as necessary. Set another breakpoint at line 19 by typing stop at AccountTest:19 (Fig. F.4). When the application runs, it suspends execution at any line that contains a breakpoint. The application is said to be in **break mode** when the debugger pauses the application's execution. Breakpoints can be set even after the debugging process has begun. Note that the debugger command stop in, followed by a class name, a period and a method name (e.g., stop in Account.credit) instructs the debugger to set a breakpoint at the first executable statement in the specified method. The debugger pauses execution when program control enters the method.

Fig. F.4 | Setting breakpoints at lines 12 and 19.

7. *Running the application and beginning the debugging process.* Type run AccountTest to execute the application and begin the debugging process (Fig. F.5). The debugger prints text indicating that breakpoints were set at lines 12 and 19. It calls each breakpoint a "deferred breakpoint" because each was set before the application began running in the debugger. The application pauses when execution reaches the breakpoint on line 12. At this point, the debugger notifies you that a breakpoint has been reached and it displays the source code at that line (12). That line of code is the next statement that will execute.

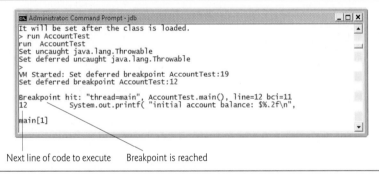

Next line of code to execute   Breakpoint is reached

Fig. F.5 | Restarting the AccountTest application.

8. *Using the **cont** command to resume execution.* Type cont. The **cont command** causes the application to continue running until the next breakpoint is reached (line 19), at which point the debugger notifies you (Fig. F.6). Note that Account-Test's normal output appears between messages from the debugger.

Another breakpoint is reached

Fig. F.6 | Execution reaches the second breakpoint.

9. *Examining a variable's value.* Type print depositAmount to display the current value stored in the depositAmount variable (Fig. F.7). The **print command** allows you to peek inside the computer at the value of one of your variables. This command will help you find and eliminate logic errors in your code. Note that the value displayed is 25.0—the value assigned to depositAmount in line 15 of Fig. F.1.

Fig. F.7 | Examining the value of variable depositAmount.

10. *Continuing application execution.* Type cont to continue the application's execution. There are no more breakpoints, so the application is no longer in break mode. The application continues executing and eventually terminates (Fig. F.8). The debugger will stop when the application ends.

Fig. F.8 | Continuing application execution and exiting the debugger.

In this section, you learned how to enable the debugger and set breakpoints so that you can examine variables with the print command while an application is running. You also learned how to use the cont command to continue execution after a breakpoint is reached.

F.3 The print and set Commands

In the preceding section, you learned how to use the debugger's print command to examine the value of a variable during program execution. In this section, you'll learn how to use the print command to examine the value of more complex expressions. You'll also learn the **set command**, which allows the programmer to assign new values to variables.

For this section, we assume that you've followed *Step 1* and *Step 2* in Section F.2 to open the **Command Prompt** window, change to the directory containing the Appendix F examples (e.g., C:\examples\debugger) and compile the AccountTest application (and class Account) for debugging.

1. *Starting debugging.* In the **Command Prompt**, type jdb to start the Java debugger.

2. *Inserting a breakpoint.* Set a breakpoint at line 19 in the source code by typing stop at AccountTest:19.

3. *Running the application and reaching a breakpoint.* Type run AccountTest to begin the debugging process (Fig. F.9). This will cause AccountTest's main to execute until the breakpoint at line 19 is reached. This suspends application execu-

tion and switches the application into break mode. At this point, the statements in lines 9–13 created an Account object and printed the initial balance of the Account obtained by calling its getBalance method. The statement in line 15 (Fig. F.1) declared and initialized local variable depositAmount to 25.0. The statement in line 19 is the next statement that will execute.

Fig. F.9 | Application execution suspended when debugger reaches the breakpoint at line 19.

4. *Evaluating arithmetic and boolean expressions.* Recall from Section F.2 that once the application has entered break mode, you can explore the values of the application's variables using the debugger's print command. You can also use the print command to evaluate arithmetic and boolean expressions. In the **Command Prompt** window, type print depositAmount - 2.0. Note that the print command returns the value 23.0 (Fig. F.10). However, this command does not actually change the value of depositAmount. In the **Command Prompt** window, type print depositAmount == 23.0. Expressions containing the == symbol are treated as boolean expressions. The value returned is false (Fig. F.10) because depositAmount does not currently contain the value 23.0—depositAmount is still 25.0.

```
Administrator: Command Prompt - jdb
main[1] print depositAmount - 2.0
 depositAmount - 2.0 = 23.0
main[1] print depositAmount == 23.0
 depositAmount == 23.0 = false
main[1]
```

Fig. F.10 | Examining the values of an arithmetic and boolean expression.

5. *Modifying values.* The debugger allows you to change the values of variables during the application's execution. This can be valuable for experimenting with different values and for locating logic errors in applications. You can use the debugger's set command to change the value of a variable. Type set depositAmount = 75.0. The debugger changes the value of depositAmount and displays its new value (Fig. F.11).

```
cm Administrator: Command Prompt - jdb                              _□ x
 depositAmount == 23.0 = false
main[1] set depositAmount = 75.0
 depositAmount = 75.0 = 75.0
main[1]
```

Fig. F.11 | Modifying values.

6. *Viewing the application result.* Type cont to continue application execution. Line 19 of AccountTest (Fig. F.1) executes, passing depositAmount to Account method credit. Method main then displays the new balance. Note that the result is $125.00 (Fig. F.12). This shows that the preceding step changed the value of depositAmount from its initial value (25.0) to 75.0.

New account balance based on altered value
of variable depositAmount

Fig. F.12 | Output displayed after the debugging process.

In this section, you learned how to use the debugger's print command to evaluate arithmetic and boolean expressions. You also learned how to use the set command to modify the value of a variable during your application's execution.

F.4 Controlling Execution Using the step, step up and next Commands

Sometimes you'll need to execute an application line by line to find and fix errors. Walking through a portion of your application this way can help you verify that a method's code executes correctly. In this section, you'll learn how to use the debugger for this task. The commands you learn in this section allow you to execute a method line by line, execute all the statements of a method at once or execute only the remaining statements of a method (if you've already executed some statements within the method).

Once again, we assume you are working in the directory containing the Appendix F examples and have compiled for debugging with the -g compiler option.

1. *Starting the debugger.* Start the debugger by typing jdb.

2. *Setting a breakpoint.* Type stop at AccountTest:19 to set a breakpoint at line 19.

3. *Running the application.* Run the application by typing run AccountTest. After the application displays its two output messages, the debugger indicates that the breakpoint has been reached and displays the code at line 19 (Fig. F.13). The debugger and application then pause and wait for the next command to be entered.

Fig. F.13 | Reaching the breakpoint in the `AccountTest` application.

4. *Using the **step** command.* The **step command** executes the next statement in the application. If the next statement to execute is a method call, control transfers to the called method. The `step` command enables you to enter a method and study the individual statements of that method. For instance, you can use the `print` and `set` commands to view and modify the variables within the method. You'll now use the `step` command to enter the `credit` method of class `Account` (Fig. 3.13) by typing `step` (Fig. F.14). The debugger indicates that the step has been completed and displays the next executable statement—in this case, line 21 of class `Account` (Fig. 3.13).

Fig. F.14 | Stepping into the `credit` method.

5. *Using the **step up** command.* After you've stepped into the `credit` method, type **step up**. This command executes the remaining statements in the method and returns control to the place where the method was called. The `credit` method contains only one statement to add the method's parameter `amount` to instance variable `balance`. The `step up` command executes this statement, then pauses before line 22 in `AccountTest`. Thus, the next action to occur will be to print the new account balance (Fig. F.15). In lengthy methods, you may want to look at a few key lines of code, then continue debugging the caller's code. The `step up` command is useful for situations in which you do not want to continue stepping through the entire method line by line.

6. *Using the **cont** command to continue execution.* Enter the `cont` command (Fig. F.16) to continue execution. The statement at lines 22–23 executes, displaying the new balance, then the application and the debugger terminate.

Fig. F.15 | Stepping out of a method.

Fig. F.16 | Continuing execution of the `AccountTest` application.

7. *Restarting the debugger.* Restart the debugger by typing `jdb`.

8. *Setting a breakpoint.* Breakpoints persist only until the end of the debugging session in which they are set—once the debugger exits, all breakpoints are removed. (In Section F.6, you'll learn how to manually clear a breakpoint before the end of the debugging session.) Thus, the breakpoint set for line 19 in *Step 2* no longer exists upon restarting the debugger in *Step 7*. To reset the breakpoint at line 19, once again type `stop at AccountTest:19`.

9. *Running the application.* Type `run AccountTest` to run the application. As in *Step 3*, `AccountTest` runs until the breakpoint at line 19 is reached, then the debugger pauses and waits for the next command (Fig. F.17).

Fig. F.17 | Reaching the breakpoint in the `AccountTest` application.

10. *Using the **next** command.* Type **next**. This command behaves like the `step` command, except when the next statement to execute contains a method call. In that case, the called method executes in its entirety and the application advances to the

next executable line after the method call (Fig. F.18). Recall from *Step 4* that the step command would enter the called method. In this example, the next command causes Account method credit to execute, then the debugger pauses at line 22 in AccountTest.

```
Administrator: Command Prompt - jdb                              _ □ ×
main[1] next
>
Step completed: "thread=main", AccountTest.main(), line=22 bci=63
22            System.out.printf( "new account balance: $%.2f\n",
main[1]
```

Fig. F.18 | Stepping over a method call.

11. *Using the **exit** command.* Use the **exit** command to end the debugging session (Fig. F.19). This command causes the AccountTest application to immediately terminate rather than execute the remaining statements in main. Note that when debugging some types of applications (e.g., GUI applications), the application continues to execute even after the debugging session ends.

```
Administrator: Command Prompt                                   _ □ ×
main[1] exit

C:\examples\debugger>
```

Fig. F.19 | Exiting the debugger.

In this section, you learned how to use the debugger's step and step up commands to debug methods called during your application's execution. You saw how the next command can be used to step over a method call. You also learned that the exit command ends a debugging session.

F.5 The watch Command

In this section, we present the **watch command**, which tells the debugger to watch a field. When that field is about to change, the debugger will notify you. In this section, you'll learn how to use the watch command to see how the Account object's field balance is modified during the execution of the AccountTest application.

As in the preceding two sections, we assume that you've followed *Step 1* and *Step 2* in Section F.2 to open the **Command Prompt**, change to the correct examples directory and compile classes AccountTest and Account for debugging (i.e., with the -g compiler option).

1. *Starting the debugger.* Start the debugger by typing jdb.

2. *Watching a class's field.* Set a watch on Account's balance field by typing watch Account.balance (Fig. F.20). You can set a watch on any field during execution of the debugger. Whenever the value in a field is about to change, the debugger enters break mode and notifies you that the value will change. Watches can be placed only on fields, not on local variables.

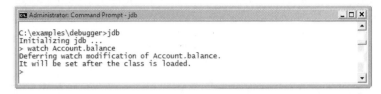

Fig. F.20 | Setting a watch on Account's balance field.

3. *Running the application.* Run the application with the command run Account-Test. The debugger will now notify you that field balance's value will change (Fig. F.21). When the application begins, an instance of Account is created with an initial balance of $50.00 and a reference to the Account object is assigned to the local variable account (line 9, Fig. F.1). Recall from Fig. 3.13 that when the constructor for this object runs, if parameter initialBalance is greater than 0.0, instance variable balance is assigned the value of parameter initialBalance. The debugger notifies you that the value of balance will be set to 50.0.

Fig. F.21 | AccountTest application stops when account is created and its balance field will be modified.

4. *Adding money to the account.* Type cont to continue executing the application. The application executes normally before reaching the code on line 19 of Fig. F.1 that calls Account method credit to raise the Account object's balance by a specified amount. The debugger notifies you that instance variable balance will change (Fig. F.22). Note that although line 19 of class AccountTest calls method credit, line 21 in Account's method credit actually changes the value of balance.

Fig. F.22 | Changing the value of balance by calling Account method credit.

5. *Continuing execution.* Type cont—the application will finish executing because the application does not attempt any additional changes to balance (Fig. F.23).

Fig. F.23 | Continuing execution of AccountTest.

6. *Restarting the debugger and resetting the watch on the variable.* Type jdb to restart the debugger. Once again, set a watch on the Account instance variable balance by typing the watch Account.balance, then type run AccountTest to run the application (Fig. F.24).

Fig. F.24 | Restarting the debugger and resetting the watch on the variable balance.

7. *Removing the watch on the field.* Suppose you want to watch a field for only part of a program's execution. You can remove the debugger's watch on variable balance by typing **unwatch** Account.balance (Fig. F.25). Type cont—the application will finish executing without reentering break mode.

Fig. F.25 | Removing the watch on variable balance.

8. *Closing the* **Command Prompt** *window.* Close the **Command Prompt** window by clicking its close button.

In this section, you learned how to use the watch command to enable the debugger to notify you of changes to the value of a field throughout the life of an application. You also learned how to use the unwatch command to remove a watch on a field before the end of the application.

F.6 The clear Command

In the preceding section, you learned to use the unwatch command to remove a watch on a field. The debugger also provides the clear command to remove a breakpoint from an application. You'll often need to debug applications containing repetitive actions, such as a loop. You may want to examine the values of variables during several, but possibly not all, of the loop's iterations. If you set a breakpoint in the body of a loop, the debugger will pause before each execution of the line containing a breakpoint. After determining that the loop is working properly, you may want to remove the breakpoint and allow the remaining iterations to proceed normally. In this section, we use the compound interest application in Fig. 5.6 to demonstrate how the debugger behaves when you set a breakpoint in the body of a for statement and how to remove a breakpoint in the middle of a debugging session.

1. *Opening the* **Command Prompt** *window, changing directories and compiling the application for debugging.* Open the **Command Prompt** window, then change to the directory containing the Appendix F examples. For your convenience, we've provided a copy of the Interest.java file in this directory. Compile the application for debugging by typing javac -g Interest.java.

2. *Starting the debugger and setting breakpoints.* Start the debugger by typing jdb. Set breakpoints at lines 13 and 22 of class Interest by typing stop at Interest:13, then stop at Interest:22 (Fig. F.26).

Fig. F.26 | Setting breakpoints in the Interest application.

3. *Running the application.* Run the application by typing run Interest. The application executes until reaching the breakpoint at line 13 (Fig. F.27).

4. *Continuing execution.* Type cont to continue—the application executes line 13, printing the column headings "Year" and "Amount on deposit". Note that line 13 appears before the for statement at lines 16–23 in Interest (Fig. 5.6) and thus executes only once. Execution continues past line 13 until the breakpoint at line 22 is reached during the first iteration of the for statement (Fig. F.28).

Fig. F.27 | Reaching the breakpoint at line 13 in the **Interest** application.

Fig. F.28 | Reaching the breakpoint at line 22 in the **Interest** application.

5. *Examining variable values.* Type print year to examine the current value of variable year (i.e., the for's control variable). Print the value of variable amount too (Fig. F.29).

Fig. F.29 | Printing year and amount during the first iteration of Interest's for.

6. *Continuing execution.* Type cont to continue execution. Line 22 executes and prints the current values of year and amount. After the for enters its second iteration, the debugger notifies you that the breakpoint at line 22 has been reached a second time. Note that the debugger pauses each time a line where a breakpoint has been set is about to execute—when the breakpoint appears in a loop, the debugger pauses during each iteration. Print the values of variables year and amount again to see how the values have changed since the first iteration of the for (Fig. F.30).

Fig. F.30 | Printing year and amount during the second iteration of Interest's for.

7. *Removing a breakpoint.* You can display a list of all of the breakpoints in the application by typing **clear** (Fig. F.31). Suppose you are satisfied that the Interest application's for statement is working properly, so you want to remove the breakpoint at line 22 and allow the remaining iterations of the loop to proceed normally. You can remove the breakpoint at line 22 by typing clear Interest:22. Now type clear to list the remaining breakpoints in the application. The debugger should indicate that only the breakpoint at line 13 remains (Fig. F.31). Note that this breakpoint has already been reached and thus will no longer affect execution.

```
amount = 1102.5
main[1] clear
Breakpoints set:
        breakpoint Interest:13
        breakpoint Interest:22
main[1] clear Interest:22
Removed: breakpoint Interest:22
main[1] clear
Breakpoints set:
        breakpoint Interest:13
main[1]
```

Fig. F.31 | Removing the breakpoint at line 22.

8. *Continuing execution after removing a breakpoint.* Type cont to continue execution. Recall that execution last paused before the printf statement in line 22. If the breakpoint at line 22 was removed successfully, continuing the application will produce the correct output for the current and remaining iterations of the for statement without the application halting (Fig. F.32).

```
        breakpoint Interest:13
main[1] cont
>    2           1,102.50
     3           1,157.63
     4           1,215.51
     5           1,276.28
     6           1,340.10
     7           1,407.10
     8           1,477.46
     9           1,551.33
    10           1,628.89

The application exited

C:\examples\debugger>
```

Fig. F.32 | Application executes without a breakpoint set at line 22.

In this section, you learned how to use the clear command to list all the breakpoints set for an application and remove a breakpoint.

F.7 Wrap-Up

In this appendix, you learned how to insert and remove breakpoints in the debugger. Breakpoints allow you to pause application execution so you can examine variable values with the debugger's print command. This capability will help you locate and fix logic errors in your applications. You saw how to use the print command to examine the value of an expression and how to use the set command to change the value of a variable. You also learned debugger commands (including the step, step up and next commands) that can be used to determine whether a method is executing correctly. You learned how to use the watch command to keep track of a field throughout the life of an application. Finally, you learned how to use the clear command to list all the breakpoints set for an application or remove individual breakpoints to continue execution without breakpoints.

Self-Review Exercises

F.1   Fill in the blanks in each of the following statements:
a) A breakpoint cannot be set at a(n) _____.
b) You can examine the value of an expression by using the debugger's _____ command.
c) You can modify the value of a variable by using the debugger's _____ command.
d) During debugging, the _____ command executes the remaining statements in the current method and returns program control to the place where the method was called.
e) The debugger's _____ command behaves like the step command when the next statement to execute does not contain a method call.
f) The watch debugger command allows you to view all changes to a(n) _____.

F.2   State whether each of the following is *true* or *false*. If *false*, explain why.
a) When application execution suspends at a breakpoint, the next statement to be executed is the statement after the breakpoint.
b) Watches can be removed using the debugger's clear command.
c) The -g compiler option must be used when compiling classes for debugging.
d) When a breakpoint appears in a loop, the debugger pauses only the first time that the breakpoint is encountered.

Answers to Self-Review Exercises

F.1   a) comment. b) print. c) set. d) step up. e) next. f) field.

F.2   a) False. When application execution suspends at a breakpoint, the next statement to be executed is the statement at the breakpoint. b) False. Watches can be removed using the debugger's unwatch command. c) True. d) False. When a breakpoint appears in a loop, the debugger pauses during each iteration.

All the news that's fit to print.
—Adolph S. Ochs

What mad pursuit? What struggle to escape?
—John Keats

Remove not the landmark on the boundary of the fields.
—Amenehope

Formatted Output

Objectives

In this appendix you'll learn:

- To understand input and output streams.
- To use `printf` formatting.
- To print with field widths and precisions.
- To use formatting flags in the `printf` format string.
- To print with an argument index.
- To output literals and escape sequences.
- To format output with class `Formatter`.

G.1 Introduction

In this appendix, we discuss the formatting features of method `printf` and class `Formatter` (package `java.util`). Class **Formatter** formats and outputs data to a specified destination, such as a string or a file output stream. Many features of `printf` were discussed earlier in the text. This appendix summarizes those features and introduces others, such as displaying date and time data in various formats, reordering output based on the index of the argument and displaying numbers and strings with various flags.

G.2 Streams

Input and output are usually performed with streams, which are sequences of bytes. In input operations, the bytes flow from a device (e.g., a keyboard, a disk drive, a network connection) to main memory. In output operations, bytes flow from main memory to a device (e.g., a display screen, a printer, a disk drive, a network connection).

When program execution begins, three streams are created. The standard input stream typically reads bytes from the keyboard, and the standard output stream typically outputs characters to a command window. A third stream, the **standard error stream** (`System.err`), typically outputs characters to a command window and is used to output error messages so they can be viewed immediately. Operating systems typically allow these streams to be redirected to other devices. Streams are discussed in detail in Chapter 17, Files, Streams and Object Serialization, and Chapter 27, Networking.

G.3 Formatting Output with `printf`

Precise output formatting is accomplished with `printf`. Java SE 5 borrowed (and enhanced) this feature from the C programming language. Method `printf` can perform the following formatting capabilities, each of which is discussed in this appendix:

1. Rounding floating-point values to an indicated number of decimal places.

2. Aligning a column of numbers with decimal points appearing one above the other.

3. Right justification and left justification of outputs.

4. Inserting literal characters at precise locations in a line of output.

5. Representing floating-point numbers in exponential format.

6. Representing integers in octal and hexadecimal format.

7. Displaying all types of data with fixed-size field widths and precisions.

8. Displaying dates and times in various formats.

Every call to printf supplies as the first argument a **format string** that describes the output format. The format string may consist of **fixed text** and **format specifiers**. Fixed text is output by printf just as it would be output by System.out methods print or println. Each format specifier is a placeholder for a value and specifies the type of data to output. Format specifiers also may include optional formatting information.

In the simplest form, each format specifier begins with a percent sign (%) and is followed by a **conversion character** that represents the data type of the value to output. For example, the format specifier %s is a placeholder for a string, and the format specifier %d is a placeholder for an int value. The optional formatting information, such as an argument index, flags, field width and precision, is specified between the percent sign and the conversion character. We demonstrate each of these capabilities.

G.4 Printing Integers

Figure G.1 describes the **integer conversion characters**. (See Appendix H for an overview of the binary, octal, decimal and hexadecimal number systems.) Figure G.2 uses each to print an integer. In lines 9–10, note that the plus sign is not displayed by default, but the minus sign is. Later in this appendix (Fig. G.14) we'll see how to force plus signs to print.

Conversion character	Description
d	Display a decimal (base 10) integer.
o	Display an octal (base 8) integer.
x or X	Display a hexadecimal (base 16) integer. X uses uppercase letters.

Fig. G.1 | Integer conversion characters.

```
1   // Fig. G.2: IntegerConversionTest.java
2   // Using the integer conversion characters.
3
4   public class IntegerConversionTest
5   {
6      public static void main( String[] args )
7      {
8         System.out.printf( "%d\n", 26 );
9         System.out.printf( "%d\n", +26 );
10        System.out.printf( "%d\n", -26 );
11        System.out.printf( "%o\n", 26 );
12        System.out.printf( "%x\n", 26 );
13        System.out.printf( "%X\n", 26 );
14     } // end main
15  } // end class IntegerConversionTest
```

Fig. G.2 | Using the integer conversion characters. (Part 1 of 2.)

```
26
26
-26
32
1a
1A
```

Fig. G.2 | Using the integer conversion characters. (Part 2 of 2.)

The printf method has the form

printf(*format-string*, *argument-list*);

where *format-string* describes the output format, and the optional *argument-list* contains the values that correspond to each format specifier in *format-string*. There can be many format specifiers in one format string.

Each format string in lines 8–10 specifies that printf should output a decimal integer (%d) followed by a newline character. At the format specifier's position, printf substitutes the value of the first argument after the format string. If the format string contains multiple format specifiers, at each subsequent format specifier's position printf substitutes the value of the next argument in the argument list. The %o format specifier in line 11 outputs the integer in octal format. The %x format specifier in line 12 outputs the integer in hexadecimal format. The %X format specifier in line 13 outputs the integer in hexadecimal format with capital letters.

G.5 Printing Floating-Point Numbers

Figure G.3 describes the floating-point conversions. The **conversion characters e** and **E** display floating-point values in **computerized scientific notation** (also called **exponential notation**). Exponential notation is the computer equivalent of the scientific notation used in mathematics. For example, the value 150.4582 is represented in scientific notation in mathematics as

1.504582×10^2

and is represented in exponential notation as

1.504582e+02

in Java. This notation indicates that 1.504582 is multiplied by 10 raised to the second power (e+02). The e stands for "exponent."

Values printed with the conversion characters e, E and f are output with six digits of precision to the right of the decimal point by default (e.g., 1.045921)—other precisions

Conversion character	Description
e or E	Display a floating-point value in exponential notation. Conversion character E displays the output in uppercase letters.
f	Display a floating-point value in decimal format.

Fig. G.3 | Floating-point conversion characters. (Part 1 of 2.)

Conversion character	Description
g or G	Display a floating-point value in either the floating-point format f or the exponential format e based on the magnitude of the value. If the magnitude is less than 10^{-3}, or greater than or equal to 10^7, the floating-point value is printed with e (or E). Otherwise, the value is printed in format f. When conversion character G is used, the output is displayed in uppercase letters.
a or A	Display a floating-point number in hexadecimal format. Conversion character A displays the output in uppercase letters.

Fig. G.3 | Floating-point conversion characters. (Part 2 of 2.)

must be specified explicitly. For values printed with the conversion character g, the precision represents the total number of digits displayed, excluding the exponent. The default is six digits (e.g., 12345678.9 is displayed as 1.23457e+07). **Conversion character f** always prints at least one digit to the left of the decimal point. Conversion characters e and E print lowercase e and uppercase E preceding the exponent and always print exactly one digit to the left of the decimal point. Rounding occurs if the value being formatted has more significant digits than the precision.

Conversion character g (or **G**) prints in either e (E) or f format, depending on the floating-point value. For example, the values 0.0000875, 87500000.0, 8.75, 87.50 and 875.0 are printed as 8.750000e-05, 8.750000e+07, 8.750000, 87.500000 and 875.000000 with the conversion character g. The value 0.0000875 uses e notation because the magnitude is less than 10-3. The value 87500000.0 uses e notation because the magnitude is greater than 10^7. Figure G.4 demonstrates the floating-point conversion characters.

```java
1   // Fig. G.4: FloatingNumberTest.java
2   // Using floating-point conversion characters.
3
4   public class FloatingNumberTest
5   {
6      public static void main( String[] args )
7      {
8         System.out.printf( "%e\n", 12345678.9 );
9         System.out.printf( "%e\n", +12345678.9 );
10        System.out.printf( "%e\n", -12345678.9 );
11        System.out.printf( "%E\n", 12345678.9 );
12        System.out.printf( "%f\n", 12345678.9 );
13        System.out.printf( "%g\n", 12345678.9 );
14        System.out.printf( "%G\n", 12345678.9 );
15     } // end main
16  } // end class FloatingNumberTest
```

```
1.234568e+07
1.234568e+07
-1.234568e+07                                          (continued...)
```

Fig. G.4 | Using floating-point conversion characters. (Part 1 of 2.)

```
1.234568E+07
12345678.900000
1.23457e+07
1.23457E+07
```

Fig. G.4 | Using floating-point conversion characters. (Part 2 of 2.)

G.6 Printing Strings and Characters

The c and s conversion characters print individual characters and strings, respectively. **Conversion characters c and C** require a char argument. **Conversion characters s and S** can take a String or any Object as an argument. When conversion characters C and S are used, the output is displayed in uppercase letters. Figure G.5 displays characters, strings and objects with conversion characters c and s. Note that autoboxing occurs at line 9 when an int constant is assigned to an Integer object. Line 15 outputs an Integer argument with the conversion character s, which implicitly invokes the toString method to get the integer value. Note that you can also output an Integer object using the %d format specifier. In this case, the int value in the Integer object will be unboxed and output.

 Common Programming Error G.1
Using %c to print a String causes an IllegalFormatConversionException—a String cannot be converted to a character.

```java
1   // Fig. G.5: CharStringConversion.java
2   // Using character and string conversion characters.
3   public class CharStringConversion
4   {
5      public static void main( String[] args )
6      {
7         char character = 'A';  // initialize char
8         String string = "This is also a string";  // String object
9         Integer integer = 1234;  // initialize integer (autoboxing)
10
11        System.out.printf( "%c\n", character );
12        System.out.printf( "%s\n", "This is a string" );
13        System.out.printf( "%s\n", string );
14        System.out.printf( "%S\n", string );
15        System.out.printf( "%s\n", integer ); // implicit call to toString
16     } // end main
17  } // end class CharStringConversion
```

```
A
This is a string
This is also a string
THIS IS ALSO A STRING
1234
```

Fig. G.5 | Using character and string conversion characters.

G.7 Printing Dates and Times

The **conversion character t** (or **T**) is used to print dates and times in various formats. It is always followed by a **conversion suffix character** that specifies the date and/or time format. When conversion character T is used, the output is displayed in uppercase letters. Figure G.6 lists the common conversion suffix characters for formatting **date and time compositions** that display both the date and the time. Figure G.7 lists the common conversion suffix characters for formatting dates. Figure G.8 lists the common conversion suffix characters for formatting times. For the complete list of conversion suffix characters, visit `java.sun.com/javase/6/docs/api/java/util/Formatter.html`.

Conversion suffix character	Description
c	Display date and time formatted as `day month date hour:minute:second time-zone year` with three characters for day and month, two digits for date, hour, minute and second and four digits for year—for example, Wed Mar 03 16:30:25 GMT-05:00 2004. The 24-hour clock is used. GMT-05:00 is the time zone.
F	Display date formatted as year-month-date with four digits for the year and two digits each for the month and date (e.g., 2004-05-04).
D	Display date formatted as month/day/year with two digits each for the month, day and year (e.g., 03/03/04).
r	Display time in 12-hour format as hour:minute:second AM|PM with two digits each for the hour, minute and second (e.g., 04:30:25 PM).
R	Display time formatted as hour:minute with two digits each for the hour and minute (e.g., 16:30). The 24-hour clock is used.
T	Display time as hour:minute:second with two digits for the hour, minute and second (e.g., 16:30:25). The 24-hour clock is used.

Fig. G.6 | Date and time composition conversion suffix characters.

Conversion suffix character	Description
A	Display full name of the day of the week (e.g., Wednesday).
a	Display the three-character name of the day of the week (e.g., Wed).
B	Display full name of the month (e.g., March).
b	Display the three-character short name of the month (e.g., Mar).
d	Display the day of the month with two digits, padding with leading zeros as necessary (e.g., 03).
m	Display the month with two digits, padding with leading zeros as necessary (e.g., 07).
e	Display the day of month without leading zeros (e.g., 3).

Fig. G.7 | Date formatting conversion suffix characters. (Part 1 of 2.)

Conversion suffix character	Description
Y	Display the year with four digits (e.g., 2004).
y	Display the last two digits of the year with leading zeros (e.g., 04).
j	Display the day of the year with three digits, padding with leading zeros as necessary (e.g., 016).

Fig. G.7 | Date formatting conversion suffix characters. (Part 2 of 2.)

Conversion suffix character	Description
H	Display hour in 24-hour clock with a leading zero as necessary (e.g., 16).
I	Display hour in 12-hour clock with a leading zero as necessary (e.g., 04).
k	Display hour in 24-hour clock without leading zeros (e.g., 16).
l	Display hour in 12-hour clock without leading zeros (e.g., 4).
M	Display minute with a leading zero as necessary (e.g., 06).
S	Display second with a leading zero as necessary (e.g., 05).
Z	Display the abbreviation for the time zone (e.g., EST, stands for Eastern Standard Time, which is 5 hours behind Greenwich Mean Time).
p	Display morning or afternoon marker in lowercase (e.g., pm).
P	Display morning or afternoon marker in uppercase (e.g., PM).

Fig. G.8 | Time formatting conversion suffix characters.

Figure G.9 uses the conversion characters t and T with the conversion suffix characters to display dates and times in various formats. Conversion character t requires the corresponding argument to be a date or time of type long, Long, **Calendar** (package java.util) or **Date** (package java.util)—objects of each of these classes can represent dates and times. Class Calendar is preferred for this purpose because some constructors and methods in class Date are replaced by those in class Calendar. Line 10 invokes static method **getInstance** of Calendar to obtain a calendar with the current date and time. Lines 13–17, 20–22 and 25–26 use this Calendar object in printf statements as the value to be formatted with conversion character t. Note that lines 20–22 and 25–26 use the optional **argument index** ("1$") to indicate that all format specifiers in the format string use the first argument after the format string in the argument list. You'll learn more about argument indices in Section G.11. Using the argument index eliminates the need to repeatedly list the same argument.

```
1   // Fig. G.9: DateTimeTest.java
2   // Formatting dates and times with conversion characters t and T.
3   import java.util.Calendar;
4
```

Fig. G.9 | Formatting dates and times with conversion characters t and T. (Part 1 of 2.)

```
5   public class DateTimeTest
6   {
7      public static void main( String[] args )
8      {
9         // get current date and time
10        Calendar dateTime = Calendar.getInstance();
11
12        // printing with conversion characters for date/time compositions
13        System.out.printf( "%tc\n", dateTime );
14        System.out.printf( "%tF\n", dateTime );
15        System.out.printf( "%tD\n", dateTime );
16        System.out.printf( "%tr\n", dateTime );
17        System.out.printf( "%tT\n", dateTime );
18
19        // printing with conversion characters for date
20        System.out.printf( "%1$tA, %1$tB %1$td, %1$tY\n", dateTime );
21        System.out.printf( "%1$TA, %1$TB %1$Td, %1$TY\n", dateTime );
22        System.out.printf( "%1$ta, %1$tb %1$te, %1$ty\n", dateTime );
23
24        // printing with conversion characters for time
25        System.out.printf( "%1$tH:%1$tM:%1$tS\n", dateTime );
26        System.out.printf( "%1$tZ %1$tI:%1$tM:%1$tS %tP", dateTime );
27     } // end main
28  } // end class DateTimeTest
```

```
Wed Feb 25 15:00:22 EST 2009
2009-02-25
02/25/09
03:00:22 PM
15:00:22
Wednesday, February 25, 2009
WEDNESDAY, FEBRUARY 25, 2009
Wed, Feb 25, 09
15:00:22
EST 03:00:22 PM
```

Fig. G.9 | Formatting dates and times with conversion characters t and T. (Part 2 of 2.)

G.8 Other Conversion Characters

The remaining conversion characters are **b**, **B**, **h**, **H**, **%** and **n**. These are described in Fig. G.10. Lines 9–10 of Fig. G.11 use %b to print the value of boolean (or Boolean) values false and true. Line 11 associates a String to %b, which returns true because it's not null. Line 12 associates a null object to %B, which displays FALSE because test is null. Lines 13–14 use %h to print the string representations of the hash-code values for strings "hello" and "Hello". These values could be used to store or locate the strings in a Hashtable or HashMap (both discussed in Chapter 20, Generic Collections). Note that the hash-code values for these two strings differ, because one string starts with a lowercase letter and the other with an uppercase letter. Line 15 uses %H to print null in uppercase letters. The last two printf statements (lines 16–17) use %% to print the % character in a string and %n to print a platform-specific line separator.

Conversion character	Description
b or B	Print "true" or "false" for the value of a boolean or Boolean. These conversion characters can also format the value of any reference. If the reference is non-null, "true" is output; otherwise, "false". When conversion character B is used, the output is displayed in uppercase letters.
h or H	Print the string representation of an object's hash-code value in hexadecimal format. If the corresponding argument is null, "null" is printed. When conversion character H is used, the output is displayed in uppercase letters.
%	Print the percent character.
n	Print the platform-specific line separator (e.g., \r\n on Windows or \n on UNIX/LINUX).

Fig. G.10 | Other conversion characters.

```
 1    // Fig. G.11: OtherConversion.java
 2    // Using the b, B, h, H, % and n conversion characters.
 3
 4    public class OtherConversion
 5    {
 6       public static void main( String[] args )
 7       {
 8          Object test = null;
 9          System.out.printf( "%b\n", false );
10          System.out.printf( "%b\n", true );
11          System.out.printf( "%b\n", "Test" );
12          System.out.printf( "%B\n", test );
13          System.out.printf( "Hashcode of \"hello\" is %h\n", "hello" );
14          System.out.printf( "Hashcode of \"Hello\" is %h\n", "Hello" );
15          System.out.printf( "Hashcode of null is %H\n", test );
16          System.out.printf( "Printing a %% in a format string\n" );
17          System.out.printf( "Printing a new line %nnext line starts here" );
18       } // end main
19    } // end class OtherConversion
```

```
false
true
true
FALSE
Hashcode of "hello" is 5e918d2
Hashcode of "Hello" is 42628b2
Hashcode of null is NULL
Printing a % in a format string
Printing a new line
next line starts here
```

Fig. G.11 | Using the b, B, h, H, % and n conversion characters.

Common Programming Error G.2

Trying to print a literal percent character using % rather than %% in the format string might cause a difficult-to-detect logic error. When % appears in a format string, it must be followed by a conversion character in the string. The single percent could accidentally be followed by a legitimate conversion character, thus causing a logic error.

G.9 Printing with Field Widths and Precisions

The size of a field in which data is printed is specified by a **field width**. If the field width is larger than the data being printed, the data is right justified in that field by default. We discuss left justification in Section G.10. You insert an integer representing the field width between the % and the conversion character (e.g., %4d) in the format specifier. Figure G.12 prints two groups of five numbers each, right justifying those numbers that contain fewer digits than the field width. Note that the field width is increased to print values wider than the field and that the minus sign for a negative value uses one character position in the field. Also, if no field width is specified, the data prints in exactly as many positions as it needs. Field widths can be used with all format specifiers except the line separator (%n).

```java
1   // Fig. G.12: FieldWidthTest.java
2   // Right justifying integers in fields.
3
4   public class FieldWidthTest
5   {
6      public static void main( String[] args )
7      {
8         System.out.printf( "%4d\n", 1 );
9         System.out.printf( "%4d\n", 12 );
10        System.out.printf( "%4d\n", 123 );
11        System.out.printf( "%4d\n", 1234 );
12        System.out.printf( "%4d\n\n", 12345 ); // data too large
13
14        System.out.printf( "%4d\n", -1 );
15        System.out.printf( "%4d\n", -12 );
16        System.out.printf( "%4d\n", -123 );
17        System.out.printf( "%4d\n", -1234 ); // data too large
18        System.out.printf( "%4d\n", -12345 ); // data too large
19     } // end main
20  } // end class RightJustifyTest
```

```
   1
  12
 123
1234
12345

  -1
 -12
-123
-1234
-12345
```

Fig. G.12 | Right justifying integers in fields.

Common Programming Error G.3

Not providing a sufficiently large field width to handle a value to be printed can offset other data being printed and produce confusing outputs. Know your data!

Method `printf` also provides the ability to specify the precision with which data is printed. Precision has different meanings for different types. When used with floating-point conversion characters e and f, the precision is the number of digits that appear after the decimal point. When used with conversion characters g, a or A, the precision is the maximum number of significant digits to be printed. When used with conversion character s, the precision is the maximum number of characters to be written from the string. To use precision, place between the percent sign and the conversion specifier a decimal point (.) followed by an integer representing the precision. Figure G.13 demonstrates the use of precision in format strings. Note that when a floating-point value is printed with a precision smaller than the original number of decimal places in the value, the value is rounded. Also note that the format specifier `%.3g` indicates that the total number of digits used to display the floating-point value is 3. Because the value has three digits to the left of the decimal point, the value is rounded to the ones position.

The field width and the precision can be combined by placing the field width, followed by a decimal point, followed by a precision between the percent sign and the conversion character, as in the statement

```
printf( "%9.3f", 123.456789 );
```

which displays 123.457 with three digits to the right of the decimal point right justified in a nine-digit field—this number will be preceded in its field by two blanks.

```
1   // Fig. G.13: PrecisionTest.java
2   // Using precision for floating-point numbers and strings.
3   public class PrecisionTest
4   {
5      public static void main( String[] args )
6      {
7         double f = 123.94536;
8         String s = "Happy Birthday";
9
10        System.out.printf( "Using precision for floating-point numbers\n" );
11        System.out.printf( "\t%.3f\n\t%.3e\n\t%.3g\n\n", f, f, f );
12
13        System.out.printf( "Using precision for strings\n" );
14        System.out.printf( "\t%.11s\n", s );
15     } // end main
16  } // end class PrecisionTest
```

```
Using precision for floating-point numbers
        123.945
        1.239e+02
        124

Using precision for strings
        Happy Birth
```

Fig. G.13 | Using precision for floating-point numbers and strings.

G.10 Using Flags in the `printf` Format String

Various flags may be used with method `printf` to supplement its output formatting capabilities. Seven flags are available for use in format strings (Fig. G.14).

Flag	Description
− (minus sign)	Left justify the output within the specified field.
+ (plus sign)	Display a plus sign preceding positive values and a minus sign preceding negative values.
space	Print a space before a positive value not printed with the + flag.
#	Prefix 0 to the output value when used with the octal conversion character o. Prefix 0x to the output value when used with the hexadecimal conversion character x.
0 (zero)	Pad a field with leading zeros.
, (comma)	Use the locale-specific thousands separator (i.e., ',' for U.S. locale) to display decimal and floating-point numbers.
(	Enclose negative numbers in parentheses.

Fig. G.14 | Format string flags.

To use a flag in a format string, place it immediately to the right of the percent sign. Several flags may be used in the same format specifier. Figure G.15 demonstrates right justification and left justification of a string, an integer, a character and a floating-point number. Note that line 9 serves as a counting mechanism for the screen output.

```
1   // Fig. G.15: MinusFlagTest.java
2   // Right justifying and left justifying values.
3
4   public class MinusFlagTest
5   {
6      public static void main( String[] args )
7      {
8         System.out.println( "Columns:" );
9         System.out.println( "0123456789012345678901234567890123456789\n" );
10        System.out.printf( "%10s%10d%10c%10f\n\n", "hello", 7, 'a', 1.23 );
11        System.out.printf(
12           "%-10s%-10d%-10c%-10f\n", "hello", 7, 'a', 1.23 );
13     } // end main
14  } // end class MinusFlagTest
```

```
Columns:
0123456789012345678901234567890123456789

     hello         7         a  1.230000

hello     7         a         1.230000
```

Fig. G.15 | Right justifying and left justifying values.

Figure G.16 prints a positive number and a negative number, each with and without the **+ flag**. Note that the minus sign is displayed in both cases, the plus sign only when the + flag is used.

```java
1   // Fig. G.16: PlusFlagTest.java
2   // Printing numbers with and without the + flag.
3
4   public class PlusFlagTest
5   {
6      public static void main( String[] args )
7      {
8         System.out.printf( "%d\t%d\n", 786, -786 );
9         System.out.printf( "%+d\t%+d\n", 786, -786 );
10      } // end main
11   } // end class PlusFlagTest
```

```
786     -786
+786    -786
```

Fig. G.16 | Printing numbers with and without the + flag.

Figure G.17 prefixes a space to the positive number with the **space flag**. This is useful for aligning positive and negative numbers with the same number of digits. Note that the value -547 is not preceded by a space in the output because of its minus sign. Figure G.18 uses the **# flag** to prefix 0 to the octal value and 0x to the hexadecimal value.

```java
1   // Fig. G.17: SpaceFlagTest.java
2   // Printing a space before non-negative values.
3
4   public class SpaceFlagTest
5   {
6      public static void main( String[] args )
7      {
8         System.out.printf( "% d\n% d\n", 547, -547 );
9      } // end main
10   } // end class SpaceFlagTest
```

```
 547
-547
```

Fig. G.17 | Printing a space before nonnegative values.

```java
1   // Fig. G.18: PoundFlagTest.java
2   // Using the # flag with conversion characters o and x.
3
4   public class PoundFlagTest
5   {
6      public static void main( String[] args )
7      {
```

Fig. G.18 | Using the # flag with conversion characters o and x. (Part 1 of 2.)

```
 8          int c = 31;      // initialize c
 9
10          System.out.printf( "%#o\n", c );
11          System.out.printf( "%#x\n", c );
12       } // end main
13    } // end class PoundFlagTest
```

```
037
0x1f
```

Fig. G.18 | Using the # flag with conversion characters o and x. (Part 2 of 2.)

Figure G.19 combines the + flag the **0 flag** and the space flag to print 452 in a field of width 9 with a + sign and leading zeros, next prints 452 in a field of width 9 using only the 0 flag, then prints 452 in a field of width 9 using only the space flag.

```
 1    // Fig. G.19: ZeroFlagTest.java
 2    // Printing with the 0 (zero) flag fills in leading zeros.
 3
 4    public class ZeroFlagTest
 5    {
 6       public static void main( String[] args )
 7       {
 8          System.out.printf( "%+09d\n", 452 );
 9          System.out.printf( "%09d\n", 452 );
10          System.out.printf( "% 9d\n", 452 );
11       } // end main
12    } // end class ZeroFlagTest
```

```
+00000452
000000452
      452
```

Fig. G.19 | Printing with the 0 (zero) flag fills in leading zeros.

Figure G.20 uses the comma (,) flag to display a decimal and a floating-point number with the thousands separator. Figure G.21 encloses negative numbers in parentheses using the (flag. Note that the value 50 is not enclosed in parentheses in the output because it's a positive number.

```
 1    // Fig. G.20: CommaFlagTest.java
 2    // Using the comma (,) flag to display numbers with thousands separator.
 3
 4    public class CommaFlagTest
 5    {
 6       public static void main( String[] args )
 7       {
```

Fig. G.20 | Using the comma (,) flag to display numbers with the thousands separator. (Part 1 of 2.)

```
 8            System.out.printf( "%,d\n", 58625 );
 9            System.out.printf( "%,.2f", 58625.21 );
10            System.out.printf( "%,.2f", 12345678.9 );
11        } // end main
12    } // end class CommaFlagTest
```

```
58,625
58,625.21
12,345,678.90
```

Fig. G.20 | Using the comma (,) flag to display numbers with the thousands separator. (Part 2 of 2.)

```
 1    // Fig. G.21: ParenthesesFlagTest.java
 2    // Using the ( flag to place parentheses around negative numbers.
 3
 4    public class ParenthesesFlagTest
 5    {
 6        public static void main( String[] args )
 7        {
 8            System.out.printf( "%(d\n", 50 );
 9            System.out.printf( "%(d\n", -50 );
10            System.out.printf( "%(.1e\n", -50.0 );
11        } // end main
12    } // end class ParenthesesFlagTest
```

```
50
(50)
(5.0e+01)
```

Fig. G.21 | Using the (flag to place parentheses around negative numbers.

G.11 Printing with Argument Indices

An **argument index** is an optional integer followed by a $ sign that indicates the argument's position in the argument list. For example, lines 20–22 and 25–26 in Fig. G.9 use argument index "1$" to indicate that all format specifiers use the first argument in the argument list. Argument indices enable programmers to reorder the output so that the arguments in the argument list are not necessarily in the order of their corresponding format specifiers. Argument indices also help avoid duplicating arguments. Figure G.22 prints arguments in the argument list in reverse order using the argument index.

```
 1    // Fig. G.22: ArgumentIndexTest.java
 2    // Reordering output with argument indices.
 3
 4    public class ArgumentIndexTest
 5    {
```

Fig. G.22 | Reordering output with argument indices. (Part 1 of 2.)

```
 6      public static void main( String[] args )
 7      {
 8         System.out.printf(
 9            "Parameter list without reordering: %s %s %s %s\n",
10            "first", "second", "third", "fourth" );
11         System.out.printf(
12            "Parameter list after reordering: %4$s %3$s %2$s %1$s\n",
13            "first", "second", "third", "fourth" );
14      } // end main
15   } // end class ArgumentIndexTest
```

```
Parameter list without reordering: first second third fourth
Parameter list after reordering: fourth third second first
```

Fig. G.22 | Reordering output with argument indices. (Part 2 of 2.)

G.12 Printing Literals and Escape Sequences

Most literal characters to be printed in a `printf` statement can simply be included in the format string. However, there are several "problem" characters, such as the quotation mark (") that delimits the format string itself. Various control characters, such as newline and tab, must be represented by escape sequences. An escape sequence is represented by a backslash (\), followed by an escape character. Figure G.23 lists the escape sequences and the actions they cause.

Common Programming Error G.4

Attempting to print as literal data in a `printf` statement a double quote or backslash character without preceding that character with a backslash to form a proper escape sequence might result in a syntax error.

Escape sequence	Description
\' (single quote)	Output the single quote (') character.
\" (double quote)	Output the double quote (") character.
\\ (backslash)	Output the backslash (\) character.
\b (backspace)	Move the cursor back one position on the current line.
\f (new page or form feed)	Move the cursor to the start of the next logical page.
\n (newline)	Move the cursor to the beginning of the next line.
\r (carriage return)	Move the cursor to the beginning of the current line.
\t (horizontal tab)	Move the cursor to the next horizontal tab position.

Fig. G.23 | Escape sequences.

G.13 Formatting Output with Class Formatter

So far, we've discussed displaying formatted output to the standard output stream. What should we do if we want to send formatted outputs to other output streams or devices, such as a JTextArea or a file? The solution relies on class Formatter (in package java.util), which provides the same formatting capabilities as printf. Formatter is a utility class that enables programmers to output formatted data to a specified destination, such as a file on disk. By default, a Formatter creates a string in memory. Figure G.24 demonstrates how to use a Formatter to build a formatted string, which is then displayed in a message dialog.

```java
1   // Fig. Fig. G.24: FormatterTest.java
2   // Formatting output with class Formatter.
3   import java.util.Formatter;
4   import javax.swing.JOptionPane;
5
6   public class FormatterTest
7   {
8      public static void main( String[] args )
9      {
10        // create Formatter and format output
11        Formatter formatter = new Formatter();
12        formatter.format( "%d = %#o = %#X", 10, 10, 10 );
13
14        // display output in JOptionPane
15        JOptionPane.showMessageDialog( null, formatter.toString() );
16     } // end main
17  } // end class FormatterTest
```

Fig. G.24 | Formatting output with class Formatter.

Line 11 creates a Formatter object using the default constructor, so this object will build a string in memory. Other constructors are provided to allow you to specify the destination to which the formatted data should be output. For details, see java.sun.com/javase/6/docs/api/java/util/Formatter.html.

Line 12 invokes method **format** to format the output. Like printf, method format takes a format string and an argument list. The difference is that printf sends the formatted output directly to the standard output stream, while format sends the formatted output to the destination specified by its constructor (a string in memory in this program). Line 15 invokes the Formatter's toString method to get the formatted data as a string, which is then displayed in a message dialog.

Note that class String also provides a static convenience method named format that enables you to create a string in memory without the need to first create a Formatter object. Lines 11–12 and line 15 in Fig. G.24 could have been replaced by

```java
String s = String.format( "%d = %#o = %#x", 10, 10, 10 );
JOptionPane.showMessageDialog( null, s );
```

G.14 Wrap-Up

This appendix summarized how to display formatted output with various format characters and flags. We displayed decimal numbers using format characters d, o, x and X; floating-point numbers using format characters e, E, f, g and G; and dates and times in various format using format characters t and T and their conversion suffix characters. You learned how to display output with field widths and precisions. We introduced the flags +, -, space, #, 0, comma and (that are used together with the format characters to produce output. We also demonstrated how to format output with class Formatter.

Summary

Section G.2 Streams
- Input and output are usually performed with streams, which are sequences of bytes.
- Normally, the standard input stream is connected to the keyboard, and the standard output stream is connected to the computer screen.

Section G.3 Formatting Output with printf
- The printf format string describes the formats in which the output values appear. The format specifier consists of argument index, flags, field widths, precisions and conversion characters.

Section G.4 Printing Integers
- Integers are printed with the conversion characters d for decimal integers, o for integers in octal form and x (or X) for integers in hexadecimal form. X displays uppercase letters.

Section G.5 Printing Floating-Point Numbers
- Floating-point values are printed with the conversion characters e (or E) for exponential notation, f for regular floating-point notation, and g (or G) for either e (or E) notation or f notation. For the g conversion specifier, the e conversion character is used if the value is less than 10^{-3} or greater than or equal to 10^7; otherwise, the f conversion character is used.

Section G.6 Printing Strings and Characters
- The conversion character c prints a character.
- The conversion character s (or S) prints a string of characters. Conversion character S displays the output in uppercase letters.

Section G.7 Printing Dates and Times
- The conversion character t (or T) followed by a conversion suffix character prints the date and time in various forms. Conversion character T displays the output in uppercase letters.
- Conversion character t (or T) requires the argument to be of type long, Long, Calendar or Date.

Section G.8 Other Conversion Characters
- Conversion character b (or B) outputs the string representation of a boolean or Boolean. These conversion characters also output "true" for non-null references and "false" for null references. Conversion character B outputs uppercase letters.
- Conversion character h (or H) returns null for a null reference and a String representation of the hash-code value (in base 16) of an object . Hash codes are used to store and retrieve objects in Hashtables and HashMaps. Conversion character H outputs uppercase letters.

- The conversion character n prints the platform-specific line separator.
- The conversion character % is used to display a literal %.

Section G.9 Printing with Field Widths and Precisions

- If the field width is larger than the object being printed, the object is right justified in the field.
- Field widths can be used with all conversion characters except the line-separator conversion.
- Precision used with floating-point conversion characters e and f indicates the number of digits that appear after the decimal point. Precision used with floating-point conversion character g indicates the number of significant digits to appear.
- Precision used with conversion character s indicates the number of characters to be printed.
- The field width and the precision can be combined by placing the field width, followed by a decimal point, followed by the precision between the percent sign and the conversion character.

Section G.10 Using Flags in the **printf** Format String

- The - flag left justifies its argument in a field.
- The + flag prints a plus sign for positive values and a minus sign for negative values.
- The space flag prints a space preceding a positive value. The space flag and the + flag cannot be used together in an integer conversion character.
- The # flag prefixes 0 to octal values and 0x to hexadecimal values.
- The 0 flag prints leading zeros for a value that does not occupy its entire field.
- The comma (,) flag uses the locale-specific thousands separator to display integer and floating-point numbers.
- The (flag encloses a negative number in parentheses.

Section G.11 Printing with Argument Indices

- An argument index is an optional decimal integer followed by a $ sign that indicates the position of the argument in the argument list.
- Argument indices enable programmers to reorder the output so that the arguments in the argument list are not necessarily in the order of their corresponding format specifiers. Argument indices also help avoid duplicating arguments.

Section G.13 Formatting Output with Class **Formatter**

- Class Formatter (in package java.util) provides the same formatting capabilities as printf. Formatter is a utility class that enables programmers to print formatted output to various destinations, including GUI components, files and other output streams.
- Formatter method format outputs formatted data to the destination specified by the Formatter constructor.
- String static method format formats data and returns the formatted data as a String.

Terminology

Self-Review Exercises

G.1 Fill in the blanks in each of the following:

a) All input and output is dealt with in the form of _____.

b) The _____ stream is normally connected to the keyboard.

c) The _____ stream is normally connected to the computer screen.

d) System.out's _____ method can be used to format text that is displayed on the standard output.

e) The conversion character _____ may be used to output a decimal integer.

f) The conversion characters _____ and _____ are used to display integers in octal and hexadecimal form, respectively.

g) The conversion character _____ is used to display a floating-point value in exponential notation.

h) The conversion characters e and f are displayed with _____ digits of precision to the right of the decimal point if no precision is specified.

i) The conversion characters _____ and _____ are used to print strings and characters, respectively.

j) The conversion character _____ and conversion suffix character _____ are used to print time for the 24-hour clock as hour:minute:second.

k) The _____ flag causes output to be left justified in a field.

l) The _____ flag causes values to be displayed with either a plus sign or a minus sign.

m) The argument index _____ corresponds to the second argument in the argument list.

n) Class _____ has the same capability as printf, but allows programmers to print formatted output to various destinations besides the standard output stream.

G.2   Find the error in each of the following and explain how it can be corrected.
   a)   The following statement should print the character `'c'`.
```
System.out.printf( "%c\n", "c" );
```
   b)   The following statement should print `9.375%`.
```
System.out.printf( "%.3f%", 9.375 );
```
   c)   The following statement should print the third argument in the argument list.
```
System.out.printf( "%2$s\n", "Mon", "Tue", "Wed", "Thu", "Fri" );
```
   d)   `System.out.printf( ""A string in quotes"" );`
   e)   `System.out.printf( %d %d, 12, 20 );`
   f)   `System.out.printf( "%s\n", 'Richard' );`

G.3   Write a statement for each of the following:
   a)   Print `1234` right justified in a 10-digit field.
   b)   Print `123.456789` in exponential notation with a sign (+ or -) and 3 digits of precision.
   c)   Print `100` in octal form preceded by `0`.
   d)   Given a `Calendar` object `calendar`, print a date formatted as month/day/year (each with two digits).
   e)   Given a `Calendar` object `calendar`, print a time for the 24-hour clock as `hour:minute:second` (each with two digits) using argument index and conversion suffix characters for formatting time.
   f)   Print `3.333333` with a sign (+ or -) in a field of 20 characters with a precision of 3.

Answers to Self-Review Exercises

G.1   a)   Streams. b) Standard input. c) Standard output. d) `printf`. e) d. f) o, x or X. g) e or E.
h) 6. i) s or S, c or C. j) t, T. k) - (minus). l) + (plus). m) 2$. n) `Formatter`.

G.2   a)   Error: Conversion character c expects an argument of primitive type `char`.
            Correction: To print the character `'c'`, change `"c"` to `'c'`.
   b)   Error: Trying to print the literal character `%` without using the format specifier `%%`.
            Correction: Use `%%` to print a literal `%` character.
   c)   Error: Argument index does not start with 0; e.g., the first argument is `1$`.
            Correction: To print the third argument use `3$`.
   d)   Error: Trying to print the literal character `"` without using the `\"` escape sequence.
            Correction: Replace each quote in the inner set of quotes with `\"`.
   e)   Error: The format string is not enclosed in double quotes.
            Correction: Enclose `%d %d` in double quotes.
   f)   Error: The string to be printed is enclosed in single quotes.
            Correction: Use double quotes instead of single quotes to represent a string.

G.3   a)   `System.out.printf( "%10d\n", 1234 );`
   b)   `System.out.printf( "%+.3e\n", 123.456789 );`
   c)   `System.out.printf( "%#o\n", 100 );`
   d)   `System.out.printf( "%tD\n", calendar );`
   e)   `System.out.printf( "%1$tH:%1$tM:%1$tS\n", calendar );`
   f)   `System.out.printf( "%+20.3f\n", 3.333333 );`

Exercises

G.4   Show what is printed by each of the following statements. If a statement is incorrect, indicate why.
   a)   `System.out.printf( "%-10d\n", 10000 );`
   b)   `System.out.printf( "%c\n", "This is a string" );`
   c)   `System.out.printf( "%8.3f\n", 1024.987654 );`

d) `System.out.printf( "%#o\n%#X\n", 17, 17 );`

e) `System.out.printf( "% d\n%+d\n", 1000000, 1000000 );`

f) `System.out.printf( "%10.2e\n", 444.93738 );`

g) `System.out.printf( "%d\n", 10.987 );`

G.5 *(Printing Dates and Times)* Write a program that prints dates and times in the following forms:

```
GMT-05:00 04/30/04 09:55:09 AM
GMT-05:00 April 30 2004 09:55:09
2004-04-30 day-of-the-month:30
2004-04-30 day-of-the-year:121
Fri Apr 30 09:55:09 GMT-05:00 2004
```

[*Note:* Depending on your location, you may get a time zone other than GMT-05:00.]

G.6 *(Rounding Numbers)* Write a program that prints the value 100.453627 rounded to the nearest digit, tenth, hundredth, thousandth and ten-thousandth.

G.7 *(Converting Fahrenheit Temperature to Celsius)* Write a program that converts integer Fahrenheit temperatures from 0 to 212 degrees to floating-point Celsius temperatures with three digits of precision. Use the formula

```
celsius = 5.0 / 9.0 * ( fahrenheit - 32 );
```

to perform the calculation. The output should be printed in two right-justified columns of 10 characters each, and the Celsius temperatures should be preceded by a sign for both positive and negative values.

G.8 Write a program that uses the conversion character g to output the value 9876.12345. Print the value with precisions ranging from 1 to 9.

Appendices on the Web

The following appendices are available from www.deitel.com/books/jhtp8/ as PDF documents:

- Appendix H, Number Systems
- Appendix I, GroupLayout
- Appendix J, Java Desktop Integration Components (JDIC)
- Appendix K, Mashups
- Appendix L, Unicode®
- Appendix M, Creating Documentation with javadoc
- Appendix N, Bit Manipulation
- Appendix O, Labeled break and continue Statements
- Appendix P, UML 2: Additional Diagram Types
- Appendix Q, Design Patterns

These files can be viewed in Adobe® Reader® (get.adobe.com/reader).

If you are not already registered at our website, go to www.deitel.com and click the **Register** link below our logo in the upper-left corner of the page. Fill in your information. There is no charge to register, and we do not share your information with anyone. We send you only account-management e-mails unless you register separately for our free *Deitel® Buzz Online* e-mail newsletter at www.deitel.com/newsletter/subscribe.html. After registering, you'll receive a confirmation e-mail with your verification code. You'll need this code to sign in at www.deitel.com for the first time. Configure your e-mail client to allow e-mails from deitel.com to ensure that the confirmation e-mail is not filtered as junk mail.

Next, go to www.deitel.com and sign in using the **Login** link below our logo in the upper-left corner of the page. Go to www.deitel.com/books/jhtp8/. You'll find the links to these appendices under the heading **Download Code Examples and Other Premium Content for Registered Users** in the left column of the page.

Index

[*Note:* Page references for defining occurrences of terms appear in **bold maroon**. Page references for web bonus appendices are listed in uppercase roman numerals. You can find the web bonus files online at www.deitel.com/books/jhtp8/.]

Symbols

^, bitwise exclusive OR **LV**
^, boolean logical exclusive OR 178, **180**
    truth table 181
^=, bitwise exclusive OR assignment
    operator LXV
_ SQL wildcard character **1192**, 1193
, (comma) formatting flag **166**
--, predecrement/postdecrement **135**, 135
-, subtraction 53, 54
!, logical NOT 178, **181**
    truth table 181
!=, not equals 57
? (wildcard type argument) **910**
?:, ternary conditional operator **112**, 137
. dot separator **77**
, flag **1454**
(flag **1454**
{, left brace 40
}, right brace 40
@ symbol **XLIII**
@Override annotation 373
* SQL wildcard character **1191**
* wildcard in a file name 78
*, multiplication 53, 54
*=, multiplication assignment operator
    134
/ forward slash in end tags **971**
/, division 53, 54
/* */ traditional comment **39**
/** */ Java documentation comment
    39, **XLIII**
//, end-of-line comment **39**
/=, division assignment operator 134
\, backslash escape sequence 46
\', single-quote-character escape
    sequence 1458
\", double-quote escape sequence 46,
    1458
\\, backslash-character escape sequence
    1458
\b, escape sequence 1458
\f, form-feed escape sequence 1458
\n, newline escape sequence 46, 1458
\r, carriage-return escape sequence 46,
    1458
\t, horizontal tab escape sequence 46,
    1458
&, bitwise AND **LV**
&, boolean logical AND 178, **180**
&&, conditional AND **178**, 179

truth table 179
&=, bitwise AND assignment operator
    LXV
character **XLIX**
flag **1454**, 1455
% conversion character **1450**
% SQL wildcard character **1192**
%, remainder 53, 54
%% format specifier 1452
%=, remainder assignment operator 134
%A format specifier **1446**
%a format specifier **1446**
%B format specifier **1450**
%b format specifier **181**, **1450**, 1451
%C format specifier **1447**
%c format specifier **1447**, 1447
%d format specifier **51**, 1444, **1444**, 1445
%E format specifier **1445**, 1445
%e format specifier **1445**, 1445
%f format specifier 68, **93**, **1445**, **1446**
%G format specifier **1446**
%g format specifier **1446**
%H format specifier **1450**
%h format specifier **1451**
%n format specifier **1451**
%o format specifier **1444**, 1445
%S format specifier **1447**
%s format specifier **47**, 1444, **1447**
%T format specifier **1448**
%t format specifier **1448**
%X format specifier **1444**
%x format specifier **1444**
- flag **1454**
+ flag **1454**
- (minus sign) formatting flag **165**
+, addition 53, 54
++, preincrement/postincrement **135**
+=, addition assignment operator **134**,
    134, 172
+=, string concatenation assignment
    operator 696
<, less than 57
<<, left shift **LV**, LXII
<<=, left shift assignment operator LXV
<=, less than or equal 57
<>, angle brackets for XML elements **971**
=, assignment operator 51
-=, subtraction assignment operator 134
== to determine whether two references
    refer to the same object 393
==, is equal to 57
>, greater than 57

>= greater than or equal to 57
>>, signed right shift **LV**, LXII
>>=, signed right shift assignment
    operator LXV
>>>, unsigned right shift **LV**, LXII
>>>=, unsigned right shift assignment
    operator LXV
|, bitwise inclusive OR **LV**
|, boolean logical inclusive OR 178, **180**
|=, bitwise inclusive OR assignment
    operator LXV
||, conditional OR 178, **179**
    truth table 180
~ (bitwise complement) **LV**
~, bitwise complement LVI

Numerics

0 flag **257**
0 format flag 319
0x (hexadecimal prefix) 1455
127.0.0.1 (localhost IP address)
    1149, 1249
15 Puzzle exercise 1010

A

abbreviating assignment expressions 134
abnormally terminate a program 260
abs method of Math 206
absolute method of ResultSet **1212**
absolute path **734**, 735, 737
absolute positioning **1266**
absolute value 206
abstract class 402, **406**, 406, 407, 408,
    425, LXXX
abstract data type (ADT) 318
Abstract Factory design pattern LXXVI,
    LXXVII, LXXXVIII
abstract implementation 879
abstract keyword **407**
abstract method **407**, 408, 411, 528, 576,
    1414
abstract superclass **406**, 528
Abstract Window Toolkit (AWT) **561**
    package **214**
Abstract Window Toolkit Event package
    214
AbstractButton class **578**, 581, 1019,
    1025
    addActionListener method 581
    addItemListener method **583**

End User License Agreement

Prentice Hall License Agreement and Limited Warranty

READ THE FOLLOWING TERMS AND CONDITIONS CAREFULLY BEFORE OPENING THIS SOFTWARE PACKAGE. THIS LEGAL DOCUMENT IS AN AGREEMENT BETWEEN YOU AND PRENTICE-HALL, INC. (THE "COMPANY"). BY OPENING THIS SEALED SOFTWARE PACKAGE, YOU ARE AGREEING TO BE BOUND BY THESE TERMS AND CONDITIONS. IF YOU DO NOT AGREE WITH THESE TERMS AND CONDITIONS, DO NOT OPEN THE SOFTWARE PACKAGE. PROMPTLY RETURN THE UNOPENED SOFTWARE PACKAGE AND ALL ACCOMPANYING ITEMS TO THE PLACE YOU OBTAINED THEM FOR A FULL REFUND OF ANY SUMS YOU HAVE PAID.

1.GRANT OF LICENSE: In consideration of your purchase of this book, and your agreement to abide by the terms and conditions of this Agreement, the Company grants to you a nonexclusive right to use and display the copy of the enclosed software program (hereinafter the "SOFTWARE") on a single computer (i.e., with a single CPU) at a single location so long as you comply with the terms of this Agreement. The Company reserves all rights not expressly granted to you under this Agreement.

2.OWNERSHIP OF SOFTWARE: You own only the magnetic or physical media (the enclosed media) on which the SOFTWARE is recorded or fixed, but the Company and the software developers retain all the rights, title, and ownership to the SOFTWARE recorded on the original media copy(ies) and all subsequent copies of the SOFTWARE, regardless of the form or media on which the original or other copies may exist. This license is not a sale of the original SOFTWARE or any copy to you.

3.COPY RESTRICTIONS: This SOFTWARE and the accompanying printed materials and user manual (the "Documentation") are the subject of copyright. The individual programs on the media are copyrighted by the authors of each program. Some of the programs on the media include separate licensing agreements. If you intend to use one of these programs, you must read and follow its accompanying license agreement. You may not copy the Documentation or the SOFTWARE, except that you may make a single copy of the SOFTWARE for backup or archival purposes only. You may be held legally responsible for any copying or copyright infringement which is caused or encouraged by your failure to abide by the terms of this restriction.

4.USE RESTRICTIONS: You may not network the SOFTWARE or otherwise use it on more than one computer or computer terminal at the same time. You may physically transfer the SOFTWARE from one computer to another provided that the SOFTWARE is used on only one computer at a time. You may not distribute copies of the SOFTWARE or Documentation to others. You may not reverse engineer, disassemble, decompile, modify, adapt, translate, or create derivative works based on the SOFTWARE or the Documentation without the prior written consent of the Company.

5. TRANSFER RESTRICTIONS: The enclosed SOFTWARE is licensed only to you and may not be transferred to any one else without the prior written consent of the Company. Any unauthorized transfer of the SOFTWARE shall result in the immediate termination of this Agreement.

6. TERMINATION: This license is effective until terminated. This license will terminate automatically without notice from the Company and become null and void if you fail to comply with any provisions or limitations of this license. Upon termination, you shall destroy the Documentation and all copies of the SOFTWARE. All provisions of this Agreement as to warranties, limitation of liability, remedies or damages, and our ownership rights shall survive termination.

7. MISCELLANEOUS: This Agreement shall be construed in accordance with the laws of the United States of America and the State of New York and shall benefit the Company, its affiliates, and assignees.

8.LIMITED WARRANTY AND DISCLAIMER OF WARRANTY: The Company warrants that the SOFTWARE, when properly used in accordance with the Documentation, will operate in substantial conformity with the description of the SOFTWARE set forth in the Documentation. The Company does not warrant that the SOFTWARE will meet your requirements or that the operation of the SOFTWARE will be uninterrupted or error-free. The Company warrants that the media on which the SOFTWARE is delivered shall be free from defects in materials and workmanship under normal use for a period of thirty

(30) days from the date of your purchase. Your only remedy and the Company's only obligation under these limited warranties is, at the Company's option, return of the warranted item for a refund of any amounts paid by you or replacement of the item. Any replacement of SOFTWARE or media under the warranties shall not extend the original warranty period. The limited warranty set forth above shall not apply to any SOFTWARE which the Company determines in good faith has been subject to misuse, neglect, improper installation, repair, alteration, or damage by you. EXCEPT FOR THE EXPRESSED WARRANTIES SET FORTH ABOVE, THE COMPANY DISCLAIMS ALL WARRANTIES, EXPRESS OR IMPLIED, INCLUDING WITHOUT LIMITATION, THE IMPLIED WARRANTIES OF MERCHANTABILITY AND FITNESS FOR A PARTICULAR PURPOSE. EXCEPT FOR THE EXPRESS WARRANTY SET FORTH ABOVE, THE COMPANY DOES NOT WARRANT, GUARANTEE, OR MAKE ANY REPRESENTATION REGARDING THE USE OR THE RESULTS OF THE USE OF THE SOFTWARE IN TERMS OF ITS CORRECTNESS, ACCURACY, RELIABILITY, CURRENTNESS, OR OTHERWISE.

IN NO EVENT, SHALL THE COMPANY OR ITS EMPLOYEES, AGENTS, SUPPLIERS, OR CONTRACTORS BE LIABLE FOR ANY INCIDENTAL, INDIRECT, SPECIAL, OR CONSEQUENTIAL DAMAGES ARISING OUT OF OR IN CONNECTION WITH THE LICENSE GRANTED UNDER THIS AGREEMENT, OR FOR LOSS OF USE, LOSS OF DATA, LOSS OF INCOME OR PROFIT, OR OTHER LOSSES, SUSTAINED AS A RESULT OF INJURY TO ANY PERSON, OR LOSS OF OR DAMAGE TO PROPERTY, OR CLAIMS OF THIRD PARTIES, EVEN IF THE COMPANY OR AN AUTHORIZED REPRESENTATIVE OF THE COMPANY HAS BEEN ADVISED OF THE POSSIBILITY OF SUCH DAMAGES. IN NO EVENT SHALL LIABILITY OF THE COMPANY FOR DAMAGES WITH RESPECT TO THE SOFTWARE EXCEED THE AMOUNTS ACTUALLY PAID BY YOU, IF ANY, FOR THE SOFTWARE.

SOME JURISDICTIONS DO NOT ALLOW THE LIMITATION OF IMPLIED WARRANTIES OR LIABILITY FOR INCIDENTAL, INDIRECT, SPECIAL, OR CONSEQUENTIAL DAMAGES, SO THE ABOVE LIMITATIONS MAY NOT ALWAYS APPLY. THE WARRANTIES IN THIS AGREEMENT GIVE YOU SPECIFIC LEGAL RIGHTS AND YOU MAY ALSO HAVE OTHER RIGHTS WHICH VARY IN ACCORDANCE WITH LOCAL LAW.

ACKNOWLEDGMENT

YOU ACKNOWLEDGE THAT YOU HAVE READ THIS AGREEMENT, UNDERSTAND IT, AND AGREE TO BE BOUND BY ITS TERMS AND CONDITIONS. YOU ALSO AGREE THAT THIS AGREEMENT IS THE COMPLETE AND EXCLUSIVE STATEMENT OF THE AGREEMENT BETWEEN YOU AND THE COMPANY AND SUPERSEDES ALL PROPOSALS OR PRIOR AGREEMENTS, ORAL, OR WRITTEN, AND ANY OTHER COMMUNICATIONS BETWEEN YOU AND THE COMPANY OR ANY REPRESENTATIVE OF THE COMPANY RELATING TO THE SUBJECT MATTER OF THIS AGREEMENT.

Should you have any questions concerning this Agreement or if you wish to contact the Company for any reason, please contact in writing at the address below.

Robin Short
Prentice Hall PTR
One Lake Street
Upper Saddle River, New Jersey 07458

License Agreement and Limited Warranty

The software is distributed on an "AS IS" basis, without warranty. Neither the authors, the software developers, nor Pearson Education make any representation, or warranty, either express or implied, with respect to the software programs, their quality, accuracy, or fitness for a specific purpose. Therefore, neither the authors, the software developers, nor Pearson Education shall have any liability to you or any other person or entity with respect to any liability, loss, or damage caused or alleged to have been caused directly or indirectly by the programs contained on the media. This includes, but is not limited to, interruption of service, loss of data, loss of classroom time, loss of consulting or anticipatory profits, or consequential damages from the use of these programs. If the media itself is defective, you may return it for a replacement. Use of this software is subject to the Binary Code License terms and conditions at the back of this book. Read the licenses carefully. By opening this package, you are agreeing to be bound by the terms and conditions of these licenses. If you do not agree, do not open the package.

Please refer to the end-user license agreements on the CD for further details.

Using the CDs

The interface to the contents of the Microsoft® Windows® CD is designed to start automatically through the AUTORUN.EXE file. If a startup screen does not pop up automatically when you insert the CD into your computer, double click on the welcome.htm file to launch the Student CD or refer to the file readme.txt on the CD.

Software and Hardware System Requirements

- 800 MHz (minimum) Pentium III or faster processor
- Windows Vista or Windows XP (with Service Pack 2)
- Minimum of 512 MB of RAM; 1 GB is recommended
- Minimum of 1.5 GB of hard disk space
- CD-ROM drive
- Internet connection
- Web browser, Adobe® Reader® and a zip decompression utility

Software Foundation; we sometimes make exceptions for this. Our decision will be guided by the two goals of preserving the free status of all derivatives of our free software and of promoting the sharing and reuse of software generally.

NO WARRANTY

11. BECAUSE THE PROGRAM IS LICENSED FREE OF CHARGE, THERE IS NO WARRANTY FOR THE PROGRAM, TO THE EXTENT PERMITTED BY APPLICABLE LAW. EXCEPT WHEN OTHERWISE STATED IN WRITING THE COPYRIGHT HOLDERS AND/OR OTHER PARTIES PROVIDE THE PROGRAM "AS IS" WITHOUT WARRANTY OF ANY KIND, EITHER EXPRESSED OR IMPLIED, INCLUDING, BUT NOT LIMITED TO, THE IMPLIED WARRANTIES OF MERCHANTABILITY AND FITNESS FOR A PARTICULAR PURPOSE. THE ENTIRE RISK AS TO THE QUALITY AND PERFORMANCE OF THE PROGRAM IS WITH YOU. SHOULD THE PROGRAM PROVE DEFECTIVE, YOU ASSUME THE COST OF ALL NECESSARY SERVICING, REPAIR OR CORRECTION.

12. IN NO EVENT UNLESS REQUIRED BY APPLICABLE LAW OR AGREED TO IN WRITING WILL ANY COPYRIGHT HOLDER, OR ANY OTHER PARTY WHO MAY MODIFY AND/OR REDISTRIBUTE THE PROGRAM AS PERMITTED ABOVE, BE LIABLE TO YOU FOR DAMAGES, INCLUDING ANY GENERAL, SPECIAL, INCIDENTAL OR CONSEQUENTIAL DAMAGES ARISING OUT OF THE USE OR INABILITY TO USE THE PROGRAM (INCLUDING BUT NOT LIMITED TO LOSS OF DATA OR DATA BEING RENDERED INACCURATE OR LOSSES SUSTAINED BY YOU OR THIRD PARTIES OR A FAILURE OF THE PROGRAM TO OPERATE WITH ANY OTHER PROGRAMS), EVEN IF SUCH HOLDER OR OTHER PARTY HAS BEEN ADVISED OF THE POSSIBILITY OF SUCH DAMAGES.

*****END OF TERMS AND CONDITIONS*****